THE LAW OF SECURITIES REGULATION

Sixth Edition

By

Thomas Lee Hazen
Cary C. Boshamer Distinguished Professor of Law
The University of North Carolina at Chapel Hill

HORNBOOK SERIES®

WEST®
A Thomson Reuters business

Mat #40675332

610 Opperman Drive
St. Paul, MN 55123
1–800–313–9378

Printed in the United States of America

ISBN: 978–0–314–18797–0

To: Lisa, George, Elliott, and Lucie

*

Preliminary Note on the Scope of the One Volume Hornbook

This Hornbook is a one volume version and a substantial abridgement of my seven volume Treatise on Securities Regulation (Practitioner's Edition). The Hornbook is designed for students but can also serve as a desk book for lawyers desiring an overview of the law. The Sixth Edition was revised in 2008 to reflect some important recent developments including the 1933 Act offering reform rules.[.5]

The Hornbook omits many sections of the Practitioner's Edition that the reader may want to consult for more in-depth analysis or for topics reserved for the Practitioner's Edition, which provides more extensive footnoting, directing the reader to primary and other secondary sources. The Hornbook provides an entry into the world of securities regulation. The Practitioner's Edition provides significantly more depth, insight, and footnoting of sources.

The Hornbook retains the section numbers[1] and footnote numbering as they appear in the multi-volume Practitioner's Edition in order to help user who decides to consult the more comprehensive treatise. The index includes all references to the Practitioner's Edition even if the sections do not appear in this Hornbook.

Preface

Securities law, especially at the federal level, was once considered a specialty that only the large Wall Street law firms had to worry about. That is certainly no longer the case. Lawyers all over the country are finding themselves in contact with many aspects of the federal securities laws. There is hardly a lawyer who himself or herself does not have either directly or indirectly some investment in the stock or bond markets. Furthermore, our clients are likely to have similar investments. There is also ever-increasing number of participants in the options, futures, and derivatives markets.

Because of the widespread possibility of federal remedies that exist for investors who are injured in the securities markets, every lawyer should have at least a passing familiarity with the federal securities laws. Conscientious lawyers should keep abreast of developments due to the burgeoning alternative investment opportunities including options, index futures and the like. Also, since the definition of securities is an expansive one, a large number of investment opportunities that are not in the traditional forms of stock or bonds may still be subject to the regulatory and protective provi-

.5 Readers desiring additional recent developments should consult the pocket part of the Practitioner's Edition.

1 Some subheadings have been deleted from the Hornbook for the convenience of the reader.

sions of both federal and state securities law. It follows that securities law has become relevant to general practitioners as well as specialists.

Additionally there are large numbers of lawyers who have a general corporate and commercial practice which touches upon both state and federal securities laws. No matter how small the business, if it is in corporate or limited partnership form, the antifraud provisions and attendant potential civil liabilities loom in the background as something for the corporate planner to keep in mind. On occasion, the securities laws may also apply to limited liability company and limited liability partnership investments.[2] Any time a company issues stock, the securities laws are implicated. The exemptions from federal and state registration requirements are not as straightforward as they may seem[3] and thus any corporate planner should be aware of the necessary precautions to secure the desired exemption.

This Hornbook, and the more comprehensive Practitioner's Edition of this treatise, is designed both for students and attorneys needing an introduction to the securities laws as well as for specialists dealing with these issues on a daily basis who seek more in-depth analysis of the law and current developments. This Hornbook, which is now in its fifth edition, is designed to give an overview of the securities laws with the understanding that the space limitations do not permit an in-depth treatment of all aspects of federal and state law. The multi-volume Practitioner's Edition has evolved and grown over the twenty years and five editions that it has been in existence. Over the years various chapters have been expanded and added to reflect the changes in the dynamic field of securities regulation.

This Hornbook is not merely a primer. The hope is to provide a firm understanding of the basics of securities law and adequate guidance as to further sources for the more esoteric aspects of the law of securities regulation.

Many areas of federal regulation are sufficiently complex so as to preclude an adequate surface treatment. The coverage of both the Hornbook and Treatise represents an attempt to strike a balance between the need for sufficient depth and the space limitations. In many instances choices have been made to allow in-depth treatment of some of the more common areas and to limit the details of the more specialized areas.

Towards these ends, a large portion of the Hornbook is devoted to discussion of the federal Securities Act of 1933[4] and the Securities Exchange Act of 1934.[5] Primary emphasis is placed upon the regulation of the securities markets as it applies to issuers of securities and to most investors. Lawyers who do not specialize in securities law are likely to come into contact with a number of areas covered by the Securities Act of 1933 and the Securities Exchange Act of 1934. These include the registration requirements for securities distributions and the various exemptions from registration. Both the 1933 and 1934 Acts provide a wide range of remedies for

2 *See* §§ 1.6[10], 1.6[11] *infra.*

3 *See* chapter 4 *infra.*

4 15 U.S.C.A. §§ 77a *et seq. See* chapters 1–7 *infra.*

5 15 U.S.C.A. §§ 78a *et seq. See* chapters 10–16 *infra.*

investors injured by fraudulent practices and material misstatements and omissions.[6] Shareholder suffrage is a major thrust of the Exchange Act's proxy regulations.[7] The Exchange Act also includes the Williams Act Amendments that contain the federal regulation of tender offers[8]—a topic often in the forefront of the financial news of the day. Another topic of current concern is the sanctions against insider trading based on nonpublic information.[9] A major developing area has been the creation of mechanisms for a national market system in order to help eliminate many of the inefficiencies of the traditional exchange and over-the-counter markets.[10]

Although regulation of the broker-dealer industry is a very important aspect of securities law, the treatment in both the Hornbook and Treatise is somewhat selective.[11] Formerly, broker-dealer law was primarily a subspecialty of interest to a relatively small number of lawyers. However, that has changed. There has been rampant fraud in many sectors of the securities industry and this has resulted in increased widespread significance of broker-dealer law. Accordingly, in the Fifth Edition, there is a significantly expanded treatment of broker-dealer regulation both by the SEC and self regulatory organizations. The previous editions' treatment of the markets generally has been revised to reflect dramatic changes that have taken place, not the least of which are due to technological developments.

In addition, there is only brief treatment of the state securities laws, in part because of the ever-increasing importance of the federal laws and also because of the high degree of jurisdictional variation and the need to consult the law of each applicable state. The Hornbook and Treatise also examine the other federal acts administered by the SEC: the Public Utility Holding Company Act of 1935,[12] the Trust Indenture Act of 1939,[13] the Investment Company Act of 1940,[14] and the Investment Advisers Act of 1940.[15] The Practitioner's Edition also contains some materials on related laws including the Securities Investor Protection Act[16] that governs broker-dealer insolvency, Article 8 of the Uniform Commercial Code[17] which governs securities transactions, the Foreign Corrupt Practices Act,[18] the Racketeering Influenced and Corrupt Organizations Act,[19] and the ever-increasing blurring of

6 *See* chapter 12 *infra*.

7 *See* chapter 10 *infra*.

8 *See* chapter 11 *infra*.

9 *See* § 12.17 *infra*.

10 *See* chapter 14 *infra*.

11 *See* chapters 14–15 *infra*. For additional discussion of the aspects of broker-dealer regulation. See Jerry W. Markham & Thomas L. Hazen, Broker–Dealer Operations Under Securities and Commodities Law: Financial Responsibilities, Credit Regulation, and Customer Protection (2d ed. 2002).

12 Pub. Law No. 74–333, 49 Stat. 803 (1935), codified as amended at 15 U.S.C.A. §§ 79–79z-6, discussed in chapter 18 *infra* [Practitioner's Edition only].

13 Act of August 3, 1939, 53 Stat. 1149, which is discussed in chapter 19 *infra*.

14 Act of Aug. 22, 1940, 54 Stat. 789, codified in 15 U.S.C.A. §§ 80a–1 through 80a–52, discussed in chapter 20 *infra*.

15 Act of Aug. 22, 1940 54 Stat. 847, codified in 15 U.S.C.A. §§ 80b–1 *et seq.*, discussed in chapter 21 *infra*.

16 Codified as amended 15 U.S.C.A. §§ 78aaa–78*lll*, discussed in § 14.24 *infra*.

17 *See* chapter 23 *infra* [Practitioner's Edition only].

18 Pub. Law 95–213, 95th Cong., 1st Sess., 91 Stat. 1494 (1977), codified in 15 U.S.C.A. §§ 78m(b), 78dd–1, 78dd–2, discussed in §§ 9.3, 22.2 *infra*.

19 Pub. Law No. 91–452, 84 Stat. 922 (1970), codified in 18 U.S.C.A. §§ 1961–1968, discussed in § 22.3 *infra*.

the lines of demarcation between investment banking and commercial banking.[20] There is also a brief overview of federal regulation of the commodities markets.[21]

As is always the case in the fast-changing world of securities regulation, there have been major changes in the law since the last edition. This Practitioner's Edition has grown from one volume in its first edition to its current six volume length.

A few of the developments over the past twenty years deserve specific mention here. The Internet has made securities investing more readily available. At the same time, it has opened up new avenues for those unscrupulous market participants wanting to engage in fraud. The changes in the law resulting from the Internet are discussed throughout both the Hornbook and the Practitioner's Edition. There have been two federal litigation reform Acts plus a total rearrangement of the jurisdictional allocation between the federal law and the states regarding securities regulation.

Disclosure obligations in many areas have changed dramatically. For example, the regulators have become increasingly concerned with the role analysts play in the securities markets and a new system has been put in place. The SEC has also instituted a new requirement of "plain English" in disclosure.

The ever-changing nature of the financial markets has also resulted in significant change. In 1999, Congress repealed the barriers that formerly existed between investment banking, commercial banking, and other financial services.[22] In 2000, Congress made revolutionary changes to commodities regulation and the law relating to derivative investments. The changes brought about by the Commodity Futures Modernization Act of 2000[23] that have had an impact on securities regulation are addressed in the Fifth Edition. Also, the terror attack of 2001 created increased focus on money laundering.[24]

The corporate scandals that emerged at the turn of the twenty-first century have had a profound impact on securities regulation. For example, in 2002, Congress adopted the Sarbanes–Oxley Act[25] in reaction to infamous corporate scandals including Enron's, Tyco's and WorldCom's. The Sarbanes–Oxley Act introduced a new federal focus on corporate governance—an area of the law that was traditionally reserved to the states. The Sarbanes–Oxley Act is discussed throughout both the Hornbook and Treatise where applicable.

[20] *See* § 22.6 *infra*.

[21] *See* § 22.7 *infra*. For more detailed discussion of the commodities laws and the derivatives markets, see Phillip McBride Johnson & Thomas Lee Hazen, Derivatives Regulation (2004).

[22] *See* the Gramm–Leach–Bliley Act, Pub. Law 106–102, 1999 U.S.C.C.A.N. (113 Stat.) 1338 (1999).

[23] Commodity Futures Modernization Act of 2000, Pub. Law 106–554, 114 Stat. 2763 (December 21, 2000).

[24] *See* § 22.5 *infra*.

[25] Sarbanes–Oxley Act of 2002, Pub. Law 107–204 (July 30, 2002).

The foregoing are but examples of the major changes that lead to the Fifth Edition. These major changes are supplemented by the significant refinements in existing doctrines in all aspects of securities regulation.

The Practitioner's Edition contains four Appendices. Appendix A contains guides to the SEC's new plain English disclosure requirements. Appendix B contains materials relating to the SEC's Regulation FD which abolished selective disclosure practices that formerly had been employed by many public companies. Appendix C consists of a helpful SEC summary of its interpretations in administering the "shareholder proposal rule" which governs the inclusion of shareholder proposals in management's proxy statement. Finally, Appendix D (which also appears as the Appendix to the Hornbook) is designed to provide an overview to researching securities law through Westlaw.

The Fifth Edition contains developments through August 2004. As was the case with previous editions, the Practitioner's Edition will be twice each year. The one-volume student Hornbook edition is considerably abridged but contains references to the Practitioner's Edition in order to facilitate further study.

The federal securities statutes along with SEC rules and forms, including the disclosure guides in Regulation S–K and S–B are found in a separate statutory supplement which is published annually by Thomson–West.

Acknowledgments

As with any work of this size there are a number of people whose hard work and support made this endeavor possible In addition to my family, which has endured the long nights and short weekends, this treatise would never have been produced without the support from the University of North Carolina School of Law. In particular I would like to thank former Dean Kenneth S. Broun for his support and encouragement as well as the support and encouragement of my current Dean Gene Nichol. During the preparation of the first edition, my former colleague and very good friend Marianne K. Smythe was most patient with my ignorance and provided me with much insight into the workings of the Securities and Exchange Commission. I would like to acknowledge the great help I received from the late Professor N. Ferebee Taylor for the hours spent parsing the intricacies of SEC Rule 10b–5 and Professor Robert G. Byrd for his insights on the law of fraud and on remedies. There also was a number of support staff whose hard work made this treatise possible and the many student assistants who have helped me over the years.

I especially want to thank my wife Lisa for her help, support, and patience.

Research Aids[26]

Researching the law in the area of securities regulation is not an easy task since a vast body of law is contained in administrative rules, interpretations and no-action letters that are not officially reported. In addition to the

26 *See also* § 1.0[2] *infra.*

database of Westlaw which contains all of the pertinent information, Thomson–West publishes a securities law library on cd-rom. The Federal Securities Law Reporter, a multiple volume looseleaf reporter published by Commerce Clearing House (CCH) is another comprehensive source; a companion CCH resource is the Blue Sky Law Reporter which addresses the various state securities regulation statutes and administrative law. The Bureau of National Affairs' Securities Regulation and Law Reporter can be very helpful in keeping lawyers up-to-date with the rapidly changing law of securities regulation. Prentice–Hall also publishes a looseleaf service. Looseleaf services in related fields include the Commodity Futures Law Reporter and the Federal Banking Law Reporter, both of which are published by Commerce Clearing House.

In addition to the Practitioner's Edition of this Treatise, secondary sources for more detail on some of the matters dealt with in this Hornbook include: James D. Cox & Thomas Lee Hazen, Cox and Hazen on Corporations (Aspen Law & Business, 2d ed.2003); Phillip McBride Johnson & Thomas Lee Hazen, Derivatives Regulation (Aspen Law & Business, 2004); and Jerry W. Markham & Thomas Lee Hazen, Broker Dealer Operations and Regulation Under Securities and Commodities Law: Financial Responsibilities, Credit Regulation, and Customer Protection (Thomson–West, 2d ed. 2002).

THOMAS LEE HAZEN

Chapel Hill, North Carolina,

December 2008

Westlaw® Overview

The Law of Securities Regulation offers a detailed and comprehensive treatment of the basic rules, principles, and issues relating to securities law. To supplement the information contained in this book, you can access Westlaw, West's computer-assisted legal research service. Westlaw contains a broad array of legal resources, including case law, statutes, expert commentary, current developments, and various other types of information.

Learning how to use these materials effectively will enhance your legal research abilities. To help you coordinate the information in the book with your Westlaw research, this volume contains an appendix listing Westlaw databases, search techniques, and sample problems.

The instructions and features described in this Westlaw overview are based on accessing Westlaw at www.westlaw.com.

THE PUBLISHER

*

Summary of Contents

*

Table of Contents

*

THE LAW OF SECURITIES REGULATION

Sixth Edition

*

Chapter 1

THE BASIC COVERAGE OF THE SECURITIES LAWS

Table of Sections

---

§ 1.0 Overview; Sources of Securities Law; Overview of this Chapter

§ 1.0[1] Overview

Securities regulation is an extremely complicated field. At the federal level, it is implemented by a myriad of statutes and regulatory rules. The statutes and rules are extremely complex and detailed. The case law is particularly perplexing because of the degree of detail and complexity the law imposes. However, it is not only the law that is difficult and elaborate. The transactions that implicate the securities laws are extremely intricate as well. This treatise tries to distill the law and its application to these transactions in an understandable manner.

Although the first laws in the United States aimed at securities regulation developed in the individual states,[1] most securities regulation today is a matter of federal law even though the states retain influence in some selected areas.

§ 1.0[2] Sources of Federal Securities Law[31]

§ 1.0[2][A] The Federal Securities Laws

Although originating as a matter of state law,[32] the vast majority of securities regulation in the United States is a matter of federal law. State law

---

§ 1.0

1. The state securities laws, also referred to as "blue sky" laws are discussed in chapter 8 *infra*.

31. This subsection is adapted from Thomas Lee Hazen & David L Ratner, Securities Regulation Cases and Materials 11–16 (6th Ed. 2003).

32. *See* § 1.2[2] *infra*.

remains significant with respect to some transactions, but federal law clearly has the most significant impact on securities regulation. Finding the law when dealing with federal securities regulation often is a difficult task as there are several sources to consult. The discussion that follows is designed to give a brief overview of the sources of federal law that are discussed throughout this treatise.

The starting point in analyzing any question of federal securities law is of course the statutes.[33] In the strictest sense, there is no federal "common law" of securities,[34] and any rights or liabilities must find their source in the statutes themselves. The statutes are, however, quite sketchy or ambiguous in many important areas, so that it is necessary to resort to supplemental sources of law. Some of the statutes and regulations are sufficiently general as to have led to what in fact does amount to a federal common law, as is the case with private remedies[35] and also with regard to insider trading.[36]

Beyond the case law in the federal courts, federal securities law exists in a large body of administrative law. The administrative law sources are of two kinds: rules and other statements of general applicability issued by the Securities and Exchange Commission[37] (or applicable self-regulatory organizations[38]) and reports of cases decided by the SEC applicable self regulatory organization).

The SEC has broad rule-making powers under the various statutes it administers and has exercised its authority by prescribing at least three different kinds of rules. One category is procedural rules, setting forth the steps to be followed in proceedings before the Commission, as well as such mundane matters as the hours the Commission is open, where papers should be filed, what size type to use, and so forth. A second important category is the type of rule the Commission writes where Congress has given it the power to fill in the terms of the statute. For example, section 14 of the 1934 Act[39] provides that no person shall solicit proxies from shareholders of a registered

33. The principal federal securities statutes are: the Securities Act of 1933, Act of May 27, 1933, c. 38, Title I, § 1, 48 Stat. 74, codified in 15 U.S.C.A. § 77a *et seq.;* the Securities Exchange Act of 1934, Act of June 6, 1934, c. 404, Title I, § 1, 48 Stat. 881, codified in 15 U.S.C.A. §§ 78a *et seq.;* the Trust Indenture Act of 1939, Act of Aug. 3, 1939 c. 411, 53 Stat. 1149, codified in 15 U.S.C.A. §§ 77aaa *et seq.*; the Investment Company Act of 1940, Act of Aug. 22, 1940, 54 Stat. 789, codified in 15 U.S.C.A. §§ 80a–1 through 80a–52; and the Investment Advisers Act of 1940, Act of Aug. 22, 1940 54 Stat. 847, codified in 15 U.S.C.A. § 80b–1 *et seq.*.

34. However, the essence of most securities litigation is grounded upon SEC Rule 10b–5 (17 C.F.R. § 240.10b–5), which is very brief and sketchy. Thus, it is fair to say that the vast body of case law under this section is a type of de facto federal common law of securities fraud. These cases and Rule 10b–5 are discussed in chapter 12 *infra.*

35. The most prominent example is the implied private right of action under 1934 Act Rule 10b–5, 17 C.F.R. § 240.10b–5 which is discussed in chapter 12 *infra.*

36. There is no statutory definition for the boundaries of permissible trading by insiders and others who may possess nonpublic information. As a result, the law has been developed by the courts. *See* § 12.17 *infra* for discussion of insider trading.

37. Alternatively referred to as the "SEC" or "the Commission."

38. Formerly the primary self regulators of the securities markets were the National Association of Securities Dealers (the NASD) and the New York Stock Exchange. In 2007 the regulatory arms of the NASD and the New York Stock Exchange merged into a single Financial Industry Regulatory Authority ("FINRA"). *See* §§ 1.1[4], 14.3 *infra.*

39. 15 U.S.C.A. § 78n.

company "in contravention of such rules and regulations as the Commission may prescribe * * *." Pursuant to that authority, the SEC has adopted a detailed set of rules (Regulation 14A) prescribing the form of proxy, the contents of the proxy statement, the procedures to be followed in proxy contests and in responding to proposals submitted by shareholders, and other matters. A third important category of rules defines some of the general terms used in the laws. A significant example of this definitional power are the rules adopted under the 1933 Act, defining the circumstances in which secondary offerings, mergers, nonpublic offerings, and intrastate offerings, will be exempt from 1933 Act registration requirements.

Supplementing the SEC's rules are its forms for the various statements and reports which issuers, broker-dealers and others are required to file under the Acts. Since disclosure is such an important part of the regulatory pattern, these forms (which have the legal force of rules) play an important part in defining the extent of the disclosure obligation.

Beyond the rules and forms, the SEC goes in for a good deal of "informal lawmaking," setting forth the views of the Commission or its staff on questions of current concern, without stating them in the form of legal requirements. The principal media for these statements are SEC "Releases" which, as the name implies, are simply statements distributed to the press, to companies and firms registered with the Commission, and to other interested persons. While Releases are also used for the proposal and adoption of rules or to meet other formal notice requirements, they are often used to set forth Commission or staff views through general statements of policy or recitation of the position taken by the Commission in various specific cases. Examples of both types will be found in this treatise. An overview of the SEC's lawmaking process is discussed below in section 1.4 of this treatise. A more detailed analysis of the SEC's operations is found in chapter 16.

In addition to general public statements of policy, the staff has, since the Commission's early days, been willing to respond to individual private inquiries as to whether a certain transaction could be carried out in a specified manner. These responses are known as "no-action" letters, because they customarily state that "the staff will recommend no action to the Commission" if the transaction is done in the specified manner.[40] Prior to 1970, these letters were not made public, leading to complaints that the large law firms which frequently corresponded with the SEC had access to a considerable body of "secret law" which was unavailable to other lawyers and their clients. As a result of these complaints, as well as recommendations from the Administrative Conference of the United States, the SEC now makes these letters and responses public, adding to the burdens of lawyers who wish to make sure they have thoroughly researched a particular point.

As noted above, technology has led to changes in the market place for securities. For example, Electronic Communication Networks (ECNs) may operate like exchanges and thus present a competing mechanism for trading securities listed on the more traditional stock exchanges.[42] In addition, Nasdq registered its national stock market, that formerly was part of the over-the-

40. No action letters are discussed in §§ 16.2, 16.32 *infra*.

42. *See* Jerry W. Markham & Daniel J. Harty, For Whom the Bell Tolls: The Demise of Exchange Trading Floors and the Growth of ECNs, 33 J. Corp. L. 865 (2008).

counter markets, as an exchange.[43] By the end of 2004 the National Stock Market was the nation's third largest stock behind the New York Stock Exchange and the NASDAQ stock market.[44] Also, in December 2004, the Archipelago Exchange accounted for twenty-two percent of the trades in Nasdaq-listed securities.[45] In 2006 most of the more widely traded over-the-counter securities became exchange traded when Nasdaq qualified its national stock market as a national exchange.

In some areas of federal securities law, notably in the registration provisions of the 1933 Act, most of the "law" is found in the rules, forms, and policy statements of the Commission, and very little in the form of decided "cases." In other areas, however, notably under the general anti-fraud provisions of the 1934 Act,[46] there is very little in the way of formal rules, and the law has developed in the traditional "common law" manner, with courts and other tribunals deciding each case on the basis of precedents.

The SEC materials include reports of decisions in several different types of proceedings. The SEC itself may proceed in a number of ways if it discovers what it believes to be a violation of the law.

If the alleged violator is a broker-dealer or investment adviser required to register with the SEC, the Commission can bring a proceeding to revoke or suspend the firm's registration or take other disciplinary action.[47] If the alleged violator is an issuer seeking to sell securities under a 1933 Act registration statement, the Securities and Exchange Commission can bring a proceeding to suspend the effectiveness of the statement.[48] And, under power granted to the Commission in 1990, it can bring a proceeding against any alleged violator of the securities laws to require that person to cease and desist from further violations. In any of these proceedings, the Commission staff acts as "prosecutor" and the Commission itself makes the final decision (after initial findings by an administrative law judge). The Commission's decision is appealable to the United States Court of Appeals in the District of Columbia or to the circuit where the registrant's principal place of business is located.

The Commission also has authority to go to court to obtain relief against alleged securities law violators. The most common type of Commission proceeding is an application to a federal district court for an injunction against future violations. In a particularly egregious case, however, the Commission may refer the matter to the Department of Justice for prosecution as a criminal violation.

The Securities and Exchange Commission is not a "collection agency." It has no statutory power to require a securities law violator to make restitution to people who have been injured by his or her violations. In a number of injunction actions, however, the SEC has requested, and the courts have

43. *See, e.g.*, Nasdaq Readying New Marketplace Meant to Replace OTC Bulletin Board, 35 Sec. Reg. & L. Rep. (BNA) 185 (Feb. 3, 2003).

44. National Stock Exchange Grows Rapidly, Reflecting State of Flux in the Securities Markets, 37 Sec. Reg. & L. Rep. (BNA) 137 (Jan. 24, 2005).

45. *See, e.g.*, National Stock Exchange Grows Rapidly, Reflecting State of Flux in the Securities Markets, 37 Sec. Reg. & L. Rep. (BNA) 137 (Jan. 24, 2005).

46. Section 10(b) of the 1934 Act, 15 U.S.C.A. § 78j(b). *See* chapter 12 *infra*.

47. Broker-dealer regulation is discussed in chapter 14 *infra*.

48. SEC powers generally and procedures are discussed in chapter 16 *infra*.

granted, as "ancillary relief," an order directing the violator to "disgorge" his profits to a depository for distribution to persons entitled to recovery. In addition, this type of ancillary disgorgement relief may be ordered as part of an SEC administrative order against someone who violates the securities laws.

People who believe they have been injured by a violation of the securities laws can bring a civil action in the courts for damages. Injured investors may sue either under the specific civil liability provisions of those laws or assert an "implied" right of action under a provision prohibiting the activity in question. There have been an enormous number of private damage actions under the federal securities laws, particularly actions asserting an implied right of action under the general anti-fraud provisions. While many of these actions relate to distinctive securities law problems, such as misleading statements or "insider trading," a substantial number have involved allegations of corporate mismanagement which might also constitute violations of state corporation law. Plaintiffs usually bring these actions under the federal securities laws to avoid restrictive state court decisions or state procedural obstacles to stockholders' derivative suits.

Prior to 1975, the United States Supreme Court reviewed very few securities cases, and when it did, it generally construed the law broadly and gave great deference to the views of the SEC. Since that time, however, the Court has taken a very restrictive view of federal securities law, particularly with respect to implied private rights of action, and has rejected the views of the SEC in a number of important cases.

Another consequence of this litigation "explosion," and the resulting uncertainties surrounding civil liability under the federal securities laws, has been increased pressure for "codification" of those laws. The American Law Institute in 1978 completed work on a nine-year project to prepare a "Federal Securities Code," designed to replace all of the federal securities laws now on the books, and to give more certainty and predictability to the provisions for civil liability. However, the proposed Securities Code was never introduced in Congress. Nevertheless, many of the proposed Code's concepts have been introduced into the current regulatory system.

§ 1.0[2][B] Where to Find the Law

Thomson/West's "Securities Regulation: Selected Statutes, Rules and Forms" should meet most lawyers' needs in studying the materials in this treatise. For advanced research, the most comprehensive and up-to-date sources for all of the federal securities laws, SEC rules, forms, interpretations and decisions, and court decisions on securities matters are the Westlaw and Lexis federal securities law libraries, and the loose-leaf Federal Securities Law Reporter published by Commerce Clearing House (CCH). Copies of the 1933 and 1934 Acts, and of the rules and forms governing the preparation of disclosure documents under those two acts, are also available through the SEC website (www.sec.gov). In addition to Westlaw (www.westlaw.com), the federal securities laws are available online through the Securities Lawyer's Deskbook (http://www.law.uc.edu/CCL/).

The official codified version of the federal securities laws is found in the United States Code (and in the United States Code Annotated) as sections 77 through 80 of Title 15. Unfortunately, whoever was in charge of numbering the Code decided that the sections of the 1933 Act (15 U.S.C. § 77) should be numbered 77a, 77b, 77c, etc. Thus 5(b)(1) of the Act becomes 15 U.S.C. § 77e(b)(1), and § 12(a)(2) becomes § 77*l*(a)(2). The 1934 Act is handled in similar fashion in 15 U.S.C. § 78. Since everyone connected with securities regulation uses the section numbers of the Acts, rather than the Code references, this treatise refers to those sections in addition to providing the official citations. If you want to find a section of the 1933 or 1934 Act in the Code you can do so easily, provided you remember the alphabet and have enough fingers to count to 26 (sections of the 1934 Act after section 26 are numbered as §§ 78aa, 78bb, and so forth). In addition, when Congress adds entirely new sections, they may be incorporated into the midst of the existing statutes with letters. Thus, for example there is a Section 8A of the 1933 Act (15 U.S.C. § 77h–1) which appears between sections 8 and 9 of that Act.

The official version of the SEC rules can be found in volume 17 of the Code of Federal Regulations. Here the numbering system is more rational than the system used by the U.S. Code for the securities laws. 1933 Act rules are found in 17 C.F.R. § 230.___ under the rule number, and 1934 Act rules can be found in 17 C.F.R. § 240.____ in the same manner. Thus 1933 Act Rule 144 is 17 C.F.R. § 230.144, and 1934 Act Rule 10b–5 is 17 C.F.R. § 240.10b–5.

SEC Releases announcing the proposal or adoption of new rules, as well as those containing significant interpretations of the law, can be found in the Federal Register for the day on which the release was issued. Other Releases are not systematically or officially published in any form other than the mimeographed releases actually distributed by the Commission, numbered serially by reference to the Act or Acts to which they related, such as Securities Act Release No. 4434. Compilations of "significant" releases under certain of the Acts are available through a number of official and unofficial compilations.

The SEC's "no-action" letters, as noted above, are now publicly available. They can be examined at the SEC office in Washington, and selected letters are published or summarized in the CCH Federal Securities Law Reporter or the BNA Securities Regulation and Law Reports (described below). Complete texts of all letters are available from several sources, including Westlaw and Lexis.

The official texts of SEC decisions in administrative proceedings brought before it are distributed as "Releases" at the time they are handed down, and are eventually printed and compiled in bound volumes of "SEC Decisions and Reports." The reports of these proceedings are available on Westlaw and Lexis and also on the SEC website (www.sec.gov).

Useful statistical and narrative information concerning the SEC's activities can be found in the Commission's "Annual Reports" to Congress. These reports are customarily available through the Government Printing Office for several years back. They are also available through the SEC's website and on Westlaw and Lexis.

Court decisions involving the federal securities laws are generally reported promptly and in full text in the CCH Federal Securities Law Reporter. Decisions of the Courts of Appeals, of course, also appear in West's Federal Reporter (F.2d & F.3d), and the more significant District Court decisions appear in the Federal Supplement (F.Supp. & F.Supp.2d). SEC briefs in cases involving the securities laws, which often contain significant statements of

Commission policy, are sometimes excerpted in the CCH Reporter. Formerly, these statements of policy were otherwise available only by request to the Commission's Office of General Counsel. Today, they are made available on the SEC website and are also collected on Westlaw and Lexis.

Up-to-date compilations of the constitutions, rules and interpretations of the major stock exchanges and the Financial Industry Regulatory Authority (FINRA, formerly the National Association of Securities Dealers (the "NASD") can be found in the loose-leaf stock exchange "Guides" and the "NASD Manual" published by CCH. They also can be found on the exchanges or FINRA's website (www.finra.org).

As far as state securities law is concerned, the most current and comprehensive compilation of statutes, rules, and administrative and court decisions is the CCH Blue Sky Law Reporter, which contains separate sections covering the law of each of the 50 states. Westlaw and Lexis also have comprehensive state securities law libraries. The securities law of any particular state can also be obtained through its published statutes, published administrative regulations (if any), and official and unofficial reports of its court decisions.

As noted above, there is a great deal of information on the Internet. For example, the official websites of the Securities and Exchange Commission all provide very useful information including regulatory rules and decisions.

Secondary sources include books, articles and current periodicals. In addition to articles and notes in the general law reviews published by law schools and bar associations, there are several publications devoted specifically to securities and related matters, including "Securities Regulation Law Journal," published by Thomson/West. Relevant secondary sources are cited throughout this treatise.

A number of programs on securities law for practicing lawyers, generally lasting two or three days but sometimes longer, are sponsored each year by various organizations. The transcripts of some of these programs, featuring lectures and panel discussions by SEC officials, securities law specialists, and others, are published in book form, and are useful sources of discussion of current problems. The outlines for many of these programs are available on Westlaw and Lexis.

Publications summarizing current developments in securities regulation on a weekly basis include Securities Regulation and Law Report, published by Bureau of National Affairs (BNA), and the summaries accompanying the weekly supplements to the CCH Federal Securities Law Reports. Of the daily newspapers, The Wall Street Journal provides the most thorough coverage, with frequent lengthier stories providing useful background information.

§ 1.0[2][C] The Securities Bar

There are no formal prerequisites for a lawyer to engage in securities practice. The SEC's rules of practice provide that any member of the bar of any state may practice before it. There are a substantial number of lawyers specializing in securities matters, and many thousands of others who deal with securities matters in the course of their practice.

As a field of practice, securities regulation is more a series of subspecialties than a single specialty. While there are common threads of doctrine and approach which run through the entire subject, securities practice tends to be divided in roughly the same way as the division in the SEC staff: disclosure, enforcement, and regulation.

Disclosure practice revolves around the preparation of the various documents that have to be filed with the SEC. Because of the great amount of time and care that goes into 1933 Act registration statements, and the substantial fees that lawyers charge for this kind of work, drafting disclosure documents has become an important sub-specialty. Legal representation of underwriters in 1933 Act offerings tends to be concentrated in a relatively small number of firms in the major financial centers. On the other hand, many lawyers who have not specialized in securities work may find themselves representing the issuer in a 1933 Act registration when a privately-owned company they have represented decides to "go public."

The second major branch of "disclosure" work grows for lawyers out of general representation of publicly-owned corporations. This work may include preparation of proxy statements and other documents in connection with annual meetings or mergers, advice to corporate officers, directors and "insiders" regarding their transactions in the corporation's securities, and preparation of other documents required by the 1934 Act.

Whereas "disclosure" work falls generally into the province of the office lawyer, "enforcement" work falls more within the province of the litigator. Enforcement work may consist of representing broker-dealers or others charged by the SEC with violations of the securities laws, but it also includes representation of plaintiffs and defendants in the rapidly increasing numbers of private damage actions alleging similar violations.

A relatively small number of lawyers specialize in the "regulation" side of the SEC's activity, representing the interests of individual firms or trade groups in SEC rule-making proceedings, Congressional hearings, and other policy-making activities.

In addition to the lawyers specializing in one or another branch of securities work, there are many thousands more engaged in general business practice who from time to time face a question of securities law, such as whether a particular transaction requires registration under the 1933 Act, or whether a defrauded client can get into federal court by adding a 1934 Act claim to his state law claims. This treatise is designed to provide a basic groundwork for the lawyers specializing in the securities field, as well as a basic familiarity with the coverage and concepts of the securities laws for those who anticipate less frequent encounters with those concepts.

§ 1.1 Overview of the Securities Markets and Their Operation

§ 1.1[1] Securities Markets and Regulation in Context[1]

Securities[2] occupy a unique and important place in American life. Securities are the instruments which evidence the financial rights, and in some

---

§ 1.1

1. Portions of this subsection were adapted from David L. Ratner & Thomas Lee Hazen, Securities Regulation: Cases and Materials ch. 1 (5th ed. 1996).

2. A "security, in business economics, [is] a written evidence of ownership conferring the right to receive property not currently in possession of the holder. The most common forms of

instances, the power to control, the corporations which own the great majority of our nation's and the world's productive facilities. Securities are the instruments through which business enterprises and governmental entities raise a substantial portion of the funds that are used to finance new capital. Securities are the instruments in which many millions of Americans (and investors all over the world) invest their savings in order to provide for their retirement income, education for their children, or in the hopes of achieving a higher standard of living for themselves and their family. And, inevitably, securities are the instruments by which unscrupulous promoters and sales people prey on those hopes and desires by selling overvalued (or even worthless) paper to many thousands of people every year.

Taken literally, the concept of a security is based on the condition of being secure and free from danger;[3] in reality this is anything but the case with respect to investment securities. The feature which distinguishes securities from most other commodities in which people deal is that securities have no intrinsic value in themselves—securities represent rights in something else. The value of a bond, note, or other promise to pay depends upon the financial position of the promisor. The value of a share of stock depends on the profitability or future prospects of the corporation or other entity which issued it. The market price of stock depends on how much other people are willing to pay for the stock, based on their evaluation of the company's prospects.

The foregoing characteristics of securities give a distinctive coloration to the regulation of transactions in securities, in contrast to the regulation of transactions in goods or commodities. Most goods are produced, distributed, and used or consumed. Governmental regulation of goods generally focuses on protecting the ultimate consumer against dangerous articles, misleading advertising, and unfair or non-competitive pricing practices. Securities are different.

The first difference is that securities are created rather than produced. Securities can be issued in unlimited amounts and virtually without any costs since securities are nothing in themselves but rather represent only an interest in something else. Therefore, an important focus of securities regulation is assuring that when securities are created and offered to the public, investors have an accurate idea of what that "something else" is and how much of an interest in that "something else" the security in question represents.

The second difference is that unlike goods, securities are not used or consumed by their purchasers. Securities become a kind of currency,[4] traded in the so-called "secondary markets"[5] at fluctuating prices. These "second-

---

securities are stocks (or shares) and bonds." The New Encyclopaedia Britannica (15th ed. Micropaedia 1998). *See also, e.g.*, Oxford English Dictionary (2d ed. 1989) (a security is "[a] document held by a creditor as guarantee of his right to payment Hence, any particular kind of stock, shares, or other form of investment guaranteed by such documents"). The statutory definition of security is discussed in § 1.6 *infra*.

3. Security has thus been defined as "the condition of being protected from or not exposed to danger; safety." Oxford English Dictionary (2d ed. 1989). *See also* footnote 2 *supra*.

4. In fact, securities are treated similarly to other cash-like "negotiable instruments under the Uniform Commercial Code." *See* Article 8 of the Uniform Commercial Code.

5. "Secondary" markets is the term used to refer to the trading of securities between buyers and sellers as opposed to investors who initially purchase the security directly from the company

ary'' transactions[6] far outweigh, in number and volume, the offerings of newly created securities (frequently referred to as initial public offerings or IPOs). A second important focus of securities regulation, therefore, is to ensure that there is a continuous flow of information about the corporation or other entity that is represented[7] by the securities being actively traded in the secondary markets.

The third difference between securities and goods involves the intangible and complex nature of securities. Since the complexity of securities invites unscrupulous people to attempt to cheat or mislead investors and traders, the securities laws contain provisions prohibiting a wide variety of fraudulent, manipulative, or deceptive practices.[8] These provisions have been applied to a wide range of activities, including trading on inside information,[9] misleading corporate publicity,[10] and improper dealings by corporate management.[11]

Fourth, and finally, since a large industry has grown up to buy and sell securities for investors and traders, securities regulation is concerned with the regulation of people and firms engaged in the business,[12] in order to assure that they do not take advantage of their superior experience and access to overreach their nonprofessional customers.

§ 1.1[2] The Securities Markets

Securities are traded through facilities known as ''markets'' which often take the form of an ''exchange.'' These markets may have physical locations, but in many instances are simply formal or informal systems of communication through which buyers and sellers make their interests known and consummate transactions. There are many different markets for securities.

Publicly held securities in the United States are traded both on formally centrally organized securities exchanges, which are operated as auction markets, and in the more loosely organized ''over-the-counter'' markets which operate through a more fragmented ''market maker'' system.[14] The largest and most prestigious national securities exchange in the United States is the New York Stock Exchange which for many years was followed both in size and in prestige by the American Stock Exchange that was acquired by the New York Stock Exchange in 2008.[15] Today the New York Stock Exchange and the Nasdaq Stock Market are the two largest securities exchanges in the United States. Both of these national exchanges are recognized and regulated

---

issuing the securities. The securities exchanges and over-the-counter markets are the secondary markets for publicly traded securities. The regulation of these markets is discussed in chapter 14 *infra*.

6. Secondary transactions are discussed in various sections throughout this treatise. *See, e.g.,* § 4.26 *infra*.

7. Securities regulation describes the corporation or entity as the ''issuer'' of the securities. *See, e.g.,* section 2(a)(4) of the Securities Act of 1933, 15 U.S.C.A. § 77b(a)(4).

8. *See, e.g.,* sections 9, 10, and 15 of the Securities Exchange Act of 1934, 15 U.S.C.A. §§ 78i, 78j, 78*o*, which are discussed in § 12.1 *infra*.

9. *See* § 12.17 *infra*.

10. *See, e.g.,* § 12.19 *infra*.

11. *See, e.g.,* § 12.20 *infra*.

12. *See* chapter 14 *infra* for discussion of broker-dealers and their regulation.

14. Market makers are discussed in § 14.10 *infra*.

15. *See* NYSE Euronext Press Release, AMEX Members Approve Acquisition of AMEX by NYSE Euronext June 18, 2008); NYSE Euronext to Acquire American Stock Exchange, Business Wire (Jan. 16, 2008).

pursuant to section 6 of the Securities Exchange Act of 1934[16] and thus are subject to supervision and oversight by the Securities and Exchange Commission.[17] The exchanges, which are modeled on an auction system, provide investor protection through the minimum standards for securities as imposed by their listing requirements and also through their requirements for broker-dealer membership. Beyond the two major national exchanges, there are seven other exchanges, many of them referred to as regional exchanges: the Boston Stock Exchange, the Chicago Board Options Exchange, the Cincinnati Stock Exchange,[18] the Chicago Stock Exchange,[19] the Philadelphia Stock Exchange,[20] and the Pacific Stock Exchange.[21] A number of the stocks traded on some regional exchanges are also traded on the New York Stock Exchange. Beginning in the 1970s, some of the regional exchanges began to focus more on options than on equity securities.[22] The American Stock Exchange became active as a securities options market. The New York Stock Exchange subsequently began listing options as well. Although the physical floor of the exchange is in theory the focus of the auction process, technology has removed a significant number of transactions from the floor of the exchange to computers.

In 2000, the SEC approved the application of the International Securities Exchange to be registered as a national securities exchange.[23] The ISE is the first attempt to adapt the auctions system applicable to securities exchange to an entirely electronic environment.[24] The number of registered securities exchanges is likely to increase even further. In 2001, NASDAQ filed an application with the SEC to be recognized as a national securities exchange.[25] In January 2006, the SEC approved the Nasdaq Stock Market's application to be registered as a national securities exchange.[26] Also, as a result of the Commodity Futures Modernization Act of 2000,[27] there could well be new

16. 15 U.S.C.A. § 78f.

17. 15 U.S.C.A. § 78f. *See* § 14.3 *infra* for a discussion of the markets' structure and regulation.

18. The Cincinnati Stock Exchange is located in Chicago, Illinois.

19. The Chicago Stock Exchange was previously known as the Midwest Stock Exchange, which in 1959 acquired the New Orleans Stock Exchange. The Chicago Stock Exchange formerly had seats much like the New York Stock Exchange but currently is fully electronic.

20. In 2008, Nasdaq acquired the Philadelphia Stock Exchange. *See* Nasdaq OMX Group Announces Completion of Phlx Acquisition, Sec. L. Daily (BNA), http://pubs.bna.com/ip/bna/sld.nsf/eh/A0B6W2H7Q5 (July 25, 2008).

21. As of 1990, there were eleven registered national securities exchanges which, in addition to the exchanges listed in the text, included the Intermountain Stock Exchange, Prior to 1991, there was a tenth registered exchange; however, the Spokane Stock Exchange became a casualty of the SEC's increased enforcement efforts with regard to penny stocks. The SEC's penny stock rules are discussed in § 14.19 *infra*.

22. For discussion of the options markets *see* SEC, Report of the Special Study of the Options Markets, 96th Cong. 1st Sess. (1978). *See also* §§ 1.5, 1.7 *infra* for discussion of the explosion of stock options and other derivative investments.

23. Approval of Application for Exchange Registration International Securities Exchange LLC, SEC News Digest 2000–36, 2000 WL 218366 (S.E.C.) (SEC February 25, 2000).

24. *See* Notice of Filing of Proposed Rule Change by the International Securities Exchange LLC, 66 FR 36353–01, 2001 WL 768983 (F.R.) (SEC July 11, 2001); Commission Grants ISE Exemption to Accommodate its Electronic Market in the Marketwide Data System, SEC News Digest 2000–101, 2000 WL 681095 (S.E.C.) (SEC May 26, 2000).

25. Fed. Sec. L. Rep. (CCH) Report Bulletin No. 1981 p. 4 (June 13, 2001).

26. *See* Approval of Nasdaq Stock Market LLC Exchange Application, 2006 WL 77691 (SEC Jan. 13, 2006).

27. Pub. Law 106–554, 114 Stat. 2763 (December 21, 2000).

exchanges recognized for the limited purpose of trading securities futures products.[28]

In 2006, the New York Stock Exchange (NYSE) expanded its electronic order execution capabilities when it merged with Archipelago which had been one of the largest electronic communications networks (ECNs).[29] Then, the NYSE eyed international expansion when it entered into an agreement to merge with Euronext, a major offshore trading facility.[30] In 2008, the New York Stock Exchange announced its decision to acquire the American Stock Exchange which at one time had been a potent rival to the NYSE.[31] The new market landscape undoubtedly has regulatory consequences.[32]

Over the years, trading on the floor of the New York Stock Exchange has become increasingly automated. By 2007, most trading functions of specialists and other floor traders had been transferred to electronic trading.[33]

The National Association of Securities Dealers (NASD) was the self-regulatory organization that was organized and governed under the oversight of the Securities and Exchange Commission pursuant to section 15 of the Securities Exchange Act of 1934.[38] In 2007, the regulatory arm of the NASD (known as NASD Regulation or NASDR) merged with the regulatory arm of the New York Stock Exchange to form the Financial Industry Regulatory Authority (FINRA) that carries out the functions formerly handled by NASDR and New York Stock Exchange Regulation.

§ 1.1[3] The Securities Industry[44]

The securities industry is characterized by great diversity, both in size and function. There are several thousand firms engaged in one or more types of securities activities, ranging from large multi-service firms engaged in brokerage, market-making, underwriting, investment advice, and fund management, as well as commodities, real estate dealings, and a variety of other financial services including banking and insurance. There also are small or even one-person firms engaged solely in selling mutual fund shares or dealing in a few securities of local or regional interest.

28. *See* Registration of National Securities Exchanges Pursuant to Section 6(g) of the Securities Exchange Act of 1934 and Proposed Rule Changes of National Securities Exchanges and Limited Purpose National Securities Associations, Sec. Exch. Act Rel. No. 34–44279 2001 WL 491727 (SEC May 8, 2001).

29. *See* NYSE, Archipelago Merger Complete; New for-Profit Company to Begin Trading, 38 Sec. Reg. & L. Rep. (BNA) 414 (March 13, 2006).

30. *See* NYSE, Euronext $20B Merger Plan Would Create World's Largest Exchange, 38 Sec. Reg. & L. Rep. (BNA) 962 (June 5, 2006). *But cf.* Italy's Stock Mart in Talks Over Possible Merger With Euronext, Sec. Reg. & L. Rep. (BNA) 1016 (June 12, 2006); Euronext Favors NYSE Proposal But Shareholders May Want Higher Offer, 38 Sec. Reg. & L. Rep. (BNA) 914 (May 29, 2006).

31. *See, e.g.,* Aaron Lucchetti, NYSE, Amex Finally Marrying, Wall St. J. p. C3, http://online.wsj.com/article/SB120060675290298637.html?mod=hps_us_whats_news (Jan. 18, 2008).

32. *See, e.g.,* Chris Brummer, Stock Exchanges and the New Market for Securities Laws, 75 U. Chi. L. Rev. 1435 (2008).

33. *See, e.g.,* Aaron Luchetti, The NYSE: Faster (and Lonelier)—Historic Electronic–Trading Shift Means Swift service for Investors, "Painful" Time for Brokers on the Floor, Wall St. J. p. C1 (Jan. 24, 2007).

38. 15 U.S.C.A. § 78*o*.

44. This subsection was adapted from David L. Ratner & Thomas Lee Hazen, Securities Regulation: Cases and Materials 3–4 (5th ed. 1996).

From the passage in 1933 of the former Glass–Steagall Act,[45] which prohibited banks from dealing in securities (except government bonds), the securities industry consisted of a relatively separate and well-defined group of firms. However, with the increasing tendency for individuals to make their equity investments indirectly through institutions, rather than trading directly in stock for their own account, securities firms came increasingly into competition with banks, insurance companies, and other financial institutions. At the same time that securities firms began offering their customers an increasing number of financial services that traditionally had been associated with commercial banking, commercial banks entered into many areas that formerly were reserved for investment bankers and securities firms. This competition placed severe strains on the existing regulatory structure under which securities firms, banks, and insurance companies are regulated by different agencies with entirely different concerns and approaches. In 1999, Congress repealed most provisions of Glass–Steagall[46] and paved the way for even more competition among and between financial institutions that can now offer a wide variety of financial services to their customers. Although the former separation of commercial and investment banking activities was eliminated in 1999, two provisions of Glass–Steagall remain in force. While there is no longer the strict prohibition against the same company engaging in commercial and investment banking, if a company does offer multiple financial services combining both investment and commercial banking aspects, it must be in the form of separate entities although they may be under the single umbrella of a financial services holding company.[47]

§ 1.1[4] The Regulatory System[48]

In addition to regulation of the securities markets, the federal securities laws regulate the companies issuing securities ("issuers"[49]) as well as purchasers and sellers of securities. Securities trading activities can be divided into two basic subgroups. Most of the day-to-day trading on both the securities exchanges and over-the-counter markets consists of "secondary" transactions between investors and involve securities that have previously been issued by the corporation or other issuer. All of the proceeds from these secondary sales, after applicable commissions to the securities brokers handling the transaction, go to the investors who are parting with their securities. None of these proceeds from secondary transactions in the securities markets flow back to the companies issuing the securities. This aspect of the secondary securities markets is frequently referred to as "trading" (as opposed to "distribution" of

45. The Banking Act of 1933, Ch. 89, 48 Stat. 184 (1933), codified in various sections of 12 U.S.C.A. (1999) *See* in particular 12 U.S.C.A. §§ 24, 378(a) (1999).

46. The Glass–Steagall Act was repealed by Pub. Law. 106–102, 1999 U.S.C.C.A.N. (113 Stat.) 1338. *See generally* Symposium, 4 N.C. Banking Inst. 1 (2000); Michael K. O'Neal, Summary and Analysis of the Gramm–Leach–Bliley Act 28 Sec. Reg. L.J. 95 (2000).

47. Section 16 of the Glass–Steagall Act amended the National Banking Act and required that the banking entity cannot engage in investment banking nor securities activities directly. 12 U.S.C.A. § 24 (seventh). Section 21 of the Glass Steagall Act prohibited securities firms from directly offering banking services and this remains in force as well. 12 U.S.C.A. § 378(a)(1). For a description of all four original section of the Glass–Steagall Act, see Securities Industry Association v. Board of Governors of the Federal Reserve System, 839 F.2d 47, 54–56 (2d Cir. 1988), *cert. denied*, 486 U.S. 1059, 108 S.Ct. 2830, 100 L.Ed.2d 931 (1988).

48. *See also* § 1.2 *infra*. For discussion of the impact of the regulatory system on the applicability of the antitrust laws, *see* § 14.1[9] *infra*.

49. Section 2(a)(4) of the 1933 Act defines "issuer". 15 U.S.C.A. § 77b(a)(4). *See* § 4.26[1] *infra*.

securities) and is regulated primarily by the provisions of the Securities and Exchange Act of 1934.[50] The regulation of the securities trading markets is termed market regulation. In 2007, the SEC division that handles in charge of market regulation changed its name from the Division of Market Regulation to the Division of Trading and Markets.[51]

The process by which securities are first offered to the public, frequently referred to as primary offerings or distributions, is governed primarily by the Securities Act of 1933.[52] This is the way in which corporate capital is raised in the public equity markets. Also covered by the Securities Act of 1933 and included within the concept of securities distributions are so-called secondary "distributions"[53] which occur, for example, when an extremely large block of securities has been placed in the hands of a private investor, institution, or group of investors and is subsequently offered by the selling shareholders to the members of the general public. As is the case with secondary transactions generally, the proceeds from secondary distributions inure to the benefit of the selling shareholder(s). In the case of both primary and secondary distributions,[54] unless an appropriate exemption is applicable, registration of the securities will be required under the Securities Act of 1933.[55] This, then, is the focus of the 1933 Act: initial public offerings, primary, and secondary distributions of securities; although some selected provisions of the Act apply to more private, non-open-market transactions. Whereas the distribution process triggers the registration provisions of the 1933 Act, for the most part the extent to which securities are widely held and actively traded triggers the jurisdictional requirements of the Securities Exchange Act of 1934.[56] Registration and periodic reporting by issuers under the 1934 Exchange Act depend generally upon the degree to which the securities are widely held.[57]

In addition to the securities markets, investors may look to the various commodities markets and the trading of commodity futures. At one time, the commodities markets were limited to agricultural and other tangible commodities such as precious metals and fossil fuels. Today, more than seventy percent of all commodity futures transactions involve financial futures. There thus has developed a wide range of overlapping or hybrid investments that have attributes of both commodities and securities. Although there have been

50. 15 U.S.C.A. § 78a *et seq.*

51. *See* SEC News Release, SEC Renames Division of Market Regulation as Division of Trading and Markets, S.E.C. 07–229, 2007 WL 3360200 (SEC Nov. 14, 2007).

52. 15 U.S.C.A. § 77a *et seq.*

53. In contrast to the secondary trading that takes place in the securities markets on a daily basis.

54. Primary and secondary distributions can occur as separate transactions or can be "piggy backed" into one registered offering. It is not uncommon for an offering to be a combination of a primary and secondary distribution. *Cf.* Moffat v. Harcourt Brace & Co., 892 F.Supp. 1431 (M.D.Fla.1994) (issuer's delay in applying for registration did not violate agreement with holder of "piggy back" registration rights).

55. *See* chapters 2, 3 *infra.*

56. An important exception is found in the general antifraud Rule 10b–5, 17 C.F.R. § 240.10b–5, the reach of which extends to purchases or sales of any securities where the facilities of interstate commerce are implicated. Rule 10b–5 and the implied private right of action thereunder are discussed in chapter 12 *infra.* In addition to Rule 10b–5, the general antifraud proscription in connection with tender offers, section 14(e), is not limited to companies subject to the 1934 Act's registration and periodic reporting requirements. 15 U.S.C.A. § 78n(e), which is discussed in § 11.6 *infra.*

57. *See* § 9.2–9.3 *infra.*

a number of jurisdictional disputes,[58] the commodities futures markets generally are regulated by the Commodity Futures Trading Commission pursuant to the Commodity Exchange Act.[59] Beginning in the 1970s and carrying through the 1980s and 1990s, the futures and commodity options markets regulated by the CFTC and the options markets regulated by the SEC have become increasingly competitive with the increased trading in derivative financial instruments, including treasury bill, foreign currency and stock index futures (as compared, for example, with the trading of stock index and foreign currency options).[60] Options on securities are regulated by the SEC, but futures and commodity options (including options on futures) are not subject to SEC regulation[61] but rather are left to the Commodity Futures Trading Commission.[62]

§ 1.2 History, Scope, and Coverage of Federal and State Securities Regulatory Schemes

§ 1.2[1] The Antecedents of Securities Regulation in the United States

As pointed out in the preceding section of this treatise,[1] securities are complex investment instruments that differ significantly from other things that are traded in commerce to the extent that securities are intangible and are neither produced nor consumed. Additionally, in large part because of their very nature, securities and the securities markets have been particularly susceptible to fraud and manipulation. The various laws that regulate securities transactions have been designed to address this susceptibility. These laws have a rich history and predate regulation in the United States.

The regulation of securities transactions began with the regulation of the dealers in securities. Over time the regulation expanded to cover the companies issuing the securities as well as the market place itself. Today there is widespread regulation of all aspects of securities transactions and the market place.

Regulation of securities brokers dates back to the thirteenth century. This early regulation authorized licensing securities brokers in London.[2] Stock exchange dealings, with speculation subject to alternate booms and panics, became a part of the English markets in the latter part of the seventeenth century. Trading in shares of stock led to periods of speculation and wild

---

58. For example, one area of current dispute is whether managed commodities accounts are securities. *See* § 1.7 *infra.*

59. 7 U.S.C.A. § 1–24. *See generally* Philip M. Johnson & Thomas L. Hazen, Derivatives Regulation (2004); Commodities Futures L.Rep. (CCH).

60. Although the form of a futures contract may differ from a listed option, their operational effect and investment strategies are very similar, if not identical, when dealing with financial options and futures.

61. In a controversial ruling, the SEC granted securities exchanges' applications to list index participation units which have some characteristics of futures but were found to be securities. Sec. Exch. Act Rel. No. 34–26709 (April 11, 1989). *See* §§ 1.5, 1.7 *infra.*

62. *See generally* Philip M. Johnson & Thomas L. Hazen, Derivatives Regulation (2004).

§ 1.2

1. *See* § 1.1[1] *supra.*

2. Statute of Edward I, in 1285. *See* S. Killik, The Work of the Stock Exchange 12 (2d ed. 1934); 1 Louis Loss & Joel Seligman, Securities Regulation § 1–A (3d ed. 1989).

fluctuations in the market.[3] This was followed by English legislation by the end of the seventeenth century, which was enacted to protect investors against unscrupulous manipulation by stock jobbers and stock brokers.[5] Investment schemes throughout Europe led to many frauds including the infamous South Sea Bubble.

The South Sea Company was one of the arch speculators in, and manipulators of, its own shares.[7] These manipulations eventually caused a great increase in the market price of its shares. The huge increase in the price of South Sea Company shares led to a tremendous wave of company promotions and to speculation in the securities of newly formed companies. On one day, for example, one thousand persons subscribed to shares in a company "for carrying on an undertaking of great importance, but nobody to know what it is."[8] In 1719, the South Sea Company launched an ambitious program to persuade investors holding government bonds and annuities to exchange them for shares of its stock. To make some funds available for speculation in its shares and to check the floatation of new companies competing for public funds, the South Sea Company inspired passage of the Bubble Act of 1720.[9] The purported objective of the Bubble Act was to prevent unwary persons from investing in fraudulent projects or undertakings. It prohibited unincorporated companies from acting as though they were corporate bodies or pretending that their shares were transferable. The South Sea Company and certain other existing companies were exempted from its prohibitions. The Bubble Act was not well drafted and failed to define clearly the practices and offenses it sought to prevent.[10] The Bubble Act was eventually repealed in 1825.[11]

The Joint Stock Companies Registration Act of 1844,[12] entitled "An Act for the Registration, Incorporation, and Regulation of Joint Stock Companies," was the first general companies act under which a joint stock company could become incorporated in England.[13] The Companies Act of 1844 also

3. Promoters of both incorporated and unincorporated companies foisted doubtful schemes on the investing public. *See* 1 James D. Cox & Thomas Lee Hazen, Cox & Hazen on Corporations § 2.2 (2d ed. 2002).

5. 8 & 9 Wm. 3, ch. 32 (1697) ("An act to restrain the number and ill practice of brokers and stock jobbers"); *see* Lane, The Years Before the Stock Exchange, 7 Hist. Today 760, 761 (1957); 1 Louis Loss & Joel Seligman, Securities Regulation § 1–A (3d ed. 1989).

7. This paragraph was adapted from 1 James D. Cox, Thomas Lee Hazen & F. Hodge O'Neal, Corporation § 2.2 (2000).

8. William Searle Holdsworth, A History of English Law 214–215 (5th ed. 1942); Leslie W. Melville, South Sea Bubble 97 (1921). *See also* John Carswell, The South Sea Bubble (1960); Virginia Cowles, The Great Swindle: The Story of the South Sea Bubble (1960).

9. 96 Geo. I, ch. 18. 2 Wood's Collyer on the Law of Partnership §§ 826, 827 at 1200, 1203 (Horace G. Wood ed. 1878).

10. The Bubble Act was a product of haste and self-interest. This ambiguous and incoherent legislation long caused great uncertainty and confusion and raised unnecessary doubts about the validity of the issuance of transferable shares by legitimate unincorporated companies. *See* 1 James D. Cox & Thomas Lee Hazen, Cox & Hazen on Corporations § 2.2 (2d ed. 2002).

11. 6 Geo. 4, ch. 91. *See* A. Dubois, The English Business Company after the Bubble Act 1720–1800 (1938).

12. 127 & 8 Vict., ch. 110.

13. "Joint stock company" was defined as a commercial partnership with more than 25 members or with capital divided into freely transferable shares. The 1844 Act compelled such companies to incorporate by registering their names, addresses, and purposes, and granted registered companies the corporate privilege of suing and being sued as entities. A company's members, however, remained subject to unlimited liability and could not absolve themselves from

enacted the first modern prospectus requirement.[14] And one of its descendants formed the basis for legislation in the United States.[15] As discussed in the next subsection of this treatise,[16] securities regulation in the United States began with the states.[17] This was followed twenty-six years later with the enactment of this nation's first federal regulation of securities transactions.

The first federal securities regulation was contained in the Securities Act of 1933 which grew out of the New Deal. The initial push for regulation in this country started years earlier in reaction to the Panic of 1907. In October 1907:

> depositors lost confidence in several New York banks which were thought to be part of a group of stock market operators who met with financial ruin when they failed to corner the market in the stock of a copper mining company they controlled. Prices on the New York Stock Exchange fell precipitously, and the bank run spread. By the time confidence was restored, the country was in a recession, many banks had closed, and many small investors had been ruined. Before long, many people came to believe that stock market operators who stood to profit from lower stock prices had engineered the price collapse. Believing that the price collapse precipitated widespread panic across the economy, these people demanded that the government intervene.
>
> In January 1908, President Theodore Roosevelt informed Congress that it would be desirable to adopt measures "to prevent at least the grosser forms of gambling in securities and commodities, such as making large sales of what men do not possess and 'cornering' the market."[18]

As pointed out above, the roots of the Securities Act of 1933 predated these events. The 1933 Act borrowed heavily from regulation that was adopted in England.[19] Federal securities regulation in the United States followed state regulation of securities[20] and several centuries of legislation in England. It has thus been observed that "the problems at which modern securities regulation is directed are as old as the cupidity of sellers and the gullibility of buyers."[21]

---

such liability to third parties even by provisions in their agreement of organization. *See* 1 James D. Cox & Thomas Lee Hazen, Cox & Hazen on Corporations § 2.2 (2d ed. 2002).

14. 7 & 8 Vict., ch. 110.

15. The definition of prospectus in the Securities Act of 1933 (1933 Act § 2(a)(10), 15 U.S.C.A. § 77b(a)(10)) was patterned on the British Companies Act of 1929. *See* Gustafson v. Alloyd Co., 513 U.S. 561, 599–600, 115 S.Ct. 1061, 131 L.Ed.2d 1 (1995) (Ginsburg, J., dissenting).

16. *See* § 1.2[2] *infra.*

17. Kans.Laws 1911, c. 133. Selective regulation predated the Kansas enactment. Some more limited securities regulation existed before the Kansas statute. For example, in 1852 Massachusetts was regulating securities issued by common carriers. *See* Harry G. Henn & John R. Alexander, Laws of Corporations 843 (3d ed. 1983).

State securities regulation was challenged as beyond the power of the states but was held to be constitutional as a valid use of police power of the states to protect the public against "speculative schemes." Hall v. Geiger–Jones Co., 242 U.S. 539, 550, 37 S.Ct. 217, 220, 61 L.Ed. 480 (1917).

18. Steve Thel, The Original Conception of Section 10(b) of the Securities Exchange Act, 42 Stan. L. Rev. 385, 395–396 (1990).

19. *See, e.g.,* Stuart Banner, Anglo–American Securities Regulation: Cultural and Political Roots, 1690–1860 (1998); Paul G. Mahoney, Essay and Review: The Pernicious Art of Securities Regulation, 66 U. Chi. L. Rev. 1373 (1999).

20. *See* § 1.2[2] *infra.* State laws are also discussed in chapter 8 *infra.*

21. Louis Loss & Joel Seligman, Securities Regulation § 1–A (3d ed. 1989). *See also, e.g.,* J. Carswell, The South Sea Bubble (1960); J. Francis, History of the Bank of England, Its Times and Traditions ch. 8 (1862); L. Melville, The South Sea Bubble viii (1921).

§ 1.2[2] The Regulatory Era Begins—State Securities Laws

Beginning in the late nineteenth century, industrialists located primarily in the eastern part of the United States found fertile ground for securities in the developing American frontier. There were many questionable promotional practices and, as a consequence, pressures arose to regulate the marketing of fraudulently valued securities. Accordingly, in 1911, Kansas passed the first state securities statutory regulatory scheme. This, like subsequent securities legislation in other states, has come to be known as a "blue sky law."

There are a number of explanations for the derivation of the "blue sky" appellation, the most common of which was because of the Kansas statute's purpose to protect the Kansas farmers against the industrialists selling them a piece of the blue sky. Or, as stated by an early decision, these state securities laws were designed to prevent "speculative schemes which have no more basis than so many feet of blue sky."[25] A number of states followed suit and blue sky laws began to spring up throughout the country. Today, all states have blue sky legislation.

As enacted, the state blue sky laws not only focused on providing investors with full disclosure of relevant facts, but also required that all securities registered thereunder "qualify" on a merit basis, evaluating the substantive terms of the securities to be offered. Blue sky laws continue to retain this dual regulatory focus. In order to rule on the merits of such investments, the state securities commissioner or administrator typically was given the power to determine whether the securities were suitable for sale. Notwithstanding the broad regulatory potential of the merit approach, the blue sky laws proved to be relatively ineffective in stamping out securities frauds, especially on a national level.[27] Following enactment of the early state securities laws, federal legislation was successfully resisted for a while. However, the stock market crash of 1929 is properly described as the straw that broke the camel's back. The era that followed ushered in federal securities regulation.[28]

The scope of state blue sky laws was significantly curtailed in 1996 with the enactment of the National Securities Markets Improvement Act of 1996.[29] These 1996 amendments to the federal securities laws reversed the pattern established under the first sixty-three years of federal securities regulation of concurrent state and federal regulation. The former regime of concurrent state and federal regulation was narrowed since the 1996 amendments explicitly preempted state law in many areas of securities regulation.[30] Particularly affected were the registration and reporting requirements applicable to securities transactions. State regulation of broker-dealers[31] and investment advis-

25. *See* Hall v. Geiger–Jones Co., 242 U.S. 539, 550, 37 S.Ct. 217, 221, 61 L.Ed. 480 (1917).

27. Although such a merit analysis exists in many states in limited form, it has not had a significant impact in eliminating unduly speculative securities from the public markets.

28. *See* § 1.2[3] *infra*.

29. Pub. L. No. 104–290, 110 Stat. 3416 (1996). *See, e.g.,* Symposium, The National Securities Markets Improvements Act–One Year Later, 53 Bus. Law. 507 (1998); Comment, The National Securities Market Improvement Act: How Improved is the Securities Market?, 36 Duq. L. Rev. 365 (1998).

30. The preemptive legislation is discussed throughout this treatise. *See* in particular the discussion in § 8.1[2] *infra*.

31. Broker-dealer regulation is discussed in chapter 14 *infra*.

ers[32] was also curtailed. The National Securities Markets Improvement Act preempts the states from imposing the specified regulatory provisions but does not preclude state law fraud actions.[33] In addition, the Securities Litigation Uniform Standards Act of 1998 preempts certain securities fraud class actions involving publicly traded securities.[34]

§ 1.2[3] The New Deal and Federal Regulation

Although the general economic conditions played a considerable role leading up to the Wall Street crash of 1929, the number of fraudulently floated securities that contributed to the great crash should not be underestimated. In fact, the congressional hearings which culminated in the first federal securities legislation are replete with examples of outrageous conduct by securities promoters that most certainly had a disastrous impact on our nation's economy. In relatively short order, Congress entered into the regulatory arena with its first major New Deal legislation—the Securities Act of 1933,[35] which became known as the "Truth in Securities" Act.[36] The federal legislation, which has been characterized as the first true consumer protection law, contained many of the features of state blue sky laws, except that it did not (and, as amended, still does not) establish a system of merit regulation. Instead, under the guidance of a federal agency, the Act focuses on disclosure. The focus on disclosure was based on the conclusion that sunlight is the best disinfectant.[38] At the time of enactment, the 1933 Act was administered by the Federal Trade Commission. The FTC's securities law jurisdiction was replaced in 1934 with the creation of the Securities and Exchange Commission.[39] The 1933 Act quite properly has been characterized as a great success in balancing the needs of investors and the public generally against the desire to maintain free and efficient markets.[40]

§ 1.2[3][A] The Securities Act of 1933

The Securities Act of 1933,[41] 8.5 as noted in the preceding section, is directed primarily at the distribution of securities. The 1933 Act does not address trading in the aftermarket once the distribution process is complete. Subject to certain enumerated exemptions, the 1933 Act generally requires the registration of offerings and distributions of securities that end up in the hands of the investing public, regardless of whether the distribution to the

---

32. Investment adviser regulation is discussed in chapter 21 *infra*.

33. Zuri–Invest AG v. Natwest Finance Inc., 177 F.Supp.2d 189 (S.D.N.Y.2001).

34. *See* §§ 7.17[2], 12.15[2] *infra*.

35. Act of May 27, 1933, c. 38, Title I, § 1, 48 Stat. 74, codified in 15 U.S.C.A. § 77a *et seq. See* chapters 2–7 *infra*.

36. Milton H. Cohen, "Truth in Securities" Revisited, 79 Harv.L.Rev. 1340 (1966).

38. This is the oft-cited phrase of Louis D. Brandeis. Louis D. Brandeis, Other People's Money ch. 5 (1914) ("sunlight is said to be the best of disinfectants electric light the most efficient policeman").

39. The organization and operation of the Securities and Exchange Commission is discussed in §§ 1.2[3][C], 1.3,–1.4, and chapter 16 *infra*.

40. *See, e.g.,* Paul G. Mahoney, The Political Economy of the Securities Act of 1933, 30 J. Leg. Stud. 1, 31 (2001) ("The Securities Act accordingly provides a useful cautionary tale about the efficacy of economic regulation. The act is generally regarded as one of the greatest success stories of the New Deal. Unlike many regulatory statutes, it has been largely untouched by claims that it raises entry barriers or enforces cartel agreements among members of the regulated industry").

41. Act of May 27, 1933, c. 38, Title I, § 1, 48 Stat. 74, 15 U.S.C.A. § 77a *et seq.*

public is accomplished through a primary or secondary offering.[42] After considerable debate, Congress decided not to follow the pattern of the state acts and eschewed the idea of a merit approach, opting instead for a system of full disclosure. The theory behind the federal regulatory framework is that investors are adequately protected if all relevant aspects of the securities being marketed are fully and fairly disclosed. The reasoning is that full disclosure provides investors with sufficient opportunity to evaluate the merits of an investment and fend for themselves. It is a basic tenet of federal securities regulation that investors' ability to make their own evaluations of available investments obviates any need that some observers may perceive for the more costly and time-consuming governmental merit analysis of the securities being offered.

The Securities Act of 1933 contains a number of private remedies for investors who are injured due to violations of the Act.[43] There are also general antifraud provisions which bar material omissions and misrepresentations in connection with the offer or sale of securities.[44] The scope of the Securities Act of 1933 is limited; first, insofar as its registration and disclosure provisions cover only distributions of securities and second, as its investor-protection reach extends only to purchasers (and not sellers) of securities.

§ 1.2[3][B] The Securities Exchange Act of 1934

In 1934, Congress enacted the Securities Exchange Act of 1934[45]1.5 which is a more omnibus regulation. The Securities Exchange Act of 1934 is referred to alternatively as the 1934 Act or as the Exchange Act. The extent of the regulation introduced by the Exchange Act was so vast that Congress felt it was not possible to continue overburdening the Federal Trade Commission with this new administrative responsibility and thus established the Securities and Exchange Commission which is now one of the most influential and well respected federal agencies, although it is relatively modest in size.4[46] The Securities Exchange Act of 1934 is directed at regulating all aspects of public trading of securities. The Act does not focus only on securities, their issuers,[48] purchasers, and sellers;[49] it also regulates the marketplace, including the exchanges, the over-the-counter markets, and broker-dealers generally.[50]

In terms of its investor-protection thrust, the Securities Exchange Act of 1934 has a much broader reach than the Securities Act of 1933. To begin with, the 1934 Act's protections extend to sellers as well as purchasers of securities. There are two distinct jurisdictional triggers for the 1934 Act's

42. *See* chapters 2, 3 *infra*. This includes not only primary distributions (sold by the issuer), but also secondary distributions wherein the securities are sold by individuals or institutions who did not acquire the securities in a public offering. *See* §§ 4.26–4.28 *infra*.

43. These are: section 11, 15 U.S.C.A. § 77k, for material misstatements and omissions in registration statements; section 12(a)(1), 15 U.S.C.A. § 77*l*(a)(1), for securities sold in violation of the registration requirements, and section 12(a)(2), 15 U.S.C.A. § 77*l*(a)(2), creating an action by purchasers against their sellers for material misstatements or omissions. *See* §§ 7.2, 7.6 *infra*.

44. Section 17(a), 15 U.S.C.A. § 77q(a). *See* § 7.11[1] *infra*.

45. Act of June 6, 1934, c. 404, Title I, § 1, 48 Stat. 881, 15 U.S.C.A. §§ 78a *et seq*.

46. *See generally* SEC, A Twenty–Five Year Summary of the Activities of the Securities and Exchange Commission 1934–1959 (1961).

48. *See* Chapter 9 *infra*. *See also* chapters 10 (proxy regulation), Chapter 11 (takeovers and tender offers), and Chapter 13 (insider reporting and short-swing profits) *infra*.

49. *See* chapter 12 *infra*.

50. *See* chapter 14 *infra*.

investor-protection provisions. First, the 1934 Act contains a general provision that bars fraud and material misstatements or omissions of material facts in connection with any purchase or sale of security.[51] The only jurisdictional limitation on this provision is that there must be the use of an instrumentality of interstate commerce.[52] Although these general antifraud proscriptions have a broad reach, the vast majority of the 1934 Act's regulation of securities issuers derives from the second jurisdictional trigger that is found in the Act's periodic reporting and disclosure requirements which emanate primarily from the fact that securities traded on a national exchange (and now most of those traded in the over-the-counter markets) must be registered with the Securities and Exchange Commission.[53]

Registration of a company's securities under the Exchange Act involves full disclosure of the company's business, financial position, and management as well as numerous periodic reporting requirements.[54] The Exchange Act also includes special provisions dealing with stock manipulation,[55] improper trading while in possession of non-public material information,[56] insider short swing profits,[57] and misstatements in documents filed with the Securities and Exchange Commission.[58] Further, because of the importance of shareholder suffrage in public issue corporations, Congress included regulation of the proxy machinery of all publicly traded corporations that are subject to the Act's reporting requirements.[59] Most of the foregoing provisions have been part of the regulatory scheme since the Act's inception in 1934. Subsequently, in 1968, Congress added the Williams Act amendments which impose candid disclosure and reporting requirements on tender offers and on other attempts to purchase control of publicly traded corporations.[60] Each of these provisions of the Exchange Act is taken up in more detail in subsequent sections of this treatise.

§ 1.2[3][C] The Securities and Exchange Commission

Since its inception, the Securities and Exchange Commission has played an important role in maintaining the efficiency and integrity of the American securities markets. However, the system is far from perfect. As the market crash of October 1987 and the market "break" of 1989 demonstrated, wild market gyrations can seriously harm investors who get caught in the squeeze. Just as the market crash of 1929 triggered the current regulatory frameworks, the 1987 crash has led to some regulatory changes, and the continued

51. Section 10(b), 15 U.S.C.A. § 78j(b). Most notable is Rule 10b–5 promulgated thereunder. 17 C.F.R. § 240.10b–5. *See* §§ 12.3, 12.4 *infra*.

52. The interstate commerce requirement has been broadly construed so as to make it highly doubtful that a case will ever be dismissed on the absence of this jurisdictional basis.

53. For purposes of the Act, the regional exchanges are regulated as national exchanges. *See* chapters 9, 14 *infra*. There is a class of securities which although not registered under the 1934 Act, are subject to the periodic reporting requirements. *See* § 9.3 *infra*.

54. *See* §§ 9.2, 9.3 *infra*.

55. Section 9, 15 U.S.C.A. § 78i; § 12.1 *infra*.

56. In addition to Rules 10b–5 and 14e–3, 17 C.F.R. §§ 240.10b–5, 240.14e–3, *see, e.g.*, sections 20A and 21(d)(2)(A), 15 U.S.C.A. § 78t–1, 78u(d)(2)(A). For a discussion of insider trading *see* § 12.17 *infra*.

57. Section 16(b), 15 U.S.C.A. § 78p(b); §§ 13.2–13.4 *infra*.

58. Section 18(a), 15 U.S.C.A. § 78r(a); § 12.19 *infra*.

59. Sections 14(a)-(c), 15 U.S.C.A. § 78n(a)-(c); chapter 10 *infra*.

60. Sections 13(d), (e), 14(d), (f), 15 U.S.C.A. § 78m(d)(e), n(d)(f); chapter 11 *infra*.

aftershocks are likely to lead to some more. The SEC, Congress, and others undertook numerous studies and investigated various ways to regulate market mechanisms in a manner that will preserve the market's efficiency and help prevent a repeat of the events of October 1987. Under the leadership of the SEC, the stock exchanges installed circuit breakers to help minimize the effect of sharp volatility in the securities markets. The 1990s brought in an expansion of trading in various types of derivative investments which resulted in struggles between the SEC and CFTC regarding jurisdiction over these investments. Also, the 1990s ushered in a new era—the use of the Internet for securities trading. This resulted in additional regulatory concerns that are considered throughout this treatise.

While no system is perfect, the SEC has had significant beneficial impact on the American securities markets and our regulatory framework has become a model for other countries. Needless to say, however, the SEC has not been without its critics.

§ 1.2[3][D] Other Federal Securities Laws

§ 1.2[3][D][1] The Public Utility Holding Company Act of 1935; the Trust Indenture Act of 1939; the Investment Company and Investment Advisers Acts of 1940; the Securities Investor Protection Act of 1970; and the Sarbanes–Oxley Act of 2002

Following the Securities Exchange Act of 1934, Congress enacted a number of additional securities laws that form part of the federal regulatory scheme. These additional five securities laws are as follows.

Public Utility Holding Company Act of 1935

The Public Utility Holding Company Act of 1935 dealt with the special problems raised by financing public issue utilities and, in particular, regulating the activities of large public utility holding company systems.[62] The Public Utility Holding Company Act affected relatively few companies which led to its repeal in 2005, seventy years after its adoption.

Trust Indenture Act of 1939

The Trust Indenture Act of 1939[64] addresses debt financing by issuing bonds to the public.[65] The substantive provisions of the Trust Indenture Act that apply to the both the indenture and debenture that comprise the corporate debt are in addition to any registration requirements under the Securities Act of 1933 or reporting or other disclosure requirements imposed by the Securities Exchange Act of 1934.

Investment Company Act of 1940

The Investment Company Act of 1940[66] provides for regulation of mutual funds and other investment companies. The Investment Company Act impos-

62. Pub.L. No. 74–333, 49 Stat. 803 (1935), codified as amended at 15 U.S.C.A. §§ 79–79z–6, discussed in chapter 18 *infra*.

64. Act of August 3, 1939, 53 Stat. 1149, codified in 15 U.S.C.A. §§ 77aaa *et seq.*and discussed in chapter 19 *infra*.

65. *See* chapter 19 *infra*.

66. Act of Aug. 22, 1940, 54 Stat. 789, codified in 15 U.S.C.A. §§ 80a–1 through 80a–52, discussed in chapter 20 *infra*.

es governance and other structural requirements as well as various antifraud and disclosure provisions. The Investment Company Act supplements the disclosure and reporting provisions of the Securities Act of 1933 and the Securities Exchange Act of 1934.

Investment Advisers Act of 1940

The Investment Advisers Acts of 1940,[68] regulates professional investment analysts in the business of generating and providing financial advice to investors. This Act covers investment advisers to institutional investors such as mutual funds, as well as investment advisers offering their services to investors generally.

Securities Investor Protection Act of 1970

In 1970, Congress added the Securities Investor Protection Act[70] which was enacted to address the increasing concern over the then increasing number of insolvent brokerage firms and broker-dealer firm failures.

Periodic Amendments to Securities Laws

The foregoing seven securities laws are amended periodically. Sometimes those amendments are ushered in by Acts with their own names. A few examples of these amending Acts are: the Williams Act[71] of 1968 which addressed tender offers, the Insider Trading Sanctions Act of 1984[73] which enhanced enforcement of insider trading prohibitions, the Private Securities Litigation Reform Act of 1995[74] which addressed many areas of private securities litigation, and the Securities Litigation Uniform Standards Act of 1998[76] which prevents most class actions based on securities fraud from being brought in state court.

Sarbanes-Oxley Act of 2002

In 2002, Congress made massive amendments when it enacted the Sarbanes–Oxley Act[79] that not only amended many provisions of the Securities Act of 1933 and the Securities Exchange Act of 1934, but also introduced some scattered stand-alone provisions into the United States Code. Since the Sarbanes–Oxley Act contained sweeping changes, it is likely that at least some observers and commentators will refer to it as the eighth federal securities law.

§ 1.2[3][D][2] The Proposed Federal Securities Code

In 1968, the Council of the American Law Institute began work on the Proposed Federal Securities Code project. Professor Louis Loss was named as the Code's chief reporter. After six tentative drafts and various revisions, in 1980, the American Law Institute endorsed the final draft of its Proposed

68. Act of Aug. 22, 1940 54 Stat. 847, codified in 15 U.S.C.A. § 80b–1 *et seq.,* discussed in chapter 21 *infra.*

70. 15 U.S.C.A. § 78aaa–78*lll*. *See* § 14.24 *infra.*

71. Pub.L. No. 90–439, 82 Stat. 454 (1968) (codified at 15 U.S.C. §§ 78m(d)–(e), n(d)–(f)).

73. Pub. L. No. 98–376, 98 Stat. 1264 (1984).

74. Pub. Law No. 104–67, 109 Stat. 737 (104th Cong. 1st Sess. December 22, 1995) (HR 1058).

76. Pub. Law No. 105–353, 112 Stat. 3227 (105th Cong.–2d Sess. November 3, 1998) (S 1260).

79. Sarbanes–Oxley Act of 2002, Pub. Law 107–204 (July 30, 2002). *See* Senate Report No. 107–205 (July 3, 2002).

Federal Securities Code.[81] The Proposed Securities Code certainly was not without its critics.[82] Although at one time the Code was endorsed by the SEC,[83] it was not even formally introduced into Congress; with the passage of time, it has become evident that the Proposed Code will not become law. Nevertheless, the Proposed Code has proven to have been a worthy project for a number of reasons. First, many of its suggestions have since become embodied in the existing regulatory scheme. Second, the drafter's comments provide an excellent analysis of the case law as of that time. In deciding cases under the existing law, some courts looked for guidance both to the body of the Proposed Code and to its comments.

§ 1.2[3][D][3] The Sarbanes–Oxley Act of 2002

The Sarbanes–Oxley Act of 2002,[91] which is discussed throughout this treatise where applicable, adopted comprehensive corporate governance reforms in response to various corporate scandals including those involving Enron and Worldcom. Many of the Sarbanes–Oxley provisions are disclosure provisions combined with enhanced criminal penalties for violations, but the clear thrust of these amendments is to improve corporate governance. The Sarbanes–Oxley Act goes further than any of the earlier securities laws and amendments in dealing directly with corporate governance—an area that had traditionally been reserved to the states. For example, the Sarbanes–Oxley Act addressed accounting and auditing reforms, the role of public corporations' audit committees, increased accountability of executive officers, and corporate attorneys, in addition to increased criminal penalties for violations of the securities laws. The Sarbanes–Oxley Act created an accounting oversight board to oversee the accounting profession and to police the self-regulatory system that previously existed.[97] The Sarbanes–Oxley Act also addressed auditor independence requirements.[98]

The Sarbanes–Oxley Act may prove to be more than a one-time reaction to major corporate scandals. It could be the beginning of a sea change by focusing federal law more and more on corporate governance and other areas of corporate law that have traditionally been left to the states.[99]

Title III of the Sarbanes–Oxley Act addressed various corporate governance concerns including the audit committee, requiring personal certifications of accuracy by the chief executive and chief financial officers of public companies.[100] The Act further prohibits loans to high ranking executives, subject to certain exceptions to be elaborated upon in SEC rulemaking. The Act also calls for enhanced financial disclosures by public companies.[101]

---

81. A.L.I., Proposed Federal Securities Code (1980).

82. *See* Lewis D. Lowenfels, The Case Against the Proposed Federal Securities Code, 65 Va.L.Rev. 615 (1979); BNA Interview: Pollack Questions the Advisability of Passing Federal Securities Code at the Time, 484 Sec.Reg. & L.Rep. (BNA) AAB1 (Jan. 3, 1979).

83. Sec. Exch. Act Rel. No. 34–17153 (Sept. 18, 1980). A year and a half later the Commission reaffirmed its endorsement. Sec. Act Rel. No. 33–6377 (Jan. 21, 1982).

91. Sarbanes–Oxley Act of 2002, Pub. Law 107–204 (July 30, 2002).

97. Sarbanes–Oxley Act of 2002, Pub. Law 107–204 tit. I (July 30, 2002). *See* § 9.6 *infra*.

98. Sarbanes–Oxley Act of 2002, Pub. Law 107–204 tit. II (July 30, 2002).

99. *See, e.g.,* Robert B. Ahdieh, From "Federalization" to "Mixed Governance" in Corporate Law: A Defense of Sarbanes–Oxley, 53 Buffalo L. Rev. 721 (2005).

100. Sarbanes–Oxley Act of 2002, Pub. Law 107–204 tit. III (July 30, 2002).

101. Sarbanes–Oxley Act of 2002, Pub. Law 107–204 tit. IV (July 30, 2002). *See* § 3.9[9] *infra*.

Titles VIII and IX of the Sarbanes Oxley Act[102] provide for enhanced criminal penalties for violations of the Act generally, and in particular, for frauds perpetrated upon shareholders of public companies. The Sarbanes–Oxley Act includes protection to corporate whistle-blowers.[103] The Act[104] provides a remedy to an aggrieved person who can establish an unfavorable personnel decision that was connected to whistle-blower activity.

Since its enactment in 2003, there has been considerable controversy concerning the burdens that the Sarbanes–Oxley Act's heightened disclosure and compliance requirements impose on public companies. The Act was drafted with the massive frauds in large companies such as Enron, Worldcom, and Tyco and a different cost benefit analysis may be appropriate when considering the Act's impact on smaller companies. The SEC has acknowledged the need to evaluate the Sarbanes–Oxley Act's impact on smaller companies. For example, in 2006, the SEC's advisory committee on smaller public companies issued a request for comments on its preliminary proposal to provide relief from some of the Sarbanes–Oxley requirements for smaller public companies.[108] It was suggested, for example, that smaller companies be given relief from section 404 of the Sarbanes–Oxley Act. However, the SEC's exemptive authority under the securities laws applies only to those laws and section 404 is not codified as part of the securities laws.[109] In the spring of 2006, the SEC announced that it would not exempt companies from section 404 but it would provide guidance to make compliance easier.[110] In July 2006, the SEC issued a concept release foreshadowing additional guidance for small companies' compliance with section 404.[111]

In 2007, the Senate defeated proposed legislation that would have made compliance with section 404 voluntary for Exchange Act reporting companies with a market capitalization of less than $700 million. However, around the same time, the SEC, on May 23, 2007, unanimously adopted interpretive guidance for evaluating internal controls and correlative rule amendments.[115]

§ 1.2[3][E] Federal Preemption of State Law

In 1996, Congress significantly limited the role of state law in securities regulation. The National Securities Markets Improvement Act of 1996[119] (NSMIA) explicitly preempts state law in many areas. An amended section 18

102. Sarbanes–Oxley Act of 2002, Pub. Law 107–204 tits. VIII, IX (July 30, 2002).

103. Sarbanes–Oxley Act of 2002, Pub. Law 107–204 § 1107 (July 30, 2002).

104. 18 U.S.C.A. § 1514A(a).

108. See Exposure Draft of Final Report of Advisory Committee on Smaller Public Companies, Sec. Act Rel. No. 33–8666; Sec. Exch. Act Rel. No. 34–53385, 71 Fed. Reg. 11090–01, 2006 WL 501877 http://www.sec.gov/rules/other/33–8666.pdf (SEC Feb. 28, 2006).

109. As was pointed out in a letter sent by a group of law professors to SEC Chairman Cox, the Sarbanes–Oxley Act does not grant the SEC exemptive authority and since section 404 of Sarbanes–Oxley is not part of the Securities Exchange Act, the SEC's exemptive authority under section 36(a) of that Act does not apply.

110. *See* SEC Announces Next Steps for Sarbanes–Oxley Implementation, SEC Press Rel. 2006–75, http://www.sec.gov/news/press/2006/2006–75.htm (SEC May 17, 2006).

111. Concept Release Concerning Managements Reports on Internal Control Over Financial Reporting, Release No. 54122, Release No. 34–54122, 2006 WL 1896710 (SEC July 11, 2006).

115. SEC, Commission Guidance Regarding Management's Report on Internal Control Over Financial Reporting Under Section 13(a) or 15(d) of the Securities Exchange Act, Sec. Act Rel. No. 33–8810, Sec. Exch. Act Rel. No. 34–55929, 2007 WL 1791162 (SEC June 20, 2007).

119. Pub. L. No. 104–290, 110 Stat. 3416 (1996). The impact on state laws is discussed further in Chapter 8 *infra*.

of the 1933 Act now provides that a number of securities offerings will be exempted from state law regulation.[120] The 1996 amendments specifically preempt state regulation that would require registration or qualification of several categories of covered securities. Those covered securities include most publicly traded securities: securities listed on the New York Stock Exchange, the American Stock Exchange, or the NASD's National Market System.[121] Although precluding the states from imposing registration or reporting requirements on issuers of covered securities, the federal act expressly preserves the states' right to require filing of documents solely for notice purposes.[122] In addition to the preemption of state laws with regard to the foregoing publicly traded securities, a number of exempt securities are also exempted from state regulation.[123] Furthermore, even for those securities and transactions not otherwise preempted and thus exempted from state regulation, sales to "qualified purchasers" as defined by the SEC are also exempted.[124]

The 1996 amendments were not limited to registration and reporting requirements. The 1996 legislation severely limits state regulation of broker-dealers.[126] The Act now also provides for exclusive federal jurisdiction over investment companies registered under the Investment Company Act of 1940.[127] In addition, there is exclusive federal jurisdiction over investment advisers to registered investment companies as well as over advisers managing more than $25 million in assets.[128]

As part of the Securities Litigation Uniform Standards Act of 1998,[129] most securities class actions involving publicly traded securities were banned from state court, making federal jurisdiction exclusive.[130] The preemption of state court actions includes state common law and securities law fraud-based claims involving covered securities which are defined to include most publicly traded securities registered with the SEC. The Uniform Standards Act (also referred to as SLUSA) does not completely eliminate state court class actions, however. Class actions involving securities that are not publicly traded may

120. 15 U.S.C.A. § 77r.

121. Section 18(b)(1)(A), 15 U.S.C.A. § 77r(b)(1)(A). The Act also gives the SEC rulemaking power to expand the exemption to other listed securities on a securities exchange that has listing standards similar to those identified in subsection (b)(1)(A). Section 18(b)(1)(B), 15 U.S.C.A. § 77r(b)(1)(B). Also exempted are securities of the same issuer with equal seniority or that are senior to the securities exempted from state regulation under subsections (1)(A) and (1)(B). Section 18(b)(1)(C), 15 U.S.C.A. § 77r(b)(1)(C).

122. Section 18(c)(2), 15 U.S.C.A. § 77r(c)(2).

123. Section 18(b)(4), 15 U.S.C.A. § 77r(b)(4).

124. Section 18(b)(3), 15 U.S.C.A. § 77r(b)(3). The SEC is empowered to define categories of qualified purchaser "consistent with the public interest and the protection of investors." *Id.*

126. Specifically, the amendments prohibit the states from regulating the extension of credit by broker-dealers as well as imposing capital, or recordkeeping requirements. This is found in section 15(h) of the 1934 Act, 15 U.S.C.A. § 78*o*.

127. Section 18(b)(2), 15 U.S.C.A. § 77r(b)(2). The Investment Company Act is considered in chapter 20 *infra*.

128. Section 203A of the Investment Advisers Act of 1940, 15 U.S.C.A. § 80b–203A. Effective, April 10, 1997, investment advisers managing more than $25 million in assets and advisers to registered investment companies fall under the exclusive jurisdiction of the SEC. Investment advisers and the Investment Advisers Act of 1940 are considered in chapter 21 *infra*.

129. Pub. Law No. 105–353, 112 Stat. 3227 (105th Cong., 2d Sess. November 3, 1998) (§ 1260).

130. 1933 Act § 16, 15 U.S.C.A. § 77; 1934 Act § 28, 15 U.S.C.A. § 78pp.

still remain in state court. The Uniform Standards Act preemptive effect does not apply to claims brought by states, their political subdivisions, or pension plans; nor does it apply to investigations and enforcement actions by state securities administrators. Further, the Uniform Standards Act applies only to class actions and thus not to individual or derivative suits, and there is an exception for certain claims involving corporate transactions that are brought in the state of incorporation.

§ 1.3 The Securities and Exchange Commission; Structure of the SEC

The Securities and Exchange Commission is a highly departmentalized federal agency, which is reflected in its wide range of authority and various types of administrative responsibilities.[1] The Commission is a true "super agency," notwithstanding its relatively small size as compared with other federal regulatory agencies. In spite of the SEC's broad range of authority and the general criticism of governmental overregulation, the Commission has been recognized as one of the most efficient and effective federal agencies.

§ 1.3[1] The SEC Commissioners

The Securities and Exchange Commission consists of five commissioners serving five-year terms.[2] The commissioners are appointed by the President, subject to the normal confirmatory action by Congress. One of the five commissioners is designated as Commission Chairman. Of the five commissioners, no more than three can be from the same political party.

The five commissioners comprise what is sometimes referred to as the full Commission, as compared with division heads and SEC staff members. The full Commission, in addition to exercising its supervisory power over all of its divisions, has direct review power of rulings and hearings before an administrative judge as well as the final authority on the promulgation of all SEC rules. The commissioners as a group necessarily fulfill the function of the final arbiter of overall SEC policy. Since there is no specific statutory provision to the contrary, SEC action is governed by common law quorum and voting rules.[3]

§ 1.3[2] The Divisions of the Commission

The adjudicatory responsibilities of the Commission are carried out through the administrative law judges, while the rest of the Commission's administrative powers are handled primarily through its four divisions (corporation finance, enforcement, market regulation, corporation finance, and investment management) that are located in the national office in Washington, D.C. The regional offices focus on examinations of broker dealers and

---

§ 1.3

1. For a more detailed discussion of the SEC *see* chapter 16 *infra* wherein the SEC, its Rules of Practice, and its structure are discussed more fully. Descriptions of current SEC activities and structure can be found in the Commission's annual reports.

2. *See* § 16.43 *infra.*

3. *See, e.g.,* Falcon Trading Group v. SEC, 102 F.3d 579 (D.C.Cir.1996) (upholding SEC rule designating two out of three commissioners to be a quorum, in the absence of all five commission positions being filled).

those enforcement matters that are not handled directly by the national office.

The Division of Enforcement is responsible for the investigation of all suspected securities laws violations.[4] Once it is believed that a violation has been committed, the result may be a SEC judicial enforcement action, reference to the Justice Department for criminal prosecution, or proceedings seeking to impose administrative sanctions to be imposed after a hearing. These enforcement actions and administrative proceedings may be brought against registered issuers, their officers and employees, registered broker-dealers, and members of exchanges or self-regulatory associations, such as the FINRA (formerly the NASD). The Division of Corporation Finance has primary responsibility for examining all registration documents for compliance with the securities laws' disclosure requirements. The Division of Corporation Finance, or "Corp Fin," also prepares various disclosure guides that are promulgated by the Commission. The Division of Corporation Finance is also extremely helpful in aiding the preparation of first-time or difficult disclosure documents. The Division of Trading and Markets (formerly known as the Division of Market Regulation) is devoted to regulatory practices and policies relating to the exchanges, the over-the-counter markets, and broker-dealers. There is some overlap with the Division of Investment Management, which is concerned with the regulation under the two 1940 Acts of the investment company industry and investment advisers. The SEC's Division of Investment Management formerly carried out the Commission's responsibilities that once existed under the former Public Utility Holding Company Act of 1935. The former Division of Corporate Regulation, which at one time had responsibility for the Public Utility Holding Company Act, had been charged with supervising bankruptcy organizations under the Federal Bankruptcy Act. The responsibilities under the Federal Bankruptcy Act have since been transferred to the Commission's regional offices.

In the Commission's hierarchy, there are various offices below the four divisions. The Office of the General Counsel is charged with the responsibility of advising both the Commission and all of its divisions on questions of law. The General Counsel also represents the Commission in litigation, both at the trial and appellate court levels, and is instrumental in preparing Commission sponsored legislation. In 1989, the Commission consolidated the functions of the Office of Opinions and Review into the Office of the General Counsel. The Office of the Accountant generates Commission policy on various accounting practices; it also represents the Commission when dealing with self-regulatory organizations, such as the Financial Accounting Standards Board (FASB) and Public Company Accounting Oversight Board (PCAOB). The Chief Economist and Directorate of Economic and Policy Analysis as their names imply, are in charge of generating various economic studies used by the Commission and its divisions. The Office of Policy Planning formerly had the task of coordinating the Commission's long term goals; this function has been transferred to the Directorate of Economic and Policy Analysis. Each Division and Office in the Washington, D.C. headquarters of the Commission has responsibility for the development, direction, and policy guidance for all operating programs under its jurisdiction.

---

4. SEC enforcement is discussed in 16.2 *infra*. The Division of Enforcement is discussed in § 16.46 *infra*.

§ 1.4 The Work of the SEC

§ 1.4[1] Overview of SEC Authority

With the creation of the Securities and Exchange Commission in 1934, Congress gave the Securities and Exchange Commission the responsibility of administering the regulation provided by all seven of the securities laws.[1] The Commission carries out that responsibility with each of the four basic administrative agency powers: rule-making, adjudicatory, investigatory, and enforcement.[2] During the late twentieth century, the Commission's enforcement powers expanded significantly. In addition to now having the ability to seek treble damage penalties for insider trading violations,[3] the Commission can impose civil penalties in administrative procedures[4] and has been given cease and desist authority.[5] The only administrative authority that the Commission does not have is the power to adjudicate disputes between individual litigants.[6]

The discussion that follows addresses the various ways in which the SEC makes law. This includes formal rule-making, interpretative releases and the no-action letter process. This is supplemented by even less formal lawmaking. A body of practices has built up over time. These practices result in a securities "lore" that supplements the law. Although these practices may be reflected in SEC releases and no-action responses, they are not always easily found as unlike with formal rules, there is no convenient indexing system.

§ 1.4[2] SEC Rulemaking

As with administrative agencies generally, there are two varieties of rule-making authority: delegated and interpretative. Much of the Commission's legislative or rule-making power derives from the certain sections of the securities laws which specifically empower the SEC to promulgate rules that have the force of statutory provisions.[7]

§ 1.4[2][A] Delegated Rulemaking

Administrative rule-making by direct legislative delegation necessarily has the effect of law so long as the rule-making has been in compliance with

§ 1.4

1. The SEC's activities are described each year in the Commission's annual report. *See generally* SEC, A Twenty Five Year Summary of the Activities of the Securities and Exchange Commission 1934–1959 (1961); SEC, The Work of the Securities and Exchange Commission (1974).

2. *See* Thomas L. Hazen, Administrative Enforcement: An Evaluation of the Securities and Exchange Commission's Use of Injunctions and Other Enforcement Methods, 31 Hastings L.J. 427 (1979).

3. Section 21A of the Exchange Act, 15 U.S.C.A. § 78u–1. *See* §§ 9.5, 13.9 *infra*.

4. Section 21B of the Exchange Act, 15 U.S.C.A. § 78u–2.

5. *E.g.*, section 21C of the Exchange Act, 15 U.S.C.A. § 78u–3. *See* § 16.5 *infra*.

6. *Compare, e.g.*, the Commodity Futures Trading Commission which through its reparations procedures can adjudicate customer/broker disputes. Section 14 of the Commodity Exchange Act, 7 U.S.C.A. § 18.

7. *See e.g.*, section 3(b) of the 1933 Act giving the Commission power to promulgate exemptions from registration, 15 U.S.C.A. § 77c(b); and section 10(b) of the 1934 Act which delegates to the Commission the responsibility to promulgate rules determining the scope of anti-fraud liability, 15 U.S.C.A. § 78j(b). For discussion of SEC rulemaking in the context of rules-based versus principle-based rulemaking, *see, e.g.*, James J. Park, The Competing Paradigms of Securities Regulation, 57 Duke L.J. 625 (2007).

the process set forth in the Administrative Procedure Act[8] and the scope of the rule does not exceed the grant of authority in the organic statute that created this administrative rule-making power.

The validity of SEC rulemaking is dependent upon the scope of the authorizing statute. Rules that go beyond the scope of the statute are therefore invalid. Major questions involving the validity of SEC rules are frequently raised in connection with rules that touch upon corporate governance, which is a matter that has traditionally been left to state law. The securities laws provide an "intelligible conceptual line excluding the Commission from corporate governance."[9] Accordingly, the D.C. Circuit Court of Appeals invalidated the Commission's attempt to regulate substantive voting rights of shareholders.[10]

SEC rules are invalid if they are arbitrary or beyond the scope of statutory authority.[11] Even if the SEC has acted within its rulemaking authority, a court may remand a rule for further consideration where the SEC fails to consider the cost of compliance with the rules.[12]

§ 1.4[2][B] Interpretative Rulemaking

Commission rule-making is not limited to legislatively delegated rules. The SEC has also promulgated a number of interpretive rules which are designed to aid corporate planners and attorneys in complying with the statutes' requirements.[19] Unlike the rules promulgated pursuant to specific statutory delegation, interpretative rules do not carry with them the force of law; they simply reflect the Commission's interpretation of the law created by the statute. Nevertheless, interpretative rules are extremely important in guiding practitioners through the regulatory maze. Equally important is that fact that when interpreting the scope of a statute, federal courts traditionally give deference to administrative interpretation.[20] The reasoning underpinning this deference is the reliability of the agency's expertise as compared to the court's general knowledge and authority.

§ 1.4[2][C] Safe Harbor Rules

A special variety of SEC interpretative rules are the so-called safe harbor rules.[21] A safe harbor rule sets forth conditions under which the SEC will take

8. 5 U.S.C.A. §§ 551 *et seq.*

9. Business Roundtable v. SEC, 905 F.2d 406 (D.C.Cir.1990).

10. Business Roundtable v. SEC, 905 F.2d 406 (D.C.Cir.1990). *See* discussion in § 10.1 *infra.* Another example of the SEC's clash with corporate governance issues arose in the context of the regulation of "going private" transactions. *See* § 11.8[2] *infra.*

11. *See, e.g.,* Chamber of Commerce of the United States of America v. SEC, 412 F.3d 133 (D.C. Cir. 2005) (upholding the statutory authority to adopt the rule).

12. *See* Chamber of Commerce of the United States of America v. SEC, 412 F.3d 133 (D.C. Cir. 2005) (SEC had authority to promulgate rules regarding independence of mutual fund directors but failed to adequately consider costs of compliance).

19. The current versions of the rules are compiled annually in volume 17 of the Code of Federal Regulations (hereinafter cited as "17 C.F.R. § ___").

20. Chevron U.S.A. v. Natural Resources Defense Council, 467 U.S. 837, 104 S.Ct. 2778, 81 L.Ed.2d 694 (1984).

21. For examples of safe harbor rules, see, e.g., Rule 144 (exemption for secondary transactions), Rule 147 (exemption for intrastate offerings), Rule 175 (forward looking statements), and 506 (exemption for offerings by an issuer not involving a public offering) of the 1933 Act, 17 C.F.R. §§ 230.144, 230.147, 230.175, 230.506.

the position that the law has been complied with. A person's compliance with a safe harbor rule will thus assure that he or she is safe from SEC prosecution with regard to the transaction in question. The SEC safe harbor rules, which are discussed throughout this treatise are designed to help provide for certainty in planning transactions in order to comply with the applicable securities laws.

§ 1.4[3] SEC Interpretive Releases; Staff Legal Bulletins

Beyond its expressly delegated and interpretative rule-making activities, the Securities and Exchange Commission disseminates unsolicited advisory opinions in the form of SEC Releases,[22] which may include guidelines or suggest interpretation of statutory provisions and rules. In addition to periodic interpretative releases, each time the Commission proposes a new rule or rule amendment, the proposal is accompanied by a release. Similarly, when new rules or amendments are adopted, the SEC's formal adoption is accompanied by an interpretative release. The SEC positions announced in interpretative releases necessarily provide less precedential and predictive value than do rules that are promulgated as a result of the more formal interpretive rule-making process.

In addition to the SEC Releases described above, the Commission will from time to time issue Accounting Releases which deal with various matters involving disclosure and presentation of financial information. Some Accounting Releases also discuss the SEC auditing requirements that apply to registered public companies. The SEC also publishes Litigation Releases which announce filings, settlements, and judgments in SEC enforcement actions that are brought in federal court.

Although having less precedential effect than the formal SEC Releases, from time to time the SEC publishes Staff Legal Bulletins. These Bulletins, which are available on the SEC's website, provide further insight into the SEC's approach to selected issues. As is the case with SEC Releases, Staff Legal Bulletins are mentioned throughout this treatise where appropriate. As is the case with no action letters that are discussed in the subsection that follows, staff legal bulletins should be given deference when interpreting the law.[23] Even though they are entitled some interpretative deference, staff legal bulletins, as is also the case with SEC staff accounting bulletins, are not given the precedential weight accorded to formal rulemaking and do not carry the force of law.[24]

§ 1.4[4] SEC No Action Letters

One step below interpretative releases, in terms of precedential hierarchy, are the Commission's "no action" letters. These no action letters are analogous to IRS private letter rulings. No action letters are SEC staff responses to

22. The Commission's releases are published in the Federal register and also appear in the various looseleaf services. This information also is available on WESTLAW.

23. Argentinian Recovery Co. v. Board of Directors of Multicanal S.A., 331 B.R. 537 (Bkrtcy. S.D.N.Y. 2005) (some degree of deference is still appropriate for SEC no action letters and staff bulletins), relying on Gryl ex rel. Shire Pharmaceuticals Group PLC v. Shire Pharmaceuticals, 298 F.3d 136 (2d Cir. 2002) and this treatise.

24. *See* Allen v. Administrative Review Board, 514 F.3d 468 (5th Cir. 2008) ("Unlike a rule promulgated by the SEC pursuant to its ruling-making authority, *see* 15 U.S.C. § 78w(a), an SEC Staff Accounting Bulletin 'does not carry with it the force of law.' "), citing Ganino v. Citizens Utilities Co., 228 F.3d 154, 163 (2d Cir.2000).

private requests for indication of whether certain contemplated conduct is in compliance with the appropriate statutory provisions and rules. Most requests for a no action letter are compliance oriented and thus are handled by the Division of Corporation Finance; although, on occasion the other divisions may render similar assistance in their areas of expertise. No action letters can be very helpful to practitioners.[25] However, it must be kept in mind that the SEC's responses are staff interpretations rather than formal Commission action and thus have extremely limited, if any, precedential weight.[26] The SEC staff position in a no action letter has been described as a statement to the effect that:

> This is my view based on the facts as you describe them. You may not rely on it as if it were a Commission decision. If you don't like it, you are at liberty to disregard it and follow your own construction, subject to the risk that I may recommend appropriate action to the Commission and the Commission may institute proceedings or take other steps if the Commission agrees with my view.[27]

A no action letter is purely a matter between the SEC staff and the party requesting it. The request for a no action letter does not bind the party requesting it to act in a certain way so as to create any protectable expectations in third parties. Accordingly, it has been held that a corporation's shareholders cannot force management to frame a transaction according to the terms of its no action request.[28] Conversely, when the Commission has responded favorably to a request for a no action letter, the SEC's interpretation will not preclude a third party from challenging the transaction. The no action position may, of course, have some persuasive effect insofar as it represents the Commission's interpretation and exhibits the SEC's current thinking on particular matters.[29] The limited precedential effect of no action letters was reinforced with the Commission's initiation of administrative proceedings to address conduct that had previously been the subject of favorable no action responses.[30] In conjunction with the initiation of the administrative proceeding, Commissioner Fleischman issued a written statement emphasizing that since no action responses are limited to the particular facts in the requesting letter, it is risky to make general conclusions from specific responses.[31] It is clear that a court will not give the same deference to

---

25. *See, e.g.,* Thomas P. Lemke, The SEC No–Action Letter Process, 42 Bus.Law. 1019 (1987).

26. *See, e.g.,* Roosevelt v. E.I. Du Pont de Nemours & Co., 958 F.2d 416, 427 n. 19 (D.C.Cir.1992) (principle of deference to agency views does not apply to no action letters as they are not formal agency positions).

27. Professional Care Services, Inc., [1973–74 Transfer Binder] Fed.Sec.L.Rep. (CCH) ¶ 79,770 at p. 84,080 (SEC No Action Letter March 15, 1974) (quoting 3 Louis Loss, Securities Regulation 1895 (2d ed. 1961)).

28. Beaumont v. American Can Co., 797 F.2d 79 (2d Cir.1986), *affirming* 621 F.Supp. 484 (S.D.N.Y.1985).

29. On occasion, the full Commission has been willing to reconsider the position taken by the staff in a no action response. *See, e.g.,* United Brotherhood of Carpenters and Joiners of America, 2002 WL 31749942 (SEC No Action Letter Dec. 6, 2002). If the Commission takes the position that the staff erred, it may nevertheless permit the company's management that relied in good faith on the staff response to act in accordance with the initial no action response. *Id.*

30. Morgan Stanley & Co., Sec.Exch.Act Rel. No. 34–28,990, Admin.Proc.File No. 3–7473 (March 20, 1991) (charging violations of limits on sale of control person stock in connection with stock sale to satisfy margin requirements).

31. As stated by Commissioner Fleischman, "since the particular letter under discussion states that it's limited to the facts of its own case and that only the addressee is protected by it,

a no action response as it would to formal rulemaking or interpretative pronouncements.[32]

Notwithstanding the absence of formal precedential effect attaching to no action letters, no action letters provide insight into the SEC's views. Furthermore, consistent no action positions may lead to reasonable reliance by third parties. Thus, the Second Circuit held that following consistent adherence to a position in no action responses, the SEC could not reverse that position in a no action response as compared to formal rulemaking.[33]

A number of commentators have criticized the "no action" letter as an inefficient method of lawmaking.[34] The no action letter as an ad hoc method of advising has been attacked as too time-consuming and cumbersome. Further, no action letters fail to provide practitioners with significant precedential or predictive aid. The value of no action letters and other mechanisms of informal Commission action is even further diminished, as described more fully below in a discussion of the registration process under the Securities Act of 1933,[35] by the availability of comment letters and less formal telephone conferences provided by the Division of Corporation Finance and various regional offices as guides for revision of documents filed with the Commission

Nevertheless, given all of its shortcomings, the no action letter process has been an influential one in forming securities law. No action letters can be of great help in shedding light on the SEC's current view of many significant issues. Relevant no action letter positions are discussed as appropriate throughout this treatise. Courts should give deference to an agency's expertise when looking to no action letters to interpret the law.[36]

§ 1.4[5] SEC Oversight and Regulatory Authority

Aside from the foregoing quasi-legislative responsibilities, the Commission also has regulatory oversight and quasi-judicial power over brokers, dealers, and exchanges that it licenses under the Exchange Act of 1934.[37] From time to time, questions have arisen concerning the effect of the SEC's regulatory and self-regulatory oversight authority on the impact of the antitrust laws. Where there is pervasive regulation either by the SEC directly or by the self regulatory organizations under the direct oversight and supervision of the SEC, then the Securities Exchange Act will operate as an implied

others claiming to be similarly situated can't be allowed to reason from the letter to derive general propositions on which the addressee itself could not rely." *Id.* (written statement of Commissioner Fleischman).

32. Amalgamated Clothing & Textile Workers Union v. Wal–Mart Stores, Inc., 821 F.Supp. 877 (S.D.N.Y.1993) (no action responses do not represent official agency positions).

33. American Federation of State, County & Municipal Employees, Employees Pension Plan v. American International Group, 462 F.3d 121 (2d Cir. 2006) (the SEC's consistent no action position over a period of time could not be changed by a no action response; instead the SEC would have to engage in formal rulemaking).

34. Louis Loss, Summary Remarks (ABA National Institute: Advisors to Management), 30 Bus.Law. 163, 164–65 (Special Issue 1975); Lewis D. Lowenfels, SEC No Action Letters: Conflicts with the Existing Statutes, Cases and Commission Releases, 59 Va.L.Rev. 303 (1973).

35. *See* chapter 3 *infra*.

36. Argentinian Recovery Co. v. Board of Directors of Multicanal S.A., 331 B.R. 537 (Bkrtcy. S.D.N.Y. 2005) (some degree of deference is still appropriate for SEC no action letters and staff bulletins).

37. 15 U.S.C.A. § 78o. *See* chapter 14 *infra*.

repeal of the antitrust laws.[38] Not all SEC regulated conduct will have such a preemptive effect on the antitrust laws. For example, conduct that is not subject to regulation under the securities laws is not immune from challenge under the antitrust laws. Also, there is authority to the effect that conduct that is not permitted by SEC Rule, self-regulatory rule, or regulation generally may be scrutinized under the antitrust laws.[39]

Correlative to the SEC's oversight responsibility is the agency's ability to impose administrative disciplinary sanctions upon those subject to its licensing authority. The SEC's disciplinary authority covers broker-dealers, investment advisers, and investment companies, as well as professionals such as attorneys or accountants who practice before the Commission. The Commission also has the power to impose administrative sanctions against other persons who violate the securities laws. In addition to direct enforcement authority, the Commission may in its discretion publish the results of its investigations.[40] One of the more controversial areas of the Commission's disciplinary authority has been exerted under Rule 102(e) of the Commission's Rules of Practice which relates to practice before the Commission and thus allows the SEC to discipline professionals such as attorneys and accountants who appear before the Commission in a representative capacity.[41] Disciplinary proceedings under Rule 102(e) relate only to practice before the Commission; more general disbarment proceedings are left to the states in their regulation of the legal and accounting professions.

§ 1.4[6] SEC Enforcement Authority

The third major administrative function carried out by the SEC, in addition to rulemaking and adjudication, is that of enforcement. Through the Division of Enforcement, the Commission investigates all potential violations of each act that it administers. Where appropriate, such violation will be addressed through the SEC's administrative sanctions referred to above, or forwarded to the Department of Justice for criminal prosecution. The Commission also performs a direct prosecutorial function by virtue of its authority to seek injunctions against alleged violators, as well as appropriate ancillary relief in the federal district courts. Originally, the ability to secure ancillary relief was implied from the court's inherent equity authority. The Commission has since been given express statutory authority to seek disgorgement of ill-gotten gains,[44] imposition of civil penalties,[45] and bar orders[46] as part of its judicial enforcement arsenal.

Congress enacted legislation in 1990 that expanded significantly the role of the Commission in enforcement matters. As part of the Securities Enforcement and Penny Stock Reform Act of 1990,[47] the Commission was given cease

38. *See* Credit Suisse Securities (USA) LLC v. Billing, 551 U.S. 264, 127 S.Ct. 2383, 168 L.Ed.2d 145 (2007).

39. *See* In re Nasdaq Market–Makers Antitrust Litigation, 1999 WL 395407 (S.D.N.Y.1999).

40. 15 U.S.C.A. § 78u(a).

41. 17 C.F.R. § 201.2(e).

44. Section 21A of the Exchange Act, 15 U.S.C.A. § 78u–1.

45. 15 U.S.C.A. § 78u–1.

46. Under appropriate circumstances, a court may order that a violator of the securities law be barred from association with a company subject to the SEC's registration and reporting requirements. Section 21(d)(2) of the Exchange Act, 15 U.S.C.A. § 78u(d)(2).

47. Pub.L. No. 101–429.

and desist power.[48] The law that gave the SEC cease and desist authority further empowers the Commission to impose civil penalties in administrative proceedings.[49] The legislation also increased civil penalties for violations of the securities laws generally[50] and empowers the SEC to go to court to secure an order barring officers and directors from associating with issuers under the Commission's jurisdiction.[51] The penalties for numerous securities violations were increased again in 2002 when Congress enacted the Sarbanes–Oxley Act[52] in reaction to many notorious corporate frauds and failures.

§ 1.5 The SEC's Subject–Matter Jurisdiction; The CFTC–SEC Division of Regulatory Authority; Financial Services

§ 1.5[1] Jurisdictional Concerns

As discussed directly above, the Securities and Exchange Commission has wide-ranging responsibility with regard to the securities markets. The expanded sophistication of the securities markets has led to sweeping changes in the regulatory role of the Commission. As discussed in the preceding sections, the heart of the Securities and Exchange Commission's jurisdiction is the regulation of securities markets and securities trading. Beginning in the 1970s, the development and diversification of derivative investment products have created overlapping jurisdiction between the SEC and the Commodity Futures Trading Commission (CFTC).

Traditionally, the futures markets were devoted to agricultural and other tangible commodities. However, those markets began to trade financial futures and other derivative instruments wherein the underlying commodities were instruments more commonly associated with the securities markets, including treasury bonds or stock index futures. When combined with foreign currency contracts and other related futures and options, it is estimated that more than seventy percent of the volume on the commodities exchanges is attributable to financial instruments as opposed to tangible commodities.

The expansion of the public trading of options on securities[1] has met with competition from the public trading of futures contracts on securities. The Commodity Exchange Act vests the CFTC with exclusive jurisdiction over futures contracts.[2] The Commodity Exchange Act further requires, however,

48. Securities Act of 1933 § 8A, 15 U.S.C.A. § 77h–1; Securities Exchange Act of 1934 § 21C, 23(d), 15 U.S.C.A. § 78u–3, 78w(d); Investment Company Act of 1940 § 9(f), 15 U.S.C.A. § 80a–9(f); Investment Advisers Act of 1940 § 203(k), 15 U.S.C.A. § 80b–3(k). *See* discussion in § 16.32 *infra*.

49. Securities Exchange Act of 1934 § 21B, 15 U.S.C.A. § 78u–2; Investment Company Act § 9(d), (e), 15 U.S.C.A. § 80a–9(d), (e); Investment Advisers Act § 203(i), 15 U.S.C.A. § 80b–3(i). *See* discussion in § 16.2 *infra*

50. Securities Act of 1933 § 20(d), 15 U.S.C.A. § 77t(d); Securities Exchange Act of 1934 § 21(d)(3), 15 U.S.C.A. § 78u(d)(3); Investment Company Act § 42(e); 15 U.S.C.A. § 80a–41(e); Investment Advisers Act § 209(e); 15 U.S.C.A. § 80b–9(e). *See* discussion in § 16.2 *infra*.

51. Securities Exchange Act of 1934 § 21(d)(2), 15 U.S.C.A. § 78u(d)(2). *See* discussion in § 16.2 *infra*.

52. Sarbanes–Oxley Act of 2002, Pub. Law 107–204 (July 30, 2002).

§ 1.5

1. *See* § 1.7 *infra*.

2. This is found in section 2(a)(1) of the Commodity Exchange Act, 7 U.S.C.A § 2. *See generally* Philip M. Johnson & Thomas L. Hazen, Derivatives Regulation (2004).

that except as otherwise expressly provided, the CFTC's jurisdiction will not interfere with the area mapped out for the SEC.[3] The increasing competition between options on securities and futures thus set the stage for continuous jurisdictional clashes between the SEC and CFTC.

§ 1.5[5] Index Participations and Other Hybrids as Securities or Commodities

In 1988, three securities exchanges filed applications to permit trading of stock index participation instruments (also known as stock baskets). A stock basket (like an index futures or option contract) allows investors to participate in gains (or losses) derived from an index based on the collective price of the underlying securities. In March 1989, the SEC granted the applications and approved trading of three types of stock baskets on the applicant securities exchanges.[50] Stock index futures have been trading on the commodities exchanges for a number of years. The SEC's recognition of these novel index participation units as securities has opened another round of the SEC/CFTC jurisdictional struggle.[51] The Chicago Mercantile Exchange challenged the SEC action, claiming that these investment instruments were futures contracts and as such were subject to the exclusive jurisdiction of the CFTC.[52] The Seventh Circuit ruled that index participations were subject to the exclusive jurisdiction of the CFTC.[53]

In holding that the CFTC had exclusive jurisdiction over these index participation units, Judge Easterbrook explained that the basic premise underlying the jurisdictional accord was that if an instrument could be classified as both a security and a futures contract, exclusive jurisdiction of its trading lies with the CFTC.[54] In the wake of the decision, the first Bush administration introduced legislation that would transfer jurisdiction over all stock index futures to the SEC.[55] Other proposals for regulatory reform that have been suggested include giving the SEC oversight responsibility with regard to the CFTC's financial and stock index jurisdiction.[56] It is thus fair to say that Congress has been reexamining the jurisdictional accord for years. For a long time, it seemed doubtful that any adjustments to the jurisdiction of the SEC and CFTC would be the result of another accord between the two agencies.[57] However, in 1999, the two agencies were close to an agreement on massive changes, including the repeal of the prohibition on futures of individ-

---

3. "[N]othing contained in this section shall (i) supersede or limit the jurisdiction at any time conferred on the Securities and Exchange Commission or other regulatory authorities under the laws of the United States or of any State, or (ii) restrict the Securities and Exchange Commission and such other authorities from carrying out their duties and responsibilities in accordance with such laws." 7 U.S.C.A. § 2.

50. Sec. Exch. Act. Rel. No. 34–26709 (SEC March 14, 1989).

51. *See* Ricks, Stock Basket Approval Stirs Court Action, Wall St. J. p. C1 (Wednesday, March 15, 1989).

52. *See* Ricks, Stock Basket Approval Stirs Court Action, Wall St. J. p. C1 (Wednesday, March 15, 1989).

53. Chicago Mercantile Exchange v. SEC, 883 F.2d 537 (7th Cir.1989), *cert. denied* 496 U.S. 936, 110 S.Ct. 3214, 110 L.Ed.2d 662 (1990).

54. *See also* the discussion in § 1.7 *infra.*

55. *See* 22 Sec.Reg. & L.Rep. (BNA) 731 (May 11, 1990).

56. *E.g.,* Report of the Presidential Task Force on Market Practices (Jan. 8, 1988).

57. *See* Brady Rules Out any Compromise on SEC–CFTC Jurisdictional Dispute, 22 Sec.Reg. & L.Rep. (BNA) 1031 (July 13, 1990).

ual securities. The legislation that was eventually enacted permits the trading of futures on individual securities and further provides that jurisdiction over securities-based swap agreements remains primarily with the CFTC except that the antifraud provisions of the securities laws are applicable to such swaps.[58]

At the same time that the CFTC was contesting the applicability of the securities laws to index participations, it exempted a number of hybrid instruments (having characteristics of both securities and commodities-related investments) from the coverage of the Commodity Exchange Act.[59] Hybrid investments qualifying for the exemption from the bulk of federal commodities law regulation include instruments that combine commodity options or futures characteristics with debt instruments, preferred equity instruments, and depository transactions.

§ 1.5[6] Registration of Exchanges and Clearing Agents

The SEC requires registration of national securities exchanges and also of clearing agents. The CFTC regulates commodities exchanges and clearing agents. Another aspect of the jurisdictional dispute arose in connection with two commodities exchanges' challenge to SEC registration of a clearing agent for an electronic trading system for options on government securities.[61] The Seventh Circuit reversed the SEC order granting clearing agent registration for an agent of an electronic system for trading options on government securities.[62] However, the victory was short-lived. On remand, the SEC ruled that the agent did not have to register as a securities exchange and reaffirmed its earlier position that it could be registered as a clearing agent.[63] The Seventh Circuit upheld the SEC's ruling.[64]

As a result of the Commodity Futures Modernization Act of 2000,[65] security futures products[66] may be traded on either securities exchanges subject to SEC regulation, or commodities contract markets or derivatives transaction execution facilities that are subject to CFTC oversight.[67]

§ 1.5[7] Financial Services

In the same year that Congress enacted the Securities Act of 1933, it also enacted the Glass–Steagall Act[68] in order to erect a barrier between commercial banking and securities activities (also known as investment banking).

---

58. Commodity Futures Modernization Act of 2000, Pub. Law No. 106–554, 114 Stat. 2763 (Dec. 21, 2000).

59. CFTC Regulations §§ 34.1–34.3, 17 C.F.R. §§ 34.1–34.3.

61. The SEC has the responsibility for registering clearing agencies for exchanges. 15 U.S.C.A § 78q–1. *See* § 14.3 *infra.*

62. Board of Trade of City of Chicago v. SEC, 883 F.2d 525 (7th Cir.1989), *appeal after remand* 923 F.2d 1270 (1991).

63. *See* 22 Sec.Reg. & L.Rep. (BNA) 56 (Jan. 12, 1990).

64. Board of Trade of City of Chicago v. SEC, 923 F.2d 1270 (7th Cir.1991).

65. Pub. Law No. 106–554, 114 Stat. 2763 (Dec. 21, 2000).

66. Futures on individual equity securities and narrow based stock index futures. *See* § 1.7[7] *infra.*

67. *See* Philip McBride Johnson & Thomas Lee Hazen, Derivatives Regulation Chapter 1 (2004).

68. The Banking Act of 1933, Ch. 89, 48 Stat. 184 (1933), codified in various sections of 12 U.S.C.A. *See* in particular 12 U.S.C.A. §§ 24, 378(a).

During the latter part of the twentieth century, banks, brokerage firms, insurance companies, and other financial institutions pushed for increased competition between the formerly separate industries. The barriers between these activities began to crumble, culminating in 1999, when Congress repealed[69] the structural impediments that were formerly imposed by the Glass–Steagall Act.

The barriers that formerly existed between commercial banking, insurance, and investment banking activities no longer exist. The current regime imposes functional regulation. This means that securities activities of banks and other financial institutions are subject to SEC jurisdiction. Banking activities are regulated by the appropriate federal or state banking agency.[71] Insurance activities are regulated by state insurance regulators.[72]

§ 1.6 Definition of "Security"

§ 1.6[1] Statutory Definition of "Security"

What do the following have in common: scotch whiskey,[13] self-improvement courses,[14] cosmetics,[15] earthworms,[16] beavers,[17] muskrats,[18] rabbits,[19] chinchillas,[20] animal breeding programs,[21] cattle embryos,[22] fishing boats,[23] vacuum cleaners,[24] cemetery lots,[25] coin operated telephones,[26] master record-

69. Gramm–Leach–Bliley Act, Pub. Law. 106–102, 1999 U.S.C.C.A.N. (113 Stat.) 1338 (1999). *See generally* Symposium, 4 N.C. Banking Inst. 1 (2000); Michael K. O'Neal, Summary and Analysis of the Gramm–Leach–Bliley Act, 28 Sec. Reg. L.J. 95 (2000).

71. *See, e.g.,* Jonathan B. Macey, The Business of Banking: Before and After Gramm–Leach Bliley, 25 J. Corp. L. 691 (2000); Michael P. Malloy, Banking in the Twenty–First Century, 25 J. Corp. L. 787 (2000).

72. *See generally* Lissa L. Broome & Jerry W. Markham, Banking and Insurance: Before and After the Gramm–Leach–Bliley Act, 25 J. Corp. L. 723 (2000). *See* Thomas Lee Hazen, Disparate Regulatory Schemes for Parallel Activities: Securities Regulation, Derivatives Regulation, Gambling, and Insurance, 24 Annual Review of Banking & Financial Law 375 (2005).

§ 1.6

13. SEC v. Glen–Arden Commodities, Inc. [1973 Transfer Binder] Fed.Sec.L.Rep. (CCH) ¶ 94,142 (E.D.N.Y.1973); SEC v. M.A. Lundy Associates, 362 F.Supp. 226 (D.R.I.1973); SEC v. Haffenden–Rimar International, Inc., 362 F.Supp. 323 (E.D.Va.1973), *affirmed* 496 F.2d 1192 (4th Cir.1974).

14. SEC v. Glenn W. Turner Enterprises, Inc., 474 F.2d 476 (9th Cir.1973), *cert. denied* 414 U.S. 821, 94 S.Ct. 117, 38 L.Ed.2d 53 (1973).

15. SEC v. Koscot Interplanetary, Inc., 497 F.2d 473 (5th Cir.1974).

16. In re Worm World, Inc., 3 Blue Sky L.Rep. (CCH) ¶ 71,414 (S.D. Dept. of Commerce & Consumer Affairs 1978).

17. Continental Marketing Corp. v. SEC, 387 F.2d 466 (10th Cir.1967).

18. State v. Robbins, 185 Minn. 202, 240 N.W. 456 (1932).

19. Stevens v. Liberty Packing Corp., 111 N.J.Eq. 61, 161 A. 193 (1932).

20. SEC v. Chinchilla, Inc., Fed.Sec.L.Rep. (CCH) ¶ 90,618 (N.D.Ill.1953); Hollywood State Bank v. Wilde, 70 Cal.App.2d 103, 160 P.2d 846 (1945).

21. United States v. Freiberg, 34 Fed.Appx. 281 (9th Cir.2002) (interests in ostrich breeding program were securities under California law); Bailey v. J.W.K. Properties, Inc., 904 F.2d 918 (4th Cir.1990) (cattle breeding program was an investment contract and hence a security; investors had little or no control over breeding operations or success of investment).

22. Eberhardt v. Waters, 901 F.2d 1578 (11th Cir.1990) (sale of cattle embryos was a security under Georgia blue sky law).

23. SEC v. Pyne, 33 F.Supp. 988 (D.Mass.1940).

24. Bell v. Health–Mor, Inc., 549 F.2d 342 (5th Cir.1977).

25. Holloway v. Thompson, 112 Ind.App. 229, 42 N.E.2d 421 (1942); In re Waldstein, 160 Misc. 763, 291 N.Y.S. 697 (1936).

26. *See* SEC v. Edwards, 540 U.S. 389, 124 S.Ct. 892, 157 L.Ed.2d 813 (2004) (pay telephone leasing program could be a security even though investors were promised a fixed rather than variable return).

ing contracts,[27] pooled litigation funds,[28] and fruit trees?[29] The answer is that they have all been held to be securities within the meaning of federal or state securities statutes. The vast range of such unconventional investments that have fallen within the ambit of the securities laws' coverage is due to the broad statutory definition of a "security." Section 2(a)(1) of the Securities Act of 1933 is representative.[31]

> The term "security" means any note, stock, treasury stock, bond, debenture, evidence of indebtedness, certificate of interest or participation in any profit-sharing agreement, collateral-trust certificate, pre-organization certificate or subscription, transferable share, investment contract, voting-trust certificate, certificate of deposit for a security, fractional undivided interest in oil, gas, or other mineral rights, any put, call, straddle, option, or privilege on any security, certificate of deposit, or group or index of securities (including any interest therein or based on the value thereof), or any put, call, straddle, option, or privilege entered into on a national securities exchange relating to foreign currency, or, in general, any interest or instrument commonly known as a "security", or any certificate of interest or participation in, temporary or interim certificate for, receipt for, guarantee of, or warrant or right to subscribe to or purchase, any of the foregoing. . . .

The statutory definition includes certain derivative investments as securities. For example, options on securities are themselves securities. In 2000, Congress amended the securities laws to exclude a security-based swap agreement from the definition of security.[34] However, securities-based swap agreements are nevertheless subject to the antifraud provisions of the securities laws.[35] Futures on individual securities are within the definition of security and can now be traded in the commodities markets provided that there has been compliance with applicable regulatory provisions.[36]

In determining the basic coverage of the securities laws, the slightly different definitions of a security in the 1933 and 1934 Acts[37] are to be treated as "virtually identical," according to the Supreme Court.[38] The statutory language is expansive and has been interpreted accordingly. The broadly drafted statutory definition has continued to give the courts problems in

---

27. *E.g.,* Kolibash v. Sagittarius Recording Co., 626 F.Supp. 1173 (S.D.Ohio 1986).

28. B.J. Tannenbaum, Jr., 18 Sec.Reg. & L.Rep. (BNA) 1826 (SEC No Action Letter Dec. 4, 1986).

29. *E.g.,* SEC v. W.J. Howey Co., 328 U.S. 293, 66 S.Ct. 1100, 90 L.Ed. 1244 (1946); SEC v. Tung Corp. of America, 32 F.Supp. 371 (N.D.Ill.1940).

31. 15 U.S.C.A. § 77b(a)(1). *See also, e.g.,* 15 U.S.C.A. § 78c(a)(10) (1976).

34. Pub. Law 106–554, 114 Stat. 2763 (December 21, 2000). *See* 15 U.S.C.A. §§ 77b–1(b)(1).

35. 1933 Act § 17(a), 1934 Act § 10(b); 15 U.S.C.A. §§ 77q(a), 78j(b). Section 17(a) of the 1933 Act is discussed in § 7.11 *infra.* Section 10(b) is discussed in chapter 12 *infra.*

36. 7 U.S.C.A. § 1a(31), added in Pub. Law 106–554, 114 Stat. 2763 (December 21, 2000).

37. For example, the 1934 Act excludes short-term commercial paper from the definition. Section 3(a)(10), 15 U.S.C.A. § 78c(a)(10). In contrast, although included in the 1933 Act's definition of security, short-term commercial paper is exempt from that Act's registration requirements. Sections 2(a)(1), 3(a)(3), 15 U.S.C.A. § 77a(1), 77c(a)(3).

38. Tcherepnin v. Knight, 389 U.S. 332, 335, 88 S.Ct. 548, 552, 19 L.Ed.2d 564 (1967). *See also, e.g.,* SEC v. Randy, 38 F.Supp.2d 657, 663 (N.D.Ill.1999) (the definition of security under the 1933 and 1934 Acts is "essentially the same").

providing predictable guidelines. Nevertheless, an attorney's failure to advise a client of the possibility of an investment offering being classified as a security can constitute legal malpractice.[40] Furthermore, it is not necessary to establish that the defendant knew that the instrument he or she was marketing was a security.[41]

In deciding whether a particular investment vehicle is a security, a number of generalizations can be made. The investors' perceptions and expectations will be a significant factor.[45] Thus, if the investment is marketed by a securities broker, it is more likely to fall under the securities laws.[46] In a close case, the existence of a parallel federal regulatory scheme may lead a court to find that the securities laws are not necessary for investor protection.[47] It must be remembered, however, that the existence of a parallel regulatory scheme subjecting the investments in question to some other regulatory agency will not preclude a finding that a security exists. Rather, the existence of such a parallel regulatory scheme simply may tip the balance against finding a security in a case that is very close to the margins.

The courts have used various tests for determining whether a security exists. One court has indicated that if the issuer registers an investment instrument as a security merely to be cautious, the investment will still not be subject to the securities laws if it fails to meet the statutory definition.[48] Thus, the issuer's determination of the character of the investment being offered will not alone determine whether the investments qualify as securities. Similarly, the fact that interests are characterized as investments will not in itself classify them as securities.[49]

§ 1.6[2] Judicial Interpretation of "Investment Contract"—The *Howey* Test

The judicial definition of security has developed primarily from interpretation of the statutory phrase "investment contract." With the lead of the Supreme Court, federal and state courts have strived to arrive at a workable definition and have formulated various tests and approaches. Throughout the

40. Popham, Haik, Schnobrich, Kaufman & Doty, Ltd. v. Newcomb Securities Co., 751 F.2d 1262 (D.C.Cir.1985).

41. *See, e.g.*, SEC v. Current Financial Services, Inc., 100 F.Supp.2d 1, 5–6 (D.D.C.2000) (defendant violated the securities laws even though he did not know that the investment vehicle he was marketing was a security).

45. *E.g.*, Reves v. Ernst & Young, 494 U.S. 56, 110 S.Ct. 945, 108 L.Ed.2d 47 (1990) (short-term notes were securities). *See also, e.g.*, SEC v. I–2001, SEC News Digest 2002–4 January 7, 2002 SECDIG 2002–4–3, 2002 WL 14394 (SEC 2002) (complaint charging online solicitation of investor funds for "guaranteed" investment).

46. *E.g.*, Pollack v. Laidlaw Holdings, Inc., 27 F.3d 808 (2d Cir.1994) (mortgage participations sold by securities broker were securities).

47. Reves v. Ernst & Young, 494 U.S. 56, 110 S.Ct. 945, 108 L.Ed.2d 47 (1990) (explicitly identifying this as a factor in determining whether a note can be excluded as short-term commercial paper); Marine Bank v. Weaver, 455 U.S. 551, 102 S.Ct. 1220, 71 L.Ed.2d 409 (1982) (bank-issued certificate of deposit not a security subject to federal securities laws since it is already federally insured and purchasers therefore do not need that extra layer of protection the laws afford).

48. Great Rivers Coop. v. Farmland Industries, Inc., 198 F.3d 685 (8th Cir.1999) ("Notwithstanding the fact that Farmland registered these instruments as securities, a registration it states was made out of caution, we agree that the characterization of the capital credits as 'rights to purchase' stock did not transform the capital credits into securities").

49. *Id.*; Teague v. Bakker, 139 F.3d 892 (4th Cir. 1998) (unpublished, text in Westlaw).

history of struggling for an appropriate definition, courts have been mindful of the fact that the bottom-line question is whether the particular investment or instrument involved is one that needs or demands the investor protection of the federal (or state) securities laws.[66]

In its first pronouncement on this issue, the United States Supreme Court focused on the general character of the investment vehicle in question.[67] Specifically, in determining whether a security existed, the Court looked to (1) the terms of the offer; (2) the plan of distribution; and (3) the economic inducements that were held out to the prospective purchaser. Courts continue to adhere to this approach today. Just three years after its initial decision, the Court set forth a more specific test that also survives to this day.

In SEC v. W.J. Howey Co.[68] the Court announced: "An investment contract for purposes of the Securities Act means a contract, transaction or scheme whereby a person [1] invests his money [2] in a common enterprise and [3] is led to expect profits [4] solely from the efforts of the promoter or a third party."[69] The *Howey* case arose from the promotion of small lots of fruit trees where the offeror also offered a "management" contract by which an affiliate of the issuer would pick and market the fruit with the profit inuring to the investor. In finding the promotional scheme to be a security, the Court pointed out that not only are formal stock certificates not required, but a nominal ownership interest in the physical assets of the enterprise, such as actually owning fruit trees, does not preclude the determination that a security in fact exists. The Court in *Howey* did not present any single determinative factor in defining "security," but rather looked to the investment package as a whole, including the ways in which the investment was marketed to investors. This aspect of the *Howey* decision is the most significant since a reading of all of the relevant cases leads to the conclusion that what is being offered may not be as important as how it is being presented.

The existence of an investment contract depends not so much on what is actually being offered as how it is being offered, and what is being promised. Thus, for example, offering and receiving money for investments that do not in fact exist violate the securities laws.[70] It is sufficient that the essential ingredients of an investment contract are being offered.[71] Fraud in describing an investment opportunity which bears the characteristics of a security can create a security even if there is no substance to the business enterprise that is described. Thus, a Ponzi scheme, which resembles a chain letter, pyramid scheme, or similar fraud will implicate the federal securities laws.[74]

66. Marine Bank v. Weaver, 455 U.S. 551, 102 S.Ct. 1220, 71 L.Ed.2d 409 (1982) (bank-issued certificate of deposit not a security subject to federal securities laws since it is already federally insured and purchasers therefore do not need that extra layer of protection the laws afford).

67. SEC v. C.M. Joiner Leasing Corp., 320 U.S. 344, 64 S.Ct. 120, 88 L.Ed. 88 (1943).

68. 328 U.S. 293, 298–99, 66 S.Ct. 1100, 1102–03, 90 L.Ed. 1244 (1946).

69. 328 U.S. 293, 298–99, 66 S.Ct. 1100, 1102–03, 90 L.Ed. 1244 (1946).

70. SEC v. Lauer, 52 F.3d 667 (7th Cir.1995); SEC v. Gallard, 1997 WL 767570, [1998 Transfer Binder] Fed. Sec. L. Rep. (CCH) ¶ 90,144 (S.D.N.Y. 1997) (fact that securities did not exist did not preclude Rule 10b–5 claim).

71. SEC v. Unique Financial Concepts, 196 F.3d 1195, 1200 (11th Cir.1999), relying on SEC v. W. J. Howey Co., 328 U.S. 293, 301, 66 S.Ct. 1100, 1104, 90 L.Ed. 1244 (1946).

74. *See, e.g.*, SEC v. George, 426 F.3d 786 (6th Cir. 2005) (Ponzi scheme violated securities law antifraud provisions and prohibitions against unregistered offerings).

§ 1.6[2][A] The Investment of Money

The Supreme Court in the *Howey* decision spoke in terms of an investor in securities being someone who "invests his money." Does this mean that avoiding an upfront investment of cash or the equivalent will avoid subjecting the investment to the securities laws? The clear answer is that it will not. Subsequent case law has taken the position that the investment of services or property, as opposed to money, can also suffice.[87] However, the mere fact that an employment agreement contains a profit sharing arrangement will not be enough to create a security.[88] On the other hand, stock appreciation rights[89] or other instruments giving the recipient the functional equivalent of stock will be a security.[90]

§ 1.6[2][B] In a Common Enterprise

Another factor under the *Howey* test for identifying an investment contract that has undergone subsequent scrutiny is the requirement that there be a common enterprise. The common enterprise requirement focuses on the question of the extent to which the success of the investor's interest rises and falls with others involved in the enterprise.[92] In contrast to the generally accepted *Howey* test, the existence of a common enterprise is not necessary under the risk capital analysis[93] that has been adopted in many states and has received at least lip service in some federal decisions.[94]

A pooling of interests among more than one investor is the clearest example of a common enterprise.[95] However, courts have also been asked to find a common enterprise when only one investor may be involved. Courts have developed the concept of "horizontal commonality" to describe the pooling of like interests among investors,[96] in contrast to "vertical commonality" where the promoter shares risk with the investor.[97] Horizontal commonality clearly satisfies the *Howey* common enterprise requirement but the courts are divided as to whether vertical commonality will suffice.[98] However, it is equally clear that when there is no common enterprise, the *Howey* test will not be satisfied.

---

87. *See, e.g.,* Popovice v. Milides, 11 F.Supp.2d 638, 643 (E.D.Pa.1998) ("several courts have held that an agreement exchanging services for stock constitutes a 'sale' under the Securities Exchange Act").

88. *E.g.,* Peyton v. Morrow Electronics, Inc., 587 F.2d 413 (9th Cir.1978).

89. *E.g.,* Sanderson v. H.I.G. P–XI Holding, Inc., 2000 WL 1042813, [1999–2000 Transfer Binder] Fed. Sec. L. Rep. (CCH) ¶ 91,047 (E.D.La.2000) (stock appreciation rights are securities).

90. *See, e.g.,* Aiena v. Olsen, 69 F.Supp.2d 521, 534 (S.D.N.Y.1999) (certificates entitling former directors payments equivalent to stock dividends could be securities).

92. *See, e.g.,* SEC v. The Infinity Group Co., 212 F.3d 180 (3d Cir.2000), *affirming* 993 F.Supp. 321, 993 F.Supp. 324 (E.D.Pa.1998) (finding an investment contract based on pooling of investments where investors were promised fixed return).

93. King v. Pope, 91 S.W.3d 314 (Tenn. 2002) (sale-leaseback arrangement was a security under risk capital test even though there was no common enterprise).

94. The risk capital test is discussed in § 1.6[3] *infra.*

95. *See, e.g.,* SEC v. Montana, 464 F. Supp.2d 772 (S.D. Ind. 2006) (high yield "trading program" satisfied the common enterprise requirement and thus was a security).

96. *See, e.g.,* SEC v. Infinity Group Co., 212 F.3d 180, 187–188 (3d Cir.2000) ("Horizontal commonality is characterized by 'a pooling of investors' contributions and distributions of profits and losses on a pro-rata basis among investors' ").

97. Many of the cases involving horizontal and vertical commonality arose in the context of deciding whether a managed brokerage account is a security.

98. *See, e.g.,* Vale Natural Gas America Corp. v. Carrollton Resources 1990, Ltd., 795 F.Supp. 795 (E.D.La.1992).

The cases examining whether vertical commonality will suffice have taken varying approaches. The Fifth Circuit adopted a broad test of vertical commonality that is satisfied by a showing that the fortunes of the investor are inextricably tied to the promoter's efforts.[100] The broad approach to vertical commonality merely requires that the success of the investment be linked to the *efforts* of the promoter.[101] The Fifth Circuit is not alone in finding vertical commonality sufficient.[102] The Eleventh Circuit similarly recognizes a broad concept of when vertical commonality will satisfy the common enterprise requirement.[103] The court explained that the common enterprise requirement is satisfied when the investor's fortunes are tied to the success of the promoter or other third party.[104] Some courts have rejected a broad definition of vertical commonality.[105] The narrower test of vertical commonality requires that the investor's fortunes be tied to the *fortunes* of the promoter.[106] A number of courts have utilized the narrow view to find that managed commodities accounts are not securities.[107] The Ninth Circuit similarly has adopted a narrow test of vertical commonality to find that no security existed with regard to a coal purchase program, the success of which was dependent upon the defendant's unique ore processing technique.[108]

§ 1.6[2][C] With an Expectation of Profit

The absence of a profit expectation will preclude finding that a security exists.[119] In United Housing Foundation, Inc. v. Forman,[120] the Supreme Court established that an insignificant profit motive will not satisfy the expectation of profit requirement. This was echoed in the Court's later decision in International Brotherhood of Teamsters v. Daniel.[121] In a questionable unpub-

100. Long v. Shultz Cattle Co., 881 F.2d 129, 140–41 (5th Cir.1989).

101. Revak v. SEC Realty Corp., 18 F.3d 81, 87–88 (2d Cir.1994), *relying on* Long v. Shultz Cattle Co., 881 F.2d 129, 140–41 (5th Cir.1989); SEC v. Comcoa, Ltd., 855 F.Supp. 1258 (S.D.Fla.1994) (finding vertical commonality with regard to service to assist application and development of FCC licenses).

102. McGill v. American Land & Exploration Co., 776 F.2d 923, 924–25 (10th Cir.1985) (finding vertical commonality sufficient with regard to joint venture and that lack of horizontal commonality with other investors did not preclude a finding of a security).

103. SEC v. Unique Financial Concepts, 196 F.3d 1195, 1199 (11th Cir.1999); SEC v. Comcoa, Ltd., 855 F.Supp. 1258 (S.D.Fla.1994).

104. SEC v. Unique Financial Concepts, 196 F.3d 1195, 1199 (11th Cir.1999).

105. Schofield v. First Commodity Corp., 638 F.Supp. 4 (D.Mass.1985), *judgment affirmed* 793 F.2d 28 (1st Cir.1986); Mechigian v. Art Capital Corp., 612 F.Supp. 1421, 1427 (S.D.N.Y.1985). *Accord* Silverstein v. Merrill Lynch, Pierce, Fenner & Smith, Inc., 618 F.Supp. 436 (S.D.N.Y. 1985).

106. Revak v. SEC Realty Corp., 18 F.3d 81, 88 (2d Cir.1994) (holding that interests in a condominium were not securities); SEC v. Pinckney, 923 F.Supp. 76 (E.D.N.C.1996) (to establish vertical commonality, investor's profits must be linked to promoters; question of fact as to whether "strict vertical commonality" test was satisfied).

107. Mordaunt v. Incomco, 686 F.2d 815 (9th Cir.1982), *cert. denied* 469 U.S. 1115, 105 S.Ct. 801, 83 L.Ed.2d 793 (1985); Brodt v. Bache & Co., Inc., 595 F.2d 459 (9th Cir.1978).

108. SEC v. Goldfield Deep Mines Co., 758 F.2d 459 (9th Cir.1985).

119. *See, e.g.*, CanAccord Capital Corp., 2002 WL 126572 (SEC No Action Letter Jan. 18, 2002) (a "Term Note" accompanying a guarantee issued under the Quebec Immigrant Investor Program for Assistance to Business was not a security).

120. 421 U.S. 837, 95 S.Ct. 2051, 44 L.Ed.2d 621 (1975) (stock in residential housing cooperative was not a security).

121. 439 U.S. 551, 99 S.Ct. 790, 58 L.Ed.2d 808 (1979) (involuntary noncontributory pension plan was not a security).

lished decision, the Fourth Circuit affirmed a district court decision holding that it is not enough that the profit motive be a significant factor, it must be the primary factor in the marketing of the investment.[122] A substantial profit motive should be sufficient to support this aspect of the *Howey* test, even if it is not the only factor motivating investors.

The expectation of a profit is not limited to participation in the proceeds of a business or enterprise. Thus, the Supreme Court has made it clear that a promise of a fixed income stream can satisfy the profit requirement.[123] In an earlier decision the Court had identified the "touchstone" of an investment contract as "the presence of an investment in a common venture premised on a reasonable expectation of profits to be derived from the entrepreneurial or managerial efforts of others," and then laid out two examples of investor interests that had previously been found to have been "profits."[124] The Court in its decision in SEC v. Edwards then made it clear that this was not an exclusive list of what constitutes a profit[125] in holding that a fixed return instrument can be an investment contract under the *Howey* test.

§ 1.6[2][D] From the Efforts of Others

Under the original formulation of the *Howey* test, in order to have a security the profits must have been expected "solely from the efforts of the promoter or a third party."[126] Subsequent case law in the circuit courts have diluted the requirement that the profits be secured "solely" from the efforts of others; it is now only required that the profits be expected to be derived "primarily" or "substantially" from the efforts of others.[127] Where the investor's efforts are significant in the success of the enterprise, an investment contract (and hence a security) will not be found to exist.[128] Where the efforts of others are *de minimis* in assuring the success of the investment, the *Howey* test will not be satisfied.[129] In contrast, the fact that investors retain some control will not be sufficient to defeat the efforts of others requirement so long as the "efforts of others" are primarily significant.[130] Thus, the fact that *some* efforts of the investor are necessary for the success of the operation,

122. Teague v. Bakker, 139 F.3d 892, 1998 WL 168876 (4th Cir.1998) (unpublished, text in Westlaw).

123. SEC v. Edwards, 540 U.S. 389, 124 S.Ct. 892, 157 L.Ed.2d 813 (2004) (holding that a promise of a fixed return from a sale-leaseback arrangement satisfied *Howey's* profit requirement).

124. United Housing Foundation, Inc. v. Forman, 421 U.S. 837, 852, 95 S.Ct. 2051, 44 L.Ed.2d 621 (1975).

125. 540 U.S. at 394–396, 124 S.Ct. at 897–898. *Cf.* Comment, SEC v. Edwards: An Opportunity to Knock on the Viability of the Howey Test as the Gatekeeper for the Federal Securities Laws, 31 Okla. City U. L. Rev. 161 (2006).

126. SEC v. W.J. Howey Co., 328 U.S. 293, 298–99, 66 S.Ct. 1100, 1102–03, 90 L.Ed. 1244 (1946).

127. *See, e.g.,* SEC v. Glenn W. Turner Enterprises, Inc., 474 F.2d 476 (9th Cir.1973), *cert. denied* 414 U.S. 821, 94 S.Ct. 117, 38 L.Ed.2d 53 (1973).

128. *E.g.,* Steinhardt Group v. Citicorp, 126 F.3d 144 (3d Cir.1997) (limited partnership interest in securitization transaction was not a security where limited partner's retention of "pervasive control" meant that he was relying extensively on his own efforts).

129. *E.g.,* SEC v. Life Partners, Inc., 87 F.3d 536 (D.C.Cir.1996), *rehearing denied* 102 F.3d 587 (D.C.Cir.1996) (viatical settlements, whereby investor receives death benefits of life insurance policy taken out on AIDS victim, were not securities since efforts of others was ministerial rather than substantive).

130. *See, e.g.,* SEC v. Unique Financial Concepts, 196 F.3d 1195, 1201–1202 (11th Cir.1999).

such as with pyramid sales arrangements,[131] licensing agreements,[132] founder-membership contracts and customer referral agreements,[133] including those denominated, at least in form, as franchise contracts,[134] does not change the scheme's character from that of an investment contract. It is clear, however, that a bona fide franchise agreement is not a security.[135] Similarly, a contract to provide bona fide services is not a sale of a security.[136] Nevertheless, a security exists when a so-called service involves a common enterprise in addition to a significant investment risk and the promoter's efforts are necessary to make the investment a success.[137] Thus, the fact that an investment may resemble a franchise in form will not insulate it from the securities laws if in substance it is a passive investment.[138]

Not every effort of the promoter (or others) will render an investment subject to the securities laws. Although in one instance, a district court held that assignments of future insurance benefits, or other contract rights, were securities where the promoter's efforts are necessary to maintain a secondary market and to assure the investor of his or her profit,[142] the ruling was reversed on appeal. The court of appeals reversed, holding that the post-purchase services of others were merely ministerial and thus not sufficient to satisfy the "efforts of others" prong of the *Howey* test.[143] In the course of its opinion the court of appeals further indicated that the efforts of others must be significant for success after the instrument is marketed. Accordingly, the fact that others efforts were significant in defining and promoting the investment vehicles was not sufficient to classify viatical[144] agreements or settlements as securities since the promoter's activities did not bear upon the

131. *E.g.,* SEC v. Glenn W. Turner Enterprises, Inc., 474 F.2d 476 (9th Cir.1973), *cert. denied* 414 U.S. 821, 94 S.Ct. 117, 38 L.Ed.2d 53 (1973) (pyramid scheme based on self-improvement course); SEC v. Koscot Interplanetary, Inc., 497 F.2d 473 (5th Cir.1974) (pyramid scheme based on cosmetic sales distributorships was a security).

132. SEC v. Aqua–Sonic Products Corp., 524 F.Supp. 866 (S.D.N.Y.1981).

133. *See, e.g.,* United States v. Holtzclaw, 950 F.Supp 1306 (S.D.W.Va.1997) (customer referral agreement in connection with gold investment program was not a security), *affirmed on other grounds*, 131 F.3d 137 (4th Cir. 1997).

134. *See* Mitzner v. Cardet International, Inc., 358 F.Supp 1262 (N.D.Ill.1973).

135. *E.g.,* Martin v. T.V. Tempo, Inc., 628 F.2d 887 (5th Cir.1980); Nash & Associates, Inc. v. Lum's of Ohio, Inc., 484 F.2d 392 (6th Cir.1973).

136. Broadview Financial, Inc. v. Entech Management Services Corp., 859 F.Supp. 444, 450–51 (D.Colo.1994) (agreement under which investment banker would render services to facilitate a merger was not a security).

137. *E.g.,* SEC v. Comcoa Ltd., 855 F.Supp. 1258 (S.D.Fla.1994).

138. SEC v. Friendly Power Co. 49 F.Supp.2d 1363 (S D.Fla.1999) (interests in a limited liability company for a franchise were securities where investors had no significant control over the enterprise).

142. *See* SEC v. Life Partners, Inc., 898 F.Supp. 14 (D.D.C.1995) (viatical settlements of life insurance policies on AIDS victims), *s.c.* 912 F.Supp. 4 (D.D.C.1996), reversed 87 F.3d 536 (D.C.Cir.1996), 102 F.3d 587 (D.C.Cir.1996).

143. SEC v. Life Partners, Inc., 87 F.3d 536 (D.C.Cir.1996), rehearing denied 102 F.3d 587 (D.C.Cir.1996).

144. A viatical agreement permits a terminally ill patient to receive a present discounted payment on his or her life insurance benefits in return for giving up the death benefits when the patient dies. These arrangements have been marketed widely, especially to H.I.V. and aids victims. A number of governments agencies have challenged these arrangements as unfair or deceptive as has the North American Securities Administrators Association. *See* Special Report, Betting on Death: Insurance Settlements Intended to Help the Dying Have Short–Changed Them and Fleeced Many Investors Instead, Consumer Reports (Feb. 2001); Viaticals Not Sure Thing, http://cnnfn.cnn.com/2001/01/16/insurance/q_viatical/.

fundamental success or failure of the underlying investment.[145] There is some authority, however, to the contrary which holds viatical contracts are securities under federal law,[146] at least where investors were sold fractional interests in the underlying insurance policies.[147]

§ 1.6[3] Alternative Interpretation of "Investment Contract"—Risk Capital Analysis

The general principles of the *Howey* investment contract analysis set forth broad guidelines as to when a security will be found to exist. Many of the cases are best understood not only in terms of the general principles but in the context of the particular type of investment involved.

Although couched in different terminology, the risk capital analysis is aimed at similar criteria as the *Howey* test, although, as noted above, under the risk capital analysis, it may not be necessary to find a common enterprise. The key is the dependency upon others for the success of the enterprise and the promotion of the activity as an investment vehicle.

The risk capital approach can be defined in terms of a four factor analysis.[158] The risk capital test will result in the finding of an investment contract when (1) the offeree provides initial value to the enterprise;[159] (2) the initial value is subject to the risks of the enterprise; (3) the initial value is induced by representations leading to a reasonable understanding that the offeree will realize a valuable benefit[160] beyond the initial value; and (4) the offeree does not exercise practical and managerial control over the enterprise.[161]

While addressing the same basic concepts as the *Howey* test, the risk capital analysis provides more flexibility and does not lead to so stringent an application as to raise questions of whether vertical commonality is sufficient or whether the profit is limited to economic benefit. Thus, for example, a managed commodities account would clearly fall within the risk capital test, while many federal circuits hold that it will not be a security under the *Howey* test without some element of vertical commonality.[162] This is the case because the elements of the risk capital test can be satisfied even though the

---

145. *E.g.*, SEC v. Life Partners, Inc., 87 F.3d 536 (D.C.Cir.1996), *rehearing denied* 102 F.3d 587 (D.C.Cir.1996) (viatical settlements, whereby investor receives death benefits of life insurance policy taken out on AIDS victim, were not securities since efforts of others was ministerial rather than substantive).

146. SEC v. Mutual Benefits Corp., 408 F.3d 737 (11th Cir. 2005), *cert. dismissed* ___ U.S. ___, 128 S.Ct. 17, 168 L.Ed.2d 793 (2007), *affirming* 323 F.Supp.2d 1337 (S.D. Fla. 2004) (viatical contract was a security).

147. *See* Wuliger v. Christie, 310 F.Supp.2d 897, 903–904 (N.D. Ohio 2004).

158. Silver Hills Country Club v. Sobieski, 55 Cal.2d 811, 13 Cal.Rptr. 186, 361 P.2d 906 (1961); Hawaii v. Hawaii Market Center, 52 Haw. 642, 485 P.2d 105, 109 (1971), *relying on* Coffey, The Economic Realities of a "Security": Is There a Meaningful Formula?, 18 W. Res. L. Rev. 366, 367 (1967).

159. This phraseology indicates that investment of value is not limited to money or cash equivalents.

160. This language seems to make clear that a benefit other than traditional profits can satisfy the test. This is in contrast to the expectation of profit requirement under the *Howey* test.

161. This parallels the *Howey* test's efforts of others requirement.

162. *See, e.g.*, Brodt v. Bache & Co., 595 F.2d 459 (9th Cir.1978) (managed commodities account is not a security).

investment does not involve a common enterprise.[163] Another example of the risk capital test's inclusiveness is demonstrated in comparison with *Howey's* expectation of profit requirement. Under the *Howey* analysis, the profit expectation must be a substantial if not primary focus of the transaction.[164] In contrast, the risk capital approach looks for a "substantial benefit." Thus, for example, an equity interest in a golf course or country club can satisfy the risk capital test when it would not be a security under the *Howey* test.[165]

§ 1.6[4] Leasing Programs as Securities

Ordinarily, leasehold interests are not securities. However, over the years there have been a variety of leasing syndications and leasing programs that have satisfied the *Howey* test and thus have been classified as securities.

A number of decisions have found that interests in leases of master video and audio recordings are investment contracts and thus held that they are securities under both federal and state law.[168] Similarly, a video production program has been held to be a security.[169] However, when the leasing program lacks a common enterprise or is dependent upon the investor's managerial efforts, a security will not be found to exist.

In SEC v. Edwards,[174] the Supreme Court held that a sale-leaseback program involving pay telephones could be a security under the *Howey* test.[175] The Court reached this result even though the arrangement promised a fixed rather than variable return.[176]

§ 1.6[5] Franchises and Distributorships—Pyramid Schemes as Securities

As is the case with leasing programs, most franchises and distributorships ordinarily are not securities.[181] This is so because in a true franchise or distribution, the efforts of the franchisee or distributor are extremely significant to the success of the enterprise.[182] However, when the efforts of the

---

163. King v. Pope, 91 S.W.3d 314 (Tenn. 2002) (sale-leaseback arrangement was a security under risk capital test even though there was no common enterprise). *See* Gregory J. Pease, Note, Bluer Skies in Tennessee—The Recent Broadening of the Definition of Investment Contract as a Security and an Argument for a Unified Federal–State Definition of Investment Contract 35 U. Mem. L. Rev. 109 (2004).

164. *See, e.g.*, Teague v. Bakker, 139 F.3d 892 (4th Cir. 1998) (unpublished, text in Westlaw).

165. *Compare, e.g.*, Silver Hills Country Club v. Sobieski, 55 Cal.2d 811, 13 Cal.Rptr. 186, 361 P.2d 906 (1961) (country club interest held to be a security under risk capital analysis), *with, e.g.*, Manchester Country Club, 31 Sec. Reg. & L. Rep. (BNA) 730 (SEC No Action Letter May 13, 1999) (country club equity interest would not be treated as a security under federal law); Bent Creek Country Club, 1993 WL 380731 (SEC No Action Letter Sept. 23, 1993) (country club equity interests did not have to be registered under federal law; no action letter was also secured from the state securities regulator).

168. Kolibash v. Sagittarius Recording Co., 626 F.Supp. 1173 (S.D.Ohio 1986) (holding that promised tax benefits satisfied the requirement that there be an expectation of a profit).

169. Nottingham v. General American Communications Corp., 811 F.2d 873 (5th Cir.1987).

174. 540 U.S. 389, 124 S.Ct. 892, 157 L.Ed.2d 813 (2004).

175. As eloquently stated by Justice O'Connor: "Opportunity doesn't always knock ... sometimes it rings. App. 113 (ETS Payphones promotional brochure). And sometimes it hangs up. So it did for the 10,000 people who invested a total of $300 million in the payphone sale-and-leaseback arrangements touted by respondent under that slogan." 540 U.S. at 391, 124 S.Ct. at 895.

176. 540 U.S. at 395–397, 124 S.Ct. at 897–898.

181. *E.g.*, Martin v. T.V. Tempo, Inc., 628 F.2d 887 (5th Cir.1980); Nash & Associates, Inc. v. Lum's of Ohio, Inc., 484 F.2d 392 (6th Cir.1973).

182. *See, e.g.*, Whole Living, Inc. v. Tolman, 344 F. Supp.2d 739 (D. Utah 2004) (distributorship was not a security; profit expectation was based in large parts on the efforts of the distributor). *See also* the discussion of the efforts of others § 1.6[2][D] *supra*.

promoter or someone associated with the promoter are the undeniably significant ones, a security will exist. If the efforts of the promoter are sufficiently significant, the fact that *some* efforts on the part of the investor are necessary for the success of the operation will not preclude a security from being found. Thus, pyramid sales arrangements,[183] licensing agreements,[184] founder-membership contracts and customer referral agreements,[185] including those denominated, at least in form, as franchise contracts,[186] have all been found to be securities under an economic reality analysis. It is clear that simply because an investment may resemble a franchise in form, the investment will not be insulated from the securities laws if in substance it is passive and its success is substantially dependent on the efforts of others.[187]

§ 1.6[6] Commodities and Managed Accounts as Securities

Another fertile area of litigation has involved the classification of commodities-related investments. Commodities themselves and commodity futures contracts are not securities. However, commodities based investments can fall under the ambit of the securities laws if certain conditions are satisfied. Based upon the extent of managerial and market-making activities offered by the seller, a gold investment has been held to be a security.[188] However, when all that is offered is the underlying commodity combined with storage and marketing services there is no security since the investor is relying upon the market price of the commodity rather than the seller's marketing or managerial efforts.[189] In contrast, when the object underlying the futures contract is itself a security, the futures contract may also be classified as a security.[190] This type of arrangement is in economic reality more like a securities option contract, which is clearly a security. However, where the subject of the futures contract is not a security but merely an index based on securities prices, a security has been held not to exist.[191] In 2000, Congress resolved some of these issues in amending the securities and commodities laws to provide that trading can now take place in futures on individual securities; and these futures contracts may be traded in both the securities and commodities markets.[192] That same legislation also provided that securi-

183. *E.g.,* SEC v. Glenn W. Turner Enterprises, Inc., 474 F.2d 476 (9th Cir.1973), *cert. denied* 414 U.S. 821, 94 S.Ct. 117, 38 L.Ed.2d 53 (1973) (pyramid scheme based on self-improvement course); SEC v. Koscot Interplanetary, Inc., 497 F.2d 473 (5th Cir.1974) (pyramid scheme based on cosmetic sales distributorships was a security).

184. SEC v. Aqua–Sonic Products Corp., 524 F.Supp. 866 (S.D.N.Y.1981).

185. *See, e.g.* Florida Discount Centers, Inc. v. Antinori, 232 So.2d 17 (Fla.1970); Hawaii v. Hawaii Market Center, Inc., 52 Hawaii 642, 485 P.2d 105 (1971).

186. *See* Mitzner v. Cardet International, Inc., 358 F.Supp. 1262 (N.D.Ill.1973).

187. SEC v. Friendly Power Co., 49 F.Supp.2d 1363 (S.D.Fla.1999) (interests in a limited liability company for a franchise were securities where investors had no significant control over the enterprise).

188. SEC v. International Mining Exchange, Inc., 515 F.Supp. 1062 (D.Colo.1981).

189. *See, e.g.,* Noa v. Key Futures, Inc., 638 F.2d 77 (9th Cir.1980). *Cf.* Dahl v. English, 578 F.Supp. 17 (N.D.Ill.1983) (artwork held not to be a security). Similarly, although a futures contract is not a security, GNMA forward contracts implicate the securities law as well as federal commodities regulation. Abrams v. Oppenheimer Government Securities, Inc., 737 F.2d 582 (7th Cir.1984).

190. Abrams v. Oppenheimer Government Securities, Inc., 737 F.2d 582 (7th Cir.1984).

191. Mallen v. Merrill Lynch, Pierce, Fenner & Smith Inc., 605 F.Supp. 1105 (N.D.Ga.1985). *See generally* David J. Gilberg, Regulation of New Financial Instruments Under the Federal Securities and Commodities Laws, 39 Vand.L.Rev. 1599 (1986). *See* § 1.7 *infra.*

192. Commodity Futures Modernization Act of 2000, Pub. Law No. 106–554, 114 Stat. 2763 (Dec. 21, 2000).

ties-based swap agreements are not securities, although they are subject to the securities laws' antifraud provisions.[193]

The Fifth[195] and Eighth[196] Circuits held that a managed brokerage account is a security. The pivotal issue is the existence of a common enterprise. The courts have analyzed this in terms of vertical or horizontal commonality. The Fifth Circuit has adopted a broad test of vertical commonality that is satisfied by a showing that the fortunes of the investor are inextricably tied to the promoter's efforts.[197] The Second Circuit has rejected the broad view of vertical commonality in favor of a stricter view.[198] The broad test of vertical commonality simply requires that the success of the investment be linked to the *efforts* of the promoter.[199] In contrast, the narrower test of vertical commonality requires that the investor's fortunes be tied to the *fortunes* of the promoter.[200] Utilizing this test, the Seventh,[201] Third[202] and Ninth Circuits[203] held that managed commodities accounts are not securities.

§ 1.6[7] Employee Benefit Plans as Securities

In International Brotherhood of Teamsters v. Daniel,[215] the Supreme Court ruled that a compulsory noncontributory defined benefit employee pension plan is not a security under the 1933 Act's definition.[216] The Court made note of not only the involuntary nature of the plan, but also the fact that there was no employee contribution (*i.e.*, no investment of money); these factors strongly negated any inference that a security was involved. The Court also noted that insofar as it was faced with a defined benefit plan, the pay-out to the employee upon retirement bore no relation to the employee's contribution in terms of time in service. Another factor considered by the Supreme Court in *Daniel* was that there was no substantial expectation of a profit.

193. Commodity Futures Modernization Act of 2000, Pub. Law No. 106–554, 114 Stat. 2763 (Dec. 21, 2000). *See* 1933 Act §§ 2A, 17(a), 15 U.S.C.A. §§ 77b–1, 77q(a).

195. SEC v. Continental Commodities Corp., 497 F.2d 516 (5th Cir.1974). *See also e.g.,* Taylor v. Bear Stearns & Co., 572 F.Supp. 667 (N.D.Ga.1983); Westlake v. Abrams, 565 F.Supp. 1330 (N.D.Ga.1983).

196. Booth v. Peavey Co. Commodity Services, 430 F.2d 132, 133 (8th Cir.1970) (indicating the presence of a remedy under the securities acts for churning in a discretionary commodities account). *Cf.* SEC v. Professional Associates, 731 F.2d 349 (6th Cir.1984) (trust agreements held to be securities).

197. This broad test has been rejected by other courts. *E.g.* Schofield v. First Commodity Corp., 638 F.Supp. 4 (D.Mass.1985), *judgment affirmed* 793 F.2d 28 (1st Cir.1986).

198. Revak v. SEC Realty Corp., 18 F.3d 81 (2d Cir.1994).

199. Revak v. SEC Realty Corp., 18 F.3d 81, 87–88 (2d Cir.1994), *relying on* Long v. Shultz Cattle Co., 881 F.2d 129, 140–41 (5th Cir.1989).

200. *See, e.g.*, Revak v. SEC Realty Corp., 18 F.3d 81, 88 (2d Cir.1994) (holding that interests in a condominium were not securities).

201. Milnarik v. M–S Commodities, Inc., 457 F.2d 274 (7th Cir.1972), *cert. denied* 409 U.S. 887, 93 S.Ct. 113, 34 L.Ed.2d 144 (1972).

202. Wasnowic v. Chicago Board of Trade, 352 F.Supp. 1066 (M.D.Pa.1972), *affirmed mem.* 491 F.2d 752 (3d Cir.1973), *cert. denied* 416 U.S. 994, 94 S.Ct. 2407, 40 L.Ed.2d 773 (1974).

203. Mordaunt v. Incomco, 686 F.2d 815 (9th Cir.1982), *cert. denied* 469 U.S. 1115, 105 S.Ct. 801, 83 L.Ed.2d 793 (1985); Brodt v. Bache & Co., Inc., 595 F.2d 459 (9th Cir.1978). *Accord* Popham, Haik, Schnobrich, Kaufman & Doty, Ltd. v. Price, 1984 WL 2395, [1983–1984 Transfer Binder] Fed.Sec.L.Rep. (CCH) ¶ 99,682 (D.D.C.1984).

215. 439 U.S. 551, 99 S.Ct. 790, 58 L.Ed.2d 808 (1979). *Accord* Coward v. Colgate–Palmolive Co., 686 F.2d 1230 (7th Cir.1982). *See also* Childers v. Northwest Airlines, Inc., 688 F.Supp. 1357, 20 Sec.Reg. & L.Rep. (BNA) 1166 (D.Minn.1988) (ESOP was not a security).

216. *See e.g.* Register v. Cameron & Barkley Co., 467 F. Supp.2d 519, 532–534 (D.S.C. 2006) (participation in compulsory noncontributory ESOP plan was not a security).

Since a large part of the eventual retirement benefits were to be derived from the employer's contribution, rather than from the reinvestment income derived from the efforts of pension plan managers, the profit aspects of the plan were too insubstantial to fall within the concept of an investment contract. Moreover, the Court focused on a number of contingencies to the plan's vesting, which in turn rendered any "profit" too speculative to justify a reasonable expectation. Because of the multiplicity of factors involved in the *Daniel* decision, it cannot be safely said that a pension plan will never be characterized as a security. In fact, benefit plans that have the investment characteristics of securities will fall under the Act. For example, a voluntary contributory plan with a variable annuity might well be found to be subject to the securities laws.[218] Similarly, interests in a voluntary employee stock option plan clearly are securities.[219] In contrast, a mandatory stock option plan completely funded by the employer is not a security.[220]

There are public policy reasons for minimizing the impact of the securities laws on certain types of employee compensation plans in order to encourage employers to offer employees a share in the profits of the business. Accordingly, stock compensation plans of non-public companies can qualify for an exemption from the 1933 Act's registration requirements.[221] Compensation to executives and other key employees of both privately held and publicly traded companies may also qualify for an exemption from registration.[222] Additionally, stock offerings to employees of publicly held companies can qualify for a very short registration form.[223]

§ 1.6[8] Variable Annuities as Securities

While variable annuity contracts come within the ambit of the securities laws,[226] fixed annuities, as is generally the case with insurance policies, do not.[227] However, the Seventh Circuit held an annuity with a minimum guarantee to be a security.[228] The Commission adopted a safe harbor rule under which qualifying annuities need not be registered as securities.[229] Those annuities qualifying for the safe harbor include annuities with guaranteed

218. *Cf.* SEC v. Variable Annuity Life Insurance Co., 359 U.S. 65, 79 S.Ct. 618, 3 L.Ed.2d 640 (1959) (variable annuity held to be a non-exempt security).

219. *E.g.,* Uselton v. Commercial Lovelace Motor Freight, Inc., 940 F.2d 564 (10th Cir.1991), *cert. denied* 502 U.S. 983, 112 S.Ct. 589, 116 L.Ed.2d 614 (1991) (contributory voluntary employee stock ownership plan was a security; ERISA did not provide sufficient protection to displace the application of federal securities laws).

220. Matassarin v. Lynch, 174 F.3d 549 (5th Cir.1999).

221. SEC Rule 701, 17 C.F.R. § 230.701, which is discussed in § 4.18 *infra.*

222. The applicable exemption here would be the one for transactions by issuers not involving a public offering. 1933 Act § 4(2), 15 U.S.C.A. § 77d(2), which is discussed in §§ 4.24, 4.25 *infra.*

223. 1933 Act Form SB8, 17 C.F.R. § 239.16b.

226. *See, e.g.,* SEC v. United Benefit Life Insurance Co., 387 U.S. 202, 87 S.Ct. 1557, 18 L.Ed.2d 673 (1967); SEC v. Variable Annuity Life Insurance Co., 359 U.S. 65, 79 S.Ct. 618, 3 L.Ed.2d 640 (1959).

227. Allen v. Lloyd's of London, 94 F.3d 923 (4th Cir.1996) (settlement of disputes and formation of reinsurance entity did not involve securities since the participants in the settlement did not stand to make any profit from the reinsurance enterprise).

228. Otto v. Variable Annuity Life Ins. Co., 814 F.2d 1127 (7th Cir.1986) (the court noted that the minimum was low and there was an expectation of a higher payout).

229. 17 C.F.R. § 230.151. *See* § 4.9 *infra. Compare, e.g.,* the proposed rules for equity indexed annuities. *See* Indexed Annuities and Other Insurance Contracts, Sec. Act Rel. No. 33–8933, Sec. Exch. Act Rel. No. 34–58022, 73 Fed. Reg. 37752–01, 2008 WL 2571221 ((SEC June 25, 2008).

purchase benefits based on the purchase price and interest credited thereto, provided further that the annuity contracts are not marketed as investments.[230] The safe harbor thus depends on the investment risk falling on the insurer rather than the insured.

§ 1.6[9] Real Estate Interests as Securities

As discussed more fully below, interests in real estate by themselves will not be securities. However, a security may be found when a real estate investment is packaged more as an investment contract, along the lines identified in the *Howey* case, which itself involved the sale of real estate interests. Thus, courts will determine whether the real estate related investment has the benchmarks of other securities.

Real estate, even when purchased for investment, ordinarily will not be a security. However, syndicated or pooled real estate interests may fall within the *Howey* test's definition of security.

In a decision that predated *Daniel*, the Supreme Court, in United Housing Foundation, Inc. v. Forman, ruled that shares of stock in a cooperative residential housing project did not fall within the Securities Act's definition.[249] As discussed in a subsequent subsection of this treatise,[250] although "stock" is expressly included in the Act's definition of security, the fact that the shares in the condominium were denominated as stock by the cooperative association was not considered dispositive of the matter since the shares had none of the traditional characteristics which investment stock generally possesses.[251] Also, analyzing the real estate interest irrespective of its denomination as stock, the Court in *Foreman* found that under the *Howey* test a security did not exist and thus upheld substance over form by focusing on the economic reality of the investment venture. The Court distinguished resort condominium cases in which someone might well be induced to purchase the property primarily for investment, since the buildings in *Forman* were used as bona fide primary residences. Although the other criteria of the four-factor *Howey* test may have been met, there was no expectation of a profit, despite promised rent deductions through profits rebated from commercial leasing. The Court found that this "return" on the commercial properties was, at best, tangential to the stock and thus the residential lease agreements were properly characterized as residential housing contracts rather than as investment contracts.[253]

Generally, a conveyance of real estate will not be subject to the securities laws.[254] Thus, for example, a condominium interest will not ordinarily be a

230. 17 C.F.R. § 230.151.

249. 421 U.S. 837, 95 S.Ct. 2051, 44 L.Ed.2d 621 (1975). *Accord* Hackford v. First Security Bank of Utah, 464 U.S. 827, 104 S.Ct. 100, 78 L.Ed.2d 105 (1983) (shares of "stock" in range land entitling owners to grazing privileges held not a security since there was no profit expectation).

250. *See* § 1.6[13] *infra*.

251. "Despite their name, they lack what the court in Tcherepnin deemed the most common feature of stock: the right to receive 'dividends contingent upon an apportionment of profits'. 389 U.S. at 339. Nor do they possess the other characteristics traditionally associated with stock: they are not negotiable; they cannot be pledged or hypothecated; they confer no voting rights in proportion to the number of shares owned; and they cannot appreciate in value." 421 U.S. at 851, 95 S.Ct. at 2060.

253. 421 U.S. at 855–58, 95 S.Ct. at 2061–63.

254. *E.g.*, Wals v. Fox Hills Development Corp., 24 F.3d 1016 (7th Cir.1994) (sale of time share unit was not sale of a security).

security.[255] However, when a transaction has the investment type indicia normally associated with investment contracts, a security may be found to exist.[256]

Sale of a real estate interest for investment or commercial purposes will be a security when the profit potential is dependent upon management of the real estate by the promoter of the real estate program.[257] For example, sale of boat slips with resale options that were marketed as an investment were held to be securities.[258] However, commercial real estate that is sold to tenants in common will not necessarily be a security if the owners are not relying primarily on the promoter's efforts for profitability.

Residential real estate can also be a security when marketed for investment purposes. Thus, for example, a security will exist where residential condominium interests are marketed with collateral agreements giving rise to a profit expectation.[260] For the same reason, an investment contract, and hence a security, will exist with respect to a real estate interest offered and sold with promises of profits from a shared rental pool in units to be managed by someone other than the investor.[261] Similarly, the currently fashionable marketing of real estate interests through time-share or shared equity programs raises securities law issues because of the possibility of finding an investment contract.[262] However, properly marketed as a vacation residence, time-share interests will not be securities. Nevertheless, when the time-share interest is offered more as an investment than as a place to stay, the securities laws are more likely to be implicated.

Fractional undivided interests in oil and mineral rights are expressly covered by the statutory definition of security.[265] However, a leasehold interest has been held to be an interest in realty and thus not a security.[266]

Country club memberships can be seen as analogous to real estate interests. Frequently country clubs raise funds through founder-memberships or the issuance of stock in lieu of an initiation fee. Country club interests may be classified as securities under some state laws,[268] but ordinarily will not be

255. Revak v. SEC Realty Corp., 18 F.3d 81 (2d Cir.1994) (condominium interest was not an investment contract and hence not a security).

256. Hocking v. Dubois, 885 F.2d 1449 (9th Cir.1989), *cert. denied* 494 U.S. 1078, 110 S.Ct. 1805, 108 L.Ed.2d 936 (1990) (question of fact as to whether rental pool arrangement was a security).

257. *See, e.g.,* Triple Net Leasing, LLC, 2000 WL 1221859 (SEC No Action Letter Aug. 23, 2000) (exchange of net real estate interest with net lease arrangement would be a security).

258. *See* Branan v. State, 285 Ga.App. 717, 647 S.E.2d 606 (2007) (applying Georgia law).

260. *See* Hocking v. Dubois, 839 F.2d 560 (9th Cir.1988).

261. SEC v. Kirkland, 521 F.Supp.2d 1281 (M.D. Fla. 2007) (sale of triplex units to be managed by promoters with profits coming out of a shared rental pool were sales of securities).

262. *See, e.g.,* David M. Fields, Real Estate Interests as Investment Contracts: An Update and a New Application: The Shared Equity Program, 12 Real Est. L.J. 307 (1984).

265. *See* SEC v. Shoreline Development Co., 149 Fed. Appx. 659 (9th Cir. 2005) (fractional undivided interests in oil and gas were securities); Cascade Energy & Metals Corp. v. Banks, 896 F.2d 1557 (10th Cir.1990), *cert. denied* 498 U.S. 849, 111 S.Ct. 138, 112 L.Ed.2d 105 (1990).

266. Deutsch Energy Co. v. Mazur, 813 F.2d 1567 (9th Cir.1987); Coal Resources, Inc. v. Gulf & Western Indus., Inc., 756 F.2d 443 (6th Cir.1985), *on remand* 645 F.Supp. 1028 (S.D.Ohio 1986).

268. *E.g.* Silver Hills Country Club v. Sobieski, 55 Cal.2d 811, 13 Cal.Rptr. 186, 361 P.2d 906 (1961).

subject to federal law because of the absence of a profit expectation.[269] However, if there is a profit potential, then the federal definition may be invoked.[270]

Outside of the real estate context, it has been held that a syndication agreement will not be subject to the securities laws where "the agreement is designed to allow the investor to *use* or *consume* the item purchased."[271] However, the result should be otherwise if the shares are marketed as an investment rather than simply a consumable.

§ 1.6[10] Partnership Interests as Securities

The applicability of the securities laws to partnerships, limited liability companies, and the like will depend upon whether the ownership interest in the business satisfies the investment contract analysis as set forth in the *Howey* test. In most instances, interests in a limited partnership are likely to fall within the statutory definition of security.[273] In some instances, joint ventures and general partnerships might also fall under the securities laws' coverage.[274]

In the case of a limited partnership interest, the Uniform Limited Partnership Act requires that, at least to some extent, the investment be a passive one. Any significant degree of control or management in the enterprise may transform the limited partner into a general partner.[275] Accordingly, any time there is a bona fide limited partnership interest, by definition, the investor puts his or her funds at risk depending primarily upon the efforts of others, *i.e.*, the managing partners. It follows that unless the limited partner exercises an unusual amount of control over the business,[276] his or her limited partnership interest will be a security.[277]

Most states permit general partnerships to register as limited liability partnerships (LLPs), thereby limiting the liability of the partners.[284] Although technically still a general partnership interest, frequently investors in LLPs are passive, with management vested in a centralized person or entity. This type of limited liability partnership more closely resembles a limited partnership and generally should be considered to be a security.[285] On the other hand,

---

269. Rice v. Branigar Organization, Inc., 922 F.2d 788 (11th Cir.1991) (sale of membership and undeveloped lots in beach club development was not the sale of a security).

270. Club at Pelican Bay, Inc., 26 Sec. Reg. & L. Rep. (BNA) 104 (SEC no action letter available Jan. 7, 1994) (refusing to issue a no action response for transferable country club interests).

271. Wabash Valley Power Association v. Public Service Co. of Indiana, 678 F.Supp. 757 (S.D.Ind.1988) (contract for construction of nuclear power plant held not a security since investor planned to use resulting power).

273. *See, e.g.,* Republic Property Trust v. Republic Properties, 540 F. Supp.2d 144, 160–161 (D.D.C. 2008) (sale of limited partnership interests generally will involve sales of securities).

274. *See, e.g.,* Consolidated Management Group, LLC v. Department of Corporations, 162 Cal.App.4th 598, 75 Cal.Rptr.3d 795 (1 Dist. 2008) (joint venture interests were securities).

275. *See, e.g.,* Weil v. Diversified Properties, 319 F.Supp. 778 (D.D.C.1970); Grainger v. Antoyan, 48 Cal.2d 805, 313 P.2d 848 (1957).

276. *See, e.g.,* Republic Property Trust v. Republic Properties 540 F. Supp.2d 144, 160–161 (D.D.C. 2008) (limited partner's ability to exercise management control precluded finding that limited partnership interest was a security).

277. *See, e.g.,* Lawrence v. Cohn, 325 F.3d 141 (2d Cir. 2003) (limited partnership interests were securities but Rule 10b–5 claim dismissed since plaintiff was neither a purchaser nor a seller).

284. *See* James D. Cox & Thomas Lee Hazen, Cox and Hazen on Corporations § 1.07[6] (2d ed. 2003).

285. *Cf.* United States v. Leonard, 529 F.3d 83 (2d Cir. 2008) (even though limited liability company membership agreement gave members the potential for member control, the reality was that the investors were passive and thus a security existed).

general partnerships where the partners play an active role may also qualify as an LLP but their interests would not be securities because of their involvement in the day-to-day operations of the business.

Since a general partnership interest and most joint ventures will ordinarily carry with them a substantial say in the management of the enterprise, they will not fall under the securities laws' purview unless there is substantial reliance on the efforts of others.[288] However, where a joint venturer or general partner does not exercise control and in essence is a passive investor, a security will be found to exist.[289] The fact that partners in a general partnership have the potential to exercise control in the enterprise will not preclude any general partnership interest from being a security.[290] The ultimate determination will depend on the ways in which the partnership interests are marketed to the investors. If it is contemplated that the partners will play a passive role while the business is managed by someone else, then the securities laws are likely to be implicated.[291]

§ 1.6[11] Limited Liability Company Interests as Securities

In the 1980s the limited liability company emerged as a new form of doing business and has continued to become increasingly popular. In fact, in many instances, the limited liability company has become the entity of choice in forming a new business. Limited liability companies are designed to give investors the benefit of pass-through tax treatment that applies to limited partnerships without imposing the limitation that limited partners may not exert too much control in the day-to-day management lest they be declared general partners and thereby lose their limited liability shield. The limited liability company has become the form of choice for non-corporate business entities. Since neither partnership interests nor shares in limited liability companies are expressly listed in the Act's definition of "security," unlike corporate stock, they qualify as securities only if they fall within the definition of an "investment contract."[295] Many limited liability companies (and hence shares in those companies) have corporate attributes, including possibly the centralization of management. Nevertheless, limited liability companies can be set up as member managed LLCs, not having a centralized management and in such cases should be treated like a general partnership which ordinarily is not a security. However, if the limited liability company agreement provides a centralized management, for the same reasons that a limited partnership interest ordinarily will be a security, interests in limited liability companies will implicate the securities laws.[297] A number of states have dealt

288. Holden v. Hagopian, 978 F.2d 1115 (9th Cir.1992) (failure to adequately allege that general partnership interest was a security).

289. Stone v. Kirk, 8 F.3d 1079 (6th Cir.1993) (joint venture interests were securities where the investors relied substantially on the expertise and managerial skills of the promoter); Reeves v. Teuscher, 881 F.2d 1495 (9th Cir.1989) (general partnership interest in real estate venture was a security).

290. *See* S.E.C. v. Merchant Capital, LLC, 483 F.3d 747, 755 (11th Cir. 2007).

291. *See, e.g.* SEC v. Friendly Power Co., 49 F.Supp.2d 1363 (S.D.Fla.1999) (limited liability company interests were securities where investors had no significant control over the enterprise).

295. *E.g.,* Robinson v. Glynn, 349 F.3d 166 (4th Cir. 2003) (applying investment contract analysis based on the particular company involved rather than trying to craft an across-the-board conclusion for all LLCs).

297. Conde v. SLS West, LLC, 2005 WL 1661747 at *8–*9 (S.D. Ind. 2005) (if facts bore out plaintiffs' allegations of centralized management, limited liability company interests would be securities).

with this nontraditional form of doing business by expressly treating limited liability companies as securities.[300]

§ 1.6[12] Beneficial Interests in Business Trusts and Real Estate Investment Trusts as Securities

In addition to the partnerships and limited liability companies which are discussed directly above, business trusts can be used as an investment vehicle. A very common example is a real estate investment trust. Although the statutory definition of security does not expressly include a business trust,[310] beneficial interests in a business trust satisfy the *Howey* test for classifying an investment contract as a security. As a passive investment in a business carried on by others, it is clear that a beneficial interest in a business trust is a security.[311] Furthermore, in its definition of equity security under the Securities Exchange Act of 1934, a business trust is expressly included.[312]

§ 1.6[13] Stock as a Security

Stock is one of the enumerated instruments in section 2(a)(1)'s definition of a security and in the 1934 Act's counterpart as well. Thus, there is a strong presumption that stock is a security and it is clear that corporate stock is a security.[314]

In United Housing Foundation v. Forman,[315] the Supreme Court held that stock in a residential housing cooperative was not a security. The Court pointed out that although stock is expressly included in the definition of security, the stock in *Forman* was not stock as that term is generally understood. The stock merely evidenced an interest in the cooperative building and a right to occupy the residential unit attached to the lease. The Court also noted that the stock was not transferable without the lease, and there was no profit incentive.[316] Thus, as a matter of the economic realities, the stock represented an interest in real estate rather than a business venture. Other certificates that are labeled stock or equity interests have been held not to be securities on similar grounds. Thus, for example, interests in an agricultural cooperative that represent the holders right to reap the commercial benefits in the cooperative are not securities.[317]

The courts and SEC no action letters holding that something labeled stock was not a security pointed out that the shares in question did not

300. *See, e.g.,* N.H. Rev. Stat. Ann. § 421–B:13 (requiring limited liability companies to indicate whether they are registering their interests as securities or are relying on an exemption); Indiana Code § 23–2–2–1 (including limited liability company within the definition of security).

310. The definition does, however, include a voting trust certificate or collateral trust certificate. 15 U.S.C.A. §§ 77b(a)(1), 78c(a)(10).

311. *See, e.g.,* SEC v. Banner Fund International, 211 F.3d 602, 614–615 (D.C.Cir.2000) (interests in offshore business trust were securities).

312. 1934 Act Rule 3a–11, 17 C.F.R. § 240.3a–11.

314. Landreth Timber Co. v. Landreth, 471 U.S. 681, 105 S.Ct. 2297, 85 L.Ed.2d 692 (1985).

315. 421 U.S. 837, 95 S.Ct. 2051, 44 L.Ed.2d 621 (1975).

316. The stock in *Forman* did not permit the holder to realize any appreciation in value. Even in more traditional cooperatives where the seller of the stock will be entitled to an appreciation in value, this appreciation would derive from the increase in the value of the real estate interest rather than any business enterprise. And, as discussed above real estate ordinarily is not a security.

317. Great Rivers Coop. v. Farmland Industries, Inc., 198 F.3d 685 (8th Cir.1999).

possess the characteristics of stock in business corporations.[324] It would follow that corporate stock (as well as options[325] on such stock) is a security. Nevertheless, utilizing the economic reality test of earlier cases, it was held that the sale of stock in a closely held corporation may not be a "security" especially if it is, in essence, a transfer of the ownership and management of the corporation's assets.[326] The circuits were in conflict as to the validity of this "sale of business" exception for including stock as a security. One court went so far as to hold that the sale of fifty percent of the outstanding shares is not a sale of securities subject to either state or federal securities regulation.[328] Many cases involving stock in closely held corporations ignored the fact that in the Supreme Court's decision in *Forman* the "stock" had none of the usual indicia of corporate shares.

The issue was eventually resolved at the federal level by the United States Supreme Court when it rejected the sale of business doctrine.[332] In companion decisions, the Supreme Court rejected outright the sale of business doctrine, reasoning that when a business enterprise elects the corporate form and offers shares with the traditional indicia of ownership, the statutory definition is satisfied. The Court's holding in *Landreth Timber* confirms that it will not aggressively utilize the economic reality test to limit applicability of the securities acts to transactions falling within a literal reading of the statute. It therefore appears that the Court's earlier restrictive ruling in *Forman* relating to stock in a government subsidized residential housing cooperative may well be *sui generis* (or close to it) and thus entitled to relatively little precedential effect except on facts very similar to those in *Forman*. Otherwise, the shares of stock will be characterized as securities.

Notwithstanding the rejection of the sale of business doctrine, a corporate acquisition that is not structured in terms of a stock transaction will not implicate the securities laws.[336] The form of a corporate acquisition thus will generally determine the extent to which the securities laws are implicated.

§ 1.6[14] Notes as Securities

Section 2(a)(1) expressly includes "any note" within the definition of a security.[346] As discussed in the discussion that follows, most of the concern over the application of the securities laws has centered around short term notes. This is because there is no exemption for long-term obligations. The broad concept of note means that even a personal loan can qualify as a security if it is not covered by the exemption for short term commercial paper.

A number of cases have addressed the issue of whether a loan agreement constitutes a security. Section 3(a)(3) of the Securities Act of 1933 exempts

324. United Housing Foundation v. Forman, 421 U.S. 837, 95 S.Ct. 2051, 44 L.Ed.2d 621 (1975); Great Rivers Coop. v. Farmland Industries, Inc., 198 F.3d 685 (8th Cir.1999).

325. It is clear that an option on a security is itself a security. *See, e.g.,* Fry v. UAL Corp., 84 F.3d 936, 937–38 (7th Cir.1996).

326. *E.g.,* Landreth Timber Co. v. Landreth, 731 F.2d 1348 (9th Cir.1984) *reversed* 471 U.S. 681, 105 S.Ct. 2297, 85 L.Ed.2d 692 (1985); Christy v. Cambron, 710 F.2d 669 (10th Cir.1983).

328. Oakhill Cemetery of Hammond, Inc. v. Tri–State Bank, 513 F.Supp. 885 (N.D.Ill.1981).

332. Landreth Timber Co. v. Landreth, 471 U.S. 681, 105 S.Ct. 2297, 85 L.Ed.2d 692 (1985); Gould v. Ruefenacht, 471 U.S. 701, 105 S.Ct. 2308, 85 L.Ed.2d 708 (1985).

336. Coal Resources, Inc. v. Gulf & Western Industries, Inc., 756 F.2d 443 (6th Cir.1985), *on remand* 645 F.Supp. 1028 (S.D.Ohio 1986), *reversed* 865 F.2d 761 (6th Cir.1989).

346. 15 U.S.C.A. § 77b(a)(1).

any "note * * * aris[ing] out of a current transaction" with a maturity not exceeding nine months.[353] In contrast section 3(a)(10) of the Securities Exchange Act of 1934 excludes such short term notes from the definition of a security.[354] For a long time the courts employed the economic reality test by asking whether the transaction under scrutiny is an investment vehicle which would trigger the securities acts' coverage or whether it is more properly characterized as a commercial venture which should not be subjected to the securities laws. This became known as the investment/commercial dichotomy. Then, in 1990, the Supreme Court focused on the economic reality and employed a similar "family resemblance test" in holding that a variable rate demand note issued by a farmers' cooperative was a security.[356]

Even in the face of the family resemblance test or the commercial-investment dichotomy, the fact that the issuer of a short-term note is a bank does not preclude the finding that a security exists.[357] Thus, when notes or loan agreements have investment attributes, the courts have found securities to exist.[358] However, the courts have been willing to find a commercial rather than investment context, especially when bank financing is involved.

Whether a note is a security depends on numerous factors that are discussed below. It is clear that with respect to any particular note, the inquiry is a highly factual one.

In Reves v. Ernst & Young,[362] the Supreme Court attempted to resolve some of the issues relating to the question of when a note will be a security. *Reves* involved variable rate demand notes that were issued by a farmers' cooperative. The Court eschewed application of the *Howey* four-factor test, reasoning that this test is limited to the definition of investment contract. The investment contract analysis is inapplicable to the other items specifically enumerated in the Act's definition of security. Instead, there is a presumption that an instrument which falls within one of the enumerated categories is a security. It follows that there is a presumption that a note is a security.

The Court in *Reves* applied the "family resemblance" test in holding that certain demand notes were securities.[365] The family resemblance test that was adopted in *Reves* to a large extent is a different way of articulating the investment-commercial dichotomy that has been employed by the circuit and district courts. In applying the family resemblance test, the Court identified four types of "notes" that do not fit within the definition of security: (1) notes delivered in connection with consumer financing, (2) a note secured by a home mortgage, (3) short-term notes to a small business secured by the business' assets, and (4) bank character loans. The more closely any particular note resembles any of these four categories, the more likely it is that the securities

---

353. 15 U.S.C.A. § 77c(a)(3).

354. 15 U.S.C.A. § 78c(a)(10).

356. Reves v. Ernst & Young, 494 U.S. 56, 110 S.Ct. 945, 108 L.Ed.2d 47 (1990).

357. Exchange National Bank of Chicago v. Touche Ross & Co., 544 F.2d 1126 (2d Cir.1976).

358. SEC v. Eurobond Exchange, Ltd., 13 F.3d 1334 (9th Cir.1994) (Eurobond investment program held to be a security); McGill v American Land & Exploration Co., 776 F.2d 923, 925 (10th Cir.1985) (note issued in connection with joint venture held to be a security).

362. 494 U.S. 56, 110 S.Ct. 945, 108 L.Ed.2d 47 (1990), *rehearing denied* 494 U.S. 1092, 110 S.Ct. 1840, 108 L.Ed.2d 968 (1990).

365. *See* Reves v. Ernst & Young, 494 U.S. 56, 110 S.Ct. 945, 108 L.Ed.2d 47 (1990). *See also, e.g.,* SEC v. Global Telecom Services LLC, 325 F.Supp.2d 94 (D. Conn. 2004) (notes were securities).

laws are not to be invoked. Just as notes are included in the definition of securities, regardless of whether issued by private issuers or governmental entities, bonds ordinarily will be securities.

The Court in *Reves* held that since "note" is one of the items enumerated in the Act's definition, there is a presumption that a note is a security.[372] However, the presumption may be rebutted by evaluation of the following four factors:

> (1) an examination of the transaction in order to assess the motivations that would prompt a reasonable lender (buyer) and creditor (seller) to enter into it—for example, was the transaction in question an investment transaction or a commercial or consumer transaction?
>
> (2) the plan of distribution used in offering and selling the instrument—for example, is the instrument commonly traded for investment or speculation?
>
> (3) the reasonable expectations of the investing public—are the notes generally perceived as investment opportunities? and
>
> (4) whether some factor such as the applicability of a parallel regulatory scheme significantly reduces the risk and thereby renders the protection of the federal securities laws unnecessary.[376]

In applying these factors, the Supreme Court Justices in *Reves* were all in agreement in finding that the uncollateralized, uninsured, unregulated notes at issue in that case were securities. However, the court was split as to whether they fell within the exemption for notes with maturities of less than nine months from the date of issuance. The majority held that although the notes were payable on demand, the demand might not come for "years or decades" in the future and accordingly, the short-term exemption should not apply.[377] The four dissenters took the position that the demand feature meant that the notes reached their maturity at issuance.[378]

The family resemblance test that was applied in *Reves* does not provide as much of a bright line as one might have hoped. Yet it does establish that since there is a presumption that a note is a security, the burden of persuasion falls on the party seeking to exclude the note from the Act's coverage. The Court in *Reves* thus announced a rule that will exclude only those instruments which, because of their terms and the way in which they are issued, do not have the basic characteristics of investment securities.[380] If the notes have been issued in a consumer or commercial context, they are not likely to fall within the definition of security.[381] Characteristics of the note may lead a court in one direction or another in determining whether a security exists. Thus, for

372. 494 U.S. at 64–66, 110 S.Ct. at 951–52, 108 L.Ed.2d at 60–61.

376. 494 U.S. at 67, 110 S.Ct. at 952.

377. 494 U.S. at 67, 110 S.Ct. at 952.

378. 494 U.S. at 76, 110 S.Ct. at 957, 108 L.Ed.2d at 67 (Rehnquist dissenting in part; Justice Rehnquist was joined by Justices White, O'Connor & Scalia).

380. *See, e.g.,* Pollack v. Laidlaw Holdings, Inc., 27 F.3d 808 (2d Cir.1994) (mortgage participations sold by securities brokers were properly characterized as investment rather than commercial and thus were securities).

381. *See, e.g.,* In the Matter of Wuerch, Administrative Proceeding File No. 3–7137, 50 S.E.C. 811, Sec. Exch. Act Rel. No. 34–30083, 50 S.E.C. Docket 623, 1991 WL 288604 n. 2 (SEC Dec. 16, 1991) (the Supreme Court "intended to exclude from the definition of security only certain types of notes which are issued in a purely commercial or consumer context").

example, the fact that a note's payout is variable rather than fixed, although not by itself determinative, may make it more likely that the note is in fact a security even if it is a demand note. The test therefore necessarily becomes highly individualized to the facts of the particular case. As the presumption indicates, issuers and sellers of notes must be aware of the potential securities law ramifications.

Under the family resemblance test announced in *Reves*, securities that most closely resemble purely commercial or banking transactions will not be classified as securities. The Second Circuit, applying the *Reves* analysis, has ruled that under the family resemblance test, participation interests in short-term commercial loans were not securities.[386] The presumption that a security exists thus may be rebutted, but the burden is on the party seeking to be excluded from the securities laws' purview. It follows that absent evidence that the note does not contain any of the benchmarks of a security as identified by the Court in *Reves,* the securities laws will apply. This presumption carries forward to commercial paper as well as to notes issued by savings and loan institutions. Therefore, for example, in the ordinary case commercial paper issued by a corporation is not likely to be a security.

§ 1.6[15] Certificates of Deposit as Securities

Related to the issue of when a note is subject to the securities laws, is the applicability of those laws to bank certificates of deposit. Section 2(a)(1)'s definition of security expressly includes "certificate of deposit for a security" within its list of investments that are subject to the 1933 Act.[393] A "certificate of deposit for a security" is similarly listed in the definition found in section 3(a)(1) of the Securities Exchange Act of 1934.[394] A certificate of deposit issued by a bank more closely resembles a bank account than an investment security. Bank accounts ordinarily are not securities.[395] Accordingly, the Supreme Court ruled that a federally insured certificate of deposit issued by a bank is not subject to the securities laws.[396] When, however, an investment firm markets certificates of deposit as liquid investments and maintains a secondary market for the certificates of deposit, their sale has been held to be subject to the securities acts.[397] Some prior and subsequent lower court decisions held that certificates of deposit issued by foreign banks are deemed to be securities.[398] The reasoning is that United States government-regulated banks and federally insured commitments do not require the protection of the securities laws

386. Banco Espanol de Credito v. Security Pacific National Bank, 973 F.2d 51 (2d Cir.1992), *cert. denied* 509 U.S. 903, 113 S.Ct. 2992, 125 L.Ed.2d 687 (1993). *Cf.* Resolution Trust Corp. v. Stone, 998 F.2d 1534 (10th Cir.1993) (enhanced automobile receivables ("EARs") were not securities).

393. 15 U.S.C.A. § 77b(a)(1).

394. 15 U.S.C.A. § 78c(a)(10).

395. However, when the banking product includes risks not traditionally associated with bank accounts in regulated and insured banking instructions, the securities laws are likely to apply. *See, e.g.,* Missouri Bankers Association, 2008 WL 3844747 (SEC No Action Letter Aug. 18, 2008) (refusing to issue a no action letter with respect to a "qualified tuition program" under IRS Section 529).

396. Marine Bank v. Weaver, 455 U.S. 551, 102 S.Ct. 1220, 71 L.Ed.2d 409 (1982), *on remand* 683 F.2d 744 (3d Cir.1982).

397. Gary Plastic Packaging Corp. v. Merrill Lynch, Pierce, Fenner & Smith, Inc., 756 F.2d 230 (2d Cir.1985).

398. Meason v. Bank of Miami, 652 F.2d 542 (5th Cir.1981), *rehearing denied* 659 F.2d 1079 (5th Cir.1981) (Grand Cayman bank).

whereas foreign instruments may. Similarly, certificates of deposit that are not subject to either United States or foreign regulation have been held to be securities.[400] Enhancements to United States certificates of deposit may also implicate the securities laws.

§ 1.7 Derivative Investments: Stock Options, Index Options, and Futures

The statutory definitions in both the 1933 and 1934 Acts make it clear that securities include not only stocks and bonds but also "any put, call, straddle, option, or privilege on any security."[1] Thus, an investment that is derivative of a security is itself a security. Derivative investments—both those based on securities and those based on commodities or other underlying values—have become a significant segment of the investment markets. Regulation of derivative investments is more fragmented than securities regulation generally. The discussion that follows addresses the applicability of the securities laws to derivative investment.

Over the past four decades, the securities markets have been infused with options trading in order to provide an alternative way to participate in short term investments in securities. Put and call options on individual securities allow investors to hedge their positions and thereby limit risk. While reducing risk may be the motivation for some investors, much options trading has been on a speculative basis. Since its inception, public trading of options on securities exchanges has been an active financial market. The success of the options markets for individual securities paved the way for expansion into markets for index options which are subject to Securities and Exchange Commission regulation and markets for futures based on stock indexes, which are subject to the jurisdiction of the Commodity Futures Trading Commission. The index markets permit investors to diversify their holdings by not tying their investments to the stock of a particular issuer. Index options and futures are broadly-based indexes the value of which is dependent upon the current per share price of the stocks comprising the index. By utilizing the index markets investors can take positions in groups of stocks tied to a publicly traded index option or futures contract. The index markets also have provided additional opportunities for the breed of arbitrageurs known as risk arbitrageurs.[3]

Primer on Options and Futures[4]

Securities options are generally described in terms of "put" and "call" options. A put option is a bilateral contract whereby one party as the option to sell (or "put") to underlying security from the counterparty at a predetermined option exercise price any time prior to the option's expiration date. In the case of a call option the option holder has the right to buy (or call the securities way from) the counterparty at a predetermined option exercise price

400. SEC v. Randy, 38 F.Supp.2d 657 (N.D.Ill.1999).

§ 1.7

1. 1933 Act § 2(a)(1), 1934 Act § 3(a)(11); 15 U.S.C. § 77b(2), 78c(a)(10).

3. *See* Thomas L. Hazen, Volatility and Market Inefficiency: A Commentary on the Effects of Options, Futures, and Risk Arbitrage on the Stock Market, 44 Wash. & Lee L.Rev. 789 (1987).

4. Part of this discussion was adapted from Thomas Lee Hazen Securities Regulation–Cases and Materials 74–76 (7th ed. 2006).

any time prior to the expiration of the option. Options on individual securities are themselves securities.[5]

The pricing of an option is based on the relationship between the current price of the underlying security and the option exercise price as well as the time value determined by the option's expiration date. A call option is considered "in the money" when the exercise price is below the current market price of the underlying security since it is economically advantageous for the option holder to exercise the option at the below market price of the security. Conversely a put option is "in the money" when the exercise price is above the current market price of the underlying security.

Publicly traded options on individual securities have standardized expiration dates—the third Friday of the month designated in the option contract. Thus, for example, an ABC Corp. $40 March 2010 call option would give the owner (i.e., the buyer of the option) the right to purchase 100 shares of ABC stock at $40 per share (plus applicable brokerage commission) any time prior to the close of trading on the third Friday of March 2010. Options on a basket of stocks (index options) also expire on the third Friday. In contrast, futures contracts[7] which also expire on the third Friday are issued in three months, rather than monthly, . Thus, four times each year–in March, June, September, and December—the last hour of trading on the third Friday (sometimes referred to as "freaky Friday") is known as the triple witching hour because there is the convergence of expiration for options on individual securities, index options and index futures contracts. The last hour of other expiration Fridays is sometimes called double witching hour because options on individual securities as well as index options expire.

Options can be used to obtain leverage or to hedge other investments. Options can be used for taking leveraged long or short positions in the underlying security. Since options are leveraged positions, a relatively small initial investment can reflect an investment position in a large block of securities. A long position exists when an investor owns a security or , in the case of options, has the option to purchase a security. An example of a short position is when an investor is a counter party to an option that could require him or her to sell a security. It is possible to use an option strategy to take the same investment position as a short sale (selling a security one does not own).[8]

When purchasing a call option, the option holder is taking a bullish position in the underlying security—that is he or she is hoping that the stock price will rise. Conversely, the seller (or writer) of a call option is taking an investment position that the price of the underlying stock will not rise.

In addition to using options as a leveraged investment, options provide an important way to hedge long positions in securities. A long position exists when an investor owns securities, as opposed to a short position when an investor has sold options or securities thereby obligating him or her to purchase them at a later date. For example, an investor owning 1000 shares of ABC Co. stock which is currently trading at $12 per share may want to limit

5. *See, e.g.,* Wharf (Holdings) Ltd. v. United International Holdings, Inc., 532 U.S. 588, 121 S.Ct. 1776, 149 L.Ed.2d 845 (2001) (oral option is a security subject to the federal securities laws).

7. Futures contracts are traded in the markets and are subject to the jurisdiction of the Commodities Futures Trading Commission.

8. Short sales are discussed in § 14.22 *infra*.

the risk of a price decline. In such a case, an appropriate hedge strategy would be to buy put options with a strike price of $10 per share. This would guarantee that at any time until the expiration date the investor could sell the stock for $10 per share. Buying the puts will cause the investor to incur the cost of the premium that the market has placed on the put and thereby the investor increases his or her total cost but limits the risk of loss.

Another example of an option strategy occurs when the investor believes that the market is likely to decline and therefore he or she maintains a large cash balance. In order to hedge against the possibility that their negative market outlook is wrong, investors may want to purchase call options, in selected stocks or broader-based index options, which would allow participation in a market rise. The purchase of call options involves less cash than investing in the underlying stocks but also is much more speculative as the investor stands to lose his or her entire investment if the option expires when the stock price is below the option exercise price.

In 2000, Congress opened the door for a futures market place to parallel the securities option markets that are subject to SEC regulation. The 2000 amendments to the Commodity Exchange Act granted for the first time to the Commodity Futures Trading Commission jurisdiction over futures contracts on individual securities.[11] This has opened the door for a futures market in securities subject to CFTC jurisdiction that will parallel the securities options markets that are regulated by the SEC.

§ 1.7[5] "New Exotics"—Swaps and Other Hybrid Derivatives

During the 1980s a host of novel and exotic investment products developed. A number of commercial banks and investment banks began to develop specialized financial products geared to the investment objectives of particular clients.[43] Among these "new exotics" were interest-rate swaps, followed by foreign currency swaps and, eventually, by equity-or commodity-based swaps. Also, during the 1980s, these hybrid and derivative instruments flourished, interrelating all sorts of financial variables to permit sophisticated hedging strategies. At the same time, many institutional investors got in over their heads. One of the most infamous incidents involved Orange County California's tremendous losses as a result of these investments.

Swap transactions have become an important part of the international economy. For example, interest rate swaps are frequently used to manage credit risks. The prevalence of swap agreements means that there are large amounts of money tied up in these arrangements most of which are largely unregulated.

In 2000, Congress amended the securities and commodities laws regarding hybrid investments.[53] Among other things, these amendments resulted in securities-based swap agreements being excluded from the definition of security but nevertheless subjected to the securities laws antifraud provisions.[54]

11. 7 U.S.C.A. § 1a(31) as added by Pub. Law 106–554, 114 Stat. 2763 (December 21, 2000). Previously, the CFTC only had jurisdiction over stock index futures. *See* § 1.5 *supra*. *Cf.* Peter J. Chepucavage, Short Sales and Securities Futures: The Need for Comprehensive Short Sale Regulation, 21 Fut. & Deriv. L. Rep. 12 (Sept.2001).

43. For a detailed discussion of the new exotics, *see* 1 Phillip McBride Johnson & Thomas Lee Hazen, Derivatives Regulation § 1.02[8][A] (2004).

53. Pub. Law 106–554, 114 Stat. 2763 (December 21, 2000).

54. *See* 15 U.S.C.A. §§ 77b–1(b)(1), 78c–1(b)(1) (excluding "security-based swap agreements" from the definition of "security"); 15 U.S.C.A. §§ 77b–1(a), 78c–1(a) (excluding "non-security-

Also, the 2000 legislation expressly provides that swaps that are not security-based do not fall with either the registration or antifraud provisions of the securities laws. Furthermore, there is authority to support the proposition that the 2000 modernization legislation does not preclude the states from regulating swap transactions as securities.[55] These amendments were part of a massive overhaul of the Commodity Exchange Act and the regulation provided by the CFTC.

Even though they are not subject to direct SEC regulation, the securities laws nevertheless can impact investments in various commodities-related derivative instruments. Item 305 of Regulation S–K requires that filings with the SEC reveal the extent of a company's exposure to risks due to derivative investments.[61] Also, brokers' failure to disclose risks of securities related derivative investments can also result in liability.[62]

§ 1.7[6] Unregulated Over-the-Counter Derivatives

At the heart of the Commodity Exchange Act was the contract market monopoly required by section 4 of that Act.[70] This meant that commodity–related instruments that fall within the exclusive jurisdiction of the CFTC had to be traded on a registered commodities contract market or exchange absent some exemption or exclusion from the Act. As a result, unlike the securities markets, there was no public over-the-counter market for commodity-related investments. If an instrument fell within the Act's exclusive jurisdiction but was exempt from the contract market monopoly requirement, then the instruments could be traded off-exchange. However, since such exempt commodity-related investments still fall under the Act's exclusive jurisdiction, the SEC cannot assert jurisdiction. As discussed more fully elsewhere in this treatise,[71] the Commodity Futures Modernization Act of 2000[72] created a revolution in commodities regulation when it largely eliminated the contract market monopoly. In addition to various exemptions from CFTC regulation, there are exclusions from the Commodity Exchange Act's coverage, such as for forward contracts[73] as opposed to futures contracts. As such, forward contracts are not subject to the act and thus may be traded over-the-counter, other than through an organized contract market.

based swap agreements" from the definition of "security"). *See also*, 15 U.S.C.A. §§ 77b(a)(1), 78c(a)(10) (definition of security); 15 U.S.C.A. §§ 77q(a), 78i(a) 78j(b) (antifraud and manipulation provisions).

55. Integrated Research Services, Inc. v. Illinois Secretary of State, Securities Dept., 328 Ill.App.3d 67, 262 Ill.Dec. 304, 765 N.E.2d 130 (2002) (foreign currency contracts were held to be securities under the Illinois Securities Act).

61. 17 C.F.R. § 229.305.

62. *See also, e.g.,* Former BT Broker Settles SEC Case Over Transactions with Gibson Greetings, 28 Sec. Reg. & L. Rep. (BNA) 754 (June 14, 1996).

70. 7 U.S.C.A. § 6. *See* 1 Philip McBride Johnson & Thomas Lee Hazen, Derivatives Regulation § 1.07 (2004).

71. *See* § 22.7 *infra*.

72. Pub. Law 106–554, 114 Stat. 2763 (December 21, 2000).

73. A forward contract is a contract calling for a future delivery where the parties to the contract engage in a trade or business that utilizes the underlying commodity. See 1 Phillip McBride Johnson & Thomas Lee Hazen, Derivatives Regulation § 1.02[5], 1.02[8][B] (2004). For example, a farmer who sells his or her crops to a distributor with a future delivery date and delivery of the farmer's crops is in fact anticipated, then the contract is classified as a forward rather than futures contract and thus not subject to the Act's regulatory provisions.

As discussed above, swap transactions have been the subject of regulatory controversy. Swap transactions, like any hybrid instruments containing commodities components, are likely to be categorized as subject to the CFTC's exclusive jurisdiction. The CFTC and Congress provided exemptions from the Act for many swap transactions involving institutional and other sophisticated participants.[75] This created an over-the-counter market among sophisticated participants for certain commodity-related investments. The widespread use of these derivatives has created an enormous derivatives risk, with as much as eighty-one trillion dollars in derivatives risk being held by the twenty-five largest banks.[78] These unregulated derivatives contributed heavily to the 2008 credit crisis.

§ 1.7[7] Security Futures Products

In a reversal of prior law, the Commodity Futures Modernization Act of 2000[81] permits the trading of futures contracts on single stocks and narrow-based security indexes. Securities futures products may be traded on either securities or commodities exchanges. In establishing this co-regulatory system, the Commodity Futures Modernization Act directs the SEC and CFTC to coordinate their regulatory oversight over securities futures. A stock future is defined as a security, which makes the Securities Exchange Act of 1934 generally applicable to trading in securities futures.[82] Securities futures can be traded only on common stock registered under section 12 of the Securities Exchange Act of 1934.[83] Those securities are subject to the detailed SEC periodic reporting requirements.[84]

In 2001, the CFTC adopted listing standards for equity security futures products including narrow-based indexes.[85] In 2006, the SEC and CFTC adopted rules permitting trading in futures on narrow-based debt security indexes and debt security futures.[86] A debt security index will not be considered narrow-based when: each index component is a security that is a note, bond, debenture, or evidence of indebtedness and none is an equity security; the index comprises more than nine securities issued by more than nine non-affiliated issuers; the securities of any issuer included in the index do not comprise more than 30 percent of the index's weighting; the securities of any five non-affiliated issuers included in the index do not comprise more than 60 percent of the index's weighting; and the issuer of a security included in an

75. 7 U.S.C. § 16(e)(2). Parts 34, 35 of the CFTC Regulations, 17 C.F.R. §§ 34.1–34.2, 35.1–35.2.

78. *See, e.g.,* Milton Recht, Derivative Amounts–and Risk–Increase at Banks, Complinet, http://www.complinet.com/us/news/news/article.html?ref=63165 & ephigh= & high=derivatives (Sept. 28, 2004).

81. Pub. Law 106–554, 114 Stat. 2763 (December 21, 2000).

82. State gambling laws and blue sky laws are preempted with respect to stock futures.

83. 5 U.S.C. § 78*l*.

84. *See* chapter 9 *infra* for general discussion of the 1934 Act's registration and periodic reporting requirements.

85. *See* Listing Standards and Conditions for Trading Security Futures Products, 66 Fed. Reg. 55,078, 2001 WL 1337418 (CFTC Nov. 1, 2001).

86. *See* SEC–CFTC, Joint Final Rules: Application of the Definition of Narrow–Based Security Index to Debt Securities Indexes and Security Futures on Debt Securities, Sec. Exch. Act Rel. No. 34–54106 (SEC–CFTC July 6, 2006). *See also, e.g.,* Kenneth M. Raisler & David J. Gilberg, SEC and CFTC Propose Rules to Permit the Trading of Futures on Debt Indeces, 26 Fut. & Deriv. L. Rep. 3 (May 2006).

index satisfies specified additional requirements.[87] The rules for narrow-based debt security indexes differ from those applicable to equity securities. The SEC–CFTC adopting release noted that "the modified criteria addressing diversification and public information about, and marketing familiarity with, the issuers of the securities underlying a debt securities index will reduce the likelihood that a future on such an index would be readily susceptible to manipulation and thus are more appropriate criteria for debt securities indexes."[88]

The Commodity Futures Modernization Act permits trading of securities futures either on a national securities exchange registered with the SEC or a commodities contract market that is registered with the CFTC. A commodities contract market that trades security futures must be cross-registered with the SEC. Conversely, a securities exchange that trades securities futures has its primary regulation by the SEC but must be cross-registered with the CFTC.

Additional regulations are imposed as a prerequisite to trading in securities futures. For example suitability requirements are imposed on a commodities contract market.[89] The suitability requirements for securities futures traded on a contract market must be comparable to the suitability requirements imposed by a national securities association.[90]

87. *Ibid.* The applicable rules are CFTC Reg. §§ 41.15, 41.21, 17 C.F.R. §§ 41.15, 41.21 and 1934 Act Rules 3a55–4 and 6h–2, 17 C.F.R. §§ 240.3a55–4, 240.6h–2.

88. SEC–CFTC, Joint Final Rules: Application of the Definition of Narrow–Based Security Index to Debt Securities Indexes and Security Futures on Debt Securities, Sec. Exch. Act Rel. No. 34–54106 (SEC–CFTC July 6, 2006).

89. Pub. Law 106–554, 114 Stat. 2763 (December 21, 2000).

90. Pub. Law 106–554, 114 Stat. 2763 (December 21, 2000). The suitability requirements for securities are discussed in § 14.16 *infra*.

Chapter 2

REGISTRATION REQUIREMENTS OF THE SECURITIES ACT OF 1933

Table of Sections

§ 2.0 Overview of 1933 Act Registration

Sometimes mistakenly people refer to securities that are registered under the 1933 Act. This reflects a misunderstanding of the how the 1933 Act operates since it is the transaction offering the securities, not the securities themselves, that are registered. Although securities are registered under the 1934 Act,[1] 1933 Act registration is transaction based. The 1933 Act registration statement covers an offering of securities. 1933 Act registration does not cover the securities beyond the offering nor does it apply to the company beyond the registered offering. In contrast, the Securities Exchange Act of 1934[2] imposes periodic disclosure requirements on publicly held companies, including companies that have gone public through a 1933 Act registration statement.[3]

When companies go public and register their offerings of securities under the 1933 Act,[5] they must pay attention to both the process and the law. In particular, this means that participants in the offering must be familiar with the mechanics of the offering process. Participants must also be familiar with the law's requirements regarding the disclosures that must be made in the registration statement that is filed for the offering as well the disclosure obligations that follow once the company is public. 1933Act registration requires filing a disclosure document with the SEC and also prescribes limitations on both the type and manner of offers until the registration becomes effective.

§ 2.0

1. Act of June 6, 1934, c. 404, Title I, § 1, 48 Stat. 881, codified in 15 U.S.C.A. §§ 78a *et seq.* 1934 Act Registration is discussed in chapter 9 *infra*.

2. 15 U.S.C.A.§§ 78a *et seq.*

3. 15 U.S.C.A. § 78m(a).

5. Act of May 27, 1933, c. 38, Title I, § 1, 48 Stat. 74, codified in 15 U.S.C.A. §§ 77a *et seq.*

The requirements that are imposed by section 5 establish limits on what companies and their representatives may say during the registration process. As part of this process there is a mandated disclosure document, known as the prospectus.[12] Section 5 of the Act thus restricts both oral and written communications and also limits actual sales to the post-effective period. In addition to the mechanics of the offering process, the 1933 Act imposes significant disclosure obligations.

§ 2.1 The Underwriting Process

Underwriters form an essential link in the process of offering securities for public consumption. Underwriting practices have varied over time. There is no single universally accepted underwriting mechanism; instead, there are a variety of underwriting arrangements. The particular underwriting arrangement for any offering will generally be a reflection of the financial exigencies of the situation.

There are a number of methods by which an issuer can raise capital, both for starting out its business and for expansion and/or continuation of an existing concern. Financing can be carried out by the issuer directly or through an intermediary or underwriter. Perhaps the simplest method is direct financing: that is, without an investment banker, underwriter, promoter, or other intermediary. Although direct financing may be simpler, the vast majority of public offerings are underwritten.

§ 2.1[1] Direct Offerings

While it is relatively rare, direct financing does have its place in the securities markets, albeit a small one. Generally, there are said to be five basic methods of direct financing, although additional variations may exist.

First, there can be a direct public offering by the issuer. Such a direct offering can be used for both small and large public offerings. Traditionally, direct public offerings have been especially rare because most issuers do not have the wherewithal or expertise in the financial industry to market their shares to a large number of investors. Marketing a full-scale public offering ordinarily requires a broker-dealer network and sales persons registered with the SEC and the Financial Industry Regulatory Authority (FINRA (formerly the National Association of Securities Dealers (NASD)). Accordingly, public offerings traditionally have been unsuitable for direct distribution by the issuer. However, the increased availability of the Internet has made many direct offerings more feasible.

A second variation of the direct offering by an issuer, and one is traditionally slightly more common than general direct offerings, is an offering to existing security holders where it is contemplated that only existing shareholders will purchase the new securities being offered, thus eliminating the necessity for a promotional or retailing sales effort. A variation is a direct offering exclusively to employees of the issuer.

The third and perhaps most common type of direct financing, utilizing traditional debt and equity securities, is the direct private placement whereby

12. "Prospectus" is defined in section 2(a)(10) of the Act, 15 U.S.C.A. § 77b(a)(10). The content of the prospectus is dictated by section 10 of the Act and the registration requirements generally. 15 U.S.C.A. § 77b. *See also* sections 6 and 7, 15 U.S.C.A. §§ 77f, 77g. The prospectus delivery requirements are discussed in §§ 2.4, 2.5 *infra*.

the issuer turns to a bank, financial institution, or significant private investor to raise all desired capital. For many endeavors, especially established concerns with good track records, such qualified willing investors are readily available and the issuer need not avail itself of an underwriter or promoter in order to stimulate investor interest. The fourth, relatively rarely used technique is the distribution of securities through public sealed bidding. The fifth and final type of direct financing is generally associated with commercial lenders and consists of directly secured bank loans, mortgage loans, equipment loans, and sale-leaseback arrangements.

§ 2.1[2] Nature and Varieties of Underwriting Arrangements

As noted above, most financing that involves any significant selling effort is conducted through promoters, investment bankers, or underwriters. Although generally associated with public offerings, underwriting arrangements are also common with relatively wide-spread unregistered exempt offerings.[17] There are various ways in which an investment banker's expertise and services may be used in connection with the raising of capital. First, and most common with regard to public offerings of securities in this country, is the negotiated underwriting agreement with an investment banker, or group of investment bankers, to handle a public offering, which is usually conducted pursuant to full-fledged federal registration. The negotiated underwriting agreement is also common in connection with a limited or qualified public offering that may take place in reliance upon one of the qualified exemptions from the registration requirements of the 1933 Act.[18] Another less frequently used method of securing an underwriter for public offering is the use of sealed bids. A variation on the competitive bidding is the "Dutch auction," where prospective underwriters bid for a portion of an upcoming offering. Occasionally, the Dutch auction is also used as a method for selling and pricing securities to the public. Under a Dutch auction, the issuer typically sets a price range and potential investors submit their bids, reflecting the price at which they are willing to purchase the securities. Dutch auction offerings are more common in Europe but have been used in the U.S.[20]

The term "underwriter" derives its meaning from former British insurance practices. When insuring their cargo shippers would seek out investors to insure their property. The insurers would add their signatures and would write their names under those of the shippers; hence the term "underwriters." Both in terms of the insurance industry and the securities markets, the concept of underwriting has expanded significantly since its inception. In many instances, underwriting no longer reflects pure insurance but may be in

§ 2.1

17. *See* Sec. Act Rel. No. 33–1256 (1937). *See generally* chapter 4 *infra*.

18. *See* sections 3 and 4 of the 1933 Act, 15 U.S.C.A. §§ 77c, 77d.

20. In the spring of 2004, Google announced that it planned to conduct an IPO via a Dutch auction. The IPO took place in August 2004. There have been successful "Dutch auctions" such as the one held for American Express Co.'s adjustable rate preferred stock (also referred to as "money market preferred"). *See* Securities Week p. 5 (October 22, 1984). *See also, e.g., Matthias Hild, The Google IPO, 3 J. Bus. L. & Technology 41 (2008). See* Peter B. Oh, The Dutch Auction Myth, 42 Wake Forest L. Rev. 853 (2007) (discussing the pros and cons of Dutch auction offerings); Lucas C. Townsend, Global Resolution "Prevent Spinning? A Critical Evaluation of Current Alternatives," 34 Seton Hall L. Rev. 1121 (2004) (recommending increased use of the Dutch auction); Note, Auctioning New Issues of Corporate Securities, 71 Va.L.Rev. 1381 (1985).

the form of various types of either best efforts or firm commitment agreements.

Most, if not all, underwriters of any securities offering will generally be broker-dealers who are members of the Financial Industry Regulatory Authority (FINRA (formerly National Association of Securities Dealers (NASD)).Underwriting agreements are subject to the FINRA's Rules of Fair Practice which deal, *inter alia*, with the distribution of shares, over allotment options (also known as "green shoe" provisions), and "compensation factors." Underwriting agreements and registration materials must be filed with FINRA's Corporate Financing Department in Washington, D.C. Upon filing, FINRA may respond with a letter of comment.

There are three basic varieties of negotiated underwriting arrangements in the securities industry. Those three are: (1) strict underwriting, (2) firm-commitment underwriting, and (3) best efforts underwriting.

§ 2.1[2][A] Strict Underwriting

Strict underwriting, also known as "old-fashioned" or "stand by" underwriting, is insurance in its strictest sense. In lieu of utilizing an investment banker as an agent to resell the securities to the public, the issuer turns to an "insuring house" which will advertise and receive subscriptions and applications for shares from the public. When the subscription lists are closed, the issuer in turn allots the securities to the applicants secured by the insuring house. In a strict underwriting arrangement, the underwriters guarantee to purchase the unsold portion of the allotment. This method is relatively rare in the United States and is generally found only in connection with offerings to existing security holders.

§ 2.1[2][B] Firm–Commitment Underwriting

The second,and most common, arrangement in this country is firm-commitment underwriting. Under a typical firm commitment agreement the issuer sells the entire allotment outright to a group of securities firms represented by one or more managers, managing underwriters or principal underwriters. In a firm-commitment underwriting agreement, the underwriting group, headed by the managing or principal underwriters, agrees to purchase the securities from the issuer. The term "firm commitment" is somewhat misleading since it is common practice to have a "market out" clause which excuses the underwriters from the obligation to purchase in the event of a substantial change in the issuer's financial condition.[26] Typically, the principal underwriters will sign the firm-commitment underwriting agreement. These managers or principal underwriters in turn contact other broker-dealers to become members of the underwriting group who are to act as wholesalers of the securities to be offered. In many instances the securities distribution network will include the use of a selling group of other investment bankers or brokerage houses. Members of the selling group generally do

26. A typical "market out" clause provides that the underwriters are excused from their firm commitment should there be "a material adverse event affecting the issuer that materially impairs the investment quality of the offered securities." *See, e.g.*, First Boston Corp., [1985–1986 Transfer Binder] Fed.Sec.L.Rep. (CCH) ¶ 78,152 (SEC No Action Letter Sept. 2, 1985). *Compare* Walk–In Medical Centers, Inc. v. Breuer Capital Corp., 818 F.2d 260 (2d Cir.1987) (affirming $33 million judgment against an underwriter who claimed that "adverse market conditions" excused performance of underwriting agreement).

not share the underwriters' risk and are thus retailers who are compensated with agents' or brokers' commissions rather than by sharing in the underwriting fee.

Section 2(a)(3) of the 1933 Act[27] excludes from its definition of "offer to sell" preliminary negotiations and agreements between the underwriter and the issuer and among underwriters in privity with the issuer. However, absent an exemption, prior to the filing of the registration statement, no offers can be made to members of the investing public; nor can there be sales or contracts for sale prior to the effective date. Although section 2(a)(3)'s exclusion probably includes the final contract between the underwriter and the issuer, it may be wise not to have more than an understanding and to reserve formal execution of the final contract until immediately after the filing of the registration statement. In fact, the typical practice is to follow such a course.

There is no definitive ruling on how "preliminary" the negotiations and agreements must be in order to qualify for exclusion.[28] Generally, the issue will be a question of fact depending upon the participants in the negotiations.[29] Also, the construction of the statutory language may raise the question as to what agreements between the issuer and underwriter or among underwriters will qualify as "preliminary." In most instances, questions regarding "agreements" are merely academic since it is common practice for the final underwriting agreement to be signed on the eve of the offering. Prior to that time, the issuer and managing underwriter generally operate under a non-binding letter of intent.[30]

Underwriting arrangements may contain an escape clause which permits the underwriting group to terminate the underwriting agreement if there has been a substantial change in the issuer's operation or, for example, if there has been a change in "operating political or marketing conditions." While this is broader than the traditional force majeure clause found in other industries, it is not generally abused. The underwriter's ability to exit from an offering is protected even beyond such escape clauses. For example, where the issuer's prospectus is misleading, the underwriting contract has been held unenforceable, entitling the underwriter to withdraw from the distribution.[31]

§ 2.1[2][C] Best Efforts Underwriting

The third basic type of underwriting arrangement commonly used in the United States is known as a "best efforts" underwriting and does not put the underwriter at risk in the event that investors do not purchase the entire

27. 15 U.S.C.A. § 77b(a)(3). *See* § 5.3 *infra*.

28. The legislative history explains that "the sole purpose * * * is to make clear that the usual agreement among underwriters as well as the agreement between the underwriters and the issuer (or controlling person, as the case may be) may be made before the registration statement has been filed." S.Rep. No. 1036, 83 Cong., 2d Sess. 11 (1954).

29. SEC v. Cavanagh, 155 F.3d 129, 135 (2d Cir.1998) (upholding district court's determination that the exclusion for preliminary negotiations did not apply to the negotiations in question).

30. A letter of intent containing an agreement to underwrite an offering is not a binding contract for the sale of securities. Cafe La France, Inc. v. Schneider Securities, Inc., 281 F.Supp.2d 361 (D.R.I. 2003) (letter of intent regarding underwriting of planned IPO was not a binding contract; underwriter could withdraw prior to IPO and did not owe a fiduciary duty to the company since the underwriting agreement clearly permitted withdrawal).

31. Kaiser–Frazer Corp. v. Otis & Co., 195 F.2d 838 (2d Cir.1952), *cert. denied* 344 U.S. 856, 73 S.Ct. 89, 97 L.Ed. 664 (1952).

allotment being offered to the public.[32] Best efforts underwriting is generally used by less established issuers that cannot find an investment banker who is willing to make a firm commitment because of the speculative nature of the distribution. In some instances, even established companies may try to avail themselves of best efforts underwriting arrangements in order to save on the cost of distribution since the underwriter's fee may be lower in an offering where the underwriter is not taking the risk of absorbing all or part of an unsold allotment. With a best efforts underwriting agreement, the investment banker or brokerage firm sells the securities for the issuer merely as an agent, rather than buying them from the issuer for resale to the public,. Under such best efforts arrangements, the underwriter is generally paid in the form of an agent's commission on actual sales rather than from a dealer's profit or a fee based on a percentage of the overall proceeds of the offering.

§ 2.1[2][D] Underwriting by Auction

There are numerous variations on the foregoing three basic types of underwriting arrangements.[33] For example, competitive bidding by potential underwriters traditionally has been the most common method for offerings involving financing by municipalities, other state governmental agencies, and public utilities.[34] A variation of this in the private sector is the relatively infrequently used "Dutch auction." Investment bankers continue to develop variations on the foregoing methods.

§ 2.1[3] Underwriters' Compensation; FINRA Review

As discussed above, the underwriting agreement is the result of negotiations between the managing or lead underwriter and the company issuing the securities to be offered. Setting the underwriters' compensation is an important part of the process. The Financial Industry Regulatory Authority (formerly the National Association of Securities Dealers (NASD)) is the self-regulatory organization that is intimately involved with broker-dealer regulation generally.[36] FINRA requires that it receive a filed copy of most 1933 Act registration statements for public offerings so it can review the underwriters' compensation.

FINRA's standards for underwriters' compensation are found in its corporate and financing rules.[37] The standards are complex and, at the same time, leave a great deal to FINRA's discretion. The following explanation is designed to provide a basic understanding of the FINRA review process and the standards for judging the reasonableness of the underwriters' compensation.

32. *See* Harold I. Freilich & Ralph S. Janvey, Understanding "Best Efforts" Offerings, 17 Sec.Reg.L.J. 151 (1989).

33. Delayed registered offerings (shelf registrations) are a relatively new development in the history of public offerings and are examples of practices that were generated by the investment banking industry. *See* 1 Louis Loss & Joel Seligman, Securities Regulation 353–372 (1987). *See also* § 3.11 *infra.*

34. *See* 1 Louis Loss & Joel Seligman, Securities Regulation 343–352 (1987). *See* § 14.6 *infra* for a discussion of municipal securities dealers.

36. *See* § 14.3 *infra.*

37. FINRA Rule 5110, formerly NASD Rule 2710 (Underwriting Terms and Arrangements).

§ 2.2 The Operation of Section 5 of the Securities Act of 1933

§ 2.2[1] Operation of Section 5—Overview

§ 2.2[1][A] Section 5 Overview

The core of the 1933 Act's registration requirements are found in section 5 of the Act.[1] Unless there is an applicable exemption, section 5's prohibitions are implemented by regulating the scope of all offers as well as sales of securities so long as there is sufficient use of interstate commerce. Section 5, by its terms, is a criminal provision but criminal prosecutions for section 5 violations are quite rare. Section 5 violations are generally redressed in SEC civil actions, including SEC administrative proceedings At least in the context of an enforcement action, any person who is a "necessary participant" or a "substantial factor" in a sale that violates section 5 will himself or herself be in violation of the Act.[3]

Absent an exemption from the 1933 Act's registration requirements,[9] section 5(c) of the Securities Act of 1933 strictly prohibits all selling efforts by making it unlawful to offer a security for sale unless a registration statement has been filed.[10] Section 5 also restricts selling efforts and absolutely prohibits sales until the registration statement has become effective. Thus, Section 5's prohibitions continue after the registration statement has been filed. Even after a registration statement has been filed, it remains unlawful to sell the securities until the registration statement has become effective.[11] Further, even after the registration statement has been filed, and even after it has become effective, section 5 restricts the types of written offers to sell that may be made.[12] Offers and sales in contravention of section 5 result in a violation even if the defendant did not know that he or she was marketing securities in violation of the Act.[13] This is the case because section 5 is not based on common law fraud[14] and thus does not require that the defendant have acted

§ 2.2

1. 15 U.S.C.A. § 77e.

3. *See*, e.g., SEC v. Rogers, 790 F.2d 1450, 1456 (9th Cir. 1986) ("A defendant may be held liable under section 5 of the 1933 Act if he is 'directly responsible' for the distribution of unregistered securities").

9. Section 3 of the Act sets forth a list of securities that are exempt from the 1933 Act's registration provisions. 15 U.S.C.A. § 77c. Section 4 sets forth transactions that are exempt from registration. 15 U.S.C.A. § 77d. Section 28 gives the SEC the power to exempt persons, transactions, and securities from any of the Act's provisions. 15 U.S.C.A. § 77z–3. Exempt securities and exempt transactions are discussed in chapter 4 *infra.*

10. Section 5(c), 15 U.S.C.A. § 77e(c). *See* § 2.3 *infra* for discussion of the restrictions during the pre-filing period.

11. Section 5(a), 15 U.S.C.A. § 77e(a). *See* § 2.4 *infra* for discussion of the waiting period. *See also, e.g.,* SEC v. Zubkis, [1999–2000 Transfer Binder] Fed. Sec. L. Rep. (CCH) ¶ 90,769 (S.D.N.Y. 2000) (summary judgment finding sale of unregistered securities).

12. This emanates from the prospectus delivery requirements of section 5(b), 15 U.S.C.A. § 77e(b). *See* section 2(a)(10) of the Act, 15 U.S.C.A. § 77b(a)(10) for the definition of prospectus. *See also* the discussion in §§ 2.3, 2.4 *infra*.

13. *See, e.g.,* SEC v. Current Financial Services, Inc., 100 F.Supp.2d 1, 5–6 (D.D.C.2000) (defendant violated the securities laws even though he did not know that the investment vehicle he was marketing was a security).

14. In contrast, SEC Rule 10b–5 is limited to fraudulent conduct. *See, e.g.,* Santa Fe Industries, Inc. v. Green, 430 U.S. 462, 476, 97 S.Ct. 1292, 1302, 51 L.Ed.2d 480 (1977); Ernst & Ernst v. Hochfelder, 425 U.S. 185, 96 S.Ct. 1375, 47 L.Ed.2d 668 (1976).

with scienter.[15] All that is required is that a defendant willfully offer securities. The Act does not expressly require that the defendant intended to violate the registration requirement. Nevertheless, a criminal conviction would appear to require at least a minimal amount of *mens rea*.[16] In other words, section 5 is a strict liability provision.

Section 5 divides the registration process into three time periods: the pre-filing, waiting, and post-effective periods. Once the public offering is contemplated, the time prior to the completion of the initial registration statement and filing is known as the *pre-filing period*.[20] After the registration statement has been filed with the SEC, there is a statutory twenty-day *waiting period* prior to the effective date of the registration statement. Sales of the securities can occur after the effective date.[21] The statutory language is not reflective of what really happens since the actual waiting period is rarely the twenty-day period specified in the statute.[22] Section 5's requirements do not end with the effective date but continue through the *post-effective* period until the distribution of securities has been completed.[23] These limitations take the form of the prospectus requirements which are discussed below.

In the fall of 2004, the SEC proposed and subsequently adopted rules to relax the restrictions on communications during the pre-filing period.[24] Among other things, the new rules which became effective in December 2005, permit increased communications by publicly held companies that are already subject to the periodic reporting requirements of the Securities Exchange Act of 1934.[25] This public offering reform introduced a major philosophical shift with respect to the amount of and types of information that can be disseminated immediately prior to and during a registered public offering. The offering reform provisions are discussed below and throughout this chapter.

The basic purpose of the 1933 Act's registration requirement, as well as section 5's prohibitions and limitations on permissible offers to sell securities, is to assure that the investor has adequate information upon which to base his or her investment decision. It is generally conceded to be a fiction that each investor or potential investor reads the prospectus from cover to cover; and thus, it has been suggested by some observers that most disclosures that are required by the securities laws are not in fact relevant to the majority of investors.[26] However, investment professionals, such as research analysts, investment advisers and broker-dealers, when viewed as a group, read all publicly disseminated information in addition to other available information.

15. *See e.g.*, SEC v. Current Financial Services, Inc., 100 F.Supp.2d 1, 5–6 (D.D.C.2000); SEC v. Friendly Power Co., 49 F.Supp.2d 1363, 1367 (S.D.Fla.1999); SEC v. Parkersburg Wireless LLC, 991 F.Supp. 6, 8–9 (D.D.C.1997). For discussion of the derivation of the scienter requirement in securities fraud actions, *see* § 12.8 *infra*.

16. *See, e.g.*, United States v. Lindo, 18 F.3d 353 (6th Cir.1994) (upholding conviction for sale of unregistered securities where defendant had reason to know that he was involved in an illegal transaction).

20. *See* § 2.3 *infra*.

21. Section 8(a) of the 1933 Act, 15 U.S.C.A. § 77h(a).

22. *See* § 2.4 *infra*.

23. *See* § 2.5 *infra*.

24. *See* Registration Under the Advisers Act of Certain Hedge Fund Advisers, Inv. Co. Act Rel. No. IA—2333, 2004 WL 2785492 (SEC 2004).

25. *See* Securities Offering Reform, Sec. Act Rel. No. 33–8591; Sec. Exch. Act Rel. No. 34–52056; Inv. Co. Act Rel. No. IC–26993, 70 Fed. Reg. 44722–01, 2005 WL 1811282 (SEC Aug. 3, 2005).

26. *See, e.g.*, Homer Kripke, A Search for a Meaningful Securities Disclosure Policy, 31 Bus.Law. 293 (1975); Symposium, New Approaches to Disclosure in Registered Securities Offerings: A Panel Discussion, 28 Bus.Law. 505 (1973).

The opinions of these market professionals, frequently reflected in terms of buy or sell recommendations, create an informed and supposedly efficient market which, in turn, prices the securities at an appropriate level. Accordingly, it is asserted that notwithstanding the absence of significant lay investor interest in the bulk of the SEC disclosure documents, the relevant information nonetheless is filtered into the market and is reflected by the price established by an informed market.[27] Other observers have disagreed, expressing the view that disclosure requirements are directly meaningful to investors.[28]

§ 2.2[2] Operation of Section 5—The Basic Prohibitions of the Pre–Filing, Waiting, and Post–Effective Periods

As noted above, section 5 divides the registration process into three parts: the pre-filing period, the waiting period, and the post-effective period. Section 5(a)(1) prohibits the use of the mails or other facility of interstate commerce to sell a security prior to the effective date of the 1933 Act registration statement.[60] Taken literally, section 5(a)(1)'s language could possibly be read to include merely making offers to sell. However, when section 5(a)(1) is read in conjunction with sections 5(b) and 5(c), it is clear that section 5(a)(1) was designed to prevent the use of the mails or other instrumentalities to make a binding contract (as opposed to something less, such as simply an offer to sell). Section 5(a)(1)'s prohibitions cover the use of the mails, "through the use or medium of any prospectus or otherwise."[61] As discussed more fully below, the Act defines prospectus to include a written offer to sell,[62] and section 5(b)(1)[63] expressly permits the use of certain forms of prospectuses during the waiting period.[64] Accordingly, it would not make sense to read section 5(a)(1) as prohibiting any form of prospectus prior to the effective date.

Section 5(a)(2)[65] prohibits the delivery of any security for sale unless a registration statement is in effect, extending its prohibitions into the waiting period. Section 5(b)[66] imposes prospectus requirements and thereby prescribes the types of prospectuses that may be used for offers during the waiting

27. *Cf.* Wielgos v. Commonwealth Edison Co., 892 F.2d 509 (7th Cir.1989) (indicating that at least with a well seasoned, actively followed issuer, the more important audience for the registration disclosures is the sophisticated analyst and that disclosures may be tailored accordingly).

28. In one influential decision the Eastern District Court of New York held that there are three audiences to whom the registration statement is directed, and that the disclosures must be understandable for each of the following audiences: (1) the amateur investor who reads only for the broadest types of information, (2) the professional advisor and/or manager who makes a close study of the prospectus and bases his or her decisions on the conclusions drawn from this study, and (3) the analyst who relies on the prospectus as one of several sources in forming an opinion. *See* Feit v. Leasco Data Processing Equipment Corp., 332 F.Supp. 544, 565–66 (E.D.N.Y.1971).

60. 15 U.S.C.A. § 77e(a)(1).

61. 15 U.S.C.A. § 77e(a)(1).

62. 15 U.S.C.A. § 2(a)(10).

63. 15 U.S.C.A. § 77e(b)(1).

64. The 1933 Act's prospectus requirements were modeled on the English Companies Act and its predecessors which date back to 1844. *See* Joel Seligman, The Transformation of Wall Street, 62–63 (1982). The concept of the waiting period was new to the 1933 Act. *Id. See also, See* Harold S. Bloomenthal and Samuel Wolf, Securities and Federal Corporate Law § 27:37.3 (2d ed. 2000).

65. 15 U.S.C.A. § 77e(a)(2). *See* § 2.5 *infra.*

66. 15 U.S.C.A. § 77e(b). *See* §§ 2.4–2.5 *infra.*

period[67] and for offers and sales during the post-effective period.[68] Section 5(c),[69] which is the broadest in prohibitions, applies only to the pre-filing period. The following diagram depicts the operation of section 5:

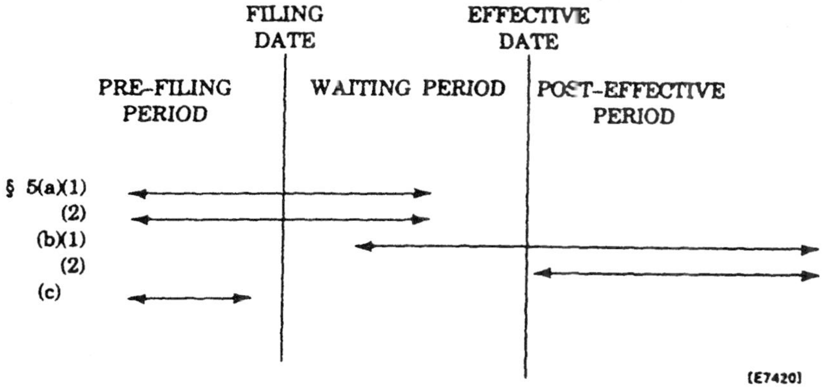

Section 5(c) prohibits all offers to sell and all offers to buy prior to the filing of a registration statement. This necessarily includes oral as well as written offers. Section 5(c) contains the only prohibition on oral offers and is also the only restriction on offers to buy. Since it covers both offers to sell and offers to buy securities, section 5(c) on its face would seem to be applicable to negotiations between issuers and underwriters. However, section 2(a)(3)[72] of the Act expressly provides an exclusion from the definition of offer to sell for preliminary negotiations between an issuer and an underwriter or among underwriters in privity with the issuer. Without such an exclusion, it would be impossible to negotiate a public offering, as the issuer would have to file the registration statement prior to even establishing either the terms of the offering or the underwriting agreement. The exclusion of preliminary underwriter negotiations and agreements is a major exception to the pre-filing prohibitions; although, as will be seen in subsequent sections of this treatise, even beyond the exclusion for preliminary underwriting negotiations and agreements, limited pre-filing publicity is permissible.[73] Section 5(c)'s prohibition[74] on offers operates during the pre-filing period, and violations of these quiet period limitations have come to be known as illegal "gun jumping."

By virtue of section 5(b) of the Act,[75] all written offers or prospectuses must conform with the statutory prospectus requirement. Section 2(a)(10) of the Act[76] defines prospectus to include any written offer[77] in addition to offers

67. The waiting period is discussed in § 2.4 *infra.*

68. The post-effective period is discussed in § 2.5 *infra.*

69. 15 U.S.C.A. § 77e(c). *See* § 2.3 *infra.*

72. 15 U.S.C.A. § 77b(a)(2).

73. *See, e.g.,* 17 C.F.R. § 230.135 which is discussed in § 2.3 *infra.*

74. 15 U.S.C.A. § 77e(c).

75. 15 U.S.C.A. § 77e(b).

76. 15 U.S.C.A. § 77b(a)(10).

77. Although not expressly covered by the statute, computer email, computer disks, and other digitally encoded communications would appear to and certainly should fall within the definition of prospectus.

made over radio or television.[78] Accordingly, oral offers to sell are not covered by section 5(b) nor are offers to buy, whether oral or in writing. Oral offers to sell and all offers to buy are thus unregulated during the waiting period; they are also unregulated during the post-effective period. Sections 10(a) and 10(b) of the 1933 Act[79] set out the requirements for permissible written offers during both the waiting and post-effective periods.[80]

Under the express terms of section 8 of the Act,[85] a registration statement becomes effective twenty days after the last amendment has been filed. This twenty-day waiting period is subject to both the Commission's authority to issue a stop order which postpones the effective date until removal of the stop order, and to the Commission's willingness to grant acceleration of the effective date upon application by the registrant.[86] The drafters of section 8 may have contemplated that ordinarily a registration statement will become effective within twenty days of its filing and that in rare cases this period would be extended by amendment to the registration statement or by the issuance of a stop order or a refusal order. However, this apparent statutory pattern is not reflective of actual SEC practice. As a practical matter, the SEC reserves the formal stop order and refusal order proceedings for woefully deficient filings. For example, where a registration statement has many material misstatements and/or omissions of material fact, the SEC is more likely to issue a formal stop order.[87] In rare instances, the SEC will use the stop order even after the registration statement has become effective.[88] The institution of stop order proceedings has collateral consequences such as imposing disclosure obligations on the registrant and also disqualifying the registrant from the use of certain exemptions from registration.[89] The SEC has also used these stop and refusal order proceedings to issue public opinions and thereby explain its views on important disclosure issues.[90]

The registration review process generally consists of correspondence between the Commission staff and the registrant.[91] Typically, the Commission staff will respond to an initial filing with a detailed letter of comments. Especially in the case of first-time registrants, this informal give and take with the SEC will generally go beyond the twenty-day statutory period. It is

78. The definition as adopted in 1933 was patterned on the British Companies Act of 1929. *See* Gustafson v. Alloyd Co., 513 U.S. 561, 599–600, 115 S.Ct. 1061, 131 L.Ed.2d 1 (1995) (Ginsburg, J., dissenting).

79. 15 U.S.C.A. § 77j(a), (b).

80. *See* §§ 2.4–2.5 *infra.*

85. 15 U.S.C.A. § 77h.

86. *See* the more detailed discussion of acceleration procedures and requirements in § 3.6[2] *infra.*

87. *See, e.g.,* In the Matter of Toks Inc. SEC News Digest 2002–6, 2002 WL 22165 (SEC Initial Decision Jan. 9, 2002) (stop order issued).

88. *Id. See, e.g.,* SEC ALJ Suspends Effectiveness of Registration Statement for IPO, 34 Sec. Reg. & L. Rep. (BNA) 49 (Jan. 14, 2002).

89. *See, e.g.,* Rules 262 and 505 which provide that a section 8 proceeding (as well as other actions under the securities laws) will disqualify registrants and underwriters from participation in Regulation A and Rule 505 offerings. 17 C.F.R. §§ 230.262, 230.505. These exemptions are considered in §§ 4.17, 4.21 *infra.* Public companies as well as those engaging in a public offering will generally have to disclose past section 8 proceedings as material events.

90. *See, e.g.,* In the Matter of Franchard Corp., 42 S.E.C. 163 (SEC 1964); In the Matter of Universal Camera Corp., 19 S.E.C. 648 (1945).

91. *E.g.,* Universal Camera Corp., 19 S.E.C. 648, 658 (1945); Sec. Act Rel. No. 33–5231, 1 Fed.Sec.L.Rep. (CCH) ¶ 057 (Feb. 3, 1972). *See* § 3.5 *infra.*

common for issuers to file delaying amendments in order to give adequate time to respond to the SEC staff's suggestions. When the informal discussions between the registrant's counsel and the Commission staff result in a registration statement that the SEC will find acceptable, it is not uncommon for the registrant to seek acceleration of the effective date.[94] The SEC's plain English requirements for disclosure documents added a new dimension to the review process.[95] In addition to substantive disclosure rules, documents are now reviewed with an eye toward plain English compliance. The SEC had always voiced a concern with the clarity of disclosures but the plain English requirements mandate particular care with respect to specified portions of the registration statement. Violations of plain English requirements will not in and of themselves render the registration statement materially misleading. However, plain English deviations may result in an enhanced SEC review process and thus a delay in the effective date.

Frequently, the pricing of an offering will not take place until just before the effective date. Although the participants planning a public offering will generally have at least a "ball park" figure for the planned offering price, general market fluctuations often require leaving the determination of a precise figure until the effective date. In these cases, it is necessary to file an amendment to the registration statement which relates to the price. Under the terms of section 8 of the Act, the filing of an amendment would ordinarily trigger an additional twenty-day statutory waiting period before the effective date. However, when such price amendments are filed, the Commission will consent to immediate effectiveness, thus, avoiding the statutory twenty-day period from running anew.[98]

The filing of a registration statement is not a step to be taken lightly. Once a registration statement has been filed, it cannot be withdrawn without Commission approval.[99] Formerly, the Commission had to act affirmatively in order to approve the request to withdraw the registration statement.[100] In 2001, the SEC amended Rule 477 to provide for automatic withdrawal of the registration statement unless the Commission objects to the request for withdrawal within fifteen days after the registrant's filing of an application to withdraw the registration statement.[101]

Although withdrawal is not guaranteed, most frequently it will be permitted. It is stated Commission policy to permit withdrawal of the registration statement if "consistent with the public interest and protection of investors."[102] In the normal course of events, the Commission will ordinarily approve a request for withdrawal. However, when it is believed that the registration process warrants imposing sanctions against the participants, the Commission might elect to refuse permission for withdrawal and go ahead

94. SEC Rule 461 sets out the requirements for acceleration. 17 C.F.R. § 230.461. *See* § 3.6[2] *infra.*

95. The plain English requirements include: use of the active rather than passive voice, short sentences, use of definite, concrete everyday words, presentation of information in tabular form or with bullet lists, the avoidance of legal jargon and highly technical business terminology, as well as the avoidance of multiple negatives. Rule 421, 17 C.F.R. § 230.421. *See* § 3.10[2] *infra.*

98. 15 U.S.C.A. § 77h(a); 17 C.F.R. § 230.430A;.17 C.F.R. § 230.475.

99. 17 C.F.R. § 230.477.

100. Former 17 C.F.R. § 230.477 (this approval requirement was amended in 2001).

101. 17 C.F.R. § 230.477.

102. 17 C.F.R. § 230.477.

with formal proceedings under section 8.[103] The SEC has been willing to use withdrawal of the registration statement as a condition to dismissal of stop order proceedings.[104] Just as the SEC does not have to grant a request to withdraw a 1933 Act registration statement, it does not have to give the registrant an opportunity to correct inaccuracies before bringing suit under the antifraud provisions.[105]

§ 2.2[3] Impact of Technology and the Internet on the Operation of Section 5

§ 2.2[3][A] Online Offerings

The ease with which potential investors can access the online resources has made the Internet fertile ground for securities offerings. In 1999, the Commission approved the use of the Internet for a public offering using online communications.[113] The Commission's approval was conditioned on safeguards designed to assure that appropriate disclosure documents were sent and received. Further, the SEC required reconfirmation of purchases by emails in order for an investor to effect a purchase of the securities.[114] In 2000, the SEC issued an interpretative release on the use of electronic media.[115] The SEC reaffirmed the necessity of taking precautions so that online offerings do not run afoul of the disclosure mandates of the 1933 Act.[117] It is clear, for example, that email communications will be treated as written communications for purposes of section 5.

§ 2.2[3][B] Electronic Delivery of "Written" Materials

As part of its public offering reform in 2005,[119] the SEC clarified that most online communications qualify as written communications.[120] There is an exception for live or real-time communications.[121]

Consent for receipt of electronic delivery may be obtained in writing, online via email, or over the telephone.[127] This consent to electronic delivery can be limited to selected documents or it can be global and thereby apply to all documents to be delivered to the investor or potential investor. The Commission has not, however, accepted the suggestion that the widespread

103. *See* the discussion of section 8 proceedings in § 3.6 *infra*.

104. *E.g.*, In the Matter of a Registration Statement of Jonathan Aerospace Materials Corp., 2001 WL 1662289, Sec. Act Rel. No. 33–8050 (SEC Dec. 31, 2001).

105. *See* SEC v. Johnson, 174 Fed. Appx. 111 (3d Cir. 2006).

113. Wit Capital Corp., 31 Sec. Reg. & L. Rep. (BNA) 993, 1999 WL 498545 (SEC No Action Letter July 14, 1999).

114. Wit Capital Corp., 31 Sec. Reg. & L. Rep. (BNA) 993, 1999 WL 498545 (SEC No Action Letter July 14, 1999).

115. Use of Electronic Media, Sec. Act Rel. No. 33–7856, 2000 WL 502290 (SEC April 28, 2000).

117. Use of Electronic Media, Sec. Act Rel. No. 33–7856, 2000 WL 502290 (SEC April 28, 2000).

119. *See* Securities Offering Reform, Sec. Act Rel. No. 33–8591, Sec. Exch. Act Rel. No. 34–52056, Inv. Co. Act Rel. No. IC–26993 70 Fed. Reg. 44722–01, 2005 WL 1692642 (SEC July 19, 2005).

120. Rule 405's definition of "written communication" expressly includes the term "graphic communication," which in turn is also defined in Rule 405. 17 C.F.R. § 230.405.

121. 17 C.F.R. § 230.405.. *See* § 2.2[3][C] *infra*.

127. Use of Electronic Media, Sec. Act Rel. No. 33–7856, 2000 WL 502290 (SEC April 28, 2000).

use of the Internet justifies an implied consent to electronic delivery or a rule that availability of information online will be treated as delivery of that information.

Another issue is the format of the information that is being used to satisfy a delivery obligation. The Commission has made it clear that use of portable delivery format (PDF files) is not too burdensome on the investing public and therefore is permitted.[130]

If an issuer decides to use a web site for prospectus delivery, the issuer must take precautions in order to assure that only permissible material is included.[131] The issuer must clearly define on the web site the document that purports to be the section 10 prospectus.[132] Any hyperlinks within that portion of the web site designated as part of the prospectus will be considered part of the prospectus. Hyperlinks that may appear elsewhere on the web site that are clearly not embodied in the prospectus will not be considered part of the prospectus.[133] As explained by the Commission, "[i]nformation on a web site would be part of a Section 10 prospectus only if an issuer (or person acting on behalf of the issuer, including an intermediary with delivery obligations) acts to make it part of the prospectus."[134] While the issuer is "in registration" there is an increasing likelihood that information in any third party web sites that are hyperlinked to the issuer's web site will be deemed to have been adopted by the issuer.[135] Additionally, the prominence of any such hyperlinks, as well as the way the information is presented will be factors in deciding whether to treat the information on the hyperlinked third party web site as having been adopted or endorsed by the issuer.

§ 2.2[3][C] Electronic Road Shows

Section 2(a)(10) of the Securities Act of 1933 defines prospectus as a written or radio or television communication.[137] Oral communications are not within the definition of prospectus and so are not regulated by section 5(b) of the Act.[138] Thus, during the waiting and post-effective periods there are no restrictions on oral communications other than those imposed by the antifraud rules. Accordingly, promoters of public offerings frequently make statements over the telephone or in person that they would not be able to make in writing during the waiting and post-effective periods.[139] It is also common for

130. Use of Electronic Media, Sec. Act Rel. No. 33–7856, 2000 WL 502290 (SEC April 28, 2000).

131. Use of Electronic Media, Sec. Act Rel. No. 33–7856, 2000 WL 502290 (SEC April 28, 2000).

132. Use of Electronic Media, Sec. Act Rel. No. 33–7856, 2000 WL 502290 (SEC April 28, 2000).

133. Use of Electronic Media, Sec. Act Rel. No. 33–7856, 2000 WL 502290 (SEC April 28, 2000).

134. Use of Electronic Media, Sec. Act Rel. No. 33–7856, 2000 WL 502290 (SEC April 28, 2000).

135. Use of Electronic Media, Sec. Act Rel. No. 33–7856, 2000 WL 502290 (SEC April 28, 2000).

137. 15 U.S.C.A. § 77b(a)(10).

138. 15 U.S.C.A. § 77e(b). However section 5(c) prohibits oral offers to sell and oral offers to buy during the pre-filing period. 15 U.S.C.A. § 77e(c). *See* § 2.3 *infra*.

139. *Cf.* Carr v. CIGNA Securities, 95 F.3d 544 (7th Cir.1996) (documents warning investors that investment was risky precluded claim based on oral assurances that the investment was safe and conservative).

promoters of public offerings to hold meetings, known as road shows, to discuss the securities being offered.[140] The SEC has also permitted road shows over the Internet without being classified as a prospectus.[141] The Commission has conditioned no action letter relief for Internet road shows as follows: (1) the road show may not exclude any material information; (2) only one version of the road show is captured for subsequent Internet transmission; and (3) the content of the road show is consistent with the information contained in the statutory prospectus.[142]

As part of its securities offering reform, the SEC codified its interpretations regarding electronic road shows. Specifically, an electronic road show that consists of a "live" broadcast is not considered to be a prospectus whereas other electronic road shows constitute a writing and therefore may be permissible as a "free writing prospectus."[144]

§ 2.3 The Pre–Filing Period

§ 2.3[1] Basic Prohibitions of the Pre–Filing Period

As written, section 5(c)[1] prohibits offers to sell and offers to buy[2] regardless of whether a public offering and registration is contemplated in the foreseeable future. It follows that section 5(c)'s prohibitions are not limited to transactions that may occur in contemplation of a registered public offering. Nevertheless, the commonly used terminology "pre-filing period" indicates that a public offering is contemplated. As discussed elsewhere in this treatise, most securities transactions that take place outside of the context of a public offering are exempt from section 5's prohibitions.[3]

Once a public offering is contemplated, section 5(c)'s prohibitions on offers to sell and offers to buy clearly come into play. When does the pre-filing period begin? There is no statutory time period to help us answer this question. The mere contemplation of a public offering in the future will not by itself trigger the 1933 Act's pre-filing obligations. The pre-filing period begins once a company decides to take concrete steps toward a public offering.[4] As a

140. *See, e.g.,* Private Financial Network, [1997 Transfer Binder] Fed. Sec. L. Rep. (CCH) ¶ 77,332 (SEC No Action Letter March 12, 1997) (video transmissions of road shows were not prospectuses).

141. *See e.g.* Charles Schwab & Co., 31 Sec. Reg. & L. Rep. (BNA) 1560 (SEC No Action Letter Nov. 12, 1999) (live presentations via Internet in password protect areas were permissible).

142. Charles Schwab & Co., 32 Sec. Reg. & L. Rep. (BNA) 235 (SEC No Action Letter Feb. 9, 2000), *clarifying* Charles Schwab & Co., 31 Sec. Reg. & L. Rep. (BNA) 1560 (SEC No Action Letter Nov. 12, 1999).

144. *See* 1933 Act Rules 164 and 433, 17 C.F.R. §§ 230.164, 230.433; Securities Offering Reform, Sec. Act Rel. No. 33–8591, Sec. Exch. Act Rel. No. 34–52056, Inv. Co. Act Rel. No. IC–26993 70 Fed. Reg. 44722–01, 2005 WL 1692642 (SEC July 19, 2005).

§ 2.3

1. 5 U.S.C.A. § 77e(c).

2. Section 5(c) is the only portion of section 5 that covers offers to buy as well as offers to sell. *See* Richard J. Morgan, Offers to Buy Under The Securities Act of 1933, 1982 Ariz. St. L.J. 809.

3. These exemptions are found in section 4 of the Act. For example, section 4(1) exempts transactions not involving an issuer, underwriter, or a dealer. 15 U.S.C.A. § 77d(1); *see* § 4.26[1] *infra.* Section 4(2) exempts transaction by an issuer not involving a public offering. 15 U.S.C.A. § 77d(2); *see* §§ 4.24, 4.25 *infra.* Section 4(3) exempts most dealer transactions in securities. 15 U.S.C.A. § 77d(3); *see* 4.31 *infra.* Section 4(4) of the Act exempts unsolicited brokers' transactions. 15 U.S.C.A. § 77d(4); *see* § 4.26[2] *infra.* Of course, absent an applicable exemption, section 5(c)'s prohibitions will apply even if no public offering is contemplated.

4. The SEC has not addressed the duration of the pre-filing period but it indicated long ago that "in registration" means "at least from the time an issuer reaches an understanding with the

practical matter, in planning transactions, planners should consider the prohibitions applicable to the pre-filing period to apply at least the thirty days immediately preceding the filing of the registration statement.

Section 5(c)[5] sets forth the basic prohibitions for the pre-filing period. There can be neither legal offers to buy nor offers to sell securities until a registration statement has been filed. Section 5(c) is the broadest proscription because it covers all offers—whether written or oral and whether to buy or to sell. Section 5(c)'s reference to an offer to sell is clarified in section 2(a)(3)[6] where an offer to sell is defined broadly as any conduct that is reasonably calculated to generate a buying interest. A violation of section 5(c) does not depend upon an actual sale so long as there have been illegal offers.[8]

Section 5(c)'s prohibitions are broader than the prospectus requirements that apply during the waiting and post effective periods. In contrast to section 5(c)'s prohibitions on offers to sell and offers to buy in the absence of a registration statement having been filed, the prohibitions for both the waiting and post-effective periods apply only to a prospectus which includes written, radio, or television offers to sell as defined by section 2(a)(10) of the Act,[9] and not to oral offers to sell nor to any offers to buy. In addition to the prohibition against offers during the pre-filing period. Since it is an offer to sell prohibited by section 5(c), absent an exemption, a prospectus cannot be used during the prefiling period.[10] In addition, section 5(a)[11] bars all sales of securities during both the pre-filing and waiting periods.

An understanding of the definition of offer to sell is crucial to an understanding of section 5(c)'s prohibitions. Preliminary negotiations and agreements between an issuer and underwriters (and among underwriters who will be in privity with the issuer) are excluded from section 2(a)(3)'s definition of sell or offer to sell[12] and thus do not violate the "gun jumping" prohibitions contained in section 5(c); nor do they implicate the prospectus requirements of section 5(b) or the sale prohibition of section 5(a).

Therefore, absent an exemption or the exclusion for underwriters' preliminary negotiations and agreements, offers to buy, offers to sell (whether written or oral), and sales are all prohibited during the pre-filing period. Accordingly, the 1933 Act's broadest prohibitions take effect prior to filing of

broker-dealer which is to act as managing underwriter prior to the filing of a registration statement." Guidelines for Release of Information by Issuers Whose Securities are in Registration, Sec.Act Rel. No. 33–5180, 1971 WL 11224, Fed.Sec.L.Rep. (CCH) ¶ 3056 (Aug. 16, 1971). As a result of the SEC's offering reform rules, there is now a thirty day safe harbor so that most statements made more than thirty days before the filing of the registration statement will not be subject to section 5(c)'s gun-jumping prohibitions.

5. 15 U.S.C.A. § 77e(c).

6. 15 U.S.C.A. § 77b(a)(3).

8. SEC v. Cavanagh, 155 F.3d 129 135 (2d Cir.1998) ("Section 5(c) requires the filing of a registration statement prior to any offer, regardless of whether a sale occurs or the conditions of that sale").

9. 15 U.S.C.A. § 77b(a)(10). *See* § 2.1 *supra.*

10. *But see* Rule 163 permits the use of a "free writing prospectus" and thus provides a safe harbor for communications by well known seasoned issuers for offers made during the pre-filing period so long as the offer is filed with the SEC and contains a legend stating that the offering will be by prospectus. 17 C.F.R. § 230.163. The free writing prospectus is discussed later in this section.

11. 15 U.S.C.A. § 77e(a).

12. 15 U.S.C.A. § 77b(a)(3).

the registration statement. This broad reach of section 5(c) makes sense to the extent that during this time there is absolutely no public information about the upcoming offering, except for information which may have been disclosed if the issuer is already a public company and therefore subject to the 1934 Act's periodic reporting requirements. In light of the absence of reliable up-to-date information about the issuer and/or the terms of the upcoming offering, any premature sales-related activity or "gun jumping" would circumvent the purpose of the 1933 Act's registration and prospectus requirements. Such circumvention would amount to a violation of section 5.

In the fall of 2004, the SEC proposed and subsequently adopted rules significantly relaxing some of the restrictions on company communications to the public during the quite period imposed prior to filing of the registration statement.[17] The public offering reforms were adopted in 2005 and became effective in December of that year.[18] The rule proposals categorize issuers and establish different levels of permissible disclosures—expanding disclosures for existing public companies subject to the periodic reporting requirements of the Securities Exchange Act of 1934.[20] The new regime eliminated many of the gun jumping restrictions formerly applicable to public companies but retained a tighter rein on first time issuers.

§ 2.3[2] What Is an Offer to Sell?: Generating a Buying Interest

Section 2(a)(3) of the Act[23] defines offer to sell in terms of any activity that is reasonably calculated to solicit or generate a buying interest. The determination of whether there is an offer is not a matter of state contract law but rather is a question of federal law depending upon whether the challenged conduct has conditioned the offeree's or public's mind by generating a buying interest. The fact that negotiations fall short of an enforceable offer to sell under state contract law thus does not prevent the person negotiating to sell the securities in question from violating section 5 of the

17. Securities Offering Reform, Sec. Act Rel. No. 33–8591, Sec. Exch. Act Rel. No. 34–52056, Inv. Co. Act Rel. No. IC–26993 70 Fed. Reg. 44722–01, 2005 WL 1692642 (SEC July 19, 2005).

18. *See* Securities Offering Reform, Sec. Act Rel. No. 33–8501, Sec. Exch. Act Rel. No. 34–50624, Inv. Co. Act Rel. No. IC–26649, 2004 WL 2610458 (SEC Nov. 3, 2004). *See also, e.g.,* SEC Proposes Securities Offering Reform, Requires Registration of Hedge Fund Investment Advisers, http://www.sec.gov/news/press/2004–150.htm (SEC Oct. 27, 2004).

20. Under the rules there are four categories of issuers:

· A non-reporting issuer would be an issuer that is not required to file reports pursuant to Sections 13 or 15(d) of the Exchange Act.

· An unseasoned issuer would be an issuer that is required to file reports pursuant to Sections 13 or 15(d) of the Exchange Act, but does not satisfy the requirements of Form S–3 or Form F–3 for a primary offering of its securities.

· A seasoned issuer would be an issuer that is eligible to use Form S–3 or Form F–3 to register a primary offering of securities.

· A well-known seasoned issuer would be a new class of issuer that is eligible to register a primary offering of its securities on Form S–3 or Form F–3 and has either $700 million of public common equity float or, for limited purposes, has issued $1 billion of registered debt in the preceding three years.

See Securities Offering Reform, Sec. Act Rel. No. 33–8501, Sec. Exch. Act Rel. No. 34–50624, Inv. Co. Act Rel. No. IC–26649, 2004 WL 2610458 (SEC Nov. 3, 2004); SEC Proposes Securities Offering Reform, Requires Registration of Hedge Fund Investment Advisers, http://www.sec.gov/news/press/2004–150.htm (SEC Oct. 27, 2004).

23. 15 U.S.C.A. § 77b(a)(3).

1933 Act.[25] A letter or other communication that solicits investor interest prior to the filing of the registration statement will ordinarily be an illegal offer to sell.[26] The SEC has indicated that it is possible to generate a buying interest and therefore have an offer to sell in promotional material that does not even mention the upcoming offering, especially where the materials are used as part of a plan to prepare the market in advance of the dissemination of offering materials.[27] Dissemination of information in the ordinary course of business is permissible but it becomes questionable when the timing of such activities seems to be gearing up to an impending public offering.[28] Of course, not all publicly disseminated information about a company will constitute an offer to sell its securities. For example, the SEC clarified that historical information presented on a company's web is not an offer to sell securities if the information is separately identified as historical information and is located in a separate section of the company's web site that contains historical information.[29] However, the historical information may become an offer to sell if it is incorporated (by reference or otherwise) into the prospectus for a securities offering or if it is otherwise used or referred to in connection with a registered securities offering.

The initial leading authority on this point is the seminal and still leading SEC decision, In the Matter of Carl M. Loeb, Rhoades & Co.[31] In that administrative proceeding, the underwriter prepared and disseminated a press release six weeks prior to the filing of the registration statement. The press release announced that a one-person real estate venture owning over one hundred thousand acres "in the area of the gold coast" in Florida was about to go public. The press release went on to identify the investment banker that would be handling the underwriting arrangements and further named the issuer's principal officers. The press release generated a buying interest, as evidenced by the fact that over one hundred securities dealers contacted the named managing underwriter asking that they be included in the underwriting syndicate.[32] The SEC examined the press release and held that although in the form of a news item, the release disclosed much more information than was necessary to simply alert the public of a newsworthy event and thus constituted an offer to sell within section 2(a)(3)'s definition. The key to the Commission's emphazised not only the fact that more than one hundred securities firms had shown a buying interest but also that the press release

25. *See, e.g.,* SEC v. Cavanagh, 155 F.3d 129, 135 (2d Cir.1998); Diskin v. Lomasney & Co., 452 F.2d 871, 875 (2d Cir. 1971).

26. *See, e.g.,* SEC v. Commercial Investment & Development Corp., 373 F.Supp. 1153 (S.D.Fla.1974).

27. Sec. Act Rel. 33–3844 Example 1, 1957 WL 3605 (1957).

28. *See, e.g.,* Georgeson & Co., 1977 WL 13861 [1977–1978 Transfer Binder] Fed. Sec. L. Rep. (CCH) ¶ 81,118 (SEC No Action Letter Feb. 3, 1977, available Mar. 3, 1977) ("it would seem prudent and appropriate for those issuers that do not have a consistent history of such activities to defer commencing them until the registration process has been completed" and thereby avoid the inference "that an issuer is engaging in them for the purpose of priming the market for an impending securities offering").

29. *See* Securities Offering Reform, Sec. Act Rel. No. 33–8591, Sec. Exch. Act Rel. No. 34–52056, Inv. Co. Act Rel. No. IC–26993 70 Fed. Reg. 44722–01, 2005 WL 1692642 (SEC July 19, 2005). *See also,* 1933 Act Rule 168, 17 C.F.R.§ 230.168.

31. 38 S.E.C. 843, Sec. Exch. Act Rel. No. 34–5870, 1959 WL 2709 (SEC Feb. 9, 1959), noted in 1959 Duke L.J. 460; 54 Nw.L.Rev. 131 (1959). *Cf.* SEC v. Arvida Corp., [1957–1961 Transfer Binder] Fed. Sec. L. Rep. (CCH) ¶ 90,883 (S.D.N.Y. 1958) (refusing to dismiss the complaint but also refusing the SEC's request for a preliminary injunction).

32. The press release also announced the issuer's intent to embark upon a "comprehensive statement of orderly development."

identified the name of the principal underwriter, hence directing potential buyers to the selling source. The SEC has specifically cautioned that including the underwriter's name in pre-filing publicity is likely to generate a buying interest and therefore be classified as an "offer to sell."[33] Naming the underwriter will disqualify a communication from the protections of Rule 135's safe harbor for pre-filing publicity.[34]

Following the *Loeb, Rhoades* decision, there was concern that the line of demarcation between legitimate pre-filing publicity and an illegal offer to sell was a murky one. Accordingly, the SEC tried to clarify the issue when it amended Rule 135.[35] The current version of the rule enumerates the types of pre-filing publicity that will not be considered in violation of section 5(c)'s "gun jumping" prohibitions. Rule 135 is silent on the extent of its reach: that is, whether it is a safe harbor or an exclusive harbor. It is best viewed simply as a safe harbor. Nevertheless, one court[36] has indicated it to be the exclusive method for disseminating permissible pre-filing information. Presumably, this view of exclusivity is limited to press releases and other announcements geared solely to the impending public offering. The SEC has explained, for example, that the issuer should continue to make full disclosure in its 1934 Act periodic reports as well as to continue the types of publicity that the issuer undertakes as a matter of its ordinary course of business.[37]

As noted above, Rule 163A provides a safe harbor from a section 5(c) violation for communications made by or on behalf of the issuer provided the statement is made more than thirty days before the registration statement is filed. This safe harbor, among other things, is conditioned upon the absence of any reference to the upcoming offering. Pre-filing publicity that references the upcoming offering must fall within one of the permissible statements discussed in the sections that follow.

The broad definition of offer to sell in section 2(a)(3) makes it very easy for inadvertent but potentially harmful section 5(c) violations to occur during the pre-filing period. Any publicity that targets or is reasonably calculated to whet investors' interest in an upcoming offering will be problematic during the pre-filing period. For example, prior to the filing of Google, Inc.'s registration statement, the company's founders participated in an interview with Playboy magazine.[39] The SEC began an investigation to determine whether the interview violated section 5 and thereby threatened the offering.[40] The SEC eventually concluded the investigation apparently with the determination not to take any action,[41] but before the investigation was complete, the

33. Sec. Act Rel. 33–4697, 1964 WL 3660 (1964). *See also, e.g.,* Chris–Craft Industries, Inc. v. Bangor Punta Corp., 426 F.2d 569 (2d Cir.1970).

34. 17 C.F.R. § 230.135. *See* § 2.3[3] *infra.*

35. 17 C.F.R. § 230.135.

36. Chris–Craft Industries, Inc. v. Bangor Punta Corp., 426 F.2d 569 (2d Cir.1970).

37. *See, e.g.,* Guidelines for Release of Information by Issuers Whose Securities are in Registration, Sec.Act Rel. No. 33–5180, 1971 WL 11224, 1 Fed.Sec.L.Rep. (CCH) ¶ 3056 (Aug. 16, 1971).

39. Saul Hansell, Google Ready to Take Bids But New Questions Arise, N.Y. Times C2, 2004 WL 5591146 (Fri. Aug. 13, 2004).

40. *See, e.g.,* Michael Liedtke, Legal Questions?/Google Principals' Interview with PLAYBOY is a Hot Topic/SEC Frowns on Pre–IPO Puffery, and Talk in April Could Fill that Bill, 8/13/04 Houston Chronicle p. 3, 2004 WL 83657472 (Friday Aug. 13, 2004) (available on Westlaw).

41. *See, e.g.,* Michael Bobelian, SEC Plans Update of Rule That Targets Pre–IPO Talk, N.Y.L.J. p. 1, (col. 3) (Mon. Jan. 24, 2005); Andrew Countryman, SEC Won't Punish Google for Interview, Chicago Tribune P.3, 2005 WL 56606573 (Fri. Jan. 14, 2005).

company amended its registration statement to include in the risk factors, the potential risk that there could be adverse legal consequences flowing from this pre-filing interview.[42]

Additional Communications Permitted

As noted above, as part of its securities offering reform, the SEC adopted rules explicitly permitting additional communications during the quiet period by qualifying preexisting public companies. The new rules also clarify the application of section 5 to first time issuers and non-reporting companies. During the thirty days immediately preceding the public offering, all companies, including first time issuers, are permitted to publicly disseminate information that does not refer to a securities offering[45] provided the issuer takes reasonable steps to prevent further distribution of the information.[46] In addition, as part of the offering reform rule amendments, the SEC codified its preexisting interpretations that during registration a company may continue to disseminate factual information in the regular course of its business.[47] There is an additional, more expansive safe harbor for preexisting public companies that explicitly includes both "factual business information or forward-looking information."[48] This exemption applies to the types of information that the company disseminates in the regular course of business.[49] The safe harbor in Rule 168 applies to information disseminated by broker-dealers as agent of the issuer[50] but is not available to investment companies.[51]

As a practical matter, the gun-jumping prohibitions of section 5 rarely apply to the largest and most widely traded public companies that qualify as well-known seasoned issuers ("WKSIs"). A WKSI is a company that qualifies for registration on 1933 Act Form S–3 or F–3 and either: (A) as of a date within 60 days of the determination date, has a worldwide market value of its outstanding voting and non-voting common equity held by non-affiliates of $700 million or more; or (B)(1) as of a date within 60 days of the determination date, has issued in the last three years at least $1 billion aggregate principal amount of non-convertible securities, other than common equity, in

42. *See, e.g.,* Michael Liedtke, Google Proceeds with IPO Auction; The Search Engine Company Conceded in an SEC Filing That a Magazine Interview has Misleading Information, Philadelphia Inquirer p. D01, 2004 WL 87779052 (Sat. Aug. 14, 2004).

45. 1933 Act Rule 163A, 17 C.F.R. 230.163A.

46. 17 C.F.R. 230.163A. The exclusion does not apply to business combinations, shell companies, nor to investment companies. *See also* the discussion of the free writing prospectus during the waiting period in § 2.4[2][E] *infra.*

47. Rule 169, 17 C.F.R. § 230.169. Among other things, the communication must resemble communications that the company had disseminated in the past. Rule 169(d), 17 C.F.R. § 230.169(d).

48. 1933 Act Rule 168(a), 17 C.F.R. § 230.168(a). Rule 168 provides a safe harbor from the definition of offer as used in section 5(c)'s gun-jumping prohibition as well as a safe harbor from section 2(a)(10)'s definition of "prospectus" thereby preventing the application of the prohibition in Securities Act section 5(b)(1) on the use of a prospectus that is not a statutory prospectus. The prospectus requirements for the waiting period are discussed in § 2.4 *infra.*

49. 17 C.F.R. § 230.168(d)(2) ("The timing, manner, and form in which the information is released or disseminated is consistent in material respects with similar past releases or disseminations").

50. 17 C.F.R. § 230.168(b)(3) ("For purposes of this section, the release or dissemination of a communication is by or on behalf of the issuer if the issuer or an agent or representative of the issuer, other than an offering participant who is an underwriter or dealer, authorizes or approves such release or dissemination before it is made").

51. 17 C.F.R. § 230.168(d)(3).

primary offerings for cash, not exchange, registered under the Act; and (2) will register only non-convertible securities, other than common equity, and full and unconditional guarantees permitted pursuant to paragraph (1)(ii) of the WKSI definition unless, at the determination date, the issuer also is eligible to register a primary offering of its securities relying on General Instruction I.B.1. of Form S–3 or Form F–3.[52]

Rule 163 permits the use of a "free writing prospectus" and thus provides a safe harbor for communications by WKSIs for offers made during the pre-filing period so long as the offer is filed with the SEC and contains a legend stating that the offering will be by prospectus.[53] The safe harbor is not available for business combinations nor is it available for investment companies.[54] The safe harbor applies to the company itself and to broker-dealers acting as agents for the company in disseminating information.[55] In contrast, reporting companies that do not reach the WKSI threshold and non-reporting companies may not use a free writing prospectus until a registration statement has been filed.[56]

Factual Information and gun-jumping; forward-looking statements by reporting companies.

Rule 169[57] provides a safe harbor for "factual business information" that is not directed to investors but is issued as part of the company's ordinary business. Thus, for example, product advertisements are protected by the safe harbor.[58] Rule 169's safe harbor applies to non-reporting companies as well as to reporting companies. The safe harbor does not apply to communications made as part of the offering and also is limited to the types of information the company had made in the past. 1934 Act reporting companies are given a broader safe harbor in Rule 168[59] which permits not only the dissemination of factual information but also forward looking information. As is the case with Rule 169, Rule 168's safe harbor for reporting companies applies only if

52. 7 C.F.R. § 230.405. A seasoned issuer, other than a WKSI, is an issuer that uses Form S–3 or Form F–3 to register primary offerings of securities. Securities Offering Reform, Sec. Act Rel. No. 33–8591, Sec. Exch. Act Rel. No. 34–52056, Inv. Co. Act Rel. No. IC–26993 70 Fed. Reg. 44722–01, 2005 WL 1692642 (SEC July 19, 2005). "An unseasoned issuer is an issuer that is required to file reports pursuant to Sections 13 or 15(d) of the Exchange Act, but does not satisfy the requirements of Form S–3 or Form F–3 for a primary offering of its securities." *Id.*

53. 17 C.F.R. § 230.163. Other issuers may take advantage of the free writing prospectus after the registration statement has been filed. 1933 Act Rule 164, 17 C.F.R. § 230.164. *See* the discussion of the free writing prospectus during the waiting period in § 2.4[2][E] *infra*. *See also* Rule 433, 17 C.F.R. § 230.433 (conditions to permissible post-filing free writing prospectuses).

54. 17 C.F.R. § 230.163(b)(3).

55. 17 C.F.R. § 230163I ("For purposes of this section, a communication is made by or on behalf of an issuer if the issuer or an agent or representative of the issuer, other than an offering participant who is an underwriter or dealer, authorizes or approves the communication before it is made").

56. *See* the discussion in § 2.4[2][E] *infra*.

57. 17 C.F.R. § 230.169.

58. 17 C.F.R. § 230.169 (b) ("(1) Factual business information means some or all of the following information that is released or disseminated under the conditions in paragraph (d) of this section: (i) Factual information about the issuer, its business or financial developments, or other aspects of its business; and (ii) Advertisements of, or other information about, the issuer's products or services. (2) For purposes of this section, the release or dissemination of a communication is by or on behalf of the issuer if the issuer or an agent or representative of the issuer, other than an offering participant who is an underwriter or dealer, authorizes or approves such release or dissemination before it is made.").

59. 17 C.F.R. § 230.168.

"the timing, manner, and form in which the information is released or disseminated is consistent in material respects with similar past releases or disseminations."[60] Rule 168 excludes from the safe harbor both communications "containing information about the registered offering and communications released or disseminated as part of the offering activities in the registered offering."[61] The safe harbors in Rules 168 and 169 apply both to section 5(c) gun jumping and to information during the waiting and post effective periods since the rules refer to section 2(a)(10)'s definition of prospectus as well.

Even after the expiration of the pre-filing period, participants must be careful not to make written offers unless they are in compliance with the prospectus requirements of section 5(b) of the Act.[62] Thus, once the decision to go public has been made and continuing through the waiting and post-effective periods when prospectuses must be delivered, participants in a registered offering must be very careful not to make statements that will be regarded as conditioning the market.

§ 2.3[3] Safe Harbor for Permissible Pre-Filing Announcements—SEC Rule 135

Rule 135 provides that, solely for the purpose of section 5 of the Act, a notice given by an issuer or selling shareholder, to the extent that it proposes to make a registered public offering, is not an offer for sale if the notice contains only the information specified in the rule and further states that an offer can be made only through the use of a prospectus. The rule, which as written reads like a safe harbor rule,[64] applies to "a notice of a proposed offering to be registered under the Act" published by "an issuer or a selling security holder (and any person acting on behalf of either of them)."[65] Notably, the rule does not address press releases by promoters, underwriters or other participants unless they are issuing the statement on behalf of the issuer or selling shareholders. It is quite possible that the omission of underwriters and promoters from Rule 135 reflects a view that any publicity initiated by an underwriter or promoter is likely to be viewed as the type of sales effort that section 5(c) was designed to prevent.[66] It would certainly make sense to limit pre-filing publicity to the information sent out by the issuer whose interest in disseminating the information may be other than initiating the sales effort. Furthermore, limiting pre-filing publicity to the issuer is consistent with Rule 135's goal of balancing the right to disseminate newsworthy information against the risks of generating a buying interest in the security which will be registered, before adequate information is available. Notwithstanding this reading of Rule 135, it should be remembered that the prohibition is limited to participants in the offering and securities profession-

60. 17 C.F.R. § 230.168(d)(2).

61. 17 C.F.R. § 230.168(c).

62. 15 U.S.C.A. § 77e(b). *See* § 2.4 *infra*.

64. At least one decision has indicated that the rule is not merely a safe harbor but is an exclusive list of permissible pre-filing notices. Chris–Craft Industries, Inc. v. Bangor Punta Corp., 426 F.2d 569 (2d Cir.1970).

65. 17 C.F.R. § 230.135.

66. The naming of the underwriter in pre-filing publicity has been held to be a significant factor in finding an illegal selling effort. *See* In the Matter of Carl M. Loeb, Rhoades & Co., 38 S.E.C. 843, Sec. Exch. Act Rel. No. 34–5870, 1959 WL 2709 (SEC Feb. 9, 1959). *See also, e.g.*, Chris–Craft Industries, Inc. v. Bangor Punta Corp., 426 F.2d 569 (2d Cir.1970).

als in light of the exemption for transactions by persons other than issuers, underwriters, and dealers.[67]

Rule 135 publicity can legitimately contain (1) the name of the issuer; (2) the title, amount, and basic terms of the offering; (3) in the case of a rights offering to existing security holders, the subscription ratio, record date and approximate date of the proposed rights offering, as well as the subscription price; (4) where securities are exchanged for securities of another issuer, the nature and "basis" of the exchange;[68] (5) in the case of an offering to employees of the issuer or any affiliate, the class of employees and the amount proposed to be offered, including the offering price; and (6) any statement required by state law or administrative authority.

Rule 135 does not expressly permit mentioning the offering price in the pre-filing publicity for most public offerings. Only Rule 135 subsections 3 and 5, which deal with rights offerings to existing securities holders and offerings to employees, expressly permit mention of price. There is authority supporting the exclusivity of these provisions permitting reference to price. For example, within the tender offer context, in the announcement of a proposed exchange offer for which no registration statement had been filed, a valuation of securities not yet issued that were to be distributed as part of the exchange package went beyond the terms of Rule 135 and was thus held to render the press release an offer to sell the securities in violation of section 5(c).[69] The "gun jumping" problem in the course of exchange offers has to a large extent been remedied by Rule 165,[70] which was promulgated in connection with the SEC's adoption of Regulation M–A.[71] Rule 165 permits announcements of tender offers prior to the filing of the 1933 Act registration statement. Rule 165 applies not only to tender offers, but also to other business combinations, such as mergers, where the shares issued will be covered by a 1933 Act registration statement.[72] The pre-filing announcements permitted by Rule 165 need to be filed with the SEC.[73] Once the registration statement is filed, any written communications to shareholders must comply with the 1933 Act's prospectus requirements.[74]

SEC Rule 135, as noted above, refers only to pre-filing publicity by issuers and says nothing about information provided by others. By virtue of section 4(1)'s exemption,[75] persons who are not issuers, underwriters, or dealers may

67. Section 4(1), 15 U.S.C.A. § 77d(1), which is discussed in § 4.26 *infra*.

68. Rule 135(a)(4) by allowing the basis of the exchange is in contrast to subsections (3) and (5) which permit mentioning the offering price.

69. Chris–Craft Industries, Inc. v. Bangor Punta Corp., 426 F.2d 569 (2d Cir.1970). The SEC subsequently indicated that mentioning price in the context of a takeover will not always be an offer to sell. *See* Interpretations Concerning the Application of Registration Requirements to Certain Tender Offers and the Application of Tender Offer Provisions to Certain Cash Option Mergers, Sec.Act Rel.No. 33–5927, Sec. Exch. Act Rel. No. 34–14699, 14 S.E.C. Docket 894, 1978 WL 170900, 3 Fed.Sec.L.Rep. (CCH) ¶ 24,284(H) (April 24, 1978).

70. 17 C.F.R. § 230.165.

71. Regulation of Takeovers and Security Holder Communications, Sec. Exch. Act Rel. No. 34–42055, 70 S.E.C. Docket 2229, 1999 WL 969596 (SEC Oct. 22, 1999).

72. This includes, for example, combinations effectuated through registration on Form S–4 that combines the 1933 Act proxy statement with the 1934 Act Schedule 14A that is required for soliciting proxies.

73. 1933 Act Rules 135(b), 425, 17 C.F.R. §§ 230.135(b), 230.425.

74. The prospectus requirements are discussed in §§ 2.4, 2.5 *infra*.

75. 15 U.S.C.A. § 77d(1). *See* § 4.26 *infra*.

issue any pre-filing information. This exemption, of course, is subject to the caveat that anyone acting on behalf of the issuer, its affiliates, or other participants in the offering will be considered one of the underwriters[76] or their agents according to common law agency principles.[77] If Rule 135 is in fact exclusive,[78] then neither underwriters nor dealers can issue any pre-filing publicity without an exemption such as those found in Rules 137, 138, and 139,[79] which are discussed directly below.[80] Arguably, any other publicity would be a selling effort or at least reasonably calculated to stimulate a buying interest and thus within section 2(a)(3)'s definition. Even if Rule 135 is deemed not to be exclusive, any non-exempt underwriter or dealer generating pre-filing publicity would be subject to careful factual scrutiny along the lines of the *Loeb, Rhoades* analysis as to whether an illegal selling effort has taken place. In any event, the safest course is to adhere strictly to Rule 135 and thus make no disclosures beyond its terms, as well as limit the dissemination of such information to the public.[81]

Summary of pre-filing limitations on dissemination of information

As discussed above,[82] communications that are reasonably calculated to generate a buying interest can constitute an illegal offer to sell and violate section 5(c)'s pre-filing period prohibition. There are some communications that are expressly permitted during the pre-filing period. As noted above, Rule 135[83] provides a safe harbor for preliminary announcements referencing a yet-to-be filed public offering. Rule 163[84] permits the most seasoned public companies (WKSIs as defined in Rule 405[85]) to use certain written communications (a free writing prospectus) during the pre-filing period. Other issuers, subject to certain conditions, may use a free writing prospectus *after* the registration statement has been filed.[86] There is more leeway for communications that do not make reference to the upcoming offering. Rule 163A[87] provides a safe harbor from a section 5(c) violation with respect to communications made by or on behalf of the issuer provided the statement is made more than thirty days before the registration statement is filed. This safe harbor, among other things, is conditioned upon the absence of any reference to the upcoming offering.[88] Statements referencing the upcoming offering must fall within the parameters of the *Loeb Rhodes* decision[89] or Rule 135[90] or,

76. *See* section 2(a)(11); 15 U.S.C.A. § 77b(a)(11).

77. *See also* section 15's liability of controlling persons. 15 U.S.C.A. § 77*o* discussed in § 7.12 *infra.*

78. *See* Chris–Craft Industries, Inc. v. Bangor Punta Corp., 426 F.2d 569 (2d Cir.1970).

79. 17 C.F.R. §§ 230.137–230.139.

80. *See* § 2.3[6] *infra.*

81. Even where the offering is purely a secondary one, a literal reading of the rule would limit the press release to the issuer as opposed to the actual registrants. Secondary distributions are discussed in §§ 4.26–4.29 *infra.*

82. *See* § 2.3[2] *supra.*

83. 17 C.F.R. § 230.135.

84. 17 C.F.R. § 230.163; *see* § 2.3[2] *supra.*

85. 17 C.F.R. § 230.405. *See* the discussion of WKSIs in §§ 2.2[1], 2.3[2] *supra.*

86. Rules 164, 433, 17 C.F.R. §§ 230.164, 230.164. *See* § 2.4 *infra.*

87. 17 C.F.R. § 230.163A.

88. 17 C.F.R. § 230.163A. *See* § 2.3[2] *supra.*

89. 38 S.E.C. 843, Sec. Exch. Act Rel. No. 34–5870, 1959 WL 2709 (SEC Feb. 9, 1959). *See* § 2.3[2] *supra.*

90. 17 C.F.R. § 230.135.

with respect to WKSIs, qualify as a permissible pre-filing free writing prospectus under Rule 163.[91]

§ 2.3[5] The Impact of Exchange Act Reporting Requirements and Other Disclosure Obligations on the Pre–Filing Quiet Period

The pressure for affirmative disclosure that may result from the 1934 Act reporting requirements, including the proxy rules and the tender offer provisions,[101] or in the case of non-reporting companies from Exchange Act Rule 10b–5,[102] may be at odds with section 5(c)'s limitations on publicity. In such a case "[t]he Commission * * * emphasizes that there is no basis in the securities acts or in any policy of the Commission which would justify the practice of non-disclosure on the grounds that it has the securities in registration under the Securities Act of 1933."[103] By "in registration," the SEC means "at least from the time an issuer reaches an understanding with the broker-dealer which is to act as managing underwriter prior to the filing of a registration statement and [continues through] the period ... during which dealers must deliver a prospectus."[104] This is not a bright line test since the SEC indicates that this is "*at least*" when "in registration" begins; thus, depending on the activities taking place it could begin earlier. Although not explicitly addressing the question of when a company is "in registration," SEC Rule 163A provides a limited safe harbor by permitting communications that do not reference the upcoming offering so long as they are disseminated at least thirty days in advance of the registration statement and the issuer has taken reasonable steps to prevent further distribution of the communication within the thirty day period prior to the filing of the registration statement.[105]

The balance that permits the issuer to continue normal publicity[106] during the pre-filing period is necessarily is a delicate one. Accordingly, it has been held that too much disclosure will nevertheless violate section 5(c),[107] thus frequently placing the issuer between a rock and a hard place in deciding the extent of permissible pre-filing publicity. Close questions necessarily require careful examination of the gun jumping prohibitions in conjunction with the materiality requirements of the applicable affirmative disclosure requirements. For example, the shareholders who are asked in a proxy statement to approve authorization of shares for future distribution must be given more pre-filing information than would otherwise be permissible under Rule 135. The offering reform rules adopted in 2005 expanded, at least in some

---

91. 17 C.F.R. § 230.163.

101. *See* Chris–Craft Industries, Inc. v. Bangor Punta Corp., 426 F.2d 569 (2d Cir.1970).

102. 17 C.F.R. § 240.10b–5. *See* chapter 12 *infra*.

103. Guidelines for Release of Information by Issuers Whose Securities are in Registration, Sec.Act Rel. No. 33–5180, 1971 WL 11224, Fed.Sec.L.Rep. (CCH) ¶ 3056 (Aug. 16, 1971).

104. *See* Sec.Act Rel. No. 33–5180, 1971 WL 11224, Fed.Sec.L.Rep. (CCH) ¶ 3056 n.1 (Aug. 16, 1971). *Accord* Use of Electronic Media, Sec. Act Rel. No. 33–7856, 2000 WL 502290 fn. 10 (SEC April 28, 2000).

105. 17 C.F.R. § 230.163A.

106. The pre-filing "gun jumping" prohibitions "are not intended to restrict the normal communications between an issuer and its stockholders or the announcement to the public generally of information with respect to important business and financial developments." Sec. Act Rel. 33–4697, 1964 WL 3660 (1964).

107. Chris–Craft Indus., Inc. v. Bangor Punta Corp., 426 F.2d 569 (2d Cir.1970).

situations, the types of communications that can be made throughout the offering and registration process.[108] In particular, Rule 163, in allowing well-known seasoned issuers to use a "free writing prospectus"[109] during the pre-filing period, allows communications that would clearly otherwise be deemed an impermissible offer to sell.[110]

Even beyond the conflicting pulls of the 1933 Act's "gun jumping" prohibitions and the Exchange Act's call for full disclosure, "gun jumping" tensions can arise in other areas in which the issuer is engaged in the public dissemination of information. The SEC suggests that issuers establish internal controls to protect against improvident release of information while securities are in registration.[111]

Pre-filing publicity in the ordinary course of business is not limited to issuers that are already subject to the periodic reporting requirements of the Securities Exchange Act. Privately held companies that have a public persona may also continue their traditional level of publicity. However, they must be careful not to increase their public relations in such a way as to precondition the market. This issue can arise, for example, with regard to company-sponsored web sites. The SEC is of the view that once a company is "in registration" under the 1933 Act, there is a strong presumption that the company has adopted any statements contained in third party web sites that are hyperlinked to the company's web site.[116]

[For discussion of SEC Rules dealing with broker-dealer recommendations during the pre-filing period, see § 2.3[6] of the Practitioner's Edition.]

§ 2.4 The Waiting Period

§ 2.4[1] Prohibitions During the Waiting Period

Once the registration statement has been filed, the waiting period begins. Since section 5(c) is no longer in effect after filing, anyone is free to make an offer to buy the security in registration, as well as to make oral offers to sell, provided that no sale is consummated, lest there be a violation of section 5(a).[2] In addition to section 5(a)'s ban on sales prior to the effective date, the key to both the waiting and post-effective periods is found in the prospectus requirements of the 1933 Act. Section 5(b)(1)[3] makes it unlawful to utilize the mails or any instrumentality of transportation in interstate commerce to transmit any prospectus with regard to a security for which a registration statement has been filed, unless the prospectus meets the requirements of section 10 of

108. *See* § 2.4[2][E] *supra*.

109. The "free writing prospectus," which may be used more broadly during the waiting and post effective periods is defined in Rule 405, 17 C.F.R. § 230.450 and is discussed in § 2.4[2][E] *supra*.

110. 17 C.F.R. § 230.163.

111. Guidelines for Release of Information by Issuers Whose Securities are in Registration, Sec.Act Rel. No. 33–5180, 1971 WL 120474, 1 Fed.Sec.L.Rep. (CCH) ¶ 3056 (Aug. 16, 1971). *Accord* Use of Electronic Media, Sec. Act Rel. No. 33–7856, 2000 WL 502290 (SEC April 28, 2000).

116. Use of Electronic Media, Sec. Act Rel. No. 33–7856, 2000 WL 502290 (SEC April 28, 2000).

§ 2.4

2. 15 U.S.C.A. §§ 77e(a), 77e(c). *See* § 2.3 *supra*.

3. 15 U.S.C.A. § 77e(b)(1).

the Act.[4] Section 5(b)(2)[5] prohibits the delivery of a security for sale unless accompanied or preceded by a prospectus meeting the requirements of section 10(a).[6]

The broad definition of prospectus gives significant impact to section 5(b)(1)'s requirements. Section 2(a)(10)[9] defines "prospectus" to include all written offers to sell the security, in addition to any offer to sell transmitted by means of radio or television. Although section 2(a)(10) does not address the issue directly, it is now clear that web-based communications (except certain real-time communications) are written communications[11] which means, for example, that an offer to sell transmitted through electronic mail, appearing on a website, delivered on computer disk or other digitally encoded manner would qualify as a prospectus. The Commission has made it clear that the prospectus delivery requirements apply to electronic communications.[14] Issuers must take care to assure that the electronic communications comply with the prospectus delivery requirements. A web site can be used to identify prospectus materials. Any hyperlinks within the area of the web site containing prospectus materials will be considered part of the prospectus, whereas hyperlinks appearing elsewhere on the web site will not.[15]

In 1997, the SEC proposed Rule 154, which, among other things, included an Internet address within the definition of addresses for the purposes of prospectus delivery (as well as delivery of annual reports to the shareholders).[16] The rule as adopted, not only permits delivery to an electronic mailbox, but also permits delivery by traditional means to multiple people at the same address so long as they sign an appropriate consent.[17]

In line with the expansive definition applicable to offers to sell generally, the definition of prospectus is far-reaching. For example, written statements that condition the market can run afoul of the prospectus requirements.[20] Section 2(a)(10)'s definition not only includes advertisement circulars and notices which offer the securities for sale but also expressly covers communications confirming sales of securities in registration. This is an especially significant aspect of the definition of prospectus since, by virtue of Rule 10b–10 of the 1934 Act,[22] all transactions by a broker for a customer's account must be preceded by a written confirmation, which pursuant to section 5(b)(1)

4. 15 U.S.C.A. § 77j. Rule 154 permits single delivery to two or more investors living in one household provided the recipients have consented to a single delivery format. Rule 154, 17 C.F.R. 230.154. *See* Sec. Act Rel. No. 33–7766, 64 Fed. Reg. 62540 (Nov. 16, 1999); Sec. Act Rel. No. 33–7475 (SEC 1997). This process is known as "householding."

5. 15 U.S.C.A. § 77e(b)(2). Since section 5(a) prohibits sales during the waiting period, the practical impact of section 5(b)(2) is during the post-effective period.

6. The section 10(a) prospectus requirements are discussed in §§ 2.5, 3.2 *infra*.

9. 15 U.S.C.A. § 77b(a)(10).

11. Rule 405's definition of "written communication" expressly includes the term "graphic communication," which in turn is also defined in Rule 405. 17 C.F.R. § 230.405.

14. Use of Electronic Media, Sec. Act Rel. No. 33–7856, 2000 WL 502290 (SEC April 28, 2000).

15. Use of Electronic Media, Sec. Act Rel. No. 33–7856, 2000 WL 502290 (SEC April 28, 2000).

16. *See* Sec. Act Rel. No. 33–7475 (SEC 1997).

17. Rule 154, 17 C.F.R. § 230.154.

20. Crowell, Weedon & Co., 1984 WL 45229 (SEC No Action Letter April 18, 1984 available May 17, 1984) ("During the period beginning with the initial decision to make a public offering and ending when prospectus delivery requirements have been satisfied, the issuer and the underwriting group should be circumspect in making public statements about the issuer in order to avoid conditioning the market for the issuer's securities").

22. 17 C.F.R. § 240.10b–10.

must conform to section 10's disclosure requirements unless an applicable exemption can be established. Section 2(a)(10) further sets forth an important exclusion from the definition of prospectus which permits use of "identifying statements" and "tombstone ads," which are considered directly below.[23]

Section 10 of the 1933 Act sets out the requirements of a statutory prospectus—*i.e.*, one that is sufficient to avoid violation of section 5(b)'s prohibitions. Section 10(a) requires the prospectus to include all relevant information about the issuer.[24] Section 10(a)(3) further provides that whenever the prospectus is used more than nine months after the registration statement's effective date, the information must be updated so as to be accurate within a time frame of not more than sixteen months prior to *use* of the prospectus.[25]

In addition to section 10(a)'s statutory prospectus, section 10(b)[26] permits the Commission to promulgate rules that allow the use of a "summary prospectus" so as to satisfy section 5(b)(1)'s prospectus requirement. Although most section 10(b) summary prospectuses can be used during both the waiting and post-effective periods, they are valid only for section 5(b)(1)'s prospectus requirements and do not extend to section 5(b)(2)'s delivery for sale proscriptions. The Commission has exercised its rulemaking power under section 10(b) to authorize summary prospectuses under Rule 430 (the preliminary or "red herring" prospectus),[27] and Rule 431[28] which permits a summary prospectus prepared by the issuer and filed with the registration statement. The preliminary or "red herring" prospectus[29] is not explicitly grounded upon section 10(b)[30] but obviously is based upon that statutory grant of rulemaking authority.

In 2005, the SEC introduced many significant reforms to the public offering process.[31] Those reforms included the recognition of a "free writing prospectus" for use by both well seasoned issuers during the pre-filing period[32] and by additional issuers during the waiting period.[33] As discussed more fully below, a free writing prospectus enables the company to issue supplemental literature that goes beyond the disclosures mandated (and permitted) in the statutory prospectus.[34]

§ 2.4[2] Permissible Offers to Sell During the Waiting Period

Since prospectus is defined as an offer to sell, unlike during the pre-filing period, offers to buy are permitted during the waiting (and post-effective

23. *See* § 2.4[2] *infra.*

24. 15 U.S.C.A. § 77aa. *See* chapter 3 *infra.*

25. 15 U.S.C.A. § 77j(a)(3). These time periods contemplate that the information in the prospectus may be as of a date several months before the prospectus was prepared.

26. 15 U.S.C.A. § 77j(b).

27. 17 C.F.R. § 230.430.

28. 17 C.F.R. § 230.431.

29. 17 C.F.R. § 230.430.

30. *See* 1 Louis Loss, Securities Regulation 232–34 (2d ed. 1961).

31. *See* Securities Offering Reform, Sec. Act Rel. No. 33–8591, Sec. Exch. Act Rel. No. 34–52056, Inv. Co. Act Rel. No IC–26993 70 Fed. Reg. 44722–01, 2005 WL 1692642 (SEC July 19, 2005).

32. *See* 1933 Act Rules 163 and 433, 17 C.F.R. §§ 230.163, 230.433. *See* § 2.3 *supra.*

33. *See* 1933 Act Rules 164 and 433, 17 C.F.R. §§ 230.164, 230.433.

34. *See* 1933 Act Rules 164 and 433, 17 C.F.R. §§ 230.164, 230.433.

period). With regard to offers to sell, there are essentially five types of permissible offers to sell that may be made during the waiting period: oral communications, identifying statements, qualifying preliminary prospectuses, certain summary prospectuses, and a "free writing prospectus." Those five types of offers to sell are discussed directly below.

§ 2.4[2][A] Oral Offers to Sell

Section 5(b) applies only to prospectuses as defined in section 2(a)(10) which, as noted above, is limited to written, radio, and television offers to sell and thus does not include oral communications. Since section 5(c)'s prohibition on all offers to sell expressly expires upon the filing of the registration statement, there are no prohibitions on oral offers after the filing. The waiting period thus permits selling efforts with regard to securities in registration. For example, brokers, and even dealers who are members of the underwriting group, may make all offers to sell either on a face-to-face basis or over the telephone, so long as there is no final contract to purchase the security prior to the effective date. Notwithstanding the absence of section 5 implications, oral offers to sell during the waiting and post-effective periods are, of course, subject to the securities acts' general antifraud provisions.

Since oral communications are not within the definition of prospectus, there are no restrictions other than those imposed by the antifraud rules. Accordingly, it is common for promoters of public offerings and brokers to make statements over the telephone or in person that they would not be able to make in writing. It is also common for promoters of public offerings to hold meetings, known as road shows, to discuss the securities being offered. Slide and video presentations at live road shows are permissible so long as the investor is not provided with copies of the materials since such copies would qualify as a "prospectus" under the Act.[38] A video broadcast that is transmitted into a live road show is also permissible for similar reasons.[39]

The SEC has also permitted road shows over the Internet.[40] The Commission has given no action letter relief for Internet road shows on three conditions: (1) the road show may not exclude any material information; (2) only one version of the road show is captured for subsequent Internet transmission; and (3) the content of the road show is consistent with the information contained in the statutory prospectus.[41] It must be remembered that statements made at road shows (regardless of how the presentation is conducted) are subject to the securities laws' antifraud provisions.[42]

It thus is clear that oral offers do not have section 5 implications during the waiting and post-effective periods. However, where oral communications progress to an enforceable contract under state law, then there will be section 5 consequences since section 5(a)[43] prohibits sales prior to the registration

---

38. *See* Exploration, Inc., 1986 WL 67374 (SEC No Action Letter Nov. 10, 1986).

39. Private Financial Network, 1997 WL 107175 (SEC No Action Letter March 12, 1997).

40. *See* Charles Schwab & Co., 31 Sec. Reg. & L. Rep. (BNA) 1560 (SEC No Action Letter Nov. 12, 1999) (live presentations via Internet in password protect areas were permissible).

41. Charles Schwab & Co., 32 Sec. Reg. & L. Rep. (BNA) 235 (SEC No Action Letter Feb. 9, 2000), *clarifying* Charles Schwab & Co., 31 Sec. Reg. & L. Rep. (BNA) 1560 (SEC No Action Letter Nov. 12, 1999).

42. Krim v. pcOrder.com, Inc., 2002 WL 1185913, Fed. Sec. L. Rep. ¶ 91786 (W.D.Tex.2002).

43. 15 U.S.C.A. § 77e(a).

statement's effective date. In another context, the Supreme Court expressly held that oral contracts for sale are subject to the federal securities laws.[44]

§ 2.4[2][B] The "Tombstone Advertisement" and Other Identifying Statements

Section 2(a)(10)(b) of the 1933 Act expressly excludes from the definition of "prospectus" a communication if it "does no more than identify the security, state the price thereof, state by whom orders will be executed, and contains such other information as [may be required by Commission rules and regulations]" and if it specifies from whom a statutory prospectus may be obtained.[45] The Commission promulgated Rule 134[46] which specifies twelve categories of information that may be included in the tombstone ad (or other identifying statement) without running afoul of the 1933 Act's prospectus requirements. Tombstone ads may appear in newspapers or other hard print media, they may be mailed, and they may appear online. It is also perfectly permissible to follow up tombstone ads by making telephone or other oral communications to the potential investors.[50]

As part of its public offering reform that was adopted in 2005,[51] the SEC amended Rule 134 and expanded the factual information that may be contained in an identifying statement during the waiting period. Rule 134 was expanded from twelve to twenty-two categories of factual information that may be contained in an identifying statement.

Inclusion of any information not specifically permitted by Rule 134 renders the rule unavailable and thus can result in a prospectus that fails to comply with section 10's requirements,[57] resulting in a violation of section 5 of the Act. Thus, for example, while a corporate "logo," corporate symbol, or trademark of the issuer or marketing organization, or "attention getting headline" is permissible in a tombstone ad or identifying statement, pictures, illustrations, graphic designs, discussion of investment objectives, and statements regarding eligibility for securities being offered are not permitted.[59] The inclusion of excess information in the tombstone ad[60] may turn it into an impermissible selling document.[61]

---

44. Wharf (Holdings) Ltd. v. United International Holdings, Inc., 532 U.S. 588, 121 S.Ct. 1776, 149 L.Ed.2d 845 (2001) (oral option is a security subject to the federal securities laws).

45. 15 U.S.C.A. § 77j(b)(10).

46. 17 C.F.R. § 230.134. *See also* Rule 142 which defines the meaning of participating in a distribution. 17 C.F.R. § 230.142.

50. *See, e.g.,* Capital Supervisors, Inc., 1983 WL 28567 (SEC No Action Letter June 27, 1983 available August 27, 1983).

51. *See* Securities Offering Reform, Sec. Act Rel. No. 33–8591, Sec. Exch. Act Rel. No. 34–52056, Inv. Co. Act Rel. No. IC–26993 70 Fed. Reg. 44722–01 2005 WL 1692642 (SEC July 19, 2005).

57. *See, e.g.* Benham Distributors, Inc., 1991 WL 243179 (SEC No Action Letter Oct. 30, 1991) (S & P rating could not be included in tombstone ad).

59. National Association of Securities Dealers, Inc., 1984 WL 47359 (SEC No Action Letter June 23, 1984). *See also* Associates First Capital Corp., 1981 WL 25435 (SEC No Action Letter Nov. 26, 1981) ("Rule 134 does not provide for graphic illustrations in advertisements by non-investment companies").

60. *See, e.g.,* Mitchum, Jones & Templeton, 1972 WL 8404 (S.E.C. No Action Letter August 31, 1972 available Oct. 2, 1972) ("The pertinent portion of Rule 134 requires that the communication in question contain no more than certain specified items").

61. *See, e.g.,* Peoples Investment Co., 1975 WL 9630 (SEC No Action Letter Sept. 24, 1975 available Oct. 24, 1975) ("additional information would constitute a direct effort to sell the securities through the medium of the advertisement").

The information permitted in a Rule 134 identifying statement is quite limited. In contrast, during the waiting period many companies may qualify for use of the more expansive "free writing prospectus"[62] that is discussed in a subsequent section of this supplement.[63]

§ 2.4[2][C] The Preliminary ("Red Herring") Prospectus

The preliminary prospectus or so-called "red herring" is authorized by Rule 430.[64] The preliminary or "red herring" prospectus may contain substantially the same information as a full-blown section 10(a) statutory prospectus, "except for the omission of information with respect to the offering price, underwriting discounts or commissions, discounts or commissions to dealers, amount of proceeds, conversion rates, call prices, or other matters dependent upon the offering price."[65] Rule 430 thus permits, but does not require, the mention of price which may also be included in the tombstone ad used during the waiting period. In addition to the possible price exclusion, the preliminary prospectus must include a legend in red ink to the effect that a registration statement has not yet become effective and that a formal offer to sell can only be made subsequent to the effective date.

§ 2.4[2][D] The Summary Prospectus

SEC Rule 431[67] permits an additional type of summary prospectus which operates solely for the purpose of section 5(b)(1) and thus not for the delivery for sale requirements of section 5(b)(2).[68] Communications complying with Rule 431 may be used during the post-effective period for section 5(b)(1) purposes.[69] The Rule 431 prospectus must be filed with the registration statement and can be used only if the issuer is a 1934 Act registered reporting company.[70] In addition, the Exchange Act reports must be current. The summary prospectus permitted by Rule 431 must contain all of the information that is specified in the official SEC form accompanying the applicable registration statement form and further may not include any information which is not permitted in the tombstone ad, as spelled out in Rule 134(a).[72] The Rule 431 summary prospectus must also contain a caption similar to that required for the preliminary prospectus as well as a statement setting forth that copies of a more complete prospectus may be obtained from designated brokerage firms. Eight copies of the Rule 431 summary prospectus must be filed with the commission at least five working days prior to the use thereof. Issuers which qualify for use of the Rule 431 summary prospectus may use a *preliminary* summary prospectus during the waiting period.

---

62. 17 C.F.R. §§ 230.163, 230.164.

63. *See* § 2.4[2][E] *infra.*

64. 17 C.F.R. § 230.430.

65. 17 C.F.R. § 230.430(a).

67. 17 C.F.R. § 230.431. The Commission has proposed expanding the category of issuers who can use the summary prospectus. *See* 22 Sec.Reg. & L.Rep. (BNA) 899 (June 15, 1990).

68. 15 U.S.C.A. §§ 77e(b)(1), (2).

69. 15 U.S.C.A. § 77e(b)(1). However, the Rule 431 summary prospectus may not be used to satisfy section 5(b)(2). 15 U.S.C.A. § 77e(b)(2). *See* § 2.5 *infra.*

70. 17 C.F.R. § 230.431(b).

72. 17 C.F.R. § 230.134(a).

§ 2.4[2][E] The Free Writing Prospectus

In 2005, the SEC overhauled its public offering rules and significantly expanded the types of information that may be publicly disseminated during a 1933 Act registration.[73] In Rules 163 and 164, the SEC introduced the concept of a free writing prospectus that may be used by qualifying issuers during the pre-filing and waiting periods.[74] These rules permit many issuers to disseminate a free writing prospectus that has been filed with the SEC. In some cases, the free writing prospectus must be accompanied or preceded by a statutory prospectus. If the requirements of Rule 163 or 164 are satisfied, written communications that otherwise would constitute an illegal offer to sell may be used during the pre-filing and waiting periods. Rule 163 permits well-known seasoned issuers (WKSIs)[76] to use a free writing prospectus during the pre-filing period providing that the offer is filed with the SEC and contains a legend that offering will be by prospectus.[77] The safe harbor is not available for business combinations nor is it available for investment companies.[78] The safe harbor applies to the company itself and to broker-dealers acting as agent for the company in disseminating information.[79]

A free writing prospectus is a written communication (including graphic and electronic communications) that constitutes an offer to sell.[80] A free

---

73. *See* Securities Offering Reform, Sec. Act Rel. No. 33–8591, Sec. Exch. Act Rel. No. 34–52056, Inv. Co. Act Rel. No. IC–26993 70 Fed. Reg. 44722–01, 2005 WL 1692642 (SEC July 19, 2005).

74. 17 C.F.R. §§ 230.163, 230.164.

76. 17 C.F.R. § 230.405. A WKSI is a company that qualifies for registration on 1933 Act Form S–3 or F–3 and either: (A) As of a date within 60 days of the determination date, has a worldwide market value of its outstanding voting and non-voting common equity held by non-affiliates of $700 million or more; or (B)(1) As of a date within 60 days of the determination date, has issued in the last three years at least $1 billion aggregate principal amount of non-convertible securities, other than common equity, in primary offerings for cash, not exchange, registered under the Act; and (2) Will register only non-convertible securities, other than common equity, and full and unconditional guarantees permitted pursuant to paragraph (1)(ii) of this definition unless, at the determination date, the issuer also is eligible to register a primary offering of its securities relying on General Instruction I.B.1. of Form S–3 or Form F–3. *Id.*

77. 17 C.F.R. § 230.163.

78. 17 C.F.R. § 230.163(b)(3).

79. 17 C.F.R. § 230.163.

80. 17 C.F.R. § 230.405:

Free writing prospectus. Except as otherwise specifically provided or the context otherwise requires, a free writing prospectus is any written communication as defined in this section that constitutes an offer to sell or a solicitation of an offer to buy the securities relating to a registered offering that is used after the registration statement in respect of the offering is filed (or, in the case of a well-known seasoned issuer, whether or not such registration statement is filed) and is made by means other than:

(1) A prospectus satisfying the requirements of section 10(a) of the Act, Rule 430 (§ 230.430), Rule 430A (§ 230.430A), Rule 430B (§ 230.430B), Rule 430C (§ 230.430C), or Rule 431 (§ 230.431);

(2) A written communication used in reliance on Rule 167 and Rule 426 (§ 230.167 and § 230.426); or

(3) A written communication that constitutes an offer to sell or solicitation of an offer to buy such securities that falls within the exception from the definition of prospectus in clause (a) of section 2(a)(10) of the Act.

Graphic communication. The term graphic communication, which appears in the definition of "write, written" in section 2(a)(9) of the Act and in the definition of written communication in this section, shall include all forms of electronic media, including, but not limited to, audiotapes, videotapes, facsimiles, CD–ROM, electronic mail, Internet Web sites, substantially similar messages widely distributed (rather than individually distributed) on telephone answering or voice mail systems, computers, computer networks and other forms of computer data

writing prospectus may not, however, contain information that contradicts information in current SEC filings (including the 1933 Act registration statement). In addition, as a general proposition, a precondition to a company's use of a free writing prospectus is that it contain a statement to the effect that the offering is being made pursuant to a registration statement. The free writing prospectus should also indicate how the registration statement or statutory prospectus can be obtained or accessed. A written communication that complies with the more limited requirements for an identifying statement under SEC Rule 134[81] is not a prospectus and thus is not subject to the requirements for a free writing prospectus.

A company's classification based on the public trading of its securities affect the availability of the free writing prospectus. WKSIs are generally free to use free writing prospectuses regardless of whether a registration statement has been filed. The use of a free writing prospectus for other issuers is generally limited to after filing of the registration statement. With respect to non-reporting[82] and unseasoned reporting companies,[83] a free writing prospectus must be accompanied or preceded by a hard copy of the most recent statutory prospectus if (1) the free writing prospectus was prepared by or on behalf of the issuer or an offering participant, (2) payment or other consideration is provided by the issuer or an offering participant for the publication or broadcast of the free writing prospectus, or (3) section 17(b) of the 1933 Act[84] otherwise requires disclosure of consideration given in exchange for dissemination of the free writing prospectus.[85] In the case of a free writing prospectus that is delivered electronically, a hyperlink to an electronic statutory prospectus satisfies the physical delivery requirement.[86] In contrast, WKSIs and seasoned issuers[87] need not make physical delivery of a statutory prospectus.[88] Instead, it is sufficient if the person disseminating the free writing prospectus

compilation. Graphic communication shall not include a communication that, at the time of the communication, originates live, in real-time to a live audience and does not originate in recorded form or otherwise as a graphic communication, although it is transmitted through graphic means.

81. 17 C.F.R. § 230.134. *See* § 2.4[2][B] *supra*.

82. "A non-reporting issuer is an issuer that is not required to file reports pursuant to Section 13 or Section 15(d) of the Exchange Act, regardless of whether it is filing such reports voluntarily." Securities Offering Reform, Sec. Act Rel. No. 33–8591, Sec. Exch. Act Rel. No. 34–52056, Inv. Co. Act Rel. No. IC–26993 70 Fed. Reg. 44722–01, 2005 WL 1692642 (SEC July 19, 2005).

83. "An unseasoned issuer is an issuer that is required to file reports pursuant to Section 13 or Section 15(d) of the Exchange Act, but does not satisfy the requirements of Form S–3 or Form F–3 for a primary offering of its securities." Securities Offering Reform, Sec. Act Rel. No. 33–8591, Sec. Exch. Act Rel. No. 34–52056, Inv. Co. Act Rel. No. IC–26993 70 Fed. Reg. 44722–01, 2005 WL 1692642 (SEC July 19, 2005).

84. 15 U.S.C.A. § 77q(b); *see* §§ 7.11[2], 14.14[4] *infra*.

85. 17 C.F.R. § 230.433(b)(2)(i).

86. Note 1 to 17 C.F.R. § 230.433(b)(2)(i). ("The condition that a free writing prospectus shall be accompanied or preceded by the most recent prospectus satisfying the requirements of section 10 of the Act would be satisfied if a free writing prospectus that is an electronic communication contained an active hyperlink to such most recent prospectus").

87. "An unseasoned issuer is an issuer that is required to file reports pursuant to Sections 13 or 15(d) of the Exchange Act, but does not satisfy the requirements of Form S–3 or Form F–3 for a primary offering of its securities. A seasoned issuer is an issuer that uses Form S–3 or Form F–3 to register primary offerings of securities." Securities Offering Reform, Sec. Act Rel. No. 33–8591, Sec. Exch. Act Rel. No. 34–52056, Inv. Co. Act Rel. No. IC–26993, 70 Fed. Reg. 44722–01, 2005 WL 1692642 (SEC July 19, 2005).

88. 17 C.F.R. § 230.433.

relating to a WKSI or seasoned issuer includes a legend notifying the recipient that a registration statement has been filed, the web address or hyperlink to the SEC website, and a toll-free number for requesting a statutory prospectus.[89]

In many instances, before it is used, a free writing prospectus must be filed with the SEC.[90] An immaterial inadvertent failure to file the free writing prospectus with the SEC will not automatically render the communication in violation of section 5(b) of the Act.

§ 2.4[2][F] Safe Harbors for Factual Information and Forward–Looking Statements by 1934 Act Reporting Companies

As is the case during the pre-filing-filing period, Rules 168 and 169 provide safe harbors for dissemination of factual information by 1933 Act registrants and of forward-looking information by 1934 Act reporting companies.[93] These rules provide safe harbors from section 2(a)(10)'s definition of prospectus and thus apply during the waiting and post-effective periods. Rule 169 provides a safe harbor for "factual business information" that is not directed to investors but is issued as part of the company's ordinary business.[94] This includes, for example, product advertisements directed to customers.[95] The safe harbor does not apply to communications made as part of the offering and is limited to the types of information the company had made in the past. 1934 Act reporting companies are given a broader safe harbor in Rule 168 which permits not only the dissemination of factual information but also forward looking information.[96] As is the case with Rule 169, Rule 168's safe harbor for reporting companies applies only if "the timing, manner, and form in which the information is released or disseminated is consistent in material respects with similar past releases or disseminations"[97] and also excludes from the safe harbor communications "containing information about the registered offering or information released or disseminated as part of the offering activities in the registered offering."[98]

§ 2.4[3] Limited Statements After Public Announcement of Tender Offer or Business Combination

At one time, securities offered as part of an exchange tender offer were subject to the tight gun jumping limitations. This was somewhat at odds with the Williams Act approach to full disclosure in tender offers.[99] In 1999, the SEC liberalized its rules concerning communications relating to a tender offer or business combination requiring the registration of shares under the 1933

89. 17 C.F.R. § 230.433. An immaterial and inadvertent failure to provide the legend will not be fatal. *See* 17 C.F.R. § 230.164I.

90. 17 C.F.R. § 230.433(d).

93. 17 C.F.R. §§ 230.168, 169.

94. 17 C.F.R. § 230.169. Among other things, the communication must resemble communications that the company had disseminated in the past. Rule 169(d), 17 C.F.R. § 230.169.

95. 17 C.F.R. § 230.169 (b).

96. 17 C.F.R. § 230.168.

97. 17 C.F.R. § 230.168(d)(2).

98. 17 C.F.R. § 230.168(c).

99. *See Pub.L. No. 90–439, 82 Stat. 454 (1968) (codified at 15 U.S.C. §§ 78m(d)–(e), n(d)–(f)).* The Williams Act is discussed in chapter 11 *infra.*

Act.[100] Under Rule 165, communications after the effective date of a registration statement that are made prior to the public announcement of a business combination will not be deemed a prospectus for the purposes of section 5(b)(1) of the 1934 Act.[102]

§ 2.4[4] Broker–Dealer Recommendations

Rules 137, 138, and 139, which are discussed earlier in this treatise,[103] permit publication of certain recommendations by dealers, provided that each of the appropriate rule's conditions are met.[104]

§ 2.4[6] Broker–Dealer Standard of Conduct With Regard to Prospectus Delivery Requirements

Exchange Act Rule 15c2–8[110] sets forth standards of conduct for broker-dealers with regard to the 1933 Act's prospectus delivery requirements. The rule makes it a deceptive act or practice for a broker or dealer to participate in a distribution covered by a 1933 Act registration statement and not to make available to each associated person sufficient copies of the preliminary prospectus prior to any customer solicitation.[111] The rule also provides that the managing underwriter must take "reasonable steps" to assure that all participating brokers and dealers are furnished with sufficient copies of the preliminary prospectus, each amended preliminary prospectus and the final prospectus.[112] The rule further requires a participating broker or dealer to take reasonable steps to comply with written requests for a copy of the latest preliminary prospectus.[113]

As a 1934 Act rule, Rule 15c2–8 does not directly affect compliance with section 5. Violations of the rule's prospectus delivery obligations do not automatically result in a violation of section 5 of the 1933 Act. However, this does not take away from the importance of broker-dealers' complying with Rule 15c2–8.

§ 2.5 The Post–Effective Period

§ 2.5[1] Prohibitions During the Post–Effective Period

Section 5(a) of the 1933 Act[1] prohibits all sales of securities facilitated by the use of the mail or other instrumentalities of interstate commerce to effect a sale prior to the effective date of the registration statement. Once the registration statement becomes effective, section 5(a)'s prohibitions cease to apply, and the only limitation on securities sales, aside from the disclosure

---

100. *See* Regulation of Takeovers and Security Holder Communications, Sec. Act Rel. No. 33–7760, 1999 WL 969596 (SEC Oct. 22, 1999).

102. Rule 165(b), 17 C.F.R. § 230.165(b).

103. *See* § 2.3[6] *supra*.

104. 17 C.F.R. §§ 230.137–139. *See* § 2.3 *supra*.

110. 17 C.F.R. § 240.15c2–8.

111. 17 C.F.R. § 240.15c2–8(d). The rule further provides that all such persons shall immediately be sent copies of any amended preliminary prospectus.

112. 17 C.F.R. § 240.15c2–8(f).

113. 17 C.F.R. § 240.15c2–8(b).

§ 2.5

1. 15 U.S.C.A. § 77e(a).

and anti-fraud provisions, are those contained in the prospectus requirements of section 5(b) of the Act.[2] Section 5(b)(1) requires that all prospectuses (*i.e.*, written, radio, or television offers to sell) must comply with the statutory prospectus requirements of section 10.[3] Delivery via the Internet will satisfy section 5(b)(1)'s requirements.

The operation and effect of section 5(b)(1) are much the same as for the waiting period except that some of the methods of permissible offers during the waiting period are not allowed during the post-effective period. The summary prospectus that has been filed as part of the registration statement as defined in Rule 431[6] may be used during both the waiting and post-effective periods, but solely for the purpose of satisfying section 5(b)(1)'s requirements and not for the delivery before sale requirement contained in section 5(b)(2). However, the preliminary prospectus or "red herring" that is permitted by Rule 430 during the waiting period is expressly limited "for use prior to the effective date."[7] Accordingly, the "red herring" may not be used during the post-effective period either for subsection (b)(1) or (b)(2).

As discussed throughout this chapter, in 2005 the SEC ushered in significant public offering reforms.[8] As part of these reforms the former physical delivery requirement was replaced with "an access equals delivery" approach with respect to final prospectuses." Under Rule 172(b), a final prospectus is deemed to precede or accompany a security for sale for purposes of section 5(b)(2) of the Act so long as the final prospectus meeting the requirements of Securities Act section 10(a) is filed or the issuer makes a good faith and reasonable effort to file it with the SEC as part of the registration statement within the required Rule 424 prospectus filing timeframe.[9] In addition, Rule 173 implements an *access equals delivery* approach to the statutory prospectus in providing that notice of the availability of a statutory prospectus will satisfy section 5(b)'s prospectus delivery requirement.[10]

§ 2.5[2] Supplementary Sales Literature ("Free Writing")

Section 2(a)(10)(a) of the 1933 Act permits the use of supplementary sales literature after the effective date even if such literature is neither in conformance to nor contained in the statutory prospectus.

This is known as "free writing," which is expressly permitted by statute only during the post-effective period; unrestricted free writing is not permitted during the waiting period. The statutory concept of free writing is much more limited that the free writing prospectus that is no permitted by virtue of amendments to the SEC rules. In 2005, as part of its public offering reform,[12] the SEC adopted Rules 163 and 164 which allow the use of a "free writing

2. 15 U.S.C.A. § 77e(b).

3. 15 U.S.C.A. § 77j.

6. 17 C.F.R. § 230.431. *See* § 2.4 *supra*.

7. 17 C.F.R. § 230.430.

8. *See* Securities Offering Reform, Sec. Act Rel. No. 33–8591, Sec. Exch. Act Rel. No. 34–52056, Inv. Co. Act Rel. No. IC–26993 70 Fed. Reg. 44722–01, 2005 WL 1692642 (SEC July 19, 2005).

9. 17 C.F.R. § 230.172(b). *See* 17 C.F.R. § 230.424.

10. 17 C.F.R. § 230.173(a).

12. *See* Securities Offering Reform, Sec. Act Rel. No. 33–8591, Sec. Exch. Act Rel. No. 34–52056, Inv. Co. Act Rel. No. IC–26993 70 Fed. Reg. 44722–01, 2005 WL 1692642 (SEC July 19, 2005).

prospectus."[13] With respect to non-reporting[15] and unseasoned reporting companies,[16] a free writing prospectus must be accompanied or preceded by a hard copy of the most recent statutory prospectus under most circumstances. In contrast, WKSIs and seasoned issuers need not make physical delivery of a statutory prospectus.[18] In many instances, before it is used, a free writing prospectus must be filed with the SEC.[19]

Unlike the free writing prospectus, free writing materials contemplated by the statute during the post-effective period, need not be filed with the SEC. A significant limitation upon use of statutorily permitted supplementary sales literature during the post-effective period is that it must be proven by the registrant, or other person relying on the permissible use of such literature, that prior to or at the same time as receiving it, a section 10(a) statutory prospectus had been sent or given to a person receiving the supplementary sales literature.

There are no explicit statutory restrictions on the types of information that may be included in the supplementary sales literature. It must not be forgotten, however, that unduly optimistic promotional sales talk will render the supplementary sales literature in violation of the anti-fraud provisions of both the 1933 and 1934 Acts. The use of electronic media for prospectus delivery raises questions concerning free writing with respect to other material that may be on or linked to the website. The SEC has taken the position that with respect to an area of a website denominated as a prospectus, hyperlinks included within that designated area will be considered part of the prospectus whereas hyperlinks that may exist elsewhere on the web site will not be considered part of the prospectus.[21]

§ 2.5[3] Updating the Registration Statement and Prospectus During the Post–Effective Period

Another aspect of the post-effective period is that although the registration statement need not be updated for most developments subsequent to the effective date,[22] the prospectus must continue to be accurate. For example, where there has been a change of events, a change in earnings, or a revaluation of projected performance, the prospectus must be updated lest it

13. 17 C.F.R. §§ 230.163, 230.164.

15. "A non-reporting issuer is an issuer that is not required to file reports pursuant to Section 13 or Section 15(d) of the Exchange Act, regardless of whether it is filing such reports voluntarily." Securities Offering Reform, Sec. Act Rel. No. 33–8591, Sec. Exch. Act Rel. No. 34–52056, Inv. Co. Act Rel. No. IC–26993 70 Fed. Reg. 44722–01, 2005 WL 1692642 (SEC July 19, 2005).

16. "An unseasoned issuer is an issuer that is required to file reports pursuant to Section 13 or Section 15(d) of the Exchange Act, but does not satisfy the requirements of Form S–3 or Form F–3 for a primary offering of its securities." Securities Offering Reform, Sec. Act Rel. No. 33–8591, Sec. Exch. Act Rel. No. 34–52056, Inv. Co. Act Rel. No. IC–26993 70 Fed. Reg. 44722–01, 2005 WL 1692642 (SEC July 19, 2005).

18. 17 C.F.R. § 230.433. Instead, it is sufficient if the person disseminating the free writing prospectus relating to a WKSI or seasoned issuer includes a legend notifying the recipient that a registration statement has been filed, the web address or hyperlink to the SEC website, and a toll-free number for requesting a statutory prospectus. *Id.*

19. 17 C.F.R. § 230.433(d). An immaterial, inadvertent failure to file the free writing prospectus with the SEC will not automatically render the communication in violation of section 5(b) of the Act. 17 C.F.R. § 230.164(b).

21. Use of Electronic Media, Sec. Act Rel. No. 33–7856, 2000 WL 502290 (SEC April 28, 2000).

22. *See* Funeral Directors Mfg. & Supply Co., 39 S.E.C. 33, 34 (SEC 1959).

be in violation of section 10(a).[24] This is so even if there is no need to update the registration statement.[25]

Frequently, changes in the prospectus will be made by affixing stickers that contain the updated or corrected information.[26] Rule 424(c) explicitly allows for prospectus supplements, commonly referred to as "stickers," to be filed with the Commission when it becomes necessary to update the prospectus.[27]

§ 2.5[6] Exemption From Prospectus Delivery Requirements for Dealer Transactions

The prospectus requirements do not apply if an appropriate exemption from the 1933 Act registration can be established. In addition to the more general securities exemptions contained in section 3 and transaction exemptions contained in section 4 of the 1933 Act,[65] there are certain circumstances under which section 5(b)'s prospectus delivery requirements do not apply. For example, section 4(3) of the Act[66] exempts transactions by a dealer, including an underwriter no longer acting as such, for securities not constituting part of an unsold allotment provided that the transaction has not taken place prior to the expiration of forty days after the registration statement's effective date or the first date that the security was "bona fide offered" to the public, whichever is later. The statutory forty-day period for registered offerings is extended to ninety days if the issuer has not previously sold securities pursuant to an effective registration statement, unless a shorter period has been specified by the SEC.[67] This forty-or ninety-day period sometimes has been referred to as the quiet period.

As pointed out above, section 4(3) expressly authorizes the SEC to shorten the period after the effective date of the registration statement during which nonparticipating dealers must comply with the prospectus delivery requirements. The Commission has exercised this authority in Rule 174 which dispenses with the prospectus requirements prior to the expiration of the forty-or ninety-day period for dealers who are neither underwriters nor members of the selling group.[68] Rule 174 dispenses with the prospectus delivery requirements if immediately prior to the filing of the registration statement the issuer was subject to the 1934 Act periodic reporting requirements,[69] or if the registration statement of a private foreign issuer using American Depositary Receipts is on Form F–6, provided that the deposited securities need not be registered under the 1933 Act.[70] Rule 174(c)[71] further dispenses with the delivery requirements where the registration statement

24. SEC v. Manor Nursing Centers, Inc., 458 F.2d 1082 (2d Cir.1972).

25. SEC v. Manor Nursing Centers, Inc., 458 F.2d 1082, 1099 (2d Cir.1972).

26. *See, e.g.,* Investment Company Institute, [1987–88 Transfer Binder] Fed.Sec.L.Rep. (CCH) ¶ 78,683 (Feb. 25, 1988) (disclosure changes required by rule 485(a) may be made through use of stickers).

27. 17 C.F.R. § 230.424(c).

65. 15 U.S.C.A. §§ 77c, 77d. *See* chapter 4 *infra.*

66. 15 U.S.C.A. § 77d(3).

67. 15 U.S.C.A. § 77d(4)(C).

68. 17 C.F.R. § 230.174.

69. 17 C.F.R. § 230.174(b).

70. 17 C.F.R. § 230.174(a)

71. 17 C.F.R. § 230.174(c)

relates to offerings to be made from time to time,[72] and the forty-or ninety-day period specified in section 4(3) has expired.

As described above, Rule 174's exemption for nonparticipating dealers from the post-effective prospectus delivery period is limited to securities of issuers which, immediately prior to the filing of the registration statement, were subject to the 1934 Act's periodic reporting requirements.[73] Thus, the exemption does not apply to first-time issuers or issuers whose securities were not widely held prior to the filing of the registration statement.[74] In 1988, Rule 174 was amended to provide more limited relief for many of those registrants who had not previously been subject to the 1934 Act's reporting requirements.[75] Under Rule 174(d), the prospectus delivery period applicable to dealers not otherwise participating in the offering (as opposed to underwriters or participating dealers) is shortened to twenty-five days for dealers (including underwriters no longer acting as such) with regard to securities which, as of the offering date, are listed on a national securities exchange or authorized for inclusion in an automated quotation system sponsored by a registered securities association (*i.e.*, NASDAQ).[76] As is the case for the statutory post-effective delivery requirement period for registered offerings, Rule 174's twenty-five-day period begins to run from the later of (1) the registration statement's effective date or (2) the first date upon which the security was "bona fide offered to the public."[77] In light of Rule 174(d), the full statutory prospectus delivery period for nonparticipating dealers applies primarily to securities which are traded through the NASD's bulletin board system or in the pink sheets.[78] It must be remembered, that, as is the case with the other exemptions provided by Rule 174, the shorter twenty-five-day prospectus delivery period does not apply to a dealer who is acting as an underwriter.[79]

Once an underwriter has completed his underwriting commitment and the public offering is complete, the underwriter is under no duty to make continuing disclosures about the issuer.[80] Rule 174 also imposes an additional requirement for penny stock offerings.[81] In the case of a blank check penny stock offering, the ninety-day period does not begin to run until the securities are released from escrow pursuant to Rule 419.[82]

Another exemption from the prospectus delivery requirements is found in Rule 153 which deals with sales to be "preceded by a prospectus" as used in

---

72. *See* 17 C.F.R. § 230.415 which is discussed in § 3.11 *infra.*

73. 17 C.F.R. § 230.174(b).

74. The 1934 Act period reporting requirements are discussed in § 9.2 *infra.*

75. *See* Sec. Act Rel. No. 33–6763, [1987–88 Transfer Binder] Fed.Sec.L.Rep. (CCH) ¶ 84,226 (SEC April 4, 1986).

76. 17 C.F.R. § 230.174(d). *See* § 14.3 *infra* for a description of NASDAQ.

77. 17 C.F.R. § 230.174(d).

78. Quotations for securities that are neither listed on a national exchange nor traded through NASDAQ are available from pink sheets which are circulated by the market maker. *See* § 10.3 *infra.*

79. 17 C.F.R. § 230.174(f).

80. In re Chaus Securities Litigation, 1990 WL 188921 (S.D.N.Y.1990).

81. The SEC's penny stock rules are discussed in § 14.19 *infra.*

82. 17 C.F.R. § 230.174(g). *See* 17 C.F.R. § 230.419.

section 5(b)(2); this does not apply to the delivery requirements of section 5(b)(1).[83] Where a transaction involving a security in registration has been carried out on a national securities exchange,[84] Rule 153 provides that a sale is preceded by a prospectus to a member of the exchange where section 10(a) prospectuses have been delivered to the exchange for redelivery to its members upon request. Rule 153 applies to sales to members of a national exchange occurring prior to forty days after the effective date or the first date upon which the security was "bona fide offered to the public," whichever is later, provided that (a) the exchange has requested sufficient copies of the prospectus appearing reasonably necessary to comply with its members' requests and (b) the issuer or an underwriter has complied with all such requests.[85] Additionally, under Rule 153a,[86] when securities are issued pursuant to a reclassification, merger, consolidation, or acquisition of assets in a transaction subject to Rule 145,[87] section 5(b)(2)'s prospectus delivery requirement is satisfied by delivery of a qualifying proxy statement to shareholders entitled to vote or whose consent is required for the transaction.

§ 2.5[7] Broker–Dealer Compliance With Prospectus Delivery Requirements

Beyond the prospectus delivery requirements and exemptions that are discussed above, the Commission has established standards of conduct for brokers or dealers participating in the distribution of securities covered by a 1933 Act registration statement. SEC Rule 15c2–8[88] requires that each participating broker or dealer take reasonable steps to comply with all written requests for a final section 10(a) prospectus after the effective date and until the termination of the distribution or expiration of the forty-or ninety-day period provided in section 4(3). Participating brokers and dealers must also take reasonable steps to assure that all associated persons who are expected to solicit customers after the effective date shall have sufficient copies of the final section 10(a) prospectus.[89] Additionally, managing underwriters must take reasonable steps to assure that all participating brokers and dealers have, pursuant to their requests, sufficient copies of the final prospectus.[90] The SEC's prospectus delivery requirements are supplemented by the NASD and exchanges' enforcement of the obligation.[91]

83. 17 C.F.R. § 230.153.

84. *See* section 6 of the Exchange Act, 15 U.S.C.A. § 78f which is discussed in § 14.3 *infra.* The NASDAQ stock market is now a national securities exchange, which means that only the less frequently traded stocks are now in the over the counter markets.

85. 17 C.F.R. § 230.153(a)(1).

86. 17 C.F.R. § 230.153a.

87. 17 C.F.R. § 230.145. *See* § 5.2 *infra.*

88. 17 C.F.R. § 240.15c2–8(c). The rule has similar proscriptions with regard to the waiting period. *See* § 2.4 *supra.*

89. 17 C.F.R. § 240.15c2–8(e).

90. 17 C.F.R. § 240.15c2–8(g).

91. *See* In the Matter of Merrill Lynch, Pierce, Fenner & Smith, Inc. NYSE Hearing Panel Dec. No. 05–87 2005 WL 1993862 (NYSE July 21, 2005) (consent to sanctions for failure to deliver offering materials); Stuart Gittleman, Merrill Lynch Fined for Supervisory and Operational Failures, Complinet, http://www.complinet.com/us/news/news/article.html?ref=72892 (Aug. 16, 2005).

§ 2.5[8] Broker–Dealer Recommendations

As discussed in a previous section,[92] broker-dealer buy recommendations might well ordinarily qualify as offers to sell and thus would be subject to the prospectus requirements if disseminated in writing during the waiting or post-effective periods.[93] SEC Rules 137, 138, and 139 exclude certain broker-dealer recommendations from the prospectus requirements.[94]

By 2000, there was increasing concern over the independence of securities analysts.[95] In 2002, the NASD proposed and adopted new rules imposing a quiet period for analysts' recommendations when the analyst's firm participates as an underwriter.[96] The NASD rules are now embodied in the Financial Industry Regulatory Authority's (FINRA) rules and require quiet periods during which a firm acting as manager or co-manager of a securities offering may not issue a report on a company within forty days after an initial public offering or within ten days after a secondary offering.[97]

---

92. *See* the discussion in § 2.3 *supra*.

93. *See* the discussion in § 2.3[6] *supra*.

94. 17 C.F.R. §§ 230.137, 230.138, 230.139. *See* the discussion in § 2.3 *supra*.

95. *See* § 14.16[6] *infra*.

96. *See* Sec. Exch. Act Rel. No. 34–45526, 2002 WL 389246 (SEC March 14, 2002) (similar rules were also put forth by the New York Stock Exchange); NASD Announces New Rules Governing Recommendations Made by Research Analysts, http://www.nasdr.com/news/pr2002/release_02_009.html (NASDR Feb. 7, 2002). *See* National Association of Securities Dealers, Inc., Sec. Exch. Act Rel. No. 34–45526, 2002 WL 373104 (SEC March 8, 2002).

97. The rules also prohibit a firm from offering or threatening to withhold favorable research to induce business.

Chapter 3

THE 1933 ACT REGISTRATION PROCESS AND DISCLOSURE

Table of Sections

---

§ 3.1 The Decision to Go Public

§ 3.1[1] Process of Going Public—Overview

Unless a transaction is structured to fall within one of the 1933 Act's exemptions,[1] any time a company plans for financing other than through a bank loan, the financing through the issuance of securities will implicate the 1933 Act's registration provisions.[2] Of course, many capital raising plans are accomplished through exempt offerings. However, when an exemption is not available, or when a company decides to go public for other reasons, it is necessary to register the offering under the Securities Act of 1933.

The 1933 Act registration statement that must be filed with the SEC[3] is the result of a joint or team effort by a working group or team that includes, among others, the issuer, the issuer's attorneys (both inside house counsel and outside general counsel), the underwriter, the underwriter's attorneys, and the accountants who serve as auditors for the financial statements. In many cases there will also be special securities counsel whose responsibilities

---

§ 3.1

1. 15 U.S.C.A. §§ 77c, 77d; 77z–3. *See* chapter 4 *infra*.

2. 15 U.S.C.A. §§ 77f, 77g. *See* William Barker, SEC Registration of Public Offerings Under the Securities Act of 1933, 52 Bus. Law. 65 (1996).

3. There are a number of alternative forms for the 1933 Act registration statement. *See* § 3.4 *infra*.

are to help draft and supervise the preparation of the registration statement and to be watchful for SEC disclosure problems. The registration statement generally will be printed professionally and in many instances technical experts will need to be retained to prepare reports about the issuer's business. The substantial expense involved in the registration process means that issuers will frequently prefer alternative means of financing. In addition to the substantial expense, a registered offering requires strict compliance with the applicable disclosure provisions, lest there be substantial liability exposure of the key participants in the registration and offering process.[4] Additionally, particular aspects of the issuer's business or past operations may create especially problematic disclosure issues.[5]

The initial step in the registration process is the decision to embark upon public financing. Thus, the first question to be answered is whether or not the needed capital should be procured by way of a registered public offering or, alternatively, through a private placement[6] or some other exempt method of financing. As a general matter, exempt offerings entail less cost, both in terms of the actual marketing expenses as well as professional fees, printing, and other indirect costs of preparing the registration statement. Exempt offerings may also involve less exposure under the 1933 Act's civil liability provisions than registered public offerings.

In deciding whether or not to embark upon a registered offering, there are a number of advantages and disadvantages that need to be considered. The potential advantages and disadvantages must be weighed carefully in order to determine whether a public offering is the most appropriate means of financing and also whether the timing is right to embark on an IPO.

In addition to the factors discussed below, there is a consequence that occurs in the event that a company, after raising money, invests the funds in securities of other companies.[10] Investing funds in securities of other companies can result in becoming an inadvertent investment company[11] and thereby implicate the provisions of the Investment Company Act of 1940.[12]

§ 3.1[2] Advantages of Going Public

The advantages of becoming a public company include creating a public market that will allow for future public financing to provide for company expansion, diversification, increase in working capital, or retirement of preexisting debt. In many instances the company may be in need of large capital infusions and such substantial sums may not feasibly be available through bank loans or other means of private financing. The issuer may want the potential for additional equity rather than debt financing. Furthermore, the presence of a favorable climate in the public market may make a registered public offering the most efficient fundraising device. The creation of a public market for an issuer's securities will result in increased liquidity of the

---

4. *See* chapter 7 *infra.*

5. *See, e.g.,* Daniel I. Winnike & Christopher E. Nordquist, Federal Securities Law Issues for the Sticky Offering, 48 Bus.Law. 869 (1993).

6. 615 U.S.C.A. § 77d(2); 17 C.F.R. § 240.506. *See* § 4.22–4.24 *infra.*

10. Companies sometimes do this to put the investors' money to work prior to investing those funds in the business itself.

11. Inadvertent investment companies are discussed in § 20.3 *infra.*

12. 15 U.S.C.A. §§ 80a–1 through 80a–52. *See* chapter 20 *infra.*

holdings of the principal owners, as well as the holdings of the minority shareholders.

Frequently, an issuer's offering of its securities will be accompanied or followed by a secondary offering. In a secondary offering, insiders or others who have received the issuer's securities (generally as part of a previous nonpublic transaction) decide to sell their shares to the public.[16] In such a situation, the selling shareholders may be able to ride "piggy back" on a registered primary offering. Even in the absence of a registered secondary offering, with the public market created by the primary offering, existing shareholders may be able to sell their shares in the aftermarket.[18] An issuer's public financing thus may help selling shareholders who want to liquidate their holdings in whole or in part and thereby take advantage of the liquidity and favorable market conditions created by the primary offering of the issuer.[19]

Another frequent beneficial by-product of going public is that the process gives the company increasing prestige and publicity among the general public, thus providing the issuer with a more favorable image and putting it in a better competitive position for its products or services. Additionally, the fact that a corporation has a public market for its securities may create an air of financial success. In some cases, a public offering will improve the company's net worth and enhance its ability to raise additional funds in the future. There are also collateral benefits of going public such as the company's ability to adopt attractive employee stock option and/or stock purchase plans in order to attract good key employees. A further advantage to going public is that the company whose stock is publicly traded may be in a better position to acquire other companies through the means of an exchange offer using the shares of the acquiring company as consideration for the shares of the target company.[20]

§ 3.1[3] Consequences, Disadvantages, and Costs of Going Public

There are a variety of consequences, many of them potential disadvantages, to public financing. Thus, it is necessary for a company to carefully consider all aspects of the alternative means of financing. For example, notwithstanding the above-mentioned favorable aspects of public financing, it must be kept in mind that economic and market conditions may not be ripe for taking advantage of this method. A number of other potential pitfalls can be identified.

A direct consequence of going public through a 1933 Act registered offering is that the company becomes subject to the periodic reporting

16. *See* §§ 4.27, 4.28 *infra.*

18. Such shares may remain restricted after the public offering. That is, the preexisting shareholders may not be able to sell their securities without registration or an applicable exemption. *See* §§ 4.23–4.26.1. SEC Rule 144 sets forth a safe harbor for selling these shares without registration. 17 C.F.R. § 230.144 which is discussed in § 4.29 *infra.*

19. Tag-along, or piggy-back, secondary distributions frequently create disclosure problems concerning dilution of the public's investment and use of the proceeds. *See, e.g.,* In the Matter of Universal Camera Corp., Sec. Act Rel. No 33–3076, 19 S.E.C. 648 1945 WL 26104 (1945); §§ 3.9, 4.28 *infra.*

20. The converse may also be true. A public company with diluted ownership may be an easier target, albeit an expensive one for takeover by others than a company with a closely-knit ownership.

obligations of the Securities Exchange Act of 1934.[21] As noted above, among other things, this means that the company's shares can now be freely traded in the public markets. On the other hand, it also means that there are compliance costs and liability exposure that goes with public ownership.

Underwriting commissions are commonly seven percent for initial offerings and can range from four to six percent for a secondary offering.[22] Additional expenses of a registered twenty million dollar IPO are likely to range from $4000,000 to $800,000.[23]

In addition to the substantial cost of a registered offering, there is the high expense of maintaining a public company, not the least of which is the increased expense and potential liability exposure created by the registration and periodic reporting provisions of the Securities Exchange Act of 1934.[24] For example, one observer estimated that by 2007, the cost of SEC compliance for a 1934 Act reporting company with less than one billion dollars in revenue, had increased to 2.8 million dollars per year as compared to the average 1.1 million in SEC compliance costs prior to the adoption of the Sarbanes–Oxley Act amendments in 2002.[25]

Public ownership, especially when it involves common stock, frequently results in loss of control over many management matters. Dividend policy is very likely to be affected, since in order to maintain a marketable security, depending upon the industry and the practices of competing companies, the directors frequently have to be willing to declare dividends—so as to make the security marketable in competition with other securities of a similar type as well as with the higher yielding bond market. In operating the enterprise, management of a publicly held company has to pay heed to the day-to-day market activity in the stock, and thus may focus more closely on the short term, as opposed to the long term, goals of the business. Just as a publicly traded company may be in a better position to acquire other companies, the fact that a company is publicly held may make it an easier target as a takeover candidate.[26]

For some companies, especially in difficult markets, perhaps the most serious potential economic disadvantage of going public, from a financial point of view, is that contrary to the best plans and intentions of the underwriter and financial analyst, the issuer might not find a receptive market for its securities. When a public offering falls upon an unreceptive market, the result is that the stock will sell at a discount substantially below the anticipated price that was probably based on past earnings (if any) and the company's

21. Section 15(d) of the 1934 Act, 15 U.S.C.A. § 78o(d) requires periodic reports for all companies issuing securities under a 1933 Act registration statement.

22. *See* Robbert B. Robbins, William L. Horton & Phillip L. Rothenberg, Preparation of the Registration Statement, Course Materials for Fundamentals of Securities Law (ALI–ABA Savannah Ga. June 12–13, 2008).

23. *See* Robbert B. Robbins, William L. Horton & Phillip L. Rothenberg, Preparation of the Registration Statement, Course Materials for Fundamentals of Securities Law (ALI–ABA Savannah Ga. June 12–13, 2008).

24. 15 U.S.C.A. §§ 78*l*, 78m. *See* chapter 9. *See generally,* Carl W. Schneider & Jason M. Schergel, "Now That You Are Publicly Owned," 36 Bus.Law. 1631 (1981).

25. *See* Hartman, The Continued Costs of Being a Public Company, The Corporate Board (Nov.-Dec. 2007).

26. Takeovers and the tender offer provisions of the federal securities laws are discussed in chapter 11 *infra*.

book value.[27] This will in turn decrease public and investor confidence in the issuer's business. Whenever the market provides such a soft reception, the issuer and selling shareholders may find themselves with less capital than had been anticipated.

Another factor which frequently is determinative in selecting the form and method of corporate financing is the actual cost of the registration statement itself. A public offering can easily cost more than several hundred thousand dollars when one includes the printing costs, underwriter's commissions, directly resulting legal fees and auditing fees, as well as indirect costs that may be necessary to put the company in a position to withstand the public disclosures required in the registration statement. Finally, as mentioned above, the potential liabilities that may result from a problematic public offering may mitigate in favor of an exempt offering.

In 2002, Congress significantly increased the burdens on public companies when it enacted the Sarbanes–Oxley Act.[28] The Sarbanes–Oxley Act, which is discussed throughout this treatise where applicable,[29] adopted comprehensive amendments to the federal securities laws including heightened disclosure and corporate governance obligations. These reforms placed significant new compliance obligations on public companies, thus resulting in increased compliance costs.[30] For example, the Sarbanes–Oxley Act imposed heightened periodic disclosure requirements[31] as well as accounting and auditing reforms.[32]

It often asserted that increasingly onerous SEC disclosure requirements have made public financing so expensive that a number of businesses are in fact deprived of access to the public market. One response was simplification of the disclosure requirements, especially with regard to relatively small issues. These developments in disclosure eased a number of the negative aspects of public financing for many comparatively small issuers. However, the increased burdens on public companies imposed by the Sarbanes–Oxley Act of 2002 have significantly increased the cost of SEC compliance. These increased burdens and costs are likely to weigh heavily against a smaller company going public.

§ 3.1[4] Contingent Public Offerings; "All or None" and "Part or None" Offerings

Issuers who embark on public offerings frequently do so in response to general financing needs, including, for example, expansion of the business. It is not uncommon for an issuer to envision a project that requires a minimum capitalization from the offering. This type of specifically targeted financing does not cause a problem where the issuer has an established track record or there are other reasons to believe that the securities will be sold at the

27. One way to account for some of the hazards of an unreceptive offering is to embark on a contingent offering, if the circumstances so warrant.

28. Sarbanes–Oxley Act of 2002, Pub. Law 107–204 (July 30, 2002). *See* Senate Report No. 107–205 (July 3, 2002).

29. For a brief summary of the coverage of Sarbanes–Oxley, *see* § 1.2[3[D][3] *supra*. The various provisions of the Sarbanes–Oxley Act are considered throughout this treatise.

30. *See, e.g.* Dan Roberts, GE Says it Faces $30m Bill for Governance, Financial Times 1B (April 29, 2004).

31. *See* §§ 9.3 *infra*.

32. *See* § 9.6 *infra*.

offering price. However, sometimes an issuer will want to take precautions when a minimum amount of funds is needed and that raising less than that amount would not be useful to the company. In such a case, the securities may be offered on a contingent basis: contingent on a certain amount of funds being raised. In such a contingent offering, if the desired funds would not be raised by subscriptions to the offerings, the offering will be cancelled. These contingent offerings are sometimes referred to as "all or none" offerings if a full subscription is necessary to raise the minimum funds needed or "part or none" offerings if a designated portion of the proceeds being sought would be sufficient. In an "all or none" basis.[34] In an "all or none" offering, if within a specified period there is not a full subscription to all shares being offered, the offering is cancelled. A variation on the "all or none" offering is a "part or none" offering in which the offering will be cancelled if less than a specified portion of the offering has been subscribed to. In both "all or none" and "part or none" offerings, the subscribers' funds typically will be placed in an escrow account and are not made available to the issuer unless the terms of the offering have been fulfilled.[35]

Both "all or none" and "part or none" offerings put a great deal of pressure on those marketing the securities,[37] and thus these offerings may be susceptible to manipulation.[38] Issuers embarking on "all or none" and "part or none" offerings must be specific as to the offering price, the duration of the offering, and the amount of securities that must be sold to make the offering effective.[39] Also, the possibility of a refund in an offering that is not fully subscribed cannot be offered on a selective basis but must be offered to all would-be purchasers.[40] It is actionable when an issuer erroneously gives the impression that a contingent offering has been sufficiently subscribed to.[41] Issuers undertaking a contingent offering have a continuing obligation of full disclosure until the contingency is met.[42]

34. *See* Robert B. Robbins, All-or-None Offerings: An Update, 19 Rev.Sec. & Commod. Reg. 181 (1986); Robert B. Robbins, All-or-None Offerings, 19 Rev.Sec. & Commod. Reg. 59 (1986).

35. *See* Richard W. Jennings & Harold Marsh, Jr., Securities Regulation: Cases and Materials 30 (6th ed. 1987).

37. SEC v. Blinder, Robinson & Co., 542 F.Supp. 468, 476 (D.Colo.1982), *affirmed* 1983 WL 20181, [1984–85 Transfer Binder] Fed.Sec.L.Rep. (CCH) ¶ 99,491 (10th Cir.1983), *cert. denied* 469 U.S. 1108, 105 S.Ct. 783, 83 L.Ed.2d 777 (1985) ("in an 'all or none' offering of securities by a new company, whether all the securities have been sold to the public in bona fide market transactions is of particular importance because the 'all or none' contingency is the investors' principal protection. Each investor is comforted by the knowledge that unless his judgment to take the risk is shared by enough others to sell out the issue, his money will be returned"). It has been suggested, however, that the applicable SEC regulations were not imposed in response to this concern. Robert B. Robbins, All-or-None Offerings, 19 Rev.Sec. & Commod. Reg. 59, 62 (1986).

38. *See, e.g.,* C.E. Carlson, Inc. v. SEC, 859 F.2d 1429 (10th Cir.1988) (underwriter held liable for falsely creating the impression that a "part or none" offering was successful).

39. 17 C.F.R. § 240.10b–9. Manipulation in connection with offerings is discussed in chapter 6 *infra. See* in particular § 6.3 *infra.*

40. SEC Rule 10b–9 declares it to be a manipulative or deceptive act or contrivance to offer a refund unless all the securities are offered pursuant to an "all or none" or "part or none" offering. 17 C.F.R. § 240.10b–9(a). *See* §§ 6.3, 12.1 *infra.*

41. See, e.g., SEC v. Sands, 902 F.Supp. 1149 (C.D.Cal.1995) (mini-max offering whereby there was a part-or-none contingency with the remaining securities to be offered on a best efforts basis).

42. Banc One Capital Partners Corp. v. Kneipper, 67 F.3d 1187 (5th Cir.1995) (misrepresentations made after the initial subscription are actionable).

§ 3.2 Preparation of the Registration Statement

A first time registrant for an initial public offering (IPO) can expect a long and rigorous preparation process. The amount of time involved will necessarily depend upon the size and complexity of the offering but it is wise to assume that an IPO will involve a six to twelve month process. Once the registration statement is drafted, the SEC review process can take months. In addition, for a first time issuer, it will often be necessary to "sell the deal."

Once an issuer has elected to embark upon a public offering and has decided upon the type of security (*i.e.* debt or preferred stock or common stock) to be offered, the issuer in consultation with its financial advisers will fix the relative rights and preferences of the securities to be offered. The next step frequently is to meet with financial advisers, potential underwriters and counsel in order to hammer out the basic terms of the offering including the anticipated price and, if applicable, yield.

Underwriting commissions are commonly seven percent for initial offerings and can range from four to six percent for a secondary offering. Additional expenses of a registered twenty million dollar IPO are likely to range from $4000,000 to $800,000.

Selection of the underwriters can involve a number of factors. Among other things, the issuer should consider the underwriter's reputation in the investment community generally as well as the underwriter's track record both with respect to public offerings and in handling after-market trading in the shares so issued. Industry expertise can also be an important factor in selecting an underwriter. A very important item is to consider possible conflicts of interest that could compromise the underwriter's performance.

After this has been accomplished, each of the participants in the registration statement—*i.e.,* the issuer, counsel, auditors, and the prospective underwriter[4]—will embark on its respective role in the joint preparation process. Preparation of the registration statement begins with formation of the working groups which will generally include: the issuer, counsel for the issuer, directors, officers and employees who will need to be consulting in gathering information for the registration statement, the lad or managing underwriter (and co-manager if any), the counsel for the underwriters, the audit firm that will be preparing the financials, and, if there are selling shareholders, the selling shareholders and their counsel.

The underwriters will not only be engaged in the preliminary steps in forming the underwriting syndicate but will also be enmeshed in substantial factual investigation of the issuer's condition; this investigation is to ensure that the offering will be marketable and also to make certain that all disclosures are accurate. Taking reasonable steps to assure the accuracy of the registration statement is necessary to protect the underwriter from potential liability under the 1933 Act.

Each of the participants in the preparation of the registration statement has a duty of reasonable investigation.[7] The highly factual nature of the due

§ 3.2

4. As pointed out in §§ 2.1, 2.3 *supra*, the during the preparation process prospective underwriters have signed letter of intent but have not entered into a legally binding underwriting agreement. A legally binding underwriting agreement generally is not signed until the eve of the offering's effective date.

7. *See* Rule 176, 17 C.F.R. § 230.176.

diligence standard precludes a one-size-fits-all template for formulating a due diligence program so as to guarantee success in establishing that the requisite reasonable investigation has been made. Risks that may be peculiar to the issuer's business may trigger more specific duties of reasonable investigation. Notwithstanding the variable nature of the reasonable investigation requirement, a number of generalizations may be made. The following activities are examples of the steps to be taken by the lawyers involved in the registration process.

First, it is necessary to amass information concerning the issuer's operations. This entails a thorough factual investigation of all aspects of the business, including an examination of the past dealings of insiders and affiliated companies. This complete factual investigation should include both personal interviews of the issuer's key personnel and careful document reviews of the issuer's files. The inquiry should extend to conferences with the head of each division of the issuer as well as the company's principal officers and managers.

The document reviews should be used to establish a complete history of the company. Corporate minute books frequently provide a good starting point for historical investigation. There should be a comprehensive review of the shareholder and director minutes of the company as well as those of all subsidiaries and affiliates. The review of past minutes not only will help uncover factual information, but it also serves as a "legal check-up"; any past illegalities or significant improprieties will most likely have to be disclosed in the registration statement. The initial document review will help establish a precise view of the issuer's capitalization. Accounting expertise will be necessary at this stage. A review of the charter and bylaws as well as all loans and guarantees and other financing agreements (including long-term leases) will shed light upon any applicable limitations and restrictions on current and future financing. In addition, a complete review of the company's dividend policy may reveal restrictions on financing.

The registration statement's detailed disclosure requirements mandate a thorough analysis of the company's business including a detailed description of all divisions, departments and lines of business, and accounting practices. There should thus be inquiry into all major customers and suppliers, including a determination of the issuer's dependency on one or more of them, as well as of the existence of alternative major customers and suppliers. The investigation should involve a complete examination of the issuer's marketing, merchandising, and pricing methods and policies, and a description of past practices. There should be a survey of the physical plant, including an examination of all leases (copies may be necessary for the registration statement), as well as title searches, where applicable. The survey should also encompass equipment including its condition, as well as anticipated maintenance and replacement requirements.

Counsel will have to obtain copies of all significant labor agreements. Are any due to expire? Are strikes or substantially higher labor expenses likely to result? If so, these are issues that may have to be discussed in the registration statement.

The registration statement must identify and describe security arrangements including pledges, assignments, and accounts receivable. If the issuer has a parent, subsidiary, or other affiliated corporations, careful attention must be given to intra-corporate, inter-subsidiary, and parent-subsidiary transactions. Counsel has to keep a watchful eye for potential conflicts of interest that may appear in mark-ups, supply and requirements contracts, loans, salaries, and stock ownership.

There must be a thorough investigation with regard to the issuer's management structure. It is necessary to obtain detailed resumes of each officer and director encompassing the past five years. Corporate minutes may be helpful in gathering information about management. In many cases personal interviews will be advisable. There should be a detailed description of all direct and indirect management compensation, as well as any insider transactions which have occurred within the past two years.[11] Relevant insider transactions include borrowings, loans, transactions in the issuer's shares, as well as contracts between the issuer and companies controlled by the insiders. Counsel should compile a list of the issuer's securities held by its officers and directors, including all shares beneficially owned, such as those held by family members, trusts, or corporations. There should be close scrutiny of all fringe benefits. Restricted and qualified stock option plans and stock or cash bonus incentive plans should be scrutinized closely. A careful review should be made of all employment and employment-related agreements.

The pre-registration review should also encompass a study of the issuer's research and development activities—both in the past and whatever may be contemplated for the immediate future. This should include an explanation of the accounting methods, percentage and completion method, and the stage of development.

In preparing for the registration statement, the issuer should compile its operating statistics including relevant trends and ratios. There should be a description of production backlog with respect to all firm orders. There must be a complete inventory, including a breakdown by lines of business and product lines. Counsel should review past tax returns to determine whether all taxes have been paid and whether future taxes have been properly estimated and withheld. Counsel should be fully aware of all competitors' activities including industry trends, reports (if available), and the price range and relative strength of comparable products. Counsel should also inquire as to whether the issuer has been in compliance with all applicable state and federal regulatory, environmental, health and safety, and labor laws.

The team preparing the registration statement must thoroughly understand all of the issuer's financial relationships. Banking relationships must be fully examined and described in detail (including lines of credit, and revolving credit agreements). A comprehensive review of the issuer's cash flow, including the source of funds, should be undertaken Counsel with the aid of accountants should determine all contingent liabilities, including an evaluation of all pending litigation—at a minimum all pleadings should be reviewed. Current financial statements must be prepared. Most registration forms require a balance sheet at least as current as ninety days prior to filing and audited profit and loss statements for three years (or two years unaudited for an offering pursuant to Regulation A's qualified exemption for small issues).[14]

11. *See* item 404 of Regulation S–K which sets forth the types of transactions and relationships with management. Transactions with officers, directors, and affiliates draw particular attention in the registration materials. *See* § 3.9 *infra.*

14. 17 C.F.R. § 240.251 *et seq. See* § 4.17 *infra.*

Counsel should examine all significant contracts to which the issuer is a party; this includes insurance coverage. There should also be a review of all patents and trademarks. All special risk factors with regard to the issuer generally, industry-wide conditions, and the particular securities to be offered must be analyzed and described in detail in the registration statement. There should be a review of all prior offerings, both private and public. Copies of all prior registration statements and underwriting agreements should be obtained and analyzed, as should be the case with 1934 Act filings such as Forms 8–K, 10–K, 10–Q, and proxy statements.[15]

It is important that the pre-filing investigation focus not only on the issuer's business generally, but also on the specific disclosure issues that may arise from the terms of the securities to be covered by the registration statement. Counsel must ensure proper documentation of resolutions and corporate minutes authorizing the offering. It may be necessary to increase capitalization and, in some cases, a formal shareholder vote may be required. All undesired stock transfer and issuing restrictions should be eliminated from the charter and/or bylaws. It may be necessary to secure the consent of creditors or other third parties before issuing the shares in question.

There must be compliance with all corporate law requirements of the state of incorporation, as well as any state in which the issuer is qualified to do business as a foreign corporation. There must also be compliance with the blue sky laws of all states in which securities are to be offered. Finally, depending upon the nature of issuer's business, there may be state or federal administrative approval that must be obtained prior to the offering.

After the foregoing factual inquiries and document preparation have taken place, there are a number of legal tasks that must be attended to as part of the underwriting process. These will generally be performed by issuer's counsel or in some cases by underwriters' counsel. It is often necessary to hire special securities counsel to coordinate the offering and supervise preparation of the registration statement. Such special counsel should then be present at preliminary discussions between the issuer and underwriters concerning the terms of the offering. Both issuer's and underwriters' counsel will be involved in the preparation of a letter of intent between the company and managing underwriter. The letter of intent generally will set forth the number of shares to be offered, the offering price, and basic underwriting terms and will provide for pre-clearance with Nasdaq and the Financial Industry Regulatory Authority (FINRA—formerly the National Association of Securities Dealers or the NASD).[18]

Counsel will then meet with the accountants to review the financial information required for SEC filing; a timetable should be established. The issuer must select a stock transfer agent and a financial printer. It will be necessary to estimate the number of copies of both the registration statement and prospectus needed for the SEC, blue sky law compliance, broker-dealers, securities exchanges, and customers. At this point counsel should be making the factual inquiries outlined above as well as gathering all of the information necessary for the registration statement.

15. *See* chapter 9 *infra.* If the issuer is using S–1 or S–3 to integrate 1933 Act and 1934 Exchange Act disclosures, due diligence requirements may be affected. *See* §§ 3.4, 3.5, 7.4 *infra.*

18. *See* Nasdaq Rules 4300 *t seq.*, NASDAQ Manual (CCH) ¶ 2151.02. The NASD is discussed in § 14.3 *infra.*

Underwriters' counsel will be preparing the underwriters' agreement with the issuer, agreement among underwriters, and agreements for the selling group. The team putting together the registration statement must also prepare a questionnaire for underwriters to establish, among other things, sufficient financial responsibility to bear the underwriting risk. Counsel should also assist in drafting a letter inviting participation in the underwriting group.

When ready, proofs of the registration materials should be distributed to all counsel, the issuer's principal officers, the accountants and the managing underwriters, all of whom should conduct a thorough review. The issuer's directors should also receive and review copies of the registration materials. Sometime prior to sending the mock-ups to the printer, a first stage of the "due diligence" meeting[20] should be held and may need to be reconvened after thorough review and receipt of all comments. The next step is to file the registration statement along with the payment of applicable fees.[21] If certain summary or preliminary prospectuses are to be used,[22] additional SEC filings may be necessary. At this time, blue sky filings may also be necessary, as will filings with Nasdaq. In the event that the securities are to be listed on an exchange, listing applications must be prepared and filed.

Counsel's job does not end with the filing of the registration statement. There are a number of post-filing activities that must be completed, in addition to work on any amendments that must be filed. The issuer may want to prepare and distribute press releases; this may also take place prior to filing provided there are no gun jumping violations as spelled out by SEC Rule 135.[25] Provisions will have to be made for stock certificates including obtaining CUSIP (Committee on Uniform Security Identification Procedures) numbers (unless the shares will be uncertificated). Special securities counsel, along with the issuer's and underwriters' counsel will have to review the accountant's comfort[26] letter. Underwriters' counsel will have to prepare a distribution list and transmit letters to other underwriters and members of the selling group.

Once the registration materials are filed, the relevant administrative agencies (including the SEC and applicable state securities administrators) may respond with letters of comment.[27] Counsel must review SEC and Nasdaq. Counsel will then prepare replies and applicable amendments to be filed with the SEC, Nasdaq or the applicable exchange. It will often be necessary to file "delaying" amendments in order to give the registrant sufficient time to respond to the letters of comment. At this point, it is time to arrange for the due diligence meeting of counsel, management, and underwriters, where all of the filings as amended will be scrutinized. All initial prospectuses must be updated, a process which includes sending of amendments to all who received initial prospectuses. If applicable, underwriters'

20. The due diligence requirement is discussed directly below and in § 7.4 *infra*.

21. *See* § 3.5 *infra*.

22. Summary and preliminary prospectuses are discussed in § 2.4 *supra*. Also, the 2004 offering reform rules introduced a new concept of a free writing prospectus.

25. 17 C.F.R. § 230.135. *See* § 2.3 *supra*.

26. A comfort letter states that the audit is materially accurate. *See*, footnote 39 *infra*.

27. As is explained more fully in § 3.7 *infra*, the SEC employs an informal review process through letters of comment rather than resorting to formal refusal order proceedings under section 8 of the Act. 15 U.S.C.A. § 77h.

counsel will have to supervise preparation for newspaper and Nasdaq quotations. It is at this stage that tombstone ads[30] will generally be prepared. It is also necessary to prepare for Nasdaq and SEC clearance and draft notifying telegrams to blue sky commissioners. The final underwriting agreement will not generally be signed until coordination of SEC clearance time and date and all last-minute amendments such as the price amendment have been filed.

Frequently, the final step in the registration process is the pricing of the issue. In most instances, the price will be determined jointly by the underwriters and issuer. Because of their firm commitment obligations, underwriters will generally be conservative in pricing an issue. In the case of additional offerings of securities that are already publicly traded, the price ordinarily will be determined by the closing price on the day before the offering. As an alternative to a fixed price for an offering, securities may be offered "at the market" (or "at market") which means that the proceeds will be based on a fluctuating market price. While an "at market" offering may find a warmer reception in a thin market, a primary drawback is that the issuer (or selling shareholders in a secondary distribution) cannot predict exactly how much money will be raised until the distribution has been completed. "At market" offerings are particularly susceptible to manipulation.[34] Accordingly, the SEC does not permit stabilizing activity during "at market" offerings.[35] When a minimum amount of capital is needed by the issuer and there is some concern that the offering may not be fully subscribed, the shares can be offered on an "all or none" or "part or none" basis.[36] In such a case, the terms of the offering will specify the minimum number of shares that must taken by investors in order for the sale to proceed. If within a specified period there is not a full subscription to all shares being offered, the offering is canceled and any monies refunded. Alternatively, the offering may take place, provided the subscribers will be offered a refund. This latter option cannot be offered selectively but must be offered to all would-be purchasers.[37] Issuers embarking on "all or none" and "part or none" offerings must be specific as to the offering price, the duration of the offering, and the amount of securities that must be sold to make the offering effective.[38]

After filing the final amendments and the application for acceleration with the SEC, counsel should prepare a closing memorandum. A number of tasks remain. Notification telegrams and copies of the final prospectus must be sent to appropriate blue sky authorities. Transfer agent instructions must be distributed as must payment instructions.

There should then be one final review of all documents and the current status of the issuer. Generally, there will be a cold comfort letter[39] prior to

30. 17 C.F.R. § 230.134. *See* section 2(10) of the 1933 Act; 15 U.S.C.A. § 77b(10) and § 2.4 *supra.*

34. *See, e.g.,* In re Hazel Bishop Inc., 40 S.E.C. 718 (SEC 1961).

35. *See* Regulation M which is discussed in § 6.2 *infra.*

36. *See* § 6.3 *infra.*

37. 17 C.F.R. § 240.10b–9.

38. 17 C.F.R. § 240.10b–9.

39. An accountant's comfort letter generally states that it is not aware of any material changes since the most recent audit. It is frequently referred to as a cold comfort letter because the accountant does not state positively that the information is correct, only that nothing has come to his or her attention to indicate that the information is incorrect.

Joel Krieger and Dorothy Walker, Earnings Per Share, Getting the Most from Comfort Letters, 10 Insights 27 (Oct. 1993).

closing. The stock certificates must be checked and counted. All payments must be made in accordance with the prospectus's description. It may be necessary to coordinate market making activities or even stabilizing activities[40] or any planned stabilizing activities which can be carried out only if in full compliance with the SEC's Regulation M.[41] Circumstances may require post effective amendments to registration statements and the prospectus. For first time registrants, it will be necessary to file with the SEC a "Report of Sales."[42]

The foregoing steps are merely illustrative of a typical registration and may vary according to the nature of the issuer and the offering. Variations may also result from use of one of the alternative registration forms that are described briefly in the next section. Many of the steps described above will also be necessary in a registration pursuant to Regulation A's qualified exemption for small offerings[43] or in preparing offering circulars for other exempt offerings.[44] Also, much of the attorney's factual investigation will have to be made for private placements, especially those in reliance upon SEC Regulation D.[45]

Compilation of a checklist of the necessary steps can be helpful in fulfilling due diligence obligations while preparing registration materials.[46] It has also been suggested that selecting one person as a "due diligence officer" to oversee the registration process will help assure compliance.[47]

The sections that follow provide an overview of the disclosure process. The discussion is not intended to provide a step-by-step "how-to" guide. The most helpful source for framing disclosures are the Commission's Regulation S–K[48] for descriptive disclosure items and Regulation S–X[49] for accounting matters. Violations of the disclosure requirements set forth in Regulation S–K are not *per se* actionable as securities fraud,[50] but can be used to support a claim based on one of the express or implied liability provisions.[51]

---

40. Market makers are discussed in § 14.10 *infra.*

41. Where an offering of securities faces a soft market, SEC rules permit bids designed to stabilize the market price but only if in compliance with Rule 104 of Regulation M, 17 C.F.R. § 242.104. Regulation M is discussed in § 6.1 *infra*. Rule 104 is the successor to former rule 10b–7, 17 C.F.R. § 240.10b–7 (rescinded). Unless Rule 104 is fully complied with, such activity will constitute illegal stock manipulation. *See* Regulation M and section 9 of the 1934 Act. 15 U.S.C.A. § 78i; 17 C.F.R. § 242.104. *See also* §§ 6.1, 12.1 *infra.*

42. 17 C.F.R. § 230.463.

43. *See* section 3(b) of the 1933 Act; 15 U.S.C.A. § 77c(b) and § 4.16 *infra.*

44. *See, e.g.,* the informational requirements for offerings under Regulation D. 17 C.F.R. § 230.502(b). Regulation D is discussed in §§ 4.20–4.22, 4.25 *infra.*

45. 17 C.F.R. §§ 230.501–230.508, discussed in §§ 4.19–4.25 *infra.*

46. *See, e.g.,* Carlos L. Israels, Checklist for Underwriters' Investigations, 18 Bus. Law. 90 (1962), as updated in ABA, Selected Articles in Securities Law 71 (1968); Robert A. Spanner, Limiting Exposure in the Offering Process, 20 Rev. Sec. & Commod. Reg. 59 (1987).

47. *See, e.g., See, e.g.,* Carlos L. Israels, Checklist for Underwriters' Investigations, 18 Bus. Law. 90 (1962), as updated in ABA, Selected Articles in Securities Law 71 (1968); Valerie Ford Jacobs, The Due Diligence Process from the Underwriter's Perspective, PLI Corporate Law and Practice Course Handbook Series (PLI June, 2007), available on Westlaw.

48. 17 C.F.R. § 229.10 *et seq.*, 7 Fed. Sec. L. Rep. (CCH) ¶ 71,001 *et seq.*

49. 17 C.F.R. § 210.1–01 *et seq.*, 6 Fed. Sec. L. Rep. (CCH) ¶ 69,101 *et seq.*

50. Securities fraud is discussed in chapters 7, 12 *infra.*

51. *See* Feldman v. Motorola, Inc., 1994 WL 160115, [1993–1994 Transfer Binder] Fed. Sec. L. Rep. (CCH) ¶ 98,133 (N.D.Ill.1994) (private suit involving SEC Rule 10b–5).

§ 3.3 Information Required in the Registration Statement and the Statutory Prospectus

The registration statement is the basic disclosure document that must be filed with the SEC for 1933 Act registration.[1] There are a number of alternative disclosure forms which may be available to issuers for registration.[2] The availability of the various forms depends upon the nature of the issuer and/or the circumstances surrounding the offering, as well as the types of securities offered. Regardless of the registration form to be filed, it is a document that is divided into two principal sections. The information contained in the first portion of the registration statement is the same as that which will be found in the prospectus as required by section 10(a) of the 1933 Act and Schedule A.[3] The Schedule A or statutory prospectus must be delivered before the consummation of any sale pursuant to a registered offering.[4] Schedule A provides only a bare-bones outline of the types of disclosures which are required. Detailed disclosure requirements are found in the SEC's registration forms and in Regulation S–K.

The items listed in Schedule A provide the bare-bones statutory guidelines for disclosure. The actual disclosure requirements are found in the applicable 1933 Act registration forms and applicable SEC regulations. In addition to the foregoing information, the front page of the prospectus must highlight the salient points of the offering. This summary must contain, among other things, the identity of the issuer and the underwriter, description of the securities offered, whether any part of the offering is secondary (not by the issuer), the use of the proceeds, and any special risks presented by the offering that warrant prominent attention.[7] Schedule A merely provides a skeletal description of the types of information that must be disclosed. The specific items that need be disclosed are listed in the instructions and individualized line item disclosures called for by the SEC registration form.[8] The forms provide the skeletal description of what needs to be disclosed. More detailed guidance and explanation of what is required for disclosure is contained in Regulation S–K.[9] Guidelines for disclosures relating to accounting matters are found in Regulation S–X.[10]

The second part of the registration statement consists of additional information which is not sent out in the prospectus but which is available in the SEC files for public inspection. As noted at the outset of this section, Schedule A is only the starting point. It is necessary to look to the applicable registration form which will supply the bare-bones description of what has to be disclosed. It is then necessary to turn to Regulation S–K for a detailed description of the ways in which the information must be presented. In

---

§ 3.3

1. *See* 15 U.S.C.A. §§ 77f, 77g.

2. The various forms for registration are discussed in § 3.4 *infra*.

3. *See* 15 U.S.C.A. §§ 77g, 77j(a), 77aa.

4. 15 U.S.C.A. § 77e(b)(2).

7. Regulation S–K, Items 501–502, 17 C.F.R. §§ 229.501–229.502; Regulation S–B Items 501–502, 17 C.F.R. §§ 228.501–228.502. *See* §§ 3.8–3.9 *infra*.

8. *See* § 3.4 *infra* for a description of the various registration forms.

9. 17 C.F.R. § 229.10 *et seq*., 7 Fed. Sec. L. Rep. (CCH) ¶ 71,001 *et seq*.

10. 17 C.F.R. § 210.10–1 *et seq*., 6 Fed. Sec. L. Rep. (CCH) ¶ 69,101 *et seq*.

addition, Regulation S–X sets forth the disclosure guide and presentation requirements for financial information.

The 1933 Act forms and rules set forth the disclosures required for 1933 Act registration. In drafting disclosures for 1933 Act forms, additional disclosures that may be required for an analogous 1934 Act disclosure item need not be consulted.[11]

Rule 421 requires the use of clear, concise, and understandable language in prospectuses.[12] The rule proposal was part of the SEC's larger initiative to require the use of "plain English" in SEC filings and reports to shareholders and investors. The plain English initiative, which began in the mid 1990s as a pilot program, involves amendments to various provisions of Regulation S–K. In a lengthy official release, the Commission describes what it means by plain English and also provides several examples of appropriate disclosure styles. The plain English requirements include: use of the active rather than passive voice, short sentences, use of definite, concrete everyday words, presentation of information in tabular form or with bullet lists, the avoidance of legal jargon and highly technical business terminology, as well as the avoidance of multiple negatives.[13]

The SEC began the implementation of the plain English requirement for 1933 Act prospectuses. Rule 421(d) applies to the cover page as well as to the summary and risk factors sections of the prospectus. The SEC explained that in addition to mandating the foregoing for the specified portions of the prospectus, the rule gives "issuers more specific guidance on how to make the entire prospectus clear, concise, and understandable."[15] The Commission has affirmed its commitment to plain English by trying to follow the guidelines in its own rulemaking. Most notably, when revising its shareholder proposal rule, the SEC used a plain English format.[16] Notwithstanding its original commitment to adhere more closely to the plain English requirements in its own rulemaking, aside from the shareholder proposal rule, the SEC rules have not been rewritten to conform to the plain English requirements that are applicable to SEC filers.

§ 3.4 Registration Forms and Integrated Disclosure

§ 3.4[1] Overview of Disclosure Requirements

For more than fifty-five years, the SEC has administered two parallel disclosure systems: one for the registration of public offerings under the Securities Act of 1933 and the other for the periodic reporting requirements of the Securities Exchange Act of 1934.[1] The parallel systems resulted in a great

11. *See, e.g.,* In re N2K, Inc. Securities Litigation, 82 F.Supp.2d 204, 207–208 (S.D.N.Y.2000) (1934 Act Rule 12b–20 did not apply to 1933 Act disclosures).

12. Plain English Disclosure, Sec. Act Rel. No. 33–7380, 62 Fed. Reg. 3152, 1997 WL 17695 (F.R.) (SEC Jan. 21, 1997). For a more detailed discussion of the plain English initiatives, *see* § 3.10[2] *infra.*

13. Plain English Disclosure, Sec. Act Rel. No. 33–7380, 62 Fed. Reg. 3152, 1997 WL 17695 (F.R.) (SEC Jan. 21, 1997).

15. Sec. Act Rel. No. 33–7497, 63 Fed. Reg. 6370–01, 1998 WL 44199 (F.R.) (SEC Feb. 6, 1998).

16. Rule 14a–8, 17 C.F.R. § 14a–8(c). *See* Peter J. Romeo & Richard J. Parrino, The New Shareholder Proposal Rules, 31 Rev. Sec. & Commodities Reg. 203 (1998). *See* § 11.7 *infra.*

§ 3.4

1. *See* § 9.2 *infra* for a discussion of the Exchange Act's periodic reporting requirements for issuers.

deal of duplicative filings and unnecessary paperwork. In 1982, the Securities and Exchange Commission adopted an integrated disclosure system for registration of securities under the 1933 Act.[2] While some duplication remains, the institution of integrated disclosure has made great strides in easing the disclosure burden. The current system integrates and simplifies the disclosure requirements under the 1933 and 1934 securities acts.[3] The Commission has explained that its goal in adopting the integrated system was "to revise or eliminate overlapping or unnecessary disclosure and dissemination requirements wherever possible, thereby reducing burdens on registrants while at the same time ensuring that security holders, investors and the marketplace have been provided with meaningful, non-duplicative information upon which to base investment decisions."[4]

As discussed in the preceding section, Schedule A provides a skeletal outline of the types of information to be made available in connection with a registered offering of securities. Each of the registration forms provided by the SEC go into slightly more detail in describing the types of disclosures that must be made. The applicable forms frequently refer to Regulation S–K which sets forth in detail the ways in which the relevant information should be set forth. Regulation S–K addresses the presentation of disclosure items generally. A particularly important part of Regulation S–K is the Management's Discussion and Analysis (MD & A) of financial condition and results of operations. The MD & A is not limited to discussion of the existing business; it also extends to a discussion and analysis of planned operations. Regulation S–X addresses accounting matters in significant detail. Thus, in preparing for a registered offering, it is necessary to consult not only the applicable registration form, but also to become conversant with the relevant disclosure items in Regulations S–K and S–X.

As part of its small business initiatives of 1992, the SEC adopted former Regulation S–B which qualifies and with respect to many items replaces Regulation S–K as the applicable disclosure guide for small business issuers.[8] Domestic issuers having revenues of less than 25 million dollars for their most recent fiscal year formerly could qualify for use of Regulation S–B's simplified disclosures that were applicable for both 1933 and 1934 Act filings. However, effective in 2008, Regulation S–B was rescinded and scaled disclosures for smaller companies were incorporated into Regulation S–K.

§ 3.4[2] Materiality

The basic dividing line between what has to be disclosed and what information may be withheld is determined by the concept of materiality which is discussed in various sections throughout this treatise.[10] Materiality is

2. *See* Sec.Act Rel. No. 33–6383, Acc.Rel. No. 306, [1937–82 Acc't'g Rel. Transfer Binder] Fed.Sec.L.Rep. (CCH) ¶ 72,328 (March 3, 1982).

3. Unlike the 1933 Act which is directed towards securities distributions, the 1934 Exchange Act deals with day-to-day trading and the securities markets in general. *See* § 1.2 *supra,* chapters 9, 14 *infra.*

4. Special Report, 1982 Integrated Disclosure Adoptions, Fed.Sec.L.Rep. (CCH) No. 956 at p. 15 (March 11, 1982).

8. *See* Sec. Act Rel. No. 33–6949, 6 Fed.Sec.L.Rep. (CCH) ¶ 72,439 (SEC July 30, 1992); Sec. Act Rel. No. 33–6924, [1991–1992 Transfer Binder] Fed.Sec.L.Rep. (CCH) ¶ 84,931 (March 11, 1992).

10. *See, e.g.,* § 7.3[1] *infra* (section 11 of the 1933 Act), §§ 10.3[4], 10.4 *infra* (1934 Act proxy rules), § 12.9 *infra* (SEC Rule 10b–5).

highly factual and thus defies a bright-line definition. Over time, there have been an increasing number of problems in the context of an evolving definition of the concept of "materiality." Materiality consists of those facts which a reasonable investor would consider significant in making an investment decision.[12] Since the hallmark of disclosure for both the 1933 Act registration statement and all 1934 Act filings is embodied in the concept of "materiality," the problems relating to disclosure in registration statements and other required filings are quite similar. Because the primary purpose of 1933 Act registration statements is to provide full and adequate information regarding the distribution of securities, certain types of disclosures may be more sensitive and thus of more concern with regard to public offerings than to other required filings.

Materiality depends not upon the literal truth of statements, but upon the ability of reasonable investors to become accurately informed. In assessing materiality courts should not focus alone on one particular sentence that is part of a larger statement without considering the entirety the statements in question.

As discussed more fully below, a finding of materiality is based on the total mix of information available. However, the mere fact that information may be publicly available does not mean that it is necessarily incorporated into every statement made.

In assessing the total mix of information that is available, courts will look beyond filings mandated by the federal securities laws. Information that is generally circulated through the media will be considered in assessing the total mix. In evaluating the total mix of information available, the courts consider the efficiency of the market and the extent to which the available information is absorbed into the total mix and ultimately reflected in the market price.

The concept of materiality, which is interwoven with all of the issues discussed throughout this chapter, is also discussed more fully in subsequent sections of this treatise.[21]

§ 3.4[3] Integrating 1933 Act Disclosure With the 1934 Act

Many observers believed that the repetitive nature of the dual filing systems of the Securities Act of 1933 and the Securities Exchange Act of 1934 resulted in needless duplicative filings and that this needed to be remedied by a thoughtful and measured approach.[22] The proposed cure was first recommended in a seminal law review article.[23] The author suggested emphasizing the 1934 Act reporting requirements and at the same time eliminating many of the duplicative disclosures formerly required by the 1933 Act.[24] Periodic

12. *See, e.g.,* Basic Inc. v. Levinson, 485 U.S. 224, 108 S.Ct. 978, 99 L.Ed.2d 194 (1988); TSC Industries, Inc. v. Northway, Inc., 426 U.S. 438, 96 S.Ct. 2126, 48 L.Ed.2d 757 (1976). This definition has been codified in SEC Rules 17 C.F.R. § 230.405, 240.12b–2.

21. *See* §§ 7.3[1], 10.4, 12.9 *infra.*

22. *See generally* James O. Hewitt Developing Concepts of Materiality and Disclosure, 32 Bus.Law. 887 (1977); Lewis D. Lowenfels, Questionable Corporate Payments and the Federal Securities Laws, 51 N.Y.U.L.Rev. 1 (1976); A.A. Sommer, Jr. Therapeutic Disclosure, 4 Sec.Reg. L.J. 263 (1976).

23. Milton H. Cohen, "Truth in Securities" Revisited, 79 Harv.L.Rev. 1340 (1966).

24. *See also, e.g.,* Michael McDonough, *Death in One Act: The Case for Company Registration*, 24 Pepp. L. Rev. 563, 585 (1997).

reporting rather than emphasizing one-time disclosures in connection with public offerings seemed to be in the best interest of investor protection.[25]

This idea of an integrated disclosure system subsequently received the support of the American Law Institute ("ALI"), which constructed a model securities code "which would unify the disparate federal securities laws into a fully integrated disclosure system."[26] The proposed securities code containing a fully integrated system was completed and had garnered the approval of the Commission; however, Congress opted not to incorporate the proposed system after all and left the issue unresolved. Congress was not willing to replace the familiarity of the 1933 and 1934 Acts with a new and unproven system.

Despite the failure of the ALI securities code, an integrated disclosure system was partially realized. And, in 1982, the Commission adopted an integrated disclosure system in Regulation S–K.[29]

In addition to its former specialized registration forms and small business initiatives, the Commission established a three-tiered system of registration and prospectus disclosure of registrant-oriented information based upon the registrant's reporting history and market following. The integrated disclosure system recognizes that transaction-specific information, that is, information specific to the securities issuance, should always be disclosed in the registration statement and prospectus. The more general registrant-oriented information, however, may already be available in reports by the registrant under the Exchange Act and need not be duplicated unnecessarily. Exchange Act reporting companies include all issuers whose securities are traded on a national exchange as well as those with ten million dollars or more in assets and having a class of equity securities held by more than five hundred persons.[30] The framework for the three-level system is provided by three alternative registration forms: Form S–1, former Form S–2, and Form S–3. Today Form S–1 may be used for integrated disclosure as may Form S–3 for more established companies.

Due Diligence and Integrated Disclosure

A collateral issue related to integrated disclosure is the extent to which it affects the due diligence of participants in the registration process. As is discussed elsewhere,[32] the issuers, officers and directors, signers of the registration statement, underwriters, accountants, and certain experts each have due diligence obligations with regard to the accuracy of the registration materials. In many instances, the due diligence obligation includes a duty to investigate the accuracy of statements made in the registration materials. When a registration statement incorporates by reference information from other filings made with the SEC, the extent of this due diligence obligation may be affected. For example, does the auditing CPA or underwriter have equal responsibility for the information that is derived from other SEC filings? The efficiency to be achieved by integrated disclosure would appear to be undercut by requiring due diligence examination of all previous 1934 Act

25. *See Id.* at 587.

26. *Id.* This commissioned group was led by scholars in the securities field, most notably Harvard University Professor Louis Loss. *See id.*

29. *See* 17 C.F.R. §§ 229.10–229.915. Regulation S–K is discussed in § 9.4 *infra.*

30. 15 U.S.C.A. § 78*l*; 17 C.F.R. § 240.12g–1. *See* § 9.2 *infra.*

32. *See* § 3.2 *supra* and § 7.4 *infra.*

filings that become a part of the registration materials by virtue of former Form S–2 and currently available in Forms S–1 and S–3.

§ 3.4[4] 1933 Act Registration Forms[33]

§ 3.4[4][A] One Size Fits All Long–Form Disclosure—Form S–1

Form S–1 remains the basic, long-form registration statement that is generally available to issuers unless they qualify for one of the other forms. It requires complete registrant and transaction information to be provided in the prospectus.[36] As a practical matter, Form S–1 is to be used primarily by first-time issuers and smaller publicly held companies.

§ 3.4[4][C] Form S–3 for Seasoned Issuers

Form S–3 is available for seasoned issuers[41]—those companies that meet the form's qualifications with respect to a history of public trading and 1934 Act reporting. Form S–3[42] requires the least detailed level of disclosure to investors by allowing for the fullest possible incorporation by reference from Exchange Act reporting. Unless there has been a material change in the issuer's affairs, no registrant-oriented information will be required to be disclosed to investors. Only the transaction-specific description of the offering need be specified in the prospectus.

A subcategory of seasoned issuers that qualify for 1933 Act Form S–3 (and its counterpart for foreign issuers, Form F–3), are well-known seasoned issuers.[46] Well-known seasoned issuers ("WIKSIs") are larger and more widely held public companies.[47] As noted earlier, a practical matter, most of section

---

33. The discussion that follows focuses on the registration of offerings under the 1933 Act. Companies that have publicly traded securities are also subject to periodic reporting and disclosure requirements under the Securities Exchange Act of 1934. The 1934 Act's registration, reporting and disclosure requirements are discussed in chapter 9 *infra*.

36. *See* Special Report, 1982 Integrated Disclosure Adoptions, Fed.Sec.L.Rep. (CCH) No. 956 at p. 19–20 (March 11, 1982). *See* the description of 1933 Act disclosure requirements in § 3.3 *supra*.

41. A seasoned issuer is a company that qualifies for S–3 registration. In contrast, "An unseasoned issuer is an issuer that is required to file reports pursuant to Section 13 or Section 15(d) of the Exchange Act, but does not satisfy the requirements of Form S–3 or Form F–3 for a primary offering of its securities." Securities Offering Reform, Sec. Act Rel. No. 33–8591, Sec. Exch. Act Rel. No. 34–52056, Inv. Co. Act Rel. No. IC–26993 70 Fed. Reg. 44722–01, 2005 WL 1692642 (SEC July 19, 2005).

42. Form S–3 is among those for which delaying amendments are not expressly authorized for postponing the effective date.

46. *See* 17 C.F.R. § 230.405 for the definition.

47. A WKSI is a company that qualifies for registration on 1933 Act Form S–3 or F–3 and either: (A) As of a date within 60 days of the determination date, has a worldwide market value of its outstanding voting and non-voting common equity held by non-affiliates of $700 million or more; or (B)(1) As of a date within 60 days of the determination date, has issued in the last three years at least $1 billion aggregate principal amount of non-convertible securities, other than common equity, in primary offerings for cash, not exchange, registered under the Act; and (2) Will register only non-convertible securities, other than common equity, and full and unconditional guarantees permitted pursuant to paragraph (1)(ii) of this definition unless, at the determination date, the issuer also is eligible to register a primary offering of its securities relying on General Instruction I.B.1. of Form S–3 or Form F–3. 17 C.F.R. § 230.405. A seasoned issuer, other than a WKSI, is an issuer that uses Form S–3 or Form F–3 to register primary offerings of securities. Securities Offering Reform, Sec. Act Rel. No. 33–8591, Sec. Exch. Act Rel. No. 34–52056, Inv. Co. Act Rel. No. IC–26993, 70 Fed. Reg. 44722–01, 2005 WL 1692642 (SEC July 19, 2005). "An unseasoned issuer is an issuer that is required to file reports pursuant to Sections 13

5(c)'s gun-jumping prohibitions do not apply to the largest public companies that qualify as well-known seasoned issuers. As discussed in the previous chapter of this treatise, WKSIs are subject to far fewer limitations on the information they can disseminate during the course of a public offering.

Effective 2008, the SEC amended to the eligibility requirements of Forms S–3 and F–3 enabling certain domestic and foreign private issuers to use these forms for primary securities offerings without regard to the size of their public float or the rating of debt they are offering, so long as they satisfy the other eligibility conditions of the respective form, have a class of common equity securities listed and registered on a national securities exchange, and the issuers do not sell more than the equivalent of one-third of their public float in primary offerings over any period of 12 calendar months. These expanded eligibility rules for Forms S–3 and F–3 do not extend to shell companies, which are prohibited from using the new provisions until 12 calendar months after they cease being shell companies. Smaller S–3 registrants may qualify for the scaled disclosures (described in the subsection that follows) that are available for smaller public companies.

§ 3.4[4][D] Smaller Public Companies

Registration of securities under the 1933 Act is an expensive and otherwise burdensome process. Accordingly, the securities laws present barriers to small business's access to the U.S. capital markets. There is a widely recognized public policy to support small businesses as an important part of the U.S. economy. This public policy is furthered by encouraging small business to get started and to have the best possible chance for success. The policy of encouraging small business is reflected in a number of initiatives at both the federal and state levels. The existence of the Small Business Administration is but one example. The policy of encouraging small business formation and capitalization thus comes into conflict with the regulatory philosophy underlying the securities laws. Mindful of these two potentially conflicted policies–investor protection and easing the barriers faced by small businesses, the federal securities laws have provided some incentives to small businesses. These incentives are designed to provide easier access to the capital markets but at the same time not forgetting about the investor protection thrust of the federal securities laws. It follows that some barriers have been lifted both through relaxed registration requirements and special exemptions from registration for securities offerings by small businesses. The SEC formerly had specialized registration forms for small business issuers. As of 2008, the scaled disclosure requirements for small business issuers were incorporated into more general purpose SEC forms and disclosure guidelines. These streamlined disclosure requirements, which are discussed below, should be considered as an alternative to the small issue exemptions from 1933 Act registration.[53]

As noted above, in 2007, the SEC eliminated the specialized forms and Regulation S–B that formerly were available to small business issuers.[61] At the

or 15(d) of the Exchange Act, but does not satisfy the requirements of Form S–3 or Form F–3 for a primary offering of its securities." *Id.*

53. These exemptions are discussed in §§ 4.15–4.25 *infra.*

61. *See* Smaller Reporting Company Regulatory Relief and Simplification, Sec. Act Rel. No. 33–8876, Sec. Exch. Act Rel. No. 34–56994, Trust Indenture Act Rel. No. 39–2451, 2007 WL 4440393 (SEC Dec. 19, 2007). The SEC issued a guide for small business issuers to help them through the revised Regulation S–K and applicable forms. *See* Changeover to the SEC's New

same time the SEC redefined the concept of small business issuers to as to enable more companies to qualify for the new scaled disclosure requirements available under both the 1933 and 1934 Acts for smaller reporting companies. Companies with less than $75 million in public equity float now qualify for scaled disclosure requirements under Regulation S–K as amended and under the applicable 1933 and 1934 Act forms as amended.[62] Companies that do not have a calculable public equity float qualify for scaled disclosure if their revenues were below $50 million in the previous year.[63]

The concessions for smaller companies are not limited to the scaled disclosures. As discussed in a later section of this treatise,[64] section 404 of the Sarbanes–Oxley Act requires public companies management to establish a system of internal controls and to provide an evaluation and assessment of those controls.[65] There were a number of observers who urged the SEC to provide an exemption for smaller companies, but it is highly questionable whether the SEC has the power to grant permanent exemptive relief.[66]

In 2007, the Senate defeated proposed legislation that would have made compliance with section 404 voluntary for Exchange Act reporting companies with a market capitalization of less than $700 million. However, around the same time, the SEC, on May 23, 2007, unanimously adopted interpretive guidance for evaluating internal controls and correlative rule amendments.[74] The new guidance and rules are designed to encourage more cost-effective compliance with the internal control requirements.

§ 3.4[4][E] Offerings to Employees

Form S–8 is available to 1934 Act reporting companies with regard to securities offered to employees, including the employees of subsidiaries who are offered the parent's securities, pursuant to any benefit plan. Form S–8 is limited to offerings geared to compensation of employees and consultants and thus does not apply to offerings designed to raise capital for the company.[82] The SEC is vigilant in watching for abuses of Form S–8 as a subtrafuge for raising capital.

Smaller Reporting Company System by Small Business Issuers and Non–Accelerated Filer Companies–A Small Entity Compliance Guide, http://www.sec.gov/info/smallbus/secg/smrepcosysguid.pdf (SEC Jan. 25, 2008).

62. *See* Smaller Reporting Company Regulatory Relief and Simplification, Sec. Act Rel. No. 33–8876, Sec. Exch. Act Rel. No. 34–56994, Trust Indenture Act Rel. No. 39–2451, 2007 WL 4440393 (SEC Dec. 19, 2007).

63. *See* Smaller Reporting Company Regulatory Relief and Simplification, Sec. Act Rel. No. 33–8876, Sec. Exch. Act Rel. No. 34–56994, Trust Indenture Act Rel. No. 39–2451, 2007 WL 4440393 (SEC Dec. 19, 2007).

64. Sarbanes–Oxley Act of 2002, Pub. Law 107–204 § 404 (July 30, 2002), codified in 15 U.S.C.A. § 7262.

65. In other words, section 404 requires a publicly held company's management to both document and test the company's internal controls.

66. The SEC's exemptive authority extends to provisions of the Securities and Exchange Act but does not expressly apply to provisions of the Sarbanes_Oxley Act that like section 404 are not codified within the securities laws but rather exist as stand-alone provisions in the United States Code.

74. SEC, Commission Guidance Regarding Management's Report on Internal Control Over Financial Reporting Under Section 13(a) or 15(d) of the Securities Exchange Act, Sec. Act Rel. No. 33–8810, Sec. Exch. Act Rel. No. 34–55929, 2007 WL 1791162 (SEC June 20, 2007).

82. *See, e.g.,* SEC v. Phan, 500 F.3d 895 (9th Cir. 2007) ("the S–8 registration ceased to be effective once [the issuer] sought to use the shares for a capital-raising purpose") (relying in part on this treatise).

Registration for an offering to employees, advisors, and consultants under Form S–8 is much more simple and inexpensive than other registration forms. The information about the issuer that must be disclosed in an offering under Form S–8 is minimal[84] and does not provide the type of disclosures that are required by other registration forms. Additionally, unlike most other registration forms, a form S–8 registration is effective immediately and thus there is no waiting period that exists with registered offerings generally. Unlike most other registered offerings, securities offered in a Form S–8 registration may be subject to resale restrictions. Rule 701 sets forth an exemption from registration for securities offered to employees of nonpublic companies.[90]

§ 3.4[4][F] Securities Issued in Connection With a Merger or Other Corporate Reorganization—Form S–4

Form S–4 (and Form F–4 for foreign issuers)[109] may be used for registration of securities issued in mergers, combinations, consolidations, acquisitions of assets, recapitalizations, and other transactions governed by SEC Rule 145.[110]

§ 3.4[5] Disclosure Guides and Procedures—Regulations S–K and S–X

§ 3.4[5][A] Regulations S–K and S–X Distinguished

In order to facilitate understanding of the registration process, the SEC has divided the applicable disclosure rules into three categories. Regulation S–K spells out in detail with respect to the narrative portion of SEC filings what must be disclosed and the manner in which it is to be presented. Regulation C sets forth the relevant procedures. Regulation S–X provides accounting rules and requirements for the form and contents of financial statements. Regulation S–X applies to financial statements required by any of the securities acts.

§ 3.4[6] EDGAR and a Newer IDEA

The SEC has entered the electronic age through the use of its computerized system known as "EDGAR" (Electronic Data Gathering And Retrieval Project); under the EDGAR system the SEC receives electronically transmitted computerized filings. When EDGAR first became operational, the computerized or electronic filings could be transmitted by telephone or could be sent to the Commission on diskette or magnetic tape. Today, the electronic filings can be transmitted by one of three methods: internet, direct dial telecommunications lines via modem, or leased lines. After a pilot program, EDGAR was used for 1933 and 1934 Act registration statements as well as selected 1934 Act filings and for some filings under the Investment Company Act of 1940. Since its inception as a pilot program, the Commission has been expanding

84. *See* Form S–8 Part II.

90. 17 C.F.R. § 230.701. The Rule 701 exemption has a maximum amount of either $1 million or a higher number based on the outstanding securities of the class being offered to employees. *See* § 4.18 *infra*.

109. Forms S–4 and F–4 are among those forms which do not have express authorization for use of delaying amendments to postpone the effective date.

110. 17 C.F.R. § 230.145. *See* § 5.2 *infra*. Form S–4 is coordinated with disclosures in connection with shareholder votes, which are governed by the proxy regulation under the 1934 Act. 15 U.S.C.A. § 78n. *See* chapter 11 *infra*.

the EDGAR program and rules that, subject to limited exceptions such as extreme hardship, *require* electronic filings for most SEC filers and filings.

Liability for misstatements will be based on the printed version of the prospectus that is seen by the investor, not by the electronic version submitted through EDGAR.[175] However, when the investor reads the electronic version, then liability may be based on that version as well.[176] The materiality of misleading or omitted information will be based on an examination of both the hard copy and the electronic version in order to determine whether the misleading or omitted information is material in light of the "total mix" of information available.

In the summer of 2008, the SEC announced a new format to supplement EDGAR and eventually to replace EDGAR.[191] The new platform—Interactive Data Electronic Applications is known as IDEA. IDEA is designed to provide an interactive format and to provide more efficient and faster access to information filed with the Commission. It is planned that in the future IDEA will replace EDGAR but for the foreseeable future will simply be another way to access data.

§ 3.6 SEC Statutory Procedures—Section 8

§ 3.6[1] Statutory Waiting Period

Section 8 of the 1933 Act[1] sets forth the SEC machinery for dealing with a registration statement once it has been filed. Section 8 establishes only a bare bones process that is supplemented by SEC rules and administrative practices that have developed over time. Section 8 on its face does not present a very good picture of what actually happens once a registration statement is filed.

As discussed in the previous section,[2] the Securities and Exchange Commission relies heavily on an informal comment policy rather than invoking the formal procedures of section 8. Section 8(a) establishes the basic statutory rule that a registration statement becomes effective[3] twenty days after the later of the filing of the initial registration statement or the most recent amendment to the registration statement.[4] The exigencies of the offering process (or of disclosure requirements) may result in the issuer requiring more than the statutory twenty days to prepare additional material before the registration statement is in proper condition for the effective date. In such cases, there is a procedure, which is available for most registration forms that will allow for further postponement of the effective date by filing what is known as a delaying amendment. Delaying amendments are generally invoked

---

175. DeMaria v. Andersen, 153 F.Supp.2d 300 (S.D.N.Y. 2001) (inaccuracies in electronic registration statement filed through EDGAR were not relevant where the printed prospectus that plaintiff received was not inaccurate).

176. The SEC makes this explicit in its rules. 17 C.F.R. § 232 304(b).

191. *See* http://www.sec.gov/spotlight/idea.shtml.

§ 3.6

1. 15 U.S.C.A. § 77h.

2. *See* § 3.6 *supra*.

3. The restrictions of section 5 of the 1933 Act provide that it is only after the effective date that sales of the securities in registration can be made. *See* section 5(a), 15 U.S.C.A. § 77e(a). The significance of the effective date is discussed in §§ 2.1, 2.5 *supra*.

4. 15 U.S.C.A. § 77h(a).

by issuers requiring more time. Conversely, issuers not needing the twenty-day waiting period may shorten the statutory period by filing with the Commission a request for acceleration of the effective date.[6] In addition to the acceleration procedure, the SEC may consent to having the amendment relate back to the filing of the registration statement so as not to cause the twenty-day period to start anew.[7] Beyond setting forth the statutory time schedule for the waiting period, Section 8 also contains the formal SEC procedures available for delaying or suspending the effectiveness of a registration statement. Section 8(b)[8] authorizes the Commission, after notice and opportunity for a hearing, to issue an order refusing to permit the registration statement to become effective until there have been such corrective amendments as the order may require. In addition to section 8(b) refusal orders, section 8(d)[9] empowers the Commission, again after notice and opportunity for a hearing, to issue a stop order suspending the effectiveness of a registration statement. In addition, section 8(e) expressly authorizes Commission investigations to determine whether a stop order should be issued.[11] The instigation of formal section 8 proceedings has consequences beyond the adverse publicity and impact on the pending offering. Rule 262[12] provides that such formal proceedings may disqualify an issuer, underwriter or affiliate from eligibility for certain exemptions from registration.

§ 3.6[2] Acceleration of the Effective Date

Section 8(a) of the Act[15] sets forth general guidelines that the Commission should consider in determining whether to grant acceleration of the effective date. Specifically, the SEC is directed to consider: the adequacy of information made available to the public, the ease with which the terms and features of the securities to be issued can be understood, the ease of understanding the relationship of the securities to be issued to the capital structure, and the ease of understanding the rights of securities holders.[17] In addition, the Act requires that the Commission more generally consider the public interest and investor protection.[18] It would appear that Congress did not contemplate that requests for acceleration would be considered "casually" nor be granted "as a matter of course."[19] Rather, the discretion to grant acceleration was designed to be exercised "only with full regard for the Act's purpose to provide investors with the information they need to be able to protect themselves against fraud and misrepresentation."[20]

6. Section 8(a). 15 U.S.C.A. § 77h(a). Rule 461 provides the procedures for acceleration requests.

7. 15 U.S.C.A. § 77h(a). Thus, for example, it is common for an issuer not to set the price until the eve of the offering and to file a price amendment without triggering another twenty-day waiting period.

8. 15 U.S.C.A. § 77h(b).

9. 15 U.S.C.A. § 77h(d).

11. 15 U.S.C.A. § 77h(e).

12. 17 C.F.R. § 230.262.

15. 15 U.S.C.A. § 77h(a).

17. 15 U.S.C.A. § 77h(a).

18. 15 U.S.C.A. § 77h(a).

19. In the Matter of Universal Camera Corp., Sec. Act Rel. No. 33–3076, 19 S.E.C. 648, 657, 1945 WL 26104 (SEC 1945).

20. In the Matter of Universal Camera Corp., Sec. Act Rel. No. 33–3076, 19 S.E.C. 648, 657, 1945 WL 26104 (SEC 1945).

SEC Rule 461[21] supplements the foregoing statutory criteria and also sets forth the procedures and requirements for requests for acceleration of the effective date.[22] There are seven stated reasons for the denial of acceleration: (1) failure to make a genuine effort to keep the prospectus reasonably readable and concise, so as to make the information readily understandable by the investing public;[23] (2) if the preliminary prospectus that has been distributed is found to have been inadequate or inaccurate in any material respect;[24] (3) if the issuer, a person controlling the issuer, or an underwriter is under current SEC investigation;[25] (4) if, in a firm commitment underwriting, the underwriter is not in compliance with the SEC's financial responsibility and net capital requirements;[26] (5) if there have been manipulative transactions by anyone proposed to be associated with the offering where those transactions have artificially affected the price of the securities to be offered;[27] (6) in the case of a secondary offering, if the issuer has failed to take adequate steps to assure compliance with Regulation M's prohibitions[28] on purchases by participants during a distribution;[29] and (7) if the underwriter's compensation is subject to FINRA review, and the FINRA has not issued a "no objection" statement.[30] In addition, failure to comply with the undertaking required by SEC Regulation S–K[31] if there are provisions for indemnification of participants who violate the 1933 Act will render acceleration unavailable. Compliance with the SEC's plain English requirements is also a factor in deciding whether to grant a request for acceleration of the effective date.[32]

§ 3.6[3] SEC Refusal Orders

As already pointed out, section 8(b) of the Act provides for refusal orders in the event that the Commission decides to prevent the registration statement from becoming effective. As discussed earlier, the more common practice is for the Commission to rely on the less formal practice of comment letters and delaying amendments until the registrant can correct any deficiencies identified by the Commission.[33] However, there are occasions when the SEC will resort to the more formal section 8 procedures—either a refusal order or a stop order—especially when it is believed that the issuer has not been

21. 17 C.F.R. § 230.461.

22. *See also* the discussion in § 3.7[3] *infra*.

23. Rule 461(b)(1), 17 C.F.R. § 230.461(b)(1).

24. Rule 461(b)(2), 17 C.F.R. § 230.461(b)(2). In such a case, acceleration may not be granted until the Commission has received adequate assurance that appropriate corrections have been made and distributed to all underwriters and dealers who received the deficient preliminary prospectus. *Id.*

25. Rule 461(b)(3), 17 C.F.R. § 230.461(b)(3).

26. Rule 461(b)(4), 17 C.F.R. § 230.461(b)(4). The SEC net capital requirements are found in Rule 15c3–1 of the Exchange Act. 17 C.F.R. § 240.15c3–1. *See* chapter 14 *infra* for discussion of broker-dealers.

27. Rule 461(b)(5), 17 C.F.R. § 230.461(b)(5).

28. *See* § 6.1 *infra*.

29. Rule 461(b)(7), 17 C.F.R. § 230.461(b)(7).

30. Rule 461(b)(6), 17 C.F.R. § 230.461(b)(6).

31. Regulation S–K Item 512(h); Regulation S–B Item 512(e). Indemnification is discussed in § 7.14 *infra*.

32. The plain English requirements are discussed in § 3.10[2] *infra*.

33. *See* the discussion in § 3.7 *supra*.

making a good faith effort to comply with the Act's requirements.[34]

§ 3.6[4] SEC Investigations and Stop Orders

As mentioned above, section 8(e) empowers the Commission to commence an "examination" to determine whether a stop order should be issued.[38] In the course of a section 8(e) examination, the Commission has the power to take testimony and examine documents. It may make inquiries of the issuer, the underwriter, "or any other person" respecting any matter that pertains to the question of whether a stop order should be issued.[39] In addition, the SEC may require production and certification of a balance sheet or other financial statements.[40] A registrant's failure to cooperate in the course of a section 8(e) examination can lead to the issuance of a stop order.

§ 3.6[5] Withdrawal of the Registration Statement

Once the registration statement has been filed, the registrant may not withdraw from registration without the Commission's permission.[53] The registrant desiring to do cancel a planned offering and withdraw the registration statement must file an application to withdraw a 1933 Act registration statement. After filing an application to withdraw a registration, the registrant formerly had to wait for the Commission to give permission but that changed in 2001. In 2001, SEC Rule 477 was amended to provide for automatic withdrawal of the registration statement unless within fifteen days after the application to withdraw the registration statement, the Commission objects to the request for withdrawal.

Ordinarily, the Commission will accede to requests to withdraw the registration statement. It is the Commission's stated policy to permit withdrawal of the registration statement if "consistent with the public interest and protection of investors."[55] Denying permission to withdraw the registration statement and the SEC's decision to institute formal proceedings under section 8 can have significant consequences. For example, the imposition of a stop order or refusal order may disable the participants from participating in certain exempt offerings over the next five years.[56]

§ 3.7 Processing the Registration Statement After Filing

§ 3.7[1] Law versus Lore: What Really Happens—Informal Procedures

Under the terms of section 8(a) of the Act, once the registration statement has been filed, it becomes effective on the twentieth day after filing, with the twenty-day period beginning to run anew on the date that each amendment is filed.[1] As is explained more fully below, the formal statutory

---

34. *See, e.g.,* Doman Helicopters, Inc., 41 S.E.C. 431 (SEC 1963).

38. 15 U.S.C.A. § 77h(e).

39. 15 U.S.C.A. § 77h(e).

40. 15 U.S.C.A. § 77h(e).

53. 17 C.F.R. § 230.477.

55. 17 C.F.R. § 230.477.

56. *See e.g.,* 17 C.F.R. §§ 230.252; 230.505(b)(2)(iii). *See* §§ 4.15, 4.18, *infra.*

§ 3.7

1. Section 8(a); 15 U.S.C.A. § 77h(a).

time periods and procedures are rarely invoked. Section 8(b) of the 1933 Act[2] empowers the SEC to issue a refusal order for deficiencies that are apparent on the face of the registration statement, provided that the Commission acts within ten days after the filing. Section 8(d)[3] permits the SEC to issue a stop order to prevent the effective date of a registration statement, and section 8(e)[4] permits the Commission to institute investigations as to whether a stop order should be issued.

The procedures spelled out in section 8 of the Act do not provide an accurate picture of the SEC registration review process as it generally proceeds. Although Congress may have contemplated that the Commission would initiate formal section 8 proceedings whenever defective registration statements are filed, such formal proceedings are the exception rather than the rule. Instead, registration review is accomplished through the less formal means of written correspondence and telephone conversations between the SEC staff and the registrant's counsel.[5]

The Commission's reliance on the informal review process dates back to its earliest years.[6] As previously explained, the formal procedures set out in section 8 are used infrequently.

Rather than relying on the stop order and the refusal order proceedings, the Commission staff generally responds to the initial filing with a detailed "letter of comment" or "deficiency letter," advising the issuer of changes that the Commission would like to see in the registration statement. These comments are not limited to specific disclosure items but also refer to readability and the ease with which the disclosures can be understood.[11] As a practical matter, virtually all registration statements filed with the Commission require at least one amendment.[12] Failure to respond to the letter of comment (or deficiency letter), in and of itself, has no legal consequences, except that it carries with it the implied threat of the Commission's initiating a formal stop order proceeding. Accordingly, rather than risk public disclosure and adverse publicity of the deficiencies that would result from formal SEC action, most registrants will readily comply with the Commission's requests. In the event that the registration statement is about to become effective as a result of the expiration of the twenty-day period, the SEC will generally suggest that the issuer file a "delaying amendment" in order to avoid the more drastic initiation of formal administrative proceedings. Since an amendment starts a new twenty-day waiting period, even the most trivial change will operate as a delaying amendment.

2. 15 U.S.C.A. § 77h(b). For discussion of the other SEC enforcement powers *see* chapter 16 *infra*.

3. 15 U.S.C.A. § 77h(d). *See* William R. McLucas, Stop Order Proceedings Under The Securities Act of 1933: A Current Assessment, 40 Bus.Law. 515 (1985).

4. 15 U.S.C.A. § 77h(e).

5. Although not a formal process, the SEC Rules do provide a basis for the giving of informal advice. *See* 17 C.F.R. § 202.2 (prefiling assistance and interpretive advice) and 17 C.F.R. § 202.3 (processing of filings).

6. *See, e.g.* In the Matter of Universal Camera Corp., Sec. Act Rel. No. 33–3076, 19 S.E.C. 648, 659, 1945 WL 26104, [1945–1947 Transfer Binder] Fed. Sec. L. Rep. (CCH) ¶ 75,560 (SEC 1945).

11. 17 C.F.R. § 230.421. *See* § 3.10 *infra*.

12. *See, e.g.*, Richard W. Jennings & Harold Marsh, Jr., Securities Regulation 174–175 (5th ed.1982).

Sometimes either the Commission or the need for last-minute additions will require minor amendments to the registration statement after all other deficiencies have been corrected. A common procedure to prevent delaying the effectiveness of the registration due amendment is to apply to the Commission for acceleration of the effective date pursuant to section 8(a).[13] For example, it is frequently very difficult to arrive at a firm price for a new issue prior to the eve of the offering. Accordingly, it is common practice for the issuer or registrant to omit the offering price from the preliminary SEC filing. After the correction of all other deficiencies the issuer or other registrant will then file a "price amendment" followed by a request for acceleration to allow the offering to proceed as contemplated.[14]

In addition to the requirements of full disclosure and accuracy that can prevent a registration statement from becoming effective, the statute and rules provide that the prospectus must constantly be kept current, even after the effective date. A prospectus containing misleading information, even though it becomes misleading after the effective date, is not in compliance with section 10 of the Act.[15] This is true even if it would not be necessary to the registration statement and prospectus to update the full registration statement.[16] Post effective amendments are frequently made by affixing stickers that contain the updated or corrected information.[17] Stickering saves the registrant the expense of reprinting the entire prospectus. There may be some instances, however, when the changes are so significant that stickering will not be sufficient.[18] Before a prospectus containing post-effective amendments can be used, ten copies of the updated prospectus must be filed with the Commission.[19]

§ 3.7[2] SEC Review Practices

The SEC does not review the merits of the registration statement and the offering. Rather, in reviewing 1933 Act registration statements, as is the case with SEC review of filings generally, the focus is on the adequacy and clarity of the disclosure. Specifically, the SEC will consider whether the applicable disclosure items are explained in sufficient detail and with sufficient clarity. In addition to the review of the adequacy of the disclosures, the SEC will examine clarity and also will conduct a "plain English" review of those portions of the registration statement that are subject to the SEC's plain English disclosure requirements.[20]

---

13. 15 U.S.C.A. § 77h(a).

14. *See* Louis Loss, Fundamentals of Securities Regulation 130–131 (1983).

15. SEC v. Manor Nursing Centers, 458 F.2d 1082 (2d Cir.1972). *See* § 2.5 *supra*.

16. SEC v. Manor Nursing Centers, 458 F.2d 1082 (2d Cir.1972).

17. *See, e.g.,* Preferred Equities Group, Inc., [1987 Transfer Binder] Fed.Sec.L.Rep. (CCH) ¶ 78,462 (SEC No Action Letter April 7, 1987) (stickering prospectus and post effective amendments to registration statement to reflect changes in the underwriting group).

18. *See* § 2.5 *supra*. In the usual case, it is not necessary to attach them to a full prospectus before filing, although a full prospectus will usually be required to be given to investors (with an exception in some employee benefit plan contexts). Sec. Act Rel. No. 33–6714 (May 27, 1987), p. 41.

The question arises as to what types of updating require a post-effective amendment as opposed to just a sticker? Most reported references treat the two as interchangeable. Materiality is the point at which one updating, whether by way of stickering or otherwise, is required. In the Matter of Blinder, Robinson & Co., Inc., 1990 WL 321585 (April 27, 1990).

19. 17 C.F.R. § 230.424(c).

20. Plain English is discussed in § 3.10[2] *infra*.

§ 3.7[3] SEC Policies on Acceleration Requests

In the event that the issuer desires an effective date prior to the expiration of twenty days after the filing of the last amendment to the registration statement, it can file with the Commission a request for an acceleration of the effective date pursuant to Rule 461.[26] The rule provides that the issuer should advise the Commission of the request for acceleration not later than the second business day before the desired effective date. The Commission has a wide range of discretion in deciding whether or not to grant the request for acceleration. There are no express statutory guidelines for acceleration and the few guides that have been prepared by the Commission are exceedingly vague. When the SEC denies a request for acceleration of the registration statement, the denial is usually based upon incomplete or inadequate disclosure.[27] The Commission in one of its seminal decisions,[28] relied on the statutory criteria that were added to the Act in 1940 and which set forth four basic but quite generalized criteria that it will consider in deciding whether or not to grant a request for acceleration:

(1) the adequacy of the information about the issuer that was available to the public before the registration,

(2) the ease with which the nature of the securities can be understood,

(3) the ease with which the relationship of the securities to the capital structure of the issuer can be understood, and,

(4) the ease with which the rights of holders of the securities can be understood.[30]

Compliance with the plain English requirements[31] is a significant factor in granting requests for acceleration of the effective date.

The lack of definite guidelines is but one of the criticisms that has led to objections to the Commission's use of acceleration.[32] As explained by the Commission, the acceleration procedure was enacted by Congress in order to give added flexibility to the SEC and at the same time reduce the harshness that otherwise resulted from a rigid twenty-day waiting period.[33]

Due to the wide latitude that the Commission allows itself for the denial of acceleration, requests for acceleration should not be made lightly. This is especially so where the registrant is concerned about the marketability of the securities being offered. News of SEC denial of an acceleration request may alert the investment community to potential problems (both real and unreal) with the securities. Except with price amendments or relatively minor amend-

26. 17 C.F.R. § 230.461.

27. *See* 17 C.F.R. § 230.460.

28. In the Matter of Universal Camera Corp., Sec. Act Rel. No. 33–3076, 19 S.E.C. 648, 658, 1945 WL 26104 , [1945–1947 Transfer Binder] Fed. Sec. L. Rep. (CCH) ¶ 75,560 (SEC 1945).

30. In the Matter of Universal Camera Corp., Sec. Act Rel. No. 33–3076, 19 S.E.C. 648, 657–58, 1945 WL 26104, [1945–1947 Transfer Binder] Fed. Sec. L. Rep. (CCH) ¶ 75,560 (SEC 1945).

31. The plain English requirements are discussed in §§ 3.8[2], 3.10[2] *infra*.

32. *See, e.g.,* Edward N. Gadsby & Ray Garrett, Jr., Acceleration Under the Securities Act of 1933—A Comment on the A.B A.'s Legislative Proposal, 13 Bus Law. 718 (1958); John Mulford, "Acceleration" Under the Securities Act of 1933—A Reply to the Securities and Exchange Commission, 14 Bus.Law. 156 (1958).

33. Universal Camera, Sec. Act Rel. No. 33–3076, 19 S.E.C. 648, 658, 1945 WL 26104 (SEC 1945).

ments which start the twenty day period running anew, because of the customary review procedures for new issuers and the more speculative ventures, acceleration may as a practical matter be limited to more established companies.

§ 3.8 Frequent Deficiencies in Registration Statements and Other Disclosures; The Plain English Requirement

§ 3.8[1] Frequent Deficiencies

Registration statement disclosures cover a wide range of topics, including the company's business generally, the terms of the offering, as well as identification and discussion of significant risk factors. Over the years there have been various common disclosure deficiencies that have come to light. Many of the deficiencies that are commonly cited in modern day offerings were identified by the SEC in its infancy.[1] The absence of clear, bright-line tests regarding these problematic disclosures has resulted in many of these deficiencies reoccurring over time.

There are a number of areas that are particularly susceptible to inadequate or misleading disclosures.[2] First, the registration statement may fail to adequately explain the issuer's prior adverse trends in sales and in income. For example, the Commission has taken the position that it is not sufficient merely to state that the issuer's income declined due to increased expenses. The 1933 Act demands, and the SEC requires, full disclosure as to precisely which expenses were increased and the reasons for their increase. Further, the issuer should explain whether such increased costs are reasonably expected to continue and, if so, whether past performance is a reasonable guide to the future. A second common deficiency in registration statements is the failure to include information concerning the relative contribution to sales and/or income of the issuer's various products, product lines, lines of business, divisions, and subsidiaries. The Commission requires identification of the sources of income and/or losses according to division and lines of business. The allocation according to lines of business does not depend upon whether or not the issuer operates its divisions on a parent-subsidiary basis. A third frequently occurring problem is the registration statement's failure to give a full, fair, and detailed description of the use of the proceeds to be raised by the offering. The Commission requires specific identification of the use of the proceeds from the offering. A fourth common disclosure problem arises out of the registration statement's treatment of transactions between the issuer and management or principal shareholders. Because of the obvious sensitivity of insider transactions, especially when there is an actual or potential conflict of interest situation, disclosure problems frequently arise. Similar disclosure problems can arise under the Exchange Act.

A fifth common deficiency in 1933 Act disclosure documents is the registrant's failure to make the prospectus readable and understandable by

§ 3.8

1. *See, e.g.,* Commonly cited Deficiencies in Financial Statements Filed Under the Securities Act of 1933 and the Securities Exchange Act of 1934, Accounting Series Rel. No. 7, 11 Fed. Reg. 10914, 1938 SEC LEXIS 1337 (SEC May 16, 1938). *See also, e.g.,* Opinion of the Director of the Division of Forms and Regulations, Sec. Act Rel. No. 33–1503, 1937 WL 29096 (SEC July 12, 1937).

2. *See* Regulation S–K. 17 C.F.R. §§ 229.10–229.802.

the general investing public. The SEC has stated its belief that these problems are exacerbated by the failure to use simple language, tables, charts, and other pictorial visual devices.[7] A sixth common deficiency is that the 1933 Act prospectus may have either an insufficient or overly verbose introductory statement. According to the Commission, an introductory statement, when required, should include identification of all of the factors that make the particular offering speculative and also of those aspects that are unique to that offering, as opposed to the industry or type of offering in general.[8] It is the SEC's position that overly verbose statements are obscure and therefore contrary to full disclosure requirements. Lack of readability can be just as harmful as a failure to disclose enough since the material information may well get lost in the issuer's verbosity, thus negating the intended impact of the cautionary introductory statement. This concern is reflected in the "buried facts" doctrine which holds that disclosures can be obscured by burying them in footnotes or appendices.[9] The SEC has pointed out, however, that a company's failure to include everything in the summary portion of a prospectus or other disclosure document will not automatically trigger the "buried facts" doctrine.[10]

A Seventh Circuit decision raises significant questions concerning the appropriate audience for registration statements.[11] Whereas the SEC has taken the position that the registration statement should be written with the ordinary investor in mind, Judge Easterbrook in Wielgos v. Commonwealth Edison Co.[12] took the position that, at least in the case of widely-followed securities, the adequacy of disclosures should be judged by the needs of sophisticated analysts. In *Wielgos,* the registrant had a sufficiently wide market following that it used registration Form S–3. The court held that disclosure should therefore be geared to the professional investors who in effect set the price for the stock. Thus, according to Judge Easterbrook:

> Descriptions in Forms 10–K and registration statements are almost useless to individual investors. They require absorption by professional traders and investors. What these professionals need is new information specific to the issuer. Telling them over and again how the NRC works or that costs are rising in the nuclear power industry, or even that Commonwealth Edison had run into trouble with its welds (which became known a few months before this stock was sold), has nothing to do with the accuracy of prices in the market. Investors who buy 500 shares of stock rely on the market price. . . . [13]

7. *See* Sec. Act Rel. No. 33–6276 (Dec. 23, 1980); Sec. Act Rel. No. 33–6235 (Sept. 2, 1980).

8. *See e.g.,* In the Matter of Universal Camera Corp., Sec. Act Rel. No. 33–3076, 19 S.E.C. 648, 1945 WL 26104 (1945); Regulation S–K, items 502–503, 17 C.F.R. §§ 229.501–502.

9. *See* Plain English Disclosure, Sec. Act Rel. No. 33–7497, 63 Fed. Reg. 6370–01, 1998 WL 44199 (F.R.) (SEC Feb. 6, 1998) ("Under the buried facts doctrine, a court would consider disclosure to be false and misleading only if its overall significance is obscured because material information is 'buried,' for example, in footnotes or appendices"). *See also, e.g.,* Gould v. American Hawaiian Steamship Company, 331 F.Supp. 981 (D.Del 1971); Kohn v. American Metal Climax, Inc., 322 F.Supp. 1331 (E.D.Pa.1970), modified, 458 F.2d 255 (3d Cir.1972).

10. Plain English Disclosure, Sec. Act Rel. No. 33–7497, 63 Fed. Reg. 6370–01, 1998 WL 44199 (F.R.) (SEC Feb. 6, 1998).

11. *See also, e.g.,* Note, Plain English: A Reappraisal of the Intended Audience of Disclosure Under the Securities Act of 1933, 72 So. Cal. L. Rev. 851 (1999).

12. 892 F.2d 509 (7th Cir.1989). *See also* the discussion in § 3.3 *supra.*

13. 892 F.2d at 518; Kapps v. Torch Offshore, Inc., 379 F.3d 207 (5th Cir. 2004) (omissions from prospectus regarding downward trend in natural gas prices was not material).

Judge Easterbrook is most certainly correct in his assertion that registration statements should not be cluttered with useless detail.[14] In fact, the SEC has long taken this position. On the other hand, Judge Easterbrook's elitist description of the market and the inefficiency of catering to the small investor ignores the basic disclosure thrust of the securities laws and portends unfortunately narrow tests of materiality.

Another disclosure problem that has emerged, both with regard to 1933 Act registration statements and to SEC filings in general, is the issuer's failure to disclose improper transactions involving domestic political activity, including campaign contributions, or foreign involvement.[15] A number of problems have also arisen in the context of the so-called "new disclosure" concerning social issues with which the issuer has a controversial relationship. Similarly, ethical investors may want to know where their invested funds are going. The courts and the Commission have dealt with these problems in the context of an expanding definition of the concept of "materiality." Since the hallmark of disclosure for both the 1933 Act registration statement and all 1934 Act filings is embodied in the concept of "materiality," the problems relating to disclosure in registration statements and other required filings are quite similar. Because the primary purpose of 1933 Act registration statements is to provide full and adequate information regarding the distribution of securities, certain types of disclosures may be more sensitive and thus of more concern with regard to public offerings than to other required filings.

§ 3.8[2] Plain English Requirements—Overview

As discussed more fully in a subsequent section of this treatise,[21] in January 1997, the SEC proposed amendments to Rule 421 to require the use of clear, concise and understandable language in prospectuses.[22] The rule proposal was part of SEC's larger initiative to require the use of "plain English" in SEC filings and reports to shareholders and investors.[23] The plain English initiative, which started out as a pilot program, is now embodied in Rule 421.[24] In a lengthy official release,[25] the Commission describes what it means by plain English and also provides several examples of appropriate disclosure styles. The plain English requirements include: use of the active rather than passive voice, short sentences, use of definite, concrete everyday words, presentation of information in tabular form or with bullet lists, the avoidance of legal jargon and highly technical business terminology, as well as

---

14. Thus, for example, it was not actionable to fail to explain in detail the elementary economic principle that increased competition could have an adverse effect on the company's profits. O'Sullivan v. Trident Microsystems, Inc., 1994 WL 124453, [1993–1994 Transfer Binder] Fed. Sec. L. Rep. (CCH) ¶ 98,116 (N.D.Cal.1994).

15. *See, e.g.,* SEC v. Jos. Schlitz Brewing Co., 452 F.Supp. 824 (E.D.Wis.1978). *But cf.* Zaluski v. United American Healthcare Corp., 527 F.3d 564 (6th Cir. 2008) (there was no duty of disclosure when at the time certain payments were made it was not reasonably likely that those payments would render a contract voidable).

21. *See* § 3.10[2] *infra.*

22. Plain English Disclosure, Sec. Act Rel. No. 33–7380, 62 Fed. Reg. 3152, 1997 WL 17695 (F.R.) (SEC Jan. 21, 1997). *See also, e.g.,* W. Randy Eaddy, Principles for Drafting Capital Formation Disclosure Documents: Planning the Assault on Lugubrious Prolixity, 32 Sec. Reg. L.J. 284 (2004). For a more detailed discussion of the plain English initiatives, *see* § 3.6 *supra.*

23. For examples of plain English, *see* § 3.10[2] *infra.*

24. 17 C.F.R. § 230.421.

25. Plain English Disclosure, Sec. Act Rel. No. 33–7497, 63 Fed. Reg. 6370–01, 1998 WL 44199 (F.R.) (SEC Feb. 6, 1998).

the avoidance of multiple negatives. The plain English requirements also call for increased white space in prospectuses in order to make the information more readable.

§ 3.9 Common Disclosure Problems—Dilution of the Public's Investment, Business Risks, Transactions With Controlling Persons, and Projections

§ 3.9[1] Overview

Because of both the potential for self-dealing and the access to inside information, transactions by the issuer's insiders frequently require detailed disclosure in the 1933 Act registration statement. The Commission shows particular concern where a significant portion of the proceeds will not be going into the issuer's business. Whenever an investment is a speculative one, the prospectus must provide the potential investor with notice and give detailed disclosures as to the reasons therefor. The prospectus must also contain an explanation of risks peculiar to the issuer or the issuer's industry.

§ 3.9[2] Dilution of the Public's Investment, Business Risks

A vintage case which, nevertheless, still accurately reflects the Commission's disclosure policy is In the Matter of Universal Camera Corp.[1] In that case, the issuer embarked upon an offering of securities that would have resulted in the rearrangement of control in an existing corporation. The issuer was to receive just under twenty percent of the aggregate offering proceeds,[2] a figure which could possibly have increased to just under forty percent upon exercise of certain warrants.[3] The registration statement that was filed came under sharp criticism in the administrative stop order proceedings initiated by the Commission. To begin with, the SEC objected that the issuer's registration statement was deficient due to an inadequate introductory statement. Although the registrant included the required legend on the first page to the effect that the investment was a speculative one, it failed to clearly "describe the speculative aspects" so as to be "plainly evident to the ordinary investor."[4] It is certain that today the Commission would require an equally explicit introductory statement explaining the speculative nature of such an investment. Under current law, any prospectus covering a speculative offering must explain why the issue is speculative by giving all pertinent details without obscuring any of the key facts or burying them in a lengthy narrative.[5]

---

§ 3.9

1. Sec. Act Rel. No. 33–3076, 19 S.E.C. 648, 1945 WL 26104 (SEC 1945).

2. The registration statement covered a public offering of 663,500 shares of class A stock, of which 530,500 shares were being sold by existing shareholders as a secondary distribution. The selling shareholders had acquired the shares covered in the secondary offering for a total of $30,000 but they were to receive $2,100,865 from reselling them through the registered offering. The remaining 133,000 Class A shares represented a primary offering by the issuer which was to receive $524,985 in net proceeds.

3. The registration statement also covered warrants which if fully exercised would cause the issuer to receive an additional $863,500.

4. 19 S.E.C. at 652.

5. *See* Regulation S–K items 502–503, 17 C.F.R. §§ 224.502–503. *See generally* 17 C.F.R. § 231.4936 (1982) (rescinded March 3, 1982). In Sec.Act Rel. No. 33–6332 (August 6, 1981) the SEC proposed to eliminate the Guides for the Preparation and Filing of Registration Statements

Perhaps the most serious disclosure problem in Universal Camera's registration statement was the failure to adequately describe the intended use of the proceeds from the offering. This was a particularly sensitive issue on the facts before the Commission since the bulk of the securities in registration represented a secondary offering and, thus, none of the proceeds from these sales was to flow to the issuer. Specifically, the Commission pointed to the registration statement's failure to explain to the investor the significance of the low percentage of proceeds the issuer was to receive and its failure to reveal that the shareholders, who were to make a huge profit on their secondary sales, would nonetheless have retained both voting control in the corporation and a forty-three percent participation in earnings by virtue of the Class B stock which they would continue to hold.[6] Thirdly, the registration statement failed to contrast plainly the offering price with the book value of the securities offered. Finally, the registration materials discussed inadequately the potential impact of the warrants and their eventual exercise.

As is discussed more fully in a subsequent section of this treatise,[7] particularly difficult disclosure problems can arise in connection with an initial public offering of a company with substantial preexisting shareholders even where those shares are not to be offered in connection with the registered offering. By virtue of Rule 144,[8] it is possible that there will be a substantial influx of these shares into the market upon the expiration of ninety days following the public offering.[9] In such a case, the 1933 Act registration statement must adequately disclose the possibility of these sales and the downward price pressure that could result.[10]

In the course of the *Universal Camera* opinion, the Commission explicitly called for plainly phrased statements as opposed to elaborate, and hence more technical, prose. This 1948 opinion marked the beginning of an SEC impetus for readable prospectuses in order to make them understandable to less sophisticated investors.[11] The Commission is not alone in this concern as courts have also recognized the necessity to use simple language.[12]

In the late 1990s, the Commission formalized these requirements in its plain English initiatives.[13] The Commission's plain English requirements include: use of the active rather than passive voice, short sentences, use of definite, concrete everyday words, presentation of information in tabular form

---

and Reports, with limited exceptions. These guides have been replaced by Regulation S–K. Sec.Act Rel. No. 33–6384 (March 3, 1982).

6. 19 S.E.C. at 653.

7. *See* § 4.25 *infra.*

8. 17 C.F.R. § 230.144. *See* § 4.26 *infra.*

9. After there has been a registered public offering, the issuer becomes subject to the 1934 Act periodic reporting requirements. Section 15(d) of the 1934 Act, 15 U.S.C.A. § 78*o*(d). *See* § 9.3 *infra.* Once this information has been available for ninety days, unregistered securities may be sold. Rule 144(e) permits, within a three month period, public sales of unregistered securities of up to the greater of one percent of the outstanding securities or the average weekly reported trading volume. Rule 144(c) contains the informational requirements.

10. Furthermore, it is conceivable that if there is a substantial volume of these unregistered secondary sales, they might be integrated into the initial offering even though they fall within Rule 144(e)'s volume limitations on sales of restricted securities and sales of securities by affiliates. The integration doctrine is discussed in § 4.29 *infra.*

11. *See generally* Regulation S–K, 17 C.F.R. §§ 229.01 *et seq.*

12. *See, e.g.,* Feit v. Leasco Data Processing Equipment Corp., 332 F.Supp. 544, 549 (E.D.N.Y. 1971).

13. *See* § 3.10[2] *infra.*

or with bullet lists, the avoidance of legal jargon and highly technical business terminology, as well as the avoidance of multiple negatives.[14]

In addition to the misstatements and omissions relating to the issuer's financial structure and the impact of the offering upon the issuer's capital structure, Universal Camera's registration statement was further woefully deficient with regard to the description of the corporation's business. In the period immediately preceding the filing of Universal Camera's registration statement, the issuer had received the bulk of its profits from government war-related contracts for the sale of binoculars. Clearly, this enterprise was not likely to continue after the war and the registration statement did not sufficiently disclose the company's pre-war activities nor its post-war plans. The registration statement simply talked in terms of "designing and preparing improved and additional photographic products which would find a ready sale" without discussing or describing in detail the nature of such products. The Commission held that this was a significant deficiency in the registration statement, especially in light of the express requirements of the registration form that was used for the filing and which called for detailed disclosure.[15] In the course of the proceedings, the issuer agreed to amend the registration statement so as to cure its deficiencies, and accordingly the SEC, in the exercise of its power to award relief in the public interest, dismissed the Commission proceedings.

Despite its age, the *Universal Camera* decision remains instructive on a number of sensitive disclosure problems. It highlights the importance of describing the specific use to be made of the proceeds, especially with regard to a secondary offering that accompanies a primary one. The opinion further stresses the necessity to use identifying statements, such as the legend required for speculative issues to alert the reader to risky aspects of the offering. Finally, the issuer must clearly disclose the nature of its business, both in terms of the past and also with regard to future plans. The registration materials must be especially descriptive where the issuer's business is cyclical or unusually dependent upon external events. Similarly, effects of costs of compliance with regulatory requirements of environmental protection laws must also be adequately disclosed.[16]

One further noteworthy aspect of the *Universal Camera* decision is the fact that, in the course of its opinion, the SEC emphasized that "it is not this Commission's function under the Securities Act to approve or disapprove securities * * *. The Act leaves it to the investor, on the basis of the facts disclosed, to weigh the earning prospects of a registered security against the risks involved and to judge for himself whether he wishes to invest his money in it."[17] This accurately sets forth the direct impact of the 1933 Act. However, the indirect effects of full disclosure cannot be ignored. Detailed disclosures may make a particular offering so unmarketable as to have the effect of precluding a public sale. This type of merit scrutiny can be achieved directly

14. Rule 421, 17 C.F.R. § 230.421.

15. 19 S.E.C. at 655.

16. *See, e.g.,* Levine v. NL Industries, Inc., 926 F.2d 199 (2d Cir.1991) (disclosure of environmental compliance costs; action under Exchange Act Rule 10b–5).

17. 19 S.E.C. at 656, 657.

under the state securities laws that permit a merit analysis of the securities in registration.[18]

§ 3.9[3] Transactions of Controlling Persons, Management Stability and Integrity, Secondary Sales

Another instructive opinion is found in the 1964 SEC decision of In the Matter of Franchard Corp.[19] The issuer was a real estate development syndication managed by Mr. Glickman, who was the principal owner and manager of the development project. The issuer undertook a series of public offerings. All prospectuses properly showed that Glickman owned most of the Class B and a major portion of the Class A stock. However, they failed to disclose that during the period of these offerings, all of his Class B and most of his Class A stock had been pledged to banks for loans totaling four and one-quarter million dollars at interest rates up to twenty-four percent. Notwithstanding the pledges, Glickman retained his voting rights in the stock. The issue before the Commission was whether these loans to the major shareholder and manager of the enterprise ought to have been disclosed. The applicable forms for filing of the registration statement expressly provide for the disclosure of all material transactions between the issuer, its affiliates, and management.[20] It was at least arguable that the pledges of stock in question were not subject to such provisions since these were not transactions between Glickman and the issuer, but rather were between Glickman and a bank that was not affiliated with the issuer.[21] However, the Commission pointed out that an investor's evaluation of management is an important part of any investment decision, especially in a business such as real estate syndication, in which the management's know-how is the primary asset of the enterprise. Thus, any facts which would be likely to indicate a possible change of management would be material to the reasonable investor.[22] The Commission concluded that disclosure of the secured loans was necessary because it would put the investor on notice that Glickman's interest in the company might be foreclosed upon, and that the corporation's management would change as a result. In the course of its opinion in *Franchard*, the Commission also highlighted the importance of adequately disclosing questionable activities by management. Questionable dealings by management can bear upon the issue of management integrity generally, which, of course, may be a valid investor concern.[23] Item 401 of Regulation S–K requires certain disclosures relating to manage-

18. *See, e.g.,* Uniform Securities Act § 304; chapter 8 *infra.*

19. Sec. Act. Rel. No. 33–4710, 42 S.E.C. 163, 1964 WL 67454 (SEC 1964).

20. *See* Schedule A item (14); Form S–1 item 17; Form S–2 item 12.

21. Glickman, who was president of the company, had also taken personal loans from the issuer and its affiliates. These loans clearly should have been disclosed as transactions with the issuer. *Id.*

22. Additionally, nondisclosure of management rifts regarding corporate policy could be material and hence actionable. Cooperman v. Individual, Inc., 171 F.3d 43, 47 (1st Cir.1999). However, where the description of the current business plan was essentially accurate, the failure to disclose management disagreement was not an actionable omission from the registration statement.

23. SEC v. Joseph Schlitz Brewing Co., 452 F.Supp. 824 (E.D.Wis.1978) (nondisclosure of commercial kickback payments was material because it related to management integrity); In the Matter of Franchard Corp., 42 S.E.C. 163, 1964 WL 67454 (SEC 1964) (nondisclosures of off-book loans to C.E.O. related to management integrity and were material). *Compare, e.g.,* Gaines v. Haughton, 645 F.2d 761 (9th Cir.1981) (drawing distinction between director breaches of trust which are presumptively material and allegations of waste of corporate assets).

ment and control persons.[24] For example, members of management and control persons must disclose certain legal proceedings which have occurred in the preceding five years and are "material to an evaluation of the ability or integrity of any director, person nominated to become a director or executive officer of the registrant."[25]

The precise limits of the *Franchard* decision's rationale are not self-evident. The decision raises questions as to the materiality of disclosures relating to the personal aspects of the lives and dealings of key personnel. It is relatively evident that Glickman's crucial position in running the enterprise made his high risk personal financial transactions material to prospective investors. On the other hand, there are many companies which are dependent upon one or a few key executives who may be undergoing changes or pressures in their personal lives that might bear upon their management ability. At what point do these factors become material? For example, must it be disclosed that a corporate chief executive officer is in ill health? Is it a material fact that a major corporate executive is under psychiatric care and potentially suicidal? Is it relevant that a corporate executive is in the midst of a harrowing divorce and suffering severe depression which might interfere with his or her management ability? Clearly, at some point such information becomes more personal to the executive than useful to the investing public. But it is equally clear that an attorney preparing a registration statement has no bright line tests regarding which aspects of a key executive's personal life will be deemed material for disclosure purposes. When an executive's personal dealings affect the issuer's business or at least present a strong potential for doing so, the materiality threshold may be reached and therefore disclosure will probably be necessary. With increasing focus on companies adopting strong codes of conduct and ethics, there are likely to be instances in which an executive's personal indiscretions can have an impact on his or her retention by the company.

There are two other decisions that deserve mention in this discussion of transactions by controlling persons. In one case,[32] the registration statement was claimed to have been materially misleading because it failed to disclose that two major shareholders intended to dispose of their holdings shortly after the public offering. These transactions amounted to twenty-five percent of the number of shares covered by the registration statement but only four percent of the total stock that was outstanding after the offering. The federal district court held that there was a triable issue of fact as to the materiality of the alleged omission and accordingly refused to dismiss the complaint. In another case,[33] the registration statement disclosed the sale of one hundred and twenty thousand shares in a private placement that had taken place two years earlier. It was further stated that those private placement purchasers had agreed not to dispose of their shares in a transaction that would constitute a public distribution unless a registration statement covering such sales had become effective. Shortly after an unrelated registered offering, these private placement purchasers sold a total of seven thousand shares without filing a registration statement and in reliance upon the exemption provided in SEC

24. 17 C.F.R. § 229.401.

25. Reg. S–K item 401(f), 17 C.F.R. § 229.401(f).

32. Birdman v. Electro–Catheter Corp., 352 F.Supp. 1271 (E.D.Pa.1973).

33. Langert v. Q–1 Corp., 1974 WL 377, [1973–1974 Transfer Binder] Fed.Sec.L.Rep. 94,445 (S.D.N.Y.1974).

Rule 144.[34] The plaintiff alleged that these sales were contrary to the disclosures in the registration statement, and, since they had been intended all along, rendered the registration statement materially misleading. The plaintiff further claimed that although the unregistered sales may have been in compliance with Rule 144, they depressed the market price of the plaintiff's stock that had been purchased during the primary offering and thus that failure to have described this predictable impact was a material omission. The court, agreeing with the plaintiff, held that the registration statement was misleading in failing to adequately describe Rule 144 and its exemption from the registration requirements of section 5. A fair description of the effects under Rule 144 would have put the investor on notice of the possibility of insider sales that would not need to be registered and might also have an adverse effect on the market price.

The foregoing cases are illustrative of sensitive disclosure problems that may arise in connection with a registered offering. Counsel must be particularly mindful of these problems in making the pre-filing investigation into the issuer and the circumstances surrounding the offering.

§ 3.9[4] Projections and Soft Information

At one time, the SEC objected to the use of favorable projections and other "soft" information in disclosure documents on the grounds that investors would likely be misled.[39] This policy of discouraging projections came under much criticism from many constituencies.[40] It was contended, among other things, that projections by management can provide useful information to the investing public. In response to the criticism of its former policy, the Commission reconsidered its approach to soft information[41] and now not only permits but in fact encourages,[42] and in some cases mandates, the use of non-misleading projections by certain issuers.

SEC Rule 175[44] (applicable to 1933 Act disclosures) and Rule 3b–6[45] (applicable to 1934 Act disclosures) provide a safe harbor for projections by 1934 Act reporting companies[46] and for similar disclosures made in the 1933 Act registration statements. These rules, which now have their counterpart in the statutes themselves,[48] provide that there is no liability for "forward-looking statements" unless the issuer made or reaffirmed such a statement without a reasonable basis or unless the disclosure was not made in good faith.[50] Thus, a good faith statement of present intent does not become

34. 17 C.F.R. § 230.144. *See* § 4.29 *infra.*

39. *See* Carl W. Schneider, Nits, Grits, and Soft Information in SEC Filings, 121 U.Pa.L.Rev. 254 (1972). *Cf.* Goldman v. Belden, 580 F.Supp. 1373 (W.D.N.Y.1984), *judgment vacated* 754 F.2d 1059 (2d Cir.1985) ("faulty economic prognostication" did not violate antifraud provisions).

40. *E.g.*, Bruce A. Mann, Prospectuses: Unreadable or Just Unread?—A Proposal to Reexamine Policies Against Permitting Projections, 40 Geo.Wash.L.Rev. 222 (1971).

41. *See* Sec.Act Rel. No. 33–5992 (Nov. 7, 1978; rescinded in Sec.Act Rel. No. 33–6384 (March 3, 1982)). (Guides for disclosure of future economic performance). *See also* Note, Disclosure of Future–Oriented Information Under Securities Laws, 88 Yale L.J. 338 (1978).

42. *See, e.g.,* Instruction 7 to Regulation S–K Item 303(a) which provides that "forward-looking information" is "encouraged, but not required." 17 C.F.R. § 229.303(a), Instruction 7.

44. 17 C.F.R. § 230.175.

45. 17 C.F.R. § 240.3b–6.

46. *See* 15 U.S.C.A. §§ 78g, 78m(a), 78*o*(d) which are discussed in §§ 9.2, 9.3 *infra.*

48. 933 Act § 27A, 1934 Act § 21E, 15 U.S.C.A. §§ 77z–2, 78u–5. *See* § 3.9[5] *infra.*

50. 17 C.F.R. § 230.175(a).

actionable simply because of a change of intent;[51] however, the change of intent which makes the previous statement no longer accurate will give rise to an obligation to give timely notice of that change by making a corrective disclosure.[52] While a good faith statement of intent will not be actionable, a statement made without any reasonable basis may be.[53]

The fact that a projection turns out not to be realized does not, standing alone, give rise to a cause of action under the securities laws. The complaint must therefore be based on something more than the fact that the projections did not come to fruition. Projections by their very nature may or may not prove to be accurate.[56] Therefore, the issue is not whether a projection turns out not to come to fruition. The critical question is whether the projection was fraudulent when made. There must be some material misstatement or omission from the projection. As discussed below, adequate cautionary language can prevent a projection from being fraudulent.[60]

Many courts have indicated that they will tolerate a certain amount of sales puffery to the extent that reliance on such statements would not be reasonable.[62] However, nondisclosure that in the past there had been a repeated failure to meet projected performance may be actionable.[63] Similarly, a projection that is inconsistent with undisclosed facts will be actionable.[64] However, when the forecast is consistent with past performance, no action will lie.[65] Nor will a projection turn out to be actionable when the alleged undisclosed facts are not material.[66]

Overly optimistic projections can, of course, form the basis of a private civil action by purchasers injured by materially misleading statements. Similarly, forward-looking statements which fail to include projected losses may be materially misleading.[68] However, following the rules established under the common law of fraud, a mere projection, forecast, or prediction of future events is not actionable.[71] Nevertheless, when the incorrect prediction implies

51. In re Phillips Petroleum Securities Litigation, 881 F.2d 1236, 1245 (3d Cir.1989), *on remand* 738 F.Supp. 825 (D.Del.1990).

52. In re Phillips Petroleum Securities Litigation, 881 F.2d 1236, 1245 (3d Cir.1989).

53. Snap–On Inc. v. Ortiz, 1999 WL 592194, [1999–2000 Transfer Binder] Fed. Sec. L. Rep. (CCH) ¶ 90,633 (N.D. Ill. 1999) (corporate officer's statement that he intended to remain with company would be actionable if made without reasonable basis).

56. *See, e.g.,* In re VeriFone Securities Litigation, 11 F.3d 865 871 (9th Cir.1993); Wielgos v. Commonwealth Edison Co., 892 F.2d 509 (7th Cir.1989).

60. *See, e.g.,* In re N2K Inc. Securities Litigation, 202 F.3d 81 (2d Cir.2000) (sufficient cautionary language that financial performance might fall below analysts' expectations).

62. *E.g.,* In re Advanta Corp. Securities Litigation, 180 F.3d 525, 538–539 (3d Cir.1999) (optimistic statements about the future were "mere puffery").

63. *See* Schwartz v. Michaels, 1992 WL 382394, [1992–1993 Transfer Binder] Fed.Sec.L.Rep. (CCH) ¶ 97,259 (S.D.N.Y.1992).

64. *E.g.,* Malone v. Microdyne Corp., 26 F.3d 471 (4th Cir.1994).

65. *E.g.,* Bentley v. Legent Corp., 849 F.Supp. 429 (E.D.Va.1994) (statements that operations were "on plan" or "on target" were not actionable).

66. *E.g.,* Marion Merrell Dow Inc., 1994 WL 396187, [1994–1995 Transfer Binder] Fed. Sec. L. Rep. (CCH) ¶ 98,357 (W.D.Mo.1994) (undisclosed facts relating to currency fluctuations, increased competition, and government regulation were in the public domain and were not the type of firm-specific information that need be disclosed in connection with growth projections).

68. C.E. Carlson, Inc. v. SEC, 859 F.2d 1429 (10th Cir.1988) (affirming denial of summary judgment for defendant).

71. *E.g.,* Hillson Partners L.P. v. Adage, Inc., 42 F.3d 204 (4th Cir.1994) (Chief executive officer's statements in press release that the year would produce "excellent" results were merely predictions and thus not actionable misrepresentations of fact).

the presence of facts which do not exist, then an action will lie for misrepresentation.[72] The materiality of contingent events is judged in light of the magnitude of the event and its probability.[73] Possibilities that are extremely contingent or speculative are not material.[74]

Absent a specific line item disclosure requirement or the impetus of the Management's Discussion and Analysis,[75] there is no requirement that management make projections or predictions.[76] The fact that management has made internal projections and even has made confidential projections to entities outside the corporation does not in itself trigger a duty of public disclosure.[77] A company thus is not subject to a public disclosure requirement simply because it has made some private projections. The court went on to point out that the nondisclosure to the public of projections might have been actionable had the projections been "based upon existing negative factors that were known only to the company."[79] A fiduciary duty based on state law may create a duty to disclose internal projections but only if they can be deemed material.[80]

§ 3.9[5] Statutory Safe Harbor for Forward–Looking Statements

Section 27A of the 1933 Act,[81] which was part of the Private Securities Litigation Reform Act of 1995, provides a safe harbor for forward-looking statements and protects issuers from private litigation based on good faith projections.[82] As described in a number of decisions, "[i]n order to be eligible for safe harbor, the forward-looking statements must either (1) be identified as forward-looking and be accompanied by meaningful cautionary language; (2) be immaterial; or (3) not be made with actual knowledge that the statement was false or misleading."[83] Once established, the statutory safe harbor will protect the defendant from liability in a private suit. However, to ensure protection from SEC actions, an issuer must satisfy the safe harbor

72. *E.g.* Rodney v. KPMG Peat Marwick, 143 F.3d 1140 (8th Cir.1998) (question of fact whether prospectus for mortgage-related securities fund contained material misrepresentations of risk).

73. *E.g.*, Basic Inc. v. Levinson, 485 U.S. 224, 238, 108 S.Ct. 978, 987, 99 L.Ed.2d 194 (1988); United States v. Mylett, 97 F.3d 663, 667 (2d Cir.1996). See § 12.9 *infra.*

74. Klein v. General Nutrition Cos., 186 F.3d 338 (3d Cir.1999).

75. Item 303 of Regulation S–K requires management to give certain projections with regard to known material adverse or favorable trends in operations and financial condition. *See, e.g.*, Mark S. Croft, MD & A: The Tightrope of Disclosure, 45 S.C. L. Rev. 477 (1994).

76. *See, e.g.,* Proxima Corp. Securities Litigation, 1994 WL 374306, [1993–1994 Transfer Binder] Fed. Sec. L. Rep. (CCH) ¶ 98,236 (S.D.Cal.1994).

77. Levit v. Lyondell Petrochemical Co., 984 F.2d 1050 (9th Cir.1993); Glassman v. Computervision Corp., 90 F.3d 617 (1st Cir.1996) (fact that quarter's results lagged behind internal projections did not trigger a duty of disclosure).

79. 984 F.2d at 1053.

80. Walter v. Holiday Inns, Inc., 985 F.2d 1232 (3d Cir.1993) (partnership's failure to make internal projections known was not a breach of fiduciary duty since the projections were not actionable).

81. 15 U.S.C.A. § 77z–2. A parallel section was added to the 1934 Act. 15 U.S.C.A. § 78u–5(c).

82. *See, e.g.,* Helwig v. Vencor, Inc., 251 F.3d 540 (6th Cir.2001) (statements regarding effect of federal Balanced Budget Act on company's financial prospects were subject to but not protected by the statutory safe harbor for forward-looking statements, since there were insufficient cautionary statements).

83. In re Sun Healthcare Group Securities Litigation, 181 F.Supp.2d 1283, 1288 (D.N.M.2002) (decided under the 1934 Act counterpart).

requirements for soft information set forth in 1933 Act Rule 175.[84] The section 27A safe harbor allows corporate management to disclose forward-looking information and projections to investors while retaining protection under the safe harbor. Section 27A applies to 1934 Act reporting companies, persons acting on behalf of such companies, outside reviewers retained by such companies, and underwriters deriving or obtaining forward-looking information from such companies. Additionally, the statute explicitly does not impose a duty to update forward-looking statements. The statutory safe harbor applies only to forward-looking statements. It is not always easy to distinguish forward-looking statements that will get the protection of the safe harbor from statements of fact that will not.

Section 27A(b) sets out exclusions for which the safe harbor provided under subsection (c) will not apply. An issuer may not utilize the 27A safe harbor if it has been convicted of any felony or misdemeanor or has been the subject of a judicial or administrative decree involving a violation of the securities laws. Furthermore, Section 27A(b) may not be relied upon if the forward-looking statement has been made in connection with (1) a blank check offering, (2) an offering of penny stock, (3) a roll-up transaction, or (4) a going private transaction. Additionally, the statutory safe harbor does not apply to forward-looking statements contained in financial statements prepared in accordance with generally accepted accounting principles, investment company registration statements, tender offers, initial public offerings, offerings relating to partnerships or limited liability companies, and disclosures in beneficial ownership reports filed pursuant to section 13(d) of the 1934 Act.

In order to comply with the safe harbor, an issuer must satisfy at least one of its two prongs. Under the first prong, an issuer must identify all written or oral forward-looking statements as forward-looking and provide "meaningful cautionary statements" that identify important factors that could cause actual results to differ materially from those in the forward-looking statement. This prong of the safe harbor incorporates the judicially created "bespeaks caution" doctrine[91] and elements of Rule 175. Boilerplate language will not satisfy the requirement of "meaningful cautionary" language; instead, substantive information about the factors that could affect the reliability of the forward-looking statement must be provided.[93] Issuers seeking to invoke the section 27A safe harbor must identify important factors in the statements that could materially affect the projection. This does not mean an issuer must identify all factors or that if an issuer fails to identify the factor which ultimately changes the forward-looking projection, it will fall outside the safe harbor. The use of the language "meaningful" and "important factors" in section 27A is meant to provide a standard for courts in deciding what constitutes a cautionary statement. However, on appropriate facts, courts may continue to find that a forward-looking statement is immaterial and therefore, not actionable under the 1933 and 1934 Acts.

The second prong of the safe harbor provision requires a plaintiff in a private action to establish that the individual or business entity made the forward-looking statement with actual knowledge that it was false or misleading. This requirement focuses on the state of mind of the person or entity

84. 17 C.F.R. § 230.175.

91. *See* the discussion *infra. Cf.*, Erin M. Hardtke, Comment, What's Wrong With the Safe Harbor for Forward–Looking Statements? A Call to the Securities and Exchange Commission to Reconsider Codification of the Bespeaks Caution Doctrine, 81 Marq. L. Rev. 133 (1997).

93. H.R. Conf. Rep. No. 104–369, 104th Cong., 1st Sess. at 43 (1995).

making the projection rather than the content of the cautionary statements. The essence of this prong is that the intent of the speaker is more important than the misleading impact of the statement on the plaintiff. Even if the plaintiff can establish the requisite intent, his or her claim will fail if the bespeaks caution doctrine has been properly satisfied. This is so because the language of the statute also indicates that even if a statement is identified as knowingly false under the second prong of the safe harbor test, if it satisfies the first prong the forward-looking statement, it will nevertheless remain not actionable.

§ 3.9[6] The Bespeaks Caution Doctrine

As discussed above, the essence of liability for materially misleading projections is not that the prediction did not prove accurate but rather that the investor has been misled as to the reliability of the projections.[99] Thus, it is beyond question that under appropriate circumstances, warnings and disclaimers can limit investors' ability to reasonably rely on projections of future earnings.[100] A number of courts have adopted what is sometimes referred to as the "bespeaks caution" doctrine.[101] In 1995, Congress codified the bespeaks caution doctrine,[102] holds that sufficient cautionary language may preclude misstatements from being actionable. The doctrine relates to materiality since it addresses the question of whether the misstatements are materially misleading when judged in light of the total mix of information available to the investor.[104] The bespeaks caution doctrine, which applies both to material misstatements and omissions in connection with projections and predictions,[105] should not be applied too quickly.[106] Properly viewed, the bespeaks caution doctrine applies only to projections, predictions, and other "soft information"; it will not be applicable to negate material misstatements of present or historical facts.[107] Thus, a defendant must first establish that the alleged misstatement is, in fact, forward-looking. Even with regard to projections and predictions, cautionary language will not always be adequate to prevent an antifraud claim, especially if it is generalized and boiler-plate.[109] Nor should the doctrine be applied if the falsity of the statements was known to the defendants at the time of the cautionary warnings. In order for the

99. *See, e.g.,* In re Infonet Services Corp. Securities Litigation, 310 F.Supp.2d 1080, 1103 (C.D. Cal. 2003) (citing this treatise).

100. Harris v. Ivax Corp., 182 F.3d 799 (11th Cir.1999) (projections of future losses were protected by safe harbor and cautionary language).

101. For a discussion of the evolution of the doctrine, *see* In re Donald J. Trump Casino Securities Litigation, 793 F.Supp. 543 (D.N.J.1992), *affirmed* 7 F.3d 357 (3d Cir.1993).

102. 1933 Act § 27A(c)(2), 15 U.S.C.A. § 77z–2(c)(2); 1934 Act § 21E(c)(2), 15 U.S.C.A. § 78u–5(c)(2). *See* §§ 7.17, 12.15 *infra*.

104. *See, e.g.,* Asher v. Baxter International, Inc., 377 F.3d 727 (7th Cir. 2004) (discovery was necessary to determine if bespeaks caution doctrine applied).

105. *See, e.g.,* In re Donald J. Trump Casino Securities Litigation, 7 F.3d 357, 371 (3d Cir.1993).

106. *See, e.g.,* In re ValueVision International Inc. Securities Litigation, 896 F.Supp. 434, 443 (E.D.Pa.1995) ("in order to conclude that cautionary statements render the misrepresentations and omissions immaterial, a defendant must prove that the cautionary statements 'discredit the other one so obviously that the risk of deception drops to nil' "), quoting Virginia Bankshares, Inc. v. Sandberg, 501 U.S. 1083, 1097, 111 S.Ct. 2749, 2760, 115 L.Ed.2d 929 (1991).

107. Shaw v. Digital Equipment Corp., 82 F.3d 1194 (1st Cir.1996) (bespeaks caution doctrine would not apply if statements referred to present facts rather than the future).

109. Gray v. First Winthrop Corp., 82 F.3d 877 (9th Cir.1996) (cautionary language was not sufficiently specific to invoke bespeaks caution doctrine).

bespeaks caution doctrine to justify the dismissal of fraud claims, the cautionary language must be sufficient to negate any reasonable reliance on predictions that may appear optimistic. The bespeaks caution doctrine may not be invoked when the warnings are given while the speaker is in possession of nonpublic facts inconsistent with the projections being made. In such a case, the cautionary language itself may be a materially misleading statement.[113]

§ 3.9[7] Management's Discussion and Analysis

In addition to these voluntary projections, an issuer must disclose in the registration statement material changes in financial condition and operations that are expected to take place as a result of the financing to be raised by the offering covered by the 1933 Act registration.[131] Similarly, soft information relating to asset valuations may be mandated material disclosures under the Securities Exchange Act of 1934. Even more striking is the soft information required by item 303 of Regulation S–K in the course of its Management's Discussion and Analysis (MD & A) of financial condition and report of operations, requiring management to disclose and discuss both adverse and favorable trends and uncertainties. The MD & A disclosures focus not only on current operations but also on management's plans for the future. Among other things, Item 303(a) requires management to discuss "any known trends or uncertainties that have had or that the registrant reasonably expects will have a material favorable or unfavorable impact on net sales or revenues or income from continuing operations."[134] The obligation extends to trends and uncertainties that are "*known*" and it thus is not sufficient that they were simply "knowable"[135] or merely possibility.[136]

The purpose of the MD & A disclosures is to provide one portion of the prospectus or other disclosure document that is devoted to a narrative analysis of the company's financial condition.[137] Most of the discussion and disclosures in a registration statement are limited to historical facts. Factual disclosures alone cannot provide a basis for forecasting the future.[138] The MD & A disclosures are designed to give investors a better basis for assessing the future prospects of the company in making their decision to invest in the securities covered by the registration statement.

Although item 303 requires disclosure of "known trends or uncertainties," it does not alter the basic rule that projections are not required.[140] Thus,

---

113. Voit v. Wonderware Corp., 977 F.Supp. 363 (E.D.Pa.1997).

131. Regulation S–K, item 303, 17 C.F.R. § 229.303.

134. Reg. S–K Item 303(a)(3)(ii), 17 C.F.R. § 229.303(a)(3)(ii)

135. *See* J & R Marketing, SEP v. General Motors Corp., 519 F.3d 552, 558–559 (6th Cir. 2008) (failure to establish that information was in fact known as opposed to knowable).

136. *See, e.g.,* Panther Partners, Inc. v. Ikanos Communications, Inc., 538 F.Supp.2d 662 (S.D.N.Y. 2008) (registration statement was not deficient in failing to disclose possibility that the company might acquire non-saleable inventory as part of a planned acquisition).

137. *See* Management's Discussion and Analysis of Financial Condition and Results of Operations, Sec. Act Rel. No. 33–6835, 1989 WL 258977 (SEC May 18, 1989) ("The MD & A requirements are intended to provide, in one section of a filing, material historical and prospective textual disclosure enabling investors and other users to assess the financial condition and results of operations of the registrant, with particular emphasis on the registrant's prospects for the future").

138. *See, e.g.* In re Convergent Technologies Securities Litigation, 948 F.2d 507, 512–514 (9th Cir.1991).

140. Instruction 7 to Regulation S–K Item 303(a) which provides that "forward-looking information" is "encouraged, but not required." 17 C.F.R. '229.303(a), Instruction 7.

a failure to make a projection is not actionable unless there is a nondisclosure of facts or known trends that were "known only to the company."[141] Similarly, in contrast to the MD & A mandate that management make timely disclosure of known trends, it is clear that standing alone there is no duty to disclose internal projections of future performance.[142] On the other hand, disclosure would be required if the internal projections were sufficiently convincing to rise to the level of a trend. It was a violation of Item 303 to fail to disclose that for over a year the company had been considering a write down of good will to reflect significant losses in that segment of its business.[143]

Failure to disclose uncertainties resulting from volatile economic and political conditions can also violate the MD & A disclosure mandate.[146] Failure to discuss a known trend of decreasing sales will violate the MD & A requirements.[147] Similarly, it was a violation to fail to discuss the impact that a trend of decreasing sales would have on net sales, revenues, and earnings.[148] Trends that are likely to lead to a liquidity crisis also must be discussed.[151]

MD & A disclosures require management to disclose their current evaluation of trends and uncertainties, but they do not require management to foresee the future. The adequacy of the disclosures should not be judged by hindsight. Accordingly, a failure to foresee a slow down and disclose it as a trend in the MD & A was held not actionable.[155] However, a failure to discuss the impact of a production delay that the company was experiencing did violate MD & A.[156] Also, a failure to discuss the impact of accounting practices can violate the MD & A requirements.[157]

§ 3.9[8] Duties to Correct and Update

As discussed in a later section of this treatise,[171] there is no duty to disclose material information absent a line-item disclosure requirement.[172] However, once the issuer has made a statement on a topic, there is likely to be a duty to update or correct the information should it become stale or

141. Levit v. Lyondell Petrochemical Co., 984 F.2d 1050, 1053 (9th Cir.1993), relying in part on In re Convergent Technologies Securities Litigation, 948 F.2d 507, 516 (9th Cir.1991).

142. In re VeriFone Securities Litigation, 11 F.3d 865 (9th Cir.1993).

143. In re Sony Corp. & Sumio Sano, Administrative Proceeding File No. 3–9666, Sec. Exch. Act Rel. No. 34–40305, 67 S.E.C. Docket 1609, Release No. AE–10, 1998 WL 439898 (SEC Aug. 5, 1998) (also pointing to the failure to adequately attribute losses to one segment of corporation's business).

146. In re Caterpillar, Inc. Exch. Act Rel. No. 34–30532, 6 Fed.Sec.L.Rep. (CCH) ¶ 73,829 (SEC March 31, 1992) (settlement order).

147. Shared Medical Systems, Inc., Administrative Proceeding File No. 3–8295, Sec. Exch. Act Rel. No. 34–33632, 56 S.E.C. Docket 199, 1994 WL 49960 (SEC Feb. 17, 1994).

148. *See, e.g.,* Shared Medical Systems, Inc., Administrative Proceeding File No. 3–8295, Sec. Exch. Act Rel. No. 34–33632, 56 S.E.C. Docket 199, 1994 WL 49960 (SEC Feb. 17, 1994).

151. In re America West Airlines, Inc., Administrative Proceeding File No. 3–8361, Sec. Exch. Act Rel. No. 34–34047, 56 S.E.C. Docket 1787, Release No. AE–562, 1994 WL 183412 (SEC May 12, 1994) (decrease in passenger revenue combined with increased fuel costs created likelihood of liquidity crunch).

155. Steckman v. Hart Brewing, Inc., 143 F.3d 1293 (9th Cir.1998).

156. In re Presstek, Inc., Administrative Proceeding File No. 3–9515, Sec. Exch. Act Rel. No. 34–39472, 66 S.E.C. Docket 328, Release No. AE–997, 1997 WL 784548 (SEC Dec. 15, 1997).

157. *See, e.g.,* In re Skaff, Administrative Proceeding File No. 3–9877, Sec. Exch. Act Rel. No. 34–41312, 69 S.E.C. Docket 1399, Release No. AE–112, 1999 WL 228423 (SEC April 20, 1999).

171. *See* § 12.19 *infra.*

172. *E.g.,* Gallagher v. Abbott Laboratories, 269 F.3d 806 (7th Cir.2001).

inaccurate. Accordingly, once a company has made statements of fact, there is a duty to correct if it is later determined that the information was in fact materially inaccurate. The issue is more difficult with regard to earnings (or other) projections and when the issuer has an obligation to make corrective disclosures when it becomes evident that the projections are inadequate. The proper distinction is between correction of inaccurate factual statements—where there is a duty to correct and situations where the projections simply turn out not to come to pass. Since projections are by their nature likely not to be completely predictive of the future, the trend is to find no duty to update a projection that was proper at the time simply because as time progresses, the projection appears more likely to prove inaccurate.

§ 3.10 Presentation of Disclosure; Plain English

Regulation S–K provides detailed guidance for compliance with the line-item disclosure that is required by the various forms and schedules that have to be filed with the SEC under both the Securities Act of 1933 and the Securities Exchange Act of 1934.[1] However, those disclosure guides do not directly address drafting issues and writing style. Over the years, the Commission has been concerned with the readability of prospectuses and other disclosures.[2] It is important that disclosure filings explain rather than obscure the pertinent issues. The discussion that follows examines issues of readability and the SEC's plain English requirements.

As pointed out in an earlier section of this treatise,[19] in January 1997, the SEC proposed various amendments to require the use of clear, concise and understandable language in prospectuses.[20] The proposal was part of the SEC's larger initiative to require the use of "plain English" in SEC filings and reports to shareholders and investors. The purpose of the plain English disclosures is to make it easy for the ordinary investor to understand the disclosures.

The plain English initiative, which evolved from a pilot program into a permanent one, involves amendments to various provisions of Regulation S–K. In a lengthy and helpful official release,[22] the Commission describes what it means by plain English and also provides several examples of appropriate disclosure styles.[23]

The SEC implemented its plain English initiative and now requires that in drafting disclosure documents, registrants should be aware of the readership of the disclosures and, of course, should also familiarize themselves with

§ 3.10

1. Regulation S–K (17 C.F.R. §§ 229.10 *et seq.*) are discussed in § 3.4[4][A] *supra* and § 9.4 *infra*.

2. *See, e.g.*, Report to the SEC on Disclosure to Investors ("The Wheat Report") 54 (1969). *See also, e.g.*, Milton Cohen, "Truth in Securities" Revisited, 79 Harv. L. Rev. 1340, 1351–1352 (1966); Robert Knauss, A Reappraisal of the Role of Disclosure, 62 Mich. L. Re. 607 (1964).

19. *See* § 3.8[2] *supra*.

20. Plain English Disclosure, Sec. Act Rel. No. 33–7380, 62 Fed. Reg. 3152, 1997 WL 17695 (F.R.) (SEC Jan. 27, 1997). *See also, e.g.*, Note, Eschew Obfuscation—The Merits of the SEC's Plain English Doctrine, 31 U. Mem. L. Rev. 135 (2000); Note, Plain English: A Reappraisal of the Intended Audience of Disclosure Under the Securities Act of 1933, 72 So. Cal. L. Rev. 851 (1999).

22. Plain English Disclosure, Sec. Act Rel. No. 33–7497, 63 Fed. Reg. 6370–01, 1998 WL 44199 (F.R.) (SEC Feb. 6, 1998).

23. Plain English Disclosure, Sec. Act Rel. No. 33–7497, 63 Fed. Reg. 6370–01, 1998 WL 44199 (F.R.) (SEC Feb. 6, 1998).

the substantive requirements that determine which information needs to be disclosed. In preparing the disclosures, registrants should employ "clear writing techniques" in order provide for more effective communication of the information subject to disclosure. The Commission further explains what it means by plain English. Disclosures should be made in the active rather than passive voice. Drafters of disclosure documents should use short sentences using definite, concrete, everyday language. Drafters of disclosure documents can make the disclosures more readable by using tabular presentations and bullet lists where appropriate. The plain English release cautions against the use of legal jargon and highly technical business terminology. Finally, the SEC encourages the avoidance of multiple negatives. In addition to the foregoing stylistic lessons, the plain English release emphasizes that registrants should design and organize their disclosure documents so they are "easy and inviting to read." The plain English guidelines thus call for the increased use of white space in order to make the prospectus more readable. The Commission showed its commitment to the plain English program by following it in its own rulemaking, most notably with its revisions to the shareholder proposal rule.[24]

§ 3.11 Delayed and Continuous Offerings—Shelf Registrations

It is generally contemplated that the entire allotment of securities covered by a registered offering will be made available for purchase on the effective date. This is not always the case, however. For example, insiders, promoters or underwriters might receive securities directly from the issuer with an intent to resell at a later date.[1] Delayed offerings may also arise in connection with corporate acquisitions. Also, in light of fluctuating interest rates, it may be desirable to get a debt offering all ready to go by filing the applicable registration statement, but then wait for a propitious moment to finalize it and offer the securities for sale. These and other delayed offerings have led to what has been known for a long time as shelf registration. In a shelf registration the registration statement is filed but the securities are put on the shelf until the manner and date of the offering are determined.

For a long while, the SEC took a dim view of shelf registrations, primarily because of the potential for misleading the investing public. Section 6(a) of the 1933 Act provides that a registration statement's effectiveness is limited to securities to be offered.[4] The Commission formerly adhered to the position that "it is misleading to include in a registration statement 'more securities than are presently intended to be offered, and thus give securities offered at some remote future date at least the appearance of a registered status.' "[5] Furthermore, there was concern that permitting delayed offerings would conflict with the thrust of the Securities Act; it, thus, had been observed that "[t]he fact that the time and manner of distribution is not presently deter-

24. Rule 14a–8, 17 C.F.R. § 14a–8(c). *See* Peter J. Romeo & Richard J. Parrino, The New Shareholder Proposal Rules, 31 Rev. Sec. & Commodities Reg. 203 (1998). *See* § 10.8 *infra.*

§ 3.11

1. *See generally* Symposium, Current Problems of Securities Underwriters and Dealers, 18 Bus.Law. 27, 44–55 (1962).

4. 15 U.S.C.A. § 77f(a) ("A registration statement shall be deemed effective only as to the securities specified therein as proposed to be offered.").

5. Shawnee Chiles Syndicate, 10 S.E.C. 109, 113 (SEC 1941).

minable clashes with the theory that the registration statement must speak as of the date of its effectiveness."[6]

Over time, much of the weight behind the foregoing objections has yielded to market realities coming from various constituents of the financial community; there was an increased call for the additional flexibility in financing that would result from allowing more shelf registrations. One reason that has been advanced is that shelf registrations will promote more competitive rates among underwriters, as shelf registrations give issuers more negotiating room.[7] The SEC has now embraced shelf registration to such an extent that there is now automatic shelf registration for companies that use Form S–3 to register the offering.

As part of its public offering reform in 2005,[14] the SEC eased its shelf offering rule as generally applied and also adopted a system of automatic shelf registration for well-known seasoned issuers (WKSIs).

With respect to shelf registrations generally, the revised shelf registration rule expanded from two years to three years the time horizon for the aggregate amount of securities anticipated to be offered and thus to be put on the shelf. Restriction on "at market" offerings were also eliminated. The revisions codified and clarified the information to be included (as well as that to be excluded) from the base shelf registration statement; the rule also specifies the manner of including information in the registration statement. In addition the revised rule permits immediate takedowns of securities and also allows prospectus supplements (rather than the former requirement of post-effective amendments) for material changes in the plan of distribution that was described in the base prospectus.

The revised shelf registration rule is even more permissive for WKSIs. "Automatic shelf registration" means that when a WKSI files a shelf registration, it's effectiveness is automatic. There is a pay-as-you-go structure for registration fees. WKSIs are allowed to file skeletal base registration statements and add the details later. For example, after the effective date, WKSIs can add to their shelf registrations both additional classes of securities and eligible majority-owned subsidiaries. WKSIs do not have to specify the amount of securities to be offered pursuant to the shelf registration. Furthermore, WKSIs are allowed to omit from the shelf registration more information than is allowed for other issuers. For example, WKSIs may omit whether it is a primary or secondary offering. A description of the securities (other than identification of the class of securities) may be omitted as may the names of any selling shareholders and disclosures regarding the plan of distribution. All of this information is then to be disclosed in the prospectus supplement when the securities are to actually be taken off the shelf.

---

6. Richard W. Jennings & Harold Marsh, Jr., Securities Regulation: Cases and Materials 390 (5th ed. 1982).

7. For a detailed discussion of the pros and cons, *see* Sec. Act Rel. No. 33–6423 (Sept. 2, 1982).

14. Securities Offering Reform, Sec. Act Rel. No. 33–8591, Sec. Exch. Act Rel. No. 34–52056, Inv. Co. Act Rel. No. IC–26993 70 Fed. Reg. 44722–01, 2005 WL 1692642 (SEC July 19, 2005).

Chapter 4

EXEMPTIONS FROM 1933 ACT REGISTRATION

Table of Sections

---

§ 4.1 Securities and Transactions Exempt From the 1933 Act's Registration Requirements—Sections 3 and 4 of the 1933 Act

§ 4.1[1] Overview of Exemptions

One way of summarizing the interrelationship of the 1933 Act's registration requirements and exemptions is that an offering of securities is either registered, exempt or illegal.[1] As discussed in an earlier section of this treatise,[2] section 5 of the 1933 Act, which contains that Act's basic prohibition against offers and sales without registration, explicitly applies on its face to all offers and all sales of *any* security.[3] This broadly drafted prohibition thus is presumptively applicable to every securities transaction taking place in the United States. However, most transactions that take place on a daily basis are not subject to section 5's prohibitions and the accompanying 1933 Act's registration requirements. This is because the Act provides a number of exemptions from the operation of section 5 and, hence, from the 1933 Act's registration requirements. These exemptions from 1933 Act registration in turn provide a mechanism for rebutting the presumption that registration is necessary before any person offers or sells a security.

A starting point when considering exemptions from registration is to look at the statutory language and the above-mentioned presumption that an offer or sale of a security will implicate the provisions of section 5. As discussed more fully below, this means that in order for a transaction to be exempt, the burden of establishing the exemption falls on the person offering or selling securities without complying with the 1933 Act's registration and prospectus delivery requirements.[4] It is imperative to keep in mind that, for the most part, the 1933 Act exemptions provide only an exemption from the Act's registration requirements and thus do not affect the Act's antifraud provisions.[5]

The Securities Act of 1933 provides three statutory bases for exemption from the Act's registration provisions. Section 3 of the 1933 Act lists various categories of securities that are exempt from registration.[6] Section 4 of the act describes a variety of transactions that qualify for an exemption from registration.[7] Section 28 of the Act gives the SEC broad exemptive rulemaking power beyond that granted by the statutory exemptions that are found in sections 3

---

§ 4.1

1. Comments of Martin P. Dunn at Fundamentals of Securities Law (ALI–ABA, Savannah Ga. June 12, 2008).

2. *See* § 2.2 *supra*.

3. 15 U.S.C.A. § 77e.

4. *See, e.g.*, SEC v. Cavanagh, 445 F.3d 105, 111 (2d Cir. 2006) ("Once a prima facie case has been made, the defendant bears the burden of proving the applicability of an exemption"), relying on SEC v. Ralston Purina Co., 346 U.S. 119, 126, 73 S.Ct. 981, 97 L.Ed. 1494 (1953).

5. Ontario Public Service Employees Union Pension Trust Funds v. Nortel Networks Corp., 369 F.3d 27 (2d Cir. 2004) (citing this treatise).

6. 15 U.S.C.A. § 77c.

7. 15 U.S.C.A. § 77d.

and 4 of the Act.[8] Notwithstanding the broad exemptive authority granted by section 28, the overwhelming majority of exemptions are grounded in section 3 or 4 of the Act. Many exemptions are based on rules or regulations explaining or implementing the terms of section 3 and section 4 of the Act. In applying and interpreting the rules, it is crucial to keep in mind that the rule can be no broader than the statute enabling the rule. Accordingly, an exemptive rule under section 3 or 4 of the Act must be read in conjunction with the terms of the statute to assure that the rule is within the bounds authorized by the statute. This is not a problem, however, when the SEC exercises its authority under section 28 of the Act since the statute there does not provide restrictions on the scope or size of the exemption.

§ 4.1[4] Exempt Securities: Section 3 of the 1933 Act

Section 3 of the Securities Act of 1933[33] exempts various types of securities, most of which are dependent upon the nature of the issuer and/or terms of the security. Section 3(a) exemptions are self-executing and are not dependent upon SEC rules for their implementation. In contrast, section 3(b) is not self-implementing. Section 3(b)[36] empowers the SEC to exempt securities which, in the Commission's discretion and by virtue of either the "small amount involved" or limited character of the public offering, do not need the registration protection of the Act. The subsection (b) exemptions which are limited to five million dollars for any one issue of securities are found in Regulation A (up to $5,000,000),[37] SEC Rule 505 (up to $5,000,000)[38] and Rule 504 (up to $1,000,000).[39] The Commission also exercised its exemptive power under section 3(b) to exempt from registration employee stock compensation plans (ranging from $500,000 to $5,000,000 annually), provided that the issuer is not subject to the Securities Exchange Act's periodic reporting requirements, but the absolute five million was effectively lifted when the SEC re-promulgated the exemption under section 28's[40] more general exemptive authority.[41] Section 3(c) of the Act[42] gives the Commission similar exemptive power with regard to investment companies that are registered under the Small Business Investment Act of 1958; the Commission has exercised this power in Regulation E[43] which covers offerings up to five million dollars.

§ 4.1[5] Exempt Transactions: Section 4 of the 1933 Act

Transaction Exemptions Under Section 4

As is the case with section 3(a), section 4 sets forth a series of exemptions and is not dependent upon SEC rulemaking for their implementation. On the

8. 15 U.S.C.A. § 77z–3. *See* § 4.35 *infra.* There is parallel general exemptive authority from the provisions of the 1934 Act. 15 U.S.C.A. § 78mm. *See* § 9.2[5] *infra.*

33. 15 U.S.C.A. § 77c.

36. 15 U.S.C.A. § 77c(b).

37. 17 C.F.R. §§ 230.251–.264. *See* § 4.17 *infra.*

38. 17 C.F.R. § 230.505. *See* § 4.22 *infra.*

39. 17 C.F.R. § 230.504. *See* § 4.21 *infra.*

40. 15 U.S.C.A. § 77z–3.

41. 17 C.F.R. § 230.701, adopted in Compensatory Benefit Plans and Contracts, Sec. Act Rel. No. 33–6768, 53 Fed. Reg. 12918–02, 1988 WL 263350, [1987–1988 Transfer Binder] Fed. Sec. L. Rep. (CCH) ¶ 84,231 (April 14, 1988). *See* § 4.18 *infra.*

42. 15 U.S.C.A. § 77c(c).

43. 17 C.F.R. §§ 230.601–.610a.

other hand, an understanding of the SEC rules is crucial to an understanding of the section 4 exemptions. In contrast to the section 3 exemptions, which are expressly designated as exempt securities, section 4 of the Act contains a number of exemptions that apply to specific transactions. These include the exemption for nonpublic offerings by issuers,[44] transactions by persons other than issuers, underwriters and dealers,[45] unsolicited brokers' transactions,[46] certain dealer transactions occurring after the effective date,[47] transactions involving certain mortgage notes secured by real property,[48] and transactions up to five million dollars that are offered and sold only to "accredited investors."[49] In working with transaction exemptions, it must be remembered that the exemption extends to the transaction, not to individuals. Thus, for example, someone who himself or herself is neither an issuer, underwriter, nor dealer may be involved in a transaction that would preclude reliance on the section 4(1) exemption.[50]

Section 3 Exemptions That Operate Like Transaction Exemptions

In addition to the foregoing exemptions that are aptly denominated as transaction exemptions, a number of the so-called exempt securities are in essence transaction exemptions. This is the case with the exemption for exchanges between an issuer and its security holders,[51] the intrastate exemption for purely local offerings,[52] and the exemptions provided by SEC rules promulgated under sections 3(b) and (c).[53] These exemptions expire at the termination of the qualifying transaction. Most of the security exemptions in section 3 are couched in terms of the nature of the security and/or its issuer, and will attach so long as the security maintains the required attributes, rights, and obligations.

§ 4.1[6] General Exemptive Authority: Section 28 of the 1933 Act: Exemption by SEC Rule or Regulation

In 1996, Congress departed from the more limited exemptive authority that had traditionally been a part of the 1933 Act when it enacted a broader exemptive authority, not linked to the nature of the securities or the nature of the transaction. In 1996, section 28 of the 1933 Act was added and now provides that the Commission may exempt transactions, securities, and persons if in the public interest and consistent with investor protection.[54] The Commission's Exemptive authority under section 28 applies to any person,

44. Section 4(2), 15 U.S.C.A. § 77d(2). *See* § 4.23 *infra.*

45. Section 4(1), 15 U.S.C.A. § 77d(1). *See* § 4.26 *infra.*

46. Section 4(4), 15 U.S.C.A. § 77d(4). *See* § 4.26 *infra.*

47. Section 4(3), 15 U.S.C.A. § 77d(3). *See* § 4.31 *infra.*

48. Section 4(5), 15 U.S.C.A. § 77d(5). *See* § 4.32 *infra.*

49. Section 4(6), 15 U.S.C.A. § 77d(6). *See* § 4.20 *infra. Compare* 15 U.S.C.A. § 77b(a)(15) (definition of accredited investor). *See also, e.g.,* C. Steven Bradford, Transaction Exemptions in the Securities Act of 1933: An Economic Analysis, 45 Emory L.J. 591 (1996).

50. *E.g.,* SEC v. Softpoint, Inc., 958 F.Supp. 846 (S.D.N.Y.1997). *See also, e.g.,* SEC v. Holschuh, 694 F.2d 130, 137–38 (7th Cir.1982); United States v. Wolfson, 405 F.2d 779 (2d Cir.1968), *cert. denied* 394 U.S. 946, 89 S.Ct. 1275, 22 L.Ed.2d 479 (1969).

51. Section 3(a)(9), 15 U.S.C.A. § 77c(a)(9). *See* Thompson Ross Securities, 6 S.E.C. 1111 (SEC 1940); § 4.10 *infra.*

52. Section 3(a)(11), 15 U.S.C.A. § 77c(a)(11). *See* § 4.12 *infra.*

53. 15 U.S.C.A. §§ 77(b), (c). *See* § 4.4 *infra.*

54. 15 U.S.C.A. § 77z–3. *See* § 4.34 *infra.*

security, or transaction but is limited to an exemption by SEC rule or regulation. In contrast, the parallel general Exemptive power under the Securities Exchange Act of 1934[55] not only permits exemption by rule or regulation but also by administrative order.

The virtually unlimited power of the SEC to provide exemptions from the Act by rule or regulation frees the Commission from the more rigid parameters of the specific exemptions set forth in sections 3 and 4 of the Act. While this greater flexibility is desirable, it is hoped that the Commission will not exercise this power to gut many of the valuable investor protection requirements of the securities laws. The SEC has been proceeding cautiously.

§ 4.1[7] Applicability of State Securities Laws

Until 1996, an exemption from registration under the 1933 Act did not affect the need for an exemption or registration under any applicable state securities laws.[59] However, in 1996, Congress changed this overlapping coverage when it enacted the National Securities Markets Improvement Act of 1996.[60] Section 18(b) of the 1933 Act[61] provides a preemption of, and thus an exemption from, state securities registration requirements.

The preemption of state securities law registration requirements extends to public offerings securities that are registered with the SEC[62] and to many transactions that are exempt from SEC registration by virtue of section 3 or 4 of the 1933 Act.[63] Most of the federal exemptions set forth in section 3 of the 1933 Act trigger the preemptive provisions. The primary federal exemptions that are not preempted by the 1996 legislation are offerings subject to the intrastate exemption and the section 3(b) exemptions (most notably, Regulation A and Rules 504 and 505 of Regulation D). Many transactions that are exempt under section 4 of the 1933 Act also qualify for the federally mandated exemption from state law registration requirements.[65]

The logic behind the preemptive pattern as adopted by Congress appears to be that federally exempt transactions can be subject to state securities law registration requirements only when the securities are offered to unsophisticated purchasers or offered solely to residents of a single state. Although the legislative purpose was to preempt a great deal of state law involvement in federally exempt transactions, many federally exempt transactions will still require registration or an independent exemption under state law.[66]

55. Securities Exchange Act section 36, 15 U.S.C.A. § 78mm(a). *See* § 9.2[5] *infra*.

59. State securities laws, commonly referred to as "Blue Sky" laws, are considered in chapter 8 *infra*.

60. Pub. L. No. 104–290, 110 Stat. 3416 (1996). *See, e.g.,* Symposium, The National Securities Markets Improvements Act—One Year Later, 53 Bus. Law. 507 (1998); Comment, The National Securities Market Improvement Act: How Improved is the Securities Market?, 36 Duq. L. Rev. 365 (1998).

61. 15 U.S.C.A. § 77r.

62. 15 U.S.C.A. § 77r(b)(1).

63. 15 U.S.C.A. § 77r(b)(4).

65. Curiously, a transaction exempt under section 4(2)'s nonpublic offering exemption are not preempted unless they are in compliance with an SEC rule or regulation. This in essence delegates to the SEC the ability to determine the scope of preemption of state law with respect to nonpublic offerings.

66. *See* Rutherford B. Campbell, Jr., Blue Sky Laws and the Recent Congressional Preemption Failure, 22 J. Corp. L. 175 (1997).

§ 4.3 Securities of Governments, Banks, Insurance Companies, and Qualified Pension Plans—Section 3(a)(2)

Section 3(a)(2) of the 1933 Act[1] exempts qualified securities which are either issued or guaranteed by governmental organizations or federal reserve banks. Section 3(a)(2) also provides an exemption from 1933 Act registration for securities of certain insurance companies. The section 3(a)(2) exemption provides a laundry list of exempted securities, including, as noted above, securities issued by state, local and federal governments, including their subdivisions and administrative bodies.[3]

§ 4.3[1] Exemption for Government and Municipal Securities

§ 4.3[1][A] Scope of Exemption for Government and Municipal Securities

Section 3(a)(2) exempts securities issued by the federal government, federal agencies, states, and qualifying state government agencies (including municipalities). In addition to straight-forward, direct government financing, the section 3(a)(2) exemption also covers qualifying joint efforts of government and industry. Accordingly, the exemption covers government-guaranteed obligations. Thus, securities issued by Government National Mortgage Association (GNMA or "Ginnie Mae") or Federal National Mortgage Association (FNMA or "Fannie Mae") would qualify for the exemption, but derivative securities[4] based on these obligations, such as futures contracts, would not.[5]

Just as state and local government guarantees can qualify a security for exemption from 1933 Act registration, so can a federal guarantee. However, the fact that there is a federal guarantee will not assure the exemption when the investment involves risks not ordinarily associated with instruments issued or guaranteed by the government.[12]

§ 4.3[2] Exemption of Certain Bank Securities

Section 3(a)(2) also exempts from 1933 Act registration certain securities issued by Federal Reserve Banks, including certificates of deposit.[19] Section

§ 4.3

1. 15 U.S.C.A. § 77c(a).

3. Most of the governmental securities issued under section 3(a)(2) are not traded on exchanges or through the National Association of Securities Dealers. In order to fill this regulatory gap, Congress created The Municipal Securities Rule–Making Board to cover broker-dealers who are not registered under the 1934 Exchange Act. *See* 15 U.S.C.A. §§ 78*o*, 78*o*–4. Municipal securities regulation is discussed in § 14.6 *infra*.

4. For example, stripping a government obligation of the interest payments and marketing the "zero coupon" portion (some of which have been marketed as "TIGRs" or "GATORs"), which are sold through stock brokers will not qualify for the exemption. The exemption is not available since in these instances the government is not the issuer of the security, the broker is acting as the issuer of this derivative instrument. *Cf., e.g.,* Small Business Admin. Guaranteed Loans, [1975–1976 Transfer Binder] Fed. Sec. L. Rep. (CCH) ¶ 80,243 (SEC No Action Letter Nov. 8, 1974).

5. This is because the derivative security is not protected by a government guarantee. *See* Small Business Admin. Guaranteed Loans, [1975–1976 Transfer Binder] Fed. Sec. L. Rep. (CCH) ¶ 80,243 (SEC No Action Letter Nov. 8, 1974).

12. *See, e.g.,* J.P. Morgan Structures Obligations Corp., [1994–1995 Transfer Binder] Fed. Sec. L. Rep. (CCH) ¶ 76,906 (SEC No Action Letter July 27, 1994) (interests in swap transactions involved different risks).

19. 15 U.S.C.A. § 77c(a)(2).

3(a)(2) thus covers banking instruments which otherwise might appear to fall within a broad definition of security. Section 3(a)(2) does not cover securities issued by industrial loan companies or their subsidiaries, as those are dealt with under section 3(a)(5).[21] However, Federal Land Bank stock is covered by section 3(a)(2)'s exemption.[22]

Not every investment involving bank accounts will be exempt from the securities laws. Thus, when an investment program involving bank accounts possesses all the characteristics of a security, the securities laws will apply.[24]

The exemption for bank securities is designed to exempt bank deposits and the like. The exemption does not purport to exclude investment securities in the bank or bank holding company. Nor does it exempt other investment vehicles that the bank offers to its customers that bear the benchmarks of a security. Nor does the exemption for banks apply to accounts that include risks not traditionally associated with bank accounts in regulated and insured banking instructions.

In response to the credit crisis and problems experienced in the mortgage markets, congress enacted the Housing and Economic Recovery Act of 2008.[29] although not addressing the 1933 Act, congress added section 38 of the 1934 Act to require 1934 Act registration and reporting with respect to securities issued by the Federal National Mortgage Association ("Fannie Mae"), the Federal Home Loan Mortgage Corporation ("Freddie Mac"), and Federal Home Loan Banks.[30]

§ 4.3[3] Exemption for Pension Plans

In addition to government securities and bank securities, section 3(a)(2) further exempts from 1933 Act registration certain qualifying employee pension plans which are set up in the form of a trust or a collective trust maintained by a bank or an insurance company. In order to qualify for the exemption under the terms of the statute, the plan must be a qualified plan under section 401 or 402(a)(2) of the Internal Revenue Code.[32] The section 3(a)(2) exemption applies to all such employee plans, regardless of whether they are pension, profit sharing, or stock plans.[33]

§ 4.4 Short Term Commercial Paper—Section 3(a)(3)

Section 3(a)(3) of the Securities Act of 1933[1] provides an exemption from registration for notes, drafts, notes of exchange, or bankers' acceptances

21. 15 U.S.C.A. § 77c(a)(5) (1976). *See* § 4.6 *infra. See also, e.g.,* Bradford v. Moench, 809 F.Supp. 1473 (D.Utah 1992) (industrial loan corporations are not "banks" within the meaning of § 3(a)(2)'s exemption).

22. Dau v. Federal Land Bank of Omaha, 627 F.Supp. 346 (N.D.Iowa 1985).

24. *See, e.g.,* SEC v. Deyon, 977 F.Supp. 510 (D.Me.1997) (bank account investment program was a security). The definition of security is discussed in § 1.6 *supra.*

29. Pub. Law. 110–289, July 30, 2008, 122 Stat. 2654 (2008).

30. 1934 Act § 38, 15 U.S.C.A. § 78oo.

32. I.R.C. §§ 401, 402(a)(2). Also exempted are plans of governmental employers qualifying under I.R.C. § 414(d).

33. There are parallel exemptions from the 1934 Exchange Act. 15 U.S.C.A. §§ 78c(A)(g)(2)(H).

§ 4.4

1. 15 U.S.C.A. § 77c(a)(3). *Cf., e.g.,* Mishkin v. Peat, Marwick, Mitchell & Co., 744 F.Supp. 531 (S.D.N.Y. 1990) (banker's acceptance with maturity of less than nine months is not a security

arising "out of a current transaction" with a maturity at the time of issue of not more than nine months.[2] The nine-month limitation does not include grace periods or any renewal of the security that is limited in the same manner as the original obligation. Short term commercial paper is thus granted an exemption from 1933 Act registration although it is, nevertheless, subject to the Act's antifraud provisions. In contrast to the 1933 Act's approach of providing an exemption from registration, short term commercial paper is expressly excluded from the definition of "security" under the Securities Exchange Act of 1934[4] and thus is not subject to that Act's antifraud provisions.[5] As discussed more fully in an earlier section of this treatise,[6] in Reves v. Ernst & Young,[7] the Supreme Court applied the "family resemblance" test in holding that certain demand notes were securities.

§ 4.5 Securities of Eleemosynary Organizations—Section 3(a)(4)

Section 3(a)(4) of the Act[1] exempts from registration all securities issued by a not-for-profit issuer that is organized and operated exclusively for religious, educational, benevolent, fraternal, charitable, or reformatory purposes. Somewhat related to the section 3(a)(4) exemption is an exemption adopted for certain church plans. Section 3(a)(13) was adopted in 1996 to provide an exemption for securities "issued by or any interest or participation in any church plan, company or account" that is excluded from the definition of investment company as a church plan.[2]

In order to qualify for section 3(a)(4)'s exemption for transactions in securities of not-for-profit issuers, no part of the issuer's net earnings may inure to the benefit of "any person, private stockholder, or individual."[4] With regard to nonprofit organizations, the availability of this exemption has generally been treated as coextensive with the issuer's federal tax status.

---

under section 3(a)(10) of the Exchange Act). *See generally* Paul Lowenstein, The Commercial Paper Market and the Federal Securities Law, 4 Corp.L.Rev. 128 (1981).

2. *See, e.g.*, Wendy Gerwick Couture, The Securities Acts' Treatment of Notes Maturing in Less than Nine Months: A Solution to the Enigma, 31 Sec. Reg. L.J. 496 (2003).

4. 15 U.S.C.A. § 78c(a)(10).

5. 15 U.S.C.A. § 78c(a)(10).

6. *See* § 1.6 *supra*.

7. 494 U.S. 56, 110 S.Ct. 945, 108 L Ed.2d 47 (1990), *rehearing denied*494 U.S. 1092, 110 S.Ct. 1840, 108 L.Ed.2d 968 (1990).

§ 4.5

1. 15 U.S.C.A. § 77c(a)(4). *Cf.*, Timothy L. Horner & Hugh H. Makens, Securities Regulation of Fundraising Activities of Religious and Other Nonprofit Organizations, 27 Stetson L. Rev. 473 (1997).

2. Section 3(c)(14) of the Investment Company Act of 1940 exempts church plans described in § 414(e) of the Internal Revenue Code and "no part of the assets may be used for … other than the Exclusive Benefit Plan Participants." 15 U.S.C.A. § 80a–3(c)(14). The exemption provided by section 3(a)(13) is discussed in § 4.14 *infra*. The Investment Company Act of 1940 is discussed in chapter 20 *infra*.

4. 15 U.S.C.A. § 77c(a)(4). Section 3(a)(4) was amended by the Philanthropy Protection Act of 1995, 104th Cong., 1st Sess., (1995) to add what is now the last phrase of the section: "or any security of a fund that is excluded from the definition of an investment company under Section 3(c)(10)(B) of the Investment Company Act of 1940." The Investment Company Act is discussed in chapter 20 *infra*.

§ 4.6 Securities of Building and Loan Associations, Farmers Cooperatives and the Like—Section 3(a)(5)

Section 3(a)(5) of the 1933 Act[1] provides an exemption from registration for securities issued by savings and loan associations, building and loan associations, cooperative banks, homestead associations, and similar institutions, provided that the issuer is subject to supervision by state or federal governmental authorities. The exemption does not apply, however, where the issuer takes for itself more than three percent of the offering's face value in the form of a fee or other remuneration, either at the time of investment or termination.[2] Section 3(a)(5) further exempts securities issued by farmers cooperatives and certain corporations that qualify for the federal taxation exemption.[3]

§ 4.8 Certificates Issued Under the Bankruptcy Act by Receivers and Trustees—Section 3(a)(7)

Section 3(a)(7) exempts from registration certificates issued by trustees, receivers, or debtors in possession under the Federal Bankruptcy Act, provided that the certificates are issued pursuant to court approval.[1] Even though the exemption may apply to securities sold as part of the original issue, it does not extend to downstream sales, in which case the person selling to secondary recipients of the certificates must register unless some other independent exemption is available.[2] The statute expressly requires court approval of the issue in order to render the exemption available.

The section 3(a)(7) exemption supplements the exemptions for bankruptcy reorganizations that are included in section 3(a)(10)'s exemption for securities issued pursuant to certain administratively or judicially approved reorganizations.[3] The section 3(a)(7) exemption which applies to trustee certificates has its counterpart in the Bankruptcy Act,[4] which not only provides an exemption from section 5 of the 1933 Act but also from the Trust Indenture Act of 1939,[5] as well as from state and local laws.

In addition, section 1145(a) of the Bankruptcy Act[6] exempts from 1933 Act registration, as well as providing an exemption from state securities laws, securities of the bankrupt if they are (1) offered under a reorganization plan and are (2) exchanged for claims or interests in the debtor.

---

§ 4.6

1. 15 U.S.C.A. § 77c(a)(5).

2. 15 U.S.C.A. § 77c(a)(5).

3. *See* I.R.C. §§ 501(a), 501(c)(2), (16), 521.

§ 4.8

1. 15 U.S.C.A. § 77c(a)(7).

2. *Cf.* Sequential Information Systems, Inc., [1972–1973 Transfer Binder] Fed. Sec. L. Rep. (CCH) ¶ 79,139 (SEC 1972) (a certificate holder who exchanges certificates for stock cannot use the section 3(a)(7) exemption when reselling the stock to the public). *See also* the discussion of resales of exempt securities in §§ 4.10, 4.11 *infra*.

3. 15 U.S.C.A. § 77c(a)(10). *See* § 4.11 *infra*.

4. 11 U.S.C.A. § 364(f). These certificates can be issued by either a trustee or a debtor in possession (*see* 11 U.S.C.A. §§ 1107(a), 1108) while section 3(a)(7) also exempts certificates issued by a receiver. The exemption provided by section 364(f) of the Bankruptcy Act does not apply to downstream sales or to sales by certain underwriters. *See* 11 U.S.C.A. § 1145(b)(1).

5. 15 U.S.C.A. § 77aaa–77bbbb. *See* chapter 19 *infra*.

6. 11 U.S.C.A. § 1145(a).

As is the case with the exemptions under sections 3(a)(9)[7] (exchanges of securities exclusively between the issuer and its existing securities holders) and 3(a)(10)[8] of the 1933 Act (securities issued in certain administratively or judicially approved exchanges), the exemption from 1933 Act registration that is provided by the Bankruptcy Act does not apply to resales of the securities so issued. However, an exemption for the resales may be secured independently, including, for example, SEC Rule 144.[10]

§ 4.9 Insurance Policies and Annuity Contracts—Section 3(a)(8)

Section 3(a)(8)[1] exempts from 1933 Act registration insurance policies and annuity contracts issued by corporations that are subject to the supervision of a state insurance commissioner, bank commissioner, or agency or officer performing a similar regulatory function. The Commission has pointed out that if the insurance or annuity contract does not place upon the issuer a "meaningful mortality risk" the policy cannot be regarded as "life insurance" or an exempt "annuity."[2] Furthermore, simply taking on a "meaningful mortality risk" does not assure the issuer an exemption from registration under the securities laws, where the annuity or other insurance contract is in essence an investment contract.[3] For example, the Supreme Court held that when analyzing a variable annuity under which the entire investment risk rests with the purchaser, the section 3(a)(8) exemption does not apply.[4]

An investment product that has gained in popularity is an equity indexed annuity. By 2008, equity Indexed Annuities (or "EIA"s) became a one hundred and twenty billion dollar industry and have been frequent targets of state securities administrators. In 2005, the National Association of Securities Dealers alerted its members that securities broker-dealers should be cautious when dealing in unregistered equity index annuities.[5] In 2008, the SEC proposed a rule to provide guidance on when 1933 Act registration would be required for equity indexed annuities.[6] The rules as adopted make it clear that equity indexed annuity contracts and related products are securities and thus require registration under the 1933 Act absent some other applicable exemption.[7]

---

7. 15 U.S.C.A. § 77c(a)(9). *See* § 4.10 *infra.*

8. 15 U.S.C.A. § 77c(a)(10). *See* § 4.11 *infra.*

10. 17 C.F.R. § 230.144 which is discussed in § 4.29 *infra.*

§ 4.9

1. 15 U.S.C.A. § 77c(a)(8).

2. General Statement of Policy Regarding Exemptive Provisions Relating to Annuity and Insurance Contracts, Sec. Act Rel. No. 33–6051, 44 Fed. Reg. 21626 (April 5, 1979). *See* SEC v. United Benefit Life Insurance Co., 387 U.S. 202, 211, 87 S.Ct. 1557, 1562, 18 L.Ed.2d 673 (1967).

3. General Statement of Policy Regarding Exemptive Provisions Relating to Annuity and Insurance Contracts, Sec. Act Rel. No. 33–6051, 44 Fed. Reg. 21626 (SEC April 5, 1979).

4. SEC v. Variable Annuity Life Insurance Co., 359 U.S. 65, 79 S.Ct. 618, 3 L.Ed.2d 640 (1959).

5. *See* NASD Notice to Members 05–50, Member Responsibilities for Supervising Sales of Unregistered Equity–Indexed Annuities, http://www.finra.org/web/groups/rules_regs/documents/notice_to_members/p014821.pdf, 2005 WL 1915787 (NASD Aug. 2008).

6. *See* Indexed Annuities and Other Insurance Contracts, Sec. Act Rel. No. 33–8933, Sec. Exch. Act Rel. No. 34–58022, 2008 WL 2549796 (SEC June 25, 2008).

7. Rule 151A, 17 C.F.R. § 230.151A. *See* Indexed Annuities and Other Insurance Contracts, Sec. Act Rel. No. 33–8933, Sec. Exch. Act Rel. No. 34–58022, 2008 WL 2549796 (SEC June 25,

As is the case with any question asking whether an investment contract exists,[9] the expectations of the policyholder must be viewed in light of an "economic reality" test, and the court's inquiry thus is not limited to the policy on its face.[10] Ordinarily, a fixed annuity will qualify for section 3(a)(8)'s exemption.[11] In contrast, most equity indexed annuities will not satisfy the exemption[12]

§ 4.10 Securities Exchanged Exclusively With Existing Security Holders—Section 3(a)(9)

Section 3(a)(9) provides an exemption from 1933 Act registration for securities exchanged by the issuer exclusively with its existing security holders, so long as no commission or other remuneration is paid for promotional activities in soliciting the exchange.[1] The exemption is not available for securities exchanged in the course of Bankruptcy Act proceedings that would be governed by 11 U.S.C.A. § 1145.[2] Section 1145 provides its own exemption from state securities laws, securities of the bankrupt qualify if they are (1) offered under a reorganization plan and are (2) exchanged for claims or interests in the debtor. The Bankruptcy Act exemption is supplemented by section 3(a)(7) of the 1933 Act.[3]

The exemption provided by section 3(a)(9) is limited to exchanges taking place solely between the issuing company and its existing securities holders. The requirement that the exchange be exclusively with existing holders does not, however, mean that all securities holders must be included. It is only required that persons who are not shareholders do not participate in the exchange.

§ 4.11 Securities Issued in Judicially or Administratively Approved Reorganizations—Section 3(a)(10)

Section 3(a)(10)[1] of the 1933 Act exempts from registration securities issued in exchange for other securities, where the issuance has been approved by a court or an appropriate administrative body. The section 3(a)(10)

2008). Proposed rule 151A was designed to make it clear that equity indexed annuities would not be classified as annuity contracts or optional annuity contracts for purposes of the section 3(a)(9) exemption, even if issued by an insurance company. *See id.*

9. *See* § 1.6 *supra.*

10. *See* Associates in Adolescent Psychiatry, S.C. v. Home Life Insurance Co., 941 F.2d 561 (7th Cir.1991), *cert. denied* 502 U.S. 1099, 112 S.Ct. 1182, 117 L.Ed.2d 426 (1992).

11. *E.g.,* Otto v. Variable Annuity Life Insurance Co., 611 F.Supp. 83 (N.D.Ill.1985). *See also, e.g.,* SKJ Commodities Corp. [1987–1988 Transfer Binder] Fed. Sec. L. Rep. (CCH) ¶ 78,675 (SEC No Action Letter Nov. 13, 1987) (annuity contract offered by a registered commodity trading advisor did not involve the sale of a security).

12. *See* Indexed Annuities and Other Insurance Contracts, Sec. Act Rel. No. 33–8933, Sec. Exch. Act Rel. No. 34–58022, 2008 WL 2549796 (SEC June 25, 2008). ("Indexed annuities are not entitled to rely on the safe harbor of rule 151 because they fail to satisfy the requirement that the insurer guarantee that the rate of any interest to be credited in excess of the guaranteed minimum rate will not be modified more frequently than once per year.").

§ 4.10

1. 15 U.S.C.A. § 77c(a)(9).

2. 11 U.S.C.A. § 1145.

3. 15 U.S.C.A. § 77c(a)(7). *See* § 4.8 *supra.*

§ 4.11

1. 15 U.S.C.A. § 77c(a)(10).

exemption is used primarily with respect to securities issued in an exchange pursuant to business combinations and reorganizations that are subject to regulatory approval,[3] securities exchanged pursuant to settlement of litigation, and exchanges of securities in connection with bankruptcy proceedings that are not subject to Chapter 11 of the Federal Bankruptcy Code.[5] The exchange of securities need not be limited to securities—it may partly involve cash.[6]

In order for the section 3(a)(10) exemption to apply, the administrative or judicial approval must be after a "hearing * * * at which all persons to whom it is proposed to issue securities * * * shall have the right to appear."[7] Absent another exemption, all downstream public sales of securities acquired under the exemption must be registered under the 1933 Act. The section 3(a)(10) exemption is a relatively narrow one, as not all approved reorganizations are covered.

§ 4.12 The Exemption for Purely Intrastate Offerings—Section 3(a)(11); SEC Rule 147

§ 4.12[1] Intrastate Offerings—The Statutory Exemption—Section 3(a)(11)

An issuer may embark upon a public offering of its securities and avoid the federal registration requirements under the intrastate exemption provided that all aspects of the offering are within the confines of a single state and are purely local in nature. The intrastate exemption from 1933 Act registration is found in section 3(a)(11) which exempts "[a]ny security which is part of an issue offered and sold only to persons resident within a single State or Territory, where the issuer of such security is a person resident and doing business within, or, if a corporation, incorporated by and doing business within, such State or Territory."[2] Both the courts and the SEC have narrowly interpreted the scope of the intrastate offering exemption, thus making it a feasible alternative only in a relatively few situations. The statutory exemption speaks in terms of "part of an issue" which seems to imply that the exemption may be available only for primary offerings. There is authority supporting the interpretation that the intrastate exemption does not apply to secondary offerings.[3] However, other exemptions which utilize the "part of an issue" concept may apply to secondary offerings.[4] To the extent that an

3. This can include approval by a foreign governmental body. *See, e.g.,* Gilat Satellite Networks Ltd., 2002 WL 31863756 (SEC No Action Letter Dec. 19, 2002) (approval by Israeli court under the Israeli Corporations Code).

5. Securities issued in federal bankruptcy proceedings can qualify for the exemption under section 3(a)(7) of the 1933 Act. 15 U.S.C.A. § 77c(a)(7). *See* § 4.3 *supra.*

6. *See, e.g.,* UBO Bancorp., 1982 WL 30461 (SEC No Action Letter July 8, 1982) Bayswater Realty & Inv. Trust, 1981 WL 26640 (SEC No Action Letter Aug. 13, 1981).

7. 15 U.S.C.A. § 77c(a)(10).

§ 4.12

2. 15 U.S.C.A. § 77c(a)(11).

3. *E.g.,* SEC v. Tuchinsky, 1992 WL 226302, [1992 Transfer Binder] Fed. Sec. L. Rep. (CCH) ¶ 96,917 (S.D.Fla.1992), relying on III Louis Loss & Joel Seligman, Securities Regulation 1142–44 & fns. 5–6 (3d ed. 1989) and cases cited therein.

4. *See* Regulation A, which is a section 3(b) exemption that utilizes the "part of the issue" language, but is expressly applicable to secondary offerings. 17 C.F.R. § 230.251(b).

exempt intrastate offering is a public one, it will be subject to the state's blue sky registration requirements.

The intrastate offering exemption is found in section 3 of the Act, and thus couched in terms of exempt securities as compared with the language of section 4's transaction exemptions.[6] However, in actuality, the intrastate exemption operates more like a transaction exemption since it is tied to the particular transaction in question and therefore is not limited to the security itself in regard to the nature of the issuer's rights and obligations thereunder. Unlike most of the other section 3(a) exemptions for certain types of securities, such as those for securities issued or guaranteed by a governmental subdivision, bank deposits, short term commercial paper, and securities of non-profit, charitable organizations, the section 3(a)(11) intrastate exemption will attach only if the transaction meets certain transactional requirements, although there is no change in the terms of the underlying security. While the exemption is dependent upon the premise that all securities which form a part of the offering will come to rest in the hands of local residents, an out-of-state resale seven months after the primary offering to residents may not void the intrastate exemption for the original offering.[7]

The title "intrastate" exemption may be misleading to the extent that it may indicate a lack of sufficient interstate contact so as to deprive the SEC of jurisdiction. The exemption is aimed at offerings that are local in character and for which all interested parties, including the issuer and all offerees, reside in that locality. The exemption is not in any way dependent upon the absence of the 1933 Act's jurisdictional requirement that the sale of a security be conducted through a means or instrumentality of interstate commerce.[9]

The choice of a state's boundaries is a somewhat arbitrary line for the limits of the locality, considering the exemption's purpose. However, it is one of convenience, as it eliminates what otherwise might be difficult factual questions in determining the scope of the local offering exemption. Despite the purpose of the exemption as evidenced by the legislative history, a corporation located in the heart of New York City may not rely on the local "intrastate" exemption for issuance of stock to a New Jersey resident directly across the river, while an issuer in Amarillo, Texas may rely on the exemption for sale to a resident of the southernmost tip of Texas. Because of its geographical contours, the intrastate exemption has proven to be more useful in the Western portion of the United States where there are fewer intrastate metropolitan areas.

Section 3(a)(11) is not a detailed statutory provision providing a great deal of guidance as to how to ensure compliance with the exemption's requirements. Persons deciding to rely on the exemption have to draw from the relatively scant judicial precedent and SEC interpretive releases and rules available. Prior to SEC Rule 147[10] most precedential guidance was found in SEC no action letters. Because of the close factual questions involved, it became common practice for issuers deciding to rely on the intrastate exemp-

6. *See* § 4.1 *supra.*

7. Busch v. Carpenter, 598 F.Supp. 519 (D.Utah 1984), *judgment affirmed in part, reversed in part* 827 F.2d 653 (10th Cir.1987).

9. If the tests were purely jurisdictional, no exemption would be necessary since by definition the transaction would be beyond the reach of the federal securities laws.

10. 17 C.F.R. § 230.147.

tion to request a no action letter[11] from the Commission before proceeding. However, the no action letter is a very inefficient method of administrative lawmaking. Furthermore, reliance upon no action letters, which by their very nature are expressly confined to the facts as given, provides little precedential value and thus little comfort to the corporate planner trying to tailor the transaction to the exemption. In response to the uncertainty surrounding the scope of the exemption, the SEC promulgated Rule 147 as a "safe harbor rule." Full compliance with the rule will give the issuer and anyone else relying on it safety from claims that the transaction in question has gone beyond the bounds of section 3(a)(11). However, like the other safe harbor rules,[12] Rule 147 is not exclusive and failure to comply with the rule does not even raise a presumption that the statutory exemption is not available. Accordingly, the pre-Rule 147 case law and SEC interpretations continue to be relevant today.

From the face of the statute, it is apparent that in order to qualify for a section 3(a)(11) exemption, not only all purchasers but also all offerees of the securities in question must be residents within a single state. Furthermore, the issuer must be a resident of the same state and be doing business there. In the case of a corporation, in addition to the requirement that its principal place of business be within the state, it is also necessary that the state be the corporation's place of incorporation. This last requirement necessarily eliminates the vast number of corporations which, while doing business in one state, select some other jurisdiction such as Delaware to be the state of incorporation in order to take advantage of that state's more attractive corporation laws. Section 3(a)(11) does not expressly address whether other business entities such as limited partnerships, limited liability companies, and business trusts must be organized in the state in order to qualify as an issuer under the intrastate exemption. However, the rule of domestic incorporation for corporate issuers should apply by analogy to other forms of doing business. In its safe harbor rule, the SEC expressly extends the requirement of in-state organization to a "limited partnership, trust or other form of business organization."[15] A limited partnership with in-state investors and in-state business will not be disqualified from relying on the intrastate exemption solely because the corporate general partner is a wholly-owned subsidiary of a corporation incorporated outside of the state.[16]

Even where the above-mentioned statutory requirements in section 3(a)(11) have been satisfied, the issuer still is not perfectly safe under the intrastate exemption. For example, it has been held that where an offering was made only to Minnesota residents and the issuer, a Minnesota corporation, had its only office in Minnesota, the fact that the proceeds would be used outside of the state was sufficient in and of itself to make the intrastate exemption unavailable.[17] The decision raises significant questions about the

11. The no action letter process for informal SEC advice is discussed in § 1.4[4] *supra* and § 16.32 *infra*.

12. *E.g.,* Rules 506 and 144 which are discussed in §§ 4.25, 4.29 *infra*.

15. Rule 147(c)(1)(i); 17 C.F.R. § 230. 147(c)(1)(i).

16. GHM/Massachusetts Health Care Partners–I Limited Partnership, 1988 WL 234449, [1988 Transfer Binder] Fed. Sec. L. Rep. ¶ 78,808 (SEC No Action Letter May 31, 1988).

17. SEC v. McDonald Investment Co., 343 F.Supp. 343 (D.Minn.1972). Compare Rule 147 which imposes an eighty percent minimum on the proceeds to be used within the state. 17 C.F.R. § 230.147(c)(2)(iii).

exemption's application to any issuer with out-of-state operations and if the offering proceeds may be even indirectly attributed to that portion of the business.[18] This use of the proceeds requirement is not as troubling if it is viewed in terms of the overall business operations,[19] but it seems to be overreaching if it will void the exemption for securities of an issuer who derives substantial income from in-state operations. For example, an issuer using the proceeds of the offering to purchase wine outside the state for resale within the state can still satisfy the in-state business requirement.[20]

Similarly, a local company that planned to use eighty-five percent of the proceeds from an intrastate offering to pay off a loan to an out-of-state bank that had been used to finance purchase of an in-state bank dealing primarily with in-state customers was allowed to rely on the exemption.[21] Use of a subsidiary or other device to segregate independent out-of-state operations by a subsidiary may also avoid running afoul of the requirement that the principal business be within the state of the offering.[22] In contrast, it is clear that where the issuer's income-producing operations are located outside of the state, the intrastate exemption will not be available.[23]

As is the case with other exemptions, where two or more purportedly separate transactions are in fact part of a single issue, the two transactions will be integrated.[24] In such cases, all offers made for the transactions to be integrated must qualify for the exemption.

§ 4.12[2] Intrastate Offerings—The SEC's "Safe Harbor"—Rule 147

As is the case with SEC policy and court decisions on issuer residence, in order to qualify for the safe harbor of Rule 147, both the issuer's place of incorporation or organization and its "principal office" must be located within the same state; and, if an individual, his or her principal residence must be located within that state.[26] Rule 147 further requires that in order for an

---

18. The issuer planned to use the proceeds for loans secured by real property outside of the state. Although the loan contracts were to be governed by Minnesota law and despite the fact that the issuer had in-state income as well, the court denied the exemption. In its broadest reading, the decision can be seen as adding to the statutory doing-business requirement a rule that the proceeds from the particular offering be used in the state. *Compare, e.g.,* Master Financial, Inc., 1999 WL 343087 (SEC No Action Letter May 27, 1999) (intrastate exemption was available where offering was used to fund company's in-state lending operations, notwithstanding the fact that more than 20 percent of the Company's gross revenue is interest and other payments received on a portfolio of loans made to out-of state borrowers).

19. *See* SEC v. Truckee Showboat, Inc., 157 F.Supp. 824 (S.D.Cal.1957); 17 C.F.R. § 230.147(c)(2).

20. Adventures in Wine, [1976–1977 Transfer Binder] Fed. Sec. L. Rep. (CCH) ¶ 80,952 (SEC 1977).

21. Fina Bancorp., Inc., 19 Sec.Reg. & L.Rep. (BNA) 961 (SEC No Action Letter June 15, 1987). The SEC staff reasoned that since the issuer's business was primarily in-state, paying off the existing loan to an out of state lender was not inconsistent with Rule 147(2)(c)(iii)'s doing business requirement. *See* 17 C.F.R. § 230.147(c)(2)(iii).

22. Fidelity Credit Corp., 1988 WL 234463 (SEC No Action Letter June 23, 1988) (transferring out-of-state assets to a subsidiary operating outside of the state and not integrated with the operations of the parent company may enable the in-state parent to continue to have intrastate offerings without having the exemption jeopardized by the out-of-state subsidiary's operations).

23. *See, e.g.,* Busch v. Carpenter, 827 F.2d 653, 658 (10th Cir.1987); Chapman v. Dunn, 414 F.2d 153, 158–59 (6th Cir.1969); SEC v. Truckee Showboat, Inc., 157 F.Supp. 824 (S.D.Cal.1957).

24. *See* § 4.36 *infra* for discussion of integration generally.

26. 17 C.F.R. § 230.147(c)(1).

issuer to be deemed doing business within the state it must have derived at least eighty percent of its gross revenues per annum as well as eighty percent of its assets (including those of its subsidiaries on a consolidated basis) from activities and/or real property located within the state over the past fiscal year.[27] This eighty percent requirement is not included within the statute but indicates the Commission's position that the statutory concept of "doing business" means that something more than having the state as the location of the principal office and the place of incorporation or organization is necessary.

Rule 147 imposes a condition that eighty percent of the net proceeds of the offering be used in the state.[28] When taking a look at the face of the statute, there is at least a question as to whether either of the rule's eighty percent requirements is an overreaching interpretation. Nevertheless, they are interpretations which have not yet met successful challenges either at the administrative or judicial level. Since Rule 147 is a safe harbor rule, such challenges are unlikely. The eighty percent test nevertheless is evidence of the SEC's position that something more than the principal office requirement is necessary. Thus, it is fair to assume that issuers falling significantly below the eighty percent threshold may have difficulty establishing the statutory exemption.

Both under the statutory exemption and pursuant to Rule 147, downstream sales of part of an intrastate issue to nonresidents can destroy the availability of the intrastate exemption. Obviously, an issuer cannot select an in-state resident to operate as a conduit or underwriter[29] and thereby avoid the limitations of the exemption. However, even inadvertent downstream sales to nonresidents, at least those taking place within a reasonably short period after the distribution for which the exemption is claimed, will destroy the exemption for all sales made pursuant to the exemption. The safe harbor guidelines for limitation on resales is found in Rule 147(e)[30] which prohibits all resales to nonresident purchasers within nine months "from the date of the last sale by the issuer of such securities." Even outside of the safe harbor rule, it is clear that a limited number of nonresident resales will render the exemption inapplicable to the entire offering.[31] In such a case, even the resident purchasers will be placed in a position of being able to claim that the securities they purchased were sold in violation of section 5, thus giving them a right of rescission under section 12(a)(1).[32] It has long been the Commission's position, however, that once securities sold pursuant to the intrastate exemption have finally come to rest in the hands of residents, subsequent isolated resales to nonresidents will not destroy the prior exemptions.[33] In

27. 17 C.F.R. § 230.147(c)(2)(i), (ii).

28. 17 C.F.R. § 230.147(c)(2)(iii).

29. The term "underwriter" is defined in section 2(a)(11), 15 U.S.C.A. § 77b(a)(11). The underwriter definition is a rather broad concept. *See* § 4.27 *infra*.

30. 17 C.F.R. § 230.147(e). A shorter period might still be permitted under the case law interpreting the scope of the statutory exemption.

31. *See* Hillsborough Investment Corp. v. SEC, 276 F.2d 665 (1st Cir.1960), *see also* 173 F.Supp. 86 (D.N.H.1958).

32. Section 3(a)(11) Exemption for Local Offerings, Sec. Act Rel. No 33–4434, 1961 WL 3670, 1 Fed. Sec. L. Rep. (CCH) ¶ 2270–2277 (SEC Dec. 6, 1961). *See* 15 U.S.C.A. § 77*l* (a)(1) which is discussed in § 7.2 *infra*.

33. Section 3(a)(11) Exemption for Local Offerings, Sec. Act Rel. No 33–4434, 1961 WL 3670, 1 Fed. Sec. L. Rep. (CCH) ¶ ¶ 2270–2277 (SEC Dec. 6, 1961). *See also* Busch v. Carpenter, 827 F.2d 653 (10th Cir.1987), *affirming in part* 598 F.Supp. 519 (D.Utah 1984); Commonwealth

terms of planning such transactions, the nine-month safe harbor guidelines of Rule 147 provide a good rule of thumb.

Notwithstanding Rule 147's detail as to the requirements of residency so far as the issuer is concerned, the rule is much more open with regard to purchasers' and offerees' residence. The test applicable to an individual is "his principal residence,"[34] which seems to limit each individual to one state, thus eliminating vacation homes and the like. A similar test has been adopted under the statute.[35] Business entities including corporations, trusts, and partnerships qualify as resident offerees and purchasers if they have their principal office in the state.[36] There is no requirement that the offeree be organized under the laws of that state, although it would have to be so organized in order to qualify as an issuer. Furthermore, the rule's eighty percent revenue and asset tests do not apply to offerees and purchasers as they apply only to issuers. The rule also provides that where a corporation, partnership, or trust is formed *for the purpose* of purchasing the securities in question, *all* of its beneficial owners must be residents.[37] It thus appears that a bona fide preexisting entity may qualify as a purchaser although it has nonresident owners. As to such entities, the SEC has opined that a nonresident trustee of a resident's individual retirement account will not disqualify the trust as a resident purchaser.[38] Similarly, with regard to partnerships, it has been held that the fact that one partner resided in another state was not in itself sufficient to prevent the partnership from being a resident for purposes of section 3(a)(11).[39] The SEC has indicated that Rule 147 would be available for limited partnership interests to be offered solely to residents of the partnership's state of organization even though the general partner was wholly owned by an out-of-state corporation.[40]

Another key factor in an intrastate offering and in deciding whether or not reliance is to be placed upon Rule 147 is the integration doctrine which operates to telescope two or more transactions into one and also applies to other exemptions under the Act.[41] The integration doctrine is the Commission's counterpart of the IRS' step-transaction analysis under which transactions that appear to be separate in form will be scrutinized closely as to substance in order to determine whether or not in fact they should be treated as two distinct transactions. Specifically, with regard to the intrastate exemption contained in section 3(a)(11), the question of the exemption's availability

Equity Trust, 19 Sec.Reg. & L.Rep. (BNA) 355 (SEC No Action Letter Feb. 20, 1987); First National Bank & Trust Co. (SEC No Action Letter Dec. 19, 1985); Scientific Manufacturing, Inc. (SEC No Action Letter June 13, 1983).

34. 17 C.F.R. § 230.147(d)(2).

35. *See generally* J. William Hicks, Exempted Transactions Under the Securities Act of 1933 ch. 4 (1980 rev. ed.).

36. 17 C.F.R. § 230.147(d)(3).

37. 17 C.F.R. § 230.147(d)(3).

38. Fair Valley Properties No. 2, [1981–1982 Transfer Binder] Fed. Sec. L. Rep. (CCH) ¶ 77,003 (SEC No Action Letter 1981).

39. Grenader v. Spitz, 390 F.Supp. 1112 (S.D.N.Y.1975), *reversed on other grounds* 537 F.2d 612 (2d Cir.1976), *cert. denied* 429 U.S. 1009, 97 S.Ct. 541, 50 L.Ed.2d 619 (1976).

40. GHM/Massachusetts Health Care Partners–I Limited Partnership, 20 Sec.Reg. & L.Rep. (BNA) 936 (SEC No Action Letter available May 31, 1988).

41. *See, e.g.,* Sidney Sosin, The Intrastate Exemptions, Public Offering and the Issue Concept, 16 W.Res.L.Rev. 110 (1974). The integration doctrine has particular impact with regard to Regulation A offerings (*see* § 4.17 *infra*) and Regulation D's exemptions (*see* §§ 4.19–4.25 *infra*). *See also* § 4.36 *infra*.

arises in the context of determining whether a given security transaction is "part of an issue" within the meaning of the statute. The determination of which transactions constitute an "issue" or "part of an issue" is a matter of federal rather than state law.[42] In determining whether the integration doctrine will apply and whether the transaction is to be considered part of a certain issue, the Commission will consider a number of factors: "(1) are the offerings part of a single plan of financing; (2) do the offerings involve issuance of the same class of security; (3) are the offerings made at or about the same time; (4) is the same type of consideration to be received; and (5) are the offerings made for the same general purpose."[43] Rule 147 in its preliminary notes expressly adopts this five factor test and points out that "any one or more of the * * * factors may be determinative."[44] The rule establishes a six-month safe harbor for avoiding integration with out-of-state sales.[45]

§ 4.15 The Small Issue Exemptions

The succeeding sections discuss the small issue exemptions. The chart on pages 172 and 173 summarizes some of the most frequently used exemptions.[22] The chart does not include section 3(a)(11)'s intrastate exemption which is not limited either in the number of offerees nor in the dollar amount of the offering.[23] Nevertheless the intrastate exemption may prove to be an effective exemption for offerings by local small business issuers.

42. Section 3(a)(11) Exemption for Local Offerings, Sec. Act Rel. No 33–4434, 1961 WL 3670, 1 Fed. Sec. L. Rep. (CCH) ¶ ¶ 2270–2277 (SEC Dec. 6, 1961).

43. Section 3(a)(11) Exemption for Local Offerings, Sec. Act Rel. No 33–4434, 1961 WL 3670, 1 Fed. Sec. L. Rep. (CCH) ¶ ¶ 2270–2277 (SEC Dec. 6, 1961).

44. Preliminary note to Rule 147; 17 C.F.R. § 230.147.

45. 17 C.F.R. § 230.147(b)(2). *See* the nine-month limit on resales in Rule 147(e). *See also* Busch v. Carpenter, 598 F.Supp. 519 (D.Utah 1984), *affirmed in part and reversed in part* 827 F.2d 653 (10th Cir.1987) (out-of-state resale occurring seven months after intrastate offering did not destroy the exemption for the intrastate sales).

22. This chart is derived from Sec. Act Rel. No. 33–6389 (March 8, 1982).

23. 15 U.S.C.A. § 77c(a)(11). *See* § 4 12 *infra*.

Comparison Item	Reg. A	Rule 504	Rule 505	4(2) Rule 506	Sec. 4(6)
Aggregate Offering Price Limitation	$5 million by issuer (every 12 months) ($1.5 million/person other than the issuer).	$1.0 million (every 12 months).	$5.0 million (every 12 months).	Unlimited.	$5.0 million.
Number of Investors	Unlimited	Unlimited	35 + unlimited accredited investors.	35 + unlimited accredited investors.	Unlimited accredited.
Investor Qualification	None.	None.	Accredited or none required.	All purchasers must be sophisticated and wealthy (alone or with purchaser representative) "Accredited" purchaser is presumed to be qualified. [Query whether § 4(2)'s offeree qualifications must also be read into rule 506).	ONLY Accredited.
Limitations on Manner of Offering	Offering Circular. Some limited advertising or announcement.	None.	*General solicitation*: there cannot be a general solicitation unless either (1) the issuer has registered under state law that requires the public filing and distribution of a substantive disclosure document or (2) the offering is exempt under state law that permits a general solicitation.	General soliciation not permitted.	General solicitation not permitted.
Limits on Resale	None.	Securities issued in a Rule 504 offering are subject to the resale restrictions of Rule 144 (17 C.F.R. § 230.144) unless either (1) the issuer has registered under state law that requires the public filing and distribution of a substantive disclosure document or (2) the offering is exempt under state law that permits a general solicitation.	Restricted.	Restricted.	Restricted.
Issuer Qualifications	Only U.S. and Canadian issuers. No investment companies or "development stage" companies. No issuers or underwriters which are disqualified by Reg. A wrongdoing rules.	No investment companies. Not available to 1934 Act reporting companies. No blank check companies. But see rule 504s.	No investment companies or issuers which are disqualified under Reg. A's wrongdoing rules.	None.	None.
Notice of Sales to SEC	Form 1–A: 7 copies to National or Regional Office. Sales material—7 copies—to Regional Office 5 days before use. Form 2–A to report sales.	Form D: 5 copies filed within 15 days of first sale, every 6 months after first sale and 30 days after last sale.	Form D: 5 copies filed within 15 days of first sale, every 6 months after 1st sale, and 30 days after last sale.	Form D: 5 copies filed within 15 days of first sale, every 6 months after 1st sale, and 30 days after last sale.	Form D (Form 4(6) was rescinded 4/15/82).

Comparison Item	Reg. A	Rule 504	Rule 505	4(2) Rule 506	Sec. 4(6)
Information Requirements	Offering Circular—See rule 253.	No information.	1. If purchased solely by accredited, no information specified. 2. If purchased by non-accredited: a. *Non-reporting companies must furnish:* i. Offerings up to $2.0 million: the same kind of information required in a Regulation A offering. ii. Offerings up to $7.5 million: information in part 1 of Form S–18 or available registration, 2 year financials, 1 year audited—if undue effort or expense, issuers other than limited partnerships only balance sheet as of 120 days before offering must be audited. If limited partnership and undue effort or expense, financials may be tax basis. iii. Offerings over $7.5 million [not applicable to rule 505]. b. *Reporting Companies:* i. Rule 14a–3 annual report to shareholders, definitive proxy statement and 10–K, if requested, plus subsequent reports and other updating information or ii. Information in most recent Form S–1 or Forms 10 or Form 10–K plus subsequent reports and other updating information. c. *Issuers must make avail. prior to sale:* 1. Exhibits ii. Written information given to accredited investors iii. Opportunity to ask questions & receive answers	1. If purchased solely by accredited, no information specified. 2. If purchased by non-accredited: a. *Non-reporting companies must furnish:* i. Offerings up to $2.0 million: the same kind of information required in a Regulation A offering. ii. Offerings up to $7.5 million: information in part 1 of Form S–18 or available registration, 2 year financials, 1 year audited—if undue effort or expense, issuers other than limited partnerships only balance sheet as of 120 days before offering must be audited. If limited partnership and undue effort or expense, financials may be tax basis. iii. Offerings over $7.5 million: information in part 1 of available registration—if undue efforts or expenses, issuers other than limited partnerships only balance sheet as of 120 days before offering must be audited—if limited partnership and undue effort or expense, financials may be tax basis. b. *Reporting Companies:* i. Rule 14a–3 annual report to shareholders, definitive proxy statement and 10–K, if requested, plus subsequent reports and other updating information or ii. Information in most recent Form S–1 or Forms 10 or Form 10–K plus subsequent reports and other updating information. c. *Issuers must make avail. prior to sale:* 1. Exhibits ii. Written information given to accredited investors iii. Opportunity to ask questions & receive answers	No information specified.

§ 4.16 Qualified Exemptions for Small Issues; Sections 3(b), 4(6), and 3(c)

§ 4.16[1] Limited Offerings—Section 3(b)

Section 3(b) of the 1933 Act[1] empowers the SEC to promulgate rules and regulations exempting issues of securities where the aggregate per issue offering price to the public does not exceed five million dollars.[2] The only

§ 4.16

1. 15 U.S.C.A. § 77c(b).

2. In 1992, the SEC recommended to Congress that the section 3(b) limit be increased from $5 million to $10 million. Although no such amendment has been made to date, as pointed out below,

statutory limitation on the creation of the exemption is that the Commission must find "that the enforcement of [the Act] with respect to such securities is not necessary in the public interest and for the protection of investors by reason of the small amount involved or the limited character of public offering."[3] Over the years, section 3(b), which when enacted in 1933 had a $100,000 cap, has to some extent kept up with inflation.[4] The statutory limit was increased in 1980 to the current five million dollars. In the 1990's, the SEC was engaged in a number of small issues initiatives which were designed to make offerings of small issues and by small issuers more efficient without sacrificing the goal of investor protection. With this in mind, in 1992, the Commission recommended that Congress increase section 3(b)'s ceiling to ten million dollars. This proposal was never adopted and has since been rendered moot. Notwithstanding the inflation that has taken place over the nearly twenty-five years since the current five million dollar ceiling was adopted, Congress has not acted to raise it. However, in 1996, Congress granted the SEC the authority to effectively raise the limit. As a general proposition, the SEC was granted expanded rulemaking discretion in 1996 when Congress enacted section 28 of the 1933 Act, discussed below, which allows the SEC to exempt any person, security, or transaction when it believes that it is in the public interest to do so.[5]

Section 3(b) is significantly different from the other major exemptions from 1933 Act registration as it is not self-executing. It is dependent upon SEC rules for implementation. It is not simply the size of the offering that leads to the exemption; it is compliance with the guidelines established by the applicable SEC rules.

The section 3(b) exemptions include the qualified exemptions for offerings up to five million dollars sanctioned by Regulation A,[6] and Rule 504's exemption for offerings not exceeding one million dollars.[7] Section 3(b) also empowers Rule 505's exemption for certain offerings up to five million dollars, sold to no more than thirty-five "unaccredited investors," but which may also include an unlimited number of "accredited investors."[8] Additionally, the section 3(b) exemptions for small issues should be read in conjunction with Rule 506's non-exclusive safe harbor for exempt transactions that do not involve a public offering.[9] The Commission has also exercised its exemptive power under section 3(b) to exempt from registration employee and consultant stock compensation plans (ranging from $500,000 to $5,000,000 annual-

---

the SEC can accomplish the same result under its general exemptive authority that was subsequently granted in section 28, 15 U.S.C.A. § 77z–3.

3. 15 U.S.C.A. § 77c(b).

4. The maximum amount was increased from $100,000 in 1933 to $300,000 in 1945, and to $500,000 in 1970. Notwithstanding the increases, there was a clamoring for additional exemptions from federal registration for small issues. Accordingly, in recent years, the upward limits of the exemption have been significantly expanded: from $500,000 to 1.5 million dollars in 1978 and then again to two million dollars within the same year.

5. 15 U.S.C.A. § 77z–3. *See* § 4.35 *infra*. The exemption must be by rule or regulation. This is in contrast to the 1934 Act's general exemptive authority which may also be implemented by SEC order. 15 U.S.C.A. § 78mm.

6. 17 C.F.R. §§ 230.251–263. *See* § 4.17 *infra*.

7. 17 C.F.R. § 230.504. *See* § 4.21 *infra*.

8. 17 C.F.R. § 230.505. *See* § 4.22 *infra*.

9. 17 C.F.R. § 230.506. *See* § 4.25 *infra*.

ly), provided that the issuer is not subject to the Securities and Exchange Act's periodic reporting requirements.[10]

§ 4.16[2] Limited Offerings Solely to Accredited Investors—Section 4(6)

In conjunction with the 1980 amendments that increased the dollar amount in section 3(b) to the current five million dollar ceiling, Congress enacted section 4(6)[20] to further expand the exemptions available for small issues. Section 4(6) exempts offers and sales made by an issuer[21] to "accredited investors" where the aggregate amount sold does not exceed the dollar limit of section 3(b) (*i.e.*, five million dollars). The only conditions to a section 4(6) exemption are (1) that offers are made only to accredited investors, (2) there is no public advertising or solicitation for the offering, and (3) that an appropriate notice of reliance on the exemption be filed with the SEC. SEC Form 4(6), which originally was the appropriate document for filing a section 4(6) notice, was rescinded in 1982 and has been replaced by Form D.

The section 4(6) exemption is available only for sales of securities that have been offered only to "accredited investors" as defined in section 2(a)(15) of the Act.[22] The statutory definition of this term expressly includes a number of institutional investors, including banks, insurance companies, and investment companies that are registered under the Investment Company Act of 1940, small business investment companies licensed by the Small Business Administration, and employee benefit plans that are subject to ERISA. Additionally, the definition of an accredited investor states that "any person who, on the basis of such factors as financial sophistication, net worth, knowledge, and experience in financial matters, or amount of assets under management qualifies as an accredited investor under rules and regulations which the Commission shall prescribe."[23]

Section 2(a)(15)'s concept of an accredited investor[31] is incorporated into Regulation D's small issue exemptions.[32] Section 4(6) was designed as a companion to the exemptions available under section 3(b). This has been accomplished through the Commission's inclusion of the accredited investor concept into Regulation D.

§ 4.17 Regulation A—Qualified Exemption for Offerings Up to $5,000,000 Per Year

§ 4.17[1] Overview of Regulation A

The oldest, and at one time most widely used of the section 3(b)[1] exemptions for small issues, is the qualified exemption from registration

10. 17 C.F.R. § 230.701, adopted in Compensatory Benefit Plans and Contracts, Sec. Act Rel. No. 33–6768, 53 Fed. Reg. 12918–02, 1988 WL 263350, SECDIG 96–82–1, 1996 WL 219749, [1987–1988 Transfer Binder] Fed. Sec. L. Rep. (CCH) ¶ 84,231 (April 14, 1988). *See* § 4.18 *infra.*

20. 15 U.S.C.A. § 77(d)(6).

21. As is the case with § 4(2)'s exemption for non-public offerings, § 4(6) speaks in terms of transactions by an issuer and thus does not apply to secondary sellers.

22. 15 U.S.C.A. § 77b(a)(15).

23. 15 U.S.C.A. § 77b(a)(15)(ii). *See* 17 C.F.R. § 230.215.

31. 15 U.S.C.A. § 77b(a)(15). *See also* 17 C.F.R. § 230.215.

32. *See* Rule 501(a), 17 C.F.R. § 230.501(a). Regulation D is discussed in §§ 4.19–4.22, 4.25 *infra.*

§ 4.17

1. 15 U.S.C.A. § 77c(b). *See* § 4.16 *supra.*

established pursuant to Regulation A, which is embodied in SEC Rules 251 through 263.[2] The exemption provided in Regulation A is dependent upon the securities being offered through the use of an offering circular, in a manner similar to the use of a prospectus in a registered offering. In order to use the Regulation A exemption, an issuer may not offer securities that exceed an aggregate amount of five million dollars in any one year.[3] As has been the case with section 3(b),[4] the dollar ceiling for a Regulation A offering has increased over time. Regulation A has been used relatively infrequently when compared to the exemptions from registration available under Regulation D.

In order to qualify for the Regulation A exemption, the issuer (and selling shareholders in the case of a secondary distribution) must comply with the Regulation's notification and disclosure requirements, including the offering circular delivery requirements that, in essence, have the same effect as a "mini registration." The Regulation A disclosure statements contain much of the information that would be included in a full-blown registration statement, and Rule 253's provisions for an offering circular are analogous to the section 5(b) prospectus delivery requirements.[6] Similarly, Rule 255 provides for the use of a preliminary offering circular prior to the date on which the offering becomes qualified for Regulation A sales.[7] As compared with a registered offering, Regulation A has broader provisions for prefiling gun-jumping sales solicitations. In particular, Rule 254 permits a solicitation of investor interest prior to the use of an offering statement.[8] This procedure is colloquially referred to as testing the waters. It is to be recalled that any comparable testing in the context of a registered offering would constitute an illegal offer to sell in violation of section 5 of the Act.[9]

As outlined above, and discussed more fully below, in order to comply with Regulation A, the qualifying issuer must follow steps similar to those required in a full-fledged registration. Nevertheless, the Regulation A offering will prove to be significantly less expensive than registration, especially in terms of legal, printing, underwriting and accounting fees.

There are a number of advantages to relying upon a Regulation A offering rather than one of the other exemptions or, alternatively going through a full-fledged 1933 Act registration. For example: (1) Unlike a registered public offering, securities issued in a Regulation A offering are not automatically subject to the periodic reporting requirements of the Securities Exchange Act of 1934.[18] (2) General solicitations of purchasers are permitted in Regulation A

2. 17 C.F.R. §§ 230.251 thru 230.263.

3. 17 C.F.R. § 230.254.

4. The maximum amount was increased from $100,000 in 1933 to $300,000 in 1945, and to $500,000 in 1970. Notwithstanding the increases, there was a clamoring for additional exemptions from federal registration for small issues. Accordingly, over the years, the upward limits of the exemption have been significantly expanded: from $500,000 to 1.5 million dollars in 1978 and then again to two million dollars within the same year. In 1980, the ceiling was raised to the current $5 million, and in 1992 the SEC proposed that Congress raise it again to $10 million.

6. 17 C.F.R. § 230.253. The prospectus requirements are discussed in §§ 2.4, 2.5 *supra*.

7. 17 C.F.R. § 230.255.

8. 17 C.F.R. § 230.254.

9. 15 U.S.C.A. § 77e. *See* § 2.3 *supra*.

18. Section 15(d) of the 1934 Act provides that the periodic reporting requirements apply to issuers who have registered an offering under the Securities Act of 1933. 15 U.S.C.A. § 78*o*(d). *See* § 9.3 *infra*.

offerings. (3) There are no required restrictions on resales of securities offered under Regulation A. (4) Unlike a 1933 Act registration, Regulation A does not require that the financial statements be audited (unless the company already has audited financials). (5) The issuer in a Regulation A offering may test the waters to see if there is sufficient investor interest in the offering before embarking on the offering process.[19] (6) An issuer under Regulation A has three choices of format for the required disclosures. (7) Regulation A offerings are far less expensive than registered offerings (and perhaps even less costly than other exemptions from registration).

Regulation A also offers a number of advantages over other exemptions. Unlike most of the other transaction exemptions, general solicitations and advertising is permissible and there are no restrictions on the resale of securities initially sold under Regulation A.[21] Additionally, unlike many of the other exemptions, Regulation A imposes no offeree or purchaser qualification requirements; in other words, anyone can be an offeree or purchaser in a Regulation A offering.

Regulation A is not simply a safe harbor from 1933 Act registration; it is an exclusive harbor, as there is no self-executing statutory exemption. Accordingly, deviations from the rules' requirements will result in loss of the exemption. The SEC has provided, however, that trivial deviations do not necessarily result in loss of the Regulation A exemption. As is also the case with Regulation D,[22] insignificant deviations from Regulation A will not result in a loss of the exemption, provided that there has been a good faith attempt to comply and the deviation does not involve "a condition or requirement directly intended to protect the individual or entity" challenging the transaction.[23] The exception for insignificant deviations does not apply in an SEC administrative proceeding under Rule 258 to suspend the Regulation A qualification.[24]

Many issuers who might otherwise rely on a Regulation A exemption may avail themselves of the scaled disclosure requirements available to smaller issuers.

§ 4.17[2] Issuers Eligible for Regulation A

The Regulation A exemption is not available to every issuer. Regulation A may be used only by an issuer which is organized under the laws of the United States or Canada and which has its principal place of business in the United States or Canada.[28] Furthermore, the issuer must not have been subject to the 1934 Act's periodic reporting requirements immediately before the Regulation A offering.[29] The issuer's business may also be a disqualifica-

19. Rule 254, 17 C.F.R. § 230.254.

21. However, in order to assure true liquidity for Regulation A securities, issuers may need to voluntarily subject themselves to the 1934 Act's periodic reporting requirements. *See* chapter 9 *infra*. Alternatively, the issuer can provide adequate public information to enable registered broker-dealers to trade in the securities. *See* 1934 Act Rule 15c2–11, 17 C.F.R. § 230.15c2–11.

22. *See* Rule 508, 17 C.F.R. § 230.508. *See* Carl W. Schneider, A Substantial Compliance Defense ("I and I") Defense and Other Changes Are Added to SEC Regulation D, 44 Bus. Law 1207 (1989).

23. Rule 260, 17 C.F.R. § 230.260.

24. Rule 260(c), 17 C.F.R. § 230.260(c). *See* 17 C.F.R. § 230.258.

28. Rule 251(a)(1), 17 C.F.R. § 230.251(a)(1).

29. Rule 251(a)(2), 17 C.F.R. § 230.251(a)(2).

tion from the Regulation exemption. The exemption is unavailable for the offer or sale of: (1) fractional undivided interests in oil, gas, or mineral rights,[30] or (2) for securities issued by registered investment companies.[31] Additionally, Regulation A may not be used by "development stage" companies, which are those issuers that have no specific business plan.[32] It is further provided that a plan to merge with unidentified companies does not qualify as a specific business plan.[33] The rationale behind the business plan requirement is to make Regulation A unavailable for "blank check" companies and other common vehicles for initial offerings in the penny stock markets.[34]

Regulation A contains so-called "bad boy" provisions which deny the availability of the exemption where the issuer, its predecessors, or any affiliated issuer has been subject to proceedings stemming from violations of the federal securities laws.[35]

§ 4.17[3] Regulation A—Disqualification Provisions

By virtue of Rule 262,[36] Regulation A is not available where there have been disclosure or other SEC related problems in the past. Specifically, the exemption presumptively is inapplicable where the issuer, its predecessors or affiliated issuers: (1) have filed a registration statement which is currently subject to examination pursuant to section 8 of the 1933 Act,[37] (2) were subject to a refusal order or stop order within the past five years,[38] or (3) were subject to any proceeding pursuant to Rule 258 (which empowers the SEC to issue sanctions similar to those under section 8 with regard to Regulation A)[39] within five years prior to the filing of the Regulation A notification.[40] The rule also disqualifies an issuer from using Regulation A where any of the issuer's predecessors or affiliated issuers have been convicted within the previous five years of any felony or misdemeanor in connection with any security transaction.[41] Thus, for example, an issuer will be disqualified from using Regulation A if its predecessors or any affiliated issuer has been convicted within five years of any crime involving the making of any false filing with the SEC. Similarly, court orders entered within the previous five years, permanently or temporarily restraining or enjoining the issuer from violating the securities

30. Rule 251(a)(5), 17 C.F.R. § 230.251(a)(5). There is a separate exemption for these interests. *See* Regulation B and SEC Rule 300, 17 C.F.R. § 230.300.

31. Rule 251(a)(4), 17 C.F.R. § 230.252(a)(4). The Investment Company Act is discussed in chapter 20 *infra.*

32. Rule 251(a)(3), 17 C.F.R. § 230.251(a)(3).

33. Rule 251(a)(3), 17 C.F.R. § 230.251(a)(3).

34. Penny stocks and the SEC's initiatives to regulate the penny stock markets is discussed in § 14.19 *infra.*

35. Rule 262, 17 C.F.R. § 230.262, which is discussed *infra* in this section. These "bad boy" provisions are also incorporated into Rule 505's section 3(b) exemption. Rule 505, 17 C.F.R. § 230.505; *see* § 4.21 *infra.*

36. 17 C.F.R. § 230.262.

37. Rule 262(a)(1), 17 C.F.R. § 230.262(a)(1). Section 8 is the provision that empowers the Commission to prevent the effectiveness of a 1933 Act registration. 15 U.S.C.A. § 77h. *See* § 7.1 *infra;* § 3.6 *supra.*

38. Rule 262(a)(1), 17 C.F.R. § 230.262(a)(1).

39. 17 C.F.R. § 230.258.

40. Rule 262(a)(2), 17 C.F.R. § 230.262(a)(2).

41. Rule 262(a)(3), 17 C.F.R. § 230.262(a)(3).

laws or from engaging in any act in connection with the purchase or sale of any security involving false filings with the Commission, will disqualify the issuer from using Regulation A. Rule 262's issuer disqualification is not limited to violations of the federal securities laws and thus applies if state blue sky laws or other relevant statutes such as the Federal Mail Fraud Act[42] have been violated. Rule 262 will also disqualify an issuer subject to any order issued by the United States Postal Service against the issuer for false representation.[43]

The disqualifications are not limited to the issuer and its affiliated entities. Similar "bad boy" prohibitions are supplied by Rule 262(b)[44] if the issuer's officers, directors, general partners, or ten-percent beneficial owners have been subject to similar SEC sanctions or court orders. Rule 262(c)[45] creates a comparable disability if the Regulation A issuer uses an underwriter who has been subject to similar proceedings within the past five years.[46] The prohibition relating to underwriters also will render the exemption unavailable if the SEC finds that the issuer used a disqualified *de facto* underwriter.[47]

Rule 262's disqualifications by their terms apply to offerings exempt under Regulation A. However, the SEC has extended them to other exemption transactions. Thus, Rule 505's exemption[48] for certain offerings up to five million dollars also is subject to Rule 262's disqualification provisions.[49]

Rule 262's disqualifications are not absolute. Application may be made to the Commission to waive the "bad boy" disqualification provisions. The Commission may lift any of the foregoing "bad boy" disqualifications "upon a showing of a good cause, that it is not necessary under the circumstances that the exemption be denied." The SEC has used its no action letter process for granting exemptions from Rule 262's Regulation A disqualifications.

§ 4.17[4] Regulation A—Limitations on Dollar Amount of the Offering

An issuer which is not subject to any of the disqualifications listed in Rule 262 may then qualify for Regulation A, provided that the aggregate offering price of all securities so offered, including any other securities sold under Regulation A, does not exceed five million dollars. In addition, there is a further limit with regard to secondary offerings; no more than one and one-half million dollars may be attributable to the offering price of securities offered by all selling shareholders. However, there can be no resales by affiliates if the issuer has not had a net income from continuing operations in at least one of its last two fiscal years.[55]

42. Mail and wire fraud are discussed in § 22.4 *infra*.

43. Rule 262(a)(5), 17 C.F.R. § 230.262(b).

44. 17 C.F.R. § 230.262(b).

45. 17 C.F.R. § 230.262(c).

46. *But cf.* Stephens, Inc., 30 Sec. Reg. & L. Rep. (BNA) 1795 (SEC No Action Letter Nov. 23, 1998) (broker-dealer's settlement of civil "play to pay" charges would not be disqualifying).

47. In the Matter of Shearson, Hammill & Co., Sec. Act Rel. No. 7743 (Nov. 12, 1965).

48. 17 C.F.R. § 230.505. The Rule 505 exemption is discussed in § 4.21 *infra*.

49. 17 C.F.R. § 230.505(a).

55. Rule 251(b), 17 C.F.R. §§ 230.251(b).

§ 4.17[5] Integration With Other Offerings

Formerly, the Regulation A dollar ceiling would be decreased by any other section 3(b) securities sold within the past year, as well as any securities sold in violation of section 5(a). This was of particular importance because any Regulation A offering which occurs within a year of an offering made in reliance upon another exemption is subject to being overturned if the exemption relied upon for the earlier offering is somehow destroyed or otherwise unavailable. In such a case, all securities sold in reliance on Regulation A would also have been sold in violation of section 5(a), since the sales will not have been exempt from registration. Although this method of calculation continues under two other section 3(b) exemptions—Rules 504 and 505[57]—it is no longer the case under Regulation A. As of the 1992 amendments, Regulation A's five million dollar ceiling includes other securities offered within the past twelve months under Regulation A, but there is no aggregation for securities sold under the other section 3(b) exemptions or in violation of section 5. Beyond the dollar computation question, Regulation A provides a safe harbor from integration for prior offers and sales of securities and for subsequent offers or sales where the subsequent transactions involve: (1) securities sold under a registration statement,[58] (2) securities offered as part of an incentive plan pursuant to the exemption provided in Rule 701,[59] (3) securities sold pursuant to an employee benefit plan,[60] (4) sales of securities outside the United States that are exempt under Regulation S,[61] or (5) any sales made more than six months after the Regulation A offering is completed.[62] Even if transactions do not qualify for the safe harbor from integration, integration may be avoided if the transactions satisfy the test for integration generally.[63]

§ 4.17[6] Regulation A—Filing and Notification Requirements

Rules 252, 256, and 257[64] contain Regulation A's filing and notification requirements. Seven copies of notification, now known as an offering statement, must be filed on Form 1–A at the Commission's national office in Washington, DC. At one time, Regulation A filings could be made in SEC Regional offices, but as of October 1, 1996, the Regional Offices ceased accepting these filings. Instead, they must be made with the small business office at the Commission's national headquarters in Washington.[65] The Commission has provided two alternative formats for Form 1–A. First, there is a narrative format that parallels the traditional registration form under the

57. 17 C.F.R. §§ 230.504, 505. *See* §§ 4.21, 4.22 *infra.*

58. Rule 251(c)(2)(i), 17 C.F.R. § 230.251(c)(2)(i).

59. Rule 251(c)(2)(ii), 17 C.F.R. § 230.251(c)(2)(ii). The Rule 701 exemption is discussed in § 4.18 *infra.*

60. Rule 251(c)(2)(iii), 17 C.F.R. § 230.251(c)(2)(iii).

61. Rule 251(c)(2)(iv), 17 C.F.R. § 230.251(c)(2)(iv). Regulation S (Rules 901 *et seq.*) is discussed in § 17.4 *infra.*

62. Rule 251(c)(2)(v), 17 C.F.R. § 230.251(c)(2)(v). There is an analogous six month safe harbor from integration in Regulation D. *See* § 4.20[3] *infra.*

63. *See* Non–Public Offering Exemption Sec. Act Rel. No. 33–4552, 1962 WL 3573, 1 Fed.Sec.L. Rep. (CCH) ¶ 2781 (Nov. 6, 1962). Integration is discussed in § 4.36 *infra.*

64. 17 C.F.R. §§ 230.252, 256, 257.

65. *See* Sec. Act Rel. No. 33–7373, 1996 WL 722986 (SEC Dec. 16, 1996).

Act. In an attempt to make the process easier for many issuers, the Commission has also established an alternative form in question and answer format. Regardless of which format is used, the offering statement must be signed by the issuer, its chief executive and financial officers, a majority of its board of directors,[66] and all persons for whose account any of the securities are to be offered.[67] There is a nonrefundable five hundred dollar initial filing fee, with no subsequent fees for amendments.[68] All amendments to the initial notification must be filed together with three additional copies and must be signed in the same manner as the original filing. Paralleling the procedure for 1933 Act registrations, absent a delaying notation, the offering statement becomes effective on the twentieth calendar day following its filing.[69] Filing of amendments begins the twenty-day period anew.[70]

§ 4.17[7] Regulation A—Testing the Waters

Rule 254 expressly permits the issuer, prior to the filing of the offering statement, to test the waters in order to obtain indications of interest from potential investors.[86] Solicitations that would otherwise be illegal offers to sell may be made prior to the filing of the offering circular so long as the solicitation does no more than solicit indications of investor interest and makes clear that offers and sales can only be made after filing of the offering statement pursuant to an offering circular. Although it is not a condition of the exemption, Rule 254(b) provides that such solicitations of investor interest be on file with the SEC on or before its use. The rule further sets forth specific warnings and disclaimers that should be in the prefiling solicitation. Specifically, it must be explained that no money is being solicited or will be accepted, and that sales will be made only by use of an offering circular.[87] The solicitation of interest must also make it clear that an indication of interest does not result in an obligation of any kind.[88] The solicitation should also identify the issuer's business and also must name its chief executive officer.[89] In order to take advantage of the testing the waters procedure, the materials used for testing the waters should be submitted to the SEC for review on or before the first day they are used.[90]

As noted above, these solicitations can take place only prior to the filing of the offering statement. Accordingly, no sales can take place for at least twenty days from the date of the last such testing of the waters. Presumably, this minimum twenty calendar day cooling-off period, which generally will be longer, will give investors sufficient opportunity to receive, read, and evaluate the materials in the Regulation A disclosure documents.

66. This parallels the requirements for a registration statement. *See* chapter 3 *supra*.

67. Rule 252(d), 17 C.F.R. § 230.252(d).

68. Rule 252(f), 17 C.F.R. § 230.252(f).

69. Rule 252(g)(1), 17 C.F.R. § 230.252(g)(1).

70. Rules 252(g)(3), 252(h)(1), 17 C.F.R. §§ 230.252(g)(3), (h)(1).

86. 17 C.F.R. § 230.254.

87. Rule 254(b)(2)(iii), 17 C.F.R. § 230.254(b)(2)(iii).

88. Rule 254(b)(2)(i), (ii) 17 C.F.R. §§ 230.254(b)(2)(i), (ii)

89. Rule 254(b)(2)(iv), 17 C.F.R. § 230.254(b)(2)(iv).

90. Rule 254(b)(1), 17 C.F.R. § 230.254(b)(1).

§ 4.18 Rule 701—Exemption for Employee Compensation Plans of Issuers Not Subject to Exchange Act Periodic Reporting Requirements

§ 4.18[1] Background and Overview of Rule 701

In 1988, the Commission exercised its exemptive power under section 3(b) to exempt from registration employee stock compensation plans (ranging from five hundred thousand dollars to five million dollars annually), provided that the issuer is neither subject to the Securities Exchange Act's periodic reporting requirements nor an investment company which is (or is required to be) registered under the Investment Company Act of 1940.[1] In 1999, the Commission eliminated the five million dollar annual ceiling that formerly applied to Rule 701 offerings so that the exemption is now available for offerings that do not exceed the greater of one million dollars (rather than the former $500,000 limit) or fifteen percent of the issuer's total assets, or fifteen percent of the outstanding securities of that class.[2] Issuers relying on Rule 701's exemption are not precluded from also relying on other exemptions.[3]

§ 4.18[2] Issuer Qualification for Rule 701

Since the Rule 701 exemption is limited to securities of non-reporting companies, it is not available to issuers whose securities are traded on a national exchange or on the more active over-the-counter markets.[6] A subsidiary of a public company may rely on Rule 701 for issuing its securities to its employees, at least when the nonpublic subsidiary's securities are issued to consultants and advisers who are not insiders of the parent.[7] Rule 701 is limited to offerings by issuers and thus does not apply to secondary offerings by resellers. Accordingly, since the exemption is available only to issuers, it cannot be relied upon by affiliates or anyone else reselling securities on the issuer's behalf.[8]

§ 4.18[3] Rule 701—Qualifying Compensation Plans

The exemption set out in Rule 701 applies to a wide variety of compensation plans. It applies to purchase plans, option plans, bonus plans, stock appreciation rights, profit sharing, thrift, incentive, or similar plans.[9] The Rule 701 exemption is conditioned on the securities being issued pursuant to a written compensatory plan or contract. The requirement of a written plan or contract does not mean that this must be a detailed plan. Although the plan

---

§ 4.18

1. 17 C.F.R. § 230.701, adopted in Sec. Act Rel. No. 33–6768, [1987–1988 Transfer Binder] Fed. Sec. L. Rep. (CCH) ¶ 84,231 (April 14, 1988). The Investment Company Act is discussed in chapter 20 *infra*.

2. Rule 701(d)(2), 17 C.F.R. § 230.701(d)(2). *See* Sec. Act Rel. No. 33–7645 (SEC Feb. 25, 1999). The Commission was able to raise Rule 701's dollar limit by amending the rule in reliance on section 28's general exemptive authority. 15 U.S.C. § 77z–3.

3. "Attempted compliance with the rule does not act as an exclusive election; the issuer can also claim the availability of any other applicable exemption." 17 C.F.R. § 230.701, preliminary note 3.

6. The Exchange Act's periodic reporting requirements are discussed in §§ 9.2, 9.3 *infra*.

7. American Bar Association, 1999 WL 592214, 31 Sec. Reg. & L. Rep. (BNA) 1186 (SEC No Action Letter Aug. 3, 1999).

8. 17 C.F.R. § 230.701 preliminary note 4.

9. 17 C.F.R. § 230.701(b)(2).

need not be detailed, something in writing must be delivered to the plan recipients prior to the issuance of the securities.[10]

Rule 701 permits an issuer to offer securities pursuant to a written contract or written compensation plan to its employees, directors, general partners, trustees, officers, consultants, or advisers.[12] The securities can be issued only in return for bona fide services but not in return for services rendered in connection with a capital raising transaction involving securities.[13] Thus, the exemption is not available for compensation of underwriters or most promoters.

In its preliminary notes to Rule 701, the Commission observes that "[t]he exemption provided by the rule is not available to any issuer for any transaction which, while in technical compliance with such rule, is part of a plan or scheme to evade the registration requirements of the Act."[14] Thus, issuers must be careful to document the bona fide nature of any compensation plan which they seek to bring within the exemption.

§ 4.18[4] Limitation on Dollar Amount of Rule 701 Offerings

The maximum amount of securities that can be offered within a twelve-month period pursuant to a compensation plan varies from one million dollars to a larger amount, depending upon the size of the company and number of shares already outstanding.

An offering under Rule 701 may exceed the one million dollar limit based on either the issuer's net assets or previously outstanding securities of the same class. The issuer may rely on Rule 701 for an amount up to the greater of (1) fifteen percent of the total assets of the issuer,[18] measured at the issuer's most recent balance sheet date, if no older than its last fiscal year end[19] or (2) fifteen percent of the outstanding amount of the class of securities being offered and sold in reliance on this section, measured at the issuer's most recent balance sheet date, if no older than its last fiscal year end.[20] Although the Commission has lifted the former five million dollar ceiling, offerings under Rule 701 in excess of five million dollars must be made with the use of a disclosure document.[21]

§ 4.18[5] Integration Doctrine Not Applicable to Rule 701 Offerings

When successive offerings are part of a single plan of financing, ordinarily the Commission may invoke the integration doctrine in order to integrate the

---

10. *See, e.g.,* Jackson, Tufts, Cole & Black, Fed. Sec. L. Rep. ¶ 78,807, 1988 WL 234420 (SEC No Action Letter available May 25, 1988).

12. 17 C.F.R. § 230.701(b)(1).

13. 17 C.F.R. § 230.701(b)(1).

14. 17 C.F.R. § 230.701, preliminary note 6. In such a case registration would be required. *Id.*

18. Or of the issuer's parent if the issuer is a wholly-owned subsidiary and the securities represent obligations that the parent fully and unconditionally guarantees.

19. Rule 701(d)(2)(ii), 17 C.F.R. § 230.701(d)(2)(ii).

20. Rule 701(d)(2)(iii), 17 C.F.R. § 230.701(d)(2)(iii). The $1 million ceiling is calculated on the basis of a twelve month period. *See, e.g.,* Subcommittee on Employee Benefits and Executive Compensation, Fed. Sec. L. Rep. ¶ 78,889, 1988 WL 234836 (SEC No Action letter available Sept. 6, 1988).

21. Rule 701(e), 17 C.F.R. § 230.701(e).

multiple transactions into one.[22] Unlike the other exemptions, there is an express exclusion[23] from the integration doctrine for Rule 701 offerings. Additionally, unlike some of the section 3(b) exemptions,[24] securities sold pursuant to the remaining section 3(b) exemptions need not be counted in Rule 701's dollar ceiling.

§ 4.18[6] Restrictions on Resale Following Rule 701 Offerings

Securities acquired pursuant to a Rule 701 offering are deemed to be restricted securities within the meaning of Rule 144.[25] The securities may not be resold unless in compliance with the Act's registration requirements or pursuant to an exemption.[26] In the event that the issuer becomes an Exchange Act reporting company, after ninety days of reporting company status, non-affiliates of the issuer are permitted to resell the securities acquired in a Rule 701 offering by following the guidelines set forth in Rule 144, but without having to comply with Rule 144's informational requirements, one-year holding period,[27] limitations on amount of securities to be sold, or notification requirements.[28] In such a case, affiliates may also resell their stock under Rule 144 but must comply with all of the rule's limitations except for the holding period.

§ 4.18[8] "Going Public" Through Rule 701 Offerings

Notwithstanding the restrictions on resale and other limitations placed on companies in Rule 701 offerings, over time companies issuing securities to their employees may evolve into public companies, thus subjecting them to many of the provisions of the Securities Exchange Act of 1934. In particular, as a company grows and the number of employees and others who receive the company's securities increases, the company may cross the threshold for 1934 Act registration and reporting. As discussed more fully in a later chapter,[31] by virtue of section 12(g)(1) of the Securities Exchange Act of 1934 and Rule 12g–1, 1934 Act registration must be filed by issuers which have both a class of equity securities having more than five hundred shareholders of record and more than ten million dollars in total assets.[32] Section 12 registration in turn subjects the company to the 1934 Act's periodic reporting and, among other

22. Integration is discussed in § 4.36 *infra.*

23. "Offers and sales exempt pursuant to this § 230.701 are deemed to be part of a single, discrete offering and are not subject to integration with any other offering or sale whether registered under the Act or otherwise exempt from the registration requirements of the Act." Rule 701(f), 17 C.F.R. § 230.701(f).

24. Regulation A, which is discussed in § 4.17 *supra;* Rule 504, which is discussed in § 4.21 *infra;* and Rule 505, which is discussed in § 4.22 *infra.*

25. Rule 701(g)(1), 17 C.F.R. § 230.701(g)(1). *See* Rule 144, 17 C.F.R. § 230.144.

26. Rule 701(g)(2), 17 C.F.R. § 230.701(g)(2).

27. Rule 144 imposes a one-year holding period for securities of issuers that are not subject to the 1934 Act's periodic reporting requirements but a shorter six month period for companies required to file 1934 Act reports. *See* Revisions to Rules 144 and 145, Sec. Act Rel. No. 33–8869, 2007 WL 4270700 (Dec. 6, 2007).

28. Rule 701(g)(3), 17 C.F.R. § 230.701(g)(3).

31. *See* chapter 9 *infra.*

32. The statute requires registration for companies with assets of more than one million dollars but Rule 12g–1 exempts issuers with assets under ten million dollars. 15 U.S.C.A. § 78*l*(g)(1); 17 C.F.R. § 240.12g–1. The ceiling was raised from five to ten million in the spring of 1996. *See* Relief From Reporting by Small Issuers, Sec. Exch. Act Rel. No. 34–37157 (SEC May 9, 1996).

requirements, proxy regulation,[33] tender offer and other takeover regulation,[34] and reporting of insider transactions in the company shares.[35] Once a company becomes a 1934 Act reporting company as a result of this accretion in the number of record shareholders, Rule 701's restrictions on resale[36] would cease to apply except that executives and others owning a large amount of stock might still need a 1933 Act registration in order to sell their shares.[37]

In 2007, the SEC provided some relief from the 1934 Act for companies relying on Rule 701 for employee compensation plans. The exemption from 1934 Act registration is limited to employee stock options issued under a written stock option plan.[38] The exemption does not apply to the issuance of stock directly but only to qualifying stock option plans and is also subject to other conditions, including limiting the permissible recipients to persons listed in 1933 Act Rule 701(c).[39] Offerings under Rule 701 of stock or of options not qualifying for the 1934 Act registration exemption may still lead to a company needing to comply with the 1934 Act's periodic reporting requirements.

§ 4.19 Coordination of the Small Issue and Limited Offering Exemptions: Regulation D—An Overview

In promulgating Regulation D,[1] the SEC adopted a comprehensive scheme for exemptions relating to small issues and small issuers. Regulation D was "designed to simplify and clarify existing exemptions, to expand their availability, and to achieve uniformity between federal and state exemptions."[2] The exemptions of Regulation D combine many of the elements of section 3(b)'s qualified exemptions for small issues,[3] section 4(6)'s exemption for offerings to "accredited investors,"[4] and section 4(2)'s exemption for issuer transactions not involving a public offering.[5]

Although embodied in one regulation, it is imperative to keep in mind that Regulation D is not a single integrated exemption but rather consists of three separate but interrelated exemptions.[6] Rule 504, promulgated under

33. *See* 1934 Act §§ 14(a), 14(b), 14(c), 15 U.S.C.A. §§ 78n(a), 78n(b), 78n(c). Proxy regulation is discussed in chapter 10 *infra.*

34. See 1934 Act §§ 13(d), 13(e), 14(d), 14(e), 14(f), 15 U.S.C.A. §§ 78m(d), 78m(e),m 78n(d), 78n(e), 78n(f). For discussion of takeover regulation under the 1934 Act, *see* chapter 11 *infra.*

35. Section 16 of the 1934 Act (15 U.S.C.A. § 78(p)) is discussed in chapter 13 *infra.*

36. *See* § 4.18[6] *supra.*

37. *See* the discussion of resales of securities in § 4.27[4] *infra.*

38. SEC Rule, 12h–1, 17 C.F.R. § 240.12h–1(f). *See* Exemption of Compensatory Employee Stock Options From Registration Under Section 12(g) of the Securities Exchange Act of 1934, Sec. Exch. Act Rel. No. 34–56887, Rel. No. IS—1305, 2007 WL 4236379 (SEC Dec. 3, 2007).

39. SEC Rule, 12h–1, 17 C.F.R. § 240.12h–1(f).

§ 4.19

1. 17 C.F.R. §§ 230.501–230.506.

2. Sec. Act Rel. No. 33–6389, [1981–1982 Transfer Binder] Fed. Sec. L. Rep. (CCH) ¶ 83,106 (March 8, 1982).

3. 15 U.S.C.A. § 77c(b). *See* § 4.16 *supra.*

4. 15 U.S.C.A. § 77d(6). *See* § 4.23 *infra.*

5. 15 U.S.C.A. § 77d(2). *See* § 4.24 *infra.* Rule 506 provides a safe harbor for the section 4(2) exemption. 17 C.F.R. § 230.506. For a chart depicting the basic coverage of Regulation D *see* § 4.15 *supra.*

6. Regulation D consists of three basic exemptions as set out in Rules 504, 505 and 506. 17 C.F.R. §§ 230.504–230.506. *See* §§ 4.19–4.22, 4.25 *infra.*

section 3(b), provides an exemption for certain offerings not exceeding one million dollars within a twelve-month period.[7] Rule 505, which similarly is a section 3(b) exemption, exempts certain offerings not exceeding five million dollars within a twelve-month period.[8] The third exemption, Rule 506, promulgated under section 4(2), permits nonpublic offerings to qualified purchasers without any limitation on dollar amount.[9] Although Regulation D contains a number of common definitions and requirements for the three exemptions set forth in Rules 504, 505, and 506, it is best to consider each exemption on its own terms rather than attempting to define a common thread that runs throughout. This is because the three rules are aimed at three different types of transactions. For example, although Rules 504 and 505 are both section 3(b) exemptions, Rule 504 contemplates that there may be a public offering within the confines of an exempt Rule 504 offering within the one million dollar limit.[10] On the other hand, general solicitations are prohibited by both Rules 505 and 506. Since Rule 505 is a section 3(b) exemption, it is subject to the five million dollar ceiling while Rule 506 is not. Finally, to the extent that the Rule 506 exemption is derived from the section 4(2) exemption, it is dependent upon the offering limitations imposed on that exemption by the Supreme Court.[11]

§ 4.20 Regulation D: Definitions, Conditions, and Filing Requirements—SEC Rules 501, 502, and 503

§ 4.20[1] Overview of Regulation D

Regulation D is a series of six rules establishing three small issue or limited offering exemptions from the registration requirements of the 1933 Securities Act.[1] Rules 501 through 503 set forth the definitions, terms, and conditions that apply to the three exemptions provided in Rules 504, 505, and 506. The rules provide exemptions for offerings that are limited in the type and number of offerees as well as for those limited in dollar amount. The definitions in Rules 501 through 503 consolidate, clarify, and expand terms that had been used in former SEC Rules 146, 240, and 242, all of which were rescinded effective June 30, 1982.[3]

§ 4.20[2] Regulation D—Definitions

Rule 501 sets forth eight definitions applicable throughout Regulation D. Briefly, they are as follows.

---

7. 17 C.F.R. § 230.504. In a rule 504 offering, no more than $500,000 of the aggregate offering price may be attributable to securities sold without registration under state law. 17 C.F.R. § 230.504(b)(2)(i). *See* § 4.21 *infra.*

8. 17 C.F.R. § 230.505. *See* § 4.23 *infra.*

9. 17 C.F.R. § 230.506. *See* § 4.25 *infra.*

10. *See, e.g.,* Katherine Killingsworth, A History of General Solicitation Under the 1933 Act and Why Additional Guidance is Needed for the Future, 33 Sec. Reg. L.J. 47 (2005).

11. SEC v. Ralston Purina Co., 346 U.S. 119, 73 S.Ct. 981, 97 L.Ed. 1494 (1953). *See* § 4.24[1] *infra.*

§ 4.20

1. 17 C.F.R. §§ 230.501–230.506.

3. *See* Revision of Certain Exemptions From Registration for Transactions Involving Limited Offers and Sales, Sec. Act Rel. No. 33–6389, 47 Fed. Reg. 11251–01, 1982 WL 125672 (SEC March 8, 1982).

An "accredited investor,"[18] a term which is also defined in section 2(a)(15) of the Act,[19] is any person who in fact comes within, or whom the issuer reasonably believes comes within, any of eight categories of investors at the time securities are sold to him or her. Generally, these categories include wealthy and/or financially sophisticated investors such as banks, insurance companies, tax-exempt organizations, directors and executive officers of the issuer, and natural persons who have considerable net worth or large annual incomes. The Regulation D exemptions either limit or exclude offerings made to any nonaccredited persons. The concept of accredited investor is also relevant to the amount and type of information the issuer must furnish to purchasers during a Regulation D offering.[20] Additionally, section 4(6) of the Act[21] exempts offerings of up to five million dollars where all offerees and purchasers are accredited investors. Failure to take adequate precautions to screen accredited investors is likely to result in the loss of an exemption.[22]

An "affiliate"[23] is a person who controls, is controlled by, or is under common control with the person with whom he or she is affiliated.[24] This definition captures the same concept that is found in the definition of control person under SEC Rule 405.[25]

"Aggregate offering price"[26] is defined to include all consideration, including non-cash items, received by an issuer for the issuance of its securities. The definition includes a comment regarding how to determine the price of securities sold in whole or in part for non-cash consideration. Determination of the aggregate offering price is important for Rules 504 and 505,[27] which have dollar ceilings of one million and five million dollars, respectively.[28]

Rule 501 further provides the method for calculating the number of purchasers involved in an exempt offering.[31] This computation is relevant to the exemptions provided by Rules 505 and 506,[32] which are limited to thirty-five purchasers. However, in making the thirty-five purchaser computation, accredited investors[33] are not included.[34] Accordingly, there can be more than

18. 17 C.F.R. § 230.501(a).

19. 15 U.S.C.A. § 77b(a)(15); 17 C.F.R. § 230.215.

20. *See* 17 C.F.R. § 230.502(b).

21. 15 U.S.C.A. § 77d(6). *See* § 4.23 *infra.*

22. *See, e.g.,* SEC v. Interlink Data Network of Los Angeles, Inc., 1993 WL 603274, [1993–1994 Transfer Binder] Fed. Sec. L. Rep. (CCH) ¶ 98,049 (C.D.Cal.1993).

23. 17 C.F.R. § 230.501(b). Rule 405 defines control as "The possession, direct or indirect, of the power to direct or cause the direction of management and policies * * * whether through the ownership of voting securities, by contract or otherwise." 17 C.F.R. § 230.405.

24. 17 C.F.R. Pt. 501(b).

25. 17 C.F.R. § 230.405.

26. 17 C.F.R. § 230.501(c). As explained more fully elsewhere, the aggregate offering price includes all securities sold within the preceding twelve months under section 3(b) or in violation of section 5. *See* § 4.17 *supra* and §§ 4.21, 4.22 *infra.*

27. 17 C.F.R. §§ 230.504, 230.505. *See* §§ 4.21, 4.22 *infra.*

28. Rules 505 and 506 are not available if there has been a general solicitation of offerees. Rule 504 offerings can be made with a general solicitation only if made pursuant to a state law mandated disclosure document. A general solicitation can also be used in a Rule 504 offering only to accredited investors (as that term is defined in Rule 501(a) under a state law exemption that permits a general solicitation). The concept of general solicitation is discussed *infra.*

31. 17 C.F.R. § 230.501(e).

32. 17 C.F.R. §§ 230.505(b), 230.506(b). *See* §§ 4.21, 4.25 *infra.*

33. *See* § 4.20[2][A] *supra.*

34. 17 C.F.R. § 230.501(e).

35 actual purchasers if there are accredited investors in the group of purchasers.

A "purchaser representative"[38] is defined, broadly, to be a person unaffiliated with the issuer who has such knowledge and experience in financial and business matters that he is capable of evaluating the risks and merits of a proposed offering. A purchaser representative can be used to qualify purchasers for Rule 506's safe harbor for private placements.[39]

§ 4.20[3] Conditions of Regulation D Offerings

Rule 502[40] establishes four conditions that are applicable to all Regulation D offerings. Those conditions relate to: (1) the integration doctrine, (2) the information to be supplied to offerees, (3) the manner of soliciting purchasers, and (4) limitations on resales.

In addition, Rule 501[41]4.5 provides definitions of certain terms used in Rules 502–506. Rule 503 requires that the issuer record the Regulation D transaction on Form D which should be filed with the Commission within 15 days of the commencement of the offering.[42] Additionally, 1934 Act reporting companies making sales of securities under the section 4(6) exemption must disclose those transactions in their periodic reports filed with the SEC.[43]

The first condition sets forth a safe harbor to avoid the integration of more than one exempt offering; it also provides a five-factor test to be considered for offerings that may not be protected by the safe harbor.[44] In short, there is a window that will last for at least twelve months during which the question of whether to integrate transactions will be answered according to the highly factual five-factor test.[45] In 2007, the SEC proposed shortening the six month period to ninety days.[46]

There is a safe harbor from integration for transactions taking place outside of that period. As discussed more fully in a subsequent section, Rule 502(a) provides that offers and sales taking place more than six months before the beginning of the Regulation D offering and those taking place more than six months after the completion of the offering will not be integrated into the Regulation D offering.[47] Transactions that are not integrated under either the safe harbor or the five-factor test will not destroy the exemption.

The second condition establishes the type of information that an issuer is required to supply to purchasers for an offering exempted by Regulation D.[50]

38. 17 C.F.R. § 230.501(h).

39. 17 C.F.R. § 230.502.

40. 17 C.F.R. § 230.506. *See* § 4.25 *infra.*

41. 17 C.F.R. § 230.501. *See* § 4.20 *supra.*

42. 17 C.F.R. § 230.503.

43. *See* Periodic Reporting of Unregistered Equity Sales, Sec. Exch. Act Rel. No. 34–37801, [1996–1997 Transfer Binder] Fed. Sec. L. Rep. (CCH) ¶ 85,852 (SEC Oct. 10, 1996). The Exchange Act's periodic reporting requirements are discussed in § 9.3 *infra.*

44. 17 C.F.R. § 230.502(a).

45. *See* § 4.36 *infra.*

46. *See* Revisions of Limited Offering Exemptions in Regulation D, Sec. Act Rel. No. 33–8828, Inv. Co. Act Rel. No. IC–27922, http://www.sec.gov/rules/proposed/2007/33–8828.pdf, 2007 WL 2239110 (SEC July 27, 2007).

47. 17 C.F.R. § 230.502(a).

If all of the purchasers are accredited investors as defined in Rule 501, then Rule 502 does not require that any specific information be furnished to them by the issuer. Formerly, the SEC required that if there was at least one unaccredited purchaser, all purchasers (including those who are accredited) had to be provided with the specified information. The SEC deleted this requirement and has replaced it with a *recommendation* that all purchasers be given this information. The amount and format of information required will depend on the size of the offering and whether the issuer is a reporting company under the Securities Exchange Act of 1934.[51]

Issuers subject to the 1934 Act's periodic reporting requirements are required to make available information contained in the most recent annual and quarterly reports as well as any disclosures made pursuant to the proxy rules.[52] With regard to issuers that are not subject to the 1934 Act reporting requirements, the mandated disclosures depend on the size of the offering. With regard to nonfinancial information, Rule 502(b)(2)(i)(A)[53] calls for disclosures that are comparable to the information that would be required in Part I of the registration statement that the issuer would be required to file in a public offering,[54] or, if the issuer is eligible to use Regulation A,[55] the types of information that would be required on Part II of Form 1–A. With regard to information relating to the financial statement, the degree of disclosure varies with the size of the offering. For offerings of up to two million dollars, the financial disclosures should generally conform to scaled back disclosure requirements applicable to smaller issuers that formerly were contained in Item 310 of former Regulation S–B.[56]

For offerings over seven and one-half million dollars, the issuer must make disclosures as would be required by the applicable 1933 Act registration form. Where the issuer is not a 1934 Act reporting company and cannot obtain audited financial statements without unreasonable delay and expense, it may elect to provide an audited balance sheet dated within one hundred and twenty days of the beginning of the offering.[60] With regard to limited partnership offerings by nonreporting companies, if an audited financial statement cannot be obtained without unreasonable effort or expense, then the issuer may provide a balance sheet, dated within one hundred and twenty days of the start of the offering, provided that the balance sheet has been prepared in accordance with federal income tax requirements and the balance sheet has been examined and reported on by an independent public or certified account-

50. 17 C.F.R. § 230.502(b). *See* SEC Rules 215 and 501, 17 C.F.R. §§ 230.215, 230.501 for the definition of accredited investor.

51. The 1934 Act registration and reporting requirements are discussed in §§ 9.2, 9.3 *infra*.

52. 17 C.F.R. § 230.502(b)(2)(ii).

53. 17 C.F.R. § 230.502(b)(2)(i)(A). The disclosures must contain the types of information required by Part II of Form 1–A.

54. The degree of disclosure may vary with the size of the issuer and the size of the offering. The alternative registration forms are discussed in § 3.4 *supra*.

55. Regulation A is available to issuers not subject to the 1934 Act's reporting requirements and may be used for offerings of up to five million dollars. Regulation A is discussed in § 4.17 *supra*.

56. 17 C.F.R. § 230.502(b)(2)(i)(B)(2).

60. 17 C.F.R. § 230.502(b)(2)(i)(B)(3).

ant.[61] Failure to comply with any applicable informational requirements will generally be fatal to a Regulation D offering.[62]

Rule 502(b)(1) provides that the foregoing informational requirements do not apply to offerings of up to one million dollars that are made pursuant to Rule 504. As pointed out above, the information requirements do not apply to Rule 505 or Rule 506 offerings in which all purchasers are accredited investors. However, if there are any nonaccredited investors, then each nonaccredited purchaser must receive the required information. Formerly, the Commission required that the offering circular go to *all* investors if there were any unaccredited investors. Although the SEC no longer imposes the affirmative disclosure requirements for all investors, it recommends that even accredited investors be supplied with the offering circular.

The third condition of Rule 502 prohibits the offer or sale of securities by a general solicitation or general advertising.[63] The concept of general solicitation is more concerned with the types of potential investors that are contacted rather than the number of potential investors contacted. Thus, for example, a general solicitation may exist even if relatively few potential investors are contacted if those persons contacted do no satisfy the necessary sophistication, wealth, and/or experience requirements for the offering. Similarly, contacting a large number of qualified potential investors will not constitute a general solicitation.[64] One of the benchmarks of a general solicitation is contacting potential investors with no previous relationship to the issuer or persons promoting the offering.[65] Accordingly, one way to avoid a general solicitation is to use an underwriter or other promoter who has a ready list of qualified potential investors with whom they have dealt previously.[66] Mass mailings will constitute a general solicitation,[67] as will mailings to a group of unrelated investors whose names were obtained through purchase of a mailing list.[68] Similarly, mailing lists, however compiled, will constitute a general solicitation, unless the potential investors have been properly screened as qualified for the offering.

This prohibition applies in both Rule 505 and Rule 506 offerings.[70] The prohibition against general solicitations also applies to offerings under Rule 504 unless made in compliance with applicable state laws.[71] As discussed more fully in a later section, the existence of unqualified offerees in a Rule 505 or Rule 506 offering may be sufficient to establish that a general solicitation has

---

61. 17 C.F.R. § 230.502(b)(2)(i)(B)(3).

62. *See, e.g.,* SEC v. Interlink Data Network of Los Angeles, Inc., 1993 WL 603274, [1993–1994 Transfer Binder] Fed. Sec. L. Rep. (CCH) ¶ 98,049 (C.D.Cal.1993).

63. 17 C.F.R. § 230.502(c).

64. *See, e.g.,* Iponet, 1996 WL 431821 (SEC No Action Letter July 26, 2000) (permitting use of the Internet to contact accredited investors).

65. *See, e.g.,* In the Matter of Kenman Corp., Administrative Proceeding File No. 3–6505 Release No. 34–21962, 32 S.E.C. Docket 1352, 1985 WL 548507 n. 6 (SEC April 19, 1985).

66. The statutory exemption (sometimes referred to as a naked section 4(2) exemption) was successfully established, for example, in Mary S. Krech Trust v. Lakes Apartments, 642 F.2d 98 (5th Cir.1981).

67. *See* Pennsylvania Securities Commission, 1990 WL 285794 (SEC No Action Letter January 16, 1990)

68. In the Matter of Kenman Corp., Administrative Proceeding File No. 3–6505 Release No. 34–21962, 32 S.E.C. Docket 1352, 1985 WL 548507 n. 6 (SEC April 19, 1985).

70. *See, e.g.,* SEC v. Shoreline Development Co., 149 Fed.Appx. 659 (9th Cir. 2005) (offering was not exempt under Rule 505 because there was a general solicitation of investors). *See also* §§ 4.21, 4.25 *infra*.

71. *See* § 4.21 *infra*.

occurred.[72] The existence of a general solicitation will be a significant factor in finding the exemption unavailable.[73] While there is not an across-the-board prohibition on general solicitations in Rule 504 transactions,[74] a general solicitation ordinarily will implicate state securities law registration requirements. In fact, as mentioned above, Rule 504 expressly conditions a general solicitation in a Rule 504 offering upon compliance with the applicable state securities law.[75]

Advertisements and other generally directed offers to sell clearly constitute a general solicitation. Similarly, contacting a wide variety of potential purchasers without regard to their wealth or investment sophistication will be a general solicitation. In order to avoid having a general solicitation, persons to whom inquiries are sent must be prescreened in such a way so as to assure that they do not represent a cross section of the investing public. Thus, for example, assuring that only accredited investors will receive offering materials will preclude a finding that a general solicitation has taken place, even if a large number of investors are contacted.[76] Safeguards can be imposed on online offerings to assure, through the use of passwords, that only qualified investors have access to the offering information.[77]

Finally, Rule 502(d)[81] sets forth limits on the resale of securities acquired in a Regulation D transaction. Formerly, these restrictions did not apply to offerings under Rule 504. However, in 1999, the Commission amended Rule 504 to require resale restrictions except in two situations.[82] Resale restrictions thus now apply in most Regulation D offerings.[83] As a safeguard against illegal resales, the issuer relying upon a Regulation D exemption, based on either a Rule 505 or Rule 506 offering (or a Rule 504 offering unless the resale restriction has been lifted) is required to exercise reasonable care to assure that purchasers are not underwriters as defined by section 2(a)(11) of the 1933 Act.[84] It is common for issuers to require all purchasers in a nonpublic

72. *See* § 4.26 *infra*.

73. *See, e.g.*, SEC v. Interlink Data Network of Los Angeles Inc., 1993 WL 603274, [1993–1994 Transfer Binder] Fed. Sec. L. Rep. (CCH) ¶ 98,049 (C.D.Cal.1993).

74. *See* § 4.19 *infra*.

75. 17 C.F.R. § 230.504.

76. *See, e.g.*, Lamp Technologies, Inc., 1997 WL 282988 (SEC No Action Letter May 29, 1997).

77. *See* Use of Electronic Media, Sec Act Rel. No. 33–7856, 2000 WL 502290 (SEC April 28, 2000).

81. 17 C.F.R. § 230.502(d).

82. Resale restrictions must be imposed on the securities issued in a Rule 504 transaction unless either (1) the securities are registered under state law that requires the filing and distribution of a substantive disclosure document, or (2) the securities are offered only to accredited investors under a state law exemption from registration that permits a general solicitation. Rule 504(b)(1).

83. Even without resale restrictions under Regulation D, securities acquired in any exempt transaction cannot be resold without an applicable exemption. Section 4(1)'s exemption ordinarily will apply unless the seller is an affiliate of the issuer. *See, e.g.*, Hawkins, 1997 WL 356244 (SEC No Action Letter June 26, 1997). Section 4(1), 15 U.S.C.A. § 77d(1) is discussed in §§ 4.26, 4.27 *infra*.

84. 15 U.S.C.A. § 77b(a)(11). *See* §§ 4.28–4.29 *infra*. There are no restrictions on resale in a Rule 504 transaction under certain circumstances. 17 C.F.R. § 230.504(b)(1). Since any security acquired in a Rule 504 transaction, absent an exemption for that resale, cannot be resold without registration, the purchaser may well be subject to resale limitations. *See* § 4.27 *infra*. Accordingly, although not required by Rule 504, the issuer may nevertheless want to take precautions against such resales taking place. *See* § 4.22 *infra*.

offering to sign letters of investment intent.[85] Rule 502(d) requires the issuer to take precautions against resales, including issuing appropriate transfer instructions to the transfer agent and placing a legend indicating the transfer restriction on the share certificate.[86] Section 8–204 of the Uniform Commercial Code provides that any such restrictions must appear in a prominent restrictive legend on the share certificates.[87] Failure to comply with the UCC's provisions can result in liability to transferees who acquire the securities without knowledge of the restrictions.[88]

In light of the resale restrictions that apply to securities offered under Regulation D, it is common for purchasers of significant amounts of Regulation D securities to be concerned about liquidity. Any registered secondary offering requires the issuer's cooperation. Accordingly, one way to achieve liquidity is for purchasers of Regulation D securities to bargain with the issuer for registration rights. These registration rights can be couched in a variety of ways. For example, the purchaser might exact a contractual right to participate in any public offerings by the issuer.[89] Understandably, issuers of non-public securities are reluctant to grant the purchasers the right to insist on a registration on demand. But such demand rights do appear in rare instances. Registration rights are also found in merger agreements involving the merger of a nonpublic company into a public company since in many such transactions, the shares issued in the merger will be subject to Rule 144 resale restrictions absent a registration statement covering those shares.[90]

Rule 503 sets forth requirements for maintaining a record of exempt sales. Under Rule 503, the Commission requires an initial filing within fifteen days after the first sale of securities pursuant to a Regulation D offering; subsequent notices of sales are due every six months after the first sale and thirty days after the final sale.[91] In 2008, the SEC mandated that Regulation D filings be made electronically.[92]

To a large degree it is a misnomer to refer to Form D as having a filing "requirement." Although Rule 503 says that a person selling securities in

---

85. *See* § 4.24 *infra.*

86. 17 C.F.R. § 230.502(d). As a practical matter before permitting removal of the transfer restrictions, transfer agents and the like will want an opinion of a securities counsel that it is permissible to do so. *See, e.g.,* Catton v. Defense Technology Systems, Inc., 2007 WL 3406928 at *1 (S.D.N.Y.2007).

87. *See* § 23.5 *infra.*

88. *See, e.g.,* Dean Witter Reynolds, Inc. v. Selectronics, Inc., 188 A.D.2d 117, 594 N.Y.S.2d 174 (1993) (company was liable to a transferee who acquired shares that had been issued in a private placement and thus were subject to resale restrictions which were not revealed in a restrictive legend as required by UCC § 8–204; the transferee who took thus acquired the stock without notice or knowledge of the restrictions and was entitled to recover damages associated with its attempts to sell the stock).

89. This is often referred to as "piggyback" rights as it enables the secondary sellers to piggyback on the primary registered offering by the issuer.

90. *See, e.g.,* Herrmann Holdings Ltd. v. Lucent Technologies Inc., 302 F.3d 552 (5th Cir. 2002) (upholding breach of contract claim to cause an S–3 registration to become effective as soon as practicable).

91. 17 C.F.R. § 230.503 (1995).

92. *See* Electronic Filing and Revision of Form D, Sec. Act Rel. No. 33–33–8891, Sec. Exch. Act Rel. No.34–57280; Trust Indenture Act Rel. No. 39–2453; Inv. Co. Act Rel. No. IC–28145; http://www.sec.gov/rules/final/2008/33–8891.pdf (SEC Feb. 6, 2008).

reliance on Regulation D "*shall*" make a Form D filing,[95] Rule 507 provides that Regulation D is unavailable to someone who is subject to an order or decree enjoining noncompliance with Rule 503's filing provision.[96] Thus, a failure to make the filing does not preclude reliance on Regulation D in the absence of such an order or decree.[97] Therefore, a failure to file Form D does not invalidate a Rule 506 transaction and thus does not negate the preemption of state registration requirements for the Rule 506 offering.[98]

§ 4.21 Regulation D's Exemption for Small Issues of $1,000,000 or Less—SEC Rule 504

Dollar Amount of Rule 504 Offering

Rule 504[1] provides an exemption from registration for offerings by issuers, who are not subject to the 1934 Act's periodic reporting requirements, provided the offering does not exceed $1 million in any twelve-month period.[2] It was formerly the rule that no more than five hundred thousand dollars of the aggregate offering price in a Rule 504 offering could be attributable to securities that were sold without registration under state law.[3] The SEC then amended Rule 504 so as to eliminate many of the limitations that formerly existed. Thus, Rule 504 now permits offerings of up to $1 million worth of securities regardless of registration under state law.[4] However, registration under state law will still affect the manner of the offering.

Solicitation of Rule 504 Purchasers and Other Issues

The ban on general solicitations and advertising that was formerly applicable in all Rule 504 offerings has been eliminated for some offerings. Specifically, a general solicitation is permitted for those Rule 504 offerings made where a disclosure document is delivered to purchasers pursuant to state securities law registration requirements or pursuant to an exemption under applicable state securities laws. Similarly, while there are no longer across-the-board restrictions on resale of securities purchased in a Rule 504 offering, resale restrictions will apply unless delivery of a disclosure document is required under state law.

In addition to the one million dollar limit on each offering, the Rule 504 exemption is available only to an issuer that is neither an investment company nor subject to the reporting requirements of the Securities Exchange Act of 1934.[7] In order to take advantage of the rule, offers and sales must conform to some of the terms and conditions for Regulation D offerings that

95. 17 C.F.R. § 230.503(a) ("An issuer offering or selling securities in reliance on § 230.504, § 230.505 or § 230.506 shall file with the Commission five copies of a notice on Form D (17 CFR § 239.500) no later than 15 days after the first sale of securities") (emphasis supplied).

96. 17 C.F.R. 230.507.

97. *See* Hamby v. Clearwater Consulting Concepts, LLLP, 428 F.Supp.2d 915, 920 (E.D. Ark. 2006).

98. Chanana's Corp. v. Gilmore, 539 F. Supp.2d 1299 (W.D. Wash. 2003). The National Securities Markets Improvement Act (NSMIA) preempts state regulation of Rule 506 transactions but not other Regulation D offerings. 15 U.S.C.A. § 77r(b)(4)(D). *See* § 4.1[7] *supra*.

§ 4.21

1. 17 C.F.R. § 230.504. Prior to 1988, rule 504 exempted offerings not exceeding $500,000. *See* Sec. Act Rel.No. 33–6758, [1987–1988 Transfer Binder] Fed. Sec. L. Rep. (CCH) ¶ 84,221 (March 3, 1988).

2. 17 C.F.R. § 230.504(b)(2)(i).

3. 17 C.F.R. § 230.504 (1990).

4. 17 C.F.R. § 230.504.

7. Securities Exchange Act of 1934, Pub.L. 291, 48 Stat. 881 (codified in 15 U.S.C.A. §§ 78a *et seq.*). *See* §§ 9.2–9.3 *infra*.

are set forth in Rules 501 through 503. Rule 502(a)'s safe harbor from integration[8] applies to Rule 504 offerings.[9] As discussed in an earlier section of this treatise,[10] these general conditions include a prohibition on general solicitations of purchasers,[11] and restrictions on resales of the securities by purchasers in the exempt offering.[12] Rule 504 does not provide an across-the-board prohibition on a general solicitation of purchasers. Additionally, the resale restrictions applicable to other Regulation D offerings are not imposed on all Rule 504 transactions.[13] Furthermore, Rule 502(b)(1) expressly excludes[14] Rule 504 offerings from Regulations D's informational requirements. Moreover, to the extent that a Rule 504 offering involves a general solicitation of purchasers, registration will presumably be required under applicable state blue sky laws.[15]

Resale Restrictions

As mentioned above, Rule 504 does not impose restrictions on resale for those offerings requiring disclosure documents under state law. Nor does Rule 504 require restrictions on resale for Rule 504 offerings made only to accredited investors. However, even with regard to those offerings where the restrictions on resale do not apply, purchasers in a Rule 504 transaction who subsequently decide to sell their shares will need to secure their own exemption from registration under federal law. Accordingly, at least in those instances in which the Rule 504 offering is not registered under a state blue sky law, the securities so acquired may be de facto restricted since, for example, a downstream sale by an accredited investor does not ordinarily carry with it an exemption from registration.

Moreover, since Rule 504 is a transaction exemption and securities acquired under it cannot be resold without registration or an independent exemption, the issuer using Regulation D may want to take reasonable care to assure that purchasers do not intend to dispose of securities they buy in such a way as to make those purchasers statutory underwriters.[16] Specifically, in many Rule 504 offerings, the issuer must at least (1) make reasonable inquiry to determine whether the purchaser is acquiring the securities for himself or for other persons, (2) disclose in writing before the sale to each purchaser that the securities have not been registered and, therefore, cannot be resold unless they are registered under the Act or unless an exemption from registration is available, and (3) place a legend on the securities stating that they have not been registered and reciting restrictions on their transferability and sale.[17] As noted above, these restrictions on resale are not expressly imposed in some

8. Rule 502(a), 17 C.F.R. § 230.502(a). *See* § 4.20[3][A] *supra* for discussion of Regulation D's integration provision and § 4.36 *infra* for discussion of integration generally.

9. Rule 504(b)(1), 17 C.F.R. § 230.502(1).

10. *See* § 4.19 *supra.*

11. Rule 502(c), 17 C.F.R. § 230.502(c).

12. Rule 502(d), 17 C.F.R. § 230.502(d).

13. Rule 504(b)(1), 17 C.F.R. § 230.504(b)(1).

14. Rule 504(b)(1) subjects Rule 504 offerings to the requirements of Rule 502(a) (integration), Rule 502(c) (ban on general solicitation), and Rule 502(d) (restrictions on resale). However, Rule 504(b)(1) does not make reference to Rule 502(b) (informational requirements).

15. Rule 502(b)(1), 17 C.F.R. § 230.502(b)(1).

16. 17 C.F.R. § 230.502(d).

17. *Id.* A former version of Rule 504(b)(ii) required that unless there were no restrictions on resale because of registration under state law, the restrictions must be disclosed. 17 C.F.R. § 230.504(b)(ii) (1988).

Rule 504 transactions and, thus, for example, do not apply if the securities are registered in states requiring delivery of a disclosure document.

Disclosure

There is no mandatory disclosure as a precondition to the Rule 504 exemption. This is in contrast to the informational requirements of Regulation A's qualified exemption for small issues,[18] Rule 506's safe harbor for private placements,[19] as well as Rule 505's exemption for offerings of up to five million dollars.[20]

In 1996, the Commission amended Rule 504 to make it explicit that there are no informational requirements.[21] However, the Commission reconsidered this position in light of increased concern over the use of the Internet for unregistered offerings of microcap securities.[22] In particular, the Commission was concerned with so-called "pump and dump" offerings where Rule 504 was used for internet offerings (to "pump" the securities into the market) and then creating a secondary market (so that the securities could be "dumped" by the initial purchasers). In 1999, the Commission amended Rule 504 to provide that a general solicitation can be used in a Rule 504 offering only if one of two conditions is met. A general solicitation can be used for a Rule 504 offering if the transaction is registered under a state securities law that requires public filing and delivery of a substantive disclosure document.[23] Alternatively, a general solicitation can be used for an offering only to accredited investors (as that term is defined in Regulation D)[24] under a state law exemption that permits a general solicitation.[25]

Integration

Rule 502 establishes a six-month safe harbor for the integration of Regulation D offerings and a five-factor test for determining whether offerings that fall outside the safe harbor will be integrated.[26]

No Harm, No Foul

As is discussed elsewhere in this treatise,[27] insignificant departures from Rule 504's requirements will not destroy the availability of the exemption.

§ 4.22 Regulation D's Exemption for Limited Offerings Not Exceeding $5,000,000—SEC Rule 505

SEC Rule 505[1] combines elements of the private placement exemption under section 4(2),[2] the safe harbor of Rule 506[3] and section 4(6)'s[4] exemption

---

18. 17 C.F.R. §§ 230.251–.260. *See* § 4.17 *supra.*

19. 17 C.F.R. § 230.506. *See* § 4.25 *infra.*

20. Rule 505 requires that information be furnished to investors unless all investors are accredited. 17 C.F.R. §§ 230.502(b), 230.505. *See* § 4.22 *supra.*

21. *See* Sec. Act Rel. No. 33–7300 (May 31, 1996).

22. *See* Sec. Act Rel. No. 33–7644 (SEC Feb. 25, 1999).

23. Rule 504(b)(1)(i),(ii), 17 C.F.R. § 230.504(b)(1)(i), (ii).

24. Rule 501(a), 17 C.F.R. § 230.501(a).

25. Rule 504(b)(1)(iii), 17 C.F.R. § 230.504 (b)(1)(iii).

26. 17 C.F.R. § 230.502(a).

27. 17 C.F.R. § 230.508. *See* §§ 4.20, 4.21 *supra* and § 4.25 *infra.*

§ 4.22

1. 17 C.F.R. § 230.505. For a case holding that rule 501 was satisfied by an offering of less than $5,000,000 to an accredited investor, *see* Wright v. National Warranty Co., 953 F.2d 256, 259–60 (6th Cir.1992).

2. 15 U.S.C.A. § 77d(2). *See* § 4.24 *infra.*

for offerings to "accredited investors" not exceeding five million dollars. Whereas Rule 506 has no limit on the dollar amount of an offering, Rule 505 exempts offerings only where the aggregate offering price of an issue, together with all securities previously offered pursuant to a section 3(b) exemption or in violation of section 5(a), does not exceed five million dollars within a twelve-month period.[5]

Purchasers in a 505 Offering

A Rule 505 offering may be made to an unlimited number of "accredited investors" and no more than thirty-five other "purchasers."[6] The Rule 505 exemption is conditioned on the absence of a general solicitation of investors. Unlike the safe harbor for non-public offerings under Rule 506,[8] there is no requirement that the unaccredited investors be sophisticated in order to participate in a Rule 505 offering. Furthermore, if an issuer takes reasonable steps to assure that the thirty-five unaccredited investor limit is not exceeded, the presence of an inadvertent extra unaccredited but otherwise qualified purchaser should not destroy the exemption.[9]

"Accredited investor" is defined in Rule 501 as any person who in fact comes within or whom the issuer reasonably believes comes within any of eight categories of investors at the time the securities are sold to him or her.[10] Generally, these categories include wealthy and/or financially sophisticated investors such as banks, insurance companies, tax-exempt organizations, directors and executive officers of the issuer, and natural persons who have a large net worth or very sizeable annual incomes.[11] When calculating the number of purchasers for purposes of Rule 505, one must exclude all accredited investors and certain relatives of a purchaser, and trusts, estates and corporations in which a purchaser has more than a fifty percent beneficial ownership.[12] In other instances, a corporation or other business entity will generally be counted as one purchaser,[13] as is each client of an investment adviser or broker.[14]

---

3. 17 C.F.R. § 230.506. *See* § 4.25 *infra*.

4. 15 U.S.C.A. § 77d(6). *See* § 4.23 *infra*.

5. 17 C.F.R. § 230.505(a), (b)(2)(i).

6. 17 C.F.R. § 230.505(b)(2)(ii). The following individuals and entities are not to be counted in the thirty-five purchaser ceiling: (1) any relative, spouse, or relative of the spouse of a purchaser who has the same principal residence as the purchaser, (2) any trust or estate in which a purchaser and any of the relatives just mentioned collectively have more than fifty percent of the beneficial interest, (3) any corporation or other organization which a purchaser together with his relatives and trusts and estates owns more than fifty percent of the equity securities or equity interests and (4) any accredited investor. 17 C.F.R. § 230.501(e).

8. 17 C.F.R. § 230.506. *See* § 4.25 *infra*.

9. 17 C.F.R. § 230.505(b)(2)(ii) ("there are no more than or the issuer reasonably believes that there are no more than 35 purchasers of securities. . . ."). In 1989 the Commission amended Rule 505 to include the language referring to the fact that the issuer must reasonably believe that the purchaser limitations are met.

10. 17 C.F.R. § 230.501(a). *See* §§ 4.20 *supra* and 4.23 *infra*. *See also* section 2(a)(15) and Rule 215; 15 U.S.C.A. § 77b(a)(15); 17 C.F.R. § 230.215 which are discussed in § 4.20 *infra*.

11. *See* § 4.23 *infra*.

12. 17 C.F.R. § 230.501(e)(1).

13. 17 C.F.R. § 230.501(e)(2).

14. 17 C.F.R. § 230.501(e) note.

Eligibility for Rule 505 Offerings

In order to be eligible to take advantage of the Rule 505 exemption the issuer must be neither an investment company nor be subject to any of the "bad boy" disqualification provisions contained in Rule 262(b) and(c) of Regulation A.[15] Further, all offers and sales made under Rule 505 must satisfy the terms and conditions of Rules 501 through 503 of Regulation D.[16]

Informational Requirements

In addition to defining "accredited investor," Rule 501 defines other terms used in Regulation D.[17] Rule 502 prohibits the use of general advertising or soliciting during an offering exempt under Rule 505. Further, Rule 502(b)[19] also requires the disclosure of certain information to purchasers who do not qualify as "accredited investors" as defined in Rule 501. The SEC recommends, however, that if there are any non-accredited investors, that all purchasers, including those who are accredited, receive the private placement memorandum. If all purchasers are accredited investors, then neither Rule 502 nor Rule 505 requires specific information to be disclosed to any purchasers. Rule 502 also provides a six-month safe harbor for the integration of Regulation D offerings and a five-factor test for determining whether offerings that fall outside the safe harbors will be integrated.[21]

Resale Restrictions

In addition, the SEC places limits on resales of securities acquired in a transaction under Rule 505, and, as a preventive measure, requires that issuers exercise reasonable care to determine that they are not selling to section 2(a)(11) underwriters.[22]

§ 4.23 The Statutory Exemption for Limited Offerings to "Accredited Investors"—Section 4(6)

Section 4(6)[1] exempts from the 1933 Act's registration requirements transactions in which the aggregate sales price does not exceed the maximum amount permitted by section 3(b)[2]—currently five million dollars—provided that all offers and sales are made only to "accredited investors."[3] The section 4(6) exemption is preconditioned upon the absence of general advertising or public solicitation in the offering process. The statute also requires that appropriate notice of sales made in reliance on section 4(6) be filed with the SEC. Form 4(6) was repealed in 1982 and replaced by Form D.

The term "accredited investor" is defined in section 2(a)(15)(i)[4] to include institutional investors such as banks, registered investment companies, em-

---

15. 17 C.F.R. § 230.505(a).

16. 17 C.F.R. § 230.505(b)(1). *See* 17 C.F.R. §§ 230.501–.503.

17. *See* § 4.19 *supra.*

19. 17 C.F.R. § 230.502(b).

21. 17 C.F.R. § 230.502(a). *See* § 4.19 *supra.* Integration is discussed in § 4.36 *infra.*

22. 17 C.F.R. § 230.502(d). *Compare, e.g.,* Note, Regulation A: Direct Public Offerings and the Internet, 79 Denver U.L. Rev. 229 (2001).

§ 4.23

1. 15 U.S.C.A. § 77(d)(6).

2. 15 U.S.C.A. § 77c(b). *See* § 4.16 *supra.*

3. *See* 15 U.S.C.A. § 77b(15). *See also* 17 C.F.R. § 230.215.

4. 15 U.S.C.A. § 77b(a)(15)(i).

ployee benefit plans subject to ERISA, and insurance companies. An alternative method for falling within the category of accredited investor under section 2(a)(15)(ii) is to be someone who, on the basis of factors such as financial sophistication, net worth, and knowledge and experience in financial matters, qualifies as an "accredited investor" as defined by the Commission's rules.[5]

The full effect of the section 4(6) exemption for sales to accredited investors is that it combines many of the features of a private placement[11] and that of the qualified exemption available under section 3(b).[12] The exemption also complements the private placement exemption provided by section 4(2) and Rule 506.[13]

§ 4.24 Exemption for Issuer Transactions Not Involving a Public Offering ("The Private Placement Exemption")—Section 4(2)

§ 4.24[1] Scope of the Section 4(2) Exemption

Section 4(2) of the 1933 Act[1] exempts "transactions by an issuer not involving any public offering." The exemption for transactions not involving a public offering is limited to issuers and thus cannot be relied upon by persons other than the issuer. However, non-issuers may be able to take advantage of the so-called section 4(1½) exemption, which is discussed in a later section of this treatise.[2] Over the years, the section 4(2) exemption, which is also commonly referred to as the private placement exemption, has proven useful for both closely held and public issue corporations.

The exemption for nonpublic offerings can be used by small firms, as well as by publicly held companies. Public companies issuing unregistered securities, including those issued under the section 4(2) exemption, must disclose those transactions in their periodic reports filed with the SEC.[5]

The nonpublic offering exemption was enacted for a number of reasons.[8] Congress was concerned with avoiding the cumbersome registration requirements when the benefits to the public were too remote and thus when there was no practical need for the Act's application.[9] The section 4(2) exemption was designed to apply to specific or isolated sales as well as to offerings to a very small number of securities holders so that the public interest is not involved. As will be seen from the discussion of the case law that has

5. 15 U.S.C.A. § 77b(a)(15)(ii). *See* 17 C.F.R. § 230.215.

11. 15 U.S.C.A. § 77d(2); 17 C.F.R. § 230.506. *See* § 4.25 *infra*.

12. 15 U.S.C.A. § 77c(b). *See* § 4.16 *supra*. The same combination is found in Rule 505, 17 C.F.R. § 230.505 which is discussed in § 4.22 *supra*.

13. 15 U.S.C.A. § 77d(2); 17 C.F.R. § 230.506.

§ 4.24

1. 15 U.S.C.A. § 77d(2).

2. *See* § 4.30 *infra*.

5. *See* Periodic Reporting of Unregistered Equity Sales, Sec. Exch. Act Rel. No. 34–37801, [1996–1997 Transfer Binder] Fed. Sec. L. Rep. (CCH) ¶ 85,852 (SEC Oct. 10, 1996). The Exchange Act's periodic reporting requirements are discussed in § 9.3 *infra*.

8. H.R.Rep. No. 85, 73 Cong., 1st Sess. 5–7, 15–16 (1933). *See also* H.R.Rep. No. 152, 73d Cong. 1st Sess. 1–29 (1933).

9. *See, e.g.,* Wright v. National Warranty Co., 953 F.2d 256, 259–60 (6th Cir.1992) (alternative holding, finding a nonpublic offering based on a sale to an accredited investor).

developed, as well as from the parameters of the safe-harbor rule, even today very small offerings to a limited number of purchasers will not be exempt if the offerees and purchasers do not qualify as sufficiently sophisticated (and/or wealthy) investors.

In order to provide more certainty in planning transactions, the SEC adopted the safe harbor rule contained in Rule 506. Compliance with the rule will provide an exemption, but according to the SEC, noncompliance does not raise even an inference that the exemption is unavailable.[11] Since Rule 506 is only a safe harbor rule, and is applicable only to qualifying non-public transactions, the pre-existing judicial and administrative interpretations remain an important part of the law today as they are still available to issuers who do not choose or are not able to comply with each and every provision of Rule 506.

Nature of the Offerees

In SEC v. Ralston Purina Co.,[13] the Supreme Court rejected the defendant's contention that an offering of stock that was limited to its own employees was necessarily exempt as not involving a public offering. The defendant, relying on a literal reading of the statute, maintained that an offering to a limited group could not properly be characterized as a public offering. The Court ruled that since the stock being offered was made available to all employees regardless of connection with the issuer and knowledge of the business, the offerees and purchasers represented a sufficiently large and representative slice of the investing public so as to render the exemption unavailable. In discussing the scope of the exemption, the Court announced the guidelines that have continued to form the basis for all private placement exemptions. In the first instance, all offerees must have access to the types of information that would be contained in a full-fledged 1933 Act registration statement. Secondly, the offerees must be capable of fending for themselves; in more recent cases, this has been interpreted to mean that the offerees must be sufficiently sophisticated to demand and understand the information that is available to them. Both offeree sophistication and access to information must be shown in order for the section 4(2) exemption to be established. The ability to fend for oneself is thus dependent upon access to information. It has therefore been held that the exemption will not be available even though the offerees are sufficiently sophisticated where they did not have access to the types of information that would otherwise have to be disclosed in the registration statement.[16]

The Supreme Court in *Ralston Purina* pointed out that even though the number of purchasers involved will not necessarily be the determinative factor, it is a significant one in considering the scope of the exemption. Accordingly, the fact that there were as many as five hundred employee offerees in the *Ralston Purina* case helped tip the balance against a section 4(2) exemption from registration. In addition to (1) the number of offerees, (2) the offerees' need for information and (3) the offerees' access to information, the courts will consider a fourth factor: the size of the offering, both in terms

11. Rule 506 (17 C.F.R. § 230.506) is discussed in § 4.25 *infra*.

13. 346 U.S. 119, 73 S.Ct. 981, 97 L.Ed. 1494 (1953).

16. Gilligan, Will & Co. v. SEC, 267 F.2d 461 (2d Cir.1959), *cert. denied* 361 U.S. 896, 80 S.Ct. 200, 4 L.Ed.2d 152 (1959). *See also, e.g.,* Van Dyke v. Coburn Enterprises, Inc., 873 F.2d 1094 (8th Cir.1989).

of the number of securities offered and the aggregate offering price. The number of offerees and size of the offering, as measured by the number of units offered, are significant because the larger the numbers of each, the more difficult it is to control downstream sales that would eventually filter the securities into the hands of the general investing public. As it becomes more likely that the securities sold pursuant to the private placement exemption will filter down to the investing public without a subsequent 1933 Act registration, it becomes less likely that the section 4(2) exemption will be available.

Absence of General Solicitation

In addition to the foregoing factors, the SEC has indicated that any "public advertising is inconsistent with a claim of private offering."[22] In light of the ban on public advertising, issuers frequently have to turn to investment bankers and other promoters in order to find an existing pool of potential customers. It is clearly permissible for a brokerage firm that is handling the private placement to contact its customers provided they meet the offering's suitability standard.[23] This was a common method of promoting tax shelters and is still widely used for other ventures that require a substantial investment. In such a case it is necessary to determine from the terms and risks of the offering the minimum offeree suitability standards. Where a private placement is not handled by a conduit with a ready list of potential offerees, all activities directed toward contacting the offerees will be closely scrutinized, lest the issuer run afoul of the general solicitation prohibition. The use of investment seminars and other promotional meetings have been a significant factor in denying the availability of the exemption for non-public offerings. Investment seminars (or "road shows") that are limited to qualified offerees who have been prescreened presumably would not violate the prohibition on a general solicitation. In general, where the issuer is unable to prove that there were a limited number of offerees, the uncertainty concerning the number of offerees will preclude reliance on the section 4(2) exemption.

Relevance of Investment Intent

A common practice of private placement issuers has been to require all purchasers to sign an "investment letter" attesting to their lack of intent to resell the securities to the public. Although this may still be a necessary precaution, and is required under Rule 506,[28] the fact that the issuer requires such investment letters is self-serving and thus will not in and of itself have any probative value as to the existence of the exemption or the issuer's reasonable efforts to assure that no downstream sales would occur without registration.[29]

---

22. Non–Public Offering Exemption, Sec. Act Rel. No. 33–4552, 1962 WL 69540, 1 Fed.Sec.L. Rep. (CCH) ¶ 2781 (Nov. 6, 1962).

23. Mary S. Krech Trust v. Lakes Apartments, 642 F.2d 98 (5th Cir.1981), *rehearing denied* 645 F.2d 72 (5th Cir.1981).

28. *See* 17 C.F.R. § 230.502(d).

29. SEC v. Continental Tobacco Co., 463 F.2d 137 (5th Cir.1972).

Is Investor Sophistication Really Necessary?

Questions can be raised as to the propriety of an investor sophistication requirement as a precondition to a section 4(2) exemption.[40] It is evident that the Supreme Court's primary concern in the *Ralston Purina* case was that offerees in a nonpublic offering have access to the types of information that would be available with a registered public offering.[42] However, as discussed directly above, the courts have since required that the offerees possess a certain degree of sophistication. It has been suggested by some observers that these cases took their lead from Rule 506's predecessor and that investor sophistication may not properly be an element of the section 4(2) nonpublic offering exemption. While offeree access to information is a necessary element of any transaction exempted under section 4(2), it clearly cannot be sufficient. The offerees as a class must somehow represent something other than a slice of the investing public.[43] As the Supreme Court observed in *Ralston Purina*:

> Since exempt transactions are those to which "there is no practical need for [the bill's] application," the applicability of section 4[(2)] should turn on whether the particular class of persons affected needs the protection of the Act. An offering to those who are shown to be able to fend for themselves is a transaction "not involving any public offering."[44]

In discussing the offerees' ability to fend for themselves, the Court was addressing something beyond access to information.

Accessibility of Information to Offerees

As noted above, it is clear that access to information is a precondition to any section 4(2) exemption. As the foregoing discussion points out, informational access alone may not be sufficient if the investors are not able to fend for themselves. As a safety precaution, each offeree should receive an offering circular containing full disclosure. The cases interpreting the section 4(2) exemption do not expressly require the use of an offering circular.[48] However, offering circulars, or private placement memorandums have become increasingly common. The use of an offering circular is a good way for planners of private placement transactions to assure that the initial access to information requirements are satisfied.

Section 4(2) in Context

Beyond the above-mentioned limitations on the structure of the offering, the section 4(2) exemption must be read in light of the exemptions provided

---

40. *See, e.g.,* Carl W. Schneider, Section 4(1½): Private Resales of Restricted or Control Securities, 49 Ohio St. L.J. 501, 509 (1988); Carl W. Schneider, The Statutory Law of Private Placements, 14 Rev.Sec.Reg. 869, 874–75 (1981); ABA Committee on Federal Regulation of Securities, Section 4(2) and Statutory Law, 31 Bus.Law. 485, 491 (1975). A number of commentators have taken the opposite view.

41. SEC v. Ralston Purina Co., 346 U.S. 119, 73 S.Ct. 981, 97 L.Ed. 1494 (1953).

43. To take an extreme example, consider an offering of securities to 10 individuals with red hair, when all offerees were given information comparable to that which would appear in a registration statement. Even assuming that all purchasers would be purchasing for investment rather than for resale, the section 4(2) exemption should not be available. *Cf.* SEC v. Sunbeam Gold Mines Co., 95 F.2d 699, 701 (9th Cir.1938).

44. SEC v. Ralston Purina Co., 346 U.S. 119, 125, 73 S.Ct. 981, 984, 97 L.Ed. 1494, 1498–99 (1953).

48. Van Dyke v. Coburn Enterprises, Inc., 873 F.2d 1094, 1098 (8th Cir.1989) (the exemption was available even though "[w]hile reasonable minds may disagree as to whether the appellants had been furnished the necessary information to make an informed investment decision, it is without dispute that they had access to the necessary information").

by section 4(1)[54] (exempting transactions not involving an issuer, underwriter, or dealer), section 4(4)[55] (exempting unsolicited brokers' transactions), section 4(6)[56] (exempting offerings up to five million dollars to accredited investors), and Rule 144[57] (dealing with downstream resales of securities issued under one of the aforementioned exemptions). Even if a qualified offeree purchases a security offered pursuant to a private placement, his or her subsequent downstream sale may well destroy the exemption. For example, someone reselling the security within a short period of time may be deemed an underwriter within the statutory definition provided by section 2(a)(11),[58] and thus the downstream sale would be beyond the scope of the section 4(1) exemption.[59] Further, through the doctrine of integration, downstream sales may relate back and destroy the original section 4(2) exemption.[60]

In addition to the federal and state securities law consequences, a failed private placement may have collateral implications. For example, when securities are offered in violation of section 5 due to non-compliance with the nonpublic offering exemption, the violation may render the contract unenforceable under state contract law.[64]

In summary, a review of the relevant cases reveals that an issuer relying on the statutory section 4(2) exemption, rather than upon Rule 506's safe-harbor provisions, may be subjecting itself to a great deal of uncertainty. In addition to the guidelines that appear from the judicial decisions, the planner must not lose sight of the original factors established by the *Ralston Purina* decision.[65] In evaluating the availability of the exemption, the courts and the SEC will look not only to the number and nature of the offerees and their access to the types of information that would be contained in the registration statement, but also to the relationship of the offerees to the issuer, the relationship of the offerees to each other, the manner of the offering, and the number of shares to be offered.

§ 4.25 Safe Harbor for Private Placements Under Section 4(2)—SEC Rule 506

SEC Rule 506[1] provides an exemption for the offer and sale of securities to no more than thirty-five purchasers.[2] As with the Rule 505[3] exemption,

54. 15 U.S.C.A. § 77d(1). *See* § 4.26 *infra.*

55. 15 U.S.C.A. § 77d(4). *See* § 4.26 *infra.*

56. 15 U.S.C.A. § 77d(6). *See* § 4.20 *supra.*

57. 17 C.F.R. § 230.144. *See* § 4.26 *infra.*

58. 15 U.S.C.A. § 77b(a)(11). *See* § 4.27 *infra.*

59. *See, e.g.,* Gilligan, Will & Co. v. SEC, 267 F.2d 461 (2d Cir.1959), *cert. denied* 361 U.S. 896, 80 S.Ct. 200, 4 L.Ed.2d 152 (1959); United States v. Sherwood, 175 F.Supp. 480 (S.D.N.Y.1959).

60. *See, e.g.,* 17 C.F.R. § 230.502(a).

64. See Frishman v. Maginn, 2006 WL 1075600 (Mass. Super. 2006) (presence of unaccredited investors rendered Regulation D unavailable; since offering violated the 1933 Act, the contract for the sale of stock was void and unenforceable under Massachusetts law).

65. *See* SEC v. Ralston Purina Co., 346 U.S. 119, 73 S.Ct. 981, 97 L.Ed. 1494 (1953).

§ 4.25

1. 17 C.F.R. § 230.506(b)(2)(i); 17 C.F.R. § 230.501(a), (e).

2. The following individuals and entities are not to be counted in the thirty-five purchaser ceiling: (1) any relative, spouse, or relative of the spouse of a purchaser who has the same principal residence as the purchaser, (2) any trust or estate in which a purchaser and any of the relatives just mentioned collectively have more than fifty percent of the beneficial interest, (3) any "accredited investors"[4] are not counted toward that limit.[5] Thus, for example, there could be one hundred accredited investors in addition to the thirty-five unaccredited purchasers. Even with regard to the thirty-five unaccredited investors, if an issuer takes reasonable steps to assure that the number is not exceeded, the presence of an inadvertent extra unaccredited but otherwise qualified purchaser should not destroy the exemption.[6]

Rule 506 further places qualifications on permissible purchasers. Each purchaser who is not an accredited investor himself, herself, or through a purchaser representative, must have such knowledge and experience in financial and business matters that the purchaser or qualifying representative is capable of evaluating the merits and risks of the prospective investment.[7] Rule 506 is a "safe harbor" rule. If an offering of securities fails to meet the requirements of Rule 506, the issuer may still qualify for a 4(2) exemption if it conforms to requirements developed through cases and SEC releases.[9]

Rule 506 is available to any issuer, whether or not it is an investment company, a non-reporting company, or subject to any of the disqualification provisions contained in Rule 252(c), (d), (e), or (f) of Regulation A.[10] However, all offers and sales made under Rule 506 must satisfy the terms and conditions of Rules 501, 502, and 503 of Regulation D.[11]

Purchaser Qualifications

An unsophisticated purchaser may still qualify as a Rule 506 investor through the use of an appropriate purchaser representative. "Purchaser representative" is defined by Rule 501 to be any person who satisfies or whom the issuer reasonably believes satisfies the following four conditions: (1) is not an insider of the issuer (*i.e.*, affiliate, director, officer, or beneficial owner of ten percent of a class of the issuer's equity securities), (2) has such knowledge and experience in financial and business matters that he is capable of evaluating, alone, or together with other purchaser representatives or with the purchaser, the merits and risks of the prospective investment, (3) is acknowledged by the purchaser in writing to be his purchaser representative

corporation or other organization which a purchaser together with his relatives and trusts and estates owns more than fifty percent of the equity securities or equity interests and (4) any accredited investor. 17 C.F.R. § 230.501(e).

The issuer must take reasonable steps to assure that there are no more than 35 purchasers. Rule 506(b)(2)(i), 17 C.F.R. § 230.506(b)(2)(i).

3. 17 C.F.R. § 230.505.

4. Accredited investor is defined in 17 C.F.R. § 230.501(a). *See also* 15 U.S.C.A. § 77b(a)(15).

5. 17 C.F.R. § 230.501(e)(1)(iv).

6. 17 C.F.R. § 230.506(b)(2)(i) ("there are no more than or the issuer reasonably believes that there are no more than 35 purchasers of securities. . . .").

7. 17 C.F.R. § 230.506(b)(2)(ii).

9. *E.g.*, Weprin v. Peterson, 736 F.Supp. 1124 (N.D.Ga.1988). *Cf.* SEC v. Interlink Data Network of Los Angeles, Inc., 1993 WL 603274, [1993–1994 Transfer Binder] Fed. Sec. L. Rep. (CCH) ¶ 98,049 (C.D.Cal.1993) (exemption was not available where issuer failed to screen for accredited investors, engaged in a general solicitation, and failed to comply with the informational requirements).

10. 17 C.F.R. § 230.506(a). *See* 17 C.F.R. §§ 230.251–62, 230.504(a), 230.505(a); § 4.17 *supra*. In 1987, the Commission considered but then, in 1988, rejected extending the "bad boy" disqualifications to Rule 506's safe harbor. Sec. Act Rel. No. 33–6758, [1987–1988 Transfer Binder] Fed. Sec. L. Rep. (CCH) ¶ 84,221 (March 3, 1988); Sec. Act Rel. No. 33–6683, [1986–1987 Transfer Binder] Fed. Sec. L. Rep. (CCH) ¶ 84,054 (Jan. 16, 1987).

11. 17 C.F.R. § 230.506(b)(1). *See* 17 C.F.R. §§ 230.501–.503.

with reference to each prospective investment considered, and (4) discloses to the purchaser before the purchaser's acknowledgment just mentioned any material relationship between the purchaser representative or his affiliates and the issuer or its affiliates that exists, is contemplated, or has existed within the previous two years, including any compensation received or to be received as a result.[12] Insiders of the issuer, however, are allowed to serve as purchaser representatives for certain relatives, trusts, and estates, as well as for corporations in which they have fifty percent beneficial interest.[13] The concept of purchaser representative allows the issuer to reach unsophisticated, wealthy investors who do not satisfy the "nature of purchaser requirements" of Rule 506.

As is the case with the section 4(2) exemption,[15] Rule 506 is limited to transactions by an issuer. Therefore, persons other than the issuer who seek an exemption from registration for their sales must look elsewhere.[16] The Commission has tried to present the issuer seeking a private placement exemption with a reasonable safe harbor rule. However, the Commission's efforts under Rule 506's predecessor have not gone without strong criticism on the grounds that the requirements are very difficult to comply with and, hence, the rule does not provide a sufficiently safe predictor for planners of securities transactions.[17] Also, as was seen in the preceding section,[18] a number of courts have borrowed heavily from Rule 506's predecessor in formulating the scope of the statutory section 4(2) exemption, thus adding a qualification to the Commission's statement that the rule is not exclusive.

Rule 506 does not include any offeree qualification requirements such as those found in its predecessor or the cases interpreting the section 4(2) nonpublic offering exemption. To the extent that Rule 506 is based on section 4(2), rather than section 3(b) or 4(6)—each of which has a five million dollar ceiling[21]—it is arguable that the statute requires the offeree qualifications to be read into the rule. The SEC in adopting Rule 506 wanted to ease the problems associated with offeree qualification under its predecessor—former Rule 146—but there is no indication of the SEC's statutory basis for ignoring the judicially imposed offeree requirements. In fact, the SEC has indicated that the nature and number of offerees remain relevant in determining whether there has been a general solicitation so as to render Rule 506 and section 4(2) unavailable.[22] The safe harbor protection, thus, is no longer dependent upon the issuer being able to prove that *each* offeree was qualified. On the other hand, if the issuer cannot show that it took adequate precautions against the solicitation of nonqualified offerees, it may lose the section 4(2) exemption because of the inability to show that a general solicitation did not take place. Accordingly, the effect of the deletion of the offeree qualification requirement in Rule 506 is that when an issuer takes reasonable

12. 17 C.F.R. § 230.501(h).

13. 17 C.F.R. § 230.501(h)(1)(i), (ii), (iii).

15. *See* § 4.24 *supra.*

16. *See* § 4.30 *infra* for discussion of the so-called "4(1½)" exemption.

17. *See, e.g.,* Robert A. Kessler, Private Placement Rules 146 and 240–Safe Harbor?, 44 Fordham L.Rev. 37 (1975).

18. *See* § 4.24 *supra.*

21. 15 U.S.C.A. §§ 77c(b), 77(d)(6). *See* § 4.16 *supra.*

22. Interpretive Release on Regulation D, Sec. Act Rel. No. 33–6455, 27 S.E.C. Docket 347, 1983 WL 409415, 1 Fed. Sec. L. Rep. (CCH) ¶ 2380 (SEC March 3, 1983) (answer to question 73).

precautions but somehow an unqualified offeree is given an offer, the safe harbor may still be available. It is important to recall that not all preliminary contacts with prospective offerees will constitute an offer. Thus, it is permissible to make preliminary inquiries to determine if prospective offerees are in fact qualified so long as these preliminary contacts do not give detail as to the nature and terms of the planned offering.

Rule 506(b)(2)(ii) provides that a purchaser must either be knowledgeable, act through a purchaser representative, or be qualified as an accredited investor.[26] In addition to institutional investors, the definition of accredited investor includes individuals with a net worth of more than one million dollars or an annual income in excess of two hundred thousand dollars, as well as married couples with a combined net worth of one million dollars, or a combined annual income of more than three hundred thousand dollars.[27] In so defining qualified purchasers, Rule 506 substitutes wealth as a criterion in lieu of investor knowledge and sophistication.

Number of Purchasers

Rule 501[28] also provides the method for calculating the number of purchasers under Rule 506. The following individuals and entities are not to be counted in the thirty-five purchaser ceiling: (1) any relative, spouse, or relative of the spouse of a purchaser who has the same principal residence as the purchaser, (2) any trust or estate in which a purchaser and any of the relatives just mentioned collectively have more than fifty percent of the beneficial interest, (3) any corporation or other organization which a purchaser together with his relatives and trusts and estates owns more than fifty percent of the equity securities or equity interests and (4) any accredited investor.[29]

General Solicitation not Permitted

Regulation D places limits on the manner of the offering and solicitation methods. Rule 502 prohibits the use of general advertising or soliciting during an offering exempt under Rule 506.[30] Rule 502 also recommends the disclosure of certain information to all purchasers if any one purchaser is not an "accredited investor" as defined in Rule 501.[31] If all purchasers are accredited investors, then neither Rule 502 nor Rule 506 requires specific information to be disclosed to any purchaser.[32]

26. 17 C.F.R. § 230.506(b)(2)(ii). The definition of accredited investor is found in Rule 501(a) (17 C.F.R. § 230.501(a)).

Broker-dealers must be careful in recommending private placements to their customers. *See, e.g.,* In The Matter of Tyler, 2001 WL 583157, Sec. Act Rel. No. 33–7978, Sec. Exch. Act Rel. No. 34–44314 (SEC May 17, 2001) (cease and desist order per settlement offer for unsuitable private placement recommendations). Broker-dealer suitability obligations are discussed in § 14.16 *infra.*

27. 17 C.F.R. § 230.501(a). *See* Howard Friedman, On Being Rich, Accredited, and Undiversified: The Lacunae in Contemporary Securities Regulation, 47 Okla. L. Rev. 291 (1994).

Assets held in a grantor irrevocable trust can be included in the net worth calculation. Herrick, Feinstein LLP, 2001 WL 15831, [2001–2002 Transfer Binder] Fed. Sec. L. Rep. (CCH) ¶ 78,115 (SEC No Action Letter Jan. 5, 2001).

28. Rule 501 is the general definitional provision for Regulation D. 17 C.F.R. § 230.501. *See* § 4.19 *supra.*

29. 17 C.F.R. § 230.501(e).

30. 17 C.F.R. § 230.502(c).

31. 17 C.F.R. § 230.502(b)(1). The information requirements are set forth in § 4.20 *supra.*

32. 17 C.F.R. §§ 230.502(b)(1)(i), 230.506(b)(1).

Informational Requirements

Rule 502(b)(1)[33] provides that where all Rule 506 purchasers are accredited, the issuer is not under the affirmative disclosure obligations set forth in Rule 502(b)(2).[34] Formerly, the rule required that if there was one unaccredited purchaser, *all* purchasers had to receive a private placement memorandum containing the specified information. Under the current version of the rule, there is no such mandate as the informational requirement applies only to unaccredited investors. However, the SEC recommends that in light of antifraud considerations *all purchasers* receive this information.[35] Accordingly, the failure to deliver an offering memorandum to accredited investors will not destroy the safe harbor exemption. Nevertheless, there seems little reason not to follow the Commission's advice and supply the offering circular to accredited investors if one has been prepared for unaccredited investors.

Rules 502 and 506 on their face give the reader the impression that for a private placement made solely to accredited investors there are no informational requirements. Rule 502 only addresses the issuer's need to provide a disclosure statement and does not address the additional requirement (derived from the courts' interpretation of the statute) that all purchasers in a non-public offering have access to current information about the issuer. In the *SEC v. Ralston Purina* decision,[36] the Supreme Court announced *two* prerequisites for the section 4(2) non public offering exemption. First, the offerees must have access to the same type of current information about the issuer that would be required in a registered offering. Second, the purchasers must be sufficiently sophisticated and knowledgeable to evaluate the information. Rule 506(b) permits the offeree qualification to be established if the purchaser is an accredited investor.[37] This goes to only the first part of the *Ralston Purina* test. As a section 4(2) exemption, Rule 506 cannot go beyond the parameters of the statute.[38] Since the statute, as interpreted by the Supreme Court, requires access to current issuer information, such a requirement should be read into Rule 506. Accordingly, Rule 502 should not be read as dispensing with the access to information requirement; its sole purpose is to relieve the issuer of the burden of preparing a disclosure memorandum in offerings where all purchasers are accredited.

Applicability of State Securities Laws

In 1996, Congress preempted the states' ability to apply their Blue Sky registration requirements to many transactions.[51] Some exempt transactions carry with them the state law preemption but section 4(2) does not except for those transactions exempt pursuant to an SEC rule or regulation.[52] This means that when the transaction qualifies for Rule 506's safe harbor, there is

33. 17 C.F.R. § 230.502(b)(1).

34. 17 C.F.R. § 230.502(b)(2).

35. 17 C.F.R. § 230.502(b)(2).

36. 346 U.S. 119, 73 S.Ct. 981, 97 L.Ed. 1494 (1953). *See* § 4.24 *supra.*

37. 17 C.F.R. § 230.506(b)(2)(ii). Alternatively, an unsophisticated unaccredited investor may qualify through the use of a purchaser representative. *Id.*

38. At least in theory, the SEC could invoke the general exemptive authority set forth in section 28 of the Act (15 U.S.C.A. § 77z–3) to depart from section 4(2)'s limitations. However, there has not been any indication of a movement in this direction.

51. Pub. L. No. 104–290, 110 Stat. 3416 (1996).

52. 15 U.S.C.A. § 77r(b)(4)(D).

an exemption from state law registration requirements. However, if the safe harbor or Rule 506 is unavailable or lost, then the state registration requirements are not preempted and the issuer must either register under state law or find an applicable state law exemption.

§ 4.26 An Overview of Transactions by Persons Other Than Issuers, Underwriters, and Dealers: Section 4(1); Unsolicited Brokers' Transactions—Section 4(4)

The registration requirements of the 1933 Act are not limited to offerings by the issuer. Secondary transactions—that, is sales by existing shareholders—may also trigger section 5's registration and prospectus obligations. Because of the proscription of section 5, the burden is on a seller of securities, including existing shareholders, to establish an exemption from registration.[1] Section 4(1),[2] 4(3),[3] and 4(4)[4] of the 1933 Act provide the most common exemptions available for secondary transactions.[5]

Section 4(1) of the 1933 Act[6] provides a registration exemption for "transactions by any person other than an issuer, underwriter or dealer." Section 4(1), especially when read in connection with the dealers' and unsolicited brokers' transaction exemptions in sections 4(3) and 4(4),[7] exempts most day-to-day transactions that are effected on an exchange or in the over-the-counter markets.[8] Since section 4(2)'s private placement exemption[9] is limited to issuer transactions, it has no application to the millions of shares that are traded daily on the national exchanges and NASDAQ where, although not involving a public offering, the transactions are not effected by issuers. The section 4(1) exemption helps fill this void. Section 4(1), which is also known as the exemption for nonprofessionals, exempts transactions rather than people and thus may not be available to someone who is not an issuer, underwriter or dealer but is involved in a transaction with one.[10] However, the mere involvement by a broker in a secondary transaction will not render the exemption unavailable.[11] Furthermore, unsolicited brokers' transactions are exempt under section 4(4).

---

§ 4.26

1. *E.g.*, SEC v. Ralston Purina Co., 346 U.S. 119, 126, 73 S.Ct. 981, 985, 97 L.Ed. 1494 (1953) (the burden of establishing an exemption falls on the person claiming the exemption). *See* § 4.1[3] *supra*.

2. 15 U.S.C.A. § 77d(1). *See* § 4.26[1] *infra*.

3. 15 U.S.C.A. § 77d(3). *See* § 4.31 *infra*.

4. 15 U.S.C.A. § 77d(4). *See* § 4.26[2] *infra*.

5. *See, e.g.*, Rutherford B. Campbell, Resales of Securities under the Securities Act of 1933, 52 Wash. & Lee L. Rev. 1333 (1995); William Hicks, The Concept of Transaction as a Restraint on Resale Limitations, 49 Ohio St. L.J. 417 (1988).

6. 15 U.S.C.A. § 77d(1). *See* Report, The Section "4(1½)" Phenomenon: Private Resales of "Restricted" Securities, 34 Bus.Law. 1961 (1979).

7. 15 U.S.C.A. §§ 77d(3), 77d(4).

8. Section 4(3) exempts transactions by nonparticipating dealers and underwriters no longer acting as underwriters after more than forty or ninety days after the registration statement's effective date. 15 U.S.C.A. § 77d(3).

9. 15 U.S.C.A. § 77d(2). *See* § 4.24 *supra*.

10. SEC v. Holschuh, 694 F.2d 130, 137–38 (7th Cir.1982); United States v. Wolfson, 405 F.2d 779 (2d Cir.1968), *cert. denied* 394 U.S. 946, 89 S.Ct. 1275, 22 L.Ed.2d 479 (1969).

11. Ackerberg v. Johnson, 892 F.2d 1328, 1334 n. 4 (8th Cir.1989).

The section 4(1) transaction exemption is limited to bona fide non-underwriter transactions. It is not available for sales that constitute an attempt to evade the Act's registration requirements.[12] Thus, for example, sales of stock in a blank check company through a market maker will not qualify for the exemption.[13]

§ 4.26[1] Section 4(1)—The Exemption for Nonprofessionals—Basic Definitions

Issuers, underwriters, and dealers are persons or entities who are engaged in securities transactions by virtue of their professions. Thus, one way to look at the section 4(1) exemption is as an exemption for ordinary transactions by ordinary, nonprofessional investors. A better understanding of the scope of the exemption flows from the definition of the terms "issuer," "underwriter," and "dealer."

Issuers. By its terms, section 4(1) exempts all transactions by persons who are not issuers, underwriters or dealers. Section 2(a)(4) of the Act[14] defines "issuer" to include every person who issues or proposes to issue a security. In addition, in the case of a voting trust or other trust certificates, "issuer" refers to the person or persons performing the acts and assuming the duties of depositor or manager under the provisions of the trust or other agreement.[15] The definition of issuer is not limited to initial distributions. For example, it has been held that a transaction is not exempt and the issuer concept applies to the reissue of stock that had previously been reacquired by the issuing corporation.[16] It has also been held that the concept of issuer applies to a corporation acting as a promoter by setting up a number of limited partnerships for syndication.[17] The statutory definition of issuer does not generally raise any significant problem of judicial interpretation since it is usually easy to identify the issuer for a particular security.

Underwriters. The question of who is an underwriter, which is taken up in more detail in the next section of this treatise,[18] is not nearly as simple as defining "issuer." Section 2(a)(11)[19] provides that an "underwriter" is anyone who purchases a security from the issuer with a view toward distribution of the security, as well as anyone who offers or sells for an issuer in connection with a distribution, including anyone involved in any indirect participation in such undertaking or the underwriting of the distribution. The most troubling problems the definition presents in operation arise in the context of persons who, although not denominated as underwriters in the generic sense of the term, act as conduits for placing the securities in the hands of members of the investing public. In addition to the general definition of underwriter, section 2(a)(11) further provides that anyone who sells securities on behalf of a

12. *E.g.,* NASD Regulation, Inc., 32 Sec. Reg. & L. Rep. (BNA) 207 (SEC No Action Letter Jan. 21, 2000).

13. NASD Regulation, Inc., 32 Sec. Reg. & L. Rep. (BNA) 207 (SEC No Action Letter Jan. 21, 2000) (neither section 4(1) nor Rule 144's safe harbor was available).

14. 15 U.S.C.A. § 77b(a)(4).

15. 15 U.S.C.A. § 77b(a)(4).

16. SEC v. Stanwood Oil Corp., 516 F.Supp. 1181, 1184 (W.D.Pa.1981).

17. SEC v. Holschuh, 694 F.2d 130, 138–39 (7th Cir.1982); SEC v. Murphy, 626 F.2d 633, 644 (9th Cir.1980).

18. *See* § 4.27 *infra.*

19. 15 U.S.C.A. § 77b(a)(11).

controlling person of the issuer is deemed an underwriter.[20] There are thus three ways to qualify for underwriter status: (1) purchasing from the issuer with a view towards distribution, (2) direct or indirect participation in an underwriting effort, and (3) selling securities on behalf of a control person. Underwriter status not only renders the section 4(1) exemption unavailable, but it also provides the basis for liability for misstatements in connection with a registered offering.[21]

Dealers. Section 2(a)(12) of the Act[22] defines "dealer" to include any person who for all or part of his or her time is in the business of offering, buying, selling, or otherwise dealing or trading in securities issued by others. It does not matter whether such sales activity is direct or indirect and the statutory definition of dealer further applies whether one is acting as agent, broker, or principal with regard to the securities transactions in question. Since virtually all day-to-day transactions are effected through the means of a registered broker-dealer, the section 4(1) exemption standing alone would not exclude the transactions from coverage of the Act's registration provisions. However, as noted above, section 4(1) must be read in tandem with section 4(3)'s exemption for most dealers' transactions and section 4(4)'s exemption for unsolicited brokers' transactions.

§ 4.26[2] Section 4(4)—Unsolicited Brokers' Transactions

One of the key provisions dealing with many day-to-day securities transactions is found in section 4(4)'s exemption for unsolicited brokers' transactions.[24] Section 4(4) exempts "brokers' transactions executed upon customers' orders on any exchange or in the over-the-counter market but not the solicitation of such orders." Neither the 1933 Act nor the SEC rules promulgated thereunder contain a definition of "broker," but it is clear that the concept cannot be coextensive with that of a "dealer" under section 2(a)(12). Additional learning on the meaning of the term "broker" can be gathered by reference to the Securities Exchange Act of 1934. Section 3(a)(4) of the 1934 Act[25] defines "broker" as anyone, other than a bank engaged in the business of effecting securities transactions for the account of others. The 1934 Act definition of broker comports with the generic meaning of the term and thus would seem to be equally applicable to the 1933 Act As such, brokers form a subclass of dealers and include anyone who is in the business of effecting securities transactions as agent for others. Accordingly, persons who only execute transactions on their own behalf or as principals may still be categorized as "dealers" but do not fall within the concept of "broker" within the statutory exemption from registration provided in section 4(4). The section 4(4) exemption only applies to transactions in which the broker acts as the purchaser's agent, rather than as an agent for someone else such as the issuer or underwriter.

---

20. *See, e.g.,* United States v. Wolfson, 405 F.2d 779 (2d Cir.1968), *cert. denied* 394 U.S. 946, 89 S.Ct. 1275, 22 L.Ed.2d 479 (1969); SEC v. Netelkos, 592 F.Supp. 906 (S.D.N.Y.1984); § 4.27 *infra.*

21. Section 11(a) imposes civil liability upon underwriters for damages resulting from reliance on material misstatements or omissions in the registration statement. 15 U.S.C.A. § 77k(a). *See* § 7.4 *infra.*

22. 15 U.S.C.A. § 77b(a)(12).

24. 15 U.S.C.A. § 77d(4). *See also* section 4(3) of the Act, 15 U.S.C.A. § 77d(3) which is discussed in § 4.31 *infra.*

25. 15 U.S.C.A. § 77c(a)(4).

Another significant aspect of the section 4(4) exemption is that it extends to "brokers' *transactions.*" Both the courts and the SEC have pointed out the distinction in terminology between "transactions" and the concept of a "distribution."[26] It has accordingly been held that although a particular securities sale may be at the behest of the customer and thus executed through a broker without his or her solicitation, it may nevertheless be subject to the Act's registration requirements. The brokers' transaction exemption has thus been held inapplicable if the amount of securities sold is so large as to constitute a "distribution"—as compared with the day-to-day "transaction" that the section 4(4) exemption was designed to cover.[27] The concept of distribution sufficient to confer underwriter status does not depend on a certain percentage of the market float but rather on the fact that a significant amount of shares are involved.[28] In addition to the magnitude of the sales in question, a distribution may be found to exist based on the types of selling efforts that are employed. The term "distribution" is used to describe "the entire process in a public offering through which a block of securities is dispersed and ultimately comes to rest in the hands of the investing public."[30] The existence of a distribution will depend on a number of factors relating to the magnitude of the transaction, including the number of shares for sale, the trading volume that those shares represent, the percentage of outstanding shares, and the public float. The amount of the shares being sold is not as significant as the percentage of the public float that those shares represent.[32]

The section 4(4) exemption is unavailable to a broker who has reasonable grounds to believe that the customer is a statutory underwriter.[33] The Commission has indicated that brokers receiving restricted stock have a duty of reasonable inquiry as to whether the customer entering a sell order is a statutory underwriter.[34] Furthermore, a broker or dealer who is asked to sell a substantial block of securities is under an obligation to investigate whether

26. *E.g.,* Gilligan, Will & Co. v. SEC, 267 F.2d 461, 466 (2d Cir.1959), *cert. denied* 361 U.S. 896, 80 S.Ct. 200, 4 L.Ed.2d 152 (1959), citing H.R.Rep. No. 1838, 73d Cong.2d Sess. 41 (1934).

27. *See, e.g.,* United States v. Wolfson, 405 F.2d 779 (2d Cir.1968), *cert. denied* 394 U.S. 946, 89 S.Ct. 1275, 22 L.Ed.2d 479 (1969); In the Matter of Ira Haupt & Co., Sec. Exch. Act Rel. No. 34–3845, 23 S.E.C. 589, 1946 WL 24150 (SEC 1946). *See* §§ 4.28–4.29 *infra.*

28. *See* Quinn & Co. v. SEC, 452 F.2d 943, 946 (10th Cir.1971) ("It is firmly established that an issuer cannot avoid registration of its securities for a public offering simply by limiting the number of shares sold. This Court is cognizant of the fact that the amount of Mountain shares sold by White does not form a great percentage of the total issue. However, under the circumstances, resale by White of 25,000 shares of Mountain stock constituted a public distribution").

30. Berckeley Investment Group, Ltd. v. Colkitt, 455 F.3d 195 (3d Cir. 2006) ("those courts interpreting the exemption have uniformly concluded that the term 'distribution' is synonymous with 'public offering' as set forth under Section 4(2)"), relying on Geiger v. SEC, 363 F.3d 481, 484 (D.C. Cir. 2004).

32. *See* Examination of the Registration of Securities To Be Offered and Sold on a Delayed or Continuous Basis in the Future, Sec. Act Rel. No. 33–6391, 24 S.E.C. Docket 1502, 1982 WL 529089 (SEC March 12, 1982).

33. In re Robert G. Leigh, 50 S.E.C. 189, 1990 WL 309872 [1990 Transfer Binder] Fed. Sec. L. Rep. (CCH) ¶ 84,700 (Feb. 1, 1990) (broker had reason to know that customer selling unregistered securities had acquired the shares from the issuer with a view to selling them). *Cf.,* Robert A. Barron, The Apparent Sale of Unregistered Securities—Can it be Saved?, 33 Sec. Reg. L.J. 82 (2005) (discussing the situation where after a sale has been effected, a broker receives stock certificates only to find out that the shares are restricted).

34. *Id.* (customer delivered to broker a large block of restricted stock in a little known company after telling broker that he received the stock as a finder's fee and that he intended to sell most of the shares).

the transaction involves a control person and/or underwriter; and reliance on the customer's assertions alone may not satisfy the obligation of reasonable investigation.

The SEC does not have any rules relating specifically to brokers' transactions themselves. However, Rule 144(g)'s provision relating to brokers' transactions and Rule 144(e)'s safe harbor for the amount of securities sold[37] may give some guidance as to the scope of the section 4(4) exemption.

§ 4.27 Who Is an Underwriter?—Section 2(a)(11)

Section 2(a)(11) of the Act[1] sets forth a broad-based statutory definition of "underwriter" which includes (1) persons who acquire securities of the issuer with a view towards distribution, (2) all persons who directly or indirectly participate in the offering, selling or underwriting process, as well as (3) persons selling on behalf of a control person of the issuer. The definition's significance goes beyond the section 4(1) exemption from registration.[2] For example, section 2(a)(11) also helps determine the scope of the class of persons liable for material misstatements and omissions made in connection with registered offerings.[3]

§ 4.27[1] The Underwriter Concept—Section 2(a)(11) and Applicable SEC Rules

The statutory definition sets forth three ways in which someone may fall within the definition of underwriter: (1) by purchasing from the issuer with a view towards distribution, (2) by direct or indirect participation in an underwriting effort, and (3) by selling securities on behalf of a control person. As is discussed more fully below, underwriter status requires the existence of a "distribution,"[5] which is generally interpreted to involve a large amount of securities.

Whether a transaction falls within the section 4(1) exemption by involving an "underwriter" often boils down to a question of fact as to the would-be underwriter's state of mind in acquiring the security. In addition, irrespective of a reseller's intent, conduct in the course of a distribution can qualify some as a statutory underwriter. Not every participant having a role in the distribution will fall within the definition of underwriter.[8]

One key aspect of this part of the statutory definition is that in order to be classified as a statutory underwriter, the participant must have been acting on behalf of or purchasing from an issuer. In this context, however, the statute provides that a control person is considered to be an issuer. Willfully acting as a conduit for distributing shares without registration is sufficient to create underwriter status, even though the person acting as an underwriter

37. 17 C.F.R. § 230.144(e).

§ 4.27

1. 15 U.S.C.A. § 77b(a)(11).

2. *See* 15 U.S.C.A. § 77d(1), which is discussed in § 4.29 *supra*; § 4.32 *infra*.

3. *See* 15 U.S.C.A. § 77k(a), which is discussed in § 7.3 *infra*.

5. 15 U.S.C.A. § 77b(a)(11). *See, e.g.*, United States v. Wolfson, 405 F.2d 779 (2d Cir.1968), *cert. denied* 394 U.S. 946, 89 S.Ct. 1275, 22 L.Ed.2d 479 (1969); In the Matter of Ira Haupt & Co., 23 S.E.C. 589, Sec. Exch. Act Rel. No. 34–3845, 1946 WL 24150 (SEC 1946).

8. *See, e.g.*, In re Refco, Inc. Securities Litigation, 2008 WL 140956 (S.D.N.Y. 2008) (banks' activities in connection with public offering did not classify them as underwriters).

did not intend to act as an underwriter.[9] Underwriter status thus can follow from playing an essential role in the distribution even though the underwriter was not the actual seller. The general approach to underwriter status may be summarized as follows: when a substantial amount of securities are sold on behalf of an issuer (or control person) or are purchased from an issuer (or control person) and subsequently resold within a short period of time, underwriter status may attach. On the other hand, the mere fact that a dealer sells a large amount of securities will not necessarily create underwriter status. The essence of underwriter status is establishing that the securities were acquired from the issuer or control person with an intent to resell.

The legislative history of section 2(a)(11) reveals that the congressional intent was to include as underwriters all persons who might operate as conduits for securities being placed into the hands of the investing public.[18] So long as the ultimate purchasers are members of the general public, as opposed to qualified private placement purchasers, the transaction calls for the protection of the Securities Act's registration provisions.[21] The exemption thus places great emphasis on the ultimate purchasers of the securities, rather than the nature of the person acting as a conduit for the sale of securities to the members of the public.

The concept of distribution refers to the process by which a block of privately held securities is dispersed to the investing public.[24] Although distributions normally involve a large amount of stock, that is not always the case.[25]

The statutory definition excludes members of the selling group from the definition of underwriter. Although certainly involved in the distribution process, those dealers who receive nothing more than their ordinary sales commissions are not classified as section 2(a)(11) underwriters. The exclusion of transactions in which the only remuneration is "the usual and customary distributors' or sellers' commission"[26] is designed to protect members of the selling group and nonparticipating brokers from being included in the concept of underwriter. SEC Rule 141[27] provides that a dealer's commission includes the normal spread between the offering price and the dealer's cost, whether the dealer was purchasing the security prior to reselling it or acting merely as a broker executing a customer's order.[28]

SEC Rule 142[29] excludes from the definition of underwriter persons who are not affiliated with either the underwriter or the issuer and who purchase or make a commitment to purchase all or part of any unsold allotment, so long as the securities are acquired for "investment" rather than for "distribution." The purpose of Rule 142 has been explained as recognition of "the

9. Geiger v. SEC, 363 F.3d 481 (9th Cir. 2004) (the lack of knowledge was not a defense).

18. *See* S.E.C. v. Lybrand, 200 F.Supp.2d 384, 2002 WL 987284 at *7 (S.D.N.Y.2002) (relying on this treatise); In the Matter of Lorsin, Inc., Admin. Proc. File No. 3–11310, 2004 WL 1064141 (SEC Initial decision May 11, 2004) (same).

21. H.R.Rep. No. 85, 73d Conn., 1st Sess. 13–14 (1933).

24. Geiger v. SEC, 363 F.3d 481 (9th Cir. 2004) (relying on this treatise).

25. Geiger v. SEC, 363 F.3d 481 (9th Cir. 2004); Pennaluna & Co. v. SEC, 410 F.2d 861, 865 (9th Cir.1969) (.025% of the outstanding shares constituted a distribution).

26. 15 U.S.C.A. § 77b(a)(11).

27. 17 C.F.R. § 230.141.

28. 17 C.F.R. § 230.141.

29. 17 C.F.R. § 230.142.

value of secondary capital in facilitating the flow of investment funds into industry, and of the fact that the owners of such secondary capital cannot practicably perform the duty of thorough investigation and analysis imposed by the Act on the underwriter proper."[30] Accordingly, "a person who does no more than agree with an underwriter to take over some or all of the undistributed portion of the issue, and who purchases for investment any securities which his commitment thus obliges him to take up, does not thereby subject himself to liability as an underwriter of the securities of the issue actually distributed to the public."[31]

In contrast to Rules 141 and 142's exclusions of certain transactions from the concept of underwriter, SEC Rule 140[32] expressly includes within the definition one type of indirect participation in the distribution process. Rule 140 confers underwriter status on any entity whose chief business is the purchase of securities of one issuer (or of two or more affiliated issuers) where that entity utilizes the sale of its own securities to finance the purchases. Under Rule 140, where such holding company or investment company acquires the issuer's securities, those securities will be deemed to have been acquired by an underwriter within the meaning of section 2(a)(11).[33] Beyond the above-mentioned Commission rules, the task of defining "underwriter" has for the most part been left to judicial interpretation and SEC decision-making. For example, just as ordinary brokerage transactions will not classify a broker-dealer as an underwriter, engaging in routine market-making activities, by simply acting as a conduit between broker-dealers, will not result in underwriter status.[34]

It is very common for institutional investors, as well as wealthy individuals, to purchase large blocks of both registered and unregistered offerings. When these investors subsequently sell their securities, there frequently may be a question as to the necessity for registration under the Act.[35] The problem is most likely to arise where the initial offering was not registered under the Act. Downstream sales are dealt with in Rule 144, which is not the exclusive method of compliance for either affiliates or non-affiliates of the issuer.[36] Rule 144 imposes a one year holding period for securities of companies that are not subject to the 1934 Act's periodic reporting requirements and a six month holding period for companies who are required to file 1934 Act reports, before the securities can be resold under the rule's safe harbor.[37] The rule further imposes limitations on the volume of sales after the one-year period has expired.[38] The Commission has recognized that the inherent dangers of such large block purchases filtering down to the investing public (even when in connection with a public offering) may call for additional protection under the

30. Opinion of SEC General Counsel, Sec. Act Rel. No. 33–1862, 1938 WL 31127 (SEC Dec. 14, 1938).

31. Opinion of SEC General Counsel, Sec. Act Rel. No. 33–1862 1938 WL 31127 (SEC Dec. 14, 1938).

32. 17 C.F.R. § 230.140.

33. *See* 17 C.F.R. § 230.140.

34. In re Laser Arms Corp. Securities Litigation, 794 F.Supp. 475 (S.D.N.Y.1989), *affirmed* 969 F.2d 15 (2d Cir.1992).

35. *See, e.g.,* United States v. Wolfson, 405 F.2d 779 (2d Cir.1968), *cert. denied* 394 U.S. 946, 89 S.Ct. 1275, 22 L.Ed.2d 479 (1969).

36. 17 C.F.R. § 230.144.

37. Rule 144(e), 17 C.F.R. § 230.144(e).

38. 17 C.F.R. § 230.144(e).

Act. Accordingly, the SEC formulated the "presumptive underwriter doctrine," under which anyone who purchased at least ten percent of a registered offering could be considered an underwriter, unless the purchaser was able to prove that he or she had sufficient investment intent. The ten percent threshold is not a hard and fast rule but certainly remains a significant factor in determining underwriting status under the Act. The presumptive underwriter rule has continued vitality in a "modified form" as it will still be considered in addition to other factors.[40]

§ 4.27[2] Case Law Developments—Inadvertent Underwriters

In one of the earliest judicial pronouncements on point, the Second Circuit made it clear that any substantial involvement in the distribution process would confer underwriter status, thus rendering unavailable the section 4(1) exemption from 1933 Act registration.[41] In SEC v. Chinese Consolidated Benevolent Association,[42] a not-for-profit association helped solicit investment in foreign government bonds.[43] The defendants maintained that they were not acting as securities promoters in the traditional sense, and that in promoting a worthy cause they should be exempt from the Act's coverage. Although their arguments swayed Judge Swan, who wrote a vigorous dissent, the court held that the voluntary association's sales efforts were sufficient participation in the distribution and underwriting process so as to render the defendants "underwriters" within the meaning of section 2(a)(11).[44] In his dissent, Judge Swan maintained that a logical extension of the court's opinion would make a newspaper an underwriter if a column or editorial recommends a bond in order to help a struggling government, or merely announces an impending offering.[45] The short answer to Judge Swan's contention is that it is a matter of degree. It is most certainly correct that incidental or collateral selling efforts or recommendations should not be sufficient to render someone potentially liable for violations of the Securities Act. Absent some other exemption, however, when an organization acts as a conduit for the sale of securities, such activity should be sufficient not only to confer jurisdiction but also to trigger the registration requirements, whether or not remuneration is received. This method of analysis makes each decision extremely factual, and relatively little firm footing is provided for counselors and corporate planners in relying on the available precedent.

The problems created by the "inadvertent underwriter" cases can create a nightmare for the corporate planner. The difficulty in planning was high-

40. Robert J. Ahrenholz & William E. Van Valkenberg, The Presumptive Underwriter Doctrine: Statutory Underwriter Status for Investors Purchasing a Specified Portion of a Registered Offering, 1973 Utah L.Rev. 773, 775.

41. See SEC v. Chinese Consolidated Benevolent Association, 120 F.2d 738 (2d Cir.1941), *cert. denied* 314 U.S. 618, 62 S.Ct. 106, 86 L.Ed. 497 (1941).

42. 120 F.2d 738 (2d Cir.1941), *cert. denied* 314 U.S. 618, 62 S.Ct. 106, 86 L.Ed. 497 (1941).

43. The Republic of China authorized the issuance of bonds in the aggregate of fifty million dollars. The defendant, a voluntary association organized in New York, created a committee to solicit funds for China through the sale of these bonds. The committee acted merely as a conduit, receiving no remuneration either directly or indirectly as it was participating in what it viewed to be a worthy cause. The only activity of the association was to forward the $600,000 it received to China and to distribute the bonds to the individual purchasers here in the United States.

44. *See* 120 F.2d at 741.

45. 120 F.2d at 742 (Swan, J., dissenting): "Hence, a single newspaper editorial, published without instigation by the Chinese Government and merely urging the purchase of the bonds in the name of patriotism, would make the newspaper an 'underwriter.' I cannot believe the statute should be so interpreted."

lighted by the celebrated decision in SEC v. Guild Films Co.[48] which involved the foreclosure sale of pledged securities.

In *Guild Films,* the inadvertent underwriters were banks engaging in a foreclosure sale of a substantial block of securities in Guild Films Company; the securities had been held as collateral for loans to a major shareholder of the company.[49] The Second Circuit accepted the Commission's argument that the banks were acting as underwriters under section 2(a)(11) even though the banks may have accepted the stock as collateral in good faith and had not dealt directly with the corporation that was the issuer of the securities.[50] The court reasoned that "the banks knew that they had been given unregistered stock and that the issuer had specifically forbidden that the stock be sold. * * * "[51] In the court's view, this was sufficient to put the bank in a position in which it must have either held on to the stock, found some other independent exemption,[52] or registered its sales upon foreclosure. The issue was not the bank's culpability in facilitating downstream sales, but rather whether the sales were made in such a manner as to trigger the need for the protection provided by registration. In contrast, when a bona fide pledge is made and there is no substantial likelihood that the pledgee will have to foreclose, it is unlikely that the pledgee will be found to be a statutory underwriter in the event that there is a foreclosure and the securities are sold.

The Commission has adhered to the rule that sales of pledged securities can, under certain circumstances, create underwriter status. Specifically, under Rule 144(d)(4)(D),[55] all securities sold by a bona fide pledgee are deemed to be acquired when they were acquired by the pledgor, and are aggregated with any sales by the pledgor for the purpose of calculating the rule's ceiling on resales. The rule further provides that where there is a pledge without any recourse against the pledgor, the acquisition date of the security for purposes of creating downstream selling liability is the date of the pledge rather than the date of acquisition by the pledgor.[56] In 1991, the

48. 279 F.2d 485 (2d Cir.1960), *cert. denied* 364 U.S. 819, 81 S.Ct. 52, 5 L.Ed.2d 49 (1960), noted in 48 Calif.L.Rev. 841 (1960); 60 Colum.L.Rev. 1179 (1960) 74 Harv.L.Rev. 1241 (1961); 36 N.Y.U.L.Rev. 901 (1961); 13 Stan.L.Rev. 652 (1961); 8 U.C.L.A.L.Rev. 663 (1961).

49. The shareholder was Hollywood personality Hal Roach. The shares that were used as collateral had been issued pursuant to a private placement, with the purchaser signing the necessary investment letter. The lower court found that notwithstanding the investment letter, Roach's intent was to resell the security at a later date. The bank had obtained the stock as collateral after negotiations to renew Roach's note. When it became necessary for the bank to foreclose on the note, the stock transfer agent refused to enter the sale and suit was brought to compel the transfer. At the same time the SEC brought suit to enjoin the sale on the ground that it would violate the Act's registration provisions.

50. 279 F.2d at 489–90. *See generally* James C. Sargent, The "Guild Films" case: The Effect of "Good Faith" in Foreclosure Sales of Unregistered Securities Pledged as Collateral, 46 Va.L.Rev. 1573 (1960).

51. 279 F.2d at 490. *Compare* Seattle–First National Bank v. Carlstedt, 1984 WL 2430, [1984 Transfer Binder] Fed. Sec. L. Rep. (CCH) ¶ 91,499 (W.D.Okl.1984) (bank purchasing participation in loans made to investors held not to be an underwriter).

52. *See, e.g.,* TeleHub Technologies Corp., [2000–2001 Transfer Binder] Fed. Sec. L. Rep. (CCH) ¶ 78,004, 2000 WL 1283644 (SEC No Action Letter Sept. 11, 2000) (trustee could sell pledged securities pursuant to auction where all shares would be sold to one investor showing sufficient evidence of investment intent).

55. 17 C.F.R. § 230.144(d)(4)(D).

56. *Id. Cf.* Shearson Lehman Hutton Holdings Inc. v. Coated Sales, Inc., 697 F.Supp. 639 (S.D.N.Y.1988) (stock transfer agent had no lawful basis to refuse to transfer stock to pledgee on default).

Commission instituted enforcement proceedings in connection with a broker's sale of control securities to satisfy a margin account.[57] The broker knew that the customer was a control person and apparently ignored the volume limitations applicable to such sales. The initiation of proceedings was especially significant in that the broker in question had relied on no action letters that had been given to others in the past. These proceedings highlight the precarious nature of trying to distill general principles from specific no action responses.

§ 4.27[3] Investment Intent—The Holding Period

In determining whether or not a person is a statutory underwriter, one of the key questions is whether the would-be underwriter had sufficient investment intent at the time of purchase. The issue is raised in the context of whether the securities were purchased with a view toward distribution.[62] One of the primary questions then becomes: how does one determine the seller's original intent at the time the securities were acquired? The period that the securities were held between the purchase and subsequent sale is a significant factor in determining whether they were originally purchased with the requisite investment intent. A sale closely following the acquisition of the securities is strong circumstantial evidence that an investment intent did not exist. In a leading case it was held within the context of a criminal prosecution that "[t]he passage of two years before the commencement of distribution of any of these shares is an insuperable obstacle to my finding that [defendant] took these shares with a view to distribution thereof, in the absence of any relevant evidence from which I could conclude that he did not take the shares for investment."[65]

The decisions in the Second Circuit thus formed the basis of a two-year rule of thumb for the holding period that survived for many years. Since this holding period initially arose in the context of a criminal prosecution, which carries a higher standard of proof, a more rigid rule, or even longer holding period, arguably could be applied in a civil action or SEC enforcement proceeding. However, the trend has been in the other direction. In fact, in 1997, the SEC shortened the holding period for resales of restricted securities under the safe harbor provisions of Rule 144 from two years to one.[66] Interestingly, as early as 1935, this same one year period had been suggested as creating a strong inference of investment intent.[67] In 2007, the SEC retained the one-year holding period under Rule 144 for companies not

---

57. Morgan Stanley & Co., Sec.Exch.Act Rel. No. 34–28,990, Admin.Proc. File No. 3–7473 (March 20, 1991).

62. *See e.g.*, Berckeley Investment Group, Ltd. v. Colkitt, 455 F.3d 195 (3d Cir. 2006) (purchasing securities while not disclosing intent to resell the securities in the U.S. would violate section 5 and render section 4(1) unavailable).

65. United States v. Sherwood, 175 F.Supp. 480, 483 (S.D.N.Y.1959) (defendant had purchased shares of the issuer's stock in a private placement and held it for two years). *Compare, e.g.*, Gilligan, Will & Co. v. SEC, 267 F.2d 461 (2d Cir.1959), *cert. denied* 361 U.S. 896, 80 S.Ct. 200, 4 L.Ed.2d 152 (1959) (ten-month holding period held insufficient).

66. 17 C.F.R. § 230.144 which is discussed in § 4.29 *infra*.

67. Opinion of General Counsel relating to Rule 142, Sec. Act Rel. No. 33–1862, 1938 WL 31127 (SEC Dec. 14, 1938) ("it is my opinion that if [the securities] were retained for a period as long as a year that fact would be sufficient, if not contradicted by other evidence, to create a strong inference that they had been purchased for investment. However, such an inference would be rebuttable; for example, it would fall in the face of evidence of a pre-arranged scheme to effect a distribution at the end of the year").

required to file periodic reports under the 1934 Act but shortened the holding period to six months for companies subject to the 1934 Act's periodic reporting requirements.[68]

The "Change in Circumstances" Exception

In the pre-Rule 144 case law, sales made prior to the expiration of the two-year holding period from the date of acquisition were permitted if the seller was able to demonstrate that he or she had the sufficient investment intent.[74] As a result, it became common for sellers to claim that although they had the requisite investment intent at the time of purchase, subsequent changes in their personal situations necessitated the resale of the securities.[75] Sellers of securities often took the position that since they had not purchased the securities with a view toward distribution, they should be relieved from the Act's registration requirements. Although the Commission often refused to issue no-action letters based on this "change of circumstances" defense, it was frequently relied upon by planners in permitting transactions without registration and also was acknowledged by the Commission as a legitimate way of avoiding underwriter status. The change in circumstances defense was highly factual and not easy to predict when it might be applied.

The change in circumstances defense was not available where the changed circumstances were reasonably foreseeable at the time of purchase, nor where the only change was that the issuer failed to meet the investor's expectations of success.[79] Additionally, the availability of the change in circumstances defense was directly related to the period of time for which the securities had been held; the shorter the holding period, the more compelling the evidence required.[80] The change in circumstances defense only added to the uncertainty in structuring transactions and resulted in "troublesome inconsistency."[81] Accordingly, in adopting Rule 144, the Commission purported to rescind the change in circumstances defense.[82] There is, however, a question as to the Commission's authority to make such a pronouncement beyond the context of a safe harbor rule. To the extent that the change in circumstances defense is a valid interpretation in terms of the section 2(a)(11) statutory definition of one who purchases with an intent to redistribute, the

---

68. See Revisions to Rules 144 and 145, Sec. Act Rel. No. 33–8869, 2007 WL 4270700 (Dec. 6, 2007).

74. *See, e.g.,* Vohs v. Dickson, 495 F.2d 607, 620–621 (5th Cir.1974) (considering change in circumstances as one factor in concluding that purchaser made purchase with the necessary investment intent).

75. *See* SEC, "Disclosure to Investors"—Report and Recommendations to The Securities and Exchange Commission From the Disclosure Policy Study, "The Wheat Report," 160–77 (1969).

79. *See* Gilligan, Will & Co. v. SEC, 267 F.2d 461, 462–68 (2d Cir.1959), *cert. denied* 361 U.S. 896, 80 S.Ct. 200, 4 L.Ed.2d 152 (1959); SEC, "Disclosure to Investors"—Report and Recommendations to The Securities and Exchange Commission From the Disclosure Policy Study, "The Wheat Report," 160–77 (1969).

80. SEC, "Disclosure to Investors"—Report and Recommendations to The Securities and Exchange Commission From the Disclosure Policy Study, "The Wheat Report," 167 (1969).

81. SEC, "Disclosure to Investors"—Report and Recommendations to The Securities and Exchange Commission From the Disclosure Policy Study, "The Wheat Report," 176 (1969).

82. Notice of Adoption of Rule 144 Relating to the Definition of the Terms "Underwriter" in Sections 4(1) and 2(11) and "Brokers" Transactions" in Section 4(4) of the Securities Act of 1933, Sec. Act Rel. No. 33–5223, 1972 WL 18134 (Jan. 11, 1972). *See also, e.g.,* Jerry Gardner, 1984 WL 45407 (SEC No Action Letter June 1, 1984 available July 9, 1984) ("in the aforementioned release the staff advised that the 'change in circumstances' concept should no longer be considered as one of the factors in determining whether a person is an underwriter").

SEC cannot by administrative fiat change the meaning of the statute.[83] However, if the change in circumstances defense was merely an administrative interpretation rather than a part of the statutory definition, the SEC can effectively eliminate the defense by changing its interpretation. In any event, since Rule 144 is non-exclusive, the change in circumstances defense arguably survives even if it is abolished for those relying upon the rule. Nevertheless, the SEC has taken the position that it has been abolished in all cases.[84] In making an argument on facts that would have satisfied the change in circumstances doctrine in the past, the advocate can frame his or her case in terms of facts showing that the seller had an investment intent at the time the securities were purchased. Since the terms of section 2(a)(11) clearly speak in the terms of the seller's intent at the time of purchase, facts showing a change in circumstances that justified an early sale should negate the inference that the seller had purchased with impermissible intent.

§ 4.27[4] Sales on Behalf of Controlling Persons

The last sentence of section 2(a)(11)'s statutory definition of underwriter provides that anyone who sells a security on behalf of a controlling person is an underwriter.[85] Thus, a control person of the company frequently will not be in a position to rely on the section 4(1) exemption from registration.[86] Although there is no statutory definition of "control," in Rule 405[87] the Commission defines control as "the possession, direct or indirect, of the power to direct or cause the direction of the management and policies of a person, whether through the ownership of voting securities, by contract, or otherwise."[88] Accordingly, the question of who is a control person is highly factual and is not dependent upon ownership of any specific percentage.[89] For example, it has been held that someone owning eight percent of a company's stock was not a control person; if he had been a control person this would have rendered anyone handling sales on his behalf an automatic statutory underwriter.[90] A state court held that three individuals owning thirty-eight percent of the issuer's stock did not exercise control and thus were not control persons.[91] Control is not limited to voting control and can be found to exist where it is exercised other than through stock ownership.[92] Thus, any policy-making officer falls within Rule 405's definition and would be deemed a

---

83. Berckeley Investment Group, Ltd. v. Colkitt, 455 F.3d 195 (3d Cir. 2006) (noting that the SEC purported to abolish the change of circumstances doctrine but further noting that although Rule 144 may not be available, the doctrine may still be viable in interpreting the statutory section 4(1) exemption), relying in part on this treatise.

84. Notice of Adoption of Rule 144 Relating to the Definition of the Terms "Underwriter" in Sections 4(1) and 2(11) and "Brokers" Transactions' in Section 4(4) of the Securities Act of 1933, Sec. Act Rel. No. 33–5223, 1972 WL 18134 (Jan. 11, 1972).

85. 15 U.S.C.A. § 77b(a)(11).

86. SEC v. Cavanagh, 155 F.3d 129, 134 (2d Cir.1998); S.E.C. v. Lybrand, 200 F.Supp.2d 384 (S.D.N.Y.2002).

87. 17 C.F.R. § 230.405.

88. 17 C.F.R. § 230.405(f).

89. *See* SEC v. Cavanagh, 445 F.3d 105 (2d Cir. 2006) (shareholders were affiliates and thus section 4(1) was unavailable to shield section 5 violations in connection with pump and dump scheme).

90. United States v. Sherwood, 175 F.Supp. 480 (S.D.N.Y.1959).

91. WNH Investments, LLC v. Batzel, 1995 WL 262248, [1995 Transfer Binder] Fed. Sec. L. Rep. (CCH) ¶ 98,764 (Del.Ch.1995) (section 4(1) exemption held applicable).

92. 17 C.F.R. § 230.405(f).

controlling person. The SEC has indicated that in the context of a sizable secondary distribution, the burden of proving the absence of control may be allocated to the person claiming the exemption.[93] Recognition of a controlling person for purposes of establishing underwriter status is not limited to a single individual. Thus, when a group of sellers act together in selling a large amount of securities without registration, underwriter status will attach.[94]

The holding period for restricted securities would seem to be equally relevant for classifying someone as an underwriter for having sold securities on behalf of a control person. This is the case because the issue is whether the seller had purchased the securities from an "issuer" (*i.e.*, control person) with a view to distribute. An affiliate who engages in secondary sales cannot force itself into the section 4(1) exemption by terminating their status as an affiliate immediately prior to the sale.[95]

Where a series of coordinated secondary offerings resulted in a corporation's publicly held shares shifting from nine percent of those outstanding to forty-six percent of those outstanding, the broker/dealer handling such sales on behalf of controlling persons was held to have been a statutory underwriter.[96] The Commission rejected the contention that since the transactions were executed upon the selling customer's orders they should be exempt under section 4(4)[97] as unsolicited broker's transactions.[98] The Commission reasoned that such a large infusion of privately held stock into the public market constituted a "distribution," as opposed to the type of day-to-day transaction or "trading" that section 4(4) was designed to exempt.[99] Thus, it is clear that any large block sales of securities by insiders (*i.e.*, control persons or affiliates) that have not been registered will be subject to the Act's registration requirements, absent some independent exemption.

An interesting question arises as to whether insiders or control persons must register sales of securities that they had purchased on the open market when, after a significant period of time, they decide to sell. In a somewhat analogous situation, the Commission held that even though securities issued prior to 1933 were exempt under former section 3(a)(1) of the Act,[101] a subsequent sale by controlling persons was a new distribution which went beyond the scope of the former section 3(a)(1) exemption.[102] The rationale for requiring registration of such large sales is that a large volume of sales will cause a disruption of an otherwise orderly public market and thus the

93. In the Matter of Wittow, File No. 3–2182, 44 S.E.C. 666, Release No. 34–9303, 1971 WL 11265 *4 (SEC Aug. 24, 1971).

94. SEC v. Kern, 425 F.3d 143 (2d Cir. 2005).

95. SEC v. Cavanagh, 445 F.3d 105, 115 (2d Cir. 2006).

96. In the Matter of Ira Haupt & Co., 23 S.E.C. 589, Sec. Exch. Act Rel. No. 34–3845, 1946 WL 24150 (SEC 1946), noted 14 U.Chi.L.Rev. 307 (1947).

97. 15 U.S.C.A. § 77d(4). The SEC decision in *Ira Haupt* was based on section 4(4)'s predecessor, an earlier version of section 4(2).

98. In the Matter of Ira Haupt & Co., 23 S.E.C. 589, 600–06, Sec. Exch. Act Rel. No. 34–3845, 1946 WL 24150 (SEC 1946). *Accord* United States v. Wolfson, 405 F.2d 779 (2d Cir.1968), *cert. denied* 394 U.S. 946, 89 S.Ct. 1275, 22 L.Ed.2d 479 (1969).

99. In the Matter of Ira Haupt & Co., 23 S.E.C. 589 at 600–06, Sec. Exch. Act Rel. No. 34–3845, 1946 WL 24150 (SEC 1946). *Accord* Gilligan, Will & Co. v. SEC, 267 F.2d 461, 466 (2d Cir.1959), *cert. denied* 361 U.S. 896, 80 S.Ct. 200, 4 L.Ed.2d 152 (1959), citing H.R.Rep. No. 1838, 73d Cong. 2d Sess. 41 (1934).

101. 15 U.S.C.A. § 77c(a)(1). *See* § 4.2 *supra.*

102. 23 S.E.C. at 599–600.

disclosure protections of the registration requirements are needed. Disclosure informs the market of who is selling and why they are selling. Also, registration will inform the market of the issuer's current condition. This rationale for disclosure through registration can be extended to certain large block transactions by controlling persons. Furthermore, although once public, if the securities have been privately held for a sufficiently long period of time, the impact on the market is the same as if they had never been publicly issued. Unless dealing with restricted stock, large block transactions by institutional investors are not generally registered, but in these instances the sellers presumably do not qualify as control persons and thus are not "issuers" for the purposes of section 2(a)(11)'s definition of underwriter. It arguably does not make sense to require registration solely because such a large block of unrestricted stock had been sold by a control person of the issuer. However, the insider's access to nonpublic information, which would have to be disclosed in a registration statement, can be used to distinguish insider large block sales from other large transactions in a company's shares.

In United States v. Wolfson,[103] the Second Circuit alarmed the brokerage industry when it noted that brokers were potentially liable as underwriters for selling a controlling person's securities.[104] The court held that defendant Wolfson, the control person who had siphoned his securities to the public by making sales through a number of brokers, was not exempt since such transactions were through an underwriter as defined in section 2(a)(11).[105] The court noted that section 4(1) exempts "transactions" and not classes of people. Citing the section 2(a)(11) definition of underwriter, the court pointed out that the brokers had supplied outlets for the stock of appellants who were "issuers" within the section 2(a)(11) definition of that term even if they were not "issuers" as defined by section 2(a)(4)[106] for purposes of the Act in general.[107] Thus, the brokers were "underwriters" within the meaning of section 2(a)(11), and according to the court, "the stock was sold in 'transactions by underwriters' which are not within the exception of section 4(1). * * * "[108]

The section 4(1) exemption, and hence the definition of underwriter, was not the only issue involved in the *Wolfson* case. The appellants in *Wolfson* also argued that the brokers could not be underwriters because the sales in question fell within the section 4(4) exemption for brokers' orders executed upon customers' orders on any exchange or in the over-the-counter market. The court agreed that section 4(4) exempted the brokers for their parts in the transaction, since the brokers had not solicited the orders, and were unaware at the time that the transactions were part of a distribution of securities by appellants.[114] Wolfson and his associates, on the other hand, were "control

103. 405 F.2d 779 (2d Cir.1968), *cert. denied* 394 U.S. 946, 89 S.Ct. 1275, 22 L.Ed.2d 479 (1969).

104. 405 F.2d at 782–783.

105. 405 F.2d at 782–783. Wolfson, together with members of his immediate family and his right-hand man, owned 1,149,775 shares, or over forty percent of the outstanding stock of Continental Enterprises, Inc.; the remainder being spread among some 5,000 outside shareholders. In the eighteen month period between August 1, 1960 and January 31, 1962, 633,825 unregistered shares of the forty percent block were sold through a variety of brokerage houses.

106. 15 U.S.C.A. § 77b(a)(4).

107. 405 F.2d at 782.

108. 405 F.2d at 782.

114. 405 F.2d at 782–783.

persons [who] must find their own exemptions."[115] Otherwise, the court reasoned, appellants would gain from having kept the true facts from the brokers.[116] In a situation in which the broker is not an unwitting participant, the size of the total secondary distribution may well preclude the application of section 4(4) to shield the brokers.

§ 4.29 The Safe Harbor Exemption for Secondary Transactions—SEC Rule 144

SEC Rule 144[1] contains a safe harbor from the 1933 Act's registration provisions for certain resales of securities. Rule 144 applies to securities whose resale are restricted (restricted) as well as to securities whether or not restricted that are held by affiliates of the issuer (often referred to as control securities). As explained more fully below, among other things the rule imposes a holding period of one year (six months for securities of publicly held companies) as a precondition to the safe harbor with respect to restricted securities (whether held by an affiliate or a non-affiliate). The rule also applies restrictions on resale to control securities that are not restricted securities. Although attempting to provide a bright-line guide for resales, Rule 144 can be quite complex when applied to transactions at the margins.

As noted in preceding sections of this treatise, the case law and SEC interpretations of section 2(a)(11)[3] underwriter status and the scope of the exemptions under sections 4(1)[4] and 4(4)[5] have not provided much firm practical guidance to the planner of corporate transactions involving the sale of restricted securities nor for transactions involving the sale of any securities held by control persons. Since many of the questions concerned with the need to register downstream securities sales essentially depend upon the resolution of factual issues, the decisions on point are frequently confusing and often may even appear to be inconsistent with one another. Rule 144 was adopted to provide more guidance to the planner and other participants by clarifying the answers to the question of who is an underwriter and thereby defining the scope of the statutory exemptions under sections 4(1) and 4(4).

The Commission explained that section 4(1) "was intended to exempt only trading transactions between individual investors with respect to securities already issued and not to exempt distributions by issuers or acts of other individuals who engage in steps necessary to such distributions."[10] The SEC further pointed out that the language of section 2(a)(11)'s definition of underwriter is disjunctive, and thus the mere absence of a view toward subsequent distribution when making the initial purchase from the issuer would not preclude a finding that the purchaser had underwriter status. The

115. 405 F.2d at 782.

116. 405 F.2d at 782.

§ 4.29

1. 17 C.F.R. § 230.144.

3. 15 U.S.C.A. § 77b(a)(11).

4. 15 U.S.C.A. § 77d(1).

5. 15 U.S.C.A. § 77d(4).

10. Notice of Adoption of Rule 144 Relating to the Definition of the Terms 'Underwriter' in Sections 4(1) and 2(11) and 'Brokers' Transactions' in Section 4(4) of the Securities Act of 1933, Sec. Act Rel. No. 33–5223, 1972 WL 13134 (Jan. 11, 1972) (*citing* SEC v. Chinese Consolidated Benevolent Association, 120 F.2d 738 (2d Cir.1941), *cert. denied* 314 U.S. 618, 62 S.Ct. 106, 86 L.Ed. 497 (1941).

Commission therefore reaffirmed the absence of any strict intent requirement as an element of inadvertent underwriter status.

Rule 144 operates as a safe harbor and as such is not the exclusive method by which an affiliate of the issuer may sell restricted securities in reliance upon an exemption.[14] The rule also applies to both sales of restricted securities by all persons and to sales of any securities by affiliates of the issuer. The rule is thus a safe harbor for both affiliates and non-affiliates. However, reliance on non-Rule 144 precedent will impose "a strong burden" on the person claiming the exemption. As is the case with any safe harbor rule, Rule 144 will not protect a transaction that although in technical compliance with the rule, is part of a scheme to evade the 1933 Act's registration requirements.

"Restricted securities" are defined in Rule 144 as including those securities acquired directly or indirectly from an issuer in a non-public offering, as well as securities subject to the resale restrictions imposed by the exemptions provided by Regulation D.[20]

A significant exception to the vitality of pre-Rule 144 case law and interpretations was the Commission's position that the "change of circumstances" defense no longer applies to downstream sales by persons purchasing from an issuer that had not registered the securities. However, the change in circumstances doctrine likely is still available under appropriate facts under the statutory exemption.[27]

Since Rule 144 applies differently to affiliates and non-affiliates, it is imperative to know who is an affiliate. Under the terms of the rule, affiliate status attaches to persons who directly or indirectly control, are similarly controlled by, or are under common control with the issuer.[34] Rule 405 defines "control" as the ability to influence, directly or indirectly, management decisions.[35] It follows that affiliate status is not limited to those who own stock but would certainly seem to apply to high level executives who are making decisions on behalf of management.[36]

Compliance with Rule 144 requires dissemination of sufficient current public information concerning the issuer. There are only two ways to satisfy the rule's information requirements. A company that is subject to the reporting requirements of the 1934 Exchange Act satisfies the rule, provided, of course, that all reports are accurate and up to date.[38] For companies that are not subject to the 1934 Act, the issuers must make similar information publicly available in order to qualify for Rule 144—specifically, most of the

14. 17 C.F.R. § 230.144(j).

20. 17 C.F.R. § 230.144(a)(3).

27. Berckeley Investment Group, Ltd. v. Colkitt, 455 F.3d 195 (3d Cir. 2006) (noting that the SEC purported to abolish the change of circumstances doctrine but further noting that although Rule 144 may not be available, the doctrine may still be viable in interpreting the statutory section 4(1) exemption), relying in part on this treatise.

34. 17 C.F.R. § 230.144(a)(1). *See, e.g.*, SEC v. M & A West, Inc., 538 F.3d 1043, 1052 (9th Cir. 2008) ("Where a single transaction accomplishes both a change in status from an affiliate to a non-affiliate and a transfer of stock from that person or entity, the transfer must be viewed as a transfer from an affiliate.").

35. 17 C.F.R. § 230.405(f).

36. *See, e.g.*, United States v. Sprecher, 783 F.Supp. 133, 159 (S.D.N.Y.1992).

38. 17 C.F.R. § 230.144(c)(1). The 1934 Act registration and periodic reporting requirements are discussed in §§ 9.2–9.3 *infra*.

information required by paragraph (a)(4) of SEC Rule 15c2–11 relating to the publication of quotations by broker-dealers must be disclosed.[39] It is to be noted that unlike the Rule 506 safe harbor exemption for nonpublic offerings by an issuer,[40] Rule 144's information requirements concern information that is publicly available, and does not mandate that this (or any other) information be made specifically available to offerees and purchasers of the restricted securities.

In addition to Rule 144's public information requirement, the rule imposes a holding period for resales of restricted securities. When the rule was originally adopted this was a two-year holding period but has since been reduced to one-year. By virtue of amendments in 2007, the one-year holding period applies to resale of restricted securities of companies that are not required to file periodic reports under the 1934 Act.[41] For companies that are subject to the 1934 Act's periodic reporting requirements, the holding period for resales of restricted securities is only six months.[42] Rule 144 thus applies to both affiliates of the issuer as well as to non-affiliates who have purchased restricted securities from the issuer (or other seller) and who elect to resell those securities without filing a registration statement.[43]

In determining the one-year holding period, any securities obtained by way of stock dividends, splits, recapitalization, or conversions are deemed to have been acquired when the original security was purchased from the issuer.[45] Similarly, securities which have been deposited with a pledgee in the course of a bona fide pledge are deemed to have been acquired by the pledgee on the date that they were originally acquired by the pledgor unless there is no recourse against the pledgor, in which case the pledgee's date of acquisition starts the holding period running anew.[46] When the securities in question have been purchased with a promissory note or pursuant to an installment contract, the one-year holding period does not begin to run until full payment has been made.[47] The rule further provides that securities acquired by gift (from persons other than the issuer) are treated as having been acquired by the donee on the date that the donor acquired them.[49] Once the donor ceases to be an affiliate, however, so do the non-affiliate donees.[50] Additionally, securities acquired from the settlor of a trust or held by a deceased's estate are considered to have been acquired by the trust or estate on the date that they were first acquired by the settlor or the deceased.[51]

Even beyond the expiration of the one-year holding period for restricted securities of non–1934 Act reporting companies (and six month holding period

39. 17 C.F.R. § 230.144(c)(2). *See* 17 C.F.R. § 240.15c2–11.

40. 17 C.F.R. § 230.506. *See* § 4.25 *supra.*

41. *See* Revisions to Rules 144 and 145, Sec. Act Rel. No. 33–8869, 2007 WL 4270700 (Dec. 6, 2007).

42. *See* Revisions to Rules 144 and 145, Sec. Act Rel. No. 33–8869, 2007 WL 4270700 (Dec. 6, 2007).

43. *See* 17 C.F.R. § 230.144(d)(1).

45. 17 C.F.R. § 230.144(d)(4)(A), (B).

46. 17 C.F.R. § 230.144(d)(4)(D).

47. 17 C.F.R. § 230.144(d)(2).

49. 17 C.F.R. § 230.144(d)(4)(E).

50. *See* Resales of Restricted and Other Securities, Sec. Act Rel. No. 33–6099, 17 S.E.C. Docket 1422, 1979 WL 174360 (SEC Aug. 2, 1979).

51. 17 C.F.R. § 230.144(d)(4)(F), (G).

for resale of restricted securities of reporting companies), Rule 144 places restrictions on all sales of securities by affiliates relying on the rule. These restrictions thus apply to affiliates' sales of both restricted and unrestricted securities. Rule 144(e)(1) permits sales by affiliates provided that the aggregate amount sold, combined with all sales of other securities of the same class (whether restricted or not) sold by the affiliate within the preceding three months, does not exceed the specified volume limit. The rule places a limit of (i) one percent of the shares of that class outstanding as shown by the most recent report of the issuer, or (ii) the average weekly reported volume of trading in such securities on national exchanges and/or reported through the consolidated transaction reporting system, or any automated quotation system of a registered securities association such as Nasdaq.[64] As a result of this provision, a substantial amount of secondary sales may take place following ninety days after an initial public offering.[65]

These "dribble out" provisions formerly applied to non-affiliates' sales of restricted securities after the initial one-year holding period had expired; and once the one-year holding period for restricted securities expired, the dribble-out provisions applied to non-affiliates' sales of restricted securities for an additional year. In 2007, the SEC significantly reduced the resale restrictions applicable to non-affiliates.[69] As a result of these amendments, there no longer are any restrictions on non-affiliate resales once the one year holding period has expired.[70] Rule 144(k) resale restrictions no longer apply when the securities have been beneficially owned by a non-affiliate for at least one year prior to their sale.[71] Similarly, once the one-year holding period for sales of restricted securities by non-affiliates has expired, none of the other Rule 144 conditions apply to subsequent non-affiliates' sales.[72] The dribble out provisions continue to apply to affiliates' sales regardless of how long the securities have been held by the affiliate. Furthermore, under subsection Rule 144(f),[74] many transactions by either affiliates or non-affiliates made in reliance upon the rule must be made in "brokers' transactions" as defined in section 4(4) of the Act,[75] or in transactions directly with a "market maker."[76] Under the current version of the rule, these limitations no longer apply to sales by non-affiliates once the one-year holding period has expired.[77] Also, in 2007, the SEC eliminated these "manner of sale" requirements with respect to resale of

64. 17 C.F.R. § 230.144(e)(1).

65. Once it has completed a registered public offering, the issuer becomes subject to the 1934 Act periodic reporting requirements. Section 15(d) of the 1934 Act, 15 U.S.C.A. § 78o(d). *See* § 9.3 *infra.*

69. *See* Revisions to Rules 144 and 145, Sec. Act Rel. No. 33–8869, 2007 WL 4270700 (Dec. 6, 2007).

70. *See* Revisions to Rules 144 and 145, Sec. Act Rel. No. 33–8869, 2007 WL 4270700 (Dec. 6, 2007).

71. 17 C.F.R. § 230.144(k).

72. *See* Revisions to Rules 144 and 145, Sec. Act Rel. No. 33–8869, 2007 WL 4270700 (Dec. 6, 2007).

74. 17 C.F.R. § 230.144(f).

75. 15 U.S.C.A. § 77d(4). *See* § 4.26 *supra.*

76. Market makers are dealers who qualify to maintain a trading market for over-the-counter securities. They will frequently be placing orders for their own account. *See* § 14.10 *infra.* The term is defined in section 3(a)(38) of the 1934 Exchange Act, 15 U.S.C.A. § 78c(a)(38).

77. *See* Revisions to Rules 144 and 145, Sec. Act Rel. No. 33–8869, 2007 WL 4270700 (Dec. 6, 2007).

debt securities by affiliates.[78] The person selling the security under Rule 144 may not solicit or arrange for solicitations of offers to buy securities in anticipation of the transaction, nor may he or she make any payment in connection with the offer or sale to any person other than the broker executing the transaction.[79]

The SEC summarizes the application of Rule 144 to both affiliates and non-affiliates as follows:[80]

	Affiliate or Person Selling on Behalf of an Affiliate	**Non-Affiliate (and Has Not Been an Affiliate During the Prior Three Months)**
Restricted Securities of Reporting Issuers	During six-month holding period - no resales under Rule 144 permitted. After six-month holding period - may resell in accordance with all Rule 144 requirements including: • Current public information, • Volume limitations, • Manner of sale requirements for equity securities, and • Filing of Form 144.	During six-month holding period - no resales under Rule 144 permitted. After six-month holding period but before one year – unlimited public resales under Rule 144 except that the current public information requirement still applies. After one-year holding period - unlimited public resales under Rule 144; need not comply with any other Rule 144 requirements.
Restricted Securities of Non-Reporting Issuers	During one-year holding period - no resales under Rule 144 permitted. After one-year holding period - may resell in accordance with all Rule 144 requirements, including: • Current public information, • Volume limitations, • Manner of sale requirements for equity securifies, and • Filing of Form 144.	During one-year holding period - no resales under Rule 144 permitted. After one-year holding period - unlimited public resales under Rule 144; need not comply with any other Rule 144 requirements.

Rule 144(g)[82] further defines the scope of section 4(4)'s brokers' transaction exemption for the purposes of the rule. The broker's activity must be limited to the execution of the order or orders to sell as agent for the person selling. In order for Rule 144 to apply, the broker may receive no more than the usual and customary broker's commission, and may neither solicit nor arrange for customers' orders to buy the securities that would be sold in a transaction.[83] There are three exceptions to Rule 144(g)'s ban on solicitation: (1) the broker may contact other dealers who have indicated interest in the

78. *See* Revisions to Rules 144 and 145, Sec. Act Rel. No. 33–8869, 2007 WL 4270700 (Dec. 6, 2007).

79. 17 C.F.R. § 230.144(f).

80. Revisions to Rules 144 and 145, Sec. Act Rel. No. 33–8869, 2007 WL 4270700 (Dec. 6, 2007).

82. 17 C.F.R. § 230.144(g).

83. 17 C.F.R. § 230.144(g).

securities within the past sixty days, (2) he or she may make inquiries to other customers who have shown an "unsolicited bona fide interest" in the securities within the past ten business days, and (3) the broker may publish bid and asked quotations in an inter-dealer quotation system "provided that such quotations are incident to the maintenance of a bona fide inter-dealer market for the security for the broker's own account. * * * "[84] The final prerequisite under subsection (g) is that the broker must make a reasonable inquiry as to whether the person for whose account the securities are being sold is an underwriter or whether the transaction is part of a distribution. Although subsection (g) was adopted solely pursuant to Rule 144, its terms are certainly helpful by way of analogy to anyone planning a transaction in reliance upon a section 4(4) exemption.[86]

In addition to compliance with all of the foregoing requirements of the rule, subsection (h)[87] requires a filing of notice of Rule 144 sales by affiliates.[88] Form 144 must be completed whenever the amount of securities sold in reliance on the rule within any three-month period is more than five hundred shares, or the aggregate sales price is more than ten thousand dollars.

As discussed more fully in the next section, in 1990, the SEC adopted an exemption for downstream sales to qualified institutional investors. As is the case with Rule 144, Rule 144A[92] classifies certain offers and sales as not involving a distribution, so that persons participating in such offers and sales are not considered "underwriters."

§ 4.30 The Section "4(1½)" Exemption for Downstream Sales; SEC Rule 144A

As discussed in previous sections of this treatise,[1] section 4(1)'s exemption for transactions not involving an issuer, underwriter, or a dealer,[2] and section 4(4)'s exemption for unsolicited brokers' transactions[3] both provide avenues to exempt transactions made by persons other than an issuer. In contrast, section 4(2)'s nonpublic offering exemption[4] is limited by its terms to "transactions by an issuer"[5] and thus is not available to exempt downstream sales from 1933 Act registration. The rationale underlying the section 4(2) exemption seems to support a comparable exemption for downstream sales by non-issuers.

As explained previously, two primary elements of the section 4(2) exemption are: (1) the purchaser's access to current information about the issuer

84. 17 C.F.R. § 230.144(g).

86. 15 U.S.C.A. § 77d(4). The section 4(4) exemption is discussed in § 4.26 *supra.*

87. 17 C.F.R. § 230.144(h).

88. Prior to the 2007 amendments to rule 144, non-affiliates were required to file Form 144 as well but that is no longer the case. *See* Revisions to Rules 144 and 145, Sec. Act Rel. No. 33–8869, 2007 WL 4270700 (Dec. 6, 2007).

92. 17 C.F.R. § 230.144A.

§ 4.30

1. *See* §§ 4.26–4.29 *supra.*

2. 15 U.S.C.A. § 77d(1).

3. 15 U.S.C.A. § 77d(4).

4. 15 U.S.C.A. § 77d(2). *See* § 4.24 *supra.*

5. 15 U.S.C.A. § 77d(2).

and (2) the purchaser's ability to evaluate that information.[7] In addition, in order to qualify for the section 4(2) exemption, the issuer is not permitted to engage in a general solicitation, but rather must target the offers to a discrete group of offerees.[8]

§ 4.30[1] Basis for the Section 4(1½) Exemption

The rationale underlying the nonpublic offering exemption for issues would appear to apply equally to secondary transactions. Conceptually, a sale by a person other than the issuer that meets the informational, purchaser qualification and other requirements of section 4(2) should similarly be exempt.

Consider, for example, a private placement by Issuer Co. where S and B both would qualify as purchasers for a section 4(2) offering. Assume further that at the time of the offering S had adequate funds but B did not, and S purchased stock pursuant to the section 4(2) exemption. Two months later, S decides to sell her stock and learns that B now has sufficient cash on hand. Since the presumptive one-year holding period has not yet passed, S cannot take advantage of section 4(1)'s safe harbor—Rule 144.[11] Similarly, she cannot be certain that she has satisfied the requirements of the section 4(1) exemption. Assuming that the issuer is willing to make current information available to B, there would seem to be no reason to require registration of S's sale to B as the only alternative to waiting until Rule 144's one-year holding period has elapsed.

Since, in the foregoing example, the issuer could validly issue shares directly to B as a qualified private placement purchaser, why should S not be able to take advantage of a similar exemption? The answer to this question is that, as discussed above, the statutory language of section 4(2) is limited to transactions by an issuer. It can be argued, however, that section 4(1) would support such an exemption. In the above example, S clearly is not an issuer or a dealer, so in order to qualify for the exemption, she must be able to demonstrate that she is not an underwriter. As discussed in an earlier section, an underwriter is someone who assists an issuer during a distribution or someone who has purchased securities from an issuer with a view towards distribution.[13] It would appear that a downstream sale which complies with the requirements of section 4(2) is not properly classified as a distribution and, as such, the seller is not properly qualified as an underwriter under section 2(a)(11)'s definition. Accordingly, the proper basis of any exemption for the downstream seller in the foregoing example is section 4(1); while the requirements that must be satisfied may be derived from the parameters of the section 4(2) exemption for issuers.[15] Unfortunately, the SEC no action letters that have been cited as the basis for the section 4(1½) exemption do

7. *See, e.g.,* SEC v. Ralston Purina Co., 346 U.S. 119, 73 S.Ct. 981, 97 L.Ed. 1494 (1953).

8. The *Ralston Purina* decision (SEC v. Ralston Purina Co., 346 U.S. 119, 73 S.Ct. 981, 97 L.Ed. 1494 (1953)) talks in terms of offeree access to information and offeree ability to evaluate the investment. *See* the authorities discussed in § 4.24 *supra.*

11. 17 C.F.R. § 230.144. *See* § 4.29 *supra.*

13. 15 U.S.C.A. § 77b(a)(11). *See* § 4.27 *supra.*

15. *See* ABA Committee on Federal Regulation of Securities, The Section "4(1½)" Phenomenon: Private Resales of Restricted Securities, 34 Bus.Law.1961, 1970–71 (1979); Carl W. Schneider, Section 4(1½)—Private Resales of Restricted or Control Securities, 49 Ohio St.L.J. 501 (1988); Christopher D. Olander & Margaret S. Jacks, The Section 4(1½) Exemption—Reading Between the Lines of the Securities Act of 1933, 15 Sec.Reg.L.J. 339 (1988).

not provide a consistent statement of what is necessary to satisfy the exemption.

In the situation presented by the example above, there is considerable support for what has become known as the section 4(1½) exemption. Although not expressly contained in the statute nor formally adopted by the Commission, support for the so-called section 4(1½) exemption can be found in SEC no action letters, SEC interpretative releases, the courts' decisions, and the commentators' writings. The absence of a formal SEC rule or interpretative release explaining the exemption means that it is difficult to ascertain the precise scope of the exemption.

The Eighth Circuit explained that the section 4(1½) exemption is merely an application of the section 4(1) exemption for transactions not involving an issuer, underwriter, or dealer.[30] The court explained that the section 4(1) exemption for private resales depends upon a finding that distribution has taken place and that the definition of distribution is coextensive with section 4(2)'s non-public offering exemption.

§ 4.30[2] Elements of the Section 4(1½) Exemption

What, then, are the elements of the section 4(1½) exemption? The elements of the section 4(1½) exemption are as follows. First, the purchaser must have access to the current information about the issuer similar to the types of information that would be made available through a registration statement. This requirement emanates from section 4(2), and, in fact has been characterized as the most important of the section 4(2) requirements.[35] As discussed in an earlier section, while accredited investor status may eliminate the need for offeree and purchaser qualification, it does not eliminate the access to information requirement.[36] Thus, although the issuer is not involved in the transaction directly, the issuer's willingness to make current information available is of the utmost importance in a section 4(1½) transaction.

Second, in addition to the requirement that a purchaser have access to current information about the issuer, the purchaser must meet section 4(2) qualifications. The applicable case law under section 4(2) has described the purchaser's qualifications in terms of sophistication, ability to understand the risks of the investment, and the suitability of the investment for that particular investor.[38] This definition would include institutional investors as well as experienced individuals.[39] Additionally, Regulation D provides that an unsophisticated investor can qualify as a section 4(2) purchaser through a purchaser representative having the requisite sophistication and expertise.[40] Rule 506 further provides that where the purchasers are accredited investors,

30. Ackerberg v. Johnson, 892 F.2d 1328 (8th Cir.1989).

35. *See* Carl W. Schneider, Section 4(1½): Private Resales of Restricted or Control Securities, 49 Ohio St.L.J. 501, 506, 511 (1988).

36. *See* the discussion in § 4.25 *supra*.

38. *E.g.,* SEC v. Ralston Purina Co., 346 U.S. 119, 73 S.Ct. 981, 97 L.Ed. 1494 (1953).

39. Presumably, section 2(a)(15)'s concept of an accredited investor (15 U.S.C.A. § 77b(a)(15)) which is incorporated into Regulation D as well, would operate as an alternative basis for purchaser qualification for the section 4(1½) exemption.

40. Rule 506 recognizes that the sophistication requirement can be satisfied through a purchaser representative. 17 C.F.R. § 230.506(b)(ii). *See also* 17 C.F.R. § 230.501(h) (definition of purchaser representative).

the knowledge and sophistication requirements need not be satisfied.[41] It would appear that the same tests should carry over to the section 4(1½) exemption.[42]

Third, any general solicitation of purchasers will destroy the section 4(2) exemption[43] and thus would be equally fatal to the section 4(1½) exemption. Fourth, if too many section 4(1½) sales take place within a given time frame, there is the possibility that a distribution will be found to exist. In such a case, the seller could be said to have been participating in a distribution, thus rendering the exemption unavailable.

§ 4.30[4] The Safe Harbor for Certain Sales to Qualified Institutional Buyers—SEC Rule 144A

In the fall of 1988, the SEC proposed Rule 144A to permit downstream resales of restricted securities to institutional investors.[50] Proposed Rule 144A, as is the case with Rule 144,[51] classified certain transactions as not involving a distribution, so that sellers of such restricted securities would thus not qualify as "underwriters."

Rule 144A, like Rule 144, classifies certain offers and sales as not involving a distribution, so that persons participating in such offers and sales are not considered "underwriters" under section 2(a)(11). Essentially, the exemption covers any sale to a "qualified institutional buyer," which is defined as any institution (including insurance companies, investment companies, employee benefit plans, banks, and savings and loan associations) that owns more than $100 million worth of securities of unaffiliated issuers and, in the case of banks and savings and loans, has a net worth of at least $25 million.

In addition to direct transactions among these classes of institutions, the rule also permits securities dealers to participate in transactions, either as purchasers for their own account, provided they themselves own at least $10 million worth of securities of unaffiliated issuers, or as agents for qualified institutions. Indeed, the rule contemplates the formation of an active trading market in Rule 144A securities, in which qualified institutions and dealers can enter bids and offers.

Rule 144A only applies to sales of securities of a class that is *not* listed on a national securities exchange nor traded in the NASDAQ system. In order to avoid minimizing or diluting this requirement, the rule specifies that convertible securities do not constitute a separate class of securities unless they are issued with at least a ten percent conversion premium.[56]

With respect to securities issued by companies subject to the 1934 Act reporting requirements, or by foreign issuers, use of the rule is not conditioned on the availability of any additional information about the issuer. With

41. 17 C.F.R. § 230.506(b)(2)(ii).

42. *See, e.g.,* SEC v. Cavanagh, 1 F.Supp.2d 337, 368 (S.D.N.Y.1998) (seller's failure to investigate the nature of his proposed purchasers, and failure to attempt to limit transferability, precluded application of the section 4 (1½) exemption)

43. *See* the discussion in § 4.25 *supra.*

50. Sec. Act Rel.No. 33–6806, [1988–1989 Transfer Binder] Fed. Sec. L. Rep. (CCH) ¶ 84,335 (SEC Oct. 25, 1988).

51. 17 C.F.R. § 230.144. *See* § 4.29 *supra.*

56. 17 C.F.R. § 230.144A(d)(3)(i).

respect to securities of other issuers, however, the rule is only available if the prospective purchaser has received from the issuer a brief statement of the nature of the issuer's business and certain specified financial statements.[57]

Simultaneously with the adoption of Rule 144A, the SEC approved the establishment by the National Association of Securities Dealers (NASD) of a screen-based computer and communication system called PORTAL (Private Offerings, Resales and Trading through Automated Linkages) to facilitate secondary trading of Rule 144A securities. The adoption of Rule 144A and the establishment of the PORTAL system create the potential for an active trading market in foreign securities and in unregistered debt and equity issues of domestic issuers, limited to a designated class of large institutions and dealers.

§ 4.31 The Exemption for Certain Dealers' Transactions—Section 4(3)

As noted above,[1] although dealers' transactions are not exempt from registration by virtue of section 4(1),[2] many will be exempt as unsolicited brokers' transactions within the meaning of section 4(4).[3] Section 4(3) of the Act[4] exempts additional dealer transactions from the Act's registration and prospectus delivery requirements. In terms of the number of transactions covered, section 4(3) is probably the most significant of the transaction exemptions. Section 4(3) dispenses with the registration and delivery requirements for all dealers' transactions taking place more than forty days, or in some cases ninety days, after the first date on which the security was offered to the public or after the effective date of the registration statement, whichever is later.[5] Section 4(3)'s exemption applies both to dealers and to underwriters[6] who are no longer acting as underwriters.

The forty- (or ninety-) day time period during which a dealer's transactions are *not* exempt under section 4(3)(B) is tolled for any time during which a stop order pursuant to section 8 of the Act[7] is in effect with regard to the registration statement. The forty-day period does not apply to first-time issuers who have not previously sold securities pursuant to an effective registration statement; for them, the applicable period is ninety rather than forty days after the first sale or effective date of the registration statement. The section also provides that a shorter time period may be established by the Commission as it "may specify by rules and regulations or order."[8]

---

57. 17 C.F.R. § 230.144A(d)(4)(i).

§ 4.31

1. § 4.26 *supra*.

2. 15 U.S.C.A § 77d(1). Section 2(a)(12) defines "dealer" very broadly to cover anyone in the business of making securities transactions. 15 U.S.C.A. § 77b(a)(12) ("The term 'dealer' means any person who engaged for all or part of his time, directly or indirectly, as agent, broker, or principal, in the business of offering, buying, selling, or otherwise dealing or trading in securities issued by another person").

3. 5 U.S.C.A. § 77d(4). *See* § 4.26 *supra*.

4. 15 U.S.C.A. § 77d(3).

5. 15 U.S.C.A. § 77d(3)(A), (B).

6. The definition of underwriter is discussed in § 4.27 *supra*. *See* 15 U.S.C.A. § 77b(a)(11).

7. 15 U.S.C.A. § 77h. *See* §§ 2.5 *supra*, 7.1 *infra*.

8. 15 U.S.C.A. § 77d(3)(B). Rule 174 is such a rule. 17 C.F.R. § 230.174.

Since section 4(3)'s dealers' transaction exemption is limited to the prospectus delivery requirements and comes into existence only after the effective date (or bona fide offering date), it has no bearing on pre-filing gun-jumping violations of section 5(c)[9] nor upon section 5(a)'s prohibitions against sales prior to the effective date.[10] Similarly, section 4(3) has no bearing upon section 5(b)(1)'s prospectus delivery requirements during the waiting period after filing of the registration statement but prior to the effective date.[11] Accordingly, the dealer's exemption operates only to excuse compliance with section 5(b)(1) and 5(b)(2)'s prospectus delivery requirements[12] during the post-effective period upon expiration of the forty-or ninety-day period. The vast majority of day-to-day transactions occur more than forty (or ninety) days after the securities were offered to the public. Hence, section 4(3) covers most transactions taking place in the U.S. securities markets.

Section 4(3)(C)[13] further provides that the exemption for dealer transactions does not apply to sales of securities that are either part or all of an unsold allotment to that dealer. This means that regardless of the amount of time that has elapsed since the beginning of the offering, any underwriting activity by a dealer will implicate the prospectus delivery requirements. It is to be noted, however, that once the forty-or ninety-day period has expired, a dealer, including an underwriter no longer acting as such, can take advantage of the exemption even if another dealer has an unsold allotment.

SEC Rule 174[14] expands upon the exemption provided in section 4(3) and thereby provides an additional exemption from the prospectus delivery requirements for certain dealer transactions. The rule dispenses with the delivery requirements during the forty-day period following the effective date, and during the ninety-day period for first time issuers. Rule 174 applies to securities of issuers which prior to the offering are subject to the 1934 Act reporting requirements,[15] as well as to foreign issuers whose securities are traded using American Depositary Receipts that have been registered on Form F–6.[16] Additionally, under Rule 174 the prospectus requirements do not apply to dealers' transactions for all registered offerings that are to be made from "time to time."[17] As a general matter for issuers that are subject to and current in their 1934 Act periodic reports[18] immediately prior to the public offering, there is no prospectus delivery requirement during the post effective period for nonparticipating dealers (including participating dealers whose participation has been completed).[19] For first-time issuers (and other issuers who were not subject to and current in their 1934 Act reports immediately

9. 15 U.S.C.A. § 77e(c). *See* § 2.3 *supra.*

10. 15 U.S.C.A. § 77e(a). *See* Rule 174, 17 C.F.R. § 230.174, which is discussed below.

11. 15 U.S.C.A. § 77b(i). *See* § 2.4 *supra.*

12. Section 5(b)(1) requires that any prospectus comply with section 10's statutory prospectus requirements while section 5(b)(2) requires delivery of a section 10(a) prospectus when the securities are delivered for sale. 15 U.S.C.A. § 77e(b)(1), (2), 77j. *See* §§ 2.5, 3.3 *supra.*

13. 15 U.S.C.A. § 77d(3)(C).

14. 17 C.F.R. § 230.174.

15. The 1934 Act registration and reporting requirements are discussed in §§ 9.2, 9.3 *infra.*

16. Private foreign issuers are discussed in § 17.4 *infra.*

17. 17 C.F.R. § 230.174(c). *See* § 3.11 *supra* for a discussion of shelf registration.

18. 1934 Act §§ 13, 15(d), 15 U.S.C.A. §§ 78m, 78*o*. *See* chapter 9 *infra.*

19. Rule 174(b), 17 C.F.R. § 230.174(b).

prior to the offering) whose securities are listed on a national exchange or NASDAQ, the ninety-day period that otherwise would apply for the prospectus delivery requirements for nonparticipating dealers under section 4(3) is shortened to twenty-five days.[20]

As summarized directly above, Rule 174's exemption for nonparticipating dealers from the post-effective prospectus delivery period is limited to securities of issuers which, immediately prior to the filing of the registration statement, were subject to the 1934 Act's periodic reporting requirements.[21] Thus, the exemption does not apply to first-time issuers or issuers whose securities were not widely held prior to the filing of the registration statement.[22] Under Rule 174(d), the prospectus delivery period for nonparticipating dealers is shortened to twenty-five days for dealers (including underwriters no longer acting as such) with regard to securities which, as of the offering date, are listed on a national securities exchange or authorized for inclusion in an automated quotation system sponsored by a registered securities association (*i.e.,* NASDAQ).[24] As in the case for the statutory prospectus delivery period for registered offerings,[25] Rule 174's twenty-five day period begins to run from the later of (1) the registration statement's effective date or (2) the first date upon which the security was "bona fide offered to the public."[26] In light of Rule 174(d), the full statutory prospectus delivery period for nonparticipating dealers applies only to securities which are traded through listings in the pink sheets or the NASDAQ electronic bulletin board. It must be remembered, that, as is the case with the other exemptions provided by Rule 174, the shorter twenty-five day prospectus delivery period does not apply to a dealer who is acting as an underwriter.[28]

Rule 174(e) provides that none of its exemptions from the prospectus delivery requirements apply if the registration statement was subject to a section 8 stop order;[29] nor is an exemption available if so ordered by the SEC upon application or its own motion in a particular case.[30] The rule, as is the case with the section 4(3) exemption, explicitly does not affect the obligation of an underwriter to deliver the prospectus, although it applies to dealers who, though underwriters for the offering, have sold or otherwise disposed of their allotment and thus are no longer acting as underwriters.

Rule 174(g) imposes an additional requirement for penny stock offerings.[31] In the case of a blank check penny stock offering, the ninety-day period does not begin to run until the securities are released from escrow pursuant to Rule 419.[32]

20. 17 C.F.R. § 230.174(d).

21. 17 C.F.R. § 230.174(b).

22. The 1934 Act periodic reporting requirements are discussed in §§ 9.2, 9.3 *infra.*

24. 17 C.F.R. § 230.174(d). *See* §§ 14.3, 14.10 *infra* for a description of NASDAQ and the operation of the over-the-counter markets.

25. 15 U.S.C.A. § 77d(3)(B).

26. 17 C.F.R. § 230.174(d).

28. 17 C.F.R. § 230.174(f).

29. 15 U.S.C.A. § 77h. *See* § 7.1 *infra.*

30. 17 C.F.R. § 230.174(e)

31. The penny stock rules are discussed in § 14.19 *infra.*

32. 17 C.F.R. § 230.174(g). *See* 17 C.F.R. § 230.419.

§ 4.33 Exemption for Certain Offshore Transactions in Securities of United States Issuers—Regulation S

With the growing globalization of the securities markets, there have been an increasing number of questions concerning the applicability of the United States securities laws to transactions taking place outside of the United States. To the extent that a United States issuer offers securities exclusively to non-United States citizens in offshore transactions, there is substantial question as to the propriety of requiring registration under the 1933 Act, even though there would be jurisdiction to do so.

Regulation S sets forth two safe harbors:

> One safe harbor applies to offers and sales by issuers, securities professionals involved in the distribution process pursuant to contract, their respective affiliates, and persons acting on behalf of any of the foregoing (the "issuer safe harbor"), and the other applies to resales by persons other than the issuer, securities professionals involved in the distribution process pursuant to contract, their respective affiliates (except certain officers and directors), and persons acting on behalf of any of the foregoing (the "resale safe harbor"). An offer, sale or resale of securities that satisfies all conditions of the applicable safe harbor is deemed to be outside the United States within the meaning of the General Statement and thus not subject to the registration requirements of Section 5.[10]

The safe harbors are premised on two general conditions:

> First, any offer or sale of securities must be made in an "offshore transaction," which requires that no offers be made to persons in the United States and that either: (i) the buyer is (or the seller reasonably believes that the buyer is) offshore at the time of the origination of the buy order, or (ii) for purposes of the issuer safe harbor, the sale is made in, on or through a physical trading floor of an established foreign securities exchange, or (iii) for purposes of the resale safe harbor, the sale is made in, on or through the facilities of a designated offshore securities market, and the transaction is not pre-arranged with a buyer in the United States. Second, in no event could "directed selling efforts" be made in the United States in connection with an offer or sale of securities made under a safe harbor. "Directed selling efforts" are activities undertaken for the purpose of, or that could reasonably be expected to result in, conditioning of the market in the United States for the securities being offered. Exceptions to the general conditions are made with respect to offers and sales to specified institutions not deemed U.S. persons, notwithstanding their presence in the United States.[12]

The safe harbor for issuers has three categories of securities offerings, which are based on various factors including the nationality and reporting status of the issuer and the degree of U.S. market interest in the issuer's securities.[13] The first category consists of securities of foreign issuers with no

---

10. Offshore Offers and Sales, Sec. Act Rel. No. 33–6863, Sec. Exch. Act Rel. No. 34–27942, Inv. Co. Act Rel. No. IC—17458, Rel. No. IS—122, 46 S.E.C. Docket 52, 1990 WL 311658 [1989–1990 Transfer Binder] Fed. Sec. L. Rep. 84,524 (SEC April 24, 1990) (adopting release).

12. Offshore Offers and Sales, Sec. Act Rel. No. 33–6863, Sec. Exch. Act Rel. No. 34–27942, Inv. Co. Act Rel. No. IC—17458, Rel. No. IS—122, 46 S.E.C. Docket 52, 1990 WL 311658 [1989–1990 Transfer Binder] Fed. Sec. L. Rep. 84,524 (SEC April 24, 1990) (adopting release).

13. Offshore Offers and Sales, Sec. Act Rel. No. 33–6863 Sec. Exch. Act Rel. No. 34–27942, Inv. Co. Act Rel. No. IC—17458, Rel. No. IS—122, 46 S.E.C. Docket 52, 1990 WL 311658 [1989–1990 Transfer Binder] Fed. Sec. L. Rep. 84,524 (SEC April 24, 1990) (adopting release).

substantial United States market interest (or "SUSMI"),[14] provided that the securities are offered and sold in offerings that are directed overseas,[15] as well as securities backed by the full faith and credit of a foreign government,[16] and securities issued pursuant to certain employee benefit plans. The second category includes securities of 1934 Act reporting issuers, non-reporting foreign issuers' debt securities, non-reporting foreign issuers' non-participating preferred stock, and asset-backed securities. The third category consists of securities of non-reporting United States issuers and equity offerings by non-reporting foreign issuers with a substantial United States market interest.

In order to qualify for Regulation S, the securities must be traded on a qualified foreign market.[19] In contrast, the current version of the rule lists qualifying foreign exchanges by name as well as the required characteristics of qualifying off-shore markets.[20] The SEC was willing to waive the exchange requirement for securities traded on the European Association of Securities Dealers Automated Quotation System[21] as well as for other off-shore securities exchanges. The SEC staff, using a no action letter, has listed the steps that must be taken in order for an off-shore market to qualify for the trading of Regulation S securities.[23]

§ 4.35 The SEC's General Exemptive Authority—Section 28

Until 1996, all exempt securities and transactions had to fit within the guidelines established by sections 3 and 4 of the 1933 Act.[1] However, that changed when Congress gave the SEC general exemptive authority. Added in 1996, Section 28 of the 1933 Act provides that the Commission may exempt transactions, securities, and persons if in the public interest and consistent with investor protection.[2] The SEC now has a choice of working within the statutory limitations of the exemptions set forth in sections 3 and 4 of the 1933 Act or in expanding those parameters through rulemaking deemed to be in the public interest.

Unlike the exemptions set forth in sections 3 and 4 of the Act, the exemptive authority established by section 28 is not constrained by the terms of the securities being offered, the amount of the offering, or the nature of the offering. The only meaningful limitation on the SEC's exemptive authority is that it be consistent with investor protection and in furtherance of the public interest.

This broad exemptive power permits the SEC to adopt exemptive rules and regulations and thereby frees the Commission from the more rigid

---

14. 17 C.F.R. § 240.902(n).

15. 17 C.F.R. § 240.902(j).

16. *See* 17 C.F.R. § 240.902(e).

19. 17 C.F.R. § 230.902(a).

20. 17 C.F.R. § 230.902(a).

21. Regulation S: Initial Public Offerings of Domestic Companies on European Association of Securities Dealers Automated Quotation, 31 Sec. Reg. & L. Rep. (BNA) 1059 (SEC No Action Letter July 27, 1999).

23. OM Stockholm Exchange, [2000–2001 Transfer Binder] Fed. Sec. L. Rep. (CCH) ¶ 78,010, 2000 WL 1526340 (SEC No Action Letter Sept. 27, 2000).

§ 4.35

1. 15 U.S.C.A. §§ 77c, 77d. *See* §§ 4.1–4.34 *supra*.

2. 15 U.S.C.A. § 77z–3.

parameters of the specific exemptions set forth in sections 3 and 4 of the 1933 Act. While this greater flexibility is desirable, it is to be hoped that the Commission will not exercise this power to gut many of the valuable investor protection requirements of the securities laws. To date, the Commission has used the general exemptive power sparingly. In 1999, the Commission utilized this authority to eliminate the five million dollar limit that formerly applied to certain offerings made pursuant to a compensatory benefit plan for employees and others.[4] At the time of this writing, the SEC has not, however, used this authority to lift other dollar ceilings such as the one found in Regulation A.[5]

The SEC's exemptive power under Section 28 of the 1933 Act is limited to rules and regulations.[6] There is a parallel exemptive authority in section 36 of the Securities Exchange Act of 1934.[7] In contrast to the 1933 Act formulation for the Commission's general exemptive authority, the parallel exemptive power under the Securities Exchange Act of 1934 is broader in that it permits an exemption by order in addition to one granted by a rule or regulation.[8] Exemptions by rule or regulation may be accomplished only through the formal rulemaking process mandated by the Administrative Procedure Act.[9] SEC administrative orders are not subject to the same procedures.[10]

§ 4.36 Integration of Transactions

§ 4.36[1] Overview of the Integration Doctrine

As discussed throughout this chapter, it is necessary to structure transactions carefully in order to assure that they qualify for exemption from the 1933 Act's registration requirements. It is imperative to consider not only each step in a particular offering, but also to be mindful of past and possible future transactions. Whenever there is a series of securities transactions, to ensure the exemption, it may not be sufficient that each transaction is exempt standing on its own. In addition to each transaction being able to qualify for an exemption, it must also be clear that when viewed as a whole, the series of transactions does not run afoul of the Act's registration provisions and prospectus requirements.

Under the "integration" doctrine, the SEC will examine multiple offerings to determine whether they should be treated as a single, unitary transaction. Frequently, an issuer will embark on two (or more) separate exempt transactions within a relatively short period. In such a case the Commission may give close scrutiny in order to determine whether all offers and sales from the two (or more) securities offerings should be telescoped and integrated into one transaction. When the integration doctrine is employed, it is possible that the two (or more) offerings combined will lose the attributes that entitled them to protection. The integration doctrine is not limited to multiple exempt transactions; it can also be used to integrate a would-be

---

4. Rule 701(d)(2); 17 C.F.R. § 230.701(d)(2). *See* § 4.18 *supra*.

5. Regulation A is discussed in § 4.17 *supra*.

6. The SEC may create a 1933 Act exemption "by rule or regulation." 15 U.S.C.A. § 77z–3.

7. 15 U.S.C.A. § 78mm (the exemption may be granted by "rule, regulation or order").

8. 1934 Act § 36, 15 U.S.C.A. § 78mm. There thus is no grant of power to individualize exemptions on an ad hoc basis under the 1933 Act.

9. *See* § 16.36 *infra*.

10. Exemptive orders are discussed in § 16.36 *infra*.

exempt offering with a registered offering where some of the offers or sales in the registered offering would destroy the availability of the exemption. Integration issues also arise in connection with domestic transactions and those taking place abroad. Also, integration may play a role in determining statute of limitations issues.

The integration doctrine is based on highly factual components and, as such does not provide much bright-line guidance outside of the few safe harbor rules that exist.[4] This section will discuss the various applications of the integration doctrine.

Illustrative Examples

A few examples will help illustrate the ways in which the integration doctrine can operate. Consider an intrastate offering made by a local issuer offered only to residents of the state of incorporation and principal place of business. Assume further that some of the purchasers in the intrastate offering are relatively unsophisticated; the offering would nevertheless qualify for the intrastate exemption.[5] Two weeks later, the issuer offers the same class of stock to several wealthy and sophisticated out-of-state investors in a manner that would satisfy section 4(2)'s nonpublic offering exemption.[6] If the integration doctrine were applied to these transactions, no exemption would be available because the sophisticated out-of-state purchasers would destroy the intrastate exemption while the unsophisticated in-state purchasers would render the non-public offering exemption unavailable.

Similarly, assume that a private placement is followed within two weeks by a registered public offering. If the two transactions are integrated, the private placement sales would be considered part of the registered offering and in violation of section 5.[7] Although the integration doctrine will not be applied every time two offerings take place within close proximity, the possibility must be taken into account. By taking the possibility of integration into account, the transactions can be structured in such a way as to minimize or even eliminate the possibility of the doctrine being applied.

Outside the context of the safe harbor rules, the integration doctrine is based on a multifaceted subjective test and depends on the facts of the particular transactions in question. Accordingly, the precise parameters of the integration doctrine are uncertain.

§ 4.36[2] The Integration Doctrine Explained and Defined

The integration doctrine first emerged with regard to the intrastate offering exemption[10] in the context of determining which transactions constitute "part of an *issue*" which is offered in accordance with the intrastate

---

4. *See, e.g.,* Rule 502(a) which provides a safe harbor from integration in connection with Regulation D offerings. 17 C.F.R. § 230.502(a). *See also, e.g.,* Rule 152 which provides that a subsequent public offering does not automatically negate a transaction that was exempt as a non-public offering), 17 C.F.R. § 230.152.

5. 15 U.S.C.A. § 77c(a)(11). *See* § 4.12 *supra.*

6. 15 U.S.C.A. § 77d(2). *See* §§ 4.24–4.25 *supra.*

7. This assumes that the would-be private placement sales took place prior to the registered offering's effective date or that there was noncompliance with the prospectus delivery requirements. *See* §§ 2.4, 2.5 *supra.*

10. 15 U.S.C.A. § 77c(a)(11). *See* § 4.12 *infra.*

limitations.[11] The "part of an issue" concept (and hence integration) applies to section 3(b) exemptions such as Regulation A.[12] Similarly, the issue concept has been carried over to section 3(a)(9)'s exemption[13] for exchanges of securities exclusively with existing securities holders.[14] The integration doctrine has also been applied to section 3(a)(10)'s exemption for administratively approved reorganizations.[15] The SEC has made it clear that integration applies equally to the transaction exemptions under section 4 and, in particular, section 4(2)'s exemption for transactions not involving a public offering.[16] Unless specifically excluded by the exemption,[17] integration could potentially be applied to several other exemptions.

The SEC developed a five-factor test to determine whether the integration doctrine should be applied to two or more transactions:

1. whether the sales are part of a single plan of financing;
2. whether the sales involve issuance of the same class of securities;
3. whether the sales have been made at or about the same time;
4. whether the same type of consideration is received; and
5. whether the sales are made for the same general purpose.[20]

The Commission has not provided any significant guidance on how these factors should be weighted. Accordingly, it would appear that in a particular case any one or more of the five factors could be determinative.

The foregoing guidelines with respect to the integration doctrine do not provide much certainty in planning transactions. Furthermore, because the integration doctrine's availability is essentially dependent upon questions of fact varying with the nuances of each situation, it is often difficult to glean any learning from the relatively sparse precedent that exists. Much of the relevant precedent is based on no action letters, which by their nature are of limited precedential value.

The integration doctrine is not limited to successive offerings by the same issuer—sometimes referred to as "offering integration."[31] Successive offerings

---

11. *See* Non–Public Offering Exemption Sec. Act Rel. No. 33–4552, 1962 WL 69540, 1 Fed.Sec.L. Rep. (CCH) ¶ 2781 (Nov. 6, 1962); Sec. Act Rel. No. 33–97, 11 Fed.Reg. 10,949 (Dec. 28, 1933).

12. 15 U.S.C.A. § 77c(b); 17 C.F.R. §§ 230.251 *et seq. See* §§ 4.16, 4.17 *supra. See generally*, C. Stephen Bradford, Regulation A and the Integration Doctrine: The New Safe Harbor, 55 Ohio St. L.J. 255 (1994).

See also Rules 504 and 505 (17 C.F.R. §§ 230.504, 230.505) which are discussed in §§ 4.20–4.22 *supra. But see* 17 C.F.R. § 230.701 (exemption for certain stock compensation plans) which provides that the integration doctrine does not apply. *See* § 4.18 *supra.*

13. 15 U.S.C.A. § 77c(a)(9). *See* § 4.10 *supra.*

14. *See* Richard W. Jennings & Harold Marsh, Jr., Securities Regulation: Case and Materials 442 (6th ed. 1987) ("This is accomplished by reading the word 'exclusively' as modifying both 'exchanged' and 'security holders.' ").

15. *See* ABA Committee on Federal Regulation of Securities, Integration of Offerings: Report of Task Force on Integration of Securities Offerings, 41 Bus.Law. 595, 600–02 (1986).

16. *See* Sec. Act Rel. No. 33–4552, 1 Fed. Sec. L. Rep. (CCH) ¶ ¶ 2770–2783 (Nov. 6, 1962).

17. *See, e.g.,* 17 C.F.R. § 230.701(b)(6).

20. *See* Sec. Act Rel. No. 33–4552, 27 Fed. Reg. 113161 Fed.Sec.L. Rep. (CCH) ¶ ¶ 2770–2783 (Nov. 6, 1962).

31. *See* ABA Committee on Federal Regulation of Securities, Integration of Offerings: Report of Task Force on Integration of Securities Offerings, 41 Bus.Law. 595, 617–20 (1986).

by issuers having separate forms but economic interdependence may also be integrated;[32] this has been referred to as "issuer integration."[33]

§ 4.36[3] Safe Harbors for Avoiding Integration

As noted earlier in this section, the Commission has provided safe harbors for avoiding integration. Thus, for example, Rule 502(a)[35] of Regulation D provides that offers and sales made more than six months before the start or six months after the completion of the Regulation D offering will not be integrated.[36] In 2007, the SEC proposed shortening the six month period to ninety days.[37]

The six-month safe harbor is dependent upon there being no Regulation D offers or sales of the same class of securities within both six-month periods, except that sales pursuant to an employee benefit plan are permitted.[38] This safe harbor applies to Rule 504's exemption for offerings of up to one million dollars,[39] Rule 505's exemption for offerings of up to five million dollars,[40] and Rule 506's safe harbor for nonpublic offerings.[41] In some Regulation D offerings, the issuer may not be able to rely on the safe harbor from integration because of other offers or sales within either of the six-month periods. In such situations, the Commission's normal integration rules, including the five-factor integration test, are applicable for determining whether the Regulation D exemption is available.[42] Thus, for example, where following a private placement complying with Regulation D, the issuer decides to embark on a public offering, the issuer may still rely on Rule 152[43] to avoid integration.

As is the case with Regulation D, Rule 147's safe harbor for intrastate offerings establishes a safe harbor from integration, provided there are no non-Rule 147 offers or sales within six months before the beginning of the offering or six-months after its completion.[45] However, the Rule 147 safe harbor does not exclude from the integration doctrine sales within those six-month periods made in connection with employee benefit plans, unless those plans are exempt under section 3 or 4 of the Act.[46] Following the same pattern as Regulation D, where a transaction fails to meet the safe harbor require-

32. *See, e.g.,* SEC v. Holschuh, 694 F.2d 130 (7th Cir.1982) (integrating offerings by separate coal exploration limited partnerships which acquired their leasehold rights from the same company); SEC v. Murphy, 626 F.2d 633 (9th Cir.1980).

33. *See* ABA Committee on Federal Regulation of Securities, Integration of Offerings: Report of Task Force on Integration of Securities Offerings, 41 Bus.Law. 595, 621–623 (1986).

35. 17 C.F.R. § 230.502(a).

36. 17 C.F.R. § 230.502(a).

37. See Revisions of Limited Offering Exemptions in Regulation D, Sec. Act Rel. No. 33–8828, Inv. Co. Act Rel. No. IC–27922, http://www.sec.gov/rules/proposed/2007/33–8828.pdf, 2007 WL 2239110 (SEC July 27, 2007).

38. See Revisions of Limited Offering Exemptions in Regulation D, Sec. Act Rel. No. 33–8828, Inv. Co. Act Rel. No. IC–27922, http://www.sec.gov/rules/proposed/2007/33–8828.pdf, 2007 WL 2239110 (SEC July 27, 2007).

39. 17 C.F.R. § 230.504. *See* § 4.21 *supra.*

40. 17 C.F.R. § 230.505. *See* § 4.22 *supra.*

41. 17 C.F.R. § 230.506. *See* § 4.25 *supra.*

42. 17 C.F.R. § 230.502(a) NOTE.

43. 17 C.F.R. § 230.152.

45. 17 C.F.R. § 230.147(b)(2).

46. 17 C.F.R. § 230.147(b)(2). *Compare* 17 C.F.R. § 230.502(a).

ments, the Commission's subjective five-factor test will apply.[47] In contrast to the safe harbors described above, Rule 701, a section 3(b) exemption, which provides an exemption for certain employee compensation plans,[48] states that the integration doctrine does not apply to transactions covered by the Rule 701 exemption for certain offerings to employees and consultants of nonpublic companies.[49]

Regulation A[50] contains an integration safe harbor that presents a variation of the one found in Regulation D. Transactions occurring before a Regulation A offering and those occurring more than six months after the offering will not be integrated into a Regulation A offering.[51]

§ 4.36[4] Integrating Nonpublic and Public Offerings

§ 4.36[4][A] Successive Offerings

As pointed out at the outset of this section, integration is not limited to multiple exemptions, but can also be applied to integrate a transaction made in reliance on an exemption together with a registered offering. Thus, for example, an issuer planning a public offering, under many circumstances, may not be able to engage in an offering of the same class of stock in reliance on the section 4(2) nonpublic offering exemption.[59] This is especially true when the proceeds from the private placement offering are to be used as seed money for an upcoming public offering.[60]

However, Rule 152 makes it clear that a decision to have a public offering made *after* the nonpublic offering will not destroy the exemption.[62] The protection provided by Rule 152 is quite narrow. The rule does not provide any protection to an issuer that first has planned a public offering and then embarks on a private one. Furthermore, the burden of proving an exemption rests with the person claiming the exemption. Accordingly, the person following a nonpublic offering with a public one must carry the difficult burden of proving a negative—i.e., the lack of a prior intent to go public. Thus, when a public offering follows a private one, it is wise to limit integration problems by, *inter alia,* issuing a different class of securities, being able to identify distinct purposes for the two offerings, or using a different type of consideration.

§ 4.36[4][B] Discontinued Offerings

In 2001, the SEC adopted Rule 155[89] to provide a safe harbor from integration for a discontinued or abandoned private offering followed by a registered public offering, and also for an abandoned public offering followed by a private offering. The integration safe harbors contained in Rule 155 were

---

47. 17 C.F.R. § 230.147(b)(2) NOTE.

48. 17 C.F.R. § 230.701. *See* § 4.18 *supra.*

49. 17 C.F.R. § 230.701(b)(6).

50. Regulation A is discussed in § 4.17 *supra.*

51. 1933 Act Rule 251(e)(2)(i)(v), 17 C.F.R. § 251(e)(2)(i),(v).

59. *See, e.g.,* Laser Fax, Inc., [1985–1986 Transfer Binder] Fed. Sec. L. Rep. (CCH) ¶ 78,136 (SEC No Action Letter Aug. 15, 1985).

60. *Id.*

62. 17 C.F.R. § 230.152.

89. 17 C.F.R. § 230.155.

designed to provide clarity and certainty regarding two common situations involving abandoned offerings. The SEC made it clear that the safe harbors of Rule 155 do not otherwise affect traditional integration analyses.[90] Rule 155 sets forth conditions under which an issuer that begins a private offering but sells no securities is able to abandon the private offering and begin a registered offering without having the abandoned private offering and subsequent public offering subjected to the integration doctrine. The SEC cautions that any private offering relying on safe harbor from integration must satisfy the conditions of a private offering exemption, so that the private offering is in fact bona fide.[92] In order to effectively terminate the abandoned private offering, the issuer and all persons acting on the issuer's behalf must terminate all offering activity with respect to the private offering. Any prospectus filed as part of the subsequent registration statement must include disclosures regarding abandonment of the private offering. The issuer further is required to wait thirty days after abandoning the private offering before filing the registration statement, unless the securities were offered in the private offering only to persons who were (or who the issuer reasonably believed to be) accredited investors[93] or sophisticated.[94]

In addition, Rule 155 provides a safe harbor from integration that permits an issuer that started a registered offering to withdraw the registration statement before any securities are sold,[96] and then begin a private offering.

---

90. Integration of Abandoned Offerings, Sec. Act Rel. No. 33–7943, 2001 WL 68771 (SEC Jan. 26, 2001).

92. Integration of Abandoned Offerings, Sec. Act Rel. No. 33–7943, 2001 WL 68771 (SEC Jan. 26, 2001).

93. Accredited investor is defined in section 2(a)(15) of the Act and Rules 215 and 501(a). 15 U.S.C.A. § 77b(a)(15); 17 C.F.R. §§ 230.215, 230.501(a).

94. Under Rule 155 an investor is sophisticated if the investor, either alone or with his or her representative, has such knowledge and experience in financial and business matters to be capable of evaluating the merits and risks of the prospective investment. 17 C.F.R. § 230.155. *See* Rule 506(b)(2)(ii) of Regulation D; 17 C.F.R. § 230. 506(b)(2)(ii).

96. *See* Rule 477, 17 C.F.R. § 230.477.

Chapter 5

THE THEORY OF SALE: CORPORATE RECAPITALIZATIONS, REORGANIZATIONS AND MERGERS UNDER THE 1933 ACT

Table of Sections

---

§ 5.1 Section 2(a)(3)'s Definition of Sale; 1933 Act Application to Unconventional Transactions; Gifts, Bonus Plans, and Pledges; Effect of State Law

§ 5.1[1] Statutory Definition of Sale

Section 2(a)(3) of the 1933 Act[9] defines "sale" as including "every contract of sale or disposition of a security or interest in a security, for value." The definition under the Securities Exchange Act of 1934[11] is far less detailed than its 1933 Act counterpart but has been interpreted in a similar fashion[12] even though it does not expressly speak in terms of a disposition for value.

The statutory definition of sale obviously encompasses the exchange of securities for cash, but what about less conventional transactions such as the exercise of options, mergers, exercise of conversion rights, pledges, and the like? The courts have frequently been asked to address whether these exchanges of securities for something other than cash fall within the statutory definition of sale.[13] Under the 1933 Act definition, [the definition of] a sale is implicated to the extent that there is a disposition for value.

---

9. 15 U.S.C.A. § 77b(a)(3).

11. Section 3(a)(14) of the Exchange Act simply provides: "[t]he terms 'sale' and 'sell' each include any contract to sell or otherwise dispose of." 15 U.S.C.A. § 78c(a)(14).

12. *See* §§ 12.6, 13.4 *infra*.

13. Similar problems have arisen under the 1934 Act's provision regarding the reporting of insider transactions and the disgorgement of insider short-swing profits. Section 16 of the 1934 Act, 15 U.S.C.A. § 78p. *See* §§ 13.1–13.4 *infra*.

Exchanges of securities ordinarily would implicate the definition of sale. This is because when an investor parts with one security in exchange for another, he or she is giving up value in exchange for the security to be acquired. Some exchanges of securities are exempt from the 1933 Act's registration provisions, but these exemptions[17] clearly demonstrate a Congressional intent to treat exchanges of securities as sales. However, when an exchange of securities is involuntary and does not significantly alter the rights of the securities holders, the exchange will not be treated as a sale.[18]

For many years, the SEC took the view that shares issued in connection with mergers and other qualifying corporate reorganizations did not constitute sales that would trigger the 1933 Act's registration requirements.[19] The Commission has since abandoned its former "no sale" approach to mergers and other forms of combinations in favor of 1933 Act coverage.

Additional definitional questions have arisen when attempting to decide whether stock dividends and corporate spin-offs constitute purchases and sales of securities.[21] These topics, which are discussed in the succeeding sections, have not been the only ones relating to the definition of sale. For example, questions may arise as to whether various other types of dispositions of securities qualify as sales under the statutory definition.

§ 5.1[2] Gifts and Bonus Plans

Even beyond exchanges of securities and the exercise of options or conversion rights, other definitional issues arise with regard to what constitutes a "sale." Ordinarily, a gift of securities will not constitute a sale under the securities laws. Gifts of securities have on occasion been scrutinized in order to determine whether they are in fact sales so as to trigger the application of the securities laws.

A bona fide gift will not be a sale even though some intangible or even indirect tangible benefit (such as a consequential tax deduction) inures to the donor's benefit. For example, when a charitable donor receives a tax deduction for his or her gift of securities, has there been a disposition for value? Presumably, there is ordinarily no sale in the case of a charitable contribution, even though the donor receives a tax benefit as a result of the gift. The receipt of such a tax benefit in exchange for the donation of a security is not sufficient to classify the gift as a disposition for value. There may nevertheless be securities law consequences that flow from a gift of securities. Thus, for example, after the gift has been made, if the donee sells the securities that he or she was given, that sale, as is the case with any sale of securities, will require either registration under the 1933 Act or an exemption from registration before the securities can fall into the hands of the investing public.[30]

---

17. Section 3(a)(7) (receivers' certificates), section 3(a)(9) (exchanges exclusively between an issuer and existing securities holders), section 3(a)(10) (certain administratively or judicially approved exchanges). 15 U.S.C.A. § 77c(a)(7), 77c(a)(9), and 77c(a)(10). *See* §§ 4.8, 4.10, 4.11 *supra*.

18. *See, e.g.,* In the Matter of Penn Central Securities Litigation, 494 F.2d 528, 534 n. 6a (3d Cir.1974):

19. Former Rule 133, 17 C.F.R. § 230.133 (1971) (rescinded in Registration of Certain Transactions Involving Mergers, Consolidations and Acquisitions of Assets, Sec.Act Rel.No. 33–5316, Sec. Exch. Act Rel. No. 34–9804, Pub. Util. Holding co. Act Rel. No. 35–17717, Inv. Co. Act Rel. No. IC–7405, 37 Fed. Reg. 23631, 1972 WL 121530 (SEC Oct. 6, 1972)).

21. *See* § 5.3 *infra*.

30. This is the treatment that the SEC deems appropriate in the context of the transfer of restricted securities. *See* Rule 144(d)(4)(E) ("Securities acquired from any person, other than the

The fact that a gift ordinarily is not a sale under the securities laws will not protect someone who is trying to evade the 1933 Act's registration provisions by trying to disguise a transaction as a gift. Accordingly, in those instances when the donor's "gifts" of securities are followed by widespread downstream sales of those securities, these would-be gifts may be characterized as a subterfuge to evade registration[32] and thus viewed as sales requiring either 1933 Act registration or an exemption from registration.[33] The SEC has accordingly taken the position that "value" for the disposition may be deemed received when the gift results in the creation of a public market for the issuer's securities—especially where that public market did not previously exist.[34] In such a case, registration of the would-be gift will be required unless, of course, an appropriate exemption can be found.

A calculated plan to "give" stock away as part of a sales promotion for a company's products will be viewed as a sale of the stock since the customer is paying for the product, and hence, for the securities that are part of the return consideration.[37] The Commission has gone further and has indicated that even without tying the "free" stock to a product purchase, a corporate promotion of "free" stock can be a sale. For example, the practice of offering "free" stock in exchange for visiting a company's website and registering to receive the stock has been viewed as a sale.[38]

§ 5.1[3] Employee Compensation Plans

A variation on the rule that a bona fide gift is not a sale arises in the context of bonus compensation plans. Following the rationale applicable to gifts, an employee bonus plan that is a true bonus—that is, over and above the employee's bargained-for consideration—is a gift and hence not a sale. On the other hand, when a so-called bonus plan is in fact a type of compensation for services, then there has been a disposition for value, and a "sale" will have taken place.

§ 5.1[4] Convertible Securities

Section 2(a)(1)'s definition of security[52] expressly includes conversion rights which themselves constitute securities separate and distinct from the underlying common stock or other security and, thus, must be registered for sale, absent an applicable exemption. The question arises, however, whether

issuer, by gift shall be deemed to have been acquired by the donee when they were acquired by the donor"), 17 C.F.R. § 230.144(d)(4)(E). Rule 144 is discussed in § 4.29 *supra*.

32. *See* In re H & B Carriers, Inc., 20 Sec.Reg. & L.Rep. (BNA) 742 (Utah Sec.Div. April 26, 1988).

33. This reasoning is analogous to that used in connection with corporate spin-off transactions. *See, e.g.,* SEC v. Datronics Engineers, Inc., 490 F.2d 250 (4th Cir.1973), *cert. denied* 416 U.S. 937, 94 S.Ct. 1936, 40 L.Ed.2d 287 (1974); SEC v. Harwyn Industries Corp., 326 F.Supp. 943 (S.D.N.Y.1971), both of which are discussed in § 5.3 *infra.*

34. *See, e.g.,* American Brewing Co., 31 Sec. Reg. & L. Rep. (BNA) 194 (SEC No Action Letter Jan. 27, 1999) (stock "give away" was really a sale).

37. American Brewing Co., 31 Sec. Reg. & L. Rep. (BNA) 194 (SEC No Action Letter Jan. 27, 1999) (offering a "free" share of a brewery's voting stock with each case of beer purchased at retail).

38. Andrew Jones, 31 Sec. Reg. & L. Rep. (BNA) 839 (SEC No Action Letter June 8, 1999); Vanderkam & Sanders, 31 Sec. Reg. & L. Rep. (BNA) 230 (SEC No Action Letter Jan. 27, 1999).

52. 15 U.S.C.A. § 77b(a)(1). *See* Sec.Act Rel.No. 33–3210 (April 9, 1947).

an exercise of conversion rights is itself a sale of the convertible security and a purchase of the underlying security. Section 2(a)(3)'s definition of sale requires that there be a disposition for "value" in order for a sale to take place.[53] When a conversion right is exercised, the holder of the security merely is receiving something he or she had a right to all along—the underlying security. Hence, it would seem to follow that a conversion ordinarily will not be a disposition "for value" since the owner already had those rights prior to exercising the right of conversion.[54] The SEC's safe harbor exemption from 1933 Act registration for resales of restricted securities takes the position that an exercise of a conversion right is not a sale and thus does not require registration.[55]

Other issues relating to convertible securities are considered in a subsequent section of this chapter.[57]

§ 5.1[5] Pledges

The Supreme Court, in Rubin v. United States, held that a pledge of securities is a sale for purposes of the 1933 Act's antifraud provisions.[58] Although there would seem to be no reason to expect a different result under the 1934 Act, the courts have been sharply divided.

In the aftermath of *Rubin,* most pledges of securities will qualify as sales under the securities laws. However, this does not mean that someone collaterally affected by the transaction will be considered a party to it. Accordingly, it has been held that a pledge of stock by a major shareholder to secure the margin loans of other investors did not constitute an unregistered sale of the pledgor's securities with respect to those investors.[63]

§ 5.1[6] Installment Sales

In most instances, installment payments under an installment sale of securities will not be new "sales" of the securities. However, where each payment involves a new investment decision, each payment may properly be treated as a new sale. Also, a stated policy of not enforcing unpaid subscriptions or installments may lead to the conclusion that calls for additional payments will be treated as new sales.[71] Similarly, calls for assessments on assessable stock will be offers of sale under the 1933 Act.[72]

53. 15 U.S.C.A. § 77b(3).

54. Gilligan, Will & Co. v. SEC, 267 F.2d 461 (2d Cir.1959) (the court did not question the conversion as a sale although sale of the underlying common stock after conversion was held to require registration), *cert. denied,* 361 U.S. 896, 80 S.Ct. 200, 4 L.Ed.2d 152 (1959).

55. Rule 144(d)(4), 17 C.F.R. § 230.144(d)(4).

57. *See* § 5.3 *infra.* Similar problems arise regarding the definitions of purchase and sale with regard to the 1934 Act's prohibitions against insiders' short-swing profits. 15 U.S.C.A. § 78p(b). *See* § 13.4 *infra.*

58. 449 U.S. 424, 101 S.Ct. 698, 66 L.Ed.2d 633 (1981), decided under section 17(a), 15 U.S.C.A. § 77q(a) which is discussed in §§ 7.11, 12.22 *infra.*

63. Silva Run Worldwide Ltd. v. Gaming Lottery Corp., 1998 WL 167330, [1998 Transfer Binder] Fed. Sec. L. Rep. (CCH) ¶ 90,196 (S.D.N.Y.1998).

71. *See, e.g.,* Goodman v. Epstein, 582 F.2d 388, 409–414 (7th Cir.1978), *cert. denied* 440 U.S. 939, 99 S.Ct. 1289, 59 L.Ed.2d 499 (1979); Troyer v. Karcagi, 476 F.Supp. 1142, 1148 (S.D.N.Y. 1979).

72. 1933 Act Rule 136, 17 C.F.R. § 230.136.

§ 5.2 Corporate Recapitalizations, Reorganizations, and Mergers Under the 1933 Act: Rule 145

§ 5.2[1] Reorganizations Exempt From 1933 Act Registration

As pointed out in the preceding chapter, section 3(a)(9) of the 1933 Act provides an exemption from registration for securities that are exchanged by the issuer exclusively with its existing security holders, provided that no sales commission or other remuneration is paid in connection with solicitation for the exchange.[1] The section 3(a)(9) exemption does not extend to downstream sales by the securities holders or in cases in which the exchange was made to persons who were likely to act as statutory underwriters.[2] The exemption further is limited to 1933 Act registration and thus does not address the 1934 Securities Exchange Act's applicability to solicitation of shareholders' votes needed to approve certain exchanges.[3] Also, section 3(a)(9) is limited to exchanges of securities by the same issuer and therefore has no application to mergers or other reorganizations in which the security holders receive securities of another issuer.[4]

Section 3(a)(9) is not the only 1933 Act exemption applicable to corporate reorganizations. Section 3(a)(7)[5] exempts certain certificates of interest issued in connection with bankruptcy reorganizations. Further, section 3(a)(10)[6] exempts judicially or administratively approved reorganizations where the approval is issued after a public hearing and considers the fairness of the transaction.[7] In addition, under appropriate circumstances, issuers involved in corporate reorganizations may also be able to avoid registration because the transaction qualifies for an exemption, such as the exemptions for intrastate,[8] nonpublic,[9] Regulation A,[10] or Regulation D[11] offerings. Absent an available exemption, securities issued in connection with corporate reorganizations will have to be registered under the 1933 Act.

§ 5.2[2] Rule 145

A corporation's shareholders' participation in a plan of reorganization or a merger will generally result in the corporation's exchange or issuance of

---

§ 5.2

1. 15 U.S.C.A. § 77c(a)(9). *See* § 4.10 *supra.*

2. *See* Letters of General Counsel Discussing Application of Section 3(a)(9), Sec.Act Rel. No. 33–646, 1936 WL 31995 (SEC Feb. 3, 1936); Letter of General Counsel relating to sections 3(a)(9) and 4(1), Sec. Act Rel. No. 33–2029, 1939 WL 36361 (SEC Aug. 8, 1939).

3. In such a case the exchange is not exclusively with existing security holders of the issuer.

4. Where the issuer is a 1934 Act reporting company, the federal proxy rules would govern such solicitations. 15 U.S.C.A. § 78n(a). *See* chapter 10 *infra.*

5. 15 U.S.C.A. § 77c(a)(7). *See* § 4.8 *supra.*

6. 15 U.S.C.A. § 77c(a)(10). *See* § 4.11 *supra.*

7. Stock acquired in a merger where the fairness has been passed upon by a state agency is exempt under section 3(a)(10) and the stock received by the shareholders is not restricted stock under Rule 144. *See* Borland Finance Co., 19 Sec.Reg. & L.Rep. (BNA) 1769 (SEC No Action Letter Oct. 10, 1987). The shareholders' holding period is to be determined by Rule 145(d)(2) and the shareholders are not permitted to tack on the Rule 144 holding period of the disappearing corporation's stock. *Id.*

8. 15 U.S.C.A. § 77c(a)(11); 17 C.F.R. § 230.147. *See* § 4.12 *supra.*

9. 15 U.S.C.A. § 77d(2). *See* § 4.24 *supra.*

10. 17 C.F.R. §§ 230.251 *et seq. See* § 4.17 *supra.*

11. 17 C.F.R. §§ 230.501 *et seq. See* §§ 4.19–4.22, 4.25 *supra.*

new securities.[13] To the extent that such a reorganization or merger would involve the disposition of shares for value, the solicitation of shareholder consent would seem to fall within section 2(a)(3)'s definition of "offer to sell"[14] with regard to the securities to be issued in the recapitalization, merger, or plan of exchange. Nevertheless, for a long time, the Commission took the position that whenever securities were issued as part of an exchange pursuant to a statutory merger, consolidation, or sale of corporate assets, their issuance did not involve a sale of securities within the meaning of section 2(a)(3) of the Act.[15] The "no sale" doctrine had become the focus of frequent and severe criticism and was discarded in 1972 with the Commission's adoption of Rule 145, which treats exchanges pursuant to mergers and reorganizations as sales.[17]

In adopting Rule 145, the Commission declared these share exchanges to involve sales of securities and thus in need of registration under the 1933 Act absent an exemption. Rule 145 therefore imposed registration requirements on all otherwise non-exempt business combinations involving a shareholder vote and the issuance of shares to the voting shareholders.[18] Rule 145 transactions may be registered on Form S–4, which is designed specifically for corporate combinations. The SEC was mindful of the overlapping Exchange Act coverage and thus further provided for coordination between the 1933 Act prospectus requirements and the proxy rules of the 1934 Act.[19] This type of coordination between the 1933 and 1934 Act is consistent with the 1970s initiative to implement an integrated disclosure system.[20]

The rule does not apply, however, to tender offers or open-market share acquisitions because these are not corporate reorganizations but rather involve transactions with the shareholders directly. When such a tender offer involves the issuance of securities, registration may be required but Rule 145 is not available. Also, the 1934 Act's tender offer provisions may come into play.[21]

Rule 145(a)[22] provides that there is an "offer," "offer to sell," "offer for sale," or "sale" within the meaning of section 2(a)(3) of the 1933 Act when a plan for reclassification, merger, consolidation, or transfer of corporate assets in exchange for securities of another issuer is submitted to securities holders for a vote or otherwise for their consent. An exception to Rule 145 involves a reorganization when the sole effect of the reorganization is a change of the issuer's domicile or state of incorporation. In such a case, 1933 Act registration is not required. However, any additional corporate restructuring beyond

---

13. The prominent exception is where the shareholders are cashed out. Redeemable preferred shares issued in a cash-out merger need not be registered so long as they are redeemed immediately. Cambior, Inc., 19 Sec.Reg. & L.Rep. (BNA) 240 (SEC No Action Letter Jan. 22, 1987).

14. 15 U.S.C.A. § 77b(a)(3). *See* § 5.1 *supra.*

15. 17 C.F.R. § 230.133 (1971) (rescinded by Sec.Act Rel.No. 33–5316 (Oct. 6, 1972)).

17. 17 C.F.R. § 230.145.

18. *Id. See, e.g.,* Kab Lae Kim, A Study on Rule 145 of the Securities Act of 1933: How to Provide Clarity and Predictability in Rule 145 Transactions, 40 Akron L. Rev. 131 (2007). The rule thus covers mergers, consolidations, sales of corporate assets, and share exchanges involving shareholder votes and to which the corporations are parties.

19. 15 U.S.C.A. § 78n(a). *See* Chapter 10 *infra.*

20. *See* § 3.4 *supra.*

21. Tender offers are discussed in Chapter 11 *infra.*

22. Sec.Act Rel.No. 33–5316 (Oct. 6, 1972). *See* 17 C.F.R. §§ 240.14a–2, 14a–6, 14c–5.

the change of domicile will implicate Rule 145 and, absent an exemption, will bring the 1933 Act's registration requirements into play.[25]

Rule 145 thus includes in section 2(a)(3)'s definition of sale and offer for sale most corporate combinations. Formerly, unless an exemption could be found, any communication, written or oral, designed to influence the shareholder's vote or consent would have run afoul of the 1933 Act's gun-jumping prohibitions unless a registration statement had been filed.[26] The only types of pre-filing publicity that are permitted are those that would comply with Rule 135.[27] As discussed below, Rule 135(a)(2)(D) permits limited pre-filing communications with shareholders. The prospectus requirements[28] apply to solicitations regarding the shareholder's vote or consent for Rule 145 transactions. In 1999, the SEC liberalized the types of announcements that can be made once there has been a public announcement[29] of the proposed business combination.[30]

§ 5.2[3] Rule 145 and Downstream Sales

SEC Rule 145 addresses the problem of downstream sales after the corporate combination has been approved and consummated and the new securities have been issued. Rule 145(c)[36] imposes 1933 Act obligations upon any party to a transaction covered by Rule 145(a), other than the issuer, including any person who is an affiliate of such party, at the time it is submitted for the security holders' vote or consent. Through 2007, parties to a Rule 145 transaction, including affiliates of the issuer, who offer for sale or sell the securities issued in the Rule 145 transaction were deemed to be engaged in a distribution and therefore are underwriters under section 2(a)(11) of the Act.[37] However, at the end of 2007, the SEC amended Rule 145 to do away with the presumptive underwriter doctrine except for business combinations and reclassifications involving shell companies (other than shell companies created solely for the purpose of effectuating a business combination involving non-shell companies).[38]

Rule 145(d)[39] excludes certain downstream sales from those which create underwriter status under subsection (c) of the rule. Any person selling securities acquired in a Rule 145 transaction who would otherwise be deemed

---

25. *See, e.g.,* In the Matter of Carolina Pipeline, Inc., 419 Sec.Reg.L.Rep. (BNA) C–1 (SEC Sept. 2, 1977).

26. 15 U.S.C.A. § 77e(c). *See* § 2.3 *supra.*

27. 17 C.F.R. § 230.135. *See also, e.g.,* Chris–Craft Industries, Inc. v. Bangor Punta Corp., 426 F.2d 569 (2d Cir.1970); In the Matter of Carl M. Loeb, Rhoades & Co., 38 S.E.C. 843 (SEC 1959). Compare the types of pre-filing publicity permitted under Rule 145(b), 17 C.F.R. § 230.145(b).

28. 15 U.S.C.A. § 77e(b). *See* 15 U.S.C.A. § 77b(10). A 1934 Act proxy statement will not violate the prospectus requirements. 17 C.F.R. § 230.145(b)(2). The prospectus requirements are discussed in § 2.4 *supra.*

29. "Public announcement" encompasses all communications that put the market on notice of a proposed transaction. "Public announcement" means any communication by a party to the transaction, or any person authorized to act on a party's behalf, that is reasonably designed to, or has the effect of, informing the public or security holders in general about the transaction. 1933 Act Rule 165(f)(3), 17 C.F.R. § 230.165(f)(3).

30. Rule 145(b)(1), 17 C.F.R. § 230.145(b)(1). Regulation of Takeovers and Security Holder Communications, Sec. Act Rel. No. 33–7760, 1999 WL 969596 (SEC Oct. 22, 1999).

36. 17 C.F.R. § 230.145(c).

37. 17 C.F.R. § 230.145(c).

38. 17 C.F.R. § 230.145(c). See Revisions to Rules 144 and 145, Sec. Act Rel. No. 33–8869, 2007 WL 4270700 (Dec. 6, 2007).

39. 17 C.F.R. § 230.145(d).

an underwriter under Rule 145(c)'s presumptive underwriter provision is excluded from the definition provided that the sales are in compliance with Rule 144(d)'s volume limitations[40] and are executed in unsolicited brokers transactions.[41] In order to take advantage of this exclusion, it is further required that the issuer be a 1934 Act reporting company that has made all current reports publicly available or, alternatively, has made publicly available similar information.[42] Rule 145 was amended in 1984 to clarify the scope of permissible downstream sales of securities acquired in a business combination. Non-affiliates receiving securities registered under the 1933 Act in a business combination may sell the securities without registration if they have owned the securities for one year provided that Rule 144's informational requirements have been satisfied.[43] Rule 145's presumptive underwriter provisions were significantly relaxed in 2007 when the SEC amended Rule 145 to do away with the presumptive underwriter doctrine form for most business combinations.[46] Rule 145(c)'s presumptive underwriter provision now applies only to business combinations and reclassifications involving shell companies (other than shell companies created solely for the purpose of effectuating a business combination involving non-shell companies).[47]

When securities issued in a corporate combination are not registered under the 1933 Act because of reliance on an exemption, downstream sales may trigger the Act's registration requirements, unless the downstream sales are themselves exempt.[50] Absent an exemption for downstream sales that may occur, if downstream sales are anticipated, then the Rule 145 transaction must be registered on Form S–4 or on a more general registration form when the securities so issued are to be traded by the recipients in such a large amount as to constitute a distribution. Otherwise, a merger or other form of business combination would be a convenient device for avoiding the 1933 Act's registration requirements and getting securities into the hands of the general investing public without a full-fledged registration statement.[52]

§ 5.3 Section 2(a)(3)'s Definition of Sale: Warrants, Employee Stock Plans, Stock Dividends, and Spin–Offs Under the 1933 Act

§ 5.3[1] Warrants, Conversion Rights, Options, and Security Futures Products

Section 2(a)(1)'s definition of security[5] makes it clear that options, warrants, and conversion rights themselves constitute securities separate and

40. 17 C.F.R. § 230.144(e). *See* § 4.29 *supra.*

41. 17 C.F.R. § 230.144(f), (g). *See* 15 U.S.C.A. § 77d(4); § 4.26 *supra.*

42. 17 C.F.R. § 230.144(c).

43. Rule 145(d)(2), 17 C.F.R. § 230.145(d)(2).

46. See Revisions to Rules 144 and 145, Sec. Act Rel. No. 33–8869, 2007 WL 4270700 (Dec. 6, 2007).

47. 17 C.F.R. § 230.145(c). See Revisions to Rules 144 and 145, Sec. Act Rel. No. 33–8869, 2007 WL 4270700 (Dec. 6, 2007).

50. 15 U.S.C.A. § 77d(1), (4). *See* § 4.26 *supra.*

52. *See* SEC v. Datronics Engineers, Inc., 490 F.2d 250 (4th Cir.1973), *cert. denied* 416 U.S. 937, 94 S.Ct. 1936, 40 L.Ed.2d 287 (1974); Sec.Act Rel.No. 33–4982 (SEC July 2, 1979); § 5.3 *infra.*

§ 5.3

5. 15 U.S.C.A. § 77b(a)(1).

distinct from the underlying common stock or other security. The question arises, however, whether an exercise of conversion rights is itself a sale of the convertible security and a purchase of the underlying security. Section 2(a)(3)'s definition of sale requires that there be a disposition for "value" in order for a sale to take place.[6] As pointed out earlier,[7] when the owner of a convertible security exercises a conversion right, the holder of the convertible security is receiving something he or she had a right to all along—the underlying security. Hence, it would seem to follow that the conversion was not "for value" since the owner already had those rights prior to conversion.[8] This view is supported both by the case law and by SEC rulemaking.[9]

When options or warrants are issued to security holders without consideration or in conjunction with the sale of some other security, there is no sale of the options or warrants unless they are immediately exercisable.[10] However, options, warrants, or conversion rights that are immediately exercisable will be viewed as the issuer's "offer to sell" the underlying security, which in turn will have to be registered unless an exemption can be found.[11] Additionally, options or warrants, although not immediately exercisable, if transferred for consideration, will constitute a sale since they have been disposed of for value.[12] Furthermore, even after the option has been acquired, the exercise of the option may constitute a distinct purchase.

§ 5.3[2] Stock Dividends

The original version of the 1933 Act as it appeared in the House of Representatives would have exempted stock dividends paid in the company's own shares (or shares of another company[22]) from the registration requirements. The congressional conference committee that considered the House and Senate versions of the 1933 Act deleted the exemption as unnecessary, reasoning that stock dividends "are exempt without expressed provision as they do not constitute a sale, not being given for value."[23] It follows that the declaration and issuance of stock dividends where the shareholders do not have an election to obtain cash in lieu of the stock do not constitute sales of securities. Similarly, stock splits do not constitute sales under the 1933 Act.[24] This does not mean, however, that downstream sales following a stock dividend or stock split may be made with impunity, since these resales of shares received as a stock dividend or stock split will raise potential statutory underwriter questions, especially if there are so many shares sold as to constitute a "distribution."[25]

---

6. 15 U.S.C.A. § 77b(3).

7. *See* § 5.1[3] *supra.*

8. In Gilligan, Will & Co. v. SEC, 267 F.2d 461 (2d Cir.1959), *cert. denied,* 361 U.S. 896, 80 S.Ct. 200, 4 L.Ed.2d 152 (1959), the court did not question the conversion as a sale although sale of the underlying common stock after conversion was held to require registration. *Accord,* Rule 144(d)(4). 17 C.F.R. § 230.144(d)(4).

9. *Ibid.*

10. The last sentence of section 2(a)(3) provides the same rule for conversion rights. 15 U.S.C.A. § 77b(a)(3).

11. *See* Sec.Act Rel.No. 33–97 (Dec. 28, 1933).

12. "Warrant" generally refers to an option to acquire the issuer's stock. Other stock options which are contracts between the prospective purchaser and seller can also require registration. There are several national exchanges which trade options in publicly traded stock These exchanges are supervised by the SEC. *See* § 14.3 *infra.*

22. This type of transaction frequently is referred to as a ' spin-off''. *See* § 5.3[3] *infra*

23. H.R.Rep. No. 152, 73d Cong. 1st Sess. 25 (1933).

24. *See* Gurvitz v. Bregman & Co., 379 F.Supp. 1283 (S.D.N.Y.1974).

25. *See* Hafner v. Forest Laboratories, Inc., 345 F.2d 167, 168 (2d Cir.1965).

The SEC has taken the position that when, as the result of director action, the shareholders have no election to receive the dividend in cash, or when the stock is issued in lieu of a cash dividend pursuant to an election prior to declaration of the dividend, there is no value and hence no sale.[26] This latter situation rarely arises; however, the use of a no-sale approach here is highly debatable since the shareholder is making an investment decision when the election is made.[27] In the more common situation, when a cash dividend is declared and the shareholder purchases additional shares, as is the case with a dividend reinvestment plan ("DRIP"), the shareholder is clearly parting with value in exchange for receiving the stock and such distributions of shares will be considered sales and thus subject to the 1933 Act registration requirements absent an applicable exemption.[28]

§ 5.3[3] Exchanges of Securities

As noted in a previous section,[29] there are exemptions from registration for certain exchanges of securities such as those exchanges exclusively with existing security holders,[30] or exchanges which are pursuant to certain judicial or administratively approved transactions.[31] But these exemptions, although denominated as "security exemptions" under section 3 of the 1933 Act, are nevertheless treated as transaction exemptions and thus will not apply to insulate down-stream sales of the securities issued in an exempt exchange.[32] Accordingly, absent a separate exemption, downstream sales of securities issued in an exempt exchange transaction will have to be registered under the 1933 Act.

Absent an exemption, an exchange, other than one pursuant to preexisting conversion rights,[33] of one class of securities for another will constitute a sale under the securities laws. In such a case, there is a disposition for value (the value being the receipt of the securities received in the exchange). In the case of non-exempt exchanges of securities, any change in the rights and obligations of the issuer or securities holders or amendment to the security constitutes both a sale and a new issue, regardless of whether such amendatory action is permissible under state corporation law.[34] Thus, for example, the

26. Letter of General Counsel Discussing the Question of Whether a Sale of a Security is Involved in the Payment of a Dividend, Sec.Act Rel.No. 33–929, 1936 WL 28873 (SEC July 29, 1936).

27. In order for the shareholder's opportunity to elect cash or stock as a dividend not to lead to a sale, the dividend must be declared in stock rather than cash by the directors. In making such an election, the corporation can still be seen as receiving value: the savings of the cash dividend. Nevertheless the SEC's position has been that no sale occurs presumably because it is only when the dividend is declared that it assumes the status of a debt. Letter of General Counsel Discussing the Question of Whether a Sale of a Security is Involved in the Payment of a Dividend, Sec.Act Rel.No. 33–929, 1936 WL 28873 (SEC July 29, 1936).

28. *Id.*

29. *See* §§ 4.10, 5.2[1] *supra.*

30. 15 U.S.C.A. § 77c(a)(9).

31. 15 U.S.C.A. §§ 77c(a)(6), (a)(7), (a)(10). *See* §§ 4.7–4.8, 4.11 *supra.*

32. *See, e.g.,* In the Matter of Thompson Ross Securities Co., 6 S.E.C. 1111 (SEC 1940).

33. *See* § 5.3[1] *supra.*

34. *See, e.g.,* United States v. New York, New Haven & Hartford Railroad Co., 276 F.2d 525 (2d Cir.1960), *cert. denied,* 362 U.S. 961, 80 S.Ct. 877, 4 L.Ed.2d 876 (1960); SEC v. Associated Gas & Electric Co., 99 F.2d 795 (2d Cir.1938).

SEC staff has taken the position that registration will be required if a corporation that has issued tracking stock with respect to some of its operations decides to exchange common stock in a subsidiary with holders of the tracking stock.[35]

§ 5.3[4] Spin–Off Transactions

Just as a corporation's dividends in its own shares do not constitute sales under the Securities Act of 1933,[37] the same rule applies to dividends paid in shares of other corporations, such as in the case of a split-up or spin-off transaction, since the corporation is not receiving value in return. However, the Commission has made it clear that a spin-off may not be used as a scheme to avoid registration[39] and that in such a case "value" may be found from the creation of a public market for shares that prior to the spin-off were privately held and illiquid.[40] As discussed below, registration is likely to be required when the shares will be distributed by resales after the spin-off. However, when the spun-off shares are properly restricted against resale, registration will not be required. Shell corporations have also been used to attempt to evade the 1933 Act's registration requirements.[43]

On occasion, corporations with a large number of shareholders have made use of their existing shareholders to effectuate distributions of shares in corporations that formerly were closely held. For example, in SEC v. Harwyn Industries Corp.,[44] a company with a large number of shareholders actively sought privately-held companies desiring to go public. After acquiring the shares of these privately-held companies for valid consideration, these shares would be distributed to the public company's shareholders as a stock dividend or spin-off, with the conduit company retaining some of the privately held company's shares. It was then a matter of time before the shares of the once privately held company became traded publicly. The Commission successfully sought an injunction against such transactions without registration or an exemption notwithstanding the defendants' argument that no value was received by the corporation and that hence there was no sale. The court found that not only did the transactions violate the spirit of the Act,[45] but since the transactions created a public market for the securities of the once privately-held corporation, value could be said to have accrued to that corporation.[46] Additionally, when reselling the shares so received via the stock dividend, the spun-off company's shareholders' distribution of shares constituted a disposition for value. The court further noted that the defendants in *Harwyn* acted in good faith, believing that there was a valid basis for not registering the

35. *See* Liberty Media Corp., 2001 WL 109542 (SEC No Action Letter Feb. 7, 2001).

37. 15 U.S.C.A. § 77b(a)(3). *See* § 5.3[2] *supra*.

39. *See* Application of the Securities Act of 1933 and the Securities Exchange Act of 1934 to Spin Offs of Securities and Trading in the Securities of Inactive or Shell Corporations, Sec.Act Rel.No. 33–4982, Sec. Exch. Act Rel. No. 34–8638, 1969 WL 97001 (SEC July 2, 1969)

40. *See, e.g.*, SEC v. Datronics Engineers, Inc., 490 F.2d 250 (4th Cir.1973), *cert. denied*, 416 U.S. 937, 94 S.Ct. 1936, 40 L.Ed.2d 287 (1974); SEC v. Harwyn Industries Corp., 326 F.Supp. 943 (S.D.N.Y.1971).

43. *E.g.*, SEC v. Lybrand, 200 F.Supp.2d 384 (S.D.N.Y.2002) (founders of shell corporation were underwriters and thus transactions were not entitled to section 4(1) exemption from registration).

44. 326 F.Supp. 943 (S.D.N.Y.1971).

45. 26 F.Supp. at 953.

46. 26 F.Supp. at 953.

transaction under the 1933 Act.[47] The spin-off is not always used in good faith, and has also been utilized as an intentional attempt to evade 1933 Act registration. This device has also been used to attempt to create a public market for shares without the required registration. In such instances the violation of the 1933 Act's registration requirement is even clearer than in the case of a good faith attempt to secure an exemption from registration.[48]

The decisions dealing with spin-offs and shell corporations arose in the limited context of transactions in which there was no other bona fide business purpose; in other words, the spun-off corporation was acquired solely for the purpose of spinning it off. However, the impact of these rulings is broad, as they also have a bearing on more legitimate spin-off transactions.[49] Consider, for example, a publicly held company that decides to spin-off a portion of its business. Such a spin-off may be motivated, for example, by a managerial decision that the spun-off portion of the business is no longer desired, or in order to achieve compliance with the antitrust laws. Alternatively, the spin-off may be a final step in the acquisition of a company with some undesired assets that the acquiring company decides to dispose of. In any of these cases, the spin-off transaction, although not the result of a scheme to evade registration, will nevertheless require registration under the 1933 Act or an applicable exemption from registration. The rationale underlying the 1933 Act's registration requirement is that the transaction places in the hands of the investing public shares that previously were privately held. Although the transaction by which the securities are transferred from the spinning-off corporation to its shareholders may not include value even in the sense of *Harwyn* and its progeny, the transaction is clearly part of a distribution. It is to be anticipated that the securities so distributed to the shareholders may be sold, unless resales are restricted subject to Rule 144 and related law.[50] In such cases, the spin-off transaction and subsequent resales may place the corporation in a position of participating in a distribution within the meaning of section 2(a)(11)'s definition of underwriter.[51] The value requirement of the sale definition is satisfied since the publicly held corporation's shareholders clearly receive value when they sell their spun-off shares. When such downstream sales are of sufficiently substantial magnitude so as to constitute a "distribution," the spin-off transaction would constitute a type of indirect participation in the distribution that in turn would trigger section 2(11)'s definition. However, when it is not reasonably anticipated that there will be downstream resales following the spin-off transaction, registration will not be required.[53]

The discussion above addresses the 1933 Act registration issues relating to spin-off transactions. Even if a spin-off transaction can successfully be accomplished without 1933 Act registration, the 1934 Act may still need to be

47. 326 F.Supp. at 954.

48. SEC v. Datronics Engineers, Inc., 490 F.2d 250 (4th Cir.1973), *cert. denied* 416 U.S. 937, 94 S.Ct. 1936, 40 L.Ed.2d 287 (1974).

49. *See generally,* Simon M. Lorne, The Portfolio Spin-off and Securities Registration, 52 Tex.L.Rev. 918 (1974).

50. 17 C.F.R. § 230.144. *Cf.* 17 C.F.R. § 230.145(d) (1982). *See* §§ 4.29, 5.2 *supra.*

51. 15 U.S.C.A. § 77b(11) which is discussed in § 4.27 *supra.* See, e.g., S.E.C. v. Lybrand, 200 F.Supp.2d 384, 2002 WL 987284 *7 (S.D.N.Y.2002) (sales of shares in spin-off transaction were neither protected by the § 4(1) exemption nor by Rule 144).

53. *See* Consolidated Silver Standard Mines Ltd., 17 Sec.Reg. & L.Rep. (BNA) 2034 (SEC No Action Letter Oct. 30, 1985) (spin-off by Canadian corporation with only 3.2 percent of its shares held by 148 shareholders in the United States).

considered. Thus, for example, another limitation on securities issued in unregistered spin-off transactions is found in 1934 Act Rule 15c2–11, which makes it illegal for a broker to either initiate or continue to give price quotes for a security in the absence of adequate publicly available information. This rule has the effect of preventing the creation of an informed public market with regard to any security. Thus, for example, market makers cannot make a market in unregistered securities without adequate public information.

The SEC's ability to require 1933 Act registration of spin-off transactions depends in large part upon whether the transaction results in the creation of a secondary market for shares that formerly did not exist. The distribution of a subsidiary's shares from the parent corporation to the shareholders of the parent corporation, standing alone, is not a sale. Accordingly, the corporation has not sold its shares to one of its shareholders who receives the shares directly in a spin-off transaction.[57] Since the shareholders of the parent corporation had no choice in the matter when they received the shares of the spun-off subsidiary, there is no investment decision to be made and, hence, no sale.[58] However, as pointed out above, when the spin-off transaction brings with it the likelihood of unregistered downstream sales by the shareholders receiving the shares that are spun off, it may well be necessary to register the transaction under the Securities Act of 1933, lest the transaction as a whole be considered an improper unregistered sale of securities.[59]

The SEC has eliminated the burden of registration for certain bona fide spin-offs so long as adequate information is provided to the public markets. In 1997, the SEC clarified its position on the applicability of the registration requirements to certain spin-off transactions.[60] The SEC staff has taken the position that 1933 Act registration will not be required for spin-off transactions that meet the following five conditions: (1) the stockholders of the parent corporation do not provide consideration for the shares being spun off, (2) the shares are spun off on a pro rata basis to the parent corporation's shareholders, (3) the parent corporation provides adequate information both to its shareholders and to the trading markets,[61] (4) the parent corporation has a valid business purpose for the spin-off transaction, and (5) in the event that the parent corporation is spinning off securities that are restricted within the context of SEC Rule 144, it must have held those securities for at least one year.[62] Under these circumstances, the Commission will thus permit the infusion of adequate information into the market without a formal 1933 Act registration.[63]

---

57. *See* Isquith v. Caremark International, Inc., 136 F.3d 531 (7th Cir.1998).

58. 536 F.3d at 533.

59. Chugai Pharmaceutical Co., Ltd., 2002 WL 826918 (SEC No Action Letter April 30, 2002).

60. Legal Bulletin No. 4,, SECDIG 97–179–1, 1997 WL 570534 Sec. L. Daily (BNA) (SEC Div. Corp. Fin. Sept. 17, 1997).

61. If the parent corporation is a 1934 Act reporting company, it can satisfy the informational requirement by providing essentially the same information that is required by Regulation 14A or Regulation 14C of the proxy rules. The proxy rules are discussed in Chapter 10 *infra*. In the event that the subsidiary being spun off has already been a reporting company for at least ninety days, then the information requirement is satisfied by providing stockholders with information regarding the distribution ratio, the treatment of fractional shares, and the spin-off transaction's expected tax consequences.

62. Rule 144, 17 C.F.R. § 230.144. Formerly there was a two-year holding period, but the Commission reduced this to one year. *See* § 4.29 *supra*.

63. *See, e.g.*, Isquith v. Caremark International, Inc., 136 F.3d 531, 533 (7th Cir.1998) (no action letter was issued permitting a spin-off without registration if the issuer filed an "informa-

§ 5.4 Periodic Payments; The Investment Decision Doctrine

Investments in securities typically require that the investor pay the consideration prior to receiving the securities. On occasion, however, payments are scheduled to be made on an installment basis.[1] In such instances, the question may arise as to when the sale takes place: at the time of the contract, or is there a new sale at the time of each payment? Determining that an installment payment is a sale can implicate the 1933 Act's registration provisions. The identification of the sale date(s) has been significant primarily for statute of limitations purposes.[2] Determining whether an installment payment constitutes a sale depends on the definitions of purchase and sale. Ordinarily, installment payments will not involve multiple sales.[3]

tion statement"). *Cf.* Triad Guaranty, Inc. and Collateral Investment Corp., 2005 WL 1963042 (SEC No Action Letter Aug. 12, 2005) (allowing liquidating distribution without 1933 Act registration).

§ 5.4

1. At times, this has been particularly common in the sale of certain limited partnership interests.

2. *See* § 7.10 *infra.*

3. However, a stated policy of not enforcing unpaid subscriptions or installments may lead to the conclusion that calls for additional payments will be treated as new sales. See, e.g., Goodman v. Epstein, 582 F.2d 388, 409–414 (7th Cir.1978), *cert. denied,* 440 U.S. 939, 99 S.Ct. 1289, 59 L.Ed.2d 499 (1979); Troyer v. Karcagi, 476 F.Supp. 1142, 1148 (S.D.N.Y.1979).

Chapter 6

IPO PRACTICES: MANIPULATION, STABILIZATION AND HOT ISSUES

Table of Sections

§ 6.1 Manipulation: An Overview

Securities that are offered to the public are sometimes subject to manipulation. The Securities Act of 1933 contains registration, disclosure, and antifraud provisions. The 1933 Act does not address aftermarket activities of securities offered under a 1933 Act registration statement. Generally, market regulation is the province of the Securities Exchange Act of 1934.[1] As such, the various provisions of the 1934 Act that address manipulative practices generally[2] are the primary weapons against manipulative or deceptive IPO practices.

As discussed more fully in subsequent sections of this treatise,[3] there are a number of provisions of the Securities Exchange Act of 1934 which prohibit manipulative conduct in connection with securities trading. Section 9 of the Exchange Act[4] prohibits manipulative activity in connection with securities that are traded on a national securities exchange. Section 9(e) of the Exchange Act contains an express remedy[6] to redress damages incurred by investors who have been injured by illegal manipulative conduct with regard to those exchange-listed securities. Since it is limited by its terms to securities traded on a national exchange, section 9 does not apply to the vast number of securities traded in the over-the-counter markets. Nevertheless, there are parallel provisions that prohibit manipulation of over-the-counter securities. However, unlike section 9(e), there is no express private remedy for such manipulative conduct.

§ 6.1

1. Act of June 6, 1934, c. 404, Title I, § 1, 48 Stat. 881, codified in 15 U.S.C.A. §§ 78a *et seq.*

2. *See, e.g.,* 1934 Act §§ 9, 10(b), 15(c), 15 U.S.C.A. § 78i 78j(b), 78o(c). *See also* §§ 12.1, 14.3[6] *infra.*

3. *See* §§ 6.1–6.3, 12.1, chapter 14 *infra.*

4. 15 U.S.C.A. § 78i. *See* § 12.1 *infra.*

6. 15 U.S.C.A. § 78i(e). *See* § 12.1 *infra.*

In contrast to section 9's narrower reach, section 10(b) of the Exchange Act[8] empowers the SEC to promulgate rules prohibiting manipulative and deceptive devices and contrivances in connection with purchases and sales of securities regardless of whether the securities are traded on a national exchange. The only specified jurisdictional limitation on the section 10(b) rules is that the prohibited activity must occur "directly, or indirectly, by the use of any instrumentality of interstate commerce."[10] Under the terms of section 15(c)(1) of the Exchange Act,[11] the Commission is given the power to promulgate rules prohibiting brokers and dealers from engaging in "manipulative, deceptive, or otherwise fraudulent" devices and contrivances.[12]

The essence of securities manipulation is engaging in a transaction for the sole purpose of interfering with natural market forces and thereby artificially affecting the market price of the stock or other security being manipulated. The Exchange Act's prohibitions against manipulation are designed to preclude artificial interferences with the operation of a free and open market. It is irrelevant that the conduct may be designed to help the market reflect the true value of the security.

§ 6.2 Manipulation and Price Stabilization Involving Public Offerings

§ 6.2[1] Manipulation in Public Offerings

Both during and immediately after a public offering, the market is trying to digest the securities that are part of the new issue. In the after market following an initial offering of securities, price fluctuations are common and there is the potential for price manipulation. As will be discussed in this section, under limited circumstances the issuer may artificially stabilize the price of the security being offered publicly. All other stabilizing activities that are not protected by SEC rules fall within the category of illegal manipulation.

Section 9 of the Securities Exchange Act of 1934[1] prohibits manipulative conduct relating to the trading of securities listed on a national exchange. Section 9(e) also provides an express remedy in the hands of investors who are injured as a consequence of the illegal price manipulation of an exchange-traded security.[2] Furthermore, section 10(b) of the 1934 Act[3] specifically empowers the Commission to promulgate rules defining the scope of prohibited manipulative conduct with regard to any security. Problems of secondary distributions,[4] as well as primary offerings with a soft or unreceptive market, create a climate conducive to manipulative activity aimed at keeping the security's price at an artificially high level. Often a new issue will arrive and will be welcomed with a significantly higher demand than supply. This is

8. 15 U.S.C.A. § 78j(b).

10. 15 U.S.C.A. § 78j(b).

11. 15 U.S.C.A. § 78*o*(c)(1).

12. *See* § 12.1 *infra*.

§ 6.2

1. Act of June 6, 1934, c. 404, Title I, § 1, 48 Stat. 881, codified in 15 U.S.C.A. § 78i.

2. 15 U.S.C.A. § 78i(e). *See* § 12.1[4][A] *infra*.

3. 15 U.S.C.A. § 78j(b). Section 10(b) also relates to antifraud protections and is the governing section for Rule 10–5. *See* chapter 12 *infra*.

4. *See, e.g.*, In the Matter of Hazel Bishop Inc., 40 S.E.C. 718 (SEC 1961) which is discussed in § 4.28 *supra*.

known as a "hot issue." Hot issues are not necessarily the result of manipulation, although manipulative and deceptive sales practices can create the appearance of a bona fide hot issue. Hot issues occur when the demand for a new offering exceeds the supply of securities being offered for sale. Offerings that are legitimately hot issues present an environment conducive to manipulation.[6] Furthermore, manipulation can result in giving the appearance of a hot issue (or artificially heating up a bona fide hot issue) by artificially stimulating demand for the offering or by artificially restricting the supply of securities.

Section 9(a)(6) of the Exchange Act[8] specifically prohibits any transaction that is entered into for the purpose of "pegging, fixing, or stabilizing" the price of securities unless said transactions are in accordance with the procedures set out by applicable SEC rules.[9] In 1940, the Commission issued a Securities Act release[10] in which the Commission discussed possible approaches to the stabilization problem. The SEC recognized that it had three choices in approaching securities price stabilization: (1) the Commission could outlaw all stabilization activities by insiders; (2) it could take the other extreme and permit stabilizing transactions without any limitations; or (3) it could issue piecemeal regulation that would have the effect of prohibiting only detrimental stabilizing activity. The Commission opted for the third alternative and has continued to operate under a system of piecemeal regulation ever since.

Initial Public Offerings (or IPO's) are not the only public offerings that may present an environment that is conducive to manipulation. Frequently, issuers decide to raise new capital by selling additional securities of a class that is already publicly traded. The Commission has recognized that the natural effect of the influx of new stock on the market, unless a comparable demand is created, would necessarily be to deflate the market price, at least in the short term. Arguably, stabilizing activity is necessary for some offerings in order to make the offering a viable one and to assure a greater degree of certainty in the amount of money that an issuer can expect to raise as a result of such a distribution. The Securities and Exchange Commission thus allows limited stabilizing activity in this type of situation. The stabilizing rules are highly complex in their attempt to permit only necessary activity without providing an avenue for otherwise illegal artificial price manipulation. A brief description of the anti-manipulation rules is contained in the sections that follow.

§ 6.2[3] Regulation M—Scope of Rule 101

In general, Rule 101 prohibits distribution participants and their affiliated purchasers from bidding for purchasing—or attempting to induce any person to bid for or purchase—a covered security during a specified period (restricted period).[27] Rule 101 applies only to distribution participants[28] and their affiliated purchasers[29] in connection with a distribution of securities.

6. Hot issues are discussed in § 6.2 *infra.*

8. 15 U.S.C.A. § 78k(a)(6).

9. For such a rule *see* Regulation M which is discussed in §§ 6.2[2]–6.2[8] *infra.*

10. Sec. Act Rel. No. 33–2446 (March 18, 1940).

27. 17 C.F.R. § 242.101.

28. 17 C.F.R. § 242.100.

29. 17 C.F.R. § 242.100.

A distribution of securities under Regulation M is distinguished from ordinary trading transactions by the "magnitude of the offering" and the presence of "special selling efforts and selling methods."[34] Thus, the current rule is not limited to the types of distributions generally covered by the 1933 Act registration requirements. In exploring the magnitude of the purported distribution, the SEC looks at a number of factors, including the number of shares for sale, the trading volume that those shares represent, the percentage of outstanding shares, and the public float.[35] The amount of the shares being sold is not as significant as the percentage of the public float that the sales represent.[36] The concept of distribution is to be interpreted flexibly in order to permit the anti-manipulation rules "to evolve with changes in the practices and methods of offering securities."[37]

Under Regulation M, public offerings, private placements, shelf offerings, mergers and acquisitions, exchange offers, forced conversions of securities, warrant solicitations, and at-the-market offerings are distributions.[38] With respect to shelf offerings, the Commission has taken the view that each takedown off a shelf is to be individually examined to determine whether that particular offering constitutes a distribution.[39]

The trading restrictions of Rule 101 cover securities which are either the subject of a distribution or reference securities.[40] Rule 100 sets forth the definitions that apply throughout Regulation M. Under Rule 100's definition, the term "reference security" is a security into which a subject security may be converted, exchanged, or exercised, or which, under the terms of the subject security, may in whole or in significant part determine the value of the subject security.[41] The anti-manipulative restrictions are effective only during the specifically defined restrictive period.[42] Depending on the average daily trading volume value[43] of the offered security and the public float value[44] of

34. 17 C.F.R. § 242.100.

35. *See* Review of Anti-manipulation Regulation of Securities Offerings, Sec. Act Rel. No. 33–7057, 56 S.E.C. Docket 1302, Release No. IS–657, 1994 WL 138672 (SEC April 19, 1994).

36. *See* Examination of the Registration of Securities To Be Offered and Sold on a Delayed or Continuous Basis in the Future, Sec. Act Rel. No. 33–6391, 24 S.E.C. Docket 1502, 1982 WL 529089 (SEC March 12, 1982).

37. *See* Review of Antimanipulation Regulation of Securities Offerings, Sec. Act Rel. No. 33–7057, 56 S.E.C. Docket 1302, Release No. IS–657, 1994 WL 138672 (SEC April 19, 1994).

38. Anti–Manipulation Rules Concerning Securities Offerings, SEC Rel. Nos. 33–7375; 34–38067; IC–22412, 62 Fed. Reg. 520, 526 (1997). Shelf registration is discussed in § 3.11 *supra*. At market offerings are discussed in § 6.3 *infra*.

39. *See* Sec. Exch. Rel. No. 19565, 48 Fed. Reg. 10631.

40. 17 C.F.R. § 242.101.

41. 17 C.F.R. § 242.100.

42. 17 C.F.R. § 242.101(a).

43. The average daily trade volume (ADTV) of a covered security is defined on the basis of reported worldwide average daily trading volume during a specified period prior to the filing of the registration statement or prior to the pricing of the offering, depending on the circumstances. *See* Anti-manipulation Rules Concerning Securities Offerings, SEC Rel. Nos. 33–7375; 34–38067; IC–22412 (Dec. 20, 1996), 62 Fed. Reg. 520, 546 (1997).

44. As for public float value, the Commission adopted a definition that reflects its usage in Form 10–K (i.e., the aggregate amount of common equity securities held by non-affiliates). 17 C.F.R. § 249.310. *See also*Sec. Act Rel. No. 7326 (Aug. 30, 1996) Sec. Act Rel. No. 7326 (Aug. 30, 1996), 61 Fed. Reg. 47706 (1996).

the issuer, the restricted period commences either one or five business days before the day of the pricing of the offering security and continues until the distribution is over.[45]

§ 6.2[4] Regulation M—Exclusions and Exemptions From Rule 101's Prohibitions

Rule 101 excludes from its coverage actively-traded securities.[48] The Commission believes that actively-traded securities are widely followed by the investment community, and thus aberrations in price are more likely to be discovered and quickly corrected. Moreover, actively-traded securities are generally traded on exchanges or other organized markets with high levels of transparency and surveillance.[49] The rule also excludes investment rated nonconvertible and asset backed securities;[50] "exempted securities" as defined in Section 3(a)(12) of the Exchange Act;[51] and face-amount certificates of securities issued by an open-end management investment company or unit investment trust.[52]

In addition to allowing permissible stabilizing activity under certain circumstances, which is discussed below,[53] Rule 101 provides a list of transactions to which the rule's prohibitions do not apply.[54]

§ 6.2[5] Regulation M—Scope of Rule 102

Rule 102 is similar in format to Rule 101: issuers and selling security holders, and their affiliated purchasers,[70] must refrain from bidding for, purchasing, or attempting to induce any person to bid for or purchase a covered security during the applicable restrictive period, unless an exception permits the activity.[71] The restrictive period is subject to the same definition that is applicable to Rule 101 as proscribed by the definition section of Regulation M. The Commission affords fewer exceptions in Rule 102 than in Rule 101 because issuers and selling security holders have the greatest interest in an offering's outcome, and generally do not have the same market access needs as underwriters.[72] The underwriters have the responsibility of bringing the securities public and also may be involved in other securities transactions which requires them to purchase securities while the offering is taking place. In contrast, the issuer and selling shareholders can simply refrain from purchasing securities until the distribution is complete.

45. 17 C.F.R. § 242.100.

48. Actively-traded securities are those with an ADTV value of at least $1 million that are issued by an issuer whose common equity securities have a public float value of at least $150 million. 17 C.F.R. § 242.101(c)(1).

49. *See* Anti–Manipulation Rules Concerning Securities Offering, SEC Rel. Nos. 33–7375; 34–38067; IC–22412 (Dec. 20, 1996), 62 Fed. Reg. 520, 527 (1997).

50. 17 C.F.R. § 242.101(c)(2).

51. 17 C.F.R. § 242.101(c)(3).

52. 17 C.F.R. § 242.101(c)(4).

53. 17 C.F.R. § 242.104.

54. 17 C.F.R. § 242.101(b).

70. 17 C.F.R. § 242.100.

71. 17 C.F.R. § 242.102(a).

72. *See* Anti–Manipulation Rules Concerning Securities Offerings, SEC Rel. Nos. 33–7375; 34–38067; IC–22412 (Dec. 20, 1996), 62 Fed. Reg. 520, 530 (1997).

§ 6.2[7] Regulation M—Scope of Permissible Stabilizing Activity

Rule 104 of Regulation M[89] sets forth the parameters of permissible stabilizing activity to prevent or retard a decline in the market price of a security and thus to facilitate an offering.[91] To begin with, both the possibility and existence of stabilizing activity must be disclosed to any purchaser prior to completion of each transaction.[92] An issuer may satisfy the notice to the purchaser requirement by placing a legend on the inside front cover of the prospectus.[93] Furthermore, any person who enters a bid for the purpose of stabilizing the price of any security shall notify the market on which the bid is placed and disclose the purpose of such bid to the person with whom the bid is entered.[94] Also, any person effecting a syndicate covering transaction,[95] or placing a penalty bid[96] shall disclose that fact to the self-regulatory organization that has direct oversight authority over the principal market in the United States.[97] Additionally, anyone subject to Rule 104 is required to keep the information of stabilizing activity for a period of three years.[98]

In addition to the above disclosure requirement, the SEC regulates the mechanics of all legitimate stabilizing activity. Participants in a distribution may engage in stabilizing activity only to the extent the stabilizing activity complies with Rule 104. Under the rule, no stabilizing bid may be higher than the lower of the offering price or the stabilizing bid for the security in the principal market.[99] The rule strictly regulates the first stabilizing bid made in connection with the offering.[100] Once a stabilizing bid has been initiated, it may be increased, maintained, reduced, or adjusted in accordance with the provisions of the rule.[102]

In adopting the anti-manipulation rules, the Commission was aware of the additional risks of price manipulation that can be associated with "at market" offerings.[103] Most securities offerings are marketed through a fixed price that is fixed before the offering commences. In contrast, in an at market offering, rather than the issuer setting a predetermined offering price prior to

89. 17 C.F.R. § 242.104.

91. 17 C.F.R. § 242.104. Unlike Rule 101 and 102, which applies to a "distribution," Rule 104 governs stabilizing to facilitate an "offering," a term that is broader in scope.

92. 17 C.F.R. § 242.104(h).

93. 17 C.F.R. § 242.104(h)(3).

94. 17 C.F.R. § 242.104(h)(1).

95. 17 C.F.R. § 242.100. A syndicate covering transaction is the placing of any bid or the effecting of any purchase on behalf of the sole distributor or the underwriting syndicate or group to reduce a syndicate short position.

96. 17 C.F.R. § 242.100. Rule 100 defines penalty bid to mean an arrangement that permits the managing underwriter to reclaim a selling concession otherwise accruing to a syndicate member in connection with an offering when the securities originally sold by the syndicate member are purchased in syndicate covering transactions.

97. 17 C.F.R. § 242.104(h)(2).

98. 17 C.F.R. § 242.104(i). Rule 17a–2(c)(1) sets forth the three-year period. Amendments to Rule 17a–2 under the Exchange Act require managing underwriters to keep records of syndicate covering transactions and penalty bids, in addition to stabilizing information. 17 C.F.R. § 240.17a–2.

99. 17 C.F.R. § 242.104(f).

100. 17 C.F.R. § 242.104(f).

102. 17 C.F.R. § 242.104(f)(3), (4), (5), (6).

103. *See, e.g.*, In the Matter of Hazel Bishop Inc., 40 S.E.C. 718 (SEC 1961).

the commencement of the offering, the securities are offered with a fluctuating price to be determined by the market price for securities of the same class that are already traded. Thus, each sale in an "at market" offering will be at the then prevailing market price based on the market price both within and without the United States borders.

§ 6.2[8] Regulation M—Manipulative Short Sales, Rule 105

Rule 105 is intended to prevent manipulative short selling prior to a public offering by short sellers who cover their short positions by purchasing securities in the offering, thus largely avoiding exposure to market risk.[111] Such short sale could result in a lower offering price and reduce an issuer's proceeds.[112] Under the rule, certain short sales are prohibited from being covered with securities offered by an underwriter, broker, or dealer participating in the offering. Rule 105 covers only those short sales effected in the period commencing five business days prior to the offering's pricing and ending with such pricing.

Rule 105 does not apply to short sales of derivative securities in accordance with the general approach of Regulation M.[115] The Commission may, either upon request or upon its own motion, grant an exemption from Rule 105's prohibitions.[118] Such an exemption from the short sale prohibition may be granted either unconditionally or pursuant to specified terms and conditions.[119] In 2004, the SEC adopted comprehensive regulation of short sales in Regulation SHO.[120] At the same time, the SEC issued interpretive guidance on the application of Regulation M's Rule 105 to short sales.[121] It also amended Rule 105 to eliminate the exemption for shelf offerings.[122]

In late 2006, the SEC proposed amending Regulation M to prevent short sales during a limited time period, shortly before pricing of a public offering by prohibiting contemporaneous sales and purchases, including entering into a contract of sale for such security in the offering[123] The SEC adopted the amendments to Rule 105 to eliminate perceived abuses by some short sellers during public offerings. In particular, the amendments replaced the previous restrictions on short sales by participants in a public offering with a prohibition against short sellers purchasing shares in a public offering if the short sale was made during a restricted period.[124] In order to prevent the rule from

111. 17 C.F.R. § 242.105.

112. *See* the discussion on short sales in § 14.22 *infra.*

115. The Commission is satisfied that any manipulative short sales involving derivative transactions continue to be addressed by the general anti-manipulation provisions, including Section 9(a)(2) of and Rule 10–5 under the Exchange Act. *See* Anti-manipulation Rules Concerning Securities Offerings, SEC Rel. Nos. 33–7375; 34–38067; IC–22412 (Dec. 20, 1996), 62 Fed Reg. 520, 538 (1997).

118. 17 C.F.R. § 242.105(c).

119. 17 C.F.R. § 242.105(c).

120. *See* Short Sales, Sec. Exch. Act Rel. No. 34–50103, 2004 WL 1697019 (SEC 2004) (adoption of Regulation SHO).

121. *See* Short Sales, Sec. Exch. Act Rel. No. 34–50103, 2004 WL 1697019 (SEC 2004) (adoption of Regulation SHO).

122. *See* Short Sales, Sec. Exch. Act Rel. No. 34–50103, 2004 WL 1697019 (SEC 2004) (adoption of Regulation SHO). Shelf offerings are discussed in § 3.11 *supra.*

123. *See* Short Selling in Connection With a Public Offering Sec. Exch. Act Rel. No. 34–54888, 71 Fed. Reg. 75002–01, 2006 WL 3610260 (SEC Dec. 13, 2006).

124. *See* Short Selling in Connection with a Public Offering, Sec. Exch. Act Rel. No. 34–56206, 72 Fed. Reg. 45094–01, 2007 WL 2273996 (SEC Aug. 10, 2007). *See also, e.g.,* Regulation SHO and

unduly limiting the pool of potential purchasers in secondary offerings, short sellers may participate in follow-on and secondary offerings during the restricted period so long as the seller makes a bona fide purchase before the offering is priced.[125] The amendments also clarified that Rule 105 is limited to equity securities offerings where the offering is made for cash.[126]

§ 6.3 Aftermarket Activities, IPO Practices, Hot Issues, Workout Markets, and Controlled Markets

§ 6.3[1] Initial Public Offerings and the After Market—An Overview

Setting the initial offering price for securities in a public offering can be a difficult task. If the securities are overpriced, the offering will not succeed, since there will be no demand for the supply offered at the excessive price. As discussed in the preceding section[1] of this treatise, even well-priced offerings can be met with a soft reception if the market cannot absorb all of the securities offered at once. In such a case, some of the offering will be sold but part of the initial allotment will remain unsold. Frequently, in such a case, the securities will then trade in the aftermarket at a price below the offering price because of the excess supply from the unsold initial allotment that is hanging over the market. In such an environment, it may take time for the entire initial allotment to be sold. Also, as discussed in the preceding section[2] of this treatise, under certain circumstances and subject to specified safeguards, price stabilization may be permitted in order to facilitate a smoother initial offering.[3]

The desire to raise the capital targeted by an initial public offering creates an incentive to not overprice the securities being offered lest there be a cool reception in the market. As discussed in a subsequent section[4] of this treatise, one possible response to the fear of not raising sufficient funds is to condition the offering on a certain number of shares being sold. In these part-or-none or all-or-none offerings, the offering will be cancelled unless the issuer and underwriters are able to sell the minimum number of shares

---

Rule 10a–1, Sec. Exch. Act Rel. No. 34–55970, 2007 WL 1880054 (SEC June 28, 2007). For the NASD conforming amendments, *see* NASD Notice 07–31, Short Sale Requirements, http://www.nasd.com/web/groups/rules_regs/documents/notice_to_members/nasdw_019381.pdf, 2007 WL 2020744 (NASD July 5, 2005).

125. 17 C.F.R. § 242.105. *See* Short Selling in Connection with a Public Offering, Sec. Exch. Act Rel. No. 34–56206, 72 Fed. Reg. 45094–01, 2007 WL 2273996 (SEC Aug. 10, 2007). *See also, e.g.,* Regulation SHO and Rule 10a–1, Sec. Exch. Act Rel. No. 34–55970, 2007 WL 1880054 (SEC June 28, 2007). For the NASD conforming amendments, *see* NASD Notice 07–31, Short Sale Requirements, http://www.nasd.com/web/groups/rules_regs/documents/notice_to_members/nasdw_019381.pdf, 2007 WL 2020744 (NASD July 5, 2005).

126. 17 C.F.R. § 242.105. *See* Short Selling in Connection with a Public Offering, Sec. Exch. Act Rel. No. 34–56206, 72 Fed. Reg. 45094–01, 2007 WL 2273996 (SEC Aug. 10, 2007). *See also, e.g.,* Regulation SHO and Rule 10a–1, Sec. Exch. Act Rel. No. 34–55970, 2007 WL 1880054 (SEC June 28, 2007). For the NASD conforming amendments, *see* NASD Notice 07–31, Short Sale Requirements, http://www.nasd.com/web/groups/rules_regs/documents/notice_to_members/nasdw_019381.pdf, 2007 WL 2020744 (NASD July 5, 2005).

§ 6.3

1. *See* § 6.2 *supra.*

2. *See* 6.2[7] *supra.*

3. *See* Rule 104 of Regulation M, 17 C.F.R. § 242.104.

4. *See* § 6.4 *infra.*

specified. These conditional offerings present special disclosure problems as well as the increased temptation for manipulation.[5]

The incentive not to overprice the securities being offered will often result in an offering where the initial demand exceeds the supply of shares covered by the initial offering. In such a case, the trading in the aftermarket will be at a price that exceeds the initial offering price. The benefit of the increased aftermarket price does not inure directly to the issuer but rather results in profits for the selling shareholders.

Thus, pricing of offerings is a very difficult task. Overpricing will result in a poor reception or even a failed offering. Underpricing will result in a hot issue, and it will create questions as to whether the company's management could have raised more capital. In an extreme case, significant underpricing could lead to a claim by preexisting shareholders that management breached their duty of care in pricing the shares. Thus, there is pressure not to underprice the securities being offered. At the same time, there are pressures in the other direction. The fear of a failed or unsuccessful offering is so strong that it pushes management in the direction of conservative pricing. Furthermore, even if the market takes the securities at a high initial price, declines in the aftermarket can lead to suits by investors claiming that the initial offering was overpriced and that the offering materials were materially misleading in violation of securities laws. The mechanics of pricing go beyond the scope of this treatise but the reader should keep in mind that this is as much an art as a science.

Just as stabilization can become a problem in securities offerings that appear in a soft market,[8] there are manipulation temptations that can arise in a bull market for the securities in distribution. When the offering is oversubscribed, there is frequently little doubt that once the stock begins to trade publicly in the aftermarket it will exceed the original offering price. In the case of such a "hot issue" there is great potential for abuse. Also, there may be the temptation to create the appearance of a hot issue in order to create additional buying demand and upward price pressure. The sections that follow[9] address the securities laws issues that can arise in connection with "hot issues"—those offerings when the trading in the aftermarket is at a price significantly in excess of the initial offering price.

In 1959, the Commission conducted and issued a study dealing with price increases that were found to have occurred immediately following certain public registered offerings.[10] The Commission's study found that a number of undesirable practices were taking place. In many cases, the underwriter would allot a portion of the registered offering to active trading firms which were not members of the selling group. These firms would in turn make a market for the securities contemporaneously with the public offering. In one case cited by the SEC study, a security that was initially offered at three dollars per share was selling for as much as five to seven dollars by the end of the first day following the offer.

---

5. *See* § 6.4 *infra.*

8. *See* § 6.2[7] *supra.*

9. *See* §§ 6.3[2], 6.3[3] *infra.*

10. Sec. Act Rel. No. 33–4150 (Oct. 23, 1959).

Not all abusive activities during a hot issue are based on price manipulation. For example, the Commission identified another practice where underwriters allotted portions of the securities in registration to their partners, officers, employees, and relatives in anticipation of a "hot issue" and quick profit in the stock.

The Commission went on to point out a number of the legal consequences of such activities. In the first instance, any arrangements regarding workouts, special allotments of securities, or the creation of trading firms to be used as market makers must be disclosed in detail on the registration statement. Second, any trading firms would clearly fall within the category of "underwriter" within the meaning of section 2(a)(11).[11] Third, also involved would be violations of the Act's antifraud provisions. Specifically, Rule 10–5 of the Exchange Act[12] and section 17(a) of the 1933 Act[13] would be violated in that the activities would be giving the public the impression that the entire offering has been subscribed to by the public when, in fact, a substantial portion has gone either to insiders or to trading firms.[14] Fourth, these types of workout activities would also violate Regulation M's (former Rule 10–6's) prohibitions on manipulation[15] which expressly forbid an underwriter or participant in a distribution from bidding for or purchasing securities being distributed. Fifth, the SEC has pointed out that a broker/dealer acting as a trading firm would in all likelihood be in violation of Rule 15c1–8[16] which prohibits sales on the market of securities in distribution. A sixth consequence is that any participating broker/dealer would be subject to possible sanctions imposed by the Commission, a stock exchange, or National Association of Securities Dealers (now FINRA).[17] The SEC has expressed the opinion that current regulation is adequate to curb abuses in connection with hot issues.[18]

Another problem associated with hot issues is the practice of "free riding" whereby a subscriber to the offering hopes to resell at a premium but plans to withdraw the order if the "temperature seems to go down before allotment."[19] Free riding clearly falls within the purview of manipulative conduct. Free riding as manipulative and deceptive conduct is not limited to new offerings. Illegal free riding takes place any time a purchaser of securities does not have the funds to pay for the purchase but rather intends to take a "free ride" on the securities purchased. For example, investors who open accounts and misrepresent their net worth to a number of brokerage firms

---

11. 15 U.S.C.A. § 77b(a)(11). *See* § 4.27 *supra. See also* The discussion of underwriters' compensation in § 2.1[3] *supra.*

12. 1117 C.F.R. § 240.10–5. *See* chapter 12 *infra.*

13. 15 U.S.C.A. § 77(a). *See* §§ 7.11, 12.22 *infra.*

14. Sec. Act Rel. No. 33–4150 (Oct. 23, 1959).

15. 17 C.F.R. § 240.10–6 (1996). *See* § 6.1 *supra.*

16. 17 C.F.R. § 240.15c1–8. Regulation of broker-dealers is discussed in chapter 14 *infra.*

17. *See* NASD Interpretation with Respect to "Free–Riding and Withholding," NASD Manual (CCH) ¶ 2151.06. *See also, e.g.,* SEC Approves Proposed Changes to NASD Rule Relating to "Hot Issues," 26 Sec. Reg. & L. Rep. (BNA) 1709 (Dec. 23, 1994).

18. No Need for Hot Issues Market Rules, SEC Tells Congress, 16 Sec.Reg. & L.Rep. (BNA) 1446 (Aug. 28, 1984).

19. " 'Free riding' is the practice whereby a stock is purchased without sufficient funds available to pay for it, the stock is sold prior to the settlement date of the purchase, and the proceeds of the sale are used to pay for the original purchase." In the Matter of Account Management Corp., Admin. Proc. File No. 3–885; Sec. Exch. Act Rel. No. 34–36314, 60 S.E.C. Docket 962, 1995 WL 579449 footnote 6 (SEC Sept. 29, 1995), relying on United States v. Tager, 788 F.2d 349, 350 (6th Cir.1986).

and then purchase securities without sufficient funds for payment have engaged in illegal free riding.[22] It is not uncommon to use nominee accounts to hide the true identity of the securities owners in order to facilitate a free riding scheme.[23]

Complicity by a brokerage firm in a free riding scheme is a violation of the securities laws. Thus, for example, criminal prosecutions have resulted from a brokerage firm's policy of selling IPOs to friends and celebrities and then buying those shares at a premium before reselling them to members of the public at an inflated price.[24] There have been numerous regulatory concerns over IPO allocation policies generally.

In its free riding and withholding interpretation, the NASD identifies several categories of "restricted person" who cannot receive securities during a hot issue.[29] The list of restricted persons includes, among others, any officer, director, general partner, employee, or agent of a broker-dealer or their family members, or a senior officer or certain specified employees of certain institutional investors.[30] The NASD disqualification of restricted persons "ensures that NASD members and their associated persons make bona-fide distributions to the public of securities that are part of a public offering."[31] The NASD interpretation is meant to prevent artificial restrictions on the supply of hot issue offerings.[32]

The NASD free riding and withholding interpretation is prophylactic in nature and does not require a showing of scienter.[33] The NASD interpretation also was designed to prevent withholding. Withholding securities from the market restricts supply and thus places upward pressure on the price of the new issue.[34] Preventing withholding of securities from the market is designed to ensure "that public customers who want to purchase them will not be forced to acquire them in the aftermarket at a higher price."[35] The NASD free riding and withholding interpretation is designed to prevent persons associated with the offering from withholding securities from the market. Long ago, it

22. E.g., SEC v. Teyibo, 1993 WL 144859, [1992–1993 Transfer Binder] Fed.Sec.L.Rep. (CCH) & 97,405 (D.Md.1993) (illegal free-riding in U.S. Treasury bonds).

23. *See, e.g.,* In the Matter of H.J. Meyers & Co., Administrative Proceeding File No. 3–9754, Sec. Act Rel. No. 33–7694, 70 S.E.C. Docket 74, 1999 WL 436513 (SEC June 30, 1999).

24. People v. Schwartz, 34 Sec.Reg. & L.Rep. 532 (N.Y.Sup.Ct. March 8, 2002) (guilty pleas entered; $21 million in restitution ordered).

29. NASD Rule Interpretation IM–2110–1.

30. NASD Rule Interpretation IM–2110–1.

31. In the Matter of Crute, Admin. Proc. File No. 3–9428, Sec. Exch. Act Rel. No. 34–40474, 68 S.E.C. Docket 118, 68 S.E.C. Docket 123, 1998 WL 652110 (SEC Sept. 24, 1998), relying on Sherman, Fitzpatrick & Co. Inc., 51 S.E.C. 1048, 1054 (1994).

32. In the Matter of Crute, Admin. Proc. File No. 3–9428, Sec. Exch. Act Rel. No. 34–40474, 68 S.E.C. Docket 118, 68 S.E.C. Docket 123, 1998 WL 652110 (SEC Sept. 24, 1998), relying on First Philadelphia Corp., 50 S.E.C. 360, 361 (1990).

33. In the Matter of Crute, Admin. Proc. File No. 3–9428, Sec. Exch. Act Rel. No. 34–40474, 68 S.E.C. Docket 118, 68 S.E.C. Docket 123, 1998 WL 652110 (SEC Sept. 24, 1998), relying on First Philadelphia Corp., 50 S.E.C. 360, 361 (1990).

34. Withholding is manipulative in any market since it keeps the securities at an artificially high price by arterially restricting supply. *See, e.g.,* In the Matter of Silverman, Sec. Act Rel. No. 33–45407, Sec. Exch. Act Rel. No. 34–45407, 2002 WL 185905, SEC News Digest 2002–26, 2002 WL 189036, (SEC Feb. 7, 2002) (consent order for manipulation based on withholding).

35. In the Matter of Sherman, Fitzpatrick & Co., Admin. Proc. File No. 3–7878, 51 S.E.C. 1048, Sec. Exch. Act Rel. No. 34–33928, 56 S.E.C. Docket 1356 1994 WL 148475 (SEC. April 19, 1994).

was held that undisclosed withholding of supply of securities from a public offering violates the antifraud provisions.[37] This continues to be the law.

Although firms are given considerable leeway in how they allocate IPO's, there are limits. Thus, for example, requiring the customer turn over a share of their trading profits in exchange for the allocation clearly is illegal.[40] Nor is it permissible to repurchase the securities of selected customers receiving shares from an IPO at a predetermined price before reselling those shares to members of the public.[41]

There are other prohibited manipulative practices that can occur in connection with hot issues. For example, a brokerage firm might unduly encourage its registered representatives to encourage customer purchases by giving sales people a higher commission for transactions where the customer purchases rather than sells the securities in question. Especially if undisclosed to the customer, this type of compensation for trades encourages the creation of more purchases than sales. Another practice is to pre-sell the offering in the after-market.[43] Under this manipulation, registered representatives (and in some cases unregistered sales personnel) require or encourage customers to commit to purchasing shares in the aftermarket in order to get part of the allotment out of the original issue. This, of course, generates additional aftermarket buying activity that is manipulative, in that it is designed to push the price higher once the security comes to market. Thus, soliciting offers before the offering takes place can be part of such a manipulation[45] as can taking aftermarket orders before the offering takes place.[46] In addition, combining a public offering with "boiler room" or other improper high pressure sales tactics[47] are manipulative, as they precondition the aftermarket following an initial offering.[48] For example, generating bids during a distribution is manipulative.[49] A somewhat related aftermarket practice that has been challenged is requiring "tie-in" purchases by institutional investors and thereby conditioning their participation in the IPO on an agreement to purchase in the aftermarket at higher prices.[50] These types of tie-in agree-

37. Otis & Co. v. SEC, 106 F.2d 579, 582–83 (6th Cir. 1939), affirming 18 F.Supp. 100, 101–102 (N.D.Ohio 1936) (failure to disclose agreements limiting the sale of 30 percent of the outstanding stock during a distribution at the market of 8 percent of the stock violated section 17(a) of the 1933 Act even though there was no violation of 1934 Act § 9's anti-manipulation provisions).

40. *See, e.g.,* SEC Charges CSFB with Abusive IPO Allocation Practices; CSFB Will PAY $100 Million TO Settle SEC and NASD Actions; Millions in IPO Profits Extracted From Customers in Exchange for Allocations in "Hot" Deals SEC News Digest 2002–14, 2002 WL 77626 (Jan. 22, 2002). *See also, e.g.,* NASD Fines and Suspends Two CSFB Execs for Failing to Prevent IPO Profit Sharing Paybacks, http://www.nasdr.com/news/pr2002/ release_02_039.html (NASD Aug. 15, 2002).

41. *See* People v. Wood (N.Y.Sup.Ct. March 8, 2002) (guilty pleas entered) as reported in USA Today p. 2B (March 11, 2002).

43. *See, e.g.,* NASDR, Disciplinary Actions Reported for April, 1999 WL 33176514 * 16 (NASDR April 1999).

45. *See, e.g.,* SEC v. Bouchy, Civ–96–2629–phx-srb, Litigation Release No. 16943, 2001 WL 286253 (D. Ariz. March 23, 2001).

46. *See, e.g.,* In the Matter of A.S. Goldmen & Co., 2001 WL 588039 *8, Sec. Exch. Act Rel. No. 34–44328 (SEC May 21, 2001).

47. Boiler rooms and high pressure sales tactics are discussed in § 14.18 *infra*.

48. *See, e.g.,* SEC v. Madden, CV 00 3632, Litigation Release No. 16600, 72 S.E.C. Docket 1801, 2000 WL 781334 (E.D.N.Y. June 20, 2000).

49. *See, e.g.,* In re Chatzer, 1995 WL 560153 (SEC initiation of proceedings Sept. 22, 1995).

50. *See* Billing v. Credit Suisse First Boston Corp., 33 Sec. Reg. & L. Rep. (BNA) 309 (S.D.N.Y. 2001) (antitrust suit charging illegal tie-in arrangements in connection with IPOs).

ments violate Regulation M's prohibitions against manipulation during public offerings.[51]

Another IPO-related manipulation is for participants in the offering to repurchase in the aftermarket at a premium in order to drive the market price up further.[52] Also, parking[53] part of the public offering[54] with nominees[55] in order to take advantage of the hot issue aftermarket is a manipulative practice.[56]

Yet another improper sales practice associated with hot issues is offering sales personnel extra commissions for generating customer purchases of the securities being offered. Along similar lines, offering high compensation to underwriters can be indicative of improper IPO selling efforts.[58] Manipulative activity in connection with IPOs is a serious matter and can run result in significant criminal consequences.

Although the Commission prohibits withholding securities from the market as well as channeling securities to relatives of the issuer, underwriters and participating dealers, there is no express limitation on dealers' showing favoritism towards certain customers.[67] For example, although a brokerage firm's method of allocating securities during a hot issue might be "unfair" in terms of parity among its customers, so long as the stock does not go to a select group of insiders, there is no violation of the securities laws' hot issue prohibitions.[68] As a result of these practices and other ways in which firms favor their larger customers, most investors do not have access to hot issues in the new issues market. Requiring customers to give a quid pro quo for IPO allocations violates the antifraud provisions.[69] This includes tie-in or "laddering" arrangements that require IPO purchasers to commit to purchasing

---

51. Prohibited Solicitations and "Tie-in" Agreements for Aftermarket Purchases, Staff Legal Bull. No. 10, http://www.sec.gov/interps/legal/slbmr10.htm (SEC Div. Market Reg. Aug. 25, 2001).

52. *See, e.g.,* In the Matter of Ackerly, S.E.C. 95–163, 1995 WL 471111 (SEC Aug. 10, 1995) (order instituting proceedings); In the Matter R.B. Webster Investments, Inc., Admin. Proc. File No. 3–8113, 51 S.E.C. 1269, Sec. Exch. Act Rel. No. 34–34659, 57 S.E.C. Docket 1494, 1994 WL 512475 (SEC Sept. 13, 1994).

53. Parking is discussed in § 14.23 *infra.*

54. *See, e.g.,* In the Matter of Salloum, Administrative Proceeding File No. 3–7402, Sec Exch. Act Rel. No. 34–35563, 59 S.E.C. Docket 39, 1995 WL 215268 (SEC April 5, 1995).

55. *See, e.g.,* SEC v. Kimmes, 799 F.Supp. 852 (N.D.Ill.1992) (defendant's failure to record nominee status of purchasers of IPO was not trivial matter as it occurred in connection with alleged market manipulation). In the Matter of Adams, 2001 WL 224979, Sec. Act Rel. No. 33–7963, Sec. Exch. Act Rel. No. 34–44051 (SEC Mar 08, 2001) (instituting proceedings for parking in connection with IPOs).

56. *See, e.g.,* SEC v. Lavigne, 00–CV–6024, Litigation Release No. LR–16788, 2000 WL 1643954 (E.D.N.Y. Nov. 2, 2000).

58. In the Matter of A.S. Goldmen & Co., 2001 WL 588039 *6, Sec. Exch. Act Rel. No. 34–44328 (SEC May 21, 2001) ("Providing greater than normal sales compensation arrangements pertaining to the distribution of a security is indicative of special selling efforts and selling methods").

67. *See, e.g.,* In the Matter of Unnamed FINRA Member, Complaint No. CAF030014, 2007 WL 3033626 (FINRA 2007); In the Matter of Institutional Securities of Colorado, SEC Admin. Proc. File No. 3B5104, 1978 SEC LEXIS 2544 (Aug. 14, 1978).

68. *See, e.g.,* In the Matter of Institutional Securities of Colorado, SEC Admin. Proc. File No. 3B5104, 1978 SEC LEXIS 2544 (Aug. 14, 1978). *See also, e.g.,* In the Matter of Unnamed FINRA Member, Complaint No. CAF030014, 2007 WL 3033626 (FINRA 2007).

69. *See* Lincolnshire L.P. v. Essex, LLC, 244 F.Supp.2d 912 (N.D.Ill. 2002) (Rule 10–5's in connection with requirement was satisfied by allegations that brokers took money in exchange for a promise to allocate IPO shares to the plaintiff even though this was not tied to a particular offering or securities transaction).

additional shares in the after market.[70] For the same reason, it would be improper for brokers to charge higher commissions in exchange for directing IPOs to their customers.

At times when the new issues markets are active, some brokerage firms have opted to allocate scarce issues only to those customers who commit to a certain amount of IPO purchases each year. Another development has been underwriters setting aside stock from new issues for the accounts of customers who can direct additional new issue business to the underwriters. The NASD has advised its members that this practice, referred to as "spinning"[75] or "flipping,"[76] may violate NASD rules.[77]

The NASD's IPO rules were approved by the SEC in October 2003.[87] In the first instance, NASD Rule 2790[88] replaced the former "Hot Issue" interpretations,[89] making it clear that limitations on IPO allocations requirements apply to all IPOs rather than being limited to those that involve hot issues. The new IPO rule expands and clarifies many of the NASD's policies that were already in place.

Additionally, flipping can run afoul of SEC regulation pertaining to conduct during an initial public offering.[90] Failure to disclose that purchasers in a public offering will be reselling their shares immediately will violate the antifraud provisions.[91] There can be consequences under state law as well. For example, a company's directors who allegedly received IPO allocations in exchange for directing investment banking to the investment banking firm could be sued for usurping a corporate opportunity.[92]

The Commission has held it to be unlawful for a participating dealer or underwriter to turn away subscribers to a new issue while at the same time soliciting purchasers for the unsold allotment.[127] This practice of turning away bona fide offers to purchase gives the appearance of a receptive market or even a "hot issue" since it leads the investor to believe that the offering is

---

70. *See, e.g.*, In re Initial Public Offering Securities Litigation, 241 F.Supp.2d 281 (S.D.N.Y. 2003) (upholding complaint challenging this practice).

75. *See, e.g.*, Spitzer v. McLeod, 38 Sec Reg. & L. Rep. (BNA) 298 (N.Y. Supp. Ct. 2006) (upholding civil fraud suit for undisclosed spinning in connection with IPO).

76. " 'Flipping' is the practice of buying a 'hot issue' and then selling it within a short period of time into a rising market, earning a quick profit on the transaction." In the Matter of Account Management Corp., Admin. Proc. File No. 3–885; Sec. Exch. Act Rel. No. 34–36314, 60 S.E.C. Docket 962, 1995 WL 579449 footnote 3 (SEC Sept. 29, 1995).

77. *See* NASD Sends Members Warning Concerning Allocation of Hot IPO's 29 Sec. Reg. & L. Rep. (BNA) 1667 (Dec. 5, 1997).

87. *See* In re National Association of Securities Dealers, Inc., Sec. Exch. Act Rel. No. 34–48701, 2003 WL 22438827 (SEC Oct. 24, 2003). *See the discussion in § 6.0* supra.

88. NASD (FINRA) Rule 2790.

89. *See* NASD's Free Riding and Withholding Interpretation, IM–2110–1.

90. *See, e.g.,* In the Matter of Monetta Financial Services, Inc., Administrative Proceeding File No. 3–9546 72 S.E.C. Docket 77, Release No. ID–162, 2000 WL 320457 (SEC Initial Decision March 27, 2000); In the Matter of the Applications of Sanders, Administrative Proceedings File No. 3–9195, Sec. Exch. Act Rel. No. 34–40600, 68 S.E.C. Docket 745, 1998 WL 741105 (SEC Oct. 26, 1998).

91. Birdman v. Electro–Catheter Corp., 352 F.Supp. 1271, 1272, 1274 (E.D.Pa.1973).

92. *See* In re eBay, Inc. Shareholders Litigation, 2004 WL 253521(Del.Ch.2004) (refusing to dismiss claim).

127. In the Matter of Shearson, Hammill & Co., 42 S.E.C. 811 (SEC 1965). *Cf.* Eichler v. SEC, 757 F.2d 1066 (9th Cir.1985) (sanctioning brokers for failing to fill orders from aftermarket in issue that broker had underwritten).

oversubscribed when, in fact, securities that represented part of the original allotment are still being peddled.[128] This improper withholding of securities to be offered is known as a "workout" market in which the underwriter and/or the issuer as a result of manipulative transactions are giving the appearance of a market that does not conform to reality. Workout tactics involve not only violations of the anti-manipulation provisions,[129] but also give rise to violations of the antifraud provisions.

All or none offerings, present an environment that is particularly conducive to manipulative activity.[133] For example, it is improper for a broker participating in an "all or none" or "part or none" offering to accept customer funds unless it promptly transmits those funds to an escrow agent or other entity.[134] The prompt transmission requirement is designed to safeguard the customer's right to a quick refund in the event that the offering contingency is not met. Manipulation is not the only issue, as disclosure problems can also occur in connection with "part or none," or "mini max" offerings as they are sometimes called.[135] In such offerings, the offering materials must accurately disclose the material aspects of any "all or none" or "part or none" conditions.

Other manipulative practices, that are not limited to new issues, occur in the context of controlled markets. This happens when a security with only one active market maker or multiple market makers[136] act in collusion to artificially control the market. Generically referred to as "house stocks,"[137] securities in controlled markets are particularly susceptible to manipulation.[138] Whether or not the market for a particular security is in actuality a controlled market is a question of fact.[139] An underwriter's control over the market is not in itself a violation of the Act.[140] However, it violates the antifraud provisions to fail to disclose control over the market for securities handled by the market-maker and broker-dealer in question.[141] Another manipulative practice is to

128. *Cf.* Brogren v. Pohlad, 960 F.Supp. 1401 (D.Minn.1997) (giving the appearance of a more active market than exists can be actionable under rule 10–5).

129. Sections 9, 10(b) and 15(c), 15 U.S.C.A. §§ 78i, 78j(b), 78o(c). *See* § 12.1 *infra*. *Cf.* SEC v. Sayegh, 906 F.Supp. 939 (S.D.N.Y.1995) (trader whose firm was market maker violated Rule 10–5 by consistently posting high bids and entering into cross trades for the purpose of creating the illusion of an active market).

133. *See* Rule 10–9, 17 C.F.R. § 240.10–9; Rooney, Pace, Sec. Exch.Act.Rel. No. 34–23763 (Admin.Proc.File No. 3–6332 Oct. 31, 1986), [1986–87 Transfer Binder] Fed.Sec.L.Rep. (CCH) ¶ 84,048. *See generally* Robert B. Robbins, All-or-None Offerings, 19 Rev.Sec. & Commodities Reg. 59 (1986); §§ 6.3, 12.1 *infra*.

134. 17 C.F.R. § 240.15c2–4. *See* In re Lowell H. Listrom & Co., Exch.Act. Rel. No. 34–22689, [1985–86 Transfer Binder] Fed.Sec.L.Rep. (CCH) ¶ 83,946 (SEC Dec. 5, 1985).

135. *See, e.g.*, SEC v. First Pacific Bancorp, 142 F.3d 1186 (9th Cir.1998) (CEO held accountable for profits made in mini max offering where minimum offering amount had not in fact been met).

136. Regulation of market makers and manipulative activities relating to market makers are discussed in § 14.10[5] *infra*.

137. *See, e.g.*, United States v. DiStefano, 129 F.Supp.2d 342 (S.D.N.Y.2001).

138. *See, e.g.*, Eichler v. SEC, 757 F.2d 1066 (9th Cir.1985).

139. *See, e.g.*, In the Matter of Hibbard, Brown & Co. Admin. Proc. File No. 3–8418 March 13, 1995 Release No. 34–35476, 58 S.E.C. Docket 2561, 1995 WL 116488 n. 20 (SEC March 13, 1995).

140. Pagel, Inc, 48 S.E.C. 223, 226 (1985), aff'd sub nom. Pagel, Inc. v. SEC, 803 F.2d 942 (8th Cir.1986).

141. SEC v. First Jersey Securities, 101 F.3d 1450, 1467–1468 (2d Cir.1996) (violation of 1933 Act § 17(a) and 1934 Act § 10(b)).

compensate brokers for encouraging customer purchases[142] or discouraging customers' sales[143] and thereby pushing the market price higher.[144]

As discussed elsewhere in this treatise,[145] the goal of the various statutes and rules prohibiting market manipulation is to prohibit activities that rig the market and thereby would inhibit the operation of the "natural law" of supply and demand.[146] In this way, the market price of securities will reflect—as much as is possible—a fair and just price for each security.[147] When a brokerage firm acts as an underwriter for an IPO and then acts as a market maker in the aftermarket there are delicate conflict of interest problems. Failure to adequately separate the underwriting and market making functions can result in violations of market making obligations.

---

142. *See, e.g.,* In the Matter of Olde Discount Corp., Administrative Proceeding File No. 3–9699, Sec. Act Rel. No. 33–7577, 67 S.E.C. Docket 2045, 1998 WL 575171 (SEC September 10, 1998)*amended*, 1999 WL 149774 (S.E.C. 1999).

143. *See, e.g,* In the Matter of DeMaio, Administrative Proceeding File No. 3–7912, 54 S.E.C. Docket 1509, Release No. ID–37, 1993 WL 300297 (SEC Aug. 4, 1993).

144. *See, e.g.,* In the Matter of A.S. Goldmen & Co., 2001 WL 588039, Sec. Exch. Act Rel. No. 34–44328 (SEC May 21, 2001).

145. *See* §§ 12.1, 14.10 *infra.*

146. *See, e.g.,* SEC v. First Jersey Securities, 101 F.3d 1450, 1466 (2d Cir.1996), cert. denied 522 U.S. 812, 118 S.Ct. 57, 139 L.Ed.2d 21 (1997); Varljen v. H.J. Meyers, Inc., 1998 WL 395266 (S.D.N.Y.1998).

147. *See, e.g.,* SEC v. First Jersey Securities, 101 F.3d 1450, 1466 (2d Cir.1996), cert. denied 522 U.S. 812, 118 S.Ct. 57, 139 L.Ed.2d 21 (1997); Varljen v. H.J. Meyers, Inc., 1998 WL 395266 (S.D.N.Y.1998).

Chapter 7

REMEDIES FOR VIOLATION OF THE SECURITIES ACT OF 1933 (AND OTHER CONSEQUENCES OF DEFICIENT REGISTRATION STATEMENTS)

Table of Sections

---

§ 7.1 Consequences of Deficient Registration Statements—Administrative Action, Criminal Sanctions, SEC Injunctive Relief, and Private Remedies

Violations of the 1933 Act registration, disclosure, and prospectus requirements can have a number of consequences. Many of them can be devastating. Deficiencies in the registration materials can result in administrative proceedings by the SEC, criminal sanctions brought by the Department of Justice, and injunctive relief in judicial proceedings instated by the SEC. This is supplemented by private remedies that may exist in favor of investors who purchased securities subject to the defective registration.[1] These deficiencies may take various forms. For example, the deficiency can be

---

§ 7.1

1. *See* §§ 7.2–7.9 *infra.*

the result of incomplete or misleading disclosures.[2] Failure to comply with the prospectus delivery requirements[3] can have serious consequences, as can dissemination of information in violation of the 1933 Act's gun-jumping provisions.[4] The 1933 Act's remedial and enforcement provisions must be viewed in the context of the Act's registration process. Recall, for example, that the 1933 Act's registration process consists of the preparation of the registration statement with its detailed disclosures, followed by the filing of the registration statement, and then a waiting period before the registration statement becomes effective and the securities may be sold to the public.

In order to prevent a deficient registration statement from becoming effective, the SEC can institute formal administrative proceedings for the purpose of issuing a refusal order.[5] Refusal order proceedings must be instituted within ten days of the registration statement's filing.[6] The refusal order can be issued only after the registrant has been given notice and has had an opportunity for a hearing.[7] Alternatively, when faced with material deficiencies in the registration statement, the Commission may commence formal stop order proceedings at any time.[8] But again, the order can be issued only after formal notice and opportunity for a hearing.[9] As is pointed out in an earlier section,[10] most such deficiencies are dealt with informally through the use of deficiency letters and delaying amendments. Accordingly, the formal proceedings established by section 8 provide a statutory framework that does not reflect the normal process that is used for dealing with deficient registration materials. Instead, section 8 reflects the formal process that is used only when the registrant fails to comply with the SEC's less formal procedures for processing registration statements.

Anti–Fraud Provisions

Beyond the foregoing remedies for violation of the prospectus and registration requirements, the 1933 Act imposes sanctions for fraudulent conduct in connection with securities sales. Under the general antifraud provision contained in section 17(a),[11] material misstatements and omissions may result in both criminal sanctions and an SEC civil suit. Additionally, there is sparse authority in support of an implied private remedy for violations of section 17(a).[12]

Private Remedies

Any material deficiencies in the registration statement are likely to carry over to the prospectus and thus will result in violations of section 5(b)'s

2. *See* §§ 3.4, 3.9–3.10 *supra* for discussion of the 1933 Act disclosure requirements.

3. *See* §§ 2.4–2.5 *supra* for discussion of the prospectus delivery requirements that apply after a 1933 Act registration has been filed, through both the waiting and post-effective periods.

4. *See* § 2.3 *supra* for discussion of the pre-filing or quiet period that exists before a registration statement has been filed.

5. Section 8(b), 15 U.S.C.A. § 77h(b). *See* §§ 3.6, 3.9 *supra.*

6. Section 8(b), 15 U.S.C.A. § 77h(b).

7. Section 8(b), 15 U.S.C.A. § 77h(b).

8. Section 8(d), 15 U.S.C.A. § 77h(d). *See* William R. McLucas, Stop Order Proceedings Under the Securities Act of 1933: A Current Assessment, 40 Bus.Law. 515 (1985).

9. Section 8(d), 15 U.S.C.A. § 77h(d).

10. *See* § 3.7 *supra.*

11. 15 U.S.C.A. § 77q(a). *See* § 7.11 *infra.*

12. *See* § 12.22 *infra.*

prospectus delivery requirements,[13] which call for an accurate and up-to-date prospectus.[14] Any violation of section 5 gives rise to possible criminal sanctions[15] as well as to judicially secured SEC equitable sanctions.[16] Purchasers of securities that were sold in violation of section 5 have an express civil remedy for rescission pursuant to section 12(a)(1), which permits suit against a violator who is a seller[17] of the securities in privity with the purchaser.[19] Section 12(a)(2) gives a rescission remedy against sellers who make material misstatements or omissions in connection with a sale.[20] In addition, section 11 of Act imposes express civil liability upon persons preparing and signing materially misleading registration statements.[21]

Irrespective of any such implied remedy, section 12(a)(2) of the Act[22] creates an express right of action in the hands of defrauded purchasers. There is good authority[23] to support the proposition that all of these private remedies are cumulative and further, do not preclude a parallel implied remedy under Rule 10b–5 of the Exchange Act.[24] Although, of course, double recovery will not be permitted for a single injury.

Section 13 of the Act[25] sets out the applicable statute of limitations for private remedies under the Securities Act of 1933.[26] Actions under sections 11 and 12(a)(2) must be brought within one year of the date of the actionable misstatement or omission.[27] An action under section 12(a)(1) for violation of section 5's registration and prospectus delivery requirements must be brought within one year of the date of the registration violation.[28] Notwithstanding a longer delay in discovery, actions under sections 11 and 12(a)(1) must in all instances be brought within three years after the security was first offered to the public. All section 12(a)(2) actions are similarly subject to a three year repose period so that in no event may suit be brought more than three years of the sale.[29]

In the 1990s, Congress enacted legislation to curtail suspected abuses in connection with securities class actions. In particular, the Private Securities

13. 15 U.S.C.A. § 77e(b). *See* Sections 2(a)(10), 10, 15 U.S.C.A. §§ 77b(a)(10), 77j.

14. *E.g.*, SEC v. Manor Nursing Centers, Inc., 458 F.2d 1082 (2d Cir.1972). *See* §§ 2.4, 2.6 *supra*.

15. 15 U.S.C.A. §§ 77e, 77x.

16. 15 U.S.C.A. § 77t.

17. *See, e.g.*, Pinter v. Dahl, 486 U.S. 622, 108 S.Ct. 2063, 100 L.Ed.2d 658 (1988) (discussing what is meant by the requirement that the defendant sold the securities to the plaintiff).

19. 15 U.S.C.A. § 77*l*(a)(1). *See* § 7.2 *infra*.

20. 15 U.S.C.A. § 77*l*(a)(2).

21. 15 U.S.C.A. § 77k. *See* §§ 7.3–7.4 *infra*.

22. 15 U.S.C.A. § 77l(a)(2). *See* § 7.6 *infra*.

23. Herman & MacLean v. Huddleston, 459 U.S. 375, 103 S.Ct. 683, 74 L.Ed.2d 548 (1983), *on remand* 705 F.2d 775 (5th Cir.1983). *See* chapters 10, 11, 12 *infra*.

24. 17 C.F.R. § 240.10b–5. *See* chapter 12.

25. 15 U.S.C.A. § 77m. *See* § 7.10 *infra*. The statute of limitations for implied remedies is discussed in § 12.16 *infra*.

26. In contrast, a longer statute of limitations applies to fraud claims brought under Rule 10b–5 and other antifraud provisions of the Securities Exchange Act of 1934. *See* § 12.16 *infra*.

27. 15 U.S.C.A. § 77m.

28. 15 U.S.C.A. § 77m.

29. 15 U.S.C.A. § 77m.

Litigation Reform Act of 1995[34] imposed procedural requirements and additional protection for projections and other forward-looking statements. The Securities Litigation Uniform Standards Act of 1998[35] significantly preempted the role of the states in securities litigation by precluding most securities fraud class actions from being brought in state court or under state law.

§ 7.2 Civil Liability for Failure to Comply With 1933 Act Section 5—Section 12(a)(1)'s Private Remedy

§ 7.2[1] Basic Elements of a Section 12(a)(1) Claim

Section 12(a)(1) of the 1933 Act[1] provides that anyone who offers or sells a security in violation of section 5[2] is liable in a civil action to the person purchasing such security "from him."[3] Section 12(a)(1) is not limited to violations of section 5's prospectus requirements;[4] any violation of section 5 can form the basis of a section 12(a)(1) cause of action.[5] This includes sales made before the registration statement's effective date[6] as well as offers to buy or offers to sell made prior to the filing of the registration statement.[7]

Agency principles apply in determining who is a purchaser for purposes of section 12. Thus, when an agent purchases securities for the account of the principal, the principal as the real party in interest should be able to bring suit under section 12. In contrast, when someone who purchases securities on behalf of another has sufficient indicia of ownership, that person qualifies as a purchaser under section 12 and thus can bring suit thereunder.[8] A violation of section 5 gives the purchaser a right of rescission (or rescissory damages) under section 12(a)(1).[9] Notwithstanding the statutory right of rescission, section 12(a)(1) does not interfere with the passage of title to the securities that have been sold in violation of section 5 of the Act.[10]

An action under section 12(a)(1) may be brought in either law or equity. As is the case with the other express civil actions under the 1933 Act, a section 12(a)(1) action may be brought either in state or federal court, but there is no right of removal to federal court for actions initiated in a state tribunal.[11] As a result of the Securities Litigation Uniform Standards Act of

---

34. Pub. Law No. 104–67, 109 Stat. 737 (104th Cong. 1st Sess. December 22, 1995) (HR 1058). *See* § 7.17[1], 12.15[1] *infra*.

35. Pub. Law No. 105–353, 112 Stat. 3227 (105th Cong. 2d sess. November 3, 1998) (S 1260). *See* § 7.17[2], 12.15[2] *infra*.

§ 7.2

1. 15 U.S.C.A. § 77*l*(a)(1).

2. 15 U.S.C.A. § 77e. *See* §§ 2.2–2.5 *supra*.

3. 15 U.S.C.A. § 77*l*(a)(1).

4. The prospectus delivery requirements are discussed in §§ 2.4, 2.5.

5. *See, e.g.*, Baldwin v. Kulch Associates, Inc., 39 F.Supp.2d 111. 115 (D.N.H.1998).

6. Sales prior to the effective date violate section 5(a). 15 U.S.C.A. § 77e(a). *See* §§ 2.4, 2.5 *supra*.

7. 15 U.S.C.A. § 77E(c). *See* § 2.3 *supra*.

8. *See* Monetary Management Group v. Kidder, Peabody & Co., 604 F.Supp. 764, 767 (E.D.Mo.1985) (investment adviser had standing).

9. 15 U.S.C.A. § 77*l*(a)(1).

10. Allison v. Ticor Title Insurance Co., 907 F.2d 645, 648 (7th Cir.1990), *appeal after remand* 979 F.2d 1187 (7th Cir.1992).

11. Section 22(a), 15 U.S.C.A. § 77y(a). *See* § 17.1 *infra*. The Class Action Fairness Act of 2005 (Pub.L. No. 109–2, §§ 4(a) & 5(a), 119 Stat. 4, 9–13, codified at 28 U.S.C.A. §§ 1332(d) &

1998 ("SLUSA"), private class actions with more than fifty class members in fraud-based actions under the securities laws must be brought in federal court.[12] By its terms, the preemptive provisions of SLUSA apply to actions based on misrepresentation or deception.[13] Section 12(a)(1) is not based on misrepresentation, fraud or manipulation but rather is based on a failure to comply with the registration requirements. As such, it follows that SLUSA's preemption provisions should not apply to class actions unless there are claims of misrepresentation or deception.

Damages under section 12(a)(1) are limited to the return of the purchase price of the security with interest, upon tender of the security. If the securities are no longer owned by the purchaser, the defendant is liable for damages based on the loss comprising the difference between the plaintiff's purchase price and sale price.[21] By virtue of section 13,[22] the section 12(a)(1) action must be brought within one year of the violation upon which it is based, but in no event may suit be commenced more than three years after the security was *bona fide* offered to the public.[23] For statute of limitations purposes, the sale occurs, and the statute generally begins to run, on the date the parties entered into a binding contract of sale.[24] Notwithstanding some scattered decisions to the contrary, the majority of courts have indicated that section 12(a)(1)'s one year period should not be tolled.[27]

Section 12(a)(1) on its face imposes a strict privity requirement[36] since the violator of section 5 is liable only to the person purchasing the security from him. On the other hand, section 12(a)(1) does not contain a requirement that the violation have a causal connection to any injury to the plaintiff.[37]

The objective of section 12(a)(1) is a prophylactic one rather than merely compensatory. It has thus been held that since the action is designed to enforce registration requirements, the defense of estoppel will not bar a rescission action for a violation of section 5.[41] The Fifth Circuit thus held that

1453(b)) does not affect the concurrent jurisdiction provisions of the 1933 Act. Luther v. Countrywide Home Loans Servicing LP, 533 F.3d 1031 (9th Cir.2008). Accordingly, the 1933 Act claims were not removable to federal court. *Id.*

12. 1933 Act § 16, 15 U.S.C.A. § 77p. *See* § 7.17[2] *infra.*

13. 15 U.S.C.A. § 77p(b).

21. 15 U.S.CA. § 77*l*. *See* Kilmartin v. H.C. Wainwright & Co., 580 F.Supp. 604, 607–08 (D.Mass.1984) for discussion of the tender requirement of section 12.

22. 15 U.S.C.A. § 77m.

23. The concept of being bona fide offered to the public is a question of fact as to whether the securities were in fact offered. The concept of a bona fide offer does not mean that the offering was in fact registered. Otherwise unregistered offerings would never have a limitations period since they would not fall under this strained interpretations of "bona fide." *See* Slagell v. Bontrager, 616 F.Supp. 634 (W.D.Pa.1985), affirmed 791 F.2d 921 (3d Cir.1986).

24. *E.g.*, Amoroso v. Southwestern Drilling Multi–Rig, 646 F.Supp. 141 (N.D.Cal.1986).

27. *See, e.g.,* Nolfi v. Ohio Ky. Oil Corp., 562 F.Supp.2d 904 (N. D. Ohio 2008); Hanson v. Johnson, 2003 WL 21639194 (D.Minn.2003); Hardy v. First American Bank, N.A., 774 F.Supp. 1078 (M.D.Tenn.1991).

36. The claim will be dismissed in the absence of privity. *E.g.*, Silva Run Worldwide Ltd. v. Bear Sterns & Co., 2000 WL 1672324, [2000–2001 Transfer Binder] Fed.Sec.L.Rep. (CCH) ¶ 91,255 (S.D.N.Y.2000).

37. *Compare* section 12(b) of the Act, 15 U.S.C.A. § 77*l*(b) which imposes a causation requirement in actions brought under section 12(a)(2) but does not include section 12(a)(1) actions in this causation requirement.

41. *See* Henderson v. Hayden, Stone Inc., 461 F.2d 1069 (5th Cir.1972).

only if the plaintiff had refused an unconditional tender of a refund would the defendant have been able to raise the defense of estoppel.[42] However, not all courts have agreed.[43] The better view is that estoppel, as that term is ordinarily understood, is not a defense to a section 12(a)(1) action. Similarly, the fact that the plaintiff is a sophisticated investor who can fend for himself or herself will not preclude recovery under section 12(a)(1).[45] Nevertheless, the Supreme Court in Pinter v. Dahl[46] ruled that on appropriate facts, although they may be rare, the *in pari delicto* (or equal fault) defense will be available in an action under section 12(a)(1). The Court held that the law applicable in Rule 10b–5 cases[47] carried over to section 12(a)(1) cases as well. Specifically, the *in pari delicto* defense will bar a claim under section 12(a)(1) only when the plaintiff's fault in causing the section 5 violation can be said to be equal to the defendant's. The Court further noted that this test of relative responsibility of the plaintiff and defendant is dependent on a factual inquiry, and thus its application may vary from case to case.[48] The Court additionally observed that in order for a section 12(a)(1) plaintiff's claim to be defeated by the equal fault defense, the plaintiff's role in the transaction must have been one of a promoter rather than simply of an investor.[49] As such, the *in pari delicto* defense is quite narrow and will not be applicable in most section 12(a)(1) actions.

§ 7.2[2] Who Is Liable Under Section 12(a)(1)?

The Court in *Pinter v. Dahl* indicated that a section 12 defendant must have been both an immediate and direct seller of the securities to the plaintiff.[57] The Court stressed that section 12 liability depends on the defendant having been more than a remote participant in the sale.[58] Thus, merely participating in the preparation of the registration statement does not satisfy the active participation requirement so as to render such participants in privity with a purchaser. Even substantial involvement in the preparation of registration and offering materials will not create liability unless there is also active involvement in the negotiations leading to the sale in question.[60]

42. 476 F.2d at 429–430. The fact that the defendant imposed a ten-day limit on the refund offer was sufficient to eliminate any such defense to the section 12(a)(1) action.

43. *See* Murken v. Barrow, 1989 WL 168062, [1989–1990 Transfer Binder] Fed.Sec.L.Rep. ¶ 94,815 at p. 94,413 (C.D.Cal.1989).

45. Byrnes v. Faulkner, Dawkins & Sullivan, 550 F.2d 1303 (2d Cir.1977) (Market maker may claim the protection of section 12(a)(1)).

46. 486 U.S. 622, 108 S.Ct. 2063, 100 L.Ed.2d 658 (1988). *See* Mark S. Klock, Promoter Liability and In Pari Delicto Under Section 12(a)(1), 17 Sec.Reg.L.J. 53 (1989).

47. *See* Bateman Eichler, Hill Richards, Inc. v. Berner 472 U.S. 299, 105 S.Ct. 2622, 86 L.Ed.2d 215 (1985). *See* § 12.21 *infra*.

48. 486 U.S. at 639, 108 S.Ct. at 2074, 100 L.Ed.2d at 677.

49. *Id.* at 638–39, 108 S.Ct. at 2074, 100 L.Ed.2d at 677.

57. 486 U.S. at 650, 108 S.Ct. at 2080, 100 L.Ed.2d at 684. *See* § 7.7 *infra*. *See also, e.g.,* DeMaria v. Andersen, 153 F.Supp.2d 300, 307–308 (S.D.N.Y.2001) (remote purchasers cannot sue remote sellers under section 12(a)(1)).

58. 486 U.S. at 654, 108 S.Ct. at 2082, 100 L.Ed.2d at 686.

60. *See* In re DDi Corp. Securities Litigation, 2005 WL 3090882 (C.D. Cal. 2005) (citing this treatise).

§ 7.3 Liability for Misstatements and Omissions in the Registration Statement—The Private Remedy Under Section 11 of the 1933 Act

The prospectus and 1933 Act registration statement can provide the basis of liability to purchasers of the securities covered by the registration statement. Section 11(a) of the Securities Act of 1933[1] creates an express right of action for damages[2] by securities purchasers when a registration statement contains untrue statements of material fact or omissions of material[3] fact. A section 11 claim cannot be brought on the basis of oral statements since the statute speaks in terms of misstatements and omissions in the registration statement.[4]

§ 7.3[2] Who Can Sue; Nature of Suit Under Section 11

§ 7.3[2][A] Who Can Sue Under Section 11

An action under section 11 may be brought by "any person acquiring such security" unless it can be shown that at the time of purchase the purchaser knew of the misstatement or omission. As discussed more fully below, this language has been interpreted to mean that the plaintiff must be able to trace the securities to those covered by the registration statement.[39] This is true regardless of whether the plaintiff purchased in the aftermarket or as part of the original offering.

Section 11 permits the plaintiff to bring suit either in law or equity in any court of competent jurisdiction. By virtue of section 22(a) of the Act,[42] the plaintiff has an absolute choice of forum since actions under the 1933 Act may be brought either in federal or state court, and there is no right of removal from a state tribunal to a federal one.[43] However, as a result of the Securities Litigation Uniform Standards Act of 1998 ("SLUSA"), private class actions with more than fifty class members in fraud-based actions under the securities laws must be brought in federal court.[44] Since section 11 is based on materially misleading disclosures, the mandatory federal forum would apply to all such class actions. In the aftermath of the Litigation Reform Act, plaintiffs still have a choice between a federal and state court forum with respect to individual actions, including section 11 claims as well as class actions involving fifty or fewer plaintiffs.[45]

---

§ 7.3

1. 15 U.S.C.A. § 77k.

2. The section 11 remedy is limited to damages; injunctive relief is not available. K/A & Co. v. Hallwood Energy Partners, L.P., 1990 WL 37866, [1990–1991 Transfer Binder] Fed.Sec.L.Rep. (CCH) ¶ 95,758 (S.D.N.Y.1990).

3. Normal concepts of materiality apply in section 11 actions. Materiality is discussed in § 12.9 *infra*. Thus, for example, the bespeaks caution doctrine, relating to soft information and projections is applicable in actions under section 11. In re Worlds of Wonder Securities Litigation, 35 F.3d 1407 (9th Cir.1994). Soft information is discussed in § 3.9 *supra* and § 12.9 *infra*.

4. In re Sterling Foster & Co. Securities Litigation, 222 F.Supp.2d 216, 267 (E.D.N.Y. 2002).

39. *E.g.*, Congregation of Sholom v. Blockbuster, Inc., 504 F.Supp.2d 151 (N.D.Tex. 2007).

42. 15 U.S.C.A. § 77v(a).

43. *See generally* Thomas L. Hazen, Allocation of Jurisdiction Between the State and Federal Courts for Private Remedies Under the Federal Securities Laws, 60 N.C.L.Rev. 707 (1982). *See* § 17.1 *infra*.

44. 1933 Act § 16, 15 U.S.C.A. § 77p. *See* § 7.17[2] *infra*.

45. Kelly v. McKesson HBOC, Inc., 2002 WL 88939 (Del.Super.2002) (permitting section 11 claim to proceed in state court).

§ 7.3[3] Permissible Defendants in a Section 11 Suit

Section 11(a) lists the categories of persons and entities in addition to the issuer which may be liable for misstatements or omissions in the registration statement:n (1) all signers of the registration statement;[49] (2) every director, person performing a similar function, or partner at the time of the filing of the registration statement; (3) all persons named with their consent in the registration statement as about to become a director, person performing similar functions, or partner; (4) every accountant, engineer, or appraiser, or any person whose profession gives authority to statements made by him or her, who has with consent been named in the registration statement as having prepared or certified any part of the filing, or any report or evaluation used in connection with the registration statement; and (5) every underwriter with respect to the security in registration.[50] Individuals and entities that do not fall within one of these categories do not incur liability under section 11.[51] Primary liability under section 11 is supplemented by controlling person liability.[52]

§ 7.3[4] Absence of Reliance Requirement in Section 11 Actions

When a section 11(a) plaintiff has acquired the securities more than twelve months after the effective date of the registration statement, and if the issuer has distributed an "earnings statement" for that period, the plaintiff must prove reliance on the material misstatement or omission.[58] However, the purchaser need not prove that he or she actually read the registration statement in order to establish such reliance.[59] Without proof of plaintiff's actual knowledge of the misstatement or omission at time of purchase, there is a conclusive presumption of reliance for any person purchasing the security prior to the expiration of twelve months.[60]

§ 7.3[5] Tracing Securities to the Registration Statement

In order for a purchaser of the security to succeed in an action under section 11, he or she must prove that the shares purchased are traceable to the offering covered by the registration statement.[64] In light of the statutory language, the courts have rigidly enforced the tracing requirement.

49. Section 6 sets forth who must sign the registration statement. 15 U.S.C.A. § 77f(a) (1976). The required signers include the issuer, the issuer's principal executive, financial and accounting officers and a majority of the issuer's board of directors or persons performing similar functions. *See* §§ 3.4–3.5 *supra.*

50. 15 U.S.C.A. § 77k(a).

51. *See, e.g.,* Dorchester Investors v. Peak International Ltd., 134 F.Supp.2d 569 (S.D.N.Y. 2001) (large shareholder who did not sign registration statement could not be held liable under section 11).

52. 1933 Act § 15, 15 U.S.C.A. § 77*o*. *See also* 1934 Act § 20(a), 15 U.S.C.A. § 78t(a). *See, e.g.,* Dorchester Investors v. Peak International Ltd., 134 F.Supp.2d 569 (S.D.N.Y.2001) (controlling person liability sufficiently alleged against controlling large shareholder).

58. 15 U.S.C.A. § 77k(a), last paragraph.

59. 15 U.S.C.A. § 77k(a).

60. *See, e.g.,* Barnes v. Osofsky, 373 F.2d 269 (2d Cir.1967); McFarland v. Memorex Corp., 493 F.Supp. 631, 641 (N.D.Cal.1980), *reconsideration granted* 581 F.Supp. 878 (N.D.Cal.1984).

64. *E.g.,* In re Direct General Corp. Securities Litigation, 2006 WL 2265472 (M.D. Tenn. 2006) (sufficient allegations tracing the securities; certifying class action).

Remote secondary and market transactions are not subject to section 11 claims, and thus tracing the securities back to the initial offering will not always satisfy a section 11 claim.[67] This does not mean, however, that section 11 actions are limited only to initial purchasers of shares covered by the registration statement. An investor who purchases his or her shares shortly after the offering can satisfy the section 11 tracing requirement.[68] This rule may have been brought into question by the Supreme Court's ruling in Gustafson v. Alloyd Co.,[69] which severely limited the scope of the private remedy under section 12(a)(2)[70] of the Act by ruling that the section 12(a)(2) remedy does not apply to transactions which do not occur in connection with a public offering or offering by prospectus. The policy underlying the *Gustafson* decision cannot justifiably limit an action under section 11 to plaintiffs who were initial purchasers.[72]

§ 7.3[8] Measure of Damages Under Section 11

Another key difference between section 11 and the express remedies provided by section 12 is the measure of damages. With regard to actions authorized by section 12, the appropriate measure of damages is rescission and the return of the purchase price paid by the plaintiff.[114] Section 11(e)[115] sets forth three alternative methods of computing the damages in an action under section 11 for material misrepresentations or omissions in a registration statement. Under section 11(e) a plaintiff is entitled to recover the difference between the amount paid for the securities (not to exceed the public offering price) and (1) the value at of time of suit, (2) the price at which plaintiff sold the securities prior to suit,[116] or (3) the price at which the security was sold after suit was brought but before judgment so long as the damages computed under this third alternative would be less than those based on the difference between the price paid for the security (not to exceed the offering price) and the value at the time suit was brought.[117]

As the statutory damage formulations present something other than a bright line approach, problems of proof abound in damage cases under section 11.[118] Proof problems are further exacerbated by the express provision in section 11(e) that the statutory damages shall be reduced to the extent that the defendant is able to prove that any portion of (or all of) said damages "represents other than the depreciation in value of each security resulting

67. Gould v. Harris, 929 F.Supp. 353 (C.D.Cal.1996).

68. *See* Lee v. Ernst & Young, LLP, 294 F.3d 969 (8th Cir.2002) (plaintiffs who were aftermarket purchasers could trace securities to the registration statement); Joseph v. Wiles, 223 F.3d 1155 (10th Cir.2000).

69. 513 U.S. 561, 115 S.Ct. 1061, 131 L.Ed.2d 1 (1995).

70. 515 U.S.C.A. § 77l(a)(2).

72. *See, e.g.,* Joseph v. Wiles, 223 F.3d 1155 (10th Cir.2000).

114. 15 U.S.C.A. § 77*l*.

115. 15 U.S.C.A. § 77k(e).

116. Section 11(e)(2) speaks in terms of "the price at which such security shall have been disposed of in the market before suit." The Ninth Circuit ruled disposition of stock pursuant to a merger is the equivalent of disposition "in the market." In re Broderbund/Learning Co. Securities Litigation, 294 F.3d 1201 (9th Cir.2002) (finding that plaintiff did not suffer a loss).

117. *See* Alpern v. UtiliCorp United, Inc., 84 F.3d 1525 (8th Cir.1996) (damage date for claim added by amended complaint related back to the date of filing the original complaint).

118. *See* Beecher v. Able, 435 F.Supp. 397 (S.D.N.Y.1975), *affirmed* 575 F.2d 1010 (2d Cir.1978).

from'' the misstatement or omission. Since the burden of proving the absence of a causal connection falls on the defendant, loss causation need not be shown in order for plaintiff to establish a prima facie case under section 11.[119] However, to the extent that the defendant is able to establish this negative causation defense, damages will not be recoverable under section 11.

Thus, when the entire decline in the price of the stock is attributable to external market forces, there will be no damages under section 11.

§ 7.3[9] Statute of Limitations

Section 13 of the 1933 Act[129] provides for a statutory limitations period of one year after discovery of the misstatement or omission, or after discovery should have been made by the exercise of reasonable diligence, but in no event can a section 11 action be brought more than three years after the security was ''bona fide offered to the public.'' The statute of limitations is the same for actions brought under section 11 or section 12(a)(2). In contrast, the one year statute begins to run from the date of violation for suits based on section 12(a)(1) of the Act to redress violations of section 5. Also, the three-year maximum limit for an action for fraud under section 12(a)(2) begins to run from the sale rather than offering date.

In 2002, Congress enacted an all-purpose limitations period applicable to ''a private right of action that involves a claim of fraud, deceit, manipulation, or contrivance in contravention of a regulatory requirement concerning the securities laws.''[130] The limitations period runs two years from the date of discovery, with a five-year repose period running from the date of the violation.[131] Section 13 of the 1933 Act which is applicable to section 11 and 12 of that act was not repealed and it would seem that the newer two-year/five-year limitations/repose period was not designed to supersede section 13 of the 1933 Act.[132] The better view is that the longer limitations period added by the Sarbanes–Oxley Act does not extend the one-year/three-year period imposed by section 13 of the 1933 Act.[133]

§ 7.3[10] Defenses to Section 11 Claims

The statutory list of all potential section 11 defendants is exclusive.[134] Generally, identifying at least the potential defendants for any particular section 11 action is not problematic. Room for interpretation is to be found,

---

119. *See, e.g.,* Garbini v. Protection One, Inc., 49 Fed.Appx. 169 (9th Cir. 2002) (referring to ''the broad nature of loss causation'' in the context of section 11 claims).

129. 15 U.S.C.A. § 77m. *See* In re Activision Securities Litigation, 1986 WL 15339, [1986–87 Transfer Binder] Fed.Sec.L.Rep. (CCH) ¶ 92,998 (N.D.Cal.1986) (Filing of a class action against underwriters as a class tolled the statute of limitations.)

The statute of limitations in actions under section 11 is discussed further in § 7.10 *infra.*

130. 28 U.S.C.A. § 1658(b). *See* Sarbanes–Oxley Act of 2002, Pub. Law 107–204 (July 30, 2002).

131. 28 U.S.C.A. § 1658(b). *See* Sarbanes–Oxley Act of 2002, Pub. Law 107–204 (July 30, 2002).

132. In re Alstom SA Securities Litigation, 406 F.Supp.2d 402 (S.D.N.Y. 2005) (agreeing with overwhelming majority of decisions that the longer Sarbanes–Oxley limitations period does not apply to 1933 Act claims).

133. In re Worldcom, Inc. Securities Litigation, 308 F.Supp.2d 214, 225 (S.D.N.Y. 2004); In re WorldCom, Inc. Securities Litigation, 294 F.Supp.2d 431 (S.D.N.Y. 2003).

134. *E.g.,* In re ZZZZ Best Securities Litigation, 1989 WL 90284, [1989 Transfer Binder] Fed.Sec.L.Rep. ¶ 94,485 (C.D.Cal.1989).

however, in connection with the reference to "every underwriter" in section 11(a)(5). Section 2(a)(11) of the 1933 Act[135] gives a broad statutory definition to the term underwriter, which goes far beyond the generic meaning of the term as used in connection with registered public offerings. This statutory definition of underwriter includes persons purchasing the securities from an issuer with a view to distribution, all those who offer or sell securities on behalf of an issuer in connection with a distribution, and anyone who "participates or has a direct or indirect participation in any such undertaking."[136] Although it has been indicated that "underwriter" under section 11 tracks the full scope of the statutory definition under section 2(a)(11); in order to prevail, the plaintiff must still prove the defendant's actual participation in the distribution.[137] An underwriter's liability under section 11 is limited to the extent of the aggregate price of the securities underwritten by him or her. This limitation on damages does not apply, however, if the underwriter received from the issuer some benefit that was not available to similarly situated underwriters.

As mentioned above, section 11(a)(4) creates liability for professionals who lend their services to deficient registration statements. It has been held that an accountant may not be held liable unless the misleading information is expressly attributable to that accountant.[138] Further, it has been held that "as a matter of law," an independent accountant's liability under section 11 is limited to those figures which he or she certifies.[139] Thus, unless the accountant is an auditor or otherwise lends his or her name to a statement, there is no section 11 liability. Similarly, an attorney who prepares the registration statement is not a proper section 11 defendant unless he or she is also a director or signer of the registration statement.[140] Aside from such cases, the attorney will only be liable under section 11 pursuant to a subsection (a)(4) expert opinion.[141] An attorney's activities in preparing and reviewing the registration statement do not mean that the entire registration statement has been "expertised" so as to render the attorney liable under section 11.[142] However, an attorney, whether representing the issuer or underwriter, may be liable under section 17(a), which provides the basis for SEC injunctive relief and may, according to some decisions, even give rise to civil liability based on negligence.[143] Similarly, attorneys have been held liable as "sellers"

135. 15 U.S.C.A. § 77b(a)(11).

136. 15 U.S.C.A. § 77b(a)(11). The section explicitly excludes from the definition of underwriter members of the selling group whose only remuneration is equivalent to a regular broker's commission.

137. *15 U.S.C.A. § 77b(a)(11). See* § 4.26 *supra.*

138. McFarland v. Memorex Corp., 493 F.Supp. 631, 644–47 (N.D.Cal.1980), *reconsideration granted* 581 F.Supp. 878 (N.D.Cal.1984). *See also, e.g.,* Steiner v. Southmark Corp., 734 F.Supp. 269 (N.D.Tex.1990) (sufficiently alleging liability of accountants).

139. McFarland v. Memorex Corp., 493 F.Supp. 631, 643 (N.D.Cal.1980), *reconsideration granted* 581 F.Supp. 878 (N.D.Cal.1984), citing Grimm v. Whitney–Fidalgo Seafoods, Inc., 1973 WL 495, [1977–1978 Transfer Binder], Fed.Sec.L.Rep. (CCH) ¶ 96,029 (S.D.N.Y.1973).

140. *E.g.* Kitchens v. United States Shelter, 1988 WL 108598, [1988–89 Transfer Binder] Fed.Sec.L.Rep. (CCH) ¶ 93,920 (D.S.C.1988). On occasion, attorneys have been proper defendants in a section 11 case. For examples of such cases *see* Feit v. Leasco Data Processing Equipment Corp., 332 F.Supp. 544 (E.D.N.Y.1971); Escott v. BarChris Construction Corp., 283 F.Supp. 643 (S.D.N.Y.1968).

141. *See* Austin v. Baer, Marks & Upham, 1986 WL 10098, [1986–87 Transfer Binder] Fed.Sec.L.Rep. (CCH) ¶ 92,881 (D.Or.1986).

142. *See* Ahern v. Gaussoin, 611 F.Supp. 1465, 1482 (D.Or.1985).

143. *See* §§ 7.11, 12.22 *infra.*

under section 12.[144] After identifying the proper defendants, the key issues under section 11 are the appropriate standard of care and the defenses that may be asserted under section 11(b) by all defendants other than the issuer, who is strictly liable.[145] These topics are taken up in the succeeding section.

§ 7.4 Defenses Under 1933 Act Section 11(b)—Due Diligence, Reliance on Experts, and Reasonable Investigation

Section 11(b)[1] contains three types of defenses for persons other than the issuer to an action under section 11(a)[2] for material misstatements or omissions in the registration statement. The issuer is strictly liable, and no degree of prudence will absolve the issuer of a section 11 claim for damages. The only defenses available to the issuer are the purchaser's knowledge of the inaccuracies, lack of materiality, or expiration of the statute of limitations.

§ 7.4[1] "Whistle–Blowing" Defense

The first two defenses contained in section 11(b) relate to the person who discovers the material misstatement or omission and takes appropriate steps to prevent the violation. A person other than the issuer who would otherwise be liable under section 11 is relieved of liability if, prior to the effective date, he or she resigns from the position that connects him or her with the registration statement (or takes all legal steps toward resignation, or ceases to act in that capacity) *and* if he or she has given written notice to the issuer and the SEC of such action and further disclaims all responsibility for the applicable parts of the registration statement.[3] If the registration statement becomes effective without the knowledge of a potential section 11 defendant, he or she may avoid liability by taking appropriate steps toward resignation and advising the SEC, in addition to giving "reasonable public notice that such part of the registration statement had become effective without his knowledge."[4] All the parties to a registration statement are thus put in a position where self-policing is required. Supplementing section 11's affirmative defense, the Sarbanes–Oxley Act includes protections to whistle blowers generally, imposing civil and criminal sanctions against those retaliating against whistleblowers.[5]

§ 7.4[2] Due Diligence Defenses

Section 11(b)(3) contains the most frequently used defense. It provides that any person other than the issuer who is a potential section 11(a) defendant is absolved of liability with regard to any part of the registration statement not made under the authority of an expert, provided that the defendant "had, after reasonable investigation, reasonable ground to believe

---

144. Junker v. Crory, 650 F.2d 1349, 1360 (5th Cir.1981). *See* § 7.2 *supra.*

145. With regard to the strict liability of issuers, *see, e.g.,* In re NationsMart Corp. Securities Litigation, 130 F.3d 309 (8th Cir.1997) (referring to section 11 liability as virtually absolute).

§ 7.4

1. 15 U.S.C.A. § 77k(b).

2. 15 U.S.C.A. § 77k(a). *See* § 7.3 *supra.*

3. 15 U.S.C.A. § 77k(b)(1).

4. 15 U.S.C.A. § 77k(b)(2).

5. Sarbanes–Oxley Act of 2002 § 1107, 18 U.S.C.A. § 1513; Sarbanes–Oxley Act of 2002 § 806(c), 18 U.S.C.A. § 1514A.

and did believe, at the time such part of the registration statement became effective, that the statements therein were true and that there was no omission to state a material fact * * *."[10] A person who is named in the registration statement as an expert is not liable under section 11(a) for misstatements as an expert if, after reasonable investigation, there was reasonable ground to believe, combined with an actual belief, that there was no material misstatement or omission.[11] Furthermore, the expert is not liable if the statement in the registration materials "did not fairly represent his statements as an expert or was not a fair copy of or extract" of his or her report or valuation as an expert.[12] As for persons who would otherwise be liable for statements made in reliance upon experts, there is no liability if there was reasonable ground to believe, plus an actual belief that the statement did not contain any material misstatements or omissions. Finally, as for any part of the registration statement that purports to be made by a public official or "a copy of or extract from a public official document," there is no liability for anyone who had reasonable grounds to believe and did actually believe that there were no material misstatements or omissions.[13]

Section 11(c) expressly establishes the appropriate standard of care: "the standard of reasonableness shall be that required of a prudent man in the management of his own property."[14] This is a significant departure from the traditional state law standard that applies to officers and directors, which is generally articulated in terms of that conduct which would be befitting of a reasonable officer or director or person under like circumstances.[15] By speaking in terms of the degree of care that one would use in handling one's own affairs, the 1933 Act apparently provides for a higher standard,[16] at least to the extent that it does not seem to include the shield of the business judgment rule. The due diligence defense involves mixed questions of law and fact. When the facts are not disputed, summary judgment will be appropriate, because leaving such decisions to judges rather than juries will result in more predictability and uniformity of result.[17] However, where there is a material dispute as to the facts, summary judgment will not be appropriate.

To date, the most definitive word on the scope of section 11(b)(3) defenses of due diligence and reasonable investigation has emanated from the New York federal district court decision in Escott v. BarChris Construction Corp.[21]

10. 15 U.S.C.A. § 77k(b)(3)(A).

11. 15 U.S.C.A. § 77k(b)(3)(B).

12. 15 U.S.C.A. § 77k(b)(3)(B).

13. 15 U.S.C.A. § 77k(b)(3)(D).

14. 15 U.S.C.A. § 77k(c). *See* 17 C.F.R. § 230.176.

15. *See, e.g.,* Revised Model Business Corp. Act § 8.30(a)(2)(1984); Model Business Corp. Act § 35 par. 2 (1977 Supp.).

16. *See* James D. Cox & Thomas L. Hazen, Corporations ch. 10 (2d ed. 2004).

17. *See* In re Software Toolworks, Inc. Securities Litigation, 789 F.Supp. 1489 (N.D.Cal.1992), *affirmed in part and reversed in part,* 38 F.3d 1078 (9th Cir.1994).

21. 283 F.Supp. 643 (S.D.N.Y.1968). The issuer, BarChris, was in the business of building bowling alleys for contracted customers on a highly leveraged basis. The company had two methods of financing. The primary method involved entering into a contract with a customer for construction and equipment of a bowling alley with the customer making a comparatively small down payment. Upon completion of the facility, the customer would pay the balance of the contract price in notes payable, which BarChris would discount. The alternative method of financing consisted of a sale and leaseback arrangement. After completing the interior of the bowling alley, the facility would then be sold to a factor for the full construction price. The factor would then lease the interior to a customer or to a BarChris subsidiary, which in turn would lease the facility to the customer.

The registration statement in *BarChris* contained a number of misstatements. In the first instance, there were over-statements regarding the comparison of the fiscal year 1960 to past performance, but the court found that such misstatements were not material, since the correct figures would have shown a growth potential which was virtually equivalent to that presented in the registration statement. These misstatements thus failed to cross the materiality threshold as they were not of the magnitude likely to be significant to the reasonable investor. The most substantial misstatements concerned failure to accurately disclose the increases in customer defaults in payment of the notes held by BarChris and the possibility that the issuer would have to repossess certain leased assets which would necessarily injure its cash position.[23] There were additional omissions regarding loans to certain officers of the corporation. The section 11(b) defenses also focused on the registration statement's signers' and participants' failure to ascertain and disclose the inaccuracies regarding the likelihood that the issuer would be foreclosing on several of its notes, as well as their failure to disclose that BarChris was already engaged and about to be further engaged in the actual operation of bowling alleys.

In the course of its opinion, the court in *BarChris* treated each of the classes of defendants separately, creating a sliding scale of liability. The decision makes it clear that the highest standard of care attaches to an insider who signed the registration statement, especially if the insider is one of the designated principal officers who must sign prior to SEC filing.[24] Similarly, as to directors, the majority of whom must also sign, the court was careful to draw a distinction between insiders and outsiders. The court further made clear that any expertise brought by a signer, such as a legal or accounting background, will be factored into the formula of the standard of care under the circumstances. This sliding scale of liability as elevated by expert knowledge is arguably contrary to what would appear on the face of section 11(c) to be a unitary standard of conduct, that of the "prudent man" with no mention of any special knowledge that he may possess.[25] Nevertheless, there has been neither judicial nor SEC authority that has questioned the *BarChris* sliding scale of liability.

Beyond the appropriate standard of care, the court in *BarChris* also looked at the defense of reliance upon experts and specifically disclaimed any reading of the statute that would entitle signers to point to reliance on an attorney who had read the entire registration statement, even if the attorney is a securities expert reading the papers as a check against possible disclosure problems. Specifically, the court held that the only *expertised* portion of the prospectus and registration statement were audited figures prepared by the independent accountant. It was reasoned that section 11(b)(3) is explicit in its

---

Under either method of financing BarChris received very little up-front money for construction. It was thus necessary for the company to seek public financing on a number of occasions to provide the necessary cash to cover its operations. The prospectus and registration statement in question were filed in connection with a public offering of debentures.

23. The failure to disclose customer delinquencies standing alone was a 1.35–million dollar inflation of the balance sheet. *See* 283 F.Supp. at 680.

24. Section 6 requires that the registration statement be signed by the issuer's principal executive officers, principal financial officer, comptroller or principal accounting officer and the majority of the board of directors or persons performing similar functions. 15 U.S.C.A. § 77f(a). *See* §§ 3.2, 3.5 *supra*.

25. "The standard of reasonableness shall be that required of a prudent man in the management of his own property." 15 U.S.C.A. § 77k(c).

requirement that the portion provided by an expert giving rise to justifiable reliance is limited to statements that were "parts of the registration statement which purported to be made upon the authority of an expert."[26] In so ruling, the court held that even as to other financial data that the accountants may have looked at, the prospectus and registration statement were not expertised.[27] The same rule was applied to portions of the registration statement that were prepared by attorneys. Thus, registration materials are not expertised merely because they are examined or even prepared by attorneys, accountants, or other experts.

Although the decision imposed liability on attorneys and accountants, it was based on their role as signers or as experts named in the registration materials. Thus, the *BarChris* court did not impose liability upon a professional who renders advice in connection with portions of the registration statement in the absence of a statement which purports to be made upon his or her expertise. There does not seem to be any basis for holding professionals not named as experts to be liable for any misstatement under section 11 unless they were signers, directors, or underwriters, as required by section 11(a). It is clear, however, that any participant in the registration statement's preparation is subject to other potential liabilities. Negligence will clearly be grounds for a SEC injunction under section 17(a)[29] and may create civil liability.[30] Conduct approaching fraud will create liability under SEC Rule 10b–5.[31] Additionally, active participation in any sale as a "seller" creates the potential for liability under sections 12(a)(1) and 12(a)(2).[32] Another significant aspect of the *BarChris* ruling is that neither attorneys nor accountants who are covered by section 11(a) are justified in relying upon the client; they must make their own independent "due diligence" investigation. Unfortunately, there is not a bright line test for determining when the required due diligence has been met. Since due diligence arises as an affirmative defense, the burden of establishing it falls on the defendant.[33]

Even in a situation where a defendant may attempt to avail himself or herself of the reliance on experts defense, the courts are not satisfied by blind reliance.[34] Borrowing from the standard in criminal cases generally, the appropriate requirements for a reliance on experts defense are as follows: (1) *full disclosure* of pertinent facts known by the person claiming reliance, and (2) *good faith* reliance on the opinion given.[35] With regard to portions of the

26. Escott v. BarChris Construction Corp., 283 F.Supp. at 683.

27. *Id. See also, e.g.*, In re The Warnaco Group, Inc. Securities Litigation (II), 388 F.Supp.2d 307, 314 (S.D.N.Y.2005) (auditor could not be liable under rule 10b–5 for unaudited portion of financial statements).

29. *See* Aaron v. SEC, 446 U.S. 680, 100 S.Ct. 1945, 64 L.Ed.2d 611 (1980), *on remand* 636 F.2d 5 (2d Cir.1981); §§ 7.11, 12.22 *infra*.

30. *See* § 12.22 *infra*.

31. 317 C.F.R. § 240.10b–5. *See* chapter 12 *infra*.

32. 415 U.S.C.A. §§ 77*l*(a)(1), (2). *See* §§ 7.2 *supra*, 7.6 *infra*.

33. *See, e.g.*, In re Worldcom, Inc. Securities Litigation, 346 F.Supp.2d 628 (S.D.N.Y. 2004) (denying defendant's motion for summary judgment on due diligence defense). *See also, e.g.*, In re Worldcom, Inc. Securities Litigation, 352 F.Supp.2d 472 (S.D.N.Y. 2005) (issues of fact precluded summary judgment against accountants).

34. *Cf.* King v. Livent, Inc., 161 Fed.Appx. 116 (2d Cir. 2005) (affidavit stating a *belief* that defendants relied on expert assurances is insufficient evidence of due diligence; there must be evidence, such as personal knowledge of such alleged reliance on experts).

35. *See, e.g.*, United States v. Lindo, 18 F.3d 353, 356 (6th Cir.1994); United States v. Duncan, 850 F.2d 1104, 1117 (6th Cir.1988); United States v. Phillips, 217 F.2d 435, 442 (7th Cir.1954).

registration statement that have been prepared by experts, those section 11 defendants who can reasonably rely are relieved of their reasonable investigation and due diligence obligations for the expertised portions.[36] Conversely, when the defendant fails to establish reasonable reliance on the expertised portion of the registrations statement, the burden falls on the defendant of showing the exercise of due diligence and reasonable investigation.[37] Thus, for example, an underwriter may need to look beyond the auditor's comfort letter when there are red flags indicating that there were some accounting improprieties.[38]

Officers' and Directors' Liability

Although not having the title of president, the functional chief executive officer in *BarChris*, who was also a member of the corporation's executive committee, was a signer of the registration statement. The court noted that this chief executive officer and member of the executive committee was totally familiar with all aspects of the issuer's business and was "personally in charge" of all dealings with the factors, as well as handling negotiations that included discussion of customer delinquencies. The court found that he "knew all the relevant facts" and "could not have believed that there were no untrue statements" and thus could not assert a valid due diligence defense.[40] The two founders of the business, its titular president and vice-president, had less actual involvement than the chief executive officer and were "men of limited education." The court conceded that "it is not hard to believe that for them the prospectus was difficult reading, if indeed they read it at all."[41] However, the court viewed their limited expertise as irrelevant since a signing officer's liability is dependent upon neither whether he or she has read the registration statement nor if having read it, he or she understood it at all. The test is whether the signing officer acted with due diligence under the circumstances.[42] Thus, officers must have sufficient sophistication to understand the company's financial situation.[43] This is emphasized by the Sarbanes–Oxley Act's requirement that CEOs and CFOs of public companies personally certify that they reasonably believe the financial statements to be accurate.[44]

The court in *BarChris* found a lack of due diligence in signing without having read or understood the registration statement. People who do not

36. *E.g.,* In re Software Toolworks, Inc. Securities Litigation, 50 F.3d 615 (9th Cir.1994).

37. *See* In re Worldcom, Inc. Securities Litigation, 346 F.Supp.2d 628 (S.D.N.Y. 2004) (denying underwriter's motion for summary judgment based on reliance on experts and due diligence defenses).

38. In re Worldcom, Inc. Securities Litigation, 346 F.Supp.2d 628, 672 (S.D.N.Y. 2004) ("underwriters' reliance on audited financial statements may not be blind. Rather, where 'red flags' regarding the reliability of an audited financial statement emerge, mere reliance on an audit will not be sufficient to ward off liability").

40. Escott v. BarChris Construction Corp., 283 F.Supp. at 684.

41. 283 F.Supp. at 684.

42. *See, e.g.,* In re Livent, Inc. Noteholders Securities Litigation, 355 F.Supp.2d 722 (S.D.N.Y. 2005) (officers failed to establish that they met their section 11 due diligence obligations).

43. Unfortunately, not all public company CEOs met this standard. *See, e.g.,* Erin McClam, Ex–WorldCom CEO Takes the Stand, http://story.news.yahoo.com/news?tmpl=story & cid=530 & e=4 & u=/ap/20050228/ap_on_bi_ge/ebbers_trial (Feb. 28, 2005) quoting the testimony of former World.Com CEO Bernard Ebbers: "I know what I don't know. I don't, to this day, know technology. I don't know finance and accounting."

44. 15 U.S.C.A. § 7241. *See, e.g.,* Lisa M. Fairfax, Form Over Substance?: Officer Certification and the Promise of Enhanced Personal Accountability Under the Sarbanes–Oxley Act, 55 Rutgers L. Rev. 1 (2002). *See also* § 9.3[2][A] *infra.*

possess the minimum necessary knowledge should not be serving as officers or directors. In addition, the two signing founding officers had been beneficiaries of loans from the corporation that were not disclosed in the prospectus. On the basis of all of the foregoing facts, the court held that these two signers had failed to meet their defenses of due diligence.

The treasurer and chief financial officer, "a certified public accountant and an intelligent man," was, as his job required, "thoroughly familiar" with the company's finances, including the problem of customer delinquency.[45] He was also a member of the executive committee which gave him access to information as to operations of the business that he might otherwise not be informed of by virtue of his corporate office. In addition, the treasurer worked on the actual preparation of the registration statement, including having met with the company's attorneys. The essence of his defense was that since all the facts and figures appeared in the company's books, the treasurer was justified in relying upon the auditor's expertise. After noting that this created "an issue of credibility" the court ruled that in any event he failed to prove his defense.[46]

Outside Directors' Liability

Another controversial aspect of the *BarChris* court's decision arose with respect to an outside director who was neither an officer nor employee but signed the registration statement. The outside director testified that he did not know that he was signing a registration statement but he vaguely understood that it was something "for the SEC." The court further conceded that the outside director believed all representations as to the company's business made by the insiders. Although he became a director "on the eve of the financing" and "had little opportunity to familiarize himself with the company's affairs," the court nonetheless held him liable for failing to make any investigation whatsoever before having signed the registration statement.[53] This might seem to be an extremely high burden to put upon a newly elected outside director; however, he did sign the registration statement. The court would have been much harder pressed to find liability under section 11(a)(2) of an outside director who had not signed the registration statement. The *BarChris* decision thus provides a good lesson for unwary outside directors who are asked to sign the registration statement.

Attorneys' Liabilities

One of the most controversial aspects of the *BarChris* ruling arose out of the court's holding liable a young attorney who was only four years out of law school at the time of the registration statement. He had previously been house counsel and assistant secretary and was then secretary to the corporation and a member of the board of directors. Although he was not a director at the time of the initial filing, he was fully liable under section 11. The court was willing to agree that as corporate secretary and house counsel he was not a principal officer; however, by being keeper of corporate minutes, he certainly had access to inside information.[54] Furthermore, he had examined the con-

45. Escott v. BarChris Construction Corp., 283 F.Supp. at 685.

46. 283 F.Supp. at 685.

53. Escott v. BarChris Construction Corp., 283 F.Supp. at 688.

54. Escott v. BarChris Construction Corp., 283 F.Supp. at 387.

tracts in question and had advised the issuer that certain contracts may not have been legally enforceable, a fact not recorded in the registration statement. The court conceded that this young attorney "did not know of many inaccuracies in the prospectus," but that he had sufficient knowledge of the business that he was at least put on inquiry notice of potential problems, and thus should have investigated "the truth of all the statements in the unexpertised portion of the document, which he signed."[55] Since the young attorney made no independent investigation whatsoever, he was held not to have met the burden of proving his due diligence defense. The court did not indicate how much investigation would have been sufficient to let him off the hook.

Another attorney who was hit with liability in the course of the *BarChris* decision was outside counsel who sat on the board of directors. He not only signed this and other registration statements for the issuer, but also took primary responsibility for preparing the initial drafts of one of the registration statements that formed the basis of the suit. Section 11 does not provide any bases for suing someone who simply prepares or drafts a registration statement,[56] yet since this attorney was both a director of the issuer and a signer of the registration statement, he was properly viewed as a section 11 defendant. The court made note of the fact that this was not a legal malpractice action, but "in considering Grant's [outside counsel's] due diligence defenses, the unique position he occupied cannot be disregarded."[57] This defendant as outside counsel, director and signer, claimed that he was justified in relying upon the statements of his clients, but the court held that under the statute he had a duty to make an independent investigation. The obvious lesson of this aspect of the ruling is that counsel should be hesitant to sign any registration statement since their expertise and access to inside information by virtue of their attorney-client relationship may impose an especially high standard of conduct. Furthermore, since section 11(a)(2) renders all directors liable, an attorney who sits as a director but does not sign the registration statement is equally open for potential liability, especially if he or she worked on the registration statement in any capacity. However, an attorney who helps prepare the registration statement cannot be held liable under section 11 unless he or she is an officer, director, signer of the registration statement, or expert within the meaning of section 11.

§ 7.4[2][C] Underwriters' Liabilities

As with other section 11, defendants other than the issuer who is held to strict liability, underwriters are held liable under section 11 only if they fall below the accepted standard of due diligence. In the *BarChris* opinion and elsewhere[60] the courts have made it clear that the underwriter plays a special role in the due diligence process since investors rely on the underwriter's investigation of the issuer. The underwriter's presence in the offering can act as an implied representation that the underwriter has investigated the is-

55. Escott v. BarChris Construction Corp., 283 F.Supp. at 687.

56. Nevertheless, liability may exist under other sections. *See* chapter 12 *infra*. *See also* § 7.15 *infra*.

57. Escott v. BarChris Construction Corp., 283 F.Supp. at 690.

60. *See, e.g.,* Sanders v. John Nuveen & Co., 524 F.2d 1064, 1069–1070 (7th Cir.1975), *vacated and remanded on other grounds,* 425 U.S. 929, 96 S.Ct. 1659, 48 L.Ed.2d 172 (1976).

suer.[61] Thus, for example, an underwriter cannot rely blindly on an auditor's comfort letter, when there were red flags that should have put the underwriter on notice of the alleged improprieties.[62] The underwriter is obligated to look behind the financial statements and seek verification as to their accuracy and/or currency.[63]

Much of the court's opinion in *BarChris* is devoted to the liability of the underwriters[65] and the accountants who performed the 1960 audit.[66] As for the underwriters, the facts were extremely damaging and justified a finding of liability. The partner in the underwriting firm who had primary responsibility for investigating the issuer was also a director of the issuer. Not only does this position with the issuer create a potential conflict of interest, it also gives access to certain types of inside information that might otherwise not be available to an underwriter, as the issuer and underwriter can no longer be viewed as dealing on a purely arms-length basis. Furthermore, the court noted that the only investigation made by the underwriter about the issuer was directed toward the decision whether or not to participate in the offering and was *not* directed toward compliance with the requirements of the statute's registration provisions. The court acknowledged that after the underwriter's partner was made a director of the issuer, he did make an independent investigation of the prospectus' accuracy, but as was the case with the other defendants, he failed to follow up on a number of questionable disclosures. The court further pointed out that although there was a "due diligence meeting" one week before the offering date, the underwriters failed to make any independent investigation after the meeting. The court thus held the managing underwriter liable because of its failure to meet the defense of due diligence. In contrast, where underwriters make a reasonable investigation, the defense will be available.[67]

In the course of its opinion in *BarChris*, the court chided the underwriters for failing to have looked beyond the contracts represented by the backlog figures.[68] It has been suggested by one commentator that this should not be taken to mean that underwriters always have to make an independent check of inventory backlogs.[69] In an even more troubling aspect of the *BarChris* opinion, the court pointed out that "the other underwriters, who did nothing and relied solely on directors and on the lawyers" did not establish a due diligence defense except as to the 1960 audit.[70] The court also went on to

61. Sanders v. John Nuveen & Co., 524 F.2d 1064, 1069–1070 (7th Cir.1975), *vacated and remanded on other grounds,* 425 U.S. 929, 96 S.Ct. 1659, 48 L.Ed.2d 172 (1976).

62. In re Worldcom, Inc. Securities Litigation, 346 F.Supp.2d 628, 672 (S.D.N.Y. 2004) ("underwriters' reliance on audited financial statements may not be blind. Rather, where 'red flags' regarding the reliability of an audited financial statement emerge, mere reliance on an audit will not be sufficient to ward off liability").

63. *See, e.g.,* Glassman v. Computervision Corp., 90 F.3d 617, 629 (1st Cir. 1996) ("[A] failure by the underwriters either to verify a company's statements as to its financial state or to consider new information up to the effective date of an offering would almost certainly constitute a lack of due diligence.").

65. Escott v. BarChris Construction Corp., 283 F.Supp. at 692–697.

66. *See* § 7.4[2][D] *infra.*

67. *See, e.g.,* In re Software Toolworks Inc. Securities Litigation, 50 F.3d 615 (9th Cir.1994).

68. Escott v. BarChris Construction Corp., 283 F.Supp. at 697.

69. Carlos L. Israels Checklist for Underwriters Investigation, 18 Bus.Law, 90 (1962), as updated in ABA, Selected Articles in Securities Law 71 (1968).

70. Escott v. BarChris Construction Corp., 283 F.Supp. at 697.

question whether the other underwriters can ever rely upon due diligence of the managing underwriter. In analyzing the significance of the *BarChris* decision with regard to the underwriters, it must be remembered that this underwriter's investigation was supervised by a partner who also was a director of the issuer. As such, the underwriter's investigation was not a truly independent one.

The *BarCris* decision raises questions as to the underwriter's outside counsel's standard of responsibility. In the course of its ruling that the managing underwriter failed to meet the due diligence standard, the court rejected the underwriter's reliance on counsel. The underwriter's outside counsel sent a young associate to check *BarChris'* corporate records. The associate did not check the issuer's contracts nor did he locate several executive committee minutes. The court held that this was an insufficient investigation and thus precluded reliance by the underwriter. Underwriter's counsel did not fit within the list of section 11 defendants and thus was not held liable. The court did not inquire, however, into the law firm's potential liability to its client for malpractice or any common law right of indemnity by a principal against its agent. Also, with respect to indemnification, the special role of the underwriter in the due diligence process has led courts to find a limitation of the underwriter's liability as contrary to public policy.[74]

In order to establish their due diligence, underwriters must show that they engaged in reasonable independent investigation of the issuer and of the offering. An example of an underwriter's successful due diligence defense arose in In re International Rectifier Securities Litigation.[75] There, the underwriters: (1) reviewed the issuer's internal financial forecasts, contracts, and other documents, (2) made a physical inspection of the issuer's major facilities, (3) employed analysts having expertise in the issuer's business, (4) conducted extensive interviews with eleven of the issuer's senior and middle management, (5) interviewed the issuer's major customers, outside quality consultants, auditors, and legal counsel, and (6) obtained written verification of the prospectus' accuracy and a "cold comfort" letter from the auditors that there were not material changes in the financial position since the last audit.

Accountants' Liabilities

As is the case with other section 11 defendants, the accountants have the burden of establishing their due diligence. The court in *BarChris* found that the auditors failed to establish their standard of due diligence. The field survey for the audit was performed by an individual who was not yet a CPA and had no prior knowledge of the bowling alley industry. This was his first major assignment as a senior accountant. The court conceded that although the investigator may have asked the right questions and received what he considered satisfactory answers, he failed to verify them. Further, it was apparent that there had been an increase in notes payable but nonetheless the auditor's investigator had "no conception how tight the cash position was."[77] Since the auditor's investigator had met with only one officer and had various

74. *See* Globus v. Law Research Service, Inc., 418 F.2d 1276 (2d Cir.1969), *cert. denied* 397 U.S. 913, 90 S.Ct. 913, 25 L.Ed.2d 93 (1970); Globus v. Law Research Service, 318 F.Supp. 955 (S.D.N.Y.1970), *affirmed per curiam* 442 F.2d 1346 (2d Cir.1971), *cert. denied* 404 U.S. 941, 92 S.Ct. 286, 30 L.Ed.2d 254 (1971).

75. 1997 WL 529600, [1997 Transfer Binder] Fed. Sec. L. Rep. (CCH) ¶ 99,469 (C.D.Cal.1997).

77. Escott v. BarChris Construction Corp., 283 F.Supp. at 702.

other bases of inquiry notice, the court found that the burden of establishing due diligence had not been met and that the auditors were liable for all mistakes in the 1960 audited figures.[78] Liability of accountants does not, however, extend to unaudited figures even though the accountants prepared that portion of the registration statement.[79]

Aftermath of BarChris; SEC Rule 176

The *BarChris* decision raises many questions concerning the extent of independent investigation that must be made. Specifically, how much of a factual inquiry must be made? Must attorneys, accountants, and underwriters make trips all over the country to inspect the physical plant of the issuer? Must there be at least a spot-check of company inventories? Must there be title searches of property claimed to be owned by the issuer? Must there be an eyeball review of all substantial contracts of the issuer? Must there be a complete opening of the company's files to outsiders such as the underwriters? These are just some of the questions that arise from the decision. The safe answer to each of these questions is clearly "yes." One effective way to help assure compliance with section 11's due diligence requirement is to appoint a due diligence officer to supervise the preparation of the registration statement.[85]

A second instructive decision on the scope of section 11(b) defenses arose in the context of an exchange offer in Feit v. Leasco Data Processing Equipment Corp.[86] Unlike the underwriters in the *BarChris* case, there was no interlocking directorate or relationship between the issuer and the underwriter. Accordingly, the underwriters were truly outsiders who were dealing at arm's length with the issuer. Thus, the court noted that "dealer-managers cannot, of course, be expected to possess the intimate knowledge of corporate affairs of inside directors, and their duty to investigate should be considered in light of their more limited access."[87] The same clearly could not have been said of the underwriters in *BarChris* because of their interlocking management. The court noted that the underwriters in *Feit* did comply with industry standards and made somewhat of an independent investigation. The court concluded that they "have just barely established * * * that they had reasonable ground to believe that the omission of a specific figure was justified."[88] In so ruling, the court found that unlike the underwriters in the *BarChris* case, in the *Feit* case Leasco's underwriters were justified in relying on the client's representations.

It is evident from the foregoing discussion that the courts have not been able to articulate a bright-line test as to the requisite standard of care under section 11. What has emerged, however, is the fact that courts will impose a sliding scale depending upon the defendant's knowledge, expertise, status

78. Escott v. BarChris Construction Corp., 283 F.Supp. at 643, 702.

79. Lattanzio v. Deloitte & Touche LLP, 476 F.3d 147 (2d Cir. 2007).

85. *See* Robert A. Spanner, Limiting Exposure in the Offering Process, 20 Rev.Sec. & Commod.Reg. 59 (1987) (also containing a helpful checklist of due diligence steps).

86. 332 F.Supp. 544 (E.D.N.Y.1971). *See* Note, Section 11 in the Exchange Offer Setting: An Analysis of Feit v. Leasco Data Processing Equipment Corp., 1972 Duke L.J. 1023.

87. 332 F.Supp. at 582. Compare Kitchens v. U.S. Shelter, 1988 WL 108598, [1988–89 Transfer Binder] Fed.Sec.L.Rep. (CCH) ¶ 93,920 (D.S.C.1988) (appraisal firm satisfied burden of proving due diligence).

88. 332 F.Supp. at 582.

with regard to the issuer, its affiliates or underwriters, and the degree of the defendant's actual participation in the registration process and in preparing the registration materials.

In an effort to clarify its position, the SEC promulgated Rule 176,[89] reinforces the judicial sliding scale of culpability and further provides for the necessity of a case-by-case, highly factual analysis, as is done with common law negligence.[91]

§ 7.5 Damages in Actions Under 1933 Act Section 11

Section 11 permits damages awards to injured purchasers of securities sold pursuant to a 1933 Act registration statement where the registration materials contain material misstatements or omissions of fact.[1] This remedy is in addition to the action provided by section 12(a)(2) which is not limited to registered offerings and provides the purchaser with a cause of action against a seller of securities where the seller is responsible for material misstatements or omissions.[2] Although both section 11 and section 12(a)(2) are directed at materially misleading information in connection with sales of securities, they provide for a different measure of damages. Under section 11, damages are based on a complex formula, which in essence is designed to award the difference between the purchase price and the true value of the securities, thereby reflecting the extent to which the purchase price was inflated by the material misstatements or omissions.[3] This figure is then reduced by that portion of the loss that defendant can show was attributable to factors other than the misstatements in question.[4]

Section 12(a)(2), as is the case with private actions under section 12(a)(1),[5] permits the purchaser to rescind the transaction or recover rescissory damages; this means that damages under section 12(a)(1) are not limited to those caused by the violation. In contrast to the measure of damages set forth in section 12(a)(1), in an action under section 12(a)(2) there is now an affirmative defense if the defendant can establish that the plaintiff's loss was caused by factors other than the section 12(a)(2) misstatement.[7] This is similar to the negative causation defense available in section 11 actions. Section 11 damages, as is the case with those available in an action under 1934 Act Rule 10b–5, are limited to those caused by the misrepresentation or omission. In a Rule 10b–5 action, loss causation is part of the plaintiff's prima facie case.[8] In contrast, under section 11, loss causation is not an element of the plaintiff's claim, but rather its absence is a defense with the burden of proof falling on the defendant.[9]

89. A.L.I., Proposed Federal Securities Code § 1704(g).

91. *See* In re Worldcom, Inc. Securities Litigation, 2005 WL 638268 (S.D.N.Y. 2005).

§ 7.5

1. 5 U.S.C.A. § 77k.

2. 15 U.S.C.A. § 77l(a)(2). *See* §§ 7.6, 7.7 *infra.*

3. 15 U.S.C.A. § 77k(e).

4. 15 U.S.C.A. § 77k(e).

5. 15 U.S.C.A. § 77*l*(a)(1). Section 12(a)(1) which permits actions by purchasers against sellers who violate section 5's registration requirements is discussed in § 7.2 *supra.*

7. Section 12(b), 15 U.S.C.A. § 77l(b). *See* §§ 7.6, 7.8 *infra.*

8. *See* § 12.11 *infra.*

9. *See, e.g.,* Lyne v. Arthur Andersen & Co., 772 F.Supp. 1064 (N.D.Ill.1991).

Damages under section 11(e) consist of the difference between the purchase price (but not in excess of the offering price) and the value of the security at the time of suit (if the plaintiff still owns the security) or, if the plaintiff has sold the security prior to bringing suit, the sale price.[10] In the event that the plaintiff owns the security at the time of suit[11] but sells the security prior to judgment, then damages are based on the difference between the purchase price and the sales price if that figure is less than the difference between the purchase price and the value at the time suit is brought.[12]

A section 11 plaintiff does not have the obligation to mitigate his or her damages.[13] The formula set forth in section 11(e) presents the plaintiff who has not yet sold his or her securities with a strategic decision: whether or not to sell. Under the statutory formula, a plaintiff who has not sold prior to judgment will have damages calculated based on the "value"[14] at the time of suit. If the plaintiff does not sell prior to bringing suit, and the price of the securities declines, such decline is not part of the section 11 damages, even if plaintiff sells prior to judgment. Similarly, if the price climbs after the date of suit and the plaintiff holds the securities through the judgment, damages are based on the value on the date of suit without taking account of the subsequent market rise.[15] However, if the price rises after the date that suit is brought and plaintiff sells the securities prior to judgment, damages will be limited to the lesser of the difference between the purchase price and the value on the date of suit, or the difference between the purchase price and the sale price. Accordingly, the section 11 plaintiff who continues to hold the securities can gain by a subsequent price rise (providing there is no sale prior to judgment) but will not be protected against a price decline.

In a section 11 action, a plaintiff who has not sold the security at the time suit is brought presumably carries the burden of initially proving a decline in value of the shares between the time the security was purchased and the time of sale or suit. From the terms of the statute, it would seem that the "value" of the security does not necessarily equal market price on the date of suit.[17] However, the use of "value" in section 11(e)(1) rather than "price" should not be taken as an open invitation to disregard or look too far beyond the market price. Courts should not look beyond market price on the date of suit without a compelling reason for doing so. Thus, for example, if trading has been halted, market price cannot be used as a yardstick. Similarly, if the market price had significant fluctuation on the date of suit, a court will have to determine whether the "value" is best represented by the closing price, the mean price, or some other price on that day. However, where the market price on the date of suit is both reliable and readily ascertainable, the price should be the court's focal point. In a questionable decision, one court found that the

10. 15 U.S.C.A. § 77k(e).

11. *See* Alpern v. UtiliCorp United, Inc., 84 F.3d 1525 (8th Cir.1996) (damage date for claim added by amended complaint related back to the date of filing the original complaint).

12. *See* Alpern v. UtiliCorp United, Inc., 84 F.3d 1525 (8th Cir.1996).

13. *See* Voege v. Ackerman, 364 F.Supp. 72, 73 (S.D.N.Y.1973).

14. While market price may be the best evidence of value, other factors may be considered as well.

15. This was the case for example in Beecher v. Able, 435 F.Supp. 397 (S.D.N.Y.1975), *affirmed* 575 F.2d 1010 (2d Cir.1978) where the market price continued to rise and eventually the securities climbed back to their original offering price.

17. Beecher v. Able, 435 F.Supp. 397 (S.D.N.Y.1975), *affirmed on other grounds* 575 F.2d 1010 (2d Cir.1978).

value of the security was in fact higher than the market price since there was sufficient documentation of "panic selling" prior to the date of original sale which had artificially lowered market price.[18] However, the better approach would have been to hold the defendant accountable for the panic selling which resulted from the misrepresentations and subsequent corrective disclosure.

Under section 11 and section 12(a)(2), the burden is on the defendant to prove the absence of causation rather than the more traditional approach of requiring the plaintiff to prove that his or her damages were both in fact and proximately caused by the defendant's misconduct.[23] It has been observed that section 11(e) "does not focus on the causal relationship between the misstatement and the original purchase, but rather on the relationship between the misstatement and any subsequent decline in value."[24]

§ 7.6 1933 Act Section 12(a)(2)—Liability for Material Misstatements or Omissions by Sellers of Securities

§ 7.6[1] Elements of Section 12(a)(2) Claim

Section 12(a)(2) of the 1933 Act[1] creates an express private remedy for material[2] misstatements or omissions in connection with the sale or offer for sale of a security; the offeror and seller[3] of the security is liable to the purchaser of the security.[4]

As is the case with section 12(a)(1), section 12(a)(2) is limited to liability of sellers and thus imposes a strict privity requirement. Difficult questions arise under section 12(a)(2) as to what degree of active participation in the transaction is necessary to classify someone as a section 12 "seller." Generally, issuers and underwriters are not sellers within the meaning of section 12 unless they actively participate in the negotiations with the plaintiff/purchaser. Similarly, an attorney's having worked on the offering circular will not make him or her a seller. On the other hand, a broker who deals directly with the plaintiff is a section 12 seller. In order to be a seller under section 12, the defendant must have both a direct relationship with the plaintiff, and he or she must also have been directly involved in the sale.[32]

Section 12(a)(2) renders the seller liable if he or she "shall not sustain the burden of proof that he did not know, and in the exercise of reasonable

18. Beecher v. Able, 435 F.Supp. 397 (S.D.N.Y.1975), *affirmed on other grounds* 575 F.2d 1010 (2d Cir.1978).

23. *See, e.g.,* McMahan & Co. v. Wherehouse Entertainment, Inc., 65 F.3d 1044, 1048–1049 (2d Cir. 1995); In re Worlds of Wonder Securities Litigation, 35 F.3d 1407, 1422–1423 (9th Cir. 1994) (remanding for trial *inter alia* on the issue of causation).

24. Akerman v. Oryx Communications, Inc., 609 F.Supp. 363, 368 (S.D.N.Y.1984), *affirmed* 810 F.2d 336 (2d Cir.1987).

§ 7.6

1. 15 U.S.C.A. § 77l(a)(2).

2. In re Donald J. Trump Casino Securities Litigation, 7 F.3d 357, 369 (3d Cir.1993) (materiality is the same under sections 11 and 12(a)(2) of the 1933 Act).

3. Section 12(a)(2) liability may only be imposed on "sellers" of securities as that term has been defined by the Supreme Court. Pinter v. Dahl, 486 U.S. 622, 108 S.Ct. 2063, 100 L.Ed.2d 658 (1988). *See* § 7.2[2] *supra* and § 7.7 *infra*.

4. The section 12(a)(2) remedy is limited to damages; injunctive relief is not available. K/A & Co. v. Hallwood Energy Partners, L.P., 1990 WL 37866, [1990–1991 Transfer Binder] Fed.Sec. L.Rep. (CCH) ¶ 95,758 (S.D.N.Y.1990).

32. Pinter v. Dahl, 486 U.S. 622, 108 S.Ct. 2063, 100 L.Ed.2d 658 (1988).

care could not have known, of such untruth or omission."[38] In 2005, the SEC clarified that the known or should have known requirement is to be judged as of the time of the sale.[39] The imposition of a "reasonable care" standard is different language than the "due diligence" rubric of section 11.[40] It is clear that section 12(a)(2)'s requirement of "reasonable care" imparts some sort of negligence standard and that it is not necessary for the purchaser to show any type of scienter on the seller's part.[41] Although there is not a *per se* affirmative investigation requirement, it has been held that the section 12(a)(2) standard of reasonable care may impose a duty to investigate depending upon the circumstances.[42] Reasonable care imparts a sliding scale of standards of conduct and has been held to impose a duty of *continuing investigation* in the case of the exclusive dealer of the security in question.[43] On the other hand, two former justices of the Supreme Court took the position that any imposition of an affirmative investigation requirement is a misapplication of the "reasonable care" standard since the "investigation" language of section 11 is said to call for a greater undertaking than the "care" requirement of section 12(a)(2).[44]

Reliance is generally an element of a fraud claim.[58] However, it is generally held that once the plaintiff has proved a material omission, it is not necessary for plaintiff to establish reliance in a section 12(a)(2) action.[59] Both the language of the statute itself and the teachings of Supreme Court[60] make it clear that reliance is not a precondition to stating a claim for relief under section 12(a)(2) of the 1933 Act.

The section 12(a)(2) action may be brought in either law or equity.[70] Additionally, as is the case with section 12(a)(1) but unlike section 11 or the

38. 15 U.S.C.A. § 77*l*(a)(2). *See* Mayer v. Oil Field Systems Corp., 803 F.2d 749, 756 (2d Cir.1986) (section 12(a)(2) claim dismissed for failure to show defendant should have known of the misrepresentation; also requiring scienter for aider and abettor liability).

39. 17 C.F.R. § 230.159(c) ("For purposes of section 12(a)(2) of the Act only, knowing of such untruth or omission in respect of a sale (including, without limitation, a contract of sale), means knowing at the time of such sale (including such contract of sale)."). *See* Securities Offering Reform, Sec. Act Rel. No. 33–8591, Sec. Exch. Act Rel. No. 34–52056, Inv. Co. Act Rel. No. IC–26993 70, Fed. Reg. 44722–01, 2005 WL 1692642 (SEC July 19, 2005).

40. *See* § 7.4 *supra.*

41. *See, e.g.,* Wigand v. Flo–Tek, Inc., 609 F.2d 1028 (2d Cir.1979).

42. Sanders v. John Nuveen & Co., 619 F.2d 1222, 1228 (7th Cir.1980), *cert. denied* 450 U.S. 1005, 101 S.Ct. 1719, 68 L.Ed.2d 210 (1981).

43. *See* Franklin Savings Bank v. Levy, 551 F.2d 521, 527 (2d Cir.1977) (commercial paper).

44. John Nuveen & Co. v. Sanders, 450 U.S. 1005, 101 S.Ct. 1719, 68 L.Ed.2d 210 (1981) (Powell, J., joined by Rehnquist, J.; dissenting from a denial of certiorari).

58. *See, e.g.,* Pell v. Weinstein, 759 F.Supp. 1107 (M.D.Pa.1991), *judgment affirmed* 961 F.2d 1568 (3d Cir.1992) (no section 12(a)(2) claim where plaintiff committed to transaction in question prior to seeing allegedly misleading statements).

59. Wright v. National Warranty Co., 953 F.2d 256 (6th Cir.1992) (reliance is not an element of a section 12(a)(2) claim; the fact that plaintiff was an insider did not by itself bar a section 12(a)(2) action).

60. Gustafson v. Alloyd Co., 513 U.S. 561, 576, 115 S.Ct 1061, 131 L.Ed.2d 1 (1995) (section 12(a)(2) gives "buyers a right to rescind without proof of reliance.").

70. Section 22(a) of the 1933 Act provides that suit can be brought in state or federal court and there is no right of removal to federal court for suits brought in state court. 15 U.S.C.A. § 77v(a). *See* § 17.1 *infra.* However, as a result of the Securities Litigation Uniform Standards Act of 1998, private class actions with more than fifty class members in fraud or disclosure based actions under the securities laws must be brought in federal court. 1933 Act § 16, 15 U.S.C.A. § 77p. *See* § 7.17[2] *infra.* Since a section 12(a)(2) action is premised on materially misleading disclosures, the mandatory federal forum applies to such class actions. *See id.*

implied remedy under Rule 10b–5 of the Exchange Act,[71] damages are limited to either rescission and return of the purchase price or damages based on that amount if the purchaser no longer owns the security.

§ 7.6[2] Judicially Imposed Limits on Section 12(a)(2)—The Public Offering or Batch Offering Limitation

Section 12(a)(2) has no express limits on its application except for those discussed earlier in this section. However, beginning in the 1990s, many decisions have held that section 12(a)(2) applies only to distributions of securities and not to isolated after-market transactions that are not part of a "batch offering."[79] Although not all courts concurred, subsequently the Supreme Court in a five-to-four decision concurred by imposing a public offering limitation on the scope of the section 12(a)(2) remedy.[80] The impact of the public offering limitation is twofold. In the first instance, it means that section 12(a)(2) is not available for misstatements made in connection with a small, limited, or private offering of securities. Secondly, the section 12(a)(2) remedy is no longer available for transactions occurring in the after-market regardless of whether those transactions are privately negotiated or take place in the public markets.

Those courts reaching this unfortunate and erroneous conclusion that section 12(a)(2) should be interpreted as limited to public offerings cannot find this limitation in the express language of the statute. Instead, the courts implied the limitation by relying on the statutory language of section 12(a)(2), which refers to misstatements and omissions made by "*prospectus* or oral communication."[82] The courts extrapolated from the words of the statute that the use of the term "prospectus" shows a legislative intent to limit the section's operation to the offering process. The error in this approach is due in part to the fact that the statutory definition of prospectus[83] does not have any such restriction and thus, on its face, applies to *all* written, television, or radio offers to sell securities, including a sales confirmation, and a contract to sell.

§ 7.6[2][C] The *Gustafson* Decision

Notwithstanding the above-described difficulties in arriving at a limiting interpretation of section 12(a)(2), in a sharply divided five-to-four decision in Gustafson v. Alloyd Co.,[102] the Supreme Court reached just such a result. As had been the case in the previous lower court decisions, the Supreme Court focused on the use of the term "prospectus" in section 12(a)(2).

The Court in *Gustafson* acknowledged that section 2(a)(10) broadly defines prospectus to include any written offer to sell.[103] The Court then looked to section 10 of the Act,[104] which sets forth the statutory prospectus

71. 17 C.F.R. § 240.10b–5.

79. Ballay v. Legg Mason Wood Walker, Inc., 925 F.2d 682 (3d Cir.1991), *cert. denied* 502 U.S. 820, 112 S.Ct. 79, 116 L.Ed.2d 52 (1991).

80. Gustafson v. Alloyd Co., 513 U.S. 561, 115 S.Ct. 1061, 131 L.Ed.2d 1 (1995).

82. 415 U.S.C.A. § 77l(a)(2); In re Cosi, Inc. Securities Litigation, 379 F.Supp.2d 580 (S.D.N.Y. 2005) (failure to allege that plaintiffs purchased securities in public offering).

83. 15 U.S.C.A. § 77b(a)(10).

102. 513 U.S. 561, 115 S.Ct. 1061, 131 L.Ed.2d 1 (1995).

103. 15 U.S.C.A. § 77b(a)(10). *See* § 2.4 *supra.*

104. 15 U.S.C.A. § 77j.

requirements; the Court concluded that the term, as it is used in section 12(a)(2), should be read as coextensive with the concept of prospectus in section 10. Accordingly, the Court rejected the plaintiff's contention that the contract for sale qualified as a "prospectus" under section 12(a)(2)[106] and thereby limited section 12 to offerings by prospectus.[107] The Court concluded, "the word 'prospectus' is a term of art referring to a document that describes a public offering of securities by an issuer or controlling shareholder."[108]

§ 7.11 The Securities Act's General Prohibition on Material Misstatements and Omissions—1933 Act Section 17

Section 17 of the 1933 Act,[1] explicitly defines a violation of the fact based on fraud or misrepresentation. Section 17(a) contains general antifraud and misrepresentation proscriptions that supplement section 5[3] and the express civil liability provisions.[4] Section 17(a) prohibits fraud, material misstatements, and omissions of fact in connection with the sale[6] of securities. Section 17(a) applies regardless of whether the securities are registered or whether they are exempt from registration under section 3 of the Act.[8] In 2000, section 17(a) was amended to extend its antifraud reach to security-based swap agreements even though those agreements are exempted from the definition of security.[9]

As is the case with Exchange Act Rule 10b–5,[18] section 17(a) does not impose an affirmative duty to disclose. Instead it imposes liability for omissions that make the statements made materially misleading.[19] However unlike its Exchange Act counterpart, section 17(a) applies only to sales of and *offers to sell* securities and thus to activities of the offeror or seller but not to fraud by the purchaser. Section 17(a) covers negligent material misstatements and omissions.[20]

The early decisions were divided on the question of whether section 17(a) will support an implied private remedy. The overwhelming majority of recent decisions have not been at all receptive to the private right of action.[30] The

106. Although it probably would under section 2(a)(3). 15 U.S.C.A. § 77b(a)(3); *see* § 2.3 *supra.*

107. *See also, e.g.,* Hilary A. Sale, Disappearing Without a Trace: Sections 11 and 12(a)(2) of the 1933 Securities Act, 75 Wash. L. Rev. 429 (2000).

108. 513 U.S. at 584, 115 S.Ct. at 1073–74.

§ 7.11

1. 15 U.S.C.A. § 77q. One of the major contributions of section 17(a) of the 1933 Act is that it was the model for Rule 10b–5 of the 1934 Act which has become the broadest of the antifraud proscriptions under the securities laws. *See* § 12.3 *infra.*

3. 15 U.S.C.A. § 77e. *See* §§ 2.1–2.5 *supra.*

4. Sections 11 and 12 are discussed in §§ 7.2–7.5 *supra.*

6. Section 17(a) focuses on sellers (as opposed to Rule 10b–5 which address fraud by either sellers or purchasers).

8. 15 U.S.C.A. § 77q(c). Section 3's exemptions are discussed in chapter 4 *supra.*

9. 15 U.S.C.A. § 77q(a) as amended by Pub. Law 106–554, 114 Stat. 2763 (December 21, 2000).

18. 17 C.F.R. § 240.10b–5. *See* chapter 12 *infra.*

19. United States v. Crop Growers Corp., 954 F.Supp. 335, 349–350 (D.D.C.1997). *See* § 12.19 *infra.*

20. Aaron v. SEC, 446 U.S. 680, 100 S.Ct. 1945, 64 L.Ed.2d 611 (1980).

30. *E.g.,* Bath v. Bushkin, Gaims, Gaines & Jonas, 913 F.2d 817 (10th Cir.1990). *See also* the authorities in § 12.22 *infra.*

trend against implying a remedy has been so strong that the Eighth Circuit affirmed the imposition of Rule 11 sanctions against counsel signing a complaint alleging a remedy under section 17(a).[31] Accordingly, prior to filing a section 17 claim, counsel should make a careful investigation and be confident that the issue has not been resolved clearly to the contrary in that circuit.

In addition to section 17(a)'s antifraud prohibitions, section 17(b)[34] prohibits disseminating information about a security without disclosing any consideration received or to be received, directly or indirectly, in connection with sales of the security.[35] Section 17(b) is not limited to formal offers to sell.[36] Also, like section 17(a), 17(b) applies to securities whether or not in registration or exempt under section 3.[37] Section 17(b) was designed to prevent the misleading impression of impartiality in certain recommendations. As explained in the House Report, section 17(b)'s prohibitions were "particularly designed to meet the evils of the 'tipster sheet,' as well as articles in newspapers or periodicals that purport to give an unbiased opinion but which in reality are bought and paid for."[39] Section 17(b) has been held applicable to periodicals receiving compensation for favorable recommendations notwithstanding a challenge that such regulation violates First Amendment rights of free speech.[40]

§ 7.12 Multiple Defendants—Joint and Several Liability; Liability of Controlling Persons

Section 11(f) of the 1933 Act[1] provides that multiple defendants in section 11 actions are jointly and severally liable for the damages awarded with the exception of outside directors who did not have knowledge of the misstatements or omissions. Those outside directors are held to be accountable according to proportionate liability.

Consistent with the trend in common law negligence cases, the federal courts have recognized a right of contribution among joint tortfeasors.[3] The extent of this right to contribution is a matter of federal law.[4] In addition to section 11(f), section 18(b) of the 1934 Act[5] also provides for contribution among defendants in an action for false filings under section 18(a).[6] But what about liabilities arising under other sections of the securities acts? Although both the 1933 and 1934 Acts recognize joint and several liability of controlling

31. Crookham v. Crookham, 914 F.2d 1027 (8th Cir.1990) ($10,000 sanction).

34. 515 U.S.C.A. § 77q(b).

35. The SEC has used section 17(b) to go after touting schemes conducting over the Internet. *See, e.g.,* SEC v. Volmer, 34 Fed. Appx. 570 (9th Cir. 2002) (affirming judgment finding violations of § 17(b) for Internet touting).

36. 15 U.S.C.A. § 77q(b).

37. 15 U.S.C.A. § 77q(c).

39. H.R.Rep. No. 85, 73d Cong., 1st Sess. 24 (1933).

40. SEC v. Wall Street Publishing Institute, Inc., 851 F.2d 365 (D.C.Cir.1988).

§ 7.12

1. 15 U.S.C.A. § 77k(f).

3. Globus, Inc. v. Law Research Service, Inc., 318 F.Supp. 955 (S.D.N.Y.1970), *judgment affirmed* 442 F.2d 1346 (2d Cir.1971), *cert. denied* 404 U.S. 941, 92 S.Ct. 286, 30 L.Ed.2d 254 (1971).

4. Globus, Inc. v. Law Research Serv., Inc., 318 F.Supp. 955 (S.D.N.Y.1970).

5. 15 U.S.C.A. § 78r(b).

6. 15 U.S.C.A. § 78r(a). *See* § 12.19 *infra.*

persons,[7] there is silence on whether this liability is coupled with a right of contribution. Similarly, the Acts are silent as to the existence of a right to contribution in the event of joint and several liability arising out of joint activity. The right to contribution is distinct from any contractual agreement for indemnification.

The Supreme Court ruled that there is an implied right of contribution in actions under SEC Rule 10b–5 of the 1934 Act.[19] In so ruling, the Court distinguished cases decided under other federal statutes containing an express right of action but no right of contribution. The case against an implied right of contribution is stronger where Congress created a right of action but said nothing about a right to contribution. Although a number of decisions caution against the implication of additional federal remedies,[20] once the courts have recognized an implied right of action, then it is appropriate to flesh it out so as to render it a reasonable remedy.[21] Implying a right of contribution is consistent with this goal. The Court pointed out that sections 9(e) and 18(a) of the 1934 Act,[22] both of which contain an express right of action, provide for a right of contribution. The Court concluded that the similarities between sections 9(e), 18(a), and 10(b) justify the recognition of an implied right of contribution under Rule 10b–5.

Section 21D(f)(7) of the 1934 Act[27] establishes a settlement bar rule for pretrial settlements. If a defendant settles a claim prior to trial, the court is directed to enter a bar order which will preclude all future claims for contribution against the settling defendant arising out of the action.[28] The bar order is bilateral in that it prohibits not only contribution claims against the settling defendant, but also any contribution claims the settling defendant might have except against someone whose liability was extinguished by the settlement.[29] The rule barring contribution against settling defendants applies to actions brought under section 11 of the 1933 Act.[30] The Reform Act further provides that any judgment subsequently obtained against non-settling defendants shall be reduced by the greater of (1) an amount corresponding to the settling defendant's percentage responsibility or (2) the dollar amount paid by the settling defendant to the plaintiff.[31] The specific prohibitions of the Reform Act bar contribution for liability arising out of settlements even with regard to claims where a right of contribution might be found other under provisions of the securities laws.[32] Statutory controlling person liability adds a

7. 15 U.S.C.A. §§ 77*o*, 78r.

19. Musick, Peeler & Garrett v. Employers Insurance of Wausau, 508 U.S. 286, 113 S.Ct. 2085, 124 L.Ed.2d 194 (1993).

20. *See* § 12.2 *infra.*

21. *See* 508 U.S. at 292–293, 113 S.Ct. at 2088–89, relying on Virginia Bankshares, Inc. v. Sandberg, 501 U.S. 1083, 111 S.Ct. 2749, 115 L.Ed.2d 929 (1991) and Blue Chip Stamps v. Manor Drug Stores, 421 U.S. 723, 95 S.Ct. 1917, 44 L.Ed.2d 539 (1975).

22. 15 U.S.C.A. §§ 78i(e), 78r(a). *See* §§ 12.1, 12.19 *infra*

27. 15 U.S.C.A. § 78u–4(f)(7).

28. *Id. See* Harden v. Raffensperger, Hughes & Co., 933 F.Supp. 763 (S.D.Ind.1996) (proportionate share method requires assessing relative fault of each defendant and then limiting nonsettling defendant's share of damage to his or her degree of blameworthiness).

29. 15 U.S.C.A. § 78u–4(f)(7).

30. *See* In re Cendant Corp. Securities Litigation, 139 F.Supp.2d 585 (D. N.J. 2001).

31. 15 U.S.C.A. § 78u–4(f)(7).

32. *See, e.g.,* In re Cendant Corp. Securities Litigation, 139 F.Supp.2d 585 (D.N.J. 2001) (Litigation Reform Act precludes contribution after settlement even though contribution might otherwise be permitted under section 11 of the 1933 Act).

basis for secondary liability that is unavailable to plaintiffs in fraud actions that are not based on the securities laws.[33]

Section 15 of the Act[34] imposes joint and several liability upon controlling persons for the acts of persons under their control. Section 20 of the 1934 Act has a comparable provision.[36] Notwithstanding a slight difference in language, these two provisions have been interpreted similarly.[37]

Controlling person liability, which is highly factual, will not be imposed if "the controlling person had no knowledge of or reasonable grounds to believe in the existence of the facts by reason of which the liability of the controlled person is alleged to exist."[39] This defense would not be available under common law principles of vicarious liability under the doctrine of respondeat superior. The "lack of knowledge" defense to controlling person liability has been held to relate to the basic facts underlying the course of business; therefore, standing alone, lack of knowledge of the particular transaction does not preclude controlling person liability.[40] The burden of establishing the lack of knowledge defense falls on those persons charged with controlling person liability.[41] Although controlling person liability under the 1933 and 1934 Acts is generally the same, controlling person liability under the 1933 Act has been held not to require knowledge of the misstatements in question although such knowledge is required for controlling person liability under the 1934 Act.[42]

§ 7.13 Multiple Defendants—Aiding and Abetting; Conspiracy

§ 7.13[1] Aiding and Abetting Generally[1]

§ 7.13[1][A] Aiding and Abetting's Demise

Although the Supreme Court previously had reserved the question of whether a person can be held accountable for aiding and abetting, every circuit court which faced the issue had recognized aiding and abetting as a proper basis for liability under the section 10(b) and Rule 10b–5 of the 1934 Act—that Act's generalized antifraud provisions.[10] As discussed more fully below, most of these courts refused to recognize aiding and abetting liability under section 11 or section 12 of the 1933 Act even before it became clear that there is no implied remedy against aiders and abettors under the 1934 Act.

To the surprise of many observers, in 1993, the Supreme Court granted *certiorari* on this issue of whether there is an implied right of action for aiding

---

33. In re Miller, 276 F.3d 424, 429 (8th Cir.2002).

34. *See* 15 U.S.C.A. § 77*o*.

36. 15 U.S.C.A. § 78t(a).

37. *E.g.*, Farley v. Henson, 11 F.3d 827 (8th Cir.1993); Hollinger v. Titan Capital Corp., 914 F.2d 1564, 1578 (9th Cir.1990), *cert. denied* 499 U.S. 976, 111 S.Ct. 1621, 113 L.Ed.2d 719 (1991).

39. 15 U.S.C.A. § 77*o*.

40. San Francisco–Oklahoma Petroleum Exploration Corp. v. Carstan Oil Co., 765 F.2d 962 (10th Cir.1985). *But see* Durham v. Kelly, 810 F.2d 1500 (9th Cir.1987) (corporate president's wife exercised some control but not held liable since she did not induce the misstatements in question).

41. *See, e.g.*, Mecca v. Gibraltar Corp., 746 F.Supp. 338 (S.D.N.Y.1990).

42. In re Twinlab Corp. Securities Litigation, 103 F.Supp.2d 193 (E.D.N.Y.2000); Degulis v. LXR Biotechnology, Inc., 928 F.Supp. 1301, 1315 (S.D.N.Y.1996).

§ 7.13

1. The discussion in this section focuses on aiding and abetting as it applies to claims under the 1933 Act. There is a more extensive discussion of aiding and abetting in § 12.25 *infra*.

10. *See, e.g.*, Cleary v. Perfectune, 700 F.2d 774 (1st Cir.1983).

and abetting under Rule 10b–5 of the 1934 Act.[11] In light of the 1993 decision that there is an implied right of contribution under the securities laws,[12] coupled with the long history of judicial acceptance of aider and abettor liability, many believed it would be surprising if the Court did not recognize an implied action against aiders and abettors under Rule 10b–5.[13] Nevertheless, the Supreme Court in a five-to-four decision held that there is no implied right of action to redress aiding and abetting a Rule 10b–5 violation.[14] The Court limited its holding to private rights of action and perhaps to some SEC actions. The Court in *Central Bank* recognized that the general federal aiding and abetting statute[15] makes it a criminal offense to aid and abet any substantive criminal violation. The Court further pointed to the absence of a generalized securities statute creating aiding and abetting liability in SEC actions generally (although it has that authority in actions against broker-dealers)[16] nor in private suits. Finally, the Court refused to imply aiding and abetting liability on the basis of section 10(b)'s prohibition of conduct which "directly or *indirectly*" violates the Act.

Congress, in passing the Private Securities Litigation Reform Act of 1995, declined to overrule the Supreme Court's decision in *Central Bank* with respect to private actions. However, at the same time, the 1995 legislation gave the SEC the power to bring enforcement actions against persons who knowingly provide substantial assistance to primary violators of the securities laws.[20] Therefore, in enforcement actions aiders and abettors may be held liable to the same extent as controlling persons[21] in SEC actions so long as the requisite element of knowledge is shown. Even beyond the SEC's enforcement authority, to the extent that a primary violation can be alleged, liability may still be established for participating in the transaction.

§ 7.17 Special Rules and Procedures for Securities Class Actions

In 1995 and 1998, Congress amended the securities laws to implement additional requirements for securities class actions. There are parallel provisions applicable to litigation under the 1933 and 1934 Act. The discussion that follows discusses the procedures generally and the provisions that apply to actions under sections 11 and 12 of the 1933 Act.[1]

11. Central Bank of Denver v. First Interstate Bank of Denver, 508 U.S. 959, 113 S.Ct. 2927, 124 L.Ed.2d 678 (1993).

12. Musick, Peeler & Garrett v. Employers Insurance of Wausau, 508 U.S. 286, 113 S.Ct. 2085, 124 L.Ed.2d 194 (1993).

13. *See* § 12.25 *infra.*

14. Central Bank of Denver, N.A. v. First Interstate Bank of Denver, 511 U.S. 164, 114 S.Ct. 1439, 128 L.Ed.2d 119 (1994). *See* § 12.25 *infra.*

15. 518 U.S.C.A. § 2.

16. Under section 15(b)(4) of the Exchange Act, 15 U.S.C.A. § 78*o*(b)(4), the Commission is empowered to limit broker dealer registration based on willful aiding and abetting of the securities laws. Under section 21B of that Act, 15 U.S.C.A. § 78u–2, the Commission may issue civil penalties against broker-dealers who have aided and abetted a violation of the securities laws.

20. Section 20(f) of the 1934 Act, 15 U.S.C.A. § 78t.

21. Controlling person liability is considered in § 7.12 *supra* and § 12.24 *infra.*

§ 7.17

1. 15 U.S.C.A. §§ 77k, 77*l* which are discussed elsewhere in chapter 7. The impact of the amendments on 1934 Act class actions under rule 10b–5, the proxy rules, and the Williams Act are discussed in § 12.15 *infra.*

In the 1990s, there was increasing concern with the supposed abuses of class actions involving securities law violations. As a result, Congress responded with two sets of amendments to the securities laws which are designed to curb these abuses. First, Congress enacted the Private Securities Litigation Reform Act of 1995, which addresses many areas of private litigation, including procedural reforms, enhanced pleading standards, and increased protection for disclosures involving soft information and projections. These changes are discussed in this section and throughout this Treatise as appropriate. Many of the Reform Act provisions could be avoided by bringing suit in state court. Congress responded with the Securities Litigation Uniform Standards Act of 1998 which prevents most securities fraud based class actions from being brought in state court. The Uniform Standards Act is also discussed in this section.

§ 7.17[1] Private Securities Litigation Reform Act of 1995—Overview

As part of the Private Securities Litigation Reform Act of 1995,[3] Congress imposed some significant limitations on class actions brought under the securities laws. Section 27 of the 1933 Act[4] establishes special procedures necessary for instituting private actions under the securities laws and in the process purports to discourage frivolous lawsuits. The 1995 legislation was designed to curtail suspected abuses including the use of class actions to bring strike suits for the purpose of coercing a settlement of baseless claims. The Congressional reforms contained in the 1995 Reform Act cover a number of areas, such as restrictions on the class representative, limits on attorney's fees, pretrial discovery, and the burden of proof on some issues. A parallel provision was adopted for claims arising under the Securities Exchange Act of 1934.[6]

Section 27 of the 1933 Act[11] requires that a "lead plaintiff" be appointed as the representative party in all class action suits, presumably to encourage substantial investors to gain control of suits and discourage lawyer-driven suits.[13] The lead plaintiff and lead counsel provisions are part and parcel of the Reform Act's intent to prevent the "race to the courthouse" phenomenon sometimes associated with class actions which generally determine the lead plaintiff under the first to file rule. Not all aggressive attorney conduct in forming a class action will be improper.[15] However, the clear message of the act is to limit lawyer-driven suits.[16]

Section 27(b)(4) of the 1933 Act[82] provides that all discovery be stayed during the pendency of a motion to dismiss or motion for summary judgment

3. Pub. Law No. 104–67, 109 Stat. 737 (104th Cong. 1st Sess. December 22, 1995) (HR 1058).

4. 15 U.S.C.A. § 77z–1.

6. Section 21D, 15 U.S.C.A. § 78u–4. *See* § 12.25 *infra*.

11. 15 U.S.C.A. § 77z–1. *See also* 15 U.S.C.A. § 78u–4.

13. *See* 104 H.R. Conf. Rep. No–369, 104th Cong., 1st Sess. at 33 (1995) (stating that the rules were intended to "effectively discourage the use of professional plaintiffs").

15. Knisley v. Network Associates, Inc., 77 F.Supp.2d 1111 (N.D.Cal.1999) (offering to reimburse brokerage firms for sending notice of class action to customers was neither a violation of the Reform Act nor improper attorney conduct).

16. *See, e.g.,* In re Network Associates, Inc. Securities Litigation, 31 Sec. Reg. & L. Rep. (BNA) 1574 (N.D. Cal. 1999) (condemning lawyer's conduct in defining group of lead plaintiffs).

82. 15 U.S.C.A. § 77z–1(b)(4). *See* 1934 Act § 21D(b)(3)(B), 15 U.S.C.A. § 78u–4(b)(3).

in order to alleviate discovery expenses on defendants.[83] The discovery stay is mandatory, but may be avoided in instances where undue prejudice would otherwise result.

In order to dissuade abusive litigation, the Act requires that courts perform a mandatory review once there is a final adjudication[92] of the action in order to determine whether any party or attorney violated Rule 11(b) of the Federal Rules of Civil Procedure.[93] If a court finds that an attorney or party has engaged in improper conduct in violation of Rule 11(b), the statute directs the court to impose sanctions on the attorney or party pursuant to the rule unless convinced otherwise by the violator. Prior to the imposition of sanctions, the court must give the attorney or party notice and an opportunity to respond. A presumption in favor of awarding all attorney fees and costs incurred in the action arises when a party files a complaint in violation of Rule 11(b) and a presumption in favor of awarding the prevailing party attorney fees and costs incurred as a direct result of the violation arises when a party's responsive pleading or dispositive motion violates Rule 11(b). However, rebuttal evidence may be offered that an award of attorneys' fees and costs is unreasonable or that the Rule 11 violation was de minimis. If this defense fails, sanctions are to be imposed pursuant to requirements of Rule 11.

§ 7.17[2] Securities Litigation Uniform Standards Act of 1998—Preemption

The class action procedural reforms of the 1995 Reform Act applied only to class actions brought in federal court. Under the 1933 Act's general jurisdiction provision,[98] private actions under sections 11 and 12 of the Securities Act can be brought in either federal or state court. Additionally, state securities law and common law fraud were able to provide alternative state court forums for class action plaintiffs who could thereby avoid the provisions of the 1995 Reform Act. Congress largely eliminated these alternatives in the Securities Litigation Uniform Standards Act of 1998.[99]

In short, the Uniform Standards Act mandates that most class actions involving publicly traded securities be brought in federal court. The Act applies not only to actions under the federal securities laws, but also to most fraud-based[101] class action suits brought under state securities law as well.[102]

83. S. Rep. No. 104–98, 104th Cong., 1st Sess. at 14 (1995) (finding that discovery costs often force defendants to settle securities class action claims). The discovery stay is subject to two statutory exceptions. Discovery need not be stayed if particularized discovery is necessary to either preserve evidence or to prevent undue prejudice to the moving party.

92. The statutory command for a mandatory Rule 11 review at the end of the proceedings means at the end of the district court's adjudication of the matter; it does not include exhaustion of appellate remedies. *See* DeMarco v. Depotech Corp., 131 F.Supp.2d 1185 (S.D.Cal.2001).

93. Section 27 of the 1933 Act, 15 U.S.C.A. § 77z–1; Section 21D of the 1934 Act, 15 U.S.C.A. § 78u–4. Rule 11 sanctions are discussed in § 12.4[4] *infra*.

98. 1933 Act § 22(a), 15 U.S.C.A. § 77v(a) which is discussed in § 17.1 *infra*.

99. Pub. Law No. 105–353, 112 Stat. 3227 (105th Cong.–2d Sess. November 3, 1998) (S 1260).

101. The Uniform Standards Act does not preempt all state claims. Thus, for example, conversion is not fraud based and thus is not preempted. Burns v. Prudential Securities, 116 F.Supp.2d 917 (N.D.Ohio 2000). *See also, e.g.,* Falkowski v. Imation Corp., 309 F.3d 1123 (9th Cir. 2002), opinion amended by 320 F.3d 905 (9th Cir.2003) (action by employees claiming fraud in connection with stock options involved covered securities and thus were preempted by SLUSA and had to be brought in federal court).

102. 15 U.S.C.A. § 77p(b).

The fact that a complaint is based on federal securities fraud does not preclude a plaintiff from amending the complaint to drop the federal claims and proceed only with state claims that are not preempted by SLUSA.[116] In contrast, where the amended complaint is merely an attempt to disguise a securities fraud claim as something else, SLUSA's preemptive provisions apply.[117] Even a good faith attempt to state a non-securities claim will result in SLUSA preemption if the claim could also be stated as one based in securities fraud.[118]

---

116. *See, e.g.,* Schuster v. Gardner, 319 F.Supp.2d 1159 (S.D. Cal. 2003) (remanding state claims to state court).

117. *See, e.,g.,* Sparta Surgical Corp. v. NASD, Inc., 159 F.3d 1209 (9th Cir. 1998) (the amended complaint was not an attempt to clarify state law claims but rather was an attempt to manipulate a securities law claim in order to achieve a state court forum).

118. *See* U.S. Mortgage, Inc. v. Saxton, 494 F.3d 833, 843 (9th Cir. 2007) ("[D]istrict courts that have confronted the issue [of whether amendment should be allowed after SLUSA is found to apply] have also recognized the inequity of dismissing otherwise valid and viable state law claims on the ground that plaintiff pled—perhaps inadvertently—a cause of action that may [trigger SLUSA]. In light of the statutory silence on the issue in SLUSA, the existence of competing policy rationales, and the fact that the granting or denial of leave to amend is ordinarily a matter left to the discretion of the district court, we hold that SLUSA does not prohibit amendment of the complaint after removal."); *accord* Wells Fargo Bank v. Superior Court, 159 Cal.App.4th 381, 71 Cal.Rptr.3d 506 (1st Dist. 2008).

Chapter 8

STATE SECURITIES LAWS ("BLUE SKY" LAWS)

Table of Sections

§ 8.0 State Securities Laws in Context

Most of this treatise focuses on federal law. However, the first securities regulation in the United States took place at the state level. Even after federal securities regulation was introduced, the states continued to play an important role. Even after Congress eventually preempted much of the states' former authority to regulate securities offerings,[1] the states retain a significant role in many aspects of securities regulation.

§ 8.1 State Blue Sky Laws: Their Origins, Purpose, and Basic Coverage

§ 8.1[1] State Blue Sky Laws

This treatise is addressed primarily to the federal law of securities regulation. The emphasis on federal law should not be taken to indicate, however, that the states do not play a significant role in regulating securities transactions. In fact, state law represents the genesis of U.S. securities regulation. Securities regulation in this country began as a matter of state law, and it was not until twenty-two years after the first state securities law that Congress enacted federal securities regulation.[1]

The state legislatures entered the arena of securities regulation more than twenty years before Congress. In 1911, Kansas enacted the first American legislation regulating the distribution and sale of securities.[2] A number of states followed suit, and today every state has enacted a securities act. As

§ 8.0

1. National Securities Markets Improvement Act of 1996. Pub. L. No. 104–290, 110 Stat. 3416 (104th Cong., 2d Sess. 1996). *See* Securities Investment Promotion Act of 1996, S. Rep. 104–293, 104th Cong., 2d Sess.; Conference Report on National Securities Markets Improvement Act of 1996, H.R. 104–864, 104th Cong., 2d Sess.

§ 8.1

1. Kansas adopted the first state securities law in 1911 (Kans.Laws 1911, c. 133) which was twenty-two years before the enactment of the Securities Act of 1933.

2. Kans.Laws 1911, c. 133.

noted above, the statutes, which vary widely in their terms and scope, are commonly referred to as "blue sky" laws, an appellation with several suggested origins. It has been said, for example, that the Kansas legislature was spurred by the fear of fast-talking eastern industrialists selling everything including the blue sky. As stated early on by a court, the these state securities laws were designed to prevent "speculative schemes which have no more basis than so many feet of blue sky."[7]

Although federal legislation in 1996 significantly narrowed the influence of state securities laws with respect to the state registration of public offerings of securities,[10] state securities laws remain robust in many other areas may still be invoked with respect to various securities transactions. For example, even with respect to the offer and sale of securities, state law can still have significant impact in regulating fraudulent transactions. The state laws also remain important in regulating broker-dealers and investment advisers.

Unlike the federal securities regulation, the state securities acts generally permit a merit analysis of the investment before certain securities can be offered for sale within that state's borders. The states thus have what is known as a merit approach (at least with regard to some offerings of securities), which is in contrast to federal securities law's exclusive focus on full disclosure. State law merit regulation imposes a substantive scrutiny that goes further than the full disclosure approach of the federal laws. Under the registration by qualification, state securities administrators are empowered to look into the merits of the investment being offered.[14] The state acts also generally provide for a short form registration for securities of more established issuers and for an even simpler registration by coordination where the issue is being registered at the federal level with the SEC.[16] As is the case with the federal registration provisions, the state securities acts provide numerous exemptions.[17] Although many of the state securities acts do not cover broker-dealer regulation in detail, most of the state statutes at least require state registration or, at least, notification of federal registration as a broker-dealer. State securities law, in addition to requiring registration of broker-dealers, generally prohibits fraudulent practices in connection with distributions and other securities transactions.[19] Under merit regulation, the states may impose standards that are stricter than their federal counterpart. The National Securities Markets Improvement Act of 1996 preempts only registration requirements; it does not affect the ability of the states to pursue fraud in the sale of securities. Nor does it preclude the states from providing private remedies that may be broader than those available under federal law. These stricter standards may exist, for example, with regard to private actions or in describing the types of conduct prohibited.[20] As discussed elsewhere in this

7. Hall v. Geiger–Jones, 242 U.S. 539, 550, 37 S.Ct. 217, 220, 61 L.Ed. 480 (1917).

10. Pub. L. No. 104–290, 110 Stat. 3416 (1996). *See* § 8.1[2] *infra.*

14. Uniform State Securities Act § 304 (hereinafter cited as "Uniform Act"). Revised Uniform State Securities Act § 304 (hereinafter cited as "Revised Act"). *See* § 8.2 *infra.*

16. Uniform Act § 303; Revised Act § 303.

17. Uniform Act § 402, discussed in §§ 8.3–8.5 *infra.* Revised Act §§ 401–402. The federal exemptions from registration are discussed in chapter 4 *supra.*

19. Uniform Act §§ 201–204. *See id.* § 409 (criminal penalties); *id.* § 410 (civil liabilities). Many states also regulate investment advisers. *See* Bruce H. Saul, Registration of Investment Advisers Under State Law, 25 Rev.Sec. & Commod.Reg. 41 (1992); chapter 14 *infra.*

20. *See, e.g.,* Riley v. Merrill Lynch, Pierce, Fenner & Smith, Inc., 168 F.Supp.2d 1352 (M.D.Fla.2001) (preemption of certain class actions by the Securities Litigation Uniform Standards Act did not unduly restrict the states' ability to impose more stringent requirements).

treatise,[21] the Securities Litigation Uniform Standards Act of 1998[22] preempts many class actions based on securities fraud.

Section 18(b) of the 1933 Act, as enacted by the 1996 legislation, provides that a number of securities offerings will be exempted from state law regulation in terms of registration and reporting requirements.[64] Notwithstanding the curtailing of state law regulatory jurisdiction, state antifraud provisions are preserved. Section 18(b) precludes state regulation requiring registration or qualification of several categories of covered securities: securities listed on the New York Stock Exchange securities exempted from state registration and reporting requirements; parallel preemption exists with respect to securities traded on the American Stock Exchange or through the Nasdaq National Market System.[65] Although precluding substantive registration and reporting requirements by the states, the Act expressly preserves the states' right to require filing of documents solely for notice purposes.[66] This preservation of the states' authority to require notice filings has the effect of preserving state registration by coordination of the federal registration.[67]

The preemption of state registration requirements is not limited to the above-mentioned publicly traded securities. Under the 1996 amendments, a large number of federally exempt securities and transactions are now also exempted from state regulation.[68] Additionally, even for those securities and transactions not otherwise exempted from state regulation, sales to "qualified purchasers," as defined by the SEC, are exempted from state imposed registration and reporting requirements that go beyond the federal filings.[69]

The preemptive effect of the 1996 amendments can be summarized as follows. Most publicly offered securities which are registered federally cannot be regulated by the states beyond notice and/or coordinated filings. Many federally exempt transactions and securities are also preempted. The primary federal exemptions that are not preempted by the 1996 legislation are offerings subject to the intrastate exemption, and the section 3(b) exemptions (most notably, Regulation A and Rules 504 and 505 of Regulation D).[70] Also, transactions exempt under section 4(2)'s nonpublic offering exemption are not preempted unless they are in compliance with an SEC rule or regulation.[71] The logic behind the preemptive pattern seems to be that federally exempt transactions can result in state registration requirements only when the securities are offered to unsophisticated purchasers.[72]

Even though the legislative intent behind NSMIA was to preempt a great deal of state law regarding exempt transactions, most federally exempt

---

21. *See* § 7.17[2] *supra* and § 12.15[2] *infra*.

22. Pub. Law No. 105–353, 112 Stat. 3227 (105th Cong. 2d sess. November 3, 1998)(s 1260).

64. 15 U.S.C.A. § 77r.

65. Section 18(b)(1)(A), 15 U.S.C.A. § 77r(b)(1)(A).

66. Section 18(c)(2), 15 U.S.C.A. § 77r(c)(2).

67. Registration by coordination is discussed in § 8.2[3] *infra*.

68. Section 18(b)(4), 15 U.S.C.A. § 77r(b)(4).

69. Section 18(b)(3), 15 U.S.C.A. § 77r(b)(3). The SEC is empowered to define categories of qualified purchaser "consistent with the public interest and the protection of investors." *Id.*

70. The section 3(b) exemption and Regulations A and D are discussed in § 4.17, 4.19–4.22 *supra*. The section 3(a)(11) exemption is discussed in § 4.12 *supra*.

71. SEC Rule 506 is the safe harbor for the section 4(2) exemption.

72. *See* Temple v. Gorman, 201 F.Supp.2d 1238 (S.D.Fla.2002).

transactions may still need registration or an independent exemption under state law.

Chapter 9

SECURITIES EXCHANGE ACT OF 1934—REGISTRATION AND REPORTING REQUIREMENTS FOR PUBLICLY TRADED COMPANIES

Table of Sections

§ 9.1 The Securities Exchange Act of 1934—Overview of the Act

The Securities Exchange Act of 1934[1] addresses virtually all aspects of securities transactions and the securities markets generally. This broad scope of the Securities Exchange Act of 1934 is in contrast to the Securities Act of 1933, which is focused on distributions of securities. The Securities Act deals with securities distributions and imposes registration and disclosure requirements for those transactions in addition to providing exemptions from the registration requirements. The Securities Exchange Act has a much broader focus both with regard to transactions in securities and also with respect to regulation of the markets and the securities industry.

The Securities Exchange Act of 1934 governs day-to-day securities transactions as compared with simply initial and secondary distributions–the focus of the 1933 Act. The Exchange Act imposes registration and reporting requirements upon issuers of certain securities.[2] The Exchange Act also regulates securities dealers and other market professionals,[3] national securities exchanges,[4] and self-regulatory organizations such as the FINRA (former-

§ 9.1

1. 15 U.S.C.A. §§ 78a *et seq.*
2. 15 U.S.C.A. § 78*l*(g)(1). *See* 15 U.S.C.A. §§ 78n, 78*o*(d). *See* §§ 9.2–9.3 *infra.*
3. 15 U.S.C.A. §§ 78*o*, 78*o*–1. *See* § 14.3 *infra.*
4. 15 U.S.C.A. §§ 78f, 78q, 78s. *See* § 14.3 *infra.*

ly the NASD),[5] as well as municipal securities, municipal securities dealers,[6] and government securities dealers.[7]

Registration and Periodic Reporting Requirements for Publicly Traded Companies[8]

The Securities Exchange Act's registration and periodic reporting provisions with regard to securities and issuers, in turn, trigger other reporting and remedial provisions of the Act. For example, the Exchange Act regulates the solicitation of proxies with respect to reporting companies,[9] tender offers for securities of reporting companies,[10] insider short-swing profits,[11] manipulative practices regarding publicly traded securities,[12] and prohibitions against fraud in connection with the purchase or sale of a security.[13] In addition, the Act imposes annual and periodic reporting requirements upon securities required to be registered.[14] In addition to the foregoing regulation of publicly traded securities, the Exchange Act, through SEC Rule 10b–5,[15] prohibits fraud in connection with all securities transactions, regardless of whether they are publicly traded.

Market Regulation[16]

The Exchange Act is not limited to the regulation of issuers and their securities; the Act also focuses on the structure and operation of the securities markets. This market regulation encompasses regulation of the markets themselves, as well as of the broker-dealers who participate in those markets. With regard to the market system and the broker-dealer industry, the Exchange Act requires registration of all national exchanges, as well as all professional traders, dealers and brokerage firms that are members of these exchanges.[18]

The Securities Exchange Act created Securities and Exchange Commission (the "SEC") and is the organic statute governing the wide panoply of the SEC's administrative authority. Pursuant to the SEC's oversight responsibilities for exchanges and self-regulatory organizations,[19] the Commission operates as a licensing authority for broker-dealers and is empowered to prohibit unprofessional conduct.[20] It also sets minimum capital requirements for licensed brokers and dealers.[21]

5. 15 U.S.C.A. § 78*o*–3. *See* § 14.3 *infra*. The NASD is currently the only non-exchange self-regulatory organization. From time to time consideration has been given to the formation of a municipal securities dealers' association.

6. 15 U.S.C.A. § 78*o*–4. *See* § 14.6 *infra*.

7. 15 U.S.C.A. § 78*o*–5. *See* § 14.7 *infra*.

8. *See* §§ 9.2, 9.3 *infra*.

9. 15 U.S.C.A. § 78n. *See* §§ 10.1–10.9 *infra*.

10. 15 U.S.C.A. §§ 78m(d), (e), 78n(d), (e), (f). *See* §§ 11.1–11.12 *infra*.

11. 15 U.S.C.A. § 78p. *See* §§ 13.1–13.4 *infra*.

12. 15 U.S.C.A. §§ 78k, 78j. *See* chapter 5 *supra* and §§ 12.1, 14.3[6] *infra*.

13. 15 U.S.C.A. § 78j(b); 17 C.F.R. § 240.10b–5. *See* chapter 12 *infra*.

14. 15 U.S.C.A. §§ 78n, 78*o*. *See* § 9.3 *infra*. *Cf.* Edmund Kitch, The Theory and Practice of Securities Disclosure, 61 Brook. L. Rev. 509 (1995).

15. 17 C.F.R. § 240.10b–5. *See* chapter 12 *infra*.

16. *See* chapter 14 *infra*.

18. 15 U.S.C.A. §§ 78f, 78q, 78s. *See* § 14.3 *infra*.

19. 15 U.S.C.A. § 78*o*–3. *See* § 14.3 *infra*.

20. *See* chapter 14 *infra*.

21. 17 C.F.R. § 240.15c3–1.

SEC Rulemaking[22]

SEC rulemaking is limited not only by the statutory mandate of the organic legislation that grants the rulemaking power; it is also limited by the requirement that the rulemaking bear a reasonable relationship to the purposes underlying the statutory mandate. SEC rulemaking is not the only vehicle for the agency's impact on the law, as the SEC frequently makes law in its role as prosecutor by bringing cases that the Commission believes are likely to establish helpful precedent.[26]

§ 9.2 Registration of Securities Under the Securities Exchange Act of 1934

§ 9.2[1] Registration Requirements

Section 12(a) of the Exchange Act[1] makes it unlawful for any broker or dealer to effect any transaction in a security on a national exchange unless a 1934 Act registration has been effected for the security. Accordingly, all securities traded on a national exchange must be registered with the Commission. Registration under the 1934 Act in turn triggers the Act's periodic reporting requirements,[3] proxy regulation,[4] insider trading[5] and antimanipulation[6] prohibitions, as well as the regulation of tender offers.[7]

In addition to the above-mentioned registration, reporting, and other disclosure requirements for exchange listed securities, the Securities Exchange Act of 1934 also imposes registration requirements on certain over-the-counter securities. By virtue of section 12(g)(1) of the Exchange Act and Rule 12g–1, 1934 Act registration must be filed by issuers which have both a class of equity securities having more than five hundred shareholders of record[8] and more than ten million dollars in total assets.[9] Section 12 registration requirements cease when the registered securities have fewer than three hundred shareholders of record or when there are fewer than five hundred shareholders on the last day of each of the past three years.[13] In today's

22. SEC rulemaking authority and procedures are discussed in § 1.4[2] *supra*.

26. *See* Roberta S. Karmel, Creating Law at the Securities and Exchange Commission: The Lawyer as Prosecutor, 61 Law & Contemp. Probs. 33 (Winter 1998).

§ 9.2

1. 15 U.S.C.A. § 78*l*(a) (1976). The registration requirement is set forth in section 12(g). 15 U.S.C.A. § 78*l*(g). *See* Checklist for Registration of Securities Under Section 12(g) of the Securities Exchange Act of 1934, 25 Bus.Law. 1631 (1970).

3. *See* § 9.3 *infra*.

4. 15 U.S.C.A. §§ 78n(a)-(c). *See* chapter 10 *infra*.

5. 15 U.S.C.A. § 78p. *See* chapter 13 *infra*.

6. 15 U.S.C.A. § 78i. Section 9 applies only to those securities listed on a national exchange. *Id. See also* section 10 and section 18's express antifraud remedies for false SEC filings. 15 U.S.C.A. §§ 78j, 78r. *See* §§ 12.1, 12.19 *infra*.

7. 15 U.S.C.A. §§ 78m(d)-(e), 78n(d)-(f).

8. *See* SEC Rule 12g5–1, 17 C.F.R. § 240.12g5–1 (elaborating on the concept of record holder).

9. The statute requires registration for companies with assets of more than one million dollars but Rule 12g–1 exempts issuers with assets under ten million dollars. 15 U.S.C.A. § 78*l*(g)(1); 17 C.F.R. § 240.12g–1. The ceiling was raised from five to ten million in the Spring of 1996. *See* Sec. Exch. Act Rel. No. 34–37157, Relief From Reporting by Small Issuers (SEC May 9, 1996).

13. 17 C.F.R. § 240.12g–4(a).

environment, it is somewhat curious that section 12(g)(1) focuses on shareholders of record. With many shares being held by brokerage houses in street name and also depositories such as Cede Corporation and the Depositary Trust Company, the number of beneficial owners (each of whom makes his or her own investment decisions) far exceeds the number of shareholders of record.[15] Under current ownership patterns, it would appear that beneficial ownership is a better barometer of how widely held a company truly is. There are far more beneficial owners than registered owners and it is the beneficial owner that is entitled to the investor protection provisions of the securities laws.

Section 12(f) of the Exchange Act permits unlisted trading privileges through the medium of an exchange for securities listed on another exchange or traded in the over-the-counter markets.[16] Additionally under Rule 19c–3,[17] the SEC permits off-exchange trading of exchange-listed securities.[18]

Reporting and Disclosure Requirements

The issuer's disclosure and reporting obligations do not end with the filing of the Exchange Act registration statements. Exchange-listed securities, as well as those over-the-counter equity securities subject to section 12(g)(1)'s registration requirements,[45] incur periodic reporting obligations as established by section 13(a).[46] These periodic reports include the 10–K annual report[47] and the 10–Q quarterly report.[48] Also required on Form 8–K[49] are filings of certain specified material changes in the issuer's condition or operations.[50] Supplementing the interim disclosures required by Form 8–K are the requirements of the Sarbanes–Oxley Act[51] that there be disclosure on "a rapid and current basis" of information regarding material changes in financial condition or operations, which may include trend and qualitative information and graphic presentations, as the SEC determines is necessary or useful to investors and in the public interest.[52] Regulation FD,[53] adopted by the SEC in 2000, prohibits registered issuers from making selective disclosures to securities

15. *See* Issuer Restrictions or Prohibitions on Ownership by Securities Intermediaries, Sec. Exch. Act Rel. No. 34–50758, 69 Fed. Reg. 70852–01, 2004 WL 2787357 (SEC 2004).

16. 1934 Act § 12 (f)(1)(A), 15 U.S.C.A. § 78*l*(f)(1)(A).

17. 17 C.F.R. § 240.19c–3.

18. *See, e.g., See* Jeffry L. Davis & Lois E. Lightfoot, Fragmentation Versus Consolidation of Securities Trading: Evidence from the Operation of Rule 19c–3, 41 J.L. & Econ. 209, 236 (1998).

45. Over-the-counter equity securities that have more than 500 shareholders of record and whose issuers have more than $10 million in assets must be registered under the Exchange Act. 15 U.S.C.A. § 78*l*(g), 17 C.F.R. § 240.12g–1.

46. 15 U.S.C.A. § 78m(a); § 9.3 *infra*. *See* Davis v. DCB Financial Corp., 259 F.Supp.2d 664, 672 (S.D. Ohio 2003) (no implied remedy under section 13(a) of the 1934 Act); Gray v. Furia Organization, Inc., 896 F.Supp. 144 (S.D.N.Y.1995) (section 13(a)'s periodic reporting requirements do not support an implied private right of action).

47. 17 C.F.R. § 249.10–K. *See also* Form 10–KSB for small business issuers. 17 C.F.R. § 249.10–KSB.

48. 17 C.F.R. § 249.10–Q.

49. 17 C.F.R. § 249.8–K.

50. *See* 17 C.F.R. § 240.13a–11.

51. Sarbanes–Oxley Act of 2002, Pub. Law 107–204 (July 30, 2002).

52. 15 U.S.C.A. § 78m(*l*). There is no elaboration of the necessary timing to satisfy the "rapid and current basis" requirement. Also, the Act does not specify whether such disclosures must be made on Form 8–K, but they certainly may be made on that form.

53. 17 C.F.R. §§ 243.100–243.103. *See* Selective Disclosure and Insider Trading, Sec. Exch. Act Rel. No. 34–43154, 2000 WL 1201556 (SEC Aug. 15, 2000) (adopting release).

analysts. Regulation FD thus requires that any disclosures to analysts also promptly be made public and may be done through a Form 8–K[54] filing.

Beyond setting forth the periodic reporting requirements, 1934 Act registration triggers other disclosure provisions. By virtue of section 14(a),[59] all proxy material for registered securities must be filed with the Commission. Section 14(d) requires SEC filings of almost all tender offers to purchase equity securities subject to the registration and reporting requirements.[60] As discussed in more detail elsewhere, anyone who purchases five percent of any class of 1934 Act registered equity security must file a full disclosure as to the purpose of such acquisition pursuant to section 13(d).[61] The section 13(d) filing requirement applies to transactions that put the purchaser beyond the five percent threshold. Additionally, all purchases or sales of equity securities by officers, directors, and beneficial owners of ten percent of any registered class of equity security must be recorded in filed reports of such transactions pursuant to section 16(a).[62] Beyond any implied remedies that may exist under the Exchange Act,[63] investors who are injured in reliance upon materially misleading statements in filed documents may bring suit under section 18(a).[64] 2 Liability also exists for those engaging in manipulative conduct with regard to exchange-listed securities[65] and for insider short-swing profits in connection with the purchase and sale of securities registered under the 1934 Act [66]

§ 9.2[2] Exemptions From 1934 Act Registration Requirements

Section 12(g)(2)[83] of the Exchange Act sets forth exemptions from the Act's over-the-counter equity security registration requirements. Section 12(g)(1) does not apply to: (a) securities listed and registered on national securities exchanges as those securities must be registered under section 12(a); (b) securities of issuers that are registered under the Investment Company Act of 1940;[84] (c) securities of savings and loans, building and loans associations, and similar institutions subject to state or federal authority that represent other than non-withdrawable capital issued; (d) securities of not-for-profit, charitable issuers; (e) securities issued by "cooperative associations" as defined in the Agricultural Marketing Act;[85] (f) securities issued by certain other mutual or cooperative associations; (g) certain insurance company securities; and (h) certain employee stock-bonus, pension or profit-sharing plans.[86]

---

54. Item 7.01 of Form 8–K provides the appropriate forum for disclosures required by Regulation FD. 17 C.F.R. § 249.8–K, items 5, 9.

59. 15 U.S.C.A. § 78n(a). *See* Rule 14a–6, 17 C.F.R. § 240.14a–6(j); chapter 10 *infra.*

60. 15 U.S.C.A. § 78n(d). Issuer tender offers for its own shares are covered by section 13(e). 15 U.S.C.A. § 78m(e). *See* chapter 11 *infra.*

61. 15 U.S.C.A. § 78m(d). *See* §§ 11.1, 11. 8 *infra.*

62. 15 U.S.C.A. § 78p(a). *See* § 13.2 *infra.*

63. *See* chapter 13 *infra.*

64. 15 U.S.C.A. § 78r(a). *See* § 12.19 *infra.* This may be true more in theory than in practice as liability is generally promised under Rule 10b–5 rather than section 18(a).

65. 15 U.S.C.A. § 78i(e). *See* § 12.1 *infra.*

66. 15 U.S.C.A. § 78p(b). *See* chapter 13 *infra.*

83. 15 U.S.C.A. § 78*l*(g)(2).

84. *See* section 8 of the Investment Company Act of 1940, 15 U.S.C.A. § 80a–8; chapter 20 *infra.*

85. 12 U.S.C.A. §§ 1141 *et seq.*

86. 15 U.S.C.A. § 78*l*(g)(2).

§ 9.2[5] SEC's General Exemptive Authority

In 1996, Congress gave the SEC broad exemptive authority under the Securities Exchange Act of 1934. In 1996 Congress added section 36 of the Act, which provides that the Commission may exempt persons, transactions, or securities if in the public interest and consistent with investor protection.[110] The exemption may be granted by rule, regulation, or order.[111] In 1998, the Securities and Exchange Commission adopted Rule 0–12[112] of its rules of general application to set forth the procedures for processing requests for exemptive orders under section 36 of the 1934 Act. The procedure, which follows a parallel process under the Trust Indenture Act of 1939, leaves the SEC with the sole discretion whether or not to consider the application.[113] In addition, the Commission may decide to publish in the Federal Register the fact that the application for an exemption has been made. The notice will also indicate the earliest date that the application will be acted upon, which will be at least twenty-five days following the publication of the notice.

§ 9.2[6] Sarbanes–Oxley Act—Overview

The Sarbanes–Oxley Act of 2002,[114] which is discussed throughout this treatise where applicable, adopted comprehensive corporate governance reforms in response to various corporate scandals including those involving Enron and Worldcom. A significant aspect of the Sarbanes–Oxley Act is the inroads it makes into corporate governance—an area that had traditionally been reserved to the states and not directly addressed in the federal securities laws. For example, the Sarbanes–Oxley Act addressed many accounting and auditing reforms,[117] the role of public corporations' audit committees, increased accountability of executive officers, and attorneys (both in-house and outside counsel) representing public corporations. Sarbanes–Oxley also added increased criminal penalties for violations of the securities laws. The Sarbanes–Oxley Act created an accounting oversight board to oversee the accounting profession and to police the self-regulatory system that previously existed.[122] The Sarbanes–Oxley Act also addressed auditor independence requirements.[123]

Sarbanes-Oxley and Corporate Governance

Title III of the Sarbanes–Oxley Act addressed various corporate governance concerns including the audit committee, requiring personal certifications of accuracy by the chief executive and chief financial officers of public companies.[126] The Act further prohibits loans to high ranking executives,

---

110. 15 U.S.C.A. § 78mm(a).

111. This is in contrast to the parallel exemptive power under the 1933 Act, which is limited to exemptions by rule or regulations and does not include individualized orders. 1933 Act § 28, 15 U.S.C.A. § 77z–3. *See* § 4.35 *supra*.

112. 17 C.F.R. § 240.0–12.

113. 17 C.F.R. § 240.0–12.

114. Sarbanes–Oxley Act of 2002, Pub. Law 107–204 (July 30, 2002). *See* Senate Report No. 107–205 (July 3, 2002).

117. These are discussed in § 9.6 infra.

122. Sarbanes–Oxley Act of 2002, Pub. Law 107–204 tit. I (July 30, 2002). *See* § 9.6 *infra*.

123. Sarbanes–Oxley Act of 2002, Pub. Law 107–204 tit. II (July 30, 2002).

126. Sarbanes–Oxley Act of 2002, Pub. Law 107–204 tit. III (July 30, 2002).

subject to certain exceptions to be elaborated upon in SEC rulemaking. The Act also calls for enhanced financial disclosures by public companies.[127]

Enhanced Criminal Penalties

Titles VIII and IX of the Sarbanes Oxley Act[128] provide for enhanced criminal penalties for violations of the Act generally and in particular, for frauds perpetrated upon shareholders of public companies.

§ 9.3 Annual, Periodic, and Continuous Reporting Requirements for Public Companies

The Exchange Act's periodic disclosure and reporting obligations are found in section 13(a) of the Act.[13] SEC Rule 10b–5[14] is the Exchange Act's general antifraud prohibition. That rule prohibits fraud and material misstatements in connection with the purchase or sale of a security.[16] Rule 10b–5 does not by itself impose affirmative disclosure requirements absent some independent duty to disclose, such as one imposed by a line-item disclosure requirement of an applicable SEC required filing. Mere nondisclosure, absent an independent duty such as a line-item disclosure mandate, contemporaneous insider trading,[18] or some other collateral activity, is insufficient to establish a violation of Rule 10b–5.[19]

Quarterly and Annual Reports

Section 13(a)(2) of the Exchange Act[20] requires all issuers of equity securities subject to section 12's registration requirements[21] to file annual and quarterly reports and copies thereof as provided by the applicable SEC rules. When dealing with section 12(a) registrations (for securities traded on a national securities exchange), duplicate originals of the annual and quarterly reports must be filed with the securities exchanges on which the securities are listed. For all section 12 registrations, the issuer's first annual report must be filed for the fiscal year following the last full fiscal year reported in the section 12 registration statement.[22] Most issuers must pay a nonrefundable fee upon filing of the annual report.[23]

127. Sarbanes–Oxley Act of 2002, Pub. Law 107–204 tit. IV (July 30, 2002). *See* § 3.9[9] *infra*.

128. Sarbanes–Oxley Act of 2002, Pub. Law 107–204 tits. VIII, IX (July 30, 2002). *See also* § 9.3[2][D] *infra*.

§ 9.3

13. 15 U.S.C.A. § 78m(a).

14. 17 C.F.R. § 240.10b–5.

16. 17 C.F.R. § 240.10b–5. *See* § 12.3 *infra*.

18. *See* § 12.17 *infra*.

19. *See, e.g.,* Williams v. Dresser Industries, 120 F.3d 1163, 1173 (11th Cir.1997) (mere possession of material nonpublic information does not trigger a duty to disclose).

20. 15 U.S.C.A. § 78m(a) Additional affirmative disclosure requirements are discussed in § 12.19 *infra*.

Section 13(a)'s reporting requirements do not support an implied private right of action. *E.g.* Gray v. Furia Organization, Inc., 896 F.Supp. 144 (S.D.N.Y.1995).

21. 15 U.S.C.A. § 78d(a), (g)(1). *See* § 9.2 *supra*.

22. 17 C.F.R. § 240.13a–1.

23. 17 C.F.R. § 240.13a–1.The filing fee does not apply to annual reports for issuers registered Investment Company Act of 1940. These two acts are discussed in chapters 18 and 20 *infra*.

The Sarbanes–Oxley Act of 2002[24] accelerated the deadline for filing periodic reports under the 1934 Act.[25] The accelerated filing dates are being phased in. For the first year following these new rules, the annual report on Form 10–K must still be filed within 90 days of the end of the fiscal year. The due date for the Form 10–K filing is reduced to seventy-five days in the second year and to sixty days in the third and subsequent years. Following the new rules, quarterly reports on Form 10–Q continue to be due forty-five days after the end of the quarter for the first year, but this is reduced to forty days in the second year and to thirty-five days for the third and subsequent years. Additionally, effective without any phase-in periods are the new rules for reporting of insider transactions under section 16 of the Act.[26] Formerly, insider transactions had to be filed within ten days following the month in which the insider had a change in share ownership, but now those reports reflecting changes in beneficial ownership must be filed with the SEC by the end of the second business day after the day of execution of the transaction.[27]

The general form for annual reports of issuers subject to the Exchange Act's registration and reporting requirements is Form 10–K.[28] The Commission provides alternative forms for special situation issuers. For example, employee stock purchase, savings, and similar plans must use Form 11–K.[29] Form 18–K[30] is for securities issued by foreign governments and political subdivisions. Registered management investment companies use Form N–1R,[31] while small business investment companies are to file their annual reports on Form N–5R.[32]

SEC Rule 13a–13[33] sets out the Exchange Act's quarterly reporting requirements for issuers of registered securities, which are generally to be filed on Form 10–Q.[34] By virtue of Rules 13a–13(b) and (c),[35] the quarterly reporting requirements do not apply to either (1) investment companies filing quarterly reports under Rule 13a–12[36] or (2) foreign private issuers filing reports under Rule 13a–16[37] on Form 6K. Furthermore, certain life insurance companies need not complete Part I of Form 10–Q.[38]

Scaled Disclosure for Smaller Companies

In 1992, the SEC introduced a number of small business initiatives that were designed to facilitate registration and reporting from small business

24. Sarbanes–Oxley Act of 2002, Pub. Law 107–204 (July 30, 2002).

25. *See* http://www.sec.gov/news/press/2002–128.htm. *See also* SEC Approves Rules Advancing Deadlines for Quarterly, Annual, and Insider Reports, 34 Sec. Reg. & L. Rep. (BNA) 1451 (Sept. 2, 2002).

26. 15 U.S.C.A. § 78p. Section 16 is discussed in chapter 13 *infra*.

27. 15 U.S.C.A. § 78p(a)(4). *See* Ownership Reports, Sec. Exch. Act Rel. No. 34–46313, 2002 WL 1792168 (SEC Aug. 6, 2002).

28. 17 C.F.R. § 249.10–K; 4 Fed.Sec.Law Rep. (CCH) ¶ 31,101.

29. 17 C.F.R. § 249.11–K. *See* 4 Fed. Sec. L. Rep. (CCH) ¶ 31,151.

30. 17 C.F.R. § 249.11–K. *See* 4 Fed. Sec. L. Rep. (CCH) ¶ ¶ 32,001–32,004.

31. *See* 5 Fed.Sec. Law Rep. (CCH) ¶ 52,301.

32. *See* 5 Fed.Sec. Law Rep. (CCH) ¶ 51,481.

33. 17 C.F.R. § 240.13a–13.

34. 17 C.F.R. § 129.10–K, 4 Fed.Sec.Law Rep. (CCH) ¶ 31,031.

35. 17 C.F.R. § 240.13a–13(b), (c).

36. 17 C.F.R. § 240.13a–12.

37. 17 C.F.R. § 240.13a–16.

38. 17 C.F.R. § 240.13a–13(c).

issuers.[39] A small business issuer was defined as a company with revenues of less than twenty-five million dollars, provided that the aggregate market value of the issuer's voting stock held by non-affiliates does not exceed twenty-five million dollars.[40] Former Regulation S–B paralleled Regulation S–K as the basic disclosure guide for small business issuers. However, Regulation S–B was rescinded, effective , as were the former specialized disclosure forms, in favor of integrating the scaled disclosure requirements for smaller issuers into Regulation S–K.[41]

Electronic Filing of Reports

EDGAR electronic filings mean that investors can have easy online access to securities filings which is supplemented by information available through the company's website. In the summer of 2008, the SEC announced a new format to supplement EDGAR and eventually to replace EDGAR.[47] The new platform—Interactive Data Electronic Applications is known as IDEA. IDEA is designed to provide an interactive format and to provide more efficient and faster access to information filed with the Commission. It is planned that eventually IDEA will replace EDGAR but for the foreseeable future will simply be another way to access data.

Interim Reports

Beyond the quarterly reports, Rule 13a–10[48] requires issuers of registered securities to file interim reports in certain situations. Under the rule, whenever an issuer changes the term of its fiscal year, an interim report must be filed not more than one hundred and twenty days following the close of the interim period. Also, Rule 13a–2[49] defines the reporting requirements for issuers who are successors to issuers of section 12 registered securities. Additional interim reporting requirements are set forth in form 8–K.

Over the years, the SEC has moved closer to a system of continuous reporting. The most significant interim disclosures are required by 1934 Act Form 8–K which is discussed directly below. There also are disclosures required by various other events such as proxy solicitations,[50] tender offers,[51] and certain large purchases of a company's shares.[52]

In addition to the quarterly reporting requirements, section 13(a)(1) of the Exchange Act[53] provides that all issuers of registered securities shall file such additional current information as the Commission shall require to keep reasonably current all statements filed pursuant to section 12 of the Act.

39. *See* Sec. Act Rel. No. 33–6949, 6 Fed.Sec.L.Rep. (CCH) ¶ 72,439 (SEC July 30, 1992). *See* § 3.4[3][D] *supra*.

40. 17 C.F.R. § 240.12b–2.

41. *See* Smaller Reporting Company Regulatory Relief and Simplification, Sec. Act Rel. No. 33–8876, Sec. Exch. Act Rel. No. 34–56994, Trust Indenture Act Rel. No. 39–2451, 2007 WL 4440393 (SEC Dec. 19, 2007).

47. *See* http://www.sec.gov/spotlight/idea.shtml.

48. 17 C.F.R. § 240.13a–10.

49. 17 C.F.R. § 240.13a–2

50. 15 U.S.C.A. §§ 78n(a). *See* chapter 14 *infra*.

51. 10 U.S.C.A. §§ 78n(d), 78n(e). *See* chapter 13 *infra*.

52. 15 U.S.C.A. §§ 78m(d), 78m(e). *See* chapter 13 *infra*.

53. 15 U.S.C.A. § 78m(a)(1).

The specifically enumerated Form 8–K line-item disclosure requirements are supplemented by the requirement added in 2002 that there be disclosure on "a rapid and current basis" of information regarding material changes in financial condition or operations, which may include trend and qualitative information and graphic presentations, as the SEC determines is necessary or useful to investors and in the public interest.[61]

In March 2004, the SEC adopted several new items for Form 8–K's mandatory disclosure.[67] As a result of these additions, the required 8–K disclosures now include the following additional items:

- entry into a material non-ordinary course agreement;
- termination of a material non-ordinary course agreement;
- creation of a material direct financial obligation or a material obligation under an off-balance sheet arrangement;
- triggering events that accelerate or increase a material direct financial obligation or a material obligation under an off-balance sheet arrangement;
- material costs associated with exit or disposal activities;
- material impairments;
- notice of delisting or failure to satisfy a continued listing rule or standard; transfer of listing; and
- non-reliance on previously issued financial statements or a related audit report or completed interim review (restatements).

In addition to the foregoing new items, the SEC transferred two disclosure items in part from the periodic reporting requirements. Specifically, a Form 8–K disclosure must now be made for unregistered sales of equity securities and material modifications to rights of security holders. Also, the SEC expanded existing required Form 8–K disclosure with respect to departure of directors or principal officers, election of directors, or appointment of principal officers, and amendments to Articles of Incorporation or Bylaws and change in fiscal year.

The expanded Form 8–K disclosures include the following items:

Item 101 Entry into a Material Definitive Agreement

Item 1.02 Termination of a Material Definitive Agreement

Item 1.03 Bankruptcy of Receivership

Item 2.01 Completion of Acquisition or Disposition of Assets

Item 2.02 Results of Operations and Financial Condition

Item 2.03 Creation of a Direct Financial Obligation or Obligation Under an Off–Balance Sheet Arrangement of a Registrant

61. 15 U.S.C.A. § 78m(*l*). There is no elaboration of the necessary timing to satisfy the "rapid and current basis" requirement. Also, the Act does not specify whether such disclosures must be made on Form 8–K, but they certainly may be made on that form.

67. *See* Additional Form 8–K Disclosure Requirements and Acceleration of Filing Date, 69 Fed. Reg 15594–01, 2004 WL 577571 (SEC March 25, 2004); SEC Votes to Adopt Additional 8–K Requirements and to Propose Amendments to Form 20–F and Fund Manager Disclosure Requirements, SEC 04–31 (SEC news release March 11, 2004), available on Westlaw.

Item 204 Triggering Events That Accelerate or Increase a Direct Financial Obligation Under an Off–Balance Sheet Arrangement

Item 205 Costs Associated with Exit or Disposal Activities

Item 2.06 Material Impairments

Item 3.01 Notice of Delisting or Failure to Satisfy a Continued Listing Rule or Standard; Transfer of Listing

Item 3.02 Unregistered Sales of Equity Securities

Item 3.03 Material Modification of Rights of Security Holders

Item 4.01 Changes in Registrant's Certifying Accountant

Item 4.02 Non–Reliance on Previously Issued Financial Statements or a Related Audit Report or Completed Interim Review

Item 5.01 Changes in Control of Registrant

Item 5.02 Departure of Directors or Certain Principal Officers: Election of Directors; Appointment of Principal Officers

Item 503 Amendments to Articles of Incorporation or Bylaws; Change in Fiscal Year

Item 504 Temporary Suspension of Trading Under Registrant's Employee Benefit Plans

Item 505. Amendments to the Registrant's Code of Ethics, or Waiver of a Provision of the Code of Ethics

Item 506 Changes in shell company Status

Section 6 (Items 6.01–6.05) Relating to Asset–Backed Securities[71]

Item 7.01 Regulation FD Disclosure[72]

Item 8.01 Other Events (at the company's option)

The expansion of the items triggering a mandatory Form 8–K filing were accompanied by a limited safe harbor under 1934 Act section 10(b)[73] and Rule 10b–5[74] for failure to timely file seven of the new items on Form 8–K.

In addition to section 13's periodic reporting requirements, further disclosures are required by the Foreign Corrupt Practices Act amendments,[80] which have a very broad reach. The Foreign Corrupt Practices Act was designed to combat international corruption and bribery and contains substantive provisions aimed directly at this conduct. The Act also introduced related disclosure obligations under the Securities Exchange Act of 1934. The amendments to the Securities Exchange Act were so broadly drafted as to require neither foreign involvement nor corrupt practices.[82] Section 13(b)(2)[83] requires all issuers subject to section 12 or section 15(d) to:

---

71. Item 6.01 (ABS Informational and Computational Material); Item 6.02 (Change of Servicer or Trustee); Item 6.03 (Change in Credit Enhancement or Other External Support); Item 6.04 (Failure to Make a Required Distribution); and Item 6.05 (Securities Act Updating disclosure).

72. Regulation FD is discussed in § 12.19[4] *infra.*

73. 15 U.S.C.A. § 78j(b).

74. 17 C.F.R. § 240.10b–5. Rule 10b–5 is discussed in chapter 12 *infra.*

80. Pub.L. No. 95–213, 91 Stat. 1494 (Dec. 19, 1977). *See* § 22.2 *infra.*

82. *See generally* Program, Practical Implications of the Foreign Corrupt Practices Act of 1977, and Recent Developments, 35 Bus.Law. 1713 (1980).

(A) make and keep books, records, and accounts, which, in reasonable detail, accurately and fairly reflect the transactions and dispositions of the assets of the issuer; and

(B) devise and maintain a system of internal accounting controls sufficient to provide reasonable assurances that:

(i) transactions are executed in accordance with management's general or specific authorization;

(ii) transactions are recorded as necessary (I) to permit preparation of financial statements in conformity with generally accepted accounting principles or any other criteria applicable to such statement, and (II) to maintain accountability for assets;

(iii) access to assets is permitted only in accordance with management's general or specific authorization; and

(iv) the recorded accountability for assets is compared with the existing assets at reasonable intervals and appropriate action is taken with respect to any difference.

When initially adopted, these internal controls requirements were the subject of considerable controversy.[84] There were several proposals to reduce the scope of the internal controls requirements. However, as noted below, the SEC has increased the obligations, as did the Sarbanes–Oxley Act.[85]

§ 9.3[2][A] CEO and CFO Certification of SEC Filings

In the wake of the massive disclosure problems involving Enron and WorldCom, there was mounting pressure to hold corporate executives accountable for misleading disclosures. For example, the Senate unanimously passed a corporate fraud bill to enhance criminal penalties for corporate fraud;[169] that bill was enacted into law.[170] The SEC proposed to accelerate the due date for periodic reports.[171] The SEC also proposed quicker disclosures of certain insider transactions via Form 8–K.[172]

While the foregoing proposals were pending, the SEC issued an order requiring that CEOs and CFOs of over 900 public companies[173] make personal

83. 15 U.S.C.A. § 78m(b)(2).

84. *See, e.g.,* Mehren, Introduction to the Foreign Corrupt Practices Act of 1970 Law Procedures and Practices, 10 Inst.Sec.Reg. 65 (1979); Program, Practical Implications of the Foreign Corrupt Practices Act of 1977, and Recent Developments, 35 Bus.Law. 1713 (1980); Note, Effective Enforcement of the Foreign Corrupt Practices Act, 32 Stan.L.Rev. 561 (1980); Note, Accounting for Corporate Misconduct Abroad: The Foreign Corrupt Practices Act of 1977, 12 Corn.Int'l L.J. 293 (1979).

85. Sarbanes–Oxley Act of 2002, Pub. Law 107–204 (July 30, 2002).

169. Public Company Accounting Reform and Investor Protection Act of 2002, S. 2673, 107th Congress. *See* Public Company Accounting Reform and Investor Protection Act of 2002, Sen. Rep. No. 107–205 (July 3, 2002).

170. Sarbanes–Oxley Act of 2002, Pub. Law 107–204 (July 30, 2002).

171. *See* Acceleration of Periodic Report Filing Dates and Disclosure Concerning Website Access to Reports, Sec. Exch. Act Rel. No. 34–8089 (SEC April 12, 2002).

172. *See* Form 8–K Disclosure of Certain Management Transactions, Sec. Exch. Act Rel. No. 34–8090 (SEC April 12, 2002).

173. The Order applied to public companies with revenues of at least $1.2 billion in their last fiscal year. *See* Order Requiring the Filing of Sworn Statements Pursuant to Section 21(a)(1) of the Securities Exchange Act of 1934, SEC Order File No. 4–460, http://www.sec.gov/rules/other/4–460.htm (SEC June 27, 2002).

certifications under oath as to the accuracy of past Exchange Act filings.[174] The certification requirement increases CEO and CFO accountability by allowing for criminal sanctions in the event that there are false affirmations of accuracy. Among other things, the certification requirements make clear what should have been apparent under prior law–that a public company's chief executive officer must be sufficiently knowledgeable and sophisticated so as to enable him or her to understand financial statements.

In essence, the certification requirement deprives these high ranking officers of a deniability defense to false filings. It is noteworthy that the certification requirement was imposed by order rather than by formal SEC rulemaking. Among other things, the SEC order was effective immediately which would not have been the case had the Commission resorted to the formal rulemaking procedures. The imposition of the certification requirement without resort to formal rulemaking procedures did not occur without objection.[177] However, the certification requirement was implemented and subsequently codified into far-reaching amendments to the securities laws that occurred in the summer of 2002.[178]

The Sarbanes–Oxley Act codifies the certification requirements by mandating that the SEC adopt rules requiring that public companies' principal executive and financial officers certify in each annual and quarterly report (1) that these officers have reviewed the report, (2) that, based on their knowledge, the report does not contain any untrue statement of material fact or omit any material fact necessary to make the statements, in light of the circumstances in which they were made, not misleading, (3) that, based on their knowledge, the financial statements and information contained in the report fairly present, in all material respects, the financial condition and results of operations of the company and (4) various disclosures relating to the company's internal controls.[180] The certification provisions require that the certification state that in all material respects the financial statements "fairly present" the company's financial condition, results of operations and cash flows. This means that there are now two standards for the financial statements. First, they must conform to Generally Accepted Accounting Principles (GAAP) and second they must satisfy this "fairly presents" standard. It does not necessarily follow that these are two different standards, however, as the "fairly presents" language is consistent with that generally found in accounting firms' audit letters.

Certification of SEC filings does not create strict liability for all misstatements in the filing.[187] As with other misrepresentations under Rule 10b–5, civil liability for a false certification requires a showing of scienter.[188] Thus, in

174. *See* Order Requiring the Filing of Sworn Statements Pursuant to Section 21(a)(1) of the Securities Exchange Act of 1934, SEC Order File No. 4–460, http://www.sec.gov/rules/other/4–460.htm (SEC June 27, 2002).

177. *See* Lawyers Question SEC's Use of § 21(a) to Impose CEO Certification Requirement, 34 Sec. Reg. & L. Rep. (BNA) 1185 (July 22, 2002).

178. Sarbanes–Oxley Act of 2002, Pub. Law 107–204 (July 30, 2002).

180. 15 U.S.C.A. § 7241.

187. *Cf.* In re Hypercom Corp. Securities Litigation, 2006 WL 1836181 (D.Ariz. 2006) (failure to conduct internal audit after company recognized absence of effective internal controls and consequential improper accounting was not evidence that the chief financial officer acted with scienter when certifying the company's internal controls).

188. Central Laborers' Pension Fund v. Integrated Electrical Services Inc., 497 F.3d 546 (5th Cir. 2007) (failure to allege scienter of officers signing Sarbanes–Oxley's required certifications).

addition to the falsity of the underlying financial report, the plaintiff must allege that the certifying officer knew of the falsity or else acted in reckless disregard of the truth.[189] On the other hand, the certification may provide evidence that the certifying officer acted with scienter with respect to the false statements.[190] However, the fact that an officer made the certification with respect to misleading financials is not sufficient to establish scienter.[191] Specific criminal penalties are imposed for CEOs and CFOs who knowingly file false certifications.[192] In addition to criminal penalties, the Act requires disgorgement of executive compensation that was not properly reported. Specifically, if a company is required to restate its financials due to "material noncompliance of the issuer, as a result of misconduct" with reporting requirements, the CEO and CFO must reimburse the company for (1) any bonus or other incentive-or equity-based compensation received during the 12 months following the first public release of the document containing the financials which were later restated and (2) any profits from the sale of securities during those 12 months.[193]

§ 9.3[2][B] Periodic Review of Company Filings

The Sarbanes–Oxley Act also requires the SEC to review a reporting company's periodic disclosures systematically and at least once every three years.[195] The factors the SEC must consider in determining the frequency of review include whether the company has made a material restatement,[196] significant stock price volatility, companies with the largest market capitalization, being an emerging company with "disparities in price-earnings ratios" or having operations which significantly affect material sectors of the economy.[197]

§ 9.3[2][C] Executive Officer Loans Prohibited

Another requirement imposed by the 2002 legislation is the prohibition of most loans to corporate officials. As enacted by section 402 of the Sarbanes–Oxley Act,[199] section 13(k) of the 1934 Act prohibits loans by a company to directors and executive officers, but there are exceptions for limited categories

189. *See, e.g.*, Hall v. The Children's Place Retail Stores, Inc., 2008 WL 2791526 at *9 (S.D.N.Y.) ("for these certifications to be materially false, it is insufficient for the financial statements themselves to have been false-defendants must also have had knowledge of that falsity" and then finding plaintiff's allegations were sufficient with respect to certifications in case involving options backdating).

190. *See, e.g.*, In re Ramp Corp. Securities Litigation, 2006 WL 2037913 (S.D.N.Y. 2006) (insufficient allegations of loss causation with respect to audit and allegations relating to management integrity) (upholding Rule 10b–5 complaint based on certification).

191. Garfield v. NDC Health Corp., 466 F.3d 1255 (11th Cir. 2006) (the certification required by Sarbanes–Oxley Act "is only probative of scienter if the person signing the certification was severely reckless in certifying the accuracy of the financial statements"; merely signing the certification was not evidence of scienter).

192. 18 U.S.C.A. § 1350 (up to $1 million and ten years in prison for a false certification; up to $5 million and twenty years in prison for "willfully" making a false certification).

193. 15 USCA § 7243. The Act does not specify the applicable standard of culpability–namely whether negligence is sufficient or alternatively whether knowing misconduct is required.

195. 15 U.S.C.A. § 7266.

196. *See* the SEC's guidance on restatement of financials in SEC Staff Accounting Bulletin No. 108, No. SAB–108, 2006 WL 2689624 (SEC Sept. 13, 2006).

197. 15 U.S.C.A. § 7266.

199. Sarbanes–Oxley Act of 2002, Pub. Law 107–204 (July 30, 2002) § 402, amending section 13 of the 1934 Act, 15 U.S.C.A. § 78m.

of loans issued in the ordinary course of the company's business for existing loans, so long as they are not renewed or materially modified.[200] Section 402 has aptly been described as "an unusual federal override of state corporate law concerning internal corporate affairs."[201]

Also, questions have been raised as to the extent to which the loan prohibition will have possible unintended consequences. For example, the provision may come into play with respect to cashless stock option exercises and in many other situations, such as when a company makes an advance payment of indemnification for its officers and directors to pending litigation. Since in many cases the payment is contingent on a successful resolution of the underlying litigation, the advance could be viewed as a loan in violation of section 13(k) of the Exchange Act. However, there is some authority to support the view that a bona fide advance is not a loan subject to the Sarbanes–Oxley Act's prohibition on loans.[206] Other types of arrangements that may be implicated by section 402's prohibition on loans include "split dollar" insurance arrangements[207] and officers' personal expenses that are charged to company credit cards.[208]

§ 9.3[2][E] Forfeiture of Certain Bonuses and Profits

Section 304 of the Sarbanes–Oxley Act[216] requires disgorgement of certain payments to the CEO or CFO. Specifically, when a company issues an accounting restatement as a result of material noncompliance with the disclosure and accounting requirements, the company's CEO and CFO must disgorge any bonuses or incentive-based compensation during the twelve-month period following the filing of the disclosures that were subsequently restated.[217] In addition the CEO and CFO must disgorge any profits realized from the sale of company securities during that twelve-month period.[218] On their face, these disgorgement provisions do not require that either the CEO or CFO have culpability for the noncompliance in question.[219] Also, the SEC is given the authority to provide exemptions from these disgorgement provisions.[220] Although the statute explicitly empowers the SEC to pursue disgorgement, it is silent on whether the prohibition on loans may be enforced by a private party. Keeping in line with the general approach to implied reme-

200. 15 U.S.C.A. § 78m(k).

201. 4 Alan R. Bromberg & Lewis D. Lowenfels on Securities Fraud § 7:428 (2d ed. Westlaw database updated May 2008).

206. *See* Envirokare Tech, Inc. v. Pappas, 420 F. Supp.2d 291 (S.D.N.Y. 2006) (Sarbanes–Oxley Act did not prohibit advancing defense expenses to CEO).

207. *See, e.g.,* John D. Dadakis And Scott H. Jacobs, Split–Dollar Life Insurance and the Sarbanes–Oxley Act, N.Y.L.J. p.4, col.4 (Jan. 31, 2003); Arthur D. Postal Will SEC Exempt Split–Dollar From Ravages Of Sarbanes–Oxley Loan Rules? 14 Insurance Chronicle p.3 (Jan. 13, 2003).

208. 2 Robert J. Haft, Venture Capital and Small Business Financings § 12:64 (2008).

216. Sarbanes–Oxley Act of 2002, Pub. Law 107–204 § 304 (July 30, 2002), codified in 15 U.S.C.A. § 7243.

217. 15 U.S.C.A. § 7243(a)(1). *See also, e.g.,* John Patrick Kelsh, Section 304 of the Sarbanes–Oxley Act of 2002: The Case for a Personal Culpability Requirement, 59 Bus. Law. 1005 (2004).

218. 15 U.S.C.A. § 7243(a)(2).

219. It has been suggested, however, that culpability should be a prerequisite of the disgorgement obligation. *See* John Patrick Kelsh, Section 304 of the Sarbanes–Oxley Act of 2002: The Case for a Personal Culpability Requirement, 59 Bus. Law. 1005 (2004).

220. 15 U.S.C.A. § 7243(b).

dies,[221] there is no basis for implying a private right of action to enforce section 304's disgorgement provisions.[222]

§ 9.4 Disclosure Guidelines—Regulation S–K

§ 9.4[1] Background of Regulation S–K

As discussed throughout this treatise, the SEC administers and oversees two parallel disclosure systems.[1] The Securities Act of 1933 (the "1933 Act"), which focuses on the registration of public offerings and the Securities Exchange Act of 1934 (the "1934 Act"), which imposes registration and periodic reporting requirements on mostly publicly held companies.[2] These are two parallel systems that when followed, often created duplicative filings and superfluous paperwork. Although the duplicative disclosures were often "provided at different times and under different circumstances, disclosure under both Acts flowed from a common core of information."[3] Accordingly, many observers believed that the repetitive nature of the dual filing system was a thorn in the side of corporate activity, and one that needed to be remedied by a thoughtful and measured approach.

The idea of integrated and hence more efficient disclosure was first noted in 1966, by Milton H. Cohen, when he wrote the article, *Truth in Securities Revisited*,[7] wherein he suggested emphasizing the 1934 Act reporting requirements and at the same time eliminating many of the duplicative disclosures formerly required by the 1933 Act. Focusing on periodic reporting, rather than emphasizing one-time disclosures in connection with public offerings, appeared to be in the best interest of investor protection.[9]

In adopting Regulation S–K,[15] the Commission was trying to ease the burden of duplicative disclosures and "sought to define (1) what information is material in securities transactions, and (2) when and how such information should be disclosed to investors and the market."[16] It was determined that much of the same information that was material under one Act was also going to be material under the other. Further, the Commission concluded that the amount and nature of the disclosure required was inextricably tied to the investors' pre-existing knowledge and familiarity with the security involved. It was with this backdrop that the Commission adopted Regulation S–K.

---

221. *See* § 12.2 *infra.*

222. *E.g.*, Pirelli Armstrong Tire Corp. Retiree Medical Benefits Trust v. Raines, 534 F.3d 779, 793 (D.C. Cir. 2008) ("The problem is that § 304 does not create a private right of action. And contrary to the suggestion in plaintiffs' brief, which relies on 1970s-era cases, courts today rarely create implied private rights of action; courts generally deem it Congress's prerogative to make that decision").

§ 9.4

1. *See, e.g.*, § 3.4 *supra.*

2. *See* §§ 9.2, 9.3 *supra.*

3. Michael McDonough, Death in One Act: The Case for Company Registration, 24 Pepp. L. Rev. 563, 585 (1997) (quoting Harold S. Bloomenthal et al., Securities Law Handbook 23, 60–61 (1995)).

7. Milton H. Cohen, "Truth in Securities" Revisited, 79 Harv.L.Rev. 1340 (1966).

9. *See* Michael McDonough, Death in One Act: The Case for Company Registration, 24 Pepp. L. Rev. 563, 587 (1997).

15. 17 C.F.R. §§ 229.10–229.915.

16. Gerald S. Backman & Stephen E. Kim, A Cure For Securities Act Metaphysics: Integrated Registration, Insights, May 1995, at 18, 19.

§ 9.4[2] Overview of Regulation S–K

§ 9.4[3] Structure of Regulation S–K

Regulation S–K is divided into ten subparts (Subpart 1—Subpart 1000). Subpart 1 sets out the Commission's procedures on two volitional disclosure issues—projections or forward looking statements and security ratings. Subpart 100 itemizes disclosures regarding the business of the registrant, while Subpart 200 sets forth disclosure requirements for the registrant's securities. Subpart 300 provides guidance for disclosing information regarding the registrant's financial information, and Subpart 400 deals with management and certain security holders. Subpart 500 requires disclosure concerning the issuer's registration statement and prospectus, while Subpart 600 lists required exhibits to various filings. Subpart 700 provides for "miscellaneous" disclosures regarding unregistered securities and indemnification of directors and officers. Subpart 800 speaks to the industries guide for the 1933 Act and 1934 Act Filings, and Subpart 900 articulates disclosure responsibilities concerning roll-up transactions. Subpart 1000, which was adopted as Regulation M–A, applies to mergers and acquisitions.

§ 9.6 Accounting and Auditing Requirements

§ 9.6[1] Accounting Requirements

§ 9.6[1][A] Financial Matters Generally; Accounting Standards

In addition to its disclosure requirements, the Exchange Act imposes numerous financial reporting and accounting requirements. Regulation S–X[2] sets forth the SEC's accounting rules for the preparation of SEC filings and the audited financial statements required by the 1933 and 1934 Acts. The Commission's general approach to financial reporting has been to rely upon Generally Accepted Accounting Principles (GAAP) and Generally Accepted Auditing Standards (GAAS). Generally Accepted Accounting Principles are adopted by the Federal Accounting Standards Board (FASB). Generally Accepted Auditing Standards are adopted by the American Institute of Certified Public Accountants (AICPA). Particularly, it has been observed that the General Accounting Practice does not consist of a rigid set of rules, but rather encompasses a range of reasonable alternative treatments.

As a result of the Sarbanes–Oxley Act of 2002,[5] a company's CEO and CFO must make personal certifications with respect to the company's financial information. Specifically, the Act requires that company CEOs and CFOs personally certify that the financial statements "fairly present" the company's financial condition, results of operations, and cash flows.[6] It is likely that this is simply a reaffirmation of the statements' accuracy rather than a standard to be applied in addition to GAAP and GAAS, since the "fairly

§ 9.6

2. 17 C.F.R. §§ 210.1–01–210.12–29. *See also* 17 C.F.R. §§ 256.00–1–256a.37 (Uniform System of Accounts for Mutual Service Companies and Subsidiary Service Companies under the Public Utility Holding Company Act of 1935). The Public Utility Holding Company Act is discussed in chapter 18 *infra*.

5. Sarbanes–Oxley Act of 2002, Pub. Law 107–204 (July 30, 2002). *See also* the discussion below.

6. 15 U.S.C.A. § 7241. *See* § 9.3[2] *supra*.

presents" language that is found in the Sarbanes–Oxley Act is consistent with that generally found in accounting firms' audit letters. The requirement that the auditor certify that the financials "fairly present" the true picture is not limited to quantitative data but applies as well to a qualitative analysis of the financials.[7]

The Commission believes that departures from GAAP can be harmful to investors. The SEC has cautioned against the use of pro forma financial information that varies from Generally Accepted Accounting Practices. The SEC explained that although pro forma financial information can be useful to investors, it can be misleading, and therefore, harmful, if it differs from the results that would be announced under GAAP accounting.[8] There have been a number of massive investigations resulting from accounting irregularities in recent years. One consequence was the proposal that there be more regulatory oversight of the accounting profession. In 2002, this became law as part of the Sarbanes–Oxley Act,[11] which created the Public Company Accounting Oversight Board.[12] The five-member Public Company Accounting Oversight Board is charged with the obligation of overseeing the auditing of public companies and adopting auditing, quality control, ethics, independence, and other standards regarding auditing.[13] The Act further requires the Oversight Board to adopt rules relating to work paper retention, second audit partner review and approval of audit reports, and testing by auditors of companies' internal control systems (with a report to be contained in the audit report on the auditors' findings and evaluation of these systems). It is illegal for an accounting firm to audit public companies unless the accounting firm is registered with the Board.

The Sarbanes–Oxley Act directed the SEC to adopt rules providing that 10–Ks and 10–Qs are to disclose all material off-balance sheet transactions, arrangements, obligations (including contingent obligations) and other relationships with unconsolidated entities and others that may have a current or future material effect on the financial condition, changes in financial condition, results of operation, liquidity, capital expenditures, capital resources or significant components of revenues or expenses.[14]

The Sarbanes–Oxley Act also mandates that the SEC promulgate rules requiring that pro forma financial information included in SEC reports or press releases be presented so as to (1) not be misleading and (2) reconcile the pro forma information with the financial condition and results of operations of the company under GAAP.[15]

---

7. *See, e.g.,* In the Matter of KPMG, LLP, Sec. Exch. Act Rel. No. 34–50564, Release No. AE–2125, 2004 WL 2359310 (SEC 2004) (As part of settlement, KPMG agreed to censure and $10 million payment to the issuer's shareholders).

8. Sec. Act Rel. No. 33–8039, Sec. Exch. Act Rel. No. 34–45124, Rel. No. FR–59, 2001 WL 1545743 (SEC Dec. 4, 2001).

11. Sarbanes–Oxley Act of 2002, Pub. Law 107–204 (July 30, 2002).

12. 15 U.S.C.A. § 7211. *See, e.g.,* Elliott J. Weiss, Some Thoughts on an Agenda for the Public Company Accounting Oversight Board, 53 Duke L.J. 491 (2003).

13. The statutory authorization of the PCAOB, which was established by the Sarbanes–Oxley Act of 2002, was challenged as in supposed violation of the separation of powers. However, a divided three-judge panel upheld the stator scheme. Free Enterprise Fund v. Public Company Accounting Oversight Board, 537 F.3d 667, 669 (D.C. Cir. 2008).

14. 15 U.S.C.A. § 78m(j). The Sarbanes–Oxley Act mandates a study to improve the transparency of reporting of off-balance sheet items.

15. Sarbanes–Oxley Act of 2002, Pub. Law 107–204 § 401(July 30, 2002).

The SEC adopted rules implementing section 404 of the Sarbanes–Oxley Act[18] mandate to require that a company's annual report address (1) management's responsibility for establishing and maintaining an adequate system of internal controls for financial reporting and (2) management's year-end assessment of the internal control system's effectiveness.

Also, the auditors must attest to and report on management's assessment of the internal controls' effectiveness in accordance with standards established by the Public Company Accounting Oversight Board. The SEC rules as adopted specify the details of the required statement and auditor certification.[21]

Since its enactment in 2002, there has been considerable controversy concerning the burdens that the Sarbanes–Oxley Act's heightened disclosure and compliance requirements impose on public companies. Sarbanes–Oxley was drafted with the massive frauds in large companies such as Enron, Worldcom, and Tyco. Therefore, a different cost benefit analysis may be appropriate when considering the Act's impact on smaller companies. The SEC has acknowledged the need to evaluate the Sarbanes–Oxley Act's impact on smaller companies. For example, in 2006, the SEC's advisory committee on smaller public companies issued a request for comments on its preliminary proposal to provide relief from some of the Sarbanes–Oxley requirements for smaller public companies, including section 404's internal controls requirements.[24] It was thus suggested, for example, that smaller companies be given relief from Section 404 of the Sarbanes–Oxley Act. However, the SEC's exemptive authority under the securities laws applies only to those laws, and Section 404 is not codified as part of the securities laws.[25] In the spring of 2006, the SEC announced that it would not exempt companies from section 404, but it would provide guidance to make compliance easier.[26] In August 2006, the SEC announced the promised relief in the form of: 1) Relief from Section 404 Compliance Dates for Smaller Companies (Non–Accelerated Filers); 2) Relief from Section 404(b) Compliance Date for Certain Foreign Private Issuers; and 3) Proposed Transition Relief for Newly Public Companies.[27] In 2007, the SEC offered additional guidance[28] and the Public Company Accounting Oversight Board proposed guidance in auditing standard number 5 that would further address audit standards regarding internal controls.[29]

---

18. Sarbanes–Oxley Act section 404, Pub. L. 107–204, 116 Stat. 745 (2002). 15 U.S.C.A. § 7262.

21. *See* SEC News Digest 2003–101, 2003 WL 21223853 (SEC May 28, 2003).

24. *See* Exposure Draft of Final Report of Advisory Committee on Smaller Public Companies, Sec. Act Rel. No. 33–8666, Sec. Exch, Act Rel. No. 34–53385, 71 Fed. Reg. 11090–01, 2006 WL 501877 http://www.sec.gov/rules/other/33–8666.pdf (SEC Feb. 28, 2006).

25. As was pointed out in a letter sent by a group of law professors (including the author) to SEC Chairman Cox, the Sarbanes–Oxley Act does not grant the SEC exemptive authority and since section 404 of Sarbanes–Oxley is not part of the Securities Exchange Act, the SEC's exemptive authority under section 36(a) of that Act does not apply.

26. *See* SEC Announces Next Steps for Sarbanes–Oxley Implementation, SEC Press Rel. 2006–75, http://www.sec.gov/news/press/2006/2006–75.htm (SEC May 17, 2006).

27. Internal Control Over Financial Reporting in Exchange Act Periodic Reports of Foreign Private Issuers that Are Accelerated Filers, Sec. Act Rel. No. 33–8730, Sec. Exch. Act Rel. No. 34–54294, 2006 WL 2285552 (SEC Aug. 9, 2006).

28. *See* Commission Guidance Regarding Management's Report on Internal Control Over Financial Reporting Under Section 13(a) or 15(d) of the Securities Exchange Act of 1934, Sec. Act Rel. No. 33–8810, Sec. Exch. Act Rel. No. 34–55929, 2007 WL 1791162 (SEC June 20, 2007).

29. *See* Public Company Accounting Oversight Board; No. 5, an Audit of Internal Control Over Financial Reporting that is Integrated with an Audit of Financial Statements, and Related

Occasionally, the SEC has adopted different accounting standards for use in its disclosure documents.[30] The extent of an auditor's compliance with GAAS and GAAP is relevant in determining the scope of liability for material[31] misstatements or omissions. Failure to follow GAAP or best practices will not, however, be sufficient to establish scienter.[33] Significantly more than a failure to follow proper procedures is required to establish scienter. A reckless or intentional failure to comply with applicable accounting standards can result in significant liability.[34]

§ 9.6[1][D] Non–GAAP Financial Measures

Section 401 of the Sarbanes–Oxley Act[89] directed the SEC to adopt rules addressing public companies' disclosure or release of certain financial information that is calculated and presented on the basis of methodologies other than in accordance with generally accepted accounting principles. In response, the SEC adopted a new disclosure regulation, Regulation G to require public companies that disclose or release such non-GAAP financial measures to include a presentation of the most directly comparable GAAP financial measure and a reconciliation of the disclosed non-GAAP financial measure to the most directly comparable GAAP financial measure.[90] The SEC also amended Item 10 of Regulation S–K to provide additional guidance to those registrants that include non-GAAP financial measures in Commission filings.[91] The SEC further amended Form 8–K[92] so as to require registrants to furnish to the Commission earnings releases or similar announcements.[93]

The SEC defines non-GAAP financial measures as numerical measures of either historical or future financial performance, financial position, or cash flow that either: (1) effectively excludes amounts that would be included in

Independence Rule and Conforming Amendments, Sec. Exch. Act Rel. No. 34–55876, 2007 WL 2031580 (SEC June 7, 2007).

30. *Cf.* Checkosky v. SEC, 23 F.3d 452 (D.C.Cir.1994) (the SEC appeared to give its own interpretation of GAAS and GAAP, but the court remanded for further explanation).

31. Materiality is not simply a matter of the numbers, it depends on the surrounding facts and circumstances. *See, e.g.,* Staff Accounting Bulletin No. 99–Materiality, Release No. SAB 99, 64 Fed. Reg. 451250–01 (Aug. 12, 1999). *See, e.g.,* Bruce A. Hitler, The SEC's New Materiality Regime, 32 Rev. Sec. & Commod. Reg. 187 (1999); Comment, Staff Accounting Bulletin No. 99: Another Ill–Advised Foray Into the Murky World of Qualitative Materiality, 95 Nw. U.L. Rev. 361 (2000). Materiality is discussed in § 12,9 *infra.*

33. *See, e.g.,* In re Doral Financial Corp. Securities Litigation, 563 F.Supp.2d 461 (S.D.N.Y. 2008).

34. *See, e.g.,* In re American Business Financial Services, Inc. Noteholders Litigation, 2008 WL 3405580 (E.D.Pa. 2008); (sufficient allegations of "red flags" so as to sustain pleadings with respect to auditor's alleged recklessness).

89. Sarbanes–Oxley Act of 2002, Pub. Law 107–204 (July 30, 2002) § 401, amending section 13 of the Exchange Act, 15 U.S.C.A. § 78m.

90. 17 C.F.R. §§ 244.100 *et seq. See* Conditions for Use of Non–GAPP Financial Measures, Sec. Act Rel. No. 33–8176, Sec. Exch. Act Rel. No. 34–47226, 2003 WL 161117 (SEC Jan. 22, 2003).

91. *See* Conditions for Use of Non–GAPP Financial Measures, Sec. Act Rel. No. 33–8176, Sec. Exch. Act Rel. No. 34–47226, 2003 WL 161117 (SEC Jan. 22, 2003).

92. Form 8–K is the form used by the SEC for items that are subject to continuous (or real time) disclosure as compared to the quarterly disclosure requirements of Forms 10–Q and 10–K. *see* § 9.3 *supra.*

93. *See* Conditions for Use of Non–GAPP Financial Measures, Sec. Act Rel. No. 33–8176, Sec. Exch. Act Rel. No. 34–47226, 2003 WL 161117 (SEC Jan. 22, 2003).

the most directly comparable GAAP accounting measure or (2) effectively includes amounts that would be excluded in the comparable GAAP measure.[94]

Another Sarbanes–Oxley provision that arose out of the Enron and related scandals is the requirement in section 401 that the SEC adopt rules to require disclosure of off-balance sheet arrangements.[95] The SEC implemented this requirement in 2003.[96] The new requirements introduced by Sarbanes–Oxley include requiring a public company to provide an explanation of its off-balance sheet arrangements in a separately captioned subsection of the "Management's Discussion and Analysis" ("MD & A") section of required SEC filings. The amendments also require public companies (but not small business issuers) to provide an overview of certain known contractual obligations in a tabular format.[97]

§ 9.6[2] Audit Requirements

Section 10A of the 1934 Act[98] details the audit requirements of issuer financial statements by independent public accountants.[99] Section 10A(a) requires that audits be conducted within generally accepted auditing standards and that procedures be designed to uncover illegal acts having direct and material effects on financial statements. The SEC does not have to prove scienter in order to establish a violation of section 10A's requirements for the auditor to take action, if certain irregularities are discovered.[100] Furthermore, with respect to auditor liability in general, as is the case with any SEC enforcement action, the SEC need only establish responsibility for the misstatement; it does not have to establish reliance by investors.[101]

In addition, section 10A(b) requires independent public accountants who become aware of any information suggesting that illegal acts have or may have occurred to perform an investigation and inform the management of the issuer. If an auditor determines that a detected illegal action is material[102] and management has taken no action to remedy it, the auditor is required to

94. *See* Conditions for Use of Non–GAPP Financial Measures, Sec. Act Rel. No. 33–8176, Sec. Exch. Act Rel. No. 34–47226, 2003 WL 131117 (SEC Jan. 22, 2003).

95. Sarbanes–Oxley Act of 2002, Pub. Law 107–204 (July 30, 2002) § 401, amending section 13 of the Exchange Act, 15 U.S.C.A. § 78m by adding a new subsection (j).

96. Disclosure in Management's Discussion and Analysis About Off–Balance Sheet Arrangements and Aggregate Contractual Obligations, Sec. Act Rel. No. 33–8182, Sec. Exch. Act Rel. No. 34–47264, 2003 WL 175446 (SEC Jan. 28, 2003).

97. *See* Disclosure in Management's Discussion and Analysis About Off–Balance Sheet Arrangements and Aggregate Contractual Obligations, Sec. Act Rel. No. 33–8182, Sec. Exch. Act Rel. No. 34–47264, 2003 WL 175446 (SEC Jan. 28, 2003).

98. 15 U.S.C.A. § 78j–1. *See, e.g.,* Andrew W. Reiss, Note, Powered by More Than GAAS: Section 10A of the Securities Litigation Reform Act Takes the Accounting Progression for a New Ride, 25 Hofstra L. Rev. 1261 (1997).

99. *See, e.g.,* Paul R. Brown, Jeanne A. Calderon & Baruch Lev, Administrative and Judicial Approaches to Auditor Independence, 30 Seton Hall L. Rev. 445 (2000).

100. SEC v. Solucorp Industries, Ltd., 197 F.Supp.2d 4 (S.D.N.Y.2002). *See also, e.g.,* Gary DiBianco & Andrew M. Lawrence, Investigation and Reporting Obligations Under Section 10A of the Securities Exchange Act, 40 Rev. Sec. & Commod. Reg. 25 (Feb. 7, 2007).

101. *See, e.g.,* SEC v. KMPG, LLP, 2005 WL 3540252 (S.D.N.Y. 2005) (engagement partners had responsibility for allegedly improper audit and thus could be held accountable in SEC action even in the absence of investor reliance).

102. Although materiality in accounting terms may have a different meaning, under the securities laws a matter is material if it is something to which an investor would attaching significance in determining whether to make an investment decision. Materiality is discussed in §§ 10.4, 12.9 *infra*.

report the illegal act to the board of directors. Issuers receiving such reports from auditors must, not later than one business day after receipt of the report, inform the Commission and provide the auditor with notice and a copy of the report submitted to the Commission. If an auditor does not receive notice from the issuer within one business day, the auditor must either resign or provide the Commission with a copy of the report not later than one business day after the failure to receive notice. Section 10A(c) provides that independent public accountants will not be held liable in a private action for any statement, findings, or conclusions made in the report.[103] However, section 10A(d) allows civil penalties to be imposed for the willful conduct of auditors in failing to provide the Commission with reports under sections 10A(c) and (d).

The statutory auditing requirements focus primarily on three aspects of the audit. First, as is the case under generally accepted auditing standards, the auditor must have in place procedures that are reasonably designed to detect illegal activities that have a direct and material effect on the figures in the financial statements. If the auditor becomes aware that an illegal act may have occurred, the auditor is required to make several determinations. The auditor must determine the likelihood that the illegal act occurred, as well as the potential effect of the illegal act on the issuer's financial statements.[104] Unless it is determined that the illegal activity is clearly immaterial, the auditor must inform appropriate members of management and assure that the audit committee is also informed.

A second focus of the statutory auditing requirements deals with related party transactions.[105] The auditors must have procedures reasonably designed to detect related party transactions that are material to the issuer's financial statements or that otherwise would require disclosure in the financial statements. Third, the auditor must make an evaluation of whether there is substantial doubt concerning the issuer's ability to continue operating, as a going concern during the upcoming fiscal year.

Auditor Independence

Whenever the SEC imposes requirements that financial information be audited, the SEC applies its own definition of auditor independence in order to determine whether the audit is in fact an independent audit. The issue has become increasingly complex over time as the services that accounting firms provide have expanded, thus creating additional possibilities for relationships that could compromise auditor independence.[106] After considerable controversy, in 2000, the Commission adopted its revised rules on auditor indepen-

103. *Cf.* Wells v. Monarch Capital Corp., 129 F.3d 1253 (1st Cir.1997) (unpublished opinion) (although accounting firm made a number of mistakes in an audit, there was not showing of scienter); Brown v. Benchmark Power Corp., 94 F.3d 650 (9th Cir.1996) (accounting firm performing audit had no duty to disclose to investors company's accounting improprieties; accountants had no active participation in dissemination of information to the public).

104. This includes contingent effects such as fines, penalties, and damages resulting from the illegal activity.

105. Related party transactions have come under heightened focus in the wake of scandals such as Tyco's, which involved massive loan forgiveness, huge bonuses, and use of corporate funds for personal purposes. The prohibition of executive loans in the Sarbanes–Oxley Act of 2002, Pub. Law 107–204 (July 30, 2002) is but one example of this concern. *See* § 9.7[4] *infra*.

106. *See, e.g.,* KMPG LLP, [2000–2001 Transfer Binder] Fed. Sec. L. Rep. (CCH) ¶ 91,252 (SEC No Action Letter 2000) (accounting firm could divide operations into distinct accounting and consulting firms and retain required independence).

dence.[107] Many observers believed that accounting firms had previously been permitted too much leeway in determining whether they in fact satisfied the independence requirements, while other observers feared SEC rules that would be too stringent. Under the current auditor independence rules as amended in 2000, the SEC identifies four situations in which an accountant lacks sufficient independence to act as an auditor for financial statements. First, an accountant does not have sufficient independence to act as an auditor if the accountant has either a mutual or conflicting interest with the client. Second, the necessary independence is lacking if the accounting firm audits the client's work (as opposed to merely performing financial audits). Third, the accounting firm lacks independence if it (or its employees) acts as an employee or manager of the client, such as would be the case if the accountant assumes outsourced management responsibilities. Fourth, an accounting firm lacks sufficient independence to act as an SEC auditor if the accounting firm acts as an advocate for the client.

The SEC's auditor independence requirements are based on both fact and appearance. The SEC's auditor independence requirements establish a general standard of auditor independence based on whether the accountant is not, or if a reasonable investor knowing all relevant facts and circumstances would conclude that the accountant is not capable of exercising objective and impartial judgment on all of the issues encompassed within the accountant's engagement.[109] Independence may depend in large part on the non-audit services that are provided by the company's principal accountant. The SEC has approved of the following factors[110] that the company's audit committee should consider in determining whether the SEC independence requirements are satisfied:

> Whether the non-audit service facilitates the performance of the audit, improves the company's financial reporting process, or otherwise is in the public interest;
>
> Whether the audit committee performs the non-audit service;
>
> The effects of the non-audit service on audit effectiveness and on the timeliness and quality of the company's financial reporting process;
>
> Whether the non audit personnel and specialists who routinely provide recurring audit support perform the audit service and whether such activity enhances the audit personnel's knowledge of the company's business and operations;
>
> Whether the audit personnel's role in [performing the non-audit service is inconsistent with the auditor's role];
>
> Whether the audit firm's personnel would be assuming a management role or have a mutuality of interest with the company's management;

---

107. *See* Revision of the Commission's Auditor Independence Requirements, Sec. Exch. Act Rel. No. 34–43602, 2000 WL 1726933 (SEC Nov. 21, 2000) (adopting release).

109. *See* Revision of the Commission's Auditor Independence Requirements, Sec. Exch. Act Rel. No. 34–43602, 2000 WL 1726933 (SEC Nov. 21, 2000) (adopting release); Revision of the Commission's Auditor Independence Requirements, Sec. Exch. Act Rel. No. 34–42994, 65 FR 43148–01, 2000 WL 950197 (SEC July 12, 2000) (proposing release).

110. *See* Revision of the Commission's Auditor Independence Requirements, Sec. Exch. Act Rel. No. 34–43602, 2000 WL 1726933 (SEC Nov. 21, 2000) (adopting release). These factors were adopted from the Blue Ribbon Committee on Improving the Effectiveness of Corporate Audit Committees.

Whether in effect the auditors would be in the position of auditing their own figures and numbers;

Whether the non-audit project must be started and completed quickly;

Whether the audit firm has unique expertise with regard to the non-audit service; and

The size of the fee charged for the non-audit service.

The Sarbanes–Oxley Act of 2002[118] mandated reforms that have a significant impact on audit committees. This legislation supplements the existing SEC rules as well as the rules of the stock exchanges. First, with respect to committee composition, the Act requires that the audit committee must be composed solely of independent directors.[119] Subject to exemptions that may be granted by SEC rulemaking, independence under the Act requires that the audit committee member not receive any consulting or other fees other than board or committee fees.[120] Nor can an audit committee member be "an affiliated person" of the company or its subsidiaries.[121] Section 303 of the Act prohibits "any officer or director of an issuer, or any other person acting under the direction thereof, to take any action to fraudulently influence, coerce, manipulate, or mislead any independent public or certified accountant engaged in the performance of an audit of the financial statements of that issuer for the purpose of rendering such financial statements materially misleading."[122]

The Sarbanes–Oxley Act also mandates that the SEC issue rules requiring companies to disclose in their periodic reports whether or not (and if not, why not) the audit committee has at least one member who is a "financial expert."[123] In defining "financial expert," the SEC must consider whether a person has, through education and experience as an auditor or a principal financial officer, comptroller or principal accounting officer of a company, an understanding of generally accepted accounting principles and financial statements, experience in the preparation of financial statements of generally comparable companies, experience with internal accounting controls, and an understanding of audit committee functions.[124]

The audit committee is to be "directly responsible for the appointment, compensation and oversight" of the auditor.[125] This includes the resolution of disagreements between management and the auditor regarding financial reporting. The Act makes it explicit that the auditor must report directly to the audit committee.[126]

118. Sarbanes–Oxley Act of 2002, Pub. Law 107–204 (July 30, 2002).

119. 15 U.S.C. 78j–1(m).

120. 15 U.S.C. 78j–1(m).

121. Accordingly, audit committee membership cannot include a director who owns a controlling stock interest in the company and may also exclude officers or directors of controlling shareholders.

122. Sarbanes–Oxley Act § 303, codified at 15 U.S.C.A. § 7242.

123. 15 USCA § 7265.

124. The SEC's implementation of the financial expert requirement are discussed in § 9.7[3] *infra*.

125. 15 U.S.C. 78j–1(m). *See also, e.g.,* Gary Simon, New Audit Committee Rules, 37 Rev. of Sec. & Commodities Reg. 167 (2004).

126. 15 U.S.C. 78j–1(m).

Members of a corporation's audit committee are thus subject to high standards of oversight of the company's financial situation. Accordingly, when there are accounting irregularities, audit committee members may be exposed to controlling person liability.[127] Audit committee members will not easily escape liability simply by claiming that they relied on the audit firm.[128]

The Sarbanes–Oxley Act requires that all auditing services be approved in advance by the audit committee,[129] including comfort letters[130] and statutory audits. There are nine specified categories of non-audit services that auditors may not provide audit clients. These include financial information systems design and implementation, internal audit outsourcing, and any other service that the Public Company Accounting Oversight Board determines is impermissible. In addition, permitted non-audit services must be approved in advance by the audit committee,[132] although there is a limited de minimis exception to this preapproval requirement.

Audit committees must be granted the authority to engage independent counsel and other advisors, as they determine necessary, to carry out their duties, and appropriate funding, as determined by the audit committee, for compensating such advisors, as well as the accounting firm for its audit services.

§ 9.7 Corporate Governance and the Federal Securities Laws; Codes of Ethics, Compensation Limitations, and Listing Standards

§ 9.7[1] Overview of Corporate Governance Provisions

As a general proposition, the federal securities laws are focused on disclosure, while matters relating to corporate governance are relegated to state corporate law.[1] Over the years, however, there have been various provisions of the securities laws that have at least an indirect impact on corporate governance. In 2002, the Sarbanes–Oxley Act[3] introduced major corporate governance reforms that now are a matter of federal law. For example, the securities laws now require disclosures with respect to corporate codes of ethics.[4] There are new independence requirements for auditors and members of the audit committee.[5] There are also controls on executive

127. In re Lernout & Hauspie Securities Litigation, 286 B.R. 33 (D. Mass. 2002). Controlling person liability is discussed in § 12.24 *infra*.

128. In re Lernout & Hauspie Securities Litigation, 286 B.R. 33 (D. Mass. 2002).

129. 15 U.S.C. 78j–1(m).

130. A comfort letter is a letter from an independent auditor in connection with a 1933 Act registered offering which states that, while a full audit has not been undertaken, the auditor has done a 'review' sufficient to assure that financial statement information in the registration statement is correctly prepared to the best of the auditor's knowledge.

132. The audit committee may delegate the authority to grant preapprovals to one or more members, whose decisions must be presented to the full committee at its scheduled meetings.

§ 9.7

1. *See generally* James D. Cox & Thomas Lee Hazen, Cox and Hazen on Corporations (2d ed. 2003).

3. Sarbanes–Oxley Act of 2002, Pub. Law 107–204 (July 30, 2002).

4. Sarbanes–Oxley Act of 2002, Pub. Law 107–204 (July 30, 2002) §§ 406, 407, codified in 15 U.S.C.A. §§ 7264, 7265. *See* § 9.7[2] *infra*.

5. Sarbanes–Oxley Act of 2002, Pub. Law 107–204 (July 30, 2002) § 301, amending section 10A of the 1934 Act, 15 U.S.C.A. § 78j–1. *See* § 9.7[3] and § 9.6 *supra*. *See also, e.g.*, Gary Simon, New Audit Committee Rules, 37 Rev. of Sec. & Commodities Reg. 167 (2004).

compensation.[6] Additionally, the listing standards of the stock exchanges and the Nasdaq also impose corporate governance limits on publicly held corporations.[7] The Sarbanes–Oxley provisions imposed significant new compliance obligations on public companies.

§ 9.7[2] Codes of Ethics

Section 406 of the Sarbanes–Oxley Act directed the SEC to develop rules requiring disclosures relating to public companies' codes of ethics.[10] Neither the statute nor the SEC rules expressly mandate that a public company has a code of ethics, but the disclosure requirements clearly provide a strong incentive since companies that do not adopt a code of ethics will have to make that disclosure and will appear out of line with the companies that have adopted such a code.[11] As such this is an indirect intervention in corporate governance rather than a mandate on any particular structure.

In adopting the code of ethics disclosure requirements,[12] the SEC requires companies to disclose whether they have adopted a corporate "code of ethics" that covers the conduct of the company's principal executive and senior financial officers.[13] If the company has not adopted a code of ethics, it must explain why it has not done so.[14] It is very likely that this will have the effect of shaming companies into adopting a code of ethics. If a company has adopted a code of ethics, it must make the code available to the public. In addition, the company must make disclosures when it amends its code of ethics or when it grants specific waivers from the code's requirements.

In order to qualify as a "code of ethics," the code must include "written standards that are reasonably designed to deter wrongdoing."[15] In addition, the code of ethics must be designed to promote honest and ethical conduct. Honest and ethical conduct includes how the company handles actual and apparent conflicts of interest between personal and professional relationships.[16] The code of ethics must also be designed to promote full, fair, accurate, and timely disclosures in the company's SEC filings as well as in the company's public communications generally. The code of ethics must be designed to promote compliance with laws, rules, and regulations applicable to the company's business. The code of ethics must identify appropriate reporting procedures within the organization with respect to code violations. In

---

6. *See* § 9.7[4] *infra.*

7. NYSE Corporate Governance Rule Proposals, http://www.nyse.com/pdfs/corp_gov_pro_b.pdf. *See* § 9.7[3] *infra.*

10. 15 U.S.C.A. § 1764; Sarbanes–Oxley Act of 2002, Pub. Law 107–204 (July 30, 2002) § 406.

11. Corporate codes of conduct existed before Sarbanes–Oxley. *See, e.g.,* Harvey L. Pitt & Karl A. Groskaufmanis, Minimizing Corporate Civil and Criminal Liability: A Second Look at Corporate Codes of Conduct, 78 Geo. L.J. 1559 (1990).

12. *See* Disclosure Required by Sections 406 and 407 of the Sarbanes–Oxley Act of 2002, Sec. Act Rel. No. 33–8177, Sec. Exch. Act Rel. No. 34–47235, 2003 WL 164269 (SEC Jan. 23, 2003).

13. Regulation S–K, Item 406.

14. Regulation S–K, Item 406.

15. Reg. S–K Item 406.

16. Codes of ethics thus can bring up the relevance of the personal activities of corporate executives. *Cf.* Dave Carpenter, Boeing Fires CEO for Improper Relationship, http://story.news.yahoo.com/news?tmpl=story & cid=530 & e=1 & u=/ap/20050307/ap_on_bi_ge/boeing_ceo (Associated Press March 7, 2005) (CEO was dismissed "for what the company said Monday was a violation of the company's code of business conduct stemming from a relationship the married [CEO] had with a female executive"). The personal life of a high level executive is not only subject to a company's code of ethics, it may also trigger disclosure obligations. *See* § 9.3[3] *supra.*

particular, the code must identify "appropriate person or persons" to whom reports of violations should be made. It is also essential that a code of ethics adequately provides a system of accountability to assure compliance with the code's substantive provisions. As noted above, the company is not required to have a code of ethics with each of these attributes. However, the New York Stock Exchange and Nasdaq Stock Market both proposed rules to require listed companies to have these codes of ethics.[17] Those rules were adopted so that the New York Stock Exchange[18] and the Nasdaq[19] market go beyond the SEC's disclosure impetus requiring listed companies to have a code of ethics.[20] In any event, if a public company either has no code of ethics or has one that lacks any of these components, then under Item 406 of Regulation S–K, the company must disclose that it does not have a code of ethics.

In adopting its rules dealing with corporate codes of ethics, the SEC also adopted rules addressing the composition of audit committees. Section 407 of the Sarbanes–Oxley Act[21] requires disclosures with respect to the audit committee and "financial experts" serving on that committee.[22]

§ 9.7[3] Audit Committees; Financial Experts

As discussed in a previous section,[23] the SEC places particular emphasis on public companies' audit committees. Amendments to section 10A of the 1934 Act strengthened the requirement that audit committee members be independent.[24] Those provisions are discussed in an earlier section of this treatise.[25] In addition, section 407 of the Sarbanes–Oxley Act[26] mandated that the SEC require disclosures relating to the presence of a financial expert on the audit committee.[27] In particular, the company must disclose whether it has an "audit committee financial expert" in the audit committee and if not, why it does not.[29] As is the case with the code of ethics requirement discussed above,[30] this is likely to shame most companies into having a financial expert on the audit committee. Companies having a financial expert on the audit committee must disclose the name of the financial expert and whether he or she is independent of management.[31]

17. *See* Sec. Exch. Act Rel. No. 34–48125, 80 S.E.C. Docket 1647, 2003 WL 21523894 (No. SR–NASD–2002–139) (SEC July 2, 2003).

18. NYSE Manual § 303A.10.

19. NASD Rule 4350(n).

20. *See* Sec. Exch. Act Rel. No. 34–48125, 80 S.E.C. Docket 1647, 2003 WL 21523894 (No. SR–NASD–2002–139) (SEC July 2, 2003) which stated the purpose of the rule as follows:

21. 15 U.S.C.A. § 1765; Sarbanes–Oxley Act of 2002, Pub. Law 107–204 (July 30, 2002) § 407.

22. *See* Disclosure Required by Sections 406 and 407 of the Sarbanes–Oxley Act of 2002, Sec. Act Rel. No. 33–8177, Sec. Exch. Act Rel. No. 34–47235, 2003 WL 164269 (SEC Jan. 23, 2003); § 9.7[3] *infra*.

23. *See* § 9.6[2] *supra*.

24. Section 301 of the Sarbanes–Oxley Act prohibits audit committee members from receiving any compensation from the company other than their director fees. Sarbanes–Oxley Act of 2002, Pub. Law 107–204 (July 30 2002) § 301, codified as amendments to 15 U.S.C.A. § 78j–1

25. *See* § 9.6[2] *supra*. *See also, e.g.,* Gary Simon, New Audit Committee Rules, 37 Rev. of Sec. & Commodities Reg. 167 (2004).

26. 15 U.S.C.A. § 1765; Sarbanes–Oxley Act of 2002, Pub. Law 107–204 (July 30, 2002) § 407.

27. *See* Disclosure Required by Sections 406 and 407 of the Sarbanes–Oxley Act of 2002, Sec. Act Rel. No. 33–8177, Sec. Exch. Act Rel. No. 34–47235, 2003 WL 164269 (SEC Jan. 23, 2003).

29. Reg. S–K Item 401.

30. *See* § 9.7[2] *supra*.

31. Reg. S–K Item 401.

The SEC sets forth various criteria for determining whether someone qualifies as an "audit committee financial expert" as that term is used with respect to the audit committee disclosure requirements. The SEC describes a financial expert as someone who has an understanding of financial statements and generally accepted accounting principles and is able to assess the general application of these principles.[32] The financial expert must also have an understanding of internal controls and financial reporting procedures as well as an understanding of the functions and role of an audit committee. In addition to the foregoing qualifications relating to understanding and knowledge, the SEC specifies the types of experience that a financial expert should have. This experience includes preparing, auditing, analyzing, or evaluating financial statements presenting accounting issues that are "generally comparable" in terms of depth and complexity to those that can reasonably be expected to arise in connection with the company's financial statements.[34] This experience requirement may also be satisfied by having actively supervised[35] anyone performing those functions.[36] The SEC further provides the ways in which the audit committee financial expert may acquire the required attributes described above.[37] For example, in addition to qualifications acquired through education, experience as a senior financial officer, accountant or auditor, as well as experience in similar positions will help qualify someone as an audit committee financial expert.[38] This also includes experience "actively supervising" a senior financial officer, accountant or auditor, or persons performing similar functions.[39] These are simply examples of ways to acquire the necessary attributes, the SEC also permits the company to look to "other relevant experience." In the event that the company is relying on "other relevant experience" to qualify someone as an audit committee financial expert, Instruction 2 to Item 401 of Regulations S–K and S–B require a brief listing of that relevant experience.

As discussed in an earlier section,[40] a director's liability under the securities laws will be heightened by any special expertise that he or she has. Item 401 to Regulation S–K provides a safe harbor to clarify that an audit committee financial expert is not deemed an "expert" for any purpose.[41] The SEC also explains that designation as an audit committee expert does not

32. This understanding must extend to accounting for estimates, accruals, and reserves.

34. *See* Disclosure Required by Sections 406 and 407 of the Sarbanes–Oxley Act of 2002, Sec. Act Rel. No. 33–8177, Sec. Exch. Act Rel. No. 34–47235, 2003 WL 164269 (SEC Jan. 23, 2003).

35. The ability to acquire the necessary attributes by actively supervising rather than actually performing the activities in question was added to the requirements as proposed before the new provisions were adopted. Disclosure Required by Sections 406 and 407 of the Sarbanes–Oxley Act of 2002, Sec. Act Rel. No. 33–8177, Sec. Exch. Act Rel. No. 34–47235, 2003 WL 164269 (SEC Jan. 23, 2003).

36. Disclosure Required by Sections 406 and 407 of the Sarbanes–Oxley Act of 2002, Sec. Act Rel. No. 33–8177, Sec. Exch. Act Rel. No. 34–47235, 2003 WL 164269 (SEC Jan. 23, 2003).

37. Disclosure Required by Sections 406 and 407 of the Sarbanes–Oxley Act of 2002, Sec. Act Rel. No. 33–8177, Sec. Exch. Act Rel. No. 34–47235, 2003 WL 164269 (SEC Jan. 23, 2003).

38. Disclosure Required by Sections 406 and 407 of the Sarbanes–Oxley Act of 2002, Sec. Act Rel. No. 33–8177, Sec. Exch. Act Rel. No. 34–47235, 2003 WL 164269 (SEC Jan. 23, 2003).

39. Disclosure Required by Sections 406 and 407 of the Sarbanes–Oxley Act of 2002, Sec. Act Rel. No. 33–8177, Sec. Exch. Act Rel. No. 34–47235, 2003 WL 164269 (SEC Jan. 23, 2003).

40. *See* § 7.2 *supra.*

41. Consider, for example, section 11 of the 1933 Act (15 U.S.C.A. § 77k) which places heightened liability on "experts" for material misstatements and omissions in a registration statement.

impose any duties, obligations, or liabilities beyond those already imposed on audit committee members.[42]

§ 9.7[4] Executive and Director Compensation; Prohibition on Certain Loans to Executives; Extraordinary Payments

The federal securities laws require that directors of public companies who serve on audit committees be independent.[55] Thus, section 301 of the Sarbanes–Oxley[56] Act prohibits directors who serve on audit committees from receiving any payments from the company except for director fees.[57]

Section 402 of the Sarbanes–Oxley Act[58] prohibits certain loans made by companies to their directors and executive officers. As enacted by section 402 of the Sarbanes–Oxley Act, section 13(k) of the Securities Exchange Act of 1934 expressly prohibits most loans by a company to its directors and executive officers or its subsidiary's directors and executive officers.[59]

Section 402 has aptly been described as "an unusual federal override of state corporate law concerning internal corporate affairs."[60] The prohibitions on loans created considerable concern because of its broad reach.

Section 402's prohibition on loans to a company's directors and executive officers (or to its subsidiary's directors and executive officers) applies not only to the initiation of loans but also to the extension of loans already in existence at the time of the 2002 amendment to the Act.[62] The prohibition on loans does not extend to loans made in the ordinary course of the company's business.[63] Thus, for example, a bank may make mortgage loans to its directors and executives and a brokerage firm may make margin loans to its directors and executives.[64] Also, the SEC implemented exemptions which it deemed appropriate.[65]

§ 9.8 Controls on Attorney Practice[a]

§ 9.8[1] Regulating Administrative Practice of Attorneys; The Sarbanes–Oxley Lawyer Conduct Rules

When representing clients of regulated industries, lawyers play various roles in dealing with the applicable administrative agencies. Administrative

42. *See* Disclosure Required by Sections 406 and 407 of the Sarbanes–Oxley Act of 2002, Sec. Act Rel. No. 33–8177, Sec. Exch. Act Rel. No. 34–47235, 2003 WL 164269 (SEC Jan. 23, 2003).

55. 1934 Act § 10A(m)(3), 15 U.S.C.A. § 78j–1(m)(3), as amended by section 301 of the Sarbanes–Oxley Act § 301, Pub. Law 107–204 (July 30, 2002) § 301.

56. Sarbanes–Oxley Act of 2002, Pub. Law 107–204 (July 30, 2002) § 301.

57. Sarbanes–Oxley Act of 2002, Pub. Law 107–204 (July 30, 2002) § 301.

58. Sarbanes–Oxley Act of 2002, Pub. Law 107–204 (July 30, 2002) § 402, amending section 13 of the 1934 Act, 15 U.S.C.A. § 78m.

59. 15 U.S.C.A. § 78m(k)(1).

60. 4 Alan R. Bromberg & Lewis D. Lowenfels on Securities Fraud § 7:428 (2d ed. Westlaw database updated May 2008).

62. 15 U.S.C.A. § 78m(k)(1).

63. 15 U.S.C.A. § 78m(k)(2).

64. 15 U.S.C.A. § 78m(k)(2).

65. Thus, for example, the SEC exempted foreign banks from the insider lending prohibitions. *See* Rule 13k–1, 17 C.F.R. § 240.13k–1.

§ 9.8

a. This section was adapted from Thomas Lee Hazen, Administrative Law Controls on Attorney Practice–A Look at the Securities and Exchange Commission's Lawyer Conduct Rules, 55 Admin. Law. Rev. 323 (2003).

agencies frequently function as tribunals and as such may implement rules regulating the practice of law before the agency. Since 1935,[2] the Securities and Exchange Commission has regulated the conduct of lawyers who practice before it. The SEC adopted the predecessor to its current Rule 102(e) of its Rules of Practice[4] "in order to protect the integrity of its processes from incompetent, unethical, or dishonest professionals, including attorneys."[5] The SEC has explained that the rule is premised not only on its "inherent authority"[6] but also on its statutory authority to adopt rules "as may be necessary or appropriate to implement the [securities laws]."[7]

Rule 102(e) and its predecessors have had a controversial history. In 2002, in response to the corporate governance crisis unearthed by high profile investigations such as the one involving Enron Corporation, Congress enacted numerous amendments to the federal securities laws under the aegis of the Sarbanes–Oxley Act of 2002.[9] Section 307 of that Act directed the SEC to adopt rules defining proper client representation in SEC matters.[10]

§ 9.8[3] SEC Rule 102

The SEC Rules of Practice contain a broad definition of what constitutes practice before the Commission.[37] Rule 102 applies not only to lawyers and accountants but also to other professionals who practice before the Commission.[38] The rule has been used primarily against lawyers and accountants. A key difference between the role of lawyers and accountants is that accountants act as certifiers of financial statements and thus are specifically subject to independence requirements.[39]

The concept of practice before the Commission is a broad one. SEC practice is not limited to administrative hearings or representation in connection with SEC investigations, but rather also extends to transacting any business with the Commission, including preparation of documents for filing with the SEC.[40]

§ 9.8[4] Role of Lawyers in SEC Practice

Although administrative agencies' regulation of lawyer conduct is not new, in the 1990s, in response to the lawyers' role in various financial frauds,

2. 1 Fed.Reg. 1753 (1936) (Rule II(k)). See also 1 SEC Ann.Rep. 45 (1935).

4. 17 C.F.R. § 201.102(e). In 1995, Rule 102(e) appeared as a recodification for former Rule 2(e).

5. *See* In re Keating, Muething & Klekamp, Sec. Exch. Act Rel. No. 34–15982, 1979 WL 186370 *17 (SEC July 2, 1979).

6. *See* In re Keating, Muething & Klekamp, Sec. Exch. Act Rel. No. 34–15982, 1979 WL 186370 *17 (SEC July 2, 1979).

7. Section 23(a)(1) of the Securities Exchange Act of 1934, 15 U.S.C. § 78w.

9. Sarbanes–Oxley Act of 2002, Pub. Law 107–204 (July 30, 2002), codified in 15 U.S.C. § 7245 (2002 supp.). *See* Senate Report No. 107–205 (July 3, 2002). Sarbanes–Oxley Act of 2002, Pub. Law 107–204 sec. 307 (July 30, 2002).

10. Sarbanes–Oxley Act of 2002, Pub. Law 107–204 (July 30, 2002), codified in 15 U.S.C. § 7245 (2002 supp.).

37. 17 C.F.R. § 201.102(f). *See* § 9.8[5] *infra*.

38. This includes engineers and other experts who may be acting on the behalf of a company or other person involved in SEC proceedings. *See* 17 C.F.R. § 201.102(f).

39. 15 U.S.C. § 78j–1 (2000).

40. 17 C.F.R. § 201.102.

there was an expansion of the rules regarding attorney conduct when practicing before certain administrative agencies.[76]

The federal securities laws' primary concern is with full disclosure in the securities markets. The Securities and Exchange Commission is the agency charged with administering the securities laws. Lawyers play a crucial role in advising clients and in drafting disclosures. Since 1935, the SEC has regulated the standards of professionals who practice before the Commission.[78] Section 307 of the Sarbanes–Oxley Act[79] mandated that the SEC specify standards of conduct for attorneys practicing before the Commission. In November 2002, the SEC announced its rule proposals relating to attorney conduct.[80]

The role lawyers play in facilitating securities frauds, albeit unwittingly in many cases, should not be ignored. There has been recent concern of the roles lawyers play as a result of failures such as Enron, Worldcom, and Tyco.[81] However, this is not a new concern. For example, as was explained long ago,

> [J]ust as a fine, natural football player needs coaching in the fundamentals and schooling in the wiles of the sport, so, too, it takes a corporation lawyer with a heart for the game to organize a great stock swindle or income tax dodge and drill the financiers in all the precise details of their play.
>
> Otherwise, in their natural enthusiasm to rush in and grab everything that happens not to be nailed down and guarded with shotguns, they would soon be caught offside and penalized, and some of the noted financiers who are now immortalized as all-time all-America larcenists never would have risen beyond the level of the petty thief or short-change man.[82]

Similarly, Judge Friendly wrote: "In our complex society the accountant's certificate and the lawyer's opinion can be instruments for inflicting pecuniary loss more potent than the chisel or the crowbar."[83]

In writing about the lawyers' role in the savings and loan scandals of the 1980s, Judge Stanley Sporkin[84] asked:

---

76. *E.g.,* 12 C.F.R. § 513.4. See Jonathan R. Macey & Geoffrey P. Miller Reflections on Professional Responsibility in a Regulatory State, 63 Geo. Wash. L. Rev. 1105, 1106–1107 (1995).

78. 1 Fed.Reg. 1753 (1936) (Rule II(k)). See also 1 SEC Ann.Rep. 45 (1935). *See* In re Keating, Muething & Klekamp, Sec. Exch. Act Rel. No. 34–15982, 1979 WL 186370 note 15 (SEC July 2, 1979). *See also, e.g.,* Simon M. Lorne & W. Hardy Callcott, Administrative Actions Against Lawyers Before the SEC, 50 Bus. Law. 1293 (1995).

79. Sarbanes–Oxley Act of 2002, Pub. Law 107–204 (July 30, 2002). *See* Senate Report No. 107–205 (July 3, 2002).

80. *See*Implementation of Standards of Professional Conduct For Attorneys, File No. S7–45–02, Sec. Act Rel. No. 33–8150, Sec. Exch. Act Rel. No. 34–46868, 2002 WL 31627090 (SEC Nov. 21, 2002).

81. Testimony of Susan P. Koniak, Professor of Law, Boston University School of Law Before the Senate Judiciary Committee February 6, 2002 ("Where were the Lawyers? Behind the Curtain Wearing their Magic Caps Hearing on Accountability Issues: Lessons Learned From Enron's Fall").

82. Westbrook Pegler, New York World Telegram Jan. 19, 1923 at p. 19, quoted in William O. Douglas, Directors Who Do Not Direct, 47 Harv. L. Rev. 1305, 1329 n.65 (1934).

83. United States v. Benjamin, 328 F.2d 854, 863 (2d Cir.), *cert. denied* 377 U.S. 953, 84 S.Ct. 1631, 12 L.Ed.2d 497 (1964).

84. Prior to serving on the federal bench, Judge Sporkin was Director of the SEC Division of Enforcement. It was under his watch that the SEC became especially vigilant over the roles of lawyer.

> Where were these professionals, a number of whom are now asserting their rights under the Fifth Amendment, when these clearly improper transactions were being consummated?
>
> Why didn't any of them speak up or disassociate themselves from the transactions?[85]

Quite properly, the SEC for a long time has held the view that lawyers should be made accountable for failing to prevent the client from complying with the securities laws' disclosure requirements.[86] For example, in the *National Student Marketing* case,[87] the SEC took the position that lawyers participated in a fraudulent scheme when they "failed to refuse to issue their opinions * * * and failed to insist that the financial statements be revised and shareholders be resolicited, and failing that, to cease representing their respective clients and, under the circumstances, notify the plaintiff Commission concerning the misleading nature of the nine month financial statements."[88] The court agreed that the lawyers had an obligation to do something.

§ 9.8[6] Increasing Attorney Accountability—Sarbanes–Oxley Section 307 and Its Background

On March 7, 2002, a group of law professors sent a letter to SEC Chairman Harvey Pitt urging the SEC to amend its Rules of Practice to better define what constitutes proper representation of public companies.[127] In particular, the letter asked that the Commission adopt a rule to conform to Rule 1.13 of the American Bar Association's Model Rules of Professional Conduct.[128] In relevant part, Rule 1.13 requires that when an attorney who is representing a corporation is made aware of serious wrongdoing, the attorney must take steps to correct the problem. Those steps include what is sometimes referred to as "climbing the corporate ladder"—reporting the violation to someone within the corporation in a position of authority to take corrective action. The Model Rule requires the attorney to continue to climb the ladder, even to the Board of Directors, until the attorney is satisfied that the matter will be attended to properly. The letter to Chairman Pitt asked that the SEC adopt a rule indicating that a lawyer who does not take this action can be suspended from practice before the SEC. On March 28, David Becker, the SEC's General Counsel responded on Chairman Pitt's behalf that since 1981, the SEC "has not brought Rule 102(e) proceedings against on allegations of professional conduct, or otherwise used the Rule to establish professional

---

85. Lincoln Savings and Loan Ass'n v. Wall, 743 F.Supp. 901, 920 (D.D.C. 1990).

86. In re Carter and Johnson, Sec. Exch. Act Rel. No. 34–17597, 1981 WL 36552, 36553 (SEC Feb. 28, 1981):

> When a lawyer with significant responsibilities in the effectuation of a company's compliance with the disclosure requirements of the federal securities laws becomes aware that his client is engaged in a substantial and continuing failure to satisfy those disclosure requirements, his continued participation violates professional standards unless he takes prompt steps to end the client's noncompliance.

87. SEC v. National Student Marketing Corp., 457 F.Supp. 682 (D.D.C.1978).

88. SEC v. National Student Marketing Corp., 360 F.Supp. 284, 290 (D.D.C. 1973).

127. March 7, 2002 letter to Chairman Pitt from Richard Painter, *et al.*, at http://www.abanet.org/buslaw/corporateresponsibility/ responsibility_relatedmat.html. *See also, e.g.,* Sung Hui Kim, The Banality of Fraud: Re–Situating the Inside Counsel AS Gatekeeper, 74 Fordham L. Rev. 983 (2005).

128. ABA Model Rules of Professional Conduct Rule 1.13.

responsibilities of lawyers."[129] Mr. Becker's letter further stated that "[t]here is a strong view among the bar that these matters are more appropriately addressed by state bar rules ..." Later in the spring of 2002, Senator John Edwards' office submitted a proposed provision that was made part of the Sarbanes–Oxley Act as section 307 of that Act.[130] The Act thus requires the SEC to impose the obligations to report the wrongdoing within the corporation. The Act does not require the attorney to blow the whistle outside of the corporate entity. However, in the late 1970s, the SEC took the position that reporting violations to the SEC might be required at some point. This was a controversial position that was opposed by the American Bar Association because of its perceived conflict with the attorney's obligation of confidentiality and was never implemented.

§ 9.8[7] The SEC Rules—Climbing the Corporate Ladder

Section 307 of Sarbanes–Oxley mandates only a climbing the ladder requirement within the corporate entity and thus does not implicate the attorney client privilege. However, in its proposed rules, the SEC went even further in calling for a noisy withdrawal from representation and notification to the SEC if the attorney is not satisfied that the course taken by the client would correct the wrongful conduct. The SEC recognized that this proposal went beyond the mandate of the statute and in light of the anticipated controversy, specifically solicited comments on this expansion.[134] As expected, the noisy withdrawal requirement met with opposition from large portions of the securities bar.[135]

On January 23, 2003, the SEC adopted a modified version of the proposed rules.[143] In the first instance, the Commission deferred for further consideration the most controversial aspect of the rule proposal—the noisy withdrawal requirement. In doing so, the SEC solicited additional comments on the noisy withdrawal requirement.

The SEC rules as adopted contain the up the ladder requirement mandated by section 307 of Sarbanes–Oxley, but at the same time the rules diluted the threshold for triggering the internal reporting requirement. In particular, the original rules spoke in terms of requiring the lawyer to begin climbing the ladder, if the attorney "reasonably believes" that a material violation might have occurred. In place of this "reasonably believes" trigger, the SEC substituted a threshold formulated as a double negative:[145] the internal reporting

129. March 28 letter from David Becker to Painter, *et al.*, at http://www/abanet.org/buslaw/corporateresponsibility/responsibility_relatedmat.html.

130. Sarbanes–Oxley Act of 2002, Pub. Law 107–204 sec. 307 (July 30, 2002), codified at 15 U.S.C.A. § 7245.

134. Implementation of Standards of Professional Conduct For Attorneys, File No. S7–45–02, Sec. Act Rel. No. 33–8150, Sec. Exch. Act Rel. No. 34–46868, 2002 WL 31627090 (SEC Nov 21, 2002).

135. *See, e.g.*, Letter from Edward E. Fleischman et al to the Securities Exchange Commission (Nov. 25, 2002); Tamara Loomis, 75 Law Firms Weigh In With Letter to SEC on Disclosures, N.Y.L.J. p.1 (Dec. 18, 2002); Attorneys Call for Delay, More Discussion of SEC Rule Proposals on Noisy Withdrawal, 34 Sec. Reg. & L. Rep. (BNA) 2045 (Dec. 23, 2002).

143. SEC Press Release, SEC Adopts Attorney Conduct Rule Under Sarbanes–Oxley Acthttp://www.sec.gov/news/press/2003–13.htm (Jan. 23, 2003).

145. It is ironic that in drafting this standard, the SEC violated one of its own drafting principles. Specifically, in its plain English requirements that apply to many SEC filings by public companies, the SEC admonishes against the use of double negatives. *See, e.g.*, Plain English Disclosure, Sec. Act Rel. No. 33–7380, 62 Fed. Reg. 3152, 1997 WL 17695 (F.R.) (SEC Jan. 27, 1997).

requirement is triggered by "credible evidence based upon which it would be *unreasonable*, under the circumstances, for a prudent and competent attorney *not to conclude* that a material violation has occurred, is ongoing, or is about to occur."[146] This is a difficult standard to prove in an enforcement action. A more troublesome problem with this high threshold of proof is that it may actually operate to discourage communication of information to attorneys so as to create deniability. In other words, as one commentator has suggested, under the rules as adopted, ignorance may be bliss.[147]

The "up the ladder" reporting operates as follows. Under Rule 205.3(b), an attorney who is practicing before the SEC in representation of a public company who becomes aware of a material violation must "report such evidence to the issuer's chief legal officer (or the equivalent thereof) or to both the issuer's chief legal officer and its chief executive officer (or the equivalents thereof) forthwith."[150] Since the reporting is within the corporation, the attorney-client privilege is in no way diminished.

The first step of the ladder thus is the report to the company's chief legal officer or equivalent officer.[153] The chief legal officer (or equivalent) must then investigate the situation[154] (or turn the matter over to a Qualified Legal Compliance Committee (QLCC)[155] within the corporation). If the chief legal officer (CLO) concludes that a material violation "has occurred, is ongoing, or is about to occur, he or she shall take all reasonable steps to cause the issuer to adopt an appropriate response, and shall advise the reporting attorney thereof."[156]

If the attorney making the original report is satisfied that the CLO has taken appropriate action, then nothing further needs to be done by the reporting attorney. If however, the reporting attorney is not satisfied that appropriate action has been taken, the reporting attorney must climb the next rung of the corporate ladder.

146. Rule 205.2(e) 17 C.F.R. § 205.2(e).

147. See, e.g., John C. Coffee, Corporate Securities, Myth & Reality: SEC's Proposed Attorney Standards, N.Y.L.J. p. 5, col. (Jan. 15, 2003).

150. 17 C.F.R. § 205.3(b).

153. If the reporting attorney believes that it would be futile to report to the CLO, then the reporting attorney should proceed directly to the second step of the ladder as set forth in Rule 205.3(b)(3) (17 C.F.R. § 205.3(b)(3)). This bypass is found in Rule 205.3(b)(4), 17 C.F.R. § 205.3(b)(4).

154. 17 C.F.R. § 205.3(b)(2).

155. Rule 205.3(c) permits, but does not require, a corporation to establish a reporting system as an alternative to reporting to the chief legal officer or equivalent.

156. 17 C.F.R. § 205.3(b)(2).

Chapter 10

SHAREHOLDER SUFFRAGE—PROXY REGULATION

Table of Sections

§ 10.1 The Regulation of Shareholder Suffrage Under the Exchange Act—Section 14 and the Proxy Rules: Introduction; Regulation of Voting Rights

With the passage of the Securities Exchange Act in 1934, Congress took note that a number of the great corporate frauds had been perpetrated through management solicitation of proxies that did not indicate to the shareholders the nature of any matters to be voted upon. Accordingly, section 14 of the 1934 Act[1] was included in the legislation in order to regulate the shareholder voting machinery for companies that are subject to both the registration requirements of section 12 of the Act[2] and the reporting requirements of section 13.[3] Although focusing on the voting process, the federal proxy rules do not address substantive voting rights, which remain a matter of state law and are generally determined by the law of the state of incorporation.

There are four primary aspects of SEC proxy regulation. First, by virtue of section 14(a) there must be full and fair disclosure of all material facts with regard to any management submitted proposals that will be subject to a shareholder vote. Second, material misstatements, omissions, and fraud in

§ 10.1

1. 15 U.S.C.A. § 78n.
2. 15 U.S.C.A. § 78*l*. *See* § 9.2 *supra*.
3. 15 U.S.C.A. § 78m. *See* § 9.3 *supra*.

connection with the solicitation of proxies are prohibited,[6] and the courts have recognized implied private remedies in the hands of injured investors.[7] Third, the federal proxy regulation facilitates shareholder solicitation of proxies as management is not only required to submit relevant shareholders proposals in its own proxy statements,[8] but also to allow the proponents to explain their position in the face of any management opposition.[9] Fourth, the proxy rules mandate full disclosure in non-management proxy materials[10] and thus are significant in corporate control struggles and contested take-over attempts.[11]

§ 10.1[2] Substantive Regulation of Voting Rights

In contrast to the Exchange Act's disclosure approach, the securities exchanges have traditionally imposed rules affecting voting rights of listed companies' shares.[19] In 1988, the SEC broke with tradition and introduced its voting rights rule to protect against the dilution of shareholder rights,[20] a matter previously regulated only by virtue of exchange rules. As discussed more fully below, the SEC's rule was struck down as not supported by the Commission's statutory grant of power. The exchange and Nasdaq shareholder voting rules were not affected and thus continue to apply.

The applicable exchange and Nasdaq rules not only govern the dilution of voting rights but also mandate a shareholder vote under certain circumstances. Thus, for example, under the New York Stock Exchange's so-called twenty percent rule,[21] a shareholder vote is required for any action by an issuer which would result in the issuance of additional shares having a significant diluting effect. If the issuance of shares would increase the outstanding shares of a class of exchange listed securities by more than twenty percent, the issuer must seek formal shareholder approval even though no approval would otherwise be required under the law of the state of incorporation or any other state law.[22] The American Stock Exchange has a similar rule[23] as does the National Association of Securities Dealers for securities traded through its Nasdaq automated quotation system.[24]

Under the New York Stock Exchange's one share/one vote rule, all New York Stock Exchange listed shares had to be given voting rights, and they must be equal voting rights.[25] The American Stock Exchange required that

---

6. 17 C.F.R. § 240.14a–9.

7. J.I. Case Co. v. Borak, 377 U.S. 426, 84 S.Ct. 1555, 12 L.Ed.2d 423 (1964). *See* § 10.3 *infra.*

8. 17 C.F.R. § 240.14a–8. *See* § 10.8 *infra.*

9. 17 C.F.R. § 240.14a–8(b).

10. *See* 17 C.F.R. § 240.14a–2.

11. *See generally* Edward R. Aranow & Herbert A. Einhorn, Proxy Contests for Corporate Control (2d ed. 1968).

19. *See,* N.Y.S.E. Company Manual §§ 312.00, 313.00; American Stock Exchange Listing Standards, Policies and Requirements § 122, Am. Stock Exch. Guide (CCH) ¶ 10,022.

20. 17 C.F.R. § 240.19c–4 which is discussed below. *See* Sec.Exch. Act Rel. No. 34–25891, [1987–1988 Transfer Binder] Fed.Sec.L.Rep. (CCH) ¶ 84,247 (July 7, 1988); Sec.Exch. Act Rel. No. 34–24623, [1987 Transfer Binder] Fed.Sec.L.Rep. (CCH) ¶ 84,140 (June 22, 1987).

21. N.Y.S.E. Company Manual § 312.00.

22. N.Y.S.E. Company Manual § 312.00.

23. American Stock Exchange Listing Standards, Policies and Requirements § 122, Am. Stock Exch. Guide (CCH) ¶ 10,022.

24. NASDAQ Marketplace Rules 4310(c)(25)(G)(i)(d), 4320(e)(21)(G)(i)(d), and 4460(i)(1)(D).

25. The one share/one vote rule prohibits the listing of shares with less than full voting rights. N.Y.S.E. Listed Company Manual § 313.00(C), (D).

common stock be voting stock but did not limit dual class voting.[26] Traditionally, the NASD and the over-the-counter markets did not have limitations on nonvoting or dual class voting stock. However, as described below, the NASD subsequently agreed with the New York and American exchanges upon a uniform voting rights rule.

This issuance of weighted voting stock has become a common anti-takeover maneuver.[27] Such unequal voting rights violate the New York Stock Exchange's one share/one vote rule. However, in light of the increasing use of this defensive tactic, the exchange undertook a reevaluation of its one share/one vote rule and suspended enforcement of the rule.[28] Under a compromise solution drafted by the New York Stock Exchange, which required SEC approval, listed companies could have created a class of shares with unequal voting rights provided that the recapitalization be approved by both a majority of independent directors and a majority of the shareholders.[29]

The SEC was concerned that some action be taken and urged the exchanges and the NASD to adopt a uniform voting rights rule that would limit dual class voting that is instituted as a defensive anti-takeover maneuver. Despite this attempt to resolve the problem through self regulation, the exchanges and the NASD were unable to reach an accord. The SEC then responded by proposing its own rule. Although the Commission's authority to adopt such a rule had been questioned, Rule 19c–4 became effective in 1988. However, just two years after the adoption of the SEC's rule, as described more fully below, it was ruled invalid.[34]

The D.C. Circuit Court of Appeals in Business Roundtable v. SEC ruled that the Commission lacked statutory authority to promulgate a rule regulating substantive voting rights.[42] Accordingly, Rule 19c–4 was declared invalid. The court noted that shareholder voting rights traditionally have been a matter of state corporate law, but that they could be regulated by the Commission but only on the basis of an appropriate grant of statutory authority. The court reviewed the various statutory provisions put forth by the Commission as a basis for the regulation. Section 19(c)[43] set forth three bases for regulation: (1) assurance of fair administration of self regulatory organizations, (2) conformity to the requirements of the Exchange Act, and (3) promulgation of rules "otherwise in furtherance of the" Act's purpose. The SEC relied on the third basis. Section 14 of the Act[44] expressly states that the regulation of the proxy process is to ensure "fair shareholder suffrage." The court noted, however, that the legislative purpose must be defined in terms of the *means* of regulation selected and section 14 regulates the proxy process, *not* substantive voting rights. The court further pointed out that

26. American Stock Exchange Listing Standards, Policies and Requirements § 122, Am. Stock Exch. Guide (CCH) ¶ 10,022.

27. Defensive tactics to takeovers are discussed in § 11.10 *infra.*

28. *See* New York Stock Exchange Initial Report of the subcommittee on Shareholder Participation and Qualitative Listing Standards, "Dual Class Capitalization" (Jan. 3, 1985); Roberta S. Karmel, Is One Share, One Vote Archaic? N.Y.L.J. p. 1 (Feb. 26, 1986).

29. *See* NYSE "Reluctantly" Adopts Dual Share Classification: SEC Approval Needed, 18 Sec.Reg. & L.Rep. (BNA) 998 (July 11, 1986).

34. Business Roundtable v. SEC, 905 F.2d 406 (D.C.Cir.1990).

42. Business Roundtable v. SEC, 905 F.2d 406 (D.C.Cir.1990).

43. 15 U.S.C.A. § 78s(c).

44. 15 U.S.C.A. § 78n.

reading section 19(c) as broadly as the Commission suggested could give the SEC power to regulate many matters of corporate management traditionally left to state law.[45] This simply would be too broad an interpretation of section 19(c)'s residual power. The court thus reasoned that if Rule 19c–4 is to survive, the SEC's power to regulate the substantive voting rights must be distinguished from other matters of corporate governance. The court concluded that there was no support for a "special and anomalous exception to the Act's otherwise intelligible conceptual line excluding the Commission from corporate governance."[46]

The long history of the New York Stock Exchange's one share/one vote rule was held not to constitute a sufficient basis for reading SEC regulatory authority into the Act. In December of 1994, a uniform rule that had been agreed upon by these three self regulatory organizations was approved by the SEC.[53]

Notwithstanding the development of exchange and Nasdaq voting rights rules, the primary source of shareholder voting rights remains the law of the state of incorporation. Many state statutes permit shareholders to have disparate voting rights.[54] However, although disparate voting rights may be permitted by statute, management's fiduciary obligations to its shareholders may place limits on weighted voting as a defensive tactic.[55]

§ 10.2 Full Disclosure in the Solicitation of Proxies

§ 10.2[1] Overview of Proxy Disclosure Requirements

Subject to limited exceptions[1] and exemptions,[2] section 14(a) of the Exchange Act[3] makes it unlawful to solicit proxies with respect to any non-exempt security registered under section 12 of the Exchange Act[4] in contra-

45. For example, could the SEC properly require independent directors or set shareholder quorum and vote requirements?

46. 905 F.2d at 413.

53. *See* SEC Approves New Voting Rights Rule, Adopts Rule Streamlining SRO Regulation, 26 Sec. Reg. & L. Rep. (BNA) 1708 (Dec. 23, 1994).

54. *See, e.g.,* Jeffrey N. Gordon, Ties that Bond: Dual Class Common Stock and the Problem of Shareholder Choice, 76 Calif.L.Rev. 1 (1988); Note, Dual Class Recapitalizations and Shareholder Voting Rights, 87 Colum.L.Rev. 106 (1987).

55. *See* Packer v. Yampol, 1986 WL 4748 (Del.Ch.1986) (variable voting rights plan may be subject to judicial interference if its operation appears to be unfair). *See also* Asarco Inc. v. Court, 611 F.Supp. 468 (D.N.J.1985). *See generally* Note, Dual Class Recapitalizations and Shareholder Voting Rights, 87 Colum.L.Rev. 106 (1987).

§ 10.2

1. The proxy rules do not apply where the securities are beneficially held in the name of or held as nominee by the person soliciting. Rule 14a–2(1), (2), 17 C.F.R. § 240.14a–2(a)(1), (2). Also excluded from the proxy rules are solicitations involving a 1933 Act registration, solicitations pursuant to a bankruptcy reorganization, and solicitations that were subject to the former Public Utility Holding Company Act, which was repealed in 2005. *Id.* § 240.14aB2(a)(3)B(5).

2. Many foreign private issuers are exempt from the proxy rules. *See* Rule 3a12–3, 17 C.F.R. § 240.3a12–3. The exemption does not, however, extend to the Williams Act tender offer and share acquisition disclosure requirements. The Second Circuit upheld Rule 3a12–3 as a valid exercise of the SEC's rulemaking authority. Schiller v. Tower Semiconductor Ltd., 449 F.3d 286 (2d Cir. 2006).

3. 15 U.S.C.A. § 78n(a).

4. 15 U.S.C.A. § 78k. Registered reporting companies are those issuers having a class of securities traded on a national securities exchange, as well as those issuers having assets of at least $10,000,000 and also having a class of equity securities with more than 500 shareholders. 15

vention of such rules and regulations as the SEC shall establish. The proxy rules are concerned with assuring full disclosure to investors of matters likely to be considered at shareholder meetings. In addition, as discussed more fully below, in the event that proxies will not be solicited, shareholders must nevertheless receive a management information statement that will provide the disclosures that would have been contained in the proxy statement had proxies been solicited. Also, as discussed more fully below, the proxy rules impose disclosure obligations not only on management but on any shareholder or third party that decides to solicit proxies or otherwise influence shareholder votes.[5] In addition to proxy solicitation materials, Rule 14a–3(b) requires the sending of an annual report of the company's operations to shareholders.[6]

SEC Rule 14a–16[10] permits, and for the two years beginning in 2008 is phasing in a mandatory posting of proxy materials on the Internet. This will notify the shareholders entitled to vote of the ability to access the proxy statement and the proxy on the Internet.

§ 10.2[2] Proxy Solicitations: The Nature and Scope of Federal Proxy Regulation

Regulation 14A consists of a series of SEC rules that set forth the applicable disclosure requirements. In Rules 14a–3 through 14a–15[11] the Commission sets forth the types of information that must be contained in public companies' proxy solicitations subject to the Act. These requirements are discussed in the sections that follow. The discussion directly below provides an overview of regulatory concerns.

The regulation of proxy disclosure has been a major item on the SEC's agenda over the past two decades. In 1990, Congress enacted the Shareholder Communication Act, which extends the applicability of the proxy rules that apply to reporting companies generally to mutual funds and other investment companies that are registered under the Investment Company Act of 1940.[13] In 1992, the Commission enacted major revisions to the proxy solicitation rules in order to facilitate communications by and between institutional holders of shares of 1934 Act reporting companies.[14] The rules adopted in 1992 included the relaxation of the definition of proxy solicitation, the elimination of a pre-filing requirement for proxy materials, permitting preliminary proxy materials to be used before the filing of the definitive proxy statement, and other changes to facilitate institutional shareholder involvement in corporate governance.

U.S.C.A. § 78*l*; 17 C.F.R. § 240.12g–1. The proxy rules thus do not apply to issuers who are required to file periodic reports under section 15(d), 15 U.S.C.A. § 78, which applies to securities not subject to section 12's registration requirements, but which were issued pursuant to a 1933 Act registration statement. The 1934 Act registration and reporting requirements are discussed in §§ 9.2, 9.3 *supra*.

5. Third parties do not, however, have an obligation to disclose in advance their intent to utilize the proxy machinery. *See* Azurite Corp. v. Amster & Co., 844 F.Supp. 929 (S.D.N.Y.1994).

6. 17 C.F.R. § 240.14a–3(b). *See* § 10.6[2] *infra*.

10. 17 C.F.R.§ 240.14a–16.

11. 17 C.F.R. §§ 240.14a–3C240.14a–15.

13. 15 U.S.C.A. § 78n(b).

14. Exch. Act Rel. 34–31326 (SEC Oct. 22, 1992).

The Securities and Exchange Commission makes a distinction between the proxy itself and solicitation materials. The proxy itself is any shareholder consent or authorization regarding the casting of that shareholder's vote.[17]

The applicable Securities and Exchange Commission rule takes a broad view of the terms "solicit" and "solicitation" so as to include in the definition "any request for a proxy whether or not accompanied by or included in a form of any request to execute or not to execute, or to revoke, a proxy; [and] the furnishing of any communication to security holders under circumstances reasonably calculated to result in the procurement, withholding or revocation of a proxy."[18] This definition has been liberally interpreted by the courts to include materials such as open letters to regulatory bodies, which although not directed toward shareholders, are reasonably calculated to affect a reasonable shareholder's voting decision.[19] Along the same lines, a press release challenging the integrity of a limited partnership's managers and urging holders of limited partnership interests to vote in a certain way met the basic definition of proxy solicitation.[20] A company's newsletter urging shareholders not to vote until they received revised proxy materials was quite properly held to have been a proxy solicitation.[21] Similarly, a newsletter urging shareholders to reject a shareholder proposal was a solicitation subject to the SEC filing requirements.[22] Communications which clearly serve another function, even when occurring around the same time as a shareholder vote, will not be subject to the proxy rules simply because of their timing and possible tangential effect on a voting decision. Thus, for example, research recommendations by brokerage firms may not implicate the proxy rules even though they contain reference to issues that may be relevant to any upcoming vote by the shareholders of a company mentioned in the research report.[23]

As part of an effort to increase shareholder participation in corporate governance, in 1992, the Commission amended the proxy rules to provide that a shareholder may announce how it intends to vote on a matter and explain the reasons for the vote without having to comply with the proxy rules.[24] The

17. The Commission also explains that "[T]he consent or authorization may take the form of failure to object or dissent." 17 C.F.R. § 240.14a–1.

18. 17 C.F.R. § 240.14a–1(f).

19. Long Island Lighting Co. v. Barbash, 779 F.2d 793 (2d Cir.1985) (proxy rules can cover advertisement indirectly addressed to shareholders that appears in publications having a general circulation); Brown v. Chicago, Rock Island & Pacific Railroad Co., 328 F.2d 122 (7th Cir.1964) (open letter to ICC to garner public support for approval of railroad merger held not to be a proxy solicitation); Union Pacific Railroad Co. v. Chicago & North Western Railway Co., 226 F.Supp. 400 (N.D.Ill.1964) (progress report on company's condition, sent out prior to shareholder meeting during takeover battle).

20. Capital Real Estate Investors Tax Exempt Fund Limited Partnership v. Schwartzberg, 929 F.Supp. 105 (S.D.N.Y.1996) (the press release failed to fall within the safe harbor of Rule 14a–1 since the proxy solicitation had begun prior to the press release in question).

21. Krauth v. Executive Telecard, Ltd., 870 F.Supp. 543 (S.D.N.Y.1994), s.c. 890 F.Supp. 269 (S.D.N.Y.1995).

22. Shoen v. AMERCO, 885 F.Supp. 1332 (D.Nev.1994).

23. Merrill Lynch, Pierce, Fenner & Smith, Inc., 1997 WL 720940 (SEC No Action Letter Oct. 24, 1997) (indicating that the proxy rules would not apply to research reports complying with either Rule 138 or 139 of the 1933 Act). For treatment of broker-dealer research department investment recommendations under the 1933 Act, *see* § 2.4, *supra*.

24. Rule 14a–1; 17 C.F.R. § 240.14a–1. *See* Regulation of Communications Among Shareholders, Sec. Exch. Act Rel. No. 34–31326, 52 S.E.C. Docket 2028, 1992 WL 301258 (SEC Oct. 16, 1992).

1992 amendments also brought in a number of other reforms, including an exemption from the rules for certain communications.[25]

The proxy rules provide an exemption for shareholders desiring to communicate with one another so long as proxies are not actually being solicited.[26] The purpose of this exemption was to permit institutional shareholders to communicate with one another without having to comply with the filing requirements. There also is an exemption from the proxy rules for solicitations by persons other than the issuer where no more than ten persons are solicited.[27] Owners of more than five million dollars of the issuer's securities must give public notice of their intent to engage in this type of soliciting activity.[28]

Another important exemption from the definition of proxy solicitation was adopted in 2007 in order to facilitate online shareholder forums and discussion groups.[31] Participants in an electronic forum are not soliciting proxies within the meaning of the federal proxy rules if the communication is sufficiently in advance of the meeting—more than sixty days in advance of the date announced for the company's annual or special meeting (or in the case of companies announcing the meeting less than sixty days in advance of the meeting, the communication may not occur more than two days after announcement of the meeting).[32] Although the exemption does not affect preexisting third-party forums such as those operated by Yahoo or Motley Fool, it could impact company-specific chat rooms.[33]

§ 10.2[3] Proxy Solicitations: Required Disclosures

SEC Rule 14a–3[37] sets forth the types of information that must be included in materials used for proxy solicitations. All nonexempt proxy solicitations must be accompanied or preceded by the information required in Schedule 14A.[39] Schedule 14A requires the following information, in addition to the date, time, and place of the meeting.[40] The first page of the proxy statement must disclose the approximate date on which the proxy statement and the form of proxy were first given to securities holders.[41] The proxy statement must include the deadline for submitting shareholder proposals for inclusion in the proxy statement and form of proxy for the next annual meeting.[42] In addition, the proxy statement must state the last date for

25. *See* Regulation of Communications Among Shareholders, Sec. Exch. Act Rel. No. 34–31326, 52 S.E.C. Docket 2028, 1992 WL 301258 (SEC Oct. 16, 1992).

26. Rule 14a–2(b)(1), 17 C.F.R. § 240.14a–2(b)(1).

27. Rule 14a–2(b)(2), 17 C.F.R. § 240.14a–2(b)(2).

28. Rule 14a–2(b)(1), 17 C.F.R. § 240.14a–2(b)(1).

31. Electronic Shareholder Forums, Sec. Exch. Act Rel. No. 34-57172, Inv. Co. Act Rel. No. IC-28124, 2008 WL 170875 (SEC Jan. 18, 2008).

32. *See* Rule 14a–2(b)(6), 17 C.F.R. § 240.14a–2(b)(6). *See also* Rule 14a–17, 17 C.F.R. § 230.14a–17.

33. *See* Electronic Shareholder Forums, Sec. Exch. Act Rel. No. 34-57172, Inv. Co. Act Rel. No. IC-28124, 2008 WL 170875 (SEC Jan. 18, 2008).

37. 17 C.F.R. § 240.14a–3. *Cf.* Shidler v. All American Life & Financial Corp., 775 F.2d 917 (8th Cir.1985) (rejecting strict liability as the proper standard under the proxy rules).

39. 17 C.F.R. § 240.14a–101.

40. Schedule 14A, item 1(a).

41. Schedule 14A, item 1(b).

42. Schedule 14A, item 1(c). *See* Rule 14a–5(e)(1), 17 C.F.R. § 240.14a–5(e)(1). SEC Rule 14a–8 sets for the requirements and procedures for the inclusion of shareholder proposals in management's proxy statement. 17 C.F.R. § 240.14a–8 which is discussed in § 10.8 *infra.*

submission of shareholder proposals for the next annual meeting irrespective of their inclusion in management's proxy statement.[43] The proxy statement must also disclose whether the proxies solicited are revocable[44] and if so, the manner in which it may be revoked.[45] The proxy statement must identify and explain the availability of statutory dissenters rights of appraisal for any proposals to be voted upon.[46] This includes an explanation of whether the failure to vote against the proposal will result in a waiver of statutory appraisal rights.[47] The proxy statement must contain a description of the person making the solicitation, including identifying who is bearing the cost of the solicitation.[48] The proxy statement must contain disclosures relating to interests of directors, officers, and "participants"[49] in matters to be voted upon.[50]

The proxy statement must also list all of the company's voting securities and principal holders thereof.[51] The record date for determining which shareholders are entitled to vote and explanation of cumulative voting rights, if any, must also be disclosed in the proxy statement.[52] If any action is to be taken with respect to election of directors, the proxy statement must disclose and explain the nominees' relationship to affiliated companies and interest in issuer's activities.[53]

Management's proxy statement must disclose the compensation of the company's executive officers and directors.[54] Each year the shareholders of a publicly held company are entitled to disclosure of the following: (1) the direct and indirect compensation paid to the top executives; (2) a comparison chart, comparing the company's executive compensation stock price performance with that of comparable companies over the past five years; and (3) the compensation committee's report of policies and criteria used in fixing executive compensation.[55] In addition, in a reversal of its past policy, the SEC staff now takes the position that shareholder proposals relating to executive compensation may not automatically be excluded from management's proxy statement on the grounds that they relate to the ordinary business of the issuer.[56] The proxy related disclosures regarding management compensation

43. Schedule 14A, item 1(c). *See* Rule 14a–5(e)(2), 17 C.F.R. § 240.14a–5(e)(2).

44. Under state law, proxies generally are revocable unless coupled with an interest. *See* James D. Cox & Thomas Lee Hazen, Corporations § 13.23 (2d 3d 2004).

45. Schedule 14A, item 2.

46. Schedule 14A, item 3.

47. Schedule 14A, item 3, instruction 1.

48. Schedule 14A, item 4.

49. "Participant" is defined in Instruction 3 to Item 4 of Schedule 14A to include directors, nominees, persons sponsoring the solicitation, persons financing the solicitation, anyone extending credit for the solicitor, and anyone taking an active role in any of the above. 17 C.F.R. § 240.14a–101.

50. Schedule 14A, item 5.

51. Schedule 14A, item 6.

52. Schedule 14A, item 6.

53. Schedule 14A, item 7 is quite complex in requiring detailed disclosures. 17 C.F.R. § 240.14a–101 item 7. *See* § 10.2[5] *infra* for discussion of the disclosures relating to elections.

54. Schedule 14A, item 8.

55. Schedule 14A, item 8.

56. *See* § 10.8 *infra* which discusses the shareholder proposal rule (Rule 14a–8, 17 C.F.R. § 240.14a–8).

are supplemented by the enhanced disclosure requirements regarding executive compensation that is found in Item 402 of Regulation S–K.[57]

The proxy statement must also disclose relationships with any independent public accountant providing services in connection with the solicitation or matters to be acted upon, including shareholder approval of independent auditors.[58] The proxy statement must disclose the aggregate fees that the auditor billed the company for each of the following types of services: (a) audit and review of the company's financial statements, (b) financial information systems design and implementation services performed by the company's principal accounts, and (c) all other services provided by the company's principal accountants.[59]

The proxy statement must describe in detail any bonus, profit sharing, and other benefit plans to be voted upon.[60] Similar information is required with regard to any pension or retirement plans to be acted upon.[61] The disclosures relating to compensation and pension plans must include detailed descriptions of any options, warrants, or rights to be voted upon.[62]

The proxy statement must describe in detail any securities to be authorized for issuance.[63] In the case of any modification or exchange of securities, the proxy statement must contain detailed disclosures.[64] If the proxy statement is seeking authorization for the issuance of securities or for the modification or exchange of securities, the proxy statement must provide financial statements relating to any such transactions.[65]

The proxy statement must describe extraordinary transactions that are up for shareholder consideration. In the case of mergers, consolidations, and acquisitions, the proxy statement must provide detailed disclosures relating to any mergers, consolidations, or acquisitions to be voted upon.[66]

If property is to be acquired or disposed of as a result of a shareholder vote, there must be a description of any property to be acquired or disposed of upon a shareholder vote.[67] There must also be a description of the terms of the transaction.[68]

The proxy statement must contain a restatement of any accounts that would be made necessary by the actions to be voted upon.[69] If applicable, the proxy statement must identify and describe any reports to be acted upon.[70]

---

57. 17 C.F.R. § 229.402. *see* § 9.4[8][B] *supra*.

58. Schedule 14A, item 9.

59. Schedule 14A, item 9.

60. Schedule 14A, item 10.

61. Schedule 14A, item 10.

62. Schedule 14A, item 10.

63. Schedule 14A, item 11.

64. Schedule 14A, item 12.

65. Schedule 14A, item 13.

66. Schedule 14A, item 14. *See also* Regulation M–A, which is part of Regulation S–K, 17 C.F.R. §§ 229.1001 et seq.

67. Schedule 14A, item 15.

68. Schedule 14A, item 15.

69. Schedule 14A, item 16.

70. Schedule 14A, item 17.

If shareholder action is to be taken with respect to any matters that are not required to be submitted to the shareholders, the proxy statement must contain an explanation of why shareholder approval is being sought.[71] If the proxy solicitation involves amendments to the articles of incorporation, charter, or other documents requiring shareholder approval, the proxy statement must provide the reasons for any such proposed amendments.[72]

In the event that any matters not specified above are being submitted to the shareholders for a vote, the proxy statement must contain disclosures in the same degree of detail as would be required by the enumerated disclosure requirements.[73]

When many items are to be submitted for shareholder consideration, they must be clearly identified so that shareholders can make informed decisions on how to vote. With respect to all matters to be voted upon, the proxy statement must set forth the vote required for approval for each matter submitted to the shareholders.[75]

Schedule 14A's disclosure requirements apply both to management's proxy statement and proxy solicitations by others.[76] When the proxy solicitation relates to the annual meeting of security holders, where directors are to be elected, an annual report must accompany or precede a proxy solicitation on behalf of the issuer.[77] The proxy rules permit presentation of a "short slate" of directors.[78] The SEC's decision to permit short slates of directors was designed to encourage shareholder participation in the election process by providing a more likely opportunity for minority representation on the board.

Proxy solicitation materials must clearly discuss each item for which shareholder votes are solicited. Combining (or "bundling") two or more items together can be materially misleading and will interfere with the proper exercise of shareholder suffrage.[80]

Rule 14a–4[83] sets forth the appropriate form for the proxy itself as opposed to solicitation materials. For example, boldface type must indicate whether or not the proxy is solicited on behalf of the issuer's management. The proxy must also provide the person solicited with an opportunity to vote for or against proposals (management may indicate which proposals it supports) as well as the ability to abstain or withhold authority from voting as to any matters.[84] In the case of a shareholder election of directors, the proxy must leave room for write-in candidates.[85] In addition to seeking proxies on

71. Schedule 14A, item 18.

72. Schedule 14A, item 19.

73. Schedule 14A, item 20.

75. Schedule 14A, item 21.

76. *See, e.g.,* IBS Financial Corp. v. Seidman & Associates, L.L.C., 954 F.Supp. 980 (D.N.J. 1997), *affirmed in part, reversed in part,* 136 F.3d 940 (3d Cir.1998) (Schedule 14A by group of dissident shareholders contained adequate disclosures).

77. 17 C.F.R. § 240.14a–3(b). *See* § 10.6[2] *infra.*

78. Rule 14a–4(b)(2), 17 C.F.R. § 240.14a–4(b)(2).

80. Koppel v. 4987 Corp., 167 F.3d 125 (2d Cir.1999). *But cf., e.g.,* Koppel v. 4987 Corp., 2001 WL 47000, [2000–2001 Transfer Binder] Fed. Sec. L. Rep. (CCH) ¶ 91,306 (S.D.N.Y. 2001).

83. 17 C.F.R. § 240.14a–4.

84. *See, e.g.,* Shoen v. AMERCO, 885 F.Supp. 1332 (D.Nev.1994) (issuer must disclose that shareholder proposals may be brought up at the meeting and that the proxy will be voted on such matters as the proxy holder sees fit).

85. 17 C.F.R. § 240.14a–4(b)(2)(iii).

specific issues, the proxy rules permit the solicitation of discretionary proxies.[86]

Technological advancements have continuing significant impact on proxy solicitations. For example, it is now technologically possible for the corporation to receive proxies by telephone. In addition to the mechanics of voting which is a matter of the applicable state corporate law, technology has affected the delivery of the disclosure documents under federal law. The SEC permits electronic delivery of documents that need to be delivered to investors.[89] In order for the electronic delivery to satisfy the securities laws' disclosure obligations, the investor must previously have consented to electronic rather than hard copy delivery.[90]

Rule 14a–5[91] provides guidance as to the presentation of information in a proxy statement, including the size and form of printed material. In many cases, five preliminary copies of each proxy statement and the form of the proxy to be used must be filed with the SEC at least ten business days prior to the first date on which they are to be sent; however, the preliminary copies need not be filed if the proxy solicitation pertains to the regular annual meeting (or a special meeting held in lieu of the annual meeting) and the only matters to be considered are the election of directors, or approval or ratification of auditors and/or shareholder proposals.[92]

The advance filing requirements of Rule 14a–6 for the proxy statement were designed to promote full disclosure and complete dissemination of information in order to achieve the desired result of informed shareholder voting. It has been held that a violation of this rule can result in an implied private right of action.[97]

Rule 14a–10 prohibits the solicitation of undated, predated, or postdated proxies.[101] Rule 14a–12, permits proxy solicitation subject to certain conditions and prior to the furnishing of a proxy statement. Under Rule 14a–12 either there must be a description of the participants in the solicitation[102] or, alternatively, there must be a prominent legend in clear, plain language advising security holders where they can obtain information about the participants.[103] All sources of financing behind the solicitation must also be disclosed. Former Rule 14a–11[104] set forth special requirements relating to the solicitation of shareholders' votes in connection with the election of directors;

86. *See, e.g.,* Union of Needletrades v. May Department Stores Co., 26 F.Supp.2d 577 (S.D.N.Y.1997) (discretionary authority was obtained validly and could be used even though company knew proponent of shareholder proposal was planning on launching his own proxy campaign).

89. Use of Electronic Media, Sec. Act Rel. No. 33–7856, 2000 WL 502290 (SEC April 28, 2000).

90. Use of Electronic Media, Sec. Act Rel. No. 33–7856, 2000 WL 502290 (SEC April 28, 2000). *See* § 9.5[2] *supra.*

91. 17 C.F.R. § 240.14a–5.

92. 17 C.F.R. § 240.14a–6(a).

97. Morris v. Bush, 1999 WL 58857, [1999 Transfer Binder] Fed. Sec. L. Rep. (CCH) ¶ 90,430 (N.D. Tex. 1999).

101. 17 C.F.R. § 240.14a–10.

102. 17 C.F.R. § 240.14a–12(a)(1)(i). *See* Instruction 3 to Item 4 of Schedule 14A, 17 C.F.R. § 240.14a–101.

103. 17 C.F.R. § 240.14a–12(a)(1)(i).

104. 17 C.F.R. § 240.14a–11. (1999) (rescinded).

however, that rule was made unnecessary by many of the provisions of Rule 14a–12.[105]

In 2007, the SEC amended its rules to require the use of the Internet for proxy solicitations.[106] The Internet posting requirement is to be phased in over a two-year period (the compliance date is January 1, 2008 for large companies and for all other affected companies, mutual funds and other soliciting persons the Internet posting is required as of January 1, 2009). Companies have two options for Internet posting of proxy solicitations and notice of meetings. Companies may either provide for "full set delivery" of proxy materials online or, alternatively, must post online notice.[107] The notice must be in "plain English" and must be posted, at least forty days before the meeting.

§ 10.3 Rule 14a–9 and the Implied Remedy for Material Misstatements and Omissions in Proxy Materials; Standing to Sue; Scienter vs. Negligence; Attorneys' Fees

§ 10.3[1] The Implied Private Remedy for Material Misstatements in the Solicitation of Proxies

Rule 14a–9 prohibits material misstatements and omissions in connection with the solicitation of proxies.[1] Rule 14a–9's prohibitions against material misstatements and omissions in proxy solicitations apply to all proxy solicitations and thus are not limited to management's proxy materials.

The Supreme Court has repeatedly recognized an implied remedy for violation of Rule 14a–9's antifraud provisions.[2] In fact, the Rule 14a–9 private remedy was the first Exchange Act implied right of action to be recognized by the Court.[3] Although the Court has not been generous in granting additional implied rights of action, there have been indications that the Rule 14a–9 remedy continues to be relatively expansive. In contrast, it has been held that there is no private remedy for violation of SEC Rule 14b–1[6] which imposes on brokerage firms the duty to transmit proxy materials to their customers.[7]

§ 10.3[2] Standing to Sue Under Rule 14a–9

Since it is an implied remedy, there is no express provision regarding appropriate plaintiffs in private actions under the proxy rules. Presumably, all

---

105. *See* Regulation of Takeovers and Security Holder Communications, Sec. Exch. Act Rel. No. 34–42055, 1999 WL 969596 (SEC Oct. 22, 1999).

106. Rule 14a–16, 17 C.F.R. § 240.14a–16. See Shareholder Choice Regarding Proxy Materials, Sec. Exch. Act Rel. No. 34–56135, Inv. Co. Act Rel. No. IC–27911, 72 Fed. Reg. 42222–01, 2007 WL 2186104 (SEC Aug. 1, 2007).

107. Rules 14a–3(a), 14a–16, 17 C.F.R. §§ 240.14a–3, 14a–16.

§ 10.3

1. 17 C.F.R. § 240.14a–9.

2. TSC Industries, Inc. v. Northway, Inc., 426 U.S. 438, 96 S.Ct. 2126, 48 L.Ed.2d 757 (1976); Mills v. Electric Auto–Lite Co., 396 U.S. 375, 90 S.Ct. 616, 24 L.Ed.2d 593 (1970); J.I. Case Co. v. Borak, 377 U.S. 426, 84 S.Ct. 1555, 12 L.Ed.2d 423 (1964); 17 C.F.R. § 14a–9.

3. J.I. Case Co. v. Borak, 377 U.S. 426, 84 S.Ct. 1555, 12 L.Ed.2d 423 (1964).

6. 17 C.F.R. § 240.14b–1. *See* § 10.10 *infra*.

7. Pundaleeka v. Fidelity Brokerage Services, Inc., [1999–2000 Transfer Binder] Fed. Sec. L. Rep. (CCH) ¶ 90,905, 1999 WL 412615 (N.D.Ill.1999).

a private plaintiff need show in a Rule 14a–9 action is that he or she was injured in connection with a proxy solicitation covered by the Exchange Act's regulation, regardless of whether there was either a purchase or sale of securities[12] involved.

Thus, for example, a corporation or a shareholder has standing to complain of a proxy rule violation so long as it can show injury and a causal connection between the violation and the injury.[14] The federal proxy rules were designed to protect the right of a shareholder to a fully-informed vote on matters with regard to which proxies have been solicited. Even in the case of management misstatements in connection with a shareholder proposal, standing is not limited to the shareholder whose proposal was the subject of the alleged violations.

Any shareholder entitled to vote on the proposal has a right to full disclosure and thus may sue to redress such a violation of the proxy rules.[15] Since the federal proxy regulations are designed to protect shareholder voting rights, standing should be limited to shareholders who had a right to vote.[16] Courts should be careful in giving too broad a reading to this limitation on standing to sue under the proxy rules. It is one thing to say that a proxy contestant whose only interest is in gaining control of a corporation should not be given standing under the proxy rules, since federal proxy regulation was designed to protect full disclosure in the exercise of shareholder suffrage and not to guarantee rights to would-be control acquirers. It would be quite another, however, to deny standing to shareholders seeking to protect their interest through a proxy battle simply because they are proxy contestants with regard to the vote in question.

While courts should strive to protect the rights of shareholders whose interest in the corporation is likely to be affected by proxy rule violations, the courts should be mindful of potential misuse and abuse of proxy litigation. Accordingly, a shareholder having ulterior reasons for challenging a vote under the proxy rules should not be granted standing.[20]

A shareholder who did not have shareholder status at the time of the alleged proxy violations does not have standing to sue under Rule 14a–9.[21] In contrast, although it was argued that standing in proxy cases should be limited to shareholders, it has been held that a director had standing to bring suit challenging an election based on alleged misstatements in the proxy

12. The courts have imposed a purchaser/seller standing requirement in private damage actions under SEC Rule 10b–5. *E.g.,* Blue Chip Stamps v. Manor Drug Stores, 421 U.S. 723, 95 S.Ct. 1917, 44 L.Ed.2d 539 (1975), *rehearing denied* 423 U.S. 884, 96 S.Ct. 157, 46 L.Ed.2d 114 (1975). *See* § 12.7[1] *infra.*

14. *See* Stahl v. Gibraltar Financial Corp., 967 F.2d 335 (9th Cir.1992) (plaintiff need not show that he or she voted in reliance on the alleged misstatements).

15. United Paperworkers International Union v. International Paper Co., 985 F.2d 1190 (2d Cir.1993); Krauth v. Executive Telecard, Ltd., 890 F.Supp. 269, 286 (S.D.N.Y.1995).

16. Royal Business Group v. Realist, Inc., 933 F.2d 1056 (1st Cir.1991), affirming 751 F.Supp. 311 (D.Mass.1990) (section 14(a) action dismissed since plaintiff was not a shareholder and thus any injury that may have been due to alleged proxy rule violations could not be challenged under the Act).

20. *See* AMR Corp. v. UAL Corp., 781 F.Supp. 292 (S.D.N.Y.1992) (airline industry competitor with minimal interest in target company was denied standing since the apparent reason for seeking to enjoin the transaction was to gain a competitive advantage).

21. Murray v. Hospital Corp. of America, 682 F.Supp. 343 (M.D.Tenn.1988). *See also* Gabrielsen v. BancTexas Group, Inc., 675 F.Supp. 367, 373–74 (N.D.Tex.1987).

materials.[22] The court reasoned that "[s]tanding depends on injury, and we believe that one who alleges that he has been wrongfully ousted from a Board of Directors because management improperly persuaded other shareholders not to vote for him, has articulated an injury cognizable under section 14(a)."[23] While the court's decision granting proxy rule standing to directors certainly furthers the integrity of the voting process, it is at odds with Supreme Court cases holding that implied remedies are limited to members of an especial class which the legislation is designed to protect.[24] This extension of proxy rule standing to directors seems to be contrary to the current direction of implied remedies.

Ordinarily, a candidate for a director position will not have standing to challenge proxy solicitations under the proxy rules. Nevertheless, when the defeated director candidate is also a shareholder, he or she may be able to state a federal proxy claim.[26] However, it would seem that for such standing to exist, the claim must be couched in terms of the plaintiff's rights as a shareholder to full disclosure rather than in terms of the would-be director's rights to a fair election.

As discussed elsewhere in this treatise,[27] reliance on the misstatements traditionally is an element of any fraud claim. However, this does not seem to be the case with respect to fraud actions based on the federal proxy rules. For example, it was held that a shareholder has standing to challenge a misleading proxy statement upon allegations of direct injury notwithstanding the absence of allegations of actual reliance.[28] Accordingly, it is not necessary to allege that the shareholder bringing suit relied on the misstatements, provided he or she can show a causally related injury.[29]

§ 10.3[3] The Standard of Culpability Under Rule 14a–9: Negligence Versus Scienter

It is an elementary principle of common law fraud that the defendant committing the fraud must have acted with a state of mind amounting to scienter.[30] Scienter also is required to prove a violation of SEC Rule 10b–5.[31]

---

22. Palumbo v. Deposit Bank, 758 F.2d 113 (3d Cir.1985).

23. 758 F.2d at 116.

24. *E.g.* Piper v. Chris–Craft Industries, Inc., 430 U.S. 1, 97 S.Ct. 926, 51 L.Ed.2d 124 (1977), *rehearing denied* 430 U.S. 976, 97 S.Ct. 1668, 52 L.Ed.2d 371 (1977) (competing tender offeror does not have standing under the Williams Act; if there is such an especial class, it is the target company and its shareholders). *See* §§ 11.10, 12.2 *infra.*

26. Morris v. Bush, 1999 WL 417928, [1999 Transfer Binder] Fed. Sec. L. Rep. (CCH) ¶ 90,521 (N.D. Tex. 1999) (sustaining § 124(a)(9) claim by former board members against ousted chairman of the board).

27. *See* § 12.10 *infra.*

28. Bradshaw v. Jenkins, 1984 WL 2457, [1984 Transfer Binder] Fed.Sec.L.Rep. (CCH) ¶ 91,645 (W.D.Wash.1984).

29. Stahl v. Gibraltar Financial Corp., 967 F.2d 335 (9th Cir.1992) (plaintiff did not rely on misstatements but alleged a proximately caused loss; this was sufficient to permit standing in a suit brought after the transaction in question—the court believed this result was compelled by the Supreme Court decision in Virginia Bankshares, Inc. v. Sandberg, 501 U.S. 1083, 111 S.Ct. 2749, 115 L.Ed.2d 929 (1991)).

30. *E.g.,* Derry v. Peek, 14 App.Cas. 337 (House of Lords 1889). *See generally* W. Page Keeton, Dan B. Dobbs, Robert E. Keeton & David G. Owen, Prosser and Keeton on Torts § 107 (5th ed. 1984).

31. Aaron v. SEC, 446 U.S. 680, 100 S.Ct. 1945, 64 L.Ed.2d 611 (1980); Ernst & Ernst v. Hochfelder, 425 U.S. 185, 96 S.Ct. 1375, 47 L.Ed.2d 668 (1976).

However, scienter is not required to establish a violation of Rule 14a–9's prohibitions against material misstatements and omissions in connection with a proxy solicitation. For example, a number of federal courts of appeals and district courts have upheld private 14a–9 claims based on negligence, thus not requiring scienter.[33] The reasoning underlying the Supreme Court's ruling in Aaron v. SEC[36] mandates that a showing of negligent conduct will suffice.

§ 10.3[4] Materiality Under Rule 14a–9

In order to be actionable under Rule 14a–9, the misstatement or omission must have been a material one. As discussed more fully in a later section of this treatise,[42] the concept of materiality under the proxy rules is much the same as under the securities laws generally.[43] This means that the misstatement or omission must be of a character that there is "a substantial likelihood that a reasonable shareholder *would* consider it important in deciding how to vote."[44] Ordinarily, judgment on the pleadings or summary judgment based on a finding of no materiality will not be appropriate.[45]

§ 10.3[5] Causation Under Rule 14a–9

The Supreme Court in Virginia Bankshares, Inc. v. Sandberg[50] has narrowed the type of causation that will suffice for a private plaintiff to establish a claim under the proxy rules. The Court in *Virginia Bankshares* held, in a five-to-four decision, that a private right of action did not lie for alleged deficiencies in proxies related to a shareholder vote that was not required to effectuate the transaction in question. *Virginia Bankshares* involved a vote taken under a state corporate law conflict of interest statute that applies to transactions between a corporation and interested directors. In an earlier decision, the Supreme Court had indicated by way of dictum that something less than but-for causation might support a claim for violation of the proxy rules.[51] The Court's subsequent decision in *Virginia Bankshares* indicates that but-for causation is in fact required.

Following the decision in *Virginia Bankshares*, it is clear that a shareholder cannot complain of alleged violations in connection with a proxy solicitation when the state law does not require the shareholder vote as a necessary step in the consummation of the transaction.[52] But what about the situation where a shareholder vote is required but the management soliciting the proxies controls sufficient votes to assure the success of the vote? As discussed more fully in a subsequent section of this treatise,[53] there is

33. *E.g.* In re Exxon Mobil Corp. Securities Litigation, 500 F.3d 189, 196 (3d Cir. 2007).

36. 446 U.S. 680, 100 S.Ct. 1945, 64 L.Ed.2d 611 (1980).

42. *See* § 12.9 *infra*.

43. *E.g.*, In re DNAP Securities Litigation, 2000 WL 1358619, [2000–2001 Transfer Binder] Fed. Sec. L. Rep. (CCH) ¶ 91,215 (N.D.Cal. 2000) (proxy statement for merger was not materially misleading).

44. TSC Industries, Inc. v. Northway, Inc., 426 U.S. 438, 449, 96 S.Ct. 2126, 2132, 48 L.Ed.2d 757 (1976) (emphasis added). *Accord* Basic Inc. v. Levinson, 485 U.S. 224, 108 S.Ct. 978, 99 L.Ed.2d 194 (1988).

45. *E.g.*, Marks v. CDW Computer Centers, Inc., 122 F.3d 363, 369–70 (7th Cir.1997).

50. 501 U.S. 1083, 111 S.Ct. 2749, 115 L.Ed.2d 929 (1991), *appeal after remand* 979 F.2d 332 (4th Cir.1992), *opinion vacated* 1993 WL 524680 (4th Cir.1993).

51. Mills v. Electric Auto–Lite Co., 396 U.S. 375, 90 S.Ct. 616, 24 L.Ed.2d 593 (1970).

52. *See, e.g.*, Dominick v. Marcove, 809 F.Supp. 805 (D.Colo.1992).

53. *See* § 10.5 *infra*. *See also, e.g.*, Stahl v. Gibraltar Financial Corp., 967 F.2d 335 (9th Cir.1992).

considerable authority for the proposition that even in such a case a plaintiff can sue if it can be shown that the transaction would have taken a different form had it not been for the misstatements or omissions in question.[54] Thus, for example, it has been held that a shareholder who claimed interference with a statutory right of appraisal was able to maintain a claim under the proxy rules.[55] However, where the defendants had sufficient votes to assure the consummation of the transaction in question, Rule 10b–5 could not be used to provide a remedy for the alleged unfairness of the merger.[56] Also, there is language in the *Virginia Bankshares* decision that could support the conclusion that proof that the required number of votes were assured may be sufficient to defeat a claim for violation of the proxy rules.[57] For example, in Grace v. Rosenstock[58] the Second Circuit held that minority shareholders were unable to establish that material misstatements in the proxy materials caused the freeze-out transaction that they challenged. In that case, the plaintiff minority shareholders had voted against the merger and thus were entitled to dissenters' appraisal rights under state law as their exclusive remedy.

In any event, the causal connection between the alleged violations and the ultimate transaction and/or injury must be direct.[61] It follows, for example, that a claim for misstatements made in connection with the directors' election was too remote from the injury that resulted from alleged director misconduct after the election in question.[62]

Courts have broken down causation in securities cases into two separate but related concepts. Causation consists of both: (1) *transaction causation*, which is designed to demonstrate that the misstatements or omissions were causally related to the occurrence of the transaction and (2) *loss causation*, which is a connection between the misstatements and the actual economic harm resulting from the transaction.[66]

§ 10.3[6] Relief Other Than Damages in Actions Under Rule 14a–9

In addition to an action for damages, Rule 14a–9 will support a claim for injunctive relief in actions brought by private parties or brought by the SEC.[67] For example, courts have been willing to order that a new meeting be held in

54. Wilson v. Great American Industries, Inc., 979 F.2d 924 (2d Cir.1992); Cowin v. Bresler, 741 F.2d 410 (D.C.Cir.1984) (election of directors); Schlick v. Penn–Dixie Cement Corp., 507 F.2d 374, 384 (2d Cir.1974), *cert. denied* 421 U.S. 976, 95 S.Ct. 1976, 44 L.Ed.2d 467 (1975). *See also, e.g.,* Howing Co. v. Nationwide Corp., 972 F.2d 700 (6th Cir.1992).

55. Wilson v. Great American Industries, Inc., 979 F.2d 924 (2d Cir.1992).

56. Boone v. Carlsbad Bancorporation, Inc., 972 F.2d 1545 (10th Cir.1992).

57. Thouret v. Hudner, 1996 WL 38824, [1995–1996 Transfer Binder] Fed. Sec. L. Rep. (CCH) ¶ 99,037 (S.D.N.Y.1996) (no private right of action since the minority shareholder's and others' votes were totally irrelevant to the passage of the company's slate of directors).

58. 228 F.3d 40 (2d Cir.2000).

61. General Electric Co. v. Cathcart, 980 F.2d 927 (3d Cir.1992) (too attenuated a connection between misstatements concerning directors' election and subsequent misconduct in office).

62. General Electric Co. v. Cathcart, 980 F.2d 927 (3d Cir.1992).

66. Schlick v. Penn–Dixie Cement Corp., 507 F.2d 374, 380–381 (2d Cir.1974), *cert. denied* 421 U.S. 976, 95 S.Ct. 1976, 44 L.Ed.2d 467 (1975). *See also, e.g.,* Hershfang v. Knotter, 562 F.Supp. 393, 398 (E.D.Va.1983).

67. *See, e.g.,* CNW Corp. v. Japonica Partners, L.P., 874 F.2d 193 (3d Cir.1989) (reversing lower court and issuing preliminary injunction against shareholder vote until corrective disclosures in Schedule 14B).

the face of proxy violations that have tainted shareholder votes.[68] This enables both sides to resolicit proxies, albeit at considerable expense. On appropriate facts, a court may issue an injunction that restores the status quo prior to the tainted shareholder vote.[70] On the other hand, once a transaction has been implemented, courts are understandably reluctant to try to unscramble the eggs and put the parties back where they were before the tainted proxy solicitation and ensuing shareholder vote.

If suit is brought in advance of the meeting where the shareholder vote is to take place, a court may require corrective disclosures prior to any vote taking place. When such corrective disclosures are possible, this is a far less expensive route than requiring a new vote. Accordingly, corrective disclosures should be favored in cases where the shareholders can be given adequate time to digest and evaluate the new information before casting their votes.

§ 10.7 Security Holders' Access to the Proxy System: Right to Information; Shareholder List

State law generally gives shareholders a right to reasonable inspection of corporate books and records.[1] This right ordinarily includes the right to access shareholder lists for the purpose of communicating with other shareholders.[2] The state law rights are supplemented by those set forth in SEC Rule 14a–7[3] which also gives shareholders a way to communicate with other shareholders regarding matters related to corporate governance.

Upon a proper request by a shareholder, Rule 14a–7 gives a publicly held corporation the choice of providing the shareholder a list of shareholders or, alternatively, mailing the shareholder's communication at the shareholder's expense.[4] An issuer subject to the Securities Exchange Act's registration and reporting requirements[5] and thus to the SEC proxy rules, must comply with written shareholder requests for information with regard to matters to be voted on at a shareholder meeting.[6] Specifically, Rule 14a–7(a) requires the issuer to provide the following information upon request by a shareholder: (1) a statement of the approximate number of security holders who have been or are to be solicited on behalf of the issuer; and (2) an estimate of the cost of mailing a specified proxy statement including cost of bankers, brokers or other persons acting on the issuer's behalf.[7] Also, if a security holder so requests, the issuer must either provide the shareholder with a list of shareholders or mail, at the security holder's expense, any material relating to matters to be voted upon at the meeting to all holders that were solicited by the issuer or someone acting on the issuer's behalf.[8] In the case of roll-up

68. *E.g.* Fradkin v. Ernst, 571 F.Supp. 829 (N.D.Ohio 1983).

70. *See, e.g.*, Crouch v. Prior, 905 F.Supp. 248 (D.Vi.1995) (restoring management as it existed prior to vote).

§ 10.7

1. *E.g.*, Del. Gen. Corp. L. Tit. 8 § 220; Model Business Corp. Act (ABA) § 16.02.

2. *E.g.*, Del. Gen. Corp. L. Tit. 8 § 220; Model Business Corp. Act (ABA) § 16.02.

3. 17 C.F.R. § 240.14a–7

4. Rule 14a–7(a)(1)(i), 27 C.F.R. § 240.14a–7(a)(1)(i).

5. 15 U.S.C.A. §§ 78*l*, 78m. *See* §§ 9.2, 9.3 *supra*.

6. 17 C.F.R. § 240.14a–7.

7. 17 C.F.R. § 240.14a–7(a).

8. 17 C.F.R. § 240.14a–7(a).

reorganizations[9] and going private transactions subject to SEC Rule 13e–3,[10] the requesting shareholder (rather than the corporation) can make an election to receive a mailing list or to have the issuer make the mailing at the shareholder's expense.[11]

The federal proxy rules' guarantee of security holders' access to the proxy machinery is supplemented by shareholders' common law and statutory inspection rights that are provided by state corporate law.[14] Put in its most general terms, corporate shareholders have a right to inspect relevant corporate books and records pursuant to a request stating a proper purpose therefor.

§ 10.8 Security Holders' Access to the Proxy System: Shareholder Proposals and the Shareholder Proposal Rule

Scope of the Shareholder Proposal Rule

One of the most highly publicized aspects of proxy rules' impact on corporate governance and shareholder input is found in the shareholder proposal rule, which is embodied in SEC Rule 14a–8.[4] Over the years, there has been a continuing controversy as to the proper role for the federal securities laws in corporate governance. Shareholder access to the proxy process in general, and in particular to management's proxy statement, has been a major focus of the struggle to define the appropriate line of demarcation between corporate governance issues that properly fall within the purview of state law and investor-protection concerns that more appropriately fit with the federal regulatory scheme for transactions in securities. The SEC and the courts have struggled with these issues, as has Congress. Thus, for example, as part of the National Securities Markets Improvement Act of 1996, Congress directed the Securities and Exchange Commission to study shareholder suffrage and the securities laws, including the extent to which shareholders should be entitled to present proposals at shareholder meetings relating to corporate involvement in social issues.[5] Corporate involvement in social issues is just one of the issues that is addressed by the SEC's shareholder proposal rule.

The thrust of the shareholder proposal rule has not resulted in a significant change in the success of shareholder proposals. Shareholders wanting to challenge management in a proxy vote ordinarily need to wage their own proxy campaign in order to achieve the votes necessary to sustain their position. Having the shareholder proposal appear in management's proxy statement is unlikely by itself to have a significant impact on the outcome of a vote. Nevertheless, the SEC and the courts for a long time have

---

9. A roll-up reorganization is a transaction in which the issuer changes the form of doing business such as by rolling up a limited partnership into a corporation. *See* Item 901 of Reg. S–K.

10. 17 C.F.R. § 240.13e–3. The SEC's going private rules are discussed in § 11.8[2] *infra*.

11. Rule 14a–7(b), 17 C.F.R. § 240.14a–7(b) as amended in Exch. Act Rel. no. 34–31326 (SEC October 22, 1992).

14. Ordinarily this would be determined by the law of the corporation's state of incorporation. *See generally* James D. Cox & Thomas L. Hazen, Corporations §§ 13.2–13.11 (2d ed. 2004).

§ 10.8

4. 17 C.F.R. § 240.14a–8.

5. Pub. L. No. 104–290, section 510(b) (1996).

recognized the importance of shareholder access to management's proxy statement, even though shareholder proposals typically fail miserably.

If the shareholder proposal is not a proper matter for consideration under the state of incorporation's corporate governance rules, then the federal law permits management to exclude the proposal from management's proxy statement.[9] In reading the discussion that follows, the reader should keep in mind that while a shareholder proposal that may be valid under state law is properly excludable, it must nevertheless be described in the issuer's proxy statement.[10] Notwithstanding some narrowing of the scope of the rule over time, the shareholder rule gives the proponents of shareholder proposals significant access to management's proxy statement. The basic thrust of Rule 14a–8 is that, subject to certain enumerated exceptions, a shareholder proposal which is proper for consideration at a shareholder meeting under state law must be included in the management's proxy statement along with a brief statement explaining the shareholder's reason for supporting the proposal's adoption, provided that it is submitted to the issuer in a timely fashion.

There are relatively few judicial decisions dealing with the shareholder proposal rule. Interpretations of the shareholder proposal rule have constantly been refined through the SEC's no action letter process.[16] These no action letters are publicly available and generally are not subject to judicial review.[18] Most no action letters are signed by a single staff member and thus do not reflect action of the full Commission although the Commission does give guidance to the staff on how to respond to various issues.[19] On rare occasions, the Commission may agree to review a staff no action position but reconsideration of the staff position through a full review is appropriate only when the request for full Commission review involves "matters of substantial importance and where the issues are novel or highly complex."[20]

Each year, the Commission is faced with hundreds of requests for no action letters. In addition to giving initial responses through the no action letter process, in appropriate instances, the SEC staff will reconsider its position after receiving additional information. Although the case-by-case approach of no action letters may not be the most efficient lawmaking process, it does provide a good source of insight into the SEC's current views. In most cases, however, the SEC staff adheres to its original position.[22]

Shareholders are not without redress for a company's refusal to act in compliance with the shareholder proposal rule. The Second Circuit has recognized the existence of a private right of action by shareholders to enforce

9. Rule 14a–8(i)(1), 17 C.F.R. § 240.14a–8(i)(1), which is discussed in § 10.8[2] *infra.*

10. Schedule 14A, item 21.

16. No action letters provide a vehicle for seeking SEC advice on particular securities law issues. The interpretations are issued by staff members in response to specific requests. The no action letters and SEC responses are publicly available.

18. *See* Amalgamated Clothing & Textile Workers Union v. SEC, 15 F.3d 254 (2d Cir.1994) (shareholder could not obtain judicial review of SEC no action letter permitting management to exclude shareholder proposal as the SEC letter did not represent a "final order"); Kixmiller v. SEC, 492 F.2d 641 (D.C.Cir.1974) (judicial review of SEC action is confined to orders issued by the Commission and does not extend to no action letter responses).

19. Those guidelines are not publicly available.

20. 17 C.F.R. § 202.1(d).

22. See, e.g., PG & E Corp., 2005 WL 723853 (SEC No Action Letter March 25, 2005) (finding no basis for reconsidering earlier position); Hercules, Inc., 2005 WL 701618 (SEC March 23, 2005) (finding no reason to reconsider the position taken in earlier no action letter response).

their rights under Rule 14a–8.[23] If management wrongfully refuses to disclose a shareholder proposal, a court may enjoin the upcoming meeting.[24] In addition, material misstatements in management's opposition to a shareholder proposal can result in a voiding of the vote and an order that the proposal be resubmitted to the shareholders at the next annual meeting.[25] Management's ability to exclude shareholder proposals regarding social issues is limited.

SEC Staff Legal Bulletin Numbers 14A, 14B, and 14C[28] provide useful guidance to both companies and their shareholders dealing with the SEC's shareholder proposal rule.

Shareholder Eligibility Requirements

Each year, management's proxy statement for the annual meeting must disclose the deadline for submitting shareholder proposals for inclusion in the proxy statement and form of proxy for the next annual meeting.[29] In addition, management's proxy statement must state the last date for submission of shareholder proposals for the next annual meeting irrespective of the process set forth in the shareholder proposal rule.[30]

In order to preclude the proposal from being subject to exclusion from management's proxy materials, the shareholder submitting the proposal must meet certain eligibility requirements. In order to qualify for protection under the shareholder proposal rule, the proponent of the proposal must be a beneficial owner of a class of security that would be entitled to vote on the proposal at the shareholder meeting.[31] When a company has multiple classes of stock, the proponent must be clear in identifying his or her ownership interest with respect to a properly identified class of shares entitled to vote. Some corporations have imposed disclosure requirements on some shareholder proponents, such as a requirement that proponents disclose any hedging activity.[33] Additionally, Rule 14a–8 applies only if the proponent has owned the securities for at least one year and meets or exceeds the rule's minimum ownership requirement (the lesser of one percent or one thousand dollars in market value of such securities).[34] In addition to the minimum ownership and holding period requirements, the proponent of a shareholder proposal must continue to be a security holder through the date on which the meeting is held.[35] If the proponent dies prior to the meeting, the eligibility requirements

23. Roosevelt v. E.I. Du Pont de Nemours & Co., 958 F.2d 416 (D.C.Cir.1992).

24. New York City Employees' Retirement System v. Dole Food Co., 795 F.Supp. 95 (S.D.N.Y. 1992), *appeal dismissed, opinion vacated* 969 F.2d 1430 (2d Cir.1992) (preliminary injunction).

25. United Paperworkers International Union v. International Paper Co., 801 F.Supp. 1134 (S.D.N.Y.1992), *affirmed and modified* 985 F.2d 1190 (2d Cir.1993).

28. Staff Legal Bulletin 14A, http://www.sec.gov/interps/legal/cfslb14a.htm (July 12, 2002); Staff Legal Bulletin No. 14 (CF) (SEC Div. of Corp. Fin. July 13, 2001); Staff Legal Bulletin 14B, http://www.sec.gov/interps/legal/cfslb14b.htm (Sept. 5, 2004); Staff Legal Bulletin 14C, http://www.sec.gov/interps/legal/cfslb14c.htm (June 28, 2005).

29. Schedule 14A item 1(c). *See* Rule 14a–5(e)(1), 17 C.F.R. § 240.14a–5(e)(1).

30. Schedule 14A item 1(c). *See* Rule 14a–5(e)(2), 17 C.F.R. § 240.14a–5(e)(2).

31. 17 C.F.R. § 240.14a–8(a)(1). *Cf.* Randall S. Thomas & Kenneth J. Martin, Should Labor be Allowed to Make Shareholder Proposals?, 73 Wash. L. Rev. 41 (1998).

33. Form 8–K filings in 2008 by Sara Lee Corp. (March 28, 2008) and Coach. Inc. (Feb. 14, 2008) revealed bylaw amendments requiring such disclosure.

34. 17 C.F.R. § 240.14a–8(a)(1).

35. 17 C.F.R. § 240.14a–8(a)(1).

have not been met and management can exclude the proposal from its proxy statement.[36] The same would of course be true if the proponent ceases to be a shareholder for any other reason prior to the meeting.

Even if the shareholder continues to meet the eligibility requirements, nonattendance at the meeting (either in person or through a representative) will render the proposal excludible from management's proxy statement.[37] Nonattendance by the proponent at meetings where he or she submitted a proposal in the past will also justify management in excluding a proposal from management's proxy statement.[38] Non-attendance at the previous meeting where a proposal was submitted may be excused for good cause but the shareholder carries the burden of establishing that in fact there was good cause for missing the meeting.[39] Additionally, management may exclude a shareholder proposal introduced by a shareholder who would not be entitled to vote on the proposal.[40] Even if the proposal shareholder owns a class of shares that would be entitled to vote on the proposal, management may exclude a shareholder proposal if the shareholder submitting it turns out only to be a nominal proponent for someone else's proposal [41]

If management makes a request, the proponent of a shareholder proposal for inclusion in management's proxy statement must provide documentary evidence that the minimum ownership requirements have been satisfied.[42] The proponent's refusal to document sufficient ownership to satisfy the eligibility criteria may justify management in excluding the proposal from the proxy statement.[43] In addition, a shareholder's failure to respond with a statement that the one-year holding period for eligibility has been met provides sufficient basis for management's exclusion of the shareholder's proposal from management's proxy statement.[44] Management may also exclude the shareholder proposal if the proponent fails to provide a written statement that he or she intends to hold the company's stock through the date of the shareholder meeting.[45]

§ 10.8[2] Grounds for Exclusion—Impropriety Under the Law of the State of Incorporation

§ 10.8[2][A] State Law Generally

The corporate law of the state of incorporation is the ultimate source for the answer to the question of whether a proposal is a proper matter for

36. Oregon Trail Financial Corp., [1999–2000 Transfer Binder] Fed. Sec. L. Rep. (CCH) ¶ 77,874, 2000 WL 821710 (SEC No Action Letter June 26, 2000) (management could exclude the proposal under Rule 14a–8(f)).

37. Rule 14a–8(h)(1), 17 C.F.R. § 240.14a–8(h)(1).

38. *E.g.,* Crown Holdings, Inc., 2008 WL 116419 (Sec No Action Letter Jan. 9, 2008) (allowing management to exclude the proposal due to proponent's past nonattendance).

39. *See, e.g.,* Crown Holdings, Inc., 2008 WL 116419 (Sec No Action Letter Jan. 9, 2008) (shareholder failed to established good cause for past nonattendance and thus the proposal could be excluded).

40. Media General, Inc., 2001 WL 138964 (SEC No Action Letter Feb. 10, 2001) (shareholder proponent held a class of stock not entitled to vote on the proposal).

41. PG & E Corp., 2002 WL 471701 (SEC No Action Letter March 1, 2002).

42. Rule 14a–8(f), 17 C.F.R. § 240.14a–8(f).

43. Rule 14a–8(f), 17 C.F.R. § 240.14a–8(f).

44. *E.g.,* AT & T Corp., 2001 WL 70431 (SEC No Action Letter Jan. 24, 2001).

45. *E.g.,* Exxon Mobil Corp. 2001 WL 65680 (SEC No Action Letter Jan. 23, 2001).

shareholder consideration. Under the SEC's shareholder proposal rule, management may exclude a proposal which is not proper under the law of the issuer's state of incorporation if the issuer is a corporation.[72] If the issuer is not a corporation but rather has a different form, such as a limited partnership, then the rule looks to the state of organization.[73] The state law's allocation of governing power within the company may thus determine whether the proposal relates to a proper exercise of that power.

Whether the shareholder meeting in question is an annual or special meeting may bear upon whether a particular shareholder proposal is a proper matter for consideration under state law. For example, under Delaware law, where a shareholder meeting is called to conduct specific business, shareholders' proposals regarding unrelated matters are not proper proposals under state law and thus may be excluded from management's proxy statement.[77] If a proposal is proper under state law, then Rule 14a–8(i)(1) cannot be relied upon as a basis for excluding the proposal from management's proxy statement. It is to be remembered that state law may give a broad definition of proper matters for shareholders. In deciding whether a proposal is excludible as relating to a matter that would violate state law, the Commission staff may decide to rely on opinion of counsel contained in the no action letter request.[80] Alternatively, some states such as Delaware,[81] allow the SEC to certify questions to the state supreme court.

Mandatory Versus Recommended Action

State law defines the respective roles of shareholders and directors in corporate governance. In its notes to the shareholder proposal rule, the SEC points out that the wording of the proposal may determine whether it is a proper matter under state law. Under the law of most states, only the board of directors may initiate amendments to the articles of incorporation,[85] and it follows that a shareholder proposal to amend the articles, as opposed to a proposal merely recommending to the directors that they propose an amendment to the articles, is not proper and thus may be excluded from management's proxy statement.[86] A similar result follows for other corporate action.

Bylaw Amendments; Shareholder Rights Plans

Many state laws permit shareholder initiative on bylaw amendments.[98] Under such a regime, proposals for amendment rather than merely recommending that the board make such amendments will be permissible shareholder proposals.[99] The SEC indicated that in the absence of clear Delaware

72. Rule 14a–8(i)(1), 17 C.F.R. § 240.14a–8(i)(1).

73. Rule 14a–8(i)(1), 17 C.F.R. § 240.14a–8(i)(1).

77. *See, e.g.,* J.P. Morgan & Co., 2000 WL 1877573 (SEC No Action Letter Dec. 22, 2000).

80. *See, e.g.,* General Dynamics Corp., 2001 WL 246749 (SEC No Action Letter March 5, 2001).

81. *See* Section 11(8) of Article IV of the Delaware Constitution, Del. Const, Art. 4, s 11.

85. *E.g.* Del Code § 242(b)(1); Model Bus. Corp. Act § 10.03.

86. *E.g.,* PSB Holdings, Inc., 2002 WL 201870 (SEC No Action Letter Jan. 23, 2002).

98. *E.g.,* Del. § 109; Model Bus. Corp. Act § 10.20.

99. *See, e.g.,* Genzyme Corp., 2007 WL 490942 (SEC No Action Letter, Feb. 8, 2007) (management could not rely on Rule 14a–8(i)(2), 14a–8(i)(3) nor 14a–8(i)(6) to exclude a proposal that would amend the bylaws to provide for the election of directors by a majority of the votes cast in an uncontested election and require directors to submit an irrevocable resignation

law on point, it was unable to conclude that the mandatory bylaw amendment was excludible under rule 14a–8(i)(1).[101] This was an apparent reversal of the Commission's previous position as to the propriety of mandatory bylaw amendments under Delaware law. The Delaware Chancery Court refused to consider the issue on procedural grounds.[102] In contrast to Delaware, the Oklahoma Supreme Court applied Oklahoma law to uphold the propriety of a shareholder initiated bylaw limiting the use of poison pills or other shareholder rights plans.[103] Even under Delaware law, framing the shareholder proposal regarding limitations on poison pills and shareholder rights plans in terms of a recommendation should eliminate management's grounds for excluding the proposal.[104] However, in one no action response, a proposal recommending that no rights plans be adopted without shareholder approval was deemed to be excludible as violative of Delaware law.[105]

§ 10.8[3] Grounds for Exclusion—Impropriety Under Law Generally

Management may exclude a shareholder proposal from the proxy statement if the proposal would violate any state, federal, or foreign law to which the company is subject.[110] Thus, if the substance of the proposal would violate state or federal law, such as requiring the company to breach existing contracts, the proposal may be excluded.[111] Similarly, a proposal calling for improper discrimination may be excluded.[112] The Commission notes, however, that exclusion from management's proxy statement on the grounds that the shareholder proposal involves a violation of foreign law is not appropriate if compliance with that foreign law in question would result in a violation of domestic state or federal law.[113] Also, management desiring to exclude the shareholder proposal has the burden of establishing that the proposal would involve a violation of state law. If management does not establish that the proposal would violate other law, the proposal may not be excluded on the basis of Rule 14a–8(i)(2).[115]

---

contingent upon the failure to receive a majority of the votes cast in an uncontested election and the acceptance of the resignation by the board of directors).

101. *See, e.g.,* Honeywell International Inc., 2002 WL 1052001 (SEC No Action Letter April 19, 2002).

102. General Datacomm Industries, Inc. v. State of Wisconsin Investment Board, 1999 WL 66533 (Del.Ch.1999).

103. International Brotherhood of Teamsters General Fund v. Fleming Companies, 975 P.2d 907 (Okla.1999).

104. *See, e.g.,* Electronic Data Systems Corp., 2005 WL 171366 (SEC No Action Letter Jan. 24, 2005).

105. General Dynamics Corp., 2001 WL 246749 (SEC No Action Letter March 5, 2001).

110. Rule 14a–8(i)(2), 17 C.F.R. § 240.14a–8(i)(2).

111. *E.g.,* Cendant Corp., 2004 WL 187657 (SEC No Action Letter Jan. 16, 2004).

112. *See, e.g.,* Churchill Downs Inc., 2004 WL 1637290 (SEC No Action Letter March 2, 2004) (management could exclude proposal seeking to impose a ten–year ban upon any and all Japanese horse owners attempting to enter their horse in a Churchill Downs Incorporated facility for a Kentucky Derby/Triple Crown race event).

113. Note to Rule 14a–8(i)(2), 17 C.F.R. § 240.14a–8(i)(2).

115. *See, e.g.,* SBC Communications Inc., 2001 WL 125056 (SEC No Action Letter Jan. 31, 2001).

§ 10.8[4] Grounds for Exclusion—Materially Misleading Proposals, Proposals in Violation of the Proxy Rules, and Overly Vague Proposals

A shareholder proposal is excludible if it violates the federal proxy rules.[126] Most commonly, this basis for exclusion is invoked when the shareholder proposal is materially misleading in violation of Rule 14a–9. If the alleged misstatement is cured, then the proposal will not be excludable. The Commission has indicated in a number of no action responses that if the proposal itself is not materially misleading but the shareholder's statement supporting the proposal contains materially misleading statements, management may exclude the materially misleading statements,[129] but must include the proposal and the non-misleading portions of the supporting statement.[130] In addition to materially misleading statements, management may exclude a shareholder proposal under Rule 14a–8(i)(3) if the proposal is too vague or indefinite.[131]

§ 10.8[5] Grounds for Exclusion—Personal Grievance

Management may exclude a shareholder proposal from management's proxy statement if the proposal relates to a personal claim or grievance of the shareholder.[139] The application of this basis for exclusion applies either because of the proposal on its face or, alternatively, the motivation of the shareholder proponent.[140] A personal grievance as a basis for exclusion from management's proxy statement applies regardless of whether the personal claim or grievance is against the issuer or against any other person.[141] The burden is on management desiring to exclude the proposal to establish that it is based on a personal grievance rather than proper shareholder concerns about corporate matters. The use of a nominee to sponsor the proposal to mask the identity of the true proponent will not limit management's ability to omit the proposal as relating to a personal grievance.[143]

§ 10.8[6] Grounds for Exclusion—Not Significantly Related to the Issuer's Business

Rule 14a–8(i)(5) permits management to exclude from management's proxy statement a shareholder proposal if the proposal is not significantly related to the issuer's business.[153] This basis for exclusion has both an objective and subjective test.

A shareholder proposal is not excludible from management's proxy statement on the grounds of relevance if it relates to more than five percent of the company's business.[155] The shareholder proposal rule permits exclusion of a

126. Rule 14a–8(i)(3), 17 C.F.R. § 240.14a–8(i)(3).

129. *See, e.g.,* Raytheon Co., 2001 WL 204745 (SEC No Action Letter Feb. 26, 2001).

130. *E.g.,* UnitedHealth Group Inc., 2001 WL 25785 (SEC Jan. 8, 2001).

131. *See, e.g.,* Ryland Group, Inc., 2005 WL 148036 (SEC No Action Letter Jan. 19, 2005).

139. Rule 14a–8(i)(4), 17 C.F.R. § 240.14a–8(i)(4).

140. *See, e.g.,* Waste Management, Inc., 2002 WL 537980 (SEC No Action Letter March 11, 2002).

141. Rule 14a–8(i)(4), 17 C.F.R. § 240.14a–8(i)(4).

143. *E.g.,* MGM Mirage, 2001 WL 294174 (SEC No Action Letter March 19, 2001).

153. Rule 14a–8(i)(5), 17 C.F.R. § 240.14a–8(i)(5).

155. 17 C.F.R. § 240.14a–8(i)(5).

proposal if it "relates to operations which account for less than 5 percent of the company's total assets at the end of its most recent fiscal year, and for less than 5 percent of its net earnings and gross sales for its most recent fiscal year, and *is not otherwise related to the company's business*."[156] By virtue of this last clause, the five-percent threshold operates as a safe harbor for management seeking to exclude a shareholder proposal from the proxy statement only if the proposal is not otherwise significant to the company's business.

A shareholder proposal ordinarily must be included (unless there is some other basis for exclusion) if the proposal relates to operations above the five-percent threshold, but it must also be included if it is significantly related to the issuer's business even if the quantitative threshold is not met. Thus, for example, activities which relate to social responsibility may be the subject of shareholder proposals even if they fall below the five percent threshold. Thus, for example, a proposal that a company reexamine its method of treating animals was deemed socially significant and thus not excludible even though the operations in question fell below the five percent thresholds.[158] Proposals relating to socially relevant issues may be excluded, however, if they do not relate to significant issues concerning the company's business.

§ 10.8[7] Grounds for Exclusion—Beyond the Issuer's Power

A shareholder proposal is excludible from management's proxy statement if the proposal relates to matters beyond the issuer's control.[170] Thus, "[i]f the company would lack the power or authority to implement the proposal," it is excludible.[171] This includes situations in which an attempt to implement the proposal would violate the law. Rule 14a–8(i)(6) thus supplements subsections (i)(1) and (i)(2) which permit exclusion of proposals that are contrary to law.[173] Rule 14a–8(i)(6) also permits exclusions of proposals that cannot be accomplished within traditional strictures of corporate governance.

A shareholder proposal may be excluded by management if it relates to the ordinary business of the issuer.[199] The determination of what is in the ordinary course of business may be difficult to determine and the SEC staff positions sometimes appear inconsistent.

The SEC's ordinary business basis for excluding shareholder proposals from management's proxy statement has had a long and checkered history. As the following discussion indicates, it is not always easy to identify a clear

156. 17 C.F.R. § 240.14a–8(i)(5).

158. Lovenheim v. Iroquois Brands, Ltd., 618 F.Supp. 554 (D.D.C.1985) (granting preliminary injunction against exclusion of shareholder proposal that the directors form a committee to consider termination of distribution of pate de foie gras until a more humane production method is developed). *See also, e.g.,* Wendy's International, Inc., 2005 WL 323190 (SEC No Action Letter Feb. 8, 2005) (management could not rely on rule 14a–8(i)(7) to exclude a proposal requesting that the board issue a report to shareholders on the feasibility of Wendy's requiring its chicken suppliers to phase in controlled-atmosphere killing within a reasonable timeframe).

170. Rule 14a–8(i)(6), 17 C.F.R. § 14a–8(i)(6).

171. 17 C.F.R. § 14a–8(i)(6).

173. Rules 14a–8(i)(1) and 14a–8(i)(2), 17 C.F.R. §§ 240.14a–8(i)(1), 14a–8(i)(2), are discussed in §§ 10.8[2], 10.8[3] *supra.*

199. 17 C.F.R. § 240.14a–8(i)(7). *See, e.g.,* Yahoo! Inc., 2007 WL 1125491 (SEC No Action Letter April 5, 2007) (management could rely on Rule 14a–8(i)(7) to exclude a proposal seeking a report on the company's rationale for supporting certain public policy measures concerning regulation of the internet, particularly "net neutrality" measures).

demarcation between which proposals are excludible from management's proxy statement and which are not. Furthermore, there are a number of topics for which the SEC has changed its position over time.

Rule 14a–8(i)(7)'s ordinary business basis for exclusion has been the most utilized basis for exclusion in recent years. The SEC's approach to shareholder proposals is extremely fact specific. Subtle variations in wording can determine whether management may exclude the proposal or not.

Over the years shareholders have enjoyed considerable success in having their proposals included in the proxy statement notwithstanding management's initial opposition. The success may be due in part to the fact that each proxy season there are new issues that add to the proposals that recur over the years.

Quite frequently proposals relate both to social issues and to ordinary business operations. In those instances, corporate managers and the SEC staff are often faced with a daunting task in trying to decide whether a shareholder proposal is excludable: it must be determined whether in fact the proposal focuses on day-to-day business matters.[217] If the primary focus is found to be on ordinary business operations, then it likely will be excludible, as compared those instances in which significant policy issues outweigh the impact on day-to-day operations.[220] The fact that a proposal mentions significant policy issues will not be sufficient to preclude management exclusion from the proxy statement where the true focus of the proposal is on day-to-day operations.[221]

Proposals related to regulatory compliance or legal compliance generally or management of the workplace[225] ordinarily will be excludible from management's proxy statement. In contrast, proposals relating to the company's ethics in conducting business are likely to be a legitimate matter of shareholder concern and hence not excludible from management's proxy statement,[226] especially when they relate to matters "over and beyond" legal compliance issues.[227] However, if the proposal relates to implementation of specific poli-

---

217. *See, e.g.*, Wells Fargo & Co., 2006 WL 399723 (SEC No Action Letter Feb. 16, 2006) (management could rely on Rule 14a–8(i)(7) to exclude a proposal requesting that the executive compensation committee of the board of directors establish a pay-for-superior-performance standard in the company's executive compensation plan for senior executives by incorporating principles set forth in the proposal).

220. *See, e.g.*, Certain Fidelity Funds, 2008 WL 223122 (SEC No Action Letter Jan. 22, 2008) (management could not rely on Rule 14a–8(i)(7) nor on Rule 14a–8(i)(3) to exclude the following proposal: "In order to ensure that Fidelity is an ethically managed company that respects the spirit of international law and is a responsible member of society, shareholders request that the Fund's Board institute oversight procedures to screen out investments in companies that, in the judgment of the Board, substantially contribute to genocide, patterns of extraordinary and egregious violations of human rights, or crimes against humanity").

221. *See, e.g.*, Walt Disney Co., 2007 WL 4305668 (SEC No Action Letter Nov. 30, 2007) (management could rely on Rule 14a–8(i)(7) to exclude a proposal requesting a report on steps the company is taking to avoid the use of negative and discriminatory racial, ethnic and gender stereotypes in its products).

225. *E.g.*, Merck & Co., 2008 WL 162838 (SEC No Action Letter Jan. 11, 2008).

226. *See, e.g.*, Certain Fidelity Funds, 2008 WL 223122 (SEC No Action Letter Jan. 22, 2008).

227. Bank of America Corp., 2008 WL 591024 (SEC No Action Letter Feb. 29, 2008) (Management could not rely on Rule 14a–8(i)(7) to exclude a proposal to amend the bylaws to establish a board committee that will review the implications of company policies, above and beyond matters of legal compliance, for the human rights of individuals in the United States and worldwide).

cies, such as a conflict of interest policy, the proposal may be excluded as relating to the ordinary business.[228]

The essence of the rule as it relates to ordinary business operations is that shareholder proposals relating to the day-to-day managerial decisions concerning how the nuts and bolts of the business is carried out may be excluded from management's proxy statement even though extraordinary matters may not be excluded. For example, a shareholder proposal asking management to establish a customer satisfaction panel was deemed to relate to the company's ordinary business and thus could be excluded from management's proxy statement.[266] Similarly, a proposal recommending that the company have annual meetings for customers was considered to relate to the ordinary business and thus could be excluded.[267] Even when the proposal relates to an important issue such as customer safety, management may exclude it if it relates to the company's day-to-day operations.[268] However, proposals relating to major consumer related policies may not be excluded.[269]

A shareholder proposal addressing the date[286] or location[287] of the annual meeting relates to the ordinary business operations and thus may be excluded by management. Shareholder proposals concerning procedures for conducting the meeting also relate to the ordinary business and may be excluded from management's proxy statement.[288]

Proposals directed to the company's method of raising capital often have been excluded as concerning the ordinary business operations of the issuer.[314] Similarly, management was permitted to exclude a proposal asking the company to institute a program for repurchasing some of its shares.[315] Deci-

228. The Williams Cos., 2008 WL 353400 (SEC No Action Letter Feb. 6, 2008).

266. Bank of America Corp., 2005 WL 517870 (SEC No Action Letter March 3, 2005)(management could exclude a proposal relates to the adoption of a "Customer Bill of Rights" and the creation of the position of "Customer Advocate."); Deere & Co., 2002 WL 31588852 (SEC No Action Letter Nov. 29, 2002) (management could exclude a shareholder proposal relating to settling "longstanding ... product quality concern[s]" through a "company buy-back."); Deere & Co., 2000 WL 1762368, 32 Sec. Reg. & L. Rep. (BNA) 1733 (SEC No Action Letter Nov. 30, 2000). *Cf.* Hilton Hotels Corp., 2001 WL 246760 (SEC March 7, 2001) (proposal related to linking compensation to franchisee satisfaction could have been excluded as duplicative under Rule 14a–8(i)(10)).

267. Wal–Mart Stores, Inc., 2001 WL 310419 (SEC No Action Letter March 27, 2001).

268. *See, e.g.*, Wal–Mart Stores, Inc., 2006 WL 851291 (SEC No Action Letter March 24, 2006) (management could rely on Rule 14a–8(i)(7) to exclude a requesting that the board publish a report evaluating the company's policies and procedures for minimizing customers' exposure to toxic substances in products).

269. *See, e.g.*, Bank of America, Inc., 2006 WL 851290 (SEC No Action Letter March 29, 2006) (management could not rely on Rule 14a–8(i)(3), 14a–8(i)(7), nor 14a–8(i)(10) to exclude a proposal requesting that the board develop higher standards for the securitization of subprime loans to preclude the securitization of loans involving predatory practices). Wal–Mart Stores, Inc., 2006 WL 851291 (SEC No Action Letter March 24, 2006) (management could rely on Rule 14a–8(i)(7) to exclude a requesting that the board publish a report evaluating the company's policies and procedures for minimizing customers' exposure to toxic substances in products).

286. Verizon Communications Inc., 2001 WL 125043 (SEC No Action Letter Jan. 30, 2001) (management could exclude shareholder proposal relating to the date of the annual meeting).

287. Northeast Utilities, 2008 WL 591030 (SEC No Action Letter March 3, 2008).

288. *See, e.g.*, Blockbuster, Inc., 2007 WL 817463 (SEC No Action Letter March 12, 2007) (management could rely on Rule 14a–8(i)(7) to exclude a proposal urging the board to adopt a policy that shareholders be given the opportunity at each annual meeting to vote on an advisory resolution to ratify the compensation of the named executive officers set forth in the summary compensation table of the company's proxy statement).

314. Irvine Sensors Corp., 2001 WL 8319 (SEC No Action Letter Jan. 2, 2001) (proposal requesting that company raise future capital primarily through offerings to existing shareholders instead of relying on private placements).

315. *See* Pfizer, Inc., 2005 WL 310442 (SEC No Action Letter Feb. 4, 2005) (management could rely on Rule 14a–8(i)(7) to exclude a proposal that would have the company increase its dividend rather than repurchase $5 billion of the company's shares in 2005).

sions relating to the company's existing debt, including bonds, relate to the ordinary business and thus related proposals may be excluded from management's proxy statement.[316] Proposals focused on the company's issuance of stock options and other derivative securities have also been considered excludible as relating to the company's ordinary business.[320] However, management may not be able to exclude proposals relating to stock option policy rather than day-to-day administration of stock option programs.[321]

As the foregoing discussion indicates, the gist of the balance struck by the SEC is that shareholder proposals relating to day-to-day financing or administration issues will be excludible,[331] while proposals relating to matters of corporate policy will not.[332] It follows, for example, that although proposals relating to the time and amount of dividends may be excludible as relating to the company's ordinary business,[333] the decision whether to declare dividends can be framed as a policy matter, and proposals to that effect may not be excluded from management's proxy statement.[334]

§ 10.8[8][E] Ordinary Business—Proposals Relating to Employment Practices

The SEC generally takes the position that proposals relating to employment practices, including the termination, hiring, or promotion of employees may be excluded as relating to ordinary business operations.[339] The SEC staff generally considers proposals relating to the evaluation of employees to be within the company's ordinary business. Thus, for example, proposals relating to the promotion and retention of employees will ordinarily be excludible.[341] This is true even with respect to proposals relating to senior management.[342]

316. *See* Vishay Intertechnology, Inc., 2008 WL 886024 (SEC No Action Letter March 28, 2008) (management could rely on Rule 14a–8(i)(7) to exclude a proposal urging the company to eliminate its long term debt by taking actions that are specified in the proposal).

320. *See, e.g.,* Sempra Energy, 2001 WL 109541 (SEC No Action Letter Jan. 30, 2001).

321. *See, e.g.,* Cintas Corp., 2004 WL 1846205 (SEC No Action Letter Aug. 13, 2004) (management could not exclude a shareholder proposal urging the board to adopt a policy that the cost of employee and director stock options be recognized in the company's income statement).

331. *E.g.,* Tyco International Ltd., 2000 WL 1874063 (SEC No Action Letter Dec. 21, 2000).

332. Kmart Corp., 2001 WL 286894 (SEC No Action Letter March 16, 2001) (management could not rely on "ordinary business" grounds to exclude shareholder proposal relating to principles defined by the International Labor Organization).

333. *E.g.,* Synovus Financial Corp., 2004 WL 414579 (SEC No Action Letter March 1, 2004).

334. Exxon Mobil Corp., 2007 WL 861169 (SEC No Action Letter March 19, 2007) (management could not rely on Rule 14a–8(i)(7) or 14a–8(i)(13) to exclude a proposal requesting that the board consider providing, in times of above-average cash flow, a more equal ration of the amounts spent on stock repurchases relative to the amounts paid out as dividends).

339. *See, e.g.,* Merrill Lynch & Co., 2008 WL 384380 (SEC No Action Letter Feb. 12, 2008) (management could rely on Rule 14a–8(i)(7) to exclude a proposal requesting that the board of directors initiate the appropriate process to amend the company's corporate governance guidelines to adopt and disclose a written and detailed succession planning policy, including features specified in the proposal; the no action response noted that the proposal related to the company's "ordinary business operations (i.e., the termination, hiring, or promotion of employees)").

341. *See, e.g.,* The McGraw Hill Cos., 2008 WL 376143 (SEC No Action Letter Feb. 7, 2008) (noting that it related to "ordinary business operations (i.e., the termination, hiring, or promotion of employees)," the SEC staff allowed management to exclude a proposal requesting that the board of directors and the audit committee adopt a policy that the company shall not employ any individual within one year of that individual being employed by any client; the company shall rotate the lead analyst for a client; and the audit committee shall manage potential conflicts of interests with clients and audit the company's compliance with this policy).

342. The MONY Group Inc., 2004 WL 434374 (SEC No Action Letter March 1, 2004) (management could exclude a proposal recommending the board promptly conduct an investigation into and a possible replacement of the company's chief executive officer and its president and chief operating officer).

However, when employment practices significantly implicate broader social issues, then there may be an argument that management may not exclude the shareholder proposal from management's proxy statement.[344]

In 1992, the SEC, in its controversial *Cracker Barrel* no action letter, permitted exclusion of a shareholder proposal regarding the company's hiring practices on the basis that the proposal related to the company's ordinary business.[345] The *Cracker Barrel* no action letter favoring exclusion of shareholder proposals dealing with discriminatory employment policies sparked controversy both within and outside the SEC. In 1997, the Commission proposed reversing the *Cracker Barrel* policy.[346] Shortly thereafter, the *Cracker Barrel* approach was repudiated by the SEC.[347] The Commission decided to revert to its former practice and explained that shareholder proposals relating to employment practices would no longer automatically be eligible for inclusion.[348] Thus, the SEC once again follows its pre-*Cracker Barrel* practice of reviewing each proposal relating to employment practices to determine if it relates to the ordinary business as opposed to more far-reaching social issues.[349]

Management may exclude from its proxy statement shareholder proposals relating to the specifics of employee compensation[362] since those proposals are properly considered as relating to ordinary business operations.[363] Proposals limited to senior executives' compensation are less likely to be excludible than proposals relating to a wider range of employees.[367] There have been an increasing number of proposals aimed at giving shareholders a "say on pay." To the extent that such proposals are focused on the shareholders in an

---

344. *E.g.*, McDonald's Corp., 2007 WL 895066 (SEC No Action Letter March 22, 2007) (management could not rely on Rules 14a–8(i)(3), 14a–8(i)(4), 14a–8(i)(6), 14a–8(i)(7), or 14a–8(i)(10) to exclude a proposal urging the board to adopt, implement and enforce a revised company-wide code of conduct, inclusive of suppliers and sub-contractors, based on the International Labor Organization's conventions, including the four principles set forth in the proposal, and prepare a report concerning the implementation and enforcement of the policy).

345. Cracker Barrel Old Country Store, Inc., [1992–1993 Transfer Binder] Fed. Sec. L Rep. ¶ 76,418 (SEC No Action Letter October 13, 1992).

346. Amendments to Rules on Shareholder Proposals, Sec. Exch. Act Rel. No. 34–39093, 62 Fed. Reg. 50682–01 (SEC Sept. 26, 1997).

347. Amendments to Rules on Shareholder Proposals, Release Act No. 34–40018, 63 Fed. Reg. 29,106, 29,108, 1998 WL 266441 (SEC May 28, 1998). *See, e.g.*, Note, Roll Out the Barrel: the SEC Reverses its Stance on Employment–Related Shareholder Proposals Under SEC Rule 14a–8—Again, 25 Del. J. Corp. L. 277 (2000).

348. *See,* Amendments to Rules on Shareholder Proposals, Release Act No. 34–40018, 63 Fed. Reg. 29,106, 29,108, 1998 WL 266441 (SEC May 28, 1998).

349. *See,* Amendments to Rules on Shareholder Proposals, Release Act No. 34–40018, 63 Fed. Reg. 29,106, 29,108, 1998 WL 266441 (SEC May 28, 1998).

362. *See, e.g.,* General Electric Co., 2004 WL 187659 (SEC No Action Letter Jan. 15, 2004).

363. *E.g.*, Citigroup, Inc., 2007 WL 4593350 (SEC No Action Letter Dec. 31, 2007) (Management could rely on Rule 14a–8(i)(7) to exclude a proposal relating to granting a post retirement supplement to pension payments of current eligible retirees).

367. *See, e.g.,* SBC Communications, Inc., 2005 WL 148042 (SEC No Action Letter Jan. 18, 2005).

advisory role, there is a better chance that the proposal will not be excludible from management's proxy statement.[369]

Proposals relating to healthcare benefits will ordinarily be classified as relating to the ordinary business and thus will be excludible from management's proxy statement.[376] However, when the proposal relates to the company's support for universal healthcare, the issue is transformed into one with significant social impact and the SEC is likely to refuse to allow management to exclude the proposal.[377]

§ 10.8[9] Grounds for Exclusion—Proposals Relating to Election to Office

A shareholder proposal may be excluded if it relates to election to a corporate office.[539] This basis for exclusion is broadly stated and has been interpreted to exclude proposals that would have an impact on a pending corporate election[540] but not to proposals that relate to the process and do not impact a pending election.

The purpose of this basis for exclusion is to recognize the adversary nature of contested elections but it is sometimes difficult to decide whether a proposal should be excludible on this ground or whether it relates to an election in a way that is legitimately a matter of shareholder concern rather than taking part in a particular election.

However, the Second Circuit held that in light of the SEC's early interpretations of the rule, it would not follow the SEC's current view of permitting exclusion of shareholder proposals to provide access to management's proxy statement for shareholder nominated directors.[560] Accordingly, absent formal SEC rulemaking, proposals recommending increased access to management's proxy statement for shareholder nominated directors will not be excludible solely on the basis that they relate to director elections.

In 2007, the SEC proposed alternative rules for dealing with shareholder access regarding director nominations.[562] The commissioners were sharply divided on what would be the best approach to take and decided to solicit comments on two alternative proposals.[563] One proposal would amend Rule 14a–8(i)(8) to preclude management from excluding from management's proxy

369. *See, e.g.*, Allegheny Energy, Inc., 2008 WL 353395 (SEC No Action Letter Feb. 5, 2008) (management could not rely on either Rule 14a–8(i)(6) or 14a–8(i)(7) to exclude a proposal requesting the board to adopt a policy that shareholders be given the opportunity at each annual meeting to vote on an advisory resolution to ratify the compensation of the named executive officers set forth in the Summary Compensation Table of the company's proxy statement).

376. *See, e.g.*, Wyeth, 2008 WL 527451 (SEC No Action Letter Feb. 25, 2008).

377. *See, e.g.*, UnitedHealth Group Inc., 2008 WL 902895 (SEC No Action Letter April 2, 2008) (management could not rely on Rule 14a–8(i)(7) to exclude a proposal urging the directors to adopt principles for health care reform based upon principles specified in the proposal).

539. 17 C.F.R. § 240.14a–8(i)(8). Properly interpreted, this means that individual election campaigns cannot be conducted in this manner but proposals relating to general criteria for officeholders will be deemed proper. *See* Rauchman v. Mobil Corp., 739 F.2d 205 (6th Cir.1984).

540. *See* Sonoma Valley Bancorp, 2007 WL 582651 (SEC No Action Letter Feb. 20, 2007).

560. American Federation of State, County & Municipal Employees, Employees Pension Plan v. American International Group, 462 F.3d 121 (2d Cir. 2006).

562. *See, e.g.,* On Proxy Access, SEC Votes 3–2 Twice, Issuing Two Diametrically Opposed Proposals, Sec. L. Daily (BNA), http://pubs.bna.com/ip/bna/ccd.nsf/eh/A0B4Z2F6C2 (Aug. 6, 2007).

563. *See* On Proxy Access, SEC Votes 3–2 Twice, Issuing Two Diametrically Opposed Proposals, Sec. L. Daily (BNA), http://pubs.bna.com/ip/bna/ccd.nsf/eh/A0B4Z2F6C2 (Aug. 6, 2007).

statement a proposed bylaw that would establish procedures for shareholder nominations of directors, provided the group proposing the bylaw amendment owns five percent of the company's stock.[564] The alternative proposal would codify the SEC's interpretation since 1980 that management could exclude bylaws relating to director nominations.[565] As noted previously, as the spring 2008 proxy season approached, it became clear that with the four member Commission there was not sufficient support to adopt the more expansive shareholder access rule. Accordingly, in late 2007, the SEC adopted amendments to Rule 14a–8(i)(8) to codify the interpretations that were struck down by the Second Circuit.[566] The rule, which is viewed by the Commission was an interim rule to provide certainty for the 2008 proxy season, provides that management may exclude shareholder proposals relating to directors' nominations, including bylaw amendments relating to procedures.[567]

§ 10.8[10] Grounds for Exclusion—Shareholder Proposals Contradicting Management Proposals

Management may exclude a shareholder proposal that contradicts a proposal submitted by management.[623] The rationale here is that the matter is already before the shareholders and the appropriate response of shareholders who disagree with management is to vote against the proposal. The SEC notes that in seeking a no action letter, management should specify the points of conflict between the shareholder proposal and management's proposal.[624]

§ 10.8[11] Grounds for Exclusion—Mootness

Management may omit a shareholder proposal from management's proxy statement if the subject of the proposal has become moot.[625] Management can exclude a shareholder proposal if it has already substantially been implemented.[626]

§ 10.8[12] Grounds for Exclusion—Duplicative Proposals

Management may exclude a shareholder proposal that substantially duplicates another proposal submitted for the same shareholder meeting.[635] This basis for exclusion is designed to prevent shareholders from harassing management through the use of repetitive proposals.[636] The fact that the matter is already before the shareholders is sufficient to satisfy the proxy rules basis for exclusion.

---

564. See Shareholder Proposals, Sec. Exch. Act Rel. No. 34-56160, Inv. Co. Act Rel. No. IC–27913, http://www.sec.gov/rules/proposed/2007/34-56160.pdf, 2007 WL 2175940 (SEC July 27 2007).

565. Shareholder Proposals Relating to the Election of Directors, Sec. Exch. Act Rel. No. 34–56161, Inv. Co. Act Rel. No. IC—27914, http://www.sec.gov/rules/proposed/2007/34–56161.pdf, 2007 WL 2175941 (SEC July 27, 2007).

566. *See* Shareholder Proposals Relating to the Election of Directors, Sec. Exch. Act Rel. No. 34–56914, Inv. Co. Act Rel. No. IC–28075, 2007 WL 4270705 (SEC Dec. 6, 2007).

567. Rule 14a–8, 17 C.F.R. § 240.14a–8.

623. Rule 14a–8(i)(9). 17 C.F.R. § 240.14a–8(i)(9).

624. Note to Rule 14a–8(i)(9). 17 C.F.R. § 240.14a–8(i)(9).

625. 17 C.F.R. § 240.14a–8(i)(10).

626. *Id.*

635. 17 C.F.R. § 240.14a–8(i)(11).

636. Airborne Freight Corp. 2000 WL 217938 (SEC No Action Letter Feb. 14, 2000) (management could exclude duplicative proposal).

§ 10.8[13] Grounds for Exclusion—Resubmissions

Management may exclude a shareholder proposal if it is substantially the same as one that was submitted in the past year and did not receive a significant number of votes.[639] This is designed to permit management to exclude proposals that the shareholders have recently resoundingly defeated. The proposal may be excluded if it is substantially the same; it is not necessary that the proposal be identical to a previous one.[641] However, a significant difference from a previous proposal will preclude management's ability to exclude it from its proxy statement.[642] Rule 14a–8(i)(12) looks to the preceding five years and permits the exclusion of the proposal if it did not cross a specified threshold of shareholder support the last time it was submitted for shareholder consideration.[644]

§ 10.8[14] Grounds for Exclusion—Relating to Dividends

Management may exclude a shareholder proposal if it relates to a specific amount of dividends.[647] Since stock splits are essentially dividends paid in stock rather than cash, the rationale for permitting exclusion of shareholder proposals relating to the specific amount of dividends extends to proposals relating to recommendations regarding stock splits.[648] Similarly, management may exclude a proposal relating to the administration of a dividend reinvestment plan since it relates to the company's ordinary business operations.[649] The ordinary business[650] basis for exclusion thus supplements Rule 14a–8(i)(13)'s reference to dividend proposals that focus on the amount of the dividend. However, a proposal that relates to a change in capital structure involves more than a stock dividend and thus may not be excluded as a proposal relating to a specific dividend payment.[651]

§ 10.8[15] Consequences of Excluding Shareholder Proposals; Practical Considerations

Notwithstanding the shareholder proposal rule's permission to management to exclude proposals under certain circumstances, in close cases, the proposals should be included since, practically speaking, management in most instances will nevertheless have to make reference to the shareholder proposal in its proxy statement. Management has little to lose by including most shareholder proposals, as they have virtually no chance of success and generally receive less than three percent of the vote. Under many circumstances, management should give serious thought to voluntary inclusion of a shareholder proposal.[661] Inclusion of the proposal saves the time and expense

639. 317 C.F.R. § 240.14a–8(i)(12).

641. Chevron Corp., 31 Sec. Reg. & L. Rep. (BNA) 415 (SEC No Action letter March 4, 1999).

642. In re Emerson Electric Co., 16 Sec.Reg. & L.Rep. (BNA) 1982 (SEC No Action Letter Nov. 21, 1984) (shareholder proposal that issuer report on military sales is different from prior proposal for formulation of "ethical criteria" for defense contracts).

644. 17 C.F.R. § 14a–8(i)(12).

647. 17 C.F.R. § 14a–8(i)(13).

648. *E.g.*, NVR, Inc., 2001 WL 40393 (SEC No Action Letter Jan. 11, 2001).

649. *See* Prudential Financial, Inc., 2008 WL 142619 (SEC No Action Letter Jan. 11, 2008) (management could rely on Rule 14a–8(i)(7) to exclude a proposal providing that the company make a dividend reinvestment program available).

650. Rule 14a–8(i)(7)'s ordinary business provision is discussed in § 10.8[8] *supra*.

651. *See, e.g.*, Urstadt Biddle Properties Inc., 1998 WL 886893 (SEC No Action Letter Dec. 17, 1998).

661. *See, e.g.*, PG & E Corp., 2002 WL 253882 (SEC No Action Letter Jan. 21, 2002) (company decided to include the proposal).

of dealing with the SEC and also may garner some good will for the company. Companies should balance inclusion against the risk of feeling overwhelmed by too many shareholder proposals.

Even if the issuer properly excludes the proposal and supporting statement, it must nevertheless describe the proposal, assuming that under state law[662] it is a proper matter for shareholder action. Item 20 of schedule 14A requires the proxy statement to include identification of any action to be taken at the shareholder meeting that is not otherwise described in the proxy statement.[663] Furthermore, if the issuer's management decides to solicit proxies that will be voted against a shareholder proposal, the antifraud proscriptions will require disclosure of the proposal and intention to vote against it.[664] Management violates the proxy rules if it fails to disclose in its proxy statement that a shareholder plans to submit proposals at the upcoming shareholder meeting.[665]

§ 10.9 Disclosure in Lieu of Proxy Solicitation—Section 14(c)

Can management avoid the disclosure requirements of the proxy rules by not soliciting proxies (or consents)? As pointed out below, the clear answer is that it cannot. If an issuer subject to the registration requirements of section 12 of the Exchange Act does not solicit proxies, its security holders are still guaranteed information by virtue of section 14(c).[1] The issuer must file with the SEC and send to its security holders information similar to that which is required for a proxy solicitation. These informational requirements are set out in Regulation 14C[2] and Schedule 14C.[3]

§ 10.10 Securities Held in Street Name; Broker–Dealers and Federal Proxy Regulation—Section 14(b)

Increasingly large numbers of securities are being held in the name of broker-dealers for their customers' accounts.[1] By 1999, between seventy and

662. For some of the leading state law cases, *see, e.g.,* Campbell v. Loew's, Inc., 36 Del.Ch. 563, 134 A.2d 852 (1957); In the Matter of Auer v. Dressel, 306 N.Y. 427, 118 N.E.2d 590 (1954).

663. "If any action is to be taken with respect to any matter not specifically referred to above, describe briefly the substance of each such matter in substantially the same degree of detail as is required by Items 5 to 20, inclusive * * *." Schedule 14A, item 20, *see* United Mine Workers of America v. Pittson Co., 1989 WL 201060, [1989–1990 Transfer Binder] Fed.Sec.L.Rep. 94,946 (D.D.C.1989).

664. Even if the proxy does not contain a specific reference to the proposal, there is generally a request to give a proxy for "such other matters" as may come up for a shareholder vote. If the proxy is sought in this manner, full disclosure should require a description of any such matter known to the persons soliciting the proxy and how they intend to vote thereon. *See* Idaho Power Co., [1996–1997 Transfer Binder] Fed. Sec. L. Rep. (CCH) ¶ 77,224 (SEC No Action Letter March 13, 1996) (management could not vote against shareholder proposal without adequate disclosures in management's proxy statement as to its reason for opposition and its intent to vote against; also the proposal must appear on the proxy card).

665. *See* Shoen v. AMERCO, 885 F.Supp. 1332 (D.Nev.1994).

§ 10.9

1. 15 U.S.C.A. § 78n(c).

2. 17 C.F.R. §§ 240.14c–1 through 14c–7.

3. 17 C.F.R. § 240.14c–101.

§ 10.10

1. SEC, Street Name Study (1976).

eighty percent of publicly held securities were held in street name.[2] Holding the customer's stock or other securities in street name is not only a matter of convenience, but also may be necessary for the extension of credit pursuant to the margin requirements.[3] Additionally, with the time for settlement of transactions moving from five to three business days, it is becoming increasingly cumbersome for customers to hold their share certificates since there is less time to deliver them for sale.[4]

The self regulatory organizations became concerned about brokerage firm voting of shares where the beneficial owner does not direct how the shares are to be voted. In the absence of a regulatory rule to the contrary, since the brokerage firm is the record owner, the firm is free to vote the shares as the firm pleases unless directed otherwise by the beneficial owner. However, New York Stock Exchange Rule 452, as amended in 2003, does not permit discretionary voting on certain "non-routine" matters such as mergers.[7] The New York Stock Exchange created a Proxy Working Group to review this and other exchange rules regulating the proxy voting process and in 2006, the Working Group issued its report.[8] The report made a number of recommendations, including amending Rule 452 to categorize election of directors as a non-routine matter and thus no longer permit brokerage firms to vote street-name and other shares held in a fiduciary capacity without specific instructions from the beneficial owner.[9] The Working Group recommended that the rule apply even when the election of directors is uncontested. In May 2007, the New York Stock Exchange proposed implementing the suggested expansion of non-routine matters to include director elections.[10]

Section 14(b) of the Exchange Act[11] requires all broker-dealers who are members of a national exchange or national security association[12] to forward proxy solicitation materials to their customers in whose account the securities are held. The statute makes it unlawful to fail to comply with such rules as the commission may promulgate.[13] The Commission has exercised the rule-making power delegated by section 14(b).[14] The rules relating to shareholder

2. *See* 23A Jerry W. Markham & Thomas Lee Hazen, Broker–Dealer Operations Under Securities and Commodities Law § 8.11[2] (22 ed. 2004).

3. 15 U.S.C.A. § 78g. Margin requirements are discussed in § 14.9 *infra*.

4. *See, e.g.,* Issuer Restrictions or Prohibitions on Ownership by Securities Intermediaries, Sec. Exch. Act Rel. No. 34–50758, 69 Fed. Reg. 70852–01, 2004 WL 2787357 (SEC 2004).

7. NYSE Rule 452.

8. See Report and Recommendations of the Proxy Working Group to the New York Stock Exchange, http://www.nyse.com/pdfs/REVISED_NYSE_Report_6_5_06.pdf (June 5, 2006).

9. Report and Recommendations of the Proxy Working Group to the New York Stock Exchange, http://www.nyse.com/pdfs/REVISED_NYSE_Report_6_5_06.pdf (June 5, 2006).

10. See NYSE Files Proposal to Eliminate Discretionary Broker Voting for Directors, 5 Corporate Accountability Report (BNA) 560, http://pubs.bna.com/ip/BNA/car.nsf/cbeebd717c2395bb85256b5200778094/ed9ee6c2987d22b5852572ec0079b188?OpenDocument (No. 5 June 1, 2007).

11. 15 U.S.C.A. § 78n(b).

12. The rule also applied to broker-dealers regulated directly by the SEC, a category abolished effective December, 1983. In other words section 14(b) applies to all broker-dealers who are subject to Exchange Act regulation and oversight by the SEC. *See* chapter 14 *infra*.

13. 15 U.S.C.A. § 78n(b).

14. *See* 17 C.F.R. § 240.14b–1 *et seq.* For an early view of the problem *see* Edward R. Aranow & Herbert A. Einhorn, Corporate Proxy Contests: Solicitation and Validity of Brokers' Proxies, 23 U.Chi.L.Rev. 640 (1956).

communications have been extended to banks and other entities holding securities in their names as fiduciaries for the beneficial owners.[15]

15. Pub.L. No. 99–222, 99 Stat. 1737 (1985), amending 15 U.S.C.A. § 78n(b). *See* 17 C.F.R. § 240.14b–2.

Chapter 11

TENDER OFFER AND TAKEOVER REGULATION

Table of Sections

§ 11.1 Federal Regulation of Tender Offers and Other Control Transactions—The Williams Act; The Terminology of Takeovers

During the 1960s, the securities markets witnessed a substantial increase in the use of tender offers—publicly announced offers to purchase the shares of a target company—as a means of effecting corporate combinations. The tender offer was used to replace or supplement what had at the time been the more conventional route of statutory merger or consolidation. The increased use of tender offers was due in part to the fact that most target companies subject to the Exchange Act's reporting requirements were required to hold a shareholder vote and to comply with the Act's proxy rules[2] when participating in a statutory merger or consolidation.[3] Bypassing or delaying the merger and

§ 11.1

2. 15 U.S.C.A. § 78n(a); 17 C.F.R. §§ 240.14a–9 *et seq.*

3. *See* chapter 10 *supra.*

accompanying shareholder vote until control had been acquired allowed the control transfer to take place without detailed, if any, disclosures to investors.

The competitive atmosphere and vociferousness with which such takeover battles were waged became extreme both in terms of public and private ramifications. The terminology that is used to describe takeover tactics reflects the intensity of takeover battles.[4]

The federal securities laws contained a regulatory gap. By and large, there were no disclosure provisions applicable to tender offers. As such, shareholders of target companies were frequently given very little information about outsiders desiring to take control of their company. Investment decisions surrounding pending takeovers thus had to be made without the types of information that Congress intended investors to generally have available.

The war-like nature of corporate takeovers and the regulatory gap for tender offers led to Congressional action. In 1968, Congress adopted the tender offer and takeover provisions of the Williams Act amendments[5] to the Exchange Act.

§ 11.1[1] The Terminology of Takeovers

The intensity with which corporate takeover battles are waged is illustrated by the jargon that has developed to describe various takeover tactics—both offensive and defensive maneuvers. For example, aggressors may use the surprise element through a quickly assembled offer known as a "midnight special."[6] A "bear hug" involves an initial "friendly" approach to management of the target company with an express or implied choice of coming quietly now or being dragged along later. "Smoking gun" refers to a mistake that impedes the progress of the tender offer or defensive tactic.[7] A "show stopper" is a mistake so drastic that it results in the offer's failure. "White knights" may be brought in by the target company to fend off an unwanted suitor; "gray knights" are competing suitors who are not solicited by the target company but are viewed as preferable to the initial aggressor, and "black knights" are competing suitors who are less attractive. "Shark repellent" refers to preventive measures by companies viewed as potential targets in order to fend off unwanted suitors.[8] "Shark repellent" may also be used to refer to state tender offer statutes that may present additional impediments to takeovers.[9] Many of these state laws have been held preempted by the federal tender offer provisions found in the Williams Act.[10]

The "wounded list" refers to executives who have lost their jobs or their health during the course of a takeover campaign. Takeovers can also involve "shootouts" and eventually some resolution through "hired guns" (the attorneys). Also important in the world of takeovers are the "arbs" or arbitrageurs

4. *See* § 11.1[1] *infra.*

5. Pub.L. No. 90–439, 82 Stat. 454 (1968) (codified at 15 U.S.C. §§ 78m(d)–(e), n(d)–(f)).

6. For a vivid example of a midnight special, *see* Wellman v. Dickinson, 475 F.Supp. 783 (S.D.N.Y.1979).

7. Defensive tactics are discussed in § 11.10 *infra.*

8. A common device has been the use of protective charter provisions such as high vote requirements for a merger.

9. *See* § 11.11 *infra.*

10. *See* § 11.13 *infra.*

whose predictions of a tender offer's success may become a self-fulfilling prophecy.

A relatively novel financing development in the 1980s, frequently referred to as "junk bonds" (euphemistically described solely as "high yield" bonds), were low quality, non-investment grade corporate debt obligations. These highly speculative debt instruments often were used to finance leveraged buy-outs (also known as "LBOs") of target companies. A variation of the LBO is the MBO, or management buyout, where existing management takes over the company by taking it private.[13]

Another common takeover device is the two-tiered offer. Under the prototypical front-end loaded, two-tiered offer, the offeror makes an offer for a limited number of target company shares with notice that a second step of the acquisition will follow at a lower price.[14] This second step is frequently referred to as the "cram down." A front-end loaded two-tier offer can be seen as coercing shareholders to tender their shares for fear of being forced out at the lower price to be offered during the second step of the transaction. It has fairly been said that a front-end loaded offer followed by a cram down places the shareholders in a "prisoner's dilemma," while the acquiring corporation is able to purchase control at a "blended price."[15]

Additionally, as defensive tactics[16] to thwart hostile takeovers continue to abound, new and colorful names are devised. A number of these terms have developed over the years. Consider, for example, the Pac–Man defense (named after the video game), which consists of the target company's attempt to acquire the predator would-be acquirer. A number of public companies have authorized or adopted "poison pills," which involve the issuance of preferred stock, debt securities, or rights to acquire such securities that have a high buy-back price, which is triggered by a hostile acquisition of the target company. A variation on the poison pill is the "poison put," which entitles shareholders of the target company to "put" their shares to the acquirer at a high price. As discussed in a later section of this treatise, many of these poison pills and poison puts have come under attack but have frequently been upheld.[17] "Greenmail" is the term that has come to be used for premiums paid out of the corporate treasury to buy back the hostile bidder's shares at a premium above the price that he or she paid. "Golden parachutes" are compensation agreements with the target company's top management, which provide for high severance payments in the event of a change in control. "Tin parachutes" are similar arrangements that may be made available to less senior executives. Under the "scorched earth" defense of its turf, a target company makes itself so unattractive for acquisition that the acquirer becomes uninterested.

---

13. The SEC's going private rules are discussed in § 11.8[2] *infra.*

14. Several states, following the lead of Maryland, enacted "fair price" statutes that prohibit the use of unfriendly front-end loaded two-tiered offers. Md. Corp's & Ass'ns Code §§ 3–602, 3–603. *See* §§ 11.12–11.13 *infra.*

15. *See generally* Two–Tier Tender Offer Pricing, Sec.Exch. Act Rel. No. 34–21,079, [1984 Transfer Binder] Fed.Sec.L.Rep. (CCH) ¶ 83,637 (SEC June 21, 1984).

16. *See* § 11.11 *infra.*

17. *See, e.g.,* Minstar Acquiring Corp. v. AMF Inc., 621 F.Supp. 1252 (S.D.N.Y.1985) (holding non-transferrable dividend right to be violative of New Jersey law). *See* § 11.20 *infra.*

§ 11.1[2] Overview of the Regulation Imposed by the Williams Act

The Williams Act amendments to the Securities Exchange Act of 1934 introduced sections 13(d), 13(e), 14(d), 14(e), and 14(f) to the Exchange Act.[18] As is the case with federal proxy regulation,[19] the filing requirements of the Williams Act are limited to securities registered under section 12 of the Act.[20] Both section 13(d)[21] and section 13(e),[22] as is the case with sections 14(d)[23] and 14(f),[24] apply only to securities subject to the Exchange Act registration requirements and accompanying reporting requirements.[25] Registered reporting companies are those issuers having a class of securities traded on a national securities exchange, as well as those issuers having assets of at least $10,000,000 and also having a class of equity securities with more than 500 shareholders of record.[26] The filing and reporting provisions of the Williams Act do not apply to those issuers who, although not having to register under section 12 of the Exchange Act, nevertheless are required to file periodic reports under section 15(d).[27] In contrast to the other provisions of the Williams Act, section 14(e)[28] by its terms applies to *any* tender offer utilizing an instrumentality of interstate commerce, even if the target company is not subject to the Exchange Act's registration and reporting requirements.

Section 13(d) of the 1934 Act[29] focuses on creeping, open market, and privately negotiated acquisitions of securities subject to the 1934 Act's registration[30] and reporting requirements. Any person who acquires, directly or indirectly, more than a five percent beneficial ownership interest in any class of equity security subject to the Exchange Act's registration requirements must file a statement of ownership with the Commission within ten days after reaching the five percent threshold.[31] The purpose of section 13(d)'s notice requirement is to provide an early warning and thereby put both investors and the target company's management on notice of a possible impending takeover attempt. However, the purchaser has ten days between the crossing of the five percent threshold and the disclosure date. This provides a ten day

18. 15 U.S.C.A. §§ 78m(d), 78m(e), 78m(d), 78n(e), 78n(f).

19. *See* §§ 10.1–10.2 *supra*.

20. 15 U.S.C.A. § 78*l*. *See* § 9.2 *supra*. For discussion of the applicability of the Williams Act to foreign tender offers, *see* Jill E. Fisch, Imprudent Power: Reconsidering U.S. Regulation of Foreign Tender Offers, 87 Nw.U.L.Rev. 523 (1993).

21. 15 U.S.C.A. § 78m(d).

22. 15 U.S.C.A. § 78m(e).

23. 15 U.S.C.A. § 78n(d).

24. 15 U.S.C.A. § 78n(f).

25. *See* §§ 9.2, 9.3 *supra*.

26. 15 U.S.C.A. § 78*l*; 17 C.F.R. § 240.12g–1. Note that the 500 shareholder threshold is based on record owners and this does not look through to the beneficial owners of shares held by brokerage firms in street name or other forms of nominee ownership.

27. 15 U.S.C.A. § 78*o*(d). Section 15(d) reporting companies include issuers that have issued securities pursuant to a 1933 Act registration statement and have at least 300 security holders of that class of securities. *Id.* the periodic reporting requirements are discussed in § 9.3 *supra*.

28. 15 U.S.C.A. § 78m(e).

29. 15 U.S.C.A. § 78m(d). *See, e.g.*, William Robinson & J. Daniel Mahoney, Schedule 13D: Wild Card in a Takeover Bid, 27 Bus.Law. 1107 (1972). *See* § 11.2 *infra*.

30. *See* § 9.2 *supra*.

31. The filing requirements are triggered not only by purchases of securities, but also by the formation of a group to exercise control in common. *See* § 11.2 *infra*.

window for additional undisclosed acquisitions of the target company's stock. This permits the acquisition of considerably more stock than the five percent threshold before any disclosure need be made. As such, this early warning mechanism has its defects. Despite numerous attempts to close it, the ten day window remains open.[32]

The Schedule 13D is the appropriate form for section 13(d) filings, and the person (or group) responsible for the filing must disclose information about itself, its officers, directors, and principal business, as well as any financing arrangements that have been entered into to finance the purchase.[33] Furthermore, the Schedule 13D must contain a statement of the purchaser's future intentions with regard to the target company.[34] For example, the purchaser must disclose whether a public tender offer, statutory merger, consolidation or other form of corporate fusion or combination is possible or likely to take place. As an alternative, the purchaser may merely state that its purchase was for purely investment purposes, if that is in fact the case.

Section 13(e) of the Act[35] makes it unlawful for issuers subject to the Exchange Act's registration requirements to purchase their own shares in contravention of SEC rules which, as discussed in a later section of this chapter,[36] require SEC filings. Furthermore, since the Schedule 13D and Schedule TO (which replaced former 13E–4)[37] are filed documents, any material misstatement or omission will give rise to a private cause of action under 18(a) of the Exchange Act to an investor who purchases or sells the security and actually relies on that information.[38]

In addition to regulatory gaps in corporate takeovers, the SEC was concerned about the trend for some companies to reduce the number of shareholders so the company would no longer be subject to the Exchange Act's periodic reporting requirements. These transactions are known as "going private" transactions regardless of the form they take. The SEC has promulgated its going private rules[39] pursuant to section 13(e).[40] These going private rules are designed to protect security holders of issuers engaging in transactions that will result in cessation of 1934 Act reporting requirements.[41] The rules assure adequate disclosures in connection with going private transactions regardless of the form that the transaction may take.

In contrast to section 13(d)'s focus on open-market and privately negotiated acquisitions, sections 14(d)[42] and 14(e)[43] are directed at "tender offers."

---

32. *See, e.g.,* D'Amato Introduces Comprehensive Proposal for Tender Offer Reform, 19 Sec.Reg. & L.Rep. (BNA) 84 (Jan. 24, 1987).

33. 17 C.F.R. § 240.13d–101.

34. See, e.g., Levie v. Sears Roebuck & Co., 2006 WL 756063 (N.D.Ill. 2006) (refusing to dismiss Rule 10b–5 claim that owner failed to adequately state his intention in section 13(d) filing).

35. 15 U.S.C.A. § 78m(e). *See* § 11.7 *infra.*

36. *See* § 11.8 *infra.*

37. 17 C.F.R. § 240.14d–100; 17 C.F.R. § 240.13e–4 (filing required by a company's tender offer for its own shares).

38. 15 U.S.C.A. § 78r(a). *See* § 12.18 *infra.*

39. 17 C.F.R. §§ 240.13e–1–13e–4.

40. 15 U.S.C.A. § 78m(e).

41. *See* § 11.17 *infra.*

42. 15 U.S.C.A. § 78n(d).

43. 15 U.S.C.A. § 78n(e).

The term "tender offer" is not defined anywhere in the Act nor in the SEC rules and regulations, however, and the absence of a statutory definition gave rise to much litigation and proposed administrative or statutory amendment.

Section 14(d) of the Act[46] requires that any person planning a "tender offer" for any class of equity security subject to the registration and reporting requirements of the Exchange Act must file with the Commission all solicitations, advertisements, and any other material to be used in connection with the tender offer. This filing must take place prior to the distribution of the tender offer material. In addition, the tender offeror must file with the SEC a long form Schedule TO,[47] disclosing information about the offeror and the offer similar to that required in the Schedule 13D. For example, the Schedule TO must disclose information about the tender offeror, its officers, directors, and principal business, as well as any financing arrangements that have been entered into to finance the offer. Furthermore, the Schedule TO must contain a statement of the purchaser's future intentions with regard to the target company.

The Williams Act filing requirements are not limited to the tender offeror (or "bidder"). Anyone who contacts shareholders or makes a public statement in support of or in opposition to a tender offer, must do so with appropriate disclosures on SEC Form 14D–9.[51]

Section 14(e)[52] prohibits fraud, deceit, and material misrepresentation or omissions "in connection with any tender offer or request or invitation for tenders, or any solicitation of security holders in opposition to or in favor of any such offer, request or invitation." Section 14(e) is the only provision of the Williams Act that applies across the board and is not limited to tender offers directed at the securities of 1934 Act registered reporting companies. Furthermore, although the Supreme Court held that section 14(e) will not support a private right of action in the hands of a competing tender offeror,[53] it remains open the extent to which a shareholder of the target company or the target company itself retains an implied private right of action.[54] Similarly, it is unclear whether a private remedy can be implied for violations of sections 13(d), 13(e), and 14(d), although most courts recognize at least a potential for injunctive relief.[55]

The final provision of the Williams Act, section 14(f),[56] requires a tender offeror or someone acquiring shares in a transaction requiring a section 13(d) filing, to publicly disclose, on appropriate SEC filing forms, the names and descriptions of persons to be elected directors or any agreements affecting directors during the transfer of management control that are connected with a tender offer for equity securities subject to the Act's reporting requirements.

---

46. 15 U.S.C.A. § 78n(d). *See* § 11.14 *infra.*

47. 17 C.F.R. § 240.14d–100.

51. 17 C.F.R. § 240.14d–101.

52. 15 U.S.C.A. § 78n(e). *See* § 11.15 *infra.*

53. Piper v. Chris–Craft Indus., Inc., 430 U.S. 1, 97 S.Ct. 926, 51 L.Ed.2d 124 (1977), *rehearing denied* 430 U.S. 976, 97 S.Ct. 1668, 52 L.Ed.2d 371 (1977).

54. *See* § 11.10 *infra.*

55. *See* § 11.9 *infra.*

56. 15 U.S.C.A. § 78n(f). *See* § 11.16 *infra. See generally* David L. Ratner, Section 14(f): A New Approach to Transfers of Corporate Control, 54 Cornell L.Rev. 65 (1968).

§ 11.2 Filing Requirements for Acquisition of More Than Five Percent of Equity Securities of an Exchange Act Reporting Company—Section 13(d)

§ 11.2[1] Section 13(d)'s "Early Warning" Filing Requirements

Section 13(d) of the 1934 Act[1] was enacted as part of the Williams Act to give investors and the public markets an early warning of a major stock acquisition that could be a first step in acquiring control of the target company. Any person, other than the issuer, who directly or indirectly acquires beneficial ownership of more than five percent of a class of equity security registered pursuant to section 12 of the 1934 Act,[2] must file appropriate disclosures with the SEC pursuant to section 13(d).[3] An issuer's purchases of its own shares, directly or through an affiliate, are subject to similar disclosure requirements by virtue of section 13(e).[4] The purpose of the section 13(d) filing is to give early warning of the existence of a person or a group that may be in a position to exert control over the corporation.[5]

The language of the statute provides that any person acquiring five percent of a class of voting equity securities must, within ten days after reaching the five percent threshold, file with the Commission six copies of a statement reflecting the information required by section 13(d)(1). The purchaser thus has a ten-day window between the crossing of the five percent threshold and the disclosure date. This ten-day period provides a window of opportunity for acquiring considerably more than the five percent threshold before section 13(d)'s early warning disclosures must be made. An SEC advisory group recommended amending the rules to require filing in advance of the five percent purchase[15] but no such change has taken place. Accordingly, there frequently will be a flurry of purchases after the five percent threshold has been crossed. A major consequence of the section 13(d) filing obligation is that it places the person making the filing under a continuing obligation to update the filing for additional purchases or for material new information.

The normal filing required by section 13(d) is embodied in Schedule 13D.[17] However, some large investors who would otherwise be required to make a Schedule 13D filing may qualify for a shorter form Schedule 13G.[18] By virtue of Rule 13d–1(b),[19] qualifying institutional investors, and other "passive investors"[20] whose intent is not to acquire or influence the control of the

§ 11.2

1. 15 U.S.C.A. § 78m(D).

2. 15 U.S.C.A. § 78*l*.

3. 15 U.S.C.A. § 78m(d)(*l*). Section 12, 15 U.S.C.A. § 78*l*, is discussed in § 9.2 *supra*.

4. 15 U.S.C.A. § 78m(e); 17 C.F.R. § 240.13e–3. *See* § 11.17 *infra*.

5. The Seventh Circuit has explained that the purpose of section 13(d) was to provide early warning of control motivated transactions. Edelson v. Ch'ien, 405 F.3d 620 (7th Cir. 2005).

15. *See* 15 Sec.Reg. & L.Rep. (BNA) 156 (June 17, 1983).

17. 17 C.F.R. § 240.13d–1. Schedule 13D is found in 17 C.F.R. § 240.13d–101.

18. 17 C.F.R. § 240.13d–102.

19. 17 C.F.R. § 240.13d–1(b).

20. The rule was amended in 1998, to expand the availability of Schedule 13G to "passive investors" owning less than twenty percent of the company and not intending to acquire or influence control of the company. The Schedule 13G can no longer be used if the passive investors cross the twenty percent threshold or changes its intent regarding control. *See* Sec. Exch. Act Rel. No. 34–39538, [1998 Transfer Binder] Fed. Sec. L. Rep. (CCH) ¶ 86,002 (SEC Jan. 12, 1998).

target company qualify to use Schedule 13G. This passive investor rule permits the acquisition of up to twenty percent of the target company's securities without having to comply with the more detailed disclosure requirements of Schedule 13D. If the passive investor decides to exert control,[21] then he or she must make a Schedule 13D filing, and there is a ten-day cooling off period before he or she can act in accordance with the new disclosure regarding control. Filing a Schedule 13G and withholding the intent to acquire control is a violation of the Act.[22] Certain institutional investors that are able to file Schedule 13G may also have to make annual filings under section 13(f).[23]

Schedule 13D disclosures are designed to alert the investing public to significant acquisitions of securities and the intentions of the person making the acquisitions. Specifically, Schedule 13D requires disclosure of the identity and background[24] of the person acquiring the target company securities. The Schedule 13D must reveal the source and amount of funds or other consideration being used to acquire the target securities.[25] The section 13(d) filing must also describe the purpose of the transaction[26] that triggers the Schedule 13D filing obligation. The Schedule 13D must reveal the interest of all persons making the filing in the target securities of the issuer.[27] Disclosures also must be made with respect to contracts and other arrangements between the persons making the Schedule 13D filing and any other persons concerning the target securities of the issuer, including voting agreements, options, and distributions of profits.[28]

§ 11.2[2] Who Must File Under Section 13(d); Formation of a "Group"

Formation of a "Group"

By virtue of section 13(d)(3),[35] when two or more people or entities get together to act as a partnership, limited partnership, syndicate, or other group for the purpose of acquiring, holding, or disposing of a target company's securities, the syndicate or group is deemed to be a "person" for the purposes of section 13(d).[36] Accordingly, a Schedule 13D must be filed when members of such a "group" in the aggregate acquire five percent of a class of equity

---

21. *See, e.g.,* Hallwood Realty Partners, L.P. v. Gotham Partners, 95 F.Supp.2d 169 (S.D.N.Y. 2000) (failure to disclose intent to exercise control and liquidate company).

22. *See* Hallwood Realty Partners, L.P. v. Gotham Partners, 95 F.Supp.2d 169 (S.D.N.Y.2000).

23. 15 U.S.C.A. § 78m(f). *See* § 11.3 *infra.*

24. Schedule 13D, item 2, 17 C.F.R. § 240.13d–101. This includes disclosure of criminal convictions and of suits involving securities law violations within the preceding 5 years. Schedule 13D, item 2(c), (d).

25. Schedule 13D, item 3, 17 C.F.R. § 240.13d–101.

26. Schedule 13D, item 4, 17 C.F.R. § 240.13d–101.

27. Schedule 13D, item 5, 17 C.F.R. § 240.13d–101.

28. Schedule 13D, item 6, 17 C.F.R. § 240.13d–101.

35. 15 U.S.C.A. § 78m(d)(3).

36. *See, e.g.,* Global Intellicom, Inc. v. Thomson Kernaghan & Co., 1999 WL 544708, [1999 Transfer Binder] Fed. Sec. L. Rep. (CCH) ¶ 90,534 (S.D.N.Y.1999).

The Second Circuit extended the group concept to the definition of person to section 16 of the Act which governs reporting of insider trades and disgorgement of short-swing profits. Morales v. Quintel Entertainment, Inc., 249 F.3d 115 (2d Cir.2001); Morales v. Freund, 163 F.3d 763 (2d Cir.1999). *See* § 13.3 *infra.*

securities subject to the Act's reporting requirements.[37] In light of both the statutory language of section 13(d) and the legislative history and purpose of the provision, in order for a group to qualify as a "person" under section 13(d), the Second Circuit takes the position that each member of the group must be a beneficial owner of securities.[38] The court's rationale seems clearly supported by the statutory purpose—namely to give advance warning of beneficial ownership.

The Second Circuit also held that the determinative factor is whether a group has been established which holds the securities, pursuant to an express or implied agreement, thus presenting the *potential* for a shift in control; no agreement to buy further securities is necessary.[39] It is not necessary that the agreement to act together be in writing.[40] Nor is it necessary that the agreement be one to gain or exert control; it is sufficient that the agreement include the acquisition of securities.[41] It is not necessary that the agreement be unconditional or subject to specific terms.[42] The members' agreement to acquire control may be established by the pattern of purchases leading up to the five percent threshold.[43] Thus, hovering just hundredths of a percentage point below the five percent threshold can be evidence of a conscious decision to act together prior to the group crossing the five percent threshold.[44] When there is evidence showing the possibility that a group existed, there is a triable issue and thus the case is not suitable for summary judgment.[45]

Derivative Securities and Beneficial Ownership

In CSX Corporation v. The Children's Investment Fund Management (UK) LLP,[51] the court held that someone with a long position in a cash settled equity swap regarding shares in a publicly held company had section 13(d) filing obligations. The court made this finding notwithstanding the defendant hedge funds' argument that as holders of swaps, they lacked voting power with respect to the shares. The court did not reach the question of whether in other cases the absence of voting power would defeat a section 13(d) filing

37. *See* IBS Financial Corp. v. Seidman & Associates, LLC, 136 F.3d 940 (3d Cir.1998) (inadequate disclosures concerning the formation of a group). *See also, e.g.*, Steel Partners II, L.P. v. Aronson, 2006 WL 1044818 (D.N.J. 2006) (upholding claim that group existed with respect to Schedule 13D filing obligations). *Cf.* Azurite Corp. v. Amster & Co., 844 F.Supp. 929 (S.D.N.Y. 1994) (having filed as a group, there was no need to disclose preliminary exploration of whether to engage in a proxy fight).

38. Rosenberg v. XM Ventures, 274 F.3d 137, 147 (3d Cir.2001).

39. GAF Corp. v. Milstein, 453 F.2d 709 (2d Cir.1971).

40. SEC v. Drexel Burnham Lambert Inc., 837 F.Supp. 587 (S.D.N.Y.1993).

41. *See, e.g.,* Roth v. Jennings, 489 F.3d 499, 508 (2d Cir. 2007) ("Although a common purpose to acquire control of the issuing company would be an indicium of collective action within the meaning of § 13(d), it is not an essential."), *relying on* Morales v. Quintel Entertainment, Inc., 249 F.3d 115, 124–25 (2d Cir.2001).

42. *See, e.g.,* Roth v. Jennings, 489 F.3d 499, 508–509 (2d Cir. 2007), *relying on* Wellman v. Dickinson, 682 F.2d 355, 363 (2d Cir.1982).

43. Corenco Corp. v. Schiavone & Sons, Inc., 488 F.2d 207, 215 (2d Cir.1973). *See also* Wellman v. Dickinson, 475 F.Supp. 783 (S.D.N.Y.1979).

Broker-dealers recommending an attractive takeover candidate may be considered part of a group. In the Matter of Katz, [1984 Transfer Binder] Fed.Sec.L.Rep. (CCH) ¶ 83,618 (SEC April 25, 1984).

44. Corenco Corp. v. Schiavone & Sons, Inc., 488 F.2d 207, 215 (2d Cir.1973).

45. Roth v. Jennings, 489 F.3d 499 (2d Cir. 2007), *reversing* Roth v. Jennings, 489 F.3d 499 (S.D.N.Y. 2007).

51. 562 F.Supp.2d 511 (S.D.N.Y. 2008).

obligation since, per Rule 13b–3(b),[52] on the facts before the court, it found a scheme to evade compliance with the filing requirement.[53]

The *CSX* case was the first to address the problem of decoupling of ownership and voting control through the use of equity swap arrangements. This has been an increasingly popular device used by hedge funds to try to garner more voting power without making the total investment necessary for outright stock ownership.[54] The United Kingdom's Financial Services Authority has adopted rules with respect to its comparable filing requirements.[56] Unless the applicable SEC rules are amended it will remain for the courts to determine when equity swaps or other hedging positions will trigger section 13(d) filing obligations. If such positions are used in an attempt to increase voting control, then section 13(d) should be invoked.

§ 11.2[4] Exemptions From Section 13(d) Filing Requirements

Section 13(d)(6) of the 1934 Act exempts certain acquisitions from section 13(d)'s and 13(g)'s filing requirements.[78] These filing requirements do not apply to an offer to acquire securities in consideration for securities to be issued under a 1933 Act registration statement. Also exempt are all acquisitions of beneficial interest which, considered with all other acquisitions by the same person over the preceding twelve months, do not exceed two percent of that class of equity securities. Section 13(d)(6) further exempts any acquisition of an equity security by the issuer of that security and any other acquisition or proposed acquisition that the commission shall exempt by its rules. The purchase of securities by the issuer is governed by section 13(e) and rules promulgated thereunder.[79]

§ 11.3 Reports of Institutional Investment Managers—Section 13(f)

Section 13(f)(1)[1] requires disclosure by institutional investment managers which exercise control over accounts containing significant portfolio holdings of equity securities, subject to the Exchange Act's filing requirements. These institutional investors must file Form 13F upon acquiring equity securities, subject to the registration requirements of section 12 of the 1934 Act[2] or the

---

52. 17 C.F.R. § 240.13d–3(b).

53. CSX Corp. v. The Children's Investment Fund Management (UK) LLP, 562 F.Supp.2d 511 (S.D.N.Y. 2008) ("Rule 13d–3(b) under the Exchange Act provides in substance that one who creates an arrangement that prevents the vesting of beneficial ownership as part of a plan or scheme to avoid the disclosure that would have been required if the actor bought the stock outright is deemed to be a beneficial owner of those shares. That is exactly what the defendants did here in amassing their swap positions. In consequence, defendants are deemed to be the beneficial owners of the referenced shares.').

54. *See* Henry T.C. Hu & Bernard Black, Equity and Debt Decoupling and Empty Voting II: Importance and Extensions, 156 U. Pa. L. Rev. 625 (2008).

56. *See* Financial Services Authority, Consultation Paper 07/20, Disclsoure of Contracts for Difference, http://www.fsa.gov.uk/pubs/cp/cp07_20.pdf (July 2008); Financial Services Authority, Policy Update on Disclosure of Contracts for Difference (CfDs) http://www.fsa.gov.uk/pubs/cp/cp07_20_update.pdf (July 2008).

78. 15 U.S.C.A. § 78m(d)(6).

79. 15 U.S.C.A. § 78m(e). *See* § 11.8 *infra.*

§ 11.3

1. 5 U.S.C.A. § 78m(f)(1).

2. 15 U.S.C.A. § 78*l*. *See* § 9.2 *supra.*

Investment Company Act[3] when the aggregate fair market value of all such equity securities exceeds one hundred million dollars.[4] The purpose of this legislation, which was adopted in 1975, was "to create a central depository of historical and current data about the activities of institutional investment managers."[5]

§ 11.4 Definition of Tender Offer

Section 13(d)'s early warning filing requirements are aimed at creeping acquisitions of substantial amounts of stock using open market or privately negotiated large block purchases.[1] In contrast, section 14's Williams Act filing and disclosure provisions are called into play when there is a "tender offer." "Tender offer" is not defined in the Williams Act. Both the courts and the SEC have broadly construed the term, providing a flexible definition. The statutory meaning of "tender offer" is important in that it determines the applicability of section 14(d)'s[2] filing requirements, section 14(e)'s[3] general antifraud proscriptions, and section 14(f)'s[4] disclosure requirements relating to new directors.

Absence of Definition by Rulemaking

On more than one occasion, Congress has considered and rejected[5] objective definitions of tender offer, such as the one embodied in the proposed Federal Securities Code.[6] The federal legislative pattern indicates either indecision or a congressional intent to retain a flexible definition and to leave the resolution of the issue to the SEC and the federal judiciary. The SEC has seized upon this flexibility (intended or not). In contrast, most state tender offer statutes contain objective definitions.[7]

In the past, the SEC declined to set objective standards[8] to determine the existence of tender offers. This position was "premised upon the dynamic nature of [the] transactions [involved] and the need for the Williams Act to be interpreted flexibly."[9] Needless to say, what the SEC views as needed flexibility is viewed by corporate planners as resulting in an unnecessary lack of predictability.

---

3. *See* § 20.3 *infra.*

4. *See* 17 C.F.R. § 240.13f–1.

5. Securities Acts Amendments of 1975, Pub.L. No. 94–29, House Conf.Rep. No. 94–229 at 109 (1975).

§ 11.4

1. 15 U.S.C.A. § 78m(d). *See* §§ 11.1, 11.2 *supra,* § 11.8 *infra.*

2. 15 U.S.C.A. § 78n(d). *See* § 11.5 *infra.*

3. 15 U.S.C.A. § 78n(e). *See* §§ 11.6, 11.10 *infra.*

4. 15 U.S.C.A. § 78n(f). *See* § 11.7 *infra.*

5. *See, e.g.,* Full Disclosure of Corporate Equity Ownership and in Corporate Takeover Bids, Hearings on S.510 Before the Subcomm. on Securities of the Senate Comm. on Banking and Currency, 90th Cong., 1st Sess. 131 (1967).

6. The proposed Code would have required an offer or solicitation directed towards more than thirty-five persons. *See* A.L.I.Fed.Sec.Code § 292 (1979); *Id.* § 299.9(a) (Tent.Draft No. 1 1972). The comments explain that although the present law has a "public connotation" of "tender offer," it is too vague and open-ended.

7. *See, e.g.,* 8 Del.Code § 203(c)(2). *See generally* Report, State Takeover Statutes and The Williams Act, 32 Bus. Law. 187 (1976).

8. *See, e.g.,* Sec.Act Rel. No. 33–5731 (Aug. 2, 1976).

9. *Id.*

The Eight Factor Test

Even in the absence of a formal rule expressly defining the term, the SEC has developed an eight-factor test to determine whether a tender offer exists. The eight factors can be summarized as follows:

(1) active and widespread solicitation of public shareholders;

(2) solicitation for a substantial percentage of the issuer's stock;

(3) whether the offer to purchase is made at a premium over prevailing market price;

(4) whether the terms of the offer are firm rather than negotiable;

(5) whether the offer is contingent on the tender of a fixed minimum number of shares;

(6) whether the offer is open only for a limited period of time;

(7) whether the offerees are subject to pressure to sell their stock; and

(8) the existence of public announcements of a purchasing program that precede or accompany a rapid accumulation of stock.[15]

These factors are simply broad guidelines. They are factors to be weighed not simply counted numerically. Hence, whatever predictability does exist must be gleaned not from the factors alone but from the cases and SEC rulings that are discussed below.

The Developing Interpretation and Case Law

In an early release, the Commission took the position that a "special bid"—the placement of a fixed-price bid on an exchange for a specified large number of shares—constitutes a tender offer.[17] Thus although ordinary open market purchases are not to be classified as tender offers,[18] use of the facilities of an exchange will not automatically preclude the finding of a "tender offer."[19] Ordinarily, open market purchases will not constitute a tender offer. In fact, as discussed below, there are no federal cases finding a tender offer on the basis of open-market purchases. An early federal district court decision held that a large block purchase of shares made without the intent to obtain control is not a tender offer under the Williams Act The court looked to the legislative history, which "made clear that the type of activity intended to be regulated ... is the acquisition of control of a corporation by outsiders through the purchase of its shares."[20] According to the legislative history, a tender offer occurs when a target company shareholder must decide whether or not to sell shares in connection with a transfer of control.[21]

15. The eight-factor test which is not contained in an official SEC rule or release has evolved over a period of time and is discussed in Wellman v. Dickinson, 475 F.Supp. 783 (S.D.N.Y.1979); Hoover Co. v. Fuqua Industries Inc., 1979 WL 1244, [1979–1980 Transfer Binder] Fed.Sec.L.Rep. (CCH) ¶ 97,107 (N.D.Ohio 1979).

17. Sec.Exch.Act Rel. No. 34–8392 (Aug. 30, 1968).

18. *Id.*

19. Adoption of Amendments to Temporary Rules and Regulations Under Section 13(d), Sec. Exch. Act Rel. No. 34–8392, 1968 WL 87251 (SEC Aug. 30, 1968).

20. Dyer v. Eastern Trust & Banking Co., 336 F.Supp. 890, 907 (D.Me.1971).

21. *See* S.Rep. No. 550, 90th Cong., 1st Sess. 2 (1967); H.R.Rep. No. 1711, 90th Cong., 2d Sess. 2 (1968).

Arguably, a series of control-related open market purchases would fall within the tender offer definition as well. The cases, however, have taken a contrary view. Notwithstanding the weight of current case law to the contrary, purchasers engaged in a series of open market transactions as a first step in acquiring control should be aware of the risk, albeit a small one, that courts may find against them on the "tender offer" issue. Open market purchases combined with secretive, high pressure private transactions could well fall within the Act's purview.

Under section 13(d), open market purchases will trigger disclosure obligations within ten days of the acquisition of five percent or more of a company's securities.[23] In contrast, section 14(d)'s filing requirements begin with the commencement of the offer.[24] Therefore, if a series of open-market purchases constitutes a tender offer, full disclosure must be made simultaneously with the first purchase. There have been many proposals before the SEC to require advance filing under section 13(d) as well.[25] Adoption of this position would, in large part, eliminate the significance of the open market purchase controversy with the very important exception that a "tender offer" triggers potential liability under section 14(e)'s antifraud proscriptions.[26]

A plan of successive open market purchases has been held not to be a tender offer where the aggregate amount of shares so purchased fell short of the five percent threshold.[27] Even where the five percent threshold was exceeded, an attempt to exercise voting control after a series of open market purchases has been held insufficient to make the acquisition a tender offer.[28] Similarly, the purchase of twenty-five percent of a company's stock in a two-day period was held not to be a tender offer where only one of the SEC's eight factors was present.[29] A "street sweep" for a target's own shares, consisting of large block purchases within a short period of time,[30] was not a tender offer even though it was designed to defeat a hostile third-party offer.[31] The most compelling case to date for characterizing a series of open-market purchases as a tender offer was Hanson Trust PLC v. SCM Corp.,[32] which held that a street sweep and a group of privately negotiated purchases for twenty-five percent of the target company's outstanding stock was not a tender offer, even though these purchases occurred on the heels of the withdrawal of a publicly announced tender offer.[33] The court refused to find these transactions

23. 15 U.S.C.A. § 78m(d). *See* § 11.1 *supra.*

24. 15 U.S.C.A. § 78n(d).

25. *See,* 15 Sec.Reg.L.Rep. (BNA) No. 24 at 1156 (June 17, 1983). The SEC proposed such legislation to Congress. *See* 16 Sec. Reg. & L.Rep. (BNA) 793 (May 11, 1984). Closing the ten-day window in section 13(d) has proven to be a difficult, if not impossible, task.

26. 15 U.S.C.A. § 78n(e).

27. Gulf & Western Industries, Inc. v. Great Atlantic & Pacific Tea Co., 356 F.Supp. 1066 (S.D.N.Y.1973), *affirmed* 476 F.2d 687 (2d Cir.1973).

28. Water & Wall Associates, Inc. v. American Consumer Industries, Inc., 1973 WL 383, [1973 Transfer Binder] Fed.Sec.L.Rep. (CCH) ¶ 93,943 (D.N.J.1973). *Accord* SEC v. Carter Hawley Hale Stores, Inc., 760 F.2d 945 (9th Cir.1985).

29. Brascan Ltd. v. Edper Equities Ltd., 477 F.Supp. 773 (S.D.N.Y.1979).

30. For example, within a two-hour trading period, the target company purchased 6.5 million of its own shares (approximately 18%); this was part of a defensive repurchase program that would have resulted in acquisition of 18.5 million shares (more than half of the company's outstanding stock).

31. SEC v. Carter Hawley Hale Stores, Inc., 760 F.2d 945 (9th Cir.1985).

32. 774 F.2d 47 (2d Cir.1985).

33. These purchases were made within hours of the withdrawal of the tender offer.

to constitute a tender offer because, among other things, the price of the purchases was at the market price and the privately negotiated purchases were accomplished without any pressure or secrecy. The result also might have been different had the withdrawal of the tender offer been part of a plan designed to evade the protections of the Williams Act.[35]

The courts' findings that these open market purchase programs are not tender offers have relied on the legislative history in distinguishing large scale stock acquisitions from tender offers. For example, it has been observed that the Williams Act was not intended to "subject any ... extensive market acquisition program to immediate characterization as a tender offer."[36] For similar reasons, courts have found that open market purchases are not tender offers under analogous state statutes.[37]

The cases involving both open market and privately negotiated stock purchases seem to turn on whether or not the "pressure-creating characteristics of a tender offer"[38] accompany the transactions. Thus, where a publicly announced intention to acquire a substantial block of stock was followed by rapid acquisition of shares, the court held that a tender offer had occurred.[39] In contrast, where acquisition proceeded more slowly and none of the SEC's eight factors were present, the court found no more than "a particularly aggressive and successful open market [and privately negotiated] stock buying program."[40]

A number of decisions have discussed whether privately negotiated transfers of a controlling block of shares can constitute a tender offer. The cases conflict, but most hold that privately negotiated transactions are susceptible of being categorized as tender offers even though most privately negotiated purchases will not fall within the definition of tender offer.[41] Any privately negotiated purchase that interferes with a shareholder's "unhurried investment decision" and "fair treatment of ... investors"[42] defeats the protections of the Williams Act and is, most likely, a tender offer. In Wellman v. Dickinson,[43] a company formed a subsidiary, LHIW [Let's Hope It Works],

---

35. *Cf.* Field v. Trump, 850 F.2d 938 (2d Cir.1988), *cert. denied* 489 U.S. 1012, 109 S.Ct. 1122, 103 L.Ed.2d 185 (1989), wherein the court found that a privately negotiated purchase sandwiched between the withdrawal of one tender offer and the initiation of a second, both at a lower price, was part of a single tender offer.

36. Ludlow Corp. v. Tyco Laboratories, Inc., 529 F.Supp. 62, 69 (D.Mass.1981). *Cf.* SEC v. Carter Hawley Hale Stores, Inc., 760 F.2d 945 (9th Cir.1985) (issuer's open market repurchase program in response to a tender offer was not a tender offer).

37. *E.g.* Condec Corp. v. Farley, 578 F.Supp. 85 (S.D.N.Y.1983) (purchase of 8.7% of the target company's stock was not a tender offer under the New York Takeover Disclosure Act).

38. Ludlow Corp. v. Tyco Laboratories, Inc., 529 F.Supp. 62, 68 (D.Mass.1981).

Subsequently it was held that a highly publicized cash merger proposal at a premium above the market price constituted a tender offer. Zuckerman v. Franz, 573 F.Supp. 351 (S.D.Fla.1983).

39. S–G Securities, Inc. v. Fuqua Investment Co., 466 F.Supp. 1114 (D.Mass.1978) (twenty-eight percent of target company). *Compare, e.g.*, SEC v. Carter Hawley Hale Stores, Inc., 760 F.2d 945 (9th Cir.1985).

40. Ludlow Corp. v. Tyco Laboratories, Inc., 529 F.Supp. 62, 67 (D.Mass.1981). *See also, e.g.*, Hanson Trust PLC v. SCM Corp., 774 F.2d 47 (2d Cir.1985).

41. *See, e.g.*, Brown v. Kinross Gold, U.S.A., 378 F.Supp.2d 1280 (D. Nev. 2005) (sales by institutional investors were not a tender offer themselves nor part of a tender offer and thus were not subject to the "best price" rule).

42. Cattlemen's Investment Co. v. Fears, 343 F.Supp. 1248 (W.D.Okl.1972) (finding a tender offer to have occurred).

43. Wellman v. Dickinson, 475 F.Supp. 783 (S.D.N.Y.1979).

through which it made simultaneous secret offers to twenty-eight of the target company's largest shareholders. These shareholders represented a total of thirty-five percent of the company's outstanding shares. The identity of the actual tender offeror was not disclosed. Further, the target shareholders were given a short period of time—from one-half hour to overnight—in which to make a decision. The court held that a tender offer had taken place.[44] In a subsequent case, a firm agreement to purchase fifty-one percent (majority control) of a company was held to be a privately negotiated sale of stock outside the scope of section 14's tender offer provisions because of the absence of most of the SEC's eight factors.[45] In addition, the Second Circuit held that where the tender offeror and the solicited shareholder agree on secrecy and the private nature of the transaction, the acquisition of nearly ten percent of a target company's outstanding shares does not constitute a tender offer.[46] Unlike the *Wellman* decision discussed above, this case did not involve a hostile, high pressure move to take control such that the interests of investor protection called for section 14(d)'s advance notice and filing requirements. Similarly, the Second Circuit held that absent special facts, five privately negotiated purchases which, combined with one open market purchase, totaled twenty-five percent of an issuer's outstanding stock did not constitute a tender offer.[47] For similar reasons, it is extremely unlikely that large block purchases would constitute a tender offer.[48]

The theme that emerges from the foregoing cases is that when a privately negotiated attempt to take control of a company raises problems that the Williams Act was designed to ameliorate (such as secrecy and high pressure), a tender offer may exist. This is a significant broadening of the tender offer definition, especially since it brings many transactions that are not subject to the filing requirements of section 13(d) within the reach of section 14(e)'s antifraud provisions. Among the key factors to look for in privately negotiated transactions are high pressure tactics, such as the "midnight special" and "bear hug" tactics used in the *Wellman* case.

Clearly, a tender offer need not be hostile in order to be subject to section 14(d)'s requirements. Where the target company's management supports the shift in control, abuses may arise that will necessitate the application of the tender offer definition.[50] It has been opined that a tender offeror's decision to extend an existing tender offer to an additional number of shares does not create a new tender offer so as to start the filing requirements of section 14(d) anew.[51] Along similar lines, shares purchased prior to the commencement of a tender offer will not be integrated into that tender offer.[52]

---

44. *Id.*

45. Astronics Corp. v. Protective Closures Co., Inc., 561 F.Supp. 329 (W.D.N.Y.1983).

46. Kennecott Copper Corp. v. Curtiss–Wright Corp., 584 F.2d 1195 (2d Cir.1978).

47. Hanson Trust PLC v. SCM Corp., 774 F.2d 47 (2d Cir.1985).

48. *See, e.g.,* E.ON AG v. Acciona, S.A, 468 F.Supp.2d 559 (S.D.N.Y. 2007) (discussing the definition of tender and the likelihood that the SEC would not take an overly broad approach in interpreting the term).

50. Smallwood v. Pearl Brewing Co., 489 F.2d 579 (5th Cir.1974), *cert. denied* 419 U.S. 873, 95 S.Ct. 134, 42 L.Ed.2d 113 (1974).

51. American General Insurance Co., [1971–1972 Transfer Binder] Fed.Sec.L.Rep. (CCH) ¶ 78,588 (SEC Staff Reply Dec. 22, 1971).

52. Lerro v. Quaker Oats Co., 84 F.3d 239 (7th Cir.1996).

As the foregoing discussion illustrates, in the absence of an SEC rule or statutory amendment, the definition of tender offer remains elusive. The cases have established some limits to the flexible definition. The inquiry, however, is highly factual and is handled on an ad hoc basis.

§ 11.5 Filings, Disclosures and Procedures for Tender Offers—Section 14(d) and Regulation 14D

§ 11.5[1] Overview of Section 14(d)'s Filing and Disclosure Requirements

Section 14(d) of the Exchange Act[1] and applicable SEC rules require the filing of tender offers along with certain mandated disclosures. Filing requirements are not limited to the tender offeror but apply to anyone who is recommending in favor of or against a tender offer covered by the Act. In addition, there are certain substantive requirements for any tender offer subject to section 14(d), but those do not extend to the fairness of the tender offer.[2] The basic thrust of section 14(d) is disclosure. Section 14(d) requires that the tender offer be fairly and fully described, but it does not require that the price offered be a fair one.[3]

Section 14(d)(1) of the Exchange Act[4] requires that all "tender offer material" for equity securities subject to the registration requirements of section 12 be filed with the Commission and accompanied by the appropriate disclosures.[5] The filing requirements do not apply to issuers whose periodic reporting obligations arise under section 15(d).[6] Section 14(d) requires disclosures of the type specified in Schedule 13D under section 13(d)[7] in addition to such other information as the SEC may require. As is the case with a Schedule 13D filing for acquisition of five percent or more of a class of a target company's stock,[8] the section 14(d) filings must be updated to reflect material changes and developments.[9] Section 14(d) does not apply to an issuer's acquisition of its own shares,[10] as those transactions are covered by section 13(e), which by virtue of SEC rulemaking imposes regulations for issuer tender offers that are comparable to Regulation 14D's rules for third party offers.[11]

---

§ 11.5

1. 15 U.S.C.A. § 78n(d).

2. *Cf.* Santa Fe Industries Inc. v. Green, 430 U.S. 462, 97 S.Ct. 1292, 51 L.Ed.2d 480 (1977) (the federal securities laws were not designed to regulate fairness; the focus is on disclosure). *See* § 12.20 *infra.*

3. Wardrop v. Amway Asia Pacific Ltd., 2001 WL 274067, [2000–2001 Transfer Binder] Fed. Sec. L. Rep. (CCH) ¶ 91,346 (S.D.N.Y. 2001).

4. 15 U.S.C.A. § 78n(d)(1).

5. 15 U.S.C.A. § 78n(d)(1).

6. 15 U.S.C.A. § 78*o*(d). Section 15(d) applies to issuers not subject to section 12 whose securities were issued pursuant to a 1933 Act registration statement. The periodic reporting requirements are discussed in § 9.3 *supra.*

7. 15 U.S.C.A. § 78m(d) which is discussed in § 11.2 *supra.*

8. 15 U.S.C.A. § 78n(d).

9. 15 U.S.C.A. § 78n(d).

10. 15 U.S.C.A. § 78n(d)(1).

11. 15 U.S.C.A. § 78m(e). In 1986, the SEC amended Rules 13e–4 and 14e–1 so as to subject issuer self-tenders to the same time periods and substantive regulation as third-party offers that are covered by section 14(d) and Regulation 14D. 17 C.F.R. §§ 240.13e–3, 240.14e–1.

Regulation 14D sets forth the Commission's filing and disclosure requirements under section 14(d). Rule 14d–1[12] provides the basic definitions for covered tender offers and further incorporates by reference all general definitions applicable under other provisions of the Exchange Act. In addition to the long-form filing set out in Schedule TO[13] the tender offeror must file copies of all additional tender offer material with the Commission no later than the date upon which it is first published or disseminated.[15] These constitute filed documents within the context of section 18(a)'s imposition of liability[16] upon those responsible therefor to injured purchasers or sellers relying on materially misleading information contained therein.

The filing requirements apply to the formal tender offer. Bidders are permitted to make a pre-commencement announcement of the offer.[17] However, it is fraudulent to make such an announcement without an intent to commence the tender offer within a reasonable time.[18]

The filing requirements are not limited to the first formal filing of the initial offer. All other documents used in the tender offer and solicitation must thus be on file with the commission prior to their use.[20]

§ 11.5[2][B] Schedule TO

The information that a tender offeror must disclose at the time of the commencement of the offer depends to some extent upon the terms of the offer that is being made. All "bidders" must file the Schedule TO. "Bidder" is defined as any person who makes a tender offer or on whose behalf a tender offer is made, except that an issuer seeking to acquire its own securities is not within the definition. Further, for the purpose of determining whether or not a tender offer has been made, two or more persons who act as a partnership, limited partnership, syndicate, or other "group" for the purpose of acquiring, holding, or disposing of the target company[32] must file eight copies of the Schedule TO,[33] including exhibits, with the Commission prior to the commencement of the tender offer. The information required by the Schedule TO for third party bidders is the same as required for issuer self-tenders. In addition to prescribing the form of the tender offer statement, Regulation 14D imposes certain substantive procedures on the mechanics and terms of the tender offer.[35]

The Schedule TO begins with a summary term sheet, as required by item 1001 of Regulation M–A.[36] The summary term sheet is not required if the

12. 17 C.F.R. § 240.14d–1.

13. 17 C.F.R. § 240.14d–100.

15. 17 C.F.R. § 240.14d–3(b).

16. 15 U.S.C.A. § 78r(a) which is discussed in § 12.19 *infra.*

17. *Cf.* Gas Natural v. E.ON AG, 468 F.Supp.2d 595, 613 (S.D.N.Y. 2006) (section 14(e)'s antifraud proscription applies to pre-tender offer announcements concerning a tender offer).

18. Rule 14e–8, 17 C.F.R. § 240.14e–8.

20. 17 C.F.R. § 240.14d–3.

32. 15 U.S.C.A. § 78n(d)(2). A similar provision is found in section 13(d)(3), 15 U.S.C.A. § 78m(d)(3). *See* § 11.2 *supra.*

33. 17 C.F.R. § 240.14d–100.

35. *See* § 11.6 *infra.*

36. Schedule TO item 1. *See* Regulation M–A item 1001, 17 C.F.R. § 229.1001. The summary term sheet must highlight the material terms of the transaction and "must provide securities holders with sufficient information to understand the essential features and significance of the proposed transaction." *Id.*

information is contained in a prospectus pursuant to a 1933 Act registration statement for the securities to be issued pursuant to the tender offer.[37] Schedule TO requires disclosure of the name of the bidder, name of the target company, and the title of the class of securities being sought.[38] It also requires that all "persons" reporting under the Schedule provide their names and addresses, as well as disclosing whether or not they belong to a "group" within the meaning of section 14(d)(2).[39] Further, it is necessary to disclose the source of funds to be used in connection with the tender offer[40] and the identity and background of the person filing the document, including the disclosure of any criminal conviction within the past five years of the person presenting the tender offer.[41]

The Schedule TO must describe the terms of the tender offer.[42] The tender offer filing must also disclose all past contracts, transactions, or negotiations between the tender offeror and the target company, the purpose of the tender offer and the bidder's plans and proposals for the future with regard to the target company.[43] The Schedule TO must divulge the bidder's current interest and holdings of securities of the target company.[44] The Schedule TO filing must identify all persons retained, employed, or compensated in connection with the tender offer,[45] as well as the bidder's financial statements[46] when the bidder's financial structure is material to an investor's decision whether or not to tender shares in the target company. For example, any tender offer involving an exchange of the target company's securities for the tender offeror's shares would necessarily trigger the financial statement requirement.[48] Additionally, if financing conditions are involved in the tender offer, the bidder's financial statements will be material.[49] Disclosure of the bidder's financial condition may also be required for cash offers if the bidder is not an Exchange Act reporting company. In addition to the disclosure items specified in Schedule TO, additional disclosures may be required if necessary to make the statements made not materially misleading.[51]

---

37. Schedule TO, item 1. The 1933 Act prospectus requirements are discussed in chapter 2 *supra*. The applicable 1933 Act disclosure requirements are discussed in chapter 3 *supra*.

38. Schedule TO item 2, 17 C.F.R. § 240.14d–100. *See* Item 1002(a) through (c) of Regulation M–A. 17 C.F.R. §§ 229.1002(a)–1002(c).

39. *See* 15 U.S.C.A. § 78n(d)(2). A similar provision is found in section 13(d)(3), 15 U.S.C.A. § 78m(d)(3). *See* § 11.2[2] *supra.*

40. Schedule TO item 7, 17 C.F.R. § 240.14d–100. *See* Items 1007(a), (b) and (d) of Regulation M–A, 17 C.F.R. §§ 229.1007(a), 229.1007(b), 229.1007(d).

41. *Id.*

42. Schedule TO item 4. *See* Items 1004(a) through (b) of Regulation M–A, 17 C.F.R. §§ 229.1004(a)–229.1004(b).

43. Schedule TO item 5, 17 C.F.R. § 240.14d–100. *See* Items 1005(a) (b) and (e) of Regulation M–A. 17 C.F.R. §§ 229.1005(a), 229.1005(b), 229.1005(e).

44. Schedule TO item 8, 17 C.F.R. § 240.14d–100. *See* Item 1008 of Regulation M–A, 17 C.F.R. § 229.1008.

45. Schedule TO item 9, 17 C.F.R. § 240.14d–100. *See* Item 1009(a) of Regulation M–A, 17 C.F.R. § 229.1009(a).

46. Schedule TO item 10. *See* Items 1010(a) and (b) of Regulation M–A, 17 C.F.R. §§ 229.1010(a), 229.1010(b).

48. *See* Instructions 1 and 2 to Schedule TO item 10, 17 C.F.R. § 240.14d–100.

49. *See* Instructions 1 and 2 to Schedule TO item 10, 17 C.F.R. § 240.14d–100.

51. *See* Schedule TO item 11, *See* Instructions 1 and 2 to Schedule TO item 10, 17 C.F.R. § 240.14d–100. *See* Instructions 1 and 2 to Schedule TO item 10, 17 C.F.R. § 240.14d–100 Regulation M–A item 1011, 17 C.F.R. § 229.1011.

In addition to the disclosures above, the Schedule TO filing must list any present or proposed material contracts, arrangements, understandings, or relationships between the bidder, its officers, directors, controlling persons, or subsidiaries and the target company or any of its officers, directors, controlling persons, or subsidiaries that would bear upon the target company shareholders' decision whether or not to tender his or her shares. Further, steps toward compliance with necessary administrative approval for the offer must be disclosed, as must the applicability of the antitrust laws, or the margin requirements as well as the pendency of material legal proceedings. When there have been material misstatements in a Schedule TO filing, they can be cured by subsequent correction, provided that adequate prominence is given to the curative changes.[54]

§ 11.5[3] Other Requirements Imposed by Regulation 14D

Section 14(d)(3) of the Act[67] provides that in determining the applicable percentage of outstanding shares of any class of equity securities, securities held by the issuer or its subsidiary must be excluded from the computation. Also, section 14(d)(4)[68] requires full disclosure according to such rules as the Commission may promulgate with regard to any solicitation or recommendation to a target company's securities holders either to accept or reject a tender offer or request for tender made by someone else. These disclosure requirements are set out in Schedule 14D–9.[69] Schedule 14D–9 is the disclosure document that must be filed in connection with any other solicitation or recommendation for or against tender offers. The Schedule 14D–9 is in essence a short form of the Schedule TO requiring similar disclosures with regard to anyone making recommendations concerning a bidder's offer. As is the case with an offeror's Schedule TO, material changes must be reflected by "prompt" amendment to the Schedule 14D–9.[71]

§ 11.5[3][A] Bidders' Right of Access to Target Company's Shareholders

SEC Rule 14d–5 spells out the target company's obligation to respond to requests for a shareholder list in connection with tender offers.[72] Briefly, if the bidder or other person presents the request according to the rule's requirements, the target company's management must comply, but the reasonable cost of compliance is to be charged to the bidder. Faced with such a request, the target company has the option of mailing the bidder's materials, within three business days of receipt, to the target company's holders.[73] Alternatively,

---

54. *See, e.g.,* American Insured Mortgage Investors v. CRI, Inc., 1990 WL 192561, [1990–1991 Transfer Binder] Fed.Sec.L.Rep. (CCH) ¶ 95,730 (S.D.N.Y.1990) (material changes had to be highlighted through the use of boldface and italic typeface).

67. 15 U.S.C.A. § 78n(d)(3).

68. 15 U.S.C.A. § 78n(d)(4).

69. 17 C.F.R. § 240.14d–101.

71. *See* In re Revlon, Inc., Exch. Act Rel. No. 34–23320, [1986 Transfer Binder] Fed.Sec. L.Rep. (CCH) ¶ 84,006 (June 16, 1986) (original 14D–9 filed by target company disclosed that merger negotiations with others might take place, discussions began on September 26 and a 14D–9 amendment filed on October 2 was held not to have discharged the target company's obligation to "promptly" amend its filing).

72. 17 C.F.R. § 240.14d–5.

73. 17 C.F.R. § 240.14d–5(b). The bidder is to be informed of the progress of any such mailing undertaken by the target company.

the target company may, within three business days, deliver the stockholder lists to the bidder making the request.[74] The SEC dictates the proper form for the bidder's written request.[75] Also, a bidder's request for such shareholder lists subjects the bidder to certain requirements, including the return of any lists furnished by the target company.[76]

§ 11.5[3][B] Shareholders' Withdrawal of Tendered Securities

Section 14(d)(5) of the Act[77] provides that all securities deposited pursuant to a tender offer may be withdrawn by or on behalf of the depositor at any time until the expiration of seven days after the first publication of the formal tender offer (or request or invitation) and at any time after sixty days from the date of the original tender offer or request for invitation unless a different period is provided for by SEC rules. Rule 14d–7,[78] which formerly limited withdrawal rights to fifteen days after the commencement of the tender offer or ten days after the commencement of a competing offer, has been amended to provide that withdrawal rights may be exercised throughout the period that the tender offer remains open, which must be for at least twenty business days.[79] Any increase or decrease in the consideration offered under the tender offer triggers the requirement that the tender offer be open for ten business days from the date of change in consideration.[80] The rule also sets out the appropriate form of the notice of withdrawal. Shareholders who tendered shares prior to receiving notice of offeror's Schedule 14D–1 (the predecessor of the current Schedule TO[81]) amendment relating to the source of funds being used for the offer were held entitled, under the former version of Rule 14d–7, to withdrawal rights for fifteen days from the notice.[82] Under the current rule, the duration of the tender offer is the appropriate extension of time for withdrawal rights.[83] By virtue of Rule 14e–1(a),[84] all tender offers by persons other than the issuer must remain open for twenty business days.[85] The same twenty-day period is applicable to issuer self-tenders.[86]

§ 11.5[3][C] Pro Rata Acceptance of Tendered Shares; Extensions of the Tender Offer

Section 14(d)(6) of the Act[87] requires pro rata acceptance of shares tendered where the tender offer by its terms does not obligate the tender

---

74. 17 C.F.R. § 240.14d–5(c).

75. 17 C.F.R. § 240.14d–5(e).

76. 17 C.F.R. § 240.14d–5(f).

77. 15 U.S.C.A. § 78n(d)(5).

78. 17 C.F.R. § 240.14d–7.

79. 17 C.F.R. § 240.14e–1.

80. 17 C.F.R. §§ 240.13e–4(f)(1)(ii), 240.14e–1(b).

81. 17 C.F.R. § 240.14d–100.

82. Cardiff Acquisitions, Inc. v. Hatch, 751 F.2d 917 (8th Cir. 1984).

83. 17 C.F.R. § 240.14d–7.

84. 17 C.F.R. § 240.14e–1(a).

85. 17 C.F.R. § 240.14e–1(a).

86. 17 C.F.R. § 240.13e–4(f)(1)(i). As is the case with third party offers, any increase or decrease in the consideration offered requires that the offer remain open at least ten business days from the notice thereof. 17 C.F.R. § 240.13e–4(f)(1)(ii).

87. 15 U.S.C.A. § 78n(d)(6).

offeror to accept all shares tendered. This takes pressure off the target company's shareholders who would otherwise have to make a quick decision were acceptance to be on a first come basis. Rule 14d–8[88] extends the pro rata requirements to the entire period of the tender offer. A tender offeror may not extend the proration period after expiration of the offer where the effect would be to alter the pro rata acceptance of the shares tendered.[89]

Section 14(d)(7) of the Act[90] provides that whenever a person varies the terms of a tender offer or request before the expiration thereof by increasing the consideration offered to the holders of the securities sought, the person making such an increase in consideration must pay to all persons tendering securities pursuant to their requests that same price whether or not the securities were tendered prior to the variation of the tender offer's terms.[91] This can be especially important if a series of transactions are integrated and held to be parts of a single tender offer.[92] Thus, for example, it has been held that a privately negotiated purchase entered into on the heels of the purported withdrawal of a tender offer was part of the same control-related transaction and thus violated the prohibition on discriminatory pricing of purchases in the course of a single tender offer.[93]

§ 11.5[3][D] The "All Holders" Rule

The SEC rules under the Williams Act are designed to ensure that shareholders of the target company are treated equally during the pendency of a tender offer. A 1985 Delaware Supreme Court decision upheld a tender offer by an issuer that excluded a hostile tender offeror.[94] However, under equal treatment rules adopted by the SEC, such exclusion is prohibited; at the same time that the Commission adopted these equal treatment rules, the SEC adopted "best price" requirements.[95] Although the equal treatment and best price rules are based on different sections, the validity of these requirements may be questionable in light of the Supreme Court ruling that section 14(e) can regulate manipulative conduct only to the extent of protecting against deception.[96]

There is an explicit exception in the "all holders" requirement for tender offers that exclude one or more shareholders in compliance with a constitutionally valid state statute.[102] In addition to reserving general exemptive power under the "all holders" rules,[103] the SEC has promulgated a specific but limited exemption for "odd-lot tender offers" by issuers—an odd-lot offer is

88. 17 C.F.R. 240.14d–8.

89. Pryor v. United States Steel Corp., 794 F.2d 52 (2d Cir.1986).

90. 15 U.S.C.A. § 78n(d)(7).

91. *See*, e.g., Field v. Trump, 850 F.2d 938 (2d Cir.1988) (recognizing private remedy for violations of section 14(d)(7)).

92. *Id.*

93. *Id.*

94. Unocal Corp. v. Mesa Petroleum Co., 493 A.2d 946 (Del.1985).

95. 17 C.F.R. §§ 240.13e–4(f), 240.14d–10.

96. Schreiber v. Burlington Northern, Inc., 472 U.S. 1, 105 S.Ct. 2458, 86 L.Ed.2d 1 (1985). *See* § 11.6 *infra.*

102. 17 C.F.R. §§ 240.13e–4(f)(9)(ii), 240.14d–10(b)(2). The SEC questions, however, whether such state statutes are in fact constitutional. *See* Exch.Act Rel. No. 34–23421 (July 11, 1986). For a discussion of the constitutionality of state statutes affecting tender offers, *see* 11.13 *infra.*

103. 17 C.F.R. §§ 240.13e–4(h)(8), 240.14d–10(e).

one that is limited to security holders owning less than a specified number of shares under one hundred.[104]

The "all holders" rule will support a private right of action.[108]

§ 11.5[3][E] The Equal Treatment and "Best Price" Requirements

As noted above, the Commission also adopted a "best price" rule that requires equal treatment[110] for all securities holders, and thus entitles anyone receiving payment under the tender offer to the highest consideration paid to any other security holder at any time during such tender offer.[111] Rule 14d–10's best price requirements have been held to support an implied private right of action.[112]

The SEC best price requirement applies only to shares purchased during a single tender offer.[113] A press release announcing an impending tender offer is not necessarily the commencement of the offer for purposes of the best price rule; accordingly the price paid for shares purchased after the press release but prior to the commencement of the tender offer did not affect the price at which the tender offer could be made.[114] As such, unlike state "fair price" statutes,[115] the SEC best price rule does not regulate two-tiered offers consummated in two distinct steps. On appropriate facts, two transactions that are distinct in form only may be integrated into a single transaction for the purpose of enforcing the best price and equal treatment requirements. The best price requirement cannot be avoided, for example, by delaying additional payments to selected insiders until after the close of the tender offer.[116] Thus, the equal treatment rule has been applied even beyond the bidder's self-proclaimed expiration date.[117] Therefore, the rule applied when a payment was made to the CEO before the tendering shareholders were paid for their shares, even though the expiration date listed in the offer had passed.[118] A payment to an executive, although labeled as in exchange for something other than shares (such as for a covenant not to compete), will be

104. 17 C.F.R. § 240.13e–4(h)(5). However, both the all holders and best price requirements will apply to the terms of the odd-lot tender offer.

108. *See, e.g.,* In re Digital Island Securities Litigation, 357 F.3d 322 (3d Cir. 2004); Polaroid Corp. v. Disney, 862 F.2d 987 (3d Cir.1988).

110. *See* 15 U.S.C.A. § 78n(d)(7).

111. 17 C.F.R. §§ 240.13e–4(f)(8)(ii), 240.14d–10(a)(2).

112. Epstein v. MCA, Inc., 50 F.3d 644 (9th Cir.1995) (suit by shareholders who were treated less favorably than others).

113. *See, e.g.,* Lerro v. Quaker Oats Co., 84 F.3d 239 (7th Cir.1996) (shares purchased prior to commencement of tender offer were not subject to best price requirement), *affirming* 897 F.Supp. 1131 (N.D.Ill.1995) (best price requirement did not apply to agreement signed one day before tender offer was announced).

114. Kahn v. Virginia Retirement System, 783 F.Supp. 266 (E.D.Va.1992). As observed in § 11.5[2][A] *supra*, the press release announcing the tender offer will be considered the commencement of the tender offer for many purposes. *See also, e.g.,* Gerber v. Computer Associates International, Inc., 303 F.3d 126 (2d Cir.2002) (looking to the date of the press release as the commencement of the tender offer).

115. *See* § 11.12 *infra.*

116. Millionerrors Investment Club v. General Electric Co. PLC, 2000 WL 1288333, [1999–2000 Transfer Binder] Fed. Sec. L. Rep. (CCH) ¶ 90,994 (W.D.Pa.2000).

117. Gerber v. Computer Associates International, Inc., 303 F.3d 126 (2d Cir.2002).

118. Gerber v. Computer Associates International, Inc., 303 F.3d 126 (2d Cir.2002).

examined pragmatically to determine if at least a portion of that payment should be treated as compensation for shares under the tender offer.[119]

As pointed out directly above, difficult questions can arise when company officials subject to a tender offer receive additional compensation. It is often difficult to determine the extent to which such payments should be characterized as executive compensation as compared to consideration under the tender offer that would have to be considered in applying the best price rule. In 2006, the SEC amended the best price rule in order to provide a safe harbor for certain compensation payments.[120] Rule 14d–10 as amended specifically exempts employment compensation and severance payments from the best price calculations if two conditions are met.[121] First, the amount paid as compensation must be based on past services already performed, future services to be performed, or future services that the employee must refrain from performing (such as in a covenant not to compete). Second, the compensation must not be based on the number of shares tendered or to be tendered. Under the safe harbor created by Rule 14d–10, payments will be considered compensation if the payments are approved by the target company's board of directors or by the tender offeror's board if the directors of the tender offeror company are a party to the compensation agreement.[122] One consequence of the amendments to the best price rule is to level the playing field between the choice of a merger or tender offer to effectuate a business combination. The former version of the best price rule created problems in structuring compensation of target company employees. The former disincentives to use a tender offer have been eliminated.[123]

The SEC best price requirements do not prohibit different types of consideration, and the different consideration need not be substantially equivalent in value so long as the tender offer permits the security holders to elect among the types of consideration offered.[124] However, offering tax favored preferred shares to some shareholders but not others can violate the equal treatment requirement.[125] Not all payments in connection with a tender offer will implicate the best price rule.

When different types of consideration are offered to all shareholders, the tender offeror may limit the availability and offer it to tendering shareholders on a pro rata basis.[127] As is the case with the "all holders" requirements, the Commission has reserved for itself the power to grant exemptions from the operation of the "best price" requirement.[128]

119. Gerber v. Computer Associates International, Inc., 303 F.3d 126 (2d Cir.2002) (upholding jury instruction on apportionment of payment).

120. *See* Amendments to the Tender Offer Best–Price Rules, Sec. Exch. Act Rel. No. 34–54684, Inv. Co. Act Rel. No. IC—27542, 2006 WL 3103705 (SEC Nov. 1, 2006).

121. 17 C.F.R. § 240.14d–10.

122. 17 C.F.R. § 240.14d–10.

123. *See* SEC Acts to Reduce Disincentives to Structuring Mergers as Tender Offers, 38 Sec. Reg. & L. Rep. (BNA) 1761 (Oct. 23, 2006).

124. 17 C.F.R. §§ 240.13e–4(f)(10), 240.14d–10(c).

125. Epstein v. MCA, Inc., 50 F.3d 644 (9th Cir.1995) (preferred shares offered in form outside of tender offer could still violate Rule 14d–10's equal treatment requirements).

127. 17 C.F.R. §§ 240.13e–4(f)(10), 240.14d–10(c).

128. 17 C.F.R. §§ 240.13e–4(h)(8), 240.14d–10(e).

The integration doctrine was developed under the 1933 Act to address multiple transactions that appear to be separate in form but in substance are part of a single transaction.[129] The same approach could be applied to integrating two successive tender offers. For example, it might be argued that successive tender offers by the same bidder, although distinct in form, are part of a single transaction and thus should be subject to the best price requirement. However, the Seventh Circuit has given a narrow reading to Rule 14d–10(a)(2)'s best price requirement and permitted a higher price to be paid to controlling shareholders immediately before the commencement of the tender offer to other shareholders.[131] The court reached this conclusion notwithstanding the fact that a higher price to the controlling shareholder was integral to the entire transaction when viewed as a whole. The court's opinion, written by Judge Easterbrook, reasoned that the language of the SEC best price rule calls for a bright line test for determining what constitutes the pendency of a tender offer for the purposes of the rule. Judge Easterbrook believed that the rule of equal treatment for all shareholders should yield to what he viewed as the practicalities of the situation. It is arguable, however, that the purpose of the best price rule and other equal treatment rules during the pendency of the offer were designed to assure that all shareholders be treated the same in what is in essence a single transaction. Should the rule of the Seventh Circuit be sustained, it will then be necessary that the ensuing tender offer adequately describe the terms of the transaction to the controlling group. In contrast to the Seventh Circuit's approach, other courts have taken a broad view of the integration concept. For example, it has been held that compensation incentives could be so inexorably entwined with a tender offer that they would be subject to the Williams Act's best price and equal treatment requirements.[134]

§ 11.5[3][F] Prompt Payment for Shares Tendered

SEC Rule 14e–1(c), which is not a part of Regulation 14D and therefore applies to all tender offers, requires that the bidder pay the consideration offered or return the tendered securities "promptly" after the termination or withdrawal of the tender offer. The rule does not define "promptly." Nevertheless, the SEC has explained that the standard for promptness may be determined by the practices of the financial community, including current settlement practices.[138] In most instances, the current settlement practice is for the payment of funds and delivery of securities no later than the third business day after the date of the transaction.[139] The Commission considers payment within these time periods as "prompt" under Rule 14e–1(c).[140] The Commission has indicated that waiting as long as thirty days does not satisfy the prompt payment requirement.[141]

129. *See* § 4.36 *supra.*

131. Lerro v. Quaker Oats Co., 84 F.3d 239 (7th Cir.1996).

134. Katt v. Titan Acquisitions, Ltd., 133 F.Supp.2d 632 (M.D.Tenn.2000).

138. *See* Sec. Exch. Act Rel. No. 34–16384, 44 Fed. Reg. 70326 (SEC Nov. 29, 1979).

139. *See* 1934 Act Rule 15c6–1(a), 17 CFR 240.15c6–1(a).

140. *See* Commission Guidance on Mini–Tender Offers and Limited Partnership Tender Offers, Release No. 34–43069, 2000 WL 1050530 (SEC July 24 2000).

141. *Id.*

§ 11.5[3][G] Post Tender Offer Extensions of Time for Tendering

Rule 14d–11,[142] which was adopted in 1999, permits the tender offeror to extend the offer for shareholders who did not tender their shares during the original offer.[143] Pursuant to Rule 14d–11, a tender offeror has the option of allowing non tendering shareholders to tender their shares for a period of at least three business days and not more than twenty business days following the closing of the offer.[144] Target company shareholders tendering during this post-offer period have the right to withdraw their shares once they are tendered.[145]

§ 11.5[3][I] Exemptions From Regulation 14D

Section 14(d)(8) of the Act[163] exempts certain tender offers or request for tenders from the scope of section 14(d)'s requirements. When the acquisition of the securities sought together with all other acquisitions by the same person of securities of the same class within the preceding twelve months does not exceed two percent of the outstanding securities of the class, section 14(d) does not apply.[164] Similarly, section 14(d) does not apply where the tender offeror is the issuer of the security.[165] The Act also gives the SEC exemptive power by rule, regulation or order from transactions "not entered into for the purpose of, and not having the effect of, changing or influencing the control of the issuer or otherwise as not comprehended within the purposes of this subsection."[166]

1§ 11.5[3][J] Unregulated Mini–Tender Offers

Section 14(d) of the 1934 Act[167] by its terms does not apply its filing and other requirements to third party tender offers where after the completion of the offer, the tender offeror does not wind up with more than five percent of the class of equity securities that are the subject of the tender offer.

In the 1990s, an unscrupulous practice developed whereby some people tried to take advantage of this absence of regulation by making mini-tender offers to shareholders at a price below the then current market price. The hope in these offers was to lure unsophisticated shareholders into thinking that this was a takeover attempt and thereby lure them into tendering their shares below the market price for the securities. In a number of cases, the SEC instituted administrative proceedings, which resulted in finding that since targeted shareholders were denied material information, such as the below market price nature of the offer and the absence of withdrawal rights

142. Rule 14d–11, 17 C.F.R. § 240.14d–11.

143. Under the terms of SEC Rule 14e–1, 17 C.F.R. § 240.14e–1, a tender offer must remain open for at least twenty business days. *See* § 11.6 *infra.*

144. Rule 14d–11, 17 C.F.R. § 240.14d–11.

145. Rule 14d–11, 17 C.F.R. § 240.14d–11. *Compare* the withdrawal rights that tendering shareholders get pursuant to section 14(d)(5) and Rule 14d–7. 15 U.S.C.A. § 78n(d)(5), 17 C.F.R. § 240.14d–7.

163. 15 U.S.C.A. § 78n(d)(8).

164. 15 U.S.C.A. § 78n(d)(8)(A).

165. 15 U.S.C.A. § 78n(d)(8)(B). *See* § 11.9 *infra.*

166. 15 U.S.C.A. § 78n(d)(8)(C).

167. 15 U.S.C.A. § 78n(d).

once the shares were tendered, these mini-tender offers violated the antifraud prohibitions.[176]

In addition to instituting administrative enforcement actions, the SEC issued a set of guidelines to be followed in mini-tender offers. These guidelines in essence provide that in mini-tender offers the bidder should act in accordance with the rules that would apply if the offer were subjected to section 14(d) regulation.[177]

§ 11.6 Unlawful Tender Offer Practices—Section 14(e) and Regulation 14E

§ 11.6[1] Section 14(e)—Antifraud and SEC Rulemaking

The foregoing provisions of the Williams Act are limited to transactions with respect to equity securities that are subject to the Securities Exchange Act's registration and reporting requirements. In sharp contrast, section 14(e) of the Exchange Act[1] prohibits material misstatements, omissions, and fraudulent practices in connection with tender offers regardless of whether the target company is subject to the Exchange Act's reporting requirements. Thus, for example, section 14(e) and SEC rules promulgated thereunder can be applied to an unregistered tender offer; it is not necessary that the target company be a public company.[3] Although there may be policy reasons not to include tender offers for the shares of companies that are not registered under the Exchange Act, the language of section 14(e) justifies federal regulation so long as the transaction in question involves a tender offer. Section 14(e) requires full and fair disclosure of the tender offer's terms; it does not require that the price be substantively fair.[4]

Materiality issues under the Williams Act are to be decided in much the same way as under the other disclosure provisions of the securities laws. Adapting the approach taken elsewhere, a fact is material if there is "a substantial likelihood that a reasonable shareholder would consider it important."[5] Courts are not inclined to engage in judicial "nit-picking" by requiring such stringent materiality scrutiny that would eventually work against shareholder interests.[6] Accordingly, subjective motivation behind fully disclosed transactions need not be spelled out.[7]

---

176. *E.g.*, In the Matter of City Investment Group, LLC, 2000 WL 745333 (SEC 2000) (violation of section 14(e)).

177. Commission Guidance on Mini–Tender Offers and Limited Partnership Tender Offers, Release No. 34–43069, 2000 WL 1050530 (SEC July 24, 2000).

§ 11.6

1. 15 U.S.C.A. § 78n(e).

3. Clearfield Bank & Trust v. Omega Financial Corp., 65 F.Supp.2d 325, 336 (W.D.Pa.1999). Section 14(e)'s jurisdictional reach thus parallels SEC Rule 10b–5 which similarly is not limited to publicly traded securities. 17 C.F.R. § 240.10b–5. *See* § 12.3 *infra.*

4. Wardrop v. Amway Asia Pacific Ltd., 2001 WL 274067, [2000–2001 Transfer Binder] Fed. Sec. L. Rep. (CCH) ¶ 91,346 (S.D.N.Y. 2001), relying on Santa Fe Industries, Inc. v. Green, 430 U.S. 462, 97 S.Ct. 1292, 51 L.Ed.2d 480 (1977) (the federal securities laws were not designed to regulate fairness; the focus is on disclosure). *See* § 12.20 *infra.*

5. TSC Industries, Inc. v. Northway, Inc., 426 U.S. 438, 449, 96 S.Ct. 2126, 2132, 48 L.Ed.2d 757 (1976). *Accord* Basic Inc. v. Levinson, 485 U.S. 224, 108 S.Ct. 978, 99 L.Ed.2d 194 (1988).

6. Macfadden Holdings, Inc. v. JB Acquisition Corp., 802 F.2d 62, 71 (2d Cir.1986), relying on Data Probe Acquisition Corp. v. Datatab, Inc., 722 F.2d 1, 5 (2d Cir.1983), *cert. denied,* 465 U.S. 1052, 104 S.Ct. 1326, 79 L.Ed.2d 722 (1984).

7. Diamond v. Arend, 649 F.Supp. 408, 415–16 (S.D.N.Y.1986).

Another issue is the standard of culpability necessary to establish a violation of section 14(e). Rule 10b–5 requires a showing of scienter;[27] section 17(a) of the 1933 Act[28] and the proxy antifraud provision of section 14a(9) of the Exchange Act[29] do not.[30] Most courts have held that in order to establish a violation of section 14(e), and therefore the rules promulgated thereunder, it must be established that the defendant acted with scienter.[32]

In what could be a very far-reaching decision, the Supreme Court in Schreiber v. Burlington Northern, Inc.,[33] limited the scope of section 14(e). *Schreiber* involved a claim that the defendant target company's renegotiation of the terms of a tender offer was manipulative and hence in violation of section 14(e).[34] Rather than directly face the issue of defining manipulative conduct,[35] the Court held that "[w]ithout misrepresentation or nondisclosure section 14(e) has not been violated."[36]

The Supreme Court held that there is no private remedy in the hands of a competing tender offeror.[40] However, most lower courts have recognized a remedy in the hands of the target company or one of its shareholders,[41] as well as the right of a competing tender offeror to seek injunctive relief.[42] The question of the availability of private remedies under the Williams Act is taken up in detail in a subsequent section of this treatise.[43]

§ 11.6[2] Regulation 14E and Other Tender Offer Regulations

§ 11.6[2][A] Duration of Tender Offer

Rule 14e–1[45] requires that any person making a tender offer hold the offer open for at least twenty business days from the date upon which it is first

27. 17 C.F.R. § 240.10b–5. *See* § 12.8 *supra.*

28. 15 U.S.C.A. § 77q(a). *See* § 7.11 *supra.*

29. 15 U.S.C.A. § 78n(a)(9). *See* §§ 10.3–10.4 *supra.*

30. *E.g.,* Aaron v. SEC, 446 U.S. 680, 100 S.Ct. 1945, 64 L.Ed.2d 611 (1980) (section 17(a)(2),(3) of the 1933 Act does not require a showing of scienter). *See* § 12.8 *infra.*

32. Clearfield Bank & Trust v. Omega Financial Corp., 65 F.Supp.2d 325, 342–344 (W.D.Pa. 1999) (and authorities cited therein). *See* § 11.10 *infra.*

33. 472 U.S. 1, 105 S.Ct. 2458, 86 L.Ed.2d 1 (1985). *See, e.g.,* Norman S. Poser, Stock Market Manipulation and Corporate Control Transactions, 40 U.Miami L.Rev. 671 (1986).

34. Burlington Northern had made a hostile tender offer to purchase 25.1 million shares of El Paso Gas for $24 per share. After negotiations with El Paso management, the original offer was withdrawn, El Paso management was given "golden parachute" severance payments, and a new tender offer was made for 21 million shares from the public and 4.1 million shares from El Paso at $24 per share. It was claimed that a combination of El Paso management's golden parachutes and a decision to reduce the size of the offer to the public in order to infuse more cash into El Paso (presumably to pay for the golden parachutes) artificially affected the price of the El Paso stock and thus constituted manipulation.

See also, e.g., Sullivan & Long v. Scattered Corp., 47 F.3d 857, 864 (7th Cir.1995) (section 14(e) is violated only by deceptive conduct).

35. *See* the discussion in § 11.11 *infra.*

36. 472 U.S. at 12, 105 S.Ct. at 2465, 86 L.Ed.2d at 10.

40. Piper v. Chris–Craft Industries, Inc., 430 U.S. 1, 97 S.Ct. 926, 51 L.Ed.2d 124 (1977). The Court held that recognized principles of implying federal rights of action did not warrant the remedy sought by the *Piper* plaintiff. *Id.* at 33, 97 S.Ct. at 944.

41. *See, e.g.,* Seaboard World Airlines, Inc. v. Tiger International, Inc., 600 F.2d 355 (2d Cir.1979) (recognizing the 14(e) remedy but finding no substantive violation).

42. *See, e.g.,* Humana, Inc. v. American Medicorp, Inc., 445 F.Supp. 613 (S.D.N.Y.1977). *Cf.* Rondeau v. Mosinee Paper Corp., 422 U.S. 49, 95 S.Ct. 2069, 45 L.Ed.2d 12 (1975).

43. *See* §§ 11.9, 11.10 *infra.*

45. 17 C.F.R. § 240.14e–1(a).

published. The twenty-day waiting period formerly did not apply, however, where the tender offer was by the issuer and was not made in anticipation of, or in response to, another person's takeover attempt.[46] As a result of amendments that became effective on March 1, 1986, Rule 14e–1's time periods apply to all issuer self-tenders.[47] Once the period during which a tender offer closes, the tender offeror now has the option of extending the offering period from between three and twenty business days for those shareholders of the target company who did not tender their shares during the tender offer.[48] However, shareholders who tender during this optional post tender offer period do not have withdrawal rights.[49]

Rule 14e–1(b) further provides that the tender offeror may not increase or decrease the terms of the offer, the type of consideration, or the dealer's soliciting fee unless the tender offer remains open for at least ten business days from the publication of the notice of such increase.[51] It is also declared to be an unlawful practice for a tender offeror to fail to pay the consideration offered or return the securities tendered promptly after either the withdrawal or termination of the tender offer.[52] Rule 14e–1(d)[53] makes it unlawful to extend the length of the tender offer without issuing a notice of such extension by press release or other public announcement, and a notice must give sufficient detail of the time period of the tender offer and its extension.

Prior to 1999, there was uneven treatment for exchange offers as compared with cash tender offers. This was because, in an exchange offer, there is a twenty-day waiting period from the filing of the 1933 Act registration statement until the effective date of the registration statement.[54] Under the 1933 Act, sales cannot be made until after the effective date; section 5(a)(1) of the 1933 Act[55] could be violated if tenders were solicited prior to the effective date of an exchange offer. This resulted in a disparity of treatment since with a cash tender offer, Exchange Act Rule 14e–1(a)'s twenty business day period begins to run from the filing of the tender offer. However, an exchange offer requires a 1933 Act filing as well, which generally takes considerably more time to prepare than the Schedule TO that must be filed under the 1934 Act. Under the tender offer rules as amended in 1999, an exchange offer can commence on the date that the 1933 Act registration statement is filed with the SEC.[56]

The *Schreiber* decision,[57] discussed above, requires deception as an element of any section 14(e) violation. To the extent that the reasoning carries

46. 17 C.F.R. § 240.14e–1 (1985).

47. *See* Sec. Exch. Act Rel. No. 34–22788 (Jan. 14, 1986).

48. Rule 14d–11, 17 C.F.R. § 240.14d–11.

49. Rule 14d–11, 17 C.F.R. § 240.14d–11. In contrast shareholders who tender their shares during the pendency of a tender offer may withdraw their shares prior to the closing of the tender offer.

51. 17 C.F.R. § 240.14e–1(b). *See also* 17 C.F.R. § 240.13e–4(f)(1)(ii) (imposing the same requirement for tender offers by issuers).

52. 17 C.F.R. § 240.14e–1(c).

53. 17 C.F.R. § 240.14e–1(d).

54. *See* 1933 Act § 8(a), 15 U.S.C.A. § 77h(a). The 1933 Act registration requirements are discussed in chapter 2 *supra*.

55. 15 U.S.C.A. § 77e(a)(1).

56. *See* Regulation of Takeovers and Security Holder Communications, Exch. Act Rel. No. 34–42055, 1999 WL 969596 (SEC Oct. 22, 1999).

57. Schreiber v. Burlington Northern, Inc., 472 U.S. 1, 105 S.Ct. 2458, 86 L.Ed.2d 1 (1985).

over to the SEC rulemaking power, that decision casts a cloud over the validity of Rule 14e–1 because the rule regulates the duration of the offer and thus goes beyond mandating full disclosure.[58] For example, what is it about a tender offer that remains open for only nineteen business days that makes it more deceptive than one which is open for the twenty business day period mandated by Rule 14e–1? It can, of course, be argued that the SEC's power to mandate a period during which the tender offer must remain open is justified, since it gives investors and the market the time necessary to digest the information mandated by the Williams Act's affirmative disclosure requirements.[59]

§ 11.6[2][B] Target Company's Management Response to a Third–Party Tender Offer

Whenever a tender offer is made for a target company's shares, the target company has ten business days from the first date upon which the tender offer is published to respond.[60] Rule 14e–2[61] requires that the target company's management make one of the following responses within the ten-day period: (1) a recommendation of acceptance or rejection of the tender offer; (2) an expression of no opinion with a decision to remain neutral towards the offer; or (3) that it is not able to take a position with respect to bidder's offer. The Rule 14e–2 statement must also include all reasons for the position taken, or the stance of neutrality, as well as any explanation of the inability to take a position. In setting forth its reasons, the target company's management is, of course, subject to all of the rules concerning materiality as well as the potential civil and criminal liabilities for material misstatements.

§ 11.6[2][C] Insider Trading Prohibited

Rule 14e–3[65] prohibits insider trading during a tender offer.[66] The Rule 14e–3 prohibitions expressly apply not only to insiders of the target company but also to anyone else:

> who is in possession of material information relating to such tender offer which information he knows or has reason to know is nonpublic and which he knows or has reason to know has been acquired directly or indirectly from (1) the offering person, (2) the issuer of the securities sought or to be sought by such tender offer, or (3) any officer, director, partner or employee or any other person acting on behalf of the offering person or such issuer. . . .[67]

The rule goes on to state that there is no violation if the transaction was an independent investment decision rather than based on knowledge of material

58. *But see* Polaroid Corp. v. Disney, 862 F.2d 987 (3d Cir.1988), which upheld the SEC's "all holders" rule (Rule 14d–10, 17 C.F.R. § 240.14d–10), reasoning that requiring the offer be made to all shareholders furthers the disclosure goals of the Williams Act.

59. *Cf.* Polaroid Corp. v. Disney, 862 F.2d 987 (3d Cir.1988).

60. 17 C.F.R. § 240.14e–2.

61. 17 C.F.R. § 240.14e–2.

65. 17 C.F.R. § 240.14e–3.

66. *See* § 12.17 *infra* for a discussion of insider trading generally. *See also* chapter 13 *infra* for treatment of the Act's short-swing profit provisions.

67. 17 C.F.R. § 240.14e–3(b). Rule 14e–3 was promulgated to fill a gap in the law created by the Supreme Court in Chiarella v. United States, 445 U.S. 222, 100 S.Ct. 1108, 63 L.Ed.2d 348 (1980). *See* § 12.17 *infra*.

non-public information. Rule 14e–3 supplements the insider trading prohibitions that are found in Rule 10b–5,[68] as well as in the insider trading legislation enacted by Congress in 1984 and in 1988.[69]

It has been held that Rule 14e–3 will support a private remedy in the hands of the target company.[70] A preliminary injunction was issued against a tender offer where the tender offer was based upon the alleged misappropriation of information by a former target company officer.[71] The Ninth Circuit held that a private remedy seeking disgorgement of illegal profits made in violation of Rule 14e–3 can be brought only by contemporaneous traders[72] as provided in section 20A's remedy for insider trading.[73] A number of courts, including the Supreme Court, have upheld the validity of Rule 14e–3.[74] The courts are divided as to weather a violation of Rule 14e–3 requires a showing of a willful breach of a known fiduciary duty.[75]

§ 11.6[2][D] Prohibition of Contemporary Purchases During Tender Offer

Rule 14e–5 prohibits tender offerors from purchasing shares subject to a tender offer and related securities during the term of a tender offer.[77] As discussed in a previous section of this treatise,[78] the tender offer commences once the Schedule TO is filed with the SEC. Rule 14e–5's prohibition against trading along side of a tender offer depends upon the existence of a tender offer.[80] On appropriate facts, the Commission has been willing to recognize exemptions from 14e–5's prohibitions on purchases outside of the tender offer.[81] It has been held that violations of Rule 14e–5's predecessor (former

---

68. 17 C.F.R. § 240.10b–5.

69. The Insider Trading Sanctions Act of 1984 (ITSA), among other things, allows the SEC to recoup three times the insider's profits. *See* § 12.17 *infra.* The Insider Trading and Securities Fraud Enforcement Act of 1988 is discussed in § 12.17 *infra.*

70. Burlington Industries, Inc. v. Edelman, 1987 WL 91498, [1987 Transfer Binder] Fed.Sec. L.Rep. (CCH) ¶ 93,339 (4th Cir.1987), *affirming on the opinion below* 666 F.Supp. 799 (M.D.N.C. 1987).

71. Private remedies under section 14(e) are discussed in § 11.10 *infra.*

72. Brody v. Transitional Hospitals Corp., 280 F.3d 997 (9th Cir.2002).

73. 15 U.S.C.A. § 78t–1(a). *See* § 12.17[7][B] *infra.*

74. *E.g.,* United States v. O'Hagan, 521 U.S. 642, 117 S.Ct. 2199, 138 L.Ed.2d 724 (1997).

75. *See, e.g.,* United States v. Cassese, 428 F.3d 92 (2d Cir. 2005) (evidence that defendant received copy of confidentiality agreement pertaining to proposed transaction, which specifically warned him that trading upon information received pursuant to merger negotiations might violate federal securities laws, was not sufficient to support jury's finding). The dissent in the *Cassese* case pointed out that such an interpretation varies from the SEC's view. *Id.* (Raggi, J. dissenting) ("Because the language of Rule 14e–3(a) does not support, and the SEC's interpretative release specifically rejects, a construction of the rule that would require proof of a relationship-knowledge element, a court cannot, in essence, rewrite the rule by adding a relationship-knowledge requirement to the willfulness element of a criminal charge."). *Cf., e.g.,* See, e.g., SEC v. Thrasher, 152 F.Supp.2d 291 (S.D.N.Y. 2001) (violation of Rule 14e–3 does not require a showing that defendant knowingly violated a fiduciary duty).

77. 17 C.F.R. § 240.14e–5

78. *See* § 11.5[2] *supra.*

80. Simon DeBartolo Group, L.P. v. Richard E. Jacobs Group, Inc., 186 F.3d 157, 175 (2d Cir.1999) (no tender offer where the proposal did not include the acquisition of an equity interest; hence Rule 10b–13 did not apply).

81. *E.g.,* Pearson PLC, [2000–2001 Transfer Binder] Fed. Sec. L. Rep. (CCH) ¶ 78,019 (SEC No Action Letter Aug. 3, 2000) (exemption for purchases of stock options during tender offer for common stock where option holders who were not eligible for the tender offer would receive consideration comparable to that offered for the common stock under the tender offer).

Rule 10b–13[82]) supported a private damage action,[83] but not all courts seem to agree that such a private remedy exists.[84]

Rule 14e–5 prohibits not only purchases of the securities subject to a tender offer, but also of any securities immediately convertible into such security. In contrast, the purchase of an option or security futures product is allowed, since it is not immediately convertible into the underlying security.[90] However, if the futures contract expires before the termination of the tender offer then the purchase of a security futures product will be precluded under Rule 14e–5.[91]

§ 11.6[2][E] Short Tendering and Hedged Tendering Prohibited

Short tendering of securities during a tender offer is the practice of tendering or guaranteeing securities not owned by the person making the tender or guarantee.[92] The SEC originally adopted former Rule 10b–4,[93] which addressed short tendering, but that rule has since been redesignated as part of Regulation 14E. Rule 14e–4 prohibits short tendering.[94] The SEC amended Rule 14e–4's predecessor to not only outlaw short tendering but also to prohibit "hedged tendering" by market professionals in tender offers for less than all of the target company's outstanding stock.[95]

The prohibition against short tendering means that during a tender offer, it is illegal to tender shares that you do not own. Thus, it is necessary that anyone tendering shares during a tender offer either actually be the owner or be a bona fide beneficial owner of the shares being tendered. Hedged tendering consists of tendering shares that are encumbered by a call option or some other obligation to sell the shares to someone other than the tender offeror. The prohibitions against short tendering and hedged tendering are designed to eliminate related manipulative practices in connection with a tender offer.

Hedged tendering occurs when market professionals sell on the open market that portion of their target company holdings that they estimate will not be accepted by the tender offeror. Rule 14e–4 is designed to prevent tendering shares that are not actually owned. Where a shareholder responded to a tender offer for less than all of the target's shares by tendering his entire holdings coupled with a short sale, the rule was not violated.[96] The court

82. 17 C.F.R. § 240.10b–13 (1998).

83. *E.g.*, City National Bank v. American Commonwealth Financial Corp., 801 F.2d 714 (4th Cir.1986), *cert. denied* 479 U.S. 1091, 107 S.Ct. 1301, 94 L.Ed.2d 157 (1987).

84. *See* Beaumont v. American Can Co., 797 F.2d 79 (2d Cir.1986) (questioning the existence of a private remedy).

90. *See* In re Commission Guidance on Application of Certain Provisions of Securities Act of 1933, Securities Act of 1934, Rules Thereunder to Trading in Security Futures Products, Sec. Act Rel. No. 33–8107, Sec. Exch. Act Rel. No. 34–46101, 2002 WL 1357820 (SEC June 27, 2002).

91. *Id.*

92. *See* Merrill Lynch, Pierce, Fenner & Smith, Inc. v. Bobker, 636 F.Supp. 444 (S.D.N.Y. 1986), *reversed* 808 F.2d 930 (2d Cir.1986) (denying proration to shareholder who sold short while tendering).

93. 17 C.F.R. § 240.10b–4 (1989).

94. 17 C.F.R. § 240.14e–4.

95. *See* 16 Sec.Reg. & L.Rep. (BNA) 575–576 (March 30, 1984) (amending Rule 10b–4, 17 C.F.R. § 240.10b–4).

96. Merrill Lynch, Pierce, Fenner & Smith, Inc. v. Bobker, 808 F.2d 930 (2d Cir.1986).

reasoned that since he tendered only his actual holdings, the tendering shareholder did not improve his proration position, but rather was taking "a separate gamble" that the stock price would decline after the proration date.[97] Also, it has been held that, at least where shareholders could not allege that their offers of tender were diluted, there is no implied private remedy for short tenders in violation of Rule 14e–4.[98] Security futures products will be counted in someone's long position for purposes of Rule 14e–4 only upon the contract settlement, when the futures product ceases trading and the owner in essence owns the underlying security.[99]

§ 11.6[2][F] Two–Tiered Tender Offers Permitted

Sometimes a tender offeror decides to make a tender offer for control of a company and then follows the tender offer by a merger of the target company into the acquiring company at a price below that which was paid in the tender offer. This is commonly referred to as a two-tiered front-end loaded offer. There is nothing under federal law to prohibit such offers so long as the first step adequately discloses any plans for a second step merger. In contrast, a number of states have adopted fair price statutes that place insurmountable barriers on these front-end loaded offers.[100] The SEC, for some time, had considered taking action that would curtail suspected unfairness and abuses in connection with the pricing of two-step or two-tiered tender offers.[101] Such substantive limitations on the scope and terms of tender offers would be difficult to support under section 14(e) in light of the *Schreiber* decision. However, section 14(d) might support some limitations.[102]

§ 11.6[2][G] Exemption for Closed–End Investment Companies

SEC Rule 14e–6[103] provides an exemption for closed-end registered investment companies.[104] A closed-end investment company repurchases its own shares from investors wanting to sell their investment company shares. This option ordinarily is constantly open to closed-end company shareholders. In order to avoid unnecessary entanglement with the tender offer laws, Rule 14e–6 exempts most closed-end investment companies from the requirements of Rules 14e–2 and 14e–3.[105]

---

97. *Id.* at 935.

98. John Olagues Trading Co. v. First Options of Chicago, Inc., 588 F.Supp. 1194 (N.D.Ill. 1984).

99. *See* In re Commission Guidance on Application of Certain Provisions of Securities Act of 1933, Securities Act of 1934, Rules Thereunder to Trading in Security Futures Products, Sec. Act Rel. No. 33–8107, Sec. Exch. Act Rel. No. 34–46101, 2002 WL 1357820 (SEC June 27, 2002).

100. *See* the discussion in § 11.4 *infra*.

101. Sec.Exch. Act Rel. No. 34–21079 (June 21, 1984).

102. 15 U.S.C.A. § 78n(d)(1), which empowers the Commission to require "such additional information as the Commission may by rules and regulations [prescribe] as necessary or appropriate in the public interest or for the protection of investors" *See* § 11.5 *supra*.

103. 17 C.F.R. § 240.14e–6.

104. Investment company regulation is discussed in chapter 20 *infra*.

105. 17 C.F.R. §§ 240.14e–1, 240.14e–2.

§ 11.6[2][H] Roll-Up Transactions

SEC Rule 14e–7 imposes special rules for tender offers in connection with roll-up transactions.[106] This was promulgated in response to section 14(h) of the Exchange Act.[107]

§ 11.6[2][I] Prohibition Against False Statements of Intent to Make Tender Offer

SEC Rule 14e–8 prohibits anyone from announcing a planned tender offer if the tender offeror does not have the intention to announce and complete the offer within a reasonable time.[108] This rule was adopted in 1999 when the SEC eliminated its gun jumping provisions prior to the commencement of a tender offer.[109] Rule 14e–8 does not require the tender offeror to have financing in place, but the would-be tender offeror's ability to finance the proposed tender offer will be considered in determining whether any pre-tender announcement is in compliance with the rule.[110]

§ 11.6[2][J] Target's Defensive Tactics Not Prohibited

As discussed in a later section of this treatise,[111] frequently management will want to oppose a third-party tender offer and will do so by engaging in defensive tactics. State law may place significant restrictions on the target company's management's ability to fend off a hostile offer. For a while, there was some question as to whether federal law would have an impact in curtailing these defensive tactics. It is now clear that this is entirely within the purview of state law. A significant judicial development under section 14(e) was the Sixth Circuit's ruling that a defensive lock-up arrangement may be struck down as a manipulative arrangement.[112] This controversially expansive holding had the potential of opening new frontiers for the federal regulation of tender offers, although it represented a minority view.[113] The *Schreiber* decision[114] now makes it clear that defensive tactics cannot violate section 14(e), even if manipulative, unless there has been a material misrepresentation or omission.

§ 11.7 Arrangements Affecting Director Turnover in Connection With a Tender Offer—Section 14(f)

As is the case with any transfer of corporate control, tender offers will frequently result in a shift in corporate management. Accordingly, it is not uncommon to find tender offers containing agreements relating to manage-

---

106. 17 C.F.R. § 240.14e–7.

107. 15 U.S.C.A. § 78n(h).

108. 17 C.F.R. § 240.14e–8.

109. *See* Regulation of Takeovers and Security Holder Communications Exch. Act Rel. No. 34–42055, 1999 WL 969596 (SEC Oct. 22, 1999). *See also, e.g.,* § 11.5 *supra.*

110. *See* Regulation of Takeovers and Security Holder Communications Exch. Act Rel. No. 34–42055, 1999 WL 969596 (SEC Oct. 22, 1999).

111. *See* § 11.4 *infra.*

112. Mobil Corp. v. Marathon Oil Co., 669 F.2d 366 (6th Cir.1981). *See, e.g.,* Elliot J. Weiss, Defensive Responses to Tender Offers and the Williams Act's Prohibition Against Manipulation, 35 Vand.L.Rev. 1087 (1982).

113. *See, e.g.,* Radol v. Thomas, 772 F.2d 244 (6th Cir.1985), *cert. denied,* 475 U.S. 1086, 106 S.Ct. 1469, 89 L.Ed.2d 724 (1986) (two-tiered, front-end loaded tender offer is not manipulative under either the Williams Act or Rule 10b–5).

114. Schreiber v. Burlington Northern, Inc., 472 U.S. 1, 105 S.Ct. 2458, 86 L.Ed.2d 1 (1985). *See, e.g.,* Norman S. Poser, Stock Market Manipulation and Corporate Control Transactions, 40 U.Miami L.Rev. 671 (1986).

ment turnover and the election of new directors. These control transfers can raise problems under state law relating to invalid control premiums and other breaches of fiduciary duty. The Williams Act superimposes certain disclosure obligations. Under section 14(f) of the Exchange Act,[3] when a tender offer for equity securities subject to the Act's reporting requirements contains agreements concerning the designation of new directors otherwise than through a formal vote at a meeting of securities holders, there must be full disclosure. Contemplated management turnover, including any arrangement regarding the make-up of the majority of directors, also must be disclosed.[4] Thus, for example, where a stock purchase agreement permits the purchaser to designate a majority of the issuer's directors, section 14(f)'s disclosure obligation is triggered.[5] When the agreed-upon shift in control occurs, a second filing obligation arises.[6]

§ 11.8 Issuer Purchases of Its Own Stock—Section 13(e) and the Going Private Rule; Issuer Self–Tender Offers

§ 11.8[1] Issuer's Share Repurchases

§ 11.8[1][A] Issuer Share Repurchases in Response to Someone Else's Tender Offer

Rule 13e–1[7] applies to an issuer's purchases of its own stock after a third party has filed a tender offer for its securities. An issuer of securities subject to the Exchange Act's registration and reporting requirements may not purchase its own securities once a third party tender offer has been made unless the issuer files with the Commission eight copies of a statement containing the following information: (1) a description of the securities to be purchased; (2) the names and classes of persons from whom the securities are to be purchased; (3) the purposes for which they are being purchased; and (4) the source of all funds used to finance the purchases.[8] This filing is supplemented by Schedule 14D–9[9] which requires a statement to be filed by an issuer making a solicitation or recommendation to security holders to accept or reject the tender offer and Rule 14e–2's[10] provisions requiring the issuer to send to the security holders a statement recommending acceptance or rejection of the tender offer or expressing no opinion toward it. Issuer purchase of its own shares is just one of the possible responses to a tender offer. An issuer's filings under Rule 13e–1 with regard to defensive share repurchases do not alleviate the need for making filings under Rule 13e–3 or Rule 13e–4 if the transaction is likely to result in the cessation of 1934 Act reporting obligations or constitute a tender offer.[12]

---

§ 11.7

3. 15 U.S.C.A. § 78n(f).

4. 15 U.S.C.A. § 78n(f). *See* 17 C.F.R. § 240.14f–1.

5. Drobbin v. Nicolet Instrument Corp., 631 F.Supp. 860 (S.D.N.Y.1986).

6. Drobbin v. Nicolet Instrument Corp., 631 F.Supp. 860 (S.D.N.Y.1986).

§ 11.8

7. 17 C.F.R. § 240.13e–1.

8. *Id.*

9. 17 C.F.R. § 240.14d–101.

10. 17 C.F.R. § 240.14e–2. *See* § 11.6 *supra.*

12. Maynard Oil Co. v. Deltec Panamerica S.A., 630 F.Supp. 502 (S.D.N.Y.1985). *See also* § 11.8 *supra* (discussing third party tender offers).

§ 11.8[1][B] Manipulation in Connection With Issuer Repurchases

Purchases by an issuer or affiliate of its own securities, if not properly handled, can raise questions of manipulation.[16] Rule 14e–5[17] prohibits purchases by persons making a tender offer other than pursuant to the terms of the tender offer.

Rule 10b–18 provides a safe harbor from the antimanipulation rules for qualifying purchases by the issuer and affiliates.[23] Purchases pursuant to issuer purchases or tender offers governed by either Rule 13e–1 or 13e–4 are excluded from Rule 10b–18's safe harbor.[24] There also are exclusions from the safe harbor for merger-related transactions. Among other things, Rule 10b–18's safe harbor depends upon both the trading volume and the price at which the issuer's bids are placed.[26]

Rule 10b–18 has four basic requirements for the safe harbor to apply. First, the transactions may be effected only through a single broker.[27] Second, there are limitations on the timing of the purchase.[28] Third, the price must not be better than published prices for the stock.[29] Fourth, the purchases must fall within the Rule's volume limitations, which in substance limit the safe harbor purchases on any given day to twenty-five percent of the average daily trading volume.[31]

Rule 10b–18 requires companies to make disclosures in their quarterly and annual reports that will list all repurchases of their equity securities. This disclosure obligation exists with respect to repurchases in open market transactions as well as to privately negotiated purchases. However, privately negotiated purchases are not subject to Rule 10b–18's more substantive provisions.[42] Disclosure is required irrespective of whether the repurchases were made pursuant to Rule 10b–18's safe harbor. Rule 10b–18 is only a safe harbor from manipulation charges and compliance with the rule does not insulate the company from exposure for other securities law violations in connection with the repurchase of shares.

§ 11.8[2] The Going Private Rule

In its so-called "going private" rules, the Commission regulates an issuer's purchases of its own shares outside of the contested tender offer milieu. The SEC's going private rules supplement the state law remedies that

16. Sections 9 and 10 of the Exchange Act prohibit manipulation. 15 U.S.C.A. §§ 78i, 78j. Manipulation is considered in § 12.1 *infra*.

17. 17 C.F.R. § 240.14e–5. *See* 11.6[2][D] *supra*.

23. 17 C.F.R. § 240.10b–18.

24. 17 C.F.R. § 240.10b–18(a)(3).

26. The rule is quite complex. 17 C.F.R. § 10b–18. *See* Sec.Exch.Act Rel. No. 34–17222 (Nov. 4, 1980). The volume computation is made on a daily basis. *See, e.g.,* Answers to Frequently Asked Questions Concerning Rule 10b–18 ("Safe Harbor" for Issuer Repurchases), answer to question 5, *http://www.sec.gov/divisions/marketreg/r10b18faq0504.htm* (SEC 2004).

27. Rule 10b–18(b)(1), 17 C.F.R. § 240.10b–18(b)(1).

28. Rule 10b–18(b)(2), 17 C.F.R. § 240.10b–18(b)(2).

29. Rule 10b–18(b)(3), 17 C.F.R. § 240.10b–18(b)(3).

31. Rule 10b–18(b)(4), 17 C.F.R. § 240(b)(4).

42. *See, e.g.,* Answers to Frequently Asked Questions Concerning Rule 10b–18 ("Safe Harbor" for Issuer Repurchases), answer to question 8, *http://www.sec.gov/divisions/marketreg/r10b18faq0504.htm* (SEC 2004).

exist for breaches of fiduciary duties in connection with freeze-out and going private transactions.

Rule 13e–3,[50] which applies primarily to issuers subject to section 12's registration requirements,[51] defines the types of transactions covered. A Rule 13e–3 transaction is one of a series of transactions that involves either (1) the purchase or tender offer by an issuer or its affiliates of any equity security subject to the Act's reporting requirements, or (2) a proxy solicitation subject to Regulation 14A,[52] or a distribution of information subject to Regulation 14C,[53] to the holders of equity securities subject to the Act's reporting requirements that is sent out by the issuer or affiliate in connection with a merger, consolidation, reclassification, recapitalization reverse stock split, or similar transaction. Any of the foregoing Rule 13e–3 transactions are covered by the Schedule 13E–3 disclosure and filing requirements if the effect of the transaction or transactions is the cessation of the reporting obligations under the Exchange Act. A difficult problem is judging the point at which the issuer should be able to predict a reasonable likelihood of such a result.[54] It is not always easy to determine at what point a transaction or series of transactions is likely to result in the issuer having fewer than three hundred shareholders. It has been held that an open market purchase program in response to a hostile takeover did not trigger Rule 13e–3's filing requirements because crossing the three hundred shareholder threshold was primarily dependent upon the success of plaintiff's hostile tender offer.[55] The going private rules require that the issuer must file a Schedule 13E–3,[56] which requires disclosures similar to those required under Schedule 13D[57] and Schedule TO.[58]

Prior to the Supreme Court decision in Santa Fe Industries, Inc. v. Green,[89] the Commission proposed a series of going private rules, one of which would have given the SEC power to prohibit such transactions merely on the basis of unfairness to the shareholders.[90] Although it would appear that the *Santa Fe* decision precludes scrutiny of transactional fairness,[91] the SEC continued to take the position that it has the power to regulate the fairness of going private transactions.[92] In 1977, the Commission included the fairness requirement in its post-*Santa Fe* version of its going private rules. However, when the going private rules were adopted, and as currently enforced, the SEC deleted the fairness requirement, noting that it "believes the question of

50. 17 C.F.R. § 240.13e–3.

51. There is limited application to section 15(d) reporting companies.

52. 17 C.F.R. §§ 240.14a–1–14a–103 *See* §§ 10.1–10.2 *supra*.

53. 17 C.F.R. §§ 240.14c–1–14c–101. *See* § 10.9 *supra*.

54. *See* Sec.Exch.Act Rel. No. 34–16075 (Aug. 2, 1979). *See also* Shamrock Associates v. Horizon Corp., 632 F.Supp. 566 (S.D.N.Y.1986) (fact that delisting might only be temporary did not preclude the necessity of a Rule 13e–3 filing).

55. Maynard Oil Co. v. Deltec Panamerica S.A., 630 F.Supp. 502 (S.D.N.Y.1985).

56. 17 C.F.R. § 240.13e–100.

57. 17 C.F.R. § 240.13d–101. *See* § 11.2 *supra*.

58. 17 C.F.R. § 240.14d–100. *See* § 11.5 *supra*.

89. 430 U.S. 462, 97 S.Ct. 1292, 51 L.Ed.2d 480 (1977). *See* § 12.20 *infra*.

90. Sec.Act Rel. No. 33–5567 (Feb. 6, 1975); 40 Fed.Reg. 7947 (1975) (proposed Feb. 24, 1975).

91. 430 U.S. at 474–77, 97 S.Ct. at 1301–03.

92. *See, e.g.,* Going Private Transactions by Public Companies or Their Affiliates, Sec.Act. Rel. No. 33–5884, Sec. Exch. Act Rel. No. 4–14185, Inv. Co. Act Rel. No. IC—10015, 1977 WL 187732 (Nov. 17, 1977).

regulation should be deferred until there is an opportunity to determine the efficacy of [the rules as adopted].''[93]

§ 11.8[3] Issuer Self–Tender Offers

Issuers on occasion will make a tender offer for their own shares. These are commonly known as issuer self-tender offers. Third party tender offers most frequently arise in the context of an attempt to gain control of the target company. In contrast, issuer self-tender offers are frequently used for other reasons as well. For example, issuers may want to offer their shareholders the convenience and savings of being able to sell back to the corporation odd-lot shareholdings.[95]

Rule 13e–4[96] sets out the filing and disclosure requirements for tender offers by a reporting company for its own shares. Schedule TO's disclosure requirements are the same as those which apply to third party tender offers.[98] Thus, issuer self-tender offers that are covered by Rule 13e–4[99] are subject to the same rules that apply to third parties under Regulations 14D[100] and 14E.[101] The issuer making a self-tender offer must file a Schedule TO.[102]

The filing requirements and other rules set forth in SEC Rule 13e–4 apply to defensive tender offers, as well as to other issuer tender offers. A target company that responds with a self-tender without responding to the third-party offer in good faith may run afoul of state law, and the self-tender may be enjoined.[104]

§ 11.9 Private Remedies Under the Williams Act—Remedies for Violations of Sections 13(d), 13(e), 14(d)

Sections 13(d),[6] 13(e),[7] and 14(d)[8] of the Securities Exchange Act create various obligations in connection with covered corporate control transactions. This section addresses the extent to which they can support an implied private right of action. Most of the litigation concerning the question of the existence of implied private rights of action under the Williams Act has arisen in the context of section 14(e)'s general antifraud proscriptions.[9] The courts

93. Going Private Transactions by Public Companies or Their Affiliates, Sec.Act. Rel.No. 33–6100, No. 34–16075, 1979 WL 195252 (Aug. 2, 1979).

95. In 1996, the SEC relaxed some of its rules relating to such odd-lot tender offers. *See* Odd–Lot Tender Offers by Issuers, Sec. Act Rel. No. 33–7376, Sec. Exch. Act Rel. No. 34–38068, Inv. Co. Act Rel. No. IC—22413, 63 S.E.C. Docket 1190, 1996 WL 734258 (SEC Dec. 20, 1996).

96. 17 C.F.R. § 240.13e–4.

98. *See* § 11.5 *supra.*

99. 17 C.F.R. § 240.13e–4.

100. 17 C.F.R. §§ 240.14d–1–14d–101. *See* SEC v. Carter Hawley Hale Stores, Inc., 760 F.2d 945 (9th Cir.1985) (issuer's open market purchase program in response to third party tender offer was not a tender offer within the meaning of section 13(e)).

101. 17 C.F.R. §§ 240.14e–1–14e–3.

102. 17 C.F.R. § 240.14d–100.

104. Plaza Securities Co. v. Fruehauf Corp., 643 F.Supp. 1535 (E.D.Mich.1986) (Michigan law).

§ 11.9

6. 15 U.S.C.A. § 78m(d). *See* § 11.8 *supra.*

7. 15 U.S.C.A. § 78m(e). *See* § 11.8 *supra.*

8. 15 U.S.C.A. § 78n(d). *See* § 11.5 *supra.*

9. 15 U.S.C.A. § 78n(e). *See* §§ 11.6 *supra,* 11.10 *infra.*

seem to be consistent in favoring the existence of at least a limited implied remedy under section 14(e), at least when the suit is brought by a target company shareholder in furtherance of the interests of target company shareholders generally.[10] However, that remedy, as is the case with any remedy that would exist under sections 13(d), 13(e) and 14(d), must be considered more questionable in light of the decline in federal implied remedies generally.[11]

Since sections 13(d), 13(e), and 14(d) all apply to issuers subject to the Exchange Act's registration and reporting requirements,[12] and involve mandatory filings with the Commission, there are a number of other remedies for material misstatements. For example, any investor who is injured by reliance upon material misstatements in the Schedule 13D,[13] Schedule 13E–3,[14] Schedule TO[15] (the successor to Schedule 14D–1[16]), or Schedule 14D–9,[17] may sue for damages under the express remedy provided in section 18(a) of the Act.[18] It is to be remembered, however, that the section 18(a) remedy is an extremely limited one insofar as it requires the investor to have actually relied upon the documents filed with the Commission.[19] In addition to the express liability provisions of section 18(a), any material misstatements or omissions that give rise to an injury in connection with the purchase or sale of a security will state a cause of action under SEC Rule 10b–5.[20] Furthermore, material misstatements and omissions in documents required by sections 13(d), 13(e), and 14(d) will give rise to the potential for criminal penalties as well as for SEC enforcement actions.[21] These remedial and criminal penalties also apply to failures to file or delays in filing. However, no private remedy would exist under Rule 10b–5 for mere delay. The question of an independent implied remedy under the Williams Act's filing requirements thus becomes significant. The cases are in conflict, but there have been a number of decisions that have held that the relevant provisions of sections 13 and 14 in and of themselves provide a basis for at least limited private relief. One pattern that has emerged is the availability of injunctive relief[23] as opposed to damages. However, some courts have recognized the availability of an action for damages.[24] In 2002, the Second Circuit ruled that there is no private damage remedy to be implied under section 13(d).[25] At the same time that the court

---

10. *See* § 11.10 *infra. Cf.* Piper v. Chris–Craft Industries, Inc., 430 U.S. 1, 97 S.Ct. 926, 51 L.Ed.2d 124 (1977) (competing tender offeror did not have standing to bring suit under section 14(e)).

11. *See* § 12.2 *infra. See* § 1.8 *supra* for an overview of the private remedies available under the 1933 and 1934 Acts.

12. 15 U.S.C.A. §§ 78*l*, 78m(a). *See* §§ 9.2, 9.3 *supra.*

13. 17 C.F.R. § 240.13d–101. *See* § 11.5 *supra.*

14. 17 C.F.R. § 240.13e–100. *See* § 11.8 *supra.*

15. 17 C.F.R. § 240.14d–100.

16. 17 C.F.R. § 240.14d–100 (1998). *See* § 11.5 *supra.*

17. 17 C.F.R. § 240.14d–101. *See* § 11.5 *supra.*

18. 15 U.S.C.A. § 78r(a).

19. *See* § 12.18 *infra* for discussion of the section 18(a) remedy.

20. 17 C.F.R. § 240.10b–5 which is discussed in chapter 12 *infra.*

21. 15 U.S.C.A. § 78aa.

23. *E.g.* International Broadcasting Corp. v. Turner, 734 F.Supp. 383 (D.Minn.1990).

24. *See* Field v. Trump, 850 F.2d 938 (2d Cir.1988).

25. Hallwood Realty Partners, L.P v. Gotham Partners, L.P., 286 F.3d 613 (2d Cir.2002).

denied the existence of a damage remedy, the court stressed that it continued to adhere to its earlier view that injunctive relief may be had on appropriate facts.

In Rondeau v. Mosinee Paper Corp.,[33] the Supreme Court indicated that a target company may have standing to complain of delays by a purchaser in filing a Schedule 13D where it can show a resultant injury. The Court held that due to the absence of substantial share acquisitions by the purchaser after the date upon which the Schedule 13D was due, the target company had failed to show an injury sufficient to support a cause of action for the defendant's delay. Following the opening that was left by this Supreme Court decision, many subsequent cases have held that a target company has standing to seek injunctive relief to bar additional purchases until the Schedule 13D has been filed.[34] However, there have also been some decisions to the contrary, holding that no private remedy exists even for injunctive relief.[35] While the shareholders of the target company may be able to bring suit, the shareholders of the acquiring company may not base a claim under section 13(d).[36]

Even in the cases recognizing an implied right to private injunctive relief, not every violation will support such relief. It has been held, for example, that in determining whether to issue a preliminary injunction for violation of section 13(d)'s filing requirements, the court should consider whether there has been injury to the shareholders and the investing public as well as to the target company.[37] Quite properly, the courts are reluctant to interfere with highly contested takeover attempts where any relief will have a substantial impact on the market,[38] but in an appropriate case a preliminary injunction will be issued.[39] Courts have indicated that a preliminary injunction should "ordinarily" be issued to remedy a defective section 13(d) filing in order to protect investors.[40] Additionally, curative amendments to the Schedule 13D filing will warrant the lifting of any injunctive relief that had previously been granted.[41]

Since time is of the essence in takeover battles, frequently the relief sought in an action under 13(d), 13(e), or 14(d) will be one for preliminary injunctive relief. Plaintiffs in such actions bear an especially high burden in light of the dual requirement that they prove both a substantial likelihood of success on the merits and irreparable injury if the preliminary injunction is not issued. Failure to meet either a substantial likelihood of success or

---

33. 422 U.S. 49, 95 S.Ct. 2069, 45 L.Ed.2d 12 (1975).

34. *E.g.*, CNW Corp. v. Japonica Partners, L.P., 874 F.2d 193 (3d Cir.1989).

35. *E.g.*, Kalmanovitz v. G. Heileman Brewing Co., 769 F.2d 152 (3d Cir.1985).

36. In re Dow Chemical Securities Bhopal Litigation, 2000 WL 1886612, [2000–2001 Transfer Binder] Fed. Sec. L. Rep. (CCH) ¶ 91,282 (S.D.N.Y. 2000).

37. *See* Mid–Continent Bancshares, Inc. v. O'Brien, 1981 WL 1404, [1982 Transfer Binder] Fed.Sec.L.Rep. (CCH) ¶ 98,734 (E.D.Mo.1981).

38. *See, e.g.,* NACCO Industries, Inc. v. Applica, Inc., 2006 WL 3762090 (N.D.Ohio 2006) (denying temporary restraining order based on alleged violations of section 13(d) and section 14(a)'s proxy provisions).

39. *See* Life Investors, Inc. v. Ago Holding, N.V., 1981 WL 15483, [1981–1982 Transfer Binder] Fed.Sec.L.Rep. (CCH) ¶ 98,356 (8th Cir.1981) (decided under section 14(d)).

40. E.ON AG v. Acciona, S.A., 468 F.Supp.2d 537 (S.D.N.Y. 2006).

41. ICN Pharmaceuticals, Inc. v. Khan, 2 F.3d 484, 489 (2d Cir. 1993).

irreparable injury will result in a denial of preliminary relief.[46] However, serious violations will warrant preliminary relief, since waiting until a full trial on the merits will usually mean that the challenged transaction will take place years before the case is resolved. As one court has put it, "[e]ffectively the only relief available to an issuer, under the prevailing view, is an order requiring the five percent owner to file a corrected 13D and perhaps enjoining further acquisitions pending the corrections."[47] Courts will enjoin a vote or other major action only in extreme circumstances. A delay in filing that may have made success on a vote easier is not in itself enough to warrant a preliminary injunction.[48]

On appropriate facts, some courts have recognized the potential for an implied remedy for damages for violations of section 14(d). Thus, for example, shareholders denied a tender offer premium because of the tender offeror's wrongful interference with their proration rights could recover in an action under section 14(d)(6).[59] The courts have recognized an implied right of action under Rule 14a–10's[60] all holders requirement.[61] Additionally, the Sixth Circuit has recognized a private remedy for violation of section 13(e)'s going private provisions which allegedly resulted in the loss of plaintiff's state law appraisal remedy due to material misstatements or omissions.[62] With the foregoing exceptions, the law seems clear that private damage remedies will not be implied solely on the basis of section 13 or 14's filing requirements. To the extent that a plaintiff can establish that the filing contained material misstatements or omissions, then an action may lie either under section 18(a) of the Exchange Act[63] or under SEC Rule 10b–5.[64]

§ 11.10 Private Remedies Under the Williams Act—Is There an Implied Remedy Under Section 14(e)?

Congress, in enacting the Williams Act's tender offer provisions, did not provide any express remedy for injured investors. Any investor injured by reliance upon a materially misleading SEC filing has an express remedy under section 18(a).[1] Anyone so injured as a purchaser or seller of a security may also have a remedy implied under Rule 10b–5.[2] Whether the Williams Act

46. *See* Cardiff Acquisitions, Inc. v. Hatch, 751 F.2d 917 (8th Cir.1984).

47. Hubco, Inc. v. Rappaport, 628 F.Supp. 345, 354 (D.N.J.1985).

48. *See* CSX Corporation v. The Children's Investment Fund Management (UK) LLP, 562 F.Supp.2d 511 (S.D.N.Y. 2008).

59. Pryor v. USX Corp., 1991 WL 346368, [1991–1992 Transfer Binder] Fed.Sec.L.Rep. (CCH) ¶ 96,630 (S.D.N.Y.1991) (unpublished case). Section 14(d)(6) and proration rights are discussed in § 11.5 *supra*.

60. 17 C.F.R. § 240.14a–10. The all holders rule is discussed in § 11.5[3][D] *supra*.

61. *See, e.g.,* In re Digital Island Securities Litigation, 357 F.3d 322 (3d Cir. 2004); Polaroid Corp. v. Disney, 862 F.2d 987 (3d Cir.1988). The requirement that the claim be pleaded with particularity applies to all holders claims. In re Digital Island Securities Litigation, 357 F.3d 322 (3d Cir. 2004). The particularity requirements are discussed in § 12.13 *infra*.

62. Howing Co. v. Nationwide Corp., 972 F.2d 700 (6th Cir.1992), *cert. denied* 507 U.S. 1004, 113 S.Ct. 1645, 123 L.Ed.2d 266 (1993) (decided under section 13(e)'s going private rules).

63. 15 U.S.C.A. § 78r(a). As noted elsewhere, the section 18(a) remedy is a relatively limited one. *See* § 12.18 *infra*.

64. 17 C.F.R. § 240.10b–5. *See* §§ 12.2–12.13 *infra*.

§ 11.10

1. 15 U.S.C.A. § 78r(a). However, this remedy is relatively narrow in scope. *See* § 12.18 *infra*.

2. 17 C.F.R. § 240.10b–5. *See* chapter 12 *infra*.

provides its own antifraud remedy for damages is somewhat questionable, especially in light of the decline of implied remedies generally.[4] However, most courts that have considered the issue have recognized an implied remedy under section 14(e) in the hands of the target company or a target company shareholder.[5] For example, it has been held that a nontendering target shareholder has standing to sue both the target and acquiring corporations.[6]

In Piper v. Chris–Craft Industries, Inc.,[7] the Supreme Court held that a competing offeror cannot maintain a private right of action under section 14(e)'s general antifraud proscriptions. In so deciding, the majority of the Justices did not rule out any private remedy; in fact, the opinion held out much hope for the recognition of a section 14(e) private right of action in the hands of the target company or its shareholders. The majority opinion in *Piper* reasoned that the purpose of the Williams Act was to further investor protection by serving the shareholders of the target company, not competing tender offerors who, at best, were collateral beneficiaries of the tender offer provisions.[8] Even if the legislation was directed at a special class of persons so as to warrant the implication of a private remedy,[9] a competing tender offeror was not a member of that special class. The Court's opinion in *Piper* pointed out that section 14(e) was directed toward "full and fair disclosure for the benefit of investors,"[10] and thus "Congress was seeking to broaden the scope of protection afforded to shareholders confronted with competing claims."[11] The precise scope of the *Piper* ruling is far from clear. Justice Blackmun in his concurrence took the position that the *Piper* decision would have been better placed on standing and other elements of the claim rather than the absence of an implied remedy but then would have found an absence of damages fatal to the claim, while agreeing with the dissent that the plaintiffs had standing to sue.[13] Justice Stevens in his dissent pointed out that since the plaintiff had

---

4. *See* § 12.2 *infra.*

5. *See, e.g.,* Clearfield Bank & Trust v. Omega Financial Corp., 65 F.Supp.2d 325 (W.D.Pa. 1999).

6. Plaine v. McCabe, 797 F.2d 713 (9th Cir.1986).

7. 430 U.S. 1, 97 S.Ct. 926, 51 L.Ed.2d 124 (1977). The 14(e) claim was but one facet of the voluminous litigation which emerged out of this bitterly waged tender offer battle. In the initial go-round, Chris–Craft, although being denied the requested injunctive relief, secured a determination that Bangor Punta's May 8, 1969 press release announcing its upcoming exchange offer violated the gun jumping prohibitions of section 5(a) of the 1933 Act. Chris–Craft Industries, Inc. v. Bangor Punta Corp. 426 F.2d 569 (2d Cir.1970) (en banc); 15 U.S.C.A. § 77e(a) (1970). *See also* SEC Rule 135, 17 C.F.R. § 230.135. Both the earlier stage of the litigation as well as the case at the Supreme Court level involved the claim that Bangor Punta's open market purchases of Piper stock during the pendency of the registered exchange offer constituted a violation of Rule 10b–6. 17 C.F.R. § 240.10b–6. The 10b–6 claim and discussion of 10b–13 are contained in the Court's opinion in 430 U.S. at 42–46, 97 S.Ct. at 949–52. *See* Warren v. Bokum Resources Corp., 433 F.Supp. 1360 (D.N.M.1977) (recognizing the existence of an implied private action under Rule 10b–13).

8. 430 U.S. at 31–34, 97 S.Ct. at 944–46.

9. This is one of the factors that the Court has stressed with regard to implied remedies generally. Implied remedies are discussed in § 12.2 *infra.*

10. 430 U.S. at 31, 97 S.Ct. at 944 (quoting 113 Cong.Rec. 24664 (Aug. 30, 1967) (remarks of Sen. Williams)). *See* Rondeau v. Mosinee Paper Corp., 422 U.S. 49, 58, 95 S.Ct. 2069, 2075, 45 L.Ed.2d 12 (1975).

11. 430 U.S. at 34, 97 S.Ct. at 945. *See also, e.g.,* Metropolitan Securities v. Occidental Petroleum Corp., 705 F.Supp. 134 (S.D.N.Y.1989) (debenture holder lacked standing notwithstanding conversion to stock after public announcement of tender offer).

13. 430 U.S. at 48–53, 97 S.Ct. at 952–55.

already acquired the target company's shares, it could be viewed as a shareholder with standing to sue under the Act.[14]

There are a number of federal circuit court decisions recognizing a target shareholder's right to sue for violation of section 14(e), at least where the injury is not premised on the loss of an opportunity to control the target company.[15] In order to challenge misstatements or omissions, must the plaintiff show actual reliance? A number of decisions under the proxy rules indicate that actual reliance would not be required so long as a causally-related injury could be shown.[16] Thus a shareholder who did not tender his or her shares should not be precluded from challenging the tender offer. Reliance remains an element of the claim even in those cases that a plaintiff is not put to the test of actual reliance. This means that there must have been a material misstatement on which a reasonable investor could have relied in making an erroneous decision of whether to tender shares.[17]

Additionally, a target company's management may seek private injunctive relief for violations of section 14(e).[18] And, it has further been held that, although unable to claim damages in light of the *Piper* decision, a competing offeror may sue for injunctive relief.[19] The plaintiff's dual burden of proving a substantial likelihood of success on the merits as well as irreparable injury makes it very difficult to secure preliminary injunctive relief; courts are mindful of the time premiums involved in tender offers and are thus reluctant to interfere.

Although tender offers necessarily involve the purchase or sale of securities, a Rule 10b–5 claim in connection with a tender offer will fail if it does not further investor protection. Accordingly, a competing tender offeror generally cannot state a 10b–5 claim when section 14(e) has not been violated.[26] Furthermore, even in suits brought by the target company or its shareholders, where there could be an overlap between the section 14(e) and Rule 10b–5 claims, there are advantages to pressing the 14(e) claim, if it exists. Rather than Rule 10b–5's purchaser/seller standing limitation,[27] a section 14(e) claim would seem to depend upon whether the plaintiff was the target of a tender offer solicitation or opposition to a tender offer, rather than whether he or she was an actual purchaser or seller.[28] Also, it is arguable that since section 14(e)

14. 430 U.S. at 56–59, 97 S.Ct. at 956–58. The majority's response was that even if standing were to be found, the plaintiff's claim lacked the requisite causation since the injury complained of was the loss of an opportunity to gain control rather than any typical investor-oriented injury. *Id.* at 36, 97 S.Ct. at 946.

15. *See, e.g.,* Schlesinger Investment Partnership v. Fluor Corp., 671 F.2d 739 (2d Cir.1982).

16. *E.g.,* Western District Council of Lumber Production and Industrial Workers v. Louisiana Pacific Corp., 892 F.2d 1412 (9th Cir.1989).

17. *See, e.g.,* Salsitz v. Peltz, 227 F.Supp.2d 222 (S.D.N.Y. 2002) (failure to establish detrimental reliance; court refused to presume reliance).

18. *E.g.* Polaroid Corp. v. Disney, 862 F.2d 987 (3d Cir.1988) (granting target company's request for preliminary relief but limiting standing under Rule 14d–10's all holders rule to target company shareholders); Florida Commercial Banks v. Culverhouse, 772 F.2d 1513 (11th Cir. 1985); Prudent Real Estate Trust v. Johncamp Realty, 599 F.2d 1140 (2d Cir.1979).

19. *E.g.* Mobil Corp. v. Marathon Oil Co., 669 F.2d 366 (6th Cir.1981).

26. *See* Luptak v. Central Cartage, 1979 WL 1280, [1981 Transfer Binder] Fed.Sec.L.Rep. (CCH) ¶ 98,034 (E.D.Mich.1979), construing Piper v. Chris–Craft Industries, Inc., 430 U.S. 1, 42–46, 97 S.Ct. 926, 949–52, 51 L.Ed.2d 124 (1977).

27. Blue Chip Stamps v. Manor Drug Stores, 421 U.S. 723, 95 S.Ct. 1917, 44 L.Ed.2d 539 (1975), *rehearing denied* 423 U.S. 884, 96 S.Ct. 157, 46 L.Ed.2d 114 (1975). *See* § 12.7 *infra*.

28. Western District Council of Lumber Production and Industrial Workers v. Louisiana Pacific Corp., 892 F.2d 1412 (9th Cir.1989).

does not have the "deceptive device" language that is present in Rule 10b–5 by virtue of section 10(b),[29] section 14(e)—as is the case with section 17(a)(2) and (3) of the 1933 Act[30]—may not require a showing of scienter.[31] Although section 14(e) does prohibit manipulative, fraudulent, and deceptive acts, that prohibition is in addition to its prohibition of material misstatements and omissions. However, some courts have nonetheless found that scienter is required for a violation of section 14(e).[32] The Supreme Court's ruling in Schreiber v. Burlington Northern Inc.,[33] emphasizes that disclosure is not only the primary but probably the sole focus of section 14(e). Since section 17(a) of the 1933 Act, another disclosure-oriented provision, has been held to be violated upon a showing of negligence,[34] it is arguable that the *Schreiber* decision permits a no scienter approach to section 14(e). However, the Supreme Court's narrow reading of section 14(e) in *Schreiber* strongly favors a scienter requirement.[36]

§ 11.12 State Regulation of Tender Offers

§ 11.12[1] State Tender Offer Regulation—Overview

Prior to the adoption of the Williams Act in 1968, there was virtually no specialized regulation of tender offers at either the federal or state level. Most states have statutes that regulate tender offers. In less than twenty years, the states went through three generations of takeover statutes.[4] To paraphrase Oliver Wendell Holmes,[5] it may fairly be said that three generations of takeover statutes is enough.[6] Investor protection has not been the motivating factor behind these statutes. In most instances, state tender offer acts have been passed at least in part to protect incumbent management and other employees of local companies that were potential takeover targets. As a result, rather than merely supplementing the federal legislation, most state statutes impose more impediments to the takeover, thus inhibiting or at least slowing down any transaction.[7] In tender offer jargon, these acts are often referred to as "shark repellent" because of their deterrent effect.

29. 15 U.S.C.A. § 78j(b). *See* § 12.20 *infra.*

30. 15 U.S.C.A. § 77q(a)(2) and (3).

31. Caleb & Co. v. E.I. DuPont de Nemours & Co., 599 F.Supp. 1468 (S.D.N.Y.1984) (scienter is not required in suit for violation of Rule 14e–1(c)'s prompt payment requirement).

32. Pryor v. United States Steel Corp., 591 F.Supp. 942 (S.D.N.Y.1984), *affirmed in part, reversed in part* 794 F.2d 52 (2d Cir.1986).

33. 472 U.S. 1, 105 S.Ct. 2458, 86 L.Ed.2d 1 (1985).

34. Aaron v. SEC, 446 U.S. 680, 100 S.Ct. 1945, 64 L.Ed.2d 611 (1980), *on remand* 666 F.2d 5 (2d Cir.1981).

36. *See, e.g.,* Orlett v. Cincinnati Microwave, Inc., 953 F.2d 224 (6th Cir.1990) (claim failed since scienter not shown).

§ 11.12

4. *See* Thomas L. Hazen, State Antitakeover Legislation—The Second and Third Generations, 23 Wake Forest U.L.Rev. 77 (1988).

5. Buck v. Bell, 274 U.S. 200, 207, 47 S.Ct. 584, 71 L.Ed. 1000 (1927) ("Three generations of imbeciles are enough").

6. See Thomas L. Hazen, State Antitakeover Legislation—The Second and Third Generations, 23 Wake Forest U.L.Rev. 77, 80 (1988) (paraphrasing Justice Holmes).

7. The most prominent example is the imposition of waiting periods between the filing and effective date of the tender offer. *See, e.g.,* 8 Del.Code § 203(a)(1); Ohio Rev.Code § 1707.041(B)(1).

The federal legislation embodied in the Williams Act attempts to strike a balance between the need for disclosure and investor protection on the one hand, and, on the other, the fear of eliminating too many potential tender offerors from the market place. Much of the state legislation to date has probably gone too far in the direction of deterring bidders from participating in the tender offer market. The Supreme Court held that when the state law limitations on tender offers prove too restrictive and conflict with the basic policy of the Williams Act, these laws are invalid because they impose an unconstitutional burden on interstate commerce.[8] Other federal courts have used the preemption doctrine to invalidate state tender offer statutes under appropriate circumstances.[9] Both the preemption and Commerce Clause issues are discussed in the next section of this treatise.[10] The discussion that follows is designed to present an overview of existing legislation.

Although there are some basic and general similarities between many of the state tender offer statutes, their lack of uniformity is far greater than that of state blue sky laws.[11] Accordingly, compliance with multiple statutes is a significant hurdle and can be a nightmare for the tender offeror. Because there is such a wide variance in statutory terms and provisions, the discussion that follows is merely a broad overview. The applicable statutes must be carefully scrutinized in order to master their individual regulatory provisions. In the words of one commentator, "State takeover acts are similar to snowflakes—if you think you have found identical ones, you are probably not looking closely enough."[12]

§ 11.12[2] Scope of State Tender Offer Regulation

The various state statutes employ a wide range of jurisdictional provisions. It is thus possible that more than one state act will apply to any particular tender offer. The majority of the state acts base jurisdiction on the target company's incorporation within the state, or on the location within the state of the target company's principal place of business and/or substantial target company assets.[13] Some statutes take a less well-defined approach by looking to substantial contacts with the state.[14] Another variation among the

8. *See* Edgar v. MITE, 457 U.S. 624, 102 S.Ct. 2629, 73 L.Ed.2d 269 (1982). *See* § 11.13 *infra.*

9. *See, e.g.,* Great Western United Corp. v. Kidwell, 577 F.2d 1256 (5th Cir.1978), *vacated on other grounds sub nom.* Leroy v. Great Western United Corp., 443 U.S. 173, 99 S.Ct. 2710, 61 L.Ed.2d 464 (1979).

10. *See* § 11.13 *infra.*

11. *See* chapter 8 *supra.*

12. Note, State Regulation of Tender Offers, 3 J.Corp.Law 603, 603 (1982) (footnote omitted).

See generally Edward Ross Aranow & Herbert A. Einhorn, State Securities Regulation of Tender Offers, 46 N.Y.U.L.Rev. 767 (1971); Harold S. Bloomenthal, The New Tender Offer Regimen, State Regulation, and Preemption, 30 Emory L.J. 35 (1981); Donald C. Langevoort, State Tender Offer Legislation: Interests, Effects and Political Competence, 62 Cornell L.Rev. 213 (1977); Report, State Takeover Statutes and the Williams Act, 32 Bus.Law. 387 (1976); Symposium, The Risks and Rewards of Regulating Corporate Takeovers, 1988 Wis.L.Rev. 353; Symposium, Controlling Corporate Takeover Bids: State Regulation and the Ohio Approach, 21 Case Wes.Res.L.Rev. 605 (1970); Note, The Utah Takeover Disclosure Act: Constitutional and Practical Considerations, 1979 Utah L.Rev. 583; Comment, The North Carolina Tender Offer Disclosure Act: Congenitally Defective?, 14 Wake Forest L.Rev. 1035 (1978).

13. *See, e.g.,* Conn.Gen.Stat.Ann. § 36b–41(1); M.S.A. § 80B.01; N.J.Stat.Ann. § 49.5–2; NY–McKinney's Bus.Corp.L § 1601; Ohio Rev.Code § 1707.041(A)(1).

14. *See, e.g.,* Iowa Code Ann. § 502.321A.

Target company means a corporation, limited partnership, or other issuer of securities which is or may be involved in a takeover offer relating to any class of equity securities if the issuer:

states arises in the context of subject matter jurisdiction by virtue of the elusive definition of "tender offer." There is no universally accepted definition of tender offer, although most acts are brought into play by virtue of securities transactions that fall within that category under federal law. While the federal act contains no statutory definition, the state statutes generally include precise but diverse statutory definitions including the number of solicited target company shareholders required before the act applies.

§ 11.12[3] First Generation State Tender Offer Statutes

§ 11.12[3][A] Types of First Generation Statutes

Major variations among the state tender offer statutes are found in the qualification requirements. Following the pattern of the state blue sky laws, many of the state tender offer statutes go beyond the disclosure philosophy of the Williams Act by giving the state administrator the power to review the merits of the tender offer[18] or the adequacy of the disclosure.[19] The state administrator is often empowered to hold hearings which may be initiated by the administrator,[20] the target company,[21] or a certain percentage of the target company's shareholders.[22] Thus, even where merit analysis is not permitted, the tender offer could be tied up in administrative hearings. The procedures vary among the statutes as to who may or must appear at such hearings and the extent of allowable pre-hearing discovery.

Even state regulation that is limited to full disclosure, as opposed to a merit or substantive review of the terms of the offer, may impose burdens beyond those created by the federal legislation. The most prominent example is the commonly found state-imposed waiting period between the filing of the tender offer and the date on which it becomes effective. Not only are such waiting periods not a part of the federal statute, but, in 1979, the SEC, by promulgating Rule 14d–2(b),[30] purported to preempt all such waiting periods. Although the preemptive effect of Rule 14d–2(b) has not specifically been decided, the Supreme Court held that waiting periods may contribute to a state statute's invalidity as an undue burden on interstate commerce.[32]

§ 11.12[4] Second Generation State Takeover Statutes

Following the Supreme Court's ruling in Edgar v. MITE Corp.,[44] a number of states enacted "second generation" takeover statutes that were designed to overcome the constitutional infirmities of the Illinois statute that was struck down in *MITE.* The basic thrust of these statutes is to regulate

---

(A) Is organized under the laws of this state or has its principal offices in this state; or

(B) Has equity security holders resident in this state who own a majority in interest of any class of equity securities.

18. *See, e.g.,* N.J.Stat.Ann. 49:5–4(a).

19. *E.g.* Ark.Stat. § 23–43–111; 70 Pa.Stat. § 74(d).

20. *E.g.* Vernon's Ann.Mo.Stat. § 409.521.

21. *E.g.* 70 Pa.Stat. § 74(d).

22. *E.g.* Conn.Gen.Stat.Ann. § 36b–44 (aggregate owners of ten percent of the outstanding equity securities of the class involved in the tender offer may petition the commissioner to schedule a hearing).

30. 17 C.F.R. § 240.14d–2(b) (1979).

32. Edgar v. MITE Corp., 457 U.S. 624, 102 S.Ct. 2629, 73 L.Ed.2d 269 (1982). *See* § 11.13 *infra.*

44. 457 U.S. 624, 102 S.Ct. 2629, 73 L.Ed.2d 269 (1982). *See* § 11.13 *infra.*

tender offers through state law rules relating to corporate governance rather than through state securities laws and administrative regulations. The basic approach of such statutes is substantive regulation of tender offers. Ohio was the first state to adopt second generation legislation.[46]

The Ohio Act, which governs all forms of takeovers and is not limited to tender offers, applies to Ohio corporations having fifty or more shareholders and a principal place of business, principal offices, or substantial assets within the state.[49] The act then classifies takeover transactions by the percentage of shares owned by the acquiring person, with each control zone triggering the act's substantive requirements. Acquiring persons must deliver to the target company a disclosure statement describing the proposed acquisition. The target company's board then has ten days to call a special shareholders' meeting which must take place within fifty days At that meeting, the transaction requires approval of a majority of the disinterested shares not owned or controlled by the acquiring person or any affiliate. Prior to the Supreme Court decision upholding the Indiana Control Share Act,[51] the Ohio statute had been struck down as violative of the Commerce Clause.[52]

In contrast to the Ohio approach, Maryland took a more structural approach in regulating share acquisitions. The Maryland statute requires that any takeover be approved by at least eighty percent of the shares and two-thirds of the disinterested shares unless all shareholders receive the "best price" paid by the acquiring person within a two-year period.[56] The best price approach, patterned after fair price charter amendments adopted by many corporations in other states as a defensive anticipatory tactic, is to fend off two-tiered offers. The Maryland Act excludes "friendly" offers from its coverage. A number of states have adopted fair price statutes, some of which vary the terms of the Maryland Act.

Ohio and Indiana have expanded the factors directors may consider in opposing takeovers.[60] Other states have adopted similar "constituency" or "stakeholder" statutes, which permit management to consider interests other than those of the shareholders in making decisions. Target management in these states thus may rely on interests other than shareholder wealth maximization as a basis for resisting a takeover. These statutes generally make it clear that although management may consider other interests, it does not have to. Still another approach taken in some of the second generation statutes is to give dissenters' rights to a wide variety of control transactions.

§ 11.12[5] Third Generation Takeover Statutes

Once one of the second generation state takeover statutes—the Indiana Control Share Act—had passed constitutional scrutiny in the Supreme

46. Ohio Rev.Code § 1701.832. *See* Gary P. Kreider, Fortress Without Foundation? Ohio Takeover Act II, 52 U. Cin.L.Rev. 108 (1983); Note, Has Ohio Avoided the Wake of MITE? An Analysis of the Constitutionality of the Ohio Control Share Acquisition Act, 46 Ohio St.L.J. 203 (1985).

49. Ohio Rev.Code § 1701.83.1.

51. CTS Corp. v. Dynamics Corp. of America, 481 U.S. 69, 107 S.Ct. 1637, 95 L.Ed.2d 67 (1987).

52. Fleet Aerospace Corp. v. Holderman, 796 F.2d 135 (6th Cir.1986), *vacated* 481 U.S. 1026, 107 S.Ct. 1949, 95 L.Ed.2d 521 (1987).

56. Md. Corp's & Ass'ns Code §§ 3–602, 3–603.

60. West's Ann.Ind.Code § 23–1–35–1(d) (Burns Supp.1986); Ohio Rev.Code § 1701.59 (Baldwin Supp.1986).

Court,[65] the third generation of tender offer statutes began to appear.[66] One form that such statutes took was to apply the law of the host state to corporations incorporated elsewhere. Such statutes, in regulating what has been called pseudo-foreign corporations, raise additional constitutional and policy questions. North Carolina was the first state to adopt a third generation statute aimed at regulating foreign corporations,[67] and a number of other states followed suit.[68] North Carolina has since repealed the extraterritorial reach of its antitakeover laws.[69] The New Hampshire legislature adopted a statute that applies to foreign target companies[70] The New Hampshire Supreme Court upheld that statute's application to a New Hampshire company and did not reach the issue of whether it would be constitutional if applied to corporations not incorporated in New Hampshire.[71]

Although the third generation statutes purporting to regulate foreign corporations are generally based upon substantial contacts within the state, the rationale of the *CTS* decision strongly indicates that such statutes may not withstand constitutional scrutiny.[72] In fact, the Oklahoma statute was struck down by a federal district court on the grounds that it was unconstitutional to the extent that it applied to non-Oklahoma corporations.[73] Similarly, the Arizona takeover statute purporting to apply to corporations incorporated elsewhere was declared an unconstitutional burden on interstate commerce.[74]

65. CTS Corp. v. Dynamics Corp. of America, 481 U.S. 69, 107 S.Ct. 1637, 95 L.Ed.2d 67 (1987). *See* § 11.13 *infra.*

66. For yet another suggested approach for state legislation, *see* Stephen M. Bainbridge, Redirecting State Takeover Laws at Proxy Contests, 1992 Wis.L.Rev. 1071.

67. In adopting both a best price and control share statutes, North Carolina purported to apply its law not only to corporations incorporated in the state, but also to corporations incorporated elsewhere having more than forty percent of its domestic assets in the state and more than four percent of its domestic employees in the state. N.C.Gen.Stat. § 55–9–01 *et seq.* ("Shareholder Protection Act"); *Id.* § 55–9A–01 *et seq.* ("Control Share Acquisitions Act"). It is further provided that neither the North Carolina best price nor control share statutes apply to corporations if in express conflict with the laws of the state of incorporation. *Id.*

In 1990, the North Carolina legislature eliminated the application of these acts to corporations not incorporated in the state.

68. Ariz.H.R.Res. 2002, 38th Leg., 3d Sess., 1987 Ariz.Legis.Serv. 32–45; 1987 Fla.Laws 87–257; Mass.Gen.Laws Ann. ch. 110D, 110E.

69. N.C.Gen.Stat. §§ 55–9–01 *et seq.,* 55–9A–01 *et seq.*

70. N.H. Rev. Stat. § 421–A:2 (applying takeover statute to target companies having more than 100 shareholders and its principal office or substantial assets in the state and having either (1) more than 10 percent of its shareholders resident in the state; (2) more than 10 percent of its shares owned by New Hampshire residents; or (3) ten thousand shareholders resident in New Hampshire).

71. New England Dragway, Inc. v. M–O–H Enterprises, Inc., 149 N.H. 188, 817 A.2d 288 (2003).

72. For example, the Court in *CTS* expressly noted that the state of incorporation has a special interest in regulating the internal affairs of its corporations:

> The Indiana statute imposes no such problem [presenting an undue burden on interstate commerce]. So long as each state regulates voting rights *only in the corporations it has created,* each corporation will be subject to the law of only one state.

107 S.Ct. at 1649, 95 L.Ed.2d at 85 (emphasis supplied).

73. TLX Acquisition Corp. v. Telex Corp., 679 F.Supp. 1022 (W.D.Okl.1987). *Cf.* Veere, Inc. v. Firestone Tire & Rubber Co., 685 F.Supp. 1027 (N.D.Ohio 1988) (indicating that there was no problem with constitutionality of Ohio statute since it applied only to target companies incorporated in Ohio).

74. Rocket Acquisition Corp. v. Ventana Medical Systems Inc., 2007 WL 2422082 (D. Ariz. 2007), relying on Tyson Foods Inc. v. McReynolds, 865 F.2d 99, 101 (6th Cir. 1989).

Another variety of third generation takeover statute is modeled on the New York "freeze" statute,[75] also known as a business combination statute. The idea behind such statutes is to delay any transaction that would complete the second step of a two-step acquisition, in those instances in which the first step was not agreed to by the target company's management. Thus, for example, the New York statute prohibits a merger or other business acquisition within five years of the control acquisition date unless the transaction was approved by the target company's directors *prior* to the control acquisition date. Other states have followed the New York lead,[76] including Delaware, which has adopted a three-year-freeze statute.[77] Based on earlier Supreme Court doctrine, there would appear to be considerable question whether such statutes can withstand constitutional scrutiny.[78] Nevertheless, the Delaware statute has withstood challenges at the preliminary injunction stage because of the failure to show a likelihood of success on the merits of the constitutional challenge, but the court noted that although the statute was probably constitutional, the constitutionality issue is not an easy one.[79] The Wisconsin freeze statute has been upheld by the Seventh Circuit.[80] There thus is mounting authority in support of these questionable freeze statutes.

§ 11.13 Validity of State Tender Offer Statutes—The Commerce Clause and the Preemption Problem; SEC Rule 14d–2(b)

State tender offer legislation has frequently been challenged under the Supremacy[1] and Commerce[2] Clauses of the Constitution. Under the Supremacy Clause, to the extent Congress has exercised its legislative power, a state may not enact inconsistent legislation.[3] Hence, state laws are preempted when either explicitly prohibited by,[4] or directly in conflict with,[5] federal legislation. Not every challenge to a takeover statute will be ripe. For example, shareholders of a potential target company did not have standing to challenge a state's

75. N.Y.Bus.Corp.Law § 912.

76. Ariz.Rev.Stat. §§ 10–2741–10–2742 (three-year delay); Minn.Stat.Ann. § 302A.673 (five-year delay); Vernon's Ann.Mo.Stat. § 351.459(3)(b) (five-year delay); N.J.Stat.Ann. § 49.5–1 (five-year delay); Wash.S.B. No. 6084, 1987 Wash.Leg.Serv. (No. 10) 11 (five year delay); Wis.Stat.Ann. § 180.1130 (three year delay).

77. Del.Corp.Code § 203.

78. *Cf.* Hyde Park Partners, L.P. v. Connolly, 839 F.2d 837 (1st Cir.1988) (Massachusetts statute imposing one-year moratorium on takeover attempts as a sanction for violation of the statute's disclosure provisions held likely to be preempted by Williams Act).

79. RP Acquisition Corp. v. Staley Continental, Inc., 686 F.Supp. 476 (D.Del.1988); BNS, Inc. v. Koppers Co., 683 F.Supp. 454 (D.Del 1988).

80. Amanda Acquisition Corp. v. Universal Foods Corp., 877 F.2d 496 (7th Cir.1989).

§ 11.13

1. "This Constitution, and the Laws of the United States . . shall be the Supreme Law of the Land." U.S. Const. art. VI, cl. 2. *See* John E. Nowak, Ronald D. Rotunda & J. Nelson Young, Constitutional Law 18–20 (2d ed. 1983).

2. "The Congress shall have the power ... [t]o regulate commerce ... among the several States." U.S. Const. art. I, § 8, cl. 3.

3. Swift & Co. v. Wickham, 382 U.S. 111, 86 S.Ct. 258, 15 L.Ed.2d 194 (1965).

4. *See, e.g.,* Rice v. Santa Fe Elevator, 331 U.S. 218, 236, 67 S.Ct. 1146, 1155, 91 L.Ed. 1447 (1947) (Federal Warehouse Act expressly preempts all concurrent state regulation).

5. Florida Lime and Avocado Growers, Inc. v. Paul, 373 U.S. 132, 142–43, 83 S.Ct. 1210, 1217, 10 L.Ed.2d 248 (1963), *rehearing denied* 374 U.S. 858, 83 S.Ct. 1861, 10 L.Ed.2d 1082 (1963) ("A holding of federal exclusion of state law is inescapable ... where compliance with both federal and state regulation is a physical impossibility....").

takeover statute prior to the commencement of a tender offer or other takeover attempt.[6]

§ 11.13[1] Preemption Challenges to State Takeover Statutes

Preemption is largely a matter of congressional intent.[7] State legislation may be implicitly preempted when there is an overriding federal interest in the subject of the legislation,[8] or when the federal regulations are so pervasive as to create an inference that Congress intended to "occupy the field" completely.[9] Similarly, state law may be invalid if it conflicts indirectly with the federal law by standing as an obstacle to the full accomplishment of federal regulatory objectives.[10] In any case, a balancing of state and federal interests is required.[11]

The Williams Act does not expressly prohibit state regulation of tender offers. Furthermore, because corporate law regulation has not generally been considered to be a matter of overriding federal concern,[12] and because the Williams Act is not a detailed comprehensive regulatory scheme, but rather a minimum standard,[13] there is no inference that Congress intended to preempt all state tender offer regulation.[14] In the absence of an explicit or implicit prohibition of state regulation, supremacy clause questions focus on whether state takeover laws conflict either directly or indirectly with the operation of the Williams Act.

§ 11.13[2] Commerce Clause Challenges to State Takeover Legislation

A state statute which survives preemption analysis may nonetheless be unenforceable under the Commerce Clause. State legislation is valid only if it

---

6. Armstrong World Industries, Inc. v. Adams, 961 F.2d 405 (3d Cir.1992).

7. California v. Zook, 336 U.S. 725, 69 S.Ct. 841, 93 L.Ed. 1005 (1949); Head v. New Mexico Board of Examiners, 374 U.S. 424, 83 S.Ct. 1759, 10 L.Ed.2d 983 (1963).

8. *See, e.g.,* Pennsylvania v. Nelson, 350 U.S. 497, 76 S.Ct. 477, 100 L.Ed. 640 (1956) (Congressional enactment of internal security laws to safeguard against overthrow of the government by force reflected overriding federal interest requiring preemption of supplementary state anti-communist legislation).

9. Rice v. Santa Fe Elevator, 331 U.S. 218, 230, 67 S.Ct. 1146, 1152, 91 L.Ed. 1447 (1947); City of Burbank v. Lockheed Air Terminal, Inc., 411 U.S. 624, 93 S.Ct. 1854, 36 L.Ed.2d 547 (1973).

10. Hines v. Davidowitz, 312 U.S. 52, 67, 61 S.Ct. 399, 404, 85 L.Ed. 581 (1941).

11. *See id.* at 73–74, 61 S.Ct. at 407–08. *See generally* Note, The Preemption Doctrine: Shifting Perspectives on Federalism and the Burger Court, 75 Colum.L.Rev. 623 (1975).

12. Corporation law has traditionally been primarily state law but largely because of the federal securities statutes a "Federal Corporations Law" has been developing. *See generally* William L. Cary & Melvin A. Eisenberg, Cases and Materials on Corporations, 13–14 (5th ed.1980).

13. *See* Note, Securities Law and the Constitution: State Tender Offer Statutes Reconsidered, 88 Yale L.J. 510, 519–20 (1979). *But cf.* Diane S. Wilner & Craig A. Landy, The Tender Trap: State Takeover Statutes and Their Constitutionality, 45 Fordham L.Rev. 1, 29–30 (1976) (the Williams Act, taken as a whole with the 1934 Act into which Congress integrated it, is comprehensive).

14. In fact, it has been argued that Congress implicitly accepted the prospect of state regulation by adding the Williams Act to the 1934 Act without also amending section 28(a) of the Act, 15 U.S.C.A. § 78bb(a), which provides that "Nothing in this chapter shall affect the jurisdiction of the securities commission ... of any state over any security or any person insofar as it does not conflict with provisions of this chapter or the rules and regulations thereunder." But the applicability of this provision to state tender offer legislation is, at best, questionable. *See* Donald C. Langevoort, State Tender–Offer Legislation: Interests, Effects, and Political Competency, 62 Cornell L.Rev. 213, 247 (1977).

regulates even-handedly to effectuate a legitimate local public interest, affects interstate commerce only incidentally, and imposes burdens on such commerce not clearly excessive in relation to the putative local benefits.[15] The protection of local incumbent management from foreign "raiders" is not a legitimate local interest in itself; however, regulation of the internal affairs of domestic corporations and the protection of local target corporations and shareholders from fraud and overreaching in the course of tender offers are clearly bona fide state concerns.[16] Thus, the vulnerability of state tender offer acts under the commerce clause is due largely to their extraterritorial coverage and the resulting cumulative burden on interstate commerce.[17]

§ 11.13[2][A] The Early Cases

In Great Western United Corp. v. Kidwell,[18] the Fifth Circuit became the first federal appellate court to consider the constitutionality of a state tender offer act. In *Kidwell,* the tender offeror was a Delaware corporation with its principal offices in Dallas, Texas. The target was organized under the laws of the state of Washington with shareholders across the United States. The Idaho takeover statute required that a registration statement be declared effective by the director of the state's Department of Finance prior to the commencement of any tender offer for an Idaho target company.[19] The offeror was required to mail a copy of the statement to the target, and the material terms of the offer had to be publicly disclosed no later than the filing date. Within twenty days of the filing, the director could hold a discretionary hearing if he thought it necessary to ensure full disclosure and equal treatment of all shareholders.[20] A hearing was required if the target company requested it, and the director's determination as to the adequacy of the registration statement had to be announced within thirty days of filing unless more time was needed.[21] The Act's jurisdictional provisions were triggered by target companies having substantial assets located in Idaho or that were either incorporated or had principal offices in the state and had securities registered under the Idaho Code or the 1934 Act.[22] Although its disclosure requirements were more stringent than those of the Williams Act, Idaho's provisions for withdrawal rights, pro rata acceptance, and price increases merely duplicated the corresponding federal provisions.[23]

The Fifth Circuit found it unnecessary to determine whether the true purpose of the takeover law was to protect investors as Idaho contended, or to

15. Pike v. Bruce Church, Inc., 397 U.S. 137, 90 S.Ct. 844, 25 L.Ed.2d 174 (1970).

16. *See* Donald C. Langevoort, State Tender–Offer Legislation: Interests, Effects, and Political Competency, 62 Cornell L.Rev. 213, 242 (1977).

17. *E.g.* CTS Corp. v. Dynamics Corp. of America, 481 U.S. 69, 107 S.Ct. 1637, 95 L.Ed.2d 67 (1987). *See* Diane S. Wilner & Craig A. Landy, The Tender Trap: State Takeover Statutes and Their Constitutionality, 45 Fordham L.Rev. 1, 22–23 (1976).

18. 577 F.2d 1256 (5th Cir.1978), *reversed on other grounds sub nom.* Leroy v. Great Western United Corp., 443 U.S. 173, 99 S.Ct. 2710, 61 L.Ed.2d 464 (1979), *on remand* 602 F.2d 1246 (5th Cir.1979).

19. Idaho Code § 30–1503(1).

20. Idaho Code § 30–1503(4)–(5). The statute did not authorize the director to review the merits of the offer.

21. Idaho Code § 30–1503(4), (5).

22. Idaho Code § 30–1501(6).

23. *Compare* Idaho Code §§ 30–1503(2)(C), 30–1506(2)–(4) *with* 15 U.S.C.A. §§ 78m(d), 78n(d)(5)–(7).

protect incumbent management as the district court had found.[24] In either case Congress had rejected Idaho's "fiduciary approach" to investor protection, which relied upon the business judgment of corporate directors with a fiduciary duty to their shareholders. Instead, recognizing that investors often benefit from tender offers, Congress had chosen the "market approach" wherein the function of federal regulation was to let the investor, on a fully informed basis, decide for himself or herself after allowing both the offeror and incumbent management to fully present their arguments.[25] The court found that the Idaho law benefited target companies by giving them advance notice of tender offers and the power to postpone offers indefinitely by insisting on a hearing. Moreover, Idaho gave preferential treatment to target companies by not regulating target defensive tactics as stringently as the offeror's activities. Indeed, the target board could exclude the offer from state regulation completely by simply approving the offer.[26] The court reasoned that the state law clearly "disrupted the neutrality indispensable for the proper operation of the federal approach to tender offer regulation,"[27] and thus stood as "an obstacle to the accomplishment and execution of the full purposes and objectives of the Williams Act" and was necessarily preempted.[28]

Following the Fifth Circuit's opinion in *Kidwell,* state and federal district court rulings on the constitutionality of state tender offer statutes remained contradictory.[29] Most courts, however, agreed with the Fifth Circuit's conclusion that the Williams Act was intended both to protect shareholders and to maintain a neutral balance between incumbent management and the offeror.[30] Hence, following the *Kidwell* reasoning, to the extent that state statutes provided management with the weapon of delay, they were most often found to disrupt the neutral balance and hinder achievement of the objectives of the Williams Act. On the other hand, a minority of courts held that the sole purpose of the Williams Act was to protect investors, and that Congress had no intention to legislate neutrality into tender offers. Neutrality, they concluded, was simply one characteristic of the legislation.

In response to the mounting confusion and the increasing number of tender offers, the SEC adopted tender offer rules which were intended to preempt state regulation by creating a direct conflict with most state statutes.[31] Before those new rules could be tested, however, the Fourth and

24. 577 F.2d at 1278–79 (citing Appellants Brief at 39–42 and the district court's opinion, 439 F.Supp. at 437).

25. 577 F.2d at 1279. *But cf.* North Star International v. Arizona Corporation Commission, 720 F.2d 578 (9th Cir.1983).

26. 577 F.2d at 1278.

27. *Id.* at 1279–80.

28. *Id.* at 1280, 1281. The court pointed out that by requiring more extensive disclosure than the Williams Act, Idaho might actually be harming investors. Too much data could hide relevant disclosures and create unnecessary confusion, thus inhibiting the offeror's efforts to communicate material information.

29. *Compare, e.g.,* Dart Industries, Inc. v. Conrad, 462 F.Supp. 1 (S.D.Ind.1978) (Delaware statute preempted by the Williams Act) *with* AMCA International Corp. v. Krouse, 482 F.Supp. 929 (S.D.Ohio 1979) (Ohio takeover law not preempted).

30. *See* MITE Corp. v. Dixon, 633 F.2d 486, 495 (7th Cir.1980), *affirmed sub nom.* Edgar v. MITE Corp., 457 U.S. 624, 102 S.Ct. 2629, 73 L.Ed.2d 269 (1982). The neutrality principle was reaffirmed by the Supreme Court in CTS Corp. v. Dynamics Corp. of America, 481 U.S. 69, 107 S.Ct. 1637, 95 L.Ed.2d 67 (1987).

31. *See* Sec.Act Rel. No. 33–6022 (SEC Feb. 5, 1979); Sec.Act Rel. No. 33–6158 (SEC Nov. 29, 1979); Sec.Act Rel. No. 33–6159 (SEC Nov. 29, 1979).

Seventh Circuits reached opposite results in controversies involving the takeover statutes of Virginia[32] and Illinois[33] respectively. The Supreme Court decided to review the Illinois case, and in Edgar v. MITE Corp.,[34] the constitutionality of state tender offer legislation was squarely before the Court for the first time.

§ 11.13[2][B] The *MITE* Decision

MITE Corporation, organized under the laws of Delaware with its principal office in Connecticut, initiated a tender offer for all outstanding shares of an Illinois corporation. MITE complied with the requirements of the Williams Act but did not comply with the Illinois Act,[35] electing instead to file suit in district court in Illinois, seeking declaratory and injunctive relief from the statute's enforcement.

Under the Illinois Business Takeover Act, an offer became effective twenty days after filing with the Secretary of State and notifying the target of the terms of the offer, unless the Secretary of State called a hearing to determine the fairness of the offer.[36] During the waiting period, the offeror could not communicate with the target shareholders, although the target was free to contact shareholders as it pleased.[37] Target companies were defined by the Act as any corporation of which ten percent of the class of securities subject to the tender offer was owned by Illinois residents, or for which any two of the following conditions were met: the corporation had its principal place of business located in Illinois, was organized under Illinois law, or had at least ten percent of its stated capital and paid-in surplus represented within the state.[38]

The Supreme Court agreed with the Seventh Circuit that the Illinois law was invalid under the Commerce Clause because it imposed an excessive indirect burden on interstate commerce.[39] Illinois derived no benefit from protecting non-resident investors, and the state's asserted interest in investor protection was seriously undermined by the fact that the target company's competing offer for its own shares was completely exempt from the coverage of the Act.[40] The substantive protections provided by the Illinois Act were essentially equivalent to those provided by the Williams Act. The Court noted that the additional disclosure requirements of the Illinois Act might not substantially enhance the shareholders' ability to make a decision and concluded that the protections the Illinois Act afforded resident shareholders were for the most part "speculative."[41]

---

32. Telvest v. Bradshaw, 618 F.2d 1029 (4th Cir.1980).

33. MITE Corp. v. Dixon, 633 F.2d 486 (7th Cir.1980), *affirmed sub nom.* Edgar v. MITE Corp., 457 U.S. 624, 102 S.Ct. 2629, 73 L.Ed.2d 269 (1982).

34. 457 U.S. 624, 102 S.Ct. 2629, 73 L.Ed.2d 269 (1982).

35. Under the Illinois Act any takeover offer for the shares of a target company had to be registered with the Secretary of State. Ill.–S.H.A. ch. 121½, § 137.54.A (repealed).

36. Ill.–S.H.A. ch. 121½, § 137.54.E (repealed).

37. Ill.–S.H.A. ch. 121½, § 137.58.1 (repealed).

38. Ill.–S.H.A. ch. 121½, § 137.52.10 (repealed).

39. Edgar v. MITE Corp., 457 U.S. 624, 642, 102 S.Ct. 2629, 2641, 73 L.Ed.2d 269 (1982). *Accord e.g.,* Mesa Petroleum Co. v. Cities Service Co., 715 F.2d 1425 (10th Cir.1983) (Oklahoma takeover statute ruled unconstitutional); Batus, Inc. v. McKay, 684 F.Supp. 637 (D.Nev.1988) (invalidating Nevada statute).

40. 457 U.S. at 645, 102 S.Ct. at 2642.

41. *Id.* at 645, 102 S.Ct. at 2642.

A plurality of the Court would also have invalidated the Illinois Act as an impermissible direct regulation of interstate commerce.[42] The plurality found a substantial difference between state blue sky laws which regulate transactions taking place within the state, and the Illinois law which could conceivably apply to tender offers involving no Illinois shareholders at all.[43] The Commerce Clause precluded the application of a state statute to commerce occurring entirely outside the state's borders whether or not the commerce had effects within the state.[44] Three of the six Justices reaching the merits in *MITE* would have affirmed the Seventh Circuit on supremacy clause grounds as well.[45] The Justices agreed with the lower court that in imposing the requirements of the Williams Act, Congress had adopted a "policy of evenhandedness."[46]

§ 11.13[2][C] The *CTS* Decision

In CTS Corp. v. Dynamics Corp. of America,[78] the Supreme Court upheld the Indiana control share statute, pointing out that, unlike the Illinois statute which was struck down in *MITE,* the Indiana statute was not balanced in favor of incumbent management.[79] It is thus significant that state takeover statutes maintain a position of neutrality, rather than favoring target management. The Supreme Court's decision in *CTS* has far-reaching implications in permitting states to control the takeover arena by regulating corporate internal affairs.

Although the *CTS* decision does not address the issue, there is a strong argument that best price statutes will withstand constitutional scrutiny. On the other hand, since most best price statutes may be waived by the board of directors, it is arguable that they do not protect the independent shareholder against incumbent management. Giving incumbent management the power to block the hostile takeover by waiving the statute's barrier to permit a friendly defensive arrangement can be viewed as violating the *CTS* neutrality requirement.[82] As the Court pointed out in the *CTS* decision, the control share acquisition statute disenfranchises both the person seeking control and target company management, and thus preserves the neutrality mandated by the Williams Act.

With regard to the Commerce Clause issue, the teaching of the Supreme Court in *CTS* seems to be contained in a three-factor analysis. First, antitakeover legislation enacted by the states must preserve the neutrality of the

42. *Id.* at 641–644, 102 S.Ct. at 2640–41.

43. *Id.* at 643, 102 S.Ct. at 2641. The plurality noted that while blue sky laws affect interstate commerce in securities only incidentally, the Illinois Act directly regulated transactions taking place across state lines. *Id.* at 641–644, 102 S.Ct. at 2640–41.

44. *Id.* at 643, 102 S.Ct. at 2641.

45. *Id.* at 632–42, 102 S.Ct. at 2635–40.

46. *Id.* at 633, 102 S.Ct. at 2636 (citing Piper v. Chris–Craft Industries, 430 U.S. 1, 97 S.Ct. 926, 51 L.Ed.2d 124 (1977)).

78. 481 U.S. 69, 107 S.Ct. 1637, 95 L.Ed.2d 67 (1987).

79. *Id.* at 81–82, 107 S.Ct. at 1645, 95 L.Ed.2d at 80.

82. *Cf., e.g.,* RTE Corp. v. Mark IV Industries, Inc., 1988 WL 75453, [1987–1988 Transfer Binder] Fed.Sec.L.Rep. (CCH) ¶ 93,789 (E.D.Wis.1988) (Unpublished Case) (Wisconsin statute held unconstitutional because it gave incumbent management the power to block a tender offer).

The SEC took the position in *amicus* briefs that the presence of a director opt-out provision interferes with the statute's neutrality. On the other hand, it can be argued that the absence of an opt-out provision sets up an impermissible burden on interstate commerce.

Williams Act and thus cannot favor target management in its defense of hostile takeovers. Second, the state legislation must leave to the shareholders the decision whether to accept the offer. Third, the Court seems to be more receptive to burdens on interstate commerce arising out of the regulation of internal corporate affairs, at least when the law in question is from the state of incorporation.

Chapter 12

MANIPULATION AND FRAUD—CIVIL LIABILITY; IMPLIED PRIVATE REMEDIES; SEC RULE 10B–5; FRAUD IN CONNECTION WITH THE PURCHASE OR SALE OF SECURITIES; IMPROPER TRADING ON NONPUBLIC MATERIAL INFORMATION

Table of Sections

---

§ 12.1 Market Manipulation and Deceptive Practices—Sections 9, 10, 14(e), 15(c)

§ 12.1[1] Anti–Manipulation Rules—Overview

The overwhelming majority of the securities laws' liability provisions (both civil and criminal) focus on disclosure and registration requirements. In addition, there is a group of provisions geared to preventing artificial market activity and practices designed to have the effect of setting manipulated—and hence, artificial—security prices. These are provisions that are specifically directed to address market manipulation. The purpose of the various statutes and rules prohibiting market manipulation is to prevent activities that rig the market and to thereby facilitate operation of the "natural law" of supply and demand.[1] In this way, market price will reflect, as much as possible, the fair and just price for each security.[2] Although it can take many forms, manipulation consists of any intentional interference with supply and demand.[3]

What Constitutes Manipulative Conduct?

Section 9 of the Exchange Act outlaws manipulative practices in connection with the trading of exchange-listed securities and also provides a private remedy for investors injured by the prohibited manipulative conduct.[8] In 2000, section 9(a)'s anti-manipulation provisions (but not section 9(e)'s private right of action) were extended to securities-based swap agreements even though those agreements are not securities under the Act.[9] The reach of section 9's manipulation provisions were significantly expanded in 2006 when the NASDAQ national stock market was registered as a national securities exchange.[10]

---

§ 12.1

1. *See, e.g.,* SEC v. First Jersey Securities, 101 F.3d 1450, 1466 (2d Cir.1996), *cert. denied,* 522 U.S. 812, 118 S.Ct. 57, 139 L.Ed.2d 21 (1997); Varljen v. H.J. Meyers, Inc., 1998 WL 395266 (S.D.N.Y.1998).

2. *See, Id.*

3. Brooklyn Capital & Securities Trading, Inc., 52 S.E.C. 1286, Sec. Exch. Rel. No. 34–38454, 64 S.E.C. Docket 483, 1997 WL 144843 *3 (SEC 1997) (manipulation is the "intentional interference with the forces of supply and demand") (quoting Pagel, Inc., 48 S.E.C. 223, 226 (1985), *aff'd,* 803 F.2d 942 (5th Cir. 1986)).

8. 15 U.S.C.A. § 78i. Sections 10 and 15 of the Securities Exchange Act cover manipulation with regard to NASDAQ listed securities or others in the over-the-counter markets. Cowen & Co. v. Merriam, 745 F.Supp. 925 (S.D.N.Y.1990). Some commentators have questioned the efficiency of prohibiting manipulative activities. *See, e.g.,* Daniel R. Fischel & David J. Ross, Should the Law Prohibit "Manipulation" in Financial Markets?, 105 Harv.L.Rev. 503 (1991). However, these prohibitions are necessary in order to maintain accurate pricing by the markets. *See also, e.g.,* Steve Thel, $850,000 in Six Minutes—The Mechanics of Securities Manipulation, 79 Cornell L. Rev. 219 (1994).

9. 15 U.S.C.A. § 78i(a) as amended by Pub. Law 106–554, 114 Stat. 2763 (December 21, 2000); 15 U.S.C.A. §§ 77b–1(b)(1), 78c–1(b)(1) (both of which exclude "security-based swap agreements" from the definition of "security"), added by Pub. Law 106–554, 114 Stat. 2763 (December 21, 2000).

10. Prior to that registration Nasdaq was solely an over-the-counter market.

Section 9's prohibitions are supplemented by section 10(b),[11] which empowers the SEC to promulgate rules barring manipulative as well as deceptive conduct, and also by section 15(c),[12] which prohibits fraudulent and manipulative conduct by broker-dealers. The language of section 9 limits its application to manipulation of securities that are subject to the Exchange Act's registration and reporting requirements[14] by virtue of being listed on a national exchange. However, section 10(b) is not so limited and applies to all securities transactions utilizing an instrumentality of interstate commerce. Unlike most other provisions of the 1934 Act, section 9 is limited to securities on a national exchange and does not apply to the securities of the many registered reporting companies that are traded in the over-the-counter markets.[17] Section 15(c) of the Act—in prohibiting fraudulent broker-dealer practices—covers securities traded in the over-the-counter markets, in addition to municipal securities.[18]

In interpreting the relevant Exchange Act provisions, the courts have recognized the concept of manipulation as a narrow one. In the first instance, there is a specific intent requirement.[19] Manipulation, as that term is used in the securities laws, does not extend to many acts and practices that have the effect of manipulating the price of a security but are not specifically intended to do so. Presumably, manipulation has the same meaning under each of the Exchange Act provisions. In order to prevail in a suit charging manipulation, it must be proven that the defendant's primary intent in entering the transaction was price manipulation.[21] It is not sufficient that the challenged conduct simply had the effect of artificially affecting the price of the security. The Supreme Court has repeatedly stated that manipulation is "a term of art" limited to certain types of transactions specifically designed to artificially affect the price of a security.[22] Therefore, the fact that the conduct in question affects the price of a security will not by itself mean that it was an illegal manipulative act.[23] The presence of manipulative intent, however, renders conduct that affects price illegal manipulation.[24]

Two common examples of manipulation are wash sales and matched orders.[30] A wash sale is a fictitious sale where there is no change in beneficial ownership and thus no true economic consequence.[31] A matched order occurs

11. 15 U.S.C.A. § 78j(b).

12. 15 U.S.C.A. § 78*o*(c). Broker-dealer regulation and selected fraudulent and manipulative practices including churning, scalping, and boiler room operations are discussed in chapter 14 *infra*.

14. 15 U.S.C.A. §§ 78*l*, 78m(a). *See* §§ 9.2, 9.3 *supra*.

17. 15 U.S.C.A. § 78i(a). *See* §§ 9.2–9.3 *supra* for discussion of the 1934 Act's registration and periodic reporting requirements.

18. 15 U.S.C.A. § 78n(c)(1).

19. *See, e.g.,* Schreiber v. Burlington Northern, Inc., 472 U.S. 1, 105 S.Ct. 2458, 86 L.Ed.2d 1 (1985).

21. *E.g.,* S.E.C. v. U.S. Environmental, Inc., 155 F.3d 107 (2d Cir.1998).

22. Santa Fe Industries, Inc. v. Green, 430 U.S. 462, 476, 97 S.Ct. 1292, 1302, 51 L.Ed.2d 480 (1977); Ernst & Ernst v. Hochfelder, 425 U.S. 185, 199, 96 S.Ct. 1375, 1383, 47 L.Ed.2d 668 (1976). *Accord* Schreiber v. Burlington Northern, Inc., 472 U.S. 1, 105 S.Ct. 2458, 86 L.Ed.2d 1 (1985).

23. *See, e.g.,* Charter Communications, Inc. Securities Litigation, 443 F.3d 987 (8th Cir. 2006).

24. *E.g.,* Markowski v. SEC, 274 F.3d 525 (D.C.Cir. 2001).

30. *See, e.g.,* Edward J. Mawod & Co. v. SEC, 591 F.2d 588 (10th Cir.1979).

31. *See, e.g.,* Ernst & Ernst v. Hochfelder, 425 U.S. 185, 205, n. 25, 96 S.Ct. 1375, 47 L.Ed.2d 668 (1976); Dietrich v. Bauer, 76 F.Supp.2d 312, 339 (S.D.N.Y.1999).

when orders are entered simultaneously to buy and sell the same security.[32] Other illegal manipulative practices include: transferring record ownership of securities in order to hide the true identity of the beneficial owner, which is known as "parking";[33] executing a planned series of securities purchases that is specifically designed to artificially restrict the supply and thereby raise prices;[34] entering limit orders for the purpose of changing the published bid and asked prices;[35] and placing orders without an intent to follow through with the transaction.[36]

Manipulation can take many forms, but often has a number of common characteristics. For example, the following factors are "classic elements" of a market manipulation: (i) restriction of the "float" or floating supply of the securities in the public market; (ii) price leadership by the manipulator; (iii) dominating and controlling the market for the security; and (iv) a collapse of the market for the security after the manipulative activity has ceased.[38] The foregoing factors are indicia of market manipulation, but are not necessarily present in every manipulation case.[39]

Subjective intent combined with deceptive conduct can establish manipulation.[45] Manipulative conduct is not limited to conduct that actually causes a rise (or fall) in the stock price. It includes conduct that retards a decline in price that would otherwise result from supply and demand forces.[46]

§ 12.1[3] Manipulative and Deceptive Acts and Practices—Section 10; Section 15(c)

§ 12.1[3][A] Overview of Anti–Manipulation Provisions

A later chapter of this treatise[95] discusses in more detail the various SEC and NASD prohibitions that address fraudulent and deceptive practices generally as well as particular types of misconduct by broker-dealers. Broker-dealers and their employees are, of course, subject to Rule 10b–5's general

32. Dietrich v. Bauer, 76 F.Supp.2d 312, 340 (S.D.N.Y.1999) ("A market manipulation claim can also be based on matched orders—'orders for the purchase/sale of a security that are entered with the knowledge that orders of substantially the same size, at substantially the same time and price, have been or will be entered by the same or different persons for the sale/purchase of such security' ") (quoting Ernst & Ernst v. Hochfelder, 425 U.S. 185, 205, n. 25, 96 S.Ct. 1375, 47 L.Ed.2d 668 (1976)).

33. *See, e.g.,* Yoshikawa v. SEC, 192 F.3d 1209 (9th Cir.1999).

34. *See, e.g.,* SEC v. National Bankers Life Ins. Co., 334 F.Supp. 444, 446 (N.D.Tex.1971), *affirmed*, 477 F.2d 920 (5th Cir.1973).

35. In the Matter of Yoshikawa, Admin. Proc. File No. 3–12057, Release No. 34–53731, 2006 WL 1113518 (SEC 2006).

36. This is sometimes referred to as spoofing.

38. *See, e.g.,* SEC v. Resch–Cassin & Co., 362 F.Supp. 964, 976 (S.D.N.Y.1973).

A similar type of manipulation can take place with regard to mutual funds. "Marking the close" consists of making purchases of portfolio securities prior to the close of trading in order to raise the fund's closing price; this is known as "portfolio pumping" when this coincides with the end of a fiscal accounting period. *See, e.g.,* In the Matter of Parlin, 2001 SECDIG 2001–155–3, 2001 WL 898677 (SEC 2001). Marking the close is discussed at the end of this subsection.

39. In the Matter of Swartwood, Hesse, Inc., 50 S.E.C. 1301, 1307, Admin. Proc. No. 3–6985, Sec. Act Rel. No. 34–31212, 52 S.E.C. Docket 1557, 1992 WL 252184 (SEC 1992).

45. *See, e.g.,* Nanopierce Technologies, Inc. v. Southridge Capital Management LLC., 2002 WL 31819207 *8, Fed. Sec. L. Rep. ¶ 92253 (S.D.N.Y. 2002) (relying on Internet Law Library v. Southridge Capital Mgmt., 223 F.Supp.2d 474 (S.D.N.Y. 2002)).

46. In the Matter of Faherty, 2003 WL 1125247 (SEC 2003).

95. *See* §§ 14.3[6], 14.10[5], 14.14–14.23 *infra*.

anti-fraud proscriptions that prohibit any person from engaging in deceptive conduct in connection with a purchase or sale of a security.[96] SEC Rule 15c1–2[97] is a rule specifically tailored to broker-dealers and generally prohibits fraudulent, manipulative and deceptive practices in connection with securities brokerage transactions. The types of specific conduct that are addressed in other broker-dealer rules include market manipulation,[98] high pressure sales tactics,[99] deceptive recommendations,[100] generation of excessive commissions,[101] unauthorized trading,[102] improper order executions,[103] improper extension of credit for securities transactions,[104] and misuse of customer funds or securities.[105] Manipulation can arise in many respects in connection with a public offering of securities.[106] For example, SEC Regulation M[107] severely regulates purchases of publicly offered securities by participants in a public offering.

Beyond the above-mentioned specific manipulative broker-dealer activities and the general anti-manipulation and deception rules, the SEC makes it clear that violation of its rified SEC rules, but rather covers all conduct that operates as a deceptive or manipulative device.[108] In addition to the applicable statutes and SEC rules, the rules of the various self-regulatory organizations (the stock exchanges and the National Association of Securities Dealers) impose standards of conduct on broker dealers. Finally, these requirements may be supplemented in appropriate cases by fiduciary duty principles.[110] Because they result from artificial activity, manipulated prices are in and of themselves unfair.[111]

Section 10(a) of the 1934 Act[112] prohibits "short sales" and "stop loss" orders in violation of SEC rules.[113] Section 10(b), which is much broader, provides that it is unlawful "to use or employ [utilizing any means or instrumentality of interstate commerce], in connection with the purchase or sale of any security * * * any manipulative or deceptive device or contrivance in contravention of such rules and regulations as the Commission may prescribe as necessary or appropriate in the public interest or for the protec-

96. 17 C.F.R. § 240.10b–5. *See* §§ 12.3–12.12 *infra*.

97. 17 C.F.R. § 240.15c1–2.

98. *See* §§ 6.2–6.3 *supra* (manipulation in connection with public offerings), § 12.1 *supra* (manipulation generally), and § 14.10[5] *infra* (manipulation by market makers).

99. *See* § 14.18 *infra*.

100. *See* §§ 14.15–14.18 *infra*.

101. *See* § 14.20 *infra*.

102. *See* § 14.21 *infra*.

103. *See* § 14.13 *infra*.

104. *See* § 14.9 *infra*.

105. *See* § 14.8[2] *infra*.

106. *See* § 6.2 *supra* (discussing Regulation M and manipulation and stabilization during a distribution) and § 6.3 *supra* (discussing hot issues and work-out markets).

107. 17 C.F.R. §§ 242.101 *et seq.*

108. Rule 15c1–2(c), 17 C.F.R. § 240.15c1–2(c).

110. *See* § 14.15 *infra*.

111. *See, e.g.,* Universal Heritage Investments Corporation, 47 S.E.C. 839, 843 (1982).

112. 15 U.S.C.A. § 78j(a).

113. Rule 10a–1, 17 C.F.R. § 240.10a–1, formerly sets out the SEC's position. Rule 10a–1 was suspended when the SEC adopted Regulation SHO governing short sales. *See, e.g.,* Short Sales, Sec. Exch. Act Rel. No. 34–50103, 2004 WL 1697019 (SEC 2004) and was eventually repealed. *See* § 14.22 *infra*.

tion of investors."[114] The SEC, following the legislative mandate, has invoked its rulemaking authority to prohibit a wide variety of conduct that is outlined here and discussed more fully in other sections of this book.

§ 12.1[3][B][2] The Section 10(b) Rules

Rule 10b–1[115] applies the prohibitions against market manipulation contained in section 9(a)[116] to securities exempt from section 12's registration requirements.[117] Rule 10b–3 prohibits broker-dealers from engaging in manipulative or deceptive acts and practices with regard to securities not traded on a national exchange[122] and with regard to municipal securities.[123] Rule 10b–3 thus closes a large part of the gap left by section 9, which applies only to transactions effected through a national exchange.

Rule 10b–5[128] is the broadest of the section 10(b) rules. Rule 10b–5 prohibits material misstatements and omissions as well as fraudulent acts in connection with purchases and sales of securities; it supports a broad implied private right of action.[129] Because of its broad language, Rule 10b–5 covers a wide variety of conduct that is considered throughout this chapter as well as in other portions of this treatise.

Rule 10b–9 prohibits "all or none" offerings of securities unless all such securities are "sold at a specified price within a specified time, and * * * the total amount due to the seller is received by him by a specified date."[133] The rule imposes the same requirements for offerings where all or part of the purchase price will be refunded if the offering is not fully subscribed.[134] Rule 10b–9 does not apply where an underwriter or someone else is obligated to purchase all of the securities being offered.[135] A private right of action for violation of Rule 10b–9 has been recognized by at least one court.[136]

Rule 10b–10 requires that brokers confirm all transactions in writing.[137] The confirmation must disclose the broker's commission and whether he or she is acting as principal or as an agent for someone other than the customer.[138] The written confirmation in turn qualifies as a "prospectus" under section 2(a)(10) of the Securities Act of 1933,[139] which must comply with

114. 15 U.S.C.A. § 78j(b).

115. 17 C.F.R. § 240.10b–1.

116. 15 U.S.C.A. § 78i(a).

117. 15 U.S.C.A. § 78*l*.

122. 17 C.F.R. § 240.10b–3(a).

123. 17 C.F.R. § 240.10b–3(b). Municipal securities are discussed in § 14.6 *infra.*

128. 17 C.F.R. § 240.10b–5.

129. *See* §§ 12.3–12.4 *infra.*

133. 17 C.F.R. § 240.10b–9(a)(1).

134. 17 C.F.R. § 240.10b–9(a)(2).

135. 17 C.F.R. § 240.10b–9(b). *Cf.* Becherer v. Merrill Lynch Pierce, Fenner & Smith, Inc., 43 F.3d 1054 (6th Cir.1995) (Rule 10b–9 ceases to apply once the minimum sales conditions have been satisfied).

136. Bormann v. Applied Vision Systems, Inc., 800 F.Supp. 800 (D.Minn.1992) (describing the decision as a case of first impression).

137. 17 C.F.R. § 240.10b–10.

138. 17 C.F.R. § 240.10b–10. *Cf.* Chasins v. Smith, Barney & Co., 438 F.2d 1167 (2d Cir.1970) (decided prior to adoption of 10b–10 and holding failure to disclose market-maker status violated Rule 10b–5). *See* § 14.10 *infra.*

139. 15 U.S.C.A. § 77b(a)(10).

section 5(b)(1)'s requirement that there be a statutory prospectus absent an applicable exemption.[140]

Rule 10b–16[145] requires disclosure of credit terms in connection with margin transactions.[146] Rule 10b–17 prohibits untimely announcements of dividends, stock splits, reverse stock splits, and rights or subscription offerings.[147] The announcement must be in compliance with applicable exchange rules[148] or be given to the National Association of Securities Dealers (NASD)[149] at least ten days prior to the record date and must describe the nature of the distribution or offering.

Rule 10b–18 sets out a safe harbor rule for issuer purchases of its own shares.[150] Compliance with Rule 10b–18 precludes a finding of manipulative conduct.[151]

§ 12.1[3][C] Anti-Manipulation Rules Under Section 15 of the Exchange Act

Section 15(c) prohibits brokers and dealers from participating in manipulative, deceptive or fraudulent acts and practices in connection with sales, or attempts to induce purchases or sales, of securities.[187] This prohibition extends to dealings in municipal securities[188] and transactions in connection with the procedures set up to facilitate a national market system.[189] As is the case with section 10(b), the rules promulgated under section 15(c) span a wide variety of conduct.[193]

§ 12.1[4] Manipulation: Private Remedies

§ 12.1[4][A] Manipulation of Exchange Listed Securities—Section 9(e)'s Express Remedy

Section 9(e) gives a private remedy in damages to any investor who is injured by conduct in violation of section 9,[228] which is limited to securities on a national exchange. Section 9 requires that the plaintiff's injury arise out of the purchase or sale of a manipulated security; it is not sufficient that the plaintiff retained the security that was the subject of the alleged manipulation.[230] In addition to costs and reasonable attorneys' fees, the plaintiff is entitled to damages based on the difference between the actual value and the

140. 15 U.S.C.A. § 77e(b)(1), 77j. *See* §§ 2.4, 2.5 *supra.*

145. 17 C.F.R. § 240.10b–16.

146. *See* § 14.9 *infra.*

147. 17 C.F.R. § 240.10b–17.

148. 17 C.F.R. § 240.10b–17(b)(3).

149. 17 C.F.R. § 240.10b–17(b)(1).

150. 17 C.F.R. § 240.10b–18.

151. 17 C.F.R. § 240.10b–18.

187. 15 U.S.C.A. §§ 78*o*(c)(1), (c)(2).

188. 15 U.S.C.A. § 78*o*(c)(2). *See* § 14.6 *infra.*

189. 15 U.S.C.A. § 78*o*(c)(6). *See* § 14.2 *infra.*

193. Many of these rules are discussed in other sections of this book. *See* especially chapter 14 *infra.*

228. 15 U.S.C.A. § 78i(e). As discussed *infra,* section 9(e)'s express remedy is limited to exchange-listed securities.

230. Lowe v. Salomon Smith Barney, Inc., 206 F.Supp.2d 442 (W.D.N.Y.2002) (dismissing plaintiff's manipulation claim).

price as affected by the manipulative conduct.[231] Liability under section 9(e) is expressly limited to persons "willfully" participating in the manipulative conduct; willfulness would seem to be an even stricter requirement than scienter, which is required generally in suits under Rule 10b–5.[232] It must be remembered that, in addition to the defendant's willful participation, the substantive violation requires proof of manipulative intent. In addition, to recover for manipulative conduct, the plaintiff must show that his or her injury was a direct, rather than remote, consequence of the prohibited activity. All of the foregoing factors combine to make the section 9(e) private remedy a very limited one.

§ 12.1[4][B] Manipulation: Implied Remedies

The Fifth Circuit initially held that manipulative activity that comes within the scope of section 9 cannot give rise to a Rule 10b–5 action independently; plaintiff had to establish that all of section 9's elements had been met.[236] Quite properly, however, that decision was vacated and remanded[237] for further consideration in light of Herman & MacLean v. Huddleston,[238] which held that the remedies under Rule 10b–5 and section 11 of the 1933 Act[239] are cumulative. In light of that Supreme Court ruling, it seems implausible that the section 9 and Rule 10b–5 remedies are mutually exclusive.[240] In other words, a plaintiff injured by the defendant's manipulative conduct may sue under either or both sections.[241] Accordingly, it is clear that manipulation can form the basis of a Rule 10b–5 claim, provided that all of the elements of a 10b–5 claim can be established.

§ 12.2 Implied Remedies in the Federal Courts

§ 12.2[1] The Trend Limiting Implied Remedies

Although the securities laws provide a wide variety of express statutory remedies for injured investors,[1] powerful private enforcement weapons have arisen out of implied rights of action. However, for more than thirty years the Supreme Court has been narrowing the number of implied remedies available under federal statutes.[2] This narrowing trend has resulted in limiting the

231. 15 U.S.C.A. § 78i(e).

232. *See* § 12.8 *infra.*

236. Chemetron Corp. v. Business Funds, Inc., 682 F.2d 1149 (5th Cir.1982), *vacated and remanded*, 460 U.S. 1007, 103 S.Ct. 1245, 75 L.Ed.2d 476 (1983), *on remand*, 718 F.2d 725 (5th Cir.1983).

237. *Id.*

238. 459 U.S. 375, 103 S.Ct. 683, 74 L.Ed.2d 548 (1983).

239. 15 U.S.C.A. § 77k. *See* §§ 7.3, 7.4 *supra.*

240. *See also, e.g.,* Marc I. Steinberg, The Propriety and Scope of Cumulative Remedies Under the Federal Securities Laws, 67 Cornell L.Rev. 557 (1982).

241. *See, e.g.,* Chemetron Corp. v. Business Funds, Inc., 718 F.2d 725 (5th Cir.1983).

§ 12.2

1. Sections 11, 12(a)(1), and 12(a)(2) of the 1933 Act, 15 U.S.C.A. §§ 77k, 77*l*(a)(1), (2); *see* §§ 7.2–7.6 *supra* (dealing with, respectively, misleading registration materials, failure to comply with that Act's prospectus requirements, and material misstatements by sellers of securities); Sections 9(e), 16(b), and 18(a) of the Exchange Act, 15 U.S.C.A. §§ 78i(e), 78p(b), 78r(a) (dealing with manipulation of exchange-listed securities, disgorgement of insider short-swing profits, and material misstatements and omissions in SEC filings).

2. *See, e.g.,* Correctional Services Corp. v. Malesko, 534 U.S. 61, 67, n.3, 122 S.Ct. 515, 151 L.Ed.2d 456 (2001) ("we have retreated from our previous willingness to imply a cause of action

remedies that continue to be recognized. Since it is clear that private remedies will not lightly be read into the statutes, it is questionable whether additional new remedies will be recognized. On the other hand, there are some firmly entrenched implied rights of action for securities law violations; however, even they have been significantly narrowed since the mid 1970s.

The restrictive trend of the implication cases generally has not bypassed the securities laws. The Supreme Court has reaffirmed its past recognition of implied private rights of action for violations of Rule 10b–5 and section 10(b) of the Securities Exchange Act of 1934[3] and the proxy disclosure requirements of section 14(a) of the Act.[4] At the same time, there has been a narrowing of the scope of these remedies.[5] The Supreme Court denied the existence of an implied remedy for damages under the anti-fraud provision of the Investment Advisers Act of 1940,[8] and found no such remedy under section 17(a) of the Securities Exchange Act of 1934.[9] Also, in another case, the Court held that a competing tender offeror does not have an implied remedy for violation of the Exchange Act's anti-fraud provisions with regard to tender offers, but nevertheless indicated that a private remedy may exist in the hands of a more appropriate plaintiff.[10]

The Supreme Court ruled that there is no implied right of action against aiders and abettors of securities laws violations.[11] Notwithstanding these and other narrowing decisions, the Court held that the Rule 10b–5 remedy is cumulative and applies even though there may be express remedies covering the transaction in question.[12]

---

where Congress has not provided one.... Just last Term it was noted that we 'abandoned' the view of *Borak* decades ago, and have repeatedly declined to 'revert' to 'the understanding of private causes of action that held sway 40 years ago.' ") (quoting Alexander v. Sandoval, 532 U.S. 275, 287, 121 S.Ct. 1511, 149 L.Ed.2d 517 (2001)).

3. 15 U.S.C.A. § 78j(b); 17 C.F.R. § 240.10b–5.

4. 15 U.S.C.A. § 78n(a); 17 C.F.R. § 240.14a–9.

5. *See, e.g.,* Central Bank of Denver v. First Interstate Bank of Denver, 511 U.S. 164, 114 S.Ct. 1439, 128 L.Ed.2d 119 (1994) (there is no implied remedy against aiders and abettors); Santa Fe Industries, Inc. v. Green, 430 U.S. 462, 97 S.Ct. 1292, 51 L.Ed.2d 480 (1977) (Rule 10b–5 covers only deceptive conduct), *on remand*, 562 F.2d 4 (2d Cir.1977); Ernst & Ernst v. Hochfelder, 425 U.S. 185, 96 S.Ct. 1375, 47 L.Ed.2d 668 (1976), *rehearing denied*, 425 U.S. 986, 96 S.Ct. 2194, 48 L.Ed.2d 811 (1976) (a violation of Rule 10b–5 requires a showing of scienter); Blue Chip Stamps v. Manor Drug Stores, 421 U.S. 723, 95 S.Ct. 1917, 44 L.Ed.2d 539 (1975), *rehearing denied*, 423 U.S. 884, 96 S.Ct. 157, 46 L.Ed.2d 114 (1975) (plaintiff must have been a purchaser or seller).

8. Transamerica Mortgage Advisors, Inc. v. Lewis, 444 U.S. 11, 100 S.Ct. 242, 62 L.Ed.2d 146 (1979). The Court there did, however, recognize an implied right of rescission. The Investment Advisers Act is discussed in chapter 21 *infra.*

9. Touche Ross & Co. v. Redington, 442 U.S. 560, 99 S.Ct. 2479, 61 L.Ed.2d 82 (1979), *on remand*, 612 F.2d 68 (2d Cir.1979).

10. Piper v. Chris–Craft Industries, Inc., 430 U.S. 1, 97 S.Ct. 926, 51 L.Ed.2d 124 (1977), *rehearing denied*, 430 U.S. 976, 97 S.Ct. 1668, 52 L.Ed.2d 371 (1977). Section 14(e) is discussed in §§ 11.6, 11.10 *supra.*

11. Stoneridge Investment Partners v. Scientific Atlanta, ___ U.S. ___, 128 S.Ct. 761, 169 L.Ed.2d 627 (2008); Central Bank of Denver v. First Interstate Bank of Denver, 511 U.S. 164, 114 S.Ct. 1439, 128 L.Ed.2d 119 (1994), which is discussed in § 12.25 *infra. See also, e.g.,* Gustafson v. Alloyd Co., 513 U.S. 561, 115 S.Ct. 1061, 131 L.Ed.2d 1 (1995) (giving a tortured and narrow reading to the express remedy under section 12(2) of the 1933 Act); the *Gustafson* case is discussed in § 7.6 *supra.*

12. Herman & MacLean v. Huddleston, 459 U.S. 375, 103 S.Ct. 683, 74 L.Ed.2d 548 (1983), *on remand*, 705 F.2d 775 (5th Cir.1983). *See* §§ 7.3, 7.4, *supra* and 12.18 *infra.*

§ 12.3 Section 10(b) and the Evolution of the Implied Remedy Under SEC Rule 10b–5

§ 12.3[1] The Statutory Context

The primary private remedy for fraud available under the Securities Exchange Act has been the one implied in SEC Rule 10b–5,[1] which prohibits fraudulent conduct in connection with a purchase or sale of securities. Although several Supreme Court cases have limited the scope of the 10b–5 private right of action, it continues to be a significant weapon against securities fraud. To put the Rule 10b–5 remedy in its proper perspective, it must be viewed in conjunction with the other modes of private relief provided by the securities laws. Some of the concurrent antifraud provisions are found in the Securities Act of 1933.

The 1933 Act contains two sections providing for express private damage remedies for misrepresentation in connection with the sale of a security.[4] These supplement the 1933 Act's general antifraud provision embodied in section 17(a).[5] Section 17(a) does not create an express right of action, but, although there is considerable authority to the contrary, it has been held by some courts to support an implied private remedy. In contrast to these provisions in the 1933 Act, the express remedies available under the Securities Exchange Act of 1934 are much more limited in scope. Section 9(e) of the Exchange Act[7] confers a private right of action upon an injured investor against one who has willfully engaged in market manipulation of securities subject to the 1934 Act's registration and reporting requirements[8] by virtue of those securities listed on a national exchange.[9] Section 18(a) of the Act[10] sets out a private right of action for an investor who has been injured due to reliance on materially misleading statements or omissions of material facts in documents required to be filed with the Commission. Section 16(b)'s disgorgement of insider short-swing profits[11] is the third express private remedy contained in the 1934 Act. A fourth private remedy was created by The Insider Trading and Securities Fraud Enforcement Act of 1988.[12]

The express remedies under the 1933 Act apply only to fraud in connection with the sale of securities, thus providing protection only to injured purchasers and not to injured sellers. The 1934 Act s express remedies do not distinguish between purchasers and sellers. The 1934 Act's express remedies are restricted, however, to securities subject to the Act's reporting require-

---

§ 12.3

1. 17 C.F.R. § 240.10b–5.

4. Sections 11 and 12(a)(2). 15 U.S.C.A. §§ 77k, 77*l*(a)(2). *See* §§ 7.2–7.6 *supra.* This is in addition to section 12(a)(1), which provides a right of rescission for all securities sold in violation of the Act's registration provisions. 15 U.S.C.A. § 77l(a)(1). *See* § 7.2 *supra.*

5. 15 U.S.C.A. § 77q(a).

7. 15 U.S.C.A. § 78i(e). *See* § 12.1 *supra.*

8. The scope of the Exchange Act's issuer registration and reporting requirements is discussed in §§ 9.2–9.3 *supra.*

9. *See* section 6 of the 1934 Act, 15 U.S.C.A. § 78f. Section 9 is thus more limited than most of the 1934 Act's liability and reporting provisions, which apply equally to many over-the-counter securities. 15 U.S.C.A. § 78*l*. *See* §§ 9.2, 9.3 *supra.*

10. 15 U.S.C.A. § 78r(a). *See* § 12.18 *infra.*

11. 15 U.S.C.A. § 78p(b). *See* chapter 13 *infra.*

12. Section 20A, 15 U.S.C.A. § 78t–1. *See* § 12.17 *infra.*

ments.[13] These express remedies are also subject to a number of other limiting factors that are discussed in earlier sections of this book. Section 10(b)[14] and Rule 10b–5[15] do not have many of these limiting factors. Although arguments have been made to the contrary, the overwhelming majority of decisions agree that the Rule 10b–5 remedy is cumulative with the express remedies noted above.[16]

§ 12.3[2] History of Rule 10b–5

A proper perspective on Rule 10b–5 also requires an examination of the rule's history and development. The general antifraud provision of the 1934 Act is contained in section 10(b), which provides that it is unlawful "to use or employ [utilizing any means or instrumentality of interstate commerce], in connection with the purchase or sale of any security * * * any manipulative or deceptive device or contrivance in contravention of such rules and regulations as the Commission may prescribe as necessary or appropriate in the public interest or for the protection of investors."[18] In Rule 10b–5 it fashioned its most encompassing antifraud prohibition.

Promulgated in 1942, Rule 10b–5 was patterned directly upon section 17(a) of the 1933 Act.[22] However, 10b–5 further extends to misstatements and omissions occurring in connection with either a *purchase or sale* of securities, while the parent section is limited to fraudulent sales and offers to sell. The rule prohibits: (1) fraudulent devices and schemes, (2) misstatements and omissions of material facts, and (3) acts and practices which operate as a fraud or deceit.[23] When it adopted Rule 10b–5, the Commission, without even realizing its eventual reach, created a powerful antifraud weapon.[24] According to one account, the decision to adopt the rule and model it on section 17(a) was arrived at without any deliberation, with the only official discussion consisting of one SEC Commissioner reportedly observing, "we are against fraud, aren't we?"[25] Given this background, it is clear that not much can be gleaned from the history of the rule, although the courts frequently refer to the legislative history behind the statute. The clear purpose of Rule 10b–5 is to provide protection against investors being duped into purchasing or selling securities.

---

13. The same is also true of some implied remedies. For example, the implied remedy under proxy Rule 14a–9 protects shareholders injured in connection with shareholder votes and does not necessarily involve either a purchase or sale. 17 C.F.R. § 240.14a–9. *See, e.g.,* J.I. Case Co. v. Borak, 377 U.S. 426, 84 S.Ct. 1555, 12 L.Ed.2d 423 (1964).

14. 15 U.S.C.A. § 78j(b).

15. 17 C.F.R. § 240.10b–5. *See* §§ 12.3–12.21 *infra.*

16. *See, e.g.,* Herman & MacLean v. Huddleston, 459 U.S. 375, 103 S.Ct. 683, 74 L.Ed.2d 548 (1983), *on remand,* 705 F.2d 775 (5th Cir.1983).

18. 15 U.S.C.A. § 78j(b). *See generally* Steve Thel, The Original Conception of Section 10(b) of the Securities Exchange Act, 42 Stan.L.Rev. 385 (1990); Symposium, Happy Birthday 10b–5: 50 Years of Antifraud Regulation, 61 Fordham L.Rev. S1 (1993).

22. 15 U.S.C.A. § 77q(a).

23. 17 C.F.R. § 240.10b–5.

24. *See* Sec.Exch. Act Rel. No. 34–3230 (May 21, 1942) ("The new rule closes a loophole in the protections against fraud administered by the commission by prohibiting individuals or companies from buying securities if they engage in fraud in their purchase").

25. *See* Milton Freeman, in Conference on Codification of the Federal Securities Laws, 22 Bus.Law. 793, 922 (1967).

§ 12.3[3] The Development of the Implied Rule 10b–5 Remedy

In 1946, a federal district court held that, notwithstanding the absence of an express private right of action, Rule 10b–5 gives rise to a private remedy in the hands of injured investors.[27] The implied remedy started to grow and flourish in the district and circuit courts but did not receive formal Supreme Court approval until twenty-four years later.[28] Over the years, there seems to have been a general demise of implied remedies in the federal courts.[29] Nevertheless, the Rule 10b–5 remedy remains firmly entrenched. The Rule 10b–5 action has, however, been cut down in scope in many respects.

In the 1970s and 1980s, a series of Supreme Court cases limited the scope of the private right of action under Rule 10b–5; this trend continues. First, the Court ruled that, in order to maintain an action, the plaintiff must be either a purchaser or seller of the securities in question.[32] Second, a showing of negligent conduct will not suffice; the defendant must have acted with scienter.[33] Third, the conduct complained of must be "deceptive."[34] Notwithstanding these limiting decisions, which are discussed in later sections, the Rule 10b–5 implied remedy remains an important one in appropriate cases for a number of reasons.

It is quite easy to establish federal jurisdiction to support a Rule 10b–5 claim. All that is required is for some aspect of the securities transaction under attack to have been carried out through the use of an instrumentality of interstate commerce. For example, even an intrastate telephone call is sufficient to satisfy the jurisdictional requirements of Rule 10b–5.[38] While a face-to-face conversation itself will not satisfy the jurisdictional requirements, there may be 10b–5 jurisdiction if the conversations are part of a transaction that utilizes an instrumentality of interstate commerce.[39] Also, although it might be argued that the language of section 10(b) and Rule 10b–5 require otherwise, it seems to be the majority rule that it is not necessary that the misrepresentation be communicated through an instrumentality of interstate commerce, so long as there is a connection between the use of the jurisdictional means and the fraud. Thus, for example, a telephone conversation that followed face-to-face delivery of the offering memorandum was sufficient to trigger federal jurisdiction for a Rule 10b–5 action.[41] The court pointed out

27. Kardon v. National Gypsum Co., 69 F.Supp. 512 (E.D.Pa.1946).

28. Superintendent of Insurance v. Bankers Life & Casualty Co., 404 U.S. 6, 92 S.Ct. 165, 30 L.Ed.2d 128 (1971), *on remand*, 401 F.Supp. 640 (S.D.N.Y.1975). In the course of one of its subsequent limiting 10b–5 decisions, the Court observed that 10b–5 represented a legislative acorn that had grown into a judicial oak badly in need of pruning. Blue Chip Stamps v. Manor Drug Stores, 421 U.S. 723, 737, 95 S.Ct. 1917, 1926, 44 L.Ed.2d 539 (1975), *rehearing denied*, 423 U.S. 884, 96 S.Ct. 157, 46 L.Ed.2d 114 (1975).

29. *See* § 12.2 *supra*.

32. Blue Chip Stamps v. Manor Drug Stores, 421 U.S. 723, 95 S.Ct. 1917, 44 L.Ed.2d 539 (1975). *See* § 12.7 *infra*.

33. Ernst & Ernst v. Hochfelder, 425 U.S. 185, 96 S.Ct. 1375, 47 L.Ed.2d 668 (1976).

34. Santa Fe Industries, Inc. v. Green, 430 U.S. 462, 97 S.Ct. 1292, 51 L.Ed.2d 480 (1977).

38. Loveridge v. Dreagoux, 678 F.2d 870 (10th Cir.1982); Dupuy v. Dupuy, 511 F.2d 641 (5th Cir.1975).

39. Leiter v. Kuntz, 655 F.Supp. 725 (D.Utah 1987) (mailing of financial statement by defendant's attorney plus use of telephone to change face-to-face meeting held sufficient to support Rule 10b–5 jurisdiction).

41. Lopes v. Vieira, 543 F Supp.2d 1149, 1172–73 (C.D. Cal. 2008) (the court noted that in addition, drafts of the offering memorandum allegedly were circulated through an instrumentality of interstate commerce).

that " 'the crookedness need not appear at all in the instrumentality used' "and that it is " 'sufficient if it were shown that fraud was used or employed *in connection with* the use of instruments of interstate commerce or the mails.' "[42]

Additionally, through the doctrine of pendent or supplemental jurisdiction,[43] a plaintiff with a Rule 10b–5 claim may bring related state statutory or common law claims into the federal court. The significance of pendent jurisdiction has diminished because of the Securities Litigation Uniform Standards Act of 1998, which preempted state law with regard to class actions of fifty persons or more involving securities fraud.[46] Individual actions, class actions on behalf of fewer than fifty persons, and derivative actions may still have parallel state law claims.[47]

The Rule 10b–5 remedy may be used in a wide variety of factual contexts. The 10b–5 action has been used to address the problems of material corporate misstatements or nondisclosures,[51] insider trading,[52] and corporate mismanagement problems that arise in the context of transactions in shares or other securities.[53] Furthermore, a parallel antifraud remedy has been implied under proxy Rule 14a–9.[54] There will frequently be cumulative Rule 10b–5 and 14a–9 remedies available in the case of mergers and corporate reorganizations, which involve both a shareholder vote and securities transactions.[55] Similarly, Rule 10b–5 has a role to play in the tender offer context, which involves the sale of target company stock.[56] In addition, the fact that securities may be exempt from registration under the Securities Act of 1933[57] will not preclude an action under Rule 10b–5. Thus, for example, a 10b–5 action may be brought for fraud in connection with United States Treasury securities,[58] or with regard to municipal securities.[59] One exception is short term commercial paper, which is expressly excluded from the 1934 Act's definition of a security.[60] Rule 10b–5 will not apply to transactions involving short term commercial paper falling within the statutory exclusion.

42. Lopes v. Vieira, 543 F. Supp.2d 1149, 1173 (C.D. Cal. 2008) (quoting from Errion v. Connell), 236 F.2d 447, 455 (9th Cir.1956).

43. *See* United Mine Workers of America v. Gibbs, 383 U.S. 715, 86 S.Ct. 1130, 16 L.Ed.2d 218 (1966). *See* § 17.1[4] *infra.*

46. 1934 Act § 28(f), 15 U.S.C.A. § 78bb(f); 1933 Act § 16(f), 15 U.S.C.A. § 77p(f). *See* §§ 12.15[2], 17.1[6] *infra.*

47. *See* § 12.15[2] *infra.* Additionally, suits charging breaches of fiduciary duty are carved out of the federal preemption. *Id. See, e.g.,* Derdiger v. Tallman, 75 F.Supp.2d 322 (D.Del.1999); Lalondriz v. USA Networks, Inc., 31 Sec. Reg. & L. Rep. (BNA) 1007 (S.D.N.Y. 1999).

51. *See* § 12.9 *infra.*

52. *See* § 12.17 *infra.*

53. *See* § 12.20 *infra.*

The private remedy under Rule 10b–5 also has been used to seek redress against various pernicious broker-dealer practices. *See, e.g.,* § 14.20 *infra* for a discussion of churning.

54. 17 C.F.R. § 240.14a–9. *See* J.I. Case Co. v. Borak, 377 U.S. 426, 84 S.Ct. 1555, 12 L.Ed.2d 423 (1964).

55. *See, e.g.,* SEC v. National Securities, Inc., 393 U.S. 453, 468, 89 S.Ct. 564, 573, 21 L.Ed.2d 668 (1969) (The overlap is "neither unusual nor unfortunate").

56. *See also* section 14(e) of the Williams Act, 15 U.S.C.A. § 78n(e); §§ 11.6, 11.10 *supra.*

57. *See* § 4.1 *supra.*

58. *E.g.,* Kahn v. Salomon Brothers, Inc., 813 F.Supp. 191 (E.D.N.Y.1993). The regulation of government securities dealers is discussed in § 14.7 *infra.*

59. The regulation of municipal securities dealers is discussed in § 14.6 *infra.*

60. 5 U.S.C.A. § 78c(a)(10). *See* § 4.4 *supra.*

§ 12.4 Rule 10b–5 Overview; Summary of the Principal Elements

There are five principal elements for stating a claim under Rule 10b–5. The plaintiff must show: (1) fraud or deceit (2) by any person (3) in connection with (4) the purchase or sale (5) of any security. Furthermore, since Rule 10b–5, like its parent section, requires deceit or fraud, the elements of common law fraud—materiality, reliance, causation, and damages—thus must be part of any Rule 10b–5 claim.

Fraud or Deceit—the Deception Requirement

Since section 10(b) speaks in terms of deceptive acts, "deception" is a necessary element of any Rule 10b–5 violation.[22] Thus, Rule 10b–5 focuses on disclosure and misrepresentation and does not cover all transactions that cause injury or otherwise result in unfairness to investors.[23]

Purchase or Sale

An important corollary to the "purchase or sale" requirement is that, in order to have standing to sue, a 10b–5 plaintiff in a private damages action must have been either a purchaser or seller of the securities that form the basis of the material omission, misstatement, or deceptive conduct.[24] Most courts allow a remedy for a corporation (or in a shareholder derivative suit) for certain transactions in its own shares, including corporate repurchases of its own shares at an inflated price, or an additional issuance of corporate shares on an unfavorable basis.[25]

By Any Person

As pointed out directly above and as discussed in a subsequent section of this treatise,[26] a plaintiff in a private damage action under Rule 10b–5 must have been a purchaser or seller of the security forming the basis of the complaint.[27] There is no parallel requirement for defendants in Rule 10b–5 actions.

The courts generally have assumed that it is not necessary for the defendant to have been a purchaser or seller of securities in order to be held to have violated Rule 10b–5.[28] Any statement reasonably calculated to affect

§ 12.4

22. *See, e.g.,* Schreiber v. Burlington Northern, Inc., 472 U.S. 1, 105 S.Ct. 2458, 86 L.Ed.2d 1 (1985); Santa Fe Industries, Inc. v. Green, 430 U.S. 462, 97 S.Ct. 1292, 51 L.Ed.2d 480 (1977); Ernst & Ernst v. Hochfelder, 425 U.S. 185, 96 S.Ct. 1375, 47 L.Ed.2d 668 (1976).

23. *See, e.g.,* Schreiber v. Burlington Northern, Inc., 472 U.S. 1, 105 S.Ct. 2458, 86 L.Ed.2d 1 (1985); Santa Fe Industries, Inc. v. Green, 430 U.S. 462, 97 S.Ct. 1292, 51 L.Ed.2d 480 (1977); § 12.20 *infra.*

24. Blue Chip Stamps v. Manor Drug Stores, 421 U.S. 723, 95 S.Ct. 1917, 44 L.Ed.2d 539 (1975), *rehearing denied,* 423 U.S. 884, 96 S.Ct. 157, 46 L.Ed.2d 114 (1975). The purchaser/seller standing requirement is discussed in § 12.7 *infra.*

25. Alabama Farm Bureau Mutual Casualty Co. v. American Fidelity Life Ins. Co., 606 F.2d 602 (5th Cir.1979), *cert. denied,* 449 U.S. 820, 101 S.Ct. 77, 66 L.Ed.2d 22 (1980) (repurchase of shares); Bailes v. Colonial Press, Inc., 444 F.2d 1241 (5th Cir.1971) (issuance of shares); Ruckle v. Roto American Corp., 339 F.2d 24 (2d Cir.1964) (issuance of shares).

26. *See* § 12.7 *infra.*

27. *E.g.,* Blue Chip Stamps v. Manor Drug Stores, 421 U.S. 723, 95 S.Ct. 1917, 44 L.Ed.2d 539 (1975), *rehearing denied,* 423 U.S. 884, 96 S.Ct. 157, 46 L.Ed.2d 114 (1975).

28. *See, e.g.,* Basic Inc. v. Levinson, 485 U.S. 224, 108 S.Ct. 978, 99 L.Ed.2d 194 (1988) (upholding liability for misleading statement but not directly addressing whether defendant's not being a purchaser or seller precluded liability).

the investment decision of a reasonable investor will satisfy the "in connection with" requirement even if the defendant was not a purchaser or seller.[29] Thus, for example, a non-seller who makes statements that induce the sale in question may be liable even though not an actual seller of the securities in question.[30] This does not mean, however, that liability for Rule 10b–5 violations will extend to all collateral participants. Although aiders and abettors can be held liable in criminal[31]and SEC enforcement actions,[32] aiders and abettors are not subject to liability in private damages actions.[33] Thus, in private suits, only primary violators can be held liable.[34] In determining who is a primary violator, the Supreme Court made it clear that it is not sufficient to have knowingly participated in a scheme, there must have been some basis on which the plaintiff can be said to have relied on the defendant's participation or conduct.[35]

Of Any Security

Rule 10b–5 applies to any purchase or sale by any person of *any* security. The fact that a security is exempt from 1933 or 1934 Act registration does not affect the applicability of Rule 10b–5's proscriptions.[36] The rule applies regardless of whether the security is registered under the 1934 Act, and regardless of whether the company is publicly-held or closely-held. Rule 10b–5 applies even to government and municipal securities, and in fact, to any kind of entity that issues something which can be called a "security." Because of this broad scope, the rule may be invoked in many situations. As a result of the Commodity Futures Modernization Act of 2000,[37] section 10(b) now applies to security-based swap agreements even though those instruments are not securities.[38]

Scienter

One of the essential elements of a fraud claim is demonstrating that the defendant acted with scienter. In its strictest sense, scienter means an intent to deceive, but there is substantial authority under common law that making statements in reckless disregard of the truth will suffice to establish scienter.[40] In 1976, the Supreme Court held that a valid claim for damages under Rule

29. SEC v. Texas Gulf Sulphur, 401 F.2d 833 (2d Cir.1968), *cert. denied*, 394 U.S. 976, 89 S.Ct. 1454, 22 L.Ed.2d 756 (1969) (misstatements in a corporate press release were made "in connection with" purchases and sales made by shareholders in the open market and violated Rule 10b–5, even though corporation itself was not buying nor selling shares).

30. Keeling v. Telehub Communications Corp., 2001 WL 688495, [2000–2001 Transfer Binder] Fed. Sec. L. Rep. (CCH) ¶ 91,330 (N.D. Ill. 2001).

31. 18 U.S.C.A. § 2. *See, e.g.,* United States v. Bradstreet, 135 F.3d 46 (1st Cir.1998) (upholding criminal conviction for aiding and abetting).

32. 15 U.S.C.A. § 78t(e).

33. Central Bank of Denver, N.A. v. First Interstate Bank of Denver, 511 U.S. 164, 114 S.Ct. 1439, 128 L.Ed.2d 119 (1994). *See* § 12.25 *infra.*

34. *See* § 12.25[3] *infra.*

35. Stoneridge Investment Partners, LLC v. Scientific–Atlanta, Inc., ___ U.S. ___, 128 S.Ct. 761, 169 L.Ed.2d 627 (2008).

36. Ontario Public Service Employees Union Pension Trust Funds v. Nortel Networks Corp., 369 F.3d 27 (2d Cir. 2004) (citing this treatise).

37. Pub. Law 106–554, 114 Stat. 2763 (December 21, 2000).

38. 15 U.S.C.A. § 78j(b).

40. *See* the authorities in § 12.18 *infra.*

10b–5 must establish that the defendant acted with scienter.[41] The Court, however, did not decide whether a showing of reckless conduct would satisfy the scienter requirement. Nevertheless, the majority of lower court decisions have found that recklessness is sufficient to state a claim under Rule 10b–5.[43] In the wake of the Private Securities Litigation Reform Act of 1995,[44] scienter is generally interpreted to require a showing of extreme recklessness, which belies a bright-line test and ordinarily requires a fact-intensive analysis.[45]

Duty to Disclose

Since Rule 10b–5 is a fraud-based rule, in order to impose liability for a material omission, it is necessary to establish that the alleged violator was in fact under a duty to disclose.[46] Rule 10b–5(b) provides that an omission of fact violates the rule when the omitted fact would be "necessary to make the statements made, in light of the circumstances under which they were made, not misleading."[47] This means that absent a statement or separate SEC rule requiring disclosure, there is no affirmative duty to disclose facts simply because they are material. Accordingly, in the absence of an SEC line-item disclosure requirement or a duty created by improper insider trading,[48] there is no duty to speak. In other words, absent such a duty, "silence is golden."[49]

Materiality

In order for a misstatement or omission to be actionable under Rule 10b–5, it must be a material one. The Supreme Court has defined materiality in terms of the type of information that a reasonable investor would consider significant in making an investment decision.[50] The materiality of a particular item is based on a highly factual inquiry and is to be determined within the total mix of information that is publicly available.[51]

---

41. Ernst & Ernst v. Hochfelder, 425 U.S. 185, 96 S.Ct. 1375, 47 L.Ed.2d 668 (1976). In 1980, the Court held that the scienter standard applies under Rule 10b–5 regardless of whether the action is a private damage action or an enforcement action brought by the Commission. Aaron v. SEC, 446 U.S. 680, 100 S.Ct. 1945, 64 L.Ed.2d 611 (1980), *on remand*, 666 F.2d 5 (2d Cir.1981). *See* § 12.8 *infra* for a discussion of the scienter requirement.

43. *See* § 12.8 *infra*.

44. The Private Securities Litigation Reform Act ("PSLRA") is discussed in detail in § 12.15[1] *infra*. Its applicability to pleading and proving scienter is discussed in § 12.8[4] *infra*. *See* Tellabs, Inc. v. Makor Issues & Rights, Ltd., 551 U.S. 308, 127 S.Ct. 2499, 168 L.Ed.2d 179 (2007).

45. *See* Dolphin and Bradbury, Inc. v. SEC, 512 F.3d 634, 639 (D.C. Cir. 2008) (quoting this treatise).

46. Chiarella v. United States, 445 U.S. 222, 100 S.Ct. 1108, 63 L.Ed.2d 348 (1980).

47. 17 C.F.R. § 240.10b–5(b).

48. *See* § 12.17 *infra* for discussion of the "disclose or abstain" rule as it relates to trading on non-public information.

49. *See* Corporate Property Associates 14 Inc. v. CHR Holding Corp., 2008 WL 963048 at *1 (Del. Ch. Ct. 2008).

50. Basic Inc. v. Levinson, 485 U.S. 224, 108 S.Ct. 978, 99 L.Ed.2d 194 (1988) (decided under Rule 10b–5); TSC Industries, Inc. v. Northway, Inc., 426 U.S. 438, 96 S.Ct. 2126, 48 L.Ed.2d 757 (1976) (decided under the proxy rules).

51. As materiality questions are highly fact-specific, summary judgment will rarely be appropriate. Materiality is discussed in § 12.9 *infra*.

Reliance

Following the basic requirements for proving common law fraud, reliance is an element of any Rule 10b–5 claim.[52] In a sharply divided decision, the Supreme Court recognized the fraud-on-the-market presumption of reliance[53] under which a showing that a material misstatement or omission adversely affected the market price creates a presumption of reliance.[54] Defendant may rebut the presumption of reliance or show that reliance was unreasonable.[55]

Causation

Again, as is the case with common law fraud, in addition to scienter, materiality, and reliance, causation is an element of a Rule 10b–5 action. Many courts have divided causation into two subparts: transaction causation and loss causation. Transaction causation requires a showing that, but-for the violations in question, the transaction would not have occurred (at least in the form that it took). Loss causation requires a showing of a causal nexus between the transaction and the plaintiff's loss.[56]

Damages

Also, as is the case with any fraud claim, the plaintiff must be able to establish damages. In most Rule 10b–5 litigation, the appropriate measure of damages is the out-of-pocket loss proximately caused by the material misstatement or omission.[57]

Statute of Limitations

As part of the Sarbanes–Oxley Act,[60] Congress enacted a longer statute of limitations (two years from discovery but not more than five years after the violation) for "a claim of fraud, deceit, manipulation, or contrivance in contravention of a regulatory requirement concerning the securities laws."[61]

Cumulative Remedies

In Herman & MacLean v. Huddleston,[62] the Supreme Court held that the remedies under Section 11 of the 1933 Act, for misstatements in registration materials, and Rule 10b–5 are cumulative. Presumably, Rule 10b–5 remedies are cumulative with other express remedies as well.

§ 12.5 "In Connection With" the Purchase or Sale of Any Security

The courts have generally assumed it is not necessary that the defendant have been a purchaser or seller of securities in order to be held to have violated Rule 10b–5.[1] It is sufficient that the material misstatement, omission,

52. Reliance is discussed in § 12.10 *infra*.

53. Basic Inc. v. Levinson, 485 U.S. 224, 108 S.Ct. 978, 99 L.Ed.2d 194 (1988).

54. The availability of the fraud-on-the-market presumption is premised on the existence of a relatively liquid and, hence, efficient market for the securities in question. *See* § 12.10 *infra*.

55. *See* § 12.10 *infra*.

56. Causation is discussed in § 12.11 *infra*.

57. *E.g.*, Wool v. Tandem Computers Inc., 818 F.2d 1433 (9th Cir.1987). Damages are discussed in § 12.12 *infra*.

60. Sarbanes–Oxley Act of 2002, Pub. Law 107–204 (July 30, 2002).

61. 28 U.S.C.A. § 1658(b).

62. 459 U.S. 375, 103 S.Ct. 683, 74 L.Ed.2d 548 (1983).

§ 12.5

1. *See, e.g.*, Basic Inc. v. Levinson, 485 U.S. 224, 108 S.Ct. 978, 99 L.Ed.2d 194 (1988), *on remand*, 871 F.2d 562 (6th Cir.1989) (upholding liability for misleading statement, but not

or fraudulent act, in the words of both the statute and the rule, be "in connection with the purchase or sale of any security * * *."[2] This means that there must be some connection between the misstatements or conduct in question and a transaction in securities.

Any statement that is reasonably calculated to affect the investment decision of a reasonable investor will satisfy the "in connection with" requirement.[6]

As a general proposition, dissemination to the public through a medium of communication upon which the reasonable investor would rely will satisfy the "in connection with" requirement.[11] Even a technical advertisement in a specialized journal could be said to be in connection with a purchase or sale of a security if it is likely to affect the readers' investment decisions about the company's securities. Thus, for example, advertisements in a medical journal concerning a new drug could form the basis of a securities fraud claim.[12] This result is not without controversy.

Public announcements and other dissemination of information can be in connection with the purchase or sale even if the speaker or disseminator is not a purchaser or seller. Although the existence of a public market at the time of any news release by itself is not sufficient to satisfy the "in connection with" requirement,[15] if the news release relates to matters likely to affect the stock price significantly, the requirement is satisfied.[16] Similarly, information contained in periodic SEC filings such as the annual or quarterly report will be considered to have been in connection with the purchase or sale of a security where the material disclosed relates to the types of information that an investor would use in deciding to purchase or sell a security.[17] Press releases and other statements directed to issues that investors deem important in making investment decisions are likely to be considered to have been made in connection with the purchase or sale of a security.

The "in connection with" requirement will not support a Rule 10b–5 action for any wrongdoing that just happens to involve securities.[21] It has thus been held that a *de minimus* "touch" test is not sufficient to satisfy the "in connection with" requirement.[22]

By analogy, a 1987 Supreme Court decision under the federal mail fraud statute[50] supports a broad reading of Rule 10b–5's "in connection with" requirement. The mail fraud statute covers any person who causes the mail to

directly addressing the question of whether defendant's not being a purchaser or seller precluded liability).

2. 15 U.S.C.A. § 78j(b); 17 C.F.R. § 240.106–5.

6. *E.g.*, Pelletier v. Stuart–James Co., 863 F.2d 1550 (11th Cir.1989).

11. *See, e.g.*, Semerenko v. Cendant Corp., 223 F.3d 165 (3d Cir.2000).

12. In re Carter–Wallace, Inc. Securities Litigation, 150 F.3d 153 (2d Cir.1998) (refusing to dismiss claim).

15. SEC v. Texas Gulf Sulphur, 401 F.2d 833 (2d Cir.1968) (Hayes, J., concurring in part and dissenting in part), *cert. denied*, 394 U.S. 976, 89 S.Ct. 1454, 22 L.Ed.2d 756 (1969).

16. 401 F.2d 833 (opinion of the court).

17. *See, e.g.*, Semerenko v. Cendant Corp., 223 F.3d 165 (3d Cir.2000).

21. *See* Levitin v. PaineWebber, Inc., 159 F.3d 698 (2d Cir.1998), *affirming*, 933 F.Supp. 325 (S.D.N.Y.1996).

22. Head v. Head, 759 F.2d 1172, 1175 (4th Cir.1985).

50. 18 U.S.C.A. § 1341.

be used to further the wrongful conduct. The Supreme Court in Carpenter v. United States[51] held that a scheme by a reporter to give advance notice to his friends concerning upcoming columns in the Wall Street Journal depended upon the dissemination of the Wall Street Journal and that this was a sufficient connection to invoke the mail fraud statute.[52] This is a surprising rationale, since the defendants did not utilize the mail themselves but rather the newspaper when published utilized the mails. The Court's expansive reading of the Mail Fraud Act's jurisdictional requirement may be used to support an equally broad reading of Rule 10b–5's "in connection with" requirement. The connection to the mails in *Carpenter* was at best tangential in comparison with the more substantial "in connection with" requirement that traditionally has been required under Rule 10b–5.

In United States v. O'Hagan, the Supreme Court held that a Rule 10b–5 violation does not require that the fraud be linked to identifiable purchasers or sellers of securities.[54] A breach of duty to the source of confidential information will support a Rule 10b–5 violation so long as the confidential information is misused in connection with securities trading. It thus is not necessary that the source of the information to whom the duty was owed have been a purchaser, seller or issuer of the securities in question.

The broad interpretation of the "in connection with" requirement in *O'Hagan* was reaffirmed by the Supreme Court in SEC v. Zandford.[55] In *Zandford*, the SEC sued a stock broker who emptied his client's account and converted the proceeds. The defendant contended that since there was no fraud in connection with specific securities transactions, Rule 10b–5 could not be used to challenge the broker's actions. The Supreme Court rejected this argument, reasoning that the purpose of the federal securities laws was to assure the existence of honest securities markets and to promote investor confidence. The court explained that there was the requisite deception insofar as the broker failed to disclose the challenged embezzlement out of a securities account to his customer and that this was sufficient connection to establish securities fraud.[56] The *Zandford* decision is significant in that it establishes a broad test for the reach of the securities laws. Rather than simply focus on a specific transaction, if the fraud involves securities in any meaningful way, then the securities laws are implicated.[57] It is also noteworthy that the Justices, who are generally divided in securities decisions, were unanimous in the *Zandford* holding.

The Supreme Court's decision in *Zandford* makes it clear that Rule 10b–5 is violated when there has been a failure to adequately disclose past misconduct even though the misconduct itself did not involve a purchase or sale of securities. Thus, the failure to disclose the embezzlement of cash from a securities brokerage account was sufficient to satisfy the "in connection with" requirement on the facts before the Court in *Zandford*. Similarly, a Rule 10b–

---

51. 484 U.S. 19, 108 S.Ct. 316, 98 L.Ed.2d 275 (1987).

52. 484 U.S. at 28, 108 S.Ct. at 322, 98 L.Ed.2d at 285. *See* § 12.11, 12.17 *infra.*

54. United States v. O'Hagan, 521 U.S. 642, 117 S.Ct. 2199, 138 L.Ed.2d 724 (1997). The *O'Hagan* decision is discussed in § 12.17 *infra.*

55. 535 U.S. 813, 824–25 122 S.Ct. 1899, 1905–06, 153 L.Ed.2d 1 (2002).

56. 535 U.S. 813, 824–25 122 S.Ct. 1899, 1905–06, 153 L.Ed.2d 1 (2002).

57. *See, e.g.*, Shaw v. Charles Schwab & Co., Inc., 2003 WL 1463842, Fed. Sec. L. Rep. ¶ 92,413 (Cal. Super. 2003) (the "in connection with" requirement is satisfied even if the misstatement does not directly relate to the value of the security).

5 violation was stated on the basis of a securities brokerage firm's alleged failure to disclose that it engaged in a pay-for-play scheme under which it offered investment services in exchange for cash payments and campaign donations.[58]

Another broad interpretation of the "in connection with" requirement was given by the Supreme Court in Merrill Lynch, Pierce Fenner & Smith v. Dabit.[63] The broad interpretation was used to limit the scope of private remedies. The Court in *Dabit* held that state class actions by holders (as opposed to purchasers or sellers of securities) with fifty or more class members are preempted by the Securities Litigation Uniform Standards Act (SLUSA).[64] The Court noted that although the "in connection" with requirement did not confer a private right of action on mere holders of securities, that same language in SLUSA was broad enough to preclude state law suits brought by plaintiffs who were neither purchasers nor sellers.[65] In contrast to *Dabit*, the Seventh Circuit in an opinion by Judge Posner held that where wrongdoing causes an injury after the purchase or sale, the "in connection with" requirement is not satisfied and SLUSA preemption does not apply.[66]

§ 12.6 "Purchase or Sale"—Identifying Purchases and Sales Under Rule 10b–5

§ 12.6[1] Definitions of Purchase and Sale

Rule 10b–5 applies to fraud and misstatements or omissions in connection with the *purchase* or *sale* of any security.[1] The definitions of purchase and sale go far beyond garden-variety cash for stock transactions. However, not every transfer of securities will constitute a sale.

The securities laws contain various formulations of the definitions for purchase and sale, but each is designed to identify a transaction in which the securities are acquired or disposed of for value. Thus, for example, section 2(a)(3) of the 1933 Act[4] defines "sale" as including "every contract of sale or disposition of a security or interest in a security, for value." In most situations, this definition will encompass transactions such as exercise of options, mergers, exercise of conversion rights, pledges, and the like.[5] On its face, the 1934 Act definition may be even broader as there is no explicit requirement that the security be disposed of for value. Thus, for example, it is not necessary to show that there is consideration in the traditional sense.[6] As

---

58. SEC v. Santos, 292 F.Supp.2d 1046 (N.D. Ill. 2003).

63. 547 U.S. 71, 126 S.Ct. 1503, 164 L Ed.2d 179 (2006).

64. SLUSA is discussed in § 12.15[2] *infra*.

65. Merrill Lynch, Pierce Fenner & Smith v. Dabit, 547 U.S. 71, 126 S.Ct. 1503, 164 L.Ed.2d 179 (2006).

66. Gavin v. AT & T Corp., 464 F.3d 634 (7th Cir. 2006).

§ 12.6

1. 17 C.F.R. § 240.10b–5.

4. 15 U.S.C.A. § 77b(a)(3).

5. *See, e.g.,* In re Zoran Corp. Derivative Litigation, 511 F.Supp.2d 986, 1011–12 (N.D. Cal. 2007) ("A stock option is a sale of securities sufficient to fulfill the 'in connection with requirement' ").

6. Seolas v. Bilzerian, 951 F.Supp. 978, 986–87 (D.Utah 1997) (relying in part on Rathborne v. Rathborne, 683 F.2d 914, 920 (5th Cir.1982)); International Controls Corp. v. Vesco, 490 F.2d 1334, 1346 (2d Cir.1974) ("[W]e find the rote emphasis on consideration inconsistent with the

one court explained, "[t]he fact that no 'value' was paid is not necessarily dispositive."[7] Section 3(a)(14) provides: "[t]he terms 'sale' and 'sell' each include any contract to sell or otherwise dispose of [a security]."[8] It is noteworthy that the definition "includes" contracts to sell but does not purport to be exclusive and thus limited by the express examples of what is a sale that are given in the statute. The Exchange Act contains a parallel definition of "purchase."[9] The definition of purchase or sale includes a "contract of sale" even though the sale does not take place and no securities are transferred.[10] Furthermore, the "in connection with" requirement does not require identification of the specific security, or a demonstration that money was actually invested in securities, to qualify plaintiff as a purchaser of the securities within the meaning of Rule 10b–5.[11]

Concepts of purchase and sale are to be construed flexibly in order to accomplish the purpose of the securities laws.[12] The courts will consider the economic reality of the transaction and whether it lends itself to fraud in the making of an investment decision. As one court explained, "several factors have so far emerged in this inquiry: (1) whether a transfer of ownership or control of the security occurred; (2) whether consideration or value was given; (3) whether, in appropriate contexts, there was a change in the fundamental nature of the security; and (4) whether the transaction had a direct effect on the conduct of the securities market."[15]

Whether or not a contract of sale is binding will ordinarily depend on state law.[17] Thus, an oral contract of sale, including an oral option contract, is a sale of a security subject to the federal securities laws.[18]

§ 12.6[4] Convertible Securities

A voluntary conversion of convertible securities can satisfy Rule 10b–5's purchase or sale requirement.[28] Rule 10b–5 is not limited, however, to voluntary exchanges.

§ 12.6[6] Pledges of Securities

Although there appear to be some decisions to the contrary, ordinarily, a pledge of securities will constitute a sale.[39]

broad scope of protection under § 10(b) for those who engage in transactions eventuating in the acquisition or disposition of securities").

7. Seolas v. Bilzerian, 951 F.Supp. 978, 986–87 (D.Utah 1997).

8. 15 U.S.C.A. § 78c(a)(14).

9. Section 3(a)(13), 15 U.S.C.A. § 78c(a)(13) ("The terms 'buy' and 'purchase' each include any contract to buy, purchase, or otherwise acquire . . .").

10. *E.g.*, Falkowski v. Imation Corp., 320 F.3d 905 (9th Cir. 2003).

11. Grippo v. Perazzo, 357 F.3d 1218 (11th Cir. 2004).

12. In re American Continental Corp., 49 F.3d 541 (9th Cir.1995).

15. Seolas v. Bilzerian, 951 F.Supp. 978, 987 (D.Utah 1997).

17. *See* § 5.1[7] *supra*.

18. The Wharf (Holdings) Ltd. v. United International Holdings, 532 U.S. 588, 121 S.Ct. 1776, 149 L.Ed.2d 845 (2001).

28. FS Photo, Inc. v. PictureVision, Inc., 61 F.Supp.2d 473 (E.D.Va.1999).

39. *See, e.g.,* Rubin v. United States, 449 U.S. 424, 101 S.Ct. 698, 66 L.Ed.2d 633 (1981); SEC v. Digital Lightwave, Inc., 196 F.R.D. 698 (M.D. Fla. 2000).

§ 12.6[7] Gifts

Ordinarily, a gift will not be a sale under the securities laws.[51] However, there may be a basis on appropriate facts for characterizing a gift as a sale under the Act. In one case, the complaint was that the plaintiff made a gift of securities that the defendant fraudulently led him to believe were worth much less than their true value. The court ruled that since such misrepresentations might need the protections of the securities laws, it would not dismiss the claim.[52]

§ 12.6[8] Periodic Payments; The Investment Decision Doctrine

Ordinarily, securities transactions require that the investor pay the consideration prior to or at the time he or she is to receive the securities. On occasion, however, payments may be set up on an installment basis. In such instances, does the sale occur at the time of the contract's making or is there a new sale at the time of each payment? The answer to this question may, of course, be significant for statute of limitations purposes. It is generally said that a purchase and sale do not take place until "the parties to the transaction are committed to each other."[56] Under what is known as the "investment decision" doctrine, when every payment involves a new investment decision, each payment will be treated as a sale.[58] In contrast, when the contract involves a single decision with subsequent periodic payments, there is only one sale.

§ 12.7 Standing to Sue Under SEC Rule 10b–5

§ 12.7[1] The Purchaser/Seller Requirement

Rule 10b–5's applicability is premised upon a transaction that is "in connection with" a "purchase or sale" of a security. Six years after the initial recognition of an implied private 10b–5 remedy,[5] the Second Circuit held, in Birnbaum v. Newport Steel Corp.,[6] that a 10b–5 plaintiff in a private damages action must have been either a purchaser or seller of the securities that form the basis of the material omission, misstatement, or deceptive conduct. The *Birnbaum* decision was adopted by the Supreme Court nearly twenty years later in Blue Chip Stamps v. Manor Drug Stores.[7] Both *Birnbaum* and *Blue Chip Stamps* have been followed by a number of inroads in and clarifications to the purchaser/seller standing requirement.

---

51. *See, e.g.,* Sanderson v. H.I.G. P–XI Holding, Inc., [1999–2000 Transfer Binder] Fed. Sec. L. Rep. (CCH) ¶ 91,047, 2000 WL 1042813 (E.D.La. 2000).

52. Berk v. Maryland Publick Banks, Inc., 6 F.Supp.2d 472 (D.Md.1998).

56. *E.g.,* Kahn v. Kohlberg, Kravis, Roberts & Co., 970 F.2d 1030, 1040 (2d Cir.1992), *cert. denied,* 506 U.S. 986, 113 S.Ct. 494, 121 L.Ed.2d 432 (1992).

58. *E.g.,* Department of Economic Development v. Arthur Andersen & Co., 683 F.Supp. 1463, 1475 (S.D.N.Y.1988).

§ 12.7

5. Kardon v. National Gypsum Co., 69 F.Supp. 512 (E.D.Pa.1946).

6. 193 F.2d 461 (2d Cir.1952), *cert. denied,* 343 U.S. 956, 72 S.Ct. 1051, 96 L.Ed. 1356 (1952).

7. Blue Chip Stamps v. Manor Drug Stores, 421 U.S. 723, 95 S.Ct. 1917, 44 L.Ed.2d 539 (1975).

The Securities Litigation Uniform Standards Act's (SLUSA's)[16] preemption of state class actions precludes using state law to circumvent the requirement in a class action with more than fifty class members.[17]

The purchaser/seller standing limitation does not necessarily carry over to state law claims. For example, the California Supreme Court held that shareholders could state a claim under common law fraud based on the allegation that they were induced not to sell their shares. However, other states have disagreed and refused to recognize a claim by holders who neither purchased nor sold in reliance on the fraudulent statement.

After the purchaser/seller standing rule was developed, it soon became clear that a plaintiff shareholder satisfies the purchaser/seller standing requirement in a shareholder derivative suit brought on behalf of a corporation defrauded in connection with its purchase or sale of securities.[46] While a shareholder can bring a derivative suit in a representative capacity for the corporation, other members of the corporate community cannot. Thus, for example, a corporate director cannot bring a claim based on a transaction by the corporation.[47] Similarly, Rule 10b–5 standing does not extend to non-shareholder officers.[48] Even being a shareholder will not assure standing to sue. In order to state a 10b–5 claim based on the corporation's purchase or sale of a security, the shareholder must be suing in a derivative rather than individual capacity.[49]

Share exchanges or cash-out transactions pursuant to a corporate merger or other business combination will ordinarily constitute purchases and sales for Rule 10b–5 purposes. However, when the merger is in fact a matter of form rather than substance, a purchase and sale will not result from the share exchange.[61]

When shareholders receive stock as a dividend, can they maintain a suit for alleged fraud under Rule 10b–5? The Seventh Circuit held that they cannot.[71] The court held that shares issued pro rata to shareholders in a spin-off transaction[72] are not "purchased" since no consideration is paid by the shareholders.[73] The court, per Chief Judge Posner, rejected the argument that the shareholders receiving the dividend purchased the spun-off shares since the value of the parent corporation's stock was reduced as a result of the spin-

16. Pub. Law No. 105–353, 112 Stat. 3227 (105th Cong.–2d sess. November 3, 1998), codified in 1934 Act § 28(f), 15 U.S.C.A. § 78bb(f).

17. *Id. See* Merrill Lynch, Pierce Fenner & Smith v. Dabit, 547 U.S. 71, 126 S.Ct. 1503, 164 L.Ed.2d 179 (2006).

46. *E.g.,* Frankel v. Slotkin, 984 F.2d 1328 (2d Cir.1993). For discussion of derivative suits generally, *see* 2 James D. Cox & Thomas L. Hazen on Corporations, ch. 15 (2d ed. 2003).

47. Brannan v. Eisenstein, 804 F.2d 1041 (8th Cir.1986). *Cf., e.g.,* Linsey v. E.F. Hutton & Co., 675 F.Supp. 1 (D.D.C.1987) (bishop could not maintain suit against broker for alleged fraud against his church).

48. Powers v. British Vita, P.L.C., 842 F.Supp. 1573 (S.D.N.Y.1994).

49. *See, e.g.,* Smith v. Ayres, 845 F.2d 1360 (5th Cir.1988).

61. Goldberg v. Hankin, 835 F.Supp. 815 (E.D.Pa.1993) (shareholder of bank that was transformed into bank holding company was not a purchaser as a result of the exchange of shares pursuant to the bank holding company's formation).

71. Isquith v. Caremark International, Inc., 136 F.3d 531 (7th Cir.1998).

72. Spin-off transactions are discussed in § 5.3 *supra.*

73. Isquith v. Caremark International, Inc., 136 F.3d 531 (7th Cir.1998).

off.[74] Other courts have similarly held that a stockholder who receives shares as a dividend has not purchased the securities.[75]

A pledge of securities generally is held to be a sale under the Exchange Act, and accordingly, the pledgees are "purchasers" able to maintain a Rule 10b–5 cause of action—although there is some conflict on this point.[76]

§ 12.7[2] Standing to Seek Injunctive Relief

There is authority to the effect that a person need be neither a purchaser nor a seller of the securities in order to maintain an action for injunctive relief under Rule 10b–5. There is also some authority to the contrary. Some courts take the position that the equitable relief exception to the purchaser/seller requirement applies only where the relief sought is prophylactic. Furthermore, even among those courts that do not require the plaintiff in an injunction action to have been a purchaser or seller, the plaintiff must still be able to show some direct injury resulting from the alleged Rule 10b–5 violation.

§ 12.7[3] Variations on the Purchaser/Seller Requirement

Following the Second Circuit's decision in Birnbaum v. Newport Steel Corp.,[97] the courts created a number of doctrines (or exceptions) to give 10b–5 standing to persons who would not otherwise directly qualify as purchasers or sellers.

When a shareholder is frozen out of a corporation or otherwise put in the position of a "forced seller," Rule 10b–5 standing ordinarily will exist even though there was no voluntary investment decision.[102] It has been said that the forced-seller doctrine should be interpreted narrowly in light of *Blue Chip Stamps*.[103] Forced purchasers also have standing under Rule 10b–5.[104] In order to invoke the forced-seller doctrine, the plaintiff must establish that the transaction resulted in a disposition of the plaintiff's ownership interest.[105]

Most of the inroads on the purchaser/seller doctrine seem to survive the Supreme Court's adoption of the purchaser/seller standing requirement in Blue Chip Stamps v. Manor Drug Stores.[107] In that case, the Court held that the plaintiffs had a right to purchase the securities in question under an antitrust consent decree. The plaintiffs refrained from purchasing the securities, allegedly relying on misleading statements made by the defendants designed to deter the planned purchase; the Court held that these would-be

74. *Id.*

75. *E.g.*, In re Adelphia Communications Corp. Securities and Derivative Litigation, 398 F. Supp.2d 244, 261 (S.D.N.Y. 2005).

76. *E.g.*, Madison Consultants v. FDIC, 710 F.2d 57 (2d Cir.1983).

97. 193 F.2d 461 (2d Cir.1952), *cert. denied*, 343 U.S. 956, 72 S.Ct. 1051, 96 L.Ed. 1356 (1952).

102. *See, e.g.*, Alley v. Miramon, 614 F.2d 1372 (5th Cir. 1980) Greenstein v. Paul, 400 F.2d 580 (2d Cir.1968); Vine v. Beneficial Finance Co., 374 F.2d 627 (2d Cir.1967), *cert. denied*, 389 U.S. 970, 88 S.Ct. 463, 19 L.Ed.2d 460 (1967).

103. *See* Jacobson v. AEG Capital Corp., 50 F.3d 1493, 1499 (9th Cir.1995) ("forced sale doctrine does not cut a wide swath"; shareholder who participated in bankruptcy reorganization could not qualify as a forced-seller).

104. *E.g.*, Zweig v. Hearst Corp., 594 F.2d 1261 (9th Cir.1979).

105. *See, e.g.*, Brown v. Kinross Gold, U.S.A., 343 F. Supp.2d 957, 962–63 (D. Nev. 2004) (plaintiffs never parted with their shares and thus lacked standing).

107. 421 U.S. 723, 95 S.Ct. 1917, 44 L.Ed.2d 539 (1975).

purchasers could not state a 10b–5 cause of action.[108] For the same reasons, the holder of an unexercised right of first refusal to purchase securities does not have standing under Rule 10b–5.[109] A binding contract right to purchase securities will support Rule 10b–5 standing even if the right to purchase is contingent.[110] However, the absence of a binding contract will preclude Rule 10b–5 standing.[111] A decision to release a claim to purchase securities does not support Rule 10b–5 standing[112] since the plaintiff is nothing more than a frustrated or would-be purchaser. A necessary corollary to these holdings would seem to be that mere "would-be" sellers cannot raise 10b–5 claims.[113] *Blue Chip Stamps* is best described as a case of the frustrated purchaser since the plaintiff had a right to purchase the securities under the terms of a consent decree. It would seem that, for similar reasons, the former exception to the *Birnbaum* doctrine for the "frustrated seller"[114] most likely does not survive *Blue Chip Stamps.*[115] Someone who has been fraudulently induced to retain their investment interest does not have standing under Rule 10b–5 and, as discussed earlier, class actions involving state law claims by mere holders are likely to be preempted.[121]

Contract rights to purchase (or sell) securities can classify the holder as a purchaser or seller of the underlying security, or may themselves be securities.[132] Thus, for example, a preemptive right to purchase shares is a contract to purchase and can provide the basis for Rule 10b–5 standing.[133] Similarly, an executory contract to acquire shares pursuant to an employment agreement can form the basis of a Rule 10b–5 claim.[134] A contract creating a conditional right to purchase securities has been held to confer standing even though the would-be purchaser received cash in lieu of securities in connection with a merger.[135]

---

108. *See also, e.g.,* Cohen v. Stratosphere Corp., 115 F.3d 695 (9th Cir.1997) (plaintiffs did not have binding contracts to purchase securities and thus lacked standing under Rule 10b–5).

109. Union Pacific Resources Group, Inc. v. Rhone–Poulenc, Inc., 45 F.Supp.2d 544 (N.D.Tex. 1999), *affirmed in part, reversed in part,* 247 F.3d 574 (5th Cir.2001) (right of first refusal that was not exercised did not constitute a purchase or sale of a security).

110. Griggs v. Pace American Group, Inc., 170 F.3d 877 (9th Cir.1999).

111. Cohen v. Stratosphere Corp., 115 F.3d 695 (9th Cir.1997).

112. Lawrence v. Cohn, 325 F.3d 141 (2d Cir. 2003).

113. *E.g.,* Calenti v. Boto, 24 F.3d 335 (1st Cir.1994).

114. *See* Neuman v. Electronic Speciality Co., 1969 WL 2828, [1969–1970 Transfer Binder] Fed.Sec.L.Rep. (CCH) ¶ 92,591 (N.D.Ill.1969); Stockwell v. Reynolds & Co., 252 F.Supp. 215 (S.D.N.Y.1965). *But see* Iroquois Industries, Inc. v. Syracuse China Corp., 417 F.2d 963 (2d Cir.1969), *cert. denied,* 399 U.S. 909, 90 S.Ct. 2199, 26 L.Ed.2d 561 (1970) (frustrated purchaser does not have standing). *Contra* Morrow v. Schapiro, 334 F.Supp. 399 (E.D.Mo.1971); Berne Street Enterprises, Inc. v. American Export Isbrandtsen Co., 1970 WL 268, [1969–1970 Transfer Binder] Fed.Sec.L.Rep. (CCH) ¶ 92,711 (S.D.N.Y.1970).

115. The aborted or frustrated-seller basis for standing was rejected in Weiner v. Rooney, Pace Inc., 1987 WL 11281, [1987 Transfer Binder] Fed.Sec.L.Rep. (CCH) ¶ 93,174 (S.D.N.Y.1987). *See also* Merrill Lynch, Pierce, Fenner & Smith v. Dabit, ___ U.S. ___, 126 S.Ct. 1503, 164 L.Ed.2d 179 (2006).

121. Merrill Lynch, Pierce Fenner & Smith v. Dabit, 547 U.S. 71, 126 S.Ct. 1503, 164 L.Ed.2d 179 (2006).

132. *See also, e.g.,* Fry v. UAL Corp., 84 F.3d 936 (7th Cir.1996), *affirming,* 895 F.Supp. 1018, 1030 (N.D.Ill.1995) (option trader had standing under Rule 10b–5).

133. Brennan v. EMDE Medical Research, Inc., 652 F.Supp. 255 (D.Nev.1986).

134. Technology Exchange Corp. of America, Inc. v. Grant County State Bank, 646 F.Supp. 179 (D.Colo.1986).

135. *See, e.g.,* Griggs v. Pace American Group, Inc., 170 F.3d 877 (9th Cir.1999).

§ 12.8 Rule 10b–5 and the Scienter Requirement; Section 17(a) and Rule 14a–9 Compared

§ 12.8[1] Rule 10b–5's Scienter Requirement; Section 17(a) Compared

Rule 10b–5 describes the type of conduct proscribed but it does not set out the appropriate standard of culpability. The question has thus arisen as to whether the securities laws reach negligent misconduct or are limited to intentional misstatements and omissions. In 1976 after twenty years of conflicting cases, the Supreme Court held in Ernst & Ernst v. Hochfelder[2] that, in order to establish a valid claim for damages under Rule 10b–5, it must be proven that the defendant acted with scienter. The Supreme Court subsequently held in Aaron v. SEC[3] that the scienter standard applies under Rule 10b–5 regardless of whether the action is one for damages or an enforcement action brought by the Commission. In the context of a criminal case, in addition to scienter, the prosecution must establish that the defendant acted willfully, which means that he or she acted with a realization that the acts were wrongful.[5]

The Supreme Court in Aaron v. SEC[11] held that scienter is not an element of an SEC claim for injunctive relief under sections 17(a)(2) and (a)(3) of the 1933 Act.[12] The Court reasoned that, although the language of Rule 10b–5 is identical in all relevant parts to that of section 17(a) of the 1933 Act, section 10(b)'s overall scope is statutorily limited to manipulative or deceptive conduct.[13] "Manipulation" is a term of art that is limited to certain specific types of trading practices and thus is not applicable in most antifraud cases.[14] In fact, there is a considerable question of whether the concept of manipulation can validly play any role with regard to Rule 10b–5.[15] The statutory deception requirement has been held to mandate a showing of scienter in order to state a 10b–5 claim because deception connotes common law fraud and common law fraud requires scienter.[16] One corollary of Rule 10b–5's deception and scienter requirements is that, as is the case with fraud generally, the complaint must be pleaded with specificity and sufficient particularity.

§ 12.8[2] The Standard of Culpability Under the Proxy Rules

Section 14(a) of the Exchange Act and Rule 14a–9 promulgated thereunder give rise to an implied antifraud remedy in connection with a proxy

---

§ 12.8

2. 25 U.S. 185, 96 S.Ct. 1375, 47 L.Ed.2d 668 (1976).

3. 446 U.S. 680, 100 S.Ct. 1945, 64 L.Ed.2d 611 (1980), on remand, 666 F.2d 5 (2d Cir.1981).

5. *E.g.*, United States v. Stewart, 305 F Supp.2d 368 (S.D.N.Y. 2004).

11. 446 U.S. 680, 100 S.Ct. 1945, 64 L.Ed.2d 611 (1980).

12. See 15 U.S.C.A. § 77q(a)(2), (3). The Court also held that scienter must be shown in an action under section 17(a)(1).

13. 15 U.S.C.A. § 78j(b).

14. See, e.g., Santa Fe Industries, Inc. v. Green, 430 U.S. 462, 476, 97 S.Ct. 1292, 1302, 51 L.Ed.2d 480 (1977).

15. Schreiber v. Burlington Northern, Inc., 472 U.S. 1, 105 S.Ct. 2458, 86 L.Ed.2d 1 (1985), held that manipulative conduct does not violate section 14(e) unless there has been deception in terms of a material misstatement or omission. See §§ 11.15, 12.1 supra.

16. Ernst & Ernst v. Hochfelder, 425 U.S. 185, 197, 96 S.Ct. 1375, 1382, 47 L.Ed.2d 668 (1976), rehearing denied, 425 U.S. 986, 96 S.Ct. 2194, 48 L.Ed.2d 811 (1976).

solicitation.[19] Section 14(a) does not expressly impose the limitation that SEC rules address conduct that is manipulative or deceptive. A number of courts have held that the absence of a similar deception requirement in the language of section 14(a)[20] results in a finding that negligence is sufficient to state a claim under the proxy rule's antifraud provisions.[21] The reasoning of the Supreme Court in *Aaron* seems to compel a finding that scienter is not required in an action under the proxy rules.

§ 12.8[3] Recklessness as Scienter

It is clear that the scienter requirement is satisfied by a showing of intentional misrepresentation made with the intent to deceive. But what about conduct that falls short of knowingly made misrepresentations? In reaching its decisions in *Hochfelder* and *Aaron*, the Court did not decide whether a showing of reckless conduct would satisfy the scienter requirement.[24] It has long been the rule at common law that, at least under certain circumstances, the showing of reckless disregard of the truth or the making of a statement with no belief in its truth constitutes scienter in an action for deceit.[25] While the recklessness question remained unsettled at the Supreme Court level, the vast majority of the circuit and district court decisions have found that recklessness is sufficient to state a claim under 10b–5.

§ 12.8[4] Pleading and Proving Scienter

Scienter is based on the defendant's state of mind and, as is true in many cases, may be difficult to prove with direct evidence. On appropriate facts, a court may be willing to permit an inference that the defendant acted with the requisite scienter. There must be a factual basis for making an inference of scienter and it should not be made lightly. In making the determination of culpability, the court should consider all inferences and weigh them together in determining whether the defendant acted with scienter.[57] Thus, the presence of some facts that could lead to an inference of scienter may be negated by other inferences that could be made.[58] Scienter should be inferred only when the fact pattern indicates that the defendants must have been acting with the requisite state of mind. The pleading standard can be explained in

19. 15 U.S.C.A. § 78n(a); 17 C.F.R. § 240.14a–9. E.g., J.I. Case & Co. v. Borak, 377 U.S. 426, 84 S.Ct. 1555, 12 L.Ed.2d 423 (1964). See § 10.3 supra.

20. Section 14(a), like section 17(a) of the 1933 Act, is not limited to deceptive and manipulative acts and practices. Section 14(a) provides that it is unlawful to solicit proxies with regard to securities registered under section 12 (15 U.S.C.A. § 78l; see § 9.2 supra) "in contravention of such rules and regulations as the Commission may prescribe as necessary or appropriate in the public interest or for the protection of investors." 15 U.S.C.A. § 78n(a).

21. *E.g.*, In re Rockefeller Center Properties, Inc. Securities Litigation, 311 F.3d 198, 211 (3d Cir. 2002); In re NAHC, Inc. Securities Litigation, 306 F.3d 1314, 1329 (3d Cir. 2002).

24. 425 U.S. at 193–94 n. 12, 96 S.Ct. at 1381 n. 12; 446 U.S. at 690–91, 100 S.Ct. at 1952.

25. E.g., Derry v. Peek, 14 App.Cas. 337 (House of Lords 1889). See generally W. Page Keeton, Dan B. Dobbs, Robert E. Keeton & David G. Owen, Prosser and Keeton on Torts § 107 (5th ed. 1984).

57. Tellabs, Inc. v. Makor Issues & Rights Ltd., 551 U.S. 308, 127 S.Ct. 2499, 2502 168 L.Ed.2d 179 (2007) ("in determining whether the pleaded facts give rise to a 'strong' inference of scienter, the court must take into account plausible opposing inferences."); Gompper v. VISX, Inc., 298 F.3d 893 (9th Cir.2002) (affirming finding of no scienter).

58. Tellabs, Inc. v. Makor Issues & Rights Ltd., 551 U.S. 308, 127 S.Ct. 2499, 168 L.Ed.2d 179 (2007).

terms of whether there is at least a "highly likely" inference that the defendants acted with scienter.[60]

Although the Private Securities Litigation Reform Act reinforced the specificity requirement with respect to pleading scienter, that Act did not provide specific statutory guidance as to what constitutes a strong inference of scienter so as to withstand a motion to dismiss. The courts have struggled to provide guidelines, with some apparent disagreements as to some of the factors to be considered, such as the relevance of motive and opportunity in establishing scienter. The absence of specific statutory guidelines has left the courts to determine the sufficiency of pleadings involving scienter on a case-by-case basis.

The Supreme Court elaborated on the requirements for pleading scienter in Tellabs, Inc. v. Makor Issues & Rights Ltd.[78]

The strong inference of scienter must be more than a plausible one, it must be "cogent."[80] This means that the inference of scienter must be more than merely reasonable and must be persuasive in light of the particular facts of the case.[81] As explained by the First Circuit, under the "at least as compelling" test, if the inferences of scienter and the absence of scienter are equally compelling, a tie results in a finding that scienter has been sufficiently alleged.[82] The inference of scienter must be at least as likely as other reasonable inferences that could be drawn from the facts as pleaded.

The *Tellabs* decision did not impose an unreasonably rigid pleading standard and much of the prior case law is likely to survive. For example, reliance on inferences of scienter and confidential sources is still permissible so long as the allegations of scienter are specific.[90] In fact, on remand in *Tellabs*, the Seventh Circuit reaffirmed its earlier position that the allegations in that case were sufficient but at the same time evidenced skepticism with respect to the value of anonymous confidential sources.[91] The presence of inquiry notice or "red flags" of material misstatements can be the basis for pleading sufficient recklessness to establish scienter.[92]

Many of the cases discussed above involving scienter focus on individual liability. Issues also can arise as to a corporation's liability under Rule 10b–5 and the ability to establish that the corporation acted with scienter. Corporate scienter "is necessarily derived from its employees"[150] or directors. In the first

60. Ezra Charitable Trust v. Tyco, International, Ltd., 466 F.3d 1 (1st Cir. 2006).

78. Tellabs, Inc. v. Makor Issues & Rights Ltd., 551 U.S. 308, 127 S.Ct. 2499, 168 L.Ed.2d 179 (2007).

80. *Id.*

81. *Id.*

82. ACA Financial Guaranty Corp. v. Advest, Inc., 512 F.3d 46, 59 (1st Cir. 2008).

90. However, the courts are likely to be more rigorous than they were in the past. *See* Indiana Electrical Workers' Pension Trust Fund IBEW v. Shaw Group, Inc., 537 F.3d 527 (5th Cir. 2008) (failure to allege a strong inference of scienter; "[f]ollowing Tellabs, courts must discount allegations from confidential sources."), relying on . Higginbotham v. Baxter International Inc., 495 F.3d 753, 756–57 (7th Cir.2007).

91. Makor Issues & Rights, Ltd. v. Tellabs Inc., 513 F.3d 702 (7th Cir. 2008). *See also, e.g.*, Jonathan W. Miller & Lyle Roberts Collective Scienter' in Securities Fraud Cases, NYLJ 4, (col. 4) (Feb. 8, 2008) (urging the courts to reject collective scienter).

92. *See, e.g.*, Katz v. Image Innovations Holdings, Inc., 542 F. Supp.2d 269 (S.D.N.Y. 2008) (sufficient allegations of scienter).

150. In re Marsh & McClennan Cos. Securities Litigation, 501 F. Supp.2d 452, 481 (S.D.N.Y. 2006). *Accord* In re Monster Worldwide, Inc. Securities Litigation, 549 F. Supp.2d 578, 583

instance, the law of agency will allow the scienter of corporate officials acting on behalf of the corporation to be imputed to the corporation.[152] It thus is clear that the knowledge of a corporate officer or agent acting within the scope of authority is attributable to the corporation.[153] Some courts have adopted a collective scienter approach in holding that scienter can be attributed to the corporation from a group of agents or officers.[155] Nevertheless, the Second[156] and Fourth Circuits rejected the collective scienter test in ruling that in order to attribute scienter to a corporate entity, there must be at least one individual who acted with the requisite state of mind.[157]

§ 12.9 Materiality in Rule 10b–5 Actions

§ 12.9[1] Materiality in Context

In a common law action for fraud or deceit, in addition to proving the requisite degree of culpability (*i.e.,* scienter),[1] the successful plaintiff must prove a material[2] misstatement or omission and reliance[3] upon the misstatement or omission in question. As is the case with scienter, the materiality[5] and reliance[6] requirements carry over to 10b–5 actions. As explained below, in order to be materially misleading, there must be a significant element of inaccuracy[7] or obfuscation. Technically accurate information can still be materially misleading if the significant facts are buried in the disclosure document and thus not readily apparent to the average reader. Thus, under the "buried facts" doctrine, disclosures can be obscured by burying them in footnotes or appendices.[8]

(S.D.N.Y. 2008) (noting that "a corporate defendant has no mind of its own" and finding genuine issues of fact as to corporate scienter).

152. *See, e.g.,* Teamsters Local 445 Freight Pension Fund v. Dynex Capital, Inc., 531 F.3d 190 (2d Cir. 2008) ("To prove liability against a corporation, of course, a plaintiff must prove that an agent of the corporation committed a culpable act with the requisite scienter, and that the act (and accompanying mental state) are attributable to the corporation.").

153. *See, e.g.,* City of Monroe Employees Retirement System v. Bridgestone Corp., 399 F.3d 651 (6th Cir. 2005).

155. *See* Southland Sec. Corp. v. INSpire Ins. Solutions, Inc., 365 F.3d 353 (5th Cir. 2004).

156. Teamsters Local 445 Freight Pension Fund v. Dynex Capital, Inc., 531 F.3d 190 (2d Cir. 2008).

157. Teachers' Retirement System of Louisiana v. Hunter, 477 F.3d 162 (4th Cir. 2007).

§ 12.9

1. *See* § 12.8 *supra.*

2. As developed more fully in this section, a term is material if it is sufficiently important to a reasonable investor to have a substantial impact on his or her decision to invest.

3. The reliance requirement, which is closely related to the concept of materiality, is discussed in § 12.10 *infra.*

5. It has been observed that "[f]or the securities lawyer 'materiality' is the name of the game." Richard W. Jennings & Harold Marsh, Jr., Securities Regulation: Cases and Materials 1023 (5th ed. 1982). *See* Yvonne Ching Ling Lee, the Elusive Concept of "Materiality" Under U.S. Federal Securities Laws, 40 Willamette L. Rev. 661 (2004).

6. *See* § 12.10 *infra.*

7. *See, e.g.,* Karacand v. Edwards, 53 F.Supp.2d 1236, 1252 (D.Utah 1999).

8. *See* Plain English Disclosure, Sec. Act Rel. No. 33–7497, 63 Fed. Reg. 6370–01, 1998 WL 44199 (F.R.) (SEC Feb. 6, 1998) ("Under the buried facts doctrine, a court would consider disclosure to be false and misleading only if its overall significance is obscured because material information is 'buried,' for example, in footnotes or appendices"). *See also, e.g.,* Gould v. American Hawaiian Steamship Company, 331 F.Supp. 981 (D.Del.1971); Kohn v. American Metal Climax, Inc., 322 F.Supp. 1331 (E.D.Pa.1970), modified, 458 F.2d 255 (3d Cir.1972).

The test of materiality depends not upon the literal truth of statements, but upon the ability of reasonable investors to become accurately informed.[11] This is sometimes referred to as the mosaic misrepresentation thesis.[12] Courts should not focus alone on one particular sentence that is part of a larger statement without considering the entirety the statements in question.[13] Accordingly, when there is adequate cautionary language warning investors as to certain risks, optimistic statements are not materially misleading.[14] However, cautionary language will not result in elimination of liability for material factual inaccuracies.[15] As discussed more fully below, a finding of materiality is based on the total mix of information available.[16] However, the mere fact that information may be publicly available does not mean that it is necessarily incorporated into every statement made.[17] Thus, for example, it was held that even though information in a company's Form 10–K filing and annual report to shareholders might have clarified alleged misstatements in a proxy solicitation, the alleged misstatements in the company's proxy statement might nevertheless be actionable.[18] The Second Circuit reasoned that for shareholders making their determination of how to vote based on the proxy statement, the information contained in the 10–K and annual report were not part of the total mix reasonably available to the shareholders who would be voting.[19]

§ 12.9[2] Factual Nature of Materiality

It has repeatedly been held that the concept of materiality cannot be distilled into a bright-line test.[32] Determinations of materiality relating to accounting matters are not determined on a mathematical basis alone; misstatements may otherwise be important to shareholders.[41]

§ 12.9[3] Materiality Defined and Explained

Materiality depends on whether the plaintiff can establish "a substantial likelihood that a reasonable shareholder *would* consider it important."[50] The

11. *E.g.,* McMahan & Co. v. Wherehouse Entertainment, Inc., 900 F.2d 576, 579 (2d Cir.1990), *cert. denied*, 501 U.S. 1249, 111 S.Ct. 2887, 115 L.Ed.2d 1052 (1991).

12. In re Genentech, Inc., Securities Litigation, 1989 WL 137189 [1989–1990 Transfer Binder] Fed.Sec.L.Rep. 94,813 (N.D.Cal.1989).

13. *See, e.g.,* Kapps v. Torch Offshore, Inc., 379 F.3d 207 (5th Cir. 2004).

14. *See, e.g., Id.*; In re Worlds of Wonder Securities Litigation, 35 F.3d 1407 (9th Cir.1994).

15. *See, e.g.,* Berson v. Applied Signal Technology, Inc., 527 F.3d 982 (9th Cir. 2008).

16. *See, e.g.,* Madden v. Deloitte & Touche, LLP, 118 Fed.Appx. 150 (9th Cir. 2004).

17. *See, e.g.,* Berry v. Valence Technology, Inc., 175 F.3d 699, 706 (9th Cir.1999).

18. United Paperworkers International Union v. International Paper Co., 985 F.2d 1190 (2d Cir.1993).

19. *Id.*

32. *E.g.,* Basic Inc. v. Levinson, 485 U.S. 224, 108 S.Ct. 978, 99 L.Ed.2d 194 (1988); Ganino v. Citizens Utilities Co., 228 F.3d 154 (2d Cir.2000).

41. In re Unisys Corp. Securities Litigation, 2000 WL 1367951, [2000–2001] [Transfer Binder] Fed. Sec. L. Rep. (CCH) ¶ 91,218, (E.D. Pa. 2000) (misstatements relating to less than 1% of income could be material), *relying on* In re Westinghouse Securities Litigation, 90 F.3d 696, 714–715 (3d Cir.1996) (misstatement of loan reserves amounting to .54% of total income could have been material but was not, since it was not demonstrated that this was otherwise important to investors); SEC v. Joseph Schlitz Brewing Co., 452 F.Supp. 824 (E.D.Wis.1978) (nondisclosure of kickback scheme was material because, inter alia, it reflected on the lack of management integrity).

50. TSC Industries, Inc. v. Northway, Inc., 426 U.S. 438, 449, 96 S.Ct. 2126, 2132, 48 L.Ed.2d 757 (1976) (emphasis added). *Accord* Basic Inc. v. Levinson, 485 U.S. 224, 108 S.Ct. 978, 99 L.Ed.2d 194 (1988).

test of materiality is whether a reasonable investor would have considered the matter significant;[51] it is not necessary to show that the investor *would* have acted differently.[52] It is not sufficient to show that a shareholder might have found the information to be of interest.[53] Once materiality is established, however, the investor still has to show a causal connection between the violation, the transaction, and any loss which he or she suffered.[54] It has been said that "materiality" encompasses those facts "which in reasonable and objective contemplation might affect the value of the corporation's stock or securities."[55]

In an early leading case involving Rule 10b–5, the Second Circuit looked to the Restatement of Torts in defining materiality in terms of whether a reasonable person "would attach importance [to the fact misrepresented] in determining his choice of action in the transaction in question."[56] When a defendant targets unreasonably naive or careless investors, the more objective reasonable person standard will not preclude a finding of materiality.[57] Such misstatements can thus be the subject of SEC or criminal action.[58] In a private action, the unreasonableness of the plaintiff's reliance could be argued as a defense to damages but the intentional targeting of such a victim should preclude the defense of unreasonable reliance.

As noted earlier, the materiality determination is to be made in light of the total mix of information available.[60] Thus, for example, oral statements will be considered in light of available written information.[61] Focusing on the total mix of information available means that plaintiffs may not base a claim on nondisclosure of publicly-known information.[62]

The fact that materiality is to be determined in context means that a purchaser or seller is not necessarily entitled to all information relating to each of the circumstances surrounding the transaction.[63]

---

51. *See, e.g.,* United States v. Peterson, 101 F.3d 375 (5th Cir.1996).

52. Folger Adam Co. v. PMI Industries, Inc., 938 F.2d 1529 (2d Cir.1991), *cert. denied,* 502 U.S. 983, 112 S.Ct. 587, 116 L.Ed.2d 612 (1991).

53. Milton v. Van Dorn Co., 961 F.2d 965 (1st Cir.1992). *See also, e.g.,* United States v. Bingham, 992 F.2d 975 (9th Cir.1993) (defendant's use of false identity and hiding the fact that he was an officer and director, in connection with sale of security was not a Rule 10b–5 violation).

54. *See* § 12.11 *infra.*

55. Kohler v. Kohler Co., 319 F.2d 634, 642 (7th Cir.1963).

56. List v. Fashion Park, Inc., 340 F.2d 457, 462 (2d Cir.1965), *cert. denied,* 382 U.S. 811, 86 S.Ct. 23, 15 L.Ed.2d 60 (1965).

57. United States v. Davis, 226 F.3d 346, 358 (5th Cir.2000) ("the naivety, carelessness, negligence, or stupidity of a victim" does not preclude criminal liability for fraud).

58. *See* United States v. Davis, 226 F.3d 346, 358 (5th Cir.2000).

60. *See, e.g.,* Shawmut Bank, N.A. v. Kress Associates, 33 F.3d 1477 (9th Cir.1994).

61. *E.g.,* Ambrosino v. Rodman & Renshaw, Inc., 972 F.2d 776 (7th Cir.1992) (written disclosures precluded action based on oral statements at variance with the writing); Casella v. Webb, 883 F.2d 805, 808 (9th Cir.1989) ("Statements made in the course of an oral presentation 'cannot be considered in isolation,' but must be viewed 'in the context of the total presentation' ").

62. Sailors v. Northern States Power Co., 4 F.3d 610 (8th Cir.1993).

63. Acito v. IMCERA Group, Inc., 47 F.3d 47 (2d Cir.1995) (deficiencies found by FDA inspectors at one of over thirty business locations was not material). *See also, e.g.,* Wilensky v. Digital Equipment Corp., 903 F.Supp. 173 (D.Mass.1995), *affirmed in part, reversed in part,* 82 F.3d 1194 (1st Cir.1996) (failure to disclose details of new marketing strategy was not actionable).

Today, almost all SEC filings are made electronically. Additionally, investors can view the filings online through the SEC website[96] and also frequently through the company's own website. The materiality of misleading or omitted information will be based on an examination of both the hard copy and the electronic version in order to determine whether the misleading or omitted information is material in light of the "total mix" of information available.[97] The electronic filing process cannot reproduce graphic images contained in the hard copy but instead must include "a fair and accurate narrative description, tabular representation or transcript of the omitted material."[98] A good-faith attempt to provide an accurate narrative or tabular description satisfies the antifraud rules.[99]

Not every miniscule inaccuracy in public statements or SEC filings will be actionable.[100] Thus, for example, the mere fact that a company's disclosures are not consistent with generally accepted accounting practices does not mean that they are actionable under the securities laws.[101] However, reckless departures from accepted accounting practices can be material[102] and made with scienter.[103]

In the context of an insider trading case, the time at which insiders begin to trade is strong circumstantial evidence of materiality.[104]

Management's motives frequently will not be material and therefore need not be disclosed.[109] Information tending to show conflicts of interest of directors, officers, or other major participants is likely to be material.[110] Similarly, facts pertaining to management integrity are likely to be material.[111] Disputes within management are likely to be material.[112] However, it has been held that a description of the company's business plan was accurate and not materially misleading despite a failure to disclose that the board of directors and CEO were divided as to the wisdom of the strategy.[113]

---

96. *See* http://www.sec.gov/edgar.shtml.

97. Demaria v. Andersen, 318 F.3d 170 (2d Cir. 2003).

98. EDGAR Rule 304(a), 17 C.F.R. § 232.304(a).

99. 17 C.F.R. § 232.304(b)(2).

100. *See, e.g.,* ABC Arbitrage Plaintiffs Group v. Tchuruk, 291 F.3d 336 (5th Cir.2002) (the misstatements concerned amounts of money that were too small to have been material); Press v. Quick & Reilly, Inc., 218 F.3d 121 (2d Cir.2000) (broker-dealer's alleged nondisclosure of conflict of interest did not violate Rule 10b–5 or Rule 10b–10).

101. In re Carter–Wallace, Inc. Securities Litigation, 150 F.3d 153 (2d Cir.1998) (company's departure from GAAP was not securities fraud).

102. *E.g.,* In re Datastream Systems, Inc. Securities Litigation, 2000 WL 33176025, [1999–2000 Transfer Binder] Sec. Reg. L. Rep. (CCH) ¶ 90,907 (D.S.C. 2000).

103. *E.g.,* In re Sunbeam Securities Litigation, 89 F.Supp.2d 1326 (S.D. Fla. 1999) (sufficient allegations of accountant's scienter in reviewing company's books); Chalverus v. Pegasystems, Inc., 59 F.Supp.2d 226 (D.Mass.1999) (sufficient allegations in addition to GAAP violations to establish scienter).

104. *See* SEC v. Texas Gulf Sulphur Co., 401 F.2d 833 (2d Cir.1968), *cert. denied*, 394 U.S. 976, 89 S.Ct. 1454, 22 L.Ed.2d 756 (1969).

109. *See, e.g.,* Ward v. Succession of Freeman, 854 F.2d 780 (5th Cir.1988).

110. *See, e.g.,* Kahn v. Wien, 842 F.Supp. 667 (E.D.N.Y.1994) (proxy solicitation).

111. *E.g.,* SEC v. Enterprise Solutions, 142 F.Supp.2d 561 (S.D.N.Y. 2001) (concealment of founder/consultant's criminal past was material).

112. Cooperman v. Individual, Inc., 171 F.3d 43 (1st Cir.1999).

113. *Id.*

§ 12.9[4] Immateriality of Vague Statements; Sales Talk and "Puffing"; Statements of Opinion and Intent

Summary judgment or dismissal of a securities fraud complaint is appropriate when the statements are too vague to be actionable.[123] Similarly, nondisclosure of extremely contingent or highly speculative possibilities (as compared to probabilities) will be immaterial as a matter of law.[124] Additionally, as discussed directly below, if there are adequate cautionary warnings, claims based on projections and other forward looking statements[126] may be subject to dismissal or summary judgment.[127]

As a general proposition both under the common law and under Rule 10b–5, statements of opinion are not actionable[128] unless they relate to management's assessment of the company or to other material facts. Thus, for example, general statements of optimism are not actionable.[130]

Borrowing from the common law of misrepresentation in certain cases the courts have tolerated some degree of "puffing" or "sales talk."[132] However, given the importance of full candor, courts should be reluctant to permit misrepresentation under the guise of puffing. Misrepresentation by implying the existence of certain facts cannot be disguised as mere puffing.[134] Reading the relevant securities cases yields the following general rule: while a good faith opinion (or even "puffing") is not material, a statement of opinion made with no belief in its truth is actionable. This is consistent with the general rule that merely because statements are couched as opinion does not preclude a finding that there is an express or implied misrepresentation of fact.[137] Similar results follow with regard to statements of intent. It is clear that a good faith statement of present intent does not become actionable simply because of a change of intent.[138]

---

123. *See, e.g.,* Fishbaum v. Liz Claiborne, Inc., 189 F.3d 460 (2d Cir.1999) (unpublished opinion) (vague statements of optimism are not actionable). Werbowsky v. American Waste Services, Inc., 172 F.3d 51 (6th Cir.1998) (general statements relating to growth potential for industry were not material misrepresentations of company's growth prospects).

124. *E.g.,* Klein v. General Nutrition Cos., 186 F.3d 338 (3d Cir.1999); In re John Alden Financial Corporation Securities Litigation, 249 F.Supp.2d 1273, 1283–1284 (S.D. Fla. 2003).

126. *See, e.g.,* In re Copper Mountain Securities Litigation, 311 F.Supp.2d 857 (N.D. Cal. 2004) (forward looking statements in press release were not actionable).

127. Parnes v. Gateway 2000, Inc., 122 F.3d 539 (8th Cir.1997); Olkey v. Hyperion 1999 Term Trust, Inc., 98 F.3d 2 (2d Cir.1996).

128. *See, e.g.,* Marsh Group v. Graff, 46 Fed.Appx. 140, 2002 WL 1997949 (4th Cir. 2002) (statements that dividend were "sacred" or "sacrosanct" were immaterial).

130. *See, e.g.,* City of Monroe Employees Retirement System v. Bridgestone Corp., 399 F.3d 651 (6th Cir. 2005) ("loosely optimistic" statements that are too unspecific are not material).

132. *E.g.,* Freedman v. Value Health, Inc., 34 Fed. Appx. 408, 2002 WL 825982 (2d Cir.2002) (unpublished disposition) (statement by CEO of a merger target in a press release that the company's business was "thriving" was supported by evidence, and was, at worst, non-actionable puffery); Nathenson v. Zonagen, Inc., 267 F.3d 400 (5th Cir.2001) (statements in press release that drug was a "fast-acting" "improved formulation" was inactionable puffery but statements concerning the scope of patents were materially misleading).

134. *E.g.,* In re Medimmune, Inc. Securities Litigation, 873 F.Supp. 953 (D.Md.1995) (statement that "there was absolutely no question about the efficacy" of a product could be actionable); In re Gupta Corp. Securities Litigation, 900 F.Supp. 1217 (N.D. Cal. 1994) (explanations of reasons for past success could be actionable, but generalized optimism about future was not).

137. *See, e.g.,* Searls v. Glasser, 64 F.3d 1061 (7th Cir.1995) (statement that company was recession-proof was too vague to be actionable).

138. *E.g.,* In re Phillips Petroleum Securities Litigation, 881 F.2d 1236, 1245 (3d Cir.1989).

§ 12.9[5] Materiality of Contingent Events

As discussed elsewhere in this treatise, disclosures relating to contingent events may be actionable.[144] In such cases, materiality is judged in light of the magnitude of the event in question and the probability of its occurrence.[145] The greater the magnitude and the greater the probability of the event, the more likely it is that it will be material. Thus, for example, relatively uncertain contingencies that would have a great impact on the company may be material. Conversely, a virtually certain event with substantially less significance may also be material. However, too much uncertainty will result in a finding of immateriality.[146]

§ 12.9[6] Materiality of Merger Negotiations

Especially difficult questions of materiality relate to the question of whether preliminary merger negotiations or other control-related transactions must be disclosed.[148] It is the general view that Rule 10b–5 does not impose an affirmative duty of disclosure, and thus silence cannot be actionable.[149] Thus, absent some independent basis for the duty, the existence of preliminary negotiations will not have to be disclosed. However, when a material development is covered by a line-item in a document that needs to be filed with the Commission or otherwise publicly disseminated, silence will not suffice and it must be decided whether preliminary negotiations need be disclosed. Similarly, once an issuer, rather than maintaining silence, voluntarily makes a statement—such as in response to an inquiry from the press or securities analysts—all statements must be totally devoid of material misstatements. As the Supreme Court has pointed out, arguments based on the premature nature of the disclosure are not pertinent in determining the materiality of a particular misstatement; "[t]he secrecy rationale is merely inapposite to the definition of materiality."[152] In addition to the corporation's disclosure obligations, the materiality of merger negotiations can be important in determining whether insiders have traded in violation of the securities laws.[153]

Some courts were of the view that preliminary acquisition negotiations need not be disclosed until there has been an agreement in principle as to the transaction's price and structure.[154] However, the SEC and many courts took a

---

144. *See* § 3.9 *supra.*

145. United States v. Mylett, 97 F.3d 663, 667 (2d Cir.1996), relying on Basic Inc. v. Levinson, 485 U.S. 224, 238, 108 S.Ct. 978, 987, 99 L.Ed.2d 194 (1988).

146. Abromson v. American Pacific Corp., 114 F.3d 898 (9th Cir.1997) (nondisclosure of disagreement regarding effect of early loan repayment was not material in light of extremely low probability).

148. *E.g.,* SEC v. Poirier, 140 F.Supp.2d 1033 (D.Ariz.2001) ("By failing to disclose their control of [the corporation, the defendants] made a material omission in connection with the offer of securities; reasonable investors would find the existence of a control group important when deciding whether to purchase Garcis stock"); *relying on* Nelson v. Serwold, 576 F.2d 1332 (9th Cir.1978) (failure to disclose the existence of a control group that is the driving force behind a public company is a material omission that violates the anti-fraud provisions).

149. *E.g.,* Taylor v. First Union Corp. of South Carolina, 857 F.2d 240 (4th Cir.1988). *See* § 12.19 *infra.*

152. Basic Inc. v. Levinson, 485 U.S. 224, 235, 108 S.Ct. 978, 985, 99 L.Ed.2d 194, 211 (1988).

153. *See* Blanchard v. EdgeMark Financial Corp., 1999 WL 59994, [1999 Transfer Binder] Fed. Sec. L. Rep. (CCH) ¶ 90,439 (N.D. Ill. 1999). Insider trading is discussed in § 12.17 *infra.*

154. *E.g.,* Flamm v. Eberstadt, 814 F.2d 1169 (7th Cir.), *cert. denied*, 484 U.S. 853, 108 S.Ct. 157, 98 L.Ed.2d 112 (1987) (applying price and structure to find preliminary negotiations not material); Greenfield v. Heublein, Inc., 742 F.2d 751 (3d Cir.1984), *cert. denied*, 469 U.S. 1215,

contrary position reasoning the "price and structure" threshold frequently would provide too late a materiality date, especially when the issue is a denial of such negotiations that in fact were taking place.[155] In Basic Inc. v. Levinson,[156] the Supreme Court rejected the price and structure threshold in accepting the SEC's view in holding that whether preliminary merger negotiations have crossed the materiality threshold is a question of fact. Whether a fact is material depends upon whether a reasonable investor would consider it significant in making his or her investment decision.[157] As discussed earlier, materiality generally is based on a highly factual inquiry and thus is difficult to predict. The thrust of the Supreme Court decision in *Basic* seems to favor a finding of materiality in borderline cases of preliminary negotiations.[158] It is clear that the fact that the impending merger is contingent does not preclude a finding of materiality and reliance.[159] The ultimate decision on materiality in this context depends upon an evaluation of the magnitude of the event discounted by the improbability of occurrence.[160]

Questions concerning the need to disclose information may also arise when the issuer, its officers, or directors are questioned by the press or by securities analysts. In such situations a "no comment" response will avoid liability.[161] "No comment" is the only safe harbor (other than giving a full and honest disclosure), as any other response will trigger the highly factual materiality inquiry.[162] While it is true that there are business reasons for keeping certain information confidential, it does not follow that management should be allowed to respond to inquiries with "white lies." As a result of the *Basic* decision, it is imperative that issuers maintain control of their information.[163] It is wise to limit the people who are authorized to speak on the issuer's behalf and to instruct everyone else to follow a "no comment" policy.

§ 12.9[7] Predictions, Projections, and Other "Soft" Information; Management's Discussion and Analysis

Another issue relating to materiality that is getting increased attention is with regard to predictions and other "soft information." There are two

105 S.Ct. 1189, 84 L.Ed.2d 336 (1985) (no duty under Rule 10b–5 to disclose merger negotiations where price had not yet been worked out).

155. *E.g.*, In re Carnation Co., Exch.Act Rel. No. 34–22214, 1985 WL 547371 [1985–1986 Transfer Binder] Fed.Sec.L.Rep. (CCH) ¶ 83,801 (July 8, 1985).

156. 485 U.S. 224, 108 S.Ct. 978, 99 L.Ed.2d 194 (1988).

157. 485 U.S. 224, 108 S.Ct. 978, 99 L.Ed.2d 194 (1988).; TSC Industries, Inc. v. Northway, Inc., 426 U.S. 438, 96 S.Ct. 2126, 48 L.Ed.2d 757 (1976). Materiality under the proxy rules is discussed in § 11.4 *supra*.

158. *See* Glazer v. Formica Corp., 964 F.2d 149 (2d Cir.1992) (reversing finding of immateriality as a matter of law; however, silence was not actionable).

159. Semerenko v. Cendant Corp., 223 F.3d 165, 180 (3d Cir.2000).

160. *See, e.g.,* United States v. Mylett, 97 F.3d 663, 667 (2d Cir.1996).

161. As stated by Delaware Chancellor Leo Stryne, "[t]he maxim silence is golden is not simply a goad to good manners at the local move theater, it is good advice in many realms of life. For example, those are truly words of wisdom when you are not under a duty to speak and someone asks you a question that potentially touches upon information that you would rather not divulge." Corporate Property Associates 14 Inc. v. CHR Holding Corp., 2008 WL 963048 at *1 (Del. Ch. Ct. 2008).

162. *See e.g.,* In re Western Waste Securities Litigation, 1994 WL 561165 [1994–1995 Transfer Binder] Fed. Sec. L. Rep. (CCH) ¶ 98,378 (C.D.Cal.1994).

163. Maintaining control of information is also important in order to prevent insider trading problems. Insider Trading is discussed in § 12.17 *infra*.

questions that frequently arise regarding disclosure of soft information. One question is the extent to which there is an obligation to make a prediction or other disclosures of soft information. A second issue that arises is whether an incorrect opinion, projection, or prediction is actionable.[168] This latter question occurs because of the lesson from the common law of fraud that pure opinion and prediction are not generally actionable.

Following the traditional common law rule, vague opinions and predictions[170] are not actionable.[171] However, the MD & A disclosures required in SEC filings, and discussed in the next section and elsewhere in this treatise, mandate disclosure of known trends or uncertainties that are expected to have a material impact on operations, earnings or sales.[174]

§ 12.9[7][B] Management Discussion & Analysis

There have been significant changes in the Commission's attitude towards projections. There currently are many line-item disclosure requirements that call for certain types of soft information. For example, under Item 303 of Regulation S–K,[193] in the course of its Management's Discussion and Analysis (MD & A) of financial condition and report of operations, management is directed to analyze operations. This analysis must include disclosure of trends and uncertainties likely to have a material effect on the company. Among other things, Item 303 requires management to discuss "any known trends or uncertainties that have had or that the registrant reasonably expects will have a material favorable or unfavorable impact on net sales or revenues or income from continuing operations."[196] The obligation extends to trends and uncertainties that are "*known*" and it thus is not sufficient that they were simply "knowable."[197]

Although the MD & A disclosures contained in Item 303 or Regulation S–K require disclosure of "known trends or uncertainties," MD & A does not alter the basic rule that projections are not required.[205]

§ 12.9[7][C] Safe Harbor for Forward–Looking Statements

As part of the Private Securities Litigation Reform Act of 1995,[212] Congress enacted section 21E of the 1934 Act,[213] which provides a safe harbor for

168. *See, e.g.,* Hillson Partners L.P. v. Adage, Inc., 42 F.3d 204 (4th Cir.1994) (Chief executive officer's statements in press release that the year would produce "excellent" results were merely predictions and thus not actionable misrepresentations of fact).

170. *See, e.g.,* Poth v. Russey, 99 Fed. Appx. 446 (4th Cir. 2004) (predictions relating to share price of anticipated IPO was not actionable as fraud).

171. *See, e.g.,* In re Adams Golf, Inc. Securities Litigation, 381 F.3d 267, 279 (3d Cir. 2004) (generalized forward looking statements were not actionable).

174. Regulation S–K item 303, 17 C.F.R. § 229.303.

193. Regulation S–K contains the SEC's basic disclosure guidelines. 17 C.F.R. §§ 228.10, 229.10 et seq., 7 Fed. Sec. L. Rep. (CCH) ¶¶ 71,001 et seq. Violations of Regulation S–K or S–B disclosure requirements are not *per se* actionable but can be used to support a Rule 10b–5 claim. *See* Feldman v. Motorola, Inc., 1994 WL 160115 [1993–1994 Transfer Binder] Fed. Sec. L. Rep. (CCH) ¶ 98,133 (N.D.Ill.1994).

196. Reg. S–K Item 303(a)(3)(ii), 17 C.F.R. § 229.303(a)(3)(ii).

197. *See* J & R Marketing, SEP v. General Motors Corp., 519 F.3d 552, 558–559 (6th Cir. 2008) (failure to establish that information was in fact known as opposed to knowable).

205. *E.g.,* Glassman v. Computervision Corp., 90 F.3d 617 (1st Cir.1996) (fact that quarter's results lagged behind internal projections did not trigger a duty of disclosure).

212. Pub. Law No. 104–67, 109 Stat. 737 (104th Cong. 1st Sess. December 22, 1995) (HR 1058).

213. 15 U.S.C.A. § 78u–5(c). A parallel provision was added to the 1933 Act. 15 U.S.C.A. § 77z–2.

forward-looking statements. Section 2 is premised on 1933 Act Rule 175,[215] 1934 Act Rule 3b–6,[216] and the "bespeaks caution" doctrine[217] created by the federal courts. The safe harbor is an example of trend of encouraging management to share with the public, its projections and predictions about the company. Section 21E applies to 1934 Act reporting companies, persons acting on behalf of such companies, outside reviewers retained by such companies, and underwriters deriving or obtaining forward-looking information from such companies. Section 21E applies to forward looking statements[221] but not to statements of fact. It has been held, for example, that a statement that a company was "on target" to meet its expectations for the quarter was a statement of present fact and therefore was not a forward-looking statement subject to the protection of the safe harbor.[223] The fact that a statement is forward-looking in part does not bring the safe harbor into play for factual statements.[224] In other words, "[i]n order to be eligible for safe harbor, the forward-looking statements must either (1) be identified as forward-looking and be accompanied by meaningful cautionary language; (2) be immaterial; or (3) not be made with actual knowledge that the statement was false or misleading."[225] Once established, the statutory safe harbor will protect the defendant from liability in a private suit. In an enforcement action, the defendant can seek protection from the safe harbor provided in Rule 3b–6.

§ 12.9[7][D] Analysts' Opinions and Estimates

Ordinarily, a company's management will not be held responsible for opinions, projections, and estimates of security analysts even though management may have supplied the analysts with some of the information they used to formulate their estimates.[240] A company will be held responsible if it passes on misinformation to analysts with the intention that the analysts communicate the misinformation to the market.[241] In the absence of such an intent to defraud the market, a company will not be held accountable for analysts' opinions unless the company has "adopted or endorsed" the analysts' re-

---

215. 17 C.F.R. § 230.175

216. 17 C.F.R. § 240.3b–6.

217. As discussed in § 12.9[8] *infra*, prior to the enactment of section 27A, at least five of the federal circuits courts had endorsed the "bespeaks caution" doctrine. *See* In re Worlds of Wonder Securities Litigation, 35 F.3d 1407 (9th Cir.1994).

221. *See, e.g.,* Lawrence v. Zilog, Inc., 242 F.3d 382 (9th Cir.2000) (table, opinion in Westlaw) (statement about likelihood of merger related to a contingent event and was protected by the safe harbor for forward-looking statements).

223. In re Secure Computing Corp. Securities Litigation, 120 F.Supp.2d 810 (N.D.Cal.2000).

224. *See, e.g.,* In re Stone & Webster, Inc., Securities Litigation, 414 F.3d 187, 213 (1st Cir. 2005).

225. In re Sun Healthcare Group Securities Litigation, 181 F.Supp.2d 1283, 1288 (D.N.M. 2002).

240. Raab v. General Physics Corp., 4 F.3d 286, 288 (4th Cir.1993) ("The securities laws require [a company] to speak truthfully to investors; they do not require the company to police statements made by third party for inaccuracies, even if the third party attributes the statement to [the company]").

241. *See e.g.,* Cooper v. Pickett, 137 F.3d 616 (9th Cir.1997).

ports[242] or unless the company or its management influenced or controlled the analysts' projections.[243] Thus, for example, it has been said that neither an issuer nor its management will be held accountable for an analyst's projection unless the issuer has adopted the projection or has otherwise "entangled" itself with the analyst's opinions.[244]

A statement by a company official that he is "comfortable" with analysts' estimates can form the basis of liability for over-optimism.[251] Such a statement can operate as an adoption of the analyst's opinion.[252] Also, management's statement that it is comfortable with analysts' projections may not be protected by the safe harbors discussed above.[253] However, merely stating that it is comfortable with analysts' estimates does not make the company liable simply because the estimate turns out to be wrong.[254]

§ 12.9[8] The "Bespeaks Caution" Doctrine and Materiality

A number of courts adopted what is sometimes referred to as the "bespeaks caution" doctrine. Congress codified the bespeaks caution doctrine as part of the Private Securities Litigation Reform Act of 1995.[262]

The doctrine holds that sufficient cautionary language may preclude misstatements from being actionable. Since the test of materiality is based upon the total mix of information, it follows that cautionary language should be considered even outside the context of projections. Thus, whether under the rubric of bespeaks caution or the normal test of materiality, cautionary language may go a long way towards defeating a Rule 10b-5 claim. The doctrine has frequently been referred to in the context of judging whether the plaintiff's reliance is reasonable, but it also necessarily relates to materiality in the sense that it addresses the question of whether the misstatements are materially misleading when judged in light of the total mix of information available to the investor.[267]

---

242. In re Burlington Coat Factory Securities Litigation, 114 F.3d 1410, 1428–29 (3d Cir. 1997).

243. Warden v. Crown American Realty Trust, 1999 WL 476996, [1999 Transfer Binder] Fed. Sec. L. Rep. (CCH) ¶ 90,525 (W.D. Pa. 1999) (analysts' statements could not be attributed to company's management).

244. Eisenstadt v. Allen, 113 F.3d 1240 (9th Cir. 1997) (unpublished opinion) (entanglement not found where there is no evidence that corporate insiders reviewed or endorsed analysts' projections in articles before publication); In re Syntex Corp. Securities Litigation, 95 F.3d 922 (9th Cir.1996) (explicit statement that analysts' statements should not be attributed to company and one-way flow of information sufficient to avoid entanglement); Elkind v. Liggett & Myers, 635 F.2d 156 (2d Cir.1980) (policy of examining projections but refraining from comment were not sufficient entanglement to impose duty to correct false information).

251. In re Burlington Coat Factory Securities Litigation, 114 F.3d 1410, 1428 (3d Cir.1997), *relying on* Virginia Bankshares, Inc. v. Sandberg, 501 U.S. 1083, 111 S.Ct. 2749, 115 L.Ed.2d 929 (1991), for the proposition that opinions of management can be actionable.

252. In re Burlington Coat Factory Securities Litigation, 114 F.3d 1410, 1429 (3d Cir.1997).

253. *See e.g.,* In re QLT Inc. Securities Litigation, 312 F.Supp.2d 526, 533 (S.D.N.Y. 2004).

254. Plevy v. Haggerty 38 F.Supp.2d 816 (C.D.Cal.1998) (statement that company was "comfortable" with analysts' estimates did not make company liable in absence of showing that it made material misrepresentations to the analysts).

262. Section 21E(c)(2), 15 U.S.C.A. § 78u–5(c)(2).

267. *See, e.g.,* Gray v. First Winthrop Corp., 82 F.3d 877 (9th Cir.1996) (cautionary language was not sufficiently specific to invoke bespeaks caution doctrine); Warshaw v. Xoma Corp., 74 F.3d 955 (9th Cir.1996) (question of fact as to whether cautionary language was sufficient to cancel optimism about FDA approval); In re Worlds of Wonder Securities Litigation, 35 F.3d 1407 (9th Cir.1994) (bespeaks caution doctrine is an application of the materiality concept); In re

The cases invoking the bespeaks caution doctrine generally have involved projections or other soft information,[270] and it is thus highly doubtful that the doctrine will have more general application. The many courts have held that the bespeaks caution doctrine is limited to projections and thus will not offset material misstatements regarding hard facts.[272] The 1995 legislation that codified the bespeaks caution doctrine expressly applies the doctrine to both oral and written "forward-looking statements,"[273] and should not be extended to material misstatements or omissions of fact.[274]

Boiler-plate generalized cautionary disclaimers will not be sufficient to invoke the bespeaks caution doctrine.[283] Thus, the cautionary statements must be meaningful and generic, which means that vague or boilerplate cautions will not suffice.[284] A corollary of this is that specific cautionary language that puts investors on notice that identified projections may not come to pass will be sufficient.[285] Thus, the cautionary language should specifically identify the factors that may make the projections unreliable.[286]

A review of disclosure documents both before and after the 1995 legislation revealed widespread use of cautionary language in both 1933 and 1934 Act filings.[295] Unfortunately, most such statements were couched in such general terms as to render them ineffective. As noted above, it is not sufficient to simply use a caution to the effect that projections and the like may not reflect actual performance. Similarly, trying to cover all disclosures with a general cautionary statement is unlikely to be effective. In order to be effective, the cautionary language should not only alert the reader to the risk factors.[298] The cautionary language must directly relate to the alleged misstatements in question.[301] As is the case with issues of materiality generally,

Donald J. Trump Casino Securities Litigation–Taj Mahal Litigation, 7 F.3d 357, 371 (3d Cir.1993).

270. *See, e.g.,* Miller v. Champion Enterprises, Inc., 346 F.3d 660 (6th Cir. 2003) (bespeaks caution doctrine precluded claim based on forward-looking statements in CEO's letter to shareholders).

272. *E.g.,* Livid Holdings, Ltd. v. Salomon Smith Barney, Inc., 403 F.3d 1050 (9th Cir. 2005) (bespeaks caution doctrine does not apply to factual representations); Shaw v. Digital Equipment Corp., 82 F.3d 1194 (1st Cir.1996) (bespeaks caution doctrine would apply only if statements related to future events rather than present facts); Harden v. Raffensperger, Hughes & Co., 65 F.3d 1392 (7th Cir.1995) (bespeaks caution doctrine does not apply to hard facts).

273. 1933 Act § 27A(c)(2), 15 U.S.C.A. § 77z–3(c)(2); 1934 Act § 21E(c)(2), 15 U.S.C.A. § 78u–5(c)(2).

274. *See, e.g.,* EP Medsystems, Inc. v. EchoCath, Inc., 235 F.3d 865 (3d Cir.2000).

283. *See, e.g.,* Yanek v. Staar Surgical Co., 388 F. Supp.2d 1110, 1123 (C.D. Cal. 2005) (cautionary language was not "meaningful").

284. *See, e.g.,* In re Sepracor, Inc. Securities Litigation, 308 F.Supp.2d 20, 34 (D. Mass. 2004).

285. *See, e.g.,* In re Metropolitan Securities Litigation, 532 F.Supp.2d 1260, 1291 (E.D.Wash. 2007) ("The bespeaks caution doctrine is thus a corollary to materiality.")(citing this treatise).

286. *See e.g.,* Rombach v. Chang, 355 F.3d 164 (2d Cir. 2004).

295. Bar Association of the City of New York, Committee on Securities Regulation, A Study of Current Practices–Forward–Looking Statements and Cautionary Language After the 1995 Private Securities Litigation Reform Act, 53 Record 725 (1998); SEC Report to the President on the Private Securities Litigation Reform Act of 1995, Fed. Sec. L. Rep. (CCH) Bull. 1763 (April 23, 1997).

298. Bar Association of the City of New York, Committee on Securities Regulation, A Study of Current Practices—Forward–Looking Statements and Cautionary Language After the 1995 Private Securities Litigation Reform Act, 53 Record 725, 743 (1998).

301. In re Donald J. Trump Casino Securities Litigation, 7 F.3d 357, 371 (3d Cir.1993).

the adequacy of a particular cautionary statement will thus be a highly factual determination.

§ 12.9[9] Materiality in Financial Statements; Accounting Issues

Accountants have their own definition of materiality in the context of the presentation of financial information. While the accountants' concept of materiality is significant with the profession, materiality under the securities laws is determined by the same test of materiality that applies to other disclosure issues. In particular, the test of materiality is whether a reasonable investor would consider the information significant in making an investment decision.[302] The financial disclosures form an important part of any securities disclosure filing, as investors need to be able to have faith in the numbers put forth by management in their SEC reports and filings. The securities laws underscore the importance of financial disclosures through the requirement that there be audited financial statements.[303]

In 1999, the Commission issued Staff Accounting Bulletin no. 99 to clarify its position on accounting and materiality issues.[304] Following the highly factual approach to materiality generally, the SEC in SAB No. 99 reinforced the "facts and circumstances" test of materiality. Although more frustrating than a bright-line test would be, the SEC approach properly recognizes the difficulties of generalizing rules for materiality. The SEC release offered significant guidance for evaluating materiality in the context of financial statements.

The SEC rejects a numerical test of materiality of accounting items. This includes rejection of the five-percent threshold that frequently is cited in the accounting profession. Instead, the Commission reaffirms that even relatively small deviations can be material, especially if they are intentional.[305] The potential materiality of even relatively small accounting errors is not a new development, as it reflects the long-standing views of the courts and the SEC.[306] However, not every financial misstatement will cross the materiality threshold.

§ 12.9[10] Duty to Correct or Update

Absent a specific line-item requirement in an SEC filing, there is no affirmative duty to disclose merely because a fact is material. This result is mandated by the terms of Rule 10b–5, which prohibits omissions of a material fact only if the fact was "necessary to make the statements made," not materially misleading.[314] The rule thus does not address the omission of facts in the absence of affirmatively making a statement. However, once a state-

302. Basic Inc. v. Levinson, 485 U.S. 224, 108 S.Ct. 978, 99 L.Ed.2d 194 (1988); TSC Industries, Inc. v. Northway, Inc., 426 U.S. 438, 449, 96 S.Ct. 2126, 2132, 48 L.Ed.2d 757 (1976).

303. The accounting and auditing requirements are discussed in § 9.6 *supra*.

304. Staff Accounting Bulletin No. 99—Materiality, Release No. SAB 99, 64 Fed. Reg. 451250–01 (Aug. 12, 1999).

305. Staff Accounting Bulletin No. 99—Materiality, Release No. SAB 99, 64 Fed. Reg. 451250–01 (Aug. 12, 1999).

306. *See, e.g.,* SEC v. Jos. Schlitz Brewing Co., 452 F.Supp. 824 (E.D.Wis.1978) (nondisclosure of kickback scheme was material because, inter alia, it reflected on the lack of management integrity).

314. Rule 10b–5(b), 17 C.F.R. § 240.10b–5(b).

ment of fact (as opposed to a projection[315]) has been made, the person making the statement is then under a duty to correct any misstatements that person also perhaps has a duty to update the public as to any material changes.[316] The courts have drawn a distinction between the duty to correct misinformation and the absence of a duty to update information that was accurate when disseminated.[317]

The duty to correct arises with respect to statements made by the person so obligated or those for which some responsibility can be attributed to the person charged with a duty to correct. In contrast, ordinarily there is no duty to correct statements made by others[318] unless there is some degree of responsibility for those third-party statements.

The Private Securities Litigation Reform Act of 1995 expressly addresses the absence of a duty to update. Section 21E(d) of the 1934 Act[320] specifically states that no person making a forward-looking statement is under any duty to update the statement.

There are times when a company's disclosures will trigger a duty to update. There is an important but difficult distinction to be made, however, between the duty to correct misleading factual information and the absence of a duty to update a forward looking statement. Thus, for example, there is a duty to correct when the factual information contained therein remains "alive" in the minds of investors.[322] When projections are made there is no implication that they will be updated. Instead, the only implication is that they were made on a reasonable basis[324] and in good faith.[325] Even if the law does not impose a duty to make corrective disclosures, the need to maintain investor confidence in the company and its management will generally dictate that corrective disclosures be made.

---

315. 1933 Act section 27A(d), 15 U.S.C.A. § 7z–2(d) ("Nothing in this section shall impose upon any person a duty to update a forward-looking statement"). *Accord* 1934 Act section 21E(d), 15 U.S.C.A. § 78u–5(d). *See also, e.g.,* Mercury Air Group, Inc. v. Mansour, 237 F.3d 542, 547 (5th Cir.2001) (failure to update projections did not violate Rule 10b–5).

316. *See e.g.,* Weiner v. Quaker Oats Co., 129 F.3d 310 (3d Cir.1997) (company had duty to update debt-equity ratio that would result from pending purchase of another company; however, slight variation from original projection was immaterial); Stransky v. Cummins Engine Co., 51 F.3d 1329 (7th Cir.1995) (stating cause of action for failure to update after predictions of better profit margins).

317. Gallagher v. Abbott Laboratories, 269 F.3d 806 (7th Cir.2001) ("a statement may be 'corrected' only if it was incorrect when made").

318. *See, e.g.,* Electronic Specialty Co. v. International Controls Corp., 409 F.2d 937 (2d Cir.1969) (no duty for company to correct published misstatement not directly attributable to it).

320. 15 U.S.C.A. § 78u–5.

322. *See* In re Burlington Coat Factory Securities Litigation, 114 F.3d 1410, 1432 (3d Cir.1997).

324. *See, e.g.,* In re 2TheMart.com, Inc. Securities Litigation, 114 F.Supp.2d 955 (C.D. Cal. 2000) (projections that on-line auction site would soon be operational lacked reasonable basis where there were no agreements to design or construct the site).

325. In re Burlington Coat Factory Securities Litigation, 114 F.3d 1410, 1433 (3d Cir.1997) ("A judicially created rule that triggers a duty of disclosure of all material information every time a single specific earnings forecast is disclosed would likely result in a drastic reduction in the number of such projections. It is these specific earnings projections that are most useful to investors in deciding whether to invest in a firm's securities").

§ 12.10 Reliance in Rule 10b–5 Actions; Fraud on the Market

The reliance requirement is a corollary of materiality[3] and is closely related to causation issues that are considered in a subsequent section.[4] As is true under the common law, the reliance requirement applies in securities fraud cases. For example, as was observed by the Second Circuit, "to the requirement that the individual plaintiff must have acted upon the fact misrepresented, is added the parallel requirement that a reasonable man would also have acted upon the fact misrepresented."[7] Thus, in order to recover damages in an action under Rule 10b–5, the reliance element must be satisfied.

Reliance is an element of a private suit under Rule 10b–5, but not in enforcement actions brought by the government. Thus, it is not necessary for the SEC to establish reliance. Similarly, reliance need not be shown in a criminal prosecution. Furthermore, even in private suits, in some instances that are discussed below the courts have not required proof of *actual* reliance.[12] Proof of reliance is an especially difficult problem in an omission case where the question is how the plaintiff would have acted had the required information been disclosed.[14] If the transaction takes place prior to the disclosures in question, reliance cannot be established.[15]

Following the same pattern as cases involving materiality, questions of reliance are highly factual and thus courts are properly reluctant to dismiss on the pleadings.[34] Similarly, claims that reliance was unreasonable will often be highly factual and thus inappropriate for dismissal before trial.[35]

The Supreme Court in Affiliated Ute Citizens of Utah v. United States[42] held that in a face-to-face transaction between seller and purchaser where the defendant purchaser failed to state material facts, the plaintiff's reliance can be presumed from the materiality of the omissions. The Court there held that upon a finding of materiality it is then up to the defendant to prove that the plaintiff had not in fact relied on the material omissions. Many subsequent district court and court of appeals decisions have followed this presumption of reliance in omission cases but have refused to extend this ruling to the extent of eliminating the reliance requirements from the securities laws even in the case of face-to-face transactions. The *Affiliated Ute* presumption arose in the context of an omission case. Some courts have held that this presumption of

---

§ 12.10

3. *See, e.g.,* Semerenko v. Cendant Corp., 223 F.3d 165, 180 (3d Cir.2000) (relying on this treatise).

4. *See* § 12.11 *infra.*

7. List v. Fashion Park, Inc., 340 F.2d 457, 462 (2d Cir.1965), *cert. denied,* 382 U.S. 811, 86 S.Ct. 23, 15 L.Ed.2d 60 1965. Therefore, there must be some connection between the alleged fraud and the transaction under attack. *See, e.g.,* Jackvony v. RIHT Financial Corp., 873 F.2d 411 (1st Cir.1989). *See also* § 12.11 *infra.*

12. *See, e.g.,* Fulco, Inc. v. American Cable Systems, 1989 WL 205356 [1989–1990 Transfer Binder] Fed.Sec.L.Rep. 94,980 (D.Mass.1989) (limited partners need not show reliance since they were forced sellers). However, in other contexts actual reliance must be shown. *E.g.,* Levine v. Prudential Bache Properties, Inc., 855 F.Supp. 924 (N.D.Ill.1994) (complaint failed to plead actual reliance on prospectus).

14. *See, e.g.,* Affiliated Ute Citizens v. United States, 406 U.S. 128, 150–54, 92 S.Ct. 1456, 1470, 1472, 31 L.Ed.2d 741 (1972), *rehearing denied,* 407 U.S. 916, 92 S.Ct. 2430, 32 L.Ed.2d 692 (1972) (applying a presumption of reliance in an omission case).

15. Integrated Technology & Development, Inc. v. Rosenfield, [1999–2000 Transfer Binder] Fed. Sec. L. Rep. (CCH) ¶ 91,038 (E.D.N.Y. 2000).

34. *See, e.g.,* Provenz v. Miller, 102 F.3d 1478 (9th Cir.1996)

35. *See, e.g.,* Castellano v. Young & Rubicam, Inc., 257 F.3d 171 (2d Cir.2001).

42. 406 U.S. 128, 153–154, 92 S.Ct. 1456, 1472, 31 L.Ed.2d 741 (1972), *rehearing denied,* 407 U.S. 916, 92 S.Ct. 2430, 32 L.Ed.2d 692 (1972).

reliance is limited to cases involving a materials omission does not apply in the case of misstatements (as opposed to omissions) to the extent that the plaintiff is in a position to prove reliance.[47] It has been reasoned that the presumption is based on the difficulty of proving a negative—namely, the fact that someone relied on something that was not said.[49]

In what was described as "an absurdity"[51] in light of its cost and impracticability, the Second Circuit once indicated that in a class action separate trials might be necessary in order to resolve the issue of reliance with regard to transactions in a faceless market.[52] On the other hand, typicality for class action purposes does not mean that the claims must be identical; and class actions will be permitted to proceed unless it is clear that the common questions of fact do not predominate.[53] Plaintiffs in a class action, for example, may not be proper representatives with regard to transactions and statements made subsequent to the plaintiff's purchases.[54]

The clear trend is that in doubtful cases courts seem to favor continuation of the class. For example, it has been pointed out that the question of whether individual trials on the reliance issue are necessary is itself a question that is common to the whole class.[56] Accordingly, the proper approach is to let the litigation continue as a class action until it becomes apparent that the common issues no longer predominate.[57] There may be cases, however, where it is clear from the outset that because of reliance issues the common questions do not predominate and a class action is not appropriate.[58]

Actively traded public markets are generally efficient markets. In an efficient market, securities prices are determined by the total mix of available information. The integrity of the securities markets is premised on the dissemination of accurate information about companies and their securities. When misleading information is injected into the market, it can move securities prices in an artificial manner. Investors in publicly traded securities rely on securities prices as the reflection of accurate pricing mechanisms. When the pricing mechanisms are rendered inaccurate because of material misinformation, something that is tantamount to a fraud has taken place. Thus, for example, in an efficient market the materiality of a statement can be judged

47. *See* Joseph v. Wiles, 223 F.3d 1155 (10th Cir.2000).

49. Binder v. Gillespie, 184 F.3d 1059, 1063 (9th Cir.1999).

51. Richard W. Jennings & Harold Marsh, Jr., Securities Regulation: Cases and Materials 1049 (5th ed. 1982).

52. Green v. Wolf Corp., 406 F.2d 291 (2d Cir.1968), *cert. denied*, 395 U.S. 977, 89 S.Ct. 2131, 23 L.Ed.2d 766 (1969).

53. *E.g.,* In re Retek, Inc. Securities Litigation, 236 F.R.D. 431 (D. Minn. 2006).

54. *See, e.g.,* In re Donald J. Trump Casino Securities Litigation, 793 F.Supp. 543, 565 (D.N.J.1992).

56. *E.g.,* In re Western Union Securities Litigation, 120 F.R.D. 629 (D.N.J.1988).

57. In re The Loewen Group Securities Litigation, 233 F.R.D. 154 (E.D. Pa. 2005) (class action allowed to proceed, noting, among other things that "the interests of justice require that in a doubtful case"), quoting Kahan v. Rosenstiel, 424 F.2d 161, 169 (3d Cir. 1970) and Esplin v. Hirschi, 402 F.2d 94, 101 (10th Cir.1968).

58. In re Initial Public Offering Securities Litigation, 471 F.3d 24 (2d Cir. 2006) (securities action based on misstatements in the prospectus created individualized proof of reliance and thus the common issues did not predominate; the fraud on the market presumption is not applicable to initial public offerings).

by the market's reaction immediately following the disclosure.[65] Just as an efficient market has an impact on materiality issues, it can come to bear on reliance. Fraud on the market recognizes the impact of false information by providing a presumption of reliance for investors who are able to establish the other elements of securities fraud. The fraud on the market presumption can be applied to any publicly disseminated statements and is not limited to statements made by the company or its representatives.[66]

In applying the presumption of reliance and economic theory, a number of courts fashioned a fraud-on-the-market presumption for proving reliance.[73] Simply put, the courts find that the reliance requirement in a securities fraud action can be satisfied by a showing that the market price was affected by the misstatement or omission and the plaintiff's injury is due to a purchase or sale at the then fraudulently induced market price.

The fraud-on-the-market presumption of reliance has three basic requirements. First, the information in question must have been material.[75] Second, the market must have been sufficiently active to be deemed to be efficient.[76] Third, the misinformation must have been disseminated publicly.[77] In deciding whether to certify a class, a court may look beyond the allegations of the complaint in evaluating the fraud-on-the-market presumption.[78]

The fraud on the market theory was adopted by the Supreme Court in a sharply divided opinion. In Basic, Inc. v. Levinson,[82] the Supreme Court adopted the fraud-on-the-market theory for cases involving affirmative misrepresentations. *Basic* involved alleged materially misleading denials of preliminary merger negotiations. The Court viewed the fraud-on-the-market presumption of reliance as a natural inference "supported by common sense and probability."[83] The Court also recognized the importance of the fraud on the market presumption in allowing class action claims to proceed.[84]

The fraud-on-the-market presumption of reliance is a driving force that permits a finding that common issues predominate in class actions based on publicly disseminated statements.[89] For example in fraud-on-the-market cases, some courts have held that proof that the market price was affected will prove reliance by the market,[90] even if the plaintiff never saw the statements in question.[91] The fraud-on-the-market analysis does not conclusively establish reliance. It merely serves as a presumption of reliance that, for example, can

65. *See, e.g.,* In re Merck & Co. Securities Litigation, 432 F.3d 261 (3d Cir. 2005).

66. In re Salomon Analyst Metromedia Litigation, 544 F.3d 474 (2d Cir. 2008).

73. *E.g.*, Hayes v. Gross, 982 F.2d 104 (3d Cir.1992).

75. Nonmaterial misstatements do not violate Rule 10b–5. *See* § 12.9 *supra*.

76. *See, e.g.,* Feinman v. Dean Witter Reynolds, Inc., 84 F.3d 539 (2d Cir.1996).

77. West v. Prudential Securities, Inc., 282 F.3d 935 (7th Cir.2002).

78. Gariety v. Grant Thornton, LLP, 368 F.3d 356 (4th Cir. 2004).

82. 485 U.S. 224, 108 S.Ct. 978, 99 L.Ed.2d 194 (1988).

83. *Id.* at 246, 108 S.Ct. at 991, 99 L.Ed.2d at 218.

84. The Court quoted the district court in explaining that "the presumption of reliance created by the fraud-on-the-market theory provide[s] 'a practical resolution to the problem of balancing the substantive requirement of proof of reliance in securities cases against the procedural requisites of [Fed.Rule Civ Proc.] 23.' " *Id.* at 242, 108 S.Ct. at 989, 99 L.Ed.2d at 215. *See also, e.g.,* Seidman v. American Mobile Systems, Inc., 813 F.Supp. 323 (E.D.Pa.1993).

89. *See, e.g.*, Pinker v. Roche Holdings Ltd., 292 F.3d 361 (3d Cir.2002).

90. *E.g.*, Zweig v. Hearst Corp., 594 F.2d 1261, 1271 (9th Cir.1979).

91. In re Control Data Corp. Securities Litigation, 933 F.2d 616 (8th Cir.1991).

be rebutted by proof that the plaintiff would have purchased the stock even if the information had been fully and accurately disclosed.[92] Merely establishing a material misrepresentation, however, will not trigger the fraud-on-the-market presumption unless it can also be shown that the market reacted to the misstatements.[93] Thus, for example, sufficient cautionary information available to the public may preclude a fraud-on-the-market claim.[94] However, once the presumption is established, the defendant must show that the price was not causally affected.[95] Conversely, evidence of a precipitous decline in the stock upon disclosure of the facts that were previously misstated will support the fraud-on-the-market presumption of reliance.[96]

The fraud-on-the-market presumption is borrowed from economic theory and the Efficient Capital Market Hypothesis.[97] A necessary element of the hypothesis is that the market is in fact efficient.[98] An efficient market means that the market must react quickly in processing information and enabling it be to be reflected in the market price.[100] It is axiomatic that the fraud-on-the-market presumption depends on the existence of an active market.[105]

It would appear that the absence of an efficient market should be sufficient to rebut any presumption of reliance based solely on market impact. However, the Eleventh Circuit held that even undeveloped markets can provide a basis for the "fraud-on-the-market" presumption of reliance, at least where the defendants knew that there would be no market but for their scheme to defraud.[136] This type of claim does not really involve a fraud *on* the market but rather a fraudulent scheme depicting the existence of a market which in fact would not exist upon full and accurate disclosure. Some courts have referred to this as a fraud-created-the-market theory of recovery.[137] Some federal courts have rejected the fraud-created-the-market theory of recovery.[140] In fact, the Second Circuit held that since there is no preexisting market and hence no efficient market, fraud on the market presumption may not be invoked with respect to fraud in connection with an initial public

92. *E.g.,* In re K Mart Corp. Securities Litigation, 1996 WL 924811 [1997 Transfer Binder] Fed. Sec. L. Rep. (CCH) ¶ 99,511 (E.D. Mich. 1996).

93. *See* Lee v. Sierra On-Line, 1994 WL 655898 [1994–1995 Transfer Binder] Fed. Sec. L. Rep. (CCH) ¶ 98,420 (E.D.Cal.1994).

94. Kaplan v. Rose, 49 F.3d 1363 (9th Cir.1994).

95. Basic Inc. v. Levinson, 485 U.S. 224, 248, 108 S.Ct. 978, 992, 99 L.Ed.2d 194 (1988).

96. Greenberg v. Crossroads Systems, Inc., 364 F.3d 657 (5th Cir. 2004).

97. Broadly speaking, the hypothesis maintains that in an efficient market, pricing will be reflective of the sum total of investors' and analysts' evaluation of publicly available information about the company. For discussion of the hypothesis, *see, e.g.,* Thomas L. Hazen, Rational Investments, Speculation, or Gambling: Derivative Securities and Financial Futures and Their Effect on the Underlying Capital Markets, 86 Nw.U.L.Rev. 987 (1992); Donald C. Langevoort, Theories, Assumptions, and Securities Regulation: Market Efficiency Revisited, 140 U.Pa.L.Rev. 151 (1992).

98. *See, e.g.,* Bell v. Ascendant Solutions, Inc., 422 F.3d 307 (5th Cir. 2005).

100. In re PolyMedica Corp. Securities Litigation, 432 F.3d 1, 14, 19 (1st Cir. 2005).

105. *See, e.g.,* In re PolyMedica Corp. Securities Litigation, 432 F.3d 1 (1st Cir. 2005).

136. Shores v. Sklar, 844 F.2d 1485 (11th Cir.1988), *rehearing granted and opinion vacated,* 855 F.2d 722 (11th Cir.1988).

137. *See, e.g.,* Joseph v. Wiles, 223 F.3d 1155 (10th Cir.2000), relying on Ockerman v. May Zima & Co., 27 F.3d 1151, 1160 (6th Cir.1994) and Ross v. Bank South, 885 F.2d 723, 729 (11th Cir.1989) (en banc) ("[T]he fraud must be so pervasive that it goes to the very existence of the bonds and the validity of their presence on the market.").

140. Eckstein v. Balcor Film Investors, 8 F.3d 1121 (7th Cir.1993).

offering.[141] The Tenth Circuit accepted the fraud-created-the-market theory, but only if the plaintiff establishes that the securities were in fact unmarketable or worthless but for the fraud.[142]

A number of courts have referred to a "truth on the market" defense to a fraud-on-the-market theory of liability.[147] The origins of this defense can be found in the Supreme Court decision in Basic, Inc. v. Levinson.[148] In *Basic,* the Court noted that even in the face of materially misleading statements, if accurate information "credibly entered the market and dissipated the effects of the misstatements," then the misstatements would not be actionable.[149] Although sounding more like a question of causation or materiality, many courts have labeled the availability of adequate accurate public information as a truth-on-the-market defense.[152] Regardless of the nomenclature of the defense, a showing that the misstatements or nondisclosures did not affect the market price will rebut the fraud-on-the-market presumption of reliance.[153] The fact that the true information is publicly available will not preclude liability when that information is not easily accessible.[154] Furthermore, it must be established that the truth in the market was sufficient to counteract the alleged fraudulent impact of the statements in question.[155]

Any reliance by the plaintiff must be reasonable.[157] actual reliance will not necessarily be sufficient to establish a securities fraud claim.[158] The circumstances surrounding the transaction must be such as to sufficiently establish at least a reasonable basis[159] for relying on the alleged misstatement when

141. *See,* In re Initial Public Offering Securities Litigation, 471 F.3d 24 (2d Cir. 2006).

142. Joseph v. Wiles, 223 F.3d 1155 (10th Cir.2000) ("Thus we require the securities to be unmarketable in order to invoke the presumption of reliance based on fraud creating the market;" plaintiff failed to meet that burden).

147. *See, e.g.,* In re Seagate Technology II Securities Litigation, 843 F.Supp. 1341, 1368–69 (N.D.Cal.1994). *See also, e.g.,* Heliotrope General, Inc. v. Ford Motor Co., 189 F.3d 971 (9th Cir.1999).

148. 485 U.S. 224, 108 S.Ct. 978, 99 L.Ed.2d 194 (1988), *on remand,* 871 F.2d 562 (6th Cir.1989).

149. 485 U.S. at 248–49, 108 S.Ct. at 992.

152. *See, e.g.,* In re Seagate Technology II Securities Litigation, 802 F.Supp. 271, 275 (N.D.Cal.1992), *relying on* In re Convergent Technologies Securities Litigation, 948 F.2d 507, 513 (9th Cir.1991) *and* In re Apple Computer Securities Litigation, 886 F.2d 1109, 1115 (9th Cir.1989).

153. Heliotrope General, Inc. v. Ford Motor Co., 189 F.3d 971 (9th Cir.1999); Fine v. American Solar King Corp., 919 F.2d 290, 299 (5th Cir.1990); In re Seagate Technology II Securities Litigation, 843 F.Supp. 1341 (N.D.Cal.1994).

154. *See* Berry v. Valence Technology, Inc., 175 F.3d 699, 706 (9th Cir.1999) (statement in a magazine article criticizing a company and its stock did not demonstrate that the market already knew of the company's fraud).

155. Ganino v. Citizens Utilities Co., 228 F.3d 154 (2d Cir.2000) (reversing dismissal based on truth-on-the-market defense); In re Ribozyme Pharmaceuticals, Inc. Securities Litigation, 119 F.Supp.2d 1156, 1163 (D. Colo. 2000) (the true facts were not sufficient to counteract the defendants' false statements); In re Resource America Securities Litigation, 2000 WL 1053861, [1999–2000 Transfer Binder] Fed. Sec. L. Rep. (CCH) ¶ 91,029 (E.D. Pa. 2000) (failure to adequately allege truth-on-the-market defense to action based on fraud-on-the-market presumption of reliance). *See also, e.g.,* In re Yukos Oil Company Securities Litigation, 2006 WL 3007036 (S.D.N.Y. 2006) (numerous articles in the press resulted in truth on the market defense for alleged omissions regarding the CEO's political activity; but sustaining the complaint as to alleged misrepresentation of tax liability).

157. *See* Starr ex rel. Estate of Sampson v. Georgeson Shareholder, Inc., 412 F.3d 103 (2d Cir. 2005).

158. *See, e.g.,* CMNY Capital, L.P. v. Deloitte & Touche, 821 F.Supp. 152, 159 (S.D.N.Y.1993).

159. Gochnauer v. A.G. Edwards & Sons, Inc., 810 F.2d 1042 (11th Cir.1987).

entering into the transaction in question.[160]

Issuing warnings as to the reliability of information may preclude a showing of reasonable reliance on the information.[166] It has been held, for example, that a plaintiff claiming reliance on alleged material misstatements will be charged with knowledge of warnings in the private placement memorandum concerning the investment risks, thus making reliance unreasonable.[167] In contrast, oral statements minimizing the significance of the written materials will still be actionable.[168] Although general blanket disclaimers of reliance will not be effective,[169] a specific disclaimer will preclude a fraud action.[170] This is especially true where the specific disclaimers are a result of face-to-face negotiations.[171] Similarly, warnings in connection with a merger will negate reliance on the statements that were the subject of the warnings.[172]

As noted earlier, many courts have referred to the effect of warnings as the "bespeaks caution" doctrine which, on appropriate facts, will preclude a finding of reasonable reliance.[173] However, blanket warnings and disclaimers in offering materials cannot preclude reliance on otherwise materially misleading statements. The cautionary language must be sufficient to adequately negate any reasonable implication to the contrary from the projection or prediction.[175]

The Tenth Circuit, which has been followed in many other circuits, summarized the relevant factors considered by the courts in assessing the reasonableness of reliance:

> the following are all relevant factors in determining whether reliance was justifiable: (1) the sophistication and expertise of the plaintiff in financial and securities matters; (2) the existence of long standing business or personal relationships; (3) access to the relevant information; (4) the existence of a fiduciary relationship; (5) concealment of the fraud; (6) the opportunity to detect the fraud; (7) whether the plaintiff initiated the stock transaction or sought to expedite the transaction; and (8) the generality or specificity of the misrepresentations.[177]

---

160. Atari Corp. v. Ernst & Whinney, 981 F.2d 1025, 1030 (9th Cir.1992); Teamsters Local 282 Pension Trust Fund v. Angelos, 762 F.2d 522, 530 (7th Cir.1985); Zobrist v. Coal–X Inc., 708 F.2d 1511, 1517 (10th Cir.1983).

166. *See* discussion of the bespeaks caution doctrine in § 12.9[8] *supra.*

167. Ambrosino v. Rodman & Renshaw, Inc., 972 F.2d 776 (7th Cir.1992).

168. *See, e.g.,* Parkhurst v. North American Financial Services Cos., 919 F.Supp. 270 (E.D.Mich.1996).

169. *See, e.g.,* In re National Century Financial Enterprises, Inc., 541 F. Supp.2d 986, 1004 (S.D. Ohio 2007) (disclaimers were not sufficient).

170. *See, e.g.,* Chavin v. McKelvey, 182 F.3d 898 (2d Cir.1999).

171. Chavin v. McKelvey, 182 F.3d 898 (2d Cir.1999).

172. *See* Kaplan v. Lazard Freres & Co., 2000 WL 145958, [1999–2000 Transfer Binder] Fed. Sec. L. Rep. (CCH) ¶ 90,760 (S.D.N.Y. 2000), *affirmed in relevant part, reversed in part,* 234 F.3d 1262 (2d Cir.2000).

173. The genesis of the bespeaks caution doctrine is found in Polin v. Conductron Corp., 552 F.2d 797, 806 n. 28 (8th Cir.), *cert. denied,* 434 U.S. 857, 98 S.Ct. 178, 54 L.Ed.2d 129 (1977) (the cautionary language were words which "bespeak caution in outlook and fall far short of the assurance required for a finding of falsity or fraud").

175. *E.g.,* Rubinstein v. Collins, 20 F.3d 160 (5th Cir.1994).

177. Zobrist v. Coal–X, Inc., 708 F.2d 1511, 1516 (10th Cir.1983).

A plaintiff's sophistication will be considered a factor in determining whether his or her reliance was reasonable.[182] However, the fact that an investor is sophisticated will not preclude a finding that he or she reasonably relied on the misstatements in question.[183] Sophisticated investors will, however, be held to a high burden of proof regard the reasonableness of their reliance. The courts will consider the surrounding circumstances in determining the extent to which an investor's sophistication will bear upon the reasonableness of any reliance. The objective requirement of reasonable reliance may not apply when the defendant intentionally targets a naive or careless investor. The naivety or carelessness of a targeted investor will not preclude a finding of materiality when the defendant knew or should have known of the investor's frailties.[186]

§ 12.11 Causation in Actions Under Rule 10b–5

As in other areas of the law, causation embodies two distinct concepts: (1) cause in fact and (2) legal cause. Legal cause is frequently dealt with in terms of proximate cause. Cause-in-fact questions are frequently stated in terms of the sine qua non rule: but for the act or acts complained of, the injury would not have occurred. Legal cause represents the law's doctrinal basis for limiting liability even though cause in fact may be proven. Courts in both tort and contract cases frequently speak in terms of foreseeability in order to determine the extent of proximate or legal cause.[9] Causation in securities law involves the same analysis of cause in fact and legal cause that was developed under the common law.[10] However, notwithstanding the similarity of analysis, the courts have developed their own rubric for causation in securities cases.

Courts have broken down the causation analysis in securities cases into two categories: "transaction causation" and "loss causation."[11] As is true with any causation analysis, these concepts are but a means to an end. As developed more fully below, transaction causation and loss causation can be difficult concepts, and careless use of these terms is likely to hinder rather than facilitate understanding.[14]

One prong of the causation requirement in a securities fraud case requires plaintiff to prove "transaction causation," which means that, but for the wrongful conduct, the transaction would not have gone through, at least in the form that it eventually took.[26] The concept of transaction causation has been properly characterized as "nothing more than 'but for' causation," and more questionably as "merely another way of describing reliance."[27] Although

182. *See, e.g.,* ATSI Communications, Inc. v. Shaar Fund, Ltd., 493 F.3d 87, 105 (2d Cir. 2007) (plaintiff's sophistication was a factor in finding failure to establish reliance in securities fraud suit).

183. Rubin v. Schottenstein, Zox & Dunn, 143 F.3d 263 (6th Cir.1998).

186. United States v. Davis, 226 F.3d 346, 358 (5th Cir.2000) ("the naivety, carelessness negligence, or stupidity of a victim" does not preclude criminal liability for fraud).

§ 12.11

9. *E.g.,* Berckeley Investment Group, Ltd. v. Colkitt, 455 F.3d 195, 222 (3d Cir. 2006).

10. *E.g.,* First Interstate Bank of Nevada v. Chapman & Cutler, 837 F.2d 775 (7th Cir.1988).

11. *E.g.,* In re Daou Systems, Inc., 411 F.3d 1006 (9th Cir. 2005).

14. *See* LHLC Corp. v. Cluett, Peabody & Co., 842 F.2d 928, 931 (7th Cir.1988) (citing this treatise).

26. *See, e.g.,* Gannon v. Continental Insurance Co., 920 F.Supp. 566 (D.N.J.1996).

27. Castellano v. Young & Rubicam, Inc., 257 F.3d 171, 186 (2d Cir.2001).

reliance and causation constitute distinct elements of a Rule 10b–5 claim, transaction causation may be established by facts that establish reliance.[28] The Supreme Court has acknowledged the close relationship between reliance and causation. For example, conduct that is too remote may preclude a finding of both causation and reliance.[29]

Transaction causation does not represent the strictest form of "but for" causation because it requires only that the terms of the transaction have been significantly affected by the material misstatement or omission.[30] It is not necessary to prove that the transaction would not have occurred but for the alleged 10b–5 violation.[31] It must be shown, however, that there was a direct causal nexus between the alleged violation and the resulting transaction.[32] When the facts are compelling, courts have been willing to infer or presume transaction causation once it has been established that an omission of fact is material.[34]

A Supreme Court decision involving causation under the proxy rules undoubtedly has implications for fraud actions brought under Rule 10b–5. In Virginia Bankshares, Inc. v. Sandberg,[42] the Supreme Court held that alleged misstatements that were made in connection with a shareholder vote that was not required to effectuate the transaction in question could not form the basis of a private damage action.[43] The Court therefore held that material misstatements or omissions which affect the transaction only in a collateral sense fail to establish the type of direct causal connection that is required to state a claim under the proxy rules. The Court thus applied a rule that seems to call for a requirement of direct transaction causation as a precondition to liability.

Once the plaintiff has proven the requisite transaction causation, it will be necessary to prove loss causation. Difficult problems of proof may arise regarding the causal relationship of the conduct to both the transaction and injury in question.[47] In large part, the problems of proving loss causation are the same as those involved in demonstrating the extent of the plaintiff's actual loss. In many cases the requirement of loss causation will include the necessity of showing a link between the fraud in question and the effect on the value of the securities. In other words, the plaintiff must establish that the fraudulent conduct was the proximate cause of the plaintiff's economic loss.[54] As noted by the Second Circuit, the concept of loss causation under the

28. Arduini/Messina Partnership v. National Medical Financial Services Corp., 74 F.Supp.2d 352, 360 (S.D.N.Y.1999) ("Plaintiffs may satisfy the element of transaction causation by pleading either direct reliance on misrepresentations or omissions, or indirect reliance through an allegation of 'fraud on the market' ").

29. *See* Stoneridge Investment Partners, LLC v. Scientific–Atlanta, Inc., 552 U.S. 148, 128 S.Ct. 761, 169 L.Ed.2d 627 (2008) ("reliance is tied to causation, leading to the inquiry whether respondents' acts were immediate or remote to the injury"). *Stoneridge Partners* is discussed in § 12.25[3], *infra*.

30. *See, e.g.,* Suez Equity Investors, L.P. v. Toronto–Dominion Bank, 250 F.3d 87 (2d Cir.2001).

31. *See, e.g.,* Schutzky Distributors, Inc. v. Kelly, 643 F.Supp. 57 (N.D.Cal.1986).

32. *E.g.,* Grace v. Rosenstock, 228 F.3d 40 (2d Cir.2000).

34. Castellano v. Young & Rubicam, Inc., 257 F.3d 171, 186 (2d Cir.2001) (noting that transaction causation is presumed when claim rests on material omission), relying on Affiliated Ute Citizens v. United States, 406 U.S. 128, 153–54, 92 S.Ct. 1456, 31 L.Ed.2d 741 (1972); Litton Indus., Inc. v. Lehman Bros. Kuhn Loeb Inc., 967 F.2d 742, 747–48 (2d Cir.1992).

42. 501 U.S. 1083, 111 S.Ct. 2749, 115 L.Ed.2d 929 (1991).

43. *See* 501 U.S. 1083, 111 S.Ct. 2749, 115 L.Ed.2d 929 (1991).

47. *See, e.g.,* Berson v. Applied Signal Technology, Inc., 527 F.3d 982 (9th Cir. 2008).

54. *See* Dura Pharmaceuticals, Inc. v. Broudo, 544 U.S. 336, 125 S.Ct. 1627, 161 L.Ed.2d 577 (2005); ATSI Communications, Inc. v. Shaar Fund, Ltd., 493 F.3d 87 (2d Cir. 2007).

securities laws imposes stricter requirements than the proximate cause rules that would apply to fraud actions generally.[56] In fact, the heightened causation requirement for securities fraud is codified in section 27D(b)(4) of the Exchange Act.[57]

The Second Circuit indicated that allegations of an inflated price were not sufficient to support loss causation in a case where plaintiffs had alleged material misstatements.[72] In contrast, the Ninth Circuit held that specific allegations of such a price correction resulting from disclosure of the true facts is not required.[76] The Supreme Court granted a petition for certiorari[77] and eventually reversed the Ninth Circuit, holding that a plaintiff cannot establish loss causation merely by alleging that security price was inflated because of misrepresentation.[78] Although an inflated price may contribute to a loss, it is not necessarily the *cause* of the loss. Thus, it must be shown that the fraudulent conduct was the proximate cause of the plaintiff's economic loss.[80] To hold otherwise would be treating the securities laws as investor insurance rather than protecting them from misrepresentations in the market place.[81]

§ 12.12 The Measure of Damages in Rule 10b–5 Actions

The assessment of damages in Rule 10b–5 cases, like any quantification of economic loss, has been a challenging task for the courts. Evaluating the current state of the law is also difficult because most 10b–5 litigation does not proceed to final judgment on the merits. As a result, there is a relative paucity of decisions dealing with the question of damages. In addition, the courts have taken a number of approaches to the damages issue. The variety of approaches, combined with the scarcity of cases, makes it difficult to identify solid trends in the law of damages in securities cases.

Notwithstanding the various approaches to damages in Rule 10b–5 actions, a few generalizations can be made. First, the cases agree that punitive damages are not available in Rule 10b–5 suits. Even in the absence of a state law permitting punitive damages, punitive damages may be awarded in an arbitration proceeding.[20]

56. *See* Merrill Lynch & Co. Inc. v. Allegheny Energy, Inc., 500 F.3d 171, 183 (2d Cir. 2007).

57. 15 U.S.C.A. § 78u–4(b)(4).

72. Emergent Capital Investment Management, LLC v. Stonepath Group, Inc., 343 F.3d 189 (2d Cir. 2003). *See also, e.g.*, Semerenko v. Cendant Corp., 223 F.3d 165 (3d Cir. 2000).

76. Broudo v. Dura Pharmaceuticals, Inc., 339 F.3d 933 (9th Cir. 2003) (complaint stated loss causation element of claim despite not showing corrective disclosure followed by stock price drop).

77. Dura Pharmaceuticals, Inc. v. Broudo, 542 U.S. 936, 124 S.Ct. 2904, 159 L.Ed.2d 811 (2004).

78. Dura Pharmaceuticals, Inc. v. Broudo, 544 U.S. 336, 125 S.Ct. 1627, 161 L.Ed.2d 577 (2005). The court pointed out, for example, that "[o]ther things being equal, the longer the time between purchase and sale, the more likely that this is so, *i.e.,* the more likely that other factors caused the loss." *Id.* at 343..

80. *See, e.g.,* In re Gilead Sciences Securities Litigation, 536 F.3d 1049 (9th Cir. 2008) (complaint established loss causation; the stock price reacted to corrective disclosures). *Seer also, e.g.,* Majer v. Sonex Research, Inc., 541 F. Supp.2d 693 (E.D. Pa. 2008).

81. Dura Pharmaceuticals, Inc. v. Broudo, 544 U.S. 336, 125 S.Ct. 1627, 161 L.Ed.2d 577 (2005).

§ 12.12

20. *See, e.g.,* Mastrobuono v. Shearson Lehman Hutton, Inc., 514 U.S. 52, 115 S.Ct. 1212, 131 L.Ed.2d 76 (1995) (a state procedural rule barring punitive damages in arbitration proceedings

The plaintiff's measure of recovery under federal securities law is limited to damages actually and proximately caused by the violations in question.[25] Limiting recovery to actual damages is required by the terms of section 28(a) of the Exchange Act.[27] The fact that damages are limited to actual damages means, for example, that a plaintiff will not be able to participate in a double recovery.[28]

There is no universally recognized unitary theory of damages in actions brought under SEC Rule 10b–5. As one court put it, "Anyone researching the issue of Rule 10b–5 damages would be immediately confronted with the repeated observation that this is a confused area of the law where courts, forced to rely on their own wits, have crafted a myriad of approaches."[42] The proper measure of damages at common law is an equally elusive concept.[43] Under common law fraud, "benefit-of-the-bargain" damages will be allowed on appropriate facts.[44] In Rule 10b–5, cases most courts have rejected a benefit-of-the-bargain measure of damages in lieu of an out-of-pocket measure,[46] in large part because in most instances proof of benefit-of-the-bargain damages is speculative.[47] However, in appropriate cases some courts have looked to the benefit-of-the-bargain.[48] Thus, for example, when a stock broker fails to deliver the securities reflected in the account, the customer may be able to recover the value of those securities even though over the years, the customer may have taken more funds out of the account than were initially invested.[49] There have been still other approaches to Rule 10b–5 damages. Some other courts in federal securities cases have adopted a rescission measure[52] while still others in insider trading cases require the disgorgement of ill-gotten gains.[53]

The measure of damages adopted in any particular case is dependent to a large extent upon the theory of recovery. When the essence of the plaintiff's claim is fraud in the inducement—namely, that he or she would not have

---

must yield to the procedural rules of the Federal Arbitration Act which permit the award of punitive damages).

25. *E.g.*, Abbey v. Control Data Corp., 933 F.2d 616 (8th Cir.1991), *cert. denied,* 502 U.S. 967, 112 S.Ct. 438, 116 L.Ed.2d 457 (1991).

27. 15 U.S.C.A. § 78bb(a).

28. Ambassador Hotel Co. v. Wei–Chuan Investment, 189 F.3d 1017 (9th Cir.1999).

42. Koch v. Koch Industries, Inc., 6 F.Supp.2d 1192, 1204–1205 (D.Kan.1998).

43. *See* W. Page Keeton, Dan B. Dobbs, Robert E. Keeton & David G. Owen, Prosser and Keeton on Torts § 110 (5th ed. 1984).

44. *E.g.,* Farley v. Henson, 11 F.3d 827 (8th Cir.1993) (benefit of bargain was appropriate in common law fraud action in connection with merger).

46. Wool v. Tandem Computers Inc., 818 F.2d 1433 (9th Cir.1987) (awarding out-of-pocket loss).

47. *See, e.g.,* Panos v. Island Gem Enterprises, Ltd., 880 F.Supp. 169, 175 (S.D.N.Y. 1995)

48. Ausa Life Insurance Co. v. Ernst & Young, 39 Fed.Appx. 667, 671 (2d Cir. 2002) (discussing benefit of the bargain but affirming denial of that measure on the facts of the case); McMahan & Co. v. Wherehouse Entertainment, Inc., 65 F.3d 1044 (2d Cir.1995) (benefit-of-the-bargain damages are available under Rule 10b–5 but not under section 11 of the 1933 Act).

49. Visconsi v. Lehman Brothers Inc., 244 Fed.Appx. 708 (6th Cir. 2007), affirming 2006 WL 290520 (E.D. Ohio 2006); Fazio v. Lehman Brothers, NYSE Arb. Docket No. 2003–014766, 2004 WL 3008652 (Oct. 20, 2004).

52. *See, e.g.*, Bosley v. Special Devices Corp., 130 Fed. Appx. 143 (9th Cir. 2005) (upholding $175,000 in rescission damages under Rule 10b–5 and $150,000 in punitive damages under California law).

53. *See* Financial Industrial Fund, Inc. v. McDonnell Douglas Corp., 474 F.2d 514 (10th Cir.), *cert. denied,* 414 U.S. 874, 94 S.Ct. 155, 38 L.Ed.2d 114 (1973).

entered into the transaction but for the defendant's fraud, rescission is arguably the proper measure of damages. In such a case, rescission would restore the status quo.[67] Rescission would not be appropriate, however, when the defendant is not on the other side of the transaction (either as a broker or principal). When the essence of the claim is not that the defendant induced the transaction, but rather, that the plaintiff's injury is attributable to the defendant's fraudulent inflation or deflation of the security's price, then the appropriate remedy would seem to be the out-of-pocket measure.[68] In other words, rescission rests on a claim that the transaction should be undone due to fraud in the inducement, while a claim for fraud generally leads to out-of-pocket recovery.[69] Rescission has been rejected in favor of out-of-pocket loss when other factors contributed to the diminution in value of the stock.[70]

There are additional instances in which a measure of damages other than out-of-pocket loss may be available. Disgorgement of ill-gotten gain may be appropriate when the remedy is based in terms of restitution, and unjust enrichment rather than any compensable loss to the plaintiff. Thus, for example, a suit against someone who has traded on inside information in breach of a duty to the plaintiff is often said to be in the nature of restitution, and thus disgorgement of profits is the proper measure.[74] When the plaintiff can state a claim under more than one provision of the securities laws, he or she is entitled to the measure of damages that will result in the higher recovery.[75]

There is a Supreme Court ruling that comes to bear on the effects of tax consequences in securities damage actions. In Randall v. Loftsgaarden,[79] the Court held that intangible tax benefits are to be treated differently from tangible property and thus are not income which needs to be deducted in the calculation of rescissory damages under section 12 of the 1933 Act. Along the same lines, the Court held that, in awarding rescissory damages under Rule 10b–5, damages were not to be offset by tax benefits received by the plaintiff/investor while owning the security.

---

67. Hatrock v. Edward D. Jones & Co., 750 F.2d 767, 773 (9th Cir.1984).

68. *See, e.g.,* In re Home Theater Securities Litigation, 1997 WL 820968, [1997 Transfer Binder] Fed. Sec. L. Rep. (CCH) ¶ 99,576 (C.D. Cal. 1997) (out-of-pocket measure should be computed based on the average of the stock's value over the five days following its delisting from securities exchange; the appropriate measure was not to be based on the stock price on the last day of exchange trading).

69. Soderberg v. Gens, 652 F.Supp. 560, 565 (N.D.Ill.1987).

70. *E.g.,* Huddleston v. Herman & MacLean, 640 F.2d 534 (5th Cir.1981), *affirmed in part and reversed in part on other grounds*, 459 U.S. 375, 103 S.Ct. 683, 74 L.Ed.2d 548 (1983). Green v. Occidental Petroleum Corp., 541 F.2d 1335 (9th Cir. 1976).

74. This is also the measure adopted for computing the civil penalty in SEC enforcement actions under the Insider Trading Sanctions Act of 1984. 15 U.S.C.A. § 78u(d)(3)(B). The disgorgement measure has also been incorporated into the private right of action in the hands of contemporaneous traders, which was enacted as part of the Insider Trading and Securities Fraud Enforcement Act of 1988. 15 U.S.C.A. § 78t–1. *See* § 12.17 *infra.*

75. Cyrak v. Lemon, 919 F.2d 320 (5th Cir.1990) (plaintiff with claims under section 12(2) of the 1933 Act and Rule 10b–5 may recover the higher amount, and then in order to avoid double recovery, the lesser claim is extinguished), *relying on* Grogan v. Garner, 806 F.2d 829, 839 (8th Cir.1986); Aboussie v. Aboussie, 441 F.2d 150, 157 (5th Cir.1971) (plaintiff entitled to higher of common law and Rule 10b–5 claim).

79. 478 U.S. 647, 106 S.Ct. 3143, 92 L.Ed.2d 525 (1986) (damages returned to investor obtaining rescission was not subject to offset for tax benefits received while holding the investment, even if the investment was sold as tax shelter). *See also* the discussion in § 7.8 *supra.*

§ 12.13 Heightened Pleading Requirements; Pleading Fraud With Particularity

§ 12.13[1] Heightened Pleading Requirements in Fraud Actions

§ 12.13[1][A] The Particularity Requirement

Although pleading rules in federal court are generally quite permissive, special rules apply in the case of fraud. By virtue of Rule 9(b) of the Federal Rules of Civil Procedure,[1] fraud must be pleaded with particularity.[2] Many elements of the enhanced pleading requirements in civil actions[3] have been also codified in the Private Securities Litigation Reform Act of 1995.[4]

The particularity requirement has been said to serve three purposes.[11] First, sufficient particularity is necessary to provide defendants with adequate notice so as to permit them to formulate a response to the charges.[12] Second, the particularity requirement prevents fishing expeditions designed to uncover suspected but unknown wrongs. Third, the particularity requirement is designed to protect defendants from baseless accusations of wrongful and immoral conduct. Courts should be cautious not to impose too stringent a pleading requirement. After all, the pleading requirements that arise prior to pretrial discovery should not be held to the same rigor as the standard on a motion to dismiss that is applied once there is a trial on the merits.[13]

The particularity requirement in pleading has been analogized to the basic rules of good journalism. This means that the pleadings should specify the "who, what, when, where, and how."[14]

§ 12.15 Securities Class Actions; Litigation Reform

Congress enacted the litigation reform legislation in response to perceived abuses involving securities class actions.[6] First, the Private Securities Litiga-

§ 12.13

1. Fed.R.Civ.P. 9(b).

2. The heightened pleading requirements of Federal Rule of Civil Procedure 9(b) apply to SEC enforcement as well. *See, e.g.*, SEC v. Tambone, 417 F.Supp.2d 127 (D. Mass. 2006) (SEC failed to plead fraud with sufficient specificity).

3. The enhanced pleading requirements do not apply to a criminal case. *See* United States v. Schiff, 538 F.Supp.2d 818, 829–830 (D.N.J. 2008). Nevertheless in addition to due process notice requirements "in a criminal case, the Court must still ensure that a theory of liability meets the legal standards for the alleged crime." *Id.* at 830.

4. Pub. Law No. 104–67, 109 Stat. 737 (104th Cong. 1st Sess. December 22, 1995) (HR 1058). *See, e.g.,* Desaigoudar v. Meyercord, 223 F.3d 1020 (9th Cir.2000) (failure to plead claim resulted in dismissal with prejudice). The 1995 Litigation Reform Act is discussed in § 12.15[1] *infra.*

11. In re Checkers Securities Litigation, 858 F.Supp. 1168, 1175 (M.D.Fla.1994).

12. *See, e.g.,* In re Juniper Networks, Inc., 158 Fed. Appx. 899 (9th Cir. 2005).

13. Liberty Ridge LLC v. RealTech Systems Corp., 173 F.Supp.2d 129, 137 (S.D.N.Y.2001) ("at this early stage in the proceedings, plaintiffs' pleadings should not be judged by the standard to be applied on the trial of the ultimate merits"), quoting Rich v. Touche Ross & Co., 68 F.R.D. 243, 247 (S.D.N.Y.1975).

14. *E.g.,* Cathedral Trading v. Chicago Board Options Exchange, 199 F.Supp.2d 851, 856 (N.D.Ill.2002), relying on DiLeo v. Ernst & Young, 901 F.2d 624, 627 (7th Cir.1990) ("This means the who, what, when, where, and how: the first paragraph of any newspaper story").

§ 12.15

6. *See, e.g.,* In re VISX, Inc. Securities Litigation, 2001 WL 210481, [2000–2001 Transfer Binder] Fed. Sec. L. Rep. (CCH) ¶ 91,336 (N.D. Cal. 2001) ("Congress enacted the PSLRA to deter

tion Reform Act of 1995[7] addressed many areas of private securities litigation including procedural reforms, enhanced pleading standards, and increased protection for disclosures involving soft information and projections. Second, Congress enacted the Securities Litigation Uniform Standards Act of 1998,[8] which prevents most class actions based on securities fraud from being brought in state court. Each of the changes to the securities laws brought in by the litigation reform initiatives are discussed in this section throughout this treatise as appropriate.

§ 12.15[1] Private Securities Litigation Reform Act of 1995

A number of observers had become increasingly concerned with abuses of class actions in securities litigation. Among other things, there was concern over the use of then-existing class action procedures to bring strike suits[9] in order to exact "extortionate settlements."[10] The Private Securities Litigation Reform Act of 1995 added section 21D of the 1934 Act,[11] which is designed to

---

opportunistic private plaintiffs from filing abusive securities fraud claims"), quoting In re Silicon Graphics Inc. Securities Litigation, 183 F.3d 970, 973 (9th Cir.1999).

The Reform Act's reach is limited to securities claims. Thus, for example, the Act's provisions do not apply to claims under the Racketeer Influenced Corrupt Organizations Act (RICO) that are not based on securities fraud. Flood v. Makowski, [2004–2005 Transfer Binder] Fed. Sec. L. Rep. (CCH) ¶ 92,899, 2004 WL 1908221 (M.D. Pa. 2004) (PSLRA does not apply to RICO claims not based on securities fraud). *But cf.* Hollinger International, Inc. v. Hollinger, [2004–2005 Transfer Binder] Fed. Sec. L. Rep. (CCH) ¶ 93,012 (N.D. Ill. 2004) (RICO claims that sounded in fraud were covered by PSLRA). RICO is discussed in § 22.3 *infra*.

7. Pub. Law No. 104–67, 109 Stat. 737 (104th Cong. 1st Sess. December 22, 1995) (HR 1058).

8. Pub. Law No. 105–353, 112 Stat. 3227 (105th Cong.–2d Sess. November 3, 1998) (S 1260).

9. *See, e.g.*, Charles M. Yablon, Essay, A Dangerous Supplement? Longshot Claims and Private Securities Litigation, 94 Nw. U. L. Rev. 567 (2000) (suggesting the importance of making a distinction between nuisance suits and "long shot" suits).

10. H.R. Conf. Rep. No. 104–369, 104th Cong., 1st Sess. at 31–32 (1995).

11. 15 U.S.C.A. § 78u–4(e). A parallel provision was added to the 1933 Act. *See* § 7.17 *supra*. The 1995 Act contained other provisions which are discussed elsewhere. For example, there is now a statutory safe harbor for financial projections. *See* §§ 3.9, 12.9 *supra*.

For discussion of the Reform Act, *see generally* James D. Cox, Making Securities Fraud Class Actions Virtuous, 39 Ariz. L. Rev. 497 (1997); Jill E. Fisch, Class Action Reform: Lessons From Securities Litigation, 39 Ariz. L. Rev. 533 (1997); Sharon M. Glenn & J. Allen Maines, The Private Securities Litigation Reform Act: Corporations Finally Get Their Day in Court, 25 Sec. Reg. L.J. 276 (1997); John F. Olson et al, Pleading Reform, Plaintiff Qualification and Discovery Stays Under the Reform Act, 51 Bus. Law. 1101 (1996); Julie Rubin, Comment, Auctioning Class Actions: Turning the Tables on Plaintiffs' Lawyers' Abuse or Stripping the Plaintiff Wizards of Their Curtain, 52 Bus. Law. 1441 (1997); Richard H. Walker, David M. Levine & Adam C. Pritchard, The New Securities Class Action: Federal Obstacles, State Detours, 39 Ariz. L. Rev. 641 (1997); Note, The Private Securities Litigation Reform Act of 1995: Friend or Foe of the Investor, 47 Fla. L. Rev. 841 (1995). *Cf.* Andre Douglas Pond Cummings, "Ain't No Glory in Pain": How the 1994 Republican Revolution and the Private Securities Litigation Reform Act Contributed to the Collapse of the United States Capital Markets, 83 Neb. L. Rev. 979 (2005) (criticizing the PSLRA and calling for repealing many of its provisions).

Most courts that faced the issue held that the 1995 Act does not apply retroactively to private actions filed before its effective date. *See* Gerber v. MTC Electronic Technologies Co., Ltd., 329 F.3d 297 (2d Cir. 2003) (PSLRA provisions on settlement do not apply retroactively); Mathews v. Kidder, Peabody & Co., 161 F.3d 156 (3d Cir.1998) (Reform Act provision relating to RICO predicate acts did not apply retroactively); Gubitosi v. Zegeye, 28 F.Supp.2d 298 (E.D.Pa.1998) (same); McKowan Lowe & Co. v. Jasmine, Ltd., 976 F.Supp. 293 (D.N.J.1997) (Act did not apply to defendants added after the Act's effective date because action had been commenced prior to the effective date); Pozzi v. Smith, 952 F.Supp. 218, 227 (E.D.Pa.1997); Vennittilli v. Primerica, Inc., 943 F.Supp. 793 (E.D.Mich.1996) (Reform Act RICO provisions do not apply to actions filed before the Act's effective date). *Accord* Zeid v. Kimberley, 973 F.Supp. 910 (N.D.Cal.1997), *vacated and remanded on other grounds*, 201 F.3d 446 (9th Cir.1999) (unpublished decision). *See also, e.g.*, Havenick v. Network Express, Inc., 981 F.Supp. 480 (E.D.Mich.1997) (although Reform Act does not apply to action filed before the Act's effective date, it does apply to conduct before the

discourage frivolous lawsuits by establishing special procedures for instituting private class actions under the securities laws. Section 21D of the Exchange Act covers a wide range of topics, including restrictions on the class representative, limits on attorneys' fees, pleading requirements, pretrial discovery, and the burden of proof on some issues. There are parallel provisions for claims made under the Securities Act of 1933. It is highly questionable whether the Reform Act has served its intended purpose. There is no discernable decrease in reported class actions.[14] It is clear that the issues for litigation have shifted, with increased focus on class representation and pleading issues. However, it is not clear that PSLRA resulted in a reduction in litigation.[15] In fact, the Reform Act has added issues to be litigated and thus in a real sense has not decreased the amount of securities litigation as its sponsors had hoped.

§ 12.15[1][A] Qualifications of Lead Plaintiff

The traditional approach in class actions is to determine the lead plaintiff by looking to the first claim that is filed. The lead plaintiff and lead counsel provisions are part and parcel of the Reform Act's intent to prevent the "race to the courthouse" phenomenon sometimes associated with the first-to-file rule.[19] The Litigation Reform Act creates a presumption in favor of the shareholder with the largest financial interest as lead plaintiff; this is designed to encourage the appointment of institutional investors as lead plaintiffs.

effective date where the action was not filed until later); Edge Partners, L.P. v. Dockser, 944 F.Supp. 438 (D.Md.1996) (claim that had been dismissed with leave to amend was held to be pending at the time of the amendments' effective date thus making the amendments inapplicable to the subsequently filed amended complaint); Vennittilli v. Primerica, Inc., 943 F.Supp. 793 (E.D.Mich.1996) (Reform Act RICO provisions do not apply to actions filed before the Act's effective date).

Although the Reform Act does not apply retroactively to actions for damages, it has been held to apply to prospective relief even if the action was pending at the time of the Act's passage. Mathews v. Kidder, Peabody & Co., 161 F.3d 156 (3d Cir.1998), *affirming*, 947 F.Supp. 180 (W.D.Pa.1996) (Reform Act did not apply to RICO damage action pending when Act became law, but it did apply to prevent the court from awarding prospective injunctive relief). *See also, e.g.,* Hockey v. Medhekar, 1997 WL 203704, [1997 Transfer Binder] Fed. Sec. L. Rep. (CCH) ¶ 99,465 (N.D.Cal.1997) (Reform Act's procedural and substantive provisions apply to all actions commenced after the Act's effective date); ABF Capital Management v. Askin Capital Management, L.P., 957 F.Supp. 1308, 1318–20 (S.D.N.Y.1997) (rejecting contention that Reform Act's RICO provisions should not apply to cases filed after the statute but based on conduct prior to enactment).

Notwithstanding the foregoing decisions, a number of courts have ruled to the contrary and have given retroactive effect to the Reform Act's provisions limiting the scope of private RICO actions. *E.g.,* Kolfenbach v. Mansour, 36 F.Supp.2d 1351 (S.D.Fla.1999) (RICO amendments applied retroactively); Krear v. Malek, 961 F.Supp. 1065 (E.D.Mich.1997) (the Reform Act's limitations on RICO apply retroactively); Rowe v. Marietta Corp., 955 F.Supp. 836 (W.D.Tenn. 1997) (Reform Act § 107 requiring conviction where predicate RICO act was securities fraud was intended to be applied retroactively); ABF Capital Management v. Askin Capital Management, L.P., 957 F.Supp. 1308, 1318–20 (S.D.N.Y.1997) (rejecting contention that Reform Act's RICO provisions should not apply to cases filed after the statute but based on conduct prior to enactment).

14. *See, e.g.,* Jordan Eth & Daniel Drosman, The Private Securities Litigation Reform Act: Five Years Young, 34 Rev. Sec. & Commod. Reg. 153 (2001).

15. *Id.*

19. "The PSLRA, according to its legislative history, was enacted in response to perceived abuses of federal securities class actions through which a race to the courthouse often resulted in non-representative plaintiffs and their attorneys controlling the litigation and reaping disproportionate fee awards at the end of the case." California Public Employees' Retirement System v. The Chubb Corp., 127 F.Supp.2d 572, 575, [2000–2001 Transfer Binder] Fed. Sec. L. Rep. (CCH) ¶ 91,299 (D.N.J. 2001), relying on In re Lucent Technologies, Inc., Securities Litigation, 194 F.R.D. 137, 144 (D.N.J.2000).

§ 12.15[1][B] Selection of Lead Counsel

Frequently, the same transaction will give rise to multiple class action filings in various federal district courts. This results not only in several candidates for lead plaintiff, but also in several candidates for lead counsel. In addition to the selection of the most appropriate lead plaintiff, issues arise as to how to select the lead counsel.[88] The presumptive lead plaintiff's choice of lead counsel is not automatic.[89] Although the selection of the lead plaintiff will often determine who is lead counsel,[90] the court must use independent judgment in determining whether the proffered lead counsel is the appropriate one.[91] Court approval is required for change of lead counsel even if that change is to be made on appeal.[92]

There are a number of possible approaches a court could take in selecting or approving lead counsel. One possible approach would be to approve whichever counsel is selected by the plaintiff who is selected to lead the class.[93] An alternative is for the court to appoint a consortium of counsel from the various plaintiffs in the consolidated actions.[94] While some courts have appointed a team of lead counsel,[95] others have recognized the extra cost involved[96] and have refused to do so.[97]

§ 12.15[1][C] Attorneys' Fees

The 1995 Reform Act also addressed the issue of attorneys' fees in securities class actions. Section 21D(a)(6)[119] states that attorneys' fees in class action cases are limited to a reasonable amount, but discretion in determining what is reasonable is left to the courts.[120] Attorneys' fees may be calculated according to the lodestar approach—multiplying an attorney's hours by a

---

88. For example, a conflict of interest will disqualify an attorney from serving as lead counsel. A lawyer may not be able to represent two different classes suing the same defendant, but he or she may represent two different classes in two different actions where each action is suing different defendants. *See* Dietrich v. Bauer, 192 F.R.D. 119 (S.D.N.Y.2000).

89. *See, e.g.,* In re Comdisco Securities Litigation, 141 F.Supp.2d 951 (N.D.Ill.2001) (potential lead counsel was required to file competitive bid).

90. *See* 15 U.S.C. § 78u–4(a)(3)(B)(v) ("The most adequate plaintiff shall, subject to the approval of the court, select and retain counsel to represent the class.").

91. *Id.*

92. In re Merck & Co. Securities Litigation, 432 F.3d 261 (3d Cir. 2005) (approving change of counsel).

93. The determination of lead plaintiff and lead counsel are two separate decisions. *See, e.g.,* Mayo v. Apropos Technology, Inc., 2002 WL 193393, Fed. Sec. L. Rep. ¶ 91,717 (N.D.Ill.2002) (lead plaintiff appointed, lead counsel to be appointed after hearing).

94. Metro Services Inc. v. Wiggins, 158 F.3d 162 (2d Cir.1998) (upholding appointment of co-lead plaintiffs).

95. *See, e.g.,* In re Lernout & Hauspie Securities Litigation, 138 F.Supp.2d 39 (D.Mass.2001) (appointing three lead counsel to represent group consisting of three lead plaintiffs); In re Tyco International, Ltd., 2000 WL 1513772 (D.N.H.2000) (appointing four co-lead counsel).

96. In re Nortel Networks Corp. Securities Litigation, 34 Sec. Reg. & L. Rep. (BNA) 346 (S.D.N.Y. 2002) (eliminating co-lead counsel in favor of single lead counsel since co-counsel created extra cost and also confusion); Sherleigh Associates LLC v. Windmere–Durable Holdings, Inc., 186 F.R.D. 669 (S.D.Fla.1999) (conducting auction rather than appoint a committee of lead counsel).

97. Weltz v. Lee, 199 F.R.D. 129, [2000–2001 Transfer Binder] Fed. Sec. L. Rep. (CCH) ¶ 91,342 (S.D.N.Y. 2001).

119. 15 U.S.C.A. § 78u–4(a)(6).

120. *E.g.,* Powers v. Eichen, 229 F.3d 1249 (9th Cir.2000) (district court failed to adequately explain the reasonableness of a fee based on 30% of the settlement fund).

reasonable fee and increasing the amount due to any risk or other relevant factors.[121] Class action settlements are subject to court approval, as is the allocation of attorneys' fees out of the settlement fund. The Private Securities Litigation Reform Act of 1995 does not mandate a particular method of calculating the attorneys' fees.[122]

§ 12.15[1][D] Pretrial Motions and Pretrial Discovery

The Reform Act attempts to limit the use of pretrial discovery as a fishing expedition. Section 21D(b)(3)[124] provides that all discovery be stayed during the pendency of a motion to dismiss or a motion for summary judgment, in order to alleviate discovery expenses on defendants.[125] Unlike many other provisions of PSLRA, the discovery stay applies to derivative claims as well as to class actions.[126] The stay is mandatory.[127] However, the stay will be lifted if necessary to avoid "undue prejudice."[128]

§ 12.15[1][E] Projections and Forward Looking Statements

Section 27A of the 1933 Act[139] and Section 21E of the 1934 Act[140] provide a safe harbor for forward-looking statements and the "bespeaks caution" doctrine created by the federal courts. The safe harbor allows corporate management to disclose forward-looking information and projections to investors with a presumption that there was a reasonable basis[141] for the projections.[142] The bespeaks caution doctrine provides that specific cautionary language can render inaccurate projections not actionable.[143]

§ 12.15[1][F] Enhanced Pleading Requirements Regarding Defendants' State of Mind

In suits involving money damages predicated on proof that a defendant acted with a certain state of mind, plaintiffs must plead with particularity that the defendant acted with such state of mind with respect to each act or omission.[144] Plaintiffs further must provide facts that indicate a "strong

121. *See, e.g.*, Williams v. MGM–Pathe Communications Co., 129 F.3d 1026 (9th Cir.1997).

122. Powers v. Eichen, 229 F.3d 1249 (9th Cir.2000) (section 21D of the 1934 Act does not mandate that fees be based on net recovery rather than the gross amount).

124. 15 U.S.C.A. § 78u–4(b)(3).

125. S. Rep. No. 104–98, 104th Cong., 1st Sess. at 14 (1995) (finding that discovery costs often force defendants to settle securities class action suits).

126. *See, e.g.*, Brown v. Kelly, 2006 WL 3411868 (N.D.Cal. 2006) (issuing order staying discovery in derivative actions); In re Altera Corp. Derivative Litigation, 2006 WL 2917578 (N.D.Cal. 2006) (same).

127. SG Cowen Securities Corp. v. U.S. District Court, 189 F.3d 909, 31 Sec. Reg. & L. Rep. (BNA) 1199 (9th Cir.1999) (limited discovery order was improper in light of mandatory stay of all discovery).

128. "Undue prejudice" has been interpreted to include something less than irreparable injury. Vacold LLC v. Cerami, 2001 WL 167704 *6, [2000–2001 Transfer Binder] Fed. Sec. L. Rep. (CCH) ¶ 91,334 (S.D.N.Y. 2001) (lifting discovery stay).

139. 15 U.S.C.A. § 77z–2.

140. 15 U.S.C.A. § 78u–5(c).

141. *See, e.g.*, Ehlert v. Singer, 245 F.3d 1313 (11th Cir.2001).

142. *See* SEC Rules 175 and 3b–6, 17 C.F.R. §§ 230.175, 240.3b–6.

143. *See, e.g.*, Powers v. Eichen, 977 F.Supp. 1031 (S.D.Cal.1997).

144. 1934 Act § 21D(b)(2), 15 U.S.C. § 78u–4(b)(2).

inference" that a defendant acted with a particular state of mind.[145] A "reasonable inference" of scienter is not sufficient.[146] In order to withstand the scrutiny imposed by the Private Securities Litigation Reform Act of 1995, the inference of scienter must be both reasonable and strong.[147]

§ 12.15[1][H] Security Deposit

In private suits involving class action claims, the court may require an undertaking from the attorneys for the plaintiff or defendant, the parties themselves, or both. The court may use equitable principles to ascertain whether to require an undertaking and to determine the relevant proportions.

§ 12.15[1][I] Review of Proceedings for Possible Sanctions

In order to dissuade abusive litigation, courts are directed to perform a mandatory review at the final adjudication of the action to determine whether any party or attorney violated Rule 11(b) of the Federal Rules of Civil Procedure.[167]

§ 12.15[1][J] Calculation of Damages

The 1995 Reform Act contained a provision designed to assure that damages are limited to losses caused by the material misstatement or omission. Section 21D(e) sets forth the method for calculating damages in civil actions, which is based on the mean trading price of the security at issue.[176] The mean trading price includes the original value of the security on the date the plaintiff purchased or sold the security and the value of the security during the 90–day period after corrective information has been disseminated. If during the 90–day period the plaintiff sells or repurchases the security,

---

145. The Conference Committee intended to strengthen the pleading standard for securities actions and modeled the standard on Second Circuit case law. S. Rep. No. 104–98, 104th Cong., 1st Sess. at 15 (1995).

146. Tellabs, Inc. v. Makor Issues & Rights Ltd., 551 U.S. 308, 127 S.Ct. 2499, 168 L.Ed.2d 179 (2007); Greebel v. FTP Software, Inc., 194 F.3d 185 (1st Cir.1999).

147. *See, e.g.,* Gompper v. VISX, Inc., 298 F.3d 893 (9th Cir.2002) (allegations did not satisfy the Reform Act's standards for pleading scienter); Burroughs v. Northrop Grumman Corp., 32 Fed.Appx. 360 (9th Cir.2002) (unpublished opinion, text in WESTLAW) (failure to satisfy heightened pleading requirements); In re Vantive Corp. Securities Litigation, 283 F.3d 1079 (9th Cir.2002) (heightened pleading requirements were not satisfied); Coates v. Heartland Wireless Communications, Inc., 100 F.Supp.2d 417 (N.D.Tex.2000).

According to the Second Circuit:

> Although litigants and lower courts need and should not employ or rely on magic words such as "motive and opportunity," we believe that our prior case law may be helpful in providing guidance as to how the "strong inference" standard may be met. Therefore, in applying this standard, district courts should look to the cases and factors discussed . . . above to determine whether plaintiffs have pleaded facts giving rise to the requisite "strong inference." These cases suggest, in brief, that the inference may arise where the complaint sufficiently alleges that the defendants: (1) benefited in a concrete and personal way from the purported fraud, (2) engaged in deliberately illegal behavior; (3) knew facts or had access to information suggesting that their public statements were not accurate; or (4) failed to check information they had a duty to monitor.

Novak v. Kasaks, 216 F.3d 300, 315 (2d Cir.2000) (references omitted). *See also, e.g.,* Note, Seeking Enlightenment From Above: Circuit Courts Split on the Interpretation of the Reform Act's Heightened Pleading Requirement, 66 Brook. L. Rev. 501 (2000). *Cf., e.g.,* Booth v. Verity, Inc., 124 F.Supp.2d 452 (W.D.Ky.2000) (enhanced pleading standards of federal Litigation Reform Act were incorporated into Kentucky blue sky law).

167. Section 27 of the 1933 Act, 15 U.S.C.A. § 77z–1; Section 21D of the 1934 Act, 15 U.S.C.A. § 78u–4. Rule 11 sanctions are discussed in § 12.14[4] *supra.*

176. 15 U.S.C.A. § 78u–4(e).

damages are determined according to the price of that transaction and the value of the security immediately following the dissemination of the corrective information.

§ 12.15[2] Securities Litigation Uniform Standards Act of 1998

The class action procedural reforms of the 1995 Reform Act apply only to class actions[224] brought in federal court. Private actions under sections 11 and 12 of the Securities Act of 1933 can be brought in either federal or state court.[225] Jurisdiction over 1934 Act claims is exclusively federal;[226] however, state securities law and common law fraud could provide alternative forums for class action plaintiffs trying to avoid the provisions of the 1995 Reform Act. Congress largely eliminated these alternatives in the Securities Litigation Uniform Standards Act of 1998,[228] which mandates that most class actions, with more than fifty class members, involving publicly traded securities be brought in federal court.[229]

Class actions involving state securities law and class actions based on common law fraud with regard to covered securities are preempted if there are more than fifty class members. Covered securities are defined in such a way as to include most publicly traded securities.[236]

The Uniform Standards Act is not complete in its elimination of state court class actions since the Act preempts only those actions involving publicly traded securities.[240] The Act also applies only to fraud or misrepresentation claims that are based on conduct "in connection with the purchase or sale"[241] of a covered security.[242] Preemption is to be determined by the nature of the facts and the alleged wrong. Whether a complaint involves a covered class action to be preempted by SLUSA depends on if it is based on "a misrepresentation or omission of a material fact in connection with the purchase or sale of a covered security"[243] regardless of whether the complaint is based on fraud or some other basis for relief such as breach of contract or breach of fiduciary duty.[244]

It is important to note further that the Uniform Standards Act applies only to class actions and thus not to individual or derivative suits.[272] There also is an exclusion for actions brought in the state of incorporation involving

224. *See, e.g.,* Behlen v. Merrill Lynch, 311 F.3d 1087 (11th Cir. 2002).

225. 1933 Act § 22(a), 15 U.S.C.A. § 77v(a) which is discussed in § 17.1 *infra.*

226. 1934 Act § 27, 15 U.S.C.A. § 78aa.

228. Pub. Law No. 105–353, 112 Stat. 3227 (105th Cong.–2d Sess. November 3, 1998) (S 1260).

229. 15 U.S.C.A. § 78bb(f).

236. 15 U.S.C.A. § 78bb(f)(5)(E) refers to section 18(b) of the 1933 Act for the definition of covered securities.

240. Thus, for example, the National Securities Markets Improvement Act of 1996, which preempted certain types of state substantive regulation, did not preempt state law fraud actions. Zuri–Invest AG v. Natwest Finance Inc., 177 F.Supp.2d 189 (S.D.N.Y.2001).

241. *See, e.g.,* Sofonia v. Principal Life Insurance Co., 465 F.3d 873 (8th Cir. 2006).

242. *See, e.g.,* Ring v. AXA Financial, Inc., 483 F.3d 95 (2d Cir. 2007).

243. 1933 Act § 16(b)(1), 15 U.S.C.A. § 77p(b)(1); 1934 Act § 28(f)(1), 15 U.S.C.A. § 78bb(f)(1).

244. *See e.g.,* Gray v. Seaboard Securities, Inc., 126 Fed.Appx. 14 (2d Cir. 2005) (although complaint was framed in terms of an action for breach of contract, the underlying alleged wrong was fraud in connection with securities transactions and thus the SLUSA preemption applied).

272. *See, e.g.,* Sung v. Wasserstein, 2006 WL 435449 (S.D.N.Y. 2006).

certain corporate transactions. The preemption only applies to fraud related claims and thus does not preclude state law claims on other theories such as conversion,[273] breach of contract,[274] or breach of fiduciary duty.[275]

The Supreme Court held that SLUSA preempts holder's (as opposed to seller's) claims.[336] among other things, the Court reasoned that when it enacted SLUSA, Congress desired to eliminate the duplicative litigation that would result from holding that such claims are not within the broadly construed "in connection with" requirement.[337] As a result of the *Dabit* ruling, state claims by holders may still proceed but only if they are not brought in the form of a class action with fewer than fifty class members.

§ 12.16 Statutes of Limitations in Rule 10b–5 Actions

For most of its history, the 1934 Act did not set forth a statute of limitations applicable to implied rights of action such as suits under Rule 10b–5. The courts thus had to imply the applicable limitations period. However, this changed in 2002 when Congress enacted a two-year statute of limitations and a five year repose period in cases where tolling the limitations period is appropriate.[1]

§ 12.17 Insider Trading and Rule 10b–5

§ 12.17[1] Overview

For nearly half a century, there have been many celebrated cases involving trading in securities based on nonpublic confidential or proprietary information. There have been some highly publicized insider trading cases. Defendants in insider trading cases have not been limited to corporate insiders and have included a wide range of people, including psychiatrists,[3] football coaches,[4] former athletes,[5] newspaper columnists,[6] printers,[7] leading arbitrageurs,[8] golfing partners,[9] and most unfortunately, lawyers.[10] Several instances have involved law firms. In one situation a partner of a big-city law

---

273. Burns v. Prudential Securities, 116 F.Supp.2d 917 (N.D.Ohio 2000).

274. Green v. Ameritrade, Inc., 279 F.3d 590 (8th Cir.2002).

275. *See, e.g.,* Paru v. Mutual of America Life Insurance, 2006 WL 1292828 (S.D.N.Y. 2006).

336. Merrill Lynch, Pierce, Fenner & Smith v. Dabit, 547 U.S. 71, 126 S.Ct. 1503, 164 L.Ed.2d 179 (2006).

337. The "in connection with" requirement is discussed in § 12.5 *supra.*

§ 12.16

1. 28 U.S.C.A. § 1658(b), which was enacted as part of the Sarbanes–Oxley Act of 2002, Pub. Law 107–204 (July 30, 2002).

§ 12.17

3. *See* United States v. Willis, 737 F.Supp. 269 (S.D.N.Y.1990).

4. *See* SEC v. Switzer, 590 F.Supp. 756 (W.D.Okl.1984).

5. *See* SEC v. Tarkenton, 2000 WL 63477, 71 S.E.C. Docket 1219, Release No. AE–12, (SEC Accounting & auditing Enforcement Rel. 2000).

6. *See* United States v. Carpenter, 791 F.2d 1024 (2d Cir.1986), *affirmed by an equally divided court,* 484 U.S. 19, 108 S.Ct. 316, 98 L.Ed.2d 275 (1987).

7. Chiarella v. United States, 445 U.S. 222, 100 S.Ct. 1108, 63 L.Ed.2d 348 (1980); SEC v. Materia, 745 F.2d 197 (2d Cir.1984), *cert. denied,* 471 U.S. 1053, 105 S.Ct. 2112, 85 L.Ed.2d 477 (1985).

8. *See* In re Ivan F. Boesky Securities Litigation, 36 F.3d 255 (2d Cir.1994), *affirming* 825 F.Supp. 623 (S.D.N.Y.1993).

9. *See, e.g.,* SEC v. King, Civ. Action No. 7:00CV00622, 32 Sec. Reg. & L. Rep. (BNA) 1140 (W.D. Va. 2000).

10. *E.g.,* United States v. O'Hagan, 521 U.S. 642, 117 S.Ct. 2199, 138 L.Ed.2d 724 (1997)

firm with an active tender offer practice frequently made purchases in the targets of his firm's client's takeover attempts.[12] The partner was not working on any part of the takeovers, but the information somehow filtered down to him. Although these facts raise questions about the internal controls at law firms and other businesses dealing with confidential inside information, no action was taken against the firm.

In analyzing the law of what traditionally has been called insider trading, many cases do not involve corporate insiders but rather deal with outsiders.[13] Outsider trading involves what has for a long time been referred to as trading on market information.[14] This occurs when someone who is not an insider of the company whose shares are traded finds out information that will affect the market price of the shares. This can happen for example when someone has advance knowledge of a pending tender offer[15] or an impending news article that is likely to affect the company's stock.[16] It is in such instances of outsider trading that the courts have come to rely on the misappropriation theory[17] for imposing liability under SEC Rule 10b–5.

The SEC has repeatedly declared that the eradication of trading on inside information is one of its top priority enforcement targets. Trading on inside information destroys the integrity of the market place by giving an informational advantage to a select group of corporate insiders and others having an informational advantage. The practice of insider trading is especially pernicious in light of the federal securities laws' thrust of full disclosure, which is designed to create and maintain an informed market and a level playing field in securities transactions. Some commentators have argued that insider trading does not have significant adverse market impact,[21] but fortunately, the

---

12. *Id.*.

13. *See, e.g.,* Ian Ayres & Stephen Choi, Internalizing Outsider Trading, 101 Mich. L. Rev. 313 (2002).

14. *See, e.g.,* Chiarella v. United States, 445 U.S. 222, 231, 100 S.Ct. 1108, 1116, 63 L.Ed.2d 348 (1980) (The "market information upon which he relied did not concern the earning power or operations of the target company, but only the plans of the acquiring company").

15. *Compare, e.g.,* United States v. O'Hagan, 521 U.S. 642, 117 S.Ct. 2199, 138 L.Ed.2d 724 (1997) *with* United States v. Chestman, 947 F.2d 551 (2d Cir.1991), *cert. denied*, 503 U.S. 1004, 112 S.Ct. 1759, 118 L.Ed.2d 422 (1992).

16. United States v. Carpenter, 791 F.2d 1024 (2d Cir.1986), *affirmed by an equally divided court*, 484 U.S. 19, 108 S.Ct. 316, 98 L.Ed.2d 275 (1987).

17. *See* § 12.17[4] *infra.*

21. Briefly put, it is claimed that, in light of the average trading volume, insider trading has no discernible impact on other investors, individually or in the aggregate. Because of the faceless market, the victims of insiders (or "know nothings") are selected randomly. It has even been suggested that trading on inside information performs a useful function by preparing the market and getting it started in the proper direction before the information is publicly announced. Otherwise, it is argued, major announcements will cause wide price fluctuations that not only disrupt an orderly market but will cause more injury to outside investors than would the insider trading. *See, e.g.,* Henry G. Manne, Insider Trading and the Stock Market (1966); Jeffrey F. Jaffe, The Effect of Regulation Changes on Insider Trading, 5 Bell.J.Econ. & Mgt.Sci. 93 (1974); Henry G. Manne, Insider Trading: Hayek, Virtual Markets, and the Dog that Did Not Bark, 31 J. Corp. L. 167 (2005); Hsin–Kwang Wu, An Economist Looks at Section 16 of The Securities Exchange Act of 1934, 68 Colum.L.Rev. 260 (1968). *See also, e.g.,* Stephen Bainbridge, The Insider Trading Prohibition: A Legal and Economic Enigma, 38 U.Fla.L.Rev. 35 (1986); William J. Carney, Signalling and Causation in Insider Trading, 36 Cath.U.L.Rev. 863 (1987); James D. Cox & Kevin S. Fogarty, Bases of Insider Trading Law, 49 Ohio St.L.J. 353 (1988); David D. Haddock & Jonathan R. Macey, A Coasian Model of Insider Trading, 80 Nw.U.L.Rev. 1449 (1986); Robert J. Haft, The Effect of Insider Trading Rules on the Internal Efficiency of the Large Corporation, 80

courts, Congress and the SEC have not joined in that position. On the other hand, it is generally recognized that there is a positive value in encouraging corporate officers, directors, and other employees to invest in the shares of their company. Accordingly, there are a number of instances in which trading by insiders is permissible. Unfortunately, the law regarding the use of nonpublic material information when trading in shares has not developed systematically. Nor has it evolved in such a way as to produce bright-line tests of when it is permissible to trade.

It is ironic that, as important as regulating trading on the basis of inside information may be under the securities laws, there is no express statutory prohibition. Therefore, most insider trading cases are based on Rule 10b–5's general antifraud provisions,[24] which do not specifically mention insider trading. Section 16(b)'s prohibition against *short-swing* profits by designated statutory insiders[25] is the one of three sections in the Exchange Act that expressly deal with insider trading. The remaining two sections deal only with remedies for insider trading rather than addressing the substantive question of what types of conduct comprise improper trading on nonpublic information. In 1984, Congress enhanced the SEC's enforcement capabilities and bolstered the penalties for insider trading.[26] In 1988, Congress supplemented Rule 10b–5 with an express private right of action.[27] Nevertheless, the fact remains that there is no statutory definition to precisely identify which types of insider trading are permissible and which are not. Since the vast majority of the federal law on insider trading has developed under Rule 10b–5, the courts have in essence created a federal common law of insider trading based on the judge made interpretations of Rule 10b–5 which does not even mention insider trading explicitly.

As discussed more fully below, the prohibition of 10b–5(c) has been utilized to craft a rule of law that subjects certain persons in possession of material nonpublic information to a "disclose or abstain" rule. The disclose or abstain rule means that when potential securities traders have obtained the material information in such a way as to subject them to Rule 10b–5's reach, they must either abstain from trading or disclose the information prior to trading.[37] In most instances, disclosure is not a reasonable option; therefore, the practical mandate is to abstain from trading until the information has been disclosed. Since insider trading prohibitions are based on a rule that does not even mention insider trading, the courts for years have been plagued with the difficulties of trying to ascertain the proper scope of insider trading

Mich.L.Rev. 1051 (1982); Thomas H. Noe, Insider Trading and the Problem of Corporate Agency, 13 J.L. Econ. & Org. 287 (1997).

For an excellent rebuttal of the economic arguments favoring insider trading, *see* James D. Cox, Insider Trading and Contracting: A Critical Response to the "Chicago School," 1986 Duke L.J. 628. *See also* Thomas L. Hazen, Commentary, 36 Cath.U.L. Rev. 987, 993–96 (1987).

24. 17 C.F.R. § 240.10b–5.

25. 15 U.S.C.A. § 78p(b).

26. Pub. L. No. 98–376, 98 Stat. 1264 (1984). The 1984 legislation that was supported by the SEC includes a fine based on treble damages against certain persons trading on inside information.

27. 15 U.S.C.A. § 78t–1. *See* Pub.L. No. 100–704, 102 Stat. 4677 (1988).

37. Trading on inside information does not violate Rule 10b–5 unless there is a duty to abstain from trading. *See, e.g.,* Abrams v. Prudential Securities, Inc., 2000 WL 390494, [2000–2001 Transfer Binder] Fed. Sec. L. Rep. (CCH) ¶ 91,292 (N.D.Ill.2000).

prohibitions. One consequence is that the law continues to change as the courts' view of insider trading evolves.

§ 12.17[2] The Basis of the Prohibition: The Development of Rule 10b–5's "Disclose or Abstain" Rule in Insider Trading Cases

In the seminal decision of Cady, Roberts & Co.,[74] the Securities and Exchange Commission imposed disciplinary sanctions against a registered broker-dealer who directed his customers to liquidate their holdings in Curtiss–Wright stock because he had advance knowledge of a pending dividend cut. The broker, tipped by a corporate insider, was merely a tippee who in turn tipped his customers. The SEC found that the broker's conduct "violated [10b–5(c)] as a practice which operated as * * * fraud or deceit upon the purchasers."[75] The Commission's opinion explained that "analytically, the obligation [to disclose or abstain from trading] rests on two principal elements; first, the existence of a relationship giving access, directly or indirectly, to information intended to be available only for a corporate purpose and not for the personal benefit of anyone, and second, the inherent unfairness involved where a party takes advantage of such information knowing it is unavailable to those with whom he is dealing."[76]

After the SEC's *Cady, Roberts* decision, the Second Circuit in SEC v. Texas Gulf Sulphur Co.[77] held that corporate insiders who purchased stock on the open market with knowledge of a valuable mineral find that had not yet been publicly announced had violated Rule 10b–5 because the information not disclosed at the time of the transactions would have been "material" to a reasonable person's investment decision. The fact that the insiders began purchasing stock and options raised a strong inference that they considered the information material.[79] One lesson that can be learned from the court's reasoning is that when purchasing the shares of their own company, corporate insiders should adopt a regular and periodic plan of purchases. Otherwise, it is likely that the fact finder might infer that the information available to the insider was in fact material,[80] and thus induced illegal insider trading. Another lesson is that insiders should avoid options trading and other speculative trading strategies that may be an indicia of trying to take advantage of nonpublic information.[81]

Following the lead of *Texas Gulf Sulphur*, some courts held that a tip of inside information will give rise to liability for a fraud on the market.[82] One

74. 40 S.E.C. 907, 1961 WL 60175 (SEC 1961).

75. 40 S.E.C. at 913.

76. 40 S.E.C. at 912.

77. 401 F.2d 833 (2d Cir.1968), *cert. denied*, 394 U.S. 976, 89 S.Ct. 1454, 22 L.Ed.2d 756 (1969).

79. In determining the "materiality date" of the insiders' information, the court relied heavily on substantial increases in insider trading, reasoning that this presented circumstantial evidence that at least the insider deemed the information to be material.

80. *See, e.g.*, SEC v. Ginsburg, 362 F.3d 1292 (11th Cir. 2004) (pattern of trades made by father and brother after calls from principal created fact issue for jury).

81. *See, e.g.,* United States v. Mooney, 401 F.3d 940 (8th Cir. 2005) (upholding conviction of corporate officer who sold stock in his margin account and purchased of call options in corporation's stock shortly before a merger was announced).

82. Shapiro v. Merrill Lynch, Pierce Fenner & Smith, Inc., 495 F.2d 228 (2d Cir.1974). *Accord, e.g.,* Elkind v. Liggett & Myers, Inc., 635 F.2d 156 (2d Cir.1980).

court even held that non-insider tippees who sell in reliance on confidential inside information will be liable and held accountable by disgorging their profits.[83]

In 1988, Congress supplemented any implied remedy that might or might not exist under Rule 10b–5 with an express private right of action by contemporaneous traders against persons making improper use of material, nonpublic information.[95] Under this express remedy, contemporaneous traders are permitted to sue for a disgorgement of the improper profits (or loss avoided).

§ 12.17[3] Causation in Insider Trading Cases—"Use" Versus "Possession"

Another question that has arisen is to what extent it must be shown that the inside information in fact caused the transactions in question. This issue has arisen, for example, in the context of the argument that it must be shown that the trader in fact used the information in question; namely, that he or she would not have traded but-for the confidential information. This debate arose in the course of Congressional deliberation over whether to define insider trading.[101] The Second Circuit indicated that actual use need not be shown; rather, it was sufficient to show that the trader, under a duty of confidentiality, entered into the transactions while *knowingly possessing*[102] material nonpublic information.[103] However, as discussed directly below, this ruling has been altered by SEC rulemaking. In a decision following the SEC rulemaking, the Seventh Circuit did not reach the question of whether trading while in knowing possession of the information was sufficient to establish liability because, on the facts presented to the jury and under the instruction given by the judge, one could infer use from possession.[104] The court went on to say that the defendant can point to a legitimate reason for entering into the trades in question is not sufficient to counteract other evidence from which one could reasonably infer that the defendant actually used the nonpublic information in making the decision to trade.[105]

In a subsequent decision, the 11th Circuit held that it is not sufficient to establish that the defendant possessed inside information when the trades in

83. Financial Industrial Fund, Inc. v. McDonnell Douglas Corp., 474 F.2d 514 (10th Cir.1973), *cert. denied*, 414 U.S. 874, 94 S.Ct. 155, 38 L.Ed.2d 114 (1973).

95. 15 U.S.C.A. § 78t–1. *See* Pub.L. No. 100–704, 102 Stat. 4677 (1988).

101. *See, e.g.,* Comment, The Insider Trading Sanctions Act of 1984: Did Congress and the SEC Go Home Too Early?, 19 U.C.D.L.Rev. 497 (1986).

102. Whether or not the defendant acted in knowing possession of material nonpublic information may depend upon the extent to which a reasonable person would have realized that the information was nonpublic. *See, e.g.,* SEC v. Thrasher, 152 F.Supp.2d 291, [2000–2001 Transfer Binder] Fed. Sec. L. Rep. (CCH) ¶ 91,367 (S.D.N.Y.2001). Ordinarily, the determination will be highly factual, making summary judgment inappropriate. *Id. See also, e.g.,* Jesse M. Fried, Insider Abstention, 113 Yale L.J. 455 (2003) (arguing in favor of a knowing possession rather than use test).

103. United States v. Teicher, 987 F.2d 112 (2d Cir.1993), *cert. denied*, 510 U.S. 976, 114 S.Ct 467, 126 L.Ed.2d 419 (1993).

104. SEC v. Lipson, 278 F.3d 656 (7th Cir.2002). *See also, e.g.,* SEC v. Evans, 2006 WL 3311872 (D.Or. 2006) (refusing to dismiss the complaint because there was a sufficient basis for inferring that defendant used material nonpublic information in making trades in question).

105. Judge Posner, speaking for the court, described it as "absurd" to suggest that a legitimate alternative purpose for making the trade is sufficient to negate liability. 278 F.3d at 661.

question were made.[106] Instead, it must be shown that the use of the information actually caused the trades. The Ninth Circuit followed suit in adopting a use rather than a possession test of causation in insider trading cases.[109]

Rule 10b5–1 requires that the defendant have used the information in making the challenged securities transactions.[119] The rule thus rejects liability based merely on showing that the defendant and subject to a disclose or abstain obligation merely possessed material non public information. In addition to adopting the "use" test for liability, Rule 10b5–1 presumes that someone who trades while in possession of material nonpublic information has in fact used the information in making the trade. The presumption of use that follows from trading while in possession may be rebutted by a showing that the defendant (1) had a preexisting binding contract to enter into the transaction in question, (2) executed a prior instruction to a third party to execute the transaction in question, or (3) had previously adopted a written plan specifying the transactions in question.[120]

Rule 10b5–1(c) establishes two affirmative defenses that rebut the presumption that the insider has in fact used the material nonpublic information in making the trades in question.

The first defense is set forth in Rule 10b5–1(c) protects individuals or entities, and applies in situations where material nonpublic information was not a factor in a trading decision because a trade was carried out pursuant to a pre-existing contract, instruction, or plan. Rule 10b5–1(c)(1) provides that a purchase or sale of securities is not deemed to be made on the basis of material nonpublic information if the individual or entity making the purchase or sale can show that, prior to becoming aware of the material nonpublic information, the individual or entity had entered into a binding contract for the purchase or sale of the security, or instructed a third party to purchase or sell the security for its account, or adopted a written plan for trading securities. Furthermore, the trading plan must specify the "amount" of securities to be purchased or sold and the "price" and "date" on which the securities were to be purchased or sold, or include a written formula for determining the amount, price and date of the transaction, or does not permit the individual or entity to exercise any subsequent influence over how, when and whether to conduct the purchases or sales, and delegated those decisions to a person who did not possess material nonpublic information.

Having established the existence of a trading plan, the defendant must show that the purchase or sale at issue occurred "pursuant to the contract, instruction or plan," which means that the individual or entity that entered into the trading plan did not alter or deviate from the plan or enter into or alter a corresponding or hedging transaction with respect to the securities. A trading plan may be modified at any time provided that the insider is not in possession of material nonpublic information. A defendant's ability to rely on a Rule 10b5–1(c)(1) trading plan is explicitly conditioned on the good faith of

106. SEC v. Adler, 137 F.3d 1325 (11th Cir.1998).

109. United States v. Smith, 155 F.3d 1051 (9th Cir.1998).

119. 17 C.F.R. § 240.10b5–1.

120. *Id. See* Sec. Exch. Act Rel. No. 34–42259 (SEC Dec. 20, 1999).

the individual or entity in entering into the trading plan. The affirmative defense thus is not available where the trading plan was entered into "as part of a plan or scheme to evade" the rule.

The second affirmative defense to the Rule 10b5–1 presumption of use of inside information is available only to entities and thus not to individuals. Rule 10b5–1(c)(2) permits an entity to demonstrate that a trade was not on the basis of material nonpublic information by demonstrating (1) that the individual who made the investment decision on behalf of the entity was not aware of the information, and (2) the entity had implemented reasonable policies and procedures, in light of the nature of the entity's business, to ensure that those making investment decisions on its behalf would not violate the insider trading laws.[127]

A study of insider trades reported a statistically significant higher rate of profitability from insider trades in reliance on Rule 10b5–1 plans as compared with those insiders studied who traded without a plan in place.[128] It is unclear what accounts for this apparent disparity. The results could be explained by abuse of the Rule 10b5–1 plans.[129] It conceivably could be argued, however, that executives not using Rule 10b5–1 plans were justifiably cautious in planning their trades and thus were not as good as a position as managers of the Rule 10b5–1 plans to select optimal trading strategies.

Even beyond the presumptions and defenses established by Rule 10b5–1, the SEC or a private plaintiff claiming insider trading can establish an inference that improper trading has taken place if the insider has engaged in unusual trading patterns. In such a case, the plaintiff has the burden of showing the existence of an unusual trading pattern.[131] Some courts have indicated that this requires a showing that the insiders' transactions were "dramatically different" from their prior trading patterns.[132] As explained by the Ninth Circuit, "[a]mong the relevant factors to consider are: (1) the amount and percentage of shares sold by insiders; (2) the timing of the sales; and (3) whether the sales were consistent with the insider's prior trading history."[133]

127. 17 C.F.R. § 240.10b5–1(c)(2). The "policies and procedures" may include arrangements designed to prevent individuals who make investment decisions on behalf of an entity from acquiring material nonpublic information, as well as policies designed to restrict trading by those who have come into possession of such information. The requirement that these policies and procedures be designed "to ensure" that violations do not occur does not mean that the defense is unavailable if a violation does in fact occur, but instead requires that the policies and procedures be reasonably designed to prevent insider trading.

128. *See* Alan D. Jagolinzer, Do Insiders Trade Strategically within the SEC Rule 10b5–1 Safe Harbor? (Stanford University Graduate School of Business, Working Paper, December 2006), available at http://papers.ssrn.com/sol3/papers.cfm?abstract_id=541502.

129. Professor Jagolinzer suggests three possible explanations for the better performance of the Rule 10b5–1 plans studied: (1) creating plans in advance of bad news becoming public, (2) terminating plans (and therefore of planned sales) before stock prices decrease, or (3) manipulating content or timing of material disclosures after trades had been planned. *See* Alan D. Jagolinzer, Do Insiders Trade Strategically within the SEC Rule 10b5–1 Safe Harbor? (Stanford University Graduate School of Business, Working Paper, December 2006), available at http://papers.ssrn.com/sol3/papers.cfm?abstract_id=541502.

131. In re Silicon Graphics Inc. Securities Litigation, 183 F.3d 970, 986–987 (9th Cir.1999).

132. *Id.* at 986.

133. *Id.*

§ 12.17[4] Refining Rule 10b–5's Applicability to Outsider Trading—The Misappropriation Theory

§ 12.17[4][A] A Duty–Based Obligation and the Evolving Misappropriation Theory of Liability

In Chiarella v. United States,[141] the Court held that, in a market transaction, there was no duty to disclose based solely on the possession of inside information, at least when that information was "market information" rather than fundamental information related to the issuer's condition.

The defendant, Chiarella, was an employee of a printing firm hired to produce documents for various tender offers. The target company's identity was concealed in the galleys sent to the printer in an effort to maintain confidentiality. Chiarella, however, identified the target company by reading the other information in the tender offer material. Armed with this knowledge, he purchased the target company's stock and sold it at a profit after the tender offer was publicly announced.[143] Chiarella's indictment was framed in terms of Rule 10b–5's requirement that insiders possessing confidential material information must either disclose the information or abstain from trading. The Court reversed the defendant's conviction on the grounds that he had no legal duty to speak and thus was not subject to the disclose or abstain obligation.

The Court, in *Chiarella,* first distinguished the SEC's ruling in *Cady, Roberts*[144] on the grounds that, in the later decision the SEC had imposed sanctions against a broker-dealer who had wrongfully obtained information from corporate insiders. The Supreme Court reasoned that the SEC's seminal opinion in *Cady, Roberts* "recognized a relationship of trust and confidence between the shareholder of a corporation and those insiders who have obtained confidential information by reason of their position with that *corporation.*"[145] The Court also explained that the *Texas Gulf Sulphur*[146] "disclose or abstain" rule was limited to persons—both insiders and others—who are subject to a duty to disclose apart from the mere possession of confidential inside information.[147] As noted above, another point of distinction between the facts in *Chiarella* and prior decisions recognizing 10b–5 violations is that *Chiarella* involved market information rather than information "belonging" to the target company.[148] This type of trading is often characterized as "outsider trading" because someone who is not a corporate insider is taking advantage of information that will affect the company's stock price.[149] The misappropriation theory thus permits the SEC and private plaintiffs to pursue

---

141. 445 U.S. 222, 100 S.Ct. 1108, 63 L.Ed.2d 348 (1980).

143. The defendant engaged in five similar transactions and realized an aggregated profit of approximately $30,000.

144. 40 S.E.C. 907 (SEC 1961).

145. 445 U.S. at 228, 100 S.Ct. at 1114, 1115 (footnote omitted; emphasis supplied).

146. SEC v. Texas Gulf Sulphur Co., 401 F.2d 833 (2d Cir.1968), *cert. denied,* 394 U.S. 976, 89 S.Ct. 1454, 22 L.Ed.2d 756 (1969).

147. 445 U.S. at 231, 100 S.Ct. at 1116.

148. *Id.*

149. *See, e.g.,* Ian Ayres & Stephen Choi, Internalizing Outsider Trading, 101 Mich. L. Rev. 313 (2002).

trading on nonpublic information, but only if the trader is guilty of the same type of conduct as an insider in the classic insider trading context.[150]

The Supreme Court in *Chiarella* held that the absence of a wrongful conversion or misappropriation of the information meant that no violation of Rule 10b–5 had occurred because there was no legal duty to disclose such information prior to trading.[151] The Court pointed out, however, that the only issue before it was whether a duty to disclose under 10b–5 was created vis-á-vis the target company by the mere possession of nonpublic information that would affect the price of its stock. The Supreme Court in *Chiarella* did not decide whether the printer's relationship to the acquiring corporation created a duty to abstain from trading.[152] Justice Stevens, in his concurrence, emphasized that this latter theory was not decided,[153] while Justice Brennan's concurrence[154] and the dissent[155] would have upheld the conviction had the conversion theory been presented to the jury. It thus appears that at least four of the Justices would have affirmed the conviction had these alternative theories been presented to the jury.[156] The Court's subsequent ruling in Dirks v. SEC[157] arguably provided a basis for a narrow view of the proper scope of Rule 10b–5 in insider trading cases. However, one post-*Chiarella* decision upheld an SEC complaint seeking injunctive relief and disgorgement of profits in an action against a proofreader who allegedly "misappropriated" tender offer information from a financial printer.[158] Unlike in *Dirks*, the defendant had been entrusted with information and used that information to his own advantage in breach of a duty. The essence of the misappropriation theory thus is the misuse of the information in breach of a duty to the source of the information. As the Supreme Court explained in a later decision, Rule 10b–5 is violated when, in breach of a duty to the source of confidential information, someone misappropriates that information for securities trading purposes.[160]

The disclose or abstain duty recognized under a misappropriation theory does not need to be based on any relationship with the company itself or even with a direct party to the transaction. for example, breach of the doctor-patient privilege has been held sufficient.[181] Similarly, an attorney's breach of duty to his or her law firm by acting on a client confidence will be sufficient to

150. SEC v. Yun, 327 F.3d 1263, 1273 n.27 (11th Cir. 2003).

151. 445 U.S. at 231–235, 100 S.Ct. at 1116–1118.

152. 445 U.S. at 235–36, 100 S.Ct. at 1118, 1119.

153. 445 U.S. at 238, 100 S.Ct. at 1119, 1120 (Stevens, J., concurring).

154. *Id.* at 239, 100 S.Ct. at 1120 (Brennan, J., concurring).

155. *Id.* at 240, 100 S.Ct. at 1120, 1121 (Burger, J., dissenting); *see also id.* at 245, 100 S.Ct at 1123 (Blackmun and Marshall, dissenting).

156. Justice Blackmun in his dissent, with Marshall joining, would have affirmed on the issues presented to the jury without reaching the other theories supported by Justices Brennan and Burger.

157. 463 U.S. 646, 103 S.Ct. 3255, 77 L.Ed.2d 911 (1983).

158. SEC v. Materia, 745 F.2d 197 (2d Cir.1984), *cert. denied*, 471 U.S. 1053, 105 S.Ct. 2112, 85 L.Ed.2d 477 (1985).

160. United States v. O'Hagan, 521 U.S. 642, 652, 117 S.Ct. 2199, 2207, 138 L.Ed.2d 724 (1997).

181. *See* SEC v. Willis, 825 F.Supp. 617 (S.D.N.Y.1993), s.c., 787 F.Supp. 58 (S.D.N.Y.1992) (misappropriation by broker of psychiatrist who had in turn misappropriated information from patient).

support a misappropriation analysis.[182] Someone who obtains information about a target company in his position as a director in a company not directly involved in the deal may be held accountable under the misappropriation theory.[183]

One irony of the misappropriation theory is that while the duty is premised on the ownership of the information, ordinarily the owner of the information will not have standing to raise a Rule 10b–5 claim. In order to bring a 10b–5 claim, the plaintiff must have been a purchaser or seller of the securities in question.[184] One such case was United States v. Carpenter.[185] As was the case on the *Carpenter* facts, the person from whom the confidential information was appropriated may not have been a purchaser or seller.[186] Presumably, however, a claim could be based on state law and breach of agency or other fiduciary duty. On the other hand, contemporaneous traders (to whom no duty was owed) may sue under the Act's express damage provision.[187] The Second Circuit's application of the misappropriation theory in *Carpenter* was affirmed by an equally divided Supreme Court and also finds support in the legislative history of the 1988 Insider Trading and Securities Fraud Enforcement Act.[188] One can only speculate whether the Court was divided over the misappropriation theory in general or whether it was divided as to whether 10b–5 applied in the absence of the misappropriator's employer having been a market participant. In an earlier ruling, the Court seemed to give tacit approval to the underpinnings of the misappropriation theory.[189] In any event, notwithstanding its rejection in the Fourth and Eighth Circuits,[190] the misappropriation theory remained good law in most circuits[191] and was eventually upheld by the Supreme Court.[192]

Although the Supreme Court was equally divided on the 10b–5 claim in *Carpenter,* the Court was unanimous in finding that the misappropriation of information constituted a violation of federal Mail Fraud Act.[193] In affirming

182. *See, e.g.,* United States v. O'Hagan, 521 U.S. 642, 117 S.Ct. 2199, 138 L.Ed.2d 724 (1997), *on remand*, 139 F.3d 641 (8th Cir.1998) (affirming attorney's conviction on remand); SEC v. Singer, 786 F.Supp. 1158 (S.D.N.Y.1992) (applying misappropriation theory to attorney).

183. SEC v. Talbot, 530 F.3d 1085 (9th Cir. 2008) (reversing district court's dismissal of misappropriation claim).

184. Blue Chip Stamps v. Manor Drug Stores, 421 U.S. 723, 95 S.Ct. 1917, 44 L.Ed.2d 539 (1975), *rehearing denied*, 423 U.S. 884, 96 S.Ct. 157, 46 L.Ed.2d 114 (1975). The standing limitations are discussed in § 12.7 *supra*.

185. United States v. Carpenter, 791 F.2d 1024 (2d Cir.1986), *affirmed by an equally divided court,* 484 U.S. 19, 108 S.Ct. 316, 98 L.Ed.2d 275 (1987).

186. *See, e.g.,* In re Ivan F. Boesky Securities Litigation, 36 F.3d 255 (2d Cir.1994), *affirming*, 825 F.Supp. 623 (S.D.N.Y.1993) (firm from which information was misappropriated had no standing to sue employee).

187. 1934 Act section 20A, 15 U.S.C.A. § 78t–1(a).

188. Pub.L. No. 100–704, 102 Stat. 4677 (1988). *See* Carpenter v. United States, 484 U.S. 19, 108 S.Ct. 316, 98 L.Ed.2d 275 (1987). *See* H.R.Rep. No. 100–910, 100th Cong. 2d Sess. 10–11 (1988).

189. Bateman Eichler, Hill Richards, Inc. v. Berner, 472 U.S. 299, 311–12 n. 21, 105 S.Ct. 2622, 2629 n. 21, 86 L.Ed.2d 215 (1985).

190. United States v. O'Hagan, 92 F.3d 612 (8th Cir.1996), rev'd 521 U.S. 642, 117 S.Ct. 2199, 138 L.Ed.2d 724 (1997); United States v. Bryan, 58 F.3d 933 (4th Cir.1995). *See also* United States v. ReBrook, 58 F.3d 961 (4th Cir.1995).

191. For other cases applying the misappropriation theory, *see* ICN Pharmaceuticals, Inc. v. Khan, 2 F.3d 484 (2d Cir.1993); SEC v. Cherif, 933 F.2d 403 (7th Cir.1991), *cert. denied*, 502 U.S. 1071, 112 S.Ct. 966, 117 L.Ed.2d 131 (1992); SEC v. Clark, 915 F.2d 439 (9th Cir.1990).

192. United States v. O'Hagan, 521 U.S. 642, 117 S.Ct. 2199, 138 L.Ed.2d 724 (1997), *on remand*, 139 F.3d 641 (8th Cir.1998) (affirming conviction on remand).

193. Carpenter v. United States, 484 U.S. 19, 108 S.Ct. 316, 98 L.Ed.2d 275 (1987); 18 U.S.C.A. §§ 1341, 1343.

the mail fraud conviction, the Court reasoned that the information concerning the Heard on the Street column was clearly property belonging to Dow Jones, and that the reporter had a duty to safeguard that information. The breach of that duty accordingly amounted to a deprivation of Dow Jones' property right in contravention of the Mail Fraud Act. In reaching its decision under the Mail Fraud Act, the Supreme Court embraced the rationale underlying the New York decision in Diamond v. Oreamuno[194] allowing a corporation to recover the profits of insiders who traded on confidential information.

The long wait for the Supreme Court's resolution of the issue ended in 1997 with its decision in United States v. O'Hagan,[197] which upheld misappropriation as a basis for imposing Rule 10b–5 liability for trading on nonpublic information.

O'Hagan arose out of the prosecution of a partner in a law firm that was retained by a would-be tender offeror. The attorney, after having learned of the firm's client's planned takeover, purchased call options in the target company prior to the announcement of the tender offer. The indictment charged that the attorney had violated Rule 10b–5 and Rule 14e–3, which prohibits trading in advance of a tender offer;[198] he was also charged with violating the mail fraud statute. The Eighth Circuit overturned a conviction on all three counts.[199] The court of appeals' rejection of the Rule 10b–5 claim was based on two grounds. First, the court stated that Rule 10b–5 requires a misrepresentation or nondisclosure. Secondly, the Eighth Circuit held that a duty owed to the source of the nonpublic information was not sufficient to satisfy section 10(b)'s requirement that the fraud be "in connection with the purchase or sale" of a security. The Supreme Court rejected both objections to the imposition of liability. The Court responded to the first objection by pointing out that trading on nonpublic information involves deceptive nondisclosure.[200] The deception that results from the misappropriation of information is based on a "feigning fidelity" to the source of the information and the fiduciary's failure to disclose plans to trade on the information.[201] Second, in addition to being premised on the necessary deceptive conduct, liability based on misappropriation satisfies the requirement that the violation be "in connection with the purchase or sale of *any* security" because it is not necessary to make a further link to "identifiable purchasers or sellers of securities."[202] The *O'Hagan* decision accordingly clarified that the duty which forms the basis of the Rule 10b–5 violation need not be owed to a purchaser or seller of securities. It is sufficient that the breach of duty is carried out through securities trading. The use of a securities transaction to effectuate the breach of the duty is a sufficient connection.

Were Congress to enact a statute explicitly prohibiting trading on material nonpublic information, and thereby define the scope of the prohibition, the law would be much clearer. We could then have a precise definition of when

194. 24 N.Y.2d 494, 301 N.Y.S.2d 78, 248 N.E.2d 910 (1969).

197. 521 U.S. 642, 117 S.Ct. 2199, 138 L.Ed.2d 724 (1997).

198. 17 C.F.R. § 240.14e–3. Rule 14e–3 is discussed *infra*.

199. United States v. O'Hagan, 92 F.3d 612 (8th Cir.1996), rev'd 521 U.S. 642, 117 S.Ct. 2199, 138 L.Ed.2d 724 (1997).

200. 521 U.S. at 653, 117 S.Ct. at 2208, 138 L.Ed.2d at 1274. The Court explained that the defendant's failure to disclose his personal trading to his law firm and his firm's client rendered that conduct "deceptive." *Id.*

201. 521 U.S. at 655, 117 S.Ct. at 2209, 138 L.Ed.2d at 1274.

202. 521 U.S. at 660, 117 S.Ct. at 2111, 138 L.Ed.2d at 1274.

such conduct will violate the law. However, until Congress acts, the misappropriation doctrine is a necessary evil considering the fact that Rule 10b–5 is the primary source of the insider trading prohibition. There is an unevenness in the application of the doctrine. For example, a broker who trades on information supplied by a customer has been held not to have violated Rule 10b–5[206] while a psychiatrist who trades on information supplied by a patient has violated the law. This is because there is not a duty of confidentiality attaching to the broker/customer relationship,[207] while a psychiatrist is subject to an obligation of patient confidentiality.[208] To say the least, it is strange that the securities laws uphold the Hippocratic oath and punish the psychiatrist for breaching it, but do not capture the equally guilty stock broker. The obvious irony here is that the securities laws were enacted to protect investors and regulate the brokerage industry, not to uphold concepts of medical ethics. Relying on Rule 10b–5 as the primary source of the insider trading prohibition causes this irony since the rule is based on fraud and thus requires a duty not to trade on the nonpublic information independent of the mere possession of the information. The doctor-patient relationship is only one example of a fiduciary relationship not involving the company or securities that can trigger liability for insider trading outside of the classical insider trading context. For example, a member of a grand jury who took advantage of information obtained in the course of jury duty was held accountable for misappropriating that information for securities trading.[209] Whether a particular relationship is fiduciary in nature so as to trigger Rule 10b–5's disclose-or-abstain rule can depend on the facts of the particular case.[210]

Difficult questions can arise in determining which relationships establish a fiduciary duty of confidentiality. Rule 10b5–2 provides some guidance as to when the disclose or abstain obligation will apply. Of course, not every relationship is a fiduciary one creating such a position of trust and confidence. Professional relationships such as attorney-client,[211] tax advisor-client,[212] and doctor-patient[213] create fiduciary obligations of confidentiality. However, a

206. United States v. Chestman, 947 F.2d 551 (2d Cir.1991), *cert. denied*, 503 U.S. 1004, 112 S.Ct. 1759, 118 L.Ed.2d 422 (1992). The court in *Chestman* also held that the husband/wife relationship did not create a duty of confidentiality. *Id.* This result was questioned in SEC v. Yun, 327 F.3d 1263 (11th Cir. 2003), which found that the spousal relationship on the facts before the court did create an expectation of confidentiality. *See also, e.g.,* SEC v. Rocklage, 470 F.3d 1 (1st Cir. 2006). (wife breached duty to her husband when she obtained nonpublic information with the intention to pass it on to her brother so he could trade on it to his advantage). In addition, SEC Rule 10b5–2 creates a presumption of confidentiality from a spousal relationship. 17 C.F.R. § 240.10b5–2.

207. United States v. Chestman, 947 F.2d 551 (2d Cir.1991), *cert. denied*, 503 U.S. 1004, 112 S.Ct. 1759, 118 L.Ed.2d 422 (1992).

208. SEC v. Brody, 1999 WL 1425401, [1999–2000 Transfer Binder] Fed. Sec. L. Rep. (CCH) ¶ 90,667 (D.D.C. 1999); United States v. Willis, 737 F.Supp. 269 (S.D.N.Y.1990).

209. United States v. Smith, 155 F.3d 1051, Sec. L. Daily (BNA, http://pubs.bna.com/ip/bna/sld.nsf/eh/A0B3V2M3P9 (S.D.N.Y.2006)) (grand juror pled guilty to leaking information from grand jury probe and was sentenced to 33 months in prison).

210. SEC v. Sargent, 229 F.3d 68, 75–76 (1st Cir.2000) (jury question whether defendant making a promise not to divulge the information had a preexisting fiduciary duty).

211. *See, e.g.,* United States v. O'Hagan, 521 U.S. 642, 117 S.Ct. 2199, 138 L.Ed.2d 724 (1997) (upholding conviction of attorney for trading on client's nonpublic information).

212. *See, e.g.,* SEC v. Kornman, 391 F.Supp.2d 477 (N.D. Tex. 2005) (upholding SEC complaint against tax advisor and estate planner who allegedly misappropriated information from client).

213. *See, e.g.,* United States v. Willis, 737 F.Supp. 269 (S.D.N.Y. 1990) (upholding indictment of psychiatrist broker who traded on the information provided by patient). *See also, e.g.,* SEC v. Willis, 825 F.Supp. 617 (S.D.N.Y. 1993).

corporate outsider, such as a bidder in merger negotiations, will not owe a fiduciary duty of non disclosure absent a confidentiality agreement.[214] For example in one leading case, it was held that the relationship of a customer to his stock broker did not create a duty of confidentiality.[215] In another case, the court explained that a fiduciary relationship requires "some measure of superiority, dominance, or control." The court then went on to hold that co-members of an entrepreneurs' society did not create such a relationship.[216] In so ruling, the court indicated that not every confidentiality agreement will trigger the obligation. For example, insider trading liability will not arise out of a confidentiality agreement that is not taken as legally binding but rather as a statement of ethical and moral obligation.[217]

Under Rule 10b5–2,[220] there are "three non-exclusive bases for determining that a duty of trust or confidence was owed by a person receiving information: (1) when the person agreed to keep information confidential; (2) when the persons involved in the communication had a history, pattern, or practice of sharing confidences that resulted in a reasonable expectation of confidentiality; and (3) when the person who provided the information was a spouse, parent, child, or sibling of the person who received the information, unless it were shown affirmatively, based on the facts and circumstances of that family relationship, that there was no reasonable expectation of confidentiality."[221] Family relationships thus can provide the basis for a confidential relationship sufficient to trigger insider trading liability.[222] The Eleventh Circuit did not go so far as to uphold Rule 10b5–2's presumption of confidentiality, but it nevertheless held that a family relationship can create a sufficient expectation of confidentiality so as to trigger Rule 10b–5's disclose or abstain obligation.[223] A subsequent First Circuit decision found that confidences passed on from one spouse to another are clothed with a duty of confidentiality sufficient to establish a Rule 10b–5 disclosure or abstain obligation.[224]

214. *See* Pennsylvania Ave. Funds v. Borey, 2008 WL 426509 (W.D. Wash. 2008) (dismissing Rule 10b–5 insider trading challenge since participant in merger negotiations was not required to sign and did not sign a confidentiality agreement).

215. United States v. Chestman, 947 F 2d 551 (2d Cir.1991), *cert. denied*, 503 U.S. 1004, 112 S.Ct. 1759, 118 L.Ed.2d 422 (1992).

216. United States v. Kim, 173 F.Supp.2d 1035 (N.D.Cal.2001), *amended by*, 184 F.Supp.2d 1006 (N.D.Cal.2002).

217. *Id.*

220. 17 C.F.R. § 240.10b5–2.

221. Selective Disclosure and Insider Trading, Sec. Exch. Act Rel. No. 34–42259 (SEC Dec. 20, 1999).

222. *See, e.g.,* SEC v. Yun, 327 F.3d 1263 (11th Cir. 2003) (whether communications between spouses were confidential was a jury question), *vacating*, SEC v. Yun, 130 F.Supp.2d 1348 (M.D.Fla.2001) (post-nuptial negotiations created confidential relationship so as to support insider trading liability can be based on a tip of information between husband and wife). *See also, e.g., See also, e.g.,* SEC v. Rocklage, 470 F.3d 1 (1st Cir. 2006) (wife breached duty to her husband when she obtained nonpublic information with the intention to pass it on to her brother so he could trade on it to his advantage); Ray J. Grzebielski, Friends, Family Fiduciaries: Personal Relationships as a Basis for Insider Trading Violations, 51 Cath. U. L. Rev. 467 (2002); Thomas M. Madden, O'Hagan, 10b5–2, Relationships and Duties, 4 Hastings Bus. L.J. 55 (2008).

223. SEC v. Yun, 327 F.3d 1263 (11th Cir. 2003)

224. SEC v. Rocklage, 470 F.3d 1 (1st Cir. 2006). (wife breached duty toi her husband when she obtained nonpublic information with the intention to pass it on to her brother so he could trade on it to his advantage).

§ 12.17[5] Insider Trading—Passing on Non–Public Information—Tipper and Tippee Liability

As discussed above, the Supreme Court in Dirks v. SEC[231] held that "a tippee assumes a fiduciary duty to the shareholders of a corporation * * * only when the insider has breached his fiduciary duty to the shareholders * * * and the tippee knows or should know that there has been a breach."[232] Corporate insiders do not breach a fiduciary duty unless the purpose of their passing on the information was to obtain, directly or indirectly, some personal or economic benefit.[233] The actions of the defendant in *Dirks* were major factors in exposing the massive Equity Funding fraud.[234] In *Dirks,* the insiders—former employees of the company in question—were motivated by a desire to expose the company's fraud; therefore, Dirks was not obligated to abstain from passing on the inside information disclosed to him.[235]

The application of tippee liability is not limited to information passed on by true insiders. Tippee and tipper liability also applies in the misappropriation context when others have passed on the information in breach of a fiduciary duty.[241] This is true even if the tippee is remote from the tipper so

---

231. 463 U.S. 646, 103 S.Ct. 3255, 77 L.Ed.2d 911 (1983).

232. 463 U.S. at 660, 103 S.Ct. at 3264. The Court went on to explain: "Thus, the test is whether the insider personally will benefit, directly or indirectly, from his disclosure. Absent some personal gain, there has been no breach of duty to stockholders. And absent a breach by the insider, there is no derivative breach [by the tippee]." *Id.*

233. *See, e.g.,* SEC v. Yun, 327 F.3d 1263 (11th Cir. 2003) (jury question as to whether wife who tipped husband had the requisite intent to benefit so as to trigger tipper liability; also rejecting a different standard of liability for misappropriation cases as opposed to classic insider trading cases).

234. The defendant, an investment analyst, was investigating Equity Funding Corp. After an investigation including talks with various employees he realized that the company's assets had been fraudulently inflated. As described by the Court,

> While Dirks was in Los Angeles, he was in touch regularly with William Blundell, the *Wall Street Journal's* Los Angeles bureau chief. Dirks urged Blundell to write a story on the fraud allegations. Blundell did not believe, however, that such a massive fraud could go undetected and declined to write the story. He feared that publishing such damaging hearsay might be libelous.
>
> During the two-week period in which Dirks pursued his investigation and spread word of Secrist's charges, the price of Equity Funding stock fell from $26 per share to less than $15 per share. This led the New York Stock Exchange to halt trading on March 27. Shortly thereafter California insurance authorities impounded Equity Funding's records and uncovered evidence of the fraud. Only then did the Securities and Exchange Commission (SEC) file a complaint against Equity Funding and only then, on April 2 did the Wall Street Journal publish a front-page story based largely on information assembled by Dirks. Equity Funding immediately went into receivership.
>
> The SEC began an investigation into Dirks' role in the exposure of the fraud. After a hearing by an administrative law judge, the SEC found that Dirks had aided and abetted violations of § 17(a) of the Securities Act of 1933, 15 U.S.C.A. § 77q(a), § 10(b) of the Securities Exchange Act of 1934, 15 U.S.C.A. § 78j(b) and SEC Rule 10b–5, 17 CFR § 240.10b–5 (1982), by repeating the allegations of fraud to members of the investment community who later sold their Equity Funding stock. The SEC concluded: "Where 'tippees'—(regardless of their motivation or occupation)—come into possession of material 'information that they know is confidential and know or should know came from a corporate insider,' they must either publicly disclose that information or refrain from trading." 21 S.E.C. Docket 1401, 1407 (1981) (footnote omitted) (quoting Chiarella v. United States, 445 U.S. 222, 230 n. 12, 100 S.Ct. 1108, 1115 n. 12, 63 L.Ed.2d 348 (1980)). Recognizing, however, that Dirks "played an important role in bringing [Equity Funding's] massive fraud to light," 21 S.E.C. Docket, at 1412, the SEC only censured him.

463 U.S. at 649–652, 103 S.Ct. at 3259–3260. *See also* Raymond L. Dirks & Leonard Gross, The Great Wall Street Scandal—Inside Equity Funding (1974).

235. The six-to-three decision in *Dirks* contained a vigorous dissent that would have applied the "disclose or abstain" rule.

241. *See, e.g.,* SEC v. Michel, 521 F.Supp.2d 795 (N.D. Ill. 2007) (remote tippee misappropriated information he received regarding pending takeover of accompany).

long as there is a direct tainted chain of information. Thus, a tip from a magazine employee about an upcoming article to a printer and then to three intermediaries nevertheless resulted in a Rule 10b–5 violation under the misappropriation theory.[242] In order to establish tippee liability, contact between a tipper and the tippee must be established.[243] If a tippee knows or has reason to know of the taint from the tipper, there is no additional need to show that the tippee owed a fiduciary duty to the tipper.[244]

The conflict has continued between a broad and narrow view of tipper and tippee liability. For example, some courts have fashioned the concept of "temporary insider" to deal with tippee accountability.[245] On the other hand, where defendant traded after having overheard a family conversation that conveyed inside information, there was no 10b–5 liability because the tipper had not breached a duty, and therefore there could be no derivative liability on behalf of the tippee.[246] Conversely, when the tipper has breached a duty and the tippee has reason to know of the breach, the tippee would be guilty of sufficient scienter to violate Rule 10b–5.[247] Similarly, a tippee will be held liable for trading on a tip that was a "gift" of confidential information passed on with the tippee's trading in mind.[248] Insider trading liability has been based on a tip from husband to wife and then in turn to a third party.[249]

In the words of one court, "It is not accurate to say that *Dirks* wrote the book on insider or outsider trading; it wrote one chapter with respect to one type of fraudulent trading."[250]

§ 12.17[6] Insider Trading in Advance of Tender Offers: Rule 14e–3

Following the Supreme Court's decision in Chiarella v. United States,[257] the SEC tried to avoid Rule 10b–5's duty requirement by adopting Rule 14e–3[258] to prohibit anyone other than the tender offeror from trading on the basis of advance information pertaining to a not-yet-announced tender offer. In one case, the Fourth Circuit upheld a preliminary injunction against a tender offer where the offer was based upon information that had been allegedly misappropriated from the target company, in violation of Rule 14e–3.[259] That rule,

242. United States v. Falcone, 97 F.Supp 2d 297 (E.D.N.Y.2000).

243. *See* SEC v. Truong, 98 F.Supp.2d 1086 (N.D.Cal.2000) (insider was held to have violated Rule 10b–5, but lack of proof of contact precluded liability of insider's friend).

244. SEC v. Lambert, 38 F.Supp.2d 1348, 1351 (S.D.Fla.1999).

245. SEC v. Tome, 833 F.2d 1086 (2d Cir.1987), *affirming*, 638 F.Supp. 596 (S.D.N.Y.1986); SEC v. Lund, 570 F.Supp. 1397 (C.D.Cal.1983).

246. SEC v. Switzer, 590 F.Supp. 756 (W.D.Okl.1984).

247. SEC v. Warde, 151 F.3d 42 (2d Cir.1998).

248. SEC v. Maio, 51 F.3d 623 (7th Cir.1995).

249. SEC v. Yun, 327 F.3d 1263 (11th Cir. 2003) (whether communications between spouses were confidential was a jury question).

250. United States v. Winans, 612 F.Supp. 827, 842 (S.D.N.Y.1985), *affirmed*, 791 F.2d 1024 (2d Cir.1986), *affirmed*, 484 U.S. 19, 108 S.Ct. 316, 98 L.Ed.2d 275 (1987).

257. 445 U.S. 222, 100 S.Ct. 1108, 63 L.Ed.2d 348 (1980).

258. 17 C.F.R. § 240.14e–3.

259. Burlington Industries, Inc. v. Edelman, 1987 WL 91498, [1987 Transfer Binder] Fed.Sec. L.Rep. (CCH) ¶ 93,339 (4th Cir.1987), *affirming on the basis of the opinion below*, 666 F.Supp. 799 (M.D.N.C.1987).

which has been challenged as going beyond the scope of the statute, was upheld by the Second, Seventh, and Ninth Circuits.[260]

The impact of Rule 14e–3 was further bolstered by the Supreme Court's decision in *United States v. O'Hagan*.[270] The Court there upheld the conviction of an attorney who traded on advance knowledge of a tender offer where the source of the information was a client of the firm.[271] There was a companion conviction based on the misappropriation of the information in violation of Rule 10b–5. The decision in *O'Hagan* left open a significant question concerning the scope of Rule 14e–3, as it did not reach the question of whether the SEC's power to define prohibited conduct under Rule 14e–3 is broader than its authority under Rule 10b–5.[272] However, the case certainly invites the broad reading of Rule 14e–3.[273]

Also, Rule 14e–3 has been used to capture tippers as well as those who trade on the information.[274] It is not necessary that the defendant know that the nonpublic information in his or her possession relates to a tender offer.[275] It is sufficient to establish that the defendant had reason to know that the information related to a tender offer.[276] It has further been held that if the defendant traded while in knowing possession of nonpublic information concerning a pending tender offer, it is not necessary to establish that the defendant acted in breach of a fiduciary duty.[277] In a divided decision, a three judge panel of the Second Circuit held that breach of a fiduciary duty is a precondition of a criminal conviction for violating Rule 14e–3.[278]

In order to hold someone criminally accountable for a violation of Rule 14e–3, it must be established that the defendant knew that the shares that were purchased were the target of a tender offer.[279] A violation of Rule 14e–3 can form the basis of a private right of action under section 20A of the 1934 Act.[280] The private action may be brought by contemporaneous traders who

---

260. SEC v. Maio, 51 F.3d 623 (7th Cir.1995) (reaffirming Rule 14e–3 as a valid exercise of rulemaking authority); SEC v. Peters, 978 F.2d 1162 (10th Cir.1992); United States v. Chestman, 947 F.2d 551 (2d Cir.1991), *cert. denied,* 503 U.S. 1004, 112 S.Ct. 1759, 118 L.Ed.2d 422 (1992).

270. 521 U.S. 642, 117 S.Ct. 2199, 138 L.Ed.2d 724 (1997). *See also, e.g.,* Comment, Improperly Incorporating Common Law Fiduciary Obligations Into § 14(e) of the Securities Exchange Act, 81 Minn. L. Rev. 1015 (1997).

271. The Eighth Circuit had refused to invoke Rule 14e–3 because of the absence of fraud. United States v. O'Hagan, 92 F.3d 612 (8th Cir.1996), *reversed,* 521 U.S. 642, 117 S.Ct. 2199, 138 L.Ed.2d 724 (1997). The court, in rejecting the decisions in other circuits, held that the rule as so applied is not supported by the language of the statute. The Eighth Circuit went on to hold that the Commission exceeded its rulemaking authority by promulgating Rule 14e–3 without requiring a fiduciary duty as a basis for triggering the duty to disclose or abstain. *Id.* at 626–627. The Eighth Circuit reached this result by relying upon the Supreme Court's ruling in Schreiber v. Burlington Northern, Inc., 472 U.S. 1, 105 S.Ct. 2458, 86 L.Ed.2d 1 (1985), which held that section 14(e) reaches only deceptive conduct.

272. 521 U.S. at 672, 117 S.Ct. at 2217, 138 L.Ed.2d at 1274.

273. *See, e.g.,* SEC v. Mayhew, 121 F.3d 44 (2d Cir.1997) (defendant received information about pending tender offer during an exercise walk with his neighbor who was an insider of one of the companies involved; when he traded on this information, he violated Rule 14e–3).

274. SEC v. Falbo, 14 F.Supp.2d 508 (S.D.N.Y.1998).

275. SEC v. Sargent, 229 F.3d 68, 78, 79 (1st Cir.2000).

276. United States v. O'Hagan, 139 F.3d, 641, 650 (8th Cir.1998).

277. *See, e.g.,* SEC v. Thrasher, 152 F.Supp.2d 291, [2000–2001 Transfer Binder] Fed. Sec. L. Rep. (CCH) ¶ 91,367 (S.D.N.Y. 2001).

278. United States v. Cassese, 428 F.3d 92 (2d Cir. 2005).

279. United States v. Cassese, 290 F.Supp.2d 443 (S.D.N.Y. 2003).

280. 15 U.S.C.A. § 78t–1(a). *See* § 12.17[7][B] *infra.*

sold while the illegal purchases were taking place.[281]

§ 12.17[7] Insider Trading: Private Remedies; Enhanced SEC Sanctions

One backlash of the *Chiarella* and *Dirks* decisions has been a push for congressional enactment of stronger insider trading penalties. Legislation by Congress (The Insider Trading Sanctions Act of 1984,[301] or ITSA) permits the SEC to bring suit against anyone violating the 1934 Act or rules "by purchasing or selling a security while in possession of material nonpublic information."[302] The enhanced sanctions apply not only to the person who violates the Act by trading on the information, but also to someone who violates the Act by passing on the information to someone else to facilitate his or her trading on the information. The enhanced set of remedies for illegal insider trading further provide for both the disgorgement of any profit and the imposition of a civil penalty. The civil penalty in such a suit, which can be granted in addition to disgorgement of the ill-gotten gain, can be as high as trebling the profits gained or loss avoided by the defendant. In addition, the 1984 amendments to the Exchange Act also increased the criminal penalties.

The Insider Trading Sanctions Act of 1984 raises a number of interesting questions. For example: do successive actions for civil penalties under ITSA and for criminal violations based on the same transactions violate the constitutional prohibition against double jeopardy? Since the treble damage provision is a penalty (although denominated as civil in nature), there would appear to be an argument that it should be treated as criminal so that double jeopardy would apply. On the other hand, a Supreme Court decision subsequently held that there is a strong presumption to be given to a congressional designation of a sanction as civil.[311] Under the current approach, it is doubtful that even a treble penalty for insider trading violations would be considered criminal. In any event, it is clear that double jeopardy would not apply to a criminal action followed by an SEC suit for disgorgement of profits.[312] This is the case because it is recognized that a criminal fine is a different matter from the remedial considerations underlying a disgorgement action.[313]

§ 12.17[7][C] Controlling Person Liability; Private Remedies—Insider Trading and Securities Fraud Enforcement Act of 1988

Congress bolstered the remedies provided by the Insider Trading Sanction Act amendments of 1984 when it enacted the Insider Trading and Securities Fraud Enforcement Act of 1988[318] (ITSFEA). This legislation specifically addressed liability of employers and controlling persons.[319] Under the

281. Brody v. Transitional Hospitals Corp., 280 F.3d 997 (9th Cir.2002) (the contemporaneous trader standing requirement applies to insider trading actions brought under the tender offer rules).

301. Pub. L. No. 98–376, 98 Stat. 1264 (1984).

302. 15 U.S.C.A. § 78u–1(a)(1), 78ff(a).

311. Hudson v. United States, 522 U.S. 93, 118 S.Ct. 488, 139 L.Ed.2d 450 (1997).

312. SEC v. Bilzerian, 814 F.Supp. 116 (D.D.C.1993).

313. *Id.*

318. Pub.L. No. 100–704, 102 Stat. 4677 (1988).

319. Controlling person liability under the Exchange Act generally is governed by section 20(a) of the Act. 15 U.S.C.A. § 78t(a). *See* § 12.24 *infra*.

Insider Trading and Securities Fraud Enforcement Act of 1988, a court can impose the treble damage penalties for insider trading violations on a controlling person only if: (1) the controlling person knew or acted in reckless disregard of the fact that the controlled person was likely to engage in illegal insider trading and (2) the controlling person failed to take adequate precautions to prevent the prohibited conduct from taking place.[320] It is further provided that general principles of respondeat superior and section 20(a)[321] controlling person liability do not apply to actions brought for illegal insider trading activities.[322] As is the case with any instance of controlling person liability, there must have been a primary violation of the securities laws. In other words, claims under section 20A claims "are derivative, requiring proof of a separate underlying violation of the Exchange Act."[323]

Perhaps the most significant aspect of the Insider Trading and Securities Fraud Enforcement Act is its applicability to private enforcement. The Insider Trading and Securities Fraud Enforcement Act of 1988 created an express private right of action in the hands of contemporaneous traders. Section 20A of the Exchange Act provides that anyone violating the Act or SEC rules while trading in possession of material, nonpublic information shall be liable to contemporaneous traders trading on the other side of the insider trader's transactions.[327] Thus, if the violator is selling, all contemporaneous purchasers can sue, while if the violator is purchasing, all contemporaneous sellers can sue.

Section 20A does not define precisely who qualifies as a contemporaneous trader. Arguably, in light of the remedy's prophylactic (rather than compensatory) purpose, that phrase should be construed relatively broadly. Most decisions seem to agree that establishing trading within a week of the defendant's improper trading will be sufficient to satisfy the contemporaneous trading requirement.[330] However, others have utilized a shorter period of time.[331]

There is authority to support the proposition that option holders can have standing under section 20A with regard to the defendant's contemporaneous trading in the underlying stock.[333] One court held that a plaintiff whose only trades are with the defendant may not sue under section 20A as a supplement to the Rule 10b–5 action.[334] However, when the plaintiff has other trades in addition to those with the defendant, he or she may bring a section 20A claim as a contemporaneous trader.[335]

---

320. 15 U.S.C.A. § 78u–1(b)(1).

321. 15 U.S.C.A. § 78t(a). *See* § 12.24 *infra.*

322. 15 U.S.C.A. § 78u–1(b)(2).

323. Makor Issues & Rights, Ltd. v. Tellabs, Inc., 2008 WL 2178150 (N.D. Ill. 2008).

327. 15 U.S.C.A. § 78t–1(a).

330. *See, e.g.,* Feldman v. Motorola, Inc., 1994 WL 160115, [1993–1994 Transfer Binder] Fed. Sec. L. Rep. (CCH) ¶ 98,133 (N.D.Ill.1994).

331. *E.g.,* In re MicroStrategy Securities Litigation, 115 F.Supp.2d 620 (E.D.Va.2000) (purchase of stock three days after officer's sale at higher price was not "contemporaneous").

333. Samuelson Trading Corp. v. Waksal, 2004 WL 813534 (N.D. Ill. 2004) (seller of put options could sue for insider trading).

334. Fujisawa Pharmaceutical Co. v. Kapoor, 115 F.3d 1332, 1337 (7th Cir.1997).

335. *See* Samuelson Trading Corp. v. Waksal, 2004 WL 813534 (N.D. Ill. 2004).

Damages in an action under the express insider trading private remedy are limited to the profits or losses avoided by the illegal transactions[339] and are to be diminished by any disgorgement (as opposed to penalty) ordered in an SEC enforcement action.[340] Controlling person liability in such a private suit is governed by section 20(a) of the Act[341] rather than by the specific controlling person provisions applicable to SEC enforcement actions.[342] Liability under the express private remedy for illegal insider trading extends to both tippers and tippees who violate the act; the act further provides that their liability is joint and several.[343]

Section 20A's express private remedy supplements any other existing express or implied remedies.[347] The Act also provides that the private remedy does not limit the Commission's or Attorney General's authority to recover penalties (as opposed to disgorgement of profits) for improper use of material, nonpublic information.[348]

Section 21A(e) of the Exchange Act permits the payment of a bounty of up to ten percent of the penalty to private individuals who provide information leading to the imposition of the penalty.[349] The decision to award a bounty lies in the sole discretion of the SEC, except that persons associated with the Commission, Department of Justice, or a self-regulatory organization are not eligible to receive a bounty award.[350]

§ 12.18 Liability for Material Misstatements and Omissions of Fact in Documents Filed With the SEC—Section 18(a) of the Exchange Act

Section 18(a) of the Exchange Act[13] imposes liability upon anyone responsible for material misstatement or omission of fact in connection with any document required to be filed with the Commission under any provision or rule of the Exchange Act.[14] The section 18(a) cause of action is available to any investor who, after having read the faulty document filed, *actually relies* upon statements in the document and is therefore injured.

The courts have held that section 18(a) requires an "eyeball" test; that is, the plaintiff must have actual knowledge of and reliance upon the materials

339. 15 U.S.C.A. § 78t–1(b)(1). In addition, there is a self-contained five-year statute of limitations. 15 U.S.C.A. § 78t–1(b)(4). The same five-year limitations period applies in SEC actions under ITSA. 15 U.S.C.A. § 78u–1(d)(5). The limitations period in Rule 10b–5 actions is discussed in § 12.16 *supra*.

340. 15 U.S.C.A. § 78t–1(b)(2).

341. 15 U.S.C.A. § 78t(a).

342. 15 U.S.C.A. § 78u–1(b).

343. 15 U.S.C.A. § 78t–1(c).

347. 15 U.S.C.A. § 78t–1(d).

348. 15 U.S.C.A. § 78t–1(e).

349. 15 U.S.C.A. § 78u–1(e).

350. 15 U.S.C.A. § 78u–1(e).

§ 12.18

13. 15 U.S.C.A. § 78r(a). Section 323 of the Trust Indenture Act of 1939, 15 U.S.C.A. § 77www is modeled on section 18(a). *See* § 19.2 *infra*.

See §§ 1.8, 7.0 *supra* for an overview of private remedies available under the 1933 and 1934 Acts.

14. Section 18(a) applies to documents "filed pursuant to this chapter," but does not apply to filing under the 1933 Act or any other of the securities laws. *Id.* Nor does section 18(a) apply to the annual report disseminated to shareholders under the proxy rules. 17 C.F.R. §§ 240.14a–3(c), 14c–3(b).

filed with the Commission, or a copy thereof; it is not sufficient that the plaintiff saw similar information contained in other documents prepared by the issuer.[17] Reliance based on a "fraud on the market" theory may be the foundation for a remedy under Rule 10b–5, but will not satisfy section 18(a)'s requirements.[19]

§ 12.19 Corporate Affirmative Disclosure Obligations and Accountability

§ 12.19[1] Affirmative Disclosure Obligations

When forms or schedules have to be filed with the SEC, the applicable form or schedule contains "line item" disclosure requirements. As was pointed out in an earlier chapter of this treatise,[4] issuers subject to the registration requirements of section 12 of the Exchange Act[5] must file periodic reports with the Commission pursuant to section 13 of the Act.[6] Section 16(a)[7] further requires officers, directors, and ten percent beneficial owners of registered reporting companies to file reports of all transactions in the issuer's shares. In addition, section 13(d)[8] requires filings by any person acquiring five percent of an equity security subject to the registration and reporting requirements, and section 14(d)[9] imposes filing requirements in connection with tender offers. These filings are publicly available.

In the absence of a filing requirement, there is no affirmative obligation to disclose material information until the next quarterly report is due, except for the limited number of items that must be disclosed in interim reports on Form 8–K. The mandatory disclosure items in these interim reports has expanded. Section 409 of the Sarbanes–Oxley Act of 2002[12] provides that the SEC should promulgate rules, as it deems "necessary or useful for the protection of investors and in the public interest," to provide for "real-time" disclosure of "information concerning material changes in the financial condition or operations of the issuer, in plain English, which may include trend and qualitative information and graphic presentations."[13] Even before this legislative impetus, the Commission began moving more towards a system of continuous rather than periodic reporting when it proposed expanding the items that have to be disclosed promptly on Form 8–K.[14] As of this writing,

---

17. Ross v. A.H. Robins Co., 607 F.2d 545, 552 (2d Cir.1979); Heit v. Weitzen, 402 F.2d 909, 916 (2d Cir.1968), *cert. denied*, 395 U.S. 903, 89 S.Ct. 1740, 23 L.Ed.2d 217 (1969).

19. *See, e.g.,* Ross v. A.H. Robins Co., 607 F.2d 545, 552 (2d Cir.1979); Heit v. Weitzen, 402 F.2d 909, 916 (2d Cir.1968), *cert. denied*, 395 U.S. 903, 89 S.Ct. 1740, 23 L.Ed.2d 217 (1969); Teachers' Retirement System of Louisiana v. Qwest Communications International Inc., 2005 WL 2359311 (D.Colo. 2005).

§ 12.19

4. *See* chapter 9 *supra.*

5. 15 U.S.C.A. § 78*l*. *See* § 9.2 *supra.*

6. 15 U.S.C.A. § 78m. *See* § 9.3 *supra.*

7. 15 U.S.C.A. § 78p(a). *See* § 13.2 *infra.*

8. 15 U.S.C.A. § 78m(d). *See* § 11.2 *supra.*

9. 15 U.S.C.A. § 78n(d). *See* § 11.5 *supra.*

12. Sarbanes–Oxley Act of 2002, Pub. Law 107–204, § 409 (July 30, 2002).

13. *Id.,* adding 1934 Act § 13(a) (*l*), 15 U.S.C.A. § 78m(*l*).

14. *See* Proposed Amendments to Form 8–K, Sec. Act Rel. No. 33–8106; 67 FR 42914–01, 2002 WL 1361660 (F.R.) (SEC June 25, 2002).

the Form 8–K mandatory disclosures have expanded[15] and are likely to continue to be amended to include additional items.

Any time a company disseminates information, it will be subject to scrutiny under the securities laws. This means not only the possibility of civil liability, but also the imposition of SEC sanctions and penalties.

Until the adoption of section 13(*l*) of the 1934 Act,[26] the Exchange Act did not contain an express requirement for prompt disclosure. Section 13(*l*) authorizes SEC rulemaking to require real time disclosure of material changes in financial condition,[27] but is not an across-the-board-requirement that a corporation report material information that is not otherwise required by the periodic reporting and shareholder information requirements. Thus, there is no affirmative duty to disclose many types of material developments until the next quarterly report. In contrast, the rules of the major stock exchanges expressly require corporations to make timely disclosure of all information that would be material to the reasonable investor.[28] However, the violation of the exchange listing requirements can lead only to sanctions by the exchange which have rarely been imposed for this type of violation alone. The SEC does not have enforcement power to pursue violations of the exchange listing requirements.

The above-mentioned interim prompt disclosure requirements are not supplemented by additional requirement to be implied from Rule 10b–5. Whether Rule 10b–5 alone is sufficient to trigger a similar affirmative duty of disclosure is, at most, highly doubtful. As discussed below, the language of Rule 10b–5 does not provide any basis for such an affirmative disclosure requirement. The absence of an affirmative disclosure requirement in Rule 10b–5 is particularly significant with regard to companies which are not subject to the New York or American Stock Exchange rules.

SEC Rule 10b–5 embodies the 1934 Act's general antifraud proscription. It prohibits fraud and material misstatements in connection with the purchase or sale of a security.[36] The rule does not by itself impose an affirmative duty to speak, and this most certainly is the proper view.

SEC Rule 10b–5(a) and (c)[37] deal with acts and practices that constitute fraud or deceit. Rule 10b–5(b) prohibits materially misleading statements and materially misleading omissions from statements made. Rule 10b–5 does not by itself impose affirmative disclosure requirements absent some independent duty to disclose, such as one imposed by a line-item disclosure requirement of an applicable SEC required filing.[38] Mere nondisclosure, absent an indepen-

15. *See* the discussion in § 9.3 *supra*.

26. 15 U.S.C.A. § 78m(*l*), added by the Sarbanes–Oxley Act of 2002, Pub. Law 107–204, § 409 (July 30, 2002).

27. 15 U.S.C.A. § 78m(*l*).

28. N.Y.S.E. Company Manual, Fed.Sec.L.Rep. (CCH) ¶ 23,121 (1977); American Stock Exchange Company Guide (CCH) ¶ 10,121; Sec.Exch.Act Rel. No. 34–8995 (Oct. 15, 1970).

36. 17 C.F.R. § 240.10b–5. *See* § 12.3 *supra*.

37. 17 C.F.R. § 240.10b–5(a), (c). Rule 10b–5(c) prohibits conduct that operates as a fraud. It can be argued that mere silence and nondisclosure of material information is not a fraud but nevertheless has the same impact as fraud and thus operates as a fraud in violation of Rule 10b–5(c). There is no reported decision adopting such a view. The text of Rule 10b–5 is set out in § 12.3 *supra*.

38. *See, e.g.,* Blanchard v. Edgemark Financial Corp., 2001 WL 587861 *5, [2000–2001 Transfer Binder] Fed. Sec. L. Rep. (CCH) ¶ 91,349 (N.D. Ill. 2001).

dent duty such as a line-item disclosure mandate, contemporaneous insider trading,[39] or some other collateral activity, is insufficient to establish a violation of Rule 10b–5.[40] For example, Rule 10b–5 has been interpreted to impose a "disclose or abstain rule" in insider trading cases. Nevertheless, unless a company is trading in its own shares, the disclose or abstain rule does not trigger a duty of disclosure. It follows that in the ordinary course of conducting company business, there is no duty to disclose. Even the corporate law that imposes fiduciary duties on corporate directors is not sufficient, standing alone, to impose an affirmative obligation to speak under Rule 10b–5.[42]

In relevant part, Rule 10b–5(b) provides that it is unlawful "to omit to state a material fact necessary *in order to make the statements made,* in light of the circumstances under which they were made, not misleading."[44] These words clearly seem to contemplate that in order to create liability for omission there must be some statement in which the material facts do not appear.[45] Thus, even though some observers may have taken a more expansive view of the rule and have indicated that an affirmative disclosure duty should be found to exist,[46] the company may avoid liability for keeping silent absent an independent basis for the duty to disclose the information.[47]

This absence of an affirmative company disclosure obligation under Rule 10b–5 is further strengthened by the Supreme Court's rule that the mere possession of confidential inside information is not sufficient to trigger the duty to disclose or abstain from trading.[48] As one court has aptly explained, "[a]bsent a specific duty to disclose, even the most material information imaginable may be withheld from the public."[49]

In the absence of an independent duty[52] to disclose material information, the inability of 10b–5 to impose an affirmative disclosure obligation permits continued corporate silence.[53]

---

39. *See* § 12.17 *supra.*

40. *See, e.g.,* National Union Fire Insurance Co. v. Turtur, 892 F.2d 199 (2d Cir.1989).

42. Blanchard v. Edgemark Financial Corp., 2001 WL 587861 *5, [2000–2001 Transfer Binder] Fed. Sec. L. Rep. (CCH) ¶ 91,349 (N.D. Ill. 2001).

44. 17 C.F.R. § 240.10b–5(b) (emphasis supplied).

45. In order to establish a violation of Rule 10b–5 in this context, it is necessary to identify the statement made that the omission renders materially misleading. United States v. Schiff, 538 F.Supp.2d 818 (D.N.J. 2008).

46. This was the contention of the issuer in *Texas Gulf Sulphur* with regard to why it issued a press release regarding a mineral find before all the facts were in. The court never reached this issue because it found the press release to have been materially misleading. SEC v. Texas Gulf Sulphur, 401 F.2d 833 (2d Cir.1968), *cert. denied,* 394 U.S. 976, 89 S.Ct. 1454, 22 L.Ed.2d 756 (1969).

47. Williams v. Dresser Industries, 120 F.3d 1163, 1173 (11th Cir.1997) (mere possession of material nonpublic information does not trigger a duty to disclose).

48. Dirks v. SEC, 463 U.S. 646, 103 S.Ct. 3255, 77 L.Ed.2d 911 (1983); Chiarella v. United States, 445 U.S. 222, 100 S.Ct. 1108, 63 L.Ed.2d 348 (1980).

49. Polak v. Continental Hosts, Ltd., 613 F.Supp. 153, 156 (S.D.N.Y.1985).

Aside from the duty issue, it may be argued that an issuer cannot be held in violation of Rule 10b–5 unless it was trading in its own shares. Although this point was raised in a Supreme Court dissent (Basic Inc. v. Levinson, 485 U.S. 224, 108 S.Ct. 978, 99 L.Ed.2d 194 (1988) (White, J. dissenting)), other courts have not picked up on this proffered limitation.

52. *See, e.g.,* Blanchard v. Edgemark Financial Corp., 2000 WL 433491, 2000 WL 1060827, [1999–2000 Transfer Binder] Fed. Sec. L. Rep. (CCH) ¶ 90,991 (N.D. Ill. 2000) (bank directors owned duty of disclosure to holders of voting trust certificates).

53. Cooperman v. Individual, Inc., 171 F.3d 43, 47 (1st Cir.1999).

Once a company chooses to make a statement, Rule 10b–5 comes into play. Thus, for example, once a statement has been made by the issuer or one of its representatives, there may be a continuing duty to update and/or correct the information that was previously disseminated.[66] Furthermore, when the initial disclosure has been made in an SEC filing pursuant to a line-item disclosure requirement, the curative disclosure must be made in the appropriate manner, which frequently will require the filing of an amended disclosure form.[67] The duty to correct erroneous information does not mean that once some disclosures have been made, all facts that might be of interest to investors must be disclosed. The duty of further disclosure applies only when failure to do so would make the statement previously made materially misleading in light of subsequent developments.[68] Although Rule 10b–5 standing alone may not trigger an affirmative duty to disclose, a company that wants to suppress information that would be relevant to investors must be mindful of the above-mentioned disclosure requirements.

§ 12.19[2] Responding to Market Rumors

Particularly knotty disclosure problems face publicly traded issuers when there are market rumors concerning a company's securities, its fundamental condition, or possible takeover activity.[77] As discussed above, Rule 10b–5 does not create an affirmative disclosure obligation. However, when approached by exchange officials, the press, market researchers, or securities analysts, the company and its representatives are faced with a dilemma. In light of the repeated reaffirmation of a materiality standard based upon those facts that a reasonable investor would deem significant in making an investment decision,[79] denying that negotiations are taking place is not a viable alternative.

Issuers have no independent obligation to correct rumors that cannot be traced back to the issuer or its representatives.[80] However, the situation is different when the issuer elects to speak. Once a statement has been made, the duty to correct may arise. When presented with a question about market rumors, companies have two alternatives. The company can, of course, respond with full disclosure, which in the case of preliminary negotiations or other sensitive business developments, might be counterproductive. Alternatively, the company can issue a "no comment" response. While the "no comment" response may be necessary for business reasons, as issuers develop increasing "no comment" policies, less information will be filtered into the market.[81] On the other hand, the absence of information clearly is preferable to the presence of misleading information.

Even a "no comment" response will not always be a safe harbor. If the issuer, or its agents, is responsible for leaks of sensitive information or market

66. *See, e.g.,* Stransky v. Cummins Engine Co., 51 F.3d 1329 (7th Cir.1995).

67. *See, e.g.,* Kaufman v. Cooper Cos., Inc., 719 F.Supp. 174 (S.D.N.Y.1989) (quarterly report did not cure misstatements in proxy material sent out 15 days earlier).

68. Weiner v. The Quaker Oats Co., 129 F.3d 310 (3d Cir.1997).

77. *E.g.,* In re Time Warner, Inc. Securities Litigation, 9 F.3d 259 (2d Cir.1993).

79. Basic, Inc. v. Levinson, 485 U.S. 224, 108 S.Ct. 978, 99 L.Ed.2d 194 (1988), *on remand,* 871 F.2d 562 (6th Cir.1989).

80. *See, e.g.,* Raab v. General Physics Corp., 4 F.3d 286, 288 (4th Cir.1993); Electronic Specialty Co. v. International Controls Corp., 409 F.2d 937 (2d Cir.1969).

81. *See, e.g.,* Little Can be Done to Stop Rumors, Exchange Officials, Others Tell Forum, 18 Sec. Reg. & L. Rep. (BNA) 253 (Feb. 25, 1986).

rumors, the SEC takes the position that the company is under a duty to correct any misinformation.[82] Although this proposition has not been definitively tested in the courts, it reflects a proper reading of the company's obligations. Thus, companies must take care to manage their proprietary information, not only for insider trading reasons but also to prevent being forced into premature disclosures by the existence of market rumors due to leaked information. Caution dictates that public companies not only develop information policies, including the creation of an information ombudsman, but also it is wise to limit the issuer's personnel who are authorized to divulge information or respond to outside questions.

Companies are thus placed in a very difficult position. When approached by a member of the press or a securities analyst, the issuer may not be able to get away with a "no comment" response. If a company is engaged in merger negotiations and, for example, has an upcoming meeting with securities analysts and decides to cancel the meeting, if the cancellation results in rumors, is the company in a position that it now has to come forward and clarify the facts behind the rumors? Some attorneys suggest that as a preventive measure, public companies adopt a policy of not commenting on acquisitions negotiations. Thus, when a question is posed, silence by the company can be supported by a recitation of the policy.

Periodic reporting obligations may in and of themselves trigger the duty to disclose once the materiality threshold has been reached. There is thus a different process that applies in determining the necessity of disclosure when dealing with line-item disclosures in required filings as opposed to under the antifraud provisions generally.[84]

§ 12.19[3] Adoption of and Entanglement With Statements by Third Parties

Just as issuers have no duty to respond to rumors, they do not have a duty to respond to analysts' statements so long as the issuer had no involvement with the analyst making the statement. In order to be held accountable as a primary violator, the issuer or its representative must have either created the misstatement or have had the misstatement publicly attributed to it.[85] Thus, for example, there is no duty with regard to an analyst's projection unless the issuer has adopted the projection or has otherwise "entangled" itself with the analyst's opinions.[86] However, once the company or a representative responds to the analyst's statements, liability can follow if there is sufficient involvement by the company. On the other hand, the mere fact that a third party obtained information from company insiders is not by itself sufficient to create entanglement so as to hold the company liable for the third party's materially misleading statements.[87] Entanglement is established,

---

82. *See* In re Carnation Co., Sec. Exch. Act Rel. No. 34–22214, [1985–86 Transfer Binder] Fed. Sec. L. Rep. (CCH) ¶ 83,801 (July 8, 1985).

84. *See* Joseph I. Goldstein, William E. Donnelly & Ida C. Wurczinger, Disclosure of a Potential Change in Corporate Control, 19 Rev.Sec. & Commodities Reg. 133 (1986).

85. *E.g.,* Cooper v. Pickett, 137 F.3d 616, 624 (9th Cir.1997) (company could be held liable for misleading analysts into making materially false statements).

86. *See, e.g.,* In re Navarre Corp. Securities Litigation, 299 F.3d 735 (8th Cir.2002), (failure to allege linkage between analysts' statements and the company).

87. In re Cabletron Systems, Inc. Securities Litigation, 311 F.3d 11, 38 (1st Cir. 2002) (but upholding claim of entanglement), relying on Suna v. Bailey Corp., 107 F.3d 64, 73–74 (1st Cir. 1997).

however, "when company officials 'intentionally foster a mistaken belief concerning a material fact.' "[88]

Liability can exist even without an express adoption of the analysts' or other third party statements if a company's management knowingly conveys materially misleading information to the analysts or other third party making a materially misleading statement or projection.[90] However, when the analysts' statements are based primarily on their own interpretation, vague statements of optimism by the company's executives will not make the company liable.[91] Mere allegations that management was in contact with analysts is not sufficient to hold management or the company liable for the analysts' statements.[93] However, such contact can be a first step in establishing entanglement so as to hold the company accountable for third-party statements about the company.

A statement by a company official that he or she is "comfortable" with analysts' estimates can form the basis of liability for over-optimism. Such a statement can operate as an adoption of the analyst's opinion.[95] However, merely stating that it was comfortable with analysts' estimates does not make the company liable simply because the estimate turns out to be wrong.[96]

§ 12.19[4] SEC Regulation FD—Prohibition on Selective Disclosure

SEC Regulation FD was adopted in 2000 in order to level the playing field concerning access to information about a company that comes from the company.[97] Under Regulation FD,[98] selective disclosure by a company to analysts or other third parties is no longer permitted. Regulation FD requires companies who make disclosures to analysts to make prompt public announcements so that all investors can have access to the same information. Regulation FD, although controversial,[100] is not a novel idea. For example, the New York Stock Exchange has for a long time had a policy against selective disclosure to analysts.[101]

Regulation FD applies only to "communications by the company's senior management, its investor relations professionals, and others who regularly communicate with market professionals and security holders." Further, Regulation FD applies only to a company's "communications with market profes-

88. In re Cabletron Systems, Inc., 311 F.3d 11, 38 (1st Cir. 2002), quoting from Elkind v. Liggett & Myers, Inc., 635 F.2d 156, 163–164 (2d Cir. 1980).

90. *See, e.g.,* In re Allaire Corp. Securities Litigation, 224 F.Supp.2d 319, 339–340 (D. Mass. 2002) (sufficient allegations of entanglement).

91. In re Northern Telecom Ltd. Securities Litigation, 42 F.Supp.2d 234, 236–237 (S.D.N.Y 1998).

93. In re: Number Nine Visual Technology Corp. Securities Litigation, 51 F. Supp. 2d 1 (D.Mass.1999) (general allegations of "a pattern of continuous interactions" are not sufficient to meet particularity requirement).

95. In re Burlington Coat Factory Securities Litigation, 114 F.3d 1410, 1429 (3d Cir.1997).

96. Plevy v. Haggerty, 38 F.Supp.2d 816 (C.D.Cal.1998).

97. 17 C.F.R. §§ 243.100–243.103.

98. 17 C.F.R. § 243.100–243.103.

100. For example, SEC Commissioner Unger dissented from the regulation's adoption. *See* Selective Disclosure Rule Gains Approval by Divided SEC, 32 Sec. Reg. & L. Rep. (BNA) 1089 (Aug. 14, 2000).

101. NYSE Listed Company Manual ¶ 202.02(A).

sionals, and holders of the issuer's securities under circumstances in which it is reasonably foreseeable that the security holders will trade on the basis of the information.'' Accordingly, Regulation FD does not apply when the company is communicating with the press, rating agencies, and ordinary-course business communications with customers and suppliers.

§ 12.19[5] Company Web Sites

An issue related to entanglement is the accountability of corporate management for material that appears on the Internet. It is clear that companies that maintain web sites must be careful to monitor the content of the sites. Material misstatements and omissions will satisfy the ''in connection with'' requirement. There thus can be serious securities law consequences for the content on company sponsored web sites. Another issue is the extent to which links on a company sponsored web site to third party sites will constitute an adoption of the statements contained on those sites.[124] At the very least, management should be careful to disclaim responsibility for statements that may appear in third party web sites that are linked to the company web site.

In 2000, the SEC issued an interpretative release that among other things, addressed company web sites.[125] The Commission announced that it will consider a number of factors in determining whether a hyperlink on a company sponsored web site that links to a third party's web site will operate as the company's adoption of the information contained on the third party web site. The context of the hyperlink must be considered. Specifically, does the corporation expressly adopt or endorse the statements that may be contained on the third party web site that is hyperlinked to the company web site? If there is such an endorsement, then the corporation may be held accountable by statements made on the third party web site.[126] The Commission further takes the position that if the hyperlink exists within a portion of the web site that constitutes a document that satisfies delivery requirements under the federal securities laws, the company will be deemed to have adopted the statements contained on the hyperlinked third party web site.[127] Additionally, if the company is embarking on an offering of securities and is ''in registration'' under the Securities Act of 1933, then there is a strong presumption that the company has adopted statements that are contained in web sites that are hyperlinked to the company's web site.

Another factor in determining whether information contained in a third-party web site will be attributed to the company is the likelihood of confusion. For example, if the hyperlink from the company-sponsored web site presents a separate screen announcing that the viewer is leaving the company's web site, there is less likelihood that the company will be deemed to have adopted the statements on the third party's web site.[130] Company disclaimers of liability

124. *See, e.g.,* Eileen Smith Ewing, Fraud on the Cybermarket: Liability for Hyperlinked Misinformation Under Rule 10b–5, 56 Bus. Law. 375 (2000).

125. Use of Electronic Media, Sec. Act Rel. No. 33–7856, 2000 WL 502290 (SEC April 28, 2000).

126. *Id.*

127. *Id.*

130. *Id.* Use of Electronic Media, Sec. Act Rel. No. 33–7856, 2000 WL 502290 (SEC April 28, 2000). *See also* Commission Guidance on the use of Company Web Sites, Sec. Exch. Act Rel. No.

for statements contained in hyperlinked third-party web sites will not in and of themselves insulate the company from liability if there are other indications that the company has somehow endorsed the statements.

In 2008 the SEC issued additional guidance with respect to company websites.[134] For example, there are ways a company can give online access to historical data without having a republication of that data every time the information is accessed. Companies must also take care to clarify that links to third-party websites and information are not statements being made by the company. The SEC guidance also clarifies that guidance clarifies that information posted on company websites would not generally be subject to rules under the Sarbanes–Oxley Act relating to a company's "disclosure controls and procedures." Information on company websites does not have to be "printer friendly" unless there is a specific SEC mandate to do so.

An issue related to corporate web sites is the treatment of chat rooms that allow real-time online conversations. Questions can arise with respect to comments, projections and statements that may be made in a chat room sponsored by the company. One thing is clear, however: participation by corporate employees in chat rooms can expose the company to potential liability for statements made in the chat rooms. Recall also that company chatrooms can implicate the proxy rules.[140]

§ 12.20 Rule 10b–5 and the Deception Requirement

Although directed at securities fraud and not corporate governance, Rule 10b–5 can be used to combat corporate mismanagement that results in deception in connection with a purchase or sale of securities. While the high-water mark for federal securities law as a lever in mismanagement cases seems to have passed, on appropriate facts federal law can still have some impact in regulating corporate management practices.

In 2002, Congress enacted the Sarbanes–Oxley Act,[2] which instituted various reforms in response to widely publicized corporate scandals. Some of the Sarbanes–Oxley amendments may be relevant in setting a new tone for the role of Rule 10b–5 in dealing with governance issues. In relevant part, Sarbanes–Oxley addressed corporate governance, including the role of independent directors and audit committees, as well as the establishment of corporate codes of ethics. This may signal a shift in Congressional policy, widening the door once again for the use of Rule 10b–5 and other securities law provisions to monitor corporate governance. As discussed below, the cases to date make it clear that a breach of fiduciary duty, without more, is not a securities law violation. It remains to be seen whether the pendulum will begin to swing to the other direction.

34–58288, Inv. Co. Act Rel. No. IC–28351, 73 Fed. Reg. 45862–01, 2008 WL 3049662, http://www.sec.gov/rules/interp/2008/34-58288.pdf (SEC Aug. 1, 2008).

134. *See* Commission Guidance on the use of Company Web Sites, Sec. Exch. Act Rel. No. 34–58288, Inv. Co. Act Rel. No. IC–28351, 73 Fed. Reg. 45862–01 2008 WL 3049662, http://www.sec.gov/rules/interp/2008/34-58288.pdf (SEC Aug. 1, 2008).

140. *See*, SEC Provides Guidance to Open Up Use of Corporate Websites for Disclosures to Investors, SECDIG 2008–147–1, 2008 WL 2909346 (SEC July 30, 2008).

§ 12.20

2. Sarbanes–Oxley Act of 2002, Pub. Law 107–204 (July 30, 2002). *See* 9.7 *supra* for discussion of some of Sarbanes–Oxley's impact.

As pointed out earlier in this chapter, section 10(b) prohibits "manipulative or deceptive" practices as defined by SEC rules. In 1971, in Superintendent of Insurance v. Bankers Life & Casualty Co.,[9] the Supreme Court announced that Rule 10b–5 is violated when there is deception touching the purchase or sale of a security even if the acts complained of amount to no more than corporate mismanagement. The defendants, management of an insurance company, caused the company to part with its assets that consisted of marketable securities. The Court upheld the 10b–5 claim since the corporation was forced to part with its securities and thus the "seller was duped into believing that it ... would receive the proceeds."[10] As a result of the Court's ruling, 10b–5 became a potential remedy to redress corporate mismanagement. The 10b–5 mismanagement remedy continued to garner great support[11] until the Supreme Court's ruling in Santa Fe Industries, Inc. v. Green.[12]

The *Santa Fe* case involved a claim by a minority shareholder who was frozen out by the majority pursuant to a short-form merger. The parent corporation complied with the requirements set out by the applicable Delaware short-form merger statute and disclosed all of the required information to both the minority shareholders and the independent appraiser. The plaintiff claimed that since the cash-out price was low, the transaction operated as a fraud or deceit upon him within the meaning of Rule 10b–5(c). The Supreme Court responded that, in order to state a 10b–5 claim the plaintiff must show an element of "deception" that was lacking in the allegations in *Santa Fe.* The Court pointed out that a number of states did not provide a cause of action for breaches of fiduciary duty in connection with freeze-out transactions, and thus to rule otherwise in the case at hand would be to federalize the corporate law of directors' obligation;[13] it further refused to impose a higher standard than the applicable state law.[14] Although Delaware has narrowed its state law remedy that was recognized just after *Santa Fe*,[15] many states recognize a broader judicial remedy against corporate freeze-outs.

In the wake of the *Santa Fe* decision, commentators were quick to predict a demise of 10b–5's role in the area of corporate mismanagement. However, there were five post-*Santa Fe* court of appeals decisions that took an expansive reading of Rule 10b–5 and a correspondingly narrow reading of the Supreme Court's decision.[18] Under these and other decisions, it is clear that the fact that mismanagement is involved does not preclude a Rule 10b–5 claim

---

9. 404 U.S. 6, 92 S.Ct. 165, 30 L.Ed.2d 128 (1971).

10. *Id.* at 9, 92 S.Ct. at 167.

11. *See, e.g.,* Marshel v. AFW Fabric Corp., 533 F.2d 1277 (2d Cir.1976), *vacated,* 429 U.S. 881, 97 S.Ct. 228, 50 L.Ed.2d 162 (1976).

12. 430 U.S. 462, 97 S.Ct. 1292, 51 L.Ed.2d 480 (1977).

13. 430 U.S. at 479 n. 16, 97 S.Ct. at 1304 n. 16.

14. The Court also pointed out that scrutiny of "fairness" under Rule 10b–5 is "at best a subsidiary purpose" of the federal securities laws. 430 U.S. at 478, 97 S.Ct. at 1303, 1304. Any such expansion of the 10b–5 remedy would, according to the Court, have been in conflict with restrictions on implied remedies. *See* § 12.2 *supra.*

15. Weinberger v. UOP, Inc., 457 A.2d 701 (Del.Sup.1983).

18. Healey v. Catalyst Recovery of Pennsylvania, Inc., 616 F.2d 641 (3d Cir.1980); Kidwell v. Meikle, 597 F.2d 1273 (9th Cir.1979); Alabama Farm Bureau Mutual Casualty Co. v. American Fidelity Life Insurance Co., 606 F.2d 602 (5th Cir.1979), *rehearing denied,* 610 F.2d 818 (5th Cir.1980); Wright v. Heizer Corp., 560 F.2d 236 (7th Cir.1977), *cert. denied,* 434 U.S. 1066, 98 S.Ct. 1243, 55 L.Ed.2d 767 (1978); Goldberg v. Meridor, 567 F.2d 209 (2d Cir.1977), *cert. denied,* 434 U.S. 1069, 98 S.Ct. 1249, 55 L.Ed.2d 771 (1978).

for material misrepresentations. However, it is also clear that, standing alone, a breach of fiduciary duty is not a securities law violation.

In Goldberg v. Meridor,[22] the defendant parent corporation caused a controlled subsidiary to issue common stock and convertible debentures. The offering raised seven million dollars in cash that was in turn loaned to its direct parent corporation. The public offering was followed by an exchange of assets whereby the controlling parent sold its assets to the subsidiary in return for stock in the subsidiary. After the transactions were completed, the direct parent's sole asset was the stock of the subsidiary, in which the plaintiff was a minority shareholder, and the subsidiary had acquired all of the parent's assets and liabilities (including the seven million dollar debt running to the subsidiary). The plaintiff brought suit under Rule 10b–5, claiming that the defendant caused its subsidiary to issue stock in the public offering for the benefit of the controlling parents, and that the subsequent exchange of assets was inadequate consideration and thus operated as a fraud against the subsidiary in the issuance of its own shares.[23] The Second Circuit applied the "controlling influence" doctrine.[24] Under the controlling influence doctrine, for a transaction in which the decision-makers are controlled directors, the standard of disclosure is measured by what would have been material to a disinterested director dealing at arms length. Although disclosure to the shareholders would not have directly affected the corporate decision in question, the court reasoned that, armed with material facts of the transactions, shareholders would have been able to avail themselves of a remedy at state law.[26] Accordingly, the Second Circuit in *Goldberg* held that disclosure of the unfair exchange would have been the basis of an injunction under New York law, and thus the plaintiffs were deceived into not seeking that relief.[27] As a second justification for the requisite deception and causation elements, the court pointed out that public disclosure of all relevant facts might have shamed the subsidiary's directors into voting against the transactions with its parents rather than hanging its dirty linen out in public.[28]

Four other circuit courts followed the Second Circuit's ruling that material non-disclosure that denied minority shareholders their opportunity to seek an injunction under state law is sufficient to satisfy the deception requirement of *Santa Fe*.[30] However, in a subsequent decision by Judge Posner, the Seventh Circuit indicated that it had rejected the *Goldberg* method of analysis.[31]

---

22. 567 F.2d 209 (2d Cir.1977), *cert. denied*, 434 U.S. 1069, 98 S.Ct. 1249, 55 L.Ed.2d 771 (1978).

23. 567 F.2d at 211.

24. *See* Schoenbaum v. Firstbrook, 405 F.2d 200 (2d Cir.1968), *cert. denied*, 395 U.S. 906, 89 S.Ct. 1747, 23 L.Ed.2d 219 (1969).

26. 567 F.2d at 218–19. The court also noted the allegation that the transaction involved "wholly inadequate consideration."

27. 567 F.2d. at 219–20.

28. 567 F.2d at 218–19.

30. Healey v. Catalyst Recovery of Pennsylvania, Inc., 616 F.2d 641 (3d Cir.1980); Kidwell v. Meikle, 597 F.2d 1273 (9th Cir.1979); Alabama Farm Bureau Mutual Casualty Co. v. American Fidelity Life Insurance Co., 606 F.2d 602 (5th Cir.1979), *rehearing denied*, 610 F.2d 818 (5th Cir.1980); Wright v. Heizer Corp., 560 F.2d 236 (7th Cir.1977), *cert. denied*, 434 U.S. 1066, 98 S.Ct. 1243, 55 L.Ed.2d 767 (1978).

31. Isquith v. Caremark International, Inc., 136 F.3d 531, 534 (7th Cir.1998), relying on LHLC Corp. v. Cluett, Peabody & Co., Inc., 842 F.2d 928, 931–32 (7th Cir.1988); Harris Trust & Savings Bank v. Ellis, 810 F.2d 700, 704 (7th Cir.1987).

Section 10(b)'s deception requirement received additional attention from the Supreme Court in Schreiber v. Burlington Northern, Inc.,[54] wherein it was held that manipulative conduct does not violate section 14(e)'s tender offer antifraud provision[55] unless the conduct complained of is also deceptive.[56] In so ruling, the Court emphasized that the thrust of the deception requirement is to address materially misleading statements and omissions. The *Schreiber* decision reinforces the fact that attempting to characterize a breach of fiduciary duty as manipulative will not elevate it to a Rule 10b–5 violation absent the type of deception required in the *Santa Fe Industries* case.

§ 12.21 The Effect of Plaintiff's Conduct on Implied Civil Liability; Due Diligence; In Pari Delicto

In order to recover in an action for common law fraud, plaintiffs are required to prove that their reliance was reasonable.[1] As a corollary to the reliance element, the federal courts developed a requirement that the plaintiff in a Rule 10b–5 action have acted with due diligence with regard to the transaction in question.[2] The plaintiff's due diligence requirement initially developed initially along negligence lines.[3] However, in Rule 10b–5 cases, it seems unquestionable that this has been changed by the Supreme Court's imposition of a scienter requirement upon defendant's conduct, which impliedly should carry over to the plaintiff's standard of conduct.[4] It would make little sense to say that an investor's negligence is sufficient to negate the defendant's more culpable intentional conduct.[5]

The Supreme Court in Bateman Eichler, Hill Richards, Inc. v. Berner,[15] held that the *in pari delicto* defense cannot be invoked in a Rule 10b–5 action unless it can be said that the plaintiff was indeed truly as culpable as the defendant. Although it has been suggested that this ruling abolishes the due diligence defense, the courts have not agreed.[16]

In a related development, the Supreme Court in Pinter v. Dahl[18] extended the *Bateman Eichler* rationale in defining equal fault under the Securities Act of 1933. Section 12(a)(1) of the 1933 Act[19] permits a rescission action by purchasers of securities in unregistered offerings that are not exempt from 1933 Act registration. The Supreme Court, echoing the investor-protection

---

54. 472 U.S. 1, 105 S.Ct. 2458, 86 L.Ed.2d 1 (1985).

55. 15 U.S.C.A. § 78n(e). *See* § 11.6, 11.10 *supra.*

56. *See also* the discussion in § 12.1 *supra.*

§ 12.21

1. Restatement, Second, Torts § 537 (1976); W. Page Keeton, Dan B. Dobbs, Robert E. Keeton & David G. Owen, Prosser and Keeton on Torts § 108 (5th ed. 1984). The reliance requirement is discussed in § 12.10 *supra.*

2. *E.g.*, Thompson v. Smith Barney, Harris Upham & Co., Inc., 709 F.2d 1413 (11th Cir.1983); Dupuy v. Dupuy, 551 F.2d 1005 (5th Cir.), *cert. denied*, 434 U.S. 911, 98 S.Ct. 312, 54 L.Ed.2d 197 (1977).

3. Rochez Brothers, Inc. v. Rhoades, 491 F.2d 402 (3d Cir.1973).

4. *E.g.,* Brown v. Earthboard Sports, USA, Inc., 481 F.3d 901, 921 (6th Cir.2007).

5. *See, e.g.,* Atari Corp. v. Ernst & Whinney, 981 F.2d 1025 (9th Cir.1992) (justifiable reliance is not a matter of contributory negligence).

15. 472 U.S. 299, 105 S.Ct. 2622, 86 L.Ed.2d 215 (1985).

16. Stephenson v. Paine Webber Jackson & Curtis, Inc., 839 F.2d 1095 (5th Cir.1988).

18. 486 U.S. 622, 108 S.Ct. 2063, 100 L.Ed.2d 658 (1988).

19. 15 U.S.C.A. § 77*l*(a)(1). *See* § 7.2 *supra.*

thrust of the securities laws, held that "the *in pari delicto* defense may defeat recovery in a § 12(a)(1) action only where the plaintiff's role in the offering or sale of nonexempted, unregistered securities is more as a promoter than as an investor."[20]

§ 12.22 Likely Absence of an Implied Remedy Under Section 17(a) of the 1933 Act

SEC Rule 10b–5[2] was modeled upon section 17(a) of the 1933 Act.[3] There are three principal differences between the 1934 Act rule and section 17(a). First, Rule 10b–5 applies to any "purchase or sale" of a security,[4] whereas section 17(a) covers the "offer or sale" of any security. Second, section 17(a) does not contain the phrase "manipulative or deceptive device" that is found in section 10(b) of the Exchange Act[5] and has formed a basis of the scienter[6] and deception[7] requirements. Third, by virtue of the jurisdictional provisions of the 1933 and 1934 Acts,[8] the federal courts are vested with exclusive jurisdiction over Rule 10b–5, actions,[9] while section 17(a) actions may be brought either in state or federal court with no right of removal from state to federal court.

Notwithstanding the arguments that might favor continued recognition of the section 17(a) remedy, the courts have found the contrary position to be more compelling.[25] The decline of implied remedies in the Supreme Court and elsewhere cannot be ignored and accordingly there certainly is a persuasive argument which has been accepted by an increasingly large number of courts that no section 17(a) remedy should be recognized.

§ 12.23 Waiver of Claims; Voiding of Contracts in Violation of the Securities Laws

Waiver of Claims

Under common law and equitable principles, a party who voluntarily relinquishes a known right can be found to have waived his or her claim for relief.[1] Section 14 of the Securities Act of 1933 provides that contracts and

20. 486 U.S. at 639, 108 S.Ct. at 2074, 100 L.Ed.2d at 677.

§ 12.22

2. 17 C.F.R. § 240.10b–5.

3. 15 U.S.C.A. § 77q(a).

4. In Blue Chip Stamps v. Manor Drug Stores, 421 U.S. 723, 95 S.Ct. 1917, 44 L.Ed.2d 539 (1975), *rehearing denied*, 423 U.S. 884, 96 S.Ct. 157, 46 L.Ed.2d 114 (1975), the Supreme Court held that this statutory language limited 10b–5 private-damage plaintiffs to purchasers and sellers of the securities in question. *See* § 12.7 *supra*.

5. 15 U.S.C.A. § 78j(b).

6. Ernst & Ernst v. Hochfelder, 425 U.S. 185, 96 S.Ct. 1375, 47 L.Ed.2d 668 (1976), *rehearing denied*, 425 U.S. 986, 96 S.Ct. 2194, 48 L.Ed.2d 811 (1976). *See* § 12.8 *supra*.

7. Santa Fe Industries, Inc. v. Green, 430 U.S. 462, 97 S.Ct. 1292, 51 L.Ed.2d 480 (1977). *See* § 12.20 *supra*.

8. 15 U.S.C.A. § 77v, 78aa. The jurisdictional provisions of both the 1933 and 1934 Acts are discussed in § 17.1 *infra*.

9. Securities Exchange Act of 1934 § 27, 15 U.S.C.A. § 78aa.

25. E.g., Barnes v. Resource Royalties, Inc., 795 F.2d 1359 (8th Cir. 1986); Landry v. All American Assurance Co., 688 F.2d 381 (5th Cir. 1982).

§ 12.23

1. *E.g.,* Bass v. Janney Montgomery Scott, Inc., 210 F.3d 577, 589–590 (6th Cir.2000) (but finding that defendant failed to establish a waiver).

stipulations purporting to waive compliance with any provision of the Act or SEC rules promulgated thereunder are void.[2] The Exchange Act's counterpart is found in section 29(a).[3] It is clear that the prohibition against waivers does not preclude releases of liability issued for consideration in connection with settlements of litigation or incipient suits.[4] However, to be valid, such a release must be for consideration and the parties must have had knowledge of the claim.[5] Thus, waivers that have been secured before there is reason to suspect that a claim may exist are not valid.[6]

Voiding of Contracts Waiving Compliance With the Securities Laws

Section 29(b) of the Exchange Act[29] goes further than the anti-waiver prohibitions discussed above. While the anti-waiver provisions merely preclude certain defenses to conduct that violates the securities acts, section 29(b) can be viewed as providing an affirmative remedy for parties who have entered into contracts with provisions contrary to the securities laws.[30] Section 29(b) provides that contracts involving performance that would be in violation of the Act are void.[31] In the first instance, this means that since a contract in violation of the act is void, a party to that contract will have a successful defense to an action to enforce the contract.

In addition to being used defensively, section 29(b) can be used affirmatively by a party challenging a contract in violation of the Act. The Supreme Court held that a similar provision contained in the Investment Advisers Act of 1940[33] supports a private right of action for rescission.[34] It seems clear that a correlative private remedy must exist under section 29(b) for contracts in violation of the Exchange Act or applicable SEC rules.

§ 12.24 Multiple Defendants in Actions Under the Securities Exchange Act of 1934: Controlling Person Liability

Controlling Person Liability Defined

Section 20(a) of the 1934 Act[1] states that "[e]very person who, directly or indirectly, controls any person liable under any provision of this chapter or of any rule or regulation thereunder shall also be liable jointly and severally

2. 15 U.S.C.A. § 77n.

3. 15 U.S.C.A. § 78cc(a).

4. *See, e.g.,* Petro–Ventures, Inc. v. Takessian, 967 F.2d 1337 (9th Cir.1992).

5. Hamilton v. Harrington, 807 F.2d 102, 106–7 (7th Cir.1986).

6. *See, e.g.,* McMahan & Co. v. Wherehouse Entertainment, Inc., 859 F.Supp. 743 (S.D.N.Y. 1994), *affirmed in part, reversed in part,* 65 F.3d 1044 (2d Cir.1995) ("no action" clause in debenture agreement could not preclude federal securities claim).

29. 15 U.S.C.A. § 78cc(b).

30. *E.g.,* Mills v. Electric Auto–Lite Co., 396 U.S. 375, 385–388, 90 S.Ct. 616, 622–624, 24 L.Ed.2d 593 (1970).

31. 15. U.S.C.A. § 78cc(b).

33. Section 215, 15 U.S.C.A. § 80b–15. The Investment Advisers Act is discussed in chapter 21 *infra.*

34. Transamerica Mortgage Advisors, Inc. (TAMA) v. Lewis, 444 U.S. 11, 100 S.Ct. 242, 62 L.Ed.2d 146 (1979), *on remand,* 610 F.2d 648 (9th Cir.1979).

§ 12.24

1. 15 U.S.C.A. § 78t(a).

with and to the same extent as such controlled person...."[2] Thus, for a controlling person to be liable, the person over who control was exercised must have committed a primary violation of the securities laws.[3] Otherwise, the controlled person will not be held accountable, and subsequently, the controlling person will have no liability in which to share jointly and severally.[4] Section 20(a) of the Exchange Act closely parallels section 15 of the 1933 Act,[5] except that the 1933 Act provision is limited to actions under section 11 or 12 of that Act.[6]

For a plaintiff to have a prima facie case that the defendant was a controlling person within the meaning of section 20(a), the plaintiff must show that (1) the defendant had actual power or influence over the controlled person, and (2) the defendant induced or participated in the alleged illegal activity.[16]

What Constitutes Control?

Although the term "control" is not defined in section 20(a), the SEC has defined the term "control" generally (including the terms "controlling", "controlled by", and "under common control with") to mean "the possession, direct or indirect, of the power to direct or cause the direction of the management and policies of a person whether through the ownership of voting securities, by contract, or otherwise."[33] In addition, the scope of power and degree of influence necessary to hold a defendant liable as a controlling person are not spelled out in section 20(a).[34]

The most common relationship in which control is presumed is that of the employer-employee. However, controlling person liability is limited to transactions taking place on behalf of the employer. Thus, for example, when the investor deals with an employee other than in his or her capacity as an employee without relying on any affiliation with the employer, the employer will not be held accountable as a controlling person.[41] On the other hand, when an employee is acting under the employer's auspices, controlling person liability and control depends upon control over the employee; control with regard to the particular transaction in question need not be shown.[42]

Controlling shareholders can be found to be control persons.[43] Corporate officers are usually presumed to possess the requisite power to control the

2. 15 U.S.C.A. § 78t(a).

3. *E.g.,* Rosenzweig v. Azurix Corp., 332 F.3d 854, 865 (5th Cir. 2003); Heliotrope General, Inc. v. Ford Motor Co., 189 F.3d 971 (9th Cir.1999).

4. *See, e.g.,* Suna v. Bailey Corp., 107 F.3d 64 (1st Cir.1997) (failure to adequately allege primary violation).

5. 15 U.S.C.A. § 77*o*. *See* § 7.7 *supra.*

6. 15 U.S.C.A. § 77k, 77*l*. *See* § 7.2–7.5 *supra.*

16. *See, e.g.,* Wallace v. Buttar, 239 F.Supp.2d 388 (S.D.N.Y. 2003).

33. 17 C.F.R. § 230.405.

34. Wool v. Tandem Computers Inc., 818 F.2d 1433, 1441 (9th Cir.1987).

41. *E.g.,* Kohn v. Optik, Inc., 1993 WL 169191, [1992–1993 Transfer Binder] Fed.Sec.L.Rep. (CCH) ¶ 97,435 (C.D.Cal.1993).

42. Hauser v. Farrell, 14 F.3d 1338 (9th Cir.1994) (brokerage firm was neither liable as controlling person nor was vicariously liable under respondeat superior).

43. Dietrich v. Bauer, 198 F.R.D. 397 (S.D.N.Y.2001) (denying sole shareholder's motion for summary judgment on control person liability).

actions of their employees and are often held accountable as controlling persons.[44]

In contrast to officers, corporate directors are not automatically liable as controlling persons.[45] Thus, "[t]here must be some showing of actual participation in the corporation's operation or some influence before the consequences of control may be imposed."[46]

The Eleventh Circuit adopted its own articulation of the test for controlling person liability where the primary violator is an entity.[49] The court, adopting the approach that had been taken by the district court, focused on three factors. The court explained that controlling person liability exists: (1) if the alleged control person had the power to control the general affairs of the entity at the time of the alleged securities law violations, (2) the alleged control person possessed the power to control the specific company policy that resulted in primary liability, and (3) the controlled entity committed a securities law violation.[50] This test, which would be applicable to corporate officers and directors, among others, seems to be a fair restatement of the general principles of controlling person liability.

Controlling person liability does not depend upon the actual exercise of the power to control.[51] Thus, all that is necessary is to establish the possession of the power of control over the primary violator.[52]

Defenses to Claims of Controlling Person Liability

Under the statute, a defendant has two affirmative defenses to a controlling person liability claim. First, the defendant can try to establish that he or she acted in "good faith."[76] The defendant will have the burden of proving his or her own good faith, which "requires not only the establishment of a proper system of supervision, but also its diligent enforcement."[77] Secondly, the defendant can also try to establish that he or she did not induce the alleged violation, or in other words, that he or she did not participate in the violation.[78]

§ 12.25 Multiple Defendants in Actions Under the Securities Exchange Act of 1934: Aiding and Abetting Liability

In cases involving violations of the securities laws, plaintiffs often brought suit against not only the person who was the primary violator of the

44. Wool v. Tandem Computers Inc., 818 F.2d 1433, 1441 (9th Cir.1987); In re JDN Realty Corp. Securities Litigation, 182 F.Supp.2d 1230 (N.D.Ga.2002).

45. Paracor Finance, Inc. v. General Electric Capital Corp., 96 F.3d 1151 (9th Cir.1996).

46. Burgess v. Premier Corp., 727 F.2d 826, 832 (9th Cir.1984) (quoting Herm v. Stafford, 663 F.2d 669, 684 (6th Cir.1981)).

49. Brown v. Enstar Group, Inc., 84 F.3d 393 (11th Cir.1996).

50. *Id.*

51. *E.g.,* IBS Financial Corp. v. Seidman & Associates, 136 F.3d 940 (3d Cir.1998).

52. *Id.*

76. *See, e.g.,* Ash v. Ameritreat, 189 F.3d 463 (3d Cir.1999) (no control person liability because control person acted in good faith).

77. Harrison v. Dean Witter Reynolds, Inc., 79 F.3d 609 (7th Cir.1996).

78. Federal Savings and Loan Insurance Corp. v. Shearson–American Express, 658 F.Supp. 1331, 1343 (D.Puerto Rico 1987).

specific statute, but also any persons who may have assisted in the wrongful act. Aiding and abetting finds its origin in criminal law.[6] Until 1994, private suits against aiders and abettors were commonly brought to assure a solvent defendant. Until 1994, aiders and abettors were generally held to be jointly and severally liable to plaintiffs for violations and were often viewed as better sources from which to seek monetary awards. However, a 1994 Supreme Court decision[8] eliminated private aiding and abetting claims. Aiding and abetting remains an important issue in criminal and SEC enforcement actions. In the private litigation arena, there is an increasing tendency of plaintiffs to try to characterize participants in a securities fraud as primary violators.

Distinction Between Primary and Secondary Violations

To the extent that an accountant or an attorney actually prepares documents containing materially misleading statements, then primary liability may well be appropriate. Thus, for example, when a law firm makes public materially misleading statements that investors might rely upon, the law firm may be held accountable as a primary violator.[96] An attorney's drafting of disclosure can lead to primary liability if the disclosure is found to have violated the securities laws[97] and the person drafting the disclosure created the fraud.[98] However, primary liability for violation of Rule 10b–5 necessarily depends upon knowledge or willful ignorance regarding the falsity of the statement. Auditors can be held primarily liable for the recklessness in failing to correct a materially false statement in financials covered by the audit.[100] Similarly, broker-dealers[101] and banks[102] may be sued as primary violators if they themselves make material misstatements in connection with someone else's fraud. Merely disseminating the false information is not sufficient to create liability under Rule 10b–5.[103] Liability would have to be based on the defendant's involvement in drafting or preparation of the materially misleading statements.[104]

§ 12.25

6. *See* 18 U.S.C.A. § 2.

8. Central Bank of Denver, N.A. v. First Interstate Bank of Denver, 511 U.S. 164, 114 S.Ct. 1439, 128 L.Ed.2d 119 (1994).

96. In re Enron Corp. Securities, Derivative and ERISA Litigation, 235 F.Supp.2d 549 (S.D. Tex. 2002). In contrast, the claims were dismissed against another law firm in the same case that did not make any public statements. *Id.*

97. *See, e.g., Id.*

98. *See* Annual Review of Federal Securities Regulation, 59 Bus. Law. 689, 877 (2004).

100. Overton v. Todman & Co., CPAs, P.C., 478 F.3d 479 (2d Cir. 2007) (holding that "an auditor may incur primary liability under § 10(b) and Rule 10b–5 when the auditor makes a statement in its certified opinion that is false or misleading when made, subsequently learns or was reckless in not learning that the earlier statement was false or misleading, knows or should know that potential investors are relying on the opinion, yet fails to take reasonable steps to correct or withdraw its opinion and/or the financial statements.").

101. First Interregional Equity Corp. v. Haughton, 1994 WL 364038, [1994–1995 Transfer Binder] Fed. Sec. L. Rep. (CCH) ¶ 98,339 (S.D.N.Y.1994) (even if *Central Bank* decision applies retroactively, there was ample evidence to sustain arbitration award against broker-dealer as a primary violator).

102. *See* Quaak v. Dexia S.A., 357 F.Supp.2d 330 (D.Mass. 2005) (complaint stated claim against bank as primary violator).

103. In re Mutual Funds Investment Litigation, 487 F. Supp.2d 618 (D. Md. 2007).

104. *Id.* (distinguishing cases from those in which the defendant actually "prepared, drafted, or signed the allegedly misleading prospectuses"); SEC v. Tambone, 417 F. Supp. 2d 127 (D.

Primary liability is not always dependent on the defendant having actually participated in the drafting of the materially misleading statement. For example, a chief executive officer and a chief operating officer could be classified as primary violators for having allowed the inaccurate filings to be filed.[107] Formerly, some courts required that the defendant have actually made the statement in order to be held liable as a primary violator.[108] Other courts, however, held that other types of substantial assistance can be sufficient to establish primary liability under the securities laws.[109] In 2008, in Stoneridge Investment Partners, LLC v. Scientific–Atlanta, Inc., the Supreme Court agreed, rejecting a requirement that the defendant must have actually uttered or authored the misstatement in order to be held accountable in a private damage action.[110] Nevertheless, something more than substantial assistance is required to establish primary liability. The Supreme Court explained that the deceptive conduct must have made the misrepresentations or omissions "necessary or inevitable."[111] In a private suit the conduct would have to provide a basis for establishing that the plaintiff had actual or constructive knowledge of the conduct and could be said to have relied on the deceptive conduct.[113] For example, one case held that a company's law firm "initiated and masterminded a 'workaround' " that led to securities law disclosure violations was not sufficient to establish primary liability under *Stoneridge Partners* because the law firm did not make any material misstatements nor participate in the drafting of the company's misstatements.[114] In another case,[116] the court found that a Rule 10b–5 claim could be stated against a law firm that prepared the stock subscription agreement in connection with an allegedly fraudulent stock offering.

The rise and fall of "scheme liability"

As noted above, someone who does not actually utter or author the misstatement may be charged with primary liability when that statement is publicly attributed to him or to her. The courts were divided on the question

Mass. 2006) (no primary liability where defendant did not prepare or draft the statements in question) rev'd on other grounds 550 F.3d 106 (1st Cir. 2008).

107. Kaufman v. Motorola, Inc., 1999 WL 688780, [1999 Transfer Binder] Fed. Sec. L. Rep. (CCH) ¶ 90,481 (N.D.Ill.1999).

108. *See, e.g.,* Anixter v. Home–Stake Production Co., 77 F.3d 1215, 1225 (10th Cir.1996) ("The critical element separating primary liability from aiding and abetting violations is the existence of a representation, either by statement or omission made by the defendant, that is relied on by plaintiff. Reliance only on representations made by others cannot itself form the basis of liability").

109. *See, e.g.,* SEC v. First Jersey Securities, 101 F.3d 1450, 1471 (2d Cir.1996) (primary liability may be imposed "not only on persons who made fraudulent misrepresentations but also on those who had knowledge of the fraud and assisted in its perpetration").

110. Stoneridge Investment Partners, LLC v. Scientific–Atlanta, Inc., 552 U.S. 148, 128 S.Ct. 761, 169 L.Ed.2d 627 (2008).

111. Stoneridge Investment Partners, LLC v. Scientific–Atlanta, Inc., 552 U.S. 148, 128 S.Ct. 761, 169 L.Ed.2d 627 (2008). *See also, e.g.,* In re Parmalat Securities Litigation, 2008 WL 3275643 (S.D.N.Y. 2008) (dismissing claim against banks on the basis of Stoneridge).

113. *See* Pugh v. Tribune Co., 521 F.3d 686 (7th Cir. 2008) (failure to establish scheme liability where defendant lacked knowledge of the deceptive conduct); Katz v. Image Innovations Holdings, Inc., 2008 WL 762105 (S.D.N.Y. 2008) (failure to establish reliance on conduct of some of the defendants). *See also* Matthew L. Mustokoff, Secondary Actors, Respondeat Superior and the Limitations of Corporate Scienter: The Seventh Circuit's Pugh Decision, 36 Sec. Reg. L.J. 237 (2008).

114. In re DVI Inc. Seurities. Litigation, 249 F.R.D. 196 (E.D. Pa. 2008).

116. Burket v. Hyman Lippitt, P.C.,,560 F.Supp.2d 571 (E.D.Mich. 2008).

of when primary liability could be attributed to someone who neither utters nor authors the misstatement. Thus, for example, some courts held that when someone's active participation in a *scheme* to defraud creates the necessary deception, primary liability could be found to exist. This has been referred to as "scheme liability" to distinguish those cases in which the defendant actively participated in the misstatement. Scheme liability thus expanded liability exposure beyond those who actually drafted or disseminated the misstatement.

In a five to three decision, the Supreme Court rejected scheme liability as a way to extend secondary liability under Rule 10b–5.[137] The Supreme Court ruled that the defendant's connection to the statement was not sufficient to support a claim of reliance by the plaintiff.[138] Investors must thus have some basis for relying on the defendant's participation in the alleged scheme.[139] The *Stoneridge* decision does not impose a *per se* requirement that the defendant have actually signed to drafted the disclosure in question, it is sufficient to establish a basis for the plaintiff's reliance on the defendant's participation.[141]

§ 12.26 Multiple Defendants in Actions Under the Securities Exchange Act of 1934: Joint and Several Liability; Proportional Liability

Section 21D(f) of the 1934 Act,[2] which was enacted as part of the Private Securities Litigation Reform Act of 1995,[3] changes the prior rule of joint and several liability for defendants in 1934 Act suits. The statute institutes a system of proportionate liability for defendants who do not knowingly commit violations of the Act.[4] Proportionate liability is also applicable to outside directors in actions under section 11 of the 1933 Act.[5] The fair share rule of liability that is imposed by section 21D(f) does not create a new cause of action or in any way change the requisite states of mind for 1933 or 1934 Act suits.

Defendants engaging in "knowing" violations of the securities laws are subject to joint and several liability. Knowing violations include material misrepresentations or omissions made with actual knowledge of false information, and do not include reckless conduct. Defendants not meeting the standard of knowledge are responsible only for their proportionate share of a

137. Stoneridge Investment Partners, LLC v. Scientific–Atlanta, Inc., 552 U.S. 148, 128 S Ct. 761, 169 L.Ed.2d 627 (2008).

138. Reliance is discussed in § 12.10 *supra* and fraud on the market is discussed in § 12.10[6] *supra*.

139. A Rule 10b–5 claim can be stated when the public has a basis for relying on the defendant's participation. *See* In re Bristol Myers Squib Co. Securities Litigation, 2008 WL 3884384 (S.D.N.Y. 2008) (upholding allegations against an officer who negotiated settlement that was misrepresented in public statements).

141. *See, e.g.,*In re Bristol Myers Squib Co. Securities Litigation, 2008 WL 3884384 (S.D.N.Y. 2008) (upholding allegations against an officer who negotiated settlement that was misrepresented in public statements).

§ 12.26

2. 15 U.S.C.A. § 78u–4(f). A somewhat more modest change was made with regard to liability under section 11 of the 1933 Act which applies these provisions only to outside directors, while other defendants remain jointly and severally liable unless fraud was involved.

3. Pub. Law No. 104–67, 109 Stat. 737 (104th Cong. 1st Sess December 22, 1995) (HR 1058).

4. S. Rep. No. 104–98, 104th Cong., 1st Sess. at 20 (1995).

5. 15 U.S.C.A. § 77k(f).

judgment. Courts in private actions are required to instruct juries to answer special interrogatories or make findings in non-jury suits with respect to each defendant. The court or jury must determine (1) whether each defendant violated any securities law; (2) the percentage of each defendant's responsibility; and (3) whether each defendant's violation(s) was knowing.

Non-knowing defendants may still be held jointly and severally liable under certain provisions relating to the uncollectible shares of other defendants. If a plaintiff establishes: (1) that the recoverable damages under the judgment are more than ten percent of the net worth of the plaintiff; and (2) that the net worth of the plaintiff is less than $200,000, a non-knowing defendant will be held jointly and severally liable for any uncollectible shares. Additionally, non-knowing defendants may be held jointly and severally liable for up to fifty percent of another defendant's share who is unable to pay due to insolvency.

However, defendants paying additional amounts due to uncollectible shares may, within six months of the date of payment, seek contribution. All defendants held liable in an action may seek contribution within six months of the final judgment from parties not named in the suit. Additionally, any defendant who settles prior to final judgment may not seek a right of contribution and the court is required to reduce the final judgment by the amount the settling defendant paid to the plaintiff.[6]

In addition to the foregoing rules on liability, the 1995 Reform Act requires bar orders with regard to partial settlement of securities law claims.[7]

§ 12.27 Multiple Defendants in Actions Under the Securities Exchange Act of 1934: Contribution and Indemnity

Defendants found liable for violations of securities laws are often jointly and severally liable to plaintiffs for their fraudulent acts under Rule 10b–5,[1] and consequently, the entire damage award can be collected from one or more defendants, assuming joint liability is found. Under the tort principle of contribution, the court may distribute the loss among the joint tortfeasors by requiring each defendant to pay his or her portion of the damages.[2] A person seeking contribution may do so either by the use of third party practice (impleader) or by bringing a separate action.

In Musick, Peeler & Garrett v. Employers Insurance of Wausau,[37] the Court held that a right of contribution was an appropriate part of the implied right of action that has long existed under Rule 10b–5. In so ruling, the Court distinguished cases decided under other federal statutes containing an express right of action but no right of contribution. Although a number of decisions

6. *See, e.g.,* Lucas v. Hackett Associates, Inc., 18 F.Supp.2d 531 (E.D.Pa.1998) (settling defendants denied order barring non-settling defendants' contribution claims).

7. *See* § 12.27 *infra. Cf.* State of Wisconsin Investment Board v. Ruttenberg, 300 F.Supp.2d 1210 (N.D. Ala. 2004) (PSLRA's bar order requirement does not preclude a settlement fashioning its own bar order).

§ 12.27

1. 17 C.F.R. § 240.10b–5.

2. *See, e.g.,* In re Olympia Brewing Co. Securities Litigation, 674 F.Supp. 597 (N.D.Ill.1987).

37. Musick, Peeler & Garrett v. Employers Insurance of Wausau, 508 U.S. 286, 113 S.Ct. 2085, 124 L.Ed.2d 194 (1993).

caution against the implication of additional federal remedies, once the courts have recognized an implied right of action, then it is appropriate to flesh it out so as to render it a reasonable remedy.[39] Furthermore, sections 9(e) and 18(a) of the Act[40] both contain an express right of action and further provide for a right of contribution. The Court reasoned that the similarities between sections 9(e), 18(a), and 10(b) support the recognition of an implied right of contribution under Rule 10b–5. Although the Court has recognized the existence of an implied right of contribution, other questions remain concerning the scope of such a right. For example, presumably, unlike a primary damage action under Rule 10b–5, it is not necessary that one violator seeking contribution from another have been a purchaser or seller of securities.[41] All that need be shown is that the third party may be liable for all or part of the liability incurred by the plaintiff seeking contribution.

39. *See* 508 U.S. at 292–293, 113 S.Ct. at 2089, *relying on* Virginia Bankshares, Inc. v. Sandberg, 501 U.S. 1083, 111 S.Ct. 2749, 115 L.Ed.2d 929 (1991) *and* Blue Chip Stamps v. Manor Drug Stores, 421 U.S. 723, 95 S.Ct. 1917, 44 L.Ed.2d 539 (1975).

40. 15 U.S.C.A. § 78i(e), 78r(a). *See* § 12.1, 12.8 *supra.*

41. *See* Axel Johnson, Inc. v. Arthur Andersen & Co., 830 F.Supp. 204 (S.D.N.Y.1993).

Chapter 13

INSIDER REPORTING AND SHORT–SWING TRADING—SECURITIES EXCHANGE ACT SECTION 16

Table of Sections

§ 13.1 Reporting Requirements for Insiders and Their Transactions in Shares—Section 16(a)

Overview of Section 16 Filing Requirements

By its terms section 16(a)[4] requires officers, directors, and beneficial owners of more than ten percent of any class of equity security registered under section 12 of the Act[5] to file appropriate notice with the Commission within ten days of becoming an officer, director, or beneficial owner. The section 16(a) filing must include disclosure of all ownership interest in any of the issuer's equity securities. Further, when there has been a change in an officer's, director's, or beneficial owner's share holdings, notice must also be filed with the Commission, generally on Form 4.[6] The Sarbanes–Oxley Act of 2002 mandates more rapid reporting of insider transaction than formerly was the case under section 16(a).[7] Section 16(a) was amended to require Form 4 reports of changes in beneficial ownership to be filed with the SEC by the end of the second business day after the day of execution of the transaction.[8] The Act permits the SEC to set another deadline if it determines the two-day period is not feasible.[9] Prior to this change, the deadline was the tenth day of

§ 13.1

4. 15 U.S.C.A. § 78p(a).

5. 15 U.S.C.A. § 78*l*.

6. 15 U.S.C.A. § 78p(a).

7. Sarbanes–Oxley Act of 2002, Pub. Law 107–204 (July 30, 2002). *See also, e.g.,* Ownership Reports, Sec. Exch. Act Rel. No. 34–46313, 2002 WL 1792168 (SEC Aug. 6, 2002).

8. 15 U.S.C.A. § 78p(a)(2)(C). *See also, e.g.,* Donald W. Glazer & Keith F. Higgins, Securities Exchange Act Section 16: Short Answers to Quick Questions Under the New Rules and Forms, 37 Rev. Sec. & Commodities Reg. 207 (Oct. 27, 2004).

9. 15 U.S.C.A. § 78p(a)(2)(C).

the month following the end of the month in which the ownership change occurred. The Act now also requires that Form 4 be filed electronically.

Section 16(a) reports are publicly available at the Commission's office in Washington, D.C. and are also available on EDGAR. The Commission also publishes official monthly summaries of the section 16(a) reports. Some investment analysts, by watching insider transactions, try to get a sense of how the issuer's securities are likely to fare in the future. Insider sales in the aggregate for any particular company are viewed as one indicator of the issuer's health. Similarly, on a macro level, the market's overall health is judged at least in part by the balance between aggregate insider purchases and aggregate insider sales.

In addition to its reporting requirements, section 16(a) also determines who is subject to section 16(b)'s provisions for disgorgement of insider short-swing profits.[27]

The initial section 16(a) filing must be made on Form 3, while all subsequent filings indicating a change in beneficial ownership must be filed on Form 4.[28] In 1991, the Commission adopted Form 5 to be filed annually to disclose any reportable section 16 transactions that were not reported on Form 3 or 4 because of an exemption or that should have been reported during the year on Form 3 or 4 but were not so reported.[29] If a Form 5 is due, it must be made within forty-five days after the close of the issuer's fiscal year.

In deciding whether a particular transaction is reportable on Form 4, it is important to distinguish between the various types of exemptions available under the rules. Transactions that are exempted from section 16(b)'s short-swing profit provisions need not be reported on Form 4, but if not so reported must be reported on Form 5. A limited exemption from Form 4 filings exists for acquisitions of equity securities not exceeding $10,000; these transactions do not trigger a Form 4 filing obligation, but must be reported on the next Form 4 or Form 5, whichever is due sooner.[33]

§ 13.1[2] Who Must File Section 16 Reports

Officers and Directors

There has been a good deal of litigation involving the question of who is an "officer" so as to be subject to section 16 of the Act. The revised rules take the position that section 16 should not be applied to individuals who are officers only in name. As such, the rules should put to rest a lot of the uncertainty that has previously existed in trying to determine who qualifies as an officer so as to trigger section 16 responsibilities. Rule 16a–1(f) expands upon the definition of "executive officer" used elsewhere in the rules.[46] Specifically included in the rule as revised are the president, principal financial officer, principal accounting officer,[47] any vice president in charge of a

27. 15 U.S.C.A. § 78p(b); § 13.2 *infra*

28. Rule 16a–3(a), 17 C.F.R. § 240.16a–3(a).

29. *See* Rule 16a–3(f), 17 C.F.R. § 240.16a–3(f) (1991).

33. Rule 16a–6, 17 C.F.R. § 240.16a–6.

46. Rule 3b–7, 17 C.F.R. § 240.3b–7. *See also* Rule 3b–2, 17 C.F.R. § 240.3b–2 (definition of officer).

47. Or the comptroller if there is no principal accounting officer.

principal business unit, division, or function[48] as well as any other officer or other person who performs policy-making functions.[49] However, "policy-making function" is not meant to include activities that are not significant.[50] Furthermore, officers of the issuer's parent or subsidiary who perform policy-making functions of the issuer are deemed to be officers of the issuer for section 16 purposes.[51] In the event that the issuer is a limited partnership or a trust, officers or employees of the general partner or trustee who perform duties similar to those outlined above are officers of the issuer.[52] With regard to advisory, emeritus, or honorary directors, the Commission has announced that it has carried forth its previous policy and thus does not treat them as subject to the regulation.[53]

Once it has been determined that someone is an officer or director required to file reports, what about transactions occurring before he or she takes office or after resignation? Someone who becomes an officer is not required to report transactions occurring prior to that date. In contrast, someone who has been an officer or director of a company before it became subject to section 12's registration requirements has filing obligations with respect to transactions prior to the effective date of the reporting obligation. In such a case, the officer or director must make reports with regard to transactions occurring within the six months prior to the issuer's 1934 Act registration provided those transactions occurred within six months of the transaction that triggered the Form 4 filing obligation.[54] As noted above, the revised provisions continue the former practice of requiring reports of transactions following an officer or director leaving office so long as the transaction occurred within six months of the last transaction while in office.[55]

Ten Percent Beneficial Owners

With respect to reporting based on beneficial ownership, the 1991 revisions of the section 16 reporting rules parallel the rules applicable to section 13(d) of the Williams Act.[56] The Commission notes that, as is the case with section 13(d), "[s]ection 16, as applied to ten percent holders, is intended to reach those persons who can be presumed to have access to inside information because they can influence or control the issuer as a result of their equity ownership."[57] In making the ten percent holder determination under section 16, nonvoting securities are excluded and derivative securities are included only if they are convertible or exercisable within sixty days.[58] It is clear that

48. The Commission lists sales, administration, and finance as specific examples.

49. 17 C.F.R. § 240.16a–1(f).

50. Note to 17 C.F.R. § 240.16a–1(f).

51. 17 C.F.R. § 240.16a–1(f).

52. 17 C.F.R. § 240.16a–1(f).

53. Sec.Exch. Act Rel. No. 34–28869, 1991 WL 292000, [1990–1991 Transfer Binder] Fed.Sec. L.Rep. (CCH) ¶ 84,709, n. 27 and accompanying text (Feb. 8, 1991).

54. Rule 16a–2(a), 17 C.F.R. § 240.16a–2(a).

55. Rule 16a–2(b), 17 C.F.R. § 240.16a–2(b).

56. 15 U.S.C.A. § 78m(d) which is discussed in § 11.2 *supra*. This brings with it section 13(d)'s "group theory" which is discussed *id.* The determination that a group exists for determination of ten percent ownership status does not mean that those securities are subject to the reporting and short-swing profit provisions.

57. Sec.Exch. Act Rel. No. 34–28869, 1991 WL 292000, [1990–1991 Transfer Binder] Fed.Sec. L.Rep. (CCH) ¶ 84,709 (Feb. 8, 1991).

58. Rules 13d–3(d)(1)(i), 16a–1(a)(1), 17 C.F.R. §§ 240.13d–3(d)(1)(i), 240.16a–1(a)(1).

the Commission intended to create parallel definitions of beneficial ownership under sections 16 and 13(d).

It is not always easy to determine if and when a shareholder reached the ten percent threshold. For example, in the case of issuers who periodically repurchase their shares, the threshold can be a moving target. When section 16 insider status is based on the formation of a group, only transactions occurring after formation of the group, as opposed to contemporaneously with the group's formation, will be matched against other transactions for the purpose of determining section 16 (b) liability.[73]

Rule 16a–1(a)(2)[74] begins by setting forth the basic rule that, for reporting purposes, beneficial ownership hinges upon the direct or indirect pecuniary interest in the shares,[75] and that that interest may be the result of "any contract, arrangement, understanding, relationship, or otherwise."[76] This includes the opportunity to participate, directly or indirectly, in any profit attributable to transactions in the shares in question. The rule then goes on to list examples of an "indirect pecuniary interest" that triggers section 16. Securities held by immediate family members sharing the same household are included.[77] A general partner's proportional interest in securities held by a general or limited partnership are similarly included.[78] In contrast, a shareholder does not have a pecuniary interest in the portfolio securities held by a corporation, limited partnership, or similar entity, so long as he or she is not a controlling shareholder of the entity and does not possess, either alone or with others, investment control over the entity's portfolio securities.[79]

In a case of first impression, the Second Circuit was asked to decide whether an insider's acquisition of a company that owned stock in the corporation of which he was an insider qualified as a purchase of the company's stock for section 16 purposes. The court decided that since there was no potential for speculative abuse, this derivative acquisition of the issuer's stock was not a section 16 purchase.[90]

The determination of beneficial ownership, as between an insider and spouse frequently presents difficult factual questions. For example, within the context of a 16(b) action to recover proscribed short-swing profits, it has been held that a wife's sale of securities is attributed to her husband who is a

73. Rosenberg v. XM Ventures, 129 F.Supp.2d 681 (D.Del.2001). This is the case since the purchase or other transaction that places the defendant over the 10% ownership line will not be matched against subsequent sales for section 16(b) purposes. Foremost–McKesson, Inc. v. Provident Securities Co., 423 U.S. 232, 96 S.Ct. 508, 46 L.Ed.2d 464 (1976).

74. Rule 16a–1(a)(2), 17 C.F.R. § 240.16a–1(a)(2). *See* Feder v. Frost, 220 F.3d 29 (2d Cir.2000) (upholding the validity of Rule 16a–1(a)(2)).

75. The "pecuniary interest" analysis set forth in Rule 16a–1(a)(2) applies to the determination of which transactions are subject to section 16(a)'s reporting requirements and also which transactions may be subject to section 16(b)'s disgorgement provisions. *See* Rosen v. Brookhaven Capital Management Co., 113 F.Supp.2d 615, 627–628 (S.D.N.Y.2000). This is distinct from the application of the ten percent beneficial ownership threshold to determine whether someone qualifies as a statutory insider and thus is subject to the reporting requirements and disgorgement provisions. 113 F.Supp.2d at 627–28.

76. Rule 16a–1(a)(2), 17 C.F.R. § 240.16a–1(a)(2).

77. 17 C.F.R. § 240.16a–1(a)(2)(ii)(A).

78. 17 C.F.R. § 240.16a–1(a)(2)(ii)(B).

79. 17 C.F.R. § 240.16a–1(a)(2)(iii). Portfolio securities are all securities owned by an entity except for securities issued by the entity. 17 C.F.R. § 240.16a–1(g).

90. At Home Corp. v. Cox Communications, Inc., 446 F.3d 403 (2d Cir. 2006).

director of the issuer even where the husband and wife maintain separate brokerage accounts but engaged in some joint planning.[91] As discussed above, the revised section 16 rules codify this result.

Definition of Equity Security

The former rules required inclusion in the ten percent ownership computation of all equity securities which the holder had the right to acquire by exercising presently exercisable rights, warrants, or conversion rights.[92] However, in light of the revised rules' treatment of derivative instruments generally, the requirement that there be a present right has been deleted.[93] Section 3(a)(11) and Rule 3a11–1 of the Act define "equity security" to include "any security convertible, with or without consideration" into an equity security;[94] this definition also includes warrants and rights to subscribe to or purchase an equity security. The Second Circuit held that convertible debentures do not themselves constitute a separate class of equity security for purposes of section 16.[95] The court explained that the ten percent beneficial ownership threshold for section 16 reporting is computed with regard to the underlying security assuming "full dilution" of the underlying security which would result from exercise of all conversion rights.[96] This would include other warrants and rights as well.[97] The Second Circuit's rule has been codified by the Commission.[98]

Under Rule 16a–4(a),[99] convertible securities are not considered a separate class of equity security, but rather part of the class of the underlying security which would be acquired upon the exercise of the conversion rights. This computation of ten percent beneficial ownership applies to convertible securities conversion rights, and derivative securities that are currently exercisable without contingencies.[100] However, when the conversion rights have material contingencies and therefore are not presently exercisable, the shares underlying convertible securities will not be aggregated with other direct holdings in the underlying securities.[102]

Treatment of Derivative Securities

One of the more significant changes implemented by the Commission with its revised section 16 rules is the applicability of the reporting requirements to derivative securities. The proliferation of put and call options has made it possible for investors to take a derivative position with regard to underlying equity securities. In many ways, investment positions in these derivative investment vehicles are functionally equivalent to positions in the

91. Whiting v. Dow Chemical Co., 523 F.2d 680 (2d Cir.1975). *See also* Whittaker v. Whittaker Corp., 639 F.2d 516 (9th Cir.1981).

92. Former Rule 16a–2(b), 17 C.F.R. § 240.16a–2(b) (1990).

93. *See* § 13.1[2][D] *infra.*

94. 15 U.S.C.A. § 78c(a)(11); 17 C.F.R. § 240.3a11–1.

95. Chemical Fund, Inc. v. Xerox Corp., 377 F.2d 107 (2d Cir.1967).

96. Chemical Fund, Inc. v. Xerox Corp., 377 F.2d 107 (2d Cir.1967).

97. Warrants and rights are included in the general definition of equity security under the Act. 15 U.S.C.A. § 78c(a)(11).

98. Rule, 16a–4(a), 17 C.F.R. § 240.16a–4(a).

99. Rule, 16a–4(a), 17 C.F.R. § 240.16a–4(a).

100. Rule, 16a–4(a), 17 C.F.R. § 240.16a–4(a).

102. *See* Levner v. Saud, 903 F.Supp. 452 (S.D.N.Y.1994).

underlying security in terms of the potential for trading profits. Accordingly, the Commission has reversed its long-standing policy by making the acquisition of a derivative security, rather than its exercise, the significant event for section 16 purposes.[114] Derivative securities are covered not only by the section 16(a) reporting requirements, but also by the short-swing profit provisions of section 16(b). The revised rules view transactions in derivative securities as matchable not only against each other, but also against transactions in the underlying security.[115] The revised rules thus equate ownership of a derivative security with ownership of the underlying security and recognize that, as is the case with convertible securities, exercise merely changes ownership from indirect to direct ownership of the underlying security.

§ 13.2 Disgorgement of Insider Short–Swing Profits—Section 16(b)

Overview of Section 16(b)

Section 16(b)[1] imposes liability for short-swing profits in the issuer's stock upon all persons required to file reports under section 16(a) of the Act.[2] Thus, officers, directors, and beneficial owners of ten percent of a class of equity securities subject to the Exchange Act's reporting requirements are subject to the short-swing profit prohibitions. These listed statutory insiders must disgorge to the issuer any "profit" realized as a result of a purchase and sale or sale and purchase of covered equity securities occurring within a six month period. Section 16(b) is not designed as a compensatory remedy. The preamble to section 16(b) indicates that this civil liability is imposed "for the purpose of preventing the unfair use of information which may have been obtained by such beneficial owner, director, or officer by reason of his relationship to the issuer."[4] The legislative history reveals congressional recognition of such a great potential for abuse of inside information so as to warrant the imposition of strict liability. The statute was viewed as a "crude rule of thumb" or objective method of preventing "the unscrupulous employment of [corporate] inside information."[5] Accordingly, in light of its broad remedial purpose, section 16(b) will require disgorgement of insider short-swing profits even in the absence of any wrongdoing.[6] The liability so imposed is often referred to as prophylactic in nature. Section 16(b) thus does not

114. Sec.Exch.Act Rel. No. 34–28869, 1991 WL 292000, [1990–1991 Transfer Binder] Fed.Sec. L.Rep. (CCH) ¶ 84,709 (Feb. 8, 1991). The rules contain a specific exemption for most exercises of rights and warrants. Rule 16b–6(b), 17 C.F.R. § 240.16b–6(b). However, the exercise exemption does not apply when the exercise creates a new opportunity for profit. The exercise exemption also does not apply to the exercise of out-of-the-money options. *See* Sec.Exch. Act Rel. No. 34–28869 *supra*. *Cf.* Frankel v. Slotkin, 984 F.2d 1328 (2d Cir.1993) (refusing to apply the change retroactively and holding that the granting of a put option to tender offeror in connection with a planned acquisition was not a "sale" under section 16(b), although the exercise would be).

115. Rule 16b–6(a), 17 C.F.R. § 240.16b–6(a). *See* § 13.2 *infra*.

§ 13.2

1. 15 U.S.C.A. § 78p(b).

2. *See* § 13.1 *supra*.

4. 15 U.S.C.A. § 78p(b).

5. Hearings on S.Res. 84, S.Res. 97 Before The Senate Comm. on Banking and Currency, 73d Cong., 1st Sess. pt. 15 at 6557 (1934).

6. Section 16(b) is based on deterrence rather than compensation or punishment. As a consequence, for example, it would undermine section 16(b)'s goal to allow indemnity even in a situation where the violator was not at fault. *See* Deephaven Capital Management v. Schnell, 2007 WL 101821 at *2 (D.Minn. 2007).

make moral distinctions as it penalizes insiders who commit a technical violation but are still "pure of heart" while at the same time a more culpable insider may be able to avoid liability by going beyond the letter of the statute.[7]

In 2002, Congress enacted the Sarbanes–Oxley Act to combat corporate fraud.[18] That Act contained provisions designed to strengthen the prohibitions on insider trading.[19] The Act prohibits directors and executive officers are prohibited from purchasing or selling company equity securities during black-out periods under 401(k) and other similar retirement funds.[20] The company may recover (including through a shareholder derivative-type action) any profits realized from such prohibited purchases or sales.[21] Unlike Section 16 of the 1934 Act, this disgorgement action does not require a matching transaction within the black-out period.

Issuers Covered

As noted above, the applicability of section 16(b)'s disgorgement provisions is determined by reference to section 16(a)'s reporting requirements.[26] Accordingly, section 16(b) liability attaches to officers, directors, and ten percent beneficial owners of a class of equity securities registered under section 12 of the Exchange Act.[28]

Securities Covered

Section 16(a)'s reporting provisions[35] determine the parameters of section 16(b)'s coverage.[36] By virtue of Rule 16a–10 the exemptions from 16(a) carry over to 16(b).[37] Similarly, the definition of "equity security" is equally broad under section 16(b) as under 16(a) and extends to conversion rights, warrants, and even stock appreciation rights.[38] Also, the same rules apply to the determination of beneficial ownership under sections 16(a) and 16(b).[39]

Procedural Aspects; Standing; Demand Requirement; Right to Jury Trial; Statute of Limitations

The private remedy embodied in section 16(b) is self contained, sui generis, and is a hybrid variety of derivative suit. For example, the statute on its face requires that the shareholder make a demand upon directors prior to being sued.

Standing to bring a suit under section 16(b) has three basic requirements. First, the plaintiff must be an owner of an equity security covered by section

7. *See* Magma Power Co. v. Dow Chemical Co., 136 F.3d 316, 320–21 (2d Cir.1998).

18. Sarbanes–Oxley Act of 2002, Pub. Law 107–204 (July 30, 2002).

19. 15 U.S.C.A. § 7244. As is the case with section 16(b), intent of the insider is not a precondition to recovery.

20. 15 U.S.C.A. § 7244(a)(1).

21. 15 U.S.C.A. § 7244(a)(2). This cause of action exists "irrespective of any intention on the part of the director or executive officer." *Id.*

26. 15 U.S.C.A. § 78p(a),(b).

28. 15 U.S.C.A. § 78*l*.

35. 15 U.S.C.A. § 78p(a).

36. *See* § 13.1 *supra.*

37. 17 C.F.R. § 240.16a–10.

38. *See* 15 U.S.C.A. § 78c(a)(11); 17 C.F.R. §§ 240.3a11–1.

39. *See* § 13.3 *infra*; § 13.1 *supra.*

16. Second, the security so owned must be the same class of security traded by the section 16(b) defendant. Third, the plaintiff must own the security at the time that the section 16(b) action is instituted.[42] There is no requirement comparable to derivative actions generally[43] imposing a contemporaneous ownership rule requiring that the plaintiff owned the security at the time of the violation. Instead, section 16(b) requires "only that he has 'some continuing financial stake in the litigation' so as to satisfy minimum standing requirements imposed by the jurisdictional limitations of Article III."[44]

In 1991, the Supreme Court set forth two requirements for standing under section 16(b): first, the suit must have been initiated at a time that plaintiff was a shareholder; and second, the plaintiff must have a continuing interest in the corporation (or its assets) so as to allow him or her to benefit from any recovery.[46] Applying this relatively limited standing requirement, a shareholder of a target company who was a shareholder of the acquiring company following a cash-out merger had standing to bring a section 16(b) action.

Notwithstanding the possible champerty implications, the courts have held that it is no defense to an action under section 16(b) that the suit was motivated primarily by an attorney's desire to obtain the attorneys' fees that may be awarded to the successful plaintiff.[48] Attorneys' fees are awarded out of the fund created by the recovery and are not added to the defendant's liability.[49]

It is generally a requirement of derivative suits that the plaintiff must first make a demand on directors to bring suit on behalf of the corporation. Section 16(b) contains its own demand requirement. The corporation, through its directors, then has sixty days to decide whether or not to bring suit.[54] However, no demand is required when it would be a futile gesture due to the self-interest of the directors.

The section 16(b) action may be brought either in law or in equity. It has been held that the plaintiff's failure to demand a jury trial renders the action one in equity, thus denying the defendant the right of election.[62]

The statute contains a two-year limitation period which begins to run from the date of the second transaction, that is, the one that creates the section 16(b) profits. However, the statute of limitations period may be extended until the time of reasonable discovery where there has been a failure to file timely section 16(a) reports.[64] The statute of limitations will not be tolled beyond the filing of the Form 4 or 5.

---

42. Gollust v. Mendell, 501 U.S. 115, 123–124, 111 S.Ct. 2173, 115 L.Ed.2d 109 (1991); DiLorenzo v. Edgar, 2004 WL 609374 *2 (D. Del. 2004).

43. *See* Fed. R. Civ. P. 23.1.

44. DiLorenzo v. Edgar, 2004 WL 609374 *2 (D. Del. 2004), quoting from Gollust v. Mendell, 501 U.S. 115, 125, 111 S.Ct. 2173, 115 L.Ed.2d 109 (1991).

46. Gollust v. Mendell, 501 U.S. 115, 111 S.Ct. 2173, 115 L.Ed.2d 109 (1991).

48. Magida v. Continental Can Co., 231 F.2d 843 (2d Cir.1956), *cert. denied* 351 U.S. 972, 76 S.Ct. 1031, 100 L.Ed. 1490 (1956).

49. *See* Super Stores, Inc. v. Reiner, 737 F.2d 962, 965 (11th Cir.1984).

54. Weisman v. Spector, 158 F.Supp 789 (S.D.N.Y.1958); Netter v. Ashland Paper Mills, Inc., 19 F.R.D. 529 (S.D.N.Y.1956).

62. Arbetman v. Playford, 83 F.Supp. 335 (S.D.N.Y.1949). *See also* Dottenheim v. Emerson Elec. Manufacturing Co., 7 F.R.D. 343 (E.D.N.Y.1947).

64. Tristar Corp. v. Freitas, 84 F.3d 550 (2d Cir.1996) (two-year period was tolled from time Form 4 filing became overdue until the date it was actually filed).

Section 16(b) Timing (the "Short Swing"[74])

Section 16(b) was intended to be straightforward in application, thus providing the predictability necessary for sound planning. However, the terms of the statute have given rise to much litigation. It is not always clear whether a particular person comes within the section's reach. Similarly it is frequently difficult to determine whether and when a purchase or sale occurs.[76] The computation of the six-month period has not escaped judicial scrutiny. It is clear that the prohibitions of section 16(b) extend to six months both prior and subsequent to the date of any particular transaction,[77] assuming, of course, that insider status attaches. Furthermore, the statute speaks in terms of a "period of *less* than six months" in which the transactions are prohibited and thus two transactions occurring within exactly six months of each other are not subject to section 16(b)'s disgorgement provisions.[78] In order to determine when a purchase or sale takes place, the courts look to the time at which the purchaser or seller became irrevocably obligated.[79] Thus, the relevant date is the date of the purchase even if there is a delayed date for issuing the securities, such as under an escrow arrangement.[80]

Determination of "Profit"

There has also been significant question as to the method of computing a "profit" within the meaning of section 16(b). Someone who sells stock and subsequently repurchases the amount sold for a lower price within a six-month period realizes a section 16(b) profit. One district court had held that in order for a court to require disgorgement, the defendant must have actually realized a profit rather than simply receiving an increase in value of shares held.[83] However, the Second Circuit reversed this ruling since the increase in value was due to sales by a corporation of shares that resulted in a profit within six months. Since the defendant owned all of the shares of the corporation that sold the shares in question, the defendant in fact benefited from the sale and realized the economic effects of a profit through the increase in value to the shares he owned in the selling corporation.[84]

Many courts have taken a broad view of what constitutes a section 16(b) "profit" when there have been a series of transactions within a six-month period. The apparent majority view is to match the lowest purchase price against the highest sales price within that period.[85] This method is the

---

74. Portnoy v. Seligman & Latz, Inc., 516 F.Supp. 1188, 1200 (S.D.N.Y.1981) ("It don't mean a thing if it ain't got that swing," quoting E.K. "Duke" Ellington).

76. *See* § 13.4 *infra.*

77. Gratz v. Claughton, 187 F.2d 46 (2d Cir.), *cert. denied* 341 U.S. 920, 71 S.Ct. 741, 95 L.Ed. 1353 (1951).

78. Morales v. Reading & Bates Offshore Drilling Co., 392 F.Supp. 41 (N.D.Okl.1975).

79. Riseman v. Orion Research, Inc., 749 F.2d 915 (1st Cir.1984); Seinfeld v. Hospital Corp. of America, 685 F.Supp. 1057 (N.D.Ill.1988).

80. *See* Dilorenzo v. Murphy, 322 F.Supp.2d 479, 481–482 (S.D.N.Y. 2004).

83. Feder v. Frost, 1999 WL 163174, 31 Sec. Reg. & L. Rep. (BNA) 465 (S.D.N.Y. 1999), reversed 220 F.3d 29 (2d Cir.2000).

84. Feder v. Frost, 220 F.3d 29 (2d Cir.2000).

85. Arrow Distributing Corp. v. Baumgartner, 783 F.2d 1274, 1277–78 (5th Cir.1986); Whittaker v. Whittaker Corp., 639 F.2d 516, 530–32 (9th Cir.1981), *cert. denied* 454 U.S. 1031, 102 S.Ct. 566, 70 L.Ed.2d 473 (1981); Gratz v. Claughton, 187 F.2d 46 (2d Cir.1951); Smolowe v. Delendo Corp., 136 F.2d 231 (2d Cir.1943), *cert. denied* 320 U.S. 751, 64 S.Ct. 56, 88 L.Ed. 446 (1943).

harsher of the alternative interpretations since it captures a "profit" even in situations where an out-of-pocket loss for all transactions entered into during the six-month period may exist.[86] There is a strong argument that this measure of damages is unnecessarily punitive and cannot be justified by section 16(b)'s remedial purpose. As is pointed out elsewhere,[87] punitive damages are generally not available in actions arising under the federal securities laws. Imposing liability for excess "profits" which in fact exceed actual profits can be viewed as unjustifiably punitive and thus contrary to the spirit of section 28(a) of the Exchange Act, which limits damages to actual damages.[88]

The matching problem described above applies only when there are multiple purchases and sales within a six month period. It does not arise when there is a series of purchases followed by a single sale (or vice versa). For example, when there are multiple purchases and one block sale, it is sufficient to simply aggregate the purchase price and then subtract the sum from the sale price.[89]

There is some authority to the effect that dividends declared on shares that are sold at a profit will be considered part of the section 16(b) profit, provided that the dividend recipient had insider status at the time of declaration of the dividend.[90] However, there is considerable authority to the contrary, holding that dividends are excluded from the section 16(b) computation absent evidence that the defendant manipulated the dividend.[91]

Difficult questions can arise concerning the computation of a profit when faced with transactions involving derivative securities. In 1991, the Commission addressed the computation of profits resulting from acquisitions and dispositions of derivative securities. If an acquisition of a derivative security is matched with the disposition of the same derivative security within a six-month period, the section 16(b) recovery is based on the profit received from the matching transactions.[96] If an acquisition or disposition of a derivative security is matched with a transaction in the underlying security or different derivative security, the maximum section 16(b) profit is based on the difference in the market value of the underlying security on the transaction dates, but the court may award a lesser recovery in the event the insider can demonstrate that the amount of profit was less.[97]

86. *See* Smolowe v. Delendo Corp., 136 F.2d 231, 239 (2d Cir 1943), *cert. denied* 320 U.S. 751, 64 S.Ct. 56, 88 L.Ed. 446 (1943); Feder v. Frost, 474 F.Supp.2d 520, 522–523 (S.D.N.Y. 2007).

87. *See* §§ 7.5, 7.8, 12.12 *supra.*

88. 15 U.S.C.A. § 78bb(a).

89. Mayer v. Chesapeake Ins. Co. Ltd., 877 F.2d 1154 (2d Cir.1989), *cert. denied* 493 U.S. 1021, 110 S.Ct. 722, 107 L.Ed.2d 741 (1990).

90. Western Auto Supply Co. v. Gamble–Skogmo, Inc., 348 F.2d 736 (8th Cir.1965), *cert. denied* 382 U.S. 987, 86 S.Ct. 556, 15 L.Ed.2d 475 (1966).

91. Blau v. Lamb, 363 F.2d 507, 528 (2d Cir.1966), *cert. denied* 385 U.S. 1002, 87 S.Ct. 707, 17 L.Ed.2d 542 (1967); Adler v. Klawans, 267 F.2d 840, 849 (2d Cir.1959); Morales v. Lukens, Inc., 593 F.Supp. 1209, 1214–15 (S D.N.Y.1984).

96. Rule 16b–6(c), 17 C.F.R. § 240.16b–6(c). *See also, e.g.,* At Home Corp. v. Cox Communications, Inc., 340 F.Supp.2d 404, 407 (S.D.N.Y. 2004) (the writing of a put option is "sale," and the "disposition of underlying securities at a fixed exercise price due to the exercise of a put equivalent position is exempt from the operation of section 16(b)") (quoting from 17 C.F.R. § 240.16b–6(b)).

97. Rule 16b–6(c), 17 C.F R. § 240.16b–6(c)(2).

Actual Use of Inside Information Not Necessary

In light of section 16(b)'s remedial and prophylactic purposes, it is not necessary that the defendant have utilized inside information in planning the transactions. Nor is it necessary that the transactions have resulted in injury to the issuer. The rule of the statute is absolute, imposing strict liability for short-swing profits by statutory insiders of Exchange Act reporting companies. Notwithstanding the clear congressional intent to provide a catch-all, prophylactic remedy, not requiring proof of actual misconduct,[106] the statute is not always strictly applied. When dealing with traditional cash-for-stock purchases and sales, the courts uniformly employ an objective approach, not looking beyond the terms of the statute. However, when faced with "unorthodox" transactions, the courts will look behind the transaction under a pragmatic mode of analysis.[108] Under the pragmatic approach courts will include or exclude unorthodox transactions from section 16(b)'s reach depending upon the presence or absence of the potential for speculative abuse. In any event, the section presents severe limitations on insider trading in stock subject to the Exchange Act's reporting requirements. To a large extent section 16(b) remains a trap for the unwary.

Equitable Defenses Rejected

The generally accepted rule is that equitable defenses will not defeat an action brought under section 16(b).[109] Thus, for example, equitable estoppel will not be a defense to a section 16(b) action.[110] *In pari delicto* is not a defense to section 16(b) liability.[111] Thus, the fact that the issuer has participated in the transaction does not preclude recovery,[112] even where the issuer may have been the impetus for the transaction.[113] As is the case with securities law claims generally,[114] waiver will not constitute a defense to section 16(b) liability. The anti-waiver provision does not apply to settlement of existing or threatened litigation.[116] Accordingly, release of liability under section 16 will be upheld if supported by valid consideration. However, if there is no knowledge of the section 16(b) liability at the time of the purported release, the waiver will not be effective.[117]

106. *See* Hearings on S.Res. 84, S.Res. 97 Before The Senate Comm. on Banking and Currency, 73d Cong., 1st Sess. pt. 15 at 6557 (1934).

108. *See* § 13.4 *infra.*

109. Texas International Airlines v. National Airlines, Inc., 714 F.2d 533, 536 (5th Cir.1983), *cert. denied* 465 U.S. 1052, 104 S.Ct. 1326, 79 L.Ed.2d 721 (1984); Roth v. Fund of Funds, Ltd., 405 F.2d 421, 422–23 (2d Cir.1968), *cert. denied* 394 U.S. 975, 89 S.Ct. 1469, 22 L.Ed.2d 754 (1969); Magida v. Continental Can Co., 231 F.2d 843, 846 (2d Cir.1956), *cert. denied* 351 U.S. 972, 76 S.Ct. 1031, 100 L.Ed. 1490 (1956).

110. *E.g.,* Texas International Airlines v. National Airlines, Inc., 714 F.2d 533, 536 (5th Cir.1983), *cert. denied* 465 U.S. 1052, 104 S.Ct. 1326, 79 L.Ed.2d 721 (1984).

111. *See, e.g.,* Donoghue v. Natural Microsystems Corp., 198 F.Supp.2d 487 (S.D.N.Y.2002).

112. *E.g.,* Texas International Airlines v. National Airlines, Inc., 714 F.2d 533, 536 (5th Cir.1983), *cert. denied* 465 U.S. 1052, 104 S.Ct. 1326, 79 L.Ed.2d 721 (1984).

113. *E.g.,* Roth v. Fund of Funds, Ltd., 405 F.2d 421, 422–23 (2d Cir.1968), *cert. denied* 394 U.S. 975, 89 S.Ct. 1469, 22 L.Ed.2d 754 (1969); Magida v. Continental Can Co., 231 F.2d 843, 846 (2d Cir.1956), *cert. denied* 351 U.S. 972, 76 S.Ct. 1031, 100 L.Ed. 1490 (1956).

114. *See* § 12.23 *supra.*

116. *See, e.g.,* Petro–Ventures, Inc. v. Takessian, 967 F.2d 1337 (9th Cir.1992).

117. Synalloy Corp. v. Gray, 816 F.Supp. 963 (D.Del.1993).

Exemptions From 16(b)'s Disgorgement Provisions

The SEC has provided a number of exemptions from section 16(b) liability. Section 16 does not apply to many foreign issuers.[120] Section 16(b) does not apply to transactions in registered investment company shares that are exempt from the Investment Company Act's short-swing prohibitions.[121]

Qualifying employee benefit plans, including those involving stock appreciation rights or phantom stock, may qualify for an exemption from section 16(b). SEC Rule 16b–3 divides employee benefit plan transactions into two principal categories: grant/award transactions and participant-directed transactions.[125] The grant and award of securities under qualifying plans are exempt so long as the securities are held for at least six months.[126] Shareholder approval continues to be a requirement for most exempt plans.[127] Rule 16b–3(d)(1) further provides that that stock transactions from an issuer to insiders "involving a grant, award or other acquisition" of issuer equity securities shall be exempt from Section 16(b) liability if the transaction is "approved by the board of directors of the issuer."[128] The fact that the option grants were improperly backdated does not render the director approval inoperative. And thus the Rule 16b–3(d) exemption remains available.[129] It is not necessary that each transaction be individually approved so long as the plan authorizing the transaction is approved by the board.[130]

Other exemptions from section 16(b) include securities acquired through certain issuer redemptions. There formerly was an exemption for redemption of other securities where the securities so acquired replace securities of an issuer whose assets consist of cash, government securities, and equity securities of the issuer whose securities were acquired.[131] The SEC rules continue the exemption for bona fide gifts[132] and inheritance.[133] Securities acquired in certain mergers also are exempt.[134] The SEC had indicated that Rule 16b–7's exemption is not limited to mergers and might also apply to other share exchanges effectuated through a statutory procedure.[135] This does not mean, however, that every reclassification is exempt under Rule 16b–7.[136] The court explained that the exemption applies to a limited number of transactions and only those where the acquiring company prior to the transaction owned eighty-five percent of the stock or assets of the company so acquired.[137] Rule

120. Many foreign private issuers are exempted by Rule 3a12–3(b), 17 C.F.R. § 240.3a12–3(b).

121. Rule 16b–1(a), 17 C.F.R. § 240.16b–1(a). *See* 15 U.S.C.A. § 80a–17(a).

125. *See* Sec.Exch.Act Rel. No. 34–28869, 1991 WL 292000, [1990–1991 Transfer Binder] Fed.Sec.L.Rep. (CCH) ¶ 84,709 (Feb. 8, 1991).

126. Rule 16b–3(d)(3), 17 C.F.R. § 240.16b–3(d)(3).

127. Sec.Exch.Act Rel. No. 34–28869, 1991 WL 292000, [1990–1991 Transfer Binder] Fed.Sec. L.Rep. (CCH) ¶ 84,709 (Feb. 8, 1991).

128. 17 C.F.R. § 240.16b–3(d)(1). *See* Dreiling v. American Express, Inc., 458 F.3d 942 (9th Cir. 2006) (upholding the SEC's authority to promulgate Rule 16b–3(d)).

129. Segen v. Rickey, 2008 WL 590505, Fed.Sec.L.Rep. ¶ 94,591, http://pubs.bna.com/ip/bna/sld.nsf/eh/A0B6E1J5P3 (N.D. Cal. 2008).

130. Gryl v. Shire Pharmaceuticals Group PLC, 298 F.3d 136 (2d Cir.2002).

131. Rule 16b–4, 17 C.F.R. § 240.16b–4.

132. *See* Dreiling v. Kellett, 281 F.Supp.2d 1215, 1224 (W.D. Wash. 2003) (gift exception to section 16 did not apply to transfer pursuant to escrow arrangement).

133. Rule 16b–5, 17 C.F.R. § 240.16b–5.

134. Rule 16b–7, 17 C.F.R. § 240.16b–7.

135. Interpretive Release on Rules Applicable to Insider Reporting and Trading, Exchange Act Release No. 34–18114, 46 Fed.Reg. 48147, 48176–77,1981 WL 31301 (Sept. 24, 1981).

136. Levy v. Sterling Holding Co., 314 F.3d 106 (3d Cir. 2002).

137. 314 F.3d at 114–115.

16b–7 was revised in 2005 to reject the disputed ruling and made it clear that the same conditions for exempting any merger or consolidation applies to a recapitalization—namely, that the company whose securities are being acquired or disposed of owns eighty-five percent or more of the all of the companies that are party to the transaction.[140]

Two additional exemptions are set forth in the statute. Section 16(d)[145] provides that bona fide market making transactions[146] are not subject to section 16(b), nor are they subject to section 16(a)'s reporting requirements[147] or section 16(c)'s prohibitions[148] regarding short sales and sales against the box. Section 16(e)[149] exempts from section 16 pure arbitrage transactions that are carried out in accordance with applicable SEC rules. SEC Rule 16e–1[150] exempts arbitrage transactions by ten percent beneficial owners who are not also officers and directors of the issuer, while officers' and directors' arbitrage transactions are subject to section 16(a) reporting and 16(b), disgorgement, but not to section 16(c)'s prohibitions against short sales and sales against the box.[151]

In addition to the foregoing exemptions from the disgorgement provisions, section 16(b) excludes from its coverage securities "acquired in good faith in connection with a debt previously contracted."[152] This exemption from section 16(b)'s coverage should be narrowly construed to avoid extending it to transactions where the potential for speculative abuse exists. The exemption accordingly does not apply to shares that were not necessary for retirement of the debt and thus were not directly attributable to the previously acquired debt.[153]

§ 13.3 Who Is Subject to Sections 16(a) and (b)? When Does Insider Status Attach?

Section 16(b)'s damage provisions, like section 16(a)'s filing requirements,[1] apply to officers, directors, and ten percent beneficial owners of any class of equity security subject to section 12's registration requirements.[2] Section 16 identifies three classes of persons whose relationship to the issuer is sufficiently close to conclusively presume access to inside information. The Act does not precisely define officer, director, or ten percent beneficial owner; and, as a result numerous questions have arisen as to the scope of section 16's coverage.

---

140. Ownership Reports and Trading by Officers, Directors And Principal Security Holders, Sec. Act Rel. No. 33–8600, Sec. Exch. Act Rel. No. 34–52202, Pub. Util. Holding Co. Act Rel. No. 35–28013, Inv. Co. Act Rel. No. IC–27025, 2005 WL 1843461 (SEC Aug. 3, 2005).

145. 15 U.S.C.A. § 78p(d). *See* § 12.7 *infra.*

146. Market makers are discussed in § 14.10 *infra.*

147. 15 U.S.C.A. § 78p(a). *See* § 13.1 *supra.*

148. 15 U.S.C.A. § 78p(c). *See* § 13.5 *infra.*

149. 15 U.S.C.A. § 78p(e). *See* § 12.7 *infra.*

150. 17 C.F.R. § 240.16e–1.

151. *See* § 12.7 *infra.*

152. 15 U.S.C.A. § 78p(b).

153. C.R.A. Realty Corp. v. Fremont General Corp., 5 F.3d 1341 (9th Cir.1993).

§ 13.3

1. 15 U.S.C.A. § 78p(a). *See* § 13.1 *supra.*

2. 15 U.S.C.A. § 78*l*. *See* § 9.2 *supra.*

Officers and Directors

For example, when dealing with a business trust or other unincorporated form of business association, does a trustee or partner qualify as a director under section 16? Presumably the issue would be approached by asking whether the person performs functions similar to those of a director. While there is no explicit definition of director under the Exchange Act, SEC Rule 16a–1(f) defines "officer" to include the president, principal executive and financial officers and other policymaking officers. Reasoning by analogy, "director" should include the functional equivalent regardless of title; this view is confirmed by other SEC rules.

When a person, although not holding a formal office, performs the functions of an officer and therefore has access to inside information, section 16(b) will require disgorgement of all short-swing profits.[6]

In the early cases defining "officer," the courts were faced with the issue of whether to subject a person not holding an officer's title to section 16(b) liability. In two subsequent cases the issue was whether a person, although denominated an officer by title, is properly treated as "officer" for purposes of section 16(b).

Deputization as the Basis of Insider Status

Another problem in determining who is subject to section 16(b) arises in the context of deputization. The Supreme Court has explained that where a partnership has profited from short-swing transactions in a corporation's stock and has designated or "deputized" one of its partners to sit on that corporation's board of directors, the partnership will be deemed to be a "director" under the doctrine of deputization.[23] Even in the absence of deputization, the director-partner's pro rata share of the partnership profits would necessarily have to be disgorged under section 16(b). The Court held that the mere possibility of inside information flowing to the partnership was not sufficient and gave the plaintiff the burden of proving an actual deputizing or agency relationship.[25]

The Second Circuit seems to have retreated from the Supreme Court's heavy burden of proof on the deputization issue. Where a corporation's president and chief executive officer sat on the issuer's board and where that person had a say in the corporation's investment interest, and further where the president resigned as a director of the issuer after the decision to sell within six months of a purchase, deputization was established and the corporation had to disgorge its short-swing profit.[26] The Second Circuit pointed out that although there was no actual proof of a formal or a de facto deputization, the corporation had a recurring pattern of placing a representative on the board of any company in which it owned a substantial number of shares. The defendant's representative on the issuer's board was not only its president and chief executive officer but also had participated in discussions with other corporate personnel about its investment holdings. Deputization was found notwithstanding the lack of evidence of any actual communication

6. Colby v. Klune, 178 F.2d 872, 873 (2d Cir.1949).

23. Blau v. Lehman, 368 U.S. 403, 82 S.Ct. 451, 7 L.Ed.2d 403 (1962).

25. Id.

26. Feder v. Martin Marietta Corp., 406 F.2d 260 (2d Cir.1969), *cert. denied* 396 U.S. 1036, 90 S.Ct. 678, 24 L.Ed.2d 681 (1970).

of inside information since the potential for abuse was more than a mere possibility. The Second Circuit's approach was quite realistic, given the circumstances surrounding the case.

Although it is clear that the mere presence of an interlocking director will not be sufficient to create a section 16(b) deputization,[28] the subjective or case-by-case nature of analysis means that each situation must be determined on its own facts.

Family Relationships

Somewhat akin to the question of deputization is the question whether a spouse's holdings are to be attributed to the other spouse who is a section 16(b) insider. In one case,[36] it was held that a wife's sales were to be matched against her husband's exercise of stock options where the husband was a director. The husband/director did not control the wife's investments; the couple maintained separate brokerage accounts but engaged in joint estate planning. The court reasoned that the wife, by virtue of her relationship and investment related conversations with her husband, had access to inside information. Federal rather than state law determines the question of beneficial ownership with regard to securities held by husband and wife.[37]

With regard to stock held by a spouse or child of an insider or trusts for either, the Seventh Circuit has required a "direct pecuniary benefit" to the insider in order to find section 16(b) liability. "[T]ies of consanguinity," "an enhanced sense of well-being" or the insider's being "led to reduce his gift giving" to the stock owner or its beneficiary will not alone lead to attribution under section 16(b).[38] Reading these two cases together, the courts quite properly will attribute beneficial ownership when it appears that the potential for speculative abuse exists.

Timing and Director or Officer Liability; Effect of Resignation

Another question under section 16 is the effect of the timing of the transactions with regard to an officer's or a director's assumption of office or resignation. For example, it has been held that a director who resigned prior to a sale at a profit within six months of his purchase was held subject to section 16(b).[39] Similarly, it was held that section 16(b) liability attaches to a short-swing profit where the defendant became an officer after his purchase but prior to his sale within six months of the purchase.[40] Notwithstanding some dicta to the contrary,[41] these rulings still had substantial following until subsequent SEC rulemaking.[42] Rule 16a–2 provides that under most circum-

28. *See* Popkin v. Dingman, 366 F.Supp. 534 (S.D.N.Y.1973).

36. Whiting v. Dow Chemical Co., 523 F.2d 680 (2d Cir.1975).

37. Walet v. Jefferson Lake Sulphur Co., 202 F.2d 433 (5th Cir.1953), *cert. denied* 346 U.S. 820, 74 S.Ct. 35, 98 L.Ed. 346 (1953).

38. C.B.I. Industries, Inc. v. Horton, 682 F.2d 643, 646–47 (7th Cir.1982).

39. Feder v. Martin Marietta Corp., 406 F.2d 260 (2d Cir.1969), *cert. denied* 396 U.S. 1036, 90 S.Ct. 678, 24 L.Ed.2d 681 (1970).

40. Adler v. Klawans, 267 F.2d 840 (2d Cir.1959); Marquette Cement Manufacturing Co. v. Andreas, 239 F.Supp. 962 (S.D.N.Y.1965).

41. Allis–Chalmers Manufacturing Co. v. Gulf & Western Industries, Inc., 527 F.2d 335, 346–348 (7th Cir.1975), *cert. denied* 423 U.S. 1078, 96 S.Ct. 865, 47 L.Ed.2d 89 (1976).

42. *See* Foremost–McKesson, Inc. v. Provident Securities Co., 423 U.S. 232, 243, n. 16, 96 S.Ct. 508, 515, n. 16, 46 L.Ed.2d 464 (1976).

stances, transactions effectuated by an officer or director prior to becoming subject to section 16(a)'s reporting requirements are not subject to section 16.[43] The only instance in which the reporting requirements apply to this period is when the reporting obligation began as a result of the issuer's having to comply with section 12's registration requirements.[44] Accordingly, when the reporting requirements are occasioned by the appointment or election to office, transactions occurring prior to the appointment or election need not be reported. At least one court has held that this carries over to liability under section 16(b).[45] Accordingly, it was held that shares acquired prior to the defendant becoming a director were not subject to section 16 (b) scrutiny.[46] The SEC rules go on to clarify that officers and directors remain subject to section 16's requirements for the six months following the last sale before cessation of officer or director status.[47]

Who Is a Ten Percent Beneficial Owner?

In order to be found to be a beneficial owner of the stock, the purported owner was required by the cases to have a direct pecuniary interest in those shares.[52] The SEC rules define who is considered a beneficial owner, for the purpose of matching purchases and sales, and include in the definition of beneficial owner anyone who has a direct or indirect pecuniary interest.[54] Courts have extended to concept of beneficial ownership to a group owning more than ten percent in the aggregate and that has agreed to act together in exercising control.[55] This interpretation is consistent with the purposes underlying section 16(b).

What happens if the owner is not made aware that his or her holdings have crossed the ten percent threshold? Especially in the case of issuers who periodically repurchase their shares, the threshold can be a moving target. If an owner is not at least put on inquiry notice that his or her holdings have reached the threshold, then there should be no section 16(b) liability until those facts come to light.[56] In contrast to the cases dealing with officers and directors, section 16(b) on its face provides that where insider status attaches by virtue of ten percent beneficial equity ownership, the section applies only where such person was a beneficial owner "both at the time of the purchase and sale, or the sale and purchase."[57] Notwithstanding some lower court decisions to the contrary,[58] the Supreme Court held that the threshold purchase that pushes the defendant over ten percent beneficial ownership

43. 17 C.F.R. § 240.16a–2.

44. 17 C.F.R. § 240.16a–2(a).

45. Gryl v. Shire Pharmaceuticals Group PLC, 298 F.3d 136 (2d Cir.2002) *affirming* 33 Sec. Reg. & L. Rep. (BNA) 1366 (S.D.N.Y.2001).

46. Gryl v. Shire Pharmaceuticals Group PLC, 298 F.3d 136 (2d Cir.2002) *affirming* 33 Sec. Reg. & L. Rep. (BNA) 1366 (S.D.N.Y.2001).

47. 17 C.F.R. § 240.16a–2(b).

52. Mayer v. Chesapeake Ins. Co., 877 F.2d 1154, 1160 (2d Cir.1989), *cert. denied* 493 U.S. 1021, 110 S.Ct. 722, 107 L.Ed.2d 741 (1990).

54. Rule 16a–1(a)(2), 17 C.F.R. § 240.16a–1(a)(2).

55. *See, e.g.*, Morales v. Freund, 163 F.3d 763 (2d Cir.1999).

56. C.R.A. Realty Corp. v. Enron Corp., 842 F.Supp. 88 (S.D.N.Y.1994).

57. 15 U.S.C.A. § 78p(b).

58. *E.g.* Stella v. Graham–Paige Motors Corp., 104 F.Supp. 957 (S.D.N.Y.1952), *affirmed in part and reversed in part* 232 F.2d 299 (2d Cir.1956), *cert. denied* 352 U.S. 831, 77 S.Ct. 46, 1 L.Ed.2d 52 (1956).

does not qualify as a "purchase" subject to section 16(b) and that only purchases made after that date will give rise to liability when matched with subsequent sales occurring within six months and resulting in a profit.[60] Thus, the initial purchase that places a non-officer or director shareholder over the ten percent threshold is a "lock-in event" that only gives rise to short-swing liability with respect to additional shares.[61]

In another case,[63] the Court held that where a ten percent beneficial owner first sells just enough shares to put him below the ten percent threshold, and on the next day liquidates the remainder of his holdings, the second sale cannot be subject to section 16(b) because of the statute's express "at the time of" requirement. This ruling was based on an objective reading of the statute rather than a subjective evaluation of the statutory insider's motives in so structuring the two-step sale.

Group Theory and Beneficial Ownership

As discussed in an earlier section of this treatise, when a group of shareholders agree to act together to exercise control, they are treated as a "group" and thus subject to the filing requirements of section 13(d) if their aggregate holdings exceed five percent of a class of equity securities[67] (as compared to section 16's ten percent threshold): This rationale has been extended to section 16(b). In Morales v. Freund,[68] the Second Circuit affirmed a finding that a group of shareholders acting together would be classified as a group and thus as a beneficial owner subject to section 16(b)'s disgorgement requirements. The court reasoned that the application of "group" analysis to the provisions of section 16 is consistent with the purposes of the Act. It certainly is true that if the statute presumes access to inside information because one person owns ten percent of a class of equity securities, that a group acting in concert should also be presumed to have the same access. However, a strict reading of the statutory language may lead to a different result. Section 16 of the Act defines beneficial owner in terms of "every *person* who is directly or indirectly the beneficial owner of more than 10 per centum of any class of equity security."[69]

The existence of a group depends upon a finding that the shareholders comprising the group had an agreement to acquire, hold, or dispose of the securities in question[75] or, alternatively, to exert control over the issuer of the securities.[76] The existence of a group depends an agreement among the group members concerning the control of the shares. As such, the existence of a group will often depend upon findings of fact and thus often will not be appropriate for determination on a motion to dismiss. Section 16(b) liability will attach to transactions occurring after the group has been formed but not

60. Foremost–McKesson, Inc. v. Provident Securities Co., 423 U.S. 232, 96 S.Ct. 508, 46 L.Ed.2d 464 (1976).

61. Schaffer ex rel. Lasersight, Inc. v. CC Investments, LDC., 2003 WL 22480052 (S.D.N.Y. 2003).

63. Reliance Electric Co. v. Emerson Electric Co., 404 U.S. 418, 92 S.Ct. 596, 30 L.Ed.2d 575 (1972).

67. 15 U.S.C.A. § 78m(d). *See* § 11.2 *supra.*

68. 163 F.3d 763 (2d Cir.1999).

69. 15 U.S.C.A. § 78p(a) (emphasis supplied).

75. *See* Litzler v. CC Investments, L.D.C., 411 F.Supp.2d 411 (S.D.N.Y. 2006).

76. Morales v. Quintel Entertainment, Inc., 249 F.3d 115 (2d Cir.2001).

with regard to transactions occurring contemporaneously with the group's formation.[78] A district court has held that the fact that some members of the group are exempt from section 16 will not provide an exemption unless each member of the group qualifies for an exemption.[79]

Convertible Securities

What about convertible securities? The convertible securities do not themselves qualify as a separate class of equity securities, so that ownership of ten percent of the convertible securities will not classify the holder as a ten percent beneficial owner unless it can be said that he or she is a ten percent owner of the underlying security, assuming full dilution.[92] The owner of convertible securities becomes a ten percent beneficial owner with regard to the underlying securities when his or her ownership of the underlying securities if his or her conversion rights were exercised would result in ten percent ownership of the underlying security.[93] Once that threshold is crossed, if the owner converts and then sells the underlying shares within six months, it has been held that the conversion will count as a section 16(b) purchase that can be matched against a subsequent sale within six months for the purpose of finding a section 16(b) profit.[94]

§ 13.4 The Definition of "Purchase" and "Sale" and the Pragmatic Approach Under Section 16(b)[1]

Following the same pattern as section 2(a)(3) of the 1933 Act's definition of "sale,"[2] section 3(a)(13) of the 1934 Act defines "purchase" to "include any contract to buy, purchase, or otherwise acquire."[3] The definition is not limited to normal day-to-day cash for stock transactions. Accordingly courts have had to decide whether other transactions such as exercise of stock options or conversion rights and exchanges of securities pursuant to a merger—so called "unorthodox transactions"[4]—fall within section 16(b)'s reach.

A number of early section 16(b) cases raised the question of whether a voluntary conversion of stock constituted a purchase of the new security or, alternatively, a sale of the convertible security, so as to have section 16(b)

78. Rosenberg v. XM Ventures, 129 F.Supp.2d 681 (D.Del.2001).

79. Strauss v. Kopp Investment Advisors, Inc., 1999 WL 787818, [1999–2000 Transfer Binder] Fed. Sec. L. Rep. (CCH) ¶ 90,656 (S.D.N.Y.1999).

92. Medtox Scientific, Inc. v. Morgan Capital, L.L.C., 258 F.3d 763 (8th Cir.2001) *affirming* 50 F.Supp.2d 896 (D.Minn.1999); Chemical Fund, Inc. v. Xerox Corp., 377 F.2d 107 (2d Cir.1967).

93. Medtox Scientific, Inc. v. Morgan Capital, L.L.C., 258 F.3d 763 (8th Cir. 2001) *affirming* 50 F.Supp.2d 896 (D.Minn.1999). *But see,* Levy v. Oz Master Fund, Ltd., 2001 WL 767013, [2001–2002 Transfer Binder] Fed. Sec. L. Rep. (CCH) ¶ 91,503 (S.D.N.Y. 2001) (defendant was not beneficial owner at the time of purchase).

94. Medtox Scientific, Inc. v. Morgan Capital, L.L.C., 258 F.3d 763 (8th Cir. 2001), *affirming* 50 F.Supp.2d 896 (D. Minn. 1999).

§ 13.4

1. Parts of this section were adapted from Thomas L. Hazen, The New Pragmatism Under Section 16(b) of the Securities Exchange Act, 54 N.C.L.Rev. 1 (1975).

2. 15 U.S.C.A. § 77b(a)(3).

3. 15 U.S.C.A. § 78c(a)(13).

4. The term "unorthodox" has been "applied to stock conversions, exchanges pursuant to mergers and other corporate reorganizations, stock reclassifications, and dealings in options, rights and warrants." Kern County Land Co. v. Occidental Petroleum Corp., 411 U.S. 582, 594, n. 24, 93 S.Ct. 1736, 1744, n. 24, 36 L.Ed.2d 503 (1973).

consequences. The cases were in conflict,[5] although they tended not to find a purchase or sale unless the surrounding circumstances created a potential for the type of speculative abuse that section 16(b) was designed to prevent. It was out of the conversion cases that the pragmatic or subjective trend arose, with the courts looking at the facts to determine if section 16 evils were present.

The opportunity to realize a profit begins the moment an insider purchases or is granted a derivative security. It follows that the acquisition of a derivative security not only is a reportable event under section 16(a),[11] it can be matched against dispositions of either the derivative or underlying security occurring within the preceding or following six months.[12] Thus for example, an acquisition of a call option may be matched with any disposition of either the underlying security or other equivalent call option.[13] Conversely, an acquisition of a put option may be matched with an acquisition of the underlying security or disposition of an equivalent put position.[14] Just as acquisitions of derivative securities are reportable and matchable events, dispositions of derivative securities have similar section 16 implications.[15] However, the exercise of the option at a fixed exercise price is neither a sale nor purchase for section 16 purposes.[16]

In the leading case of Kern County Land Co. v. Occidental Petroleum Corp.,[25] the Supreme Court addressed the applicability of section 16(b) to sales of the target company's shares by a defeated tender offeror. The management of Kern, the target company, had opposed the takeover by defendant Occidental, and within two weeks responded with a defensive stock for stock merger with Tenneco. Rather than sell its holdings immediately, two weeks after approval of the merger, Occidental entered into an agreement with Tenneco to issue to Tenneco an option to purchase the Tenneco preferred shares received pursuant to the merger in six months at one hundred and five dollars per share. In return, Tenneco agreed to pay Occidental a premium of ten dollars per option which would be applied to the exercise price. More than six months after both Occidental's purchase of the Old Kern stock and its acquisition via the exchange of the Tenneco stock,[26] Tenneco exercised the

---

5. *Compare, e.g.,* Heli–Coil Corp. v. Webster, 352 F.2d 156 (3d Cir.1965) (conversion is a section 16(b) purchase; applying objective test) *with* Petteys v. Butler, 367 F.2d 528 (8th Cir.1966), *cert. denied* 385 U.S. 1006, 87 S.Ct. 712, 17 L.Ed.2d 545 (1967) (finding no purchase, utilizing "pragmatic" analysis).

11. Rule 16a–4(a), 17 C.F.R. § 240.16a–4(a).

12. Rule 16a–6(a), 17 C.F.R. § 240.16b–6(a).

13. Sec.Exch.Act Rel. No. 34–28869, 1991 WL 292000, [1990–1991 Transfer Binder] Fed.Sec. L.Rep. (CCH) ¶ 84,709 (Feb. 8, 1991).

14. *Id.*

15. Thus, for example, dispositions of call positions may be matched against acquisitions of the underlying security or acquisitions of another call equivalent position. Similarly, dispositions of put positions may be matched against dispositions of the underlying security or call equivalent positions of the underlying security. *Id.*

16. 17 C.F.R. § 240.16b–6. *See, e.g.,* At Home Corp. v. Cox Communications, Inc., 446 F.3d 403 (2d Cir. 2006), *affirming*, 340 F.Supp.2d 404 (S.D.N.Y. 2004) (the writing of a put option is "sale," and the "disposition of underlying securities at a fixed exercise price due to the exercise of a put equivalent position is exempt from the operation of section 16(b)") (quoting from 17 C.F.R. § 240.16b–6(b)).

25. 411 U.S. 582, 93 S.Ct. 1736, 36 L.Ed.2d 503 (1973).

26. As a holder of Kern stock under the merger, Occidental received shares of Tenneco, one of its largest competitors.

option. The district court held that Occidental's acquisition of Tenneco stock pursuant to the Old Kern–Tenneco merger was a section 16(b) "sale" within six months of its Kern purchases pursuant to the original tender offer, and further that the subsequent option agreement was a "sale" of the revised securities and thus also within the reach of section 16(b).[27] The Second Circuit reversed since, *inter alia,* Occidental's obligation to dispose of the shares had not been fixed until Tenneco exercised the option more than six months after the purchase.

The Supreme Court affirmed the Second Circuit's ruling and its adherence to a pragmatic analysis of the transaction:

> In deciding whether borderline [unorthodox] transactions are within the reach of the statute, the courts have come to inquire whether the transaction may serve as a vehicle for the evil which Congress sought to prevent—the realization of short-swing profits based upon access to inside information—thereby endeavoring to implement congressional objectives without extending the reach of the statute beyond its intended limits.[29]

The Court's opinion recognized that Occidental was in a very difficult position at the time that the Old Kern–Tenneco merger had been announced since the only realistic alternative to participating in the exchange and subsequent sale to Tenneco would have been to dispose of the Old Kern stock on the open market via a garden variety cash-for-stock sale which clearly would have resulted in certain 16(b) liability.

Proceeding on the theory that there had not been a statutory sale by virtue of the share exchange, the next question for decision was whether Occidental "sold" its new Tenneco shares on the date of the option agreement or at the later date it was exercised. The Court reasoned that Occidental's obligation to dispose of the stock did not become fixed until Tenneco's exercise of the option on December 11. The Court also pointed out that as of June 2, Occidental had not locked in a profit since, had the stock price declined sufficiently in value by the exercise date, the defendant would have been left with Tenneco holdings worth less than the "purchase" price, notwithstanding the option premium.[31] Although this pragmatic analysis creates some uncertainty in the section 16(b) analysis, it gives the courts the ability to achieve the statute's purpose.[32]

The apex of the pragmatic approach was achieved by the Fourth Circuit in Gold v. Sloan[33] where the court held one selling director liable under section 16(b) while exonerating three others. The issue was whether an exchange of stock pursuant to a merger between the Atlantic Research and Susquehanna corporations constituted a "purchase" under 16(b).[34] Within less

---

27. Abrams v. Occidental Petroleum Corp., 323 F.Supp. 570, 579–80 (S.D.N.Y.1970), *reversed* 450 F.2d 157 (2d Cir.1971).

29. 411 U.S. at 594–95, 93 S.Ct. at 1744–45 (footnotes omitted).

31. 411 U.S. at 602, 93 S.Ct. at 1748.

32. *See* Transcontinental Realty Investors, Inc. v. Gotham Partners, L.P., 218 F.Supp.2d 415 (S.D.N.Y. 2002) (option arrangement was unorthodox transaction but was not subject to speculative abuse).

33. 486 F.2d 340 (4th Cir.1973), *cert. denied* 419 U.S. 873, 95 S.Ct. 134, 42 L.Ed.2d 112 (1974).

34. Atlantic Research Corporation had merged into the Susquehanna Corporation via an exchange of stock; the defendants in *Gold* had been holders of Atlantic stock for more than six

than six months after the merger had been consummated, the defendant insiders sold their newly acquired Susquehanna holdings at a profit. The Fourth Circuit pointed to the Supreme Court's decision in *Kern County* as having "resolved [the] conflict and adopted what had earlier been described as a 'pragmatic rather than technical' test"[35] for unorthodox transactions. It was thus necessary "to examine the particular situation of each defendant as it relates to the merger."[36] Three of the defendants had no contact whatsoever with the merger negotiations and thus were held to have had no access to Susquehanna's inside information.[37] In contrast, the fourth defendant, Atlantic's chief executive officer, had been "in complete charge of the negotiations" and "had access to the books and records * * *."[38] Accordingly, this access created a potential for abuse and thus warranted finding the merger exchange to have been a section 16(b) purchase by the inside director. Although certainly consistent with the Supreme Court's rationale in *Kern,* the *Gold* decision has been criticized as running contrary to the straightforward, crude rule of thumb that section 16(b) was designed to provide.[39] Critics of the *Gold* decision were particularly upset with the ruling that the same transaction produces differing treatment for individuals falling within the statute's objective reach. However, the pragmatic trend continued to flourish.[40]

Involuntariness is an important element of an unorthodox transaction. Therefore, since a sale pursuant to a tender offer is not involuntary, section 16(b) applies to an exchange offer.[62] Furthermore, since a sale pursuant to a *cash* tender offer is equally voluntary, the pragmatic analysis would be equally inapplicable.

§ 13.5 Prohibitions Against Short Sales by Insiders—Section 16(c)

Section 16(c) of the Exchange Act[1] prohibits certain speculative activity by insiders who must file reports under the reporting provisions of section 16(a)[2] (*i.e.*, officers, directors, and ten percent beneficial owners of any class of

months prior to the merger negotiations, thus eliminating the problem of whether the exchange was a section 16(b) "sale," which had been dealt with in the *Kern County* decision. The defendants were also officers and directors of Atlantic and under the terms of the merger agreement occupied similar positions with respect to Susquehanna, the surviving corporation.

35. 486 F.2d at 343.

36. 486 F.2d at 344.

37. 486 F.2d at 344. *Accord* Heublein, Inc. v. General Cinema Corp., 559 F.Supp. 692 (S.D.N.Y.1983), *affirmed* 722 F.2d 29 (2d Cir.1983).

38. 486 F.2d at 351–52. *Accord* Colan v. Cutler–Hammer, Inc., 516 F.Supp. 1342 (N.D.Ill. 1981).

39. *See. e.g.,* Note, Securities Exchange Act § 16(b): Fourth Circuit Harvests Some Kernels of Gold, 42 Fordham L.Rev. 852 (1974); Recent Developments, Securities-' 16(b)-Mergers as a "Purchase," 20 Wayne L.Rev. 1415 (1974).

40. *See, e.g.,* Portnoy v. Revlon, Inc., 650 F.2d 895 (7th Cir.1981) (finding no sale in merger agreement); Heublein, Inc. v. General Cinema Corp., 559 F.Supp. 692 (S.D.N.Y.1983) (no sale in defensive merger), *affirmed* 722 F.2d 29 (2d Cir.1983); Reece Corp. v. Walco National Corp., 565 F.Supp. 158 (S.D.N.Y.1981) (two-step transaction treated as one "sale" in violation of § 16(b)); Colan v. Cutler–Hammer, Inc., 516 F.Supp. 1342 (N.D.Ill.1981) (finding a sale pursuant to a merger, following the rationale of Gold).

62. Colan v. Mesa Petroleum Co., 941 F.2d 933 (9th Cir.1991), *amended* 951 F.2d 1512 (9th Cir.1991), *cert. denied* 504 U.S. 911, 112 S.Ct. 1943, 118 L.Ed.2d 548 (1992).

§ 13.5

1. 15 U.S.C.A. § 78p(c).

2. 15 U.S.C.A. § 78p(a). *See* § 13.1 *supra.*

equity securities subject to the Exchange Act's reporting requirements).[3] The section is aimed at two types of speculative transactions: (1) short sales,[4] or selling the security of the issuer without owning the underlying security, and (2) sales against the box,[5] where the seller delays in delivering the securities. In both instances, the investor's hope is that the price will decline from the time of sale, thus enabling the seller to cover at a lower price. Both short sales and sales against the box are permissible trades, provided there is compliance with the applicable SEC rules[7] and margin requirements.[8] Both short sales and sales against the box present the potential for speculative abuse where the seller has access to inside information and thus both are prohibited by section 16(c) just as short-swing profits based on long positions in securities must be disgorged under section 16(b).[9] It has been held that the section applies only to shares beneficially owned by the insider, but not to shares sold by an insider acting merely as an agent for the true owners.[10]

Section 16(c) operates to make it unlawful to sell the security if the selling insider either (1) does not own the security or (2) if he or she owns the security but does not deliver it within twenty days or deposit it in the mail within five days. The section provides that "no person shall be deemed to have violated this subsection if he proves that notwithstanding the exercise of good faith he was unable to make such delivery or deposit within such time, or that to do so would cause undue inconvenience or expense."[11]

Although they are certainly legitimate speculating devices in certain instances, the practices of selling short[12] and selling against the box are high risk transactions which, as in the case with the short-swing profit,[13] are subject to speculative abuse and are therefore declared improper for insiders.[14] It has been held that section 16(c) was not intended to create a private remedy parallel to the one provided by section 16(b).[15]

3. 15 U.S.C.A. § 78*l*. *See* § 9.2 *supra*.

4. Short sale: When a seller believes the price of a stock will fall, he or she borrows stock from a lender and sells the borrowed shares to the buyer. Later, he or she buys similar stock to pay back the lender, hopefully at a lower price than he or she received on sale to the buyer. Short sales are discussed in § 14.22 *infra*.

5. Sale against the box: When the seller anticipates a decline in the price of stock he or she owns, he or she will sell it to a buyer at the present market price, but deliver it later, when hopefully the market price will have fallen below the sales price, thus creating a paper profit for the seller.

7. Short sales are subject to Regulation SHO, *See* 17 C.F.R. §§ 242.201 *et seq.*; Short Sales, Sec. Exch. Act Rel. No. 34–50103,2004 WL 1697019 (SEC 2004) (adoption of Regulation SHO). *See* § 14.22 *infra*.

8. The margin requirements address the extension of credit for securities transactions. *See* § 14.9 *infra*. It is clearly unlawful to enter a sell order without owning the underlying security in the absence of full disclosure. *See* United States v. Naftalin, 441 U.S. 768, 99 S.Ct. 2077, 60 L.Ed.2d 624 (1979).

9. *See* § 13.2 *supra*.

10. Rogers v. Valentine, 306 F.Supp. 34 (S.D.N.Y.1969), *affirmed* 426 F.2d 1361 (2d Cir.1970).

11. 15 U.S.C.A. § 78p(c). *See* Fuller v. Dilbert, 244 F.Supp 196 (S.D.N.Y.1965), *affirmed sub nom.* Righter v. Dilbert, 358 F.2d 305 (2d Cir.1966) (seller showed inconvenience).

12. *See, e.g.,* Short Sales, Sec. Exch. Act Rel. No. 34–50103, 2004 WL 1697019 (SEC 2004) (adopting Regulation SHO that regulates short sales generally)

13. 15 U.S.C.A. § 78p(b). *See* §§ 13.1–13.4 *supra*.

14. 15 U.S.C.A. § 78p(c).

15. Executive Telecard, Ltd. v. Mayer, 941 F.Supp. 435 (S.D.N.Y.1996).

The SEC clarified the treatment of derivative securities for the purposes of section 16(c)'s short sale prohibitions. Rule 16c–4[22] provides that establishing or increasing a put equivalent position is exempt from section 16(c) so long as it is a covered position (the put position does not exceed the amount of underlying securities owned). This exemption makes clear that an uncovered put equivalent should be treated as a short sale, as, at least in the context of section 16(c)'s prohibitions, an uncovered put option is functionally equivalent from an investment standpoint.[24]

22. 17 C.F.R. § 240.16c–4.

24. *But cf.* Baker Botts, LLP, 32 Sec. Reg. & L. Rep. (BNA) 1009, 2000 WL 972990 (SEC No Action Letter July 13, 2000) (expiration of put option more than six months after it was written does not violate section 16(b); there was no mention of any impact of section 16(c)'s prohibition against insider short sales).

Chapter 14

MARKET REGULATION AND BROKER–DEALER REGULATION

Table of Sections

---

§ 14.1 Market Regulation—An Overview

Regulation of securities brokers is not new. Securities broker regulation can be traced back to the thirteenth century. This early regulation took the form of licensing securities brokers in London.[1] Notwithstanding this regulatory structure, stock exchange dealings, with speculation subject to alternate booms and panics, became a part of the English markets in the latter part of the seventeenth century. There were periods of speculation and wild fluctuations in the market.[2] This was followed by English legislation by the end of the seventeenth century, which was enacted to protect investors against unscrupulous manipulation by stock jobbers and stock brokers.[4] Many of the U.S. states adopted similar stock jobber and stock broker regulation. For example, in 1829, in reaction to speculative fever, New York enacted a Stock Jobbing Act[5] which was designed to control "the more shadowy forms of financial speculation."[6] This and similar legislation proved to be ineffective, and there was no comprehensive regulation of securities brokers in this country until the adoption of the Securities Exchange Act of 1934. Among other things, the Exchange Act created the SEC and charged this federal agency with regulating the securities markets. As discussed in the sections that follow, over the years this has developed into a comprehensive system of SEC regulation and self regulation by the securities exchanges and the Financial Industry Regulatory Authority (FINRA). Although the self-regulatory system was once fragmented with each SRO having its own regulatory arm, FINRA is now in the process of compiling a consolidated rule book.[8] Until that process is completed, preexisting NASD Regulation (NASDR) and New York Stock Exchange Regulation (NYSER) rules remain in effect.

§ 14.1[1] How the Securities Markets Operate—An Overview

SEC regulation is supplemented by its oversight of the self-regulatory organizations (SROs). An exchange is a securities market that is formally organized as an exchange in contrast to the "over-the-counter" markets which is a term that describes the trading of securities other than on a formal centralized exchange. At one time there were two major stock exchanges—The New York Stock Exchange and the American Stock Exchange—and several regional stock exchanges. In addition to exchange-traded securities, there is the over-the-counter market where non-exchange listed securities are traded. At one time, most "prestige" securities were traded on the New York Exchange, or "big board" which carries the most prestige of the United States securities markets. One reason for the higher prestige of the New York Stock Exchange is the listing requirements for securities, with the New York's listing standards being more difficult for a company to satisfy.[12] Over the years, the over-the-counter markets gained in their prestige and today many

§ 14.1

1. Statute of Edward I, in 1285.

2. Promoters of both incorporated and unincorporated companies foisted doubtful schemes on the investing public. *See* 1 James D. Cox & Thomas Lee Hazen Cox & Hazen on Corporations § 2.2 (3d ed. 2002).

4. 8 & 9 Wm. 3, ch. 32 (1697) ("An act to restrain the number and ill practice of brokers and stock jobbers").

5. Stock Jobbing Act, 1 N.Y. REV. STAT. 710, tit. 19, art. 2, § 6 (1829)

6. See The Development of the Law of Gambling 1776–1976 150 (National Institute for Law Enforcement and Criminal Justice Grant No. 74–NI–99–0030, Nov. 1977).

8. *See* FINRA Information Notice, Rulebook Consolidation Process, 2008 WL 698461, http://www.finra.org/web/groups/rules_regs/documents/notice_to_members/p038121.pdf (FINRA March 12, 2008).

12. *See e.g.,* New York Stock Exchange Manual.

"blue chip" companies in the technology field are traded in the Nasdaq market. Microsoft and Intel are two notable examples.

There are also seven regional exchanges which at one time only traded secondary stocks and provided regional trading for New York and American Exchange listed securities. Today some of the regional exchanges such as the Chicago, Pacific, and Philadelphia exchanges are major centers for options trading.

An exchange, as the name implies, provides a central clearing house for the trading of its listed securities. Originally all transactions took place physically on the floor of the exchange. While this in large part is still true today, there has been some movement towards more of a national market system with automated quotations and a consolidated tape reflecting all transactions and volume whether or not the transactions are made on the exchange floor. Trading on the exchange floor is carried out by "specialists" in each listed security, whose job it is to help maintain an orderly market.[16] By the end of the twentieth century, the mechanics of many trading processes had been automated and computerized. As pointed out below, Nasdaq has registered its stock market as a national securities exchange.

Securities not traded on one or more of the national exchanges are traded in the over-the-counter markets which are coordinated by FINRA (formerly the NASD) and operated through Nasdaq. There is no central exchange floor but merely a matching of bid and asked quotes for each security. The matching of these offers to buy and offers to sell securities is carried out by market-makers with respect to each security. With its national market quotation system, Nasdaq has moved toward a national market system.[20] This national market system has been successful in keeping many companies in the over-the-counter markets that in the past would have moved to the New York Stock Exchange. Until 2006, the Nasdaq National Stock Market was part of the over-the-counter markets since it was not a national securities exchange as that term is used in the 1934 Act. In January 2006, the SEC approved the Nasdaq Stock Market's application to be registered as a national securities exchange.[22] The Nasdaq national market thus is now a national securities exchange. As of July 1, 2006, there are now three tiers (Global Select, Global Market and National Market) rather than the two tiers (NMS and Small Cap) of Nasdaq securities that formerly existed. In another attempt to strengthen its competitive position, the NASD, through Nasdaq, acquired the American Stock Exchange. The exchange was acquired by the NASD but as a subsidiary and continued to be operated as a separate entity. In 2003, the NASD entered into an agreement to sell the American Stock Exchange to GTCR Golder Rauner LLC (GTCR), a Chicago-based private equity firm.[23] Notwithstanding this short-lived acquisition of the American Stock Exchange, which has since

---

16. *See* § 14.11 *infra.* Specialists, who are also known as downstairs or floor brokers, do not have a retail business. Compare market makers in the over-the-counter and Nasdaq markets who typically are also retail brokers. *See* § 14.10 *infra.*

20. *See* 17 C.F.R. §§ 240.11Aa–1–11Ac–2.

22. *See* Approval of Nasdaq Stock Market LLC Exchange Application, 2006 WL 77691 (SEC Jan. 13, 2006).

23. *See* NASD News Release, NASD Agrees to Principle Terms To Sell American Stock Exchange To GTCR Golder Rauner LLC, http://www.nasdr.com/news/pr2003/release_03_024.html (NASD June 2, 2003).

agreed to be acquired by the New York Stock Exchange,[24] Nasdaq acquired the Philadelphia Stock Exchange in 2008.[25]

Although a completely unified national market system might arguably benefit investors and promote market efficiency, old institutions die hard and thus the exchange system and over-the-counter markets are likely to remain the bulwarks of the securities markets for quite a long period of time. Furthermore, there are some indications that the centralized exchanges perform a function, including policing of their members and listed companies, that is not accomplished through an automated quotation system.

Technological advancements have now created an environment in which electronic trading systems can facilitate off-exchange trading. Another outgrowth of this technology was the approval, originally on a one-year pilot basis, of an Nasdaq electronic bulletin board for computerized quotations for stocks not listed on a national exchange or in the Nasdaq system.[54] The electronic bulletin board is not an established part of Nasdaq's over-the-counter network. Also, in conjunction with its adoption of Rule 144A,[55] the SEC approved the NASD's screen-based computer and communication system called PORTAL (Private Offerings, Resales and Trading through Automated Linkages) to facilitate secondary trading of Rule 144A securities.

Another major development of the securities markets has been the move toward demutualization. For most of their history, the exchanges and the Nasdaq were organized as mutual membership organizations. In the late 1990s, the New York Stock Exchange announced its intent to demutualize and transform into a profit-making corporation. When it eventually merged with Archipelago, a publicly held electronic trading platform, the regulatory arm of the exchange was transferred to a separate entity (New York Stock Exchange Regulation–NYSER) that is not part of the for-profit corporation. Previously, the NASD had demutualized and has spun off its regulatory functions to NASDR (National Association of Securities Dealers Regulation). In 2007 the NYSER and NASDR merged into a unitary self regulatory organization–The Financial Industry Regulatory Authority (FINRA). In addition, the International Securities Exchange and the Pacific Stock Exchange have demutualized.

§ 14.1[2] Options Trading and Other Derivatives

In addition to the stock and bond markets, the SEC regulates the options markets wherein there is public trading of put and call options for securities and indexes. The options themselves qualify as securities which are separate and distinct from the underlying securities.[60] Accordingly, the public trading of options contracts on stock, stock indexes, and other securities is subject to SEC regulation. Options on securities and certain indexes are publicly traded

24. *See* NYSE Euronext Press Release, AMEX Members Approve Acquisition of AMEX by NYSE (Euronext June 18, 2008); NYSE Euronext to Acquire American Stock Exchange, Business Wire (Jan. 16, 2008).

25. *See* Nasdaq OMX Group Announces Completion of Phlx Acquisition, Sec. L. Daily (BNA), http://pubs.bna.com/ip/bna/sld.nsf/eh/A0B6W2H7Q5 (July 25, 2008).

54. Sec.Exch.Act Rel. No. 34–27975, 46 S.E.C. Docket 200, 1990 WL 311827 (SEC May 1, 1990). *See* SEC Approves One–Year Pilot Program for NASD's OTC Electronic Bulletin Board, 22 Sec.Reg. & L.Rep. (BNA) 672 (May 4, 1990).

55. 17 C.F.R. § 230.144A, which is discussed in § 4.29 *supra*.

60. 15 U.S.C.A. § 77b(a)(1); 15 U.S.C.A. § 78c(a)(10). *See* § 1.6 *supra*.

on the American Stock Exchange as well as many of the regional exchanges—primarily the Midwest, Pacific, and Philadelphia Exchanges. Rather than have the exchanges separately register each option that is publicly traded, the Options Clearing Corporation files applicable disclosure documents governing the generic options—*i.e.*, put and call options on individual securities. These disclosure documents not only reveal the mechanics of options trading but also the risks peculiarly associated with options trading.[61] These options-related disclosures are also designed to help inform investors as to the various option investment strategies.

As noted elsewhere in this treatise,[64] the Commodity Futures Trading Commission (CFTC) regulates financial futures. Options and index futures have been cited as the cause of increased volatility. As a result various proposals have been considered, including earlier options and futures expiration and the disclosure of open orders.

In 2000, there was a massive overhaul of commodities and derivatives regulation.[68] The revolutionary legislation introduced three tiers of commodities markets and parallel tiers of regulation.[69] The 2000 overhaul of commodities regulation also formally recognized the over-the-counter commodities markets and these markets which are virtually unregulated except for antifraud proscriptions[70] are open only to the largest institutional investors dealing in certain types of swap and other hybrid contracts.[71] At the same time, both the securities and commodities laws were amended to provide that securities-based swap agreements are not securities,[72] although they remain subject to the securities laws' antifraud provisions.[73] The degree of CFTC involvement in derivatives markets thus depends on the nature of the investors that are permitted to participate and the types of commodities based products being offered.

Until 2001, futures instruments on individual stocks were not permitted. However, the commodities markets wanted a share of the trading volume and the Commodities Futures Trading Commission agreed. In September 2000, the SEC and CFTC agreed on a proposal for submission to Congress.[74] This

61. 17 C.F.R. § 240.9b–1 (options disclosure document). *See also* NASD Manual (CCH) 2183–84.

64. *See* § 22.7 *infra.*

68. Commodity Futures Modernization Act of 2000, Pub. Law No. 106–554, 114 Stat. 2763 (Dec. 21, 2000).

69. The highest degree of regulation remains with the designated commodities contract markets where retail futures trading takes place. The 2000 legislation created a type of contract market for the trading of futures contracts—an "exempt board of trade." An exempt board of trade can be recognized as a derivatives transaction execution facility and is subject to fewer regulatory requirements than CFTC designated contract markets. The third tier is the formal recognition of over-the-counter derivatives instruments for institutional investors. *See* § 22.6 *infra.*

70. The 2000 legislation also provided that although excluded from the definition of security under the securities acts, commodities based swap agreements are subject to the securities laws' antifraud provisions.

71. Commodity Futures Modernization Act of 2000, Pub. Law 106–554, 114 Stat. 2763 (December 21, 2000).

72. 15 U.S.C.A. §§ 77b(a)(1), 78c(a)(10).

73. 15 U.S.C.A. §§ 77q(a), 78j(b).

74. *See* Single Stock Futures Would be Securities Under Agencies' Agreement for Lifting Ban, 32 Sec. Reg. & L. Rep. (BNA) 1256, 1256 (September 18, 2000). *See also* §§ 1.5, 1.6 *supra.*

legislation was enacted in December that same year.[75] Futures on individual stocks thus are subject to both SEC and CFTC regulation.[76]

§ 14.1[3] Market Regulation—History, Background, and Overview

Background

While the Securities Act of 1933 regulates the distribution of securities,[77] the Securities Exchange Act of 1934 charges the SEC with the authority to supervise daily market activity. In addition to imposing disclosure requirements upon issuers of publicly traded securities,[78] the Exchange Act of 1934 regulates the market place. In 2007, the SEC changed the name of the division that handles market regulation changed from the Division of Market Regulation to the Division of Trading and Markets. Regulating the market place means regulating broker-dealers, securities exchanges, clearing organizations, and the over-the-counter markets. Although the SEC has direct authority, a great deal of market regulation is carried out through its oversight of national exchanges and self-regulatory organizations. The SEC oversight responsibilities include the review of rulemaking by self-regulatory organizations.

Nature of Broker–Dealer Regulation

A substantial portion of the SEC's activity is devoted to regulation of firms engaged in the securities business. The three principal capacities in which firms act in that business are as broker, dealer, and investment adviser. The 1934 Act defines a "broker" as a "person engaged in the business of effecting transactions in securities for the account of others,"[89] while a "dealer" is a "person engaged in the business of buying and selling securities for such person's own account."[90] An "investment adviser" is defined in 202(a)(11) of the Investment Advisers Act of 1940 as a "person who, for compensation, engages in the business of advising others . . . as to the advisability of investing in, purchasing or selling securities,"[91] but broker-dealers who render such advice as part of their brokerage activities are exempt from the definition.[92]

Under section 15(a) of the 1934 Act,[93] no person may engage in business as a broker or dealer in securities (unless he does exclusively intrastate business or deals only in exempted securities) unless he is registered with the Commission. Under section 15(b),[94] the SEC may revoke or suspend a broker-dealer's registration, or impose a censure, if the broker-dealer is found to have

75. Pub. Law No. 106–554, 114 Stat. 2763 (Dec. 21, 2000).

76. *Id.*

77. *See* chapters 2–3 *supra.*

78. *See* chapter 9 *supra.*

89. 1934 Act § 3(a)(4), 15 U.S.C.A. § 78c(a)(4).

90. 1934 Act § 3(a)(5), 15 U.S.C.A. § 78c(a)(5).

91. 15 U.S.C.A. § 80b–3(a). *See* § 21.2[1] *infra.*

92. 15 U.S.C.A. § 80b–2(a)(11)(C).

93. 15 U.S.C.A. § 78*o*(a).

94. 15 U.S.C.A. § 78*o*(b). Section 203 of the Investment Advisers Act of 1940 contains comparable provisions with respect to investment advisers. 15 U.S.C.A. § 80b–3.

violated any of the federal securities laws or committed other specified misdeeds.[95]

In spelling out the substantive obligations of these securities "professionals" in dealing with public investors, the SEC has proceeded largely under the general anti-fraud provisions of sections 10(b)[96] and 15(c)[97] of the 1934 Act, section 17(a) of the 1933 Act,[98] and section 206 of the Investment Advisers Act.[99] The SEC's attention has been focused on two broad areas: (a) conflicts between the firm's obligations to its customers and its own financial interests,[100] and (b) trading in or recommending securities in the absence of adequate information about the issuer.[101] Violation of the anti-fraud provisions in these two areas has given rise to lawsuits by aggrieved customers[102] as well as disciplinary actions by the SEC.[103]

A number of the sections in this chapter exemplify the approaches taken by the SEC and the courts in regulating (1) excessive prices for over-the-counter securities;[104] (2) activities of market-makers who deal directly with individual customers;[105] (3) generation of commissions by excessive trading in customers' accounts;[106] and (4) undisclosed interests of investment advisers in the stocks they recommend.[107]

Market regulation includes the establishment of fair market practices and minimum capital requirements for broker-dealers in order to minimize the risk of insolvency.[108] A major goal of this regulation is to assure orderly markets.[109] There are also severe prohibitions against fraudulent and manipulative broker-dealer conduct.[110] Additionally, the SEC and the Federal Reserve Board work together in regulating the extension of credit for securities transactions.[111]

Self Regulation[112]

SEC regulation of the industry is supplemented by a system of "self regulation". Sections 6 and 15A of the 1934 Act[113] delegate to "national securities exchanges" and "national securities associations," respectively,

---

95. *See, e.g.,* Studer v. SEC, 148 Fed. Appx. 58 (2d Cir. 2005) (upholding revocation of broker-dealer registration).

96. 15 U.S.C.A. § 78j(b). *See* § 12.1 *supra* and § 14.3[6] *infra.*

97. 15 U.S.C.A. § 78*o*(c). *See* § 12.1 *supra* and § 14.3[6] *infra*

98. 15 U.S.C.A. § 77q(a). *See* § 7.11 *supra.*

99. 15 U.S.C.A. § 80b–6. *See* § 21.4[1] *infra.*

100. *See* §§ 14.3, 14.10 *infra.*

101. *See* §§ 14.15–14.18 *infra.*

102. *See* § 14.26 and chapter 15 *infra.*

103. *See* § 14.3 *infra.* The SEC's enforcement authority generally is discussed in chapter 16 *infra.*

104. *See* § 14.14 *infra.*

105. *See* § 14.10 *infra.*

106. *See* § 14.20 *infra.*

107. *See* § 14.18 *infra.*

108. *See* § 14.8 *infra.*

109. *See* §§ 14.3, 14.10–14.11 *infra*

110. *See* §§ 14.3[6], 14.15–14.23 *infra.*

111. *See* § 14.9 *infra.*

112. *See* § 14.3 *infra.*

113. 15 U.S.C.A. §§ 78f, 15*o*–1.

substantial authority over their members, including the power to expel, suspend, or discipline them for certain specified kinds of activities or for "conduct ... inconsistent with just and equitable principles of trade." In order to exercise such powers, an exchange or association must register with the SEC, which, under section 19 of the Act,[115] is given certain oversight powers with respect to its disciplinary proceedings and adoption and amendment of its rules.

In general, a securities firm must become a member of one or more exchanges in order to execute transactions in listed securities on an exchange, and must become a member the Financial Industry Regulatory Authority (FINRA), formerly the National Association of Securities Dealers (NASD), the only registered association, to transact business effectively in the over-the-counter market.

Stock Exchanges

When Congress created the SEC in 1934, stock exchanges, as private associations, had been regulating their members for up to one hundred and forty years. Rather than displace this system of "self regulation," Congress superimposed the SEC on it as an additional level of regulation. The effect of section 5[126] is to require every "national securities exchange" to register with the SEC. Under section 6(b) of the Act,[127] an exchange cannot be registered unless the SEC determines that its rules are designed, among other things, to "prevent fraudulent and manipulative acts and practices, to promote just and equitable principles of trade,"[128] and to provide for appropriate discipline of its members for any violations of its own rules or the securities laws.

Under the authority of section 6 of the Act, the various exchanges, of which the New York Stock Exchange (NYSE) is by far the largest and most important, have maintained and enforced a large body of rules for the conduct of their members. These rules fall into two categories: rules relating to transactions on the particular exchange, and rules relating to the internal operations of the member firms and their dealings with their customers. As noted above, in 2006, the Nasdaq national market became a registered national securities exchange.

The first group consists of rules governing: criteria for listing securities on the exchange and provisions for delisting or suspension of trading in particular securities; obligations of issuers of listed securities; bids and offers on the exchange floor; activities of "specialists" (designated market-makers in listed securities); transactions by members in listed securities for their own account; conditions under which transactions in listed securities may be effected off the exchange; clearing and settlement of exchange transactions; and rules for the governance and operation of the exchange itself.[130]

In the second category are rules governing: the form of organization of member firms and qualifications of their partners or officers; qualifications of salesmen and other personnel; handling of customers' accounts; advertising;

115. 15 U.S.C.A. § 78s.

126. 15 U.S.C.A. § 78e.

127. 15 U.S.C.A. § 78f(b).

128. *See, e.g.,* In the Matter of Hazelgrove–Mulkerrins, Exchange Hearing Panel Decision 00–211, 2000 WL 33158159 (N.Y.S.E. Nov. 28, 2000).

130. *See* § 14.11 *infra.*

and financial statements and reports. In the case of firms which are members of more than one exchange, there is a kind of "pecking order" with respect to regulatory responsibility: the New York Stock Exchange (now FINRA) has principal responsibility for regulation of the internal affairs of all of its members (which includes almost all of the largest firms in the industry), the American Stock Exchange has principal responsibility for those of its members that are not also New York Stock Exchange members, and the various "regional" exchanges in cities other than New York have responsibility over their "sole" members.

Section 19 of the Exchange Act, as originally enacted, gave the SEC power to suspend or withdraw the registration of an exchange, to suspend or expel any member of an exchange, to suspend trading in listed securities, and to require changes in exchange rules with respect to a wide range of matters. However, it did not require SEC approval for changes in stock exchange rules, nor did it provide for SEC review of disciplinary actions by exchanges against their members. Section 19, as amended in 1975, expanded and consolidated the SEC's authority over *all* self regulatory organizations. The SEC's increased authority with respect to exchanges and the National Association of Securities Dealers (NASD, now part of FINRA) with respect to the over-the-counter markets is roughly comparable to, but even broader than, its previous authority over the NASD.[132] In particular, since 1975, the SEC must give advance approval for any exchange rule changes, and has review power over exchange disciplinary actions.[133]

National Association of Securities Dealers

When Congress decided to extend federal regulation over the nonexchange, or over-the-counter (OTC) market, it followed the pattern already established with respect to exchanges. Section 15A,[135] added by the "Maloney Act" of 1938,[136] authorized the establishment of "national securities associations" to be registered with the SEC. Like an exchange, any such association must have rules designed "to prevent fraudulent and manipulative acts and practices [and] to promote just and equitable principles of trade" in transactions in the over-the-counter market. Only one such association has been established, the National Association of Securities Dealers (NASD) which has since become a part of the Financial Industry Regulatory Authority (FINRA). The NASD has adopted a substantial body of "Rules of Fair Practice," dealing with various problems in the over-the-counter markets. Among the most important are: its rule that a dealer may not recommend a security unless it has reason to believe the security is "suitable" to the customer's financial situation and needs;[139] its interpretation of its "fair spread or profit" rule to bar mark-ups in excess of five percent on principal transactions;[140] its procedures for reviewing underwriting compensation and provisions for assuring that members make a bona fide public offering of underwritten securities;[141]

132. *See* Marianne K. Smythe, Self Regulation and the Antitrust Laws: Suggestions for An Accommodation, 62 N.C.L.Rev. 475, 505–506 (1984).

133. *See, e.g.,* Ho v. SEC, 2007 WL 1224027 (7th Cir. 2007).

135. 15 U.S.C.A. § 78*o*.

136. Pub. L. No. 75–719, 52 Stat. 1070 (1938).

139. *See* § 14.16 *infra*.

140. *See* § 14.14[3] *infra*.

141. NASD Manual Rule 2710 (Corporate Finance Rule) (available on Westlaw).

and its rules with respect to execution of orders in the over-the-counter market and disclosure in confirmations to customers.[142]

From time to time, FINRA (formerly the NASD) promulgates rules and issues interpretations directed to specially described prohibited practices. Although FINRA and NASD rules and interpretations identify a number of impermissible practices, those specifically identified practices do not comprise an exclusive list of prohibited practices. The rules and interpretations that identify specific practices are not exclusive. In other words, FINRA can invoke general antifraud principles as well as the general concept of just and equitable principles of trade to invalidate improper conduct that is not specifically defined in FINRA or SEC rulemaking.

The scandals following the turn of the twentieth century led to increased concern over the effectiveness of self regulation. As noted elsewhere in this chapter, one response was to adopt rules specifically directed to the abuses in connection with IPOs and with respect to research analyst recommendations. One other response was to expand the NASD's enforcement authority. In 2003, the NASD was given increased enforcement authority when it was given cease and desist powers with respect to certain securities law violations.[149]

§ 14.1[9] Antitrust Laws and Market Regulation

The federal antitrust laws are designed to curb anticompetitive activities.[210] From time to time, the anticompetitive consequences of various activities in the securities markets have been brought into question. For example, since the definition of securities manipulation depends upon artificially pegging or fixing the price of securities,[212] manipulative conduct by definition has an anticompetitive effect on securities prices.[213] The former practice of fixed brokerage commission rates imposed by the New York Stock Exchange is another example of anticompetitive activity challenged under the antitrust laws.[214] Additionally, many of the rules of the SEC and of the self regulatory organizations permit conduct that otherwise would violate the antitrust laws.[215] From time to time, antitrust challenges have been made and the question arises whether the pervasive regulatory framework imposed by the securities laws on the securities markets operates as an implied repeal of the antitrust laws. The implied repeal argument has been met with considerable success in challenging antitrust scrutiny of the securities markets.[216] On the

142. *See* § 14.13 *infra.*

149. *See* NASD Special Notice to Members 03–35, http://www.nasdr.com/pdf-text/0335ntm.txt (NASDR June 23, 2003).

210. *See, e.g.,* section 1 of the Sherman Antitrust Act, 15 U.S.C.A. § 1 which, among other things, prohibits contracts in restraint of trade. *See also, e.g.,* Section 2 of the Sherman Antitrust Act address monopolies as they violate the antitrust laws. 15 U.S.C.A. § 2. Section 5 of the Clayton Antitrust Act, 15 U.S.C.A. § 15.

212. Section 9(a) of the 1934 Act, 15 U.S.C.A. § 78i(a). *See* § 12.1 *supra* and § 14.3[6] *infra.*

213. *See, e.g.,* Friedman v. Salomon/Smith Barney, Inc., 313 F.3d 796 (2d Cir. 2002).

214. *See* Gordon v. New York Stock Exchange, Inc., 422 U.S. 659, 95 S.Ct. 2598, 45 L.Ed.2d 463 (1975).

215. For example, the market-maker regulations by imposing barriers to entry, limit which firms can act as market makers for over-the-counter securities. Market-maker regulation is discussed in § 14.10 *infra.* Similarly, the specialist system for exchange based trading is a form of permissible monopoly. Specialist and exchange trading are discussed in § 14.11 *infra.*

216. *See, e.g.,* United States v. NASD, 422 U.S. 694, 95 S.Ct. 2427, 45 L.Ed.2d 486 (1975); Gordon v. New York Stock Exchange, Inc., 422 U.S. 659, 95 S.Ct. 2598, 45 L.Ed.2d 463 (1975); In re Stock Exchanges Options Trading Antitrust Litigation, 317 F.3d 134 (2d Cir. 2003).

other hand, it is clear that the antitrust laws will not be preempted simply because the alleged anticompetitive conduct involves the securities markets.[217]

§ 14.3 Regulation of Broker–Dealers—The SEC, Self Regulatory Organizations, National Exchanges, and FINRA

§ 14.3[2] State Regulation of Broker–Dealers—Limited Preemption

Limited preemption of state broker-dealer regulation

In 1996, Congress, as part of the National Securities Markets Improvement Act of 1996,[5] took away from the states the power to regulate certain areas of broker-dealer activity. In particular, the states may not impose regulations relating to the extension of credit (margin requirements), net capital requirements, or recordkeeping and reporting requirements.[6] In 2006, Utah passed a statute that would have imposed sanctions on brokers' failure to deliver securities that go far beyond the consequences of fails to deliver under SEC regulation.[7] In February 2007, Utah repealed its short sale legislation before it was implemented.[8] The Utah statute clearly contravened the National Securities Market Improvement Act (NSMIA).[9] Utah agreed to a preliminary injunction against the implementing the statute.[10] There are a number of reasons that the Utah statute would have failed in addition to NSMIA's express mandate.

Remaining vitality of state broker-dealer regulation

Notwithstanding the preemptive legislation, many states play a significant role in broker-dealer regulation.[26] The preemption of broker-dealer regulation imposed by National Securities Markets Improvement Act of 1996 is limited. It does not affect the states' ability to regulate broker dealers

---

217. Silver v. New York Stock Exchange, 373 U.S. 341, 359, 83 S.Ct. 1246, 1258, 10 L.Ed.2d 389 (1963).

§ 14.3

5. Pub. L. No. 104–290, 110 Stat. 3416 (1996).

6. 1934 Act section 15(h), 15 U.S.C. § 78*o*(h).

7. Utah SB 3004.

8. *See* Seven Months After SIFMA Lawsuit Utah Acts to Repeal Short Selling Law, Broker–Dealer Compliance Rep. (BNA), http://pubs.bna.com/ip/bna/bdc.nsf/eh/A0B4C9C9F8 (March 7, 2007).

9. *See* Securities Industry Association Press Release, SIA Files Lawsuit To Preserve Uniform National Standards For Rules Governing Settlement, Record Keeping and Reporting, http://www.sia.com/press/2006_press_releases/29152215.html (July 28, 2006); Stuart Gittleman, Complinet, http://www.complinet.com/global/news/news/article.html?ref=82011#(July 31, 2006).

10. On July 28, the parties stipulated to a preliminary injunction against implementation of the Utah statute; the injunction expires on June 1, 2007. Securities Industry Association v. Klein, Case No. 2:06cv00624 TC (D. Utah Aug. 11, 2006). *See* Securities Industry Association Press Release, Utah "Fail to Deliver" Lawsuit–Parties Agree to Preliminary Injunction, http://www.sia.com/press/2006_press_releases/29712031.html (Aug. 11, 2006).

26. *See* New York v. Justin, 237 F.Supp.2d 368 (W.D.N.Y. 2002) (federal law does not preempt state's ability to prosecute securities broker for improper supervision of registered sales representative).

generally through registration requirements.[27] A number of states have been aggressive in enforcing their antifraud provisions in broker-dealer prosecutions. Furthermore, the existence of exclusive federal jurisdiction under the Securities Exchange Act of 1934 does not preclude state law claims against broker dealers.[30] Nor does it preempt state law fraud claims generally.[31] The only fraud claims that would be preempted would be those class actions covered by SLUSA.[32]

§ 14.3[3] Self–Regulation: The National Association of Securities Dealers and the National Exchanges

By virtue of section 15A,[41] FINRA (formerly the NASD) operates as the largest of the self regulatory organizations subject to SEC oversight. Although the Commission has, pursuant to Section 15 of the Act, the direct authority to regulate broker-dealers who are members of the NASD, as a practical matter the bulk of the day-to-day regulation is generally delegated to the self regulatory organization. The NASD (and now FINRA) has extensive rules governing its members and employees which relate both to organizational structure and standards of conduct.

By virtue of section 19 of the Act,[57] the Commission has oversight responsibility with respect to all rulemaking activity of national exchanges. Similar authority exists with regard to FINRA (formerly the NASD).[59]

Section 19(c)[63] of the Exchange Act empowers the SEC to "abrogate, add to, and delete from" the rules of self regulatory organizations. However, this power is exercised only on a very infrequent basis.

Section 19(a)(1) gives the Commission the authority to register national exchanges.[64] Under section 19(h), the Commission has the authority to discipline national exchanges for violating the securities Acts' provisions.[65] There is also the express authority of exchanges to discipline persons associated with an exchange, including power to remove from office or censure its officers or directors for willful violations of the Act.[66] The Commission has exercised its statutory authority[67] to expel a national exchange on only one occasion.[68] But the Commission has with more frequency exercised its authority under subsection (h) to uphold expulsion of members from the exchange. The power to discipline and sanction members is given directly to the exchange with a right of appeal to the SEC which may in its discretion review the record de novo.[70] The SEC decision is then subject to review by a federal court of

27. *See* A.S. Goldmen & Co. v. New Jersey Bureau of Securities, 163 F.3d 780 (3d Cir.1999) (upholding constitutionality of state registration requirements for broker-dealers doing business within the state).

30. *See* Roskind v. Morgan Stanley Dean Witter & Co., 165 F.Supp.2d 1059, 1065–1066 (N.D.Cal.2001).

31. *See* Zuri–Invest AG v. Natwest Finance Inc., 177 F.Supp.2d 189 (S.D.N.Y.2001).

32. Pub. Law No. 105–353, 112 Stat. 3227 (105th Cong.–2d sess. November 3, 1998) (S 1260), discussed in § 12.15[2] *supra*.

41. 815 U.S.C.A. § 78*o*–3. There was some movement toward establishing a self regulatory organization for dealers in municipal securities. But no such group was ever formed.

57. 15 U.S.C.A. § 78s.

59. *See* 15 U.S.C.A. § 78*o*–3.

63. 15 U.S.C.A. § 78s(c).

64. 15 U.S.C.A. § 78s(a)(1).

65. 15 U.S.C.A. § 78s(h).

66. 15 U.S.C.A. § 78f(d).

67. 15 U.S.C.A. § 78s(h)(1).

68. San Francisco Mining Exchange v. SEC, 378 F.2d 162 (9th Cir.1967).

70. 15 U.S.C.A. § 78f; *see* 15 U.S.C.A. § 78s(h).

appeals. FINRA (formerly the NASD) has similar status and authority. The Commission can suspend or revoke the securities association's registration.[72] FINRA has the power to hold hearings and issue sanctions against members and associated persons, including expulsion of its members from the association for conduct in violation of the Act or FINRA's rules.[73] The sanctions authorized by the statute are intended to protect investors and not to serve as punishment for the violations complained of.[74]

In addition to the sanctions imposed by the SROs, the Commission can institute its own proceedings. The Commission is empowered to suspend or revoke broker-dealer registration for violations of the securities laws.[75] The Commission can also bar any person from associating with a broker-dealer,[76] a member of a registered securities association (*i.e.* FINRA, formerly the NASD),[77] or an investment adviser,[78] as well as barring that person from serving in various capacities with a registered investment company.[79] Additionally, with respect to all of the powers outlined above, the Commission can, of course, impose less severe sanctions, including suspension for a definite period of not more than twelve months, or merely censuring persons involved.[80] Section 19(d) sets out the SEC's authority with regard to disciplinary actions by self regulatory organizations.[81] Sections 19(e) and 19(f) set out the standards for commission review of disciplinary proceedings and sanctions imposed by self regulatory organizations.[82] In addition, the SEC can bring its own enforcement action to enforce a self regulatory organization's imposition of a monetary sanction.[83]

Over and beyond the regulatory structure outlined above, agreements between members of self regulatory agencies that their disputes be arbitrated are generally enforceable.[87] This supplements the general rule that federal securities claims are arbitrable.[88]

Although the federal securities laws do not regulate commodities transactions directly, since stock brokers frequently trade in commodities, improper conduct can run afoul of both the federal securities and commodities regulato-

72. 15 U.S.C.A. § 78o–3(h).

73. 15 U.S.C.A. § 78s(h)(2).

74. PAZ Securities, Inc. v. SEC, 494 F.3d 1059 (D.C. Cir. 2007) (the statute "authorizes [the Commission to order] expulsion not as a penalty but as a means of protecting investors.... The purpose of the order is remedial, not penal"; finding that SEC abused its discretion in the NASD's failure to consider mitigating factors in imposing sanctions), quoting from Wright v. SEC, 112 F.2d 89, 94 (2d Cir.1940).

75. 15 U.S.C.A. § 78*o*(b)(5).

76. 15 U.S.C.A. § 78*o*(b)(6).

77. 15 U.S.C.A. § 78s(h)(3).

78. 15 U.S.C.A. § 80b–3(f).

79. 15 U.S.C.A. § 80a–9(b).

80. *See* Sec.Exch.Act Rel. No. 34–14761 (May 15, 1978).

81. 15 U.S.C.A. § 78s(d). *See* 17 C.F.R. §§ 240.19d–1, .19d–2, .19d–3. *Cf., e.g.,* Swirsky v. National Association of Securities Dealers, 124 F.3d 59 (1st Cir.1997) (SEC's refusal to review NASD decision was final order and was not subject to collateral attack).

82. 15 U.S.C.A. §§ 78s(e), s(f).

83. *See* SEC v. Markowski, 277 Fed.Appx. 903 (11th Cir. 2008) (SEC's use of 1934 Act § 21(e) to seek judicial enforcement of NASD monetary sanctions did not violate due process).

87. 15 U.S.C.A. § 78bb(b).

88. *See* chapter 15 *infra*.

ry framework.[89] In some instances commodities transactions may be directly regulated by the securities laws, such as is the case with pooled managed commodities accounts.[90]

SEC Rules 11Ac–1–1 and 11Ac–4 permit electronic communications networks ("ECN"s) for providing electronic quotations and facilitating transactions in the over-the-counter markets.[104] These and other alternative trading systems[105] have opened up competition in the electronic markets[106] but have also engendered some criticism as being too restrictive and not being as competitive as some observers had hoped. The influence of the ECNs continues to grow. For example, in December 2004, the Archipelago Exchange accounted for twenty-two percent of the trades in Nasdaq-listed securities. Also, by the end of 2004 the National Stock Market was the nation's third largest stock behind the New York Stock Exchange and the Nasdaq stock market. Although these electronic exchanges to grow in both size and number, there have been some setbacks. For example, some public companies have found regulatory burdens of multiple exchange listings to justify a delisting from the secondary exchanges.

§ 14.3[4] Substance of Self Regulation

Section 15(b)(4)[111] of the Exchange Act empowers the Commission to hold a hearing and impose disciplinary sanctions ranging from censure to revocation of the registration of broker-dealers engaging in certain types of proscribed conduct. The Act lists the following situations in which the SEC may impose sanctions after an administrative hearing: (1) when a broker-dealer makes false filings with the Commission;[113] (2) when the broker-dealer within the past ten years has been convicted of certain crimes or misdemeanors involving moral turpitude or breaches of fiduciary duty;[114] (3) when the person involved has been enjoined from being a broker-dealer or investment adviser or from engaging in or continuing to engage in any conduct or practice in connection with such activity or in connection with the purchase or sale of any security;[115] (4) when a broker-dealer has willfully violated any provision of the Securities Act of 1933, the Exchange Act of 1934, the Investment Company Act of 1940, or the Investment Advisers Act of 1940, or any rules promulgated thereunder;[116] (5) when the broker-dealer has willfully aided, abetted, counseled, commanded, induced, or procured any violation of any of

89. *See, e.g.,* Smoky Greenhaw Cotton Co. v. Merrill Lynch, Pierce, Fenner & Smith, Inc., 785 F.2d 1274 (5th Cir.1986), *on remand* 650 F.Supp. 220 (W.D.Tex.1986).

90. *See* § 1.6 *supra.*

104. 17 C.F.R. §§ 240.11Ac1–1, 11Ac1–4.

105. *See* Regulation ATS. Securities Exchange Act Release No. 40760 (Dec. 8, 1998), 63 FR 70844 (December 22, 1998) (adopting Release).

106. *See, e.g.,* NASD Rule 6540, as amended in May 2002, which permits ECNs and other alternative trading systems (ATS) to list over-the-counter bulletin board stocks provided that certain conditions are met. One of those conditions is the the ECN or ATS will have to obtain current information about a company that complies with SEC Rule 15c2–11, 17 C.F.R. § 240.15c2–11 before listing a quotation.

111. 15 U.S.C.A. § 78*o*(b)(4).

113. 15 U.S.C.A. § 78*o*(b)(4)(A).

114. 15 U.S.C.A. § 78*o*(b)(4)(B).

115. 15 U.S.C.A. § 78*o*(b)(4)(C).

116. 15 U.S.C.A. § 78*o*(b)(4)(D). This subsection also covers conduct in violation of rules of the Municipal Securities Rule–Making Board. *See* § 14.6 *infra.*

the foregoing statutes or rules;[117] (6) when the broker-dealer is subject to an SEC order barring or suspending his right to be associated with a broker or dealer;[118] and (7) when the broker-dealer has violated any foreign securities law or regulation.[119] Section 15(b)(6)[120] empowers the Commission to impose similar sanctions for the same types of conduct with regard to persons who, although not themselves broker-dealers, are associated or seek to become associated with broker-dealers.[121] Brokerage firms have a duty to supervise their personnel and can be held liable and subject to SEC or self regulatory organization sanctions for breach of the duty to supervise.[122]

Self Regulatory Disciplinary Authority

In addition to direct SEC enforcement, the self regulatory organizations—the exchanges and FINRA (formerly the NASD)—can investigate suspected violations and discipline their members for violations of self regulatory organization rules. The exchanges and FINRA are given broad investigatory and disciplinary powers.[124] Self regulatory organization disciplinary actions are subject to SEC review and, in turn, to review by a federal court of appeals. The right to appeal an SEC decision reviewing a FINRA ruling to federal court is available to someone subject to a disciplinary order but not to FNRA.[127] The D.C. Circuit Court of appeals takes the position that the NASD (now FINRA), acting in its adjudicative capacity as lower tribunal subject to SEC plenary review of its disciplinary decisions, was not "aggrieved person"

---

117. 15 U.S.C.A. § 78*o*(b)(4)(E).

118. 15 U.S.C.A. § 78*o*(b)(5)(F). *See* 15 U.S.C.A. 78*o*(b)(6).

119. 15 U.S.C.A. § 78*o*(b)(4)(G).

120. 15 U.S.C.A. § 78*o*(b)(6).

121. *See, e.g.,* Alderman v. SEC, 104 F.3d 285 (9th Cir.1997) (NASD Rule requiring associated person to conform to just and equitable principles of trade was not void for vagueness).

122. *E.g.,* Kersh v. General Council of the Assemblies of God, 804 F.2d 546 (9th Cir.1986); In the Matter of Clarence Z. Wurts, Initial Decisions Rel. No. 194, 2001 WL 1343997 (SEC Initial Decision Oct. 31, 2001) (imposing censure and 6 month supervisory suspension for supervisory violations); Leavey v. Blinder, Robinson & Co., 1986 WL 10556, [1986–1987 Transfer Binder] Fed.Sec.L.Rep. (CCH) ¶ 92,996 (E.D.Pa.1986) (imposing controlling person liability under section 12 of the Exchange Act; noting failure to adequately supervise); In the Matter of Josephthal & Co., Sec. Exch. Act Rel. No. 34–46039, 2002 WL 1286177 (SEC June 6, 2002) (consent order; imposing sanction for failing to have system for assuring that branch managers were living up to their supervisory obligations); In the Matter of the Chepak, 2000 WL 49226, Sec. Exch. Act Rel. No. 34–42356, 71 S.E.C. Docket 1203 (SEC 2000) (upholding NASD sanctions for failure to adequately supervise). *See generally* Thomas L. Taylor III & Patricia A. Gomez, Recent Trends in "Failure to Supervise" Cases, 33 Review of Securities and Commodities Regulation 251 (Dec. 12, 2000)(description of SEC and NASD priority focus on failure to supervise cases). *Cf.* SEC v. Stratton Oakmont, Inc., 1995 WL 46559, [1994–1995 Transfer Binder] Fed. Sec. L. Rep. (CCH) ¶ 98,503 (D.D.C.1995) (preliminary injunction requiring retention of independent consultant to review firm's sales practices). *But cf.* Buhler v. Audio, 807 F.2d 833 (9th Cir.1987) (no breach of duty to supervise with regard to account executive's off-book transactions). Controlling person liability generally is discussed in § 12.24 *supra. See also* § 7.12 *supra* and § 14.26[6][A] *infra.*

The Investment Advisers Act of 1940 imposes supervision standards comparable to those in the Securities Exchange Act. 15 U.S.C.A. § 80b–3. Investment adviser regulation is discussed in chapter 21 *infra. See also* Letter From the Office of Compliance, Inspections and Examinations to Registered Investment Advisers on Areas Reviewed and Violations Found During Inspections, 2000 WL 91373 (S.E.C. May 1, 2000).

SRO rules are also subject to SEC oversight. *See, e.g.,* General Bond & Share Co. v. SEC, 39 F.3d 1451 (10th Cir.1994).

124. *See, e.g.,* Gold v. SEC, 48 F.3d 987 (7th Cir.1995) (due process does not require exchange to give notice to former brokerage employee that his conduct with the firm was under investigation).

127. NASD v. SEC, 431 F 3d 803 (D.C.Cir. 2005).

so as to give a right to appeal an SEC decision reversing an NASD disciplinary adjudication.[128]

The doctrine of exhaustion of remedies applies to self regulatory organization disciplinary proceedings.[129] This means that disciplinary and other self regulatory action must proceed through the self regulatory agency's appeals process before there can be review by the SEC or by a court.[130] SEC review of FINRA and other SRO decisions is subject to the final judgment rule and therefore limited to final decisions.[131]

Broker–Dealer Operations

In addition to imposing sanctions arising out of the SEC's direct broker-dealer regulation, the Commission is charged with the supervision of a firm's structure and taking measures to ensure the broker-dealer's solvency. Section 15(b)(7) requires broker-dealers to meet such operational and financial competence standards as the Commission may establish.[171] Perhaps the most significant of these requirements is the Commission's net capital rule which sets out the minimum standards of broker-dealer solvency based on the balance sheet. The net capital rule, Rule 15c3–1, is among the longest and most complex of the Commission's rules.[172] In short, the rule requires that a broker-dealer's balance sheet reflect a sufficient asset base as well as mandating the applicable accounting standards for determining that asset base.[173] The net capital rule is complicated not only because of its formulas but also because of the rules regarding "haircuts"—the discounted value of the securities before the computation is made. The competence requirements imposed by the Act include provisions for maintenance of adequate records[174] and imposition of standards for supervisory and associated personnel, as well as a number of related requirements that go into more detail than is appropriate here. One of the other more important regulatory structures is the SEC's customer protection rule, which requires segregation of customers' funds from the brokerage firm's propriety funds and accounts.[177]

Section 15(c)(1)[178] prohibits securities broker-dealers from engaging in fraudulent practices and conduct. Section 15(c)(1) applies to all registered broker-dealers.[179] Section 15(c) may be used against unregistered broker-dealers as well.[180] The Act also specifically declares it illegal to misuse customers' funds and securities.[181]

---

128. *Id.*

129. *See, e.g.,* MFS Securities Corp. v. SEC, 380 F.3d 611, 622 (2d Cir. 2004).

130. *See* Marchiano v. NASD, 134 F.Supp.2d 90 (D.D.C.2001).

131. Section 19(d) of the Securities Exchange Act sets forth the SEC's jurisdiction to review SRO decisions. 15 U.S.C.A. § 78s(d).

171. 15 U.S.C.A. § 78*o*(b)(7).

172. 17 C.F.R. § 240.15c3–1.

173. For a more detailed analysis *see* Jerry W. Markham & Thomas L. Hazen, Broker-dealer Operations Under Securities and Commodities Law: Financial Responsibilities, Credit Regulation, and Customer Protection, ch. 5 (2001).

174. *See* the recordkeeping requirements of section 17(h).

177. SEC Rule 15c3–3, 17 C.F.R. § 240.15c3–3.

178. 15 U.S.C.A. § 78*o*(c)(1).

179. *See, e.g.,* SEC v. Montana, 464 F.Supp.2d 772, 785 (S.D. Ind. 2006).

180. *Id.*

181. 15 U.S.C.A. § 78*o*(c)(3).

Potential Conflicts of Interest and the Chinese Wall (or "Fire Wall") Requirement

Over the years, there has been an increased concern about the potential conflicts of interest resulting from the varied activities of multiservice brokerage firms. For example, when a firm acts as an underwriter or investment adviser for publicly traded issuers it will have access to nonpublic information that would be of interest to its retail customers who may be purchasing or selling the securities in question. The traditional response has been to establish a Chinese Wall (or "firewall") between the firm's various departments and thus to eliminate the potential conflict within each department. Another response to potential conflicts of interest has been for firms to place securities on a "restricted list" when the investment banking or underwriting department becomes involved in a proposed public offering or acquisition. The required information barriers go beyond separating the research and underwriting functions from each other and from the retail operations. When a broker-dealer acts as a market maker for over-the-counter securities, the market making activities must be carried on independently of other operations including the firm's own trading department as well as the departments mentioned above.

Conflicts of interest and information barriers are discussed in a later section of this treatise.[206] Broker-dealer firms encounter conflicts of interest in other areas as well. For example, conflicts of interest arise in the over-the-counter markets between a firm's retail operations and its market making functions.[207] There has been considerable controversy over the conflicts of securities analysts.[208]

Anti-Money Laundering Provisions

As major financial instructions, broker-dealers are frequently used by the unscrupulous to engage in money laundering operations. The activities that can lead to money laundering include organized crime operations, drug trafficking, and financial fraud generally. There are several federal statutes that address illegal money laundering operations.[279] As a result of increased efforts to enforce the federal anti-money laundering rules, broker-dealers, like other financial instructions, are subject to regulations and compliance programs designed to detect and in turn prevent money laundering operations from being filtered through these institutions.[280] The required compliance programs include reporting of certain transactions[281] In 2002, the New York Stock Exchange and the NASD set forth rules designed to strengthen their anti-money laundering compliance programs.[282] In particular, these rules require member firms to establish compliance programs that at a minimum: (1) establish and implement policies and procedures that can be reasonably

206. *See* § 14.12 *infra.*

207. *See* § 14.10[4] *infra.*

208. *See* § 14.16[6] *infra.*

279. *E.g.,* 18 U.S.C.A. § 1952 (the Travel Act); 31 U.S.C.A. §§ 5311–5313 (Foreign Corrupt Practices Act); 31 U.S.C.A. § 5313(a); 31 C.F.R. § 103.22(a) (Bank Secrecy Act).

280. *See generally* Jerry W. Markham & Thomas Lee Hazen, Broker–Dealer Operations Under Securities and Commodities Law ch. 11 (2d ed. 2007).

281. 31 U.S.C.A. § 5318(g).

282. Sec. Exch. Act Rel. No. 34–45487, 67 Fed. Reg. 10463–012002 SEC LEXIS 478 (SEC Feb. 28, 2002).

expected to detect and cause the reporting of transactions required under 31 U.S.C.A. § 5318(g); (2) establish and implement policies, procedures, and internal controls reasonably designed to achieve compliance with the Bank Secrecy Act; (3) provide for independent testing for compliance to be conducted by member or member organization personnel or by a qualified outside party; (4) designate, and identify to the Exchange (by name, title, mailing address, e-mail address, telephone number, and facsimile number) a person or persons responsible for implementing and monitoring the day-to-day operations and internal controls of the program and provide prompt notification to the Exchange regarding any change in such designation(s); and (5) provide ongoing training for appropriate persons.[283] The exchanges also require broker-dealers to establish anti-money laundering compliance programs.

In the wake of the terror attacks of September 11, 2001, Congress enacted the USA Patriot Act[285] which, among other things, broadens the list of financial institutions subject to the anti-money laundering laws. The Treasury Department has promulgated rules implementing the new provisions.[286] The rules apply to mutual funds that are regulated under the Investment Company Act of 1940.[287]

On July 1, 2002, The Financial Crimes Enforcement Network (FinCEN) announced some new reporting rules.[288] The rules require brokers to report suspicious transactions that are conducted or attempted by, at, or through a broker-dealer and involve or aggregate at least $5,000 in funds or other assets. Specifically, the rules identify four classes of transaction that qualify as involving suspicious activity. First, suspicious activity includes transactions involving funds derived from illegal activity or intended or conducted in order to hide or disguise funds derived from illegal activity. Second, the rule covers transactions designed, whether through structuring or other means, to evade the requirements of the Bank Secrecy Act. The third category consists of transactions that appear to serve no business or apparent lawful purpose or are not the sort of transactions in which the particular customer would be expected to engage, and for which the broker dealer knows of no reasonable explanation after examining the available facts. The fourth type of transaction that qualifies as suspicious activity includes transactions intended to further a criminal purpose, but apparently involving legally-derived funds. This fourth category is directed to cover the use of the broker-dealer to facilitate criminal activity, including terrorism.

SEC Administrative Sanctions for Broker–Dealers

Section 15(b)(4) of the Act gives the Commission authority to impose various sanctions against registered broker-dealers who violate the Act.[313] Registered brokers and dealers who violate the Act can suffer a wide range of consequences, ranging from censure to revocation of registration.[314] Depend-

283. *Id.*

285. Pub. L. No. 107–56 (2001).

286. Financial Crimes Enforcement Network; Anti–Money Laundering Programs for Financial Institutions, 67 Fed. Reg. 21,110, 2002 WL 737165 (April 29, 2002); 31 C.F.R. Part 103.

287. 15 U.S.C.A. § 80a–5(a)(1).

288. *See* Financial Crimes Enforcement Network; Amendment to the Bank Secrecy Act Regulations—Requirement that Brokers or Dealers in Securities Report Suspicious Transactions, 67 FR 44048–01, 2002 WL 1400399 (FinCEN, Treasury July 1, 2002).

313. 5 U.S.C.A. § 78*o*(b)(4).

314. *Id.*

ing on the severity of the violations, the SEC can also place limits on the registrant's activities.[315] In addition to sanctions against registered brokers and dealers, the Commission has similar authority with respect to persons associated with registered brokers and dealers. Section 15(b)(6)(A) of the 1934 Act grants the SEC broad administrative authority over such associated persons.[317] The SEC is empowered to hold hearings and impose sanctions for violations of the Act upon associated persons of broker-dealers. These sanctions can range from censure to suspension for up to twelve months and also include the power to issue an order barring the violator from associating with a broker or dealer.[318] The Commission can also place limitations on the activities of such associated persons.[319] The Commission can impose similar sanctions against municipal securities dealers[320] and government securities dealers.[321]In addition, the Commission can impose an administrative penalty for each violation of the act or rules of up to $50,000 for natural persons and $250,000 for entities.[322] The SEC also has cease and desist authority which permits cease and desist orders, after notice and opportunity for a hearing, against any person who violates the Act or rules promulgated under the Act.[323]

§ 14.3[6][A] Prohibited Practices Generally

SEC Rule 15c1–2[327] generally prohibits fraudulent, manipulative, and deceptive practices in connection with securities brokerage transactions. Broker-dealers and their employees are also subject to the anti-manipulation provisions contained in section 9 of the Exchange Act[329]as well as Rule 10b–5's general antifraud proscriptions that prohibit any person from engaging in deceptive conduct in connection with a purchase or sale of a security.[330] Because they result from artificial activity, manipulated prices are in and of themselves unfair. Conduct that is designed to artificially restrict supply is manipulative because it is meant to artificially raise prices as a result of the limited supply.

Manipulation generally does not consist of a single act, but rather is usually accomplished through a combination of various activities. As discussed below, there are virtually an infinite variety of manipulations. However, many manipulations have a number of common characteristics. For example, the following factors frequently are "classic elements" of a market manipulation: (i) restriction of the "float" or floating supply of the securities in the public market; (ii) price leadership by the manipulator; (iii) dominating and controlling the market for the security; and (iv) a collapse of the market for the security after the manipulative activity has ceased.[336] The foregoing factors are

315. 5 U.S.C.A. § 78*o*(b)(4).

317. 15 U.S.C.A. § 78*o*(b)(6)(A).

318. *Id.*

319. *Id.*

320. 15 U.S.C.A. § 78*o*–4(c)(2).

321. 15 U.S.C.A. § 78*o*–5(c)(1).

322. 15 U.S.C.A. § 78u–2.

323. 15 U.S.C.A. § 78u–3.

327. 17 C.F.R. § 240.15c1–2.

329. 15 U.S.C.A. § 78i.

330. 17 C.F.R. § 240.10b–5. *See* §§ 12.3–12.12 *supra.*

336. *See, e.g.,* SEC v. Resch–Cassin & Co., 362 F.Supp. 964, 976 (S.D.N.Y.1973); In the Matter of Monroe Parker Securities, Inc., Disciplinary Proceeding No. CAF970011, 1999 WL 33261827 (N.A.S.D.R. June 18, 1999).

indicia of market manipulation but are not necessarily present in every manipulation case.

Although it can take many forms, manipulation consists of any intentional interference with supply and demand.[343] As discussed in the subsections that follow, fictitious trades frequently form the basis of manipulative activity. However, it is not necessary that the transactions in question be fictitious. Manipulation can infect bona fide transactions.[344] The determination of whether a manipulation exists depends upon a combination of the foregoing factors.

§ 14.3[6][B] Wash Sales, Fictitious Trades, Matched Orders, Cross Trades, Marking the Close, and Painting the Tape

Section 9 of the Act not only prohibits manipulative practices generally but also certain well known manipulative practices. These include wash sales, fictitious trades, and matched orders. Related to a fictitious trade is a fictitious order or "spoof" that is designed to drive the quoted price higher.[346] Fictitious orders can also be used to artificially depress the market price of a security.[347] By their very nature, fictitious orders are deceptive.[348]

A wash sale is a fictitious sale where there is no change in beneficial ownership.[349] The evil of a wash sale is that it is a transaction without the usual profit motive and is designed to give the false impression of market activity when in fact there is none. A matched order occurs when orders are entered simultaneously to buy and sell the same security.[351] The mere fact that a broker crosses trades[352] or enters into matched orders does not violate the Act.[353] In fact, cross trades can actually benefit the firms' customers if the savings on commissions are passed on to the customers.[354] Thus, in some instances cross trades can result in price improvement for the firms custom-

343. Brooklyn Capital & Securities Trading, Inc., 52 S.E.C. 1286, Sec. Exch. Rel. No. 34–38454, 64 S.E.C. Docket 483, 1997 WL 144843 *3 (SEC 1997) (manipulation is the "intentional interference with the forces of supply and demand") (quoting Pagel, Inc., 48 S.E.C. 223, 226 (1985), aff'd, 803 F.2d 942 (8th Cir. 1986)).

344. *E.g.,* Markowski v. SEC, 274 F.3d 525, 529 (D.C.Cir.2001).

346. Spoofing is a practice whereby someone enters an order in order to drive the price up and then cancels the order before it is executed. *See* In the Matter of Monski, Administrative Proceeding File No. 3–10465, Sec. Exch. Act Rel. No. 34–44250, 2001 WL 460744 *2 (SEC May 3, 2001).

347. *See, e.g.,* In the Matter of the Application of Nickolaou, Administrative Proceeding File No. 3–5542 Sec. Exch. Act Rel. No. 34–16210, 18 S.E.C. Docket 409, 1979 WL 170308 (SEC Sept. 18, 1979) (fictitious sale orders were used to depress option prices).

348. *See* In the Matter of Jawitz, Complaint No. CMS960238, 1999 WL 1022138 (N.A.S.D.R. July 9, 1999).

349. *See, e.g.,* Ernst & Ernst v. Hochfelder, 425 U.S. 185, 205, n. 25, 96 S.Ct. 1375, 47 L.Ed.2d 668 (1976).

351. Dietrich v. Bauer, 76 F.Supp.2d 312, 340 (S.D.N.Y.1999).

352. *See, e.g.,* Michelson v. Merrill Lynch, Pierce, Fenner & Smith, Inc., 669 F.Supp. 1244, 1252 (S.D.N.Y.1987) ("A 'cross trade' is understood to mean a noncompetitive trade made by matching the orders of two customers, either directly or through an intermediary, without offering them openly").

353. In the Matter of Meehan, File No. 4–232, 2 S.E.C. 588, 1937 WL 1551 (SEC July 31, 1937). *See also, e.g.,* Yoshikawa v. SEC, 192 F.3d 1209, 1216 (9th Cir.1999).

354. *See* In the Matter of Strong/Corneliuson Capital Management, Administrative Proceeding File No. 3–8411, 57 S.E.C. Docket 394, Inv. Adv. Act Rel. No. IA–1425, 1994 WL 361971 n10 (SEC June 12, 1994).

ers. In fact, specialists and market makers may violate their best execution obligation if they interposition themselves between customer orders that could be matched or crossed for the benefit of both customers.[357]

Failure to disclose that trades entered on customer's behalf were cross trades can constitute deceptive conduct in violation of the Exchange Act.[368] Unauthorized cross trades also violate the securities laws.[369] Cross trades must be recorded as such in the broker-dealer's records.[370]

Another variety of market manipulation that can involve wash sales is "marking the close."[389] Marking the close consists of attempting to influence a security's closing price by executing purchase or sale orders at or near the close of normal trading hours.[390] If successful, the placing of an order to peg the price will artificially inflate or depress the closing price for the security and thus will determine the price of "market-on-close" orders placed by customers or other third parties.

Yet another manipulative practice that has the effect of artificially raising a stock's price is known as "painting the tape." Painting the tape consists of making a number of transactions throughout a trading day in order to give the impression that there is buying interest in the shares.[402] When these transactions are either shams[403] or solely designed to artificially raise the price, a manipulation has taken place.[404]

§ 14.3[6][C] Other Manipulative Practices: High Pressure Sales, Deceptive Recommendations, Excessive Commissions, Order Execution Obligations, Parking

The types of specific conduct that are addressed in other broker-dealer rules include market manipulation,[405] high pressure sales tactics,[406] deceptive recommendations,[407] generation of excessive commissions, [408] unauthorized

357. *See, e.g.,* In re NYSE Specialists Securities Litigation, 503 F.3d 89 (2d Cir. 2007), *affirming in relevant part and vacating and remanding in part on other grounds* 405 F.Supp.2d 281 (S.D.N.Y. 2005).

368. *See* Sartain v. SEC, 601 F.2d 1366, 1370 (9th Cir.1979).

369. *See, e.g.,* In the Matter of Bearcat, Inc., Administrative Proceeding File No. 3–10372, Sec. Exch. Act Rel. No. 34–43669, 2000 WL 1775287 (SEC Dec. 5, 2000).

370. *See, e.g.,* In the Matter of Robert Schwarz, Inc., Administrative Proceeding File No. 3–7377 No. 34–1248, 46 S.E.C. Docket 20, Release No. IA–28400 1990 WL 310672 (SEC Aug. 31, 1990) (failure to report cross trades).

389. *See., e.g.,* In the Matter of Chema, Sec. Exch. Act Rel. No. 34–40719, 68 S.E.C. Docket 1911, 1998 WL 820658 (SEC Nov. 30, 1998) (wash sales used to effectuate a marking the close manipulation).

390. *See, e.g.,* T.H.C., Inc. v. Fortune Petroleum Corp., 1999 WL 182593 *3 n. 5 (S.D.N.Y. 1999); SEC v. Schiffer, 1998 WL 226101 *1 n. 3 (S.D.N.Y.1998)

402. *See, e.g.,* SEC v. Competitive Technologies, Inc., 2005 WL 1719725 (D.Conn. 2005)

403. *See* Nanopierce Technologies, Inc. v. Southridge Capital Management LLC., 2002 WL 31819207 at *5 note 8 (S.D.N.Y. 2002).

404. *See, e.g.,* Purchases of Certain Equity Securities by the Issuer and Others, Sec. Act Rel. No. 33–6248, Sec. Exch. Act Rel. No. 34–17222, Inv. Co. Act Rel. No. IC–11403, 21 S.E.C. Docket 212, 1980 WL 20756 at *16 (SEC Oct. 17, 1980).

405. *See* §§ 6.2–6.3 *supra* (manipulation in connection with public offerings) § 12.1 *supra* (manipulation generally), and § 14.10[5] *infra* (manipulation by market makers).

406. *See* § 14.18 *infra.*

407. *See* §§ 14.16, 14.17 *infra.*

408. *E.g.,* Adonnino v. SEC, 111 Fed. Appx. 46 (2d Cir. 2004) (firm violated duty to supervise with respect to broker who was sharing profits and losses in a customer's account).

trading,[409] improper order executions,[410]improper extension of credit for securities transactions,[411] and misuse of customer funds or securities.[412]

Another manipulative practice is known as "parking" which consists of transferring record ownership of securities in order to hide the true identity of the beneficial owner.[414] All of these practices are prohibited by section 9 with regard to exchange-traded securities and by rules promulgated under sections 10(b) and 15 of the Exchange Act with regard to securities traded in the over-the-counter markets as well as on the exchanges.

Trading ahead of customers is an impermissible practice whereby a broker enters an order for his or her own account in advance of placing an order for customers. The object of this manipulative practice is to give the broker a preferential price. Trading ahead of customers ordinarily contravenes FINRA's (formerly the NASD's) fair and equitable principles of trade.[418] Front running is a manipulative practice that is based on a form of insider trading.[420] Front running exists in many forms. For example, front running can consist of trading ahead of customers' orders in order to take advantage of inside information pertaining to others that will have an effect on the price. If the broker knows of a large sell order that will move the price downward once it is entered and executed, and if the broker sells for his or her own account ahead of that order, the broker gets the advantage of the market price determined without the market's consideration of the large pending sell order. Front running is manipulative and also is inconsistent with FINRA's requirement that brokers' conduct be consistent with fair and equitable principles of trade.

Various manipulative practices can occur in connection with public offerings. For example, artificially preparing the market or stimulating the aftermarket will run afoul of the anti-manipulation rules.[424] Additionally, Regulation M[425] severely restricts purchases by persons participating in a distribution in the course of the distribution. Another deceptive practice that can take place in the context of a public offering is "free riding,"[426] which involves purchasing securities in a public offering without the intent or the funds to pay for the purchase with a view toward taking a free ride on a rising market.[427] Free riding also violates the margin requirements that govern the extension of credit for securities transactions.[428] In any context, entering an

409. *See* § 14.21 *infra.*

410. *See* § 14.13 *infra.*

411. *See* § 14.9 *supra.*

412. *See* § 14.8[2] *supra.*

414. *See, e.g.,* Yoshikawa v. SEC, 192 F.3d 1209 (9th Cir.1999); SPIC v. Vigman, 74 F.3d 932, 933 n. 3 (9th Cir.1996).

418. NASD IM–2110–2 (interpretative material prohibiting trading ahead of customer limit orders).

420. *See, e.g.,* John v. Journal Communications, Inc., 801 F.Supp. 210, 211 (E.D.Wis.1992).

424. *See* § 6.3 *supra.*

425. 17 C.F.R. §§ 242.101 *et seq.*; *See* Anti–Manipulation Rules Concerning Securities Offerings, Sec. Rel. Nos. 33–7375; 34–38076; IC–22412 (Dec. 20, 1996), 62 Fed. Reg. 520 (1997). *See* § 6.2 *supra.*

426. In the Matter of Wu, Administrative Proceeding File No. 3–9024, 70 S.E.C. Docket 386, Rel. No. ID–144, 1999 WL 518983 *13 n. 8 (SEC July 22, 1999).

427. *See* § 6.3[2] *supra.*

428. *See* § 14.9 *infra.*

order to purchase a security without any intent to pay for it other than through a free ride is deceptive conduct.[429] In contrast, where a customer's nonpayment for the securities is a simple breach of contract without deception, the securities laws will not be implicated.[430]

Beyond these specific manipulative broker-dealer activities and the general anti-manipulation and deception rules, the SEC makes it clear that violation of its rules is not limited to violation of any specified SEC rules, but rather covers all conduct that operates as a deceptive or manipulative device.[431] This broad coverage of SEC regulation thus is not limited to conduct that is specifically identified in SEC rules. Broker-dealers have an obligation to act in a professional manner and failure to do so can be a deceptive practice in violation of the generalized antifraud prohibitions.[432]

The SEC has taken the position in various contexts that it can regulate conduct that would be manipulative even if the concern is not based on activity that is explicitly prohibited by existing rules.[433]

§ 14.4 Broker–Dealer Registration; Definitions and Exemptions

Section 15(a)(1) of the Exchange Act[1] provides that securities brokers and dealers must be registered in order to conduct their business, unless their business is exclusively intrastate or unless otherwise exempted from registration.

§ 14.4[1] Broker–Dealer Registration: Definitions

Definitions of Broker and Dealer

Broker is defined in the Exchange Act to include any person in the business of buying and selling securities for others.[8] To fall within the definition, it is not necessary that the broker deal directly with customers; thus, for example, clearing brokers are subject to SEC regulation. A dealer is defined by the Exchange Act to be any person who is in the business of purchasing securities for his or her own account.[10]

The Act's registration requirements, as well as the definitions of broker and dealer, are drafted broadly to include a wide range of securities professionals. Key terminology in the definitions of broker and dealer is the phrase "engaged in the business."[11] In deciding whether a firm is acting as a broker-

---

429. A.T. Brod & Co. v. Perlow, 375 F.2d 393 (2d Cir.1967).

430. *See* A.T. Brod & Co. v. Perlow, 375 F.2d 393, 398 (2d Cir.1967).

431. Rule 15c1–2 (c), 17 C.F.R. § 240.15c1–2(c).

432. As explained in one opinion, "Under the shingle theory, investors are entitled to rely on the implied representation that they will be dealt with fairly, honestly and in accord with industry standards." In the Matter of Gartz, Administrative Proceeding File No. 3–9060, 65 S.E.C. Docket 351, Release No. ID–113, 1997 WL 441913 n. 33 (SEC Initial Decision Aug. 6, 1997) relying on Charles Hughes & Co. v. SEC, 139 F.2d 434, 437 (2d Cir.1943), *cert. denied*, 321 U.S. 786, 64 S.Ct. 781, 88 L.Ed. 1077 (1944).

433. *See, e.g.*, In the Matter of Hazel Bishop, Inc., 40 S.E.C. 718, 1961 WL 65108 (SEC 1961).

§ 14.4

1. 15 U.S.C.A. § 78*o*(a)(1).

8. 15 U.S.C.A. § 78c(a)(4)(A).

10. Section 3(a)(5)(A).

11. Sections 3(a)(4), 3(a)(5); 15 U.S.C.A. §§ 78c(a)(4), 78c(a)(5).

dealer, a number of factors are considered. The relevant factors include whether the firm (1) receives transaction-based compensation, such as commissions or referral fees, (2) is involved in negotiations between an issuer of securities and investors, (3) makes valuations as to the merits of the investment or gives advice, and (4) is active rather than passive in locating investors.[13] Participating in a public offering as an underwriter or dealer requires registration as a broker-dealer under the Exchange Act.[14]

§ 14.5 Broker–Dealer Registration Requirements

The broker-dealer registration requirements are found in section 15(b) of the Exchange Act[3] and the SEC rules promulgated thereunder. The registration process is commenced by an applicant's completion of SEC Form BD.[5] The information to be supplied in the registration materials includes a detailed description of the broker-dealer's assets and financial condition,[6] including a showing of compliance with the Commission's net capital rule.[7] Nonresident broker-dealers, general partners of broker-dealers, and managing agents of broker-dealers must file an irrevocable power of attorney designating the SEC as agent for service of process.[8]

After the Form BD has been filed, the SEC may grant or deny the registration.[9] In the event that the Commission is inclined to deny an application for registration, it is directed by statute to institute formal proceedings by giving notice of the grounds for the proposed denial and giving the applicant an opportunity to be heard.[10] Once a broker-dealer's registration has been granted, the Commission can also institute formal proceedings to revoke the registration for noncompliance with the registration or other requirements of the Act.[11] The SEC may suspend a broker-dealer's registration pending a determination of whether the registration should be revoked.[12] As an alternative to ordering a revocation of registration, for less severe violations, the Commission has the option of censuring or placing limitations upon the broker-dealer's activities.[13] Additionally, the Commission may suspend a broker-dealer for a period of up to one year.[14]

Once a broker-dealer is registered under the Act, cancellation may be

13. *See, e.g.,* SEC v. Zubkis, No. 97 Civ. 8086, 2000 WL 218393, *9 (S.D.N.Y.2000).

14. *See, e.g.,* SEC v. Milan Capital Group Inc., 2000 WL 12467 (S.D.N.Y. 2000).

§ 14.5

3. 15 U.S.C.A. § 78*o*(b).

5. 4 Fed.Sec.L.Rep. (CCH) ¶ 32,702–32,703.

6. In addition, once registered, the broker-dealer firm must file annual audited financials with the SEC pursuant to SEC Rule 17a–5, 17 C.F.R. § 240.17a–5. When the broker-dealer has just been registered and has not yet begun any business nor realized any income, then the annual financial report may be waived. *See* Spike Financial Services, LLC, 2001 WL 1512715 (DEC No Action Letter Nov. 29, 2001).

7. *See* 17 C.F.R. § 240.15c3–1.

8. 17 C.F.R. § 240.15b1–5.

9. 15 U.S.C.A. § 78*o*(b).

10. 15 U.S.C.A. § 78*o*(b)(1)(B).

11. 15 U.S.C.A. § 78*o*(b)(4).

12. 15 U.S.C.A. § 78*o*(b)(5).

13. 15 U.S.C.A. § 78*o*(b)(4).

14. *Id.*

effected by a filing of a formal withdrawal from registration.[16] Registration can also be suspended or revoked as a result of disciplinary action by the SEC or a self regulatory organization.

§ 14.6 Municipal Securities Dealers

Municipal securities, as referred to in the Securities Exchange Act of 1934, comprise a wide variety of obligations, primarily bonds issued by state, local or other political subdivisions or their agencies, including industrial development bonds.[1] Because of their governmental issue or guarantee, municipal securities are generally exempt from the registration and reporting provisions of both the 1933 and 1934 Acts.[2] Proponents of the municipal exemption from registration and reporting requirements cite several arguments in favor of the current legal status: (1) independent audits of municipal issuers and SEC registration are claimed to be undue cost burdens which would decrease municipal bond marketability and impair the municipality's ability to borrow for a public purpose; and (2) the 1934 Act sought to prevent speculative abuse, which had not occurred in the municipal area, and would not arise since institutional investors dominated that market and held the bonds for investment, not speculative, objectives.[3]

Transactions in municipal securities generally take place in more specialized markets by brokers and dealers dealing exclusively with municipal securities and who are, therefore, exempt from the general broker-dealer regulation and rules of the Securities and Exchange Commission. There is no organized exchange subject to SEC oversight nor is there FINRA coverage regarding persons dealing only in municipal securities. Furthermore, prior to 1975, the Securities and Exchange Commission had no jurisdiction over these transactions except in circumstances involving fraud. The antifraud provisions that are applicable to municipal securities provide some protection to investors, but significantly less than investors in securities of private issuers. Even with municipal securities regulation that was added to the Exchange Act in 1975, the 1933 Securities Act's exemptions and the lack of an organized exchange leave investors with less protection than with the regular securities market for private issuers. However, as discussed below, notwithstanding the exemption from 1933 Act registration, when municipal securities are initially offered to the general public, municipal securities dealers must provide a disclosure document that somewhat parallels those that would be required in a 1933 Act registration. The required disclosure document has been criticized as inadequate. In addition to the required disclosure document, although exempt from registration, municipal securities are not exempt from the antifraud provisions. Thus, for example, failure to disclose mark-ups for municipal securities transactions can support a private action for violations of SEC Rule 10b–5.[9]

---

16. 17 C.F.R. § 240.15b6–1.

§ 14.6

1. 15 U.S.C.A. § 78c(a)(29).

2. 15 U.S.C.A. §§ 77c(a)(2), 78c(a)(12). *See* § 4.3 *supra*.

3. *See* Note, Municipal Bonds, and the Federal Securities Laws: The Results of Forty Years of Indirect Regulation, 28 Vand. L. Rev. 561, 583–85 (1975).

9. Grandon v. Merrill Lynch & Co., 2001 WL 826092, [2001–2002 Transfer Binder] Fed. Sec. L. Rep. (CCH) ¶ 91,497 (S.D.N.Y.2001).

§ 14.7 Regulation of Government Securities Dealers

Brokers and dealers who deal solely in exempted securities need not register under section 15 of the Exchange Act.[1] Municipal securities dealers, who are also exempt from broker-dealer registration, are regulated through the Municipal Securities Rulemaking Board,[2] but there was no comparable regulation for government securities dealers until 1986. Following the insolvency of a number of government securities dealers, Congress enacted legislation to require the regulation of government securities dealers. The government securities dealer registration requirements more closely parallel that of broker-dealers generally than of municipal securities dealers.

Government securities are those securities which are issued or guaranteed by the federal government or a federal agency. Treasury securities, such as savings bonds, "T–Bills," and "Treasury Notes" are familiar government securities. Lesser-known government-guaranteed securities are those issued by federally-owned agencies, for example Government National Mortgage Obligations or "Ginnie Maes." Finally, there are money market instruments such as "federal funds," and "repurchase agreements." Federal funds are cash reserves which the Federal Reserve Board requires banks to maintain for liquidity purposes and which are manipulated by the Federal Reserve Board to effectuate monetary policy. "Repurchase agreements" or "repos" are investment schemes by which institutional investors and government securities dealers exchange cash for government securities.

The market for United States government securities has been described as the world's largest, most efficient and liquid securities market.[6] The United States Treasury uses the market to finance the national debt, while the Federal Reserve Board conducts monetary policy through the market.[7] As such, the market is "the cornerstone of the U.S. capital market system," and its integrity must be insured.[8] However, between July 1975 and April 1985, failures of unregistered government securities dealers threatened this integrity.[9] Certain problems were common to many of the failures. In some cases the failed firm had issued false and misleading financial statements; or in some cases a firm would mask its troubled status through complex relationships and transactions with affiliated companies; and finally, customer losses often occurred because the customer failed to secure control of or collateralize securities underlying a repurchase (or "repo") transaction with a problem dealer. Congress identified the weakness of the regulatory framework for the government securities market as a major cause of these failures.[11] To bolster this framework, Congress enacted the Government Securities Act of 1986.[12]

The Government Securities Act of 1986 added section 15C to the Exchange Act of 1934 and provided for conforming amendments to the Exchange

§ 14.7

1. 15 U.S.C.A. § 78*o*–4(c). *See* §§ 14.2, 14.4 *supra*.

2. *See* 15 U.S.C.A. § 78*o*–4.

6. Senate Report No. 99–426, S. 1416, Government Securities Act of 1986, Fed.Sec.L.Rep. (CCH) No. 1195 at 5 (Sept. 17, 1986).

7. *Id.* at 4.

8. *Id.* at 2.

9. *Id.* at 6.

11. *Id.* at 7.

12. 15 U.S.C.A. § 78o–5(a)(1)(A).

Act, the Investment Company Act of 1940, and the Investment Advisers Act of 1940.[13] The Act seeks to eliminate problems by: (1) requiring registration of government securities brokers and dealers with the Commission or with appropriate regulatory agencies; (2) establishing financial responsibility safeguards such as capital adequacy and reporting requirements; (3) mandating procedures for the acceptance and use of customers' securities; and (4) allowing on-site inspection and enforcement by federal regulators.[15] The Government Securities Act of 1986 is also designed not to impose regulation that will adversely affect the liquidity and efficiency of the government securities market.[16]

§ 14.8 Broker–Dealer Net Capital and Reserve Requirements

The solvency of broker-dealer firms has long been a concern for investors and for the investment markets in general. As discussed in a later section, in reaction to a number of brokerage firm failures, Congress enacted the Securities Investor Protection Act of 1970 to provide for customers' insurance against losses due to brokerage firm insolvency.[1] However, other regulatory protections focused on preventing brokerage firm insolvencies, have been in place much longer. For example, the SEC has had its long-standing net capital requirements for broker-dealer firms. A companion set of protections is found in the SEC reserve requirements. Both the net capital and reserve requirements are discussed below.

Net Capital Requirements

In 1942, the SEC adopted its net capital rule which is designed to assure a safe balance between a brokerage firm's securities holdings, cash, and liabilities.[2] The current net capital rule imposes extremely complicated accounting and solvency requirements for a brokerage firm's assets and liabilities.[3] The discussion that follows will present a brief overview of the net capital requirements. For more detailed discussion, the reader should consult other sources.[5]

The basic financial responsibility standards for broker-dealers are found in the "net capital" rule adopted by the SEC under authority of section 15(c)(3) of the 1934 Act.[6] Prior to the financial debacle suffered by the securities industry from 1968 to 1970, securities brokerage firms belonging to stock exchanges which had "net capital" rules deemed to be more stringent than those of the SEC were exempt from the SEC's net capital requirements. However, after the SEC and Congressional investigations showed how flexibly

13. Senate Report No. 99–426, S. 1416, Government Securities Act of 1986, Fed.Sec.L.Rep. (CCH) No. 1195 at 11 (Sept. 17 1986).

15. H. Rep. No. 99–258, 99th Cong, 1st Sess., at 17–23 (1985); S. Rep. No. 99–426, 99th Cong., 2d Sess., at 14 (1986).

16. *Id.*

§ 14.8

1. 15 U.S.C.A. §§ 78ccc *et seq. See* the discussion in § 14.24 *infra.*

2. Sec. Exch. Act Rel. No. 34–3323 (SEC Oct. 29, 1942).

3. SEC Rule 15c3–1, 17 C.F.R. § 240.15c3–1.

5. *See* 23A Jerry W. Markham & Thomas Lee Hazen, Broker–Dealer Operations Under Securities and Commodities Law: Financial Responsibilities, Credit Regulation and Customer Protection ch. 5 (2d ed. 2002).

6. 15 U.S.C.A. § 78o(c)(3).

the exchanges had interpreted their rules to allow member firms to continue business with inadequate capital, the SEC revoked this exemption and made all broker-dealers subject to its requirements.

Net Worth Test for Net Capital. Under the SEC net capital rule, if the broker-dealer opts out of the aggregate indebtedness test that is described below, a broker-dealer must maintain "net capital" of at least $250,000.[7] "Net capital" is defined as "net worth" (excess of assets over liabilities), subject to many special adjustments prescribed in the rule. One of the more important special adjustments is the "haircut" or discount that must be applied in valuing securities listed on the asset side of the balance sheet. The net capital rule requires the broker-dealer to discount securities by a specified amount; this amount varies depending on the type of security. The haircut is designed to provide an additional margin of safety in light of the volatility of securities prices.

Alternative methods for Satisfying Net Capital Requirements. There are two alternatives to the net capital rule's net worth test. The first alternative is the rule's aggregate indebtedness test under which a broker-dealer may not let its aggregate indebtedness exceed 1500% of its net capital (800% during its first year of business).[8] Also, a broker-dealer can alternatively qualify under Rule 15c3–1(d), which is designed to test its general financial integrity and liquidity, and its ability to meet its continuing commitments to its customers. This alternative, which has some enumerated exceptions,[10] is not available for all broker-dealers.[11]

On occasion, unscrupulous brokers have attempted to evade the net capital requirements by contrived and deceptive transactions known as parking. Parking, an illegal trade practice, consists of transferring securities for the purpose of hiding their true ownership.[12]

Customers' Funds and Securities: The Customer Protection Rule and the Reserve Requirements

Customers leave large amounts of cash and securities with their brokers. The cash "free credit balances"[18] arise principally from two sources: a deposit of cash by a customer prior to giving his broker a purchase order, and receipt by the broker of proceeds of a sale of securities, or interest or dividend income, which has not yet been reinvested or delivered to the customer. The securities are of two types: securities purchased "on margin"[19] (i.e., with the

---

7. Prior to 1992, there was a $25,000 minimum for active broker-dealers.

8. *See* 17 C.F.R. § 240.15c3–1(i).

10. *See* 17 , C.F.R. § 240.15c3–1(k).

11. *See* 17 C.F.R. § 240.15c3–1(k)(2).

12. *See, e.g.,* Yoshikawa v. SEC, 192 F.3d 1209 (9th Cir.1999).

18. This is the cash in a customer's margin account that can be withdrawn by the customer at any time without restriction. Moreover, this is also represents the total remaining money in a margin account after margin requirements.

19. The margin requirements are discussed in § 14.9 *infra.*

broker advancing part of the purchase price to the customer), which (under the standard margin agreement) the broker is entitled to hold as security for the loan and to repledge to secure its own borrowings; and "fully-paid" securities, which the broker holds solely as a convenience for the customer (serving as custodians) and is supposed to "segregate" from the broker's own securities.[20]

§ 14.9 The Margin Rules and Extension of Credit for Securities Transactions

Margin Transactions Explained

Not all securities are purchased in a straight cash transaction. A large number of securities transactions, especially those by speculative investors, are entered into by a broker, extending credit to the purchaser, while the lender (broker) holds the purchased securities as collateral. These securities purchases on credit are referred to as margin transactions. Margin transactions are permissible in margin accounts–namely those that have qualified for the extension of credit. A margin purchase gives the security holder (investor) leverage, and thus, while significantly increasing the risk of investment, also increases the potential gain. However, excessive credit balances in customer accounts create undue investor risk. For example, brokerage firms that extended high levels of credit in the 1920s were wiped out by the stock market crash of 1929. The margin requirements were designed to curb such excesses in the levels of credit extension to investors.

The effect of price changes of the securities purchased on credit and held in a margin account can be understood from examining how an increase in the loan value of a securities account will increase the likelihood of a margin call whereby the broker makes a demand on the customer for additional collateral in order to shore up the account's solvency. Assume that an investor has a stock portfolio consisting entirely of marginable securities with a current market value of $100,000. The less the investor borrows against his or her portfolio, the risk of a margin maintenance call is greatly reduced. For example, if the investor borrows thirty percent of the value of stocks (i.e., $30,000), the stocks must decline in value by more than fifty-seven percent before the investor would be subject to a maintenance call, assuming a margin maintenance requirement of thirty percent imposed by the investor's brokerage firm.[7] A margin involving securities consists of borrowing money from your broker to buy a stock and using your investment as collateral. Borrowing on margin provides a person with the means to leverage his/her assets to secure access to a line of credit. The credit (funds) obtained from a margin account are often used to leverage the value of existing assets to borrow money for the purchase of additional securities. The following table demonstrates the effects of margin borrowing against $100,000 worth of stock:

20. SEC Rule 15c2–1(a), 17 C.F.R. § 240.15c2–1(a).

§ 14.9

7. Although, as discussed below, the self regulatory organizations impose a 25% maintenance requirement for most securities, many brokerage firms impose a higher requirement for their own protection. The margin maintenance requirement may in fact be higher for more volatile and/or less liquid securities.

If investor borrows:	A maintenance call will be issued if the portfolio value declines to:	Percentage decline before maintenance call occurs:
$50,000 (50%)	$71,429	29%
$40,000 (40%)	$57,143	43%
$30,000 (30%)	$42,857	57%
$20,000 (20%)	$28,571	71%
$10,000 (10%)	$14,286	85%

The examples that follow demonstrate the calculation of permissible margin levels for an initial purchase of securities.

If an investor wants to buy 10,000 shares of ABC Corp. stock which is trading at $10 per share (for a total $100,000 for 10,000 shares) and wants to make the purchase with only $75,000 cash, he or she can do so by borrowing the remaining $25,000 that is necessary to complete the purchase. The margin calculation for the account would be as follows:

The investor purchases 10,000 shares of ABC Corp. at $10 per share for a total cost of $100,000. The investor would then deposit the $75,000 cash with the broker and borrow the remaining $25,000 from the broker.

$100,000 (value of stock)—($25,000) (debit balance) = $75,000 (net equity);

$75,000 (net equity) ÷ $100,000 (value of stock) = 75% net equity as the margin balance

The next example demonstrates the calculation of the maximum loan permitted under the Federal Reserve Board's fifty percent limit under its margin rules for the extension of credit. An investor wants to purchase 10,000 shares of ABC Corp. stock which is trading at $10 per share (a total of $100,000 for the 10,000 shares). The investor can purchase on fifty percent margin by purchasing the stock for $100,000, using $50,000 cash and borrowing $50,000 from the broker:

10,000 shares ABC Corp. @ $10 = $100,000 net equity [$50,000 cash + $50,000 margin loan]

This is the maximum number of shares that the investor may purchase with $50,000 cash, since it puts the investor at the Federal Reserve Board's fifty percent margin limit for the extension of credit. Specifically, each time an investor purchases additional securities on margin, it is considered another extension of credit so that the 50% maximum credit balance (or minimum fifty percent margin) will apply to each purchase. An investor can only leverage 50% of stock purchased. In other words, an Investor purchasing stock on margin must put at least 50% of money down toward the purchase of the stock. Thus, for example, after making the first purchase of the 10,000 ABC Corp. shares, if the investor now wants to purchase an additional $10,000 of stock, he or she must deposit at least an additional $5,000 cash (or at least an additional $10,000 worth of other marginable collateral) in order to make the second purchase. The margin calculation is cumulative across all stocks purchased by an investor.

The following are examples of the operation of the margin maintenance requirements of at least twenty-five percent that are imposed by the self regulatory organizations.

An investor's securities account has a $50,000 debit on which the investor will be charged interest by the lending brokerage firm. The interest on the investor's debt will in turn be added to the account's debit balance. For example, if the $10 per share price of the 10,000 shares of ABC Corp. stock remains constant, assuming 6% interest (1/2% per month), after one month the investor's account would incur an additional $250 debit. The investor's account would still consist of 10,000 shares ABC Corp. at $10 per share for a total of $100,000. There would be the initial $50,000 debit plus an additional $250 resulting from the interest charged over the first month. This would result in a total debit balance of $50,250. The margin computation would then be as follows:

$100,000 (value of stock)—$50,250 (debit balance) = $49,750 (net equity); $49,750 (net equity) ÷ $100,000 (value of stock) = 49.75% net equity (or margin)

The foregoing example would be in compliance with the self regulatory organization margin maintenance requirements but not with the Federal Reserve Board's extension of credit requirements. Assume that after the first month, the price of ABC Corp. has dropped to $8 per share. The investor's account would then consist of 10,000 shares of ABC Corp. at $8 per share for a total of $80,000. The account would have the $50,000 initial debit plus the $250 interest for a total debit of $50,250. The account would still be in compliance with the minimum margin maintenance requirement because compliance is calculated based on the initial extension of credit:

$80,000 (value of stock)—$50,250 (debit balance) = $29,750 (net equity); $29,750 (net equity) ÷ $80,000 (value of stock) = 37.1875% margin

However, if during the first month, the price of ABC has dropped to $6 (instead of the $8 per share in the previous example), then the investor's account would be computed as follows. There would be 10,000 shares of ABC Corp. at $6 per share for a total of $60,000. The account would have the $50,000 initial debit plus the $250 interest for a total debit of $50,250. The account would not be in compliance with the minimum margin maintenance requirement:

$60,000 (value of stock)—$50,250 (debit balance) = $9,750 (net equity) $9,750 (net equity) ÷ $60,000 (value of stock) = 16.25% margin

This example results in a total that is below the New York Stock Exchange (NYSE), American Stock Exchange, and FINRA (formerly NASD) minimum margin maintenance requirements and the investor would be subject to a margin call. As a result, either the investor would have to provide additional money or collateral, or the broker would liquidate the securities in the account to pay off the debit balance.

Limitations on the Extension of Credit for Securities Transactions

Section 7 of the Exchange Act sets out a complex system of regulation with regard to the extension of credit for securities transactions, but does not apply to exempt securities.[15] By virtue of section 7(a),[16] the Federal Reserve System Board of Governors is delegated the authority to promulgate rules governing the extension of credit where securities are used as collateral to secure the loan. Various regulations have been adopted with regard to broker-dealers, banks, and other persons so extending credit. Broker-dealer margin rule enforcement lies with the SEC through injunctions, criminal proceedings, revocation of registration, or suspension from membership in self regulatory

15. 15 U.S.C.A. § 78g.

16. 15 U.S.C.A. § 78g(a).

organizations. In 1996, Congress preempted the states' ability to regulate the extension of credit in securities transactions.[17]

The credit extension rules are not limited to traditional margin accounts. The credit extension rules also apply to late payments in cash accounts.[19]

The maximum limits for the extension of credit are set forth in the statute, but the statutory limits have been further cut back by the Federal Reserve Board. Section 7(a) of the Exchange Act states that the initial extension of credit may not be for an amount greater than the higher of (1) fifty-five percent of the security's then current market price or (2) one hundred percent of the lowest market price of the security during the preceding thirty-six calendar months but no more than seventy-five percent of the current market price. However, certain exempt governmental securities trade with a much higher margin. For example, United States Treasury bills can have up to a ninety percent margin at the time of purchase. This more highly leveraged transaction for federal government notes is more in line with the margin requirements for the more speculative commodity markets.[26] Notwithstanding the statutory fifty-five percent ceiling on credit, the Federal Reserve Board has imposed an even lower credit ceiling of fifty percent for the extension of credit as opposed to the margin maintenance requirements.[27]

The applicable rules of the Federal Reserve Board for broker-dealers' extension of credit are found in Regulation T.[30] Regulation U governs bank loans that are secured directly or indirectly by stock or other marginable securities.[31] Regulation X applies to margin borrowing by residents of the United States of either domestic or foreign lenders.[34] Regulation X in addition to applying to foreign lenders focuses on the borrower; the rules prohibit borrowers from entering into transactions that would violate Regulations T or U.

In order to qualify for an extension of credit under Regulation T, the securities must either be traded on a national securities exchange[38] or be actively traded in the over-the-counter market. Formerly, there was a list of margin equity securities established by the Federal Reserve Board.[39] The Federal Reserve Board now provides for the automatic marginability of stocks

17. 1934 Act section 15(h), 15 U.S.C.A. § 78o(h).

19. The settlement period for equity securities formerly was five business days but this has been shortened to three business days. Rule 15c6–1, 17 C.F.R. § 240.15c6–1. *See* Securities Transactions Settlement, Sec. Exch. Act Rel. No. 34–33023, 55 S.E.C. Docket 332, 1993 WL 403275 (SEC Oct. 6, 1993); NASD Notice to Members 93–77, 1993 WL 1434168 (Nov. 1993). Options transactions have a one-day settlement and thus must be settled on the next business day.

26. One way to achieve comparable leverage in the securities markets is to trade listed "put" and "call" options. *See* SEC Report of the Special Study of the Options Markets, 96th Cong., 1st Sess. (1978). In additional to the foregoing credit rules, option and short selling transactions will have impact on the margin regulated balance. To the extent the security customer has options positions, these positions will further limit the margin requirement. Even without credit, the margin requirement will limit the option for other positions the customer can take because they are leverage.

27. *See, e.g.,* Supplement to Regulation T, 12 C.F.R. § 220.18.

30. 12 C.F.R. § 220.1–220.131.

31. 12 C.F.R. § 221.1–221.124.

34. 12 C.F.R. § 224.1–224.3.

38. *See* section 6 of the Act, 15 U.S.C.A. § 78f. *See* § 14.2 *supra.*

39. 15 U.S.C.A. § 78g(c)(2).

that are part of the Nasdaq's National Market.[40] Additionally, foreign sovereign debt securities are marginable to the extent of their "good faith" loan value. The current level of the margin securities cannot exceed a fifty percent debit balance in connection with the purchase of any additional securities.[41] The Federal Reserve Board is statutorily empowered to impose minimum levels for maintaining margin accounts under section 7(a), as well as initial levels, but it has never exercised this authority. Accordingly, a "margin call," whereby the customer is required to come up with additional collateral lest the margined securities be sold, will never be required by operation of law unless a new security is purchased for the account. This is thus left to the broker-dealer's discretion[43] and the twenty-five percent minimum required by exchange rules and by Nasdaq and FINRA (formerly the NASD). Most brokerage firms have established their own policies for margin calls, many of which are more stringent than FINRA and exchange rules. Brokers' guidelines may also depend in part not only upon the value of the collateral but also on the diversification of the margined securities as well as their reliability.

In addition to the credit limitations for margin accounts, the margin rules require that whenever a security is purchased in a cash account, payment must be made within a specified settlement period after the date of purchase or else the broker-dealer must cancel or otherwise liquidate the transaction.[45] In mid–1993, the settlement period for most securities was shortened to three business days.[46] The settlement date for options remains the business day following the transaction. A broker's delay in liquidating the account will not relieve the customer of the obligation to pay for the securities.[47] A rapid sale of the securities before the settlement date will not enable the customer to take a free ride. Free riding is the entering into a transaction without the intent to pay with the hope that the purchase price will be covered by a quick sale. Free riding violates the securities laws. Under the Federal Reserve Board rules, if a customer sells securities within three days of purchase and without having paid for the securities, for the next ninety days, the customer cannot purchase securities unless the account contains enough cash to cover the purchase price.[49]

Margin Maintenance Requirements

The statutory (and Federal Reserve Board) limits on margin accounts apply only to the *initial* extension of credit and do not deal with an increase in the ratio of the debit of the margin account in relation to the value of the securities due to the decline in the price of securities used as collateral after their initial purchase. In other words, under both SEC and Federal Reserve

40. *See* Bd. of Governors of the Federal Reserve System Docket No. R–0512 (March 7, 1984).

41. 12 C.F.R. §§ 220.3(c), (d), 220.18(a). Regulation T does not avail itself of the fifty-five percent statutory maximum. Instead, it imposes a lower ceiling of fifty percent. Supplement to Regulation T, 12 C.F.R. § 220.18.

43. *See* SEC Report of the Special Study of the Options Markets, 96th Cong., 1st Sess. pt. 4 at 5–6 (1978). *Cf.* United States v. Tuff, 359 F. Supp.2d 1129, 1135–1136 (W.D. Wash. 2005).

45. 12 C.F.R. § 220.8(b)(1), (4).

46. Rule 15c6–1, 17 C.F.R. § 240.15c3–1.

47. Shearson Lehman Brothers, Inc. v. M & L Investments, 10 F.3d 1510 (10th Cir. 1993) (broker-dealer's failure to liquidate account after purchaser failed to pay for stock was not a defense to breach of contract action).

49. 12 C.F.R. § 220.105.

Board regulation it lies purely within the lender's discretion to decide at what point additional securities as collateral or cash will be needed to fortify a margin account where the value of the current collateral is declining. However, the exchanges Nasdaq, and FINRA (formerly the NASD) impose margin maintenance requirements. Under these margin maintenance rules, the current market value of the collateral must be at least twenty-five percent of the account's total value. Thus, there are minimum margin maintenance requirements for all accounts. Generally, brokerage firms assure compliance with the margin maintenance requirements by instituting an internal policy for "house calls" at a level above the regulatory minimum.[53] The higher house call level thus provides a safety zone in the event that the market is unusually volatile or the customer delays in providing the necessary additional collateral.

Margin Disclosure Requirements; Suitability

In addition to the substantive margin regulation set forth by the Federal Reserve Board and self regulatory organization regulations, margin accounts trigger special disclosure obligations.[56] The customer must be given a margin disclosure statement by the broker-dealer when the margin account is opened and must also receive a disclosure statement annually.[57] The disclosure statement is designed to alert customers to the risks associated with margin accounts. The required disclosure at the opening of a margin account is designed to inform the customer of margin related risks. The annual disclosure requirement is designed to remind the customer of these risks. By themselves, margin trades are high risk transactions and are not suitable for all investors.

Failure to fully inform the client of margin risks can result in broker-dealer liability for losses caused as a result thereof.[64] However, when a customer understands the nature of margin risks, he or she will not be able to state a claim for relief.[65]

The SEC has evidenced significant concern about investors' misunderstanding of the significant risks associated with margin transactions. In addition to the foregoing disclosure requirements, SEC Rule 10b–16[66] requires broker-dealers to adequately disclose the cost to the customer of any securities transaction where credit is extended. In 2001, the SEC initiated a special link on its official website to better inform investors as to the risks of purchasing securities on credit.[67]

Remedies for Violations of the Margin Rules

At one time, some courts recognized a private remedy in the hands of the customer who is injured by the broker-dealer's violation of the credit exten-

53. The brokerage firm can raise the house call level without prior notice to the customer. *See, e.g.,* Sec. Exch. Act Rel. No. 34–44223, 2001 WL 431540 (SEC April 26, 2001); NASD Rule 2341.

56. *See* NASD Rule 2341.

57. *Ibid.*

64. *See, e.g.,* Burton v. Wheat First Securities, Inc., Docket Number 99–03729, 2000 WL 33171709 (N.A.S.D. Dec. 20, 2000) (arbitration award in excess of $200,000).

65. *See, e.g.,* Podgoretz v. Evans & Co., Inc., 1997 WL 138989 (E.D.N.Y.1997).

66. 17 C.F.R. § 240.10b–16.

67. *See* http://www.tradeworx.com/sec/cgi-bin/tutorialmargin.cgi.

sion rules.[75] However, the overwhelming majority of more recent decisions is to the contrary.[76] The absence of an implied remedy under the margin rules is bolstered by the amendment to section 7(f) and ensuing Federal Reserve Board Regulation X rendering the customer himself or herself in violation of the Act.

§ 14.10 Market Makers

Market Making in Context

Formerly market makers were primarily the province of the over-the-counter markets. However, Nasdaq's national stock market, formerly an over-the-counter market is now a national securities exchange but it still thrives on the market-maker system. Traditionally, exchanges were formerly based on a system of specialists.[1] Some exchanges have completely abolished their trading floors and now operate through market makers. Although the New York Stock Exchange has kept a trading floor and the specialist system, as the markets become increasingly electronic, specialists are becoming more akin to market makers and it is likely that they will eventually be completely replaced by market makers.

Since the over-the-counter markets by definition do not have a central exchange for the entering of buy and sell orders, it is necessary to have some sort of central clearing mechanism to perform a comparable function. The National Association of Securities Dealers Automated Quotation System (Nasdaq) is merely an electronic means of transmitting, disseminating, and publicizing the latest quotes but it is not a vehicle for effecting transactions. Nasdaq generally gives both "bid" and "asked" quotes for over-the-counter securities. Several hundred of the more actively traded over-the-counter securities are listed on a "national market" with only one quoted price. As of 2006, the Nasdaq national market is registered national securities exchange. This means that as of July 1, 2006, there is a three-tiered Nasdaq market (Global Select, Global Market and National Market) rather than the former two tiers (NMS and Small Cap) of Nasdaq securities. A number of smaller over-the-counter companies listed in Nasdaq which do not qualify for the national market system have their securities listed in the Nasdaq small capitalization system.

Lower volume stocks and many of the lowest priced over-the-counter securities have their quotations listed on an electronic bulletin board or in the "pink sheets." Traditionally, quotations for securities not traded through the national market system or automated quotation system were found in the "pink sheets." The SEC approved, originally on a one-year pilot basis, a Nasdaq electronic bulletin board for computerized quotations for stocks not listed on a national exchange or in the Nasdaq system.[7] Although "pink

---

75. *E.g.* Pearlstein v. Scudder & German, 429 F.2d 1136 (2d Cir.1970), *cert. denied*, 401 U.S. 1013, 91 S.Ct. 1250, 28 L.Ed.2d 550 (1971).

76. *E.g.* Useden v. Acker, 947 F.2d 1563 (11th Cir.1991), *cert. denied*, 508 U.S. 959, 113 S.Ct. 2927, 124 L.Ed.2d 678 (1993); Bennett v. United States Trust Co., 770 F.2d 308 (2d Cir.1985), *cert. denied*, 474 U.S. 1058, 106 S.Ct. 800, 88 L.Ed.2d 776 (1986); Bassler v. Central National Bank in Chicago, 715 F.2d 308 (7th Cir.1983); Gutter v. Merrill Lynch, Pierce, Fenner & Smith, Inc., 644 F.2d 1194 (6th Cir.1981); Gilman v. FDIC, 660 F.2d 688 (6th Cir.1981).

§ 14.10

1. *See* § 14.11 *infra*.

7. Sec.Exch.Act Rel. No. 34–27975 (May 1, 1990). *See* SEC Approves One–Year Pilot Program for NASD's OTC Electronic Bulletin Board, 22 Sec.Reg. & L.Rep. (BNA) 672 (May 4, 1990).

sheets" continue to exist for some securities, many small capitalization companies that formerly would have been listed in the pink sheets are now traded through the Nasdaq bulletin board.

Most over-the-counter trades take place through online communications among securities dealers and using quotations provided by market makers. The enhanced technology presents the opportunity for magnifying the effects of human error by transferring that misinformation more rapidly and efficiently into the marketplace.

Mechanics of Market Making Activities—Some Basic Concepts

A broker-dealer acts as a market maker for a particular security or securities. Many securities have more than one market maker. A market maker for a particular security not traded on a national exchange must enter "bid" and "asked" quotes in or over the automated quotation system (Nasdaq), over the Nasdaq's bulletin board for less actively traded small capitalization stocks or in the "pink sheets" with respect to stocks not listed on an automated quotation system. There must be at least three market makers in order for a security to be listed through Nasdaq. Some market makers are more active than others in maintaining current quotations. In addition to general market maker qualifications, the Nasdaq rules provide that a market maker can qualify as a Primary Nasdaq Market Maker ("PNMM").[15]

A market maker is responsible for making "two-way" bids on the securities for which it makes a market. In other words, the market maker has the responsibility of quoting both a bid price (the price which someone is willing to pay for the security) or an offer wanted (OW) as well as an asked price (the price at which someone is willing to sell the security) or a bid wanted (BW). The difference between the bid and asked price is known as the spread and represents the market maker's compensation with respect to transactions executed at the bid and asked price. To the extent that trades are to be made in transactions that exceed the size of the bid and asked quotes, there is no published spread.

Published bid and asked quotations are qualified by the quantity of shares for any quote. In other words a bid or asked quote at a stated price would be for a stated number of shares (which could range, for example, from 100 shares to thousands of shares). As such, the market maker must be willing to stand behind these price quotations. The market maker thus must be willing and prepared to both buy the stock and sell it as principal according to the quantities covered in any bid or asked price that the market maker posts. Accordingly, the market maker is frequently in the position of holding long and short positions in the securities in which he or she makes the market. To the extent that a market maker executes transactions beyond the amount of shares currently in inventory or outside the size parameters of the

---

15. For example, there are the following thresholds for being designated as a Primary Nasdaq Market Maker: (I) it must be at the best bid or best offer as shown in the Nasdaq quotation system at least thirty-five percent of the time, (II) it must maintain a spread no greater than one hundred and two percent of the average dealer spread, and (III) no more than fifty percent of the market maker's quotation updates may occur without being accompanied by at least one unit of trading.

A firm may continue as a market maker only so long as it carries out its market making functions properly. *Cf.* In the Matter of Tower Trading, L.P., Sec. Exch. Act Rel. No. 34–47537, 2003 WL 1339179 (SEC 2003) (NASD revoked permission to act as primary market maker but SEC reversed the order, citing irregularities in the hearing process).

current quotations, the market maker is taking a risk, depending upon the demands of the market. The SEC rules require that the market maker is financially able to fulfill its market making obligations.[18] As a general proposition, market makers are subject to significant regulation by both FINRA (formerly the NASD) and SEC.[19] The SEC rules also give FINRA supervisory power over market makers which includes the ability to withdraw a broker-dealer's market making authority.[20]

Actively traded stocks have multiple active market makers. Competition for orders among active market makers results in competitive prices although there may be price variations between and among market makers.

A market maker's obligations include the posting of reliable quotations that are not the result of market manipulation. The market maker is also obligated to honor the quotations that it posts to the market. Accordingly, it is a violation of NASD (now FINRA) rules for a market maker to fail to honor posted quotes.[22]

When there are multiple market makers, the national best bid/best offer ("NBBO") is representative of the best price available based on current quotations. This is a constantly moving target which can change on a second-by-second basis. The NBBO represents the highest bid and the lowest asked quotation that is available at a particular point in time.[23] The NBBO, as is the case with any published bid or asked price, is generally qualified by the number of shares being offered. In other words, the NBBO price reflects quotations or offers with respect to a specified number of shares. The availability of the both the NBB (national best bid) and the NBO (national best offer) thus necessarily is in large part dependent upon a transaction size falling within the NBBO share quantity parameters. In rare instances, even for trades within the NBBO share quantity parameters, brokers may be able to get a better execution. For example, price improvement may be possible when there are available cross trades within the firm. It is to be noted, however, that cross trades in many situations may be problematic as they are susceptible to claims of manipulation.[24]

Traders are guilty of manipulation when they enter orders merely to inflate or deflate the NBBO. Entering small limit orders for the purpose of changing the published bid and asked prices constitutes illegal manipulation.[37] This practice has been referred to as auto execution manipulation[38] or spoofing. Regulation NMS (and former Exchange Act Rule 11Ac1–4) provides

18. 17 C.F.R. § 240.15c3–1(a)(4).

19. *See* § 14.10[4] *infra.*

20. *See* 15 U.S.C.A. § 78*o*–3(b)(7), following procedures set out in 15 U.S.C.A. § 78*o*–3(h)(1).

22. *See, e.g.,* NASD Regulation Directs Knight Securities to Pay $1.5 Million For Market Violations, *http://www.nasdr.com/news/pr2002/release_02_001.html* (Jan. 7, 2002) (imposing a $700,000 fine and requiring $800,000 in payments to customers for failing to honor posted quotes and other market making violations).

23. *See, e.g.,* Geman v. S.E.C., 334 F.3d 1183, 1186 n.5 (10th Cir. 2003) ("More specifically, the NBBO is the highest quoted bid price and lowest quoted offer price from among all quotations entered in the Consolidated Quotation Service.")

24. *See, e.g.,* SEC v. Sayegh, 906 F.Supp. 939 (S.D.N.Y.1995).

37. In the Matter of Yoshikawa, Admin. Proc. File No. 3–12057, Release No. 34–53731, 2006 WL 1113518 (SEC 2006) (placing of small limit orders in order to manipulate the National Best Bid and Offer prices violated NASD rules; NASD sanctions affirmed).

38. *Id.*

that an electronic communications network must display a customer's limit order as the new NBBO. Within seconds after placing his small limit order, the auto-execution manipulator then placed a larger order on the opposite side through a clearing system that he expected to auto-execute the trade at the new NBBO; he would then cancel the first order allowing the NBBO to return to its original price.

Premise of FINRA Regulation of Market Makers

Market makers are subject to both SEC and FINRA regulation. This regulation includes inspection of records in order to assure that they are not abusing their market making positions.[53] FINRA's oversight of market making activity includes the authority to disqualify a broker-dealer from acting as a market maker.[54]

FINRA's Rules of Fair Practice establish standards of conduct for market makers to ensure that they carry out their operations in an appropriate manner. Thus, for example, a broker-dealer who accepts payment for its decision to act as a market maker has compromised its position of neutrality and therefore will be subject to SEC sanctions. The acceptance of compensation interferes with the normal factors a broker-dealer should consider in deciding whether to act as market maker; such factors include attributes that affect the security's liquidity and intrinsic value. The market maker's obligation is to maintain an orderly market. However, when the market maker is executing customer orders, its primary obligation is to those customers.[56]

Market Makers' Conflict of Interest; Disclosure Obligations

In an attempt to promote the more efficient execution of customer orders and more accurate pricing, as well as to eliminate potential conflicts of interest, the SEC approved the FINRA's prohibition against market makers trading ahead of certain customer orders.[57] The interpretation of NASD (now FINRA) Rules of Fair Practice applies to all Nasdaq-traded securities and prohibits broker-dealers acting in their market making capacity from trading ahead of their customers' limit orders.[59]

In addition to conducting market making transactions in which the broker-dealer acts as principal, he or she may also enter into riskless transactions upon a customer's order or upon orders of other broker-dealers.[62] The

53. 17 C.F.R. § 240.17a–5(a).

54. *See* 15 U.S.C.A. § 78*o*–3(b)(7), following procedures set out in 15 U.S.C.A. § 78*o*–3(h)(i).

56. Eichler v. SEC, 757 F.2d 1066 (9th Cir.1985) (market maker's duty to execute customer orders meant that it could not base pricing and order execution on an orderly market without making full disclosure to its customers). *See* Newton v. Merrill, Lynch, Pierce, Fenner & Smith, 135 F.3d 266 (3d Cir.1998) (en banc) (upholding complaint against brokerage firms for looking only to NASD's National Best Bid and Offer rather than to private online quotations that would have given the customer a better execution price).

57. Exch. Act Rel. No. 34–34279, 59 Fed. Reg. 34,883 (SEC July 7, 1994).

59. A limit order is one in which a customer specifies a minimum price that he or she will accept in payment for securities being sold or a maximum price that he or she will pay for securities being purchased. The limit order is an alternative to an "at market" order which simply instructs a broker to purchase or sell a security at the market price.

62. "In Nasdaq, a riskless principal trade is one in which a broker/dealer, after having received an order to buy (sell) a security, purchases (sells) the security as principal, at the same price, to satisfy that order. The broker/dealer generally charges its customer a mark up, markdown, or commission equivalent for its services, which is disclosed on the confirmation required by Securities Exchange Act (Exchange Act) Rule 10b–10." *See* Guidance on Compensa-

individual risk that attaches to his or her transactions as a principal puts the market maker in a potential conflict of interest situation vis--vis his or her responsibilities as an agent for retail customers. It has been held that a broker-dealer who recommends a security without disclosing that he or she is a market maker has made a material misrepresentation so as to give rise to a private right of action for violation of Rule 10b–5.[63] In order to prevail in such an action, plaintiff must prove all the elements normally required to state a Rule 10b–5 claim. Thus, for example, nondisclosure of the market maker's acting as principal did not result in liability in the absence of proof that the price of the stock was affected.[65] It has been held, however, that a market maker who purchases stock from a customer at a price below the market will be liable for fraud in the transaction.[66]

Ordinarily broker-dealer in their retail transactions are compensated through a mark-up or commission.[67] When the same firm acts as a market maker for the securities, the broker may charge the customer a net price without differentiating the applicable mark-up, mark-down or commission. NASD Rule 2441, adopted in 2006, which is now a FINRA rule, requires customer consent before net pricing can occur.[68] Specifically, Rule 2441 requires market makers intending to trade equity securities on a net basis with their customers to provide disclosure to, and obtain written consent from, non-institutional customers on an order-by-order basis.[69]

In addition to imposing civil liability for material omissions in connection with recommendations, the SEC rules require disclosure of market maker status. SEC Rule 10b–10[76] makes it unlawful for a broker or dealer to effect a

---

tion and Mixed Capacity Trading, Special NASD Notice to Members 01–85 (Dec. 24, 2001) (question 3). For further guidance on riskless principal trade reporting obligations for Nasdaq securities, *see* NASD, Notice to Members 00–79; NASD Notice to Members 99–66; NASD Notice to Members 99–65.

This is in contrast to an agency trade: "An agency trade is a trade in which a broker/dealer, authorized to act as an intermediary for the account of its customer, buys (sells) a security from (to) a third party (e.g., another customer or broker/dealer). Such a trade is not executed in, or does not otherwise pass through, the broker/dealer's proprietary account. When executing an agency trade, the broker/ dealer generally charges the customer a commission for its services." Guidance on Compensation and Mixed Capacity Trading, Special NASD Notice to Members 01–85 (Dec. 24, 2001) (question 2).

"A riskless principal transaction occurs when a dealer receives from its customer an order to purchase (or sell) a security and purchases (or sells) that security to another person in a transaction that is proximate in time and designed to offset the customer's order." In re Lynch, Sec. Exch. Act Rel. No. 34–46439, 78 S.E.C. Docket 1055, 78 S.E.C. Docket 1058, 2002 WL 1997953 (SEC Aug. 30, 2002), relying on Strategic Resource Management, Inc., 52 S.E.C. 542, 544 n.8 (1995).

63. Chasins v. Smith, Barney & Co., 438 F.2d 1167 (2d Cir.1970). Liability was imposed even though the sales confirmation disclosed the broker's market making activity. *See also,* Magnum Corp. v. Lehman Brothers Kuhn Loeb, Inc., 794 F.2d 198 (5th Cir.1986); Bischoff v. G.K. Scott & Co., 687 F.Supp. 746 (E.D.N.Y.1986).

65. Shivangi v. Dean Witter Reynolds, Inc., 825 F.2d 885 (5th Cir.1987). *But see* Chasins v. Smith, Barney & Co., 438 F.2d 1167 (2d Cir.1970) (where the court permitted rescission without a specific showing of loss causation). *Cf.* Geman v. SEC, 334 F.3d 1183 (10th Cir. 2003) (affirming sanctions against brokerage firm for failing to disclose it was trading as principal at favorable prices).

66. Weiner v. Rooney, Pace, Inc., [1987 Transfer Binder] Fed.Sec.L.Rep. (CCH) ¶ 93,174 (S.D.N.Y.1987).

67. *See* § 14.14 *infra.*

68. FINRA Rule 2441.

69. *Id.*

76. 17 C.F.R. § 240.10b–10.

transaction for any customer or to induce any purchase or sale of a security without disclosing whether the broker is acting as the agent for the customer or as agent for someone else, including whether or not the broker is acting as a market maker or principal. It has been held that the mere fact that the dealer's role is disclosed in the transaction confirmation slip will be insufficient to preclude a violation of Rule 10b–10 if the customer does not understand the significance of the disclosure. It is to be noted, however, that not every nondisclosure of a conflict of interest will violate Rule 10b–10.[78]

A broker-dealer is subject to disciplinary sanctions for failure to disclose his or her market maker status in violation of Rule 10b–10. It is one thing to show a failure to disclose market maker or principal status in a given transaction; however, it is quite another thing for the customer to show materiality, reliance, and scienter so as to give rise to a Rule 10b–5 cause of action. In a Second Circuit decision, a 10b–5 claim was recognized for nondisclosure of market maker status in connection with a broker-dealer's recommendation since the market maker status was a material factor in the customer's decision to invest.[80] Some courts have required proof of actual loss causation in terms of a differential in market price.[81] In the context of an unsolicited transaction, it is not as significant for the investor to know that the broker-dealer effecting the customer's offer is a market maker, except perhaps for the purpose of determining the commission. When a broker's firm acts as a market maker it may be possible for the customer to get a slight break on the commission.[83]

Although Rule 10b–10 establishes disclosure obligations in connection with confirmation of securities transactions, compliance with its requirements does not preclude liability for fraud.[84] It has thus been held that compliance with Rule 10b–10 did not preclude a market maker's liability for failing to disclose allegedly excessive mark-ups.[85]

Market Makers and Manipulation

The market making obligations place market makers in control of market prices. As such, unscrupulous market makers can abuse their positions by engaging in manipulative practices.[93] Due to the potential for manipulation, regulators scrutinize market making activities. FINRA (formerly the NASD)

---

78. Press v. Quick & Reilly, Inc., 218 F.3d 121 (2d Cir.2000) (broker-dealer's alleged nondisclosure of conflict of interest did not violate Rule 10b–5 or Rule 10b–10; SEC had filed an *amicus* brief urging the court to find, as it did, that the disclosure was sufficient; the nondisclosures discussed certain fees in connection with automatic sweeps of customers' funds into money market fund).

80. Chasins v. Smith, Barney & Co., 438 F.2d 1167 (2d Cir.1970). *But see* Shivangi v. Dean Witter Reynolds, Inc., 825 F.2d 885 (5th Cir.1987).

81. Shivangi v. Dean Witter Reynolds, Inc., 825 F.2d 885 (5th Cir.1987). *See also, e.g.,* Eichler v. SEC, 757 F.2d 1066 (9th Cir.1985) (affirming disciplinary sanctions against underwriter and market maker which failed to obtain the best executions for its retail customers).

83. When a broker goes through a third party market maker they split the commission. Although a brokerage firm's market making and retail operations are distinct, acting through a broker which is also a market maker does eliminate a middleman.

84. *E.g.,* Ettinger v. Merrill Lynch, Pierce, Fenner & Smith, Inc., 835 F.2d 1031 (3d Cir.1987).

85. *Id.* (Rule 10b–10 requires disclosure of mark-ups for many transactions but not for others).

93. *E.g.,* United States v. Haddy, 134 F.3d 542 (3d Cir.1998) (manipulation found where defendants: 1) controlled the quantity of the securities available for trading, 2) generated demand for the stock, 3) raised the price of the securities, and 4) sold the securities at a large profit).

watches closely to assure that the market maker in fact maintains an orderly market and is not engaging in manipulative practices; if so, the market maker will be subject to losing approval to act as market maker. The risk of market maker manipulation is much greater when a broker-dealer acts as the sole active market maker for the stock in question. When brokerage firms have such "house stocks,"[98] there is no independent free market to gauge the legitimacy of their market making and other activities. Brokerage houses handling house stocks are thus in a very good position to manipulate the market. Thus, although there is nothing illegal per se about concentrating in house stocks, doing so is one of the common benchmarks of a controlled market manipulation. Other manipulative activities can also occur in connection with house stocks.[101] For example, account representatives may be given higher commissions for pushing "house stocks."[102] They may also be given disincentives for having customers enter sell orders in house stocks.[103] In extreme instances, customer sell orders may even be ignored.[104] These practices designed to dissuade customer sales orders constitute illegal manipulation and also violate broker-dealer standards of fair dealing.

In part because of the potential for abuse resulting from control of the market, Nasdaq stocks must be handled by at least three market makers in order to be listed on Nasdaq. Continued listing requires only two active market makers,[107] except for the largest National Market System securities, which must have at least four active market makers.[108] The presence of multiple market makers does not eliminate the potential for collusion and thus a dealer with only a small percentage of the total market float can be participating in manipulative market making practices.[109] Collusion is not the only way that one market maker can dominate the market. Some market makers may simply decide to concentrate on other stocks that they make markets in and thus remain passive with regard to securities that end up being handled by a dominant market maker. In this way one market maker can dominate the market without conscious collusion with the remaining market makers.

Control over the market is not in itself a violation of the Act.[111] However, it violates the antifraud provisions to fail to disclose control over the market for securities handled by the market-maker and broker-dealer.[112] Also, by controlling and cornering the market by reducing the market float,[115] or

98. Stocks that are traded solely among the clients of that brokerage house. *See, e.g.,* United States v. DiStefano, 129 F.Supp.2d 342 (S.D.N.Y.2001).

101. *See, e.g.,* SEC v. Hasho, 784 F.Supp. 1059 (S.D.N.Y.1992).

102. *See, e.g.,* SEC v. Wellshire Securities, 737 F.Supp. 251 (S.D.N.Y.1990).

103. *See, e.g,* In the Matter of Demaio, Administrative Proceeding File No. 3–7912, 54 S.E.C. Docket 1509, Release No. ID–37, 1993 WL 300297 (SEC Aug. 4, 1993).

104. *E.g.,* United States v. Matthews, 34 Sec. Reg. & L. Rep. (BNA) 601 (S.D.N.Y.2002).

107. NASD Rule 4310(c)(1).

108. NASD Rule 4450(e).

109. In the Matter of Hibbard, Brown & Co., Admin. Proc. File No. 3–8418, Release No. 34–35476, 58 S.E.C. Docket 2561, 1995 WL 116488 n. 20 (SEC March 13, 1995).

111. Pagel, Inc., 48 S.E.C. 223, 226 (1985), aff'd sub nom. Pagel, Inc. v. SEC, 803 F.2d 942 (8th Cir.1986).

112. SEC v. First Jersey Securities, 101 F.3d 1450, 1467–1468 (2d Cir.1996).

115. *See, e.g,* SEC v. National Bankers Life Ins. Co., 334 F.Supp. 444, 446 (N.D.Tex.1971), affirmed 477 F.2d 920 (5th Cir.1973).

executing market squeezes,[116] broker-dealers can illegally maintain artificially high prices in the stocks they are manipulating. Market domination is thus a common starting point for manipulative scheme.

Regardless of the absence of market dominance, a market maker's bad faith in publishing quotations is a breach of the market maker's obligations. Thus, for example, a market maker's pattern of backing away from published quotes can establish manipulation.[122] A market maker's backing away from published quotations will often be in violation of the so-called "firm quote" rule[123] that requires market makers to stand behind their published quotations. Market maker improprieties can easily develop into manipulative conduct. Traders are guilty of manipulation when they enter orders merely to inflate or deflate the NBBO. Entering small limit orders for the purpose of changing the published bid and asked prices constitutes illegal manipulation.[124] Not every questionable act by a market maker amounts to a manipulation. Thus, for example, although backing away from quotations may be evidence of a manipulative scheme, the mere fact that a market maker backed away is not sufficient to establish a manipulation.[127]

§ 14.11 Trading on Stock Exchanges; The Specialist System

Trading by Exchange Members

The principal function and purpose of a national securities exchange is to provide a marketplace in which member firms, acting as brokers, can purchase and sell securities for the account of their customers. The question addressed in section 11 of the Exchange Act[2] is the extent to which stock exchange members and their firms should be permitted to trade in listed securities for their own account, in view of the possibly unfair advantages they may have over public customers when engaging in such trading.

Section 11(a),[3] as amended in 1975, prohibits an exchange member from effecting any transactions on the exchange for its own account, or any account with respect to which it exercises investment discretion,[4] with certain specified exceptions, including transactions as a market maker (specialist) or odd-lot dealer, stabilizing transactions in connection with distributions, bona fide arbitrage transactions, and other transactions which the SEC concludes should be exempt from the prohibition. Traditionally, the inquiry has focused on three special categories of transactions: (a) "floor trading" and "off-floor trading" by members and their firms, (b) transactions by "odd-lot dealers," and (c) transactions by specialists. The increasing domination of New York

116. *See, e.g.,* In the Matter of Goldman, Administrative Proceeding File No. 3–7866, Sec. Exch. Act Rel. No. 34–31210, 52 S.E.C. Docket 1551, 1992 WL 252182 (SEC Sept. 22, 1992).

122. *See, e.g.,* In re The Chicago Stock Exchange, Sec. Exch. Act Rel. No. 34–48566, 81 S.E.C. Docket 490, 2003 WL 22245922 (SEC 2003).

123. The SEC's firm quote requirement is found in SEC Rule 11 Ac1, 17 C.F.R. § 240. 11 Ac1–1.–1.

124. In the Matter of Yoshikawa, Admin. Proc. File No. 3–12057, Release No. 34–53731, 2006 WL 1113518 (SEC 2006).

127. In the Matter of Elgindy, Admin. Proc. File No. 3–11145, Sec. Exch. Act Rel. No. 34–49389, 2004 WL 865791 (SEC 2004).

§ 14.11

2. 15 U.S.C.A. § 78k.

3. 15 U.S.C.A. § 78k(a).

4. 15 U.S.C.A. § 78k(a)(1).

Stock Exchange trading by institutional customers has focused attention on two additional categories: (d) "block positioning" by member firms, and (e) transactions for "managed institutional accounts."

The New York Stock exchange retains its trading floor although it is becoming increasingly electronic. Other exchanges have abandoned the physical trading floor and have transformed into electronic markets.

Specialists

For most of its history, the specialist system was the core of the New York Stock Exchange and distinguished it from other securities markets. However, with technological advancements including screen-based trading and electronic communications networks (ECNs), the traditional specialist system and floor trading practices became obsolete.[21] By 2007, it became clear that the specialist system was in need of change due to technological advancements. The changes included changing the name of specialists as they functions and operations were redefined.[22]

§ 14.12 Multiservice Brokerage Firms; Information Barriers; The Chinese Wall or Fire Wall

At the time that the federal securities laws were originally enacted, the functions of the various professionals in the securities industry were relatively distinct. However, the last quarter of the twentieth century witnessed not only the elimination of clear distinctions between the permissible activities of banks and securities firms,[1] but also the proliferation of multiservice firms providing a wide variety of financial services. Thus, for example, today, a multiservice securities firm combines the functions of investment banking and corporate counseling with investment advisory, investment management and retail broker-dealer services.[2]

Brokerage firms that offer a wide variety of services will have to separate the operations of many of those services. This separation is not limited to operations but also to accounting and recordkeeping issues. Furthermore, information barriers known as "Chinese walls" or "fire walls" may have to be established in order to avoid conflict of interest problems.

A typical multiservice firm performs numerous functions. These functions typically include: (1) investment banking (including underwriting and rendering advice to corporate issuers); (2) research (which services all of the firm's departments); (3) sales, which includes both retail sales and investment management; and (4) generally firms will have their own trading desk which operates in the over-the-counter markets and also performs arbitrage for their own account. The following simplified graphic depicts a prototypical multiservice securities brokerage firm:

21. *See generally* Jerry W. Markham & Daniel J. Harty, For Whom the Bell Tolls: The Demise of Exchange Trading Floors and the Growth of ECNs, 33 J. Corp. L. 865 (2008).

22. *See, e.g.,* Aaron Lucchetti, Hi, "Designated Market Makers," Wall St. J. p. C4 (Nov. 30, 2007) (discussing impending changes in the operation of New York Stock Exchange trading).

§ 14.12

1. *See* § 22.5 *infra.*

2. Commercial banks are subject to the same conflicts.

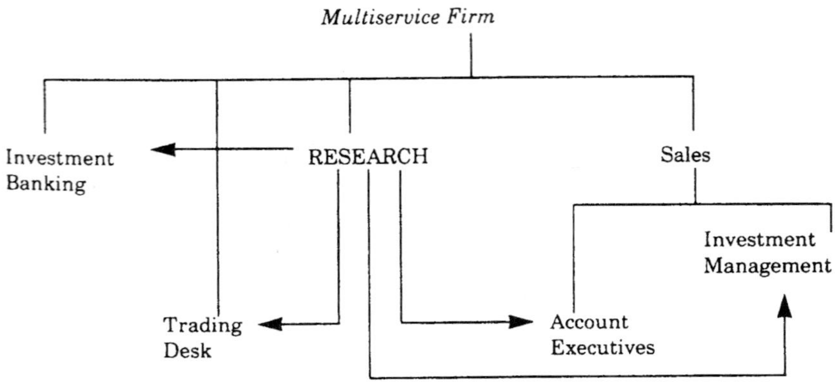

These varied functions give rise to conflicts of interest as the firm has a duty to guard the confidentiality of any non-public information it receives from a corporate client. A major problem is that while the research department is supplying information to each of the other departments, the research department should be basing its evaluation on independent research, not from confidential information acquired from the firm's other departments. The antifraud provisions of the security laws require the firm to disclose all material non-public information it has or abstain from using it in trading or recommending the security in question.[3] This "disclose or abstain" rule further obligates firms to refrain from executing or recommending transactions unless justified in light of all information known to the firm.[4] In response to these conflicting duties, multiservice financial institutions have established internal policies and procedures to restrict the flow of material nonpublic information from the department in which it originates. These procedures are colloquially referred to as "Chinese Walls" or "fire walls."

The required information barriers involve every aspect of a brokerage firms operations. Information barriers are not limited to separating the research and underwriting functions from each other and from the retail operations. When a broker-dealer acts as a market maker for over-the-counter securities, there are a number of potential conflicts of interest that can arise. For example, market makers may also be acting as underwriters with respect to a public offering. A brokerage firm's market making activities must be carried on independently of other operations including the firm's own trading department as well as the firm's other departments that are mentioned above.

§ 14.13 Execution of Customer Orders

The Best and Prompt Execution Obligations

Assuring fair execution of customer orders is a concern of the SEC in overseeing the operation of the securities markets. Customers can enter various types of orders. For example, a market order directs the broker (through the floor trader or market maker) to execute the transaction at the

3. *See, e.g.,* In re Cady, Roberts & Co., 40 S.E.C. 907 (1961) and the other authorities discussed in § 12.17 *supra*. *See also, e.g.,* Dirks v. SEC, 463 U.S. 646, 103 S.Ct. 3255, 77 L.Ed.2d 911 (1983).

4. *See* § 12.17 *supra*.

market price. As discussed below in this section, broker-dealers have obligations to ensure that customers receive a fair execution of these market orders. As an alternative to committing to purchase or sell at the market price, a customer can let the market come to him or her by placing a limit order and giving the broker specific limits. For example, a limit order would authorize purchase at a particular price or lower but in no event higher than the price specified in the limit order. Broker-dealers have duties with regards to these orders as well. For example, there is the question of priority of limit orders. There are prohibitions against broker-dealers trading ahead of their customer's limit orders.[2] Among other things, these prohibitions are designed to prevent the broker from putting its order (and therefore its interests) above that of the customer.[3]

The best execution obligation can thus be divided into two categories: those relating to market orders which have been referred to as the "plain vanilla" best execution obligation and the "sophisticated" best execution obligation that applies when a broker is given price discretion such as with a not-held[4] order.[5]

In addition to violating the trading standards noted above, undisclosed trading ahead of customers perpetrates a deception upon those customers.[7] This type of deception is in violation of a broker-dealer's obligations even in the absence of an express prohibition on undisclosed trading ahead of customer orders.[8]

Over the past several years, there has been increasing concern over whether brokers, especially in the over-the-counter markets, were securing the best order executions for their customers.[10] There were charges that brokers and market makers were conspiring on setting the spread between

---

§ 14.13

2. *See, e.g.,* NASD IM–2110–2 (available on Westlaw) (rule relating to trading ahead of customers and protection of limit orders).

3. *See* Order Approving National Association of Securities Dealers, Inc.'s Limit Order Protection on Nasdaq, File No. SR–NASD–94–62, Sec. Exch. Act Rel. No. 34–35751, 59 S.E.C. Docket 867, 1995 WL 325939 (SEC May 22, 1995).

4. As explained by one court:

> A customer placing a not-held order provides the market maker with the volume of a particular stock sought to be bought or sold and grants the market maker discretion as to price and time of execution of that trade, with the goal of achieving "best execution." On a not-held order, a market maker is not "held" to the immediacy and price requirements imposed in a market or limit order.
>
> The NASD has defined a not-held, or "working," order as "an order voluntarily categorized by the customer as permitting the member to trade at any price without being required to execute the customer order." When handling such an order, a broker-dealer "must use its brokerage judgment in the execution of the order, and if such judgment is properly exercised, the broker is relieved of its normal responsibilities with respect to the time of execution and the price or prices of execution of such an order." Although the customer bestows discretion to the broker-dealer, a customer nevertheless monitors the transaction and modifies the parameters of the order as it deems necessary.

SEC v. Pasternak, 561 F.Supp.2d 459, 482 (D.N.J. 2008) (citations omitted).

5. *Id.* at 507.

7. *See e.g.,* United States v. Dial, 757 F.2d 163, 168–169 (7th Cir.1985), *cert. denied,* 474 U.S. 838, 106 S.Ct. 116, 88 L.Ed.2d 95 (1985).

8. In the Matter of E.F. Hutton & Co., Admin. Proc. File No. 3–6490, 49 S.E.C. 829, Sec. Exch. Act Rel. No. 34–25887, 41 S.E.C. Docket 413, 1988 WL 239506 (SEC July 6, 1988).

10. *See, e.g.,* Introducing Firms Must Monitor Best Execution by Clearing Brokers, 32 Sec. Reg. & L. Rep. (BNA) 567 (May 5, 2000).

bid and asked quotes so as to deny customers the benefit of competitive quotes for stocks having multiple market makers. SEC investigation of the problem led to charges of antitrust violations.[12] On the heels of these proceedings, the SEC established a series of requirements designed to improve the execution of customer orders in the over-the-counter markets. The Commission adopted Rule 11Ac1–4,[14] known as the "display rule." Rule 11Ac1–4 requires market makers and specialists to display the price and the full size of customer limit orders that reflect buying and selling interest at a better price than a specialist's or market maker's public quote. The rule also requires market makers and specialists to increase the size of their quote for a particular security to reflect a limit order when the limit order is priced equal to the specialist's or market maker's disseminated quote and that quote is equal to the national best bid or offer.[15] The Commission also amended its "quote rule"[16] which requires market makers and specialists to publicly disseminate the best prices that they enter into an electronic communications network.[17]

In 2005, The NASD proposed amending its best execution rule (FINRA Rule 2320) to extend to orders placed by other broker-dealers as well as to orders placed by customers.[22] The amendment was approved by the SEC so that it is now clear that the NASD's best execution rule applies to all orders received by a market maker.[23] The 2006 amendments also expanded the best execution obligations in other respects. It is now clear that in checking the available market price, the broker or market maker must consider all market centers, thus expressly including ECNs[24] and the accessibility of the quotation.[25] In addition, the Rule now directs the broker to consider the terms of the order in performing the best execution.[26]

FINRA (formerly the NASD) has a specific rule prohibiting broker-dealers from trading ahead of their customers' limit orders.[30] This rule expanded upon the preexisting NASD position[31] that a market maker could not trade ahead of

12. These charges led to class action of more than 1 million plaintiffs against 37 market makers, which has since been settled. *See* Court Approves Distribution of Settlement in Nasdaq Market–Makers Antitrust Litigation, 32 Sec. Reg. & L. Rep. (BNA) 148 (Feb. 7, 2000).

14. 17 C.F.R. § 240.11Ac1–4.

15. The size must be increased only when the customer limit order is "greater than de minimis." *See* Order Execution Obligations, Sec. Exch. Act Rel. No. 34–37619A, 61 Fed. Reg. 48,290 (SEC Sept. 12, 1996).

16. Rule 11Ac1–1, 17 C.F.R. § 240.11Ac1–1.

17. *See* Order Execution Obligations, Exch. Act Rel. No. 34–37619A, 61 Fed. Reg. 48,290, 1996 WL 513729 (SEC Sept. 12, 1996). In a parallel development, designed to eliminate market fragmentation, the New York Stock Exchange rescinded its former Rule 390 that limited exchange members' ability to engage in off-exchange transactions for exchange-listed securities. *See* Order Approving Proposed Rule Change to Rescind Exchange Rule 390, Sec. Exch. Act Rel. No. 34–42758, Pub. Util. Hldg. Co. Act Rel. No. 35–42758, 72 S.E.C. Docket 889, 2000 WL 649013 (SEC May 5, 2000).

22. *See* Sec. Exch. Act Rel. No 34–51229, File No. SR–NASD–2004–026, 84 S.E.C. Docket 3069, 2005 WL 1114854 (SEC Feb. 18, 2005).

23. NASD Rule 2320(a); Sec. Exch. Act Rel. No. 34–54339, SECDIG 2006–162–7, 2006 WL 2424699 (SEC Aug. 23, 2006).

24. NASD Rule 2320(a)(3).

25. NASD Rule 2320(a)(4).

26. NASD Rule 2320(a)(5).

30. *See* Sec.Exch.Act Rel.No. 34–34279 59 Fed.Reg. 34,883, 1994 WL 319529 (SEC June 29, 1994).

31. In re E.F. Hutton & Co., Sec. Exch. Act Rel. No. 34–25887 (SEC 1988).

a customer's limit order without first informing the customer. This rule was again expanded in May 1995, to prohibit broker-dealers from trading ahead of customer limit orders they accept from other brokers.[32] Accordingly, a FINRA member firm violates the rule if it accepts a customer limit order and continues to trade for its own account at a price equal to or better than the limit order unless the customer's order is filled at the limit price or better. The rule as amended applies not only to the firm's customers, but also to orders placed as member-to-member limit orders. FINRA is also concerned with fairness in the allocation of customer orders. Although FINRA does not have a rule mandating a certain allocation system, it properly considers unfair allocation systems to be contrary to fair and equitable principles of trade and therefore in violation of a broker-dealer's FINRA (formerly NASD) obligations.[33] Although a system of procedures may be necessary to assure fairness in allocation of trades, the fact that the allocation is in accordance with pre-established procedures does not substitute for a case-by-case consideration of fairness.[34]

FINRA rules require brokers to use a variety of systems and procedures designed to establish the best execution. Related to the obligation to seek the best price are the so-called trade-through rules of the NASD and the exchanges that prohibit market makers in the over-the-counter markets (and specialists on an exchange) from trading "at a price inferior to a price displayed in another market." The trade-through rules are designed to prevent "trading at inferior prices across markets"[52] and supplement the best execution obligation in preventing orders below the best price as displayed in market quotations.[54]

In 2006, the NASD amended its best execution rule to clarify that in executing transactions, brokers must consider quotations from all market centers and the accessibility of those quotations in determining the best execution that is available.[61] The NASD's best execution rule now provides that the obligation exists to all transactions "irrespective of whether a customer order is executed by the originating broker-dealer or routed to a recipient member."[62] The NASD's rule amendments in 2006 also deleted reference to the inter-dealer market in order to clarify that the "best market" is not limited to the inter-dealer markets but rather includes all markets where the security is traded.

A corollary to the best execution obligation is the requirement that orders be executed promptly. Some leeway in this regard may exist when a customer consents to a "not held order" which grants discretion with respect to order execution. This discretion is not absolute as the best execution obligations still apply to the extent that all steps must be taken to obtain the best available price for the customer.

32. *See* Sec. Exch. Act Rel. No. 34–35751 60 Fed. Reg. 27,997 (SEC May 22, 1995).

33. Guidance on Compensation and Mixed Capacity Trading, Special NASD Notice to Members 01–85 (Dec. 24, 2001) (question 15).

34. *Id.*

52. Regulation NMS, Sec. Exch. Act Rel. No. 34–49325, 82 S.E.C. Docket 758, 2004 WL 366257 at p. *9 (SEC Feb. 26, 2004).

54. *See id.*

61. NASD (FINRA) Rule 2320(a).

62. NASD Notice to Members 06–58, Best Execution, http://www.nasd.com/web/groups/rules_regs/documents/notice_to_members/nasdw_017607.pdf (Oct. 2006).

§ 14.14 Brokerage Commissions—Disclosure, Payment for Order Flow, Excessive Mark Ups, Relationship to Recommendations, Soft Dollar Arrangements

Broker-dealers owe fiduciary duties to their customers.[1] These duties arise when brokers recommend securities to their customers.[2] Execution of these fiduciary duties and recommendations often revolve around brokers' conflicts of interest. One such conflict of interest arises from the fact that if a customer follows a broker's recommendation to buy or sell a security, the broker ordinarily receives a sales commission. Accordingly, brokers have a self-interest in encouraging customer transactions and thus are faced with a conflict of interest. Mark-ups and commissions can create disclosure issues, conflicts of interest, fraud issues and other regulatory concerns.

Disclosure of Broker–Dealer Commissions

SEC Rule 10b–10[6] requires broker-dealers to confirm securities transactions in writing before the transaction is completed. In reality, however, the confirmation is not sent until after the investor makes the investment decision and becomes committed to the transaction. Rule 10b–10 imposes certain specific disclosure requirements in the sales confirmation.[8] Among the disclosures required[9] is the compensation to be received by the broker-dealer in connection with the transaction.[10] The compensation need not be disclosed in the confirmation, however, if it is determined other than on a per transaction basis in accordance with a prior written agreement between the broker and the customer.[11] Rule 10b–10 disclosures apply to securities transactions and generally and also to transactions in mutual fund shares.

The mark-up or commission will be divided between the broker and the employing firm. Generally, commission splitting arrangements between a broker-dealer firm and its registered representatives are not of concern unless they are so unusual that they create a conflict of interest or are otherwise material, thus requiring disclosure.[21] Similarly, sales credits granted to a broker from the firm's market-making department do not ordinarily need to be disclosed.[22]

Mark-ups[26] and mark downs[27] consist of charges added to the transaction price and represent the way that sales commissions are generally described

---

§ 14.14

1. *See* § 14.15 *infra.*

2. *See* § 14.16 *infra.*

6. 17 C.F.R. § 240.10b–10.

8. A customer may waive trade-by-trade confirmations and instead receive disclosure of commissions in the periodic account statements the customer receives from the broker. *See* Confirmation of Transactions, Sec. Exch. Act Rel. No. 34–33743, 56 S.E.C. Docket 558, 1994 WL 73633 (SEC March 9, 1994).

9. Rule 10b–10 also requires disclosure of whether the broker is acting as a principal or market maker in connection with the transaction. 17 C.F.R. § 240.10b–10.

10. 17 C.F.R. § 240.10b–10(a)(2)(i)(B).

11. *Id.*

21. *See, e.g.,* NASD Notice to Members 99–81, 1999 WL 33176581 (NASDR Sept. 2, 1999).

22. *See, e.g.,* SEC v. Pasternak, 561 F.Supp.2d 459, 505 (D.N.J. 2008).

26. A mark-up is the sales commission that is added to the market price of a security when a customer purchases a security. Thus, for example, it the transaction takes place at $5 per share and the broker-dealer charges a 2% mark-up, the customer will pay a total of $5.10 for each share with respect to transactions in the over-the-counter markets. As pointed out above, Rule 10b–10 requires disclosure of mark-ups, mark-downs and commissions. However, when an order is entered on a "net" basis, there ordinarily will be no duty to disclose the mark-up, mark-down, or commission.[28]

Ordinarily, the terms commission, mark-up, and mark-down apply to payments to broker-dealers in connection with agency transactions.[29] However, commissions and commission equivalent charges can also exist when the broker-dealer firm is acting in other capacities as well.[30]

Payment for Order Flow

Brokers will charge other brokers a fee for directing orders to them. These payments, known as payment for order flow, are permissible subject to certain disclosure requirements.[55] Payment for order flow has long been a part of the equities markets but is a relatively new development in the options markets.

The SEC has indicated that it has concerns about the practice of payment for order flow as having led to less vigorous quote competition and isolation of investor limit orders.[62] The SEC's concern is reflected in various payment for order flow requirements. Rule 11Ac1–3 requires that when opening a new account, broker-dealers who will be acting as the customer's agents to make written disclosures of their policies regarding payment for order flow.[63] The NASD also indicated its concern with the practice and responded by requiring disclosure of payment for order flow on confirmations of customer transactions.[64] In addition, the SEC confirmation rule, Rule 10b–10 requires disclo-

---

of the security purchased, with the broker-dealer firm receiving a 10per share mark-up that generally will be shared with the account executive dealing with the customer.

27. A mark-down is the sales commission that is deducted from the market price of a security when a customer sells a security Thus, for example, it the transaction takes place at $5 per share and the broker-dealer charges a 2% mark-down, the customer will receive a total of $4.90 for each share of the security sold, with the broker-dealer firm receiving a 10¢ per share mark-down that generally will be shared with the account executive dealing with the customer. Note that in this context if the customer buys and sells the security at the same market price, there will be a total 20¢ in brokerage commissions—the 10¢ per share mark-up for the purchase and the 10¢ mark-down for the sale. It is further to be noted that in an over the counter market there also will be a spread between the bid and the asked price meaning that a customer wanting to purchase the security will pay a higher price than the customer will receive for selling a security. *See* the discussion of market making in § 14.10 *supra*.

28. *See, e.g.,* SEC v. Pasternak, 561 F.Supp.2d 459, 507 (D.N.J. 2008).

29. "An agency trade is a trade in which a broker/dealer, authorized to act as an intermediary for the account of its customer, buys (sells) a security from (to) a third party (e.g., another customer or broker/dealer). Such a trade is not executed in, or does not otherwise pass through, the broker/dealer's proprietary account. When executing an agency trade, the broker/dealer generally charges the customer a commission for its services." Guidance on Compensation and Mixed Capacity Trading, Special NASD Notice to Members 01–85 (Dec. 24, 2001) (question 2).

30. *E.g.,* Guidance on Compensation and Mixed Capacity Trading, Special NASD Notice to Members 01–85 (Dec. 24, 2001).

55. Rules 10b–10(a)(2)(i)(c) and 11Ac1–3, 17 C.F.R. §§ 240.10b–10(a)(2)(i)(c); 240.11Ac1–3.

62. Disclosure of Order Execution and Routing Practices, Sec. Exch. Act Rel. No. 34–43590, 2000 WL 1721163 (SEC Nov. 17, 2000) ("The Commission particularly highlighted its concerns that dealer practices such as internalization and payment for order flow have contributed to the isolation of investor limit orders and to less vigorous quote competition").

63. 17 C.F.R. § 240.11Ac1–3.

64. Notice of Amendment to Proposed Rule Change by National Association of Securities Dealers, Inc. Relating to Disclosure of Payment for Order Flow Arrangements on Customer Confirmations, Sec. Exch. Act Rel. No. 34–28774, 47 S.E.C. Docket 1475, 1991 WL 286831 (SEC Jan. 14, 1991).

sure of payment for order flow in transactions where the broker is acting as the customer's agent.[65]

Directing orders pursuant to a payment for order flow arrangement can be viewed as contrary to the broker's obligation to seek the best execution for the customer.[66] Some courts have indicated that the duties of stockbrokers are governed by federal, not state law.[67] Other courts have disagreed.[68] There is considerable authority to the effect that the Securities Exchange Act preempts any fiduciary duty claims associated with failure to inform the customer of payments for order flow.[69]

Excessive Mark–Ups

At one time, brokerage firms charged uniform commission rates. This custom ceased as we moved into a competitive era with the abolition of fixed brokerage commission rates. The absence of fixed commission rates was designed to promote competition. With regard to exchange traded securities, the commission is usually based on a percentage of the transaction price, or alternatively, in the case of discount brokers at a set fee per trade or per share block. Unlike the exchanges with a centralized trading floor, in the over-the-counter and NASDAQ markets there is no centralized exchange and shares are traded through market makers who purchase shares and then resell them.[75] The difference between the bid price[76] and asked price[77] in the over-the-counter markets and NASDAQ thus reflects a market maker's mark up, which is commonly referred to as the "spread." In ordinary parlance, the mark-up or mark-down is the retail commission that a broker charges for a trade over and beyond the market price that typically includes the market maker's spread.

Failure to disclose an excessive mark-up is fraudulent conduct that violates SEC Rule 10b–5.[82] In addition, excessive mark-ups can form the basis

65. 17 C.F.R. § 240.10b–10(a)(2)(i)(c).

66. NASD Notice 01–22, 2001 WL 278615 (NASD March 16, 2001).

67. *E.g.* Smith Barney, Inc. v. Painters Local Union No. 109 Pension Fund, 254 Neb. 758, 579 N.W.2d 518 (1998).

68. *E.g.,* Levin v. Kilborn, 756 A.2d 169 (R.I.2000) (neither Rhode Island's security law, nor federal securities law, supersedes common law causes of action regarding breach of fiduciary duty, misrepresentation, etc.).

69. Gilman v. BHC Securities, Inc., 1995 WL 747738, [1995–1996 Transfer Binder] Fed. Sec. L. Rep. (CCH) ¶ 99,051 (S.D.N.Y.1995), *vacated on the other grounds* 104 F.3d 1418 (2d Cir.1997) (section 28 of the Exchange Act dealing with the effect of the Act on existing law does not preclude preemption of inconsistent state laws; state law action against brokerage firm for acceptance of payment for order flow was preempted by federal law); McKey v. Charles Schwab & Co., 67 Cal.App.4th 731, 79 Cal.Rptr.2d 213 (Cal.App.1998); Eirman v. Olde Discount Corp., 697 So.2d 865 (Fla.App.1997) (order flow payment practices are exclusively a matter of federal law); Orman v. Charles Schwab & Co., 179 Ill.2d 282, 227 Ill.Dec. 927, 688 N.E.2d 620 (1997); Dahl v. Charles Schwab & Co., Inc., 545 N.W.2d 918 (Minn.1996); Guice v. Charles Schwab & Co., 89 N.Y.2d 31, 674 N.E.2d 282, 651 N.Y.S.2d 352. (1996); Shulick v. PaineWebber, Inc., 554 Pa. 524, 722 A.2d 148 (1998). *See also, e.g.,* Comment, Preemption in the Securities Industry: A Diminished Standard, 74 St. Jon's L. Rev. 259 (2000).

The SEC was asked to consider barring the CBOE from permitting payment for order flow in the options markets. After considering the issue, the SEC decided to let the practice continue. *See* SEC Will Not Abrogate CBOE Rule, Leaving Order Flow Program Intact, 32 Sec. Reg. & L. Rep. (BNA) 1229 (Sept. 18, 2000).

75. Market makers are discussed generally in § 14.8 *supra.*

76. The price at which the market maker is willing to purchase the securities.

77. The price at which the market maker is willing to sell the securities.

82. *See* Grandon v. Merrill Lynch & Co., 147 F.3d 184, 189–90 (2d Cir.1998).

of fraud and fiduciary duty claims under state law.[83] Some courts have held, however, that failure to disclose an excessive mark-up although in violation of the securities laws, is not actionable as common law fraud[84] Nevertheless, a scheme of undisclosed excessive mark-ups can form the basis of state criminal prosecutions for securities fraud.[85]

The SEC and self regulatory organizations seek to prevent the charging of excessive commissions. For example, the SEC not only determines the types of entities that can receive remuneration from securities trades,[98] it also imposes disclosure requirements regarding the basis of customer charges.[99] Additionally, FINRA (formerly the NASD) through its mark-up policy provides guidelines as to what would constitute an excessive brokerage commission.

The Five Percent Mark–Up Policy

The NASD established a "five percent" policy as a guide for determining the fairness of the mark-up.[110] The NASD stressed that this is a guide,[111] not a per se rule nor a safe harbor rule.[112] Thus, the markup must be considered in conjunction with other factors. For most of its history, NASD Rule 2440 and its predecessors addressed mark-ups in the over the counter markets. However, in 2006 the Nasdaq National Stock Market qualified as a registered securities exchange under the 1934 Act. In 2008, FINRA amended Rule 2440 to clarify that its rules and policies on fair prices and commissions apply to *all* transactions executed by FINRA member firms.[114]

The five percent mark-up policy does not provide a safe harbor for brokers charging less than a five percent mark-up. Although the presumption of an improper mark-up does not apply to mark-ups below the five percent level, proof of anticompetitive charges can render a less than five percent markup impermissible.[120]

---

83. *See, e.g.,* City of Vista v. Robert Thomas Securities, Inc., 84 Cal.App.4th 882, 101 Cal.Rptr.2d 237 (Cal.App. 2000).

84. Lehman Bros. Commercial Corp. v. Minmetals International Non–Ferrous Metals Trading Co., 179 F.Supp.2d 159 (S.D.N.Y.2001) (New York law); Granite Partners, L.P. v. Bear, Stearns & Co. Inc., 58 F.Supp.2d 228, 263 (S.D.N.Y.1999) (same).

85. *E.g.,* New York v. Downey, 33 Sec. Reg. & L. Rep. (BNA) 1548 (N.Y.Sup.Ct. Oct. 22, 2001) (conviction for high pressure sales and nondisclosure of excessive mark-ups).

98. *See, e.g.,* In re Financial Charters & Acquisitions, Inc., 17 Sec.Reg. & L.Rep. (BNA) 27 (SEC No–Action Letter Nov. 25, 1984) (unregistered firms may get commissions for referrals to registered broker-dealers).

99. 17 C.F.R. § 240.10b–10(a)(7), (8).

110. NASD (FINRA) Rule 2440, IM–2440.

111. *See* Lehl v. S.E.C., 90 F.3d 1483, 1488 n. 4 (10th Cir.1996) ("To guide its members in determining when a price is 'reasonably related to the current market price,' the NASD surveyed industry pricing practices, concluding that the vast majority of transactions occurred at markups of 5% or less. It then issued guidelines setting 5% as a benchmark of reasonableness, to be considered with other relevant factors. The NASD cautioned, however, that the 5% policy is a guide—not a rule'; that a 'mark-up pattern of 5% or even less may be considered unfair or unreasonable'; and that '[i]n the case of certain low-priced securities, such as those selling below $10.00, a somewhat higher percentage may sometimes be justified' "), relying on Handley Inv. Co. v. SEC, 354 F.2d 64, 65 (10th Cir.1965).

112. *See Id.*

114. *See* NASD Notice to Members 08–36, SEC Approves Amendments to Expand the Scope of NASD Rule 2440 and IM–2440–1 to All Securities Transactions, 2008 WL 2782520 (FINRA July 11, 2008), amending NASD Rule 2440 and IM–2440.

120. *See, e.g.,* In re Initial Public Offering Securities Litigation, 358 F. Supp.2d 189, 219 (S.D.N.Y. 2004).

In computing the mark-up, the best evidence of prevailing market price is the dealer's contemporaneous cost for the securities.[122] However, identifying the true mark-up is not always an easy task, especially in less liquid markets when there can be a time lag between a market maker's purchase of the security and its resale. In riskless transactions, mark-ups should be based on the cost of acquisition rather than the prevailing market price.[125] The dealer's cost will thus be the appropriate measure of market price when faced with an integrated dealer who controls the market of the securities in question. However, in such a situation, the interdealer market is a better indicator of the true market price than the price that the integrated dealer paid in a transaction with a retail customer.[127] The interdealer price ordinarily is the best indicator[128] and will be rejected only when there is reason to believe that it took place in an artificially manipulated market.[129]

Recommendations Induced by Commissions or Other Incentive

Even in the absence of excessive commissions, a commission structure can interfere with the impartiality of brokers in recommending securities for their customers. Where a brokerage firm's commission rate structure encourages sales representatives to recommend selected securities, those recommendations will run afoul of the securities laws to the extent they are motivated by the sales representative's self interest rather than the best interests of the customer.[158] Thus, for example, undisclosed differential sales commissions, when used as an incentive to recommend particular stocks, is a material omission from the broker's recommendation.[159] While it is true that neither Rule 10b–10 nor FINRA or NASD rules explicitly require disclosure of the compensation paid to individual brokers,[160] when the size of the commission on selected stocks is an incentive for brokers to recommend that stock, nondisclosure is problematic. The NASD made it clear that commissions are not limited to a portion of the transaction price charged to the customer. FINRA (formerly NASD) Conduct Rule 3040 thus defines selling compensation to include any compensation that is paid directly or indirectly from

122. *E.g.,* Lehl v. SEC, 90 F.3d 1483 (10th Cir.1996).

125. *E.g.,* G.K. Scott & Co., Inc. v. S.E.C., 56 F.3d 1531, 1995 WL 364671 (D.C.Cir.1995) (unpublished opinion on Westlaw); Orkin v. SEC, 31 F.3d 1056, 1064 (11th Cir.1994); In re Meyer Blinder, 50 S.E.C. 1215, 1221, Sec. Exch. Act Rel. No. 34–31095, 52 S.E.C. Docket 1145, 1992 WL 216702 (SEC Aug. 26, 1992).

127. In the Matter of Sanders, Administrative Proceedings File No. 3–9195, Sec. Exch. Act Rel. No. 34–40600, 68 S.E.C. Docket 745, 1998 WL 741105 (SEC Oct. 26, 1998).

128. In the Matter of Salloum, Sec. Exch. Act Rel. No. 34–35563, 59 SEC Docket 4349 (SEC April 5, 1995) ("prices paid in wholesale trades are a more reliable indication of the prevailing market price [than retail trades] because they occur between informed market professionals. . . ."). *See also* In the Matter of Palumbo, Admin. Proc. File No. 3–8348, Sec. Exch. Act Rel. No. 34–36427, 60 S.E.C. Docket 1473, 1995 WL 630926 (SEC Oct. 26, 1995); In the Matter of Amato, 51 S.E.C. 316, 317–18 (1993) ("the best evidence of the prevailing market price is the price that the dealer pays other dealers. . . . If there are no contemporaneous purchases from other dealers, purchases from retail customers may be used. . . ."), affirmed 18 F.3d 1281 (5th Cir.), *cert. denied,* 513 U.S. 928, 115 S.Ct. 316, 130 L.Ed.2d 278 (1994).

129. *See* NASD, Notice to Members 92–16.

158. *See, e.g.,* In the Matter of Flanagan, Administrative Proceeding File No. 3–9784, 71 S.E.C. Docket 1415, Release No. ID–160, 2000 WL 98210 (SEC Initial Decision Jan. 30, 2000) (weighted commissions encouraged recommendations of some mutual fund shares as opposed to others); In the Matter of Olde Discount Corp., Administrative Proceeding File No. 3–9699, Sec. Act Rel. No. 33–7577, 67 S.E.C. Docket 2045, 1998 WL 575171 (SEC Sept. 10, 1998) (special sales incentives for registered representatives were part of fraudulent recommendation scheme).

159. *See, e.g.,* In the Matter of Coram, 2007 WL 207436 (N.A.S.D.R. 2007).

160. *See, e.g.,* United States v. Alvarado, 2001 WL 1631396 at **8–9 (S.D.N.Y.2001).

whatever source as a result of the purchase or sale of a security.[162] The definition of compensation is a broad one as the NASD "intended it to include any item of value received."[163] Improper incentives are not limited to cash compensation and can also include non-cash incentives for sales of securities.[164] As is the case with other sales incentives, non-cash compensation for brokers and others recommending securities not only creates a conflict of interest, it also damages investor confidence.[165] FINRA (formerly the NASD) does, however, permit de minimis non-cash compensation of sales personnel under limited circumstances.[166]

Recommendations that are induced by compensation violate the broker-dealer's obligations that generally attach to recommendations.[176] In addition recommendations are subject to the implied representation that brokers will deal fairly and professionally with their customers. Even beyond sales incentives, high pressure brokerage firms may unduly pressure their sales representatives to solicit transactions.[178] The foregoing broker-dealer prohibitions are supplemented by section 17(b) of the Securities Act of 1933,[179] which declares illegal recommending securities for compensation without disclosing the compensation paid in connection with the making of the recommendation. A recommendation that is bought and paid for violates the securities laws. In fact, the SEC has explained that it is "egregious" for a broker to accept compensation in exchange for recommending a particular security to his customers.[182]

Section 17(b) of the 1933 Act is not invalidated by the First Amendment since the prohibition is addressed to commercial speech.[187] Among other things, the anti-touting provisions of section 17(b) are reasonably related to governmental interests in protecting the deception of investors.[188]

§ 14.15 Broker–Dealers and Fiduciary Obligations; The Shingle Theory

As discussed throughout this chapter, there are various SEC and FINRA (formerly NASD) prohibitions addressing particular types of misconduct by broker dealers. For example, SEC Rule 15c1–2[1] generally prohibits fraudulent,

162. FINRA (formerly NASD) Conduct Rule 3040. *See* In the Matter of Goldsworthy, Sec. Exch. Act Rel. No. 34–45926, 2002 WL 987627 n. 40 (SEC May 15, 2002).

163. In the Matter of Goldsworthy, Sec. Exch. Act Rel. No. 34–45926, 2002 WL 987627 (SEC May 15, 2002), quoting In the Matter of Morgan, 51 S.E.C. 622, 627, Sec. Exch. Act Rel. No. 34–32744, 54 S.E.C. Docket 1611, 1993 WL 307557 (SEC Aug. 12, 1993).

164. *See, e.g.,* SEC v. Savino, 2006 WL 375074 (S.D.N.Y. 2006) (upholding sanction for obtaining a flow of trades through a series of payments and gifts).

165. NASD Notice to Members 03–53, SEC Announces Immediate Effectiveness of Amendments to Non–Cash Compensation Provisions of Rule 2710 and Rule 2810, http://www.nasdr.com/pdf-text/0353ntm.txt (Sept. 2003).

166. *Id.*

176. *See* § 14.16 *infra.*

178. *See e.g.,* Varljen v. H.J. Meyers, Inc., 1998 WL 395266, *1 (S.D.N.Y.1998).

179. 15 U.S.C.A. § 77q(b).

182. In the Matter of DuBois, Sec. Act Rel. No. 33–8264, Sec. Exch. Act Rel. No. 34–48332, 2003 WL 21946858 (SEC Aug. 13, 2003).

187. United States v. Wenger, 427 F.3d 840 (10th Cir. 2005).

188. *Id.*

§ 14.15

1. 17 C.F.R. § 240.15c1–2.

manipulative, and deceptive practices in connection with securities brokerage transactions. Broker-dealers and their employees are also subject to Rule 10b–5's general antifraud proscriptions relating to deceptive conduct in connection with a purchase or sale of a security.[2] The types of specific conduct that are addressed in other rules include market manipulation,[3] high pressure sales tactics,[4] deceptive recommendations,[5] generation of excessive commissions,[6] unauthorized trading,[7] improper order executions,[8] improper extension of credit for securities transactions,[9] and misuse of customer funds or securities.[10] Beyond these specific activities and the general anti-manipulation and deception rules, the SEC makes it clear that violation of its rules is not limited to violation of any specified SEC rules, but rather covers all conduct that operates as a deceptive or manipulative device.[11] Even beyond SEC rules, the rules of the various self regulatory organizations impose standards of conduct on broker dealers.

In addition to SEC rules and requirements of the applicable self regulatory organizations, broker-dealers are, of course, subject to common law duties and., in many contexts, fiduciary obligations. Federal courts have recognized the existence of the fiduciary relationship in federal securities cases.[16] When a broker acts as a mere order taker, then most courts say that the only duty is to find the best and prompt execution for that order.[17] When the broker performs additional functions, then fiduciary obligations may exist. For example, when a broker has discretion with respect to executing transactions, the broker is a fiduciary.[18] Similarly when a broker recommends securities or transactions, heightened duties apply.[19] When a fiduciary duty exists a broker will be subject to heightened disclosure requirements.[20] Fiduciary duties can also result in implied representations,[21] including implied representations of expertise, which may also be referred to as the "shingle theory." It is to be remembered that accountability for the implied representations that may arise out of a fiduciary duty will not violate the securities laws' antifraud

2. 17 C.F.R. § 240.10b–5. *See* §§ 12.3–12.12 *supra*.

3. *See* §§ 6.2–6.3 *supra* (manipulation in connection with public offerings) § 12.1 *supra* (manipulation generally), and § 14.10[5] *supra* (manipulation by market makers).

4. *See* § 14.18 *infra*.

5. *See* §§ 14.15–14.18 *infra*.

6. *See* § 14.20 *infra*.

7. *See* § 14.21 *infra*.

8. *See* § 14.13 *supra*.

9. *See* § 14.9 *supra*.

10. *See* § 14.8[2] *supra*.

11. Rule 15c1–2(c), 17 C.F.R. § 240.15c1–2(c).

16. *See, e.g.,* United States v. Santoro, 302 F.3d 76 (2d Cir.2002) (broker's recommendation created "position of trust" pursuant to federal sentencing guidelines); Rolf v. Blyth Eastman Dillon & Co., Inc., 424 F.Supp. 1021, 1036 (S.D.N.Y.1977).

17. *Cf.* Press v. Chemical Investment Services Corp., 166 F.3d 529 (2d Cir.1999), affirming 988 F.Supp. 375, 386–87 (S.D.N.Y. 1997) ("naked allegation" that broker was a fiduciary of customer was insufficient to state a securities law claim).

18. *See, e.g.,* McAdam v. Dean Witter Reynolds, Inc., 896 F.2d 750, 767 (3d Cir.1990).

19. Recommendations are discussed in § 14.16 *infra*.

20. *See, e.g.,* SEC v. Pasternak, 561 F.Supp.2d 459 (D.N.J. 2008).

21. SEC v. Zandford, 535 U.S. 813, 823, 122 S.Ct. 1899, 153 L.Ed.2d 1 (2002) ("any distinction between omissions and misrepresentations is illusory in the context of a broker who has a fiduciary duty to her clients").

provisions in the absence of a showing that the defendant acted with the requisite scienter.[23]

Some courts have spoken in terms of an "inherent" fiduciary duty running from the stock broker to the customer.[25] This is so because the brokerage relationship is an agency relationship which is fiduciary in nature.[26] However, the fact that the relationship is a fiduciary one only takes one so far. They key question is to determine what actual duties arise out of the relationship. The answer to that question depends on the particular broker-customer relationship and the functions performed by the broker. Thus, for example, a clearing broker that does not perform the retail functions normally associated with introducing and full-service brokers and has been said not to owe fiduciary duties to the customer[27] unless the clearing broker has reason to know of wrongdoing by the introducing broker.[28]

Although there is authority to the contrary,[31] the apparent majority view of the cases applying state common law is that there is no blanket fiduciary relationship[32] between broker-dealer and client as a matter of law,[33] but that the surrounding circumstances can suffice to create a fiduciary duty.[34] Representing oneself to have investment and advisory expertise will give rise to fiduciary obligations.[37] A broker who misrepresents his or her expertise is guilty of a material misrepresentation.[39]

The Shingle Theory

Common law principles have been borrowed in formulating SEC policy in many areas. These common law principles may also form the basis of liability under state law. The discussion that follows focuses on the "shingle theory" which holds that by hanging up a shingle, the broker implicitly represents that he or she will conduct business in an equitable and professional manner.[98] A breach of the implied representation that a broker will deal fairly with the customer will be actionable under Rule 10b–5 only if the plaintiff can show a causal relationship between the alleged breach and an injury to the

23. In the Matter of Flanagan, Administrative Proceeding File No. 3–9784, 71 S.E.C. Docket 1415, Release No. ID–160, 2000 WL 98210 *24 (SEC Initial Decision Jan. 31, 2000).

25. French v. First Union Securities, Inc., 209 F.Supp.2d 818, 825 (M.D.Tenn.2002).

26. *Id.*

27. *E.g.,* Lesavoy v. Lane, 304 F. Supp.2d 520, 526 (S.D.N.Y. 2004) (applying New York law).

28. *See, e.g.,* Fezzani v. Bear, Stearns & Co., Inc., 2004 WL 744594 (S.D.N.Y.,2004).

31. *See e.g.,* Conway v. Icahn & Co., Inc., 16 F.3d 504 (2d Cir.1994).

32. *See, e.g.,* Press v. Chemical Investment Services Corp., 166 F.3d 529 (2d Cir.1999), affirming 988 F.Supp. 375, 386–87 (S.D.N.Y. 1997).

33. *See* Associated Randall Bank v. Griffin, Kubik, Stephens & Thompson, Inc., 3 F.3d 208 (7th Cir.1993).

34. *See, e.g.,* Press v. Chemical Investment Services Corp., 166 F.3d 529 (2d Cir.1999).

37. *See, e.g.,* Burdett v. Miller, 957 F.2d 1375, 1381 (7th Cir.1992).

39. *See* NASD Notice to Members 8–27, Misleading Communications About Expertise, 2008 WL 2156999 (FINRA May 20, 2008); NASD (FINRA) Rule 2210 (prohibiting false, misleading or exaggerated communications with the public and the omission of material facts or qualifications that would cause a communication to be misleading).

98. *See, e.g.,* Brennan v. Midwestern United Life Ins. Co., 286 F.Supp. 702, 707 (N.D.Ind 1968), *affirmed* 417 F.2d 147 (7th Cir.1969), *cert. denied,* 397 U.S. 989, 90 S.Ct. 1122, 25 L.Ed.2d 397 (1970). *Accord, e.g.,* Charles Hughes & Co., Inc. v. SEC, 139 F.2d 434 (2d Cir.1943) *cert. denied,* 321 U.S. 786, 64 S.Ct. 781, 88 L.Ed. 1077 (1944).

plaintiff.[99] A breach of fiduciary duty will not by itself support a claim under Rule 10b–5.[100] The shingle theory will thus be the basis of a Rule 10b–5 violation only to the extent that it amounts to a fraudulent implied misrepresentation in connection with the purchase or sale of a security.[101]

Although often attributed to the common law, the shingle theory is well grounded under the federal securities laws as well. The shingle theory has been applied in both SEC enforcement[102] actions and private damage actions under the federal securities laws.[103]

The shingle theory can be used in many contexts. For example, in judging the appropriate standard of care that attaches to a broker-dealer in recommending securities to his or her customers and in dealing with the customers' accounts generally, the Commission has relied upon the "shingle theory." The shingle theory is but an extension of the common law doctrine of "holding out."[104]

The shingle theory arose in the context of a broker's charging excessive mark-ups[107] but is not limited to mark-up cases.[108] When brokers hold themselves out as experts either in investments in general or in the securities of a particular issuer, they will be held to a higher standard of care in making recommendations. In applying this aspect of shingle theory, a broker who makes a recommendation is viewed as making an implied representation that he or she has adequate information on the security in question for forming the basis of the broker's opinion.[110] This concept of implied representation has also been expressed in terms of a broker-dealer "implicitly warrant[ing] the soundness of the statements of stock value,"[111] but this is too strong a statement of the rule. The concept of implied warranty has not to date been extended to brokers' recommendations, and the appropriate standard of care, whether under the shingle theory or otherwise, is necessarily based upon the broker-dealer's factual basis and reasonable belief in the opinions that form the basis of the recommendation.

The shingle theory is sometimes applied to bring activities of the broker which otherwise might not fall within the literal application of the SEC antifraud rules within the ambit of those rules. In many of these cases brokers have held themselves out as having complied with SEC regulations. These activities that have then given rise to accountability, and in some cases

99. *See, e.g.*, In re Credit Suisse First Boston Corp. (Agilent Technologies, Inc.) Analyst Reports Securities Litigation, 2005 WL 852455 (D.Mass. 2005).

100. *See* Santa Fe Industries, Inc. v. Green, 430 U.S. 462, 479–80, 97 S.Ct. 1292, 1304, 51 L.Ed.2d 480 (1977).

101. Bissell v. Merrill Lynch & Co., Inc., 937 F.Supp. 237, 246 n. 7 (S.D.N.Y.1996).

102. *See, e.g.*, Charles Hughes & Co. v. SEC, 139 F.2d 434, 437–438 (2d Cir.1943), *cert. denied*, 321 U.S. 786, 64 S.Ct. 781, 88 L.Ed. 1077 (1944); S.E.C. v. Great Lakes Equities Co., 1990 WL 260587 *6 (E.D.Mich.1990); Duker & Duker, 6 S.E.C. 386, 388, Sec. Exch. Act Rel. No. 34–2350, 1939 WL 36426 (SEC Dec. 19, 1939).

103. *See e.g.*, Granite Partners, L.P. v. Bear, Stearns & Co. Inc., 58 F.Supp.2d 228, 262 (S.D.N.Y.1999), relying on Grandon v. Merrill Lynch & Co., 147 F.3d 184, 189–90, 192–93 (2d Cir.1998).

104. *See, e.g.*, Burdett v. Miller, 957 F.2d 1375, 1381 (7th Cir.1992).

107. Charles Hughes & Co. v. SEC, 139 F.2d 434 (2d Cir.1943), *cert. denied*, 321 U.S. 786, 64 S.Ct. 781, 88 L.Ed. 1077 (1944).

108. It has thus been aptly observed that "By now—one may add 'happily'—the shingle theory not only is unchallenged but has been considerably refined . . . Moreover the potentialities of the 'shingle' theory are not exhausted by markup cases." 9 Louis Loss & Joel Seligman, Securities Regulation § 9–C–1 a at p. 3779 (3d ed. 1991).

110. *See, e.g.*, Filloramo v. Johnston, Lemon & Co., Inc., 697 F.Supp. 517 (D.D.C.1988).

111. Kahn v. SEC, 297 F.2d 112, 115 (2d Cir.1961) (Clark J., concurring).

liability, include undisclosed insolvency,[112] egregious failures to comply with SEC bookkeeping requirements,[113] and noncompliance with net capital requirements.[114]

The shingle theory intertwines with the suitability and "know your customer" doctrines that are discussed in the next section.

§ 14.16 A Broker's Obligation to Customers With Regard to Recommendations: The Know Your Security, Suitability, and Know Your Customer Obligations

Recommendations and Suitability Generally

Securities brokers and brokerage firms that render advice incidental to their brokerage activities are exempted from the coverage of the Investment Advisers Act of 1940 that regulates those persons and entities in the business of rendering investment advice.[1] Accordingly, this type of incidental advice rendered by brokerage firms is regulated pursuant to the applicable provisions of the 1934 Exchange Act, SEC rules, and the rules of the self regulatory organizations as supplemented by common law principles. Many brokerage firms also register as investment advisers (or have advisory divisions or subsidiaries) in which case the 1934 Act regulation will supplement the Investment Advisers Act.

The securities laws prohibit a broker-dealer from recommending a security unless he or she has actual knowledge of the characteristics and fundamental facts relevant to the security in question; furthermore, the recommendation must be reasonably supported by the facts.[3] In the context of a securities brokerage relationship, whenever a broker recommends a security to a customer, there is an implied representation that the broker is informed as to the security and that the recommendation has a reasonable factual basis.[5] When a broker recommends a security for purchase there is said to be an implied representation that the broker "has made a thorough investigation."[6] The obligation to have a basis for the recommendation sometimes is referred to as the "know the security" obligation. The broker's responsibilities do not end with this obligation. In addition to the implied representation that the broker making the recommendation after a reasonable independent investigation[7] has a reasonable basis for the recommendation, the broker must disclose any

112. SEC v. Resch–Cassin & Co., Inc., 362 F.Supp. 964 (S.D.N.Y.1973).

113. Joseph v. Shields, Jr., [1967–1969 Transfer Binder] Fed.Sec.L.Rep. (CCH) & ¶ 77,643 (Jan. 3, 1969).

114. SEC v. Charles Plohn & Co., 433 F.2d 376 (2d Cir.1970); Joseph v. Shields, Jr., [1967–1969 Transfer Binder] Fed.Sec.L.Rep. (CCH) ¶ 77,643 (SEC 1969).

§ 14.16

1. 15 U.S.C.A. § 80b–2(a)(11). *See* § 21.2 *infra.*

3. *See, e.g.,* United States v. Santoro, 302 F.3d 76 (2d Cir.2002).

5. *E.g.,* SEC v. Dain Rauscher, Inc., 254 F.3d 852, (9th Cir. 2001) ("A securities professional has an obligation to investigate the securities he or she offers to customers"); Franklin Savings Bank of New York v. Levy, 551 F.2d 521, 527 (2d Cir.1977) ("where a broker-dealer makes a representation as to the quality of the security he sells, he impliedly represents that he has an adequate basis in fact for the opinion he renders").

6. Alton Box Bd. Co. v. Goldman, Sachs & Co.,560 F.2d 916, 922 (8th Cir.1977).

7. *See, e.g.,* In the Matter of Merrill Lynch, Pierce, Fenner & Smith, Inc., Sec. Exch. Act Rel No. 3414149 (SEC Nov. 9, 1977). *See also, e.g.,* Hanly v. SEC, 415 F.2d 589, 596 (2d Cir.1969)

facts he or she knows that are inconsistent with the recommendation.[8] Consideration must also be given to whether the broker has a conflict of interest when making the recommendation. A broker's or securities analyst's recommendation should not be unduly influenced by special incentives from the brokerage firm or from others.[9] The suitability requirement supplements the requirement that the broker have a reasonable basis for making the recommendation. This obligation is sometimes referred to as the "know or security" obligation. It also is sometimes called "reasonable basis suitability."

In order for analysts' recommendations to be actionable, fraud or misrepresentation must be established.[19] Even though conflicts of interest may ethically compromise an analyst and may violate regulatory requirements, they are not actionable as fraud unless specifically tied to a recommendation.[20]

An example of impermissible incentive has taken the form of mutual fund payments to brokers to obtain priority in "shelf space" for particular funds.[23] Payments for more prominent shelf space involves the same type of conflict of interest issues as do differential sales commissions and other hidden incentives that brokers receive to recommend particular securities to their customers.

Limits on use of "soft dollars" to support research

Section 28(e) of the 1934 Act limits the use of funds received by money managers and broker-dealers who charge for their investment services.[32] In 2006, the SEC issued guidance restricting the circumstances under which money managers can use soft dollar commissions to fund research.[33] Specifically, the SEC clarified that the safe harbor for using soft dollars as follows.

Suitability Generally

In addition to the broker-dealer's knowledge of the security, there are also obligations imposed with regard to the broker-dealer's duty to know his or her customer. This is most commonly referred to as the suitability obligation. A suitability obligation can be derived from the antifraud rules. Specifically, it can be said that a broker's recommendation to a customer implies that the security recommended is consistent with the customer's investment objectives and thus is suitable. The obligation is also derived from the rules of the self regulatory organizations.[43] Claims of unsuitable recom-

---

8. *E.g.,* In the Matter of Frankfort, Complaint No. C02040032, 2007 WL 1559564 (NASDR 2007).

9. *See, e.g.,* In the Matter of Flanagan, Administrative Proceeding File No. 3–9784, 71 S.E.C. Docket 1415, Release No. ID–160, 2000 WL 98210 (SEC Initial Decision Jan. 30, 2000); In the Matter of Olde Discount Corp., Administrative Proceeding File No. 3–9699, Sec. Act Rel. No. 33–7577, 67 S.E.C. Docket 2045, 1998 WL 575171 (SEC Sept. 10, 1998).

19. *See* In re Credit Suisse First Boston Corp., 431 F.3d 36, 49–50 (1st Cir. 2005).

20. *See id.*

23. *See, e.g.,* In the Matter of Citigroup Global Markets, Inc., Sec. Act Rel. No. 33–8557, Sec. Exch. Act Rel. No. 34–51415, 2005 WL 673272 (SEC 2005).

32. 15 U.S.C.A. § 78b(e)(1).

33. Interpretive Guidance on Client Commission Practices, 2006 WL 2240353 (SEC No Action Letter July 18, 2006).

43. NASD (FINRA) Rule 2310(a) ("[i]n recommending to a customer the purchase, sale or exchange of any security, a member shall have reasonable grounds for believing that the recommendation is suitable for such customer upon the basis of the facts, if any, disclosed by such customer as to his other security holdings and as to his financial situation and needs."); NYSE Rule 405 (the know your customer rule).

mendations are not limited to specific securities but also can extend to unsuitable trading patterns[44] such as recommendations that result in high volume trading.[45]

The suitability obligation takes various forms depending on the applicable self regulatory organization. As noted above, unsuitability violations often result in severe administratively imposed sanctions.[56] It is unlikely that a violation of these rules without more will provide an independent basis for private relief by an injured investor, although it may be relevant in an action brought under SEC Rule 10b–5 or under state law fiduciary duty principles. The essence of a Rule 10b–5 claim is deception, which generally means misrepresentation or nondisclosure.[59] A broker's recommendation of a security will give rise to damages to the customer for an unsuitable recommendation only if the recommendation contains an express or implied material misrepresentation of the risks involved.[60] As explained by one court: "the plaintiff asserting unsuitability must show (1) the investment was incompatible with the plaintiff's investment objectives; and (2) the broker recommended the investment although (3) the broker knew or reasonably believed the investment was inappropriate."[61] Brokers and advisers who materially misrepresent risks of an investment will be held accountable for their misstatements or implied misrepresentations.[62] Not every misrepresentation of risk is actionable; investors are held to an understanding of certain fundamental concepts such as the relationship of risk to potential reward and there are basic risks that investors are presumed to know.[63]

The New York Stock Exchange has a "know your customer rule"[70] which has been used to impose an obligation on brokers that they know their customer's investment goals and risk tolerance before making a recommendation.[71] Although the know your customer rule has been used to address unsuitable recommendations, there is some evidence that its intent may have been to protect brokers from unsuitable customers and this is one reason that

44. *See, e.g.,*In the Matter of Dunbar, 2008 WL 2167905 (FINRA May 20, 2008).

45. *See, e.g.,* Jack H. Stein, Sec. Exch. Act Rel. No. 34–47335, 79 S.E.C. Docket 1777, 2003 WL 431870 (Feb. 10, 2003).

56. *See, e.g.,* In the Matter of Alacan, Admin. Proc. No. 3–10765, Sec. Act Rel. No. 33–8436, Sec. Exch. Act Rel. No. 34–49970, 2004 WL 1496843 (SEC July 06, 2004) (imposing industry bar for suitability violations).

59. *See, e.g.,* Schreiber v. Burlington Northern, Inc., 472 U.S. 1, 105 S.Ct. 2458, 86 L.Ed.2d 1 (1985).

60. *See, e.g.,* Rosati v. Bekhor, 167 F.Supp.2d 1340 (M.D.Fla.2001).

61. Keenan v. D.H. Blair & Co., 838 F.Supp. 82, 87 (S.D.N.Y.1993) (holding the plaintiffs failed to meet the required specificity in pleading since they "failed to show why the stock was incompatible with their investment aims.... Plaintiffs merely recite the stock declined in value. Such conclusory allegations are not sufficient to state an unsuitability claim with particularity.").

62. *See, e.g.,* In re Piper Capital Management, Inc., SEC Admin Proc. File No. 3–9657, 32 Sec. Reg. & L. Rep. (BNA) 1674 (SEC Initial decision 2000) (imposing $2 million fine for misrepresenting high risk mutual fund as having conservative investment strategy).

63. *See, e.g.,* Louros v. Kreicas, 367 F.Supp.2d 572 (S.D.N.Y.2005) (investor could not reasonably rely on assurance that he "could make money with no risk," since "the relationship between risk and return is one of the fundamental features of all commercial and financial dealings." The failure to disclose information "so basic that any investor could be expected to know it" is not actionable but other misrepresentations of risk could be actionable), *relying on Zerman v. Ball,* 735 F.2d 15, 21 (2d Cir.1984) and Levitin v. PaineWebber, Inc., 159 F.3d 698, 702 (2d Cir.1998).

70. NYSE Rule 405.

71. *See, e.g.,* Rolf v. Blyth, Eastman Dillon & Co., Inc., 570 F.2d 38, 49 (2d Cir. 1978).

courts have found the absence of an implied remedy unless the conduct in question amounts to fraud in violation of SEC Rule 10b–5.

FINRA (formerly the NASD) in its so-called "suitability rule" requires that in recommending a purchase or sale of a particular security to a customer, the broker-dealer must have "reasonable grounds for believing that the recommendation is suitable for such customer upon the basis of the facts, if any, disclosed by such customer as to his other security holdings and as to his financial situation and needs."[74] Interestingly, the suitability rule on its face does not impose upon the broker any affirmative duty of investigating the customer's investment objective, but merely requires the broker-dealer to act reasonably based upon the information, if any, that the customer provides. Nevertheless, the NASD in a policy statement by its Board of Governors went further by requiring the broker to obtain information concerning the customers' other securities holdings before recommending speculative, low-priced securities.

The suitability and know your customer obligations have arisen in the context of broker-dealer recommendations. There has been some suggestion that the concept should be extended to the broker's suggested obligation to monitor the investor's own decisions.[76] However, there is considerable authority to the contrary, holding that the broker does not have a duty to intercede when the investment is the customer's choice rather than on the basis of the broker's recommendation.[77]

Suitability requirements have been applied even beyond recommendations of particular securities or types of investments. For example, suitability requirements have been applied to margin accounts.[79]

The suitability obligation can exist with regard to institutional investors. The NASD issued an interpretation applying its suitability rule to advice given institutional investors.[87] Under the NASD interpretation there are two important considerations in invoking the suitability doctrine for institutional investors. The first consideration is the institutional customer's ability to comprehend and independently evaluate the risks involved. The second factor is the extent to which the customer will be exercising independent judgment in evaluating the recommendation. Suitability rules regarding recommendations to institutional investors are especially timely in light of many crises involving derivative investments.[90] Because of the high level of risk involved in hedge fund investments, in 2003, the NASD reminded its members of suitability issues regarding hedge fund recommendations.[91] As with any recommenda-

74. FINRA Rule 2310 (formerly NASD Rule 2310 , and before that Art. III, Sec. 2 NASD Rules of Fair Practice). *See, e.g.,* In the Matter of Muth, Admin. Proc. File No. 3–11346, Sec. Act Rel. No. 33–8622, Sec. Exch. Act Rel. No. 34–52551, 2005 WL 2428336 (SEC 2005).

76. *See* Hilary H. Cohen, The Suitability Doctrine: Defining Stockbrokers' Professional Responsibilities, 3 J. Corp. L. 533 (1978).

77. *See e.g.,* Associated Randall Bank v. Griffin, Kubik, Stephens & Thompson, Inc., 3 F.3d 208, 212 (7th Cir.1993) ("customer-directed transactions fall outside the 'suitability' requirements."); Wasnick v. Refco, Inc., 911 F.2d 345, 349 (9th Cir.1990) (no duty to stop customer from engaging in unsuitable commodities transactions).

79. *See* § 14.9 *supra* for a discussion of the margin rules.

87. *See* NASD Approves New Interpretation of Suitability Obligations to Institutions, 27 Sec. Reg. & L. Rep. (BNA) 1220 (July 21, 1995).

90. *See also, e.g.,* Banca Cremi, S.A. v. Alex Brown & Sons, Inc., 132 F.3d 1017 (4th Cir.1997).

91. NASD Notice to Members 03–07, http://www.nasdr.com/pdf-text/0307ntm.txt.

tion, the broker must use due diligence in investigating the security or fund being recommended.[92]

From time to time, the NASD identified investments that are particularly susceptible to suitability concerns. For example, the NASD targeted online trading and day trading, low priced securities, and mutual fund sales practices.

Online Trading and Day Trading

The growing use of the Internet for stock trades has created a new arena for fraud and for suitability issues in particular. In this regard, the NASD issued a notice to its members cautioning that the suitability requirements apply to online recommendations of securities.[137] The SEC staff echoed the NASD's reminder that the suitability obligations apply to online communications.[138]

The SEC approved NASD rules relating to day trading. Among other things, the NASD (now FINRA) rule[142] requires that the broker-dealer make an investigation into the suitability of the customer for day trading before opening an account.[143] Before approving an account for day trading, a firm must "have reasonable grounds for believing that the day-trading strategy is appropriate for the customer."[144] In making this determination, the firm must "exercise reasonable diligence to ascertain the essential facts about the customer, including his or her financial situation, tax status, prior investment and trading experience, and investment objectives."[145] The brokerage firm must also "prepare a record setting forth the basis on which the firm has approved the customer's account for day trading."[146] In addition to the suitability check, before offering a customer access to day trading facilities, the brokerage firm must provide the customer with a risk disclosure statement.

Special Suitability Problems Associated With Low Priced Securities

Over the past several years, there has been increasing concern over low priced securities that are not marketed through a national exchange or the NASDAQ national market. Many investors have been injured as a result of high pressure sales techniques in connection with these so-called "penny stocks." The SEC's penny stock regulations were implemented in 1990 and expanded in 1992. Congress reinforced the SEC's concerns with penny stocks with the enactment of the Securities Enforcement and Penny Stock Reform Act of 1990.[151] Section 3(a)(51) of the Exchange Act now provides a statutory

92. *Id.*

137. Executive summary, NASD Notice to Members 01–23 Online Suitability, 2001 WL 278614 (March 19, 2001).

138. *See* SEC Counsel Issues Suitability Warning: Rules Apply to Recommendations Online, 33 Sec. Reg. & L. Rep. (BNA) 1757 (Dec. 17, 2001).

142. NASD Rule 2360.

143. *See* Securities Exchange Act Release No. 34–43021, 2000 WL 955176 (SEC July 10, 2000).

144. *Id.*

145. *Id.*

146. *Id.*

151. Pub.L. No. 101–429 (1990). *See* H.R. Rep. No. 101–617, 101st Cong., 2d Sess. (1990).

definition of "penny stock" which excludes most exchange-listed and Nasdaq securities.[152]

Suitability and Mutual Fund Sales Practices

In 1995, the NASD issued a directive concerning the obligations of member broker-dealers with respect to mutual fund sales practices.[155] There is an obligation to assure that when recommending mutual funds all material facts be disclosed to investors. Material facts include: the fund's investment objectives, portfolio, performance history, expense ratio, and sales charges. The risks of investing in the recommended fund as compared with other investment products also is material and must be disclosed. Violation of suitability rules with regard to mutual fund investments can result in the imposition of FINRA (formerly NASD) sanctions.[156] There are also specific disclosures relating to breakpoint pricing of mutual fund shares. The SEC's rules regarding mutual fund pricing focus on disclosures sufficient to inform investors regarding breakpoint pricing.[157] Recommendations of unsuitable breakpoint pricing can result in the recommending broker's liability for excessive fees.[158] Steering mutual fund investors to unsuitable classes of mutual fund shares can result in violation of state law obligations.[159]

Suitability and Investment Advisers

In 1994, the SEC proposed a rule that would have expressly prohibited an investment adviser from making recommendations of securities that are unsuitable for his or her clients.[170] However, that rule was never adopted. In light of the proposal not having been adopted, the only formal suitability requirement would be the one that is recognized with regard to broker-dealer recommendations. Nevertheless, the Commission has taken the position that the antifraud provisions of the Investment Advisers Act can be used to enforce a suitability requirement.[172]

Recommendations and Conflicts of Interest; Analysts' Recommendations

Another problem that arises in connection with securities recommenda-

152. 15 U.S.C.A. § 78c(a)(51).

155. Special NASD Notice to Members 95–80 (Sept. 26, 1995).

156. *See, e.g.,* In the Matter of Koppel–Heath, Complaint No. C02950044, 1998 WL 1084579 (N.A.S.D.R. Jan. 6, 1998).

157. Disclosure of Breakpoint Discounts by Mutual Funds, Sec. Act Rel. No. 33–8427; Sec. Exch. Act rel. No. 34–49817; Inv. Co. Act Rel. No. IC–26464 (SEC 2004). In particular, the SEC rules require that in the prospectus mutual funds provide a brief description of arrangements resulting in sales load breakpoints. The disclosures relating to breakpoints must include a summary of eligibility requirements. Mutual fund prospectuses must also contain a description of the methods used to value accounts in order to determine whether a shareholder qualifies for sales load breakpoints. The pricing disclosures in the prospectus must also state any requirement that in order to obtain a breakpoint, it may be necessary for a shareholder to provide information and records, such as account statements, to a mutual fund or financial intermediary. In addition the SEC rules require a mutual fund to state in its prospectus whether breakpoint information is made available on the mutual fund's website.

158. *See, e.g.,* Phillips v. Wedbush Morgan Securities, NASD Docket No. 03–07340, 420 F.3d 598 (NASD 2005).

159. *See* Benzon v. Morgan Stanley Distributors, Inc., 420 F.3d 598 (6th Cir. 2005).

170. Inv. Adv. Act Rel. No. IA–1406, [1993–1994 Transfer Binder] Fed. Sec. L. Rep. (CCH) ¶ 85,327 (SEC March 16, 1994). *See also, e.g.,* MLC Limited 1997 WL 408759 n. 2 (SEC No Action Letter July 21, 1997).

172. MLC Limited, 1997 WL 408759 n. 2 (SEC No Action Letter July 21, 1997).

tions is nondisclosure of potential conflicts of interest.[175] Most brokerage firms engage in a wide variety of activities and some of those activities create internal conflicts of interest. It is improper for any person to recommend a security for the purposes of enhancing one's own investments in that security.[178] In addition, it is impermissible to receive compensation for making a recommendation of a particular security without disclosing that compensation.[179] The violation extends to nondisclosure of any economic self interest that could have an influence on the broker, analyst, or other person making the recommendation.[180]

Among other things, FINRA (and formerly NASD) rules require increased supervision of analysts in order to assure their independence and eliminate potential conflicts of interest and other improprieties.[194] First, research analysts are prohibited from directly or indirectly participating in a road show related to an investment banking services transaction, or otherwise communicating with customers in the presence of investment banking personnel or company management about an investment banking services transaction.[196] Investment banking personnel may not directly or indirectly direct a research analyst to engage in sales and marketing efforts or other communications with a current or prospective customer related to an investment banking services transaction.[197] Research analyst written and oral communications relating to an investment banking services transaction with a current or prospective customer or with internal personnel, "must be fair, balanced and not misleading, taking into consideration the overall context in which the communication is made."[198]

The rules explicitly provide than an analyst's compensation may not be tied to specific investment banking transactions. Furthermore, if the analyst's compensation is based in any degree upon the investment banking revenues, the research reports must disclose this. Disclosure is also required if the firm or its affiliates received compensation from that company within the previous 12 months; disclosure is also required if the firm or affiliates expect to receive compensation from the company within the next three months following publication of the report. Additionally, when an analyst recommends a security in a public appearance, the analyst must disclose if the issuer is a client of the firm.

The requirements regarding analysts' independence preclude a research analyst from being supervised or controlled by a firm's investment banking department. The research department must act independently of the invest-

175. *See, e.g.,* La Grasta v. First Union Securities, Inc., 358 F.3d 840 (11th Cir. 2004).

178. This practice is known as scalping, which is both fraudulent and manipulative. *See* § 14.17 *infra.*

179. Section 17(b) of the 1933 Act, 15 U.S.C.A. § 77q(b) which is discussed in § 7.11 *supra.*

180. *See, e.g.,* In re Richmark Capital Corp., Sec. Act Rel. No. 33–8333, Sec. Exch. Act Rel. No 34–48758, 2003 WL 22570712 *3 (SEC Nov. 7, 2003).

194. *See* Order Approving Proposed Rule Changes by the New York Stock Exchange, Inc., and the National Association of Securities Dealers, Inc., To Prohibit Participation by a Research Analyst in a Road Show Related to an Investment Banking Services Transaction and To Require Certain Communications About an Investment Banking Services Transaction To Be Fair, Balanced and Not Misleading, Sec. Exch. Act Rel. No. 34–51593; File Nos. SR–NYSE–2004–24; SR–NASD–2004–141 (SEC April 28, 2005).

196. FINRA Rule 2711(c)(5); NYSE Rule 472(b)(6)(i).

197. FINRA Rule 2711(c)(6); NYSE Rule 472(b)(6)(ii).

198. FINRA Rule 2711(c)(7); NYSE Rule 472(b)(6)(iii).

ment banking department and may only have reports checked for factual accuracy by either the investment banking department or the company that is the subject of the report.

The independence requirements preclude an analyst or member of the analyst's household from purchasing or receiving a company's securities prior to its IPO, if the company is engaged in the same business that the analyst follows and issues reports about. The rules also impose a trading moratorium so that no analyst or household member may trade securities issued by companies the analyst follows for thirty days prior to the issuance of the research report and ending five days after the date of the research report. The rules also prohibit analysts and household members from making trades contrary to the analyst's most current recommendations.

FINRA rules require that when making a public appearance an analyst would have to disclose (and a firm must disclose in research reports) if the analyst or a household member has a financial interest in the securities of a recommended company. Any other known conflict of interest must also be disclosed in the research report or during the public appearance. Additionally, if a firm, as of five business days before the public appearance or publication of a research report, owns one percent or more of any equity class of the company, there must be disclosure in the research report or during the appearance.

FINRA rules also impose a quiet period for securities offerings registered under the Securities Act of 1933 where the analyst's firm participates as an underwriter.[207] The rules as proposed and adopted require quiet periods, during which a firm acting as manager or co-manager of a securities offering may not issue a report on a company within forty days after an initial public offering or within ten days after a secondary offering. The rules also prohibit a firm from offering or threatening to withhold favorable research to induce business.

§ 14.17 Scalping and Related Activities

§ 14.17[1] Scalping as Securities Fraud

A fraudulent practice that has been utilized by some unscrupulous investment advisers and securities dealers is known as "scalping." Scalping consists of an investment adviser's purchasing a security in advance of making a buy recommendation, with the knowledge that a buy recommendation will help drive up the price of the stock. The stock is sold at a profit once the scalper's recommendation has been issued and the price has risen in reaction thereto.

In SEC v. Capital Gains Research Bureau, Inc.,[2] the Supreme Court held that failure to disclose an intention to scalp operates as a fraud or deceit upon an investment adviser's prospective clients under the terms of section 206 of the Investment Advisers Act of 1940.[3] The Court ruled that the concept of fraud or deceit in section 206 of the Act is not limited to material misstate-

207. *See* §§ 2.3[6], 2.4[4], 2.5[8] *supra* for discussion of broker and analyst recommendations while a security is in registration.

§ 14.17

2. 375 U.S. 180, 84 S.Ct. 275, 11 L.Ed.2d 237 (1963).

3. 15 U.S.C.A. § 80b–6. The Investment Advisers Act is discussed in chapter 21 *infra*.

ments but also extends to omissions of material fact. The Court explained: "The high standards of business morality exacted by our laws regulating the securities industry do not permit an investment adviser to trade on the market effect of his own recommendations without fully and fairly revealing his personal interest(s) in these recommendations to his clients."[4] On balance, it was held that this is a relatively low burden to place upon the investment adviser (or anyone else whose investment opinions are likely to be relied upon by others). The Court further explained that this burden is justified when viewed in relation to the necessity of preserving a climate of fair dealing that is essential to maintain confidence in the securities markets.

It is interesting to note that the Supreme Court's reasoning in *Capital Gains Research Bureau* appears to make undisclosed scalping a violation of Rule 10b–5(c)'s[5] prohibition against acts and practices that operate as a fraud as well as Rule 10b–5(b)'s proscription against making material misstatements or omissions in connection with the purchase or sale of securities.[6] The Ninth Circuit in Zweig v. Hearst Corp.[7] has followed up on the Supreme Court's lead in holding that undisclosed scalping is in violation of Rule 10b–5. The 10b–5 scalping violation is not based on the conduct alone, but rather only when the conduct is viewed together with the actionable nondisclosure of the scalper's trading in the securities being recommended. In *Zweig* the defendant, a financial columnist, received unjustifiably optimistic information about a corporation directly from the corporation's officers and directors, whom he interviewed in preparation for a column on the company. After receiving this favorable information, and apparently making no effort to investigate its accuracy, the defendant purchased five thousand shares of stock directly from the issuer at a substantial discount below the market price. Two days later in his column, the defendant published a buy recommendation for the stock in question, causing the market price of the stock to increase by more than fifty percent. The day after the column appeared, the defendant recovered his entire initial investment by selling two thousand shares, thus retaining three thousand shares as sheer profit.[8] The court, following the reasoning of *Capital Gains Research Bureau,* held that defendant's activities were in violation of Rule 10b–5, saying "[w]hile Rule 10b–5 should not be extended to require every financial columnist or reporter to disclose his or her portfolio to all of his or her readers, it does cover the activities of one who uses a column as part of a scheme to manipulate the market and deceive the investing public."[9]

The court in *Zweig* held the defendant liable in damages to those readers who had purchased the securities at the artificially high price as well as to shareholders of another company who had not read the column but had suffered a loss when the artificially high price of the recommended stock decreased the number of shares they received in a merger. The rationale was

---

4. 375 U.S. at 201, 84 S.Ct. at 287.

5. 17 C.F.R. § 240.10b–5(c).

6. *See* 17 C.F.R. § 240.10b–5(c). *See also* chapter 12 *supra.*

7. 594 F.2d 1261 (9th Cir.1979).

8. Defendant had a "long history of similar dealings." 594 F.2d at 1265. In one two-year period he purchased the stock of twenty-one companies just prior to publishing columns pertaining to those companies. In twenty-one of twenty-two sales taking place inside of five days after publication defendant profited from an increase in the price of the stock. *Id.* at 1264 n. 4.

9. *Id.* at 1271.

that the defendant had perpetrated a fraud on the market.[10] The court explained that the plaintiffs had "relied on the free and unmanipulated market that the federal securities laws were designed to foster * * *."[11] The court acknowledged that the defendant did not owe any common law duty to non-readers, but to deny them recovery while allowing the readers a recourse would be a "wholly incongruous result."[12] The defendant was thus held liable despite the fact that the plaintiffs' aggregate losses far exceeded the defendant's gain. The court couched its decision wholly in terms of the defendant's failure to disclose his purchase of the stock prior to making his recommendation.[14]

In addition to violation of the Securities Exchange Act of 1934, and the Investment Advisers Act of 1940, scalping necessarily triggers the potential for sanctions under the broker-dealer registration provisions of the Exchange Act.[18] Additionally, scalping violates the rules of self regulatory organizations such as the national exchanges and FINRA.[19] Furthermore, as the *Zweig* case indicates, scalping prohibitions are not limited to investment advisers who are subject to the Act's direct regulations, but also extend to anyone whose recommendation would be reasonably expected to affect the market price.

Section 17(b) of the Securities Act of 1933[20] outlaws practices similar to scalping. Section 17(b) prohibits the making of recommendation to sell a security without disclosing any compensation that may have been paid to the person making the recommendation.

§ 14.18 High Pressure Sales Tactics: Boiler Room Operations

In making his or her recommendation to the customer, the broker-dealer is under an obligation not only to know and consider the customer's investment objectives, but also to have some familiarity with the security being recommended.[2] High pressure sales tactics can take various forms and are carried our using a variety of tactics. For example, one unfortunate practice that has developed with some of the more unscrupulous securities brokers and dealers is a concerted high pressure sales campaign which frequently includes the cold calling of individuals who are not regular customers. Cold calling is but one example of the tactics that can create the backdrop for improper high

---

10. *Id.* at 1270. *See, e.g.,* Shores v. Sklar, 647 F.2d 462 (5th Cir.1981); Blackie v. Barrack, 524 F.2d 891, 907 (9th Cir.1975), *cert. denied,* 429 U.S. 816, 97 S.Ct. 57, 50 L.Ed.2d 75 (1976).

11. 549 F.2d at 1270.

12. *Id.* at 1270–71.

14. "We hold that [the federal securities] laws * * * require a financial columnist in recommending a security that he or she owns, to provide the public with all material information he or she has on that security, including his or her ownership, and any intent he or she may have (a) to score a quick profit on the recommendation * * *." 594 F.2d at 1271. *Cf.* SEC v. Brant, 1984 WL 2427, [1991 Transfer Binder] Fed.Sec.L.Rep. (CCH) ¶ 91,483 (SEC Litigation Rel. No. 10386, S.D.N.Y., May 16, 1984) (charging reporter with trading based on nonpublic information).

18. 15 U.S.C.A. § 78*o*. *See* § 14.3 *supra.*

19. *See, e.g.,* N.Y.S.E.Guide (CCH) ¶ 2472.40 (October 1998); Am.Stock Ex.Guide (CCH) ¶ 9491A.40 (June 6, 1997). FINRA (formerly NASD) Rule 2711(g) prohibits research analysts from buying or selling a security that the analyst is covering between 30 days before and five days after the report is published. *See* FINRA Rule 2711(g).

20. 15 U.S.C.A. § 77q(b).

§ 14.18

2. *See, e.g.,* In the Matter of Kemprowski, [1994–1995 Transfer Binder] Fed. Sec. L. Rep. (CCH) ¶ 85,469 (SEC 1994).

pressure sales campaigns by securities brokers. A more recently developed practice analogous to cold calling is sending out spam emails with stock recommendations.[3] Brokerage firms sponsoring such high pressure sales campaigns typically pressure their sales representatives to push the securities in question through the use of sales incentives or other tactics.[5]

The movie "Boiler Room"[7] accurately depicted many of the tactics used in the perpetration of securities brokers' high pressure sale frauds. The extreme measures portrayed in that movie were not exaggeration. In fact, they reflect many of the tactics found in the SEC, NASD, and FINRA decisions. These tactics are not new. In fact, similar overreaching brokerage sales programs were behind the regulation that Congress imposed in 1934. For example, many of these operations "lent a carnival tone to securities marketing."[9] In particular, Congress was concerned with sales contests for brokers, awarding liberal prizes to the brokers and/or offices with the most securities sales.[10] These types of sales campaigns are thus clearly inconsistent with the fair and equitable principles of trade that apply to securities brokers under the 1934 Act and system of self regulation that exists thereunder. Conduct that may be acceptable in other sales intensive business simply is not to be tolerated for securities brokers.[12] High pressure sales operations often result in criminal convictions and imprisonment. Injured investors have been able to recover damages in broker-dealer arbitration proceedings. Restitution may be awarded in connection with disciplinary proceedings as well as in other enforcement actions.

---

3. *See, e.g.,* SEC v. Meltzer, 440 F.Supp.2d 179 (E.D.N.Y. 2006).

5. In one case:

> H.J. Meyers sponsored incentive programs that offered rewards such as television sets for high volumes of sales. The firm also provided brokers with various scripts that could be used in cold calls to potential customers to pressure customers to purchase Palomar stock. As negative reinforcement, for example, the managers subjected brokers who did not meet target sales to a ritual called the "walk of shame," wherein the broker was required to walk around the floor of the brokerage office while other brokers threw objects at him or her. In addition, brokers were subjected to the "ten or ten" rule, meaning that they were required to make at least ten successful cold calls to sell Palomar stock, or to stay in the office until ten o'clock at night.

Varljen v. H.J. Meyers, Inc., 1998 WL 395266, *1 (S.D.N.Y.1998).

7. New Line Cinema (2000).

9. Joel Seligman, The Transformation of Wall Street 24 (1982).

10. *See,* Jerry W. Markham & Thomas L. Hazen, Broker–Dealer Operations Under Securities and Commodities Law: Financial Responsibilities, Credit Regulation, and Customer Protection pp. 1–64 (2001); Ferdinand Pecora, Wall Street Under Oath: The Story of Our Modern Money Changers 91–92 (1939). Sales contests can provide an improper inducement for brokers to recommend target securities or mutual funds. *See, e.g.,* NASD Fines Morgan Stanley for Sales Contests and Supervisory Violations, http://www.complinet.com/securities-na/dailynews/display.html?ref=49025 (Sept. 17, 2003) (settlement including fines for sales contests with respect to brokerage firm's proprietary mutual funds).

The NASD proposed a rule that would bar contests and the like that focused on specified securities or products rather than rewarding total production for all securities sold. NASD Proposes Banning Most Cash Sales Contests, NASD Press Release, http://www.nasd.com/web/idcplg?IdcService=SS_GET_PAGE & ssDocName=NASDW_013847 & ssSourceNodeId=6 (April 21, 2005) ("A broker's first responsibility is to recommend securities that are right for the investor. Sales contests, whether they pay off in cash or cruises, that favor particular securities can interfere with that responsibility.... This rule proposal would eliminate, in a clear and complete way, this potential conflict of interest."). Even in the absence of such an explicit rule, the existence of targeted sales contests can create disclosure issues as well as issues with respect to the reasonableness of the recommendation").

12. *See, e.g.,* People v. Schwartz, 34 Sec. Reg. & L. Rep (BNA) 532 (N.Y.Sup.Ct. March 27, 2002).

In the context of these problematic high pressure sales campaigns, the sales personnel making the calls typically recommend purchases of large blocks of speculative securities in new companies, predicting dramatic earnings and rapid increases in the market prices of the securities. Where there is a conscious plan of high pressure sales tactics,[16] the situation is referred to as a "boiler room" operation.[17] The term boiler room reflects the former practice of locating such operations in back rooms or boiler rooms.[18] One notable location for making telephone solicitations was from a prison cell.[19] It was observed that "In the old days, you had the boiler rooms where you had to hire 20 people to make thousands of phone calls to sell fraudulent securities. Now one person can do this by the push of a button."[20]

Sometimes the term "bucket shop" is used interchangeably with "boiler room." The bucket shop has many of the same high pressure sales tactics as a boiler room but has a different history. The bucket shops that operated long ago were based on a failure to enter customer orders on an exchange,[22] and thus turning the apparent transactions into illegal difference contracts[23] or simply wagers.[24] The essence of the bucket shop is the fictitious nature of the transactions.[25] In contrast, boiler rooms use high pressure sales with respect to real transactions.

Bucket shops and boiler room operations as high pressure sales campaigns are inconsistent with the broker-dealer's implied representation under the shingle theory to conduct its business in a professional (i.e., fair and equitable) manner.[26]

In the context of a boiler room, high pressure sales campaigns can constitute securities fraud and illegal manipulative activity.[27] Thus, for exam-

16. *See, e.g.,* United States v. Ross, 321 F.2d 61 (2d Cir.1963).

17. *See, e.g.,* Berko v. SEC, 316 F.2d 137 (2d Cir.1963).

18. *See, e.g.,* In the Matter of Josephthal & Co., Disciplinary Proceeding No. C3A990071, 2001 WL 1886873 n. 58 (NASDR May 15, 2001) ("A 'boiler room' is defined as a 'place where high-pressure salespeople use banks of telephones to call lists of potential investors (known in the trade as sucker lists) in order to peddle speculative, even fraudulent, securities. They are called boiler rooms because of the high-pressure selling.' Barron's Dictionary of Finance and Investment Terms 54 (4th ed.1995)").

In one instance, a boiler room operation was compared to high pressure television marketing campaigns. In the Matter of Blinder, Robinson & Co., Complaint No. NEW–737, 1991 WL 840282 (N.A.S.D.R. Sept. 18, 1991) ("... the managers got up and it was like a Jerry Lewis telethon. Everyone in the office was selling this blind pool. We didn't know what they were. We were given a pitch to use, and it was a sales pitch. We were sales people. We were not stockbrokers. We were told to tell people that our clients made money. And if you wanted to make money, you do this or that. We basically were boiler room people.")

19. SEC v. Monas, 33 Sec. Reg. & L. Rep. (BNA) 338 (S.D.N.Y. 2001).

20. *See* Debate in Senate on H.R. 1058 Reported by Conference Committee (2000) (James B. Adelman, former head of enforcement of the SEC's Boston office) in Harold S. Bloomenthal and Samuel Wolff, Securities and Federal Corporate Law APPENDIX B4 (2d ed. 2000).

22. *See, e.g.,* Board of Trade of City of Chicago v. Christie Grain & Stock Co., 198 U.S. 236, 246, 25 S.Ct. 637, 638, 49 L.Ed. 1031 (1905) (describing bucket shops as "places wherein is permitted the pretended buying and selling of grain, etc., without any intention of receiving and paying for the property so bought, or of delivering the property so sold.").

23. Davis v. Fleshman, 245 Pa. 224, 227, 91 A. 489, 490 (Pa.1914).

24. Streeter v. Lowe, 184 F. 263, 264 (1st Cir.1911).

25. Eldridge v. Ward, 174 F. 402 (2d Cir.1909).

26. In the Matter of Mac Robbins & Co., 41 S.E.C. 116, Release No. 34–6846, 1962 WL 67931 *2 (SEC July 11, 1962) (discussing the shingle theory in the context of boiler room operations). *See* § 14.15 *supra* for discussion of the shingle theory.

27. *See, e.g.,* United States v. Harris, 32 Sec. Reg. & L. Rep. (BNA) 1711 (C.D. Cal. 2000).

ple, boiler room activities and other high pressure sales tactics can violate SEC Rule 10b–5 and can also form the basis for FINRA (formerly NASD) disciplinary sanctions.[28] One benchmark of the boiler room variety of high pressure sales tactics is heavy reliance on telephone solicitations and usually concentrating on long-distance cold calling operations. Another common high pressure tactic that implicates the anti-manipulation rules is the use of pre-written scripts including prepared rebuttals to customer objections.[29] This is often accompanied by high commissions to sales representatives for pushing the stocks in question.[30] Many boiler room operations routinely use unregistered sales representatives.[31] Frequently, boiler room operations involve shell companies or other scam stocks.[32]

Brokers and others who sell securities are often very aggressive in their marketing techniques. However, not every instance of high pressure sales tactics will violate the securities laws.[35] Material misrepresentations and omissions can of course expose brokers and others to potential liabilities under the securities laws, but high pressure sales tactics alone will not rise to the requisite level of fraud. On the other hand, when brokers and brokerage firms cross the line between permissible accepted sales tactics and impermissible manipulative or deceptive conduct, they can be held accountable for this conduct under the securities laws. In extreme cases, customer selling orders have even been ignored.

One of the features of a boiler room operation is aggressive cold calling programs whereby a broker calls someone with whom there has been no prior business relationship and tries to enlist him or her as a client. The practice of cold calling has not been limited to boiler room operations and has been utilized by many of the more established retail brokerage firms. In 1994, Congress enacted the Telemarketing and Consumer Fraud and Abuse Prevention Act.[40] As part of that legislation the SEC was authorized to impose limitations on telephone solicitations. In 1995, the SEC approved New York Stock Exchange and NASD rules requiring member firms to maintain and preserve "do not call lists."[41] Among other things, the rules require firms to honor requests not to be called by the firm or its sales agents. The rules also contain sanctions for violations of the requirement that a list be maintained and also for failure to honor customers' requests to be left alone. Many states have their own telemarketing laws that supplement the federal law and in some cases go further.

---

28. *See, e.g.,* In the Matter of Goodman, Complaint No. C9–960013, 1999 WL 1489030 (N.A.S.D.R. Nov. 9, 1999).

29. In the Matter of Olde Discount Corp., Administrative Proceeding File No. 3–9699, Sec. Act Rel. No. 33–7577, 67 S.E.C. Docket 2045, 1998 WL 575171 (SEC September 10, 1998).

30. *See, e.g., Id.*

31. *See, e.g.,* In the Matter of M. Rimson & Co., Administrative Proceeding File No. 3–8772, 63 S.E.C. Docket 2494, Release No. ID–106, 1997 WL 93628 (S.E.C. Feb. 25, 1997).

32. *See, e.g.,* SEC v. Mersky, Civ. Ac. No. 93–CV–5200, Litigation Release No. 13812, 55 S.E.C Docket 307, 1993 WL 387105 (E.D.PA. Sept. 30, 1993). *See also, e.g.,* Gary Weiss, The Mob on Wall Street, Business Week p.92 (Dec. 16, 1996).

35. *See, e.g.,* In re Westcap Enterprises, 230 F.3d 717, 727–728 (5th Cir.2000).

40. Pub. L. No. 103–297, 108 Stat. 1545 (1994).

41. Sec. Exch. Act Rel. No. 34–35831 (SEC June 9, 1995) (approving NASD rule requiring maintenance of do not call lists); Sec. Exch. Act Rel. No. 34–35832 (SEC June 7, 1995) (approving New York Stock Exchange rule requiring maintenance of do not call list).

The SEC disclaimed that there is any *per se* violation of the antifraud provisions resulting from boiler room activities.[48] However, liability is readily imposed under either the shingle theory or the antifraud provisions.[49] The Commission requires that a broker find out certain minimum information about the customer and the security before entering into a transaction.[50] This duty of investigation prior to making a recommendation has been phrased in terms of an obligation of "due diligence." In contrast, the duty of investigation of the security is higher in a sale of unseasoned securities; in such a case, before recommending purchase (or sale), the broker should make a "searching inquiry."[51] In addition, an individual's knowing participation in a high pressure sales campaign fraught with improper sales techniques and recommendations will result in a violation of the Act notwithstanding the defense that he or she relied upon information furnished by the employer broker-dealer.[52] The cases deal mostly with SEC- or NASD-imposed sanctions on participants in boiler room activities rather than in terms of private rights of action by injured investors. Private remedies for boiler room operations can be based upon the antifraud provisions of Rule 10b–5 or sections 12(a)(2) and 17(a) of the 1933 Act,[53] provided that there have been material misrepresentations in connection therewith. Similarly, boiler room operations can result in liability for fraud.[54]

§ 14.19 Penny Stock Regulation; Microcap Fraud

Penny Stock Regulation

As discussed in the preceding section,[1] issues relating to the suitability of broker-dealer recommendations can apply to a wide variety of investments. However, suitability problems are particularly acute when dealing with low-priced securities (frequently referred to as "penny stocks"). For example, the NASD in its suitability rule highlighted the particular concern for low priced securities.[2] In August 1989, the SEC adopted the penny stock rule which became effective on January 1, 1990.[3] The penny stock regulations, which are

---

48. *E.g.,* Kahn v. SEC, 297 F.2d 112 (2d Cir.1961); In re Palombi Securities Co., 41 S.E.C. 266 (SEC 1962).

49. Richard J. Buck & Co., 43 S.E.C. 998 (1968), *aff'd sub nom.* Hanly v. SEC, 415 F.2d 589 (2d Cir.1969); In the Matter of G. Gilman Johnston, 42 S.E.C. 217 (1964).

50. *See* Sec.Exch.Act Rel. No. 34–9671 (July 26, 1972).

51. R.A. Holman & Co., 42 S.E.C. 866 (1965), *affirmed* 366 F.2d 446 (2d Cir.1966), *modified on other grounds* 377 F.2d 665 (2d Cir.1967), *cert. denied* 389 U.S. 991, 88 S.Ct. 473, 19 L.Ed.2d 482 (1967).

52. Berko v. SEC, 316 F.2d 137 (2d Cir.1963); SEC v. Macon, 28 F.Supp. 127, 129 (D.Colo. 1939).

53. 15 U.S.C.A. §§ 77*l*(a)(2), 77q(a); 17 C.F.R. § 240.10b–5. *See* chapters 7, 12 *supra.* The remedy under section 12(a)(2) of the 1933 Act is judicially limited to securities offered by prospectus. Gustafson v. Alloyd Co., 513 U.S. 561, 115 S.Ct. 1061, 131 L.Ed.2d 1 (1995); *see* § 7.6 *supra.* Any remedy under section 17(a) is highly doubtful. *See* § 12.22 *supra.*

54. *See, e.g.,* In the Matter of the Arbitration Between Johnston v. Investors Associates, Inc., Docket Number 98–03685, 2000 WL 1919877 (N.A.S.D. Arbitration Nov. 10, 2000) (arbitration award of $688,000 damages for fraud and common law fraud in connection with high pressure telephone sales).

§ 14.19

1. *See* § 14.16 *supra.*

2. NASD Rule 2310. *See also* former Art. III, Sec. 2 NASD Rules of Fair Practice.

3. Sec.Exch.Act Rel. No. 34–27160, [1989 Transfer Binder] Fed.Sec.L.Rep. (CCH) ¶ 84,440 (Aug. 22, 1989).

discussed below, contain special investor protections applicable to certain dealers in low priced securities. As observed above, although not directly applicable to all transactions involving any broker-dealers, the SEC's increased focus on suitability probably has implications, at least by analogy, for all brokers and for all recommendations.

Congress reinforced the SEC's concerns with penny stocks with the enactment of the Securities Enforcement and Penny Stock Reform Act of 1990.[19] Section 3(a)(51) of the Exchange Act now provides a statutory definition of "penny stock" which excludes most exchange-listed and Nasdaq securities.[20] However, the 1990 legislation gave the SEC rulemaking power to include as "penny stock" one that is listed only on a regional exchange or a Nasdaq security that is not listed in the national market system.[21] In addition to giving the SEC the authority to promulgate rules defining "penny stock," the 1990 amendments also imposed substantive disclosure and regulatory requirements upon broker-dealers dealing in penny stocks.

The 1990 legislation required broker-dealers entering into penny stock transactions to provide substantial risk-disclosure documents to prospective customers before any transactions can take place.[22] Broker-dealers must disclose with respect to each penny stock transaction the spread between the bid and asked price, the depth and liquidity of the market for the stock, and the broker-dealers' compensation for effectuating the transaction. The broker-dealer must also provide the customer with monthly statements indicating the value of the account's penny stock holdings. The Commission is directed to adopt rules establishing additional disclosure requirements.[23] The Commission is also given the authority to provide exemptions from the disclosure requirements "by rule, regulation, or order."[24] It is unlawful to violate any of the above disclosure requirements as well as any SEC rules "reasonably designed to prevent fraudulent, deceptive, or manipulative acts and practices with respect to penny stocks," in order to protect investors or to maintain fair and orderly markets.[25] The penny stock legislation permits the SEC to designate any section 15(c)(2)[26] rules which if violated will not result in a voidable transaction under section 29(b) of the Act.[27] The 1990 reform legislation also prevents a person subject to statutory disqualification from acting as a promoter, consultant, or broker-dealer that underwrites penny stocks.[28]

In addition to the disclosure and regulatory reform described above, the Penny Stock Reform Act enacted section 17B of the Exchange Act[31] which is designed to encourage the development of automated quotation systems for penny stocks. There were also amendments to the 1933 Act regarding "blank check" offerings. A "blank check" company is any company issuing penny

19. Pub.L. No. 101–429 (1990). *See* H.R. Rep. No. 101–617, 101st Cong., 2d Sess. (1990).

20. 15 U.S.C.A. § 78c(a)(51).

21. 15 U.S.C.A. § 78c(a)(51)(B).

22. 15 U.S.C.A. § 78*o*(g)(2).

23. 15 U.S.C.A. § 78*o*(g)(3).

24. 15 U.S.C.A. § 78*o*(g)(4).

25. 15 U.S.C.A. § 78*o*(g)(5).

26. 15 U.S.C.A. § 78*o*(c)(2).

27. 15 U.S.C.A. § 78cc(b).

28. 15 U.S.C.A. § 78*o*(b)(6)(C).

31. 15 U.S.C.A. § 78q–2.

stock as defined in section 3(a)(51) of the Exchange Act[32] that either has no specific business plan or purpose or has indicated that it plans to merge with an unidentified company or companies.[33] The 1990 legislation not only created this new definition, it also directed the Commission to promulgate rules imposing special disclosure requirements for offerings by blank check companies.[34] Furthermore, it also empowered the Commission to place restrictions on the use of the proceeds until such disclosure requirements have been met.[35] The 1990 amendments further authorized the SEC to impose a right of rescission by purchasers of securities sold in violation of the blank check company disclosure requirements.[36] As is the case with the broker-dealer disclosure requirements, the Commission was given exemptive power with regard to blank check offerings.[37]

Securities Issued by "Blank Check Companies"

In a parallel development, the Commission adopted rules regarding 1933 Act registration statements filed by "blank check" companies.[54] A "blank check" company is a company in its development stage offering penny stock where the company has no specific business plan or purpose, or where the company has indicated that its business purpose is to merge with an unidentified company or companies that is issuing penny stock as defined in Rule 3a51–1. The "blank check" company registration rules do not apply to offerings by small businesses other than blank check companies. Thus, for example, the rules do not apply to investments in limited partnerships (or other direct participation programs) involving a detailed plan of business development, even though specific investment properties are not identified.

1933 Act Rule 419[55] requires that proceeds received and securities issued in a blank check company offering must be deposited into an escrow account and held for the sole benefit of purchasers during the offering. Upon the consummation of a business acquisition in which the fair value of the acquired business represents at least eighty percent of the maximum offering proceeds, the blank check company must file a post-effective amendment to its registration statement. The post-effective amendment must disclose information concerning the acquisition. When purchasers of the blank check company receive the post-acquisition information in a prospectus, the purchasers must be given the opportunity to withdraw their deposit funds. Funds from the offering will not be released from the escrow account until the acquisition has been consummated. Furthermore, if the acquisition does not occur within eighteen months subsequent to the effective date of the initial registration statement, the proceeds from the offering must be returned to the purchasers.

Microcap Fraud

In the 1990s, "microcap" fraud stole the spotlight from the penny stock problems of the late 1980s and early 1990s. Microcap became the term that is

32. 15 U.S.C.A. § 78c(a)(51).

33. 15 U.S.C.A. § 77g(b)(3).

34. 15 U.S.C.A. § 77g(b)(1)(A).

35. 15 U.S.C.A. § 77g(b)(1)(B).

36. 15 U.S.C.A. § 77g(b)(1)(C).

37. 15 U.S.C.A. § 77g(b)(2).

54. *See* Sec. Act Rel. No. 33–6932, [1991–1992 Transfer Binder] Fed.Sec.L.Rep. (CCH) ¶ 84,937 (April 13, 1992).

55. 17 C.F.R. § 230.419.

now often used when referring to *very small* capitalization companies. The Internet has been used for many microcap offerings and has led to several abuses and securities law violations.[59] For example, the Commission became concerned with the use of the exemption from registration under 1933 Act Rule 504[60] for unregistered Internet offerings of microcap securities.[61] In particular, the Commission was concerned with so-called "pump and dump" offerings[62] where Rule 504 frequently was used for Internet offerings (to "pump" the securities into the market) and then creating a secondary market (so that the securities could be "dumped" by the initial purchasers). In 1999, the Commission amended Rule 504 to prohibit the use of the exemption for public offerings unless registered or otherwise required by state law to use a disclosure document when offering the securities for sale. The SEC has also focused enforcement efforts on microcap fraud. Another microcap abuse was the utilization of the short Form S–8 for 1933 Act registration of offerings to employees, advisors, and consultants for microcap securities.[65] In an effort to deter these microcap abuses, the Commission eliminated the availability of Form S–8 for offerings to advisors and consultants whose services involve selling or making a market in the issuer's securities.[66] Pump and dump schemes also arise outside of initial offerings, where the perpetrators of the scheme manipulate the price of a security to create a frothy market.[67]

NASD (now FINRA) Rule 2315 applies to certain recommendations of securities that are published in a "quotation medium" and are either (1) not listed on Nasdaq or a national securities exchange or (2) are listed on a regional securities exchange and are not included in transaction reports over the Consolidated Tape. The Rule applies to recommendations of a purchase or short sale of covered microcap securities, but does not apply to recommended sales out of a long position.

§ 14.20 Excessive Trading in Securities—Churning

Churning is a concept that goes beyond the securities industry. For example, it is also an abuse found in insurance sales. Churning is the practice of entering into trades for the purpose of generating commissions rather than for the customer's benefit.

SEC Rule 15c1–7[1] prohibits excessive trading by a broker for any account in which he or she holds discretionary trading powers. When a broker in a discretionary trading account enters into transactions for the purpose of

59. *See, e.g.,* Special Report, Microcap Fraud Over the Internet Seen as Trend by Enforcement Officials, 30 Sec. Reg. & L. Rep. (BNA) 1224 (Aug. 14, 1998). *See also, e.g.,* Note, "Click Here to Buy the Next Microsoft": The Penny Stock Rules, Online Microcap Fraud, and the Unwary Investor, 75 Ind. L.J. 379 (2000).

60. 17 C.F.R. § 230.504. *See* § 4.19 *supra.*

61. *See* Sec. Act Rel. No. 33–7300 (May 31, 1996).

62. *See, e.g.,* In the Matter of Scacci, Administrative Proceeding File No. 3–10012, Sec. Exch. Act Rel. No. 34–41873, 70 S.E.C. Docket 1290, 1999 WL 710848 (SEC Sept. 14, 1999).

65. Form S–8 does not impose the detailed disclosure requirements that are found with other registration forms. *See* § 3.3 *supra.* This then allowed microcap issuers taking advantage of the form to issue securities without the level of disclosure that would ordinarily be required.

66. *See* Sec. Act Rel. No. 33–7645 (SEC Feb. 25, 1999).

67. *See, e.g.,* In the Matter of Terrell, Administrative Proceeding File No. 3–10154, Sec. Exch Act Rel. No. 34–42483, 71 S.E.C. Docket 1863, 2000 WL 248549 (SEC March 2, 2000).

§ 14.20

1. 17 C.F.R. § 240.15c1–7.

generating commissions, the broker unjustifiably gains from the customer's loss or transaction costs. This practice is generally referred to as "churning" the customer's account. Rule 15c1–7 declares churning to be a "manipulative, deceptive or other fraudulent device or contrivance."[3] The SEC rule is limited by its terms to trading accounts where the broker has the discretion to enter into transactions, but the account overall need not be formally discretionary. A 1949 SEC ruling took the position that the "handling of a customer's account may become fraudulent whenever the broker or dealer is in a position to determine the volume and frequency of transactions by reason of the customer's willingness to follow the suggestions of the broker or the dealer and he abuses the customer's confidence by overtrading."[4] In contrast to a fraudulent pattern of recommendations, a churning claim requires more than asserting a pattern of the customer having followed the broker's advice; it must be shown that the broker had "control" over the account.[5] The customer may be relatively naive or unsophisticated in investment matters, having naively acquiesced in the broker's management of the account or consented to some trading, but not such excessive trading. In addition to violating the broker's standards of conduct embodied in section 15(c)(1),[6] churning can form the basis of a violations of the 1934 Act's general antifraud provisions contained in Rule 10b–5.[7] Excessive trading can violate a broker's obligations even if the requisite control is not present, if it can be shown that the excessive trading resulted from unsuitable recommendations.[8]

There are few, if any, substantive defenses to a churning claim once a prima facie case has been established. It has further been held that the customer's opportunity to complain about the transactions by virtue of his having viewed the transaction confirmations does not in itself create an estoppel so as to preclude a churning action under Rule 10b–5.[28] This is the generally accepted view since in order to succeed on the defense of laches or estoppel, the defendant must establish that the plaintiff was guilty of a lack of due diligence and that the passage of time worked to the prejudice of the defendant.[29] Similarly, in contrast to a claim for unauthorized trading, which is discussed in the next section of this treatise,[30] ordinarily it would not be a defense to a churning claim that the plaintiff's failure to object to the trades in question operated as a ratification of the trades. However, when the customer is a sophisticated investor, a failure to object to the broker's

3. 17 C.F.R. § 240.15c1–7.

4. In re Norris & Hirshberg, 21 S.E.C. 865, 890 (1946), *affirmed sub nom.* Norris & Hirshberg v. SEC, 177 F.2d 228 (D.C.Cir.1949).

5. Hotmar v. Lowell H. Listrom & Co., Inc., 808 F.2d 1384 (10th Cir.1987).

6. 15 U.S.C.A. § 78o(c)(1).

7. *E.g.,* Arceneaux v. Merrill Lynch, Pierce, Fenner & Smith, Inc., 767 F.2d 1498 (11th Cir.1985); Costello v. Oppenheimer & Co., 711 F.2d 1361 (7th Cir.1983); Armstrong v. McAlpin, 699 F.2d 79 (2d Cir.1983); Carras v. Burns, 516 F.2d 251 (4th Cir.1975); Fey v. Walston & Co., Inc., 493 F.2d 1036 (7th Cir.1974).

8. *See, e.g.,* Jack H. Stein, Sec. Exch. Act Rel. No. 34–47335, 79 S.E.C. Docket 1777, 2003 WL 431870 (Feb. 10, 2003)(finding unsuitability based on "[r]ecommending excessive activity in a customer's account."); In the Matter of Dunbar, 2008 WL 2167905 (FINRA May 20, 2008) (recommending high volume trading was unsuitable).

28. Mihara v. Dean Witter & Co., Inc., 619 F.2d 814, 822–23 (9th Cir.1980); Hecht v. Harris, Upham & Co., 430 F.2d 1202, 1208 (9th Cir.1970).

29. *See, e.g.,* Hecht v. Harris, Upham & Co., 430 F.2d 1202, 1208 (9th Cir.1970).

30. *See* § 14.21 *infra.*

discretionary trades that are reported to the investor may preclude the investor's claim for damages.[31]

In order to establish churning it generally will be necessary to prove substantial disparity between the turnover in the account in question and the normal trading activity for similar accounts. For example, in one case the plaintiff prevailed by showing that an account which amounted to less than one-tenth of one percent of the local office's portfolio value generated 4.7 percent of its commission income.[36] Although the damaging turn-over rate must necessarily be decided on a case by case basis, it appears that a given account's annual turn-over rate in excess of six times is considered generally to reflect excessive trading.[37] In addition, a court will review the patterns of trading; for example courts should scrutinize sales soon after or at the same time as purchases (or purchases soon after sales) of the same security. It also is suspicious if a broker causes one account to buy a security sold out of another account over which he exercises discretion. Courts further look at the commissions and profits of the broker with regard to the transactions under scrutiny. In such cases, where one or more of these factors are present, the burden would presumably shift to the broker to justify this activity.

The types of investments being made will also be relevant to the determination of whether there has been excessive trading. Ordinarily, a lower turnover rate will be appropriate in debt investments than in equity holdings. Similarly, a higher turnover rate ordinarily will be permitted in options as opposed to equity transactions.[38] For similar reasons a higher turnover rate may be tolerated in a speculative or trading account.

The appropriate measure of damages[50] is not always easy to identify in a churning case. The general rule appears to be that the defendant is liable only for the losses due to the excessive commissions plus accrued interest.[51] However, some courts have assessed the measure of damages as the excess of the average decline in market values over the decline in value of the plaintiff's portfolio.[52] On the other hand, it has been held by other courts that a plaintiff may also recover additional consequential losses due to changed investment strategy decisions occurring during the churning activity.[53] Since churning does not necessarily result in less prudent investments, it quite properly has been suggested that the better view would be to award damages for diminution in investment value only in situations where the broker-dealer has also violated the suitability requirements.[54] Since the evil involved is the genera-

31. *See, e.g.*, Smith v. Slade & Co., 1982 WL 1341 (D.D.C. 1982).

36. Hecht v. Harris, Upham & Co., 430 F.2d 1202 (9th Cir.1970).

37. *See* Mihara v. Dean Witter & Co , Inc., 619 F.2d 814, 821 (9th Cir.1980); Gopez v. Shin, 736 F.Supp. 51 (D.Del.1990).

38. *See, e.g.,* Leo W. Desmond & Brian Murray, Determining Excessive Trading in Options Accounts: A Synthetic Valuation Approach, 23 U. Dayton L. Rev. 15 (1997).

50. *See* § 12.12 *supra* for discussion of the measure of damages in Rule 10b–5 actions generally.

51. Hecht v. Harris, Upham & Co., 430 F.2d 1202 (9th Cir.1970); Sebbag v. Shearson Lehman Brothers, Inc., 1991 WL 12431, [1990–1991 Transfer Binder] Fed.Sec.L.Rep. (CCH) ¶ 95,775 (S.D.N.Y.1991).

52. *E.g.*, Miley v. Oppenheimer & Co., 637 F.2d 318 (5th Cir.1981).

53. *See* Miley v. Oppenheimer & Co., 637 F.2d 318 (5th Cir.1981); Fey v. Walston & Co. Inc., 493 F.2d 1036, 1044–54 (7th Cir.1974).

54. Nesbit v. McNeil, 896 F.2d 380, 385 (9th Cir.1990); Miley v. Oppenheimer & Co., 637 F.2d 318, 326 (5th Cir.1981); In re Thomson McKinnon Securities, Inc., 191 B.R. 976 (Bkrtcy.S.D.N.Y. 1996).

tion of excessive commissions, the fact that the customer's account increased in value does not preclude a churning claim.[55] At least one court has allowed consideration of the lost profits that would have accrued to the investor had the churning and accompanying unsuitable investments not occurred.[56]

§ 14.21 Unauthorized Trading

An unauthorized trade is simply the purchase or sale of stock by a broker on behalf of a customer who has not authorized the transaction. Unauthorized trading differs from churning in that under a churning claim, the plaintiff will attempt to show that excessive trading has occurred on his account simply to generate brokerage fees or commissions. The plaintiff in churning cases need not argue that the trading was per se unauthorized. Usually, the customer authorizes trading on his or her account; the evil in churning cases is the broker's excessive trading in order to generate commissions. A variation on unauthorized trading is the ignoring of customer sell orders. Ignoring customer orders obviously is not to generate sales commissions but rather may be part of a scheme to manipulate and thereby inflate the price of the stock in question.

Unauthorized trading claims can arise in many contexts. The only defense to unauthorized trading claims is that the broker in fact had the authority or discretion to execute the transactions in question. The broker can get such authority from a specific customer order or from a grant of discretionary trading authority. Grants of discretionary trading authority require prior written authorization. Specifically, NASD (FINRA) Rule of Conduct 2510 provides that a registered representative may not exercise without written authorization.[3] Unauthorized trades similarly place a broker in violation of New York Stock Exchange Rules.[4]

§ 14.22 "Short Sales" and Applicable Regulations

If an investor believes that the price of a security is likely to decline, there are several potential investment strategies. Most such strategies are linked to dealing with put and call options.[1] Another alternative is to enter an order to sell the security at the current price with the understanding that the investor is to fulfill that obligation at a later date by purchasing the security at a lower price. This practice, known as selling short, is extremely risky since

---

55. Davis v. Merrill Lynch, Pierce, Fenner & Smith, Inc., 906 F.2d 1206 (8th Cir.1990); Nesbit v. McNeil, 896 F.2d 380 (9th Cir.1990).

56. *See* Scalp & Blade, Inc. v. Advest, Inc., 765 N.Y.S.2d 92, 309 A.D.2d 219 (2003).

§ 14.21

3. FINRA Rule of Conduct 2510.

4. In the Matter of Koos, NYSE Hearing Panel Decision 01–122 2002 WL 799395 (N.Y.S.E. August 1, 2001).

§ 14.22

1. For example, by purchasing a "put" option, the investor gets the right to put the security to the option seller at the exercise price on or before the expiration date. The hope is that the security can be purchased at a low enough price to offset the premium paid for the right to "put" it (*i.e.*, sell it) to the option writer at the higher price. Options are traded on several of the national securities exchanges under the supervision of the SEC, the applicable exchange and the Options Clearing Corporation. *See* SEC, Report of the Special Study of the Options Market, 96th Cong., 1st Sess. (1979).

Another strategy, of course, is selling the security if it is owned in order to prevent loss resulting from the anticipated price deterioration.

every increase in the price causes loss to the investor until he or she covers the short sale. An alternative method is "selling against the box" where securities are borrowed as collateral for delivery for sale at a later date.

The mechanics of a short sale are as follows. The customer sells securities that he or she does not own. The customer then borrows the security from the broker in order to be able to deliver the security to the purchaser in the short sale transaction.[3] In turn, the customer pays interest on the loan[4] until he or she closes the transaction by purchasing the security in question and restoring that stock to the broker.[5] As pointed out above, an alternative method to effectuate the transaction is known as "selling against the box" where rather than borrowing securities from the broker, the customer uses securities that he or she already owns as collateral for the short sale.[6] When the customer posts collateral for the short sale or sale against the box, the brokerage firm may earn profits from the collateral so held.[7] It is not securities fraud to fail to inform the customer of these profits.[8] The clearing mechanisms for securities transactions generally and applicable SEC short sale rules in Regulation SHO are designed to make short sales transparent to buyers.

Because of the speculative nature of and potential for abuse associated with short sales and sales against the box, insiders of publicly traded securities are strictly prohibited from engaging in such transactions.[14] Also, short sales are not meant for the ordinary investor both because of the risk involved and the level of sophistication that should exist before an investor embarks upon such a transaction. An investor can take the same investment strategy with the use of options. For example, purchasing a put option on a particular security gives the investor the right (before the option expires) to sell the security at the exercise price to the writer of the put option. If the price of the security declines below the option exercise price, then the option is "in the money" since if the option is exercised and the underlying security is then sold, the investor would realize a profit. There would cease to be a profit once the price of the stock climbs above the option exercise price since the investor could purchase the security more cheaply on the open market than by exercising his or her put option.

When an investor writes (or sells) a put option, the investor takes a "short" investment position, and therefore this involves similar risks as short sales and sales against the box. However, the writing of put options is not expressly covered by the short sale regulations.

Because of the risky nature of a short sale investment strategy, a broker has a duty to explain the transaction in a manner understandable to the investor.[15] This is equally true of a short position in options. A material

3. Since the securities that are borrowed for the short sale are delivered for sale, from the purchaser's perspective a purchase of securities from a short sale is no different that an ordinary purchase.

4. The loan transaction is regulated by the margin rules which govern the extension of credit where securities are held as collateral. *See* § 14.9 *supra*.

5. *See, e.g.,* Levitin v. PaineWebber, Inc. 159 F.3d 698 (2d Cir.1998).

6. *See* Bissell v. Merrill Lynch & Co., 157 F.3d 138 (2d Cir.1998).

7. Bissell v. Merrill Lynch & Co., 157 F.3d 138 (2d Cir.1998); Levitin v. PaineWebber, Inc., 159 F.3d 698 (2d Cir.1998).

8. *See* Levitin v. PaineWebber, Inc., 159 F.3d 698 (2d Cir.1998); Bissell v. Merrill Lynch & Co., 157 F.3d 138 (2d Cir.1998).

14. 15 U.S.C.A. § 78p(c). *See* § 13.5 *supra*.

15. Vucinich v. Paine, Webber, Jackson & Curtis, Inc., 803 F.2d 454 (9th Cir.1986).

misrepresentation concerning the risks of a short sale transaction (or option transaction) can form the basis of a private suit under SEC Rule 10b–5. Additionally, short sales have lent themselves to manipulative practices.

Short selling has the potential to be manipulative and can be used as part of a scheme to manipulate the market. However, short selling by itself is not manipulative.[18] The fact that there is a large amount of short selling that necessarily has the effect of depressing a stock's price does not make the short sales manipulative.[19] As discussed elsewhere in this treatise,[20] the key question in any manipulation case is not whether the activity in fact affected the price of the stock but whether the activity was entered into for the purpose of affecting the price.

After conducting an inquiry into the effects of concentrated short selling during the market break of 1937, the Commission adopted former Rule 10a–1 in 1938 in order to restrict short selling in a declining market. The Commission's former "short sale rule," 1934 Act Rule 10a–1, was designed to restrict short sellers from effecting short sales in an exchange-traded security when the price of that security is declining and implemented what was known as the "tick test". In 2007, The SEC adopted Rule 201 of Regulation SHO that prohibits the self regulatory organizations from adopting rules regulating the price of short sales.[27]

Another concern of the regulators has been "naked short selling" which involves selling short without adequate collateral to cover the short sale. Abusive naked short sales where there is no intent to provide adequate collateral for the short position violates general antifraud proscriptions, even without rulemaking specifically targeting abusive short selling.[29] Former SEC Rule 10a–2, addressed the process of covering of short sales[30] by purchasing or borrowing the underlying security in order to effect delivery of the security that was sold short.

Rule 203[31] of Regulation SHO replaced former Rule 10a–2.[32] It could easily be questioned whether the SEC became too lax in regulation aimed at abusive short selling practices.[33] In the midst of the credit crisis of 2008 and the precipitous stock price plunge in many financial institutions and mortgage lenders, the SEC took emergency action.[34] Specifically, the Commission an-

18. *See* GFL Advantage Fund, Ltd. v. Colkitt, 272 F.3d 189, 207–210 (3d Cir.2001); Sullivan & Long, Inc. v. Scattered Corp., 47 F.3d 857, 864 (7th Cir.1995).

19. GFL Advantage Fund, Ltd. v. Colkitt, 272 F.3d 189, 209 (3d Cir.2001).

20. *See* § 12.1 *supra*.

27. 17 C.F.R. § 242.202.

29. "[A]busive "naked" short selling as part of a manipulative scheme is always illegal under the general anti-fraud provisions of the federal securities laws, including Rule 10b–5 under the Exchange Act . . ." "Naked" Short Selling Anti–Fraud Rule, Sec. Exch. Act Rel. No. 34–57511, 2008 WL 706578 (SEC March 17, 2008) (proposing a new antifraud Rule 10b–21 specifically targeting naked short sales).

30. 17 C.F.R. § 240.10a–2 (repealed 2004).

31. 17 C.F.R. § 242.242.203.

32. *See* Short Sales, Sec. Exch. Act Rel. No. 34–50103, 2004 WL 1697019 (SEC 2004).

33. *See, e.g.*, Edward D. Herlihy, Theodore A. Levine & Caitlin S. Hall, Market's Dramatic Response to Naked Short Sale Restrictions Underscores Need for Additional SEC Action (Wachtell, Lipton, Rosen & Katz Memorandum July 21, 2008).

34. *See* Cox Announces Emergency Rule To Bar Naked Short–Selling in Major Firms, Sec. L. Daily (BNA), http://pubs.bna.com/ip/bna/sld.nsf/eh/A0B6V2E6A9 (July 16, 2008).

nounced enhanced efforts against naked short selling.[35] The first measure was an emergency rule to prevent naked short selling in Fannie Mae, Freddie Mac, and other major financial institutions affected by the mortgage crises.[36] The Commission also announced its intention to initiate rulemaking focusing on short selling practices in the broader market.

Regulation SHO

Regulation SHO defines ownership of securities, specifies aggregation of long and short positions, and requires broker-dealers to identify sales in all equity securities "long," "short," or "short exempt."[38] As noted above, the "tick test" was abolished after a pilot program temporarily suspending its operation.

Regulation SHO provides further that short sellers of equity securities must locate securities to borrow before selling.[44] When it adopted Regulation SHO, the SEC issued interpretive guidance addressing sham transactions designed to evade Regulation M's provisions on manipulative purchases during a distribution.[45]

When it adopted Regulation SHO, the SEC replaced former Rule 3b–3's[46] short sale definition with Rule 200.[47] Among other things, Rule 200 requires broker dealers to identify sell orders in all equity securities as "long," "short," or "short exempt."[48]

Rule 203[49] of Regulation SHO replaced provisions that formerly were contained in Rule 10a–1 and 10a–2 regarding the covering of securities underlying a short sale. Rule 203(b) imposes a requirement that prior to effecting a short sale with respect to an equity security must "locate" securities available for borrowing.[50] As explained by the SEC, "Specifically, the rule prohibits a broker-dealer from accepting a short sale order in any equity security from another person, or effecting a short sale order for the broker-dealer's own account unless the broker-dealer has (1) borrowed the security, or entered into an arrangement to borrow the security, or (2) has reasonable grounds to believe that the security can be borrowed so that it can

35. SEC Enhances Investor Protections Against Naked Short Selling, Sec Press Release 2008–143, http://www.sec.gov/news/press/2008/2008–143.htm (SEC July 15, 2008).

36. Emergency Order Pursuant to Section 12(k)(2) of the Securities Exchange Act of 1934 Taking Temporary Action to Respond To Market Developments, Sec. Exch. Act Rel. No. 34–58166, 2008 WL 2743880 (SEC July 15, 2008).

38. *See* Short Sales, Sec. Exch. Act Rel. No. 34–50103, 83 S.E.C. Docket 1278, 2004 WL 1697019 (SEC 2004) (adoption of Regulation SHO).

44. *See* Short Sales, Sec. Exch. Act Rel. No. 34–50103, 2004 WL 1697019 (SEC 2004). Regulation SHO also imposes additional delivery requirements on broker-dealers for securities in which a substantial number of failures to deliver have occurred. *See id.*

45. *See id.* Regulation M is discussed in chapter 6 *supra*.

46. 17 C.F.R. § 240.3b–3 (repealed 2004).

47. 17 C.F.R. § 242.200.

48. 17 C.F.R. § 242.200(g). In addition, Rule 200 permits broker-dealers to calculate net positions in a particular security within defined trading units; incorporates the block-positioner exception from current Rule 10a–1(e)(13); and also codifies prior SEC interpretations related to the ownership of security futures products, and the unwinding of certain index arbitrage positions. *See* Short Sales, Sec. Exch. Act Rel. No. 34–50103, 2004 WL 1697019 (SEC July 28, 2004) (adoption of Regulation SHO).

49. 17 C.F.R. § 242.203

50. 17 C.F.R. § 242.303(b).

be delivered on the date delivery is due.''[51] The broker-dealer must satisfy this location obligation and it must be documented prior to effecting a short sale, even if seller's short position may be closed out by purchasing securities the same day.[52] Rule 203 sets forth ''some limited exceptions,''[53] including an exception for short sales effected in connection with bona-fide market making.[54]

In 2008, the SEC amended Regulation SHO in order to address abusive naked short sales.

Uncovered, or ''naked,'' short sales can be manipulative and hence in violation of the 1934 Act. The evil of a naked short sale is that when entered it misrepresents to the market that an actual or covered short sale has been made. The SEC has indicated that naked short sales can be fraudulent[60] but it has been observed that there is no firm authority holding that naked short sales are always manipulative or fraudulent.[61] Nevertheless, the SEC has indicated that it is.[62] As pointed out above, the general antifraud and antimanipulation rules can be applied to short sales as well. Thus, for example, manipulative short sales violate Rule 10b–5.[63]

So called ''naked short selling,'' which can be seen as the equivalent of selling counterfeit shares,[107] is entering into a short sale without borrowing the necessary securities to make delivery, thus potentially resulting in a ''fail to deliver'' securities to the buyer. A ''fail to deliver'' occurs when a broker-dealer fails to deliver securities to the party on the other side of the transaction on settlement date. As noted by the SEC, naked short selling is not necessarily a violation of the federal securities laws or the SEC's rules. Indeed, in certain circumstances, naked short selling contributes to market liquidity, such as when broker-dealers that make a market in a security generally stand ready to buy and sell the security on a regular and continuous basis at a publicly quoted price, even when there are no other buyers or sellers. Thus, market makers must sell a security to a buyer even when there are temporary shortages of that security available in the market. As explained by the SEC:

> One of Regulation SHO's primary goals is to reduce fails to deliver. Currently, Regulation SHO requires certain persistent fail to deliver positions to be closed out. Specifically, Rule 203(b)(3)'s close-out requirement requires a participant of a clearing agency registered with the Commission to take immediate action to close out a fail to deliver position

51. Short Sales, Sec. Exch. Act Rel. No. 34–50103, 83 S.E.C. Docket 1278, 2004 WL 1697019 (SEC July 28, 2004) (adopting release).

52. *Id.*

53. *Id.*

54. *See id.*

60. See Short Sales, Sec. Exch. Act Rel. No. 34–48709, 68 Fed. Reg. 62972, 62974 at 62975 n. 29, 2003 WL 22461522 (SEC Oct. 28, 2003), Sec. Exch. Act Rel. No. 34–6778 (SEC Apr. 16, 1962).

61. Zachary T. Knepper, Future–Priced Convertible Securities and the Outlook for ''Death Spiral'' Securities–Fraud Litigation, 26 Whittier L. Rev. 359, 380 (2004).

62. Short Sales, Sec. Exch. Act Rel. No. 34–48709, 68 Fed. Reg. 62972, 62974 at 62975 n. 29, 2003 WL 22461522 (SEC Oct. 28, 2003).

63. *E.g.*, United States v. Russo, 74 F.3d 1383 (2d Cir.1996) (fraudulent short sales in connection with stock kiting scheme, wherein defendants shifted securities from one account to another in order to create the appearance of market activity, violated Rule 10b–5).

107. *See, e.g.*, Jag Media Holdings Inc. v. A.G. Edwards & Sons Inc., 387 F.Supp.2d 691, 695 (S.D.Tex. 2004); In the Matter of Eagletech Communications, Inc., Sec. Exch. Act Rel. No. 34–54095, Admin. Proc. File No. 3–11832, 2006 WL 1835958 at *2 (SEC 2006).

> in a threshold security in the Continuous Net Settlement (CNS) system that has persisted for 13 consecutive settlement days by purchasing securities of like kind and quantity. In addition, if the failure to deliver has persisted for 13 consecutive settlement days, Rule 203(b)(3)(iii) prohibits the participant, and any broker-dealer for which it clears transactions, including market makers, from accepting any short sale orders or effecting further short sales in the particular threshold security without borrowing, or entering into a bona-fide arrangement to borrow, the security until the participant closes out the fail to deliver position by purchasing securities of like kind and quantity.[108]

Nevertheless, the Commission has indicated that under many circumstances naked short selling is a violation of the securities laws.[109] In fact, in 2008, the SEC proposed and subsequently adopted a rule in order to clarify that naked short selling when there is no intent to locate securities to borrow as collateral is a fraudulent act.[110] On the other hand, when what amounts to a naked short sale results from a fail to deliver, the settlement rules provide that if the short position is corrected within ten days after settlement there is no violation.[111]

§ 14.23 Parking

A practice that is clearly deceptive and also can be manipulative is known as "parking." Parking occurs when an investor or broker transfers his or her securities to a third party for the purpose of hiding the true ownership.[1] The SEC has described parking as "the sale of securities subject to an agreement or understanding that the securities will be repurchased by the seller at a later time and at a price which leaves the economic risk on the seller."[2] When this type of transfer occurs, it clearly qualifies as deceptive within the meaning of section 10(b) of the 1934 Act. Parking is a "sham" transaction and thus in addition to constituting deceptive conduct can also be properly characterized as manipulation.

Usually, the critical issue in a parking case is establishing whether the arrangements relating to the transactions in question involve bona fide purchases and sales, or, instead, are sham transactions designed to conceal true ownership.

§ 14.24 Customer Protection for Broker-Dealer Insolvency—The Securities Investor Protection Act

During the 1960s, a large number of brokerage firms experienced various types of severe financial problems, including insolvency. Since many investors

---

108. *See* Proposed Amendments to Regulation SHO, Sec. Exch. Act Rel. No. 34-54154, 71 Fed. Reg. 41710-01, 2006 WL 2032073 (SEC July 14, 2006).

109. Short Sales, Sec. Exch. Act Rel. No. 34-48709, 68 Fed. Reg. 62972, 62974 at 62975 n. 29, 2003 WL 22461522 (SEC Oct. 28, 2003).

110. *See* Securities and Exchange Commission OKs Three Proposals Related to ETFs, "Naked" shorting, Identity Security, Broker/Dealer Compliance Re. (BNA) 1, http://pubs.bna.com/ip/bna/bdc.nsf/eh/A0B6D6Q8D6 (March 5, 2008).

111. Rule 203(b) of Regulation SHO requires that action be taken if a fail to deliver remains open ten days after the settlement date. 17 C.F.R. § 242.203(b).

§ 14.23

1. Yoshikawa v. SEC, 192 F.3d 1209 (9th Cir.1999); SIPC v. Vigman, 74 F.3d 932, 933 n. 3 (9th Cir.1996); United States v. Jones, 900 F.2d 512, 515 (2d Cir.1990).

2. In re Barlage, 63 S.E.C. 1060, 1996 WL 733756 at *1 n. 2 (SEC 1996).

allow their securities to be held by their brokers in "street name,"[1] the broker's insolvency creates a substantial risk of harm in addition to that resulting from the broker-dealer's inability to honor or follow through with customer orders. Congress responded to these risks with the Securities Investor Protection Act of 1970.[2] The Act established the Securities Investor Protection Corporation (SIPC),[3] a nonprofit corporation whose membership is made up of most broker-dealers registered under the 1934 Exchange Act.

The Securities Investor Protection Corporation, which operates under SEC supervision,[5] has two primary functions. First, SIPC is responsible for establishing and maintaining a fund for the benefit of injured investors.[6] The SIPC fund is designed to protect customer claims for both cash and securities that are lost due to a brokerage firm's insolvency.[7]

In many respects, SIPC is similar in nature to the Federal Deposit Insurance Corporation (FDIC), which protects depositors in commercial banks.[8] SIPC becomes a party to proceedings to liquidate insolvent brokerage firms,[10] which are conducted in a manner similar to that provided under the federal bankruptcy laws,[11] including the appointment of a trustee.[12] Unlike the federal bankruptcy laws, however, there is no provision under the Securities Investor Protection Act for reorganization as an alternative to liquidation.[13] SIPC may bring suit against third parties on behalf of the customers of the insolvent brokerage firm.[14] SIPC's standing to bring suit exists notwithstanding the statute's failure to expressly list the authority to sue, since bringing a suit for damages falls within SIPC's authority to pursue the insolvent brokerage firm's revenue in the ordinary course of business.[15]

The SIPC fund is maintained by both initial and periodic assessment of the members.[16] The fund is available to provide cash advances to injured customers who have valid claims[17] against the insolvent broker-dealer in the liquidation proceedings.[18] Any such advance is limited to five hundred thousand dollars per customer, but is not to exceed one hundred thousand dollars if the customer has a claim only for cash as opposed to a claim for securities.[19] SIPC may also, in its discretion, advance to the trustee for the liquidation

§ 14.24

1. *See* SEC, Street Name Study; § 10.10 *supra.*

2. Codified as amended 15 U.S.C.A. §§ 78aaa–78*lll*. For additional information on the background and purpose of the Act, *see* S.Rep. No. 1218, 91st Cong., 2d Sess. (1970).

3. 15 U.S.C.A. § 78ccc.

5. 15 U.S.C.A. §§ 78ccc(a)(2)(B), 78ggg.

6. 15 U.S.C.A. § 78ddd. *See* 15 U.S.C.A. §§ 78fff–3, 78fff–4.

7. *See, e.g.,* In re New York Times Securities Services, Inc., 371 F.3d 68 (2d Cir. 2004).

8. *See* SEC v. Albert & Maguire Securities Co., 560 F.2d 569 (3d Cir.1977). *See also, e.g.,* SEC v. Securities Northwest, Inc., 573 F.2d 622, 624 (9th Cir.1978).

10. 15 U.S.C.A. § 78eee(d).

11. 15 U.S.C.A. §§ 78fff–1—78fff–2. *See* Redington v. Touche Ross & Co., 612 F.2d 68 (2d Cir.1979).

12. 15 U.S.C.A. § 78eee(b)(3). The trustee has the same powers and title and the same rights to avoid preferences as a trustee in bankruptcy. 15 U.S.C.A. § 78fff–1(a).

13. *See* SEC v. Securities Northwest, Inc., 573 F.2d 622 (9th Cir.1978).

14. *See, e.g.,* SIPC v. BDO Seidman, 222 F.3d 63, 68–69 (2d Cir. 2000).

15. *See, id.*

16. 15 U.S.C.A. § 78ddd(c).

17. A SIPA claim requires that the customer be able to identify cash or property held in an account by the insolvent broker-dealer in order to recover. *See, e.g.,* In re MJK Clearing, Inc., 371 F.3d 397 (8th Cir. 2004) (failure to establish SIPA claim).

18. 15 U.S.C.A. § 78fff–3.

19. 15 U.S.C.A. § 78fff–3(a)(1).

proceedings funds (1) to pay or guarantee indebtedness to a bank or other lender,[20] (2) to secure indemnification of SIPC members against cash shortages,[21] and (3) to purchase securities for the satisfaction of customer claims against the insolvent broker-dealers.[22]

The protection of the Securities Investor Protection Act is generally reserved for customers of broker-dealers. Not every transaction effected through a securities broker that may happen to involve securities will classify someone delivering securities to a broker-dealer as a customer with regard to the transaction in question.[24]

§ 14.25 Private Remedies Against Exchanges and FINRA for Damages Resulting From Nonenforcement of Their Own Rules

On occasion, a self regulatory organization will fail to enforce its own rules. In such situations can the self regulatory organization be held accountable for losses resulting from the failure to enforce? The case law under the Exchange Act is relatively sparse, although there is some authority for the existence of a private remedy in appropriate cases to redress nonenforcement of securities exchange's customer protection rules. Analogies can be made to the more substantial body of law that recognized a private remedy against commodity exchanges for enforcement lapses.[3]

The courts have been in conflict as to the existence of an implied remedy against exchanges under the Exchange Act.[4] The Third Circuit in Walck v. American Stock Exchange, Inc.,[12] denied the existence of an implied right of action against a securities exchange.[13]

§ 14.26 Private Remedies Against Market Professionals; Secondary Liability

Broker-dealers, like anyone else, can be subject to liability for a violation. Rule 10b–5's general antifraud provisions, which are discussed in chapter 12 of this treatise. It is significant that the Supreme Court has taken a broad view of Rule 10b–5's requirement that for the rule to apply the fraud be in connection with the purchase or sale of a security.[2] The fraud does not have to

20. 15 U.S.C.A. § 78fff–3(c)(1). *See* 15 U.S.C.A. § 78fff–1(b)(2).

21. 15 U.S.C.A. § 78fff–3(c)(2). *See* 15 U.S.C.A. § 78fff–2(f)

22. 15 U.S.C.A. § 78fff–3(c)(3). *See* 15 U.S.C.A. § 78fff–2(d).

24. *See, e.g.,* In re New Times Securities Services, Inc., 463 F.3d 125 (2d Cir. 2006); In re Stalvey & Associates, Inc., 750 F.2d 464 (5th Cir.1985).

§ 14.25

3. *See generally* 3 Philip McBride Johnson & Thomas Lee Hazen, Derivatives Regulation (2004).

4. *See, e.g.,* Raymond James & Associates v. National Association of Securities Dealers, 844 F.Supp. 1504 (M.D.Fla.1994) (dictum recognizing implied remedy).

12. 687 F.2d 778 (3d Cir.1982), *cert. denied* 461 U.S. 942, 103 S.Ct. 2118, 77 L.Ed.2d 1300 (1983).

13. *See also, e.g.,* Ferreri v. Mainardi, 690 F.Supp. 411 (E.D.Pa.1988) (no implied remedy against exchange for failure to enforce its own rules).

§ 14.26

2. SEC v. Zandford, 535 U.S. 813, 122 S.Ct. 1899, 153 L.Ed.2d 1 (2002).

occur with respect to a particular securities transaction, but can involve a course of conduct relating to securities transactions generally.[3] Since by definition broker-dealers' contact with their customers generally relates to securities transactions, the securities antifraud provisions are likely to be implicated.

As for violations of exchange FINRA, or NASD rules, it is generally held that violation of a rule of a self regulatory organization will not, by itself, support a private right of action.[29] However, a violation of an exchange or FINRA rule can form the basis of a 10b–5 action, provided, of course, that all of the elements of a 10b–5 claim can be established. Thus, for example, it is well established that a broker-dealer who churns a customer's account can be held accountable for damages under Rule 10b–5.[31] Broker-dealers may, of course, be held liable under Rule 10b–5 for material misstatements or omissions in connection with their customers' purchases and sales of securities.

Of particular interest in broker-dealer litigation is the extent to which the brokerage firm can be held accountable for actionable violations by its account executives or other employees. The three principal vehicles for imposing such liability are: (1) statutorily created controlling person liability[74] (2) for the brokerage's firm's culpable failure to supervise its employees, and (3) under common law principles of vicarious liability of employers generally.

In addition to the duty to supervise that exists under agency principles, the securities laws and the rules of the self regulatory organizations[109] impose upon broker-dealers a duty to supervise their employees.[110] Although this provides the basis for administrative sanctions[111] and does not extend expressly to private litigation, a failure to supervise can be the basis of controlling person liability.[112] In addition to the consequences under federal law, inadequate supervision of brokerage employees can result in violation of state law.[114]

If a brokerage firm's employees in supervisory positions are put on inquiry notice that an employee may be acting improperly, the supervisor must see that the matter is investigated promptly and then take steps to follow up on the investigation. If the supervisor does not initiate his or her own investigation, he or she must direct someone else to investigate. It, thus, is not sufficient to rely simply on the employee's representations that no

3. *Id.*

29. *See, e.g.,* Spicer v. Chicago Board Options Exchange, Inc., 977 F.2d 255 (7th Cir.1992); Craighead v. E.F. Hutton & Co., 899 F.2d 485 (6th Cir.1990); Carrott v. Shearson Hayden Stone, Inc., 724 F.2d 821 (9th Cir.1984); Jablon v. Dean Witter & Co., 614 F.2d 677 (9th Cir.1980); Colonial Realty Corp. v. Bache & Co., 358 F.2d 178 (2d Cir.1966), *cert. denied* 385 U.S. 817, 87 S.Ct. 40, 17 L.Ed.2d 56 (1966).

31. *See* cases collected in § 14.20 *supra.*

74. 15 U.S.C.A. § 77*o*, 78t. *See* §§ 7.12, 12.24 *supra.*

109. *See, e.g.,* Gliksman, Complaint No. C02960039, 1999 WL 515762 (N.A.S.D.R. March 31, 1999).

110. *See, e.g.,* Adonnino v. SEC, 111 Fed. Appx. 46 (2d Cir. 2004).

111. *See, e.g.,* Patrick v. SEC, 19 F.3d 66 (2d Cir.1994).

112. *See, e.g.,* Jairett v. First Montauk Securities Corp., 153 F.Supp.2d 562, 572–573 (E.D.Pa. 2001).

114. *See, e.g.,* New York v. Justin, 237 F.Supp.2d 368 (W.D.N.Y. 2002) (federal law does not preempt state's ability to prosecute securities broker for improper supervision of registered sales representative).

misconduct took place. The investigation should determine whether the conduct in fact occurred and whether there have been similar occurrences.

In the event that multiple supervisors may be involved, it is important to promptly and clearly define the responsibility of each of the supervisors in responding to the suspected wrongdoing. Again, it will be necessary to follow up in order to assure that appropriate investigatory and preventive measures have been taken. Additionally, simply reporting the suspected misconduct to a higher supervisor will not be sufficient unless the supervisor's superiors instruct him or her not to take any action. The Commission explained that appropriate supervisory action should be taken even after the matter is reported.

Instituting the investigation does not end the supervisor's responsibilities. Prompt action should be taken to prevent repetition of the suspected misconduct. This would include increased supervision of the suspected employee. Thus, it is not sufficient simply to tell the employee that the matter is under investigation and that his or her career may be in jeopardy.

The duty to supervise is not satisfied by the supervisor's merely relying on a trader's experience.[115] The presence of "red flags" imposes on the supervisor a duty to make an affirmative inquiry or investigation.[116] Thus, someone in a supervisory position cannot simply ignore or disregard "red flags" or "suggestions of irregularities"; instead, the supervisor must "act decisively to detect and prevent" improper activity.[117]

115. *See, e.g.,* In the Matter of Grady, Sec. Exch. Act Rel. No. 34–41309, 69 S.E.C. Docket 1392, 1999 WL 222640 (SEC Apr. 19, 1999).

116. *See, e.g.,* In the Matter of Grady, Sec. Exch. Act Rel. No. 34–41309, 69 S.E.C. Docket 1392, 1999 WL 222640 (SEC Apr. 19, 1999).

117. *Id.*

Chapter 15

ARBITRATION OF BROKER–DEALER DISPUTES

Table of Sections

§ 15.1 The Enforceability of Arbitration Agreements in Federal and State Securities Cases

§ 15.1[1] Enforcement of Broker–Dealer Arbitration Agreements

At one time, pre-dispute arbitration agreements were unenforceable with regard to claims arising under the federal securities laws. This meant that virtually all claims by customers against their securities brokers were resolved in court or by settlement. In subsequent years there was a major reversal of this earlier situation. As a result of this major shift of position by the Supreme Court,[1] most brokerage firms routinely require customers to sign agreements diverting any customer claims to arbitration. Accordingly, most disputes between customers and their brokers now are decided in arbitral forums rather than in court. One consequence of this virtual universal use of arbitration for disputes between a broker-dealer and a customer has been that much of the law relating to litigation involving broker-dealers has been placed in a state of suspended animation as it existed in the era before customer-broker disputes were so readily submitted to arbitrators as they are today.

The Financial Industry Regulatory Authority (FINRA) offers an alternative dispute resolution in the form of a non-binding mediation program. It appears that the vast majority of disputes do not result in a formal binding arbitration. For example, from 2003 to 2007, approximately seventy to eighty percent of the customer claims filed with NASD arbitration were resolved through settlement or other disposition without an arbitration panel resolution three to four percent of the filings resulted in arbitrators' decisions based on written submissions and eighteen to twenty-four of the claims resulted in a decision after a formal arbitration hearing.[10]

§ 15.1

1. *See* Rodriguez de Quijas v. Shearson/American Express, 490 U.S. 477, 109 S.Ct. 1917, 104 L.Ed.2d 526 (1989); Shearson/American Express, Inc. v. McMahon, 482 U.S. 220, 107 S.Ct. 2332, 96 L.Ed.2d 185 (1987).

10. *See* Stephen J. Choi, Jill E. Fisch & A.C. Pritchard, Attorneys as Arbitrators, at p. 10, http://papers.ssrn.com/sol3/papers.cfm?abstract_id=1086372 (Draft No. 11 Jan. 2008).

Over the years, the former bar to arbitration was weakened until it was eventually eliminated. However, The Supreme Court eventually made it clear that claims subject to a pre-dispute arbitration agreement arising under Rule 10b–5 are arbitrable.

The Court in Shearson/American Express, Inc. v. McMahon[24] pointed out that the basis of the *Wilko* former law was the belief that arbitration did not adequately safeguard the parties' interest, thus implicating the anti-waiver provisions.[25] However, as commercial arbitration has become more widely accepted, the procedures are now viewed more favorably than before. Additionally the major exchanges and the NASD had arbitration rules that are subject to SEC oversight. Accordingly, the premise of the former bar became highly suspect, at least with regard to pre-dispute arbitration agreements between brokers and customers. The Supreme Court overruled the former bar in Rodriguez De Quijas v. Shearson/American Express, Inc.[28]

The Federal Arbitration Act: Policies Favoring Arbitration

The Federal Arbitration Act[38] embodies a strong public policy favoring arbitration.[39] The Uniform Arbitration Act, which has been adopted by many states, similarly favors arbitration.[40] There are limits, however, to the Federal Arbitration Act's impact. For example, the Federal Arbitration Act does not create a basis for federal jurisdiction independent of that which might be

24. 482 U.S. 220, 107 S.Ct. 2332, 96 L.Ed.2d 185 (1987).

25. Following the *McMahon* decision, a number of courts ruled that holding Rule 10b–5 claims to be arbitrable was to be given retroactive application. *See* Peterson v. Shearson/American Express, Inc., 849 F.2d 464 (10th Cir.1988); Mayaja v. Bodkin, 824 F.2d 439 (5th Cir.1987); Noble v. Drexel, Burnham, Lambert, Inc., 823 F.2d 849 (5th Cir.1987). *But see, e.g.,* Church v. Gruntal & Co., 698 F.Supp. 465 (S.D.N.Y.1988).

28. 490 U.S. 477, 109 S.Ct. 1917, 104 L.Ed.2d 526 (1989). *See* Osterneck v. Merrill Lynch, Pierce, Fenner & Smith, Inc., 841 F.2d 508, 512 (3d Cir.1988) (1933 Act claims are not arbitrable until the Supreme Court decides otherwise); Pompano–Windy City Partners, Ltd. v. Bear, Stearns & Co., 698 F.Supp. 504 (S.D.N.Y.1988); Rosenblum v. Drexel Burnham Lambert, Inc., 700 F.Supp. 874 (E.D.La.1987); Ketchum v. Almahurst Bloodstock IV, 685 F.Supp. 786 (D.Kan.1988); McCowan v. Dean Witter Reynolds, Inc., 682 F.Supp. 741 (S.D.N.Y.1987); Schultz v. Robinson–Humphrey/American Express, Inc., 666 F.Supp. 219 (M.D.Ga.1987); Johnson v. O'Brien, 420 N.W.2d 264 (Minn.App.1988), *cert. granted and judgment vacated* 490 U.S. 1078, 109 S.Ct. 2096, 104 L.Ed.2d 658 (1989) (section 12(2) claim not arbitrable).

Rodriguez has been applied retroactively. Paulson v. Dean Witter Reynolds, Inc., 905 F.2d 1251 (9th Cir.1990); Brown v. Dean Witter Reynolds, Inc., 882 F.2d 481 (11th Cir.1989).

See generally Stephen P. Bedell & Brian A. Bosch, The *Rodriguez* Decision: A New Tradition in the Arbitration of Securities Disputes, 18 Sec.Reg.L.J. 53 (1990); J. Kirkland Grant, Securities Arbitration: Is Required Arbitration Fair to Investors?, 24 New Eng.L.Rev. 389 (1989); Ellen P Kelly, Donahue & Clark, Legal and Ethical Perspectives on the Use of Arbitration in the Securities Industry, 25 Creighton L.Rev. 1311 (1992). Perry E. Wallace, Jr., Securities Arbitration After *McMahon, Rodriguez,* and the New Rules: Can Investors' Rights Really be Protected?, 43 Vand.L.Rev. 1199 (1990); Note, Classwide Arbitration and 10b–5 Claims in the Wake of *Shearson/American Express v. McMahon,* 74 Cornell L.Rev. 380 (1989).

Following the *Rodriguez* opinion, courts have imposed Rule 11 sanctions on attorneys frivolously opposing a motion to compel arbitration. *E.g.,* Robinson v. Dean Witter Reynolds, Inc., 129 F.R.D. 15 (D.Mass.1989) (Rule 11 sanctions were appropriate with regard to memorandum of law opposing motion to compel arbitration); Mastrobuono v. Shearson Lehman Hutton, Inc., 128 F.R.D. 243 (N.D.Ill.1989) (semble).

38. Arbitration Act of Feb. 12, 1925, ch. 213, 43 Stat. 883, codified at 9 U.S.C.A. §§ 1–208.

39. *See, e.g.,* Beer v. Nutt, 2007 WL 13100 (S.D.N.Y. 2007) (ordering arbitration of customer dispute even though the challenged investment took place before the firm was a member of the NASD).

40. *See, e.g.,* Swayze v. The Huntington Inv. Co., 2005 WL 1208116 (Ohio App. 2 Dist. 2005) (noting that both Massachusetts and Ohio adopted the Uniform Arbitration Act that favors arbitration; dispute in question was arbitrable).

available under the federal securities laws.[41] Although the Federal Arbitration Act applies to claims involving interstate commerce, it does not apply to a transaction which is wholly intrastate.[42] On the other hand, when the jurisdictional reach of the Federal Arbitration Act is implicated, that act may preempt the applicable state law.[43]

§ 15.1[9] Other Factors Affecting Enforcement of Pre-dispute Arbitration Agreements

Section 2 of the Federal Arbitration Act provides that arbitration agreements can be invalidated upon such grounds as exist at law or equity for the invalidity of any contract.[137] Thus, a court cannot compel arbitration unless there is a valid contractual obligation.[138] Where the dispute relates to the existence of a valid arbitration agreement, that issue generally is left to the court to decide.[139] Brokerage customers frequently seek to avoid pre-dispute arbitration agreements by claiming that the arbitration clause is an invalid contract of adhesion.[140] The determination of whether there is an adhesion is highly factual. It is generally held that if the claims of invalidity go to the contract as a whole, they should be resolved by the arbitrator.[141] When the court must determine whether there has been fraud in the inducement (or fraud in fact) discovery related to that issue may be appropriate. Thus, for example, it was appropriate to conduct discovery on the authenticity of the signatures on the agreement to arbitrate.[142]

The contract interpretation issues will generally be determined under state law, keeping in mind the federal policy favoring arbitration. However,

41. *See* Moses H. Cone Memorial Hospital v. Mercury Construction Corp., 460 U.S. 1, 25 n. 32, 103 S.Ct. 927, 74 L.Ed.2d 765 (1983) ("The Arbitration Act is something of an anomaly in the field of federal-court jurisdiction. It creates a body of federal substantive law establishing and regulating the duty to honor an agreement to arbitrate, yet it does not create any independent federal-question jurisdiction under 28 U.S.C. § 1331 (1976 ed., Supp. IV) or otherwise.").

42. Ex parte Jones, 628 So.2d 316 (Ala.1993) (a divided Alabama Supreme Court held that since predispute arbitration agreements are not enforceable under Alabama law, arbitration was not available in a securities transaction between Alabama residents involving the securities of an Alabama corporation).

43. Olde Discount Corp. v. Tupman, 1 F.3d 202 (3d Cir.1993) (Federal Arbitration Act may preclude state action seeking rescission pending outcome of arbitration); Mayo v. Dean Witter Reynolds, Inc., 258 F.Supp.2d 1097 (N.D. Cal. 2003) (Federal Arbitration Act preempted California rule require disclosure of arbitrators' backgrounds).

A Supreme Court ruling further points out the preemptive effect of the Federal Arbitration Act. In Mastrobuono v. Shearson Lehman Hutton, Inc., 514 U.S. 52, 115 S.Ct. 1212, 131 L.Ed.2d 76 (1995), the Court ruled that a state procedural rule barring punitive damages in arbitration proceedings must yield to the procedural rules of the Federal Arbitration Act in light of the broad policy favoring arbitration under that Act. The Court held that the parties' choice of law clause meant that the state's substantive law permitting punitive damages applied but not the procedural bar.

137. 9 U.S.C.A. § 2.

138. *See, e.g.*, Jolley v. Welch, 904 F.2d 988 (5th Cir.1990), *cert. denied* 498 U.S. 1050, 111 S.Ct. 762, 112 L.Ed.2d 781 (1991) (broker failed to meet burden of establishing existence of valid arbitration agreement; broker did not introduce an arbitration agreement purporting to be signed by the investor).

139. *See, e.g.*, Ameriprise Financial Services, Inc. v. Etheredge, 277 Fed.Appx. 447 (5th Cir. 2008), relying on Banc One Acceptance Corp. v. Hill, 367 F.3d 426, 429 (5th Cir.2004)

140. *E.g.*, Zigrang v. U.S. Bancorp Piper Jaffray, Inc., 329 Mont. 239, 123 P.3d 237 (2005).

141. Houlihan v. Offerman & Co., 31 F.3d 692 (8th Cir.1994); Bhatia v. Johnston, 818 F.2d 418 (5th Cir.1987); Benoay v. Prudential–Bache Securities, Inc., 805 F.2d 1437 (11th Cir.1986); Miller v. Drexel, Burnham, Lambert, Inc., 791 F.2d 850 (11th Cir.1986).

142. Ameriprise Financial Services, Inc. v. Etheredge, 277 Fed.Appx. 447 (5th Cir. 2008).

rules of the self regulatory organizations may also affect the validity of arbitration clauses. Accordingly, failure to comply with the FINRA (formerly the NASD's) disclosure obligations and formerly those that existed under the New York Stock Exchange program, including the requirement that any agreement containing an arbitration clause be specifically acknowledged by the customer, can result in the invalidity, and hence unenforceability, of the arbitration agreement.[153]

The essence of the adhesion contract claim is that the use of arbitration clauses is an industry-wide practice and that it is unfair to force them upon customers. However, the majority of courts have held that there is nothing inherently unfair about arbitration clauses[155] and thus the clause does not place the customer in an unfair position.[156] Arbitration clauses have been upheld even when appearing on the reverse side of the brokerage agreement.[157] However, not all courts have upheld arbitration provisions, especially when it is shown that the broker was guilty of overreaching or other wrongdoing.[158]

§ 15.1[10] Judicial Review of Arbitration Decisions

Unless a different venue is selected in the agreement to arbitrate, arbitration decisions under the federal securities laws are reviewable by federal district courts.[163] The Federal Arbitration Act does not by itself create subject matter jurisdiction[164] and review may be had in state court if the arbitration agreement and arbitral forum so provide[165] but in the absence of an agreement, the federal courts have jurisdiction.[166] In addition to the statutory grounds of corruption, fraud, and evident partiality,[167] arbitration decisions are subject to the judicially created standard of "manifest disregard of the law."[168] There is an extremely high burden of establishing a manifest disregard of the law which is a "severely limited" ground for overturning an arbitration award.[169] However, this is not an insurmountable in appropriate cases. In other words not withstanding the very narrow standard of review, "[a]n arbitration award, however, is not "utterly impregnable."[170]

---

153. *See* Mueske v. Piper, Jaffray & Hopwood, Inc., 260 Mont. 207, 859 P.2d 444 (1993).

155. *See, e.g.,* Coleman v. Prudential Bache Securities, Inc., 802 F.2d 1350 (11th Cir.1986); Webb v. R. Rowland & Co., Inc., 800 F.2d 803 (8th Cir.1986).

156. Shotto v. Laub, 632 F.Supp. 516 (D.Md.1986); Peele v. Kidder Peabody & Co., 620 F.Supp. 61 (E.D.Mo.1985).

157. *See* Speck v. Oppenheimer & Co., Inc., 583 F.Supp. 325 (W.D.Mo.1984).

158. Woodyard v. Merrill Lynch, Pierce, Fenner & Smith, Inc., 640 F.Supp. 760 (S.D.Tex. 1986).

163. 9 U.S.C.A. § 9.

164. Fromm v. ING Funds Distributor, LLC, 486 F.Supp.2d 348 (S.D.N.Y. 2007).

165. *See, e.g.,* Peebles v. Merrill Lynch, Pierce, Fenner & Smith Inc., 431 F.3d 1320 (11th Cir. 2005); Baltin v. Alaron Trading Corp., 128 F.3d 1466, 1469 (11th Cir. 1997), *cert. denied,* 525 U.S. 841, 119 S.Ct. 105, 142 L.Ed.2d 84 (1998). However, notwithstanding state court jurisdiction, if there is diversity of citizenship and the amount in controversy exceeds $75,000, federal courts may have jurisdiction.

166. 9 U.S.C.A. § 9.

167. 9 U.S.C.A. § 10.

168. *E.g., See* Bauer v. Carty & Co., Inc., 246 Fed.Appx. 375 (6th Cir. 2007).

169. *See, e.g.,* Barclays Capital Inc. v. Shen, 20 Misc.3d 319, 857 N.Y.S.2d 873, 874 (Sup. Ct. 2008).

170. Kashner Davidson Securities Corp. v. Mscisz, 531 F.3d 68, 74 (1st Cir. 2008), quoting Cytyc Corp. v. DEKA Products Ltd. P'ship, 439 F.3d 27, 32 (1st Cir. 2006).

§ 15.2 Factors Relating to Enforceability of Pre–dispute Arbitration Clauses

There are two steps in establishing an enforceable pre-dispute arbitration agreement between a broker and a customer.[9] The dispute must be between a customer and an NASD member or associated person and it must arise in connection with the firm's or associated person's business activities as a securities professional.[10] The fact that an agreement designates a procedure pursuant to the rules adopted by the NASD does not necessarily require the NASD to act as the arbitral forum.[11]

Mutuality of remedies is not essential to the enforcement of a pre-dispute arbitration agreement. Thus, the fact that the agreement expressly permits the brokerage firm to pursue other remedies (including going to court), does not automatically give reciprocal rights to the customer who has signed the arbitration agreement.[12]

§ 15.2[2] Which Law Controls?

When dealing with the enforceability of pre-dispute arbitration agreements, there is an unusual mix of state and federal law. In the first instance, the policy favoring arbitration as embodied in the Federal Arbitration Act[13] mitigates in favor of enforcing pre-dispute arbitration agreements. On the other hand, interpreting the terms of any agreement between customers and securities brokers generally will be a matter of state contract law rather than federal securities or arbitration law.[14] Ordinarily, state contract law will control whether the parties have in fact agreed to submit the controversy to arbitration.[15]

9. *See* World Group Securities, Inc. v. Sanders, 2006 WL 1278738 (D.Utah 2006) ("Based on these two sections, courts have fashioned a two-part test that must be satisfied to trigger the NASD arbitration requirement. First, the claim must involve a dispute between either an NASD-member and a customer, or an associated person and a customer. Second, the dispute must arise in connection with the activities of the member or in connection with the business activities of the associated person."), relying on MONY Securities Corp. v. Bornstein, 390 F.3d 1340 (11th Cir. 2004); Vestax Securities Corp. v. McWood, 280 F.3d 1078, 1081 (6th Cir. 2002).

10. *See* World Group Securities, Inc. v. Sanders, 2006 WL 1278738 (D. Utah 2006). *Cf.* Weiss Capital Management, Inc. v. Crowder, 964 So.2d 865 (Fla.App. 4 Dist. 2007) (investment company that was parent of wholly-owned subsidiary that was an NASD member was not required to arbitrate its dispute with former employee, who was an associated person of the subsidiary which was an NASD member).

11. *See* Reddam v. KPMG LLP, 457 F.3d 1054 (9th Cir. 2006) (upholding NASD's refusal to hear arbitration but nevertheless holding that dispute had to be arbitrated in another forum per agreement).

12. *See* Huertas v. Ameritrade, Inc., 2008 WL 141106 at *4 (D.N.J. 2008) ("Though the agreement does lack mutuality of remedies, a reservation of the right to seek a remedy in a judicial forum by one party does not alone invalidate an arbitration clause"), relying on Delta Funding Corp. v. Harris, 189 N.J. 28, 48, 912 A.2d 104 (2006).

13. Arbitration Act of Feb. 12, 1925, ch. 213, 43 Stat. 883, codified at 9 U.S.C.A. §§ 1–208.

14. *See, e.g.,* Petrie v. Pacific Stock Exchange, 982 F.Supp. 1390 (N.D.Cal.1997) (no private remedy under exchange rules, suit to enforce arbitration clause was a contract law issue).

15. *See, e.g.,* PaineWebber Inc. v. Bybyk, 81 F.3d 1193, 1198 (2d Cir.1996) ("Arbitration 'is a matter of contract and a party cannot be required to submit to arbitration any dispute which he has not agreed so to submit.' ") (quoting AT & T Techs., Inc. v. Communications Workers of America, 475 U.S. 643, 648, 106 S.Ct. 1415, 1418, 89 L.Ed.2d 648 (1986)); Coleman & Co. Securities, Inc. v. Giaquinto Family Trust, 2000 WL 1683450 (S.D.N.Y.2000) ("In deciding whether the parties agreed to arbitrate a matter, the courts ordinarily apply state law principles governing the formation of contracts"). *See also, e.g.,* First Options of Chicago, Inc. v. Kaplan, 514 U.S. 938 115 S.Ct. 1920, 131 L.Ed.2d 985 (1995).

Where the arbitration agreement contains a clear choice of law provision, that provision can overcome the primacy of the Federal Arbitration Act. Thus, for example, where the contract designated Tennessee law as governing the agreement, the Tennessee rule that that enforceability of an arbitration clause in the face of a claim of fraud in the inducement is to be determined by a court rather than the arbitrators. Morgan Keegan & Co., Inc. v. Force, 2007 WL 1954025 (Ky.App. 2007).

Chapter 16

OPERATION OF THE SECURITIES AND EXCHANGE COMMISSION

Table of Sections

---

§ 16.2 Civil and Criminal Enforcement: SEC Injunctions, Investigations, Parallel Proceedings; Administrative Hearings and Disciplinary Sanctions

§ 16.2[0] Overview of Enforcement; Cooperation in Investigations

§ 16.2[0] Overview of SEC Enforcement

The Securities and Exchange Commission has a panoply of administrative powers. In fact, the Commission has all administrative powers save one: the SEC does not adjudicate disputes between private parties. The Securities and Exchange Commission has a wide variety of enforcement roles under the various securities acts.[1] With regard to registration statements under the Securities Act of 1933, the Commission has the power to issue stop orders and refusal orders that can be used for defective registration statements.[2] In addition, the Commission can impose disciplinary sanctions against broker-dealers registered under section 15 of the Exchange Act,[3] against municipal securities dealers pursuant to section 15B,[4] and against government securities dealers under section 15C.[5] Beyond these administrative enforcement powers, its oversight of regulatory and self-regulatory organizations,[6] and its rulemaking responsibilities,[7] the Commission is given broad investigatory and enforcement powers in the courts.

The SEC may cooperate with other parties or agencies in litigation under the securities laws. Section 21(g) of the 1934 Act prohibits the consolidation of

---

§ 16.2

1. The work of the SEC is discussed in § 1.4 *supra.*
2. 15 U.S.C.A. § 77h. *See* § 3.6 *supra.*
3. 15 U.S.C.A. § 78*o*–1. *See* § 14.3 *supra.*
4. 15 U.S.C.A. § 78*o*–4. *See* § 14.12 *supra.*
5. 15 U.S.C.A. § 78*o*–5. *See* § 14.13 *supra.*
6. *See* § 14.3 *supra.*
7. *See* §§ 1.3, 1.4 *supra.*

SEC actions with any other action, even though those actions involve the same factual determinations, without the Commission's consent.[9] Since section 21(g) provides for consolidation with other actions only with the SEC's consent, it is improper for a federal court in one case to enjoin an SEC injunction suit in another federal court.[10] Third parties can move to intervene in SEC actions[11] in order to protect their interests, but this does not mean that they have a right to intervene,[12] nor do third parties have a right to enforce consent decrees between the SEC and a violator of the Act.[13] Section 21(g) which, as mentioned above, precludes consolidations without the SEC's consent, has been held to preclude intervention without the Commission's consent as well.[14] Some courts have indicated that section 21(g) presents an impenetrable barrier[15] to third parties seeking to intervene in SEC litigation. But not all courts have agreed.[16] The trend is to deny such requests unless the SEC consents to the intervention.[17]

Just as the SEC may permit other parties to intervene in SEC proceedings, there are instances when the Commission may decide to participate in litigation by way of an amicus brief. The Commission, through its office of general counsel, will file an amicus brief if it believes it can further the public interest.

In 2001, the SEC announced a major shift in its enforcement program.[19] In order to encourage more self-policing by 1934 Act reporting companies, the SEC announced that it will proceed with leniency against companies that, after an internal investigation admit and correct past violations. The Commission announced that in deciding whether to seek punishment for violations of reporting requirements, the SEC would consider four factors. The SEC will consider: (1) whether a company has a system of internal controls that provides an effective self-policing mechanism; (2) whether the company promptly reported the violations in question; (3) the extent of the company's cooperation with law enforcement agencies; and (4) whether the company disciplined the persons responsible, improved internal control procedures, and compensated investors who were injured by the violations.[21]

§ 16.2[1] SEC Administrative Hearings

Section 15(b)(4) of the Act gives the Commission authority to sanction registered broker dealers by imposing a variety of consequences ranging from

---

9. 15 U.S.C.A. § 78u(g).

10. Smith v. SEC, 129 F.3d 356 (6th Cir.1997).

11. *See, e.g.,* SEC v. Kings Real Estate Investment Trust, 222 F.R.D. 660 (D. Kan. 2004).

12. *E.g.,* SEC v. Homa, [2000–2001 Transfer Binder] Fed. Sec. L. Rep. (CCH) ¶ 91,223, 2000 WL 1468726 (N.D.Ill.2000).

13. SEC v. Prudential Securities, Inc., 171 F.R.D. 1 (D.D.C.1997).

14. SEC v. Homa, [2000–2001 Transfer Binder] Fed. Sec. L. Rep. (CCH) ¶ 91,223, 2000 WL 1468726 (N.D.Ill.2000).

15. SEC v. Heartland Group, Inc., 2003 WL 103015 at *2 (N.D.Ill. 2003).

16. *See* SEC v. Kings Real Estate Investment Trust, 222 F.R.D. 660 (D. Kan. 2004).

17. *See,* e.g., SEC v. Heartland Group, Inc., 2003 WL 103015 at *2 (N.D.Ill. 2003).

19. Report of Investigation Pursuant to Section 21(a) of the Securities Exchange Act of 1934 and Commission Statement of the Relationship of Cooperation to Agency Enforcement Decisions, Sec. Exch. Act Rel. No. 34–44969, 2001 WL 1301408 (SEC Oct 23, 2001).

21. *Id.*

censure to revocation of registration.[65] Depending on the severity of the violations, the SEC can also place limits on the registrants' activities.[66] Section 15(b)(6)(A) of the 1934 Act grants the SEC broad administrative authority over persons associated with brokers and dealers.[67] In particular, the Commission is empowered to hold hearings and impose sanctions against associated persons of broker-dealers, ranging from censure to suspension for up to twelve months[68] and also including bar orders.[69] The Commission can also place limitations on the activities of such associated persons.[70] The Commission has similar administrative enforcement powers with regard to investment advisers.[71] The Commission can impose similar sanctions against municipal securities dealers,[72] government securities dealers,[73] and clearing agencies.[74] In addition to the power to impose these administrative sanctions, the Commission can impose an administrative penalty for each violation of the act or rules of up to $50,000 for natural persons and $250,000 for entities.[75] The SEC also has cease and desist authority, which permits cease and desist orders, after notice and opportunity for a hearing, against any person who violates the Act or rules promulgated under the Act.[76]

Relying on the rule applied in SEC injunctive actions in the courts, the SEC took the position that there is no statute of limitations that is generally applicable to the Commission's institution of administrative proceedings to enforce the Act.[77] However, where the SEC invokes its own administrative process by instituting an administrative proceeding to seek imposition of a civil fine or penalty, then a five-year statute of limitations applies in administrative proceedings.[78]

It is quite common for SEC enforcement actions, both those initiated in court as well as those taking the form of administrative proceedings, to end in settlement. Generally, when the defendant in an SEC enforcement proceeding consents to SEC sanctions, he or she does so without either admitting or denying guilt. It has become standard Commission policy to include a statement to the effect that the settling defendant will not deny the allegations of the complaint.

---

65. 515 U.S.C.A. § 78*o*(b)(4).

66. *Id.*

67. 715 U.S.C.A. § 78*o*(b)(6).

68. *See, e.g.*, Wonsover v. SEC, 205 F.3d 408 (D.C.Cir.2000) (six-month suspension of broker who sold unregistered securities was not an abuse of discretion).

69. 915 U.S.C.A. § 78*o*(b)(6)(A).

70. 15 U.S.C.A. § 78*o*(b)(6)(A).

71. Investment Advisers Act § 203(f), 15 U.S.C.A. § 80b–3(e). *See* § 21.1 *infra*.

72. Securities Exchange Act section 15B(c)(2), 15 U.S.C.A. § 78o–4(c)(2).

73. Securities Exchange Act section 15C(c)(1), 15 U.S.C.A. § 78o–5(c)(1).

74. Securities Exchange Act section 17A, 15 U.S.C.A. § 78q–1.

75. Securities Exchange Act section 21B, 15 U.S.C.A. § 78u–2.

76. Securities Exchange Act section 21C, 15 U.S.C.A. § 78u–3.

77. *See, e.g.*, In the Matter of Patricia A. Johnson, Exch. Act Rel. No. 34–33664, [1993–1994 Transfer Binder] Fed. Sec. L. Rep. (CCH) ¶ 85,323 (SEC 1994).

78. 24 U.S.C.A. § 2462.

§ 16.2[2] SEC Injunctions

§ 16.2[2][A] Power to Seek Injunctive Relief

The SEC has the authority to seek both temporary and permanent injunctive relief in the courts "whenever it shall appear to the Commission that any person is engaged or about to engage in any acts or practices which constitute or will constitute a violation."[81] Frequently, the SEC will announce the initiation of an enforcement action by publicly issuing a litigation release. It does not violate the defendant's due process when the SEC issues a litigation release without affording the defendant advance notice and hearing.[83]

Federal Rule of Civil Procedure 9(b) requires that fraud be pleaded with specificity.[84] This heightened pleading requirement applies in SEC actions well as in private suits. However, the enhanced pleading requirements of the Private Securities Litigation Reform Act of 1995[86] do not apply in SEC actions.[87]

Courts have observed that the injunctive power should not be used without "positive proof of a reasonable likelihood that past wrongdoing will occur" and proof that there is "something more than the mere possibility which keeps the case alive."[90] Accordingly, even in the face of proof of past violations, failure to prove a reasonable likelihood of future violations is likely to mean that an injunction will not be granted.[91]

An injunction against future violations, even without ancillary relief[92] such as a fine or disgorgement, can have serious consequences. For example, an injunction will disqualify the defendant from participating in transactions protected by certain 1933 Act exemptions.[93] In addition to the adverse publicity that will normally follow issuance of an SEC injunction, the injunction and reasons therefor will have to be disclosed in future SEC filings.

§ 16.2[2][B] Preliminary Injunctive Relief

In deciding whether to issue an injunction, courts will look to the seriousness of the securities law violations[95] and the requested injunction's impact on the defendant.[96] Other factors include the degree of the defendant's

---

81. *E.g.,* 1933 Act section 20(b), 15 U.S.C.A. § 77t(b).

83. SEC v. Rivlin, 1999 WL 1455758, [1999–2000 Transfer Binder] Fed. Sec. L. Rep. (CCH) ¶ 90,725 (D.D.C. 1999).

84. Fed. R. Civ. P. 9(b).

86. Pub. Law No. 104–67, 109 Stat. 737 (104th Cong. 1st Sess. December 22, 1995) (HR 1058). The Private Securities Litigation Reform Act is discussed in § 12.15 *supra.*

87. *See, e.g.,* SEC v. Brady, 2006 WL 1310320 (N.D.Tex. 2006), SEC v. Kornman, 391 F.Supp.2d 477, 494 (N.D.Tex.2005).

90. SEC v. Bausch & Lomb, Inc., 565 F.2d 8, 18 (2d Cir.1977) (quoting United States v. W.T. Grant Co., 345 U.S. 629, 633, 73 S.Ct. 894, 897, 97 L.Ed. 1303 (1953)).

91. *See e.g.,* S.E.C. v. Sargent, 329 F.3d 34 (1st Cir.2003).

92. Ancillary relief is discussed in § 16.2[4] *infra.*

93. *E.g.,* Regulation A (17 C.F.R. §§ 251 *et seq.*) and Rule 505 (17 C.F.R. § 230.505). *See* §§ 4.17, 4.22 *supra.*

95. SEC v. Advance Growth Capital Corp., 470 F.2d 40, 53–54 (7th Cir.1972); SEC v. Manor Nursing Centers, Inc., 458 F.2d 1082, 1102 (2d Cir.1972).

96. *E.g.,* SEC v. Manor Nursing Centers, Inc., 458 F.2d 1082, 1102 (2d Cir.1972).

culpability[97] and the length of time between the acts complained of and time of suit. In deciding whether to order a preliminary injunction, courts will thus consider "the egregiousness of the defendant's actions, the isolated or recurrent nature of the infraction, the degree of scienter involved, the sincerity of the defendant's assurances against future violations, the defendant's recognition of the wrongful nature of his conduct, and the likelihood that the defendant's occupation will present opportunities for future violations."[99] Before granting a preliminary injunction, the court will consider both the likelihood of proving the current violation as well as the likelihood of future violations.[100] In SEC v. Unifund SAL,[101] the Second Circuit reconsidered the appropriate standard for a court in deciding whether to issue preliminary relief. The court began by rejecting a requirement that the Commission establish a "strong prima facie case"[102] as a precondition to issuing a preliminary injunction. The court also rejected the SEC's contention that the test applicable to private litigants—a substantial likelihood of success on the merits in addition to a showing of irreparable harm that would result in the absence of an injunction[103]—should be utilized. Instead, the court required not only a likelihood of success on the merits, but also a showing that there is a risk of future violations and that the seriousness of the violation warrants the preliminary relief. The court made it clear that the more burdensome the relief requested, the more substantial must be the showing of violation and risk of recurrence. However, it has been held that in deciding whether to issue preliminary relief, a court should view the evidence "in a light most favorable to the Commission" and further that the SEC is "entitled to all reasonable inferences."[105]

§ 16.2[4] Ancillary Relief in SEC Injunction Actions

§ 16.2[4][A] Varieties of Ancillary Relief

The statutory enabling provisions speak solely in terms of the SEC's power to enjoin violations. However, the SEC and the courts have fashioned remedies ancillary to the traditional injunctive decree relying on "the general equitable powers of the federal courts."[147] Ancillary relief has taken many forms, ranging from disgorgement of ill-gotten profits[148] to more imaginative corrective or remedial action. Among such remedies are the appointment of an

97. *See* SEC v. Spence & Green Chemical Co., 612 F.2d 896, 903 (5th Cir.1980), *cert. denied* 449 U.S. 1082, 101 S.Ct. 866, 66 L.Ed.2d 806 (1981); SEC v. Bonastia, 614 F.2d 908 (3d Cir.1980); SEC v. Commonwealth Chemical Securities, Inc., 574 F.2d 90, 100 (2d Cir.1978); SEC v. Universal Major Industries Corp., 546 F.2d 1044, 1048 (2d Cir.1976), *cert. denied* 434 U.S. 834, 98 S.Ct. 120, 54 L.Ed.2d 95 (1977).

99. SEC v. International Heritage, Inc., 4 F.Supp.2d 1368, 1372 (N.D.Ga.1998).

100. SEC v. Princeton Economic International, Ltd., 73 F.Supp.2d 420 (S.D.N.Y.1999).

101. 910 F.2d 1028 (2d Cir.1990), *rehearing denied* 917 F.2d 98 (1990).

102. This standard had been enunciated in prior decisions. *See, e.g.,* SEC v. Management Dynamics, Inc., 515 F.2d 801, 807 (2d Cir.1975); SEC v. Boren, 283 F.2d 312, 313 (2d Cir.1960).

103. The standard applicable for private preliminary relief is discussed in §§ 11.9, 11.10 *supra.*

105. SEC v. International Heritage, Inc., 4 F.Supp.2d 1368, 1372 (N.D.Ga.1998), relying on SEC v. Blatt, 583 F.2d 1325 (5th Cir.1978).

147. James R. Farrand, Ancillary Remedies in SEC Civil Enforcement Suits, 89 Harv.L.Rev. 1779, 1781 (1976).

148. *E.g.*, SEC v. Diversified Corporate Consulting Group, 378 F.3d 1219 (11th Cir.2004).

independent majority on the board of directors,[149] the appointment of a receiver,[150] prohibitions against exercising voting control in a proxy battle,[151] the appointment of "special professionals" to assure compliance with securities laws,[152] the imposition of additional reporting requirements,[153] fashioning of orders designed to protect remaining assets,[154] and prohibitions against continued participation as an officer or director of any public company.[155] Refusal to comply with orders of ancillary relief can result in contempt of court and also can form the basis of incarceration.[156]

Ancillary relief will sometimes include relief that is designed to compensate injured investors. An example is ordering a disgorgement of profits. Although investors may thus have an interest in the outcome of SEC litigation, they are not parties to the proceedings. However, at least in the Fifth Circuit which has an admittedly lenient rule[157] for standing to appeal, an injured investor may be able to appeal an order entered in an SEC enforcement action.[158] The court applied a three-part test to grant a private party standing to appeal from an order in an SEC enforcement action. The court relied on (1) the private parties' participation in the district court proceedings by filing a notice that they were interested parties, (2) the equities weighed in their favor since they would be affected by the distribution of funds ordered below, and (3) therefore, they had a personal stake in the outcome of the SEC suit.[159]

The SEC can pursue ancillary relief against so-called "nominal defendants."[160] A nominal defendant is an intermediary who has not been a knowing participant in the securities law violation but has possession of illegally obtained funds.[161] The enforcement action against such a nominal defendant is for the purpose of collecting funds rather than to impose any sanctions against the nominal defendant.[162]

149. *See* SEC v. Vesco, 571 F.2d 129 (2d Cir.1978).

150. *E.g.,* SEC v. Bilzerian, 378 F.3d 1100 (D.C.Cir.2004).

151. *E.g.,* SEC v. Westgate California Corp., SEC Litigation Release No. 6142, 3 SEC Docket 30 (S.D.Cal. Nov. 9, 1978) (settlement order).

152. *E.g.,* SEC v. Beisinger Industries Corp., 552 F.2d 15, 18–19 (1st Cir.1977), *affirming* 421 F.Supp. 691 (D.Mass.1976); SEC v. Joseph Schlitz Brewing Co., 452 F.Supp. 824 (E.D.Wis.1978) (consent decree).

153. *See, e.g.,* James R. Farrand, Ancillary Remedies in SEC Civil Enforcement Suits, 89 Harv.L.Rev. 1779, 1792–1793(1976).

154. *E.g.,* SEC v. Hickey, 322 F.3d 1123 (9th Cir.2003) (asset freeze and disgorgement order fell within court's equitable powers).

155. SEC v. Cosmopolitan Inv. Funding Co., SEC Litigation Release No. 7366 (April 23, 1976); 42 SEC Ann.Rep. 119 (1976).

156. SEC v. Princeton Economic International Ltd., 152 F.Supp.2d 456 (S.D.N.Y.2001) (upholding continued confinement for civil contempt); SEC v. Bilzerian, 131 F.Supp.2d 10 (D.D.C. 2001) (incarceration ordered due to defendant's failure to comply with disgorgement order).

157. *See also, e.g.,* In re Beef Industry Antitrust Litigation, 589 F.2d 786, 788 (5th Cir.1979).

158. SEC v. Forex Asset Management LLC, 242 F.3d 325 (5th Cir.2001).

159. *Id.*

160. SEC v. Cavanagh, 155 F.3d 129, 136 (2d Cir.1998); SEC v. Colello, 139 F.3d 674, 675–677 (9th Cir.1998).

161. *Id.*

162. *Id.*; SEC v. Colello, 139 F.3d 674, 676 (9th Cir.1998).

§ 16.2[4][B] Disgorgement of Profits

Disgorgement of ill-gotten gain is common in insider trading cases and can be based on specific statutory authority.[164] The disgorgement remedy has been utilized in the context of other violations as well.[165] Courts have continued to become increasingly receptive to the disgorgement remedy.[166] Thus, for example, it is not necessary that the disgorgement amount be proven with absolute precision; it is sufficient to reasonably approximate the profits attributable to the illegal transaction.[167] Nevertheless, the SEC must have evidence sufficient to establish a causal connection between the violations charged and provable improper profits to be disgorged.[168] Also, disgorgement is remedial in nature and is not to be awarded for punitive purposes. The remedial nature of the remedy does not mean, however, that it is essentially compensatory in nature. The primary function of the remedy is to deny the wrongdoer the fruits of ill-gotten gains.[170] Disgorgement may be ordered not only against the wrongdoer but also against those who received proceeds of the ill-gotten gains as gifts.[171] Although distribution of the disgorgement proceeds to investors may be appropriate in many cases, disgorgement is not appropriate when there are a large number of investors with relatively small claims.[172] The SEC simply is not equipped to act as a collection agency in every case that results in compensable losses to investors. Unless distributed to investors, the disgorgement fund goes to the United States Treasury.[173]

The disgorgement remedy is not limited to violators and may be used against non-violators holding illegally obtained profits where the defendants have no legitimate claim to the proceeds.[185] Section 20(f) of the 1933 Act and section 21(d)(4) of the 1934 Act prohibit any funds received in a disgorgement action, either by the SEC in federal court or in an administrative proceeding, from being used to pay attorneys' fees in private actions seeking a distribution of the disgorged funds.[186]

§ 16.2[5] Civil Penalties in SEC Enforcement Actions

In 1990, Congress expanded the scope and amount of civil penalties that can be ordered in judicial proceedings brought by the SEC.[232] The Act gives the authority to pursue "any person" who has violated the Act or applicable rule or regulation.[233]

164. Congress has expressly empowered the SEC to seek disgorgement plus a treble damage penalty for insider trading violations. 15 U.S.C.A. § 78u–1(a)(1), 78ff(a).

165. *See, e.g.,* SEC v. Wolfson, 249 Fed. Appx. 701 (10th Cir.2007).

166. *See, e.g.,* SEC v. Warren, 534 F.3d 1368 (11th Cir. 2008).

167. *See, e.g.,* SEC v. Friendly Power Co., 49 F.Supp.2d 1363 (S.D.Fla.1999).

168. SEC v. Jones, 476 F.Supp.2d 374 (S.D.N.Y. 2007).

170. SEC v. McCaskey, 34 Sec. Reg. & L. Rep. (BNA) 559, 2002 WL 850001 (S.D.N.Y.2002) (magistrate's recommendation) (" 'the primary purpose of disgorgement [to the SEC] is not to compensate investors,' but rather to force 'a defendant to give up the amount by which he was unjustly enriched.' "), quoting SEC v. Commonwealth Chem. Sec., Inc., 574 F.2d 90, 102 (2d Cir.1978).

171. *See, e.g.,* SEC v. George, 426 F.3d 786 (6th Cir.2005), relying on SEC v. Cavanagh, 155 F.3d 129, 137 (2d Cir.1998).

172. S.E.C. v. Lange, 2002 WL 475130 (E.D.Pa.2002), relying on SEC v. Drexel Burnham Lambert, Inc., 956 F.Supp. 503, 507 (S.D.N.Y.1997).

173. *Id.*

185. SEC v. Seibald, 1997 WL 605114, [1997 Transfer Binder] Fed. Sec. L. Rep. (CCH) ¶ 99,586 (S.D.N.Y.1997).

186. 615 U.S.C.A. §§ 77t; 78u(d).

232. *See, e.g.,* 15 U.S.C.A. §§ 78u(a)(3), 80b–9(e), adopted in Pub.L. No. 101–429 (1990).

233. *E.g.,* 15 U.S.C.A. § 78u(3)(a).

Congress also gave the SEC the power to impose civil penalties in administrative proceedings.[239] While those administrative proceedings are limited to market professionals registered with or otherwise regulated under the supervision of the SEC,[240] the Commission can institute a civil action in federal court against anyone who is in violation of the securities laws or rules promulgated thereunder.

If it appears to the Commission that a person has violated an SEC rule or regulation, or a cease and desist order, other than a violation which is subject to a penalty under the Insider Trading Sanctions Act of 1984, the SEC may bring a civil action seeking a civil penalty against the violator by virtue of its general enforcement authority.[244]

Civil penalties ordinarily are payable to the United States Treasury However, section 308 of the Sarbanes–Oxley Act,[247] in what is known as "the Fair Funds provision," empowers the SEC to take penalties paid by individuals and entities in enforcement actions and combine them with disgorgement funds for the benefit of victims.[248]

§ 16.2[6] Bar Orders

The 1990 legislation also empowers the SEC to seek judicial orders prohibiting certain violators from serving as officers and directors of 1934 Act reporting companies.[260] In any action by the SEC for an injunction or criminal prosecution under section 20(b) of the 1933 Act[261] or section 21(d)(1) of the 1934 Act,[262] the court may prohibit, conditionally or unconditionally, permanently or temporarily, any person who has violated section 17(a)(1) of the 1933 Act[263] or section 10(b) of the 1934 Act,[264] from acting as an officer or director of any issuer that has a class of securities registered under the Securities Exchange Act of 1934[265] or that is required to file periodic reports under that Act.[266] The bar order may be issued if the violator's conduct demonstrates substantial unfitness to serve as an officer or director of any such issuer.[267] The SEC can also go to court to secure an order barring

239. *See* Pub.L. No. 101–429 (1990). The Commission was also given cease and desist authority.

240. The power to impose civil penalties applies to proceedings against a broker-dealer, associated person, municipal securities dealer, government securities dealer, or registered clearing agent, as well as to persons registered under the Investment Company or Investment Advisers Acts of 1940. 15 U.S.C.A. §§ 78u–2, 80a–9(d), (e), § 80b–3(i). *See* 15 U.S.C.A. §§ 78*o*(b)(4), 78*o*(b)(6), 78*o*–4, 78*o*–5, 78q–1.

244. 15 U.S.C.A. §§ 77t(d)(1), 78u(d)(3)(A), 80a–12(e)(1), 80b–9(e)(1). The SEC further has the power to impose civil penalties in the course of administrative proceedings. Section 21B, 15 U.S.C.A. § 78u–2.

247. Sarbanes–Oxley Act of 2002, Pub. Law 107–204, § 308 (July 30, 2002), codified in 15 U.S.C.A. § 7246.

248. *See* Statement of the Securities and Exchange Commission Concerning Financial Penalties, SEC Release 2006–4, SECDIG 2006–02–1, 2006 WL 14406 (SEC Jan. 4, 2006).

260. *See, e.g.,* SEC v. First Pacific Bancorp, 142 F.3d 1186 (9th Cir.1998) (CEO subjected to lifetime ban from serving as an officer of a public company).

261. 7415 U.S.C.A. § 77t(b).

262. 7515 U.S.C.A. § 78u(d)(1).

263. 15 U.S.C.A. § 77q(a).

264. 15 U.S.C.A. § 78j(b). See Chapter 12 *supra*.

265. 15 U.S.C.A. § 78g. *See* § 9.2 *supra*.

266. 15 U.S.C.A. §§ 77t(e), 78u(d)(2). *See* 15 U.S.C.A. § 78*o*(d).

267. 15 U.S.C.A. §§ 77t(e), 78u(d)(2).

violators from associating with broker-dealers.[268]

In addition to the ability to seek a bar order by judicial decree, the SEC can issue bar orders in the course of its administrative proceedings. The Commission's general sanctioning authority over associated persons of broker-dealers in section 15(b)(6) of the Act[272] contains the express authority to bar violators from associating with brokers or dealers.

§ 16.2[7] SEC Investigations

Prior to instigating formal action, the SEC generally investigates possible securities law violations that have been brought to its attention. There are generally two stages of any SEC investigation. First, the SEC staff conducts an informal investigation. There is no requirement that targets of preliminary administrative investigations be given either actual or constructive notice of the investigation.[281] Frequently, an informal investigation will lead to the second stage—an SEC order instituting a formal investigation. The SEC is vested with broad discretionary powers of investigation. The decision to commence an investigation is not a final order subject to review and, thus, it is not appropriate to enjoin a continuing investigation.[282] Similarly, the Commission's decision not to institute a proceeding is not judicially reviewable.

Formal investigations are authorized when the Commission believes that there is a likelihood of a violation. The issuance of an order authorizing a formal investigation gives the SEC staff subpoena power.[285] It has been held that the appropriate procedure for challenging an investigative subpoena is to refuse to comply and then raise the issue in the ensuing SEC enforcement action.[286] Courts will generally enforce any such subpoena unless it is shown that the Commission was not acting in good faith and, thus, enforcement would constitute an abuse of the court's process.[287] As stated by the Ninth Circuit, a subpoena directed to the target of a formal investigation will be upheld upon the SEC's showing: "(1) the agency has a legitimate purpose for the investigation; (2) the inquiry is relevant to that purpose; (3) the agency does not possess the information sought; and (4) the agency has adhered to administrative steps required by law."[288]

The SEC practice has been to invite targets of investigations to respond informally to the Commission. These responses have come to be known as

268. *See, e.g.,* Rizek v. SEC, 215 F.3d 157, [1999–2000 Transfer Binder] Fed. Sec. L. Rep. (CCH) ¶ 90,998 (1st Cir.2000) (permanently barring broker from securities industry); S.E.C. v. Zahareas, 100 F.Supp.2d 1148 (D.Minn.2000).

272. 8415 U.S.C.A. § 78o(b)(6)(A).

281. RNR Enterprises, Inc. v. SEC, 122 F.3d 93, 98 (2d Cir.1997); Wells v. SEC, 113 F.3d 1230 (2d Cir.1997) (due process does not require that target be named); Gold v. SEC, 48 F.3d 987, 991 (7th Cir.1995) ("[d]ue process does not require notice, either actual or constructive, of an administrative investigation into possible violations of the securities laws").

282. Hunter v. SEC, 1994 WL 580096, [1995 Transfer Binder] Fed. Sec. L. Rep. (CCH) ¶ 98,601 (E.D.Pa.1994).

285. 15 U.S.C.A. § 78u(b).

286. 15 U.S.C.A. § 78u(c).

287. *See, e.g.,* SEC v. Wheeling–Pittsburgh Steel Corp., 648 F.2d 118 (3d Cir.1981).

288. Jerry T. O'Brien, Inc. v. SEC, 704 F.2d 1065, 1067 (9th Cir.1983), *reversed on other grounds* 467 U.S. 735, 104 S.Ct. 2720, 81 L.Ed.2d 615 (1984), *on remand* 773 F.2d 1070 (9th Cir.1985) relying on United States v. Powell, 379 U.S. 48, 57–58, 85 S.Ct. 248, 254–55, 13 L.Ed.2d 112 (1964).

"Wells submissions."[299] This informal process[300] gives a person under investigation the opportunity to present his or her position to the SEC before the SEC decides whether to initiate formal proceedings.[301] This presents the target of an informal investigation with the opportunity to try to dissuade the Commission from proceeding further.[302] Although the SEC has indicated that the Wells submission process may be most useful in providing an opportunity to be heard with respect to law or policy,[303] Wells submissions are frequently used to deal with factual matters as well.

§ 16.2[8] Parallel Civil and Criminal Proceedings

SEC investigations that reveal wrongdoing may result in SEC injunction actions brought in federal district court. Alternatively, the SEC can refer the case to the Department of Justice to determine if criminal sanctions are appropriate.[315] There has been increasing use of criminal prosecution for securities fraud generally both against individuals[317] and the corporations.[318] The Commission and the Department of Justice may cooperate in their parallel proceedings.[319]

Double jeopardy problems will not ordinarily affect the ability to impose both SEC civil sanctions and criminal penalties in separate actions. Similarly, even though the SEC has review power over FINRA sanctions, the double jeopardy clause does not preclude the SEC from bringing an enforcement action notwithstanding prior NASD sanctions for the same activity.[321] For the same reason, the existence of a parallel criminal investigation did not excuse the targets of a FINRA investigation from responding to a subpoena compelling testimony in connection with FINRA investigation.[322]

Collateral estoppel may preclude the defendant from relitigating in an SEC enforcement action facts determined in a prior criminal action resulting in conviction for the same violations.

299. The practice was initiated in response to the recommendations of a special advisory committee appointed by the SEC that was chaired by a lawyer named John Wells. *See* Arthur F. Mathews, Effective Defense of SEC Investigations: Laying the Foundation for Successful Disposition of Subsequent Civil, Administrative and Criminal Proceedings, 24 Emory L.J. 567, 618 n. 172 (1975).

300. *See* Sec. Act Rel. No. 33–5320, 37 Fed. Reg. 23,829 (SEC Nov. 9, 1972) (discussing the process).

301. In re Initial Public Offering Securities Litigation, 2004 WL 60290 *1 (S.D.N.Y. 2004)

302. 17 C.F.R. § 202.5(c).

303. *See* Sec. Act Rel. No. 33–5310, 1972 WL 18218 *1 (SEC Sept. 27, 1972).

315. 15 U.S.C.A. § 78u(d).

317. *See, e.g.,* United States v. Rigas, 490 F.3d 208 (2d Cir.2007) (upholding convictions of founder and son for financial fraud); United States v. Ebbers, 458 F.3d 110, 125 (2d Cir.2006) (upholding conviction of CEO). *See also, e.g.,* United States v. Simon, 425 F.2d 796, 805–806 (2d Cir.1969) (upholding accountants' convictions for securities fraud).

318. In what proved to be a very controversial prosecution, the criminal action against Arthur Andersen & Co. led to the accounting firm's demise.

319. SEC v. Dresser Industries, Inc., 628 F.2d 1368 (D.C.Cir.1980), *cert. denied* 449 U.S. 993, 101 S.Ct. 529, 66 L.Ed.2d 289 (1980); United States v. Fields, 592 F.2d 638, 646 (2d Cir.1978), *cert. denied* 442 U.S. 917, 99 S.Ct. 2838, 61 L.Ed.2d 284 (1979).

321. Jones v. SEC, 115 F.3d 1173 (4th Cir.1997), *cert. denied* 523 U.S. 1072, 118 S.Ct. 1512, 140 L.Ed.2d 666 (1998).

322. D.L. Cromwell Investments, Inc. v. NASD Regulation, Inc., 132 F. Supp.2d 248 (S.D.N.Y. 2001).

§ 16.2[10] Section 21(a) Reports

Securities and Exchange Commission investigations do not always culminate in enforcement actions, even when the Commission concludes that the securities laws have been violated. The SEC can publicize the results of its investigations. Section 21(a) of the 1934 Act expressly authorizes such public reports.[353] The institution of civil litigation in a matter does not limit the Commission's ability to continue with a section 21(a) investigation parallel to the law suit.[354]

Section 21(a) thus supplements the SEC's already broad investigatory powers. Section 21(a) has formed the basis of much controversy. For example, in In re Spartek, Inc.,[356] the Commission issued a section 21(a) report of a staff investigation including the acceptance of the registrant's offer of settlement. Commissioner Karmel vigorously dissented, considering the report to be in excess of the SEC's jurisdiction.[357] She reasoned that the publicity function could not properly be used as an alternative to SEC enforcement actions.[358] Notwithstanding Commissioner Karmel's concern, the SEC has since used the section 21(a) publicity function in this manner, albeit relatively sparingly. Additionally, the SEC issued a statement of practice supporting the use of section 21(a) reports and asserting that "where it appears to be in the public interest," settlement statements given to the Commission should be submitted "with the expectation that the Commission may make the statements public."[360] Once again, Commissioner Karmel voiced her dissent, pointing, *inter alia,* to possible due process objections.[361] The SEC has used section 21(a) as a vehicle for announcing policy shifts. For example, in 2001, the SEC announced a new approach to enforcement proceedings in instance when companies' self-policing efforts led to discovery of securities law violations.[362]

In 2002, the SEC invoked the power to issue reports under section 21(a) to impose the requirement that CEOs and CFOs certify the accuracy of financial statements.[363] Some members of the bar voiced their objection to the

---

353. 15 U.S.C.A. § 78u(a).

354. *See* SEC v. F.N. Wolf & Co., [1993–1994 Transfer Binder] Fed. Sec. L. Rep. (CCH) ¶ 98,015 (S.D.N.Y.1993).

356. Sec.Exch.Act Rel. No. 34–15567, 16 S.E.C. Docket 1094, 1979 WL 173653, 491 Sec.Reg. & L.Rep. (BNA) E–1 (February 141, 1979).

357. Sec.Exch.Act Rel. No. 34–15567, 16 S.E.C. Docket 1094, 1979 WL 173653, 491 Sec.Reg. & L.Rep. (BNA) E–1 (February 141, 1979).

358. Sec.Exch.Act Rel. No. 34–15567, 16 S.E.C. Docket 1094, 1979 WL 173653, 491 Sec.Reg. & L.Rep. (BNA) E–1 (February 141, 1979).

360. The Commission's Practice Relating to Reports of Investigations and Statements Submitted to the Commission Pursuant to Section 21(a) of the Securities Exchange Act of 1934, Sec.Exch.Act Rel. No. 34–15664, 17 S.E.C. Docket 18, 1979 WL 171071, [1979 Transfer Binder] Fed.Sec.L.Rep. (CCH) ¶ 82,014 at pp. 81,557–558 (March 21, 1979).

361. The Commission's Practice Relating to Reports of Investigations and Statements Submitted to the Commission Pursuant to Section 21(a) of the Securities Exchange Act of 1934, Sec.Exch.Act Rel. No. 34–15664, 17 S.E.C. Docket 18, 1979 WL 171071, [1979 Transfer Binder] Fed.Sec.L.Rep. (CCH) ¶ 82,014 at p81,558 (March 21, 1979).

362. *See* Report of Investigation Pursuant to Section 21(a) of the Securities Exchange Act of 1934 and Commission Statement of the Relationship of Cooperation to Agency Enforcement Decisions, Sec. Exch. Act Rel. No. 34–44969, 2001 WL 1301408 (SEC Oct. 23, 2001).

363. Order Requiring the Filing of Sworn Statements Pursuant to Section 21(a)(1) of the Securities Exchange Act of 1934, SEC Order File No. 4–460, http://www.sec.gov/rules/other/4–460.htm (SEC June 27, 2002).

use of this procedure to bypass formal rulemaking.[364] The certification requirements were subsequently incorporated into the Sarbanes–Oxley Act.[365]

§ 16.2[11] Section 15(c)(4) Orders

As part of the Insider Trading Sanctions Act of 1984,[366] Congress significantly expanded the SEC's administrative powers with regard to an individual or entity who was a "cause" of a failure to comply with the act's reporting requirements. Prior to the amendment, the section 15(c)(4) power was limited in its coverage to persons who were the actual violators of the Act. The 1984 legislation thus expanded the SEC's power, after notice and opportunity for a hearing, to issue an order calling for compliance or steps toward compliance with any SEC Rule or Regulation.[367] The section 15(c)(4) order extends the SEC's administrative power beyond broker-dealers and thus gives the Commission power to issue administrative sanctions against issuers subject to the 1934 Act, as well as against officers, directors, and employees of such issuer, or anyone else responsible for, or who could have prevented, the violation. Further, since the section 15(c)(4) order applies to anyone subject to the provisions of section 12, 13, 14, or 15(d) of the Act, it also extends to persons and entities required to make Williams Act filings in connection with the acquisition of reporting company shares. The broad terms of section 15(c)(4) do not place any limits on the types of orders that the Commission may issue. Thus, for example, the SEC could rely on section 15(c)(4) to issue an order barring an individual from being associated with a 1934 Act reporting company.

§ 16.2[12] Cease and Desist Authority

A major part of the 1990 enforcement legislation was the granting to the Commission of its cease and desist power.[373] If the SEC finds, after notice and opportunity to be heard, that a regulated securities professional is violating, has violated, or is about to violate any rule or regulation, the SEC may issue a cease and desist order against that person for any current or future violations and against any other person who causes the violation due to an act or omission that the person knew or should have known would contribute to such violation.[374] The authority to issue a cease and desist order may be invoked against any person who violates the Act. In addition, the Commission may order an asset freeze if the proceeding is against a respondent who acts, or during the alleged misconduct acted, as a broker, dealer, investment advisor, investment company, municipal securities dealer, government securities broker, government securities dealer, transfer agent, or associate of any of the foregoing.[375]

---

364. *See* Lawyers Question SEC's Use of § 21(a) to Impose CEO Certification Requirement, 34 Sec. Reg. & L. Rep. (BNA) 1185 (July 22, 2002). SEC Rulemaking is discussed in § 16.36 *infra*.

365. Sarbanes–Oxley Act of 2002, Pub. Law 107–204 (July 30, 2002). *See* § 9.3[2][A] *supra*.

366. Pub. L. No. 98–376, 98 Stat. 1264 (1984).

367. 15 U.S.C.A. § 78*o*(c)(4).

373. Securities Act of 1933 § 8A, 15 U.S.C.A. § 77h–1; Securities Exchange Act of 1934 §§ 21C, 23(d), 15 U.S.C.A. §§ 78u–3, 78w(d); Investment Company Act of 1940 § 9(f), 15 U.S.C.A. § 80a–9(f); Investment Advisers Act of 1940 § 203(k), 15 U.S.C.A. § 80b–3(k).

374. *See, e.g.,* In the Matter of Haeglin, Acc. & Audit. Enforcement Rel. No. 461, Fed.Sec. L.Rep. (CCH) 73,920 (SEC 1993) (cease and desist order against CFO and President in connection with misleading financial filings).

375. 15 U.S.C.A. § 77h–1(c)(2); 15 U.S.C.A. § 78u–2; 15 U.S.C.A. § 80a–9(f)(3)(B); 15 U.S.C.A. § 80b–3(k)(3)(B).

In deciding whether a cease and desist order should issue, the administrative law judge must consider the possibility of a recurrence of the alleged violation.[376] The seriousness of the violation may also be a factor.[377] A "weak" risk of future violation will not be sufficient to support a cease and desist order.[378]

§ 16.2[13] SEC Administrative Proceedings

The SEC is empowered to hold administrative hearings in the course of exercising its supervisory authority over broker-dealers,[393] national exchanges,[394] investment companies and advisers,[395] municipal securities dealers,[396] government securities dealers,[397] and formerly with respect to public utility holding companies.[398] These are generally disciplinary proceedings.

Pursuant to section 6 of the 1934 Act, the Commission is charged with overseeing national securities exchanges.[405] Although the power has been exercised only once,[406] the SEC may suspend or revoke registration of an exchange.[407] The SEC also has the power to expel individual broker-dealers from a national exchange.[408] In addition, the SEC has the authority to revoke the registration of publicly companies, thus resulting in a permanent delisting of their shares.[409] The 1934 Act additionally charges the SEC with overseeing registered securities associations and other broker-dealer self-regulatory organizations.[410] The Commission can suspend or revoke an association's registration,[411] as well as suspend or expel a member of the association.[412] Also, by virtue of its registration of broker-dealers,[413] the Commission has the power to suspend or revoke such registration.[414] The Commission can bar any person

376. *See, e.g.,* WHX Corp. v. SEC, 362 F.3d 854 (D.C.Cir.2004).

377. *See, e.g., Id.*

378. *See, e.g., Id.*

393. 15 U.S.C.A. § 78*o*–1. *See* § 14.3 *supra.*

394. 15 U.S.C.A. §§ 78*l,* 78s. *See* §§ 14.1, 14.3 *supra.*

395. *See* 15 U.S.C.A. § 80a–1 *et seq.,* 80b–1 *et seq. See* chapters 20, 21 *infra.*

396. 15 U.S.C.A. § 78*o*–4. *See* § 14.12 *supra.*

397. 15 U.S.C.A. § 78*o*–5. *See* § 14.13 *supra.*

398. 15 U.S.C.A. § 79a *et seq.* (2004). The Public Utility Holding Company Act was repealed in 2005. *See* chapter 18 *infra.*

405. 15 U.S.C.A. § 78f.

406. San Francisco Mining Exchange v. SEC, 378 F.2d 162 (9th Cir.1967).

407. 15 U.S.C.A. § 78s(h)(1).

408. 15 U.S.C.A. § 78s(h)(2).

409. *See* § 9.2 *supra.*

410. 15 U.S.C.A. §§ 78*o*–3, 78q–1, 78s, 78c(a)(26), 78c(a)(34).

411. 15 U.S.C.A. § 78s(h)(1).

412. 15 U.S.C.A. § 78s(h)(2).

413. 15 U.S.C.A. § 78*o*.

414. 15 U.S.C.A. § 78*o*(b)(5). *See, e.g.,* Svalberg v. SEC, 876 F.2d 181 (D.C.Cir.1989) (permanently barring brokers from serving as principals in any NASD member firm). *Cf.* Antoniu v. SEC, 877 F.2d 721 (8th Cir.1989), *cert. denied* 494 U.S. 1004, 110 S.Ct. 1296, 108 L.Ed.2d 473 (1990) (nullifying Commission order permanently barring association with a broker-dealer because of public statements made by a Commissioner prior to the proceedings which indicated that he had prejudged the matter); Dlugash v. SEC, 373 F.2d 107 (2d Cir.1967) (revocation); Peoples Securities Co. v. SEC, 289 F.2d 268 (5th Cir.1961) (denial of registration); Gilligan, Will & Co. v. SEC, 267 F.2d 461 (2d Cir.1959), *cert. denied* 361 U.S. 896, 80 S.Ct. 200, 4 L.Ed.2d 152 (1959) (suspension). The Commission has parallel authority over investment advisers under the 1940 Advisers Act. 15 U.S.C.A. § 80b–3(e).

from associating with a broker-dealer,[415] a member of a registered securities association,[416] or an investment adviser,[417] or bar that person from serving in various capacities with a registered investment company.[418] In addition, in a divided decision, the SEC held that it has the power to issue collateral or industry-wide bar orders against securities professionals.[419] The Commission thus concluded that it could bar violators of the act from not only engaging in the types of activities in which the wrongful conduct occurred, but also other regulated securities-related activities.[420] With respect to all of the powers discussed above, the Commission can impose the less drastic sanction of censure.[421]

The Supreme Court held that in reviewing SEC sanctions, the courts of appeals should affirm the Commission's findings if they are supported by a preponderance of the evidence.[422] Many courts have stated the standard of review in terms of substantial evidence,[423] which requires something less than a preponderance of the evidence.[424] Also, any review of SEC decisions is to be made on a deferential basis.[425]

§ 16.2[14] Civil Penalties in Administrative Actions

The Securities Enforcement Remedies and Penny Stock Reform Act of 1990[431] empowers the Commission to impose civil penalties in administrative proceedings.[432] The power to impose civil penalties applies to proceedings against a broker-dealer,[433] associated person,[434] municipal securities dealer,[435] government securities dealer,[436] or registered clearing agent.[437] The SEC has

415. 15 U.S.C.A. § 78*o*(b)(6). *See, e.g.,* Elliott v. SEC, 36 F.3d 86 (11th Cir.1994) (barring individual convicted of 37 counts of mail fraud from associating with any broker-dealer). Berdahl v. SEC, 572 F.2d 643 (8th Cir.1978); Chatham v. SEC, 604 F.2d 1368 (D.C.Cir.1978); Collins Securities Corp. v. SEC, 562 F.2d 820 (D.C.Cir.1977); Stead v. SEC, 444 F.2d 713 (10th Cir.1971), *cert. denied* 404 U.S. 1059, 92 S.Ct. 739, 30 L.Ed.2d 746 (1972); Sec.Exch.Act Rel. No. 34–14668 (April 17, 1978); Sec.Exch.Act Rel. No. 34–14918 (July 3, 1976).

416. 15 U.S.C.A. § 78s(h)(3)

417. 15 U.S.C.A. § 80b–3(f).

418. 15 U.S.C.A. § 78a–9(b).

419. In re Blinder, SEC Admin. Proc. File No. 3–8305, No. 34–39355, 1997 WL 797524, 29 Sec. Reg. & L. Rep. (BNA) 1406 (SEC 1997).

420. *Id.*

421. *See, e.g.,* In the Matter of National Bank of Chicago Bond Department, Sec.Exch.Act Rel. No. 34–14761, 1978 WL 207853 (May 15, 1978).

422. Steadman v. SEC, 450 U.S. 91, 101 S.Ct. 999, 67 L.Ed.2d 69 (1981).

423. Brofman v. SEC, 167 Fed.Appx. 836 (2d Cir.2006).

424. "Substantial evidence, in the usual context, has been construed to mean less than a preponderance, but more than a scintilla of evidence. 'It means such relevant evidence as a reasonable mind might accept as adequate to support a conclusion.' Universal Camera v. NLRB, 340 U.S. 474, 477, 71 S.Ct. 456, 95 L.Ed. 456 (1951)." Cellular Telephone Co. v. Town of Oyster Bay, 166 F.3d 490, 494 (2d Cir.1999).

425. Valicenti Advisory Services, Inc. v. SEC, 198 F.3d 62 (2d Cir.1999).

431. Pub.L. No. 101–429.

432. Securities Exchange Act of 1934 § 21B, 15 U.S.C.A. § 78u–2; Investment Company Act § 9(d), (e), 15 U.S.C.A. § 80a–9(d), (e); Investment Advisers Act § 203(i), 15 U.S.C.A. § 80b–3(i).

433. *See* section 15(b)(4), 15 U.S.C.A. § 78*o*(b)(4).

434. *See* section 15(b)(6), 15 U.S.C.A. § 78*o*(b)(6).

435. *See* section 15B, 15 U.S.C.A. § 78*o*–4.

436. *See* section 15C, 15 U.S.C.A. § 78*o*–5.

437. *See* section 17A, 15 U.S.C.A. § 78q–1.

similar authority over persons registered under the Investment Company or Investment Advisers Act of 1940.[438] If, after notice and opportunity to be heard, the Commission finds: (1) a willful violation of the securities laws, (2) a willful violation of the rules of an applicable self regulatory organization, (3) that the respondent has willfully made material misstatements or omissions in required reports, or (4) that the respondent has willfully failed to adequately supervise persons,[439] then it may impose a civil penalty according to a three-tiered maximum, depending upon the degree of the respondent's culpability and the impact of the violations.[440] In considering whether the imposition of a penalty is warranted, and if so the appropriate amount of the penalty, the Commission is directed to consider a number of factors. The Commission must consider the degree of culpability, the harm to others, the extent to which the violator was unjustly enriched, whether the violator has previously run afoul of the securities laws (or similar laws), the need to deter such conduct, "and other matters as justice may require."[441] In considering whether to impose such a penalty, the Commission must consider any evidence the respondent chooses to introduce that relates to his or her ability to pay.[442] In addition to a penalty, the Commission is empowered to order a disgorgement or accounting of profits.[443]

§ 16.2[18] Suspension of the Right to Practice Before the Commission—SEC Rule 102(e)

Under SEC Rule of Practice 102(e)[476] the Commission may suspend, limit, or bar "*any* person" from practicing before it "in *any* way."[477] The Rule 102(e) power has been used against both accountants and lawyers. Although use of Rule 102(e)'s sanctions has been questioned in light of the absence of express statutory authority, the Second Circuit has upheld the rule as consistent with the Commission's overall statutory mandate.[481]

In 2002, Congress enacted the Sarbanes–Oxley Act in response to the corporate fraud scandals of 2001 and 2002.[490] There was considerable concern that more vigilant representation by attorneys could have prevented or at least minimized the fraud involved in such celebrated failures as Enron and WorldCom. As a result, Congress expanded attorney responsibility by calling on attorneys to report serious wrongdoing to high ranking corporate officials.[491] The Act mandates that the SEC promulgate rules setting forth minimum standards of professional conduct for attorneys appearing and practicing before the SEC in connection with their representation of issuers.[492]

438. 15 U.S.C.A. §§ 80a–9(d), (e), 80b–3(i).

439. *See* section 15(b)(4)(E), 15 U.S.C.A. § 78*o*(b)(4)(E).

440. *See* section 21B of the Exchange Act, 15 U.S.C.A. § 78u–3.

441. Section 21C, 15 U.S.C.A. § 78u–3(c).

442. Section 21C(d). 15 U.S.C.A. § 78u–3(d).

443. Section 21C(e), 15 U.S.C.A. § 78u–3(e).

476. Rule 102(e) formerly was designated Rule 2(e). Those descriptions are used interchangeably throughout this section.

477. 17 C.F.R. § 201.102(e)(3). For a more detailed discussion *see* § 16.4 *infra*.

481. Touche Ross & Co. v. SEC, 609 F.2d 570, 579 (2d Cir.1979).

490. Sarbanes–Oxley Act of 2002, Pub. Law 107–204 (July 30, 2002).

491. 15 U.S.C.A. § 7245. *See generally* Thomas Lee Hazen, Administrative Law Controls on Attorney Practice Before the Securities and Exchange Commission, 55 Admin. L. Rev. 323 (2003).

492. *See* 15 U.S.C.A. § 7245.

The SEC rules must contain a requirement that attorneys report evidence of a material violation of securities laws or breach of fiduciary duty or similar violation by a company, including an agent of the company, to the chief legal counsel or the chief executive officer and, if that officer does not respond appropriately, to the audit committee (or other committee composed entirely of outside directors).[493] The statute makes no distinction between inside and outside counsel advising a reporting company.

Rule 102(e) is not the only means for pursuing attorneys and other professionals. For example, the SEC has used its power under section 15(c)(4) of the Act[500] against attorneys who caused a violation of the securities laws.[501] The SEC has used cease and desist proceedings to sanction improper professional conduct.[504] The SEC has also used its general enforcement powers to pursue attorneys.[505]

§ 16.2[19] SEC Oversight Authority

The self regulatory organizations for the securities industry—the exchanges and FINRA—are subject to SEC oversight.[506] As part of this oversight responsibility, by virtue of section 19 of the Act,[507] the Commission has oversight responsibility with respect to all rulemaking activity of national exchanges. Similar authority exists with regard to FINRA.[509] One consequence of the SEC oversight authority is that when it provides a pervasive regulatory scheme, the regulation will operate as an implied repeal of the antitrust laws as an alternative way to scrutinize the activity in question.[510]

The self regulatory organizations have disciplinary authority over their members to redress violations of self regulatory organization rules. Self regulatory organization disciplinary actions are subject to SEC review and, in turn, to review by a federal court of appeals.[517] As is the case with judicial review of SEC decisions, when reviewing a decision of a self regulatory organization, the SEC will give deference to the findings below.[518] However, in reviewing the sanctions imposed in SRO disciplinary proceedings de novo review is appropriate.[519] The doctrine of exhaustion of remedies means that

---

493. *Id.*

500. 15 U.S.C.A. § 78*o*(c)(4) which was significantly expanded by the Insider Trading Sanctions Act of 1984, Pub. L. No. 98–376, 98 Stat. 1264 (1984). *See* § 16.2[11] *supra.*

501. In the Matter of George C. Kern, Jr. Administrative Proceeding File No. 3–6869, 52 S.E.C. Docket 451, 1988 WL 357006 (SEC Initial decision March 21, 1988), *reversed as not applying to future violations,* 1991 WL 284804, 50 S.E.C. 596, Sec. Exch. Act Rel. No. 34–29356, 49 S.E.C. Docket 422 (SEC Jun 21, 1991)

504. In The Matter of Seymour, Administrative Proceeding File No. 3–10521, 2001 WL 698371, Sec. Exch. Act Rel. No. 34–44461, Release No. AE–1413 (SEC June 21, 2001).

505. *See, e.g.,* Speech by SEC Director of Enforcement, Stephen Cutler: The Themes of Sarbanes–Oxley as Reflected in the Commission's Enforcement Program, http://www.sec.gov/news/speech/spch092004smc.htm (Sept. 20, 2004).

506. *See* § 14.3 *supra.*

507. 15 U.S.C.A. § 78s.

509. *See* 15 U.S.C.A. § 78*o*–3.

510. *See* United States v. NASD, 422 U.S. 694, 95 S.Ct. 2427, 45 L.Ed.2d 486 (1975); Gordon v. New York Stock Exchange, Inc., 422 U.S. 659, 95 S.Ct. 2598, 45 L.Ed.2d 463 (1975). *See also, e.g.,* Silver v. New York Stock Exchange, 373 U.S. 341, 83 S.Ct. 1246, 10 L.Ed.2d 389 (1963).

517. *See, e.g.,* L.H. Alton & Co. v. SEC, [1999–2000 Transfer Binder] Fed. Sec. L. Rep. (CCH) ¶ 91,021, 2000 WL 975183 (9th Cir.2000).

518. *See, e.g.,* Ho v. SEC, 2007 WL 1224027 (7th Cir.2007).

519. *See* PAZ Securities, Inc. v. SEC, 494 F.3d 1059 (D.C.Cir.2007).

disciplinary and other self regulatory action must proceed the self regulatory agency before review by the SEC or by a court.[520]

520. *See, e.g.*, MFS Securities Corp. v. SEC, 380 F.3d 611, 622 (2d Cir.2004).

Chapter 17

JURISDICTIONAL ASPECTS

Table of Sections

---

§ 17.1 Exclusive Federal Jurisdiction Under the Exchange Act; Concurrent Jurisdiction Under the 1933 and Other Securities Acts

§ 17.1[1] The Jurisdictional Mosaic

The federal securities laws provide a mosaic approach to jurisdiction. The Securities Act of 1933 and most of the other acts comprising the battery of securities laws provide for concurrent jurisdiction of federal and state courts, thus giving parties a choice of a federal or state forum[1] in the context of private causes of action. In contrast, the Securities Exchange Act of 1934 provides that jurisdiction is exclusively federal, which means that all private suits must be brought in federal court. All criminal prosecutions under the securities laws and judicial enforcement actions by the Securities and Exchange Commission must be maintained only in federal court.[3] Similarly, jurisdiction over appeals from SEC administrative decisions is exclusively federal.[4] When dealing with private remedies, however, the six securities acts present three different approaches to jurisdictional allocation.

The ability to take advantage of state court forums has been severely limited by the preemptive effect of the Securities Litigation Uniform Standards Act of 1998 (SLUSA).[15] The federal preemption is not total but it does

---

§ 17.1

1. *See generally* Thomas L. Hazen, Allocation of Jurisdiction Between the State and Federal Courts for Remedies Under the Federal Securities Laws, 60 N.C.L. Rev. 707 (1982).

3. Securities Act of 1933, § 22(a), 15 U.S.C.A. § 77v(a); Securities Exchange Act of 1934, § 27, 15 U.S.C.A. § 78aa; Public Utility Holding Company Act of 1935, § 25, 15 U.S.C.A. § 79y (repealed in 2005); Trust Indenture Act of 1939, § 322(b), 15 U.S.C.A. § 77vvv(b); Investment Company Act of 1940, § 44, 15 U.S.C.A. § 80a–43; Investment Advisers Act of 1940, § 214, 15 U.S.C.A. § 80b–14.

4. Securities Act of 1933, § 9, 15 U.S.C.A. § 77i; Securities Exchange Act of 1934, § 25, 15 U.S.C.A. § 78y; Public Utility Holding Company Act of 1935, § 24, 15 U.S.C.A. § 79x (repealed in 2005); Trust Indenture Act of 1939, § 322(a), 15 U.S.C.A. § 77vvv(a); Investment Company Act of 1940, § 43, 15 U.S.C.A. § 80a–42; Investment Advisers Act of 1940, § 213, 15 U.S.C.A. § 80b–13.

15. Pub. Law No. 105–353, 112 Stat. 3227 (105th Cong., 2d Sess. November 3, 1998) (S 1260).

extend to most securities fraud class actions involving publicly traded securities, even if the complaint includes claims under state law.[17] Even though 1933 Act claims under section [18] or 12(a)(2)[19] do not require scienter,[20] they appear to be subject to SLUSA's preemption. In contrast, section 12(a)(1)[21] is based on a violation of the 1933 Act's registration provisions and should remain removable to state court since the claim is not based on fraud or misrepresentation and thus is not subject to the language of the SLUSA's preemption.[22]

§ 17.1[2] Exclusive Federal Jurisdiction Under the Exchange Act

State courts must dismiss any claim based on the Securities Exchange Act of 1934 in light of its grant of exclusive federal jurisdiction.[47] As discussed below, there has been some disagreement as to whether this also extends to those instances in which the alleged federal violation of federal law is raised as a defense to a state law cause of action that was brought in a state court forum.

It is one thing to say that jurisdiction over affirmative claims and causes of actions is exclusively federal, and it may be another to preclude the Securities Exchange Act from being raised as a defense in a state court. Although a large number of states will entertain 1934 Act claims raised defensively,[48] a few influential courts, including Delaware's, have ruled that they lack jurisdiction in such cases.[49] This harsh minority view has been criticized,[50] as well it should be. The mere fact that the success of a state law claim may be dependent on an interpretation of an SEC rule is not sufficient to transform a state law cause of action into a federal claim.[51] Conversely, a plaintiff cannot disguise a federal claim as one under state law. The "artful pleading rule"[53] prevents a plaintiff from omitting necessary federal questions

17. 15 U.S.C.A. §§ 77p(b), 78bb(f). *See also, e.g.* § 12.15[2] *supra*.

18. 15 U.S.C.A. § 77k. *See* §§ 7.3–7.5 *supra*.

19. 15 U.S.C.A. § 77l(a)(2). *See* § 7.6 *supra*.

20. The scienter requirement is discussed in § 12.8 *supra*.

21. 15 U.S.C.A. § 77l(a)(1). *See* § 7.2 *supra*.

22. *See, e.g.,* Zia v. Medical Staffing Network, Inc., 336 F.Supp.2d 1306 (S.D.Fla. 2004); In re Tyco International Multidistrict Litigation, 322 F.Supp.2d 116 (D.N.H. 2004); In re King Pharmaceuticals, 36 Sec. Reg. & L. Rep. (BNA) 444 (E.D. Tenn. 2004); In re Waste Management Securities Litigation, 194 F.Supp.2d 590 (S.D. Tex. 2002).

47. *See, e.g.*, Evans v. Dale, 896 F.2d 975 (5th Cir.1990).

48. *See* Gregory–Massari, Inc. v. Purkitt, 1 Cal.App.3d 968, 82 Cal.Rptr. 210 (1969); Johnson, Lane, Space, Smith & Co. v. Lenny, 129 Ga.App. 55, 198 S.E.2d 923 (1973); Michigan National Bank v. Dunbar, 91 Mich.App. 385, 283 N.W.2d 747 (1979); J. Cliff Rahel & Co. v. Roper, 186 Neb. 34, 180 N.W.2d 682 (1970); Birenbaum v. Bache & Co., 555 S.W.2d 513 (Tex.Civ.App.1977). *See also* Calvert Fire Insurance Co. v. American Mutual Reinsurance Co., 600 F.2d 1228, 1231 n. 6 (7th Cir.1979); Shareholders Management Co. v. Gregory, 449 F.2d 326 (9th Cir.1971).

49. *See* Investment Associates v. Standard Power & Light Corp., 29 Del.Ch. 225, 238–39, 48 A.2d 501, 508–09 (1946), *affirmed*, 29 Del.Ch. 593, 606, 51 A.2d 572, 579 (1947); Eliasberg v. Standard Oil Co., 23 N.J.Super. 431, 92 A.2d 862 (1952), *affirmed per curiam*, 12 N.J. 467, 97 A.2d 437 (1953); Western Capital & Securities, Inc. v. Knudsvig, 768 P.2d 989, 21 Sec.Reg. & L.Rep. (BNA) 317 (Utah Ct.App.1989).

50. 2 Louis Loss, Securities Regulation at pp.973–1000 (2d ed.1961); *see generally* Thomas L. Hazen, Allocation of Jurisdiction Between the State and Federal Courts for Remedies Under the Federal Securities Laws, 60 N.C.L. Rev. 707, 722–724 (1982).

51. Petrie v. Pacific Stock Exchange, 982 F.Supp. 1390 (N.D.Cal.1997).

53. "[U]nder the artful pleading rule 'a plaintiff may not defeat removal by omitting to plead necessary federal questions in a complaint.' " ARCO Environmental Remediation, LLC v. Depart-from the complaint.[54] However, the fact that the same facts may give rise to both federal and state claims does not implicate the artful pleading doctrine so as to defeat the state court's jurisdiction.[55]

§ 17.1[4] Federal Supplemental (or Pendent) Jurisdiction Over State Claims

What about the plaintiff with 1934 Act claims and related state causes of action? All related claims can be heard together in federal court when the court invokes supplemental pendent jurisdiction over the state law claims.[72] Even after the federal claim is dismissed, a federal court can retain jurisdiction over the state claim.[73] If the federal claim fails, however, the federal court is likely to dismiss the state law cause of action.[74]

§ 17.2 Subject Matter Jurisdiction—Use of the Jurisdictional Means

The Exchange Act's registration and reporting requirements are triggered by offerings or issuers having sufficient interstate contact to support federal regulation. In contrast, the 1933 Act registration requirements are implicated by a nonexempt offer or sale of securities through an instrumentality of interstate commerce.[2] Although not required as a matter of jurisdictional limitation, Congress elected to exempt from 1933 Act registration offerings that originate and take place within the confines of a single state.[3]

The jurisdictional requirements are easily satisfied. However, in order to state a claim and establish jurisdiction, the complaint must refer to federal law.

Typically, the securities acts' antifraud provisions are triggered by the use of an instrumentality of interstate commerce.[5] The language of the other

---

ment of Health and Environmental Quality of the State of Montana, 213 F.3d 1108 (9th Cir.2000) (citing Franchise Tax Board of California v. Construction Laborers Vacation Trust for Southern California, 463 U.S. 1, 22, 103 S.Ct. 2841, 77 L.Ed.2d 420 (1983)); Herman v. Salomon Smith Barney, Inc., 266 F.Supp.2d 1208 (S.D. Cal. 2003).

54. "A state-created cause of action can be deemed to arise under federal law (1) where federal law completely preempts state law; (2) where the claim is necessarily federal in character; or (3) where the right to relief depends on the resolution of a substantial, disputed federal question." ARCO Environmental Remediation, LLC v. Department of Health and Environmental Quality of the State of Montana, 213 F.3d 1108 (9th Cir.2000).

55. *See* Lippitt v. Raymond James Financial Services, Inc., 340 F.3d 1033 (9th Cir. 2003).

72. United Mine Workers v. Gibbs, 383 U.S. 715, 86 S.Ct. 1130, 16 L.Ed.2d 218 (1966); Chapman v. Merrill Lynch, Pierce, Fenner & Smith, Inc., 1983 WL 1340, [1984–1984 Transfer Binder] Fed.Sec.L.Rep. (CCH) ¶ 99,419 at p. 96,410–11 (D.Md.1983).

73. *See, e.g.,* United International Holdings, Inc. v. Wharf (Holdings) Ltd., 210 F.3d 1207, 1219–1220 (10th Cir.2000), *affirmed on other grounds*, 532 U.S. 588, 121 S.Ct. 1776, 149 L.Ed.2d 845 (2001).

74. United Mine Workers v. Gibbs, 383 U.S. 715, 725–27, 86 S.Ct. 1130, 1138–1140, 16 L.Ed.2d 218 (1966).

§ 17.2

2. Section 5 of the Act makes it unlawful to make offers and sales "mak[ing] use of any means or instrumentality of transportation or communication in interstate commerce or of the mails to sell such security" unless the securities are registered (or exempt). 15 U.S.C.A. § 77e. *See* chapter 2 *supra.* The exemptions are discussed in chapter 4 *supra.*

3. 15 U.S.C.A. § 77c(a)(11); 17 C.F.R. § 230.147. *See* § 4.12 *supra.*

5. *E.g.,* 15 U.S.C.A. § 77*l* (referring back to violations of section 5's prohibitions); 15 U.S.C.A. § 77q(a) ("offer or sale of any securities by the use of any means or instruments of transportation

jurisdictional provisions is varied. However, the courts' focus in interpreting these provisions has centered on the use of an instrumentality of interstate commerce for some part of the transaction, not necessarily limited to the communication of the actual misstatement.[7] Furthermore, in interpreting the reach of the statute, the federal courts have taken a broad view of the securities laws' jurisdictional reach. The broad language regarding the necessary jurisdictional nexus when combined with the courts' expansive interpretation means that most securities transactions will be covered. Thus, for example, an intrastate telephone call will support jurisdiction.[8] Similarly, it has been held that the particular communication containing the actionable statement need not be made through an instrumentality of interstate commerce so long as the transaction in question was effectuated through the use of such an instrumentality.[9]

Although a face-to-face conversation, standing alone, will not satisfy the jurisdictional requirements, there may be jurisdiction under Rule 10b–5, if the conversations are part of a transaction that utilizes an instrumentality of interstate commerce.[12]

§ 17.4 Extraterritorial Application of the Securities Laws; Their Relevance to Foreign Issuers and to Transactions in Foreign Markets; Antifraud Provisions

Geographic and geopolitical borders have had increasingly less significance in the operation of securities markets around the globe. This has led to increasingly complex questions about which countries should be regulating transactions in the increasingly multinational securities markets.

Most American case law dealing with the extraterritorial application of United States securities laws focuses on the antifraud provisions of the 1934 Exchange Act.[2] The courts have developed two tests for subject-matter jurisdiction in securities fraud cases. One test is based on the conduct[3] of foreign persons within the United States; the other focuses on the effects[4] within the

---

or communication in interstate commerce or by use of the mails, directly or indirectly * * * "); 15 U.S.C.A. § 78j(b) ("by the use of any means or instrumentality of interstate commerce, or of the mails, or of any facility of any national securities exchange"); 17 C.F.R. § 240.10b–5 ("by the use of any means or instrumentality of interstate commerce, or of the mails, or of any facility of any national securities exchange"). *Cf.* United States v. Cashin, 281 F.2d 669, 673 (2d Cir.1960) (jurisdictional reach of section 12(1) and 17(a) of the 1933 Act are the same).

A defendant will not escape the jurisdictional reach solely because his or her role in a transaction implicating interstate commerce was purely intrastate. Busch v. Buchman, Buchman & O'Brien, Law Firm, 11 F.3d 1255 (5th Cir.1994).

7. *See, e.g.*, United States v. Johnson, 553 F.Supp.2d 582, 622 (E.D. Va. 2008), quoting from United States v. MacKay, 491 F.2d 616, 619 (10th Cir.1973).

8. *E.g.*, Loveridge v. Dreagoux, 678 F.2d 870, 874 (10th Cir.1982); Dupuy v. Dupuy, 511 F.2d 641, 642–44 (5th Cir.1975), *appeal after remand*, 551 F.2d 1005 (1977).

9. *See, e.g.*, Leiter v. Kuntz, 655 F.Supp. 725, 726–27 (D.Utah 1987).

12. *E.g.*, Franklin Savings Bank of New York v. Levy, 551 F.2d 521, 524 (2d Cir.1977).

§ 17.4

2. *E.g.*, 17 C.F.R. § 240.10b–5. *See* chapter 12 *supra*.

3. *See, e.g.*, Kauthar SDN BHD v. Sternberg, 149 F.3d 659 (7th Cir.1998); IIT v. Vencap, Ltd., 519 F.2d 1001, 1017 (2d Cir.1975).

4. *See, e.g.*, Des Brisay v. Goldfield Corp., 549 F.2d 133 (9th Cir.1977); Reingold v. Deloitte Haskins & Sells, 599 F.Supp. 1241 (S.D.N.Y.1984).

United States of conduct occurring in foreign countries. As discussed below, these tests do not always lead to predictable results.[5]

The increased use of the Internet for securities offerings and trading increases the potential for extraterritorial impact.[7] The Commission has taken the position that Internet communications that are targeting only foreign investors will be considered offshore so long as the web site takes precautions to guard against sales to United States residents.[8]

§ 17.4[1] Extraterritorial Jurisdiction Under the Antifraud Provisions

Federal courts can exercise jurisdiction under the federal securities laws under two different rationales, focusing on either the location of the conduct or the effects of the conduct.[9] First, jurisdiction exists, under what has become known as the "effects test," if the effect or impact of the conduct in question involves transactions and or markets in the United States.[10] The impact must be specific and not merely a generalized allegation of impact in the United States.[11] Alternatively, the federal securities laws provide jurisdiction if the conduct in question takes place in the United States, regardless of where the ultimate transaction occurs–this is known as the "conduct" test.[12]

Jurisdiction can be based on misrepresentations made here, although involving foreign securities that were traded only in foreign markets.[16] However, activities within the United States that are "merely preparatory" to the actual fraud are clearly insufficient to confer subject-matter jurisdiction.[17]

It has, thus, been said that the antifraud provisions of the federal securities laws:

> (1) Apply to losses from sales of securities to Americans resident in the United States whether or not acts * * * of material importance occurred in this country; and
>
> (2) Apply to losses from sales of securities to Americans resident abroad if * * * acts * * * of material importance in the United States have significantly contributed thereto; but

---

5. *See, e.g.,* Lewis D. Lowenfels & Alan R. Bromberg, U.S. Securities Fraud Across the Border: Unpredictable Jurisdiction, 55 Bus. Law. 1023 (2000).

7. *See, e.g.,* SEC v. Gold–Ventures Club, Case No. 1:02–CV–1434 (CAP), Litigation Release No. 17537, 2002 SECDIG 2002–103–3, 2002 WL 1058847 (N.D. Ga. 2002) (emergency order including asset freeze against foreign website attempting to lure U.S. investors through fraudulent promotion).

8. Statement of the Commission Regarding Use of Internet Web Sites to Offer Securities, solicit Securities Transactions or Advertise Investment Services Offshore, International Series Release No. 1125, Sec. Act Rel. No. 33–7516, 1998 WL 135626 (F.R.) (SEC March 27, 1998).

9. *See, e.g.,* Hannah L. Buxbaum, Multinational Class Actions Under Federal Securities Law: Managing Jurisdictional Conflict, 46 Colum. J. Trans. L. 14 (2007).

10. *See, e.g.,* Zoelsch v. Arthur Andersen & Co., 824 F.2d 27 (D.C.Cir.1987); Bersch v. Drexel Firestone, Inc., 519 F.2d 974 (2d Cir.1975), *cert. denied* 423 U.S. 1018, 96 S.Ct. 453, 46 L.Ed.2d 389 (1975).

11. *See, e.g.,* In re Alstom Securities Litigation, 406 F.Supp.2d 346, 369–370 (S.D.N.Y. 2005)

12. *See, e.g.,* Zoelsch v. Arthur Andersen & Co., 824 F.2d 27 (D.C.Cir.1987).

16. *See* Leasco Data Processing Equipment v. Maxwell, 468 F.2d 1326 (2d Cir.1972).

17. Zoelsch v. Arthur Andersen & Co., 824 F.2d 27 (D.C.Cir.1987); Bersch v. Drexel Firestone, Inc., 519 F.2d 974 (2d Cir.1975), *cert. denied* 423 U.S. 1018, 96 S.Ct. 453, 46 L.Ed.2d 389 (1975); IIT v. Vencap, Ltd., 519 F.2d 1001 (2d Cir.1975).

(3) Do not apply to losses from sales of securities to foreigners outside the United States unless acts * * * within the United States directly caused such losses.[20]

§ 17.4[2] 1933 Act Registration and 1934 Act Reporting Requirements for Foreign Issuers

A common method for domestic trading of foreign issues is through American Depositary Receipts (ADR's). The foreign securities are placed in a central depository and ADR certificates, representing a share of the depository's holdings, are traded in the American securities markets. When ADRs are first offered to the American public, registration of the depositary shares (ADSs) is required under the 1933 Act on Form F–6. ADSs registered on Form F–6 have been exempted from the 1934 Act's registration and reporting requirements.[74]

When private foreign issuers offer their equity securities, 1933 Act registration can be effectuated on Form F–1 or F–3, but not on Form F–6. Form F–6 is to be used only for ADSs.

The Commission addressed the applicability of Regulation D to transactions occurring outside the United States. As a general proposition, registration is not required for sales to nonresident purchasers where the sales are made outside of the United States and effected in a manner that should result in the securities coming to rest outside the United States.[103] This rule may be relied upon even if Regulation D sales are contemporaneously being made in the United States.[104] The Commission has made it clear in Regulation D that an issuer's providing information to journalists outside of the United States will not be deemed to have violated the requirement that the issuer not be engaged in a general solicitation of purchasers.[105] Issuers can take advantage of this provision so long as the materials or meetings offshore are in compliance with Rule 135e's safe harbor.[106]

§ 17.4[6] Multijurisdictional Disclosure System for Canadian Issuers

In 1991, the Commission adopted a multijurisdictional disclosure system (MJDS) to facilitate registration and reporting of qualifying securities of Canadian issuers.[125] In adopting the MJDS, four registration forms were added. 1933 Act registration Form F–7 is available to an issuer organized in

20. Bersch v. Drexel Firestone, Inc., 519 F.2d 974, 993 (2d Cir.1975), *cert. denied*, 423 U.S. 1018, 96 S.Ct. 453, 46 L.Ed.2d 389 (1975).

74. 17 C.F.R. § 240.12g3–2(c). *Cf.* SEC v. Great Lakes Equities Co., 1990 WL 260587 at *18, Fed.Sec.L.Rep. ¶ 95,685 (E.D.Mich.1990) (noting that Rule 12g3–2(b) is an exemption under the 1934 Exchange Act and not the 1933 Securities Act).

103. Regulation D, Preliminary Note 7, 17 C.F.R. § 230.501, relying on Sec.Act Rel. No. 33–4708 (July 9, 1964). *See also* § 4.19 *supra.*

104. Regulation D, Preliminary Note 7, 17 C.F.R. § 230.501. *Cf.* G.T. Global Financial Services, Inc., 20 Sec.Reg. & L.Rep. (BNA) 1820 (SEC No Action Letter avail. Aug. 2, 1988).

105. Rule 502(c)(2), 17 C.F.R. § 230.502(c)(2).

106. Rule 502(c)(2), 17 C.F.R. § 230.502(c)(2). *See* 17 C.F.R. § 230.135e.

125. Multijurisdictional Disclosure and Modifications to the Current Registration and Reporting System for Canadian Issuers, Sec. Act Rel. No. 33–6902, Sec.Exch.Act Rel. No. 33–6902, Inv. Co. Act Rel. No. IC—18210, International Series Rel. No. IS—291, 56 Fed. Reg. 30036, 49 S.E.C. Docket 260, 1991 WL 285685, [1991 Transfer Binder] Fed.Sec.L.Rep. (CCH) ¶ 84,812 (SEC June 21, 1991).

Canada, which is either a foreign private issuer or a Crown corporation, provided that the issuer has a class of securities listed on either the Toronto Stock Exchange, Montreal Exchange, or Senior Board of the Vancouver Stock Exchange. The required disclosures under Form F–7 consist of those disclosures that are required by the home jurisdiction to be delivered to shareholders. Form F–8 is also available to issuers qualifying for Form F–7 for mergers and other reorganization transactions. Form F–9 is designed for investment grade debt or preferred securities. Form F–10 is available to qualifying issuers for registration of any class of securities, provided that certain conditions are met. Issuers must satisfy five conditions in order to qualify for use of Form F–10.

When the Commission embarked on the Multijurisdictional Disclosure System, it was the Commission's intent to pursue similar arrangements with countries other than Canada. However, the SEC appears to have abandoned that original plan.[128] Recognizing that the Canadian securities laws bear a particular similarity to the United States law, it would appear more difficult to work out comparable agreements with other countries.

128. SEC to Tighten Reg S, Could Take Enforcement Action, Roberts Says, 26 Sec. Reg. & L. Rep. (BNA) 1387 (Oct. 21, 1994); Remarks of Commissioner Roberts as reported in CCH Fed. Sec. L. Rep. Rep. Bulletin No. 1602, p.8 (March 30, 1994).

Chapter 19

DEBT SECURITIES AND PROTECTION OF BONDHOLDERS—THE TRUST INDENTURE ACT OF 1939

Table of Sections

---

§ 19.1 Introduction to the Trust Indenture Act of 1939

Corporations, like other forms of business, frequently raise capital through debt financing. Debt represents borrowed capital that must be repaid. In essence, bonds or debentures are promissory notes, but contain more elaborate provisions than ordinary commercial loans. Corporate debentures are generally long-term obligations, but in times of fluctuating interest rates, shorter-term instruments are not uncommon. In order to borrow funds from a large number of investors, corporations and other public issuers contract with a third party to administer a bond issue. This third party acts as the indenture trustee.

There are two parts to every bond issue; there is the trust indenture (the counterpart of the loan agreement) and the separate bonds (the counterpart of the promissory note). The trust indenture has two distinct parts. The first part of the indenture sets forth all the obligations and restrictions on the bonds' issuer; the second part not only sets forth the bondholders' rights on default of the conditions set forth in the first part, but also, by tracking the standards embodied in the Trust Indenture Act of 1939, sets forth the relationship between the indenture trustee and the bondholders. The trust indenture, also contains provisions related to amendment of the indenture, as well as protection of any conversion privilege.

The contract, or "indenture," identifies the rights of all parties concerned, as well as the duties of the trustee (a third-party administrator), the obligations of the borrower, and the remedies available to the investors ("indenture securities holders").[3]

The Trust Indenture Act of 1939[18] was enacted to protect "the national public interest and the interest of investors."[19] The necessity for federal legislation became apparent after years of judicial conflict over the duties of trustees to bondholders[20] and the lack of financial protection afforded even secured bondholders in the chaos that followed the 1929 stock market crash.[21] Exculpatory clauses were included in most indentures and rendered bondholders impotent to hold trustees liable even in those instances in which the trustee's acts or omissions directly resulted in an injury.[22] In addition to the federal consequences, there is authority to the effect that a failure to comply with Trust Indenture Act's registration and reporting requirements constitutes a breach of the indenture as a matter of state law.[24]

Unlike the Securities Act of 1933 and the Exchange Act of 1934 which are generally limited to disclosure issues, the Trust Indenture Act goes beyond disclosure and imposes regulation over the substance of corporate and other private debt securities. The Act lists six separate instances wherein a public offering of private debt securities could prove harmful to investor interests: (1) when the obligor fails to provide a trustee; (2) when the trustee is without adequate rights, powers, or duties to protect and enforce the rights of investors; (3) when the trustee is without adequate resources to fulfill its duties; (4) when the flow of information from obligor to trustee is inadequate; (5) when the indenture contains misleading provisions; and (6) when the obligor prepares the indenture without investor participation or understanding.[25] The Act addresses these problems.

§ 19.2 Operation of the Trust Indenture Act of 1939; Exemptions

The Trust Indenture Act of 1939 focuses primarily upon the terms of the indenture as the means to its end of bondholder protection.[1] In the absence of the Act's coverage, rights and obligations under the indenture would be purely a matter of state law. The Trust Indenture Act applies to notes, bonds, debentures, and other evidences of indebtedness, whether or not secured, and

§ 19.1

3. *See* 15 U.S.C.A. § 77ccc(7). Substantive rights are thus governed by the indenture and the requirements of the Trust Indenture Act. In this regard, the Act differs significantly for the vast majority of federal securities laws which are generally limited to disclosure concerns. Thus, for example, by way of contrast, 1934 Act SEC Rule 10b–5 imposes disclosure obligations, it does not affect the issuer's obligations under the terms of the indenture.

18. Act of August 3, 1939, 53 Stat. 1149, codified in 15 U.S.C.A. §§ 77aaa *et seq.*

19. 15 U.S.C.A. § 77bbb(a).

20. *See, e.g.,* Sturges v. Knapp, 31 Vt. 1, 58 (1858).

21. SEC Report on the Study and Investigation of the Work, Activities, Personnel and Functions of Protective and Reorganization Committees, pt. VI Trustees Under Indentures (1936).

22. *See, e.g.,* 2 Louis Loss, Securities Regulation 719–725 (2d ed. 1961).

24. Bank of New York v. BearingPoint, Inc., 13 Misc.3d 1209(A), 824 N.Y.S.2d 752 (2006). *See also, e.g.,* AG Capital Funding Partners, L.P. v. State Street Bank and Trust Co., 896 N.E.2d 61, 11 N.Y.3d 146 (N.Y. 2008).

25. 15 U.S.C.A. § 77bbb.

§ 19.2

1. The background and purpose of the Act is considered in § 19.1 *supra.*

to all certificates representing such an interest.[2] Most of these securities, when issued, are also subject to registration under the Securities Act of 1933.[3] Thus, there is an interrelationship between the disclosure provisions of the 1933 Act and the more substantive regulation of the Trust Indenture Act. For example, if there is noncompliance with the provisions of the Trust Indenture Act, the SEC may refuse to permit the issuer's 1933 Act registration statement to become effective.[4] Once issued, the bonds are also subject to regulation under the Securities Exchange Act of 1934. Thus, 1934 Act and self regulatory rules contain rules and disclosure requirements that supplement the provisions of the Trust Indenture Act.

In 1990, Congress enacted comprehensive amendments to the Trust Indenture Act.[6] The revisions were designed to modernize the Act and to make it more efficient in light of current market conditions and industry practices.[7] Among other things, the 1990 amendments eliminated the requirement of certain boilerplate language in the trust agreements which serve only to increase administrative costs without providing additional investor protection.[8] Additionally, debenture holders will receive statutory protection notwithstanding contrary language in the indenture.

Exemptions From the Act's Coverage

Section 304 of the Trust Indenture Act exempts from its coverage a number of debt securities that would otherwise fall within the Act's purview.[9] Section 304(a)(9) of the Act[10] exempts securities issued under an indenture where the aggregate amount of debt within a thirty-six month period does not exceed ten million dollars unless the Commission prescribes a lower dollar ceiling. The Commission has exercised this rulemaking authority, to lower the ceiling, in Rule 4a–2.[11] Rule 4a–2 exempts securities issued pursuant to an indenture limiting the aggregate principal outstanding indebtedness to five million dollars and provided further that for thirty-six consecutive months the issuer has not had outstanding securities with more than five million dollars in aggregate principal indebtedness. Also exempted are most securities exempted from 1933 Act registration;[12] these include securities issued or guaranteed by the federal government (or any state or foreign government), church plans, companies or accounts that are excluded from the definition of an investment company under section 3(c)(14) of the Investment Company Act of 1940, notes with a maturity date less than nine months from the date of issuance, bonds issued by non-profit organizations, any indebtedness of a

---

2. 15 U.S.C.A. § 77ddd(a)(1). *See also,* AG Capital Funding Partners, L.P. v. State Street Bank and Trust Co., 896 N.E.2d 61, 11 N.Y.3d 146 (N.Y. 2008) (quoting this treatise).

3. 15 U.S.C.A. §§ 77a–77bbb. *See* § 19.1 and chapters 1–7 *supra.*

4. 15 U.S.C.A. § 77eee(b).

6. Pub. L. 101–550, 101st Cong. 2d Sess. *See* Fed.Sec.L.Rep. (CCH) Report Bulletin no. 1420 (Nov. 7, 1990).

7. Senate Report (Banking, Finance and Urban Affairs Committee) No. 101–155 Oct. 2, 1989 (To accompany S.1712) at 29.

8. Senate Report (Banking, Finance and Urban Affairs Committee) No. 101–155 Oct. 2, 1989 (To accompany S.1712) at 29.

9. 15 U.S.CA. § 77ddd.

10. 15 U.S.C.A. § 77ddd(a)(9). *Compare* section 4(a)(8)'s limited exemption for securities not issued under an indenture. *See* 17 C.F.R. §§ 260.0–7, 260.4a–2.

11. 17 C.F.R. § 260.4a–2, referring to Regulation A, which is discussed in § 4.17 *supra.*

12. 15 U.S.C.A. §§ 77c(a)(2), (3), (4), (5), (6), (7), (8), (11). *See* chapter 4 *supra.*

savings and loan association due to bonds issued, common carrier certificates, securities offered only within a particular state, securities issued by a trustee in bankruptcy, and commercial paper.[13]

Also exempt from the Trust Indenture Act are certificates of interest or participation in more than one security where the pooled securities have "substantially different rights and privileges."[14] Debt securities that were issued prior to six months after the Act's effective date are exempt, but the exemption does not apply to any new offering of such securities.[15] Debt securities issued under a mortgage insured under the National Housing Act[16] are exempt from the Trust Indenture Act.[17] Debt securities issued by foreign governments or their agencies, departments, subdivisions, or instrumentalities are also exempt.[18] The Act further provides an exemption for guarantees of any of the above securities exempted by section 304(a).[19]

A further exemption is provided in section 304(a)(8) of the Trust Indenture Act[22] for debt securities that are not issued under an indenture, provided that the aggregate offering of any such securities within a twelve-month period does not exceed the dollar limit established by section 3(b) of the 1933 Act[23] (which currently is five million dollars), unless the SEC sets a lower ceiling. The Commission formerly had lowered the limit in Rule 4a–1[24] so that the exemption applied only if during a period of twelve consecutive months the issuer had not had more than two million dollars aggregate principal amount of *any* securities of that issuer, but in 1992, the ceiling was raised to five million dollars.

In 1990, Congress expanded the Commission's exemptive authority under the Act. Section 304(d) of the Act now empowers the Commission to exempt from all or part of the Act any person, registration statement, indenture, security, or transaction from the Act to the extent that the exemption is "necessary or appropriate in the public interest and consistent with the protection of investors and the purposes fairly intended" by the Act.,[25] The SEC is further specifically permitted to exercise its discretion to refuse to consider an application for such an exemption.[26] SEC Rule 4d–7 sets forth the technical requirements with regard to filing an application for an exemption pursuant to section 304(d).[27] The application to the Commission requesting the exemption must contain the name, address, and telephone number of each applicant and each other person to whom questions concerning the application

13. 15 U.S.C.A. § 77ddd(a)(4). *See* 17 C.F.R. §§ 260.0–7, 260.4a–2.

14. 15 U.S.C.A. § 77ddd(a)(2). Also included in the exemption are temporary certificates of the same type.

15. 15 U.S.C.A. § 77ddd(a)(3). *See* 15 U.S.C.A. § 77ddd(c).

16. 12 U.S.C.A. §§ 1701 *et seq.*

17. 15 U.S.C.A. § 77ddd(a)(5), (a)(10).

18. 15 U.S.C.A. § 77ddd(a)(6).

19. 15 U.S.C.A. § 77ddd(a)(7).

22. 15 U.S.C.A. § 77ddd(a)(8). *Compare* section 304(a)(9)'s exemption for securities issued under an indenture provided that the aggregate principal indebtedness does not exceed five million dollars within thirty-six consecutive months, as provided in Rule 4a–2.

23. 15 U.S.C.A. § 77c(b). *See* § 4.16 *supra.*

24. 17 C.F.R. § 260.4a–1.

25. 15 U.S.C.A. § 78ddd(d).

26. 15 U.S.C.A. § 78ddd(d).

27. 17 C.F.R. § 260.4d–7.

should be directed.[28] In addition to stating the relevant facts, the application must contain a justification for the requested exemption as well as a statement of any benefits that could be expected to accrue as a result thereof to security holders, trustees, and/or obligors.[29]

In addition to the foregoing exclusions from the Trust Indenture Act of 1939, all of the transaction exemptions found in section 4 of the 1933 Act apply as well to registration under sections 305 and 306 of the Trust Indenture Act.[30] These transaction exemptions are: (1) transactions by a person other than an issuer, underwriter or dealer,[31] (2) transactions not involving a public offering,[32] (3) certain transactions by dealers,[33] (4) unsolicited brokers transactions,[34] (5) transactions involving certain real estate mortgage notes,[35] and (6) transactions involving accredited investors,[36] as defined in section 2(a)(15) of the 1933 Act.[37]

In addition, the SEC may, on application from the issuer and after a hearing, exempt debt securities issued by private foreign issuers.[38] Also, the Commission may by rule exempt securities issued by a small business investment company pursuant to the Small Business

§ 19.3 Qualification Under the Trust Indenture Act

Debt securities that are not exempt from the Trust Indenture Act by virtue of section 304,[1] whether or not also subject to the 1933 Act, must be "qualified" under the Trust Indenture Act before they may be offered for public sale.[2] In order to be so qualified under the Act, issuers must disclose, to the SEC through an application for qualification[3] and to investors through a prospectus,[4] the following information:

(1) whether the proposed trustee is eligible to serve as such;

(2) whether the trustee has a conflict of interest;[5]

---

28. 17 C.F.R. § 260.4d–8.

29. 17 C.F.R. § 260.4d–8.

30. 15 U.S.C.A. § 77ddd(b). *See* 15 U.S.C.A. §§ 77eee, 77fff.

31. 15 U.S.C.A. § 77d(1). *See* § 4.26 *supra.*

32. 15 U.S.C.A. § 77d(2). *See* 4.24 *supra.* The fact that there are only a limited number of lenders may preclude a finding that a public offering has taken place. The fact that a trustee is not covered by the 1939 Act does not affect the applicability of state law relating to indenture trustees. *See, e.g.,* In re E.F. Hutton Southwest Properties II, Ltd., 953 F.2d 963 (5th Cir.1992) (New York law characterized the trustee as an indenture trustee notwithstanding absence of a public offering; but further holding that trustee's reliance on counsel precluded a finding of liability for negligence).

33. 15 U.S.C.A. § 77d(3). *See* § 4.31 *supra.*

34. 15 U.S.C.A. § 77d(4). *See* § 4.26 *supra.*

35. 15 U.S.C.A § 77d(5). *See* § 4.32 *supra.*

36. 15 U.S.C.A. § 77d(6). *See* § 4.23 *supra.*

37. 15 U.S.C.A. § 77b(a)(15).

38. 15 U.S.C.A. § 77ddd(d). Private foreign issuers are discussed in § 17.4 *supra.*

§ 19.3

1. 15 U.S.C.A. § 77ddd. *See* § 19.2 *supra.*

2. 15 U.S.C.A. §§ 77eee–77ggg.

3. 15 U.S.C.A. § 77ggg.

4. 15 U.S.C.A. § 77fff(b) & (c).

5. As defined in 15 U.S.C.A. § 77jjj(b), discussed in § 19.4 *infra.*

(3) what will constitute a default under the indenture and under which circumstances the trustee may withhold information of such default from bondholders;

(4) the method of authentication and delivery of indenture securities and how their proceeds will be applied;

(5) provisions defining when the release or release and substitution of any property subject to the lien of indenture will be allowed;

(6) how satisfaction and discharge of the indenture will occur; and

(7) the evidence an obligor will be required to furnish in order to remain in compliance with the indenture's conditions and covenants.[6]

§ 19.4 Trustee Qualifications

Conflicts of Interest

The role of the trustee under the Act's provisions is perhaps its most controversial aspect. A qualified indenture must provide for one or more trustees, at least one of which is a corporation that is organized under the laws of the United States, or any single U.S. state, and further has a minimum combined capitalization and surplus of one hundred and fifty thousand dollars.[2] The Act further specifies that trustees may not have conflicting interests with those of indenture securities holders.[3] The statute enumerates a number of conflict of interest situations that preclude qualification of the trustee under the Trust Indenture Act. As noted below, the conflict does not arise until the bond is in default and thus does not disqualify trustees at the time that the obligations are created. The conflicting interest situations that operate to disqualify a trustee are those where:

(1) the trustees serve as trustee under other indentures of the obligor;

(2) the trustees, or any of their officers or directors, are the obligors or an underwriter for the obligor;

(3) the trustees control or are controlled by the obligor or its underwriter;

(4) the trustees, or their officers or directors, are directors or officers of the obligor or its underwriter, except that if there are more than nine directors, one may overlap;

(5) the obligor, or any of its officers or directors, beneficially owns ten percent of the trustee's voting securities, or twenty percent of such securities are owned by two such persons;

(6) the trustees beneficially own five percent of the obligor's voting securities or ten percent of any other class of securities of the obligor or the obligor's underwriter;

(7) the trustees beneficially own five percent or more of the voting securities of persons controlling or controlled by obligors or persons owning ten percent or more of the obligor's voting securities;

---

6. 15 U.S.C.A. § 77eee(a).

§ 19.4

2. 15 U.S.C.A. § 77jjj(a). Corporations serving as trustees are known as institutional trustees. *Id.* § 77jjj(a)(1).

3. 15 U.S.C.A. § 77jjj(b).

(8) the trustees beneficially own ten percent or more of any class of securities of any person who, to the trustee's knowledge, owns fifty percent or more of the obligor's voting securities; or

(9) the trustees own an aggregate of twenty-five percent or more of any class of securities in a representative capacity where beneficial ownership would constitute a conflict of interest under (6), (7), or (8) above.

Once a trustee finds that it is in a conflict of interest situation, the trustee must eliminate the conflict within ninety days or resign.[7] The trustee's resignation under these circumstances is to be effective upon the appointment of a successor.[8] If the trustee does not resign in the face of a statutorily defined conflict of interest, the trustee must notify indenture security holders within ten days of the expiration of the ninety-day period.[9] Upon such notification, "any security holder who has been a bona fide holder of indenture securities for at least six months may, on behalf of himself and all others so situated, petition any court of competent jurisdiction for the removal of such trustee, and the appointment of a successor if such trustee fails, after a written request therefore by such holder, to [eliminate the conflict of interest or resign]."[10]

The Trust Indenture Reform Act of 1990[11] amended section 310(b) to provide that a trustee's conflict of interest does not arise until there has been a default under the indenture.[12] The Act thus permits the trustee with a conflict of interest to apply to the SEC, within ninety-days of certain defaults, for permission to continue to serve as trustee.[13] This application for permission to remain a trustee beyond the ninety-day period may be made for defaults not involving principal, interest, or sinking fund payments. This application will be granted if, after an opportunity for a hearing, the applicant has demonstrated that (1) the default may be cured or waived in accordance with procedures described in the application, and (2) a stay of the duty to resign is not inconsistent with the interests of indenture security holders.[14] The contents of and procedures for such an application to the Commission are set forth in Rules 10b–4, 10b–5, and 10b–6.[15]

Trustees Who Are Also Creditors of the Issuer (Obligor)

Banks frequently serve as trustees under the Act. These banks also may be creditors of the issuer, but this relationship does not result in a per se

7. 15 U.S.C.A. § 77jjj(b)(1)(i).

8. 15 U.S.C.A. § 77jjj(b)(1)(i).

9. 15 U.S.C.A. § 77jjj(b)(1)(iii).

10. 15 U.S.C.A. § 77jjj(b)(1)(iii).

11. Pub.L. 101–550, 101st Cong. 2d Sess.

12. 15 U.S.C.A. § 77jjj(b).

13. 15 U.S.C.A. § 77jjj(b).

14. 15 U.S.C.A. § 77jjj(b).

15. Rule 10b–4 sets forth the technical filing requirements. Rule 10b–5 sets forth the contents of the application, including a statement of reasons why the exemption should be granted. Rule 10b–6 specifies the notice required and directs that the application contain a draft notice that will appear in the Federal Register and a notice for interested persons to appear to be heard. 17 C.F.R. §§ 260.10b–4—260.10b–6. Notice of applications for a stay will appear in the Federal Register. Also, the filing of an application automatically stays the duty to resign pending the Commission's decision. 15 U.S.C.A. § 77jjj(b).

disqualification under the Trust Indenture Act. The Trust Indenture Act does not consider the trustee to have a conflict of interest with bondholders substantial enough for disqualification simply because the trustee is also a creditor of the obligor.[16] This view may seem surprising since, according to the SEC, "however honest or conscientious a trustee may be, if it occupies a creditor position competitive with that of its beneficiaries, self-interest may lead to violations of fiduciary obligations."[17] The conflict of interest nevertheless is allowed in recognition of the economic realities governing the corporate and banking worlds wherein the most likely source of credit to a troubled obligor would be the institutional indenture trustee since it is already familiar with the obligor's business.[18] However, the Trust Indenture Act creates certain safeguards in order to reduce the potential abuse of debt collection by trustee creditors where an obligor has economic problems and its default or demise may be imminent. Section 311(a) of the Act[19] does not allow a trustee to retain any payment or property it receives as a creditor, whether secured or unsecured, within four months before, or any time subsequent to, a default on the issuer's obligation to the bondholders. The section contains disgorgement provisions to ensure that trustees do not receive "a greater percentage of their claims as creditors (after deducting non-preferential collections) than the investors receive on the unsecured portions of their claims."[20] These disgorgement provisions do not apply in all instances where the trustee is also a creditor of the obligor as there are exclusions in certain limited situations.[21]

§ 19.5 Qualification of the Indenture; Required Provisions

In order to qualify under the Act, the trust indenture must contain certain required provisions.[1] In cases of conflict, the statute's mandatory provisions control.[2] In 1990, Congress enacted comprehensive amendments to the Trust Indenture Act.[3] Among other things, the 1990 amendments to the Trust Indenture Act legislation eliminated the requirement of certain boilerplate language in the trust agreements which served only to increase adminis-

16. *See* 15 U.S.C.A. § 77jjj(b) ("Corporate securities * * * shall not include any note or other evidence of indebtedness issued to evidence an obligation to repay moneys lent to a person by one or more banks, trust companies or banking firms").

17. SEC, Report on the Study and Investigation of the Work, Activities, Personnel and Functions of Protective and Reorganization Committees, pt. VI, Trustees Under Indentures at 88 (1936).

18. Hearings on H.R. 2191 & H.R. 5020 before a subcommittee of the committee on Interstate and Foreign Commerce, House of Representatives, 76th Congress, 1st session pp. 159–60, 170–71, 268–9 (1939).

19. 15 U.S.C.A. § 77kkk(a).

20. John P. Campbell & Robert Zack, Put a Bullet in the Poor Beast. His Leg is Broken and His Use is Past. Conflict of Interest in the Dual Role of Lender and Corporate Indenture Trustee: A Proposal to End It in the Public Interest, 32 Bus.Law. 1705, 1711 (1977).

21. 15 U.S.C.A. § 77kkk(b). Excepted from the provisions of this section are creditor relationships arising from (1) the ownership of securities whose maturity is more than a year, (2) authorized advances made for the purpose of preserving the security, (3) minor disbursements made as trustee, and (4) certain temporary credits arising out of sales of goods and transactions in "self liquidating" paper such as drafts and acceptances. Note, The Trust Indenture Act of 1939, 25 Cornell L.Q. 105, 109 (1939).

§ 19.5

1. 5 U.S.C.A. § 77fff(a), 77ggg.

2. 15 U.S.C.A. § 77aaaa.

3. Pub. L. 101–550, 101st Cong. 2d Sess. *See* Fed.Sec.L.Rep. (CCH) Report Bulletin no. 1420 (Nov. 7, 1990).

trative costs without providing additional investor protection.[4] Additionally, debenture holders will receive statutory protection notwithstanding contrary language in the indenture.

Unless the obligor defaults, the trustee's only liability is for failure to perform those duties enumerated in the indenture.[5] Also, the indenture may not relieve the trustee from liability "for its own negligent action, its own negligent failure to act, or its own willful misconduct."[6] The trustee may, in the absence of bad faith, conclusively rely upon the truth of statements and the correctness of opinions expressed to it pursuant to indenture provisions.[7] The indenture must contain provisions:

(1) requiring the obligor to furnish the trustee with the names and addresses of all indenture security holders[8],

(2) allowing the bondholders to communicate with one another[9];

(3) requiring the trustee to issue periodic reports to the investors as to its continued eligibility, advances made by it of trust property, conflicts of interest it may have with the indenture security holders in its creditor-of-obligor status, and release (or release and substitution) of property subject to lien of indenture, any additional unreported issue(s) of indenture securities, and any action (save certain types of default) materially affecting the indenture securities[10]; and

(4) requiring the obligor to file annual reports with the trustee of such information as the obligor must provide to the SEC pursuant to the 1934 Exchange Act.[11]

In addition, where additional bonds are to be issued or secured property is to be released or substituted, section 314[12] of the Act requires "elaborate" filings in connection with liens; these filings must be made by counsel, accountants, engineers, and appraisers who must generally be "independent" experts.[13]

§ 19.6 Duties of Trustee When the Issuer Defaults

The duties of the indenture trustee change considerably upon a default by the obligor.[1] Upon default, trustees must use "the same degree of care and skill in their exercise as a prudent man would exercise or use under the circumstances in the conduct of his own affairs" to prevent injury to the

---

4. *Id.*

5. 15 U.S.C.A. § 77*ooo*(a).

6. 15 U.S.C.A. § 77*ooo*(d).

7. 15 U.S.C.A. § 77*ooo*(a).

8. 15 U.S.C.A. § 77*lll*(a).

9. 15 U.S.C.A. § 77*lll*(b).

10. 15 U.S.C.A. § 77mmm(a)(1)–(7).

11. 15 U.S.C.A. § 77nnn(a).

12. 15 U.S.C.A. § 77nnn(a).

13. *See* Semi–Tech Litigation, LLC v. Bankers Trust Co., 353 F.Supp.2d 460, 473–479 (S.D.N.Y. 2005).

§ 19.6

1. Prior to default, the trustee's obligations are not as great. *See, e.g.,* 15 U.S.C.A. § 77*ooo* (a)(2) (permitting provision in indenture allowing trustee, prior to default, to conclusively rely on opinion of counsel); Cruden v. Bank of New York, 957 F.2d 961 (2d Cir.1992) (trustee's reliance on counsel was a defense to action by debenture holders).

bondholders' interests.[2] This "prudent man" standard of conduct is mitigated, however, by section 315(d)(2),[3] which absolves a trustee for errors made in good faith.

The term "default" is nowhere defined in the Act; presumably, its characteristics are instead left to the indenture provisions.[4] Generally, the trustee must notify the bondholders of a default.[5] The indenture may permit the trustee to withhold notice of known defaults not connected with defaults in principal, interest, or sinking fund payments.[6] In the event of default, a wide assortment of alternative actions are available to the trustee. The trustee has the power to accelerate the balance due if so authorized, or it might recover a judgment against the obligor, or it might sue to enforce the covenants of the indenture. The trustee, however must also determine whether immediate resort to litigation will best serve the interests of the bondholders. A complete liquidation and sale, which is often the end result of many remedial actions, may not only destroy the obligor's business, but may also destroy much of the value of the bondholders' security.[8] The Act empowers trustees to excuse defaults on interest payments for up to three years, provided they secure the consent of seventy-five percent of the indenture security holders.[9] Upon default, the trustee must institute foreclosure proceedings whenever a majority of the bondholders instructs the trustee to institute such proceedings.[10] The trustee is insulated from liability for such actions taken at the bondholder's demand.[11] In addition to the provisions relating to trustees, the Trust Indenture Act provides that the right of bondholders to payments due shall not be impaired except in accordance with the terms of the Act.[12]

Prior to the Trust Indenture Reform Act of 1990,[13] the Trust Indenture Act gave the trustee a ninety-day grace period after a conflict of interest arose to either resign or eliminate the conflict.[14] However, under the Act as amended, a conflict does not arise until there has been a default under the indenture.[15] The Act also permits the trustee with a conflict of interest to apply within ninety days of certain defaults for permission to continue to

---

2. 15 U.S.C.A. § 77*ooo* (c).

3. 15 U.S.C.A. § 77*ooo* (d)(2).

4. *See, e.g.,* Upic & Co. v Kinder–Care Learning Centers, Inc., 793 F.Supp. 448 (S.D.N.Y. 1992).

5. 15 U.S.C.A. § 77*ooo* (b). Although the Act speaks in terms of the duty to give notice of "of all defaults known to the Trustee," is not limited to actual knowledge. Where the trustee has a statutory duty to examine the certificates of the indenture, ignorance of the contents of those certificates will not excuse a failure to give notice of default. *See, e.g.,* In re Bankers Trust Co., 450 F.3d 121 (2d Cir. 2006) (trustee failed to give notice of default; failure to examine the relevant documents does not relieve the trustee of the duty to give notice); Trust Indenture Act of 1939, § 315(b).

6. 15 U.S.C.A. § 77*ooo* (b).

8. *See* Henry F. Johnson The "Forgotten" Securities Statute: Problems in the Trust Indenture Act, 13 U. Toledo L.Rev 92, 100–101 (1981).

9. 15 U.S.C.A. § 77ppp(a)(2).

10. 15 U.S.C.A. § 77ppp(a)(1).

11. 15 U.S.C.A. § 77*ooo*(d)(3).

12. Trust Indenture Act § 316(b), 15 U.S.C.A. 77ppp(b).

13. Pub.L. 101–550, 101st Cong. 2d Sess.

14. 15 U.S.C.A. § 77jjj(b) (1982).

15. 15 U.S.C.A. § 77jjj(b).

serve as trustee.[16] The application for permission to remain a trustee beyond the ninety-day period may be made for defaults not involving principal, interest, or sinking fund payments. The Commission is directed to grant such an application if, after an opportunity for a hearing, the applicant has demonstrated that (1) the default may be cured or waived in accordance with procedures described in the application, and (2) a stay of the duty to resign is not inconsistent with the interests of indenture security holders.[17] The procedures for such an application are set forth in Rules 10b–4, 10b–5, and 10b–6.[18] Notices of applications for a stay will appear in the Federal Register. Also, the filing of an application automatically stays the duty to resign pending the Commission's decision.[19]

§ 19.7 Enforcement of the Act; Remedies for Trustees' Breaches of Duties

Enforcement of the trustee's pre-default duties is qualified by the leeway in allowing reasonable reliance by the trustee upon third parties' representations.[1] Indeed, it has been held that no fiduciary obligations in this regard are imposed on the trustee by federal law beyond those stipulated in the trust indenture.[2] A 1975 district court decision gave the bondholders a civil cause of action to enforce a trustee's liability for willful misconduct in violation of a qualified indenture's provisions.[3] The court noted that the SEC is without power to enforce the provisions of an already registered indenture,[4] and the Commission's only affirmative powers lie in the qualification of indentures and the filing of required reports.[5] The court then reasoned that since section 315(e)[6] provides for the awarding of the costs entailed in a suit to enforce the rights and remedies available under an indenture, "[t]he existence of a private right of action follows, * * * [as] Congress expressly anticipated that any liability indirectly imposed would be enforced by private civil actions, and specifically excluded the commission from an enforcement role."[7]

In 1990, Congress enacted comprehensive amendments to the Trust Indenture Act[8] that were designed to simplify compliance but, at the same

16. 15 U.S.C.A. § 77jjj(b).

17. 15 U.S.C.A. § 77jjj(b).

18. Rule 10b–4 sets forth the technical filing requirements; Rule 10b–5 sets forth the contents of the application, including a statement of reasons why the exemption should be granted; Rule 10b–6 specifies the notice required and provides that the application should contain a draft notice that will appear in the Federal Register and a notice for interested persons to appear to be heard. 17 C.F.R. §§ 260.10b–4 through 260–10b–6.

19. 15 U.S.C.A. § 77jjj(b).

§ 19.7

1. Caplin v. Marine Midland Grace Trust Co., 406 U.S. 416, 92 S.Ct. 1678, 32 L.Ed.2d 195 (1972) (failure to ascertain certain facts does not create trustee liability where trustee relied upon statutorily sanctioned certificates and opinions).

2. Browning Debenture Holders' Committee v. DASA Corp., 431 F.Supp. 959 (S.D.N.Y.1976), *affirmed in part* 560 F.2d 1078 (2d Cir.1977).

3. Morris v. Cantor, 390 F.Supp. 817 (S.D.N.Y.1975).

4. 15 U.S.C.A. § 77iii(e).

5. 15 U.S.C.A. §§ 77sss–77uuu.

6. 15 U.S.C.A. §§ 77*ooo*(e).

7. 390 F.Supp. at 822.

8. Pub.L. 101–550, 101st Cong., 2d Sess. *See* Fed.Sec.L.Rep. (CCH) Report Bulletin no. 1420 (Nov. 7, 1990).

time, not dilute the rights of bondholders. Among other things, the 1990 amendments to the Act provided that debenture holders will receive statutory protection notwithstanding contrary language in the indenture.

The only express civil liability imposed by the Trust Indenture Act is found in section 323(a) and covers material misstatements and omissions in any report filed with the SEC pursuant to the Act's filing requirements.[9] Reliance by the plaintiff is a precondition to a finding of liability.[10] Additionally, as is the case with section 18(a) of the Exchange Act,[11] section 323 liability does not attach if the defendant can prove that he or she acted in good faith and without knowledge of the materially misleading defects.[12] The section 323 claim must be brought within one year of discovery of the violation, but in no event will an action lie more than three years after the violation.[13]

Although section 323(a) presents a narrow remedy, it should be kept in mind that section 323(b)[14] expressly provides for the availability of cumulative remedies under the Securities Act of 1933,[15] the Securities Exchange Act of 1934,[16] the former Public Utility Holding Act of 1935,[17] and any remedy at law or in equity.[18] Section 323(b) of the Act has been held not to "preclude the imposition of *state* fiduciary duties on indenture trustees."[19] While there are no trustee duties under federal law beyond those stipulated in the indenture,[20] it has been held that state common law protections afforded indenture security holders should *not* be limited by the Trust Indenture Act.[21] This may be viewed as somewhat inconsistent, however, with section 315(a)'s[22] language allowing the trustee's liability to be limited to that which is specifically set out in the indenture.[23]

§ 19.8 Overview of the Trust Indenture Act's Registration and Disclosure Requirements

In addition to the indenture and trustee qualifications that are discussed above, the Trust Indenture Act imposes various informational and disclosure requirements. Section 305[1] requires disclosure in the registration statement and prospectus of information relating to the trustee's qualification and

9. 15 U.S.C.A. § 77www.

10. In re Nucorp Energy Securities Litigation, 772 F.2d 1486 (9th Cir.1985).

11. 15 U.S.C.A. § 78r(a). *See* § 12.18 *supra.*

12. 215 U.S.C.A. § 77www(a).

13. *Id.*

14. 15 U.S.C.A. § 77www(b).

15. 15 U.S.C.A. §§ 77a–77bbb. *See* §§ 7.1–7.9 *supra.*

16. 15 U.S.C.A. §§ 78a *et seq. See* chapters 12–13 *supra.*

17. 15 U.S.C.A. §§ 79a *et seq.* (2004). *See* chapter 18 *supra.* The Public Utility Holding Company Act was repealed in 2005

18. 15 U.S.C.A. § 77www(b).

19. Broad v. Rockwell International Corp., 614 F.2d 418 (5th Cir.1980), *on rehearing*, 642 F.2d 929 (5th Cir.1981) (emphasis added).

20. 15 U.S.C.A. § 77*ooo*(d).

21. Broad v. Rockwell International Corp., 614 F.2d 418, 432 (5th Cir.1980).

22. 15 U.S.C.A. § 77*ooo* (a).

23. *See* Semi–Tech Litigation, LLC v. Bankers Trust Co., 353 F.Supp.2d 460, 470 (S.D.N.Y. 2005).

§ 19.8

1. 15 U.S.C.A. § 77eee.

provisions in the indenture. With regard to debt securities being offered but not registered under the 1933 Act, unless exempt by virtue of section 304,[2] section 306[3] provides that the securities cannot be sold unless the indenture has been qualified. Although not expressly limited, section 306, as explained by the legislative history and SEC, applies to debt securities issued in a reorganization or exchange with existing securities holders even though those securities are exempted from the 1933 Act by virtue of sections 3(a)(9)[4] or 3(a)(10)[5] of that Act.[6]

Section 308 of the Trust Indenture Act[7] provides for integration of the informational requirements with those of the 1933 and 1934 Acts, as well as with the Public Utility Holding Company Act of 1935[8] which was repealed in 2004. This integration of the Trust Indenture Act with the other federal securities laws is facilitated in Trust Indenture Act filings by permitting incorporation by reference to filings under the other acts.[9]

Section 312(a)[10] of the Trust Indenture Act requires that a qualified indenture provide that the trustee receive a list of current bondholders' names and addresses at regular intervals of not more than six months. A trustee must also be able to obtain a current list at any other time in response to a written request.[11] Analogous to the 1934 Act's proxy rules' right of access to other security holders,[12] the Trust Indenture Act confers similar rights. The indenture must provide that upon receiving a written request from three or more indenture security holders, the trustee must make available to them a current list or mail information to the other security holders.[13] However, the trustee need comply with such a request only when at least three requesting security holders have been owners for six months.[14] Also, the communication must relate either to proxy solicitations or security holders' rights under the indenture.

---

2. 15 U.S.C.A. § 77ddd. *See* § 19.2 *supra.*

3. 15 U.S.C.A. § 77fff.

4. 15 U.S.C.A. § 77c(a)(9) (securities exchanged exclusively with security holders). *See* § 4.10 *supra.*

5. 15 U.S.C.A. § 77c(a)(10) (securities issued under judicially or administratively approved reorganizations). *See* § 4.11 *supra.*

6. *See* 4 Fed.Sec.L.Rep. (CCH) ¶ 42,240. Securities issued under other 1933 Act exemptions are exempt from the Trust Indenture Act by virtue of section 304(a)(4), 15 U.S.C.A. § 77ddd(a)(4). *Cf.* Trust Ind. Act Rel. No. 39–30 (Aug. 18, 1944) (dealing with securities issued under chapter X of the federal Bankruptcy Act).

7. 15 U.S.C.A. § 77hhh.

8. The former Public Utility Holding Company Act is discussed in chapter 15 *supra.*

9. 15 U.S.C.A. § 77hhh(a).

10. 15 U.S.C.A. § 77*lll*(a).

11. 15 U.S.C.A. § 77*lll*(a).

12. 17 C.F.R. § 240.14a–7. *See* § 11.7 *supra.*

13. 15 U.S.C.A. § 77*lll*(b).Following the pattern of 1934 Act proxy Rule 14a–7, the trustee has the option of providing the list or mailing the communications at the expense of the requesting security holders.

14. 15 U.S.C.A. § 77*lll*(b).

Chapter 20

FEDERAL REGULATION OF INVESTMENT COMPANIES— THE INVESTMENT COMPANY ACT OF 1940

Table of Sections

§ 20.1 The Investment Company Act of 1940: Background and Scope

The Investment Company Act of 1940[1] was enacted to protect investors entrusting their savings to others for expert management and diversification of investments which would not be available to them as individuals. The most common type of investment company is the mutual fund.[3] Investors wanting to invest in a mutual fund or investment company have relatively little protection under state law. State corporate law does not provide safeguards to the public, such as independent boards of directors and a separate investment advisor, which are among the requirements imposed by the Investment Company Act. Investment company assets most often consist of cash, securities which generally are liquid, mobile, and readily negotiable, and in some

§ 20.1

1. Act of Aug. 22, 1940, 54 Stat. 789, codified in 15 U.S.C.A. §§ 80a–1 through 80a–52.

3. *See* Donald W. Glazer, A Study of Mutual Fund Complexes, 119 U.Pa.L.Rev. 205 (1970).

cases commodity futures and options. An entity such as a corporation that is formed to provide a pooling of investment funds to permit the entity to invest in securities (including securities options) ordinarily will be considered an investment company and, unless exempt, is subject to SEC regulation. Pooled investment funds where the investment objective focuses primarily on commodity-related investments (including futures and options) are known as commodity pools. Commodity Pool Operators (CPOs) are regulated by the Commodity Futures Trading Commission.[7]

Companies subject to the Investment Company Act are also governed by the Securities Act of 1933 and the Securities Exchange Act of 1934. In 1990, Congress enacted the Shareholder Communication Act, which extends the applicability of the proxy rules under the Securities Exchange Act of 1934 that apply to reporting companies generally to mutual funds and other investment companies that are registered under the Investment Company Act.[8]

Shortly after the enactment of the Sarbanes-Oxley Act,[11] the SEC proposed[12]—and subsequently adopted-[13]rules making it clear that the CEO's and CFO's certification requirements apply to most investment companies that are registered under the Investment Company Act of 1940.[14] Rule 30a–2 requires certifications by principal executive and principal financial officers of investment companies that are subject to the 1934 Act reporting requirements,[15] but that file semi-annual reports on Form N–SAR[16] in lieu of the 10–Q quarterly reports and 10–K annual report required for other 1934 Act reporting companies. At the same time that it adopted Rule 30a–2, the SEC proposed a new Form N–CSR to be used for certifying investment company act reports.

The highly liquid nature of investment company assets creates an increased risk of management abuse that is not present with ordinary manufacturing and other operating companies. This led Congress to believe that investment companies would be easy prey for management abuse in the absence of comprehensive federal regulation.[18]

The basic impact of the Investment Company Act is to require registration of non-exempt investment companies and to protect against money managers' conflicts of interest. Section 7 of the Act[29] bars an investment company from engaging in any form of interstate commerce when there has

7. 7 U.S.C.A. §§ 6m, 6o. *See generally* Philip M. Johnson & Thomas L. Hazen, Derivatives Regulation (2004). The jurisdiction of the SEC and CFTC is discussed in § 1.5 *supra.*

8. 15 U.S.C.A. § 78n(b). The proxy rules under the Exchange Act are discussed in chapter 10 *supra.*

11. Sarbanes-Oxley Act of 2002 sec. 906, Pub. Law 107–204 (July 30, 2002).

12. *See* Certification of Management Investment Company Shareholder Reports and Designation of Certified Shareholder Reports as Exchange Act Periodic Reporting Forms, Sec. Exch. Act Rel. No. 34–46441, 2002 WL 1997955 (SEC Aug. 30, 2002).

13. Certification of Management Investment Company Shareholder Reports and Designation of Certified Shareholder Reports as Exchange Act Periodic Reporting Forms Sec. Act Rel. No. 33–8124, Sec. Exch. Act Rel. No. 34–46427, Inv. Co. Act Rel. No. IC–25722, 67 Fed. Reg. 57298–01, 2002 WL 31004871 (SEC Sept. 9, 2002).adopting Investment Company Act Rule 30a–2, 17 C.F.R. § 270.30a–2.

14. *Id.*

15. 1934 Act §§ 13(a), 15(d), 15 U.S.C.A. § 78m(a), 78o(d). *See* § 9.3 *supra.*

16. 17 C.F.R. §§ 249.330, 274.101.

18. Sen.Rep. No. 1775, 76th Cong., 3d Sess. (1940).

29. 15 U.S.C.A. § 80a–7.

been a failure to register under the Act, unless there is an applicable exemption.[30] There are criminal sanctions for willful violations of the Act,[31] and contracts of unregistered investment companies are rendered unenforceable and thus courts will not order performance by third parties.[32] The Act also regulates the investment company's relationship with its investment advisers.[33]

Interlocking Ownership of Investment Company Shares—The Antipyramiding Provisions

Another Investment Company Act provision that deserves mention is the antipyramiding rules imposed by section 12(d)(1) of the Act.[37] The thrust of the Act is to prohibit control of one investment company by another investment company.

First, section 12(d)(1) prohibits an investment company from acquiring more than three percent of the total outstanding voting securities of another investment company.[39] Second, section 12(d)(1) also prohibits an investment company from acquiring shares of another investment company when the shares so acquired would have a value in excess of five percent of the acquiring company's assets.[40] Third, section 12(d)(1) of the Investment Company Act prohibits an investment company from acquiring shares of another investment company when the aggregate of all shares in all investment companies owned by the acquiring company when calculated after the acquisition would exceed ten percent of the acquiring company's assets.[41] The antipyramiding provisions apply to share ownership by investment companies, but cannot be extended to cover situations in which affiliated investment companies are controlled by the same investment adviser even though the investment adviser decides how to vote the fund's portfolio shares.[42] In addition to focusing on the acquiring company, section 12(d) makes it unlawful for any investment company, principal underwriter, or registered broker-dealer to knowingly sell or otherwise dispose of investment company shares when the result of the transaction would be to place the investment company acquiring the shares in violation of section 12(d)'s ownership limitations.[43] It has been held that violations of section 12(d)'s antipyramiding provisions will support an implied private right of action, at least for injunctive relief[44] but not all courts have agreed.[45] There are various provisions of the Act that are

30. *See, e.g.,* Europe & Overseas Commodity Traders v. Banque Paribas London, 147 F.3d 118 (2d Cir.1998) (section 7(d) did not apply to Bahamian investment company which had fewer than 100 United States shareholders).

31. 15 U.S.C.A. § 80a–48.

32. 15 U.S.C.A. § 80a–46.

33. *See* §§ 20.2, 20.9 *infra.*

37. 15 U.S.C.A. § 80a–12(d).

39. 15 U.S.C.A. § 80a–12(d)(1)(A)(i)

40. 15 U.S.C.A. § 80a–12(d)(1)(A)(ii).

41. 15 U.S.C.A. § 80a–12(d)(1)(A)(iii).

42. *See* meVC Draper Fisher Jurvetson Fund I, Inc. v. Millennium Partners, L.P., 260 F.Supp.2d 616 (S.D.N.Y. 2003).

43. 15 U.S.C.A. § 80a–12(d)(1)(B).

44. Bancroft Convertible Fund, Inc. v. Zico Investment Holdings, Inc., 825 F.2d 731 (3d Cir.1987) .

45. *See* meVC Draper Fisher Jurvetson Fund I, Inc. v. Millennium Partners, L.P., 260 F.Supp.2d 616 (S.D.N.Y. 2003).

designed not only to assure the independence of directors but also to protect investment company shareholders from conflict of interest transactions.

§ 20.2 The Relationship Between Investment Companies, Investment Advisers, and Underwriters

Functionally, an investment company has been described as "a shell, a pool of assets consisting of securities, belonging to the shareholders of the fund."[1] Investors depend upon prudent management of the investment company's securities holdings. In theory and in practice, decisions concerning where to put the investment company's funds are made by an investment adviser to the investment company's board of directors. The investment adviser has a contractual relationship with the investment company.

Frequently, the investment adviser (or a parent company that controls the adviser) is the investment company's founder, appointing its initial board of directors[3] and providing its initial capitalization.[4] Due to the potential for abuse of this close relationship between investment company and investment adviser, section 15 of the Investment Company Act requires a written contract between the two entities which, as discussed below, must be approved by the investment company shareholders.[5] The section also requires a written contract between investment companies and underwriters,[6] but these underwriting provisions are becoming less important in practice as more investment companies have become "no-load" and sell directly to the public.[7] The underwriting function remains significant, however, during the investment company's start-up period, when a maximum of twenty-five "responsible persons" must make firm commitments to buy at least an aggregate of one hundred thousand dollars worth of securities from the investment company before any securities may be issued by it.[8] The Act also prohibits an investment company from retaining a principal underwriter unless a majority of the investment company's board of directors are not considered interested persons of the underwriter.[9]

Section 15(a) of the Act requires that the contract between an investment company and an investment adviser be approved by a majority of the investment company's outstanding voting securities.[10] Section 15(a) appears to

---

§ 20.2

1. Zell v. InterCapital Income Securities, Inc., 675 F.2d 1041, 1046 (9th Cir.1982). *See* Leland E. Modesitt, Mutual Fund—A Corporate Anomaly, 14 U.C.L.A.L.Rev. 1252 (1967).

3. *See* 2 Tamar Frankel, The Regulation of Money Managers, 212–13 (1978).

4. The Act requires a minimum $100,000 initial capitalization. 15 U.S.C.A. § 80a–14(a).

5. 15 U.S.C.A. § 80a–15(a). When an investment company selects a new investment company adviser there can be a problem relating to the "sale" of the advisory contract. *See e.g.,* Rosenfeld v. Black, 445 F.2d 1337 (2d Cir.1971), *on remand* 336 F.Supp. 84 (S.D.N.Y.1972). *See* § 20.9 *infra.*

6. 15 U.S.C.A. § 80a–15(b).

7. *See, e.g.,* James H. Ellis, Going No Load, 6 Sec.Reg.L.J. 357 (1979).

8. 15 U.S.C.A. § 80a–14(a)(3).

9. Section 10(b)(2) of the Investment Company Act, 15 U.S.C.A. § 80a–10.

10. 15 U.S.C.A. § 80a–15(a). This requirement is largely negated regarding the investment company's initial advisory contract because the investment adviser generally controls the voting shares of a start-up investment company. For a discussion of shareholder voting on subsequent advisory contracts in connection with their assignment, *see* § 20.9 *infra.* Small advisory contracts are exempted from the shareholder approval requirement altogether if the proposed adviser is not an underwriter or affiliate of the investment company, its annual compensation does not exceed certain limits, and the aggregate amount paid by the single investment company to all such advisers does not exceed a certain limit. 17 C.F.R. § 270.15a–1.

vest the investment company's board of directors with a great deal of responsibility, authority, and discretion in deciding whether or not to renew the advisory contract. While the directors clearly have a large amount of responsibility,[12] their authority and discretion are rarely exercised. For example, it would generally not be practical for an investment company to terminate its advisory contract because of the dominant role generally played by the investment adviser. Functionally, it is the adviser which "selects the fund's investments and operates its business, providing [the investment company with] expertise, personnel, and office space."[13] For many investment companies, in essence, the adviser runs the investment company.[14] Directors act primarily as "watchdogs" over adviser activity and do so for the benefit of fund shareholders.[15] This is not always the case, however, as some investment companies have more of an arm's length relationship with the investment adviser.[16] This is especially true with regard to the relatively few investment companies having more than one investment adviser.[17]

In 2003, a number of mutual fund abuses came to light that resulted in the strengthening of the roles of independent fund directors. The improper practices that came to light in these scandals included market-timing and late trading issues,[18] breakpoint pricing of transaction fees, and other fee-related concerns.[20] Late trading, which is discussed more fully below,[21] occurs when traders take advantage of open-end mutual funds' forward pricing by trading on the basis of news and events made public *after* the price of the shares has been fixed, thus allowing the late traders to take advantage of virtually guaranteed price movements in the fund shares the next day. The concern over breakpoints for transaction fees addresses pricing practices that failed to provide customers with the cheapest transaction fee consistent with their investment objectives.

§ 20.3 The Definition of "Investment Company"; The Problem of the Inadvertent Investment Company

In relevant part, Section 3(a) of the Investment Company Act defines "investment company" to be any issuer which: "(1) is or holds itself out as being engaged primarily, or proposes to engage primarily, in the business of investing, reinvesting, or trading in securities . . ."[1] As was indicated in the

12. See authorities in §§ 20.6, 20.9, infra.

13. Zell v. InterCapital Income Securities, Inc., 675 F.2d 1041, 1046 (9th Cir.1982); Burks v. Lasker, 441 U.S. 471, 481, 99 S.Ct. 1831, 1838–1839, 60 L.Ed.2d 404 (1979).

14. Report of the Securities and Exchange Commission on the Public Policy Implications of Investment Company Growth, H.R.Rep. No. 2337, 89th Cong. 2d Sess. (1966).

15. *See* § 20.6 infra for a discussion of investment company directors' duties.

16. *See* Investment Company Governance, Inv. Co. Act Rel. No. IC–26520, 2004 WL 1672374 (SEC 2004).

17. Some investment companies have more than one adviser in order to achieve diversification with regard to portfolio management as well as to portfolio diversification. This multi-adviser structure is the exception rather than the rule.

18. *See, e.g.,* SEC Chairman Donaldson Releases Statement Regarding Initiatives to Combat Late Trading and Market Timing of Mutual Funds, http://www.sec.gov/news/press/2003–136.htm (Oct. 9, 2003).

20. *See, e.g.,* Stephen J. Crimmins, David U. Gourevitch & Joseph V. Del Raso, The Mutual Fund Probes—What We Can Tell So Far, 35 Sec. Reg. & L. Rep. (BNA) 1834 (Nov. 3, 2003).

21. *See* § 20.5 *infra.*

§ 20.3

1. 15 U.S.C.A. § 80a–3(a)(1).

preceding section of this treatise, there are a number of companies inadvertently finding themselves subject to the Investment Company Act by virtue of section 3(a)(3).[2] Any company holding investment securities in excess of forty percent of its total non-cash asset value comes within the purview of section 3(a)(3).[3] By virtue of the Act's definitional sections,[4] "investment securities" do not include government securities,[5] securities issued by employees' securities companies,[6] or securities issued by non-investment company majority-owned subsidiaries of the holder.[7]

The "value of a company's total assets" as defined in section 2(a)(41) has been explained as the cost of assets acquired since the end of the preceding fiscal quarter, in addition to the market value of assets previously acquired. Accordingly, it has been observed that "assets theretofore acquired are valued at market value, if available in the case of securities, or fair value as determined by the board [of directors], if market quotations of securities are not available or if other assets are in question."[8] The "cash items" excluded from a company's total assets for purposes of section 3(a)(3)'s tabulation have been interpreted informally by the SEC to include time deposits, funds in transit, certificates of deposit, and commercial short-term notes; but accounts receivable are most probably not "cash items" to be excluded from a company's total assets.[9]

A business enterprise not intending to be an investment company is most likely to cross the forty percent threshold during its start-up period when the company invests the capital it does have in order to amass enough money to finance its own operating expenses, when it is selling off its assets and investing the proceeds pending ultimate use of them,[10] and when it is in the process of a final liquidation. The advent of Internet initial public offerings for start-up companies has added increased possibilities for inadvertent investment companies. There are, of course, other less common situations where one may encounter an inadvertent investment company. For example, an unsuccessful tender or exchange offer conceivably could turn the would-be acquirer into an inadvertent investment company.

There are a number of factors to be considered in determining whether an operating company has become an inadvertent investment company requiring registration under the Investment Company Act. The Seventh Circuit recently reaffirmed the five factors that were first identified by the SEC in 1947.[14] Those factors include: (1) the company's history, (2) the way the

2. 15 U.S.C.A. § 80a–3(a)(3).

3. The Second Circuit noted that "In effect, § 3(a)(3) creates a presumption that a company [satisfying the percentage requirements] is an investment company, which is refuted if a company demonstrates that it falls within one of the exceptions of the Act for companies that are essentially industrial corporations but have over 40% of their assets in marketable securities." SEC v. S & P National Corp., 360 F.2d 741, 746 (2d Cir.1966).

4. See § 20.3 supra.

5. Defined in section 2(a)(16), 15 U.S.C.A. § 80a–2(a)(16).

6. Defined in section 2(a)(13), 15 U.S.C.A. § 80a–2(a)(13).

7. Defined in section 2(a)(24), 15 U.S.C.A. § 80a–2(a)(24).

8. Edmund H. Kerr & Alan Appelbaum, Inadvertent Investment Companies—Ten Years After, 25 Bus.Law. 887, 888 (1970).

9. *Id.*

10. *E.g.*, SEC v. National Presto Industries, Inc., 397 F. Supp.2d 943 (N.D. Ill. 2005).

14. S.E.C. v. National Presto Industries, Inc., 486 F.3d 305 (7th Cir. 2007), relying on In re Tonopah Mining Co., 26 S.E.C. 426, 1947 WL 26116 (1947).

company represents itself to the investing public, (3) the activities of the company's officers and directors, (4) the nature of the company's assets and (5) the company's sources of its income.[15]

In 2007, the SEC staff took a controversial position that the public offerings of two well known former private equity firms[16] did not implicate the registration provisions of the Investment Company Act.[17]

Exclusions from section 3(a)(3) of the Investment Company Act are found in section 3(b).[18] Although sometimes referred to as exemptions,[19] the statutory language excludes certain categories of companies from the definition of investment company. The following are the exclusions set forth in section 3(b) even though the forty percent investment portfolio threshold has been crossed:

> (1) Any issuer primarily engaged, directly or through a wholly-owned subsidiary or subsidiaries, in a business or businesses other than that of investing, reinvesting, owning, holding, or trading in securities.
>
> (2) Any issuer which the Commission, upon application by such issuer, finds and by order declares to be primarily engaged in a business or businesses other than that of investing, reinvesting, owning, holding, or trading in securities either directly or (a) through majority-owned subsidiaries or (b) through controlled companies conducting similar types of businesses. The filing of an application under this paragraph in good faith by an issuer other than a registered investment company shall exempt the applicant for a period of sixty days from all provisions of this subchapter applicable to investment companies as such. For cause shown, the Commission by order may extend such period of exemption for an additional period or periods. Whenever the Commission, upon its own motion or upon application, finds that the circumstances which gave rise to the issuance of an order granting an application under this paragraph no longer exist, the Commission shall by order revoke such order.
>
> (3) Any issuer all the outstanding securities of which (other than short-term paper and directors' qualifying shares) are directly or indirectly owned by a company excepted from the definition of investment company by paragraph (1) or (2) of this subsection.[20]

The principal considerations used to determine whether an issuer is "primarily engaged" in non-investment company business for subsection 3(b) purposes were set out by the SEC in its vintage Tonopah Mining Co. decision.[21] In deciding whether to grant a section 3(b) exemption, the Commission explained that it will consider "(1) the company's historical development; (2) its public representations of policy; (3) the activities of its officers and

15. S.E.C. v. National Presto Industries, Inc., 486 F.3d 305 (7th Cir. 2007), relying on In re Tonopah Mining Co., 26 S.E.C. 426, 1947 WL 26116 (1947). The court in *National Presto Industries* applied these factors and reversed the district court's determination that a consumer products and munitions company had become an inadvertent investment company.

16. The two firms were the Blackstone Group L.P. and Fortress Investment Group LLC.

17. *See, e.g.,* SEC's Donohue Defends Decision Not to Deem Issuers Investment Companies, Sec. L. Daily (BNA) http://pubs.bna.com/ip/bna/sld.nsf/eh/A0B4W5T7M5 (July 12, 2007).

18. 15 U.S.C.A. § 80a–3(b).

19. Section 6 of the Act sets forth exemptions. 15 U.S.C.A. § 80a–6; see § 20.4[2] infra.

20. 15 U.S.C.A. § 80a–3(b).

21. 26 S.E.C. 426, 1947 WL 26116 (1947).

directors; and most important, (4) the nature of its present assets; and (5) the source of its present income.''[22] The Seventh Circuit applied these factors and reversed the district court's determination that a consumer products and munitions company had become an inadvertent investment company.[23]

Section 3(b)(2)'s exemptions can be implemented only upon application by the issuer and a subsequent order by the Commission.[24] The exemption has special impact for controlled companies—that is, those over which the issuer can exert a ''controlling influence''—which is assumed if twenty-five percent or more of the company's outstanding voting securities are held by the issuer.[25] Such controlled companies must be involved in a similar type of business as each other, as well as with the issuer, in order to qualify for a section 3(b)(2)(B) exemption. There is no requirement of similarity of business for the majority-owned subsidiaries of the issuer/parent company.[27]

§ 20.4 Classification of Investment Companies

Companies deemed subject to the Investment Company Act are divided into three categories by section 4 of the Act. There are (1) face-amount certificate companies, (2) unit investment trusts, and (3) management companies.[147]

The largest group of investment companies consists of management companies. The Act establishes two categories of management companies. Section 5 classifies management companies as either ''open-end,'' that is, those offering for sale already-issued redeemable securities, or ''closed-end'' which includes all other management companies.[148] As discussed in subsequent sections, there are special regulations that apply to each of these categories. Most mutual funds are open-end investment companies.[149] Trading in shares of these open-end companies is primarily through redemption and reissuance by the company at the per share net asset value.[150] Closed-end management companies typically have a fixed number of shares outstanding which are traded as any other corporate stock might be, that is, on the exchanges or over-the-counter at a price established by the market.[151] A closed-end investment company repurchases its own shares from investors

22. 26 S.E.C. at 427, 1947 WL 26116 (discussing section 3(b)(2)). *Accord* S.E.C. v. National Presto Industries, Inc., 486 F.3d 305 (7th Cir. 2007).

23. S.E.C. v. National Presto Industries, Inc., 486 F.3d 305 (7th Cir. 2007), relying on In re Tonopah Mining Co., 26 S.E.C. 426, 1947 WL 26116 (1947).

24. 15 U.S.C.A. § 80a–3(b)(2).

25. 15 U.S.C.A. § 80a–2(a)(9); American Manufacturing Co. Inc., 1963 WL 62734, 41 S.E.C. 415 (1963).

27. This approach has been followed to some extent in Rule 3a–1, 17 C.F.R. § 270.3a–1.

§ 20.4

147. All investment companies not fitting into the other categories are management companies, 15 U.S.C.A. § 80a–4(3).

148. 15 U.S.C.A. § 80a–5(a).

149. *See, e.g.,* Richard M. Philips, Deregulation Under the Investment Company Act—A Reevaluation of the Corporate Paraphernalia of Shareholder Voting and Boards of Directors, 37 Bus.Law. 903, 905 (1982).

150. *See* Comment, The Distribution of Mutual Fund Shares—Recent Developments in SEC Regulation, 1975 Wash.U.L.Q. 1153, 1190 (1975).

151. A ''closed-end'' company is one with a set number of shares as compared to ''open-end'' companies which will issue additional shares as new investors or new capital is found. 15 U.S.C.A. § 80a–5.

wanting to sell their investment company shares. This option ordinarily is constantly open to closed-end company shareholders. In order to avoid unnecessary entanglement with the tender offer laws, Rule 14e–6 of the Securities Exchange Act of 1934 exempts most closed-end management investment companies from the requirements of Rules 14e–2 and 14e–3.[152]

The Investment Company Act further categorizes companies according to the diversification of investments in their portfolios. Section 5 of the Act classifies management companies as "diversified" and 'non-diversified."[153] In the former category, seventy-five percent of the management company's assets are "limited to securities representing not more than 10 percent of the outstanding voting securities of any one company and not more than 5 percent of its total assets [may be] in the securities of any one company."[154] Contrary to the popular meaning of the term, "diversification" refers to the concentration of investments in a single issuer, not in a single industry.[155] Authorization by a majority of its outstanding voting securities is required before a diversified investment company may change its investment policy towards one of non-diversification.[156]

Another type of investment company falling within the purview of the Investment Company Act is the "special situation company."[157] A special situation company typically buys up controlling blocks of the securities of another corporation with the intent of boosting the value of these securities through more efficient management of the target corporation. Special situation companies do not have a long-term interest in managing the businesses acquired; the primary goal is to eventually sell all of the securities at a profit.[158] The SEC has taken the position that a special situation company "engages in the operation of other companies for the primary purpose of making a profit in the sale of the securities of such companies" and, as such, is subject to the provisions of the Investment Company Act.[159]

Another special category of investment companies is comprised of certain enterprises devoted to financing small businesses As part of the Small Business Incentive Act of 1980,[160] "business development companies" are afforded different treatment than regular investment companies. Business development companies principally invest in and provide managerial assistance to small, growing, and financially troubled businesses.[161] This special treatment for these companies is due to the recognition that the onerous requirements of the Investment Company Act would otherwise restrict the

152. 17 C.F.R. § 240.14e–6. Rules 14e–1 and 14e–2 are discussed in § 11.6 *supra*.

153. 15 U.S.C.A. § 80a–5(b). Even beyond the statutory definition, a fund may set its own investment policies that impact upon a fund's diversification.

154. Alan Rosenblatt & Martin E. Lybecker, Some Thoughts on the Federal Securities Laws Regulating External Management Arrangements and the ALI Federal Securities Code Project, 124 U.Pa.L.Rev. 587, 593 n. 16 (1976). A diversified company receives special treatment under Subchapter M of the Internal Revenue Code, *id.*

155. *See id.*

156. 15 U.S.C.A. § 80a–13(a)(1).

157. *See* Edmund H. Kerr, The Inadvertent Investment Company: Section 3(a)(3) of the Investment Company Act, 12 Stan.L.Rev. 29, 47 (1959).

158. Richard W. Jennings & Harold Marsh, Jr., Securities Regulation: Cases and Materials 1364 (5th ed. 1982).

159. In the Matter of Frobisher Ltd., 1948 WL 28984, 27 S.E.C. 944, 950 (1948).

160. Pub.L. 96–477, 94 Stat. 2275 (1980).

161. 5 U.S. Code Cong. and Adm. News 4800, 4801 (1980).

flow of capital to small business.[162] Companies electing to be regulated as business development companies must comply with sections 55 through 65 of the Investment Company Act,[163] the provisions of which are more relaxed than those applicable to regular investment companies.

Although money market funds are not classified as a separate type of investment company under the statute, the Commission has adopted special rules applicable to these funds.[164] One of the unique aspects of these funds is that the per share value remains constant. Variations in net asset value will thus, if anything, affect the dividends on the shares rather than the price of the shares.

In order for a company to withdraw from registration once it has been found subject to the Act's provisions, the Commission must affirmatively act to find the "investment company" classification no longer valid.[165]

§ 20.4[4] Open–End and Closed–End Funds; Exchange Traded Funds

§ 20.4[4][A] Open–End and Closed–End Funds Distinguished

As noted above, another distinction, referred to in the statute as "sub-classification"[166] of investment companies depends on a difference in structure—the difference between open-end and closed-end funds. Management companies can adopt either structure.[167] An open-end fund is one where the company will continually issue additional shares as new investors participate.[168] There ordinarily is not a secondary market for the shares of open-end companies. Liquidity in open-end companies is provided by the requirement

162. 5 U.S. Code Cong. and Adm. News at 4804, procedure of which is found at 15 U.S.C.A. § 80a–53.

163. 15 U.S.C.A. §§ 80a–54–80a–64. *See generally* Ronald L. Thomas & Paul F. Roye, Regulation of Business Development Companies Under the Investment Company Act, 55 S.Cal. L.Rev. 895 (1981).

164. For example, the Commission imposed limits on the amount of money that money market funds can invest in debt instruments of any one issuer. Rule 2a–7, 17 C.F.R. § 270.2a–7; Inv.Co.Act Rel. IC–18005, [1990–1991 Transfer Binder] Fed.Sec.L.Rep. (CCH) ¶ 84,710 (Feb. 20, 1991). *See* SEC Adopts Changes to Help Ensure Safety of Money Market Funds, 23 Sec.Reg. & L.Rep. (BNA) 193 (Feb. 15, 1991). The SEC has excluded tax exempt money market funds from the general money market fund requirement that money market fund directors approve the acquisition of securities that are either unrated or rated only by one rating agency. 17 C.F.R. § 270.2a–7. *See* Inv.Co.Act Rel. IC–18177, [1990–1991 Transfer Binder] Fed.Sec.L.Rep. (CCH) ¶ 84,741 (May 31, 1991).

When promoting money market accounts, broker-dealers or other financial institution must clearly disclose the absence of FDIC insurance that would be available for comparable bank accounts offered by banks. *See, e.g.,* In the Matter of Ford Motor Credit Co., Sec Dig. 2005–113–3, 2005 WL 1392493 (SEC June 2005). (cease and desist and $64,000 disgorgement order for distributing sales materials soliciting investment in variable denomination floating rate demand notes issued by the company and marketed as the "Ford Money Market Account" without also distributing with those sales materials a copy of the prospectus containing the detailed information about the notes included in the registration statement filed with the SEC).

165. 15 U.S.C.A. § 80a–8(f).

166. Investment Company Act § 5, 15 U.S.C.A. § 80a–5.

167. Investment Company Act § 5, 15 U.S.C.A. § 80a–5.

168. Investment Company Act § 5(a)(1), 15 U.S.C.A. § 80a–5(a)(1) ("'Open-end company' means a management company which is offering for sale or has outstanding any redeemable security of which it is the issuer").

that open-end investment company shares be redeemable.[169] A closed-end fund is a management company which has not issued any redeemable securities.[170] The liquidity in closed-end funds depends on the existence of a secondary market for the investment company shares. As noted above, most investment companies are open-end.

§ 20.4[4][B] Exchange Traded Funds (ETFs)

In recent years, a new type of mutual fund has become increasingly popular. A number of closed-end funds are now traded like stocks on the exchanges, including the New York Stock Exchange. These exchange traded funds (often referred to simply as "ETFs") allow investors to buy into a large basket of stocks. The selection of stocks in the ETF may be in order to recreate a widely followed stock index such as is done with Standard and Poor's Depositary Receipts (SPDRS).[171] ETFs can also be sector or industry funds providing investors diversity within identified industries, stocks, and/or markets. As of January 2005, assets held by ETFs traded in the United States totaled more than $222 billion.[172] ETFs are not limited to securities, if the funds include derivative investments[173] such as swaps or more traditional commodity futures contracts, they will also be subject to the jurisdiction of the Commodity Futures Trading Commission under the Commodity Exchange Act.[174]

§ 20.5 Regulating the Distribution and Pricing of Investment Company Shares

Open-end and closed-end investment companies[1] are subject to different provisions and regulations of the Investment Company Act regarding both the types of capital structure they may have and the methods they may use for the distribution and pricing of their shares. Nevertheless, there are similarities between the two types of companies. Neither type of investment company

---

169. The SEC has permitted in-kind redemptions (*i.e.*, in portfolio securities) rather than in cash. Signature Financial Group, 1999 WL 1261284 (SEC No Action Letter Dec. 28, 1999) (explaining limitations on when such redemptions would be permitted).

170. Investment Company Act § 5(a)(2), 15 U.S.C.A. § 80a–5(a)(2) ("closed-end company" means any management company other than an open-end company).

171. *See, e.g.*, Self–Regulatory Organizations; Chicago Board Options Exchange, Inc.; Notice of Filing and Immediate Effectiveness of Proposed Rule Change Relating to the Systematizing of Orders in the Standard and Poor's Depositary Receipts ("SPDR") Option Class, Sec. Exch. Act Rel. No. 34–51006, 70 Fed. Reg. 2680–03, 2005 WL 74005 (SEC Jan. 14, 2005).

172. This was according to figures released by the Investment Company Institute. *See.* Reuters News, Assets of U.S. ETFs Decline in January–ICI, http://yahoo.reuters.com/finance QuoteCompanyNewsArticle.jhtml?duid=mtfh07509_005-02-25_21-07-00 _n25155364_newsml (Feb. 25, 2005) Assets of stock index ETFs totaled $213.49 billion. Bond index ETF totaled $9.40 billion. *See id.* During January, net issuance of stock index ETFs was a positive $2.15 billion. Bond ETFs had a positive net issuance of $840 million. *See id.*

173. *See, e.g.*, Self–Regulatory Organizations; Notice of Filing of Proposed Rule Change and Amendment Nos. 1 and 2 Thereto by the New York Stock Exchange, Inc. Relating to Customer Portfolio and Cross–Margining Requirements, Sec. Exch. Act Rel. No. 34–50885, 69 Fed. Reg. 77287–01, 2004 WL 2973341 (SEC Dec. 27, 2004).

174. For discussion of the derivatives markets, *see generally,* Philip McBride Johnson & Thomas Lee Hazen, Derivatives Regulation (2004).

§ 20.5

1. In a closed-end investment company, the issuer puts out a limited number of shares; with an open-end company, additional shares are usually issued to each new investor. In a closed-end company there may or may not be active secondary markets. 15 U.S.C.A. § 80a–5. *See* § 20.3 *supra.*

may make a public offering of its securities until it has a net worth of at least one hundred thousand dollars.[2] Section 18(i) requires, with some exceptions, that every share of stock issued by a registered management company must be voting stock with equal voting rights.[3] Further similarities between open-end and closed-end management/investment companies lie in the Investment Company Act's provisions prohibiting either type of company from issuing warrants or rights for its stock,[4] and the provisions prohibiting the payment of dividends for either type of company from a source other than accumulated undistributed net income unless the dividend is accompanied by a written statement identifying the source.[5] There are, however, significant differences in the regulations applicable to closed-end and open-end investment companies.

§ 20.5[1] Distribution and Pricing of Closed–End Investment Company Shares; Repurchases of Its Own Shares

Closed-end investment companies may issue debt securities and preferred stock; open-end companies may not. Section 18(a) of the Act provides that debt securities must have an asset coverage of three hundred percent and preferred stock must have an asset coverage of two hundred percent.[6] In addition, no more than one class of preferred stock may be issued by a single closed-end company.[7] Section 23(a) of the Act requires that the consideration received by a closed-end company for any stock it issues must be cash or securities, which may include its own securities, "except [shares issued] as a dividend or distribution to its securities holders or in connection with a reorganization."[8] Unlike most corporate enterprises, past services are specifically disallowed as consideration for the issuance of closed-end investment company shares.[10]

The Investment Company Act places restrictions on the initial offering price of investment company shares. A closed-end company may not sell any shares of its common stock at a price below its current net asset value without the consent of a majority of its stockholders, or unless pursuant to a conversion privilege.[11] The stock of closed-end investment companies generally has a market price below net asset value.[12] Section 23(b) thus presents a serious impediment to additional offerings of closed-end investment company shares.

The Investment Company Act also restricts a closed-end company's repurchase of its own shares. A closed-end company may purchase any of its

2. 15 U.S.C.A § 80a–14(a). Rule 14a–3 exempts unit investment trusts from this capitalization requirement if certain preconditions are met. 17 C.F.R. § 270.14a–3.

3. 15 U.S.C.A. § 80a–18(i).

4. 15 U.S.C.A. § 80a–18(d).

5. 15 U.S.C.A. § 80a–19(a). Section 18(d) of the Investment Company Act has been held not to preclude a company from issuing a poison pill. *See* Neuberger Berman Real Estate Income Fund, Inc. v. Lola Brown Trust No. 1B, 485 F. Supp.2d 631 (D. Md. 2007).

6. 15 U.S.C.A. § 80a–18(a). "Asset coverage" is defined in 15 U.S.C.A. § 80a–18(h).

7. 15 U.S.C.A. § 80a–18(c).

8. 15 U.S.C.A. § 80a–23(a).

10. 15 U.S.C.A. § 80a–23(a).

11. 15 U.S.C.A. § 80a–23(b).

12. Among other things, this reflects the fact that the costs of liquidation will cut into the liquidation value of the assets.

own shares only upon notification to its shareholders of its intention to do so, given within the preceding six months, and in accordance with rules designated by the Commission.[14] Share repurchases may also be made pursuant to tender offers to all holders of the class of securities to be purchased and pursuant to any rules the Commission may promulgate to ensure fairness to all securities holders of the class of shares to be purchased.[15] Rule 23c–1 operates independently of section 23's provisions and allows a closed-end company to purchase its own securities for cash upon either the satisfaction of eleven stated conditions or upon application and Commission permission to do so.[16] Rule 23c–2 permits the redemption of closed-end company shares that are redeemable according to their terms, provided that there is equal treatment of and adequate notice given to all shareholders.[17] Rule 23c–3 allows repurchase offers at the net asset value at pre-established periodic intervals or, alternatively, on a discretionary basis not more than once every two years.[18]

§ 20.5[2] Distribution and Pricing of Open–End Investment Company Shares

While the provisions regulating the distribution of the shares of a closed-end investment company are relatively straightforward and have remained stable since the Investment Company Act's passage in 1940, such has not been the case for the provisions dealing with open-end investment companies. The regulation of open-end companies is particularly significant because they have replaced the closed-end company as the dominant investment company form. Section 22 of the Act regulates the distribution of open-end investment company shares. The section's complexity is partially necessitated by the fact that open-end companies are constantly issuing and distributing new shares to balance out the shares redeemed and to satisfy the demand created by new investors. The consideration requirements placed on open-end company shares are the same as those placed on the shares of closed-end companies.[20] No registered investment company may suspend the right of redemption of its securities except under the narrow circumstances delimited in section 22(e) of the Act.[21] Suspension of redemption rights is permitted only (1) when the New York Stock Exchange is closed or has restricted trading, (2) during an "emergency" rendering redemption "not reasonably practicable," or (3) in accordance with SEC rules.[22] The Commission has not provided any additional exceptions through its rule-making power.

Section 11(a) of the Act prohibits registered open-end companies and underwriters from making exchange offers to investment company shareholders on any basis other than the net asset value unless the exchange is approved by the Commission order or in accordance with applicable SEC rules.[23] In 1989, the Commission adopted Rule 11a–3 to permit exchange offers to shareholders of different funds in the same group of funds without

14. 15 U.S.C.A. § 80a–23(c).

15. 15 U.S.C.A. § 80a–23(c).

16. 17 C.F.R. § 270.23c–1.

17. 17 C.F.R. § 270.23c–2.

18. *See* Investment Co. Act Rel. No. IC–19399, [1993 Transfer Binder] Fed. Sec. L. Rep (CCH) ¶ 85,125 (SEC April 7, 1993).

20. 15 U.S.C.A. § 80a–22(g).

21. 15 U.S.C.A. § 80a–22(e).

22. 15 U.S.C.A. § 80a–22(e).

23. 15 U.S.C.A. § 80a–11(a).

seeking SEC approval.[24] Under the rule, the investment company is permitted to charge sales loads, redemption fees, administrative fees, or any combination thereof provided that certain conditions are met.

Section 22(d) of the Investment Company Act requires that the securities of all open-end investment companies be sold "at a current public offering price described in the prospectus," whether to the public directly by the fund or through an underwriter.[26] Shares are sold at the first price calculated after an order to buy or sell is received.[27] Also, shares are valued twice daily.[28] This practice, adopted in 1968, is known as "forward pricing."[29] Broker-dealers generally contract with underwriters to sell open-end investment company shares to the public.[30]

The uniformity of price requirement imposed by section 22(d) of the Act prevents price competition between dealers selling shares of the same fund.[31] Most broker-dealers belong to the National Association of Securities Dealers (NASD) and are which is now regulated by the Financial Inudstry Regulatory Authority (FINRA).[32] FINRA (and formerly the NASD) may prescribe rules for its members regarding the purchase and sale of redeemable securities from investment companies "for the purpose of eliminating or reducing so far as reasonably practicable any dilution of the value of other outstanding securities of such company" or other practice "unfair to holders of such other outstanding securities."[33] The SEC is also empowered to promulgate rules for the sale of mutual fund shares.[34] Broker-dealers belonging to the FINRA may elect to follow SEC or NASD (now FINRA) rules.[35] In the event of conflicting rules, those of the SEC prevail.[36] Another problem that arises with respect to the forward pricing of mutual fund shares is the establishment of the net asset value (NAV) when some portfolio securities have not traded and thus may not have available a current market price. As part of its response to the various mutual fund scandals, in 2003 and 2004, the SEC adopted rules designed to require funds to use fair value pricing when market quotations are not readily available.[37]

---

24. 17 C.F.R. § 270.11a–3. *See* Inv. Co. Act Rel. No. 40–17097, [1989–1990 Transfer Binder] Fed.Sec.L.Rep. ¶ 84,435 (Aug. 3, 1989).

26. 15 U.S.C.A. § 80a–22(d).

27. 17 C.F.R. § 270.22c–1.

28. NASD Rules of Fair Practice, Art. III § 26. The National Association of Securities Dealers is discussed in § 14.3 *supra*.

29. *See* Inv.Co.Act Rel. No. 5519 (1968). For a summary of the "two price system" that forward pricing eliminated *see* United States v. NASD, 422 U.S. 694, 702–709, 95 S.Ct. 2427, 2434–2438, 45 L.Ed.2d 486 (1975).

30. An underwriter may not underwrite shares not already the subject of a purchase order. *See* Comment, The Mutual Fund Industry: A Legal Survey, 44 Notre Dame Law. 732, 814 (1969) (discussing NASD Rules of Fair Practice, Art. III § 26(f)(2)).

31. James V. Heffernan & James F. Jorden, Section 22(d) of the Investment Company Act of 1940—Its Original Purpose and Present Function, 1973 Duke L.J. 975, 976 (1973).

32. *See* § 14.3 *supra* for a description of the role of the NASD in the regulation of broker-dealer activities.

33. 15 U.S.C.A. § 80a–22(a).

34. 15 U.S.C.A. § 80a–22(b)(2).

35. *Id.*

36. 15 U.S.C.A. § 80a–22(c).

37. Investment Company Act Rule 38a–1 requires a mutual fund board of directors to adopt written policies and procedures reasonably designed to prevent the fund from violating the Federal securities laws. 17 C.F.R. § 270.38a–1.

The NASD (FINRA) Rules of Fair Practice place a ceiling on the "sales load,"[38] or the sales commission, for transactions in shares of open-end companies that a broker-dealer member may charge to investors.[39] The limits placed on mutual fund sales loads are in sharp contrast to the free competition with regard to brokers' commissions generally. The ceiling on sales loads is in accordance with section 22(b)'s mandate that the price allowed by FINRA rules "shall not include an excessive sales load but shall allow for reasonable compensation for sales personnel, broker-dealers, and underwriters and for reasonable sales loads to investors."[41]

In 2004, the SEC amended its rules relating to investment company fees in order to deal with certain improper sales incentives under the Investment Company Act resulting from the practice known as directed payments.[64] In 2004, the SEC amended Investment Company Act Rule 12b–1[65] to prohibit mutual funds from paying securities brokers an added commission for directing sales of those mutual fund shares.[66] Furthermore, independent of the new rules, the SEC quite properly takes the position that any undisclosed revenue sharing between brokers and mutual funds violated the securities laws.[67]

§ 20.5[3] Secondary Markets for Investment Company Shares

This initial distribution system of mutual fund shares forms the primary market for these shares.[68] The "secondary market" for mutual funds shares refers to the trading of such shares other than through the investment company directly or its underwriter and broker-dealer network. Though still existing, elimination of this market where investors had little protection was among the primary goals of the Congress in enacting the Investment Company Act.[69] The Supreme Court held that section 22(d) of the Act does not prohibit broker-dealers from matching buy and sell orders of individual investors, nor from acting as an agent in the sale of mutual fund shares at any price the investors agree upon.[70] This order matching practice is not subject to section 22(d)'s uniform price requirement because the section speaks only of "dealer transactions," that is, when securities are bought and sold for the agent's own account.[71] When merely acting as a broker for the accounts of others, the broker-dealer is not effecting a transaction for his own account and therefore escapes section 22(d)'s provisions.[72] The Court also dealt with section 22(f)'s provision allowing a mutual fund to restrict the

38. As defined in section 2(a)(35), 15 U.S.C.A. § 80a–2(a)(35).

39. NASD (FINRA) Rule 2830 (investment company shares may not be offered with excessive sales loads).

41. 15 U.S.C.A. § 80a–22(b)(1).

64. *See* Prohibition on the Use of Brokerage Commissions to Finance Distribution, Inv. Co. Act Rel. No. IC–26591, 2004 WL 1969665 (SEC 2004).

65. 17 C.F.R. § 270.12b–1.

66. 17 C.F.R. § 270.12b–1(h). *See* Prohibition on the Use of Brokerage Commissions to Finance Distribution, Inv. Co. Act Rel. No. IC–26591, 2004 WL 1969665 (SEC 2004).

67. *See* Edward Jones to Pay $75 Million to Settle Revenue Sharing Charges, SEC News Rel, No. 04–177, http://www.sec.gov/news/press/2004–177.htm, 2004 WL 2967922 (SEC Dec. 22, 2004).

68. United States v. NASD, 422 U.S. 694, 699, 95 S.Ct. 2427, 2433, 45 L.Ed.2d 486 (1975).

69. 422 U.S. at 700, 95 S.Ct. at 2433–2434.

70. 422 U.S. at 711–19, 95 S.Ct. at 2438–2443.

71. As defined in 15 U.S.C.A. § 80a–2(a)(11).

72. As defined in 15 U.S.C.A. § 80a–2(a)(6). *See* 422 U.S. at 713, 95 S.Ct. at 2439–2440.

transferability and negotiability of its shares in conformity with legends on the shares themselves and with the fund's registration statement. SEC rules under section 22(d) allow mutual funds to regulate the secondary market by private contractual agreements between the funds, the NASD, and brokers, dealers and underwriters, as well as by the terms of the funds' registration statements.[73] The SEC had held that this private method of regulating the secondary market was preferable to the promulgating of further administrative rules in the area.[74] The Supreme Court held these arrangements to be immunized from illegality under the Sherman Antitrust Act[75] due to the broad regulatory powers over mutual fund shares granted by Congress to the SEC in section 22(f) of the Investment Company Act.[76] The importance of this aspect of the decision is minimal due to the relatively insignificant size of the secondary mutual fund market of open-end companies today.

§ 20.5[4] Improper Trading and Pricing Practices

§ 20.5[4][A] Late Trading

Investigations by former New York Attorney General Elliott Sptizer revealed a number of trading abuses involving mutual fund shares.[77] The abuses uncovered during the mutual fund investigations took various forms. Prohibited mutual fund sales practices are discussed in the pages that follow.

One of the pernicious practices that came to light in 2003 was that many mutual funds engaged in late trading of open-end fund shares. Investigations by the SEC and the New York Attorney General revealed that many reputable mutual funds were engaging in fraudulent practices. The two most visible practices were late trading schemes and market timing.[78] Open-end mutual fund shares are based on forward pricing. Open-end fund shares are priced each day based on the net asset value of the fund's assets at the close of regular trading in the securities markets (4:00 p.m. eastern time).[79] Late trading occurs when a trade is entered after the market is closed but is priced at the level fixed by the 4:00 calculation. This allows late traders to take advantage of events taking place after 4:00 that will move the net asset value either up or down. This, in turn, allows the late trader to guarantee a profit by trading on news available to everyone but at a price available only to those

73. 422 U.S. at 720–28, 95 S.Ct. at 2443–2447.

74. 422 U.S. at 720–28, 95 S.Ct. at 2443–2447.

75. 15 U.S.C.A. § 1.

76. 422 U.S. at 729–30, 95 S.Ct. at 2447–2448.

77. The investigation culminated in the leveling of substantial fines. Investigations into mutual fund sales practices have resulted in substantial fines. *See, e.g.,* Firms Settle SEC, NASD Charges Over Alleged Mutual Fund Sales Practices, 37 Sec. Reg. & L. Rep. (BNA) 553 (March 28, 2005); Milton Recht & Stuart Gittleman, Bank of America Finalizes Record Mutual Fund Trading Abuse Settlement with SEC, Complinet, http://www.complinet.com/us/news/news/print_display.html?ref=68100 (Feb. 10, 2005) ($515 million settlement).

78. *See, e.g.,* SEC Chairman Donaldson Releases Statement Regarding Initiatives to Combat Late Trading and Market Timing of Mutual Funds, http://www.sec.gov/news/press/2003–136.htm (Oct. 9, 2003); Roberto M. Braceras, Late Trading and Market Timing, 37 Rev. Sec. & Commod. Reg. 61 (2004).

79. Unscrupulous fund managers can manipulate the price by "marking the close" transactions designed to raise the closing price and therefore increase the fund's asset value. *See, e.g.,* In the Matter of Schultz Investment Advisors, Inc., Release No. 33–8650, Release No. 34–53029, Release No. IA—2470, 2005 WL 3543078 (SEC Dec. 28, 2005) (consent order imposing $100,000 fine plus disgorgement of profits for marking the close violations). Marking the close as a market manipulation is discussed in § 14.3[6][B], *supra.*

who have access to late trading. All other investors desiring to trade on the news get to trade at the price fixed at 4:00 on the *next* trading day, after that news has affected the price of the securities in the fund's portfolio. Late trading thus operates just like insider trading. A group of insiders are able to take advantage of their access based on their position. In the case of insider trading, the violation consists of taking advantage of information not generally available at a transaction price available to the investing public. Conversely, late trading allows an insider to take advantage of pricing not available to the investing public in order to take advantage of price movements resulting from information that is generally available. Late trading practices unfairly advantage participating investors and have been the subject of SEC enforcement actions.[81] In late 2003, the SEC proposed a 4:00 p.m. cut-off for mutual fund trading in order to eliminate late trading issues.[82]

Even in the absence of an express rule prohibiting late trading, the SEC has made clear that late trading is improper and violates the securities laws.[83] The evil and illegality of late trading is based on the pricing of the shares, not the timing. In other words, there is nothing wrong with agreeing to a trade after the close of trading, so long as the trade is priced to the next day's opening price.[84] Also, a contractual provision calling for late trading transactions is void and unenforceable; however, it does not necessarily void the entire contract relating to transactions in investment company shares.[85]

§ 20.5[4][B] Market Timing

Market timing of transactions in mutual fund shares is another way to take advantage of the forward pricing mechanism of open-end mutual fund shares. It provides another way for traders to take advantage of prices that have become stale because the mutual fund share price is fixed, notwithstanding events and news that will affect the fund share price once the next net asset valuation is made at the close of trading. Market timing permits traders to trade during the course of one business day and then lock in a mutual fund share price based on the previous day's close and then sell the mutual fund shares the next day once the fund shares are trading at the price that reflects the new information. The mutual fund industry segments engaging in this practice claim that although it may have been questionable, it is not illegal. Nevertheless, the SEC and the states have been pursuing certain market timing practices as securities law violations.[87] For example, misrepresentations about market timing can constitute violation of the Exchange Act's general antifraud Rule 10b–5.[88] Even in the absence of scienter, individuals

81. *See, e.g.,* SEC Sues Dallas Broker-Dealer/Adviser, Mutuals.com, for Fraud in Fund Trading, 35 Sec. Reg. & L. Rep. (BNA) 2021 (Dec. 8, 2003).

82. *See* Compliance Programs of Investment Companies and Investment Advisers, Inv. Adv. Act Rel. No. IA–2204, Inv. Co. Act Rel. No. IC–26299, 2003 WL 22971048, (SEC 2003).

83. *See* In re Compliance Programs of Inv. Companies and Inv. Advisers, Inv. Adv. Act Rel. No. IA—2204, Inv. Co. Act Rel. No. IC—26299, 81 S.E.C. Docket 2775, 2003 WL 22971048 (SEC Dec. 17, 2003).

84. *See* Prusky v. Reliastar Life Insurance Co., 445 F.3d 695, 698 n.5 (3d Cir. 2006).

85. *See id.*

87. *See, e.g.,* SEC v. Gann, 2006 WL 616005 (N.D.Tex. 2006) (SEC sufficiently alleged broker's market timing violations).

88. *See, e.g.*, S.E.C. v. Gann, 2008 WL 857633 (N.D.Tex. 2008) (misrepresentations to mutual funds regarding broker's market timing strategy violated rule 10b–5).

who cause improper market timing may be subjected to a cease and desist order.[89]

There are at least two instances in which institutional market timing of mutual fund shares is clearly improper. In the first instance, if a mutual fund, as it should, discourages short-term investment strategies but then enters into arrangements with market timers that encourage timing, the fund has breached obligations to the other fund shareholders. The second situation involves off-shore funds where the varying time zones allow market timers to take advantage of forward pricing of mutual fund shares in much the same way as late traders in the United States. Improprieties also occur when a fund fails to charge redemption fees in order to facilitate undisclosed or otherwise improper market timing by the account holder.[90] Many hedge funds engaged in improper market timing practices by waiving their market timing restrictions in exchange for consideration.[91]

In 2005, the SEC adopted a rule designed to curtail market timing abuses. Investment Company Act Rule 22c–2 requires a mutual fund's board of directors to consider imposing a redemption fee for fund shares redeemed within seven calendar days of their acquisition.[92] The rule thus mandates that the board of directors either approve the imposition of a redemption fee, not to exceed two percent, or, alternatively, make an affirmative determination that a redemption fee is neither necessary nor appropriate in order to protect the fund's investors.[93] The rule does not apply to either money market funds nor to exchange-traded funds (ETFs).

Investment Company Act Rule 22c–2 further requires covered mutual funds that redeem shares within seven days to enter into agreements with their broker-dealer or other intermediaries (such as a retirement plan administrator) obligating the intermediary to provide the fund with shareholder trading information.[94] This information provided by the intermediary will enable the funds to identify shareholders who violate the funds' market timing policies. The information further facilitates the fund in overseeing the intermediary's assessment of any applicable redemption fees. Rule 22c–2 had a delayed effective date. Although adopted in 2005.

The SEC's concern about market timing is supplemented by the actions of the self regulatory organizations. For example, FINRA (and formerly the NASD) plays an important role in policing market timing violations.[96] Also,

---

89. *See* In the Matter of Lammert, Admin Proc. File No. 3–12386, SEC Rel. No. ID—348, 2008 WL 1867960 (SEC Initial Decision 2008) (dismissing fraud claims as to all defendants but subjecting two defendants to a cease and desist order).

90. *See* In the Matter of BancOne Investment Advisers Corp., Admin. Proc. No. 3–11530, Inv. Adv. Act Rel. No. IA–2254, Inv. Co. Act Rel. No. IC–26490, 2004 WL 1472043 (SEC June 29, 2004) (settlement of cease and desist proceedings). *See also, e.g.,* Investment Company Governance, Inv. Co. Act Rel. No. IC–26520, 69 FR 46378–01, 2004 WL 1707823 (SEC Aug. 2, 2004).

91. See Registration Under the Advisers Act of Certain Hedge Fund Advisers, Inv. Adv. Act Rel. No. IA–2333, 69 Fed. Reg. 72054–01, 2004 WL 2825810 (SEC Dec. 10, 2004).

92. 17 C.F.R. § 270.22c–2.

93. 17 C.F.R. § 270.22c–2.

94. 17 C.F.R. § 270.22c–2.

96. *See, e.g.,* NASD Fines H & R Block Financial Advisors $500,000 for Enabling Deceptive Market Timing, Orders Payment of $325,000 in Restitution, http://www.nasd.com/stellent/idcplg?IdcService=SS_GET_PAGE & ssDocName=NASDW_012819 & ssSourceNodeId=13 (NASD Dec. 21, 2004).

the New York Stock Exchange imposed a substantial fine on brokers who engaged in market timing violations.[97]

§ 20.5[4][C] Breakpoint Pricing of Investment Company Shares

Mutual funds sometimes offer their shares in various classes with differing sales charges. For example, Class A mutual fund shares typically are based on front-end loaded sales charges. In contrast, sales charges on Class B shares typically are back-end loaded. The size of the investment and the investor's investment objectives can bear upon the most appropriate class for a particular investment. Breakpoint pricing requires full disclosure[99] as to the pricing differences and the effect on the customer in order for the customer to make an informed investment decision. Brokers' recommendations can also raise suitability issues.[100] Class C shares typically have back-end loaded sales charges that are lower than Class B shares. As explained by the NASD (now FINRA):

> Class A shares typically charge a front-end sales charge. When you buy Class A shares with a front-end sales charge, a portion of the dollars you pay is not invested. Class A shares may impose an asset-based charge, but it generally is lower than the asset-based sales charge imposed by the other classes.
>
> A mutual fund may offer you discounts, called breakpoints, on the front-end sales charge if you:
>
> - make a large purchase;
> - already hold other mutual funds offered by the same fund family; or
> - commit to regularly purchasing the mutual fund's shares.

* * *

> Class B shares typically do not charge a front-end sales charge, but they do impose asset-based sales charges that may be higher than those that you would incur if you purchased Class A shares. Class B shares also normally impose a contingent deferred sales charge (CDSC), which you pay when you sell your shares. For this reason, these should not be referred to as "no-load" shares. The CDSC normally declines and eventually is eliminated the longer you hold your shares. Once the CDSC is eliminated, Class B shares often then "convert" into Class A shares. When they convert, they will begin to charge the same asset-based sales charge as the Class A shares.
>
> Class B shares do not impose a sales charge at the time of purchase. So unlike Class A purchases, all of your dollars would be immediately invested. But your expenses, as measured by the expense ratio, may be

97. *See* Merrill Lynch, Pierce, Fenner & Smith Inc., Exchange Hearing Panel Decision 05–27, 2005 WL 580396 (NYSE Initial Decision March 7, 2005).

99. *See* In the Matter of Suntrust Securities, Inc., Admin. Proc. File No. 3–11924, Sec. Exch. Act Rel. No. No. 34–51700, 2005 WL 1172237 (SEC 2005) (settlement involving Rule 10b–10 violations regarding mutual fund breakpoint pricing).

100. *See, e.g.,* Phillips v. Wedbush Morgan Securities, NASD Docket No. 03–07340, 2005 WL 1140221 (NASD 2005) ($49,040.00 arbitration award for claim involving breakpoint pricing violations). Suitability generally is discussed in § 14.16 *supra.*

higher. You also may pay a sales charge when you sell your Class B shares.

If you intend to purchase a large amount of Class B shares, you may want to discuss with your financial adviser whether Class A shares would be preferable. The expense ratio charged on Class A shares is generally lower than for the Class B shares, and the mutual fund may offer large-purchase breakpoint discounts from the front-end sales charge for Class A shares.

To determine if Class A shares may be more advantageous refer to the mutual fund's prospectus, which may describe the purchase amounts that qualify for a breakpoint discount.

* * * Class C shares usually do not impose a front-end sales charge on the purchase, so the full dollar amount that you pay is immediately invested. Often Class C shares impose a small charge if you sell your shares within a short time of purchase, usually one year. Class C shares typically impose higher asset-based sales charges than Class A shares, and since their shares generally do not convert into Class A shares, their asset-based sales charge will not be reduced over time. Class C shares are often used for asset-allocation purposes.

Class C shares do not impose a sales charge at the time of purchase, but they may impose a CDSC or other redemption fees. Additionally, in most cases your expense ratio would be higher than Class A shares, and even than Class B shares if you hold for a long time.[102]

Recommendations regarding fund purchases must adequately disclose the differing sales charges.[103] Suitability issues can arise in recommending a class of shares that may not have the charges suitable for the particular investor.[104] Recommending mutual funds with less than optimal breakpoint pricing in light of the customer's objectives can result in the recommending broker's liability for excessive fees.[105] Even when disclosures as to breakpoint pricing may be sufficient under federal law, there may be state law duty breaches when a broker directs a customer to the wrong class of mutual fund shares.[106]

One response to the abuses related to pricing of mutual fund shares was additional SEC rulemaking with respect to disclosures relating to mutual fund share pricing.[111] The SEC's rules regarding mutual fund pricing focus on disclosures sufficient to inform investors regarding breakpoint pricing. In particular, the SEC rules require that in the prospectus mutual funds provide

102. NASD Investor Alert, Understanding Mutual Fund Classes (NASDR Jan. 14, 2003). *See also, e.g.,* NASD Investor Alert, Mutual Fund Breakpoints: A Break Worth Taking, http://www.nasdr.com/alert_breakpoint.htm (NASDR Jan. 14, 2003).

103. *See, e.g.,* In the Matter of Hoffman, 71 S.E.C. Docket 1247, Release No. ID–158, 2000 WL 64976 (SEC Initial Decision Jan. 27, 2000) (disclosures were adequate).

104. *See* In the Matter of Citigroup Global Markets, Inc., Sec. Act Rel. No. 33–8557, Sec. Exch. Act Rel. No. 34–51415, 2005 WL 673272 (SEC 2005).

105. *See, e.g.,* Phillips v. Wedbush Morgan Securities, NASD Docket No. 03–07340, 2005 WL 1140221 (NASD 2005) ($49,040.00 arbitration award for claim involving breakpoint pricing violations).

106. *See* Benzon v. Morgan Stanley Distributors, Inc., 420 F.3d 598 (6th Cir. 2005) (disclosures relating to class B shares did not violate federal securities laws but directing customers to those shares might violate state law obligations).

111. *See* Investment Company Governance, Inv. Co. Act Rel. No. IC–26520, 2004 WL 1672374 (SEC 2004).

a brief description of arrangements resulting in sales load breakpoints. The disclosures relating to breakpoints must include a summary of eligibility requirements. Mutual fund prospectuses must also contain a description of the methods used to value accounts in order to determine whether a shareholder qualifies for sales load breakpoints. The pricing disclosures in the prospectus must also state any requirement that in order to obtain a breakpoint, it may be necessary for a shareholder to provide information and records, such as account statements, to a mutual fund or financial intermediary. In addition, the SEC rules require a mutual fund to state in its prospectus whether breakpoint information is made available on the mutual fund's website.

§ 20.6 Investment Company Directors—Fiduciary Duties; Independent Investment Company Directors

Unlike the 1933 and 1934 securities acts, the Investment Company Act of 1940 imposes substantive rules upon an issuer's internal governance structure. This represents a significant departure from the general thrust of most federal securities laws and regulations, which is to eschew direct involvement in the corporate chartering process. For example, the Securities Exchange Act of 1934 protects shareholder interests by requiring full disclosure and regulating proxy machinery in shareholder votes. These shareholder voting safeguards alone are considered inadequate methods of protecting investment company shareholders, due both to the nature of investment company activity and the fluctuations in the number of shares owned by any single shareholder as a result of dividend payments or daily cash needs.[2]

§ 20.6[1] Composition of an Investment Company's Board of Directors

Independent directors serve primarily as "watchdogs" over an investment company to protect the interests of shareholders against abuses by investment advisers and others in a position to profit illegally from the company.[6] The SEC continues to stress the importance of investment company directors, especially in the face of scandals in the mutual fund industry.

Section 10(a) of the Investment Company Act ensures some degree of management independence by requiring registered investment companies' boards of directors to be composed of at least forty percent disinterested persons.[9] "Interested persons" are defined to include: (1) any affiliated person of the investment company; (2) the immediate family members of an affiliated natural person; (3) any person interested in the investment company's investment adviser or principal underwriter; (4) anyone who has acted as the investment company's legal counsel within the past two years; (5) certain brokers or dealers registered under the Securities Exchange Act who have a relationship to the investment company, or any affiliate thereof;[10] and (6) any person the Commission deems to be interested due to a material or professional relationship with the investment company within the previous two years.[11]

§ 20.6

2. One example of the substantive protection is the antipyramiding rule of section 12(d)(1) 15 U.S.C.A. § 80a–12(d)(1) which is discussed in § 20.1 *supra*.

6. S.Rep.No. 184, 91st Cong., 1st Sess. 32 (1969).

9. 15 U.S.C.A. § 80a–10(a).

10. *See* 17 C.F.R. § 270.2a19–1.

11. 15 U.S.C.A. § 80a–2(a)(19)(A)(i)–(vi).

An "affiliated person" is any person owning or holding with voting power five percent or more of the company's outstanding voting securities; any company of whose outstanding voting securities the investment company owns five percent or more; any person controlled by the investment company; any officer, director, partner, copartner, or employee of the investment company; and any investment adviser or member of the advisory board of the investment company.[12]

Membership on the board of directors of an investment company or ownership of less than five percent of the investment company securities does not in and of itself constitute grounds to classify a person as "interested."[13] Participation on multiple boards of funds within the same fund complex does not in itself render directors "interested" in violation of the Investment Company Act's definition of who is a disinterested director.[14] In the case of no-load mutual funds, only one member of the board need be a disinterested person with regard to the investment adviser.[15]

Control persons, affiliates, and employees of an investment company will qualify as interested persons under the Act.[16] There is a presumption that a natural person is not a control person.[17] This is a rebuttable presumption.[18] There is no comparable presumption for the more generalized concept of control person under the 1933 and 1934 Acts.[19] The independence of investment company directors will be judged by the substance of any relationship to the investment advisor rather than focusing on the form. Indirect compensation from the adviser will preclude a finding of independence. Thus, for example, a director who receives compensation from service on the board of multiple investment companies managed by a single adviser is not a disinterested person within the meaning of the Investment Company Act.[20] In contrast, when a director receives special consideration in IPO allocations, his independence may be compromised.[21]

12. 15 U.S.C.A. § 80a–2(a)(3). In 1993, the Commission adopted a rule which provides that when an investment company is set up as a limited partnership, limited partners will not be considered "affiliated persons" *solely* because of their limited partnership interests. Rule 2a3–1, 17 C.F.R. § 270.2a3–1.

13. 15 U.S.C.A. § 80a–2(a)(19).

14. Krantz v. Prudential Investments Fund Management LLC, 305 F.3d 140 (3d Cir. 2002) (failure to show fees were excessive).

15. 15 U.S.C.A. § 80a–10(d)(3). "No load" mutual funds are those where neither the investor's purchase nor sale price includes a charge for sales and promotional activities or administrative fees. *See* 15 U.S.C.A. § 80a–2(a)(35). *See generally* James H. Ellis, Going No Load, 6 Sec.Reg.L.J. 357 (1979).

16. Investment Company Act § 2(a)(9), 15 U.S.C.A. § 80a–2(a)(9); Strougo v. BEA Associates, 2000 WL 45714, [1999–2000 Transfer Binder] Fed. Sec. L. Rep. (CCH) ¶ 90,742 (S.D.N.Y. 2000).

17. Investment Company Act §§ 2(a)(3)(D), 2(a)(9), 15 U.S.C.A. §§ 80a–2(a)(3)(D), 80a–2(a)(9). *Cf., e.g.,* Migdal v. Rowe Price–Fleming Intern., Inc., 248 F.3d 321, 2001 WL 460752 (4th Cir.2001) (upholding dismissal of claim that directors lacked independence).

18. *See* Strougo v. BEA Associates, 2000 WL 45714, [1999–2000 Transfer Binder] Fed. Sec. L. Rep. (CCH) ¶ 90,742 (S.D.N.Y. 2000) (director was interested for purposes of demand requirement).

19. 15 U.S.C.A. §§ 77*o*, 78t. *See* §§ 7.12, 12.24 *supra*.

20. Strougo v. BEA Associates, 2000 WL 45714, [1999–2000 Transfer Binder] Fed. Sec. L. Rep. (CCH) ¶ 90,742 (S.D.N.Y. 2000). *See also* Strougo v. Bassini, 1 F.Supp.2d 268, 273 (S.D.N.Y. 1998).

21. *See* Monetta Financial Services, Inc., Sec. Act Rel. No. 33–8239, Sec. Exch. Act Rel. No. 34–48001, Inv. Adv. Act Rel. No. IA–2136, Inv. Co. Act Rel. No. IC–26070, 2003 WL 21310330 (SEC June 9, 2003).

In 1999, the SEC moved to expand the watchdog function of independent investment company directors. The Commission proposed rules designed to enhance the independence of investment company directors.[22] These amendments were adopted in 2001.[23] Contemporaneously with the proposal of the amendments in 1999, the Commission issued an interpretative release focusing on interpretations concerning the independence requirement.[24]

The requirement of independence requires that the directors not be so interested as to preclude an unbiased evaluation of the investment company's operations. The mere fact that directors have interlocking directorships with affiliated companies is not sufficient to establish the absence of the required degree of independence.[34] There is a rebuttable presumption that outside directors are independent.[35] The fact that the outside directors are highly compensated for serving on the board of an investment company is not sufficient in and of itself to rebut the presumption of their independence.[36] However, a director who is compensated for serving on a number of boards of investment companies managed by a single adviser was found not to be a disinterested person.[37] Compensation for serving on a number of boards of investment companies managed by a single adviser has been treated as the equivalent of being employed by the adviser.[38]

The courts have identified ten factors to be considered in determining whether the plaintiffs can overcome the rebuttable presumption[39] that outside directors are in fact independent. Those ten factors are: "(1) selection or nomination of the director by the controlling party; (2) existence of family ties; (3) social relations; (4) former business associations between the director and the controlling person; (5) the amount of time spent by directors at meetings; (6) respective ages; (7) participation in recommending, evaluating, and terminating policies; (8) independent knowledge of corporate affairs; (9) interlocking directors and officers, together with share ownerships; and (10) actual domination and operation."[40]

The U.S. Chamber of Commerce challenged the SEC's rule calling for a 75 percent independence requirement on the grounds that it exceeded SEC

22. Role of Independent Directors of Investment Companies, Inv. Co. Act Rel. No. IC–24082, 1999 WL 820633 (SEC Oct. 14, 1999).

23. *See* Role of Independent Directors of Investment Companies, Sec. Exch. Act Rel. No. 34–43786, 2001 WL 6738 (SEC Jan. 2, 2001).

24. Interpretive Matters Concerning Independent Directors of Investment Companies Inv. Co. Act Rel. No. IC–24083, 1999 WL 820629 (SEC Oct. 14, 1999).

34. *E.g.,* Krantz v. Prudential Investments Fund Management LLC, 77 F.Supp.2d 559 (D.N.J.1999).

35. Verkouteren v. Blackrock Financial Management, Inc., 1999 WL 511411, [1999 Transfer Binder] Fed. Sec. L. Rep. (CCH) ¶ 90,536 (S.D.N.Y. 1999); Olesh v. Dreyfus Corp., 1995 WL 500491, [1995–1996 Transfer Binder] Fed. Sec. L. Rep. (CCH) ¶ 98,907 (E.D.N.Y.1995). *See also, e.g.,* Acampora v. Birkland, 220 F.Supp. 527, 543 (D.Colo.1963) ("proof of control demands a presentation of evidence establishing actual domination and operation. Mere influence would fall short of this level of proof").

36. Verkouteren v. Blackrock Financial Management, Inc., 1999 WL 511411, [1999 Transfer Binder] Fed. Sec. L. Rep. (CCH) ¶ 90,536 (S.D.N.Y. 1999).

37. Strougo v. BEA Associates, 2000 WL 45714, [1999–2000 Transfer Binder] Fed. Sec. L. Rep. (CCH) ¶ 90,742 (S.D.N.Y. 2000); Strougo v. Bassini, 1 F.Supp.2d 268, 273 (S.D.N.Y.1998).

38. Strougo v. BEA Associates, 2000 WL 45714, [1999–2000 Transfer Binder] Fed. Sec. L. Rep. (CCH) ¶ 90,742 (S.D.N.Y. 2000).

39. *See* the discussion above.

40. Strougo v. BEA Associates, 188 F.Supp.2d 373, 381 (S.D.N.Y.2002), quoting Verkouteren v. Blackrock Fin. Management, Inc., 37 F.Supp.2d 256, 261 (S.D.N.Y.1999). This is a restatement of the factors set forth by the SEC in First Australian Fund, Inc., 1987 WL 108483 [1987–1988 Transfer Binder], Fed. Sec. L. Rep. (CCH) ¶ 78,551 (SEC No Action Letter Oct. 8, 1987).

rulemaking authority.[63] The court found that although the SEC has the authority to impose a 75 percent independence requirement,[64] it failed to adequately consider cost of compliance with the rules.[65] The court remanded the rule to the SEC for further consideration of the costs of compliance. The SEC need not consider every possible compliance cost but it must consider significant compliance costs that have been brought to its attention.[67] Specifically, the analysis of the three commissioners voting for the new rule failed to adequately discuss and evaluate the compliance costs suggested by numerous commentators and the two dissenting commissioners who favored a disclosure rather than mandatory approach to the independence requirements.[68] Just eight days after the Court of Appeals ruling, the SEC in a sharply divided three-to-two-vote reconsidered and once again approved the new rule.[70] Shortly after the SEC's reaffirmation of the rule, the Chamber of Commerce again challenged the rule.[71] The court of appeals responded by issuing a stay pending briefing and argument on the validity of the rule.[72] In the third trip to the D.C. Circuit Court of Appeals, the rule was vacated and was once again deferred, in order to give the SEC more time to consider additional evidence on the cost-effectiveness of the new rule.[73] In June 2006, the SEC complied with the court's decision and solicited further comment on the proposed rule.[74] In December, 2006, the SEC once again extended the comment period and the investment company corporate governance rules retained their status as proposed but not adopted.[75]

§ 20.6[2] Duties of Investment Company Directors

As in the case of any corporation, the board of directors is responsible for overseeing the investment company's general management.[76] The Act does not

63. *See* Chamber of Commerce of the United States of America v. SEC, 412 F.3d 133 (D.C. Cir. 2005).

64. Chamber of Commerce of the United States of America v. SEC, 412 F.3d 133, 142 (D.C. Cir. 2005).

65. *Id.*

67. Chamber of Commerce of the United States of America v. SEC, 412 F.3d 133 (D.C. Cir. 2005).

68. Chamber of Commerce of the United States of America v. SEC, 412 F.3d 133 (D.C. Cir. 2005).

70. Chamber of Commerce of the United States of America v. SEC, 412 F.3d 133 (D.C. Cir. 2005).

71. *See* U.S. Chamber Sues SEC Second Time Over Mutual Fund Rule, 37 Sec. Reg. & L. Rep. (BNA) 1170 (July 11, 2005). The Chamber also asked the SEC to delay implementation of the rule. *See* U.S. Chamber Asks SEC to Stay Fund Governance Rule Pending Decision, 37 Sec. Reg. & L. Rep. (BNA) 1213 (July 18, 2005). However, by a 2–2 divided vote the SEC decided not to delay implementation of the rule. By 2–2 Vote, SEC Refuses to Stay Fund Governance Rules Pending Decision, 37 Sec. Reg. & L. Rep. (BNA) 1249 (July 25, 2005).

72. Chamber of Commerce of the United States of America v. SEC, No. 05–1240 (D.C. Cir. Aug. 10, 2005); Appeals Court Stays Mutual Fund Governance Requirements, 37 Sec. Reg. & L. Rep. (BNA) 1357 (Aug. 15, 2005).

73. *See* Chamber of Commerce of the United States of America v. SEC, 443 F.3d 890 (D.C.Cir. 2006).

74. *See* Request for Additional Comment, Inv. Co. Act Rel. No. IC–27395, 71 Fed. Reg. 35366–01, 2006 WL 1666075 (SEC June 19, 2006).

75. *See* Investment Company Governance, Inv. Co. Act Rel. No. IC—27600, 2006 WL 3718282 (SEC Dec. 15, 2006).

76. SEC, Institutional Investor Study Report, H.R. Doc. No. 64, Vol. 2, 92d Cong. 1st Sess. 214 (1971); Joseph F. Krupsky, The Role of Investment Company Directors, 32 Bus.Law. 1733, 1740 (1977).

impose strict liability upon directors, so long as the fiduciary duties imposed upon them by section 36(a)[77] have been fulfilled.[78]

It has been held that section 1(b) of the Act[79] codified the common law duties and obligations of corporate directors generally and applies them to investment company directors.[80] In Burks v. Lasker,[81] the Supreme Court expressly noted that the Investment Company Act was not intended to supplant the "entire corpus of state corporation law" even where a plaintiff's cause of action arises solely out of Investment Company Act provisions.[82] *Burks* concerned the ability of investment company directors acting upon independent advice to terminate shareholder derivative suits. The Court reversed the overturning of the board action and stated that federal courts "should apply state law governing the authority of independent directors to discontinue derivative suits to the extent such law is consistent with the policies of the Investment Company Act and the Investment Advisers Act."[83] Suits claiming breaches of fiduciary duty under the Investment Company Act are derivative in nature and thus are subject to the demand requirement.[84]

The Investment Company Act of 1940 Rule 38a–1[85] requires investment company boards of directors—including a majority of the independent directors—to adopt written policies and procedures reasonably designed to prevent securities law violations. These boards should also approve the policies and procedures of the fund's investment adviser, principal underwriter, administrator and transfer agent. The compliance rules must cover pricing of portfolio securities and fund shares, processing of fund shares, identification of affiliated persons, protection of non-public information, governance procedures, and market timing safeguards.

Rule 38a–1 requires registered investment companies to adopt policies and procedures to determine whether market quotations are not reliable and do not provide a basis for determining current fair value.[86] The rule also requires registered investment companies to establish procedures that segregate investor orders received before funds price their shares from those shares that were received after the fund's shares are priced.

The rule also addresses governance of registered investment companies. The rule requires procedures designed to protect against an (1) improperly constituted board, (2) the failure of the board to properly consider matters

77. 15 U.S.C.A. § 80a–35(a); Brouk v. Managed Funds, Inc., 286 F.2d 901, 918 (8th Cir.1961), *judgment vacated* 369 U.S. 424, 82 S.Ct. 878, 8 L.Ed.2d 6 (1962).

78. *See, e.g.,* Moses v. Burgin, 445 F.2d 369 (1st Cir.1971), *cert. denied* 404 U.S. 994, 92 S.Ct. 532, 30 L.Ed.2d 547 (1971); Fogel v. Chestnutt, 533 F.2d 731 (2d Cir.1975), *cert. denied* 429 U.S. 824, 97 S.Ct. 77, 50 L.Ed.2d 86 (1976); Tannenbaum v. Zeller, 552 F.2d 402 (2d Cir.1977).

79. 15 U.S.C.A. § 80a–1(b).

80. Aldred Investment Trust v. SEC, 151 F.2d 254, 260 (1st Cir.1945), *cert. denied* 326 U.S. 795, 66 S.Ct. 486, 90 L.Ed. 483 (1946).

81. 441 U.S. 471, 99 S.Ct. 1831, 60 L.Ed.2d 404 (1979).

82. *Id.* at 478, 99 S.Ct. at 1837.

83. *Id.* at 486, 99 S.Ct. at 1841.

84. *E.g.,* Marquit v. Williams, 229 F.3d 1135 (2d Cir.2000) (table, opinion in Westlaw).

85. 17 C.F.R. § 270.38a–1.

86. Rule 38a–1 requires policies and procedures to monitor for circumstances that may necessitate the use of fair value prices (i.e., unreliable market quotations); establish criteria for determining when market quotations are no longer reliable for a particular portfolio security; provide a methodology for a fair value determination; and regularly review the appropriateness and accuracy of this methodology, making any necessary adjustments.

entrusted to it, and (3) the failure of the board to properly request and consider information required by the Investment Company Act from the fund's investment adviser and other service providers.

In addition, Rule 38a–1 requires funds to review their policies and procedures, as well as those of their service providers, annually for the same criteria. Rule 38a–1 requires registered investment companies to appoint a chief compliance officer.[87]

§ 20.6[3] Approval of the Advisory Contract

Some state courts have given undue deference to the decisions of unaffiliated boards of directors renewing advisory contracts.[88] To counteract this undue deference and potential for self-dealing, section 36(b) was added in 1970 to provide that investment advisers are also subject to a fiduciary duty to the investment company.[89] This is supplemented by section 15(c)'s requirement that the investment adviser provide the information requested by the board of directors that is reasonably necessary to evaluate the adviser's performance.[90] The investment company's board has a statutory duty to request this information and consider it in its deliberations of whether to renew the advisory contract.[91] The Investment Company Act further requires that for renewal of the advisory contract, a majority of the disinterested directors must approve the renewal in person at a special meeting called for that express purpose.[92] This approval is in addition to the majority shareholder consent that is required for the initial advisory contract or for a change in investment advisers.[93]

Investment company directorial responsibility does not diminish with a delegation of authority to an investment adviser.[94] The investment adviser's "contractual authority to direct the functions and activities of the investment company to the extent of portfolio selection,"[95] the restrictions placed upon investment company activity by section 12,[96] and the requirement of share-

87. Rule 38a–1 also provides that a Fund's board may remove a chief compliance officer if it loses confidence in his or her effectiveness. A Fund's chief compliance officer must report directly to the board and meet in executive session with the independent directors at least once each year. Furthermore, the new rule explicitly forbids a Fund's affiliates from directly or indirectly taking any action to coerce, manipulate, mislead, or fraudulently influence the Fund's chief compliance officer in the performance of his or her responsibilities under the new rule.

88. *See, e.g.,* Saxe v. Brady, 40 Del.Ch. 474, 184 A.2d 602 (1962).

89. Investment Company Amendment Act, Pub.L. No. 91–547, 84 Stat. 1413 (1970); 15 U.S.C.A. § 80a–35(b). *See* § 20.10 *infra.*

90. 15 U.S.C.A. § 80a–15(c).

91. 15 U.S.C.A. § 80a–15(c).

92. 15 U.S.C.A. § 80a–15(c).

93. 15 U.S.C.A. § 80a–15(a). Problems associated with changes in the investment adviser are discussed in § 20.9 *infra.*

94. *See* 15 U.S.C.A. § 80a–15.

95. Joseph F. Krupsky, Role of Investment Company Directors, 32 Bus.Law. 1748 (1977).

96. Section 12 places numerous limitations on investment company activities. An investment company may not: purchase securities on margin; participate in joint trading accounts; effect a short sale of any security; distribute its own securities except through an underwriter; commit to underwrite securities of other issuers if its holdings therein exceed certain percentages; own more than three percent of any other investment company's securities; own securities of another single investment company the assets of which exceed five percent of the investment company's assets; own securities of other investment companies valued in the aggregate over one hundred percent of its total assets; acquire insurance company securities, save as enumerated; or purchase securities issued by its brokers, dealers, underwriters, or investment advisers. All of these are subject to numerous exceptions. 15 U.S.C.A. § 80a–12(a)–(d).

holder approval for changes in investment policy,[97] all combine to impose upon investment company directors a duty to continually oversee the adviser's portfolio supervision throughout the year. This obligation supplements the directors' duty to annually reconsider and reevaluate investment advisory contracts that continue in effect for more than two years from the making and execution of the advisory contract.[99] A "heavy duty of disclosure is imposed upon management in order to permit the directors to exercise informed discretion [in performing their duties]" since directors are not full-time employees and therefore probably not attuned to possible problems in the fund's day-to-day operation.[100]

The actual protection afforded public shareholder interests by disinterested director requirements and shareholder voting in adopting the original advisory contract is questionable since the adviser controls the initial voting securities after it creates the fund.[105] Even with the expansion of investment company shareholders, the investment adviser continues to effectively control the company's proxy machinery. Voting rights as a protection of shareholder interests are therefore minimal, and the independent director emerges as the shareholders' only unbiased advocate.[106]

Factors to be considered by an investment company's board of directors in evaluating an advisory contract's fairness include:

(1) the costs of comparable services;

(2) a comparison of total fund expenses as a percentage of fund assets;

(3) the reduction of advisory fees to reflect economies of scale, i.e., the fact that it does not require ten times the effort by the adviser to manage a fund of ten million dollars rather than one of one million dollars;

(4) the expenses and profits of the adviser;

(5) the quality of the investment advice received, thought by some to be the most important criterion to be evaluated by the board;

(6) the quality of other services performed by the adviser for the company;

(7) a consideration of the cost and the feasibility of internalizing management; and

(8) the basis of the fee arrangement.[108]

---

97. 15 U.S.C.A. § 80a–13

99. 15 U.S.C.A. § 80a–15(a).

100. Clarke Randall, Fiduciary Duties of Investment Company Directors and Management Companies Under the Investment Company Act of 1940, 31 Okla.L.Rev. 635, 668 (1978) (discussing Moses v. Burgin, 445 F.2d 369 (1st Cir.), *cert. denied* 404 U.S. 994, 92 S.Ct. 532, 30 L.Ed.2d 547 (1971)).

105. Comment, Duties of the Independent Director in Open–End Mutual Funds, 70 Mich. L.Rev. 696, 699 (1972); Joseph F. Krupsky, Role of Investment Company Directors, 32 Bus.Law. 1733, 1743 (1977).

106. Richard M. Phillips, Deregulation Under the Investment Company Act—Reevaluation of the Corporate Paraphernalia of Shareholder Voting and Boards of Directors, 37 Bus.Law. 903, 909 (1982).

108. *See* Michael J. Radmer, Duties of Directors of Investment Companies, 3 J.Corp.L. 61, 71–81 (1977).

An investment company rarely has the option of terminating an advisory contract due to its inability to internalize management and further due to the financial disturbance which would be suffered by the fund with a change of investment advisers.[109] Indeed, a change of advisers may frustrate shareholder expectations since most shareholders decide to invest in a company based on the reputation of the adviser.[110] Therefore, the mandatory reporting of all investment adviser activity affecting the company's performance to the board of directors is the most efficacious method of keeping adviser activity honest and above board. The investment company board of directors' decision to renew an advisory contract is given only as much weight as a court deems appropriate in an action against an adviser for breach of fiduciary duty.[111]

In 2004, the SEC adopted enhanced disclosure requirements regarding approval of the investment advisory contract. The SEC rules as amended require registered mutual funds to make disclosures in their reports to shareholders regarding the material factors and the conclusions with respect to those factors that formed the basis for the board's approval of advisory contracts during the most recent fiscal half-year.[112] The SEC rules "also are designed to encourage improved disclosure in proxy statements regarding the basis for the board's recommendation that shareholders approve an advisory contract."[113]

§ 20.6[4] Other Investment Company Board Obligations

The selection and supervision of an investment adviser is not the only function of the investment company's board of directors. Investment company directors must also choose an independent accountant for the fund—a choice which must be ratified by a majority of shareholders.[114] The independent accountants aid the investment company directors in discharging their duty to evaluate portfolio securities where market quotations are not readily available, since accountants presumably have more expertise to make such evaluations.[115] The choice of accountant is also important since it is the accountant who is required to report "inadequacies in the fund's accounting system and system of internal accounting control, along with an indication of any corrective action taken or proposed" in Form NBIR that is required under section 30 of the Investment Company Act.[116] Accountants therefore act as watchdogs for the watchdogs. Directors must also choose the investment company's attorney, although there are no statutory provisions for that procedure.

Investment company directors must ensure that the reports required by the various securities laws and SEC regulations are filed in a timely and

109. Joseph F. Krupsky, Role of Investment Company Directors, 32 Bus.Law. 1749–51 (1977).

110. SEC, Public Policy Implications of Investment Company Growth, H.R. Rep. No. 2337, 89th Cong.2d Sess. 31 (1966).

111. 15 U.S.C.A. § 80a–35(b)(2).

112. Disclosure Regarding Approval of Investment Advisory Contracts by Directors of Investment Companies, Sec. Act Rel. No. 33–8433; Sec. Exch. Act Rel. No. 34–49909; Inv. Co. Act Rel. No. IC–26486 (SEC June 30, 2004) (adopting release).

113. Disclosure Regarding Approval of Investment Advisory Contracts by Directors of Investment Companies, Sec. Act Rel. No. 33–8433; Sec. Exch. Act Rel. No. 34–49909; Inv. Co. Act Rel. No. IC–26486 (SEC June 30, 2004) (adopting release).

114. 15 U.S.C.A. § 80a–31.

115. 15 U.S.C.A. § 80a–2(a)(41).

116. Michael J. Radmer, Duties of Directors of Investment Companies, 3 J.Corp.L. 61, 84 (1977).

accurate fashion. Directors of investment companies have a duty to fill board vacancies created by death or resignation prior to the expiration of a director's term.[117] However, at least two-thirds of the directors of an investment company must have been elected by the shareholders.[118] Directors are also responsible for assuring that proper proxy solicitation materials are submitted to the shareholders and the SEC, although this obligation is often satisfied by the investment adviser. Directors must also ensure that dividends are paid correctly and that conditions for maintaining Subchapter M tax treatment[119] are met. In sum, investment company directors are subjected to all common law directorial duties and a host of others by the Investment Company Act. As a means of implementing the additional duties imposed by the Act, a private cause of action will lie for breach of a director's fiduciary duty.[120]

Over the years, there has been increasing concern over the accountability of mutual fund managers to the mutual fund investors when exercising the voting rights arising out of the ownership of shares in the investment portfolio. In 2003, the SEC adopted new rules requiring investment companies to make disclosures relating to their voting of portfolio securities.[121] The SEC adopted Investment Company Act Rule 30b1–4[122] to require registered management investment companies to provide disclosure about how they vote proxies relating to portfolio securities they hold. The SEC adopted a new form N–PX for making the portfolio voting disclosures and also amended existing registration and disclosure forms to assure that similar disclosures are made at least annually. Specifically, it requires registered management investment companies to disclose the policies and procedures that they use to determine how to vote proxies relating to portfolio securities.[123] In addition, management investment companies must file with the SEC and make available to shareholders the specific proxy votes that they cast in shareholder meetings of issuers of portfolio securities.[124] The SEC adopted a parallel set of rules for investment advisers.[125]

---

117. 15 U.S.C.A. § 80a–15.

118. 15 U.S.C.A. § 80a–16(a).

119. 26 U.S.C.A. §§ 851–55.

120. 15 U.S.C.A. § 80a–35(b). *See* § 20.10 *infra*. *See* SEC v. Pimco Advisors Fund Management, LLC, 341 F. Supp.2d 454, 471 (S.D.N.Y. 2004) (SEC had jurisdiction to pursue breach of fiduciary duty claim against investment company executives).

121. *See* Disclosure of Proxy Voting, Policies and Proxy Voting Records by Registered Management Investment Companies, Sec. Act Rel. No. 33–8188, Sec. Exch. Act Rel. No. 34–47304, Inv. Co. Act Rel. No. IC–25922, 79 S.E.C. Docket 1638, 2003 WL 215451 (SEC Jan. 31, 2003).

122. 17 C.F.R. § 270.30b1–4.

123. *See* Disclosure of Proxy Voting, Policies and Proxy Voting Records by Registered Management Investment Companies, Sec. Act Rel. No. 33–8188, Sec. Exch. Act Rel. No. 34–47304, Inv. Co. Act Rel. No. IC–25922, 79 S.E.C. Docket 1638, 2003 WL 215451 (SEC Jan. 31, 2003).

124. *See* Disclosure of Proxy Voting, Policies and Proxy Voting Records by Registered Management Investment Companies, Sec. Act Rel. No. 33–8188, Sec. Exch. Act Rel. No. 34–47304, Inv. Co. Act Rel. No. IC–25922, 79 S.E.C. Docket 1638, 2003 WL 215451 (SEC Jan. 31, 2003).

125. *See* Proxy Voting By Investment Advisors, Inv. Adv. Act Rel. No. IA–2106, 79 S.E.C. Docket 1673, 2003 WL 215467 (SEC Jan. 31, 2003). Those rules require investment advisers to adopt proxy policies and procedures for voting shares held for advisory clients, to describe their proxy voting policies and procedures to their advisory clients, to furnish a copy of the voting policies and procedures upon request to advisory client; and to disclose how advisory clients can obtain information about how the adviser voted their proxies. *Id.*

§ 20.6[5] Enhanced Fiduciary Obligations; Investment Adviser Code of Ethics

As discussed earlier in this treatise, the Sarbanes–Oxley Act of 2002[126] introduced a number of corporate governance reforms applicable to publicly traded companies,[127] including disclosures relating to a company's code of ethics.[128] These disclosures apply as well to publicly traded mutual funds. In 2004, the SEC adopted rules requiring investment advisers to adopt and enforce codes of ethics applicable to persons they supervise.[129]

Investment Adviser Act Rule 204A–1 is designed to prevent fraud by reinforcing the fiduciary principles that must govern the conduct of advisory firms and their personnel.[130] Under the SEC rules, an investment adviser's code of ethics must include certain minimum provisions, as summarized by the SEC:

> Standards of Business Conduct. The code will be required to establish standards of conduct that are expected of the adviser's supervised persons and that reflect the adviser's fiduciary duties. Supervised persons will have to acknowledge, in writing, receipt of a copy of the code of ethics and any amendments.
>
> Compliance with Federal Securities Laws. An adviser's code of ethics will have to require the adviser's supervised persons to comply with applicable federal securities laws.
>
> Personal Securities Reporting. An adviser's code of ethics will have to require certain supervised persons called access persons to report their personal securities holdings and transactions, including transactions in mutual funds advised by the adviser or an affiliate.
>
> Pre–Approval of Certain Transactions. The code of ethics will have to require access persons to pre-clear any personal investments in initial public offerings and limited offerings.[131]

The SEC rules also require investment advisers to report violations of their codes of ethics. Thus, an investment adviser's code of ethics must require supervised persons to report, promptly, any violations of the adviser's code of ethics to the firm's chief compliance officer or to other designated persons.

§ 20.7 Transactions Between an Investment Company and Affiliated Persons

Section 17 of the Investment Company Act[1] regulates the activities of those who, due to their connection with an investment company, stand to gain

---

126. Sarbanes–Oxley Act of 2002, Pub. Law 107–204 (July 30, 2002).

127. *See* § 9.3[2] *supra.*

128. *See* § 9.4[8][F] *supra.*

129. Inv. Adv. Act Rule 204A–1, 17 C.F.R. § 280.204A–1. *See also* Inv. Co. Act Rule 17j–1, 17 C.F.R. § 270.17j–1; Inv. Adv. Act Rule 204–2, 17 C.F.R. § 280.204–2.

130. Disclosure of Breakpoint Discounts by Mutual Funds, Sec. Act Rel. No. 33–8427; Sec. Exch. Act rel. No. 34–49817; Inv. Co. Act Rel. No. IC–26464 (SEC 2004). *See also* § 21.4[1][F] *infra.*

131. SEC Adopts Rules on Breakpoint Disclosure and Adviser Ethics Codes, Proposes Transfer Agent Rule, http://www.sec.gov/news/press/2004–71.htm (May 26, 2004).

§ 20.7

1. 15 U.S.C.A. § 80a–17. See Note, The Application of Section 17 of The Investment Company Act of 1940 to Portfolio Affiliates, 120 U.Pa.L.Rev. 983 (1972).

personally from the manipulation of the company's investments, perhaps to the detriment of shareholders. Section 17(a) thus protects "minority interests from exploitation by insiders of their 'strategic position' "[2] and assures that interested persons deal with the investment company "at arm's length in an endeavor to secure the best possible bargain for their respective stockholders."[3] "Affiliated person" is defined in section 2(a)(3).[4] Briefly stated, the statutory definition includes persons controlling, controlled by or in common control with the investment company.[5]

Section 17 of the Act contains numerous provisions regulating the conduct of interested persons. Subsections (e) through (j) are relatively straightforward in protecting shareholders on a basic level against such things as theft of securities. In contrast, subsections (a) through (d) regulate more complex transactions between affiliated persons and the investment company. Subsection (e) prohibits affiliated persons acting as agents from accepting payment for transactions in securities or other property by an investment company except as regular salary or commission in the course of its business as an underwriter or a broker.[6] Such fees may not exceed "the usual and customary broker's commission."[7] Because of the potential conflict of interest, the prohibitions of section 17(e) should be broadly construed.[8] Thus, for example, a portfolio manager was appropriately convicted of a section 17(e) violation when she accepted the opportunity to purchase warrants from a company, the securities of which she had purchased for the pension plans she managed.[9] The conviction was upheld without proof that the warrants were purchased at a discount since the jury could reasonably have concluded that the opportunity to purchase the warrants was itself a benefit.[10]

Section 17(f)[11] of the Investment Company Act requires that securities owned by investment companies be placed in a bank, with a member of a national securities exchange (as defined in the Securities Exchange Act of

2. E.I. du Pont de Nemours & Co. v. Collins, 432 U.S. 46, 60 n. 6, 97 S.Ct. 2229, 2237 n. 6, 53 L.Ed.2d 100 (1977) (Brennan, J., dissenting), quoting SEC Report on Investment Trusts and Investment Companies, H.R. Doc. No. 279, 76th Cong., 1st Sess., 1414 (1940).

3. E.I. du Pont de Nemours & Co. v. Collins, 432 U.S. 46, 60 n. 6, 97 S.Ct. 2229, 2237 n. 6, 53 L.Ed.2d 100 (1977) See also, e.g., In the Matter of Strong/Corneliuson Capital Management, Inc., [1994–1995 Transfer Binder] Fed. Sec. L. Rep. (CCH) ¶ 85,416 (SEC 1994) (mutual funds violated section 17(a) in series of transactions with other funds managed by the same investment adviser). *Cf*, Pfeiffer v. Bjurman, Barry & Associates, 2004 WL 1903075 (S.D.N.Y. 2004) (investors alleged claim for excessive advisory fees but to prevail would have to establish "that the fees were so disproportionately large that they bore no reasonable relationship to the services actually provided and could not have been the product of arm's length negotiations"), quoting Gartenberg v. Merrill Lynch Asset Management, Inc , 694 F.2d 923, 928 (2d Cir.1982).

4. 15 U.S.C.A. § 80a–2(a)(3).

5. 15 U.S.C.A. § 80a–2(a)(3). See also § 20.6 supra.

6. 15 U.S.C.A. § 80a–17(e)(1). See Annot., When is Affiliated Person of Registered Investment Company "Acting as Agent" Within Meaning of § 17(e)(1) of Investment Company Act of 1940 (15 U.S.C.A. § 80a–17(e)(1)), Prohibiting Such Person From Accepting Compensation From Any Other Source for Purchase or Sale of Property to or for Company, 62 A.L.R.Fed. 575 (1983).

7. 15 U.S.C.A. § 80a–17(e)(2).

8. But cf. Paine/Webber Managed Investments Trusts, 26 Sec. Reg. & L. Rep. (BNA) 1168 (SEC No Action Letter available Aug. 8, 1994) (permitting sales of illiquid securities to an affiliated person; the staff response agreed that in light of the unusual nature of the transaction and representations as to the value of the securities, the protections of the Act did not require invocation of the prohibition).

9. United States v. Ostrander, 999 F.2d 27 (2d Cir.1993).

10. United States v. Ostrander, 999 F.2d 27 (2d Cir.1993).

11. 15 U.S.C.A. § 80a–17(f).

1934[12]), or with the investment company. Securities may also be deposited in a central handling system established by any registered securities exchange.[13] No investment company may act as custodian of its own securities except pursuant to Rule 17f–2.[14] Rule 17f–2 requires the securities to be physically separated at all times from those of any other person,[15] unless the securities are serving as collateral for a loan.[16] There are further restrictions under Investment Company Act Rule 17f–2. Access to the securities is through resolution of the board of directors only; a maximum of five persons may be designated for access by each resolution and each must be an officer or "responsible employee" of the investment company.[17] An investment company officer must be present when access to the securities is permitted.[18] Additional precautionary measures against larceny and embezzlement appear in section 17(g)'s bonding requirements for those with access to the investment company's securities.[19] The minimum permissible bond varies with the investment company's gross assets.[20]

Section 17(h) prohibits certain types of indemnification agreements. An investment company's charter, certificate of incorporation, articles of association, indenture of trust, or bylaws cannot indemnify or otherwise protect a director or officer against liability for "willful misfeasance, bad faith, gross negligence or reckless disregard of the duties involved in the conduct of his office."[21] Section 17(i) similarly prohibits any investment adviser or principal underwriter from contracting away its liability.[22]

Section 17(j) of the Investment Company Act[24] parallels section 10(b) of the Securities Exchange Act[25] as the general antifraud provision applicable to affiliated persons. Enacted in 1970, section 17(j) is directed at insider trading for the insider's personal account in the investment company's portfolio securities.[26] Rule 17j–1[27] is the Investment Company Act's counterpart to Rule 10b–5 in prohibiting material misrepresentation and fraudulent practices. Rule 17j–1 also requires each investment company to adopt a written code of

12. Section 6, 15 U.S.C.A. § 78f.

13. 17 C.F.R. § 270.17f–4 (1982). See § 14.2 supra.

14. 17 C.F.R. § 270.17f–2.

15. 17 C.F.R. § 270.17f–2(b).

16. 17 C.F.R. § 270.17f–2(c).

17. 17 C.F.R. § 270.17f–2(d). Certain bank officers and employees and independent public accountants may also have access to the securities jointly with the investment company officers, id.

18. 17 C.F.R. § 270.17f–2(d).

19. 15 U.S.C.A. § 80a–17(g).

20. 17 C.F.R. § 270.17g–1(d)(1).

21. 15 U.S.C.A. § 80a–17(h). Compare the SEC's approach to indemnification in connection with 1933 Act registration statements. See § 7.14 supra.

22. 15 U.S.C.A. § 80a–17(i).

24. 15 U.S.C.A. § 80a–17(j).

25. 15 U.S.C.A. § 78j(b); 17 C.F.R. § 240.10b–5. See, chapter 12 supra.

26. 1970 U.S.Code Cong. and Adm.News 4897, 4923. See generally Gerard H. Manges, The Investment Company Amendments Act of 1970–An Analysis and Appraisal After Two Years, 14 B.C. Ind. & Comm.L.Rev. 387 (1973); Gerard Manges, The Investment Company Amendments Act of 1970, 26 Bus.Law. 1311 (1971); Walter P. North, The Investment Company Amendments Act of 1970, 46 Notre Dame Law. 712 (1971).

27. 17 C.F.R. § 270.17j–1. See Inv. Co. Act Rel. No. 11421, [1980 Transfer Binder] Fed.Sec. L.Rep. (CCH) ¶ 82,679 (Oct. 31, 1980).

ethics to be followed by each of the company's "access persons."[28] The term "access persons" is defined broadly in the rule to include persons who render investment advice. Specifically it includes: (1) any director, officer, general partner, or "advisory person"[29] of an investment company or its investment adviser "primarily engaged" in advising investment companies or investment clients,[30] (2) any director, officer, or general partner of a principal underwriter who makes, participates in, or obtains information regarding the sale of securities for the investment company as part of his or her ordinary course of business, and (3) any director, officer, general partner or advisory person of an investment adviser "primarily engaged in a business or businesses other than advising registered investment companies or other advisory clients," who makes recommendations, or participates in the determination of which recommendation to make to the investment company.[31] Also included in the definition of "access persons" are those individuals or entities who obtain information concerning securities recommendations being made by the investment adviser to the investment company.[32]

§ 20.8 Registration and Disclosure Requirements; Civil Liability

§ 20.8[1] Investment Company Name

Investment Company Act Rule 35d–1[1] imposes limitations on the names of registered investment companies. The rule is designed to prevent investment companies from adopting names that are likely to mislead investors about the investment company's investments and risks.[2] Rule 35d–1 requires a registered investment company with a name that suggests the company focuses on a particular type of investment or industry[3] to invest at least eighty percent of its assets in the type of investment suggested by its name.[4] Rule 35d–1 also addresses investment company names suggesting that an investment company focuses its investments in a particular country or geographic

28. 17 C.F.R. § 270.17j–1(b).

29. As defined in 17 C.F.R. § 270.17j–1(e)(2).

30. An investment adviser is "primarily engaged in a business or businesses other than advising registered investment companies or other advisory clients" when, for each of its most recent three fiscal years or for the period of time since its organization, whichever is lesser, the investment adviser derived, on an unconsolidated basis, more than fifty percent of (A) its total sales and revenues, and (B) its income (or loss) before income taxes and extraordinary items from such other business or businesses. 17 C F.R. § 270.17j–1(e)(1)(iv).

31. 17 C.F.R. § 270.17j–1(e)(1)(i)–(iii).

32. 17 C.F.R. § 270.17j–1(e)(1)(i)–(iii).

§ 20.8

1. 7 C.F.R. § 270.35d–1.

2. Investment Company Names, Inv. Co. Act Rel. IC–24828, 66 Fed. Reg. 8509–01, 2001 WL 81473 (F.R.) (SEC Feb. 1, 2001).

3. For example, if an investment company calls itself the ABC Stock Fund, the XYZ Bond Fund, or the QRS U.S. Government Fund.

4. "A name suggesting that the Fund focuses its investments in a particular type of investment or investments, or in investments in a particular industry or group of industries, unless: (i) The Fund has adopted a policy to invest, under normal circumstances, at least 80% of the value of its Assets in the particular type of investments, or in investments in the particular industry or industries, suggested by the Fund's name; and (ii) Either the policy described in paragraph (a)(2)(i) of this section is a fundamental policy under section 8(b)(3) of the Act (15 U.S.C. 80a–8(b)(3)), or the Fund has adopted a policy to provide the Fund's shareholders with at least 60 days prior notice of any change in the policy . . ." 17 C.F.R. § 270.35d–1(a)(2).

region,[5] names indicating that a company's distributions are exempt from income tax,[6] and names suggesting that a company or its shares are guaranteed or approved by the United States government.

§ 20.8[2] Registration Requirements

As is the case with all other federal securities laws, the Investment Company Act has numerous registration, disclosure, and antifraud provisions meant to protect the investing public by requiring information relating to the issuer's policies and activities. Unless an available exemption can be found, a domestic company deemed to be an investment company within the definitions of section 3(a) of the Act[12] must register under section 8.[13] Registration is initiated by the filing of Form N–8A,[14] which is a short-form notification of registration that will be followed by more detailed disclosures in subsequent filings.

In addition, the registrant must recite and describe all of its investment policies which may change only if authorized by a shareholder vote, those policies fundamental to the company, the name and address of each affiliated person of the registrant, the name and principal address of every company of which each such person is an officer, director or partner, and a brief statement of the business experience of each officer and director of the registrant for the past five years.[17]

The Investment Company Act supplements other securities law provisions.[18] An investment company must also file such information and documents as are required under the 1933 Securities Act[19] and the 1934 Securities Exchange Act.[20] In registering under the 1933 Act, however, section 24(a) of the Investment Company Act of 1940[21] allows documents filed under the 1940 Act to suffice in lieu of some of the documents that would otherwise be required by the 1933 Act's provisions.

---

5. In order to have such a name, the investment company must have adopted a policy to invest, under normal circumstances, at least 80% of the value of its Assets in investments that are tied economically to the particular country or geographic region suggested by its name. 17 C.F.R. § 270.35d–1(a)(3)(i). Furthermore, the fund must disclose in its prospectus the specific criteria used by the Fund to select these investments. 17 C.F.R. § 270.35d–1(a)(3)(ii).

6. An investment company's name may not suggest that the Fund's distributions are exempt from federal income tax or from both federal and state income tax, unless the Fund "has adopted a fundamental policy under section 8(b)(3) of the Act (15 U.S.C. 80–8(b)(3)): (i) To invest, under normal circumstances, at least 80% of the value of its Assets in investments the income from which is exempt, as applicable, from federal income tax or from both federal and state income tax; or (ii) To invest, under normal circumstances, its Assets so that at least 80% of the income that it distributes will be exempt, as applicable, from federal income tax or from both federal and state income tax." 17 C.F.R. § 270.35d–1(4).

12. 15 U.S.C.A. § 80a–3(a). *See* § 20.3 *supra.*

13. 15 U.S.C.A. § 80a–8. Foreign investment companies register through the provisions of Section 7(d). *Id.* at § 80a–7(d).

14. 17 C.F.R. § 274.10.

17. 15 U.S.C.A. § 80a–8(b)(2)–(4). Form N–1 is used for open-end management companies, 17 C.F.R. § 274.11. Form N–2 is used for closed-end companies, 17 C.F.R. § 274.11a–1.

18. 15 U.S.C.A. § 80a–8(b)(5).

19. 15 U.S.C.A. §§ 77a *et seq. See* chapters 2–3 *supra.*

20. 15 U.S.C.A. §§ 78a *et seq.* The registration and periodic reporting requirements of sections 12 and 13(a), 15 U.S.C.A. §§ 78*l*, 78m(a), are discussed in §§ 9.2, 9.3 *supra.*

21. 15 U.S.C.A. § 80a–24(a).

As a final safety net for investors, the affirmative disclosure requirements of the Act are supplemented by broad antifraud prohibitions in Rule 8b–20.[23]

Rule 8b–2 provides a test of materiality: "the term 'material' when used to qualify a requirement for the furnishing of information as to any subject, limits the information required to those matters as to which an average prudent investor ought reasonably to be informed before buying or selling any security of the particular company."[24] The investment company must provide complete disclosure of all its relevant activities; there is, however, the disclaimer that "information required need be given only insofar as it is known or reasonably available to the registrant."[25] The issuer can be held criminally accountable[26] and civilly liable[27] for fraudulent statements made in connection with its registration and/or the reports which the investment company is required to file.[28] Failure to file registration statements properly and/or omissions of material facts are grounds for the revocation of a company's registration.[29]

The Investment Company Act contains periodic reporting requirements in addition to the initial registration. Section 30 of the Act requires issuers to file periodic reports with the SEC and to send such to their shareholders.[30] Annual reports similar to those required by section 13(a) of the Securities Exchange Act[31] must be filed by the investment company issuer.[32] Formerly, issuers were required to file quarterly reports with the Commission and supply the Commission with copies of all information sent to their shareholders within ten days of the transmission.[33] In 1985 the SEC replaced the quarterly reporting requirement with semi-annual reports.[34] The reporting form, Form N–SAR, replaced the five quarterly reporting forms that formerly were used by most registered investment companies and thus is another step in the Commission's move towards simplification.[35] Also, the amended reporting system parallels the semi-annual reports that have to be made to share-

23. 17 C.F.R. § 270.8b–20.

24. 17 C.F.R. § 270.8b–2(g). *Compare* the 1934 Act's definition of materiality in Rule 12b–2 17 C.F.R. § 240.12b–2. *See* §§ 10.4, 12.9 *supra.*

See, e.g., SEC v. Steadman, 798 F.Supp. 733 (D.D.C.1991), *vacated on other grounds and affirmed in part* 967 F.2d 636 (D.C.Cir.1992) (overstatement of net asset value was material misrepresentation).

25. 17 C.F.R. § 270.8b–21.

26. 15 U.S.C.A. § 80a–33(b).

27. False filings under the 1934 Act will result in civil liability under section 18(a). 15 U.S.C.A. § 78r(a). *See* § 12.19 *supra.*

28. 15 U.S.C.A. § 78r(a). *See* § 12.19 *supra. See, e.g.,* SEC v. Steadman, 798 F.Supp. 733 (D.D.C.1991), *vacated on other grounds and affirmed in part* 967 F.2d 636 (D.C.Cir.1992) (investment company violated § 22(c) and Rule 22c–1 by overstating net asset value).

29. 15 U.S.C.A. § 80a–8(e).

30. 15 U.S.C.A. § 80a–29.

31. 15 U.S.C.A. § 78m(a). *See* § 9.3 *supra.*

32. 15 U.S.C.A. § 80a–29(a); 17 C.F.R. § 270.30a–1.

33. 15 U.S.C.A. § 80a–30(b); 17 C.F.R. § 270.30b1–5(T) (1984).

34. 17 C.F.R. § 270.30b1–1. *See* Inv.Co.Act.Rel. No. IC–14299, [1984–1985 Transfer Binder] Fed.Sec.L.Rep. (CCH) ¶ 83,725 (Jan. 4, 1985).

35. The SEC, in yet another step towards integrated disclosure requirements, has also proposed a new form N–7 that would replace form N–8B–2 for investment trusts and would replace Form S–6 under the 1933 Act. Inv.Co.Act Rel. No. IC–15612, [1987 Transfer Binder] Fed.Sec.L.Rep. (CCH) ¶ 84,109 (March 9, 1987); Inv. Co. Act Rel. No. IC–14513, [1984–1985 Transfer Binder] Fed.Sec.L.Rep. (CCH) ¶ 83,774 (May 14, 1985).

holders. In 1990, the Shareholder Communication Act extended to mutual funds and other investment companies that are registered under the Investment Company Act the applicability of the 1934 Act proxy rules that govern Exchange Act reporting companies generally.[36]

§ 20.8[3] Reporting Requirements

Registered investment companies must send semi-annual reports to their shareholders.[37] These reports should include the following information compiled "as of a reasonably current date":[38]

(1) a balance sheet accompanied by a statement of the investments' aggregate value;

(2) a listing of amounts and values of securities owned;

(3) an itemized income statement insofar as each item of income or expense exceeds five percent of the company's total income or expense;

(4) a statement of surplus itemized for each charge or credit representing over five percent of the total charges or credits in the report period;

(5) a statement of the aggregate remuneration paid during the report period to all directors and members of an advisory board for regular compensation, to each of the foregoing for special compensation, to all officers, and to each person of whom any officer or director of the investment company is an affiliated person; and

(6) a statement of the aggregate dollar amounts of sales and purchases of investment securities, other than government securities, during the report period.

In 1993, 1933 Act Registration Form N–1A (for investment company securities) was amended to require disclosures pertaining to fund managers, a discussion of the factors and strategies that had an effect on recent fund performance, and a line graph comparing the fund's performance to an index of the over-all market over a ten-year period.[39]

An open-end management company may substitute a currently effective prospectus under the Securities Act of 1933 if the remuneration information from item (5) and financial information for the half-year are also included.[40] The financial statements filed by an investment company must be signed or certified by an independent public accountant.[41] No controlling person, employee, or principal accounting officer of a management company or face-amount certificate company may participate in the preparation of financial statements without an affirmative vote to do so by a majority of the board or of the shareholders.[42]

36. 15 U.S.C.A. § 78n(b). The Exchange Act's proxy rules are discussed in chapter 10 *supra*.

37. 15 U.S.C.A. § 80a–29(d). *Compare* the annual report requirement for 1934 Act reporting companies. 17 C.F.R. §§ 240.14a–3(b), 14c–3. *See* §§ 10.6, 10.9 *supra*.

38. 15 U.S.C.A. § 80a–29(d).

39. *See* Inv. Co. Act. Rel. IC–19382, [1993 Transfer Binder] Fed. Sec. L. Rep. (CCH) ¶ 85,123 (SEC April 6, 1993).

40. 17 C.F.R. § 270.30d–1.

41. 15 U.S.C.A. § 80a–29(e).

42. 15 U.S.C.A. § 80a–31(b).

Adoption of Rule 482 (formerly Rule 434d) under the Securities Act of 1933[43] in 1979 has allowed investment companies to advertise more freely than had been allowed previously.[44] This rule allows an investment company to advertise in newspapers and magazines and on radio and television some but not all of the information required to be included in its prospectus by section 10(a) of the Securities Act of 1933[45] so as to satisfy the requirement of section 5 of that Act requiring that statutory prospectuses be distributed to investors along with the sale of registered securities.[46] The advertisement must conspicuously state "from whom a prospectus containing more complete information may be obtained and that the investor should read that prospectus carefully before investing."[47] Any representation by a money market fund of its yield must be computed according to the formula required by Form N–1[48] and identify the last day in the period used in compiling the quotation.[49]

Investment companies are required to file periodic reports[50] with the SEC and, further, must amend their registration statements annually.[51] Registration statements of open-end management companies, unit investment trusts, and face-amount certificate companies must be amended to reflect any increase in the number of securities offered.[52] If such a company sells more than the number of securities registered, it may be required to pay a treble registration fee and the securities will be deemed to have been registered.[53] To avoid this potentially expensive filing penalty, open-end companies may register to sell "an indefinite number of the securities."[54]

Prior to the mid–1990s, shareholders of investment companies were not taxed on their investment company's gains and income that were not passed through dividends or other distributions to the investment company shareholders. This all changed when investment companies became pass-through tax entities so that the company's gains and income would be passed on to the investment company shareholders for tax purposes. One consequence of this was that between 1994 and 1999, investors in diversified stock funds were required to pay an average of fifteen percent of their annual investment company's gains to taxes.[55] In order to give mutual fund investors a more accurate picture of the return on their investment, in 2001, the SEC amended its disclosure requirements to require investment companies to provide share-

43. 17 C.F.R. §§ 230.134(d), 482. *See* § 20.8[4] *infra*.

44. 15 U.S.C.A. § 77j(a). The prospectus delivery requirements of section 5(b) of the 1933 Act, 15 U.S.C.A. § 77e(b) are discussed in §§ 2.4, 2.5 *supra*.

45. 17 C.F.R. § 230.134(d).

46. The registration and prospectus provisions of the 1933 Act are discussed in chapter 2 *supra*.

47. 17 C.F.R. § 230.434(d)(a)(4).

48. 17 C.F.R. § 274.11.

49. 17 C.F.R. § 230.434(d)(a)(6).

50. 15 U.S.C.A. § 80a–29.

51. 17 C.F.R. § 270.8b–16.

52. 15 U.S.C.A. § 80a–24(e)(1).

53. 15 U.S.C.A. § 80a–24(f).

54. *Id.* Shelf registrations generally under the 1933 Act are considered in § 3.11 *supra*.

55. *See* Disclosure of Mutual Fund After–Tax Returns, Inv. Co. Act Rel. IC–24832, 66 Fed. Reg. 9002–01, 2001 WL 89496 (F.R.) (SEC Feb. 5, 2001).

holders with after-tax performance information.[56] Mutual funds must disclose in their prospectuses the after-tax returns based on standardized formulas comparable to the formula currently used to calculate before-tax average annual total returns.[57] The amendments further require certain funds to include standardized after-tax returns in advertisements and other sales materials.

§ 20.8[5] Investment Company Sales Literature

The Securities Act of 1933 limits written materials during the waiting and post-effective periods during a 1933 Act registration to permissible prospectuses.[62] 1933 Act Rule 482[63] permits specified investment company advertising materials in compliance with the 1933 Act prospectus requirements.[64] As originally adopted, information that could be provided in advertisements was limited to the information that is permitted in a prospectus.[65] Limiting permissible advertising material to information that is in the prospectus operates as a limitation on investment company advertising, since usually not all matters are covered in the 1933 Act prospectus.[66] In 1996, Congress expanded the information that may be included in part to facilitate the advertising of funds using performance data which would not otherwise be permitted in a 1933 Act prospectus.[68]

All sales literature used by open-end management companies, unit investment trusts, and face-amount certificate companies must be filed with the Commission within ten days of its being sent.[69] "Sales literature" includes:

> any communication (whether in writing, by radio, or by television) used by any person to offer to sell or induce the sale of securities of any investment company. Communications between issuers, underwriters and dealers are included in this definition of sales literature if such communications, or the information contained therein, can be reasonably expected to be communicated to prospective investors in the offer or sale of securities or are designed to be employed in either written or oral form in the offer or sale of securities.[70]

---

56. As explained by the SEC, "Disclosure of standardized mutual fund after-tax returns will help investors to understand the magnitude of tax costs and compare the impact of taxes on the performance of different funds." *Id.*

57. Form N–1A, Item 21. Calculation of Performance Data *See* Disclosure of Mutual Fund After–Tax Returns, Inv. Co. Act Rel. IC–24832, 66 Fed. Reg. 9002–01, 2001 WL 89496 (F.R.) (SEC Feb. 5, 2001).

62. *See* §§ 2.4–2.5 *supra*.

63. 17 C.F.R. § 230.482.

64. The 1933 Act prospectus requirements are found in sections 5 and 10 of the 1933 Act. 15 U.S.C.A. §§ 77e, 77j. *See* chapter 2 *supra*.

65. 17 C.F.R. § 230.482(a)(2).

66. Testimony of Barry Barbash Concerning H.R. 1495, The Investment Company Act Amendments of 1995, Before the Subcommittee on Telecommunications and Finance, Committee on Commerce, U.S. House of Representatives 34 (Oct. 31, 1995), citing H.R. Rep. No. 1382, 91st Cong., 2d Sess. 10–11, 23–35 (1970) at 16.

68. 15 U.S.C.A. § 80a–24(g).

69. 15 U.S.C.A. § 80a–24(b). In 1988, the SEC adopted Rule 24b–3 which permits filing of sales literature with a registered national securities association (which currently only applies to FINRA), provided that the association has adopted rules providing standards for investment company advertising and further has adopted procedures to review such advertising. 17 C.F.R. § 270.24b–3. *See* Inv.Co.Act Rel. No. IC–16245, [1987–1988 Transfer Binder] Fed.Sec.L.Rep. (CCH) ¶ 84,217 (Feb. 2, 1988). *See also* Inv.Co.Act Rel. No. IC–15–315 (Sept. 17, 1986).

70. 17 C.F.R. § 230.156(c). Compare the 1933 Act's definition of "prospectus" in section 2(a)(10). 15 U.S.C.A. § 77b(a)(10).

The content of investment company literature is regulated by 1933 Act Rule 156.[71] Under this rule it is illegal for any person to make a materially misleading statement. The rule sets out specific criteria for determining whether a statement is misleading.[72] As discussed above, the issuer of the securities will be held liable if statements in the investment company's sales literature are found to be misleading.

§ 20.9 Limitations on Advisory Fees; Transfers of Control—The "Sale" of Investment Advisory Contracts

§ 20.9[1] Investment Advisory Fees

Investment advisers that manage investment companies' assets generally are compensated through a management fee based on a percentage of the fund's average asset value. Typically this fee is annualized based on between one-half and one percent of the fund's average assets. During the start-up time, the adviser's fee may be quite modest but, as the fund grows, the fee can become "enormous."[1] Prior to the shareholders' annual approval of the advisory contract there must be full disclosure of the terms of compensation.[2] The limitations on the amount of compensation are found in the Act's general imposition of fiduciary duties,[3] and prohibition against unlawful conversion of investment company assets.[4] In addition, the Act prohibits the charging of unreasonable expenses and other charges in connection with the operation of the investment company.[5]

Section 37 of the Act[6] makes it unlawful for any person to steal, unlawfully "abstract," or convert investment company assets. A violation of this section seems to require more than merely excessive compensation and thus section 37 will not be very helpful in challenging excessive advisory fees.[7] Section 36(b), which supports an express private right of action,[8] imposes fiduciary obligations upon the investment adviser. Section 36(b)'s fiduciary obligations include refraining from charging and collecting excessive investment advisory fees.

The courts have long required under general corporate law that management compensation be fair and reasonable.[9] This rule has been followed under the Investment Company Act, which "subject[s] the transaction to rigorous

---

71. 17 C.F.R. § 230.156.

72. 17 C.F.R. § 230.156(b).

§ 20.9

1. Richard W. Jennings & Harold Marsh, Jr., Securities Regulation: Cases and Materials 1398 (5th ed.1982).

2. 15 U.S.C.A. § 80a–15(a)(1) ("precisely describe all compensation to be paid thereunder").

3. 15 U.S.C.A. § 80a–35(b).

4. 15 U.S.C.A. § 80a–36.

5. 15 U.S.C.A. §§ 80a–26(e), 80a–27(i).

6. 15 U.S.C.A. § 80a–36.

7. *See, e.g.,* Brown v. Bullock, 294 F.2d 415 (2d Cir.1961).

8. 15 U.S.C.A. § 80a–35(b). *See, e.g.,* Fogel v. Chestnutt, 668 F.2d 100 (2d Cir.1981), *cert. denied* 459 U.S. 828, 103 S.Ct. 65, 74 L.Ed.2d 66 (1982); Tannenbaum v. Zeller, 552 F.2d 402 (2d Cir.1977), *cert. denied* 434 U.S. 934, 98 S.Ct. 421, 54 L.Ed.2d 293 (1977).

9. Rogers v. Hill, 289 U.S. 582, 53 S.Ct. 731, 77 L.Ed. 1385 (1933); Hingle v. Plaquemines Oil Sales Corp., 399 So.2d 646 (La.App.1981), *writ denied* 401 So.2d 987 (La.1981); Ruetz v. Topping, 453 S.W.2d 624 (Mo.App.1970).

scrutiny for fairness.''[10] As noted in one decision, ''the Court must consider the 'nature, quality and extent' of the services to the Fund in relation to the fee paid by the Fund.''[11]

Although investment company advisory fees may be high, the courts have tended to validate the compensation in light of industry practices[13] as well as looking to the size of the fund.[14] A successful challenge to advisory fees requires a showing that the fees themselves are excessive.[15] This means that the courts will scrutinize the amount of the compensation and not the method of calculation. Thus, for example, the Second Circuit upheld a fee arrangement that gave the investment advisers incentive to maximize leverage in order to increase their advisory fees.[16] Even though this fee arrangement created the potential for a conflict of interest in selecting investments, it was not a *per se* breach of fiduciary duty.[17] Furthermore, it is not sufficient to establish that the fee structure created an incentive for the fund manager to consider its own interests when making leverage decisions for the funds.[18]

Another reason for the difficulty in proving excessive fees is the fact that shareholders or the board of directors ratify the contract annually.[19] However, it is clear that ratification upon full disclosure will not preclude judicial scrutiny of the fairness of the compensation.[20] Nevertheless, there is a relatively high burden imposed for overcoming the effect of shareholder ratification.

---

10. Galfand v. Chestnutt, 545 F.2d 807, 811–812 (2d Cir.1976).

11. Gartenberg v. Merrill Lynch Asset Management, Inc., 528 F.Supp. 1038, 1047 (S.D.N.Y. 1981), *affirmed* 694 F.2d 923 (2d Cir.1982). *See also, e.g.,* Krasner v. Dreyfus Corp., 500 F.Supp. 36 (S.D.N.Y.1980); Note, Mutual Fund Advisory Fees—Too Much for Too Little?, 48 Fordham L.Rev. 530, 545 (1980).

13. *E.g.* Krinsk v. Fund Asset Management, Inc., 875 F.2d 404 (2d Cir.1989); Saxe v. Brady, 40 Del.Ch. 474, 184 A.2d 602 (1962).

14. *E.g.*, Meyer v. Oppenheimer Management Corp., 895 F.2d 861 (2d Cir.1990) (advisory and distribution fees were not excessive); Gartenberg v. Merrill Lynch Asset Management, Inc., 694 F.2d 923 (2d Cir.1982). *But see* Brown v. Bullock, 294 F.2d 415, 424 (2d Cir.1961) (Moore, J. dissenting), which is quoted in footnote 1 *supra.*

15. *See, e.g.,* Krantz v. Prudential Investments Fund Management LLC, 305 F.3d 140 (3d Cir. 2002) (failure to show fees were excessive); Migdal v. Rowe Price–Fleming Intern., Inc., 248 F.3d 321, 2001 (4th Cir.2001) (insufficient allegations of excessive fees).

A successful suit under section 36(b) requires that the excessive fees be received by the advisers. Accordingly, a claim for excessive fees in violation of Rule 12b–1 was dismissed since the fees were compensation to the brokers and thus were not received by the investment adviser. *See* Pfeiffer v. Bjurman, Barr & Associates, 215 Fed. Appx. 30 (2d Cir. 2007).

16. Green v. Fund Asset Management, L.P., 286 F.3d 682 (3d Cir.2002).

17. Green v. Fund Asset Management, L.P., 286 F.3d 682 (3d Cir.2002).

18. Green v. Nuveen Advisory Corp., 295 F.3d 738 (7th Cir. 2002).

19. *See* 15 U.S.C.A. § 80a–15(a)(2). *See also, e.g.,* Green v. Nuveen Advisory Corp., 295 F.3d 738 (7th Cir. 2002) (investment advisers did not breach any statutory fiduciary duty because they were not decision makers and disinterested board of directors approved the advisory compensation).

20. *E.g.*, Gartenberg v. Merrill Lynch Asset Management, Inc., 694 F.2d 923 (2d Cir.1982); Galfand v. Chestnutt, 545 F.2d 807, 811–812 (2d Cir.1976); Rosenfeld v. Black, 445 F.2d 1337, 1343 (2d Cir.1971), *cert. dismissed* 409 U.S. 802, 93 S.Ct. 24, 34 L.Ed.2d 62 (1972); Krasner v. Dreyfus, 90 F.R.D. 665 (S.D.N.Y.1981). The claims in *Gartenberg v. Merrill Lynch Asset Management, Inc.* were eventually dismissed after a full trial. *See* 740 F.2d 190 (2d Cir.1984) (failure to meet the burden of proving fee was unreasonable).

The Supreme Court held that when a shareholder challenges fees as excessive under section 36(b), there is no need to make a demand upon directors. Daily Income Fund, Inc. v. Fox, 464 U.S. 523, 104 S.Ct. 831, 78 L.Ed.2d 645 (1984).

Notwithstanding this difficulty, the courts will examine whether excessive advisory fees are being charged. In evaluating whether excessive fees are being charged, courts will look to six factors. First, the courts will look to both the nature and the quality of the advisory services that are being provided.[22] A second factor is the fund's profitability to the adviser.[23] Third, the court will look to the economies of scale that come into play in managing the fund as it grows larger.[24] Fourth, comparative fee structures of comparable funds are to be considered in evaluating the advisory fee.[25] Fifth, the courts look to any indirect profits that inure to the adviser that can be attributed in some way to the fund; these are known as "fall out benefits."[26] Sixth, the independence and conscientiousness of the fund's directors are a factor in evaluating the advisory fees.[27]

The Seventh Circuit takes a different approach than the cases coming out of the Second Circuit.[28] The Seventh Circuit criticized the Second Circuit for taking more of a rate regulation approach than a fiduciary duty analysis.[29] According to the Seventh Circuit, the other decisions' placing a cap on fees is a mistake and focus rather should be placed on full disclosure and ratification.[30] The Seventh Circuit's approach leaves room for abuse that the statute was designed to prevent. While the Seventh Circuit is correct to note that the Act is concerned with fiduciary obligations, the court's approach fails to recognize that ratification cannot cure all fiduciary duty breaches and, as such, the reasonableness of the compensation is a factor that needs to be considered. Considering the reasonableness of the compensation does not automatically transfer the analysis from one of fiduciary duty to one of mere rate regulation. Judge Easterbrook, speaking for the Seventh Circuit, made it explicit that he favors letting the market regulate fees and found such intent in the Investment Company Act notwithstanding the fact that over many years other courts have focused more on the fiduciary model rather than simply a full disclosure market.

§ 20.9[2] Modification or Assignment of the Advisory Contract

A basic premise of the Investment Company Act is that the public interest, and that of an investment company's investors, is adversely affected by a change in the management of an investment company without the consent of its stockholders.[32] In most instances, modifications of the advisory

22. Krinsk v. Fund Asset Management, 875 F.2d 404, 409 (2d Cir.1989); Gartenberg v. Merrill Lynch Asset Management, Inc., 694 F.2d 923, 929–930 (2d Cir.1982); Krantz v. Fidelity Management & Research Co., 98 F.Supp.2d 150, 159 (D.Mass.2000).

23. *Id.*

24. *Id.*

25. *Id.*

26. *Id.*

27. *Id.*

28. Jones v. Harris Associates L.P., 527 F.3d 627, 2008 WL 2080753 (7th Cir. 2008), *rehearing en banc denied* 537 F.3d 728, 2008 WL 3177282 (7th Cir. 2008) (five judges dissented from the denial of a rehearing en banc).

29. Jones v. Harris Associates L.P., 527 F.3d 627, 2008 WL 2080753 (7th Cir. 2008), *rehearing en banc denied* 537 F.3d 728, 2008 WL 3177282 (7th Cir. 2008).

30. *Id.* ("A fiduciary duty differs from rate regulation. A fiduciary must make full disclosure and play no tricks but is not subject to a cap on compensation. The trustees (and in the end investors, who vote with their feet and dollars), rather than a judge or jury, determine how much advisory services are worth.").

32. 15 U.S.C.A. § 80a–1(b)(6).

agreement will require approval by the investment company's shareholders. However, a reduction in advisory fees with no reduction in advisory services does not have to be approved by the fund's shareholders.[33] A number of Investment Company Act provisions operate to limit potential abuses in connection with changes in investment advisers. Section 2(a)(4) of the Act provides that any "direct or indirect" transfer of a controlling block of shares in the investment adviser constitutes an assignment of the advisory contract.[34] The investment advisory contract automatically terminates upon its assignment.[35] Approval of the new contract with the new adviser by the investment company's shareholders is required to validate the contract.[36]

Section 15(f) of the Act allows, but at the same time places express limitations upon, the receipt of a premium based on the transfer of controlling interests in an investment adviser to a mutual fund or investment company.[37] When control in the adviser is sold at a premium and the investment company shareholders and directors ratify the new advisory contract, there is considered to be express approval of the transfer of control for a premium. Absent the Investment Company Act's provisions, this premium might be prohibited by the common law of most states because the former adviser is making a profit while choosing its successor—a decision that, at least in form, lies in the hands of the investment company's directors and shareholders.[38] Section 15(f) was enacted in 1975[39] in response to the Second Circuit's decision in Rosenfeld v. Black,[40] which contained broad statements concerning the investment adviser's fiduciary duty and corresponding obligation not to profit personally from a sale of its office with the investment company.[41] Section 15(f) makes it clear that the investment adviser may make a profit either by selling a controlling block of its shares at a price above their net asset value or by facilitating the transfer of an advisory contract to a new adviser.

§ 20.10 Private Causes of Action and Civil Liability for Violations of the Investment Company Act

Implied Remedies Under the Investment Company Act

A number of Supreme Court cases have cast a looming shadow over implied remedies.[5] The trend of the recent cases is strongly against implying

33. The R.O.C. Taiwan, [1999–2000 Transfer Binder] Fed. Sec. L. Rep. (CCH) ¶ 77,698, 2000 WL 150796 (SEC No Action Letter Feb. 11, 2000) (no shareholder vote required for permanent advisory fee reduction).

34. 15 U.S.C.A. § 80a–2(a)(4).

35. 15 U.S.C.A. § 80a–15(a)(4).

36. 15 U.S.C.A. § 80a–15(a).

37. 15 U.S.C.A. § 80a–15(f).

38. *See* 2 James D. Cox & Thomas L. Hazen, Cox & Hazen on Corporations §§ 12.1–12.2 (2d ed. 2003); Harry G. Henn & John R. Alexander, Laws of Corporations § 656 (3d ed. 1983); Adolf A. Berle, The Price of Power: Sale of Corporate Control, 50 Cornell L.Q. 628 (1965); Victor Brudney, Fiduciary Ideology in Transactions Affecting Corporate Control, 65 Mich.L.Rev. 259 (1966); Hazen, *supra* footnote 19.

39. Act of June 4, 1975, Pub.L. No. 94–29, 89 Stat. 97 (1975).

40. 445 F.2d 1337 (2d Cir.1971), *cert. dismissed sub nom.* Lazard Freres & Co. v. Rosenfeld, 409 U.S. 802, 93 S.Ct. 24, 34 L.Ed.2d 62 (1972).

41. *See, e.g.,* 445 F.2d at 1343.

§ 20.10

5. *See* § 12.2 *supra.*

private remedies under the Investment Company Act.[8] There is nevertheless substantial precedent for the implication of private relief under the Act. An unregistered investment company has been held civilly liable under section 7 of the Act[9] for failure to comply with the registration requirements of section 8.[10] The sale of securities to an unregistered investment company has been held *voidable* at the seller's option, rather than automatically void under section 47 of the Act,[11] lest innocent sellers be penalized to the same extent as the culpable unregistered purchaser.[12] It is clear that an innocent shareholder/purchaser may rescind transactions with an unregistered investment company.[13] Private enforcement actions by "injured" plaintiffs have also been recognized (1) under section 17[14] for dealings between affiliates,[15] (2) under section 37[16] for the willful conversion of an investment company's assets,[17] (3) under section 35(d)[18] for misleading use of an investment company name,[19] and (4) under section 48[20] for contravention of Investment Company Act provisions through the use of a third party.[21] However, many of these cases were decided prior to the more recent Supreme Court decisions curtailing implied remedies.[22] As such, there is some question as to their continued vitality. More recently, the Second Circuit held that a plaintiff could not bring a private right of action under either section 26(f) or 27(i) to recover allegedly excessive fees charged in connection with an insurance company's sale of a variable annuity.[23]

8. *See, e.g.,* Bellikoff v. Eaton Vance Corp., 481 F.3d 110 (2d Cir. 2007).

9. 15 U.S.C.A. § 80a–7. Blatt v. Merrill Lynch, Pierce, Fenner & Smith, Inc., 916 F.Supp. 1343 (D.N.J.1996) (recognizing private remedy under section 7(d) of the Act); Carr v. Equistar Offshore, Ltd., 1995 WL 562178, [1995–1996 Transfer Binder] Fed. Sec. L. Rep. (CCH) ¶ 98,932 (S.D.N.Y.1995) (private right of action under section 7).

10. 15 U.S.C.A. § 80a–8; Cogan v. Johnston, 162 F.Supp. 907 (S.D.N.Y.1958).

11. 15 U.S.C.A. § 80a–46.

12. Avnet, Inc. v. Scope Industries, 499 F.Supp. 1121 (S.D.N.Y.1980).

13. 15 U.S.C.A. § 80a–46(b); Mathers Fund, Inc. v. Colwell Co., 564 F.2d 780, 783–84 (7th Cir.1977).

14. 15 U.S.C.A. § 80a–19. *See* DH2, Inc. v. Athanassiades, 359 F. Supp.2d 708, 714 (N.D. Ill. 2005) (section 17(j) of the Investment Company Act does not support a private right of action).

15. SEC v. General Time Corp., 407 F.2d 65, 70 (2d Cir.1968), cert. denied 393 U.S. 1026, 89 S.Ct. 637, 21 L.Ed.2d 570 (1969); Langner v. Brown, 913 F.Supp. 260, 268–69 (S.D.N.Y.1996) (section 17 claim survived motion to dismiss). *See also, e.g.,* In re ML–Lee Acquisition Fund II, L.P., 848 F.Supp. 527 (D.Del.1994) (there is an implied right of action under section 17(j) of the Investment Company Act);

16. 15 U.S.C.A. § 80a–36.

17. Brown v. Bullock, 294 F.2d 415 (2d Cir.1961) (holding directors liable for willful conversion of assets rather than for a breach of any explicit fiduciary duty).

18. 15 U.S.C.A. § 80a–34(d).

19. Taussig v. Wellington Fund, Inc., 313 F.2d 472, 475–76 (3d Cir.1963), *cert. denied* 374 U.S. 806, 83 S.Ct. 1693, 10 L.Ed.2d 1031 (1963).

20. 15 U.S.C.A. § 80a–47. *See* Strougo v. Bassini, 282 F.3d 162 (2d Cir.2002) (private action under §§ 36(a) and 48).

21. Jerozal v. Cash Reserve Management, 1982 WL 1363, [1982–1983 Transfer Binder] Fed.Sec.L.Rep. (CCH) ¶ 99,019 (S.D.N.Y.1982). *See also, e.g.,* Reeves v. Continental Equities Corp. of America, 912 F.2d 37 (2d Cir.1990) (whistle-blowing employee of investment company had no private remedy under § 48(b) for his alleged wrongful dismissal because he was not a member of a class for whose special benefit the statute was enacted).

22. *See* § 12.2 *supra* for a discussion of implied remedies and the trend of not recognizing additional remedies.

23. Olmsted v. Pruco Life Ins. Co. of New Jersey, 283 F.3d 429 (2d Cir.2002).

The issues become thornier when suit is brought for a breach of the fiduciary duties imposed upon investment company directors and advisers by section 36 of the Act[37] and implemented by section 15.[38] Section 15(a) has been held to provide investment company shareholders with a private right of action for the failure of directors to approve an investment contract in a meaningful fashion.[39] Section 15(a) has also provided a private right of action against an investment adviser charged with self-dealing,[40] but not the recovery of excessive fees which is governed by section 36(b)'s express remedy.[41]

Although federally regulated under the Investment Company Act of 1940, investment companies are incorporated or otherwise organized under state law. It follows that state law generally controls questions relating to breaches of fiduciary duty unless specifically preempted by federal law.[47] In this regard, the Third Circuit held that the Investment Company Act does not preempt state common law claims.[48] Depending on the theory underlying the claim, shareholders challenging director misconduct may be able to bring either a direct (e.g., class action) or a derivative suit.[49] The determination of whether a fiduciary duty claim with respect to investment companies is direct or derivative is a question of state law.[50]

Express Remedy Under Section 36(b)

Section 36(b) addresses excessive compensation and thus does not apply to every alleged breach of fiduciary duty by the investment adviser.[77] Section 36(b) creates an express right of action for breaches of fiduciary duty that arise out of excessive compensation payments to investment advisers and their affiliates. The section 36(b) action to recover for excessive compensation may be brought against the investment company's officers, directors, advisory board, investment adviser, or depositor. In the case of open end companies, unit investment trusts, and face amount certificate companies, the section 36(b) action may be brought against the investment company's principal underwriter.[79] Since the section 36(b) remedy is limited to excessive compensation, the implied remedies discussed above remain important with regard to other wrongdoings by investment company managers.

---

37. 15 U.S.C.A. § 80a–35.

38. 15 U.S.C.A. § 80a–15.

39. *See, e.g.,* Brown v. Bullock, 294 F.2d 415, 420–21 (2d Cir.1961).

40. Fogel v. Chestnutt, 668 F.2d 100 (2d Cir.1981), *cert. denied* 459 U.S. 828, 103 S.Ct. 65, 74 L.Ed.2d 66 (1982).

41. Tarlov v. Paine Webber Cashfund, Inc., 559 F.Supp. 429 (D.Conn.1983).

47. *See, e.g.,* Bellikoff v. Eaton Vance Corp., 481 F.3d 110 (2d Cir. 2007), *aff'g* In re Eaton Vance Mutual Funds Fee Litigation, 380 F.Supp.2d 222 (S.D.N.Y. 2005) (there was no private right of action to enforce Investment Company Act (ICA) provisions prohibiting destruction or falsification of records, breach of fiduciary duty, or control person liability; Securities Litigation Uniform Standards Act preempted state law claims against trustees and advisers).

48. Green v. Fund Asset Management, L.P., 245 F.3d 214 (3d Cir. 2001) (section 36(b) of the Investment Company Act does not preempt common law claims challenging investment advisory fees as a breach of fiduciary duty).

49. *See, e.g.,* 2 James D. Cox, & Thomas Lee Hazen, Cox & Hazen on Corporations § 15.3. (2d ed. 2003).

50. *E.g.,* Strougo v. Bassini, 282 F.3d 162 (2d Cir.2002).

77. The section 36(b) action thus requires allegations of excessive fees; the mere assertion that there was not an arm's-length bargain is not sufficient. Strougo v. BEA Associates, 1999 WL 147737, [1999 Transfer Binder] Fed. Sec. L. Rep. (CCH) ¶ 90,457 (S.D.N.Y. 1999).

79. 15 U.S.C.A. § 80a–35(a).

Liability under section 36 is based on a breach of duty to the investment company shareholders and thus will not support an action by someone else injured by the alleged wrongdoing.[105] The realm of fiduciary duties covered by section 36(b) is relatively narrow and thus does not include, for example, violations of the Investment Company Act's proxy regulations.[108]

The amount recoverable in a section 36(b) action is limited to improper compensation paid within one year before the suit was instituted.[109] Only those who actually receive compensation from the investment company for advisory services may be held liable for breach of their fiduciary duties under section 36(b).[110] In making the determination whether the compensation paid was, in fact, excessive, courts will give great weight to approval by fully informed, properly qualified independent directors.[111]

105. Index Fund, Inc. v. Hagopian, 609 F.Supp. 499, 505 (S.D.N.Y.1985).

108. *See* Schuyt v. Rowe Price Prime Reserve Fund, Inc., 622 F.Supp. 169 (S.D.N.Y.1985) (recognizing a right to sue for the proxy violations under section 20(a) of the Act).

109. Section 36(b)(3), 15 U.S.C.A. § 80a–35(b).

110. Halligan v. Standard & Poor's/Intercapital, Inc., 434 F.Supp. 1082, 1085 (E.D.N.Y.1977).

111. *E.g.,* Schuyt v. Rowe Price Prime Reserve Fund, Inc., 663 F.Supp. 962 (S.D.N.Y.1987).

Chapter 21

INVESTMENT ADVISERS ACT OF 1940

Table of Sections

§ 21.1 Regulation of Investment Advisers; Terms and Conditions in Advisory Contracts

The Securities Exchange Act of 1934 regulates market professionals through its broker-dealer registration and oversight provisions.[1] The Exchange Act does not, however, address itself directly to non-broker-dealers who are in the business of rendering investment advice. This gap is filled by the Investment Advisers Act of 1940.[2]

Professional investment advisers frequently sell their services by disseminating advice through newsletters and other publications. Others manage funds through an investment company or through custodial accounts. The Investment Advisers Act of 1940 addresses itself to many of these services.

In 1985, the Supreme Court ruled that requiring registration of newsletters rendering investment advice on an impersonal basis does not fall within the Act's definition of investment adviser.[7] The Court held that the unregistered status of such investment services did not justify restraining future publication.

Section 203(f) of the Investment Advisers Act gives the SEC the authority to hold hearings and impose sanctions against investment advisers and their associated persons who violate the securities laws. These sanctions range from censure to suspension.[9] This power includes the ability to limit the adviser's activities or to impose a bar order.[10] The Court of Appeals for the District of Columbia Circuit held that this power extends to both registered and unregistered investment advisers.[11]

---

§ 21.1

1. 15 U.S.C.A. §§ 78*o*, 78*o*–4. *See* § 14.3 *supra*.
2. Act of Aug. 22, 1940 54 Stat. 847, codified in 15 U.S.C.A. § 80b–1 *et seq.*
7. Lowe v. SEC, 472 U.S. 181, 105 S.Ct. 2557, 86 L.Ed.2d 130 (1985).
9. 15 U.S.C.A. § 80b–3(f).
10. 15 U.S.C.A. § 80b–3(f).
11. Teicher v. SEC, 177 F.3d 1016 (D.C.Cir.1999).

The Investment Advisers Act requires registration of all non-exempt investment advisers.[13] In addition to registration, non-exempt investment advisers must file periodic reports with the SEC and be available for periodic examination by the Commission.[14] Section 206 of the Act[15] prohibits material misrepresentations and fraudulent practices in connection with the rendering of investment advice. This antifraud provision applies to investment advisers even though they may be exempt from the Act's registration requirements. Section 206 applies only to investment advisors with respect to primary violations although others may be accountable in enforcement actions as aiders and abettors.[17] Section 206 applies to negligent misstatements, as well as to those made with the intent to defraud.[18]

The Act also regulates contracts between investment advisers and their clients.[19] The Act prohibits contracts whereby the adviser's compensation is dependent upon a share of the client's capital appreciation or gain.[20] Contingent fees are therefore prohibited. The theory is that such arrangements may lead the adviser to take undue risks with clients' funds.[21] The fee may be based on the total value of the fund taken at designated time periods.[22] In 1985, the SEC changed its long-time policy and now permits performance-based advisory fees for certain qualifying large advisory contracts.[23]

An advisory contract must by its terms preclude assignment of the contract unless the client or customer consents.[24] This is designed to protect the investor against an unannounced change in the quality or character of the advisory services. If the investment adviser is a partnership, the advisory contract must provide for notice within a reasonable time of all changes in the composition of the partnership.[25] The sections that follow examine the registration and disclosure provisions of the Advisers Act

13. For example, advisers acting solely on behalf of insurance companies are exempt from registration. 15 U.S.C.A. § 80b–3(b)(2). The other exemptions are found in 15 U.S.C.A. § 80b–6a. *See* § 21.2 *infra*.

14. 15 U.S.C.A. § 80b–4.

15. 15 U.S.C.A. § 80b–6. Section 207 is addressed specifically to false filings with the Commission. 15 U.S.C.A. § 80b–7.

17. *See* SEC v. Pimco Advisors Fund Management, LLC, 341 F. Supp.2d 454, 470 (S.D.N.Y. 2004) (executives of mutual fund were not investment advisers and thus could not be primary violators of section 206 but they could be accountable as having aided and abetted an investment adviser's violations of that section).

18. Morris v. Wachovia Securities, Inc., 277 F.Supp.2d 622, 644 (E.D. Va. 2003), relying on SEC v. Capital Gains Research Bureau, Inc., 375 U.S. 180, 194, 84 S.Ct. 275, 11 L.Ed.2d 237 (1963); SEC v. Blavin, 760 F.2d 706, 711 (6th Cir.1985).

19. 15 U.S.C.A. § 80b–5.

20. 15 U.S.C.A. § 80b–5(a)(1).

21. Inv.Adv.Act Rel. No. IA–721 (May 16, 1980).

22. 15 U.S.C.A. § 80b–5; 17 C.F.R. §§ 275.205–1, 275.205–2.

23. An adviser can base fees on net realized capital gains and unrealized capital appreciation of a customer's funds for advisory contracts with a client that has at least $500,000 under the adviser's management or of a client with a net worth that exceeds one million dollars. In addition to the objective financial criteria, the client must be financially sophisticated and, in particular, the client must understand both the method of compensation and the risks presented by such a performance-based system of adviser compensation. 17 C.F.R. § 275.205–3. *See* Inv.Adv.Act Rel. No. IA–996 (Nov. 14, 1985).

24. 15 U.S.C.A. § 80b–5(a)(2).

25. 15 U.S.C.A. § 80b–5(a)(3).

§ 21.2 Who Is Subject to the Advisers Act—Definitions, Exclusions, and Exemptions

Definition of Investment Advisor

Section 203(a) of the Investment Advisers Act requires registration of all investment advisers doing business through an instrumentality of interstate commerce unless exempted under section 203(b).[1] The Act defines "investment adviser" to include "any person who, for compensation, engages in the business of advising others, either directly or through publications or writings as to the value of securities or as to the advisability of investing in, purchasing, or selling securities * * *."[2] As discussed below, there are significant exclusions from the Investment Adviser Act's definition of investment adviser. Some of the more important exclusions are banks, lawyers, accountants, engineers, or teachers rendering such advice incidental to their professions.[4] Broker-dealers who render advice incidental to their broker-dealer operations are also excluded from the definition of investment adviser.[5] There is another exclusion for publications which render impersonal investment advice.[6] Also excluded from the definition are financial planners and other professionals who may render generalized advice as to how people should manage their money—including their investment activities-but do not render advice on individual securities or mutual funds. When the activities of an entity are purely administrative and do not involve rendering investment advice, the Act's definition of investment adviser will not be implicated.[7] However, the fact that an entity's primary function is not the rendering of investment advice will not preclude application of the Investment Advisers Act.[8] Thus, for example, a firm that acts as a referral service for investment advice may fall under the Act's definition.[9]

---

§ 21.2

1. 15 U.S.C.A. § 80b–3(a), (b).

2. 15 U.S.C.A. § 80b–2(a)(11). *See, e.g.,* SEC v. Washington Inv. Network, 475 F.3d 392 (D.C. Cir.2007) *affirming in relevant part,* SEC v. Bolla, 401 F.Supp.2d 43, 59–60 (D.D.C. 2005) (firm that rendered advice and held itself out as an investment adviser was within the Act's definition) *on remand,* 519 F.Supp.2d 76 (D.D.C. 2007) (issuing permanent injunction); SEC v. Kenton Capital, Ltd., 69 F.Supp.2d 1 (D.D.C.1998) (operator of "trading program" involving the hypothecation of rented treasury bills to obtain funds for trading violated investment adviser and broker-dealer registrations requirements).

See generally Fred B. Lovitch, The Investment Adviser's Act of 1940—Who is an "Investment Adviser?", 24 Kans.L.Rev. 67 (1975); Note, SEC Release 1092 of the Investment Advisers Act of 1940: Applicability of the Investment Advisers Act to Financial Planners and Other Persons Who Provide Financial Services, 45 Wash. & Lee L.Rev. 1139 (1988). *See also, e.g.,* United Methodist Foundation of Baltimore Annual Conference, Inc., 20 Sec.Reg. & L.Rep. (BNA) 1989 (SEC No Action Letter available Nov. 29, 1988) (church foundation managing funds needed to register as an investment adviser).

4. 15 U.S.C.A. § 80b–2(a)(11)(B).

5. 15 U.S.C.A. § 80b–2(a)(11)(A), (B).

6. 15 U.S.C. § 80b–2(a)(11). *See* Lowe v. SEC, 472 U.S. 181, 105 S.Ct. 2557, 86 L.Ed.2d 130 (1985).

7. *See, e.g.,* League Central Credit Union, 1987 WL 108069 (SEC No Action Letter August 21, 1987). *See also, e.g.,* National Football League Players Association, 2002 WL 100675 (SEC No Action letter Jan. 25, 2002) (union's providing a list of screened investment advisers to its members did not require union register as an investment adviser).

8. *See, e.g.,* Gary L. Pleger, 1977 WL 15164 (SEC No Action Letter September 9, 1977) (cautioning that business broker may be investment adviser); Bay Business Service, 1977 WL 14076 (SEC No Action Letter Feb. 14, 1977) (same).

9. *See* SEC v. Washington Investment Network, 475 F.3d 392, 400 (D.C.Cir. 2007).

As evidenced by the exclusions from the definition of investment adviser, simply because someone renders investment advice as part of their profession does not put them within the Investment Adviser Act's definition of investment adviser. This is true even for the professions not expressly listed in the exclusions from the Act.[15] Thus, for example, a sports agent who advises professional athletes on investment matters does not necessarily fall within the definition of investment adviser.[16] A number of factors will be considered in determining whether someone who renders investment advice as part of their profession will fall within the definition of investment adviser.

The more individualized the investment advice that is given, the more likely it is that someone will be classified as an investment adviser.[18] As pointed out above, one of the considerations is whether the person rendering the investment advice is "in the business of rendering such advice. Whether someone who renders advice is considered to be in the business of rendering investment advice depends on a number of factors. A significant factor is whether the person rendering advice holds himself or herself out as an investment adviser or someone providing investment advice.[19] A second factor weighing in favor of classifying someone as an investment adviser is whether he or she receives any separate or additional compensation representing 'a clearly definable charge' for those advisory services."[20] The rendering of investment advice without compensation is likely to take the person rendering the advice out from under the purview of the Investment Advisers Act.[22] As a third factor, if the person rendering specific investment advice does so only on "rare, isolated and non-periodic" occasions, he or she is not likely to be considered to be in the business of rendering investment advice.[23]

The definition of investment adviser depends upon the advice being rendered with regard to securities as opposed to some other type of investment. However, it is to be recalled that the definition of security is an expansive one[24] and is not limited to traditional securities such as stocks and bonds. Thus, for example, someone who offers clients advice with regard to investment vehicles, such as tax-exempt repurchase agreements, stock income agreements, or collateral loan agreements can fall within the Act's definition of investment adviser.[25]

The use of the Internet for the rendering of investment advice will classify the person rendering the advice as an investment adviser, unless he or she can fit within the exclusion for publications that render impersonal investment advice.[26] The SEC has indicated that providing a "passive" electronic bulletin board to facilitate the posting of information about securities will not qualify as rendering investment advice for the purpose of having to

15. Those listed professions include banks, lawyers, accountants, engineers, or teachers. 15 U.S.C.A. § 80b–2(a)(11)(B).

16. Zinn v. Parrish, 644 F.2d 360, 364 (7th Cir.1981).

18. *See* United States v. Elliott, 62 F.3d 1304, 1309–1311 (11th Cir.1995).

19. *See id.*

20. *Id.* at 1309–1311.

22. *See, e.g.,* Dominion Resources, Inc., 1985 WL 54428 (SEC No Action Letter 1985).

23. *See* United States v. Elliott, 62 F.3d 1304, 1311 (11th Cir.1995).

24. 15 U.S.C.A. §§ 77b(a)(1), 78c(a)(10). *See* § 1.6 *supra.*

25. *See* United States v. Elliott, 62 F.3d 1304, 1309–1310 (11th Cir.1995).

26. SEC v. Park, 99 F.Supp.2d 889 (N.D.Ill.2000).

register under the Investment Advisers Act.[27] In order to avoid having to register, the providers of passive bulletin boards (1) may not be involved in any purchase or sale negotiations arising from the bulletin board and (2) may not give advice regarding the merits or shortcomings of any particular trade.[28]

The Abortive Attempt at Hedge Fund Registration

Advisers of most hedge funds are not subject to the Act's registration requirements but that changed, albeit only momentarily, in the fall of 2004.[34] As a result of amendments adopted by a three-to-two vote of the Commissioners, hedge fund advisers were to be subject to the registration requirements of section 203 of the Act. The exclusion for advisers that have a limited number of clients was amended to provide a "look-through" approach that no longer counts a fund as one advisory client but rather looks through to the fund's investors as advisory clients.[36] The rule amendments were part of the SEC's effort to increase regulation of off-shore hedge funds.[37] The investment advisor registration requirements thus were to apply to advisers having more than fourteen advisory clients, using the new "look through" method for calculating the number of clients.[38]

In 2006, the D.C. Circuit Court of Appeals struck down the SEC's Investment Adviser Act hedge fund rule.[47] The court held that the SEC failed to adequately explain the justification for a look-through approach for the definition of "client" under the exemptive provision of the Adviser's Act in the face of contrary interpretations of client as that term is used elsewhere in the Investment Advisers Act. At least in theory, the SEC was given the opportunity to adequately explain the justification for the rule. The tenor of the opinion, however, indicates that such an explanation would be difficult, if not impossible, in light of the statute. For example, the court's opinion described the rule as "arbitrary" in its exclusion from regulation hedge funds having fewer that fifteen clients while the Investment Company Act exempts funds having fewer than one hundred shareholders.[49] This was a rather

27. *See, e.g.,* Internet Capital Corp., 1998 WL 9357 (SEC No Action Letter Jan. 13, 1998).

28. *See id.*

34. *See* Registration Under the Advisers Act of Certain Hedge Fund Advisers, Inv. Co. Act Rel. No. IA–2333, 2004 WL 2785492 (SEC 2004).

36. *See* Registration Under the Advisers Act of Certain Hedge Fund Advisers, Inv. Co. Act Rel. No. IA–2333, 2004 WL 2785492 (SEC 2004).

37. *See* SEC Proposes Securities Offering Reform, Requires Registration of Hedge Fund Investment Advisers, http://www.sec.gov/news/press/2004–150.htm (SEC Oct. 27, 2004).

38. SEC Rule 203(b)(3)–2, 17 C.F.R. § 203(b)(3)–2 (2006).

47. Goldstein v. SEC, 451 F.3d 873 (D.C. Cir. 2006).

49. *Id.* ("One might say that if Congress meant to exclude regulation of small operations, it chose a very odd way of accomplishing its objective-by excluding investment companies with one hundred or fewer investors and investment advisers having fewer than fifteen clients. But the *Hedge Fund Rule* only exacerbates whatever problems one might perceive in Congress's method for determining who to regulate. The Commission's rule creates a situation in which funds with one hundred or fewer investors are exempt from the more demanding Investment Company Act, but those with fifteen or more investors trigger registration under the Advisers Act. This is an arbitrary rule"). *See also id.* at 880 ("Here, even if the Advisers Act does not foreclose the Commission's interpretation, the interpretation falls outside the bounds of reasonableness. 'An agency construction of a statute cannot survive judicial review if a contested regulation reflects an action that exceeds the agency's authority. It does not matter whether the unlawful action arises because the disputed regulation defies the plain language of a statute or because the agency's construction is utterly unreasonable and thus impermissible.' Aid Ass'n for Lutherans v. United States Postal Service, 321 F.3d 1166, 1174 (D.C.Cir. 2003); *see also id.* at 1177–78; American Library Ass'n v. FCC, 406 F.3d 689, 699 (D.C.Cir. 2005)").

curious objection, however, since it was Congress, not the SEC, that selected the different thresholds for exemption under the Investment Company Act (one hundred fund investors)[50] and the Investment Advisers Act (fewer than fifteen advisory clients).[51]

The SEC's response to *Goldstein* was to abandon attempts to require registration under the Investment Advisers Act. Instead, in December 2006, the Commission proposed and subsequently adopted an antifraud rule aimed at hedge funds and also heightened sophistication and wealth requirements for investors qualifying for Investment Company Act and Securities Act exemptions.[53]

The pooled investment fraud rule contains an open-ended definition of fraud that is open to interpretation by the SEC, thus avoiding a roadmap by identifying certain acts and leaving room for would-be fraudsters to argue that other acts are not prohibited. The rule, which does not require a showing of scienter, does not provide a private right of action.[59]

§ 21.2[2] Exclusions From the Definition of Investment Adviser

Exclusions Generally; Exemptions Distinguished

The definition of investment adviser excludes banks, lawyers, accountants, engineers, or teachers rendering such advice incidental to their professions.[66] Also excluded from the Investment Advisers Act are advisers who render advice solely with respect to government securities of the United States government.[67] An exclusion from the definition of Investment Adviser means that there is no regulation under any of the provisions of the Investment Advisers Act. In contrast, an exemption provides only an exemption from the Act's registration provisions.[68]

Exclusion for Broker–Dealers

Another exclusion from the definition of investment adviser is any broker-dealer whose advisory service "is solely incidental to the conduct of his business as a broker or dealer" and without special compensation.[69] Once it is established that someone is a broker, the burden falls on the SEC (or other plaintiff) to show that the investment advice given was more than incidental[70] to the brokerage activities and that special compensation was received for that advice.[71] Absent proof of such special compensation, a broker-dealer will not

50. Investment Company Act § 3(c)(1), 15 U.S.C.A. § 80a–3(c)(1).

51. Investment Advisers Act § 203(b)(3), 15 U.S.C.A. § 80b–3(b)(3).

53. Prohibition of Fraud by Advisers to Certain Pooled Investment Vehicles; Accredited Investors in Certain Private Investment Vehicles, Sec. Act Rel. No. 33–8766; Inv. Adv. Act Rel. No. IA–2576, 72 Fed. Reg. 400–01, 2007 WL 13910 (SEC Jan. 4, 2007).

59. Investment Advisers Act Rule 206(4)–8, 17 C.F.R. § 275.206(4)–8.

66. 15 U.S.C.A. § 80b–2(a)(11)(B).

67. 15 U.S.C.A. § 80b–2(a)(11)(E).

68. *See, e.g.,* Teicher v. SEC, 177 F.3d 1016 (D.C.Cir.1999).

69. 15 U.S.C.A. § 80b–2(a)(11)(C).

70. *See, e.g.,* SEC v. National Executive Planners, Ltd., 503 F.Supp. 1066 (M.D.N.C.1980) (advisory activities were incidental to broker-dealer activity).

71. *See* SEC v. Kenton Capital, Ltd., 69 F.Supp.2d 1, 13 (D.D.C.1998).

be classified as an investment adviser.[72] A broker-dealer's holding himself or herself out as a financial planner will not in itself implicate the Investment Advisers Act registration provisions.[73]

In 1999, the SEC proposed clarification of the exemption with a rule that was eventually adopted, stating that a broker-dealer providing nondiscretionary advice that is solely incidental to its brokerage services would be excepted from the Investment Advisers Act regardless of whether it charges a wrap or fixed fee, or transaction-based commissions.[74] The SEC adopted its final rule in April 2005.[85] However, in 2007, a three judge panel of the D.C. Circuit Court of Appeals struck down the exemption as inconsistent with the text of the Investment Advisers Act.[86] The panel explained that section 202(a)(11)(C) provides an express exemption for broker-dealers giving incidental investment advice when no special compensation is paid for the advice.[87] The court, over a dissent, reasoned that since a wrap account fee is not transaction-based it includes compensation for the services rendered which may include investment advice. As such, the rule would have exempted broker-dealers where in fact compensation was being paid for the investment advice and this was held to be beyond the scope of the statute. The SEC announced that it did not plan to seek review of the court's ruling.

Financial Planners

The past several decades have witnessed the growth of financial planning as an industry. The emergence of the financial planning industry necessarily raises questions concerning the applicability of the Investment Advisers Act's registration provisions.[102] Financial planners who render only generalized investment advice do not have to register under the Investment Advisers Act. However, the SEC has indicated that registration may be required for a computer-generated financial planning service, although not recommending specific securities, which would nevertheless offer a service developed by an unaffiliated organization where the service identifies investments that would affect the generalized investment recommendations.[104]

Exclusion for Publications Rendering Impersonal Investment Advice

The Act expressly excludes from the definition of investment advisor "the publisher of any bona fide newspaper, news magazine or business or financial publication of general and regular circulation."[105] As one court explained,

---

72. *See, e.g.*, Darrell v. Goodson, [1979–1980 Transfer Binder] Fed. Sec. L. Rep. (CCH) ¶ 97,349, 1980 WL 1392 (S.D.N.Y.1980).

73. *See* Inv. Adv. Act Rel. No. IA–770 (Aug. 13, 1981).

74. Certain Broker–Dealers Deemed Not To Be Investment Advisers, Sec. Exch. Act Rel. No. 34–42099, Inv. Adv. Act Rel. No. IA–1845, 64 Fed. Reg. 61226–01, 1999 WL 1014717 (SEC Nov. 10, 1999) (proposing release).

85. Certain Broker–Dealers Deemed Not To Be Investment Advisers, Sec. Exch. Act Rel. No. 34–51523, Inv. Adv. Act Rel. No. IA–2376, 70 Fed. Reg. 20424–01, 2005 WL 849053 (SEC 2005).

86. Financial Planning Association v. SEC, 482 F.3d 481 (D.C. Cir. 2007).

87. 15 U.S.C.A. § 80b–2(a)(11)(C).

102. See Applicability of the Investment Advisers Act to Financial Planners, Pension Consultants, and Other Persons Who Provide Investment Advisory Services as a Component of Other Financial Services, Investment Advisers Act Release No. IA–1092, 52 Fed.Reg. 38400, 38401–02 (SEC Oct. 8, 1987).

104. In re Computer Language Research, Inc., [1985–1986 Transfer Binder] Fed.Sec.L.Rep. (CCH) ¶ 78,185 (SEC No Action Letter Dec. 26, 1985).

105. 15 U.S.C.A. § 80b–2(a)(11)(D).

"[t]he plain truth is that newspapers of general circulation like the Post are not meant to be subject to the Investment Advisers Act and no amount of casuistic ratiocination can make it otherwise."[106] The exemption does not, however, exclude every regular publication that contains investment advice.

In Lowe v. SEC,[107] the Supreme Court interpreted the exclusion for publications and investment newsletters. The Court explained that the exclusion is limited to publications that render impersonal investment advice, and then held that the publication in question did not fall within the Act's definition of investment adviser.[108] The Court reasoned that the essence of the activity which the Act seeks to regulate is the personal service of investment advising and that such regularly published investment letters are impersonal and thus not within the Act's target. The Court in relying on the statutory definition did not have to reach the question on which it originally granted certiorari—whether prohibiting publication of such newsletters without registration under the Act was an unconstitutional prior restraint, which violated the First Amendment's right of free speech. The Court noted, however, that Congress' decision to focus investment adviser regulation on the providing of personal services was motivated in part "to keep the Act free of constitutional infirmities."[110] The Court identified the Investment Adviser Act's focus as having been "designed to apply to those persons engaged in the investment advisory profession—those who provide *personalized* advice attuned to a client's concerns, whether by written or verbal communication."[111]

In defining the scope of its holding in *Lowe*, the Court pointed out that it was limited to "bona fide" newsletters rendering impersonal investment advice. The exclusion from the definition of investment adviser, thus, for example, does not apply to tout sheets designed to generate commissions for the adviser; and, thus, when used as part of a "scalping scheme," the SEC arguably should still have jurisdiction to enjoin publication.[113]

The *Lowe* decision does not mean that investment newsletters which are excluded from the Act escape all regulation under the securities laws. For example, it is clear that if a newsletter is used as part of a fraudulent or manipulative scheme, the securities laws will apply.[116] In addition, section 17(b) of the 1933 Act prohibits recommending securities without disclosing any remuneration connected with the recommendation.[117]

§ 21.2[3] Exemptions From the Investment Advisers Act

The dividing line between exclusions and exemptions is not as clear as it might be since the SEC has exercised its exemptive authority with regard to persons and entities that at least come close to falling within one of the exclusions that are discussed above that negate the applicability of the Act's investment adviser definition. The Commission has utilized its exemptive

---

106. Person v. New York Post Corp., 427 F.Supp. 1297, 1303 (E.D.N.Y.1977).

107. 472 U.S. 181, 105 S.Ct. 2557, 86 L.Ed.2d 130 (1985).

108. 15 U.S.C.A. § 80b–2(a)(11)(C).

110. 472 U.S. at 208, 105 S.Ct. at 2572, 86 L.Ed.2d at 149.

111. 472 U.S. at 208, 105 S.Ct. at 2572, 86 L.Ed.2d at 149 (emphasis supplied; footnote omitted).

113. *See* Joel D. Ferber, The Narrow Holding of the *Lowe* Case, 19 Rev.Sec. & Commodities Reg. 29 (1986).

116. *See, e.g.*, SEC v. Franklin, 265 Fed. Appx. 644, 647 (9th Cir. 2008).

117. 15 U.S.C.A. § 77q(b). *See* § 7.11 *supra*.

power to exclude persons rendering investment advice pursuant to their activities as financial planners, pension planners, and others who provide the advice "as an integral component of other financially related services."[122] The SEC issued an interpretative release which explains that many financial planners, pension consultants, sports, or entertainment representatives, and others providing financial advisory services are investment advisers and therefore subject to regulation both at the federal and state levels.[125]

In addition to the above-mentioned exclusions from the definition of investment adviser, the Act provides exemptions from registration.[126] These exemptions do not immunize the adviser from the Act's anti-fraud provisions.[127] Securities offerings to sophisticated investors are exempted from registration under the Securities Act of 1933.[128] There is no comparable exemption for investment advisers. The Investment Adviser Act thus applies to advisers who render advice only to sophisticated investors. There are three exemptions from investment adviser registration.

First, a local adviser—that is, one whose clients are residents of the state of its principal place of business—is exempt so long as the adviser does not furnish advice with regard to exchange-listed securities.[130] The exemption for local advisers became less meaningful after April 10, 1997. As of that date, advisers with less than twenty-five million dollars in assets under management who are not advisers to registered investment companies are subject to the exclusive regulatory jurisdiction of the states.[131]

The second exemption from investment adviser registration applies to advisers whose only clients are insurance companies.[132] The third exemption from investment adviser registration applies to advisers who do not have more than fifteen clients and do not hold themselves out as advisers either to the public[133] or to investment companies.[134]

§ 21.3 Investment Adviser Registration and Reporting Requirements

Federal Registration and Reporting Requirements

All non-exempt investment advisers must register pursuant to section 203(c) of the Act[1] by filing Form ADV with the Commission.[2] As discussed in

122. Inv. Adv. Act Rel. No. IA–770 (Aug. 13, 1981).

125. Inv.Act Rel. No. IA–1092, 5 Fed.Sec.L.Rep. (CCH) ¶ 56,156E (Oct. 8, 1987). *Cf.* Note, Financial Planning: Is It Time For a Self–Regulatory Organization?, 53 Brooklyn L.Rev. 143 (1987).

126. 15 U.S.C.A. § 80b–3(b).

127. 15 U.S.C.A. § 80b–6. *See* § 21.4 *infra.*

128. 1933 Act § 4(2), 15 U.S.C.A. § 77d(2). *See* § 4.24 *supra.*

130. 15 U.S.C.A. § 80b–3(b)(1).

131. Investment Advisers Act section 203A, 15 U.S.C.A. § 80b–203A.

132. 15 U.S.C.A. § 80b–3(b)(2).

133. *See, e.g.,* Lamp Technologies, Inc., 1998 WL 278984 (SEC No Action Letter May 29, 1998) (making information available on the Internet only to selected, prescreened qualified investors did not constitute "holding out to the public"). *See also, e.g.,* Lamp Technologies, Inc., 1997 WL 282988 (SEC No Action Letter May 29, 1997).

134. 15 U.S.C.A. § 80b–3(b)(3). *See* the discussion at pp. 730–731 supra regarding the failure of the SEC's look-through rule.

§ 21.3

1. 15 U.S.C.A. § 80b–3(c).

2. *See* 17 C.F.R. § 275.203–1.

the next subsection, advisers with less than $25 million under management register with their home state rather than with the SEC. Form ADV requires disclosure of the identity and background of the adviser and affiliated persons. The adviser must disclose its principal business[4] and the nature of such business.[5] It is also necessary to disclose the scope of the adviser's authority[6] and the basis of compensation,[7] and also to include a balance sheet. The adviser must further disclose any criminal record that would affect qualification for registration.[8] The disclosure must include the adviser's educational and business background,[9] as well as a description of any other business activities. Form ADV requires the adviser to set forth a list of the services provided, including a description of the types of clients served and the types of securities for which advice is rendered. Additional disclosures apply when the adviser manages discretionary accounts. As a general rule, all information in an adviser's registration statement is available to the public.[10] Much of the information disclosed in Form ADV must also be provided to existing and prospective advisory clients.[11]

After Form ADV has been filed, the SEC has forty-five days to either grant the application for registration or institute proceedings to determine whether the application should be denied.[14] The applicant is entitled to notice of the grounds being considered as the basis for denial.[15] The SEC's statutory mandate is to deny registration if it finds that the applicant, if registered, would be subject to suspension or revocation.[16]

Registered investment advisers must file annual reports with the SEC on Form ADV–S.[17] Although the Form ADV must be kept current, the Commission has also designated records that must be maintained and made available for periodic inspection.[18] These records include balance sheets, income statements, and a journal of all accounts;[19] copies of all communications sent and received relating to investment advice or the execution of orders;[20] copies of all

4. 15 U.S.C.A. § 80b–3(c)(1)(H).

5. 15 U.S.C.A. § 80b–3(c)(1)(C).

6. 15 U.S.C.A. § 80b–3(c)(1)(E).

7. 15 U.S.C.A. § 80b–3(c)(1)(F).

8. 15 U.S.C.A. § 80b–3(c)(1)(G).

9. 15 U.S.C.A. § 80b–3(c)(1)(B).

10. 15 U.S.C.A. § 80b–10(a).

11. 17 C.F.R. § 275.204–3(a). *See* Inv.Adv.Act Rel. No. IA–767 (July 21, 1981).

14. 15 U.S.C.A. § 80b–3(c)(2).

15. *Id.*

16. *Id.*

17. *See* 15 U.S.C.A. § 80b–4. 17 C.F.R. § 275.204–1(c). This is much less lengthy than the Exchange Act's annual report requirements for issuers. *See* 17 C.F.R. §§ 240–14a–3(b), 14c–3 which are discussed in § 10.6 *supra.* It has been observed that "Form ADV–S is intended to inform the SEC whether the adviser is still in business and whether the address has changed, to remind advisers to make any necessary amendments to Form ADV, and to provide a vehicle for the submission of balance sheets on an annual basis." Richard D. Harroch, Applicability of the Investment Advisers Act of 1940 to Financial and Investment Related Publications, 5 J.Corp.L. 55, 59 (1979).

18. 15 U.S.C.A. § 80b–4 (SEC is empowered to require reports by registered investment advisers); 17 C.F.R. § 275.204–2.

19. 17 C.F.R. §§ 275.204–2(a)(1), (2).

20. 17 C.F.R. § 275.204–2(a)(7).

notices, letters, reports, and advertisements distributed by the adviser to more than ten customers;[21] and records of all securities transactions.[22]

When an investment adviser wishes to deregister, he or she must file a notice to withdraw from registration.[26] Withdrawal applications are to be submitted to the SEC on Form ADV–W.[27]

The SEC has the power to impose sanctions, ranging from censure to revocation of registration, for advisers who themselves have committed certain crimes or securities law violations, or have associated with persons having committed such crimes or violations of the securities laws.[28] The disqualifying violations include false SEC filings, perjury, and crimes involving larceny, embezzlement, extortion, forgery, counterfeiting, fraud, mail fraud, and fraudulent misappropriation of funds or securities.[29] These sanctions may be imposed only after notice and a hearing and in accordance with the public interest.[30] The Commission can similarly censure, suspend, or bar persons subject to similar disqualification who seek to become associated with a registered investment adviser.[31]

There are some additional requirements beyond the above-mentioned registration and reporting requirements. Investment advisers, other than those furnishing "impersonal advisory services" through newsletters or otherwise,[32] must comply with the "brochure rule" prior to signing up prospective customers other than a registered investment company.[33] Rule 204–3 requires that prospective advisory customers be furnished with a brochure or disclosure document containing the information required in Part II of Form ADV's registration statement.[34] Advisers providing impersonal advisory services charging two hundred dollars or more must also comply with the brochure delivery requirements.[35]

Institutional investors play an important role in corporate governance. In 2003, the SEC adopted rules under the Investment Advisers Act[37] that require investment advisers to make information about their voting of portfolio securities available to advisory clients. In particular, Rule 206–4(6) provides that registered investment advisers must adopt proxy policies and procedures for voting shares held for advisory clients; to describe their proxy voting

21. 17 C.F.R. § 275.204–2(a)(11).

22. 17 C.F.R. § 275.204–2(a)(12).

26. 15 U.S.C.A. § 80b–3(h).

27. *See* 17 C.F.R. § 275.203–2.

28. 15 U.S.C.A. § 80b–3(e).

29. 15 U.S.C.A. § 80b–3(e)(2). Mail fraud is discussed in § 22.4.

30. 15 U.S.C.A. § 80b–3(e).

31. 15 U.S.C.A. § 80b–3(f).

32. Rule 204–3(g) defines "impersonal advisory services" as those not related to the investment objectives of specific individuals or accounts. 17 C.F.R. § 275.204–3(g).

33. 17 C.F.R. § 275.204–3. *See* Inv. Advisers Act Rel. No. IA–664 (Jan. 30, 1979). The relationship between investment companies registered under the Investment Company Act of 1940 and their investment advisers is discussed in §§ 20.2, 20.9 *supra.*

34. 17 C.F.R. § 275.204–3.

35. 17 C.F.R. § 275.204–3(c)(3). The SEC has adopted Rule 206(4)–4 which explicitly requires disclosure of adverse financial conditions as well as disciplinary or legal events questioning the adviser's integrity. 17 C.F.R. § 275.206(4)–4.

37. *See* Proxy Voting By Investment Advisors, Inv. Adv. Act Rel. No. IA—2106, 79 S.E.C. Docket 1673, 2003 WL 215467 (SEC Jan. 31, 2003).

policies and procedures to their advisory clients; to furnish a copy of the voting policies and procedures upon request to advisory client; and to disclose how advisory clients can obtain information about how the adviser voted their proxies.[38] The SEC also adopted a parallel set of rules under the Investment Company Act that require management investment companies to make disclosures relating to their voting of portfolio securities.[39]

§ 21.3[2] Division of Federal and State Jurisdiction

As a result of 1996 amendments to the Investment Advisers Act, there is now exclusive federal jurisdiction over larger advisers and those advising registered investment companies.[40] As of April 10, 1997, investment advisers managing more than twenty-five million in assets and advisers to registered investment companies fall under the exclusive jurisdiction of the SEC.[41] All other advisers are subject to the exclusive jurisdiction of the states. The Act further limits the regulation that can be imposed on those advisers by states other than the adviser's principal place of business. There have been attempts by some advisers covered by this exception to retain their registration under the Act.[42] Presumably, such a request is motivated by a preference for the federal rather than state regulatory regime. In 1998, the Commission amended its rules to permit federal registration of some investment advisers even though they do not reach the $25 million threshold. Investment Adviser Act Rule 203A–2 exempts advisers that otherwise would have to be registered in thirty or more states from the prohibition against SEC registration of advisers below the twenty-five million dollar threshold.[43] Thus, truly national advisers can register with the SEC regardless of the asset value of the accounts they manage. The Investment Adviser Act rule applies to newly formed investment advisers who reasonably expect that they will satisfy the thirty-state test within ninety days of registration with the SEC.[44] In 2002, the SEC amended its rules to provide that an Internet-based investment adviser that provides all of its investment advice through the Internet may register with the SEC regardless of the amount of funds under management.[45]

Investment advisers subject to the state registration requirements register electronically through the Investment Adviser Registration Depository (IARD). The registration depository is a joint effort of the SEC and the North American Securities Administrators Association (NASAA).[50]

38. *See id.*

39. *See id.*

40. Section 203A of the Investment Advisers Act of 1940, 15 U.S.C.A. § 80b–203A.

41. The SEC has considered raising the $25 million threshold for SEC-regulated investment advisers. *See* Raising $25M Registration Threshold Under Discussion at SEC, Richards Says, 37 Sec. Reg. & L. Rep. (BNA) 1799 (Oct. 31, 2005).

42. *See* Investment Advisers Seek to Remain Registered with the SEC, Fed. Sec. L. Rep. (CCH) Rep. No. 1772 (June 25, 1997).

43. 17 C.F.R. § 275.203A–2.

44. Rule 203A–2, 17 C.F.R. § 275.203A–2.

45. 17 C.F.R. § 275.203A–2(f). *See* Exemption for Certain Investment Advisers Operating Through the Internet, Inv. Adv. Act Rel. No. IA–2091, 67 Fed. Reg. 77620–01, 2002 WL 31827219 (SEC Dec. 18, 2002).

50. The IARD system is operated by FINRA as a counterpart to the FINRA's Central Registration Depository (CRD) that it uses for broker-dealer registration.

§ 21.4 Prohibited Practices; Sanctions and Penalties

§ 21.4[1] Prohibited Investment Adviser Practices

Fraudulent Practices

Section 206(1) of the Investment Adviser's Act outlaws fraudulent practices.[3] Section 206(1) of the Investment Advisers Act is virtually identical to 17(a)(1) of the Securities Act of 1933[4] which, according to the Supreme Court, is violated only when there is a showing that the defendant acted with scienter.[5] Due to the similarity in statutory language, scienter is a necessary element of any violation of section 206(1) of the Investment Advisers Act.[6] The similarity in language among the antifraud provisions also means that scienter under section 206 carries the same definition as it does under other sections: knowing or reckless conduct.[7] Section 206 Act covers a wide variety of conduct. Prohibited practices under section 206(1) include scalping[8] and misleading advertising.[9] The Act specifically outlaws aiding and abetting as well as primary violations.[10] This is significant in light of the Supreme Court's ruling that aiding and abetting liability may not be implied from the primary prohibitions of the securities laws.[11] The aiding and abetting provision can bring under the Act individuals who would not be covered as primary violators. Thus, for example, section 206 applies only to investment advisors with respect to primary violations although others may be accountable in enforcement actions as aiders and abettors.[12]

Section 206 also prohibits excessive trading,[13] undisclosed conflicts of interest,[14] and splitting fees with persons not registered under the Act.[15] In addition to fraud, the Act also prohibits conduct that "*operates* as a fraud or

---

§ 21.4

3. 15 U.S.C.A. § 80b–6(1) (prohibiting "any device, scheme or artifice to defraud any client or prospective client").

4. 15 U.S.C.A. § 77q(a)(1).

5. Aaron v. SEC, 446 U.S. 680, 100 S.Ct. 1945, 64 L.Ed.2d 611 (1980).

6. SEC v. Steadman, 967 F.2d 636 (D.C.Cir.1992).

7. *See* Vernazza v. SEC, 327 F.3d 851 (9th Cir.2003).

8. The Supreme Court held that scalping (recommending securities after they have been purchased) constitutes a violation of section 206(1). SEC v. Capital Gains Research Bureau, Inc., 375 U.S. 180, 84 S.Ct. 275, 11 L.Ed.2d 237 (1963). *See also* Courtland v. Walston & Co., 340 F.Supp. 1076 (S.D.N.Y.1972).

9. *E.g.*, SEC v. C.R. Richmond & Co., 565 F.2d 1101 (9th Cir.1977); In the Matter of Dow Theory Forecasts, Inc., 43 S.E.C. 821 (SEC 1968).

10. *See, e.g.*, In the Matter of Seaboard Investment Advisers, Inc., [1994–1995 Transfer Binder] Fed. Sec. L. Rep. (CCH) ¶ 85,419 (SEC 1994).

11. Central Bank of Denver v. First Interstate Bank of Denver, 511 U.S. 164, 114 S.Ct. 1439, 128 L.Ed.2d 119 (1994), which is discussed in § 12.25 *supra*.

12. *See* SEC v. Pimco Advisors Fund Management, LLC, 341 F. Supp.2d 454, 470 (S.D.N.Y. 2004) (executives of mutual fund were not investment advisers and thus could not be primary violators of section 206 but they could be accountable as having aided and abetted an investment adviser's violations of that section).

13. *E.g.*, In the Matter of Shearson, Hammill & Co., 42 S.E.C. 811, 1965 WL 87139 (SEC 1965).

14. *See, e.g.*, In the Matter of Smith Barney Fund Management LLC, Sec. Exch. Act Rel. No. 34–51761, Inv. Adv. Act Rel. No. IA–2390, 2005 WL 1278368 (SEC May 31, 2005).

15. Rhodes, King, Ruman & Farber, [1972–73 Transfer Binder] Fed.Sec.L.Rep. (CCH) ¶ 79,-121 (SEC 1972) (splitting fees with attorney).

deceit upon any client or prospective client.''[16] Presumably, scienter is not an element of such a violation.[17]

Section 206(3) of the Investment Adviser's Act prohibits an investment adviser from acting as a principal in a transaction with a client without disclosure and the client's consent.[18] Similarly, where the adviser represents both parties to a transaction, there must be full written disclosure and the clients' written consent must be obtained.[19] These provisions do not apply to broker-dealers giving investment advice as part of their brokerage services.[20]

Following the pattern of section 10(b) of the 1934 Exchange Act,[21] section 206(4) of the Advisers Act[22] prohibits ''fraudulent, deceptive, or manipulative'' acts or practices as defined by SEC rules. Investment Adviser Act Rule 206(4)–1[23] governs adviser advertising. In addition to forbidding material misstatements generally,[24] the SEC also prohibits the commingling of clients' funds and requires separate accounts and adequate record-keeping.[25] When funds or securities are held by the adviser, they must be kept in custodial accounts and the client is entitled to receive an itemized statement at least once every three months.[26] In addition, all such funds must be subjected to annual inspection and certification by an independent public accountant.[27]

In what could have become an extremely significant development, the SEC proposed a rule that would expressly prohibit an investment adviser from making recommendations of securities that are unsuitable for his or her clients.[28] However, that rule was never adopted. As such, the only formal suitability requirement is the one that is recognized with regard to broker-dealer recommendations. Nevertheless, the Commission has taken the position that the antifraud provisions of the Investment Advisers Act can be used to enforce a suitability requirement.[30] As is the case with broker-dealers,[31] investment advisers owe their customers a duty to obtain the best execution in transactions directed by the adviser.[32] This means that an investment

16. 15 U.S.C.A. § 80b–206(2). *See, e.g.*, Monetta Financial Services, Inc. v. SEC, 390 F.3d 952 (7th Cir. 2004).

17. *See* Sheldon Co. Profit Sharing Plan and Trust v. Smith, 828 F.Supp. 1262, 1284 (W.D.Mich.1993).

18. 15 U.S.C.A. § 80b–6(3).

19. 17 C.F.R. § 275.206(3)–2. These are known as ''agency cross transactions.''

20. 15 U.S.C.A. § 80b–6(3). Broker-dealers must disclose principal status under Exchange Act Rule 10b–10, 17 C.F.R. § 240.10b–10. *See* chapter 14 *supra* for discussion of broker-dealer obligations.

21. 15 U.S.C.A. § 78j(b).

22. 15 U.S.C.A. § 80b–6(4). Section 206(4) applies only to advisory contracts and not to collateral agreements. *See* Paul S. Mullin & Associates, Inc. v. Bassett, 632 F.Supp. 532 (D.Del.1986).

23. 17 C.F.R. § 275.206(4)–1.

24. *See* 15 U.S.C.A. § 80b–6(1).

25. 17 C.F.R. § 275.206(4)–2.

26. 17 C.F.R. § 275.206(4)–2(a)(2), (4).

27. 17 C.F.R. § 275.206(4)–2(a)(5).

28. Inv. Adv. Act Rel. No. IA–1406, [1993–1994 Transfer Binder] Fed. Sec. L. Rep. (CCH) ¶ 85,327 (SEC March 16, 1994).

30. MLC Limited, 1997 WL 408759 n. 2 (SEC No Action Letter July 21, 1997).

31. *See* § 14.13 *supra*.

32. *See, e.g.,* In the Matter of Portfolio Advisory Services, Inv. Adv. Act Rel. No. IA—2038, 2002 WL 1343823 (SEC June 20, 2002).

adviser should "periodically and systematically" evaluate the execution they are receiving for their clients.[33] Directing trades to generate commissions to a preferred broker-dealer violates this obligation.[34]

Following the decision invalidating the SEC Rule attempting to regulate hedge funds,[35] the SEC adopted a pooled investment fraud rule that contains an open-ended definition of fraud open to interpretation by the SEC, thus avoiding a roadmap by identifying certain acts and leaving room for would-be fraudsters to argue that other acts are not prohibited.[36] The rule, which does not require a showing of scienter, does not provide a private right of action.[38]

Fraudulent Advertising

Investment Adviser Act Rule 206(4)–1[40] prohibits certain types of advertisements which are deceptive or fraudulent within the meaning of section 206. The rule prohibits (1) testimonials concerning the adviser's services,[42] (2) reference to selected past recommendations,[43] (3) the use of any graphs or charts without explaining the limitations on such charting methods,[44] (4) offering free services with hidden charges,[45] and (5) the making of "any untrue statement of a material fact, or which is otherwise false or misleading."[46]

Related to the hidden charges is the question of disclosing mark-ups in connection with securities transactions. Nondisclosure of potentially excessive mark-ups violates the antifraud provisions of the securities laws.[47]

As discussed in the preceding chapter of this treatise, investment companies are subject to specific rules concerning presentation of historical performance data.[48] In contrast, there were no comparable formal rules under the Investment Adviser's Act. Formerly, the Commission took the position that it was *per se* materially misleading for an investment adviser to publish performance data without reflecting the actual fees charged to the accounts

---

33. In the Matter of Portfolio Advisory Services, Inv. Adv. Act Rel. No. IA—2038, 2002 WL 1343823 (SEC June 20, 2002), relying on Securities; Brokerage and Research Services, Sec. Exch. Act Rel. No. 34–23170, 35 S.E.C. Docket 703, 1986 WL 630442 (SEC April 23, 1986).

34. *See, e.g.,* Directed Brokerage Violations Deliberate, FINRA Panel Affirms, Sec. L. Daily (BNA), http://pubs.bna.com/ip/bna/sld.nsf/eh/A0B6K3E4J5 (May 1, 2008).

35. *See* Goldstein v. SEC, 451 F.3d 873 (D.C. Cir. 2006) which is discussed in § 21.2 *supra.*

36. Investment Advisers Act Rule 206(4)–8, 17 C.F.R. § 275.206(4)–8; Prohibition of Fraud by Advisers to Certain Pooled Investment Vehicles, Inv. Adv. Act Rel. No. IA–2628, 72 Fed. Reg. 44756–01, 2007 WL 2261336 (SEC Aug. 9, 2007).

38. Investment Advisers Act Rule 206(4)–8, 17 C.F.R. § 275.206(4)–8; Prohibition of Fraud by Advisers to Certain Pooled Investment Vehicles, Inv. Adv. Act Rel. No. IA–2628, 72 Fed. Reg. 44756–01, 2007 WL 2261336 (SEC Aug. 9, 2007).

40. 17 C.F.R. § 275.206(4)–1.

42. 17 C.F.R. § 275.206(4)–1(a)(1).

43. 17 C.F.R. § 275.206(4)–1(a)(2). The adviser may provide a list of *all* recommendations within the past year, describing the price at the time of recommendation and the current price. There must also be the following cautionary legend: "it shall not be assumed that recommendations made in the future will be profitable or will equal the performance of the securities in this list." *Id.*

44. 17 C.F.R. § 275.206(4)–1(a)(3).

45. 17 C.F.R. § 275.206(4)–1(a)(4).

46. 17 C.F.R. § 275.206(4)–1(a)(5).

47. *See* SEC v. Rauscher Pierce Refsnes, Inc., 17 F.Supp.2d 985 (D.Ariz.1998).

48. Investment company advertising is discussed in § 20.5 *supra.*

whose performance was summarized.[49] However, in 1996, the Commission reversed this policy by announcing that an adviser could use "model" fees, provided the adviser maintain a record of the way in which the model fee was calculated.[50] Also, investment advisers can have a performance-based fee structure for qualified clients and accounts.[51]

In addition to section 206's prohibitions against fraudulent conduct, section 208 sets out general prohibitions.[52] An adviser can advertise his registered status but may not imply any governmental approval of his activities.[53] It is unlawful for registered advisers to describe themselves as "investment counsel" unless that is their principal business.[54] It is also unlawful to do indirectly any act prohibited by the statute.[55]

Limitations on Cash Referral Fees

In its cash referral fee rule, the Commission limits payments by the adviser for client solicitation.[56] In the summer of 2008, the SEC issued a no action letter clarifying that the cash solicitation rule does not apply to cash payments where the payment is *solely* to compensate someone for soliciting or referring investors with respect to a privately-offered investment fund managed by the advisor.[57]

Cash solicitation fees may be paid to others by advisers rendering impersonal investment advice, but must be pursuant to a written agreement, under which they can be paid only after a client has been informed of the fee arrangements and cannot be paid to persons who have run afoul of the securities acts and other "bad boy" provisions.[58] The SEC has been willing to waive these bad actor disqualifications for paid solicitors so long as the conduct in the past did not result in conduct that would disqualify the solicitor from serving as a registered investment adviser.

Limitations on Advisory Fees

Section 205 of the Advisers Act[63] imposes a number of conditions on the advisory contract. Subject to exceptions permitted by the SEC, section 205(a)(1) of the Act prohibits performance-based compensation to the extent that the fee is based on a share of the capital gain or appreciation of the value of the client's account.[64] The adviser's compensation may, however, be based

49. Securities Industry Association, 1989 WL 246550 (SEC No Action Letter Nov. 27, 1989).

50. J.P. Morgan Investment Management, Inc., 1996 WL 282573, (SEC No Action Letter May 7, 1996).

51. *See* Rule 205–3, 17 C.F.R. § 275.205–3 (raising the eligibility requirements from clients with $1 million net worth or accounts with more than $500,000 under management to $1.5 million net worth or accounts with more than $750,000 under management).

52. 15 U.S.C.A. § 80b–8.

53. 15 U.S.C.A. § 80b–8(a), (b).

54. 15 U.S.C.A. § 80b–8(c). *See* Inv.Adv.Act Rel. No. IA–8 (Dec. 12, 1940).

55. 15 U.S.C.A. § 80b–8(d).

56. 17 C.F.R. § 275.206(4)–3.

57. Mayer Brown, LLP, 2008 WL 274193 (SEC No Action letter July 15, 2008).

58. 17 C.F.R. § 275.206(4)–3(a)(1).

63. 15 U.S.C.A. § 80b–5. *See* § 21.1 *supra*.

64. 15 U.S.C.A. § 80b–5(a)(1).

upon the average asset value of the client's account over a definite period of time.[65]

The rationale for the general rule prohibiting performance-based fees was to avoid encouraging the investment adviser to take undue risks with the client's funds.[66] In 1983, the Commission decided to reverse its early refusal to permit performance-based fees under any circumstances. Originally, the SEC had proposed that performance-based compensation be permitted with regard to accounts of more than one hundred and fifty thousand dollars when the customer meets subjective sophistication tests.[67] However, the Commission eventually selected more stringent standards when it adopted guidelines for performance-based adviser fees for clients having accounts that represent at least a seven hundred and fifty thousand dollar value and for clients having a net worth of at least one and one half million dollars.[68] The rule retained the financial sophistication test as well as the requirement that the client understand not only the method of compensation but also the risks presented by the performance-based formula.[69]

Investment Adviser Supervisory Obligations

As is the case with securities broker-dealers firms,[80] investment advisers are under an obligation to supervise their personnel.[81] In addition, in 2004 the SEC adopted rules requiring investment advisers to adopt and enforce codes of ethics applicable to persons they supervise.[82] The SEC rules also require investment advisers to report violations of their codes of ethics. Thus, an investment adviser's code of ethics must require supervised persons to report, promptly, any violations of the adviser's code of ethics to the firm's chief compliance officer or to other designated persons.

Absence of Implied Remedy for Fraud but Recognition of Implied Right of Rescission

The Supreme Court held that section 206 does not give rise to implied private remedies.[85] Enforcement of section 206's prohibitions is thus limited to criminal prosecution for willful violations,[86] SEC injunctive actions,[87] and the imposition of sanctions in an administrative hearing ranging from censure to revocation of registration.[88] These are the sanctions available for all violations of the Act. The Supreme Court has recognized an implied right of rescission

65. 15 U.S.C.A. § 80b–5(b)(1).

66. Inv.Adv. Act Rel. No. IA–721 (May 16, 1980).

67. 15 Sec.Reg. & L.Rep. (BNA) 1019 (June 3, 1983).

68. 17 C.F.R. § 275.205–3. Investment advisers who use performance data in their advertising literature must maintain records to support the advertising claims. 17 C.F.R. § 275.204–2.

69. Rule 205–3(e), 17 C.F.R. § 275.25–3(e).

80. *See* §§ 14.3, 14.26 *supra.*

81. 15 U.S.C.A. § 80b–3.

82. Inv. Adv. Act Rule 204A–1, 17 C.F.R. § 280.204A–1. *See also* Inv. Co. Act Rule 17j–1, 17 C.F.R. § 270.17j–1; Inv. Adv. Act Rule 204–2, 17 C.F.R. § 280.204–2.

85. Transamerica Mortgage Advisors, Inc. v. Lewis, 444 U.S. 11, 100 S.Ct. 242, 62 L.Ed.2d 146 (1979).

86. 15 U.S.C.A. § 80b–17.

87. 15 U.S.C.A. § 80b–9(e). *See* § 16.2 *supra.*

88. 15 U.S.C.A. § 80b–12. *See also* 15 U.S.C.A. § 80b–3(e).

under section 215 of the Act,[89] which provides that contracts in violation of the Act are void.[90] Since the section 215 remedy is rescissory, restitution under that section does not include damages for consequential losses.[91]

89. 15 U.S.C.A. § 80b–15.

90. Transamerica Mortgage Advisors, Inc. v. Lewis, 444 U.S. 11, 100 S.Ct. 242, 62 L.Ed.2d 146 (1979).

91. Washington v. Baenziger, 656 F.Supp. 1176 (N.D.Cal.1987).

Chapter 22

SPECIAL PROBLEMS AND OVERVIEW OF RELATED LAWS

Table of Sections

§ 22.1 Related Laws

Differing Coverage of State Corporate Law and Federal Securities Law

As a general proposition, federal securities law is premised on a system of full disclosure rather than scrutiny of the merits of securities that are offered and sold.[2] The SEC does not review the substance of the investment. Instead, the SEC is charged with ensuring that investors have sufficient information upon which to make an investment decision. As discussed in chapter 8 of this treatise, this is in contrast to the state securities laws which focus not only on disclosure, but may also regulate the merits or fairness of securities offered within the state.[3] State securities laws are supplemented in many respects by state corporate laws. State corporate laws focus on corporate formation, operation, and corporate governance. Corporate governance includes defining the respective roles of shareholders, officers, and directors. Among other things, state corporate law provides the rules governing shareholder voting rights, although there are the federal disclosure requirements that are discussed earlier in this treatise.[4] State law also establishes corporate officers' and directors' duty of care and loyalty[5] and defines what constitutes mismanagement.[6] These are areas that the federal securities laws have traditionally avoided.

---

§ 22.1

2. For discussion of the history, scope, and coverage of federal and state securities laws, *see* § 1.2 *supra*.

3. *See* the discussion of the approaches of state and federal securities laws in § 1.2 *supra*.

4. The federal proxy rules are discussed in chapter 10 *supra*.

5. *See e.g.,* § 11.11 *supra* discussing the states' role in regulating management's responses to takeover attempts. *See also, e.g.,* §§ 11.12–11.13 *supra* discussing the role of state tender offer legislation.

6. *See* § 12.20 *supra* for a discussion of the federal securities laws' fraud provisions' inability to address matters of corporate mismanagement.

The Sarbanes–Oxley Act of 2002

There was a departure from the traditional dichotomy of state corporate law and federal securities law in 2002 when Congress enacted the Sarbanes–Oxley Act.[8] The Sarbanes–Oxley Act, which is discussed throughout this treatise where applicable,[9] adopted comprehensive amendments to the federal securities laws and also adopted some notable corporate governance reforms in response to various corporate scandals including Enron and Worldcom. These reforms placed significant new compliance obligations on public companies. Many of the Sarbanes–Oxley provisions are disclosure requirements combined with enhanced criminal penalties for securities law violations, but the clear thrust of these amendments enhancing disclosure and accountability was to improve corporate governance.

From a long-term perspective, perhaps the most significant aspect of Sarbanes–Oxley is not the enhanced disclosure requirements or criminal penalties, but rather that the Sarbanes–Oxley Act goes further than any of the earlier federal securities laws and amendments in dealing directly with corporate governance—an area that had traditionally been reserved to the states.[12] For example, the Sarbanes–Oxley Act addressed accounting and auditing reforms, the role of public corporations' audit committees,[13] heightened disclosure obligations,[14] and increased accountability of executive officers[15] and corporate attorneys,[16] in addition to increased criminal penalties for violations of the securities laws. The Sarbanes–Oxley Act created an accounting oversight board to oversee the accounting profession and to police the self-regulatory system that previously existed.[17] The Sarbanes–Oxley Act also addressed auditor independence requirements.[18]

The following table details the provisions of the Sarbanes–Oxley Act:

Related Federal Regulatory Laws—Overview

There are a number of related federal laws that affect securities law practitioners and their clients. There may be SEC involvement in some of these related areas. For certain regulated industries,the securities of regulated issuers are subject to other federal administrative agencies.[19] For example, the

---

8. Sarbanes–Oxley Act of 2002, Pub. Law 107–204 (July 30, 2002).

9. The Sarbanes–Oxley Act is discussed in §§ 9.2[6], 9.7, 2 *supra* and throughout this treatise where applicable. For a brief summary of the coverage of Sarbanes–Oxley, *see* § 1.2[3][D][3] *supra*.

12. *See, e.g.,* the discussion of the inability to use SEC antifraud rules to regulate corporate mismanagement in § 12.20 *supra*.

A number of states have adopted their own versions of increased corporate governance controls. *See, e.g.,* Timothy A. French & Larry D Soderquist, State Responses to Corporate Corruption: Thirteen Mini Sarbanes–Oxley Acts, 32 Sec. Reg. L.J. 168 (2004).

13. *See* § 9.6 *supra*.

14. *See* chapter 9 *supra*.

15. *See* § 9.3 *supra*.

16. Sarbanes–Oxley Act of 2002, Pub. Law 107–204 § 307 (July 30, 2002), which mandates SEC rulemaking to define what constitutes proper representation by attorneys practicing before the SEC. The rules must require, *inter alia,* that once an attorney has evidence of serious corporate wrongdoing, he or she must climb the corporate ladder, possibly to the audit committee and to the board of directors, until satisfied that the problem has been attended to. *See* § 9.8 *supra*.

17. Sarbanes–Oxley Act of 2002, Pub. Law 107–204 tit. I (July 30, 2002). *See* § 9.6 *supra*.

18. Sarbanes–Oxley Act of 2002, Pub. Law 107–204 tit. II (July 30, 2002).

19. *See, e.g.,* Harry G. Henn & John R. Alexander, Laws of Corporations § 304 (3d ed. 1983).

Comptroller of the Currency has jurisdiction over the distribution of securities issued by national banks,[20] although securities issued by bank holding companies are subject to SEC jurisdiction. A similar arrangement exists with regard to securities of savings and loan associations, that are subject to regulation by the Office of Thrift Supervision (formerly the Federal Home Loan Bank Board).[21]

The SEC and the self regulatory organizations under its oversight authority provide pervasive regulation of broker-dealers and the securities markets generally.[24] Over the years various questions have arisen concerning the effect of the SEC's regulatory and self regulatory oversight authority on the impact of the antitrust laws. When the SEC directly, or the self regulatory organizations under the direct oversight and supervision of the SEC, regulate and thereby approve of the conduct in question, this regulation under the Securities Exchange Act will operate as an implied repeal of the antitrust laws.[25] Not all SEC regulation of conduct in the securities markets has a similar preemptive effect on the antitrust laws. For example, conduct that is not expressly permitted by SEC Rule, self regulatory rule, or general regulations, in appropriate cases, may be scrutinized under the antitrust laws.[26]

For securities and issuers that are subject to SEC regulation, there are a number of other related federal statutes that may come into play in addition to the federal securities laws. The more important of these laws are taken up in the sections that follow. First, the Foreign Corrupt Practices Act of 1977 was enacted in response to widespread concern over the activities of domestic companies in their dealings abroad.[27] That act has implications that go beyond foreign activities and corrupt practices.

The Racketeer Influenced and Corrupt Organizations Act (RICO) was enacted in order to make for more efficient law enforcement with regard to organized crime and racketeering activities.[28] RICO not only includes certain types of securities fraud with regard to its criminal penalties, it also includes civil actions for a fraud-based RICO violation resulting in the award of treble damages.[29]

The federal Mail Fraud Act[30] and the federal Wire Fraud Act[31] can be potent weapons in the enforcement of the securities law.[32] For example, while the Supreme Court was equally divided over criminal convictions under the

20. 12 U.S.C.A. §§ 51 *et seq.*

21. 12 U.S.C.A. §§ 1464 *et seq.*

24. *See* chapter 14 *supra.*

25. *See* United States v. NASD, 422 U.S. 694, 95 S.Ct. 2427, 45 L.Ed.2d 486 (1975); Gordon v. New York Stock Exchange, Inc., 422 U.S. 659, 95 S.Ct. 2598, 45 L.Ed.2d 463 (1975). *See also, e.g.,* Silver v. New York Stock Exchange, 373 U.S. 341, 83 S.Ct. 1246, 10 L.Ed.2d 389 (1963).

26. *See* In re Nasdaq Market–Makers Antitrust Litigation, 1999 WL 395407 (S.D.N.Y.1999); In re Nasdaq Market–Makers Antitrust Litigation, 184 F.R.D. 506 (S.D.N.Y.1999); Court Approves Distribution of Settlement in Nasdaq Market–Makers Antitrust Litigation, 32 Sec. Reg. & L. Rep. (BNA) 148 (Feb. 7, 2000).

27. Pub.L. 95–213, 95th Cong., 1st Sess. (1977). *See* § 22.2 *infra.*

28. Pub.L. No. 91–452, 84 Stat. 922 (1970).

29. 15 U.S.C.A. § 1964(c). *See* § 22.3 *infra.* (Practitioner's Edition)

30. 18 U.S.C.A. § 1341.

31. 18 U.S.C.A. § 1343.

32. *See, e.g.,* United States v. Tarallo, 380 F.3d 1174 (9th Cir. 2004) (upholding securities and mail fraud convictions).

securities laws for trading on confidential information, the Court was unanimous that the conduct was violative of the Mail Fraud Act.[33]

The federal money laundering laws have for a long time been useful in tracking organized crime activities. As discussed later in this chapter,[34] money laundering laws necessarily impose regulatory requirements on financial services firms, including securities broker-dealers. There was increased emphasis on the money laundering laws in the wake of various terrorist attacks.

During the 1960s there was a rash of stock brokerage firm bankruptcies. In response to the need for customer protection, Congress enacted the Securities Investor Protection Act of 1970.[35] As a result of that Act, the Securities Investor Protection Corporation ("SIPC") helps safeguard customer interests in cases of broker-dealer insolvency. The Securities Investor Protection Act is considered in an earlier section of this treatise.[36]

One of the hottest topics in securities regulation at the end of the twentieth century was when Congress would respond to the increasing competition between banking and more traditional securities industries. Although the Glass–Steagall Act of 1933[37] prohibited commercial and savings banks from engaging directly in various aspects of investment banking, the line between investment banking and commercial banking became increasingly blurred over time.[38] The developing competition between commercial and investment banking was highlighted not only by each offering competing services, but also by bank acquisition of stock brokerage operations and vice versa. In addition to the increased competition between the two industries, the SEC and various bank regulatory agencies, including the Comptroller of the Currency, were constantly engaged in jurisdictional disputes. In 1999, Congress eliminated the separation of commercial and investment activities that had been imposed by the Glass–Steagall Act.[39]

One other major area of jurisdictional dispute involves the regulation of commodities futures and commodities options. Although the futures market is directly regulated by the Commodity Futures Trading Commission,[40] over the years, the SEC has asserted jurisdiction over various aspects of the commodities markets.[41] For example, although there are some conflicting decisions, a number of cases have held that managed commodities accounts constitute securities.[42] Another major developing area of conflict between the securities

33. Carpenter v. United States, 484 U.S. 19, 108 S.Ct. 316, 98 L.Ed.2d 275 (1987). (Practitioner's Edition)

34. *See* § 22.5 *infra.* (Practitioner's Edition)

35. Codified in 15 U.S.C.A. §§ 78aaa–78*lll*.

36. *See* § 14.24 *supra.*

37. The Banking Act of 1933, ch. 89, 48 Stat. 184 (1933), codified in various sections of 12 U.S.C.A.

38. *See* § 22.6 *infra.* (Practitioner's Edition)

39. The Banking Act of 1933, Ch. 89, 48 Stat. 184 (1933), codified in various sections of 12 U.S.C.A. (1999) *See* in particular 12 U.S.C.A. §§ 24, 378(a) (1999). The Glass–Steagall Act was repealed by Pub. Law. 106–102, 1999 U.S.C.C.A.N. (113 Stat.) 1338.

40. 7 U.S.C.A. §§ 1–25. *See generally* Philip M. Johnson & Thomas L. Hazen, Derivatives Regulation (2004).

41. Regulation of the commodities markets is discussed in § 22.7 *infra. See also* §§ 1.5, 1.7 *supra.*

42. *E.g.,* SEC v. Continental Commodities Corp., 497 F.2d 516 (5th Cir.1974); Booth v. Peavey Co. Commodity Services, 430 F.2d 132 (8th Cir.1970). *Contra, e.g.,* Mordaunt v. Incomco, 686 F.2d

and commodities markets resulted from the development of new investment products such as financial futures, which are traded in the commodities markets, and financial index options, which are traded in the securities markets.[43] In 2000, Congress revamped regulation under the Commodity Exchange Act with the amendments brought in by the Commodity Futures Modernization Act of 2000.[44] This legislation brought with it a new regulatory framework for regulating derivative investments.

§ 22.2 The Foreign Corrupt Practices Act

In 1977, Congress enacted the Foreign Corrupt Practices Act amendments to the Securities Exchange Act of 1934.[1] These amendments were inspired by concerns over foreign kickbacks and other corrupt practices taking place abroad; in many cases the conduct, although illegal if it took place here, may not have been frowned upon in other countries.[3] The reach of the Foreign Corrupt Practices Act is not limited to domestic companies. The Foreign Corrupt Practices Act contains both substantive prohibitions against these acts,[5] as well as disclosure provisions and accounting controls that are limited neither to foreign acts nor corrupt practices.[6]

The Foreign Corrupt Practices Act's internal controls and accounting requirements sparked a great deal of controversy. For a number of years, the SEC did not take as broad a view of the Foreign Corrupt Practices Act as it once did. The SEC continues to vigorously enforce the disclosure provisions of the Foreign Corrupt Practices Act and those provisions cover a variety of matters.[8]

Substantive Prohibitions of the Foreign Corrupt Practices Act

Section 30A of the Exchange Act[14] contains the substantive provisions of the Foreign Corrupt Practices Act which applies to issuers subject to the Exchange Act's registration and periodic reporting requirements[15] and prohib-

815 (9th Cir.1982), *cert. denied*, 469 U.S. 1115, 105 S.Ct. 801, 83 L.Ed.2d 793 (1985); Milnarik v. M–S Commodities, Inc., 457 F.2d 274 (7th Cir.), *cert. denied*, 409 U.S. 887, 93 S.Ct. 113, 34 L.Ed.2d 144 (1972). The definition of security is discussed in § 1.6 *supra*.

43. *See* §§ 1.5, 1.7 *supra*.

44. Pub. Law No. 106–554, 114 Stat. 2763 (Dec. 21, 2000).

§ 22.2

1. Pub.L. 95–213, 95th Cong., 1st Sess., 91 Stat. 1494 (1977), codified in 15 U.S.C.A. §§ 78m(b), 78dd–1, 78dd–2. The 1977 amendments also contain amendments to the 1934 Act reporting requirements (The Domestic and Foreign Investment Improved Disclosure Act of 1977).

3. S.Rep. No. 114, 95th Cong., 1st Sess. 1977.

5. 15 U.S.C.A. §§ 78dd–1, 78dd–2.

6. 15 U.S.C.A. § 78m(b).

8. As discussed more fully below, the Foreign Corrupt Practices Act amendments to the Securities Exchange Act of 1934 require disclosure of internal controls imposed by companies to monitor their financial and business operations. Duties with regard to management oversight of the business are also implicated by the Management Discussion and Analysis (MD & A) disclosures required by the Exchange Act. It is to be noted however, that the Commission's increased focus on Management Discussion and Analysis of operations (*see* §§ 3.9, 9.4 *supra*) has increased the obligation to monitor and disclose trends and uncertainties that can materially affect operations.

14. 15 U.S.C.A. § 78dd–1.

15. 15 U.S.C.A. §§ 78*l*, 78m(a), 78*o*(d). *See* §§ 9.2, 9.3 *supra*. The Act's prohibitions are thus not limited to registered securities but also to securities subject to section 15(d)'s periodic reporting requirements.

its those companies from engaging in specified corrupt practices. For example, the Act makes it unlawful to use an instrumentality of interstate commerce "corruptly in furtherance of an offer, payment, promise to pay, or authorization of the payment of any money, or offer, gift, promise to give, or authorization of the giving of anything of value to (1) any foreign official"[16] and, *inter alia,* for any person to participate in diverting funds to such persons for the purposes of assisting the issuer "in obtaining or retaining business."[17] The Act prohibits both corrupt giving and offering anything of value with the purpose of improper influence peddling. Specifically prohibited is a payment or offer of payment designed to influence an official act or decision.[18]

The Foreign Corrupt Practices Act prohibits a payment or offer of payment designed to induce someone to act or fail to act in such a way as to violate that person's lawful duty.[23] The Act prohibits a payment or offer of payment designed to induce someone to influence a foreign government to act in a certain way.[24] The Act also prohibits the payment or offering of a payment designed to secure any improper advantage in order to obtain, retain, or direct business to any person.[25]

Improper payments to foreign officials can include payment of travel and entertainment expenses that are paid as a quid pro quo for special favors.[26] Section 104 of the Foreign Corrupt Practices Act[27] applies similar prohibitions to any "domestic concern"[28] other than an issuer subject to section 30A.

§ 22.2[2] Internal Controls and Disclosure Obligations

Section 30A of the Exchange Act and section 104 of the Foreign Corrupt Practices Act zero in directly on the types of conduct that led to the Act's passage—corrupt practices taking place in foreign countries. In contrast, the amendments to section 13 of the Exchange Act[36] have a much broader reach. As noted above, these disclosure and reporting requirements are not limited to corrupt practices and do not require involvement in a foreign country. The Foreign Corrupt Practices Act imposed two requirements on issuers subject to the periodic reporting requirements of sections 13(a) and 15(d) of the Exchange Act.[37] The issuer must make more accurate disclosure of corporate expenditures and also must establish a system of internal controls to monitor expenditures of corporate funds. The theory behind section 13(b) was that by imposing more stringent accounting methods, corporate management would have tighter controls on corporate expenditures and thus be able to prevent the types of conduct prohibited by section 30A of the Exchange Act and section 104 of the Foreign Corrupt Practices Act.

16. 15 U.S.C.A. § 78dd–1(a)(1).

17. 15 U.S.C.A. § 78dd–1.

18. 15 U.S.C.A. § 78dd–1.

23. 15 U.S.C.A. § 78dd–1.

24. 15 U.S.C.A. § 78dd–1.

25. 15 U.S.C.A. § 78dd–1.

26. *See, e.g.*, United States v. Metcalf & Eddy, No. 1:99CV125666 (D. Mass. Filed Dec. 14, 1999).

27. 15 U.S.C.A. § 78dd–2.

28. *See* 15 U.S.C.A. § 78dd–2(h).

36. 15 U.S.C.A. § 78m.

37. 15 U.S.C.A. §§ 78m(a), 78*o*(d).

Section 13(b)(1) of the Exchange Act empowers the Commission to prescribe reports for information required by section 13(b)(2).[42] At one time the Commission proposed extensive disclosure requirements that would have had far-reaching effects upon corporate governance.[43] These proposals raised tremendous controversy. These proposals were not adopted, and there are currently two much less controversial rules that have been promulgated and adopted under section 13(b). Rule 13b2–1 prohibits falsification of records required by section 13(b)(2)(A).[44] Rule 13b2–2 prohibits officers and directors from making material misstatements or omissions of fact in connection with any audit or preparation of reports pursuant to section 13(b)(2).[45]

The SEC views the basic thrust of these provisions of the Foreign Corrupt Practices Act as requiring more effective accounting controls,[46] and thus has backed away from more stringent corporate governance requirements.

As noted above, the Sarbanes–Oxley Act of 2002 enhanced the independence of audit committees and the auditors themselves. Sarbanes–Oxley also established a requirement that company filings be personally certified by the CEO and CFO.[59] These certifications include the accuracy of the disclosures relating to a company's internal controls and thus reinforce the requirements of the section 13(b)(2) disclosures.

§ 22.7 Derivatives Regulation Under the Commodity Exchange Act

§ 22.7[1] Overview of Commodities Markets and Regulation

Commodities Markets

Originally developed as a means for hedging by producers, manufacturers, and large-scale buyers of commodities, public trading in commodities futures contracts has become a major investment vehicle for many investors.[1] Futures contracts embody a promise to deliver underlying commodities at a future date that will then be sold at the previously agreed-upon price.[2] This promise of future delivery must be honored either by delivery of the underlying commodity or by purchasing an off-setting futures contract. Although the commodities laws do not impose a suitability requirement, it is a fact of reality that investments in commodities futures are suitable only for sophisticated investors who are able to bear the loss of their entire investment.[3] The commodities markets are highly volatile and investment is usually made with ten percent payment and ninety percent credit margin, which magnifies the

42. 15 U.S.C.A. § 78m(b)(1).

43. Sec.Exch.Act Rel. No. 34–15772 (April 30, 1979).

44. 17 C.F.R. § 240.13b2–1.

45. 17 C.F.R. § 240.13b2–2.

46. Sec.Exch.Act Rel. No. 34–17500 (Jan. 29, 1981) ("The primary thrust of the Act's accounting provisions, in short, was to require those public companies which lacked effective internal controls or tolerated unreliable recordkeeping to comply with the standards of their better managed peers. *That* is the context in which these provisions should be construed").

59. 15 U.S.C.A. § 7241.

§ 22.7

1. *See generally* 1,2 Philip M. Johnson & Thomas L. Hazen, Derivatives Regulation (2004).

2. Futures trading is thus different from the securities options market, where there is no promise to deliver; instead, there is an option which may be exercised. *See, e.g.,* Paul M. Architzel and John P. Connolly, Delivery on Futures Contracts as a Legal Requirement, 36 Bus.Law 579 (1981).

3. *See, e.g.,* 17 C.F.R. § 1.56 (risk disclosure statement to customers of futures commission merchants and introducing brokers).

speculative nature of an intrinsically volatile investment.[4] Added to the high degree of leverage are the limits on daily price movements in many commodities, the result of which can be to lock-in the investor while his or her investment tumbles.

There is wide variety in the types of publicly traded commodities contracts, providing a broad range of investment alternatives, many of which compete directly with comparable securities options.[7] The regulation of trading in commodity futures contracts has been increasing in intensity. One by-product has been the development of jurisdictional disputes between the Commodity Futures Trading Commission (CFTC) and the Securities and Exchange Commission. The discussion that follows is designed to give a very brief overview of the increasingly complex regulation of the commodities markets.

In terms of financial impact, unregulated over-the-counter derivatives transactions provide the vehicle for a huge amount of risk-shifting arrangements. For example, the widespread use of these derivatives has created an enormous derivatives risk, with as much as eighty-one trillion dollars in derivatives risk being held by the twenty-five largest banks.[9]

Overlap of Securities and Commodities Markets

The Commodity Exchange Act contains a number of provisions designed to protect investors in the highly speculative and volatile commodities markets.[10] The Act generally prohibits contracts that are designed to defraud investors.[11] The Act also prohibits certain "meretricious transactions," including wash sales, cross trades, accommodation trades and fictitious sales.[12]

From its inception, the CFTC has been in conflict with the SEC with regard to jurisdiction over conduct and transactions that could be covered by either the securities laws or the Commodity Exchange Act. For example, commodities pools are subject to regulation under both the securities laws and the Commodity Exchange Act.[14] Ordinarily, a commodity futures contract is not a security.[15] However, a security will exist when the underlying commodity is itself a security[16]—but, according to one district court decision, not where

4. *Compare* the fifty percent margin requirements that apply to the extension of credit for most securities transactions. 15 U.S.C.A. § 78g. *See* § 14.9 *supra*.

7. *See* Jerry W. Markham and David I. Gilberg, Stock and Commodity Options—Two Regulatory Approaches and Their Conflicts, 47 Albany L.Rev. 741 (1983).

9. *See, e.g.*, Milton Recht, Derivative Amounts–and Risk–Increase at Banks, Complinet, http://www.complinet.com/us/news/news/article.html?ref=63165&ephigh=&high=derivatives (Sept. 28, 2004).

10. 7 U.S.C.A. § 6a. The statute is directed, *inter alia*, to the establishment of trading or position limits, as well as to cornering the market and other abusive speculative practices. The CFTC's regulations are found in 17 C.F.R. parts 1–180.

11. 7 U.S.C.A. § 6b.

12. 7 U.S.C.A. § 6c. *Compare* the antimanipulation provisions of the Securities Exchange Act. 15 U.S.C.A. §§ 78i, 78j, 78*o*(c). *See* §§ 6.1, 6.2, 12.1 *supra*.

14. *See* H.R.Rep. no. 565 (pt. 1) 97th Cong., 2d Sess. (1982); S.Rep. no. 384, 97th Cong., 2d Sess. (1982).

15. *E.g.*, Silverstein v. Merrill Lynch, Pierce, Fenner & Smith, Inc., 618 F.Supp. 436 (S.D.N.Y.1985).

16. Abrams v. Oppenheimer Government Securities, Inc., 737 F.2d 582 (7th Cir.1984) (when the object underlying the futures contract is itself a security, the futures contract is also a security).

the underlying commodity is a stock index.[17] Also, although the courts are in conflict, there is some authority supporting the view that discretionary managed commodity accounts constitute securities.[18] There is increasing support, however, for the view that a discretionary commodities account is not a security unless there is a pooling of customers' funds.[19]

Overview of Commodities Regulation

Until 1974 there was very sparse regulation of commodities markets, but this was changed by the enactment of the Commodity Futures Trading Commission Act Amendments[26] to the Commodity Exchange Act.[27] The 1974 amendments created the Commodity Futures Trading Commission (CFTC) which has "pervasive" regulatory authority over the public futures markets, the brokers, and other professionals in the commodities markets.[28] Specifically, it is unlawful for any person to act as a commodity trading adviser or commodity pool operator unless registered with the CFTC.[29] Additionally, CFTC registration requirements extend to brokers and all persons associated with futures commission merchants who solicit or accept customer orders (or persons supervising others engaged in these activities).[30] As is the case under the securities acts, brokerage firms dealing with commodities have a duty to supervise their employees to assure compliance with the Act and applicable rules of conduct.[31]

Comparable to the SEC's regulation of national securities exchanges[32] is the CFTC's power to designate any qualifying board of trade as a "contract market."[33] These contract markets not only regulate the futures contracts offered on a retail basis to the investing public, but also professional traders and brokers who must be members of a board of trade.[34] In contrast to the SEC, the CFTC has jurisdiction to adjudicate disputes between private par-

17. *See, e.g.,* Mallen v. Merrill Lynch, Pierce, Fenner & Smith, Inc., 605 F.Supp. 1105 (N.D.Ga.1985) (stock index futures are commodities and are *not* securities).

18. *See* Smoky Greenhaw Cotton Co. v. Merrill Lynch, Pierce, Fenner & Smith, Inc., 785 F.2d 1274 (5th Cir.1986) (taking a broad view in treating managed accounts as securities).

19. *E.g.,* Lopez v. Dean Witter Reynolds, Inc., 805 F.2d 880 (9th Cir.1986); Point Landing, Inc. v. Omni Capital Int'l, Ltd., 795 F.2d 415 (5th Cir.1986) *affirmed on other grounds,* 484 U.S. 97, 108 S.Ct. 404, 98 L.Ed.2d 415 (1987) (CFTC has exclusive jurisdiction).

26. Pub.L. No. 93–463, 88 Stat. 1389 (1974).

27. 7 U.S.C.A. §§ 1–25.

28. *See* Jeffrey S. Rosen, Regulation of Commodity Pool Operators Under the Commodity Exchange Act, 40 Wash. & Lee L.Rev. 937, 939–940 (1983).

The CFTC consists of five commissioners appointed for five-year terms by the President with the advice and consent of the Senate. 7 U.S.C.A. § 4a. The CFTC's powers are broader than those of the SEC. The commission has rulemaking authority. 7 U.S.C.A. § 4a(j). The CFTC has enforcement power in the courts (7 U.S.C.A. §§ 13a–1, 15), as well as oversight responsibilities with regard to boards of trade and futures associations (7 U.S.C.A. §§ 7, 21). Additionally, commodities professionals—brokers, futures, merchants, commodity advisers and commodity pool operators—must register with the CFTC. 7 U.S.C.A. §§ 6f, 6j, 6k, 6n. The Commission has disciplinary authority with regard to members of commodities exchanges. 12 U.S.C.A. § 12c. *See* Michael S. Sackheim, Administrative Enforcement of The Federal Commodities Laws by The Commodity Futures Trading Commission, 12 Seton Hall L.Rev. 445 (1982).

29. 7 U.S.C.A. § 6n.

30. 7 U.S.C.A. § 6k.

31. 7 U.S.C.A. § 13c(b).

32. 15 U.S.C.A. § 78f. *See* §§ 14.1, 14.3 *supra.*

33. 7 U.S.C.A. § 7.

34. 7 U.S.C.A. §§ 7a, 12a. In 2000, Congress enacted two other regulatory tiers.

ties. Private parties who have been injured by fraud or other Commodity Exchange Act violations by registered commodities professionals may seek reparation in administrative proceedings before the CFTC.[35] The Supreme Court has since concurred in the Commodity Futures Trading Commission's position that, in its reparations proceedings, the CFTC has the power to adjudicate counterclaims not arising under the Commodities Act but based on common law.[36]

The CFTC's reparations proceedings' administrative remedy to resolve disputes between customers and brokers is in addition to the implied private remedy that the Supreme Court subsequently recognized for violations of the Act's general antifraud proscriptions.[37] Following the Court's recognition of implied remedies, Congress amended the Commodity Exchange Act to provide express private remedies.[38]

Not every breach of a commodities broker's fiduciary duty will give rise to a remedy under the Act, as the plaintiff must be able to show intentional or reckless misconduct.[39] Allegations of churning can form the basis of a remedy.[40] It has been observed that a higher degree of account turnover will be tolerated in commodities accounts than in securities accounts because of the volatile nature of commodities investments.[41] In a variation of what is known as scalping, the practice of "trading ahead"—a broker's trading futures contracts in advance and in anticipation of a customer's trades—constitutes common law fraud and thus the basis for a mail fraud prosecution.[42]

In contrast to the antifraud remedy, it is generally recognized that the Act's registration provisions do not provide an implied private remedy.[43] It further has been held that an exchange member has no right of action against an exchange for failure to alter the terms of a contract, but an allegation that self interest or other ulterior motives prompted the exchange's regulatory stance was held to state a cause of action.[44]

Also, like the SEC, the Commodity Futures Trading Commission has cease and desist power with regard to registered professionals.[46] The CFTC also has enforcement powers in the courts.[47] In addition to regulation of contract markets, other registered entities, and commodities professionals, the CFTC has oversight responsibilities with respect to registered futures associations.[48]

35. 7 U.S.C.A. § 18.

36. Commodity Futures Trading Commission v. Schor, 478 U.S. 833, 106 S.Ct. 3245, 92 L.Ed.2d 675 (1986).

37. Merrill Lynch, Pierce, Fenner & Smith, Inc. v. Curran, 456 U.S. 353, 102 S.Ct. 1825, 72 L.Ed.2d 182 (1982).

38. 7 U.S.C.A. § 25.

39. *E.g.,* Evanston Bank v. Conticommodity Services, Inc., 623 F.Supp. 1014, 1023–24 (N.D.Ill.1985).

40. Evanston Bank v. Conticommodity Services, Inc., 623 F.Supp. 1014 (N.D.Ill.1985).

41. Griswold v. E.F. Hutton & Co., 622 F.Supp. 1397 (N.D.Ill.1985).

42. United States v. Dial, 757 F.2d 163 (7th Cir.1985), *cert. denied,* 474 U.S. 838, 106 S.Ct 116, 88 L.Ed.2d 95 (1985).

43. Marshall v. Green Giant Co., 16 Sec.Reg. & L.Rep. (BNA) 1157 (D.C.Minn.1984).

44. Sam Wong & Son, Inc. v. New York Mercantile Exchange, 735 F.2d 653 (2d Cir.1984).

46. 7 U.S.C.A. § 13b.

47. 7 U.S.C.A. § 13a–1.

48. 7 U.S.C.A. § 22. This is analogous to the SEC's power under the Securities Exchange Act of 1934 with regard to self regulatory organizations. *See* § 14.3 *supra.*

The Commodity Exchange Act prohibits public futures transactions other than through a member of a board of trade that is registered as a "contract market."[49] Publicly traded futures and commodities options contracts formerly could be traded only through designated contract markets registered with the Commodity Futures Trading Commission. Traditionally, there was no retail over the counter market for commodities based products. In the 1980s and 1990s, various types of commodities-based investments took place between institutional investors other than through the facility of a regulated contract market, in what can only be called an over-the-counter market. Increasing trading of swap and other hybrid products took place under exemptions from the statutorily imposed contract market monopoly. The ever-changing appearance of the commodities markets and special needs of institutional and other large investors led to the most significant change in commodities regulation since 1974.

In 2000, there was a massive overhaul of commodities markets regulation when a three-tiered layer of regulation was introduced.[52] The highest degree of regulation remains with the designated contract markets where retail futures trading takes place in the more traditional commodities products, including agricultural commodities. The Commodity Futures Modernization Act of 2000[53] introduced a new category of futures markets for certain commodities-based products and is open not to retail investors generally (unless participating through a registered futures commission merchant), but only to specified qualified investors. The Modernization Act created two new categories. The Act created an "exempt board of trade" (XBOT) and also created a "derivatives transaction execution facility" ("DTEF"). DTEFs are subject to fewer regulatory requirements than CFTC-designated contract markets. DTEFs are open only to certain investors and those trading through registered futures commission merchants.[54] Permitting retail investors access only through registered futures commission merchants is designed to provide unsophisticated investors with adequate regulatory protection, should they decide to participate in this over-the-counter derivatives market.[55] In addition to limiting investor access to derivatives transaction execution facilities (as opposed to registered contract markets), the regulatory scheme ushered in by

49. 7 U.S.C.A. § 6(a).

52. Commodity Futures Modernization Act of 2000, Pub. Law No. 106–554, 114 Stat. 2763 (Dec. 21, 2000).

53. Pub. Law No. 106–554, 114 Stat. 2763 (Dec. 21, 2000).

54. The 2000 amendments to the Commodity Exchange Act introduced a new category of eligible contract participants ("ECPs") consisting of institutional and highly accredited customers. ECPs include financial institutions; insurance companies, registered investment companies; corporations, partnerships, trusts, and other entities having total assets exceeding $10,000,000; employee benefit plans subject to ERISA that have total assets exceeding $5,000,000; governmental entities; and others. Eligible commercial entity refers to a subset of ECPs including, among others, entities who have a demonstrable ability to make or take delivery of the underlying commodity, incur risk in addition to price risk related to the commodity, or are dealers regularly providing risk management or hedging services to or engaging in market-making activities with other eligible commercial entities.

Access to DTEFs must be confined to ECPs or to non-ECPs who trade through an FCM that is registered with the CFTC, is a member of a registered futures association (or, "in the case of securities futures products, a registered securities association), is a clearing member of a derivatives clearing organization, and has net capital of at least $20,000,000.

55. Perhaps, once the DTEFs are fully operational, they will operate in much the same way as NASDAQ does for over the counter securities when viewed in contrast to the national securities exchanges. For discussion of the securities markets, *see* chapter 14 *supra*.

the Modernization Act imposed limits on what products may be offered on a DTEF.[56] The 2000 amendments also formally recognized the over the counter commodities markets; but these markets—which are virtually unregulated except for antifraud proscriptions[57]—are open only to the largest institutional investors dealing in certain types of swap and other hybrid contracts. These unregulated over the counter derivatives transactions must be bilateral private transactions between eligible traders, and the transactions must be on a principal-to-principal basis.

At the same time that Congress gave formal approval to the over-the-counter commodities markets for qualified participants, both the securities and commodities laws were amended to provide that securities-based swap agreements are not securities[58]—although they remain subject to the securities laws' antifraud provisions.[59] The degree of CFTC involvement in derivatives markets thus depends on the nature of the investors and the types of commodities-based products being offered.

The Commodity Exchange Act authorizes the CFTC to coordinate its regulatory efforts with other regulatory bodies. This coordination includes cooperation with the SEC in regulating products that overlap the securities and commodities markets.[60] The CFTC cooperates with other regulatory bodies as well. Thus, for example, the Commodity Futures Trading Commission may refer any transaction or matter subject to other Federal or State statutes to any department or agency administering such statutes for investigation, action, or proceedings that that department or agency shall deem appropriate.

An unusual aspect of the Commodity Exchange Act is its reauthorization process. Under the terms of the statute, the power of the Commodity Futures Trading Commission is subject to reauthorization by Congress. Frequently, the reauthorization process results in major substantive amendments. For example, in its 1986 reauthorization legislation, Congress expanded the variety of investments by permanently authorizing trading of options on futures.[61] The 1992 amendments also were far-reaching. However, on other occasions, as in 1994, reauthorization has not resulted in major change.

As pointed out in earlier sections of this treatise,[62] the Commodity

56. DTEFs may trade only commodities—based contracts satisfying the following criteria: (1) the underlying commodity has a "nearly exhaustible" deliverable supply; (2) the underlying commodity has a deliverable supply that is sufficiently large that the contract is "highly unlikely to be susceptible" to the threat of manipulation; (3) the underlying commodity has no cash market; (4) the contract is a security futures product and the registered DTEF is a national securities exchange registered under the 1934 Act; (5) the CFTC determines, based on the market characteristics, surveillance history, self-regulatory record and capacity of the facility, that trading in the contract is highly unlikely to be susceptible to the threat of manipulation, or (6) the underlying commodity is not an agricultural commodity and trading access is limited to eligible commercial entities trading for their own accounts.

57. The 2000 legislation also provided that, although excluded from the definition of security under the securities acts, commodities-based swap agreements are subject to the securities laws' antifraud provisions.

58. 15 U.S.C.A. §§ 77b(a)(1), 78c(a)(10).

59. 15 U.S.C.A. §§ 77q(a), 78j(b).

60. *See* § 1.5 *supra*.

61. Futures Trading Act of 1986 § 102. Prior to this enactment, the CFTC had been supervising a pilot options program.

62. *See* §§ 1.7[5], 1.7[6], 1.7[7] *supra*.

Futures Modernization Act of 2000[63] permitted for the first time futures contracts on individual securities and also provided for expanded over-the-counter derivatives and swap markets that previously were questionable under the Commodity Exchange Act. In 2008, the SEC and CFTC announced increased cooperation through a memorandum of understanding.[64] Among other things, the SEC/CFTC memorandum of understanding establishes a permanent liaison between the two agencies; provides that there will be formal joint staff meetings each quarter on ongoing consultations regarding enforcement, examination, and mergers, and also to consider explicit principles to guide regulation of novel financial products.[65]

§ 22.7[2] Commodities Trading Professionals

With the increased integration of financial services, many of the major securities brokerage firms operate both as securities brokers and commodities brokers. Although the commodities brokerage relationship functions in much the same way as securities brokerage, the nomenclature and regulatory structure are quite different.

The primary retail brokerage unit in the commodities world is known as a futures commission merchant (FCM).[67] FCMs must be registered with the National Futures Association as a result of authority delegated to it by the Commodity Futures Trading Commission.[68] Employees of a futures commission merchant who function as account executives are classified as "associated persons" (APs) of the FCM, and similarly must be registered with the CFTC.[69] An alternative arrangement exists in the case of "introducing brokers" (IBs),[70] who perform much the same functions as associated persons of futures commission merchants, but elect not to be registered as an associate person of the FCM. Introducing brokers, who must also register with the National Futures Association, act as agents of the FCM.

In the commodities world, many floor traders are known as floor brokers (FBs). As is the case with other commodity trading professionals, floor brokers are subject to registration requirements.[71]

63. Pub. Law No. 106–554, 114 Stat. 2763 (Dec. 21, 2000).

64. See Press Release No. 2008–40 SEC, CFTC Sign Agreement to Enhance Coordination, Facilitate Review of New Derivative Products—Agencies Also Announce First Fruits of Collaboration: Joint Action on Gold Products, http://www.sec.gov/news/press/2008/2008–40.htm (SEC March 11, 2008).

65. See Press Release No. 2008–40 SEC, CFTC Sign Agreement to Enhance Coordination, Facilitate Review of New Derivative Products—Agencies Also Announce First Fruits of Collaboration: Joint Action on Gold Products, http://www.sec.gov/news/press/2008/2008–40.htm (SEC March 11, 2008).

67. *See* section 1a(12) of the Commodity Exchange Act, 7 U.S.C.A. § 1a(12).

68. Section 4f of the Commodity Exchange Act addresses the registration of futures commission merchants. 7 U.S.C.A. § 6f. *See generally* Philip M. Johnson & Thomas L. Hazen, Derivatives Regulation (2004).

69. Section 4k of the Commodity Exchange Act addresses the registration of associated persons. 7 U.S.C.A. § 6k.

70. *See* section 1a(14) of the Commodity Exchange Act, 7 U.S.C.A. § 1a(14) ("The term 'introducing broker' means any person, except an individual who elects to be registered as an associated person of a futures commission merchant, engaged in soliciting or accepting orders for the purchase or sale of [commodity futures and options] * * * ").

71. Section 4f of the Commodity Exchange Act addresses the registration of floor brokers. 7 U.S.C.A. § 6f. *See generally* 2Philip M. Johnson & Thomas L. Hazen, Derivatives Regulation (2004).

The commodities world's counterparts to investment companies[72] are known as commodity pools. Commodity pools are managed by commodity pool operators (CPOs). Unless they can find an exemption in the Commodity Exchange Act or the CFTC regulations promulgated thereunder, commodity pool operators must register with the National Futures Association.[73] In addition to the various exemptions, entities that are registered as investment companies under the Investment Company Act of 1940[74] are excluded from the Commodity Exchange Act's CPO registration requirements.[75]

Investment advisors who render advice with regard to commodities investments are known as commodity trading advisors (CTAs). Unless an exemption is available, commodity trading advisors are subject to registration requirements similar to those applicable to commodity pool operators.[76]

Two other varieties of commodities trading professionals deserve mention. Prior to exchange trading for commodity options, off-exchange options that originated from registered option grantors could be traded through commodity option dealers.[77] Although off-exchange commodity options may soon become a thing of the past in light of exchange trading, commodity option grantors that operated prior to exchange trading continue to operate subject to the Act's registration requirements.[78] Additionally, leverage transaction merchants (LTMs) who are registered under the Act[79] may deal in leveraged commodity contracts. Over the years, there has been a great deal of consideration given to phasing out leverage contract trading.[80]

---

72. *See* chapter 20 *supra.*

73. Section 4m of the Commodity Exchange Act addresses the registration of commodity pool operators. 7 U.S.C.A. § 6m. *See generally* Philip M. Johnson & Thomas L. Hazen, Derivatives Regulation (2004). *Cf.* In the Matter of Lake States Commodities, Inc., 936 F.Supp. 1461 (N.D.Ill.1996) (adequately alleging control of unregistered commodity pool by futures commission merchant).

74. 15 U.S.C.A. § 80a–1 et seq. *See* chapter 20 *supra.*

75. 17 C.F.R. § 4.5(a)(1). *See, e.g.,* James G. Smith, A Securities Law Primer for Commodity Pool Operators, 1996 Colum. Bus. L. Rev. 281.

76. Section 4m of the Commodity Exchange Act addresses the registration of commodity trading advisors. 7 U.S.C.A. § 6m. *See generally* 2 Philip M. Johnson & Thomas L. Hazen, Derivatives Regulation (2004).

77. *See Id.*

78. 7 U.S.C.A. § 6c(d); 17 C.F.R. §§ 32.1–32.12.

79. 7 U.S.C.A. § 23; 17 C.F.R. §§ 31.1–31.26. *See generally* 2 Philip M. Johnson & Thomas L. Hazen, Derivatives Regulation (2004).

80. *See Id.*

*

Appendix

Researching Securities Law on Westlaw

Analysis

Section 1. Introduction

The Law of Securities Regulation provides a strong base for analyzing even the most complex problem involving issues related to securities law. Whether your research requires examination of **case law, statutes, administrative materials, or expert commentary,** West books and Westlaw are excellent sources of information.

To keep you informed of current developments, Westlaw provides frequently updated databases. With Westlaw, you have unparalleled legal research resources at your fingertips.

Additional Resources

If you have not previously used Westlaw or if you have questions not covered in this appendix, call the West Reference Attorneys at 1–800–REF-ATTY (1–

800–733–2889). The West Reference Attorneys are trained, licensed attorneys, available 24 hours a day to assist you with your Westlaw search questions. To subscribe to Westlaw, call 1–800–344–5008 or access **www.westlaw.com**.

Section 2. Westlaw Databases

Each database on Westlaw is assigned an abbreviation called an *identifier*, which you can use to access the database. You can find identifiers for Westlaw databases in the online Westlaw Directory and in the printed *Westlaw Database Directory*. When you need to know more detailed information about a database, use Scope. Scope contains coverage information, lists of related databases, and valuable search tips.

The following chart lists selected Westlaw databases that contain information pertaining to securities law. For a complete list of securities law databases, see the online Westlaw Directory or the printed *Westlaw Database Directory*. Because new information is continually being added to Westlaw, you should also check the online Westlaw Directory for new database information.

Selected Securities Law Databases on Westlaw

Database	Identifier	Coverage
Combined Federal Materials		
Federal Securities–Combined Materials	FSEC-ALL	Varies by source
Federal Securities–Code and Regulations	FSEC–CODREG	Varies by source
Federal Cases		
Federal Securities–Cases	FSEC–CS	Begins with 1789
Federal Securities–Supreme Court Cases	FSEC–SCT	Begins with 1790
Federal Securities–Courts of Appeals Cases	FSEC–CTA	Begins with 1891
Federal Securities–District Courts Cases	FSEC–DCT	Begins with 1789
Financial Crisis–Cases	FC–CS	Begins with 1658
Briefs, Pleadings, Other Court Documents, and Jury Materials		
Federal Securities Briefs	FSEC–BRIEF	Begins with 1942
Andrews Derivatives Litigation Reporter Court Documents	ANDERLR–DOC	Begins with 2000
Andrews Mergers and Acquisitions Litigation Reporter Court Documents	ANMALR–DOC	Begins with 2000
Andrews Securities Litigation and Regulation Reporter Court Documents	ANSLRR–DOC	Begins with 2000

Database	Identifier	Coverage
Financial Crisis Civil Trial Filings	FC–FILING	Begins with 2006
Securities Civil Trial Filings	SEC–FILING	Begins with 1993
Securities Trial Motions	SEC–MOTIONS	Begins with 1997
Securities Trial Pleadings	SEC–PLEADINGS	Begins with 1997
Securities Combined Jury Verdicts and Settlement Summaries	SEC–JV	Varies by source
Federal Statutes, Rules, and Legislative History		
Federal Securities–U.S. Code Annotated	FSEC–USCA	Current data
Federal Commodity Futures Trading Commission–United States Code Annotated	FCFTC–USCA	Current data
Federal Securities–Rules	FSEC–RULES	Current data
Federal Securities–Legislative History	FSEC–LH	Begins with 1933
Arnold & Porter Legislative History: Government Securities Act of 1986	GOVSEC86–LH	Full history
Arnold & Porter Legislative History: Government Securities Reform Act of 1993	GOVSEC93–LH	Full history
Arnold & Porter Legislative History: Insider Trading Act	INSIDER–LH	Full history
Arnold & Porter Legislative History: Sarbanes–Oxley Act of 2002	SAROX–LH	Full history
Financial Crisis–Congressional Record	FC–CR	Begins with First Session of 99th Congress (1985)
Financial Crisis–Pending Federal Legislation	FC–BILLTXT	Begins with 104th Congress (1995)
Financial Crisis–Public Laws	FC–PL	Current data
Federal Administrative Materials		
Federal Securities–Final, Temporary, and Proposed Regulations	FSEC–REG	Varies by source

Database	Identifier	Coverage
Federal Securities–Code of Federal Regulations	FSEC–CFR	Current data
Federal Securities–Federal Register	FSEC–FR	Begins with January 1981
Federal Commodity Futures Trading Commission–Code of Federal Regulations	FCFTC–CFR	Current data
Federal Commodity Futures Trading Commission–Federal Register	FCFTC–FR	Begins with January 1981
Financial Crisis–Federal Register	FC–FR	Begins with January 1988
National Association of Securities Dealers (NASD)–Final, Temporary, and Proposed Regulations	NASD–REG	Varies by source
National Association of Securities Dealers (NASD)–Code of Federal Regulations (Title 12 and Title 17)	NASD–CFR	Current data
National Association of Securities Dealers (NASD)–Federal Register	NASD–FR	Begins with January 1981
Federal Securities–Administrative Materials	FSEC–ADMIN	Varies by source
Federal Securities–Arbitration Awards	FSEC–ARB	Begins with 1989
Federal Securities–Commodity Futures Trading Commission Decisions	FSEC–CFTC	CFTC decisions begins with 1976; administrative law judge decisions begins with 1983
Federal Securities–Commodity Futures Trading Commission Letters	FSEC–CFTCLTR	Begins with 1987
Federal Securities Exchange Commission–Miscellaneous Documents	FSEC–MISC	Begins with 1997
Federal Securities–Interpretive and Policy Letters	FSEC–IRP	Begins with 1970
Federal Securities–News Releases	FSEC–NR	SEC releases begins with November 1991;CFTC releases begins with January 1992

Database	Identifier	Coverage
SEC Enforcement Manual	FSEC–ENFMAN	Current data
Federal Securities–SEC News Digest	FSEC–DIG	Begins with July 1987
Federal Securities–SEC No–Action Letters	FSEC–NAL	Begins with 1970
Federal Securities–Securities Releases	FSEC–RELS	SEC releases and decisions begins with 1933; Staff Accounting Bulletins begins with 1976; Staff Legal Bulletins: begins with 1997
Federal Securities–Stock Exchange Disciplinary Decisions	FSEC–DISP	Exchange Hearing Panel decisions begins with 1972; Disciplinary Panel decisions: begins with 1985; National Adjudicatory Council decisions begins with 1990
Federal Securities–Sworn Certification of Financial Statements	FSEC–CERT	Begins with August 2002
Financial Crisis–Administrative Materials	FC–ADMIN	Varies by source
Financial Industry Regulatory Authority Organizational Materials	FINRA–ORG	Notices begins with 1983; *NASD Manual*, NYSE constitution and rules: current data
Nasdaq Manual	NASDAQ–MANUAL	Current data
National Association of Securities Dealers (NASD)–Arbitration Awards	NASD–ARB	Begins with 1981
National Association of Securities Dealers (NASD)–Disciplinary Decisions	NASD–DISP	Selected coverage begins with 1990; full coverage begins with 1992
National Association of Securities Dealers (NASD) Manual	NASD–MANUAL	Current data
National Association of Securities Dealers (NASD)–Notices to Members	NASD–NOTICE	Begins with 1983
National Association of Securities Dealers (NASD)–Office of Hearing Officers	NASD–OHO	Begins with 1998
Securities Regulations Suite®	SEC–REGS	Varies by jurisdiction

Database	Identifier	Coverage
Combined State Materials		
Blue Sky Statutes and Regulations–Combined	BLUESKY–COMBINED	Current data
Individual State Blue Sky Combined	XXSEC–COMBINED (where XX is a state's two-letter postal abbreviation)	Current data
50 State Survey–Securities (Statutes and Regulations)	SURVEY–SEC	Current data
State Cases		
Multistate Securities and Blue Sky Law–Cases	MSEC–CS	Varies by state
Individual State Securities and Blue Sky Law Cases	XXSEC–CS (where XX is a state's two-letter postal abbreviation)	Varies by state
Financial Crisis–Cases	FC–CS	Begins with 1658
State Statutes		
Blue Sky Statutes	BLUESKY–ST	Current data
Individual State Blue Sky Statutes	XXSEC–ST (where XX is a state's two-letter postal abbreviation)	Current data
State Administrative Materials		
Blue Sky Regulations	BLUESKY–REG	Current data
Individual State Blue Sky Regulations	XXSEC–REG (where XX is a state's two-letter postal abbreviation)	Current data
Multistate Regulatory Securities Contact Lists	SECCTL–ALL	Begins with 2006
Individual State Regulatory Securities Contact Lists	XX–SECCTL (where XX is a state's two-letter postal abbreviation)	Begins with 2006
Multistate Regulatory Securities Forms	SECFMS–ALL	Begins with 2006
Individual State Regulatory Securities Forms	XX–SECFMS (where XX is a state's two-letter postal abbreviation)	Begins with 2006
Multistate Regulatory Securities Guidelines and Manuals	SECMAN–ALL	Begins with 2006
Individual State Regulatory Securities Guidelines and Manuals	XX–SECMAN (where XX is a state's two-letter postal abbreviation)	Begins with 2006
Multistate Regulatory Securities Materials	REGSEC–ALL	Begins with 2006
Individual State Regulatory Securities Materials	XX–REGSEC (where XX is a state's two-letter postal abbreviation)	Begins with 2006

Database	Identifier	Coverage
Multistate Securities and Blue Sky Law–Administrative Decisions	MSEC–ADMIN	Varies by state
Individual State Securities Administrative Decisions	XXSEC–ADMIN (where XX is a state's two-letter postal abbreviation)	Varies by state
Securities Regulations Suite	SEC–REGS	Varies by jurisdiction
Public Records		
Dockets–Federal Securities	DOCK–FSEC	Full docket records begins with January 2000; index records begins with 1990
Dockets–Securities	DOCK–SEC	Begins with January 2000
EDGAR–SEC Filings	EDGAR	Full-text EDGAR filings begins with April 1993; records of other filings begins with 1968
Insider Stock Transactions	STOCK	Current data
Securities and Exchange Commission Corporate Filings	SEC–ONLINE	Begins with January 1987
Legal Periodicals		
Securities and Blue Sky Law–Law Reviews, Texts, and Bar Journals	SEC–TP	Varies by publication
Journals and Law Reviews	JLR	Varies by publication
Financial Crisis–Journals and Law Reviews	FC–LAWREVPRO	Varies by publication
Fordham Journal of Corporate and Financial Law	FDMJCFL	Full coverage begins with 1997 (vol. 2)
Journal of Business and Securities Law	JBSECL	Full coverage begins with 2006 (vol. 6)
Securities Regulation Law Journal	SECRLJ	Begins with 2004 (vol. 32, no. 2)
Legal Texts and Practice Materials		
Securities and Blue Sky Law–Law Reviews, Texts, and Bar Journals	SEC–TP	Varies by publication
Acquisitions and Mergers: Negotiated and Contested Transactions	SECACQMERG	Current data

Database	Identifier	Coverage
American Law Reports–Securities	ALR–SEC	Current data
Analysis of Key SEC No–Action Letters	SECKEYNAL	Current data
Anatomy of a Merger	ANATMERG	Current data
Audit Committees: Regulation and Practice	AUDCRP	Second edition
Blue Sky Law	SECBLUE	Current data
Blue Sky Practice for Public and Private Direct Participation Offerings	BSP	2008–2009 edition
Broker–Dealer Operations Under Securities and Commodities Law	SECBDOP	Current data
Broker–Dealer Regulation	PLIREF–BDR	Current data
Bromberg and Lowenfels on Securities Fraud and Commodities Fraud	SECBROMLOW	Second edition
Civil Liabilities: Enforcement and Litigation Under the 1933 Act	SECCIVIL	Current data
Commodities Regulation: Fraud, Manipulation, and Other Claims	SECCOMMREG	Current data
Corporate Anti–Takeover Defenses: The Poison Pill Device	SECPILL	Current data
Corporate Compliance Series: Securities	CORPC–SEC	Current data
Corporate Counsel's Guide to Insider Trading and Reporting	CCGINTRR	Current data
Corporate Whistleblowing in the Sarbanes–Oxley Era	PLIREF–CWSOE	Current data
Directors' and Officers' Liability	PLIREF–DIRLIAB	Current data
Disclosure and Remedies Under the Securities Laws	SECDRSL	Current data
Due Diligence–Periodic Reports and Securities Offerings	DUEDILSEC	Current data
Exempted Transactions Under the Securities Act of 1933	SECEXTRANS	Current data

Database	Identifier	Coverage
Federal Money Laundering Regulation: Banking, Corporate, and Securities Compliance	FMNYL	Current data
Federal Securities Law	FEDSECLAW	Second edition
Ferrara on Insider Trading and the Wall	INSIDETRADE	Current data
Financial Product Fundamentals: A Guide for Lawyers	PLIREF–FINP	Current edition
Georgia Securities Practice with Forms	GASECPRAC	2001 edition
Going Public and the Public Corporation	SECPUBCORP	Current data
Hedge Funds and Other Private Funds: Regulation and Compliance	SECHEDGE	Current data
Insider Trading Regulation, Enforcement, and Prevention	INSIDETRAD	Current data
International Capital Markets and Securities Regulation	SECINTCAP	Current data
Investment Adviser Regulation	PLIREF–INVEST	Current edition
Law of Securities Regulation	LAWSECREG	Fifth edition
Law of Suretyship and Guaranty	SURETY	Current data
Liability of Attorneys and Accountants for Securities Transactions	SECATTACC	Current edition
Limited Liability Company Handbook	SECLLCHB	Current data
Limited Offering Exemptions: Regulation D	SECREGD	Current data
Manual of Corporate Forms for Securities Practice	SECMCORPF	Current data
Model Documents: Mergers and Acquisitions	MODELDOC–M&A	Begins with 2000
Modern Securities Transfers	MODSECTRN	Third edition
Mortgage and Asset Backed Securities Litigation Handbook	MABSL	Current data
Mortgage–Backed Securities	MORTSEC	Current data

Database	Identifier	Coverage
Mutual Fund Regulation	PLIREF–MFR	Current data
Negotiated Acquisitions of Companies, Subsidiaries, and Divisions	NACOMP	Current data
Opinion Letters in Securities Matters: Texts–Clauses–Law	SECOPINION	Current data
Partnership Law for Securities Practitioners	SECPRAC	Current data
PLI Guide to the Sarbanes–Oxley Act	PLIREF–GSOA	Current data
PLI Securities Law Reference Books Multibase	PLIREF–SEC	Current data
Practical Guide to SEC Proxy and Compensation Rules	PGSPC	Current data
Practical Guide to Section 16: Reporting and Compliance	PGSSN	Current data
Private Activity Bond Tests	PRIVACT	Current data
Proxy Rules Handbook	PRXYRH	2008–2009 edition
Raising Capital: Private Placement Forms and Techniques	RCPPF	Third edition
Real Estate Investment Trusts Handbook	SECREITHB	Current data
Regulation of Corporate Disclosure	TROCD	Third edition
Regulation of Financial Planners	SECREGFINP	Current data
Regulation of Investment Advisers	SECREGINA	Current data
Regulation of Investment Management and Fiduciary Services	REGINVSVC	Current data
Resales of Restricted Securities	SECRESR	Current data
RIA® WGL Securities Compliance Library	WGL–SECLIB	Current data
S Corporation Handbook	SECSCORPHB	2008–2009 edition
Sarbanes–Oxley Deskbook	PLIREF–SAROX	Current data
Savings Institutions: Mergers, Acquisitions, and Conversion	SAVIMA	Current data
Section 16 of the Securities Exchange Act	SEC16	Current data

Database	Identifier	Coverage
Securities Activities of Banks	SECAB	Third edition
Securities and Federal Corporate Law	SECFEDCORP	Current data
Securities Arbitration Desk Reference	SABREF	Current data
Securities Counseling for Small and Emerging Companies	SECCOUNS	Current data
Securities Credit Regulation, Second Edition	SECCREDREG	Current data
Securities Crimes	SECCRIM	Current data
Securities Law Handbook	SECLAW–HB	Current data
Securities Law of Public Finance	PLIREF–SECFIN	Current data
Securities Law Review	SECLAWREV	2008 edition
Securities Litigation: Damages	SECLITD	Current data
Securities Litigation: Forms and Analysis	SECLITFRMS	Current data
Securities Practice: Federal and State Enforcement	SECPRACFSE	Current data
Securities: Public and Private Offerings	SECPUBPRIV	Current data
Securities Regulation Forms	SECREGFRM	Current data
Shareholder Derivative Litigation: Besieging the Board	SDLBTB	Current data
Shareholder Litigation	SHARELIT	Current data
Soderquist on Corporate Law and Practice	PLIREF–CORPL	Third edition
Soderquist on the Securities Laws	PLIREF–SECLAW	Current data
Soft Dollars and Other Brokerage Arrangements	DOLLARS	Current data
Takeover Defense	TKRDF	Sixth edition
Tax–Advantaged Securities Handbook	SECTAXAHB	Current data
U.S. Securities Law for International Financial Transactions and Capital Markets, Second Edition	SECINTFTCM	Current data
Venture Capital and Small Business Financings	SECVENTURE	Current data

Database	Identifier	Coverage
West Group® Securities Law Series Online	SECSERIES	Varies by publication
WGL Handbook of SEC Accounting and Disclosure	WGL–SECHDBK	Current data
WGL SEC Accounting and Reporting Manual	WGL–SECMAN	Current data
WGL SEC Compliance: Financial Reporting and Forms	WGL–SECFIN	Current data
Williams Act–Tender Offers and Stock Accumulations	SECWACT	Current data
News and Information		
Andrews Derivatives Litigation Reporter	ANDERLR	Begins with November 1996
Andrews Mergers and Acquisitions Litigation Reporter	ANMALR	Begins with December 1996
Andrews Securities Litigation and Regulation Reporter	ANSLRR	Begins with November 1996
Corporate Governance Expert Commentary	CORPGOV–EXP	Begins with January 2003
Edgar Prospector	EDGARPRS	Begins with September 2005
Financial Crisis–Andrews Articles	FC–ANDREWS	Begins with 1996
Financial Crisis–Aspatore Special Reports	FC–ASPSR	Begins with 2007
Financial Crisis–Miscellaneous Documents	FC–MISC	Varies by source
Financial Crisis–News	FC–NEWS	Varies by source
Futures and Derivatives Law Report	GLFDLR	Selected coverage begins with May 1996; full coverage begins with 1998
Internet Law and Strategy	INTERLSTR	Begins with January 2003
M&A Lawyer	GLMALAW	Begins with May 1997
Money Manager's Compliance Guide Newsletter	MNYMGUIDE–NWL	Begins with August 2004
PLI Compliance Counselor	PLI–CC	Begins with February 2004
Securities and Federal Corporate Law Report	SECFEDCLN	Begins with January 2003
Securities Litigation Report	GLSLR	Begins with October 2005

Database	Identifier	Coverage
Wallstreetlawyer.com: Securities in the Electronic Age	GLWSLAW	Begins with July 1997
Westlaw Topical Highlights–Securities Regulation	WTH–SEC	Current data
Directories		
West Legal Directory®–Securities	WLD–SEC	Current data

Section 3. Retrieving a Document with a Citation: Find and Hypertext Links

3.1 Find

Find is a Westlaw service that allows you to retrieve a document by entering its citation. Find allows you to retrieve documents from anywhere on Westlaw without accessing or changing databases. Find is available for many documents, including case law (state and federal), the *United States Code Annotated®* (USCA®), state statutes, administrative materials, and texts and periodicals.

To use Find, simply type the citation in the *Find this document by citation* text box at the tabbed Westlaw page and click **Go**. The following list provides some examples:

To find this document:	Type:
United States v. O'Hagan, 117 S. Ct. 2199 (1997)	**117 sct 2199**
In re SEC ex rel. Glotzer, 374 F.3d 184 (2d Cir. 2004)	**374 f3d 184**
15 U.S.C.A. § 78r	**15 usca 78r**
17 C.F.R. § 201.430	**17 cfr 201.430**
N.Y. Gen. Bus. Law § 352–c	**ny gen bus s 352–c**

For a complete list of publications that can be retrieved with Find and their abbreviations, click **Find & Print** at the top of any Westlaw page and then click **Publications List** in the left frame.

3.2 Hypertext Links

Use hypertext links to move from one location to another on Westlaw. For example, use hypertext links to go directly from the statute, case, or law review article you are viewing to a cited statute, case, or article; from a headnote to the corresponding text in the opinion; or from an entry in a statutes index to the full text of the statute.

Section 4. Searching with Natural Language

Overview: With Natural Language, you can retrieve documents by simply describing your issue in plain English. If you are a relatively new Westlaw user, Natural Language searching can make it easier for you to retrieve cases that are on point. If you are an experienced Westlaw user, Natural Language gives you a valuable alternative search method to the Terms and Connectors search method described in Section 5.

When you enter a Natural Language description, Westlaw automatically identifies legal phrases, removes common words, and generates variations of terms in your description. Westlaw then searches for the concepts in your description. Concepts may include significant terms, phrases, legal citations, or topic and key numbers. Westlaw retrieves the documents that most closely match the concepts in your description, beginning with the document most likely to match.

4.1 Natural Language Search

Access a database, such as the Federal Securities–Cases database (FSEC–CS). Click the **Natural Language** tab if it is not already selected and type a description such as the following in the *Search* text box. Then click **Search Westlaw**.

who is a ten percent beneficial owner

4.2 Browsing Search Results

Best Mode: To display the best portion (the portion that most closely matches your description) of each document in a Natural Language search result, click the **Best** arrows at the bottom of the right frame.

Term Mode: To display portions of the document that contain your search terms, click the **Term** arrows at the bottom of the right frame.

Previous/Next Document: To view the previous or the next document in the search result, click the left or right **Doc** arrow at the bottom of the right frame.

Section 5. Searching with Terms and Connectors

Overview: With Terms and Connectors searching, you enter a query consisting of key terms from your issue and connectors specifying the relationship between these terms.

Terms and Connectors searching is useful when you want to retrieve a document for which you know specific details, such as the title or the fact situation. Terms and Connectors searching is also useful when you want to retrieve all documents containing specific terms.

5.1 Terms

Plurals and Possessives: Plurals are automatically retrieved when you enter the singular form of a term. This is true for both regular and irregular plurals (e.g., **child** retrieves *children*). If you enter the plural form of a term, you will not retrieve the singular form.

If you enter the nonpossessive form of a term, Westlaw automatically retrieves the possessive form as well. However, if you enter the possessive form, only the possessive form is retrieved.

Compound Words and Abbreviations: When a compound word is one of your search terms, use a hyphen to retrieve all forms of the word. For example, the term **rule-making** retrieves *rule-making*, *rulemaking*, and *rule making*.

When using an abbreviation as a search term, place a period after each of the letters to retrieve any of its forms. For example, the term **s.e.c.** retrieves *SEC*, *S.E.C.*, *S E C*, and *S. E. C.* Note: The abbreviation does not retrieve the phrase *Securities and Exchange Commission*, so remember to add alternative terms such as **"securities and exchange commission"** to your query.

The Root Expander and the Universal Character: When you use the Terms and Connectors search method, placing the root expander (!) at the end of a root term generates all other terms with that root. For example, adding the ! to the root *fraud* in the query

fraud! /s transfer

instructs Westlaw to retrieve such terms as *fraud*, *fraudulent*, and *fraudulently*.

The universal character (*) stands for one character and can be inserted in the middle or at the end of a term. For example, the term

s* * **holder

will retrieve *shareholder* and *stockholder*. Adding three asterisks to the root *elect*

elect* * *

instructs Westlaw to retrieve all forms of the root with up to three additional characters. Terms such as *elected* or *election* are retrieved by this query. However, terms with more than three letters following the root, such as *electronic*, are not retrieved. Plurals are always retrieved, even if the plural form of the term has more than three letters following the root.

Phrase Searching: To search for an exact phrase, place it within quotation marks. For example, to search for references to *junk bond*, type **"junk bond"**. When you are using the Terms and Connectors search method, you should use phrase searching only if you are certain that the terms in the phrase will not appear in any other order.

5.2 Alternative Terms

After selecting the terms for your query, consider which alternative terms are necessary. For example, if you are searching for the term *constitutional*, you might also want to search for the term *unconstitutional*. You should consider both synonyms and antonyms as alternative terms. You can also use the Westlaw thesaurus to add alternative terms to your query.

5.3 Connectors

After selecting terms and alternative terms for your query, use connectors to specify the relationship that must exist between search terms in your retrieved documents. The connectors are described below:

Type:	**To retrieve documents with:**	**Example:**
& (and)	both search terms	**director & officer**
a space (or)	either search term or both search terms	**i.p.o. "initial public offering"**

/p	search terms in the same paragraph	**pre-empt! /p state**
/s	search terms in the same sentence	**investment /s advis*r**
+s	the first search term preceding the second within the same sentence	**burden +s proof prov!**
/n	search terms within *n* terms of each other (where *n* is a number from 1 to 255)	**limited /5 liab!**
+n	the first search term preceding the second by *n* terms (where *n* is a number from 1 to 255)	**plain +3 english**
" "	search terms appearing in the same order as in the quotation marks	**"red herring"**

Type:	**To exclude documents with:**	**Example:**
% (but not)	terms following the % symbol	**fraud % "statute of frauds"**

5.4 Field Restrictions

Overview: Documents in each Westlaw database consist of several segments, or *fields*. One field may contain the citation, another the title, another the synopsis, and so forth. Not all databases contain the same fields. Also depending on the database, fields with the same name may contain different types of information.

To view a list of fields and their contents for a specific database, see Scope for that database. Note that in some databases not every field is available for every document.

To retrieve only those documents containing your search terms in a specific field, restrict your search to that field. To restrict your search to a specific field, type the field name or abbreviation followed by your search terms enclosed in parentheses. For example, to retrieve the U.S. Supreme Court case titled *United States v. O'Hagan,* access the Federal Securities–Supreme Court Cases database (FSEC–SCT). Click the **Terms and Connectors** tab if it is not already selected and type the following query in the *Search* text box, restricting your search to the title field (ti). Then click **Search Westlaw**.

ti(u.s. "united states" & o'hagan)

The fields discussed below are available in Westlaw case law databases you might use for researching issues related to securities law.

Digest and Synopsis Fields: The digest (di) and synopsis (sy) fields summarize the main points of a case. The synopsis field contains a brief description of a case. The digest field contains the topic and headnote fields and includes the complete hierarchy of concepts used by West's editors to classify the headnotes to specific West digest topic and key numbers. Restricting your search to the synopsis and digest fields limits your result to cases in which your terms are related to a major issue in the case.

Consider restricting your search to one or both of these fields if

- you are searching for common terms or terms with more than one meaning, and you need to narrow your search; or
- you cannot narrow your search by using a smaller database.

For example, to retrieve state cases that discuss whether promissory notes are exempt from registration requirements for securities, access the Multistate Securities and Blue Sky Law–Cases database (MSEC–CS) and type the following query:

sy,di(exempt! /s regist! /p promissory /5 note)

Headnote Field: The headnote field (he) is part of the digest field but does not contain the topic names or numbers, hierarchical classification information, or key numbers. The headnote field contains a one-sentence summary for each point of law in a case and any supporting citations given by the author of the opinion. A headnote field restriction is useful when you are searching for specific statutory sections or rule numbers. For example, to retrieve headnotes from federal courts of appeals cases that cite 15 U.S.C.A. § 77k, access the Federal Securities–Courts of Appeals Cases database (FSEC–CTA) and type the following query:

he(15 +s 77k)

Topic Field: The topic field (to) is also part of the digest field. It contains the hierarchical classification information, including the West digest topic names and numbers and the key numbers. You should restrict search terms to the topic field in a case law database if

- a digest field search retrieves too many documents; or
- you want to retrieve cases with digest paragraphs classified under more than one topic.

For example, the topic Securities Regulation has the topic number 349B. To retrieve federal district court cases that discuss insider trading by officers or directors, access the Federal Securities–District Courts Cases database (FSEC–DCT) and type a query like the following:

to(349b) /p inside* /s trad! information /p officer director

To retrieve cases classified under more than one topic and key number, search for your terms in the topic field. For example, to retrieve federal cases discussing investment companies, which may be classified to such topics as Banks and Banking (52) or Securities Regulation (349B), access the FSEC–CS database and type a query like the following:

to("investment company")

For a complete list of West digest topics and their corresponding topic numbers, access the West Key Number Digest by clicking **Key Numbers** at the top of any page. Then click **West Key Number Digest Outline** under *Browse Key Numbers*. Alternatively, click **Custom Digest** at a case law database Search page.

To search for topic and key numbers, click **Key Numbers** at the top of any page. Then type terms describing your issue in the *Search for Key Numbers* text box and click **Search**.

> *Note*: Slip opinions and cases from topical services do not contain the West digest, headnote, and topic fields.

Prelim and Caption Fields: When searching in a database containing statutes, rules, or regulations, restrict your search to the prelim (pr) and caption (ca) fields to retrieve documents in which your terms are important enough to appear in a section name or heading. For example, to retrieve federal statutes regarding registration of brokers and dealers, access the Federal Securities–U.S. Code Annotated database (FSEC–USCA) and type the following query:

pr,ca(regist! & broker dealer)

5.5 Date Restrictions

You can use Westlaw to retrieve documents *decided* or *issued* before, after, or on a specified date, as well as within a range of dates. The following sample queries contain date restrictions:

da(2008) & due /5 diligence

da(aft 1998) & due /5 diligence

da(3/6/1986) & due /5 diligence

You can also search for documents *added to a database* on or after a specified date, as well as within a range of dates, which is useful for updating your research. The following sample queries contain added-date restrictions:

ad(aft 2005) & due /5 diligence

ad(aft 11/9/2001 & bef 6/23/2002) & due /5 diligence

Section 6. Searching with Topic and Key Numbers

To retrieve cases that address a specific point of law, use topic and key numbers as your search terms. If you have an on-point case, run a search using the topic and key number from the relevant headnote in an appropriate database to find other cases containing headnotes classified to that topic and key number. For example, to search for federal cases containing headnotes classified under topic 349B (Securities Regulation) and key number 60.48(3) (Fraud on the Market), access the FSEC–CS database and type the following query:

349bk60.48(3)

For a complete list of West digest topics and their corresponding topic numbers, access the West Key Number Digest by clicking **Key Numbers** at the top of any page. Then click **West Key Number Digest Outline** under *Browse Key Numbers*. Alternatively, click **Custom Digest** at a case law database Search page.

To search for topic and key numbers, click **Key Numbers** at the top of any page. Then type terms describing your issue in the *Search for Key Numbers* text box and click **Search**.

> *Note*: Slip opinions and cases from topical services do not contain West topic and key numbers.

6.1 West Key Number Digest

The West Key Number Digest, also known as the Custom Digest, contains the complete topic and key number outline used by West attorney-editors to classify headnotes. You can use the West Key Number Digest to obtain a single document containing all case law headnotes from a specific jurisdiction that are classified under a particular topic and key number.

Access the West Key Number Digest by clicking **Key Numbers** at the top of any page. Then click **West Key Number Digest Outline** under *Browse Key Numbers*. Alternatively, click **Custom Digest** at a case law database Search page. Select up to 10 topic and key numbers from the easy-to-browse outline and click **Search selected**. Then follow the displayed instructions.

For example, to research issues involving securities regulation scroll down the list of topics until topic *349B Securities Regulation* is displayed. Click the plus symbols (+) to display key number information. Select the check box next to each key number you want to include in your search, then click **Search selected**. Select the jurisdiction from which you want to retrieve headnotes and, if desired, type additional search terms and choose a date restriction. Click **Search**.

6.2 KeySearch

KeySearch is a research tool that helps you find cases and secondary sources in a specific area of the law. KeySearch guides you through the selection of terms from a classification system based on the West Key Number System® and then uses the key numbers and their underlying concepts to provide a query for you.

To access KeySearch, click **Key Numbers** at the top of any page. Then click **KeySearch** under *Browse Key Numbers*. Browse the list of topics and subtopics and select a topic or subtopic to search by clicking the hypertext links. For example, to search for sources that discuss officer and director liability under the Sarbanes–Oxley Act, click **Securities Law** at the first KeySearch page. Then click **Officers and Directors** and **Liabilities under Sarbanes–Oxley** at the next two pages. Select the source from which you want to retrieve documents and, if desired, type additional search terms. Click **Search**.

Section 7. Verifying Your Research with KeyCite

Overview: The KeyCite citation research service is a tool that helps you ensure that your cases, statutes, regulations, and administrative decisions are good law; retrieve cases, legislation, articles, or other documents that cite them; and verify the spelling and format of your citations.

7.1 KeyCite for Cases

KeyCite for cases covers case law on Westlaw, including unpublished opinions. KeyCite for cases provides the following:

- direct appellate history of a case, including related references, which are opinions involving the same parties and facts but resolving different issues

- negative citing references for a case, which consist of cases outside the direct appellate line that may have a negative impact on its precedential value
- the title, parallel citations, court of decision, docket number, and filing date of a case
- citations to cases, administrative decisions, secondary sources, and briefs and other court documents on Westlaw that have cited a case
- complete integration with the West Key Number System so you can track legal issues discussed in a case

7.2 KeyCite for Statutes and Regulations

KeyCite for statutes and regulations covers the USCA, the *Code of Federal Regulations* (CFR), statutes from all 50 states, and regulations from selected states. KeyCite for statutes and regulations provides

- links to session laws or rules amending or repealing a statute or regulation
- statutory credits and historical notes
- citations to proposed legislation affecting a statute
- citations to all drafts of bills proposed before the statute was enacted
- citations to reports, journals, *Congressional Record* documents, presidential or executive messages, and testimony relevant to the statute
- citations to cases, administrative decisions, secondary sources, and briefs and other court documents that have cited a statute or regulation

7.3 KeyCite for Administrative Materials

KeyCite for administrative materials includes materials such as the following:

- Board of Contract Appeals decisions
- Board of Immigration Appeals decisions
- Comptroller General decisions
- Environmental Protection Agency decisions
- Federal Communications Commission decisions
- Federal Energy Regulatory Commission (Federal Power Commission) decisions
- Internal Revenue Service revenue rulings, revenue procedures, private letter rulings, and technical advice memoranda
- National Labor Relations Board decisions
- *Public Utilities Reports*
- U.S. Merit Systems Protection Board decisions
- U.S. Patent and Trademark Office decisions
- U.S. patents
- U.S. Tax Court (Board of Tax Appeals) decisions

7.4 KeyCite Alert

KeyCite Alert monitors the status of your cases, statutes, regulations, and administrative decisions and automatically sends you updates at the frequency you specify when their KeyCite information changes.

Section 8. Researching with Westlaw: Examples

8.1 Retrieving Law Review Articles

Recent law review articles are often a good place to begin researching a legal issue because law review articles serve as an excellent introduction to a new topic or review for an old one, providing terminology to help you formulate a query; as a finding tool for pertinent primary authority, such as cases, statutes, and rules; and in some instances, as persuasive secondary authority.

Suppose you need to gain background information on the bespeaks caution doctrine in securities fraud claims.

Solution

- To retrieve law review articles relevant to your issue, access the Journals and Law Reviews database (JLR). Using the Natural Language search method, type a description like the following:

  application of bespeaks caution doctrine in securities fraud claim

- If you have a citation to an article in a specific publication, use Find to retrieve it. (For more information on Find, see Section 3.1 of this appendix.) For example, to retrieve the article found at 47 U. Kan. L. Rev. 495, access Find and type

  47 u kan l rev 495

- If you know the title of an article but not the journal in which it was published, access the JLR database and search for key terms in the title field. For example, to retrieve the article "A Comparative Analysis of the Application of the Bespeaks Caution Doctrine to Forward-Looking Statements," type the following Terms and Connectors query:

  ti(comparative & "bespeaks caution")

8.2 Retrieving Case Law

Suppose you need to retrieve federal district court cases discussing due diligence as a defense under section 11 of the Securities Act of 1933.

Solution

- Access the FSEC-DCT database. Type a Terms and Connectors query such as the following:

  due /5 diligence /p "section 11"

- When you know the citation for a specific case, use Find to retrieve it. For example, to retrieve *In re Countrywide Financial Corp. Securities Litigation*, 588 F. Supp. 2d 1132 (C.D. Cal. 2008), access Find and type

588 fs2d 1132

- If you find a topic and key number that is on point, run a search using that topic and key number to retrieve additional cases discussing that point of law. For example, to retrieve federal cases containing headnotes classified under topic 349B (Securities Regulation) and key number 25.21(4) (Good Faith; Due Diligence or Reasonable Investigation), access the FSEC–CS database and type the following query:

349bk25.21(4)

- To retrieve opinions written by a particular judge, add a judge field (ju) restriction to your query. For example, to retrieve federal district court cases written by Judge Pfaelzer that contain headnotes classified under topic 349B (Securities Regulation), access the FSEC–DCT database and type the following query:

ju(pfaelzer) & to(349b)

- You can also use KeySearch and the West Key Number Digest to retrieve cases and headnotes that discuss the issue you are researching.

8.3 Retrieving Statutes and Regulations

Suppose you need to retrieve federal statutes dealing with manipulative or deceptive practices with regard to securities.

Solution

- Access the FSEC–USCA database. Search for your terms in the prelim and caption fields using the Terms and Connectors search method:

pr,ca(manipulat! decepti! & securities)

- When you know the citation for a specific statute or regulation, use Find to retrieve it. For example, to retrieve 15 U.S.C.A. § 78j, access Find and type

15 usca 78j

- To look at surrounding sections, use the Table of Contents service. Click **Table of Contents** on the Links tab in the left frame. To display a section listed in the Table of Contents, click its hypertext link.

8.4 Retrieving Administrative Decisions

Suppose you need to retrieve arbitration awards involving failure to execute a limit order.

Solution

- Access the Federal Securities–Arbitration Awards database (FSEC–ARB) and type the following query:

fail! /5 execut! /p limit /3 order

8.5 Using KeyCite

Suppose one of the cases you retrieve in your case law research is *Gustafson v. Alloyd Co.,* 115 S. Ct. 1061 (1995). You want to make sure it is good law and retrieve a list of citing references.

Solution

- Use KeyCite to retrieve direct history and negative citing references for *Gustafson*. Access KeyCite and type **115 sct 1061**.
- Use KeyCite to display all citing references for *Gustafson*. Click **Citing References** on the Links tab in the left frame.

8.6 Following Recent Developments

If you are researching issues related to securities law, it is important to keep up with recent developments. How can you do this efficiently?

Solution

One of the easiest ways to follow recent developments in securities law is to access the Westlaw Topical Highlights–Securities Regulation database (WTH–SEC). The WTH–SEC databases contain summaries of recent legal developments, including court decisions, legislation, and materials released by administrative agencies. When you access WTH–SEC, you automatically retrieve a list of documents added to the database in the last two weeks.

You can also use the WestClip® clipping service to stay informed of recent developments of interest to you. WestClip will run your Terms and Connectors queries on a regular basis and deliver the results to you automatically. You can run WestClip queries in legal and news and information databases.

*

Table of Cases and Selected Administrative Materials

A

B

C

D

Dreiling v. Kellett, 281 F.Supp.2d 1215 (W.D. Wash. 2003)—**§ 13.2, n. 132**.
Drobbin v. Nicolet Instrument Corp., 631 F.Supp. 860 (S.D.N.Y.1986)—**§ 11.7, n. 5, 6**.
DuBois, Matter of, 2003 WL 21946858 (SEC 2003)—**§ 14.14, n. 182**.
Duker & Duker, 1939 WL 36426 (SEC 1939)—**§ 14.15, n. 102**.
Dunbar, Matter of, 2008 WL 2167905 (FINRA 2008)—**§ 14.16, n. 44; § 14.20, n. 8**.
Duncan, United States v., 850 F.2d 1104 (6th Cir.1988)—**§ 7.4, n. 35**.
Dupuy v. Dupuy, 511 F.2d 641 (5th Cir.1975)—**§ 12.3, n. 38; § 17.2, n. 8**.
Dupuy v. Dupuy, 551 F.2d 1005 (5th Cir.)—**§ 12.21, n. 2**.
Dura Pharmaceuticals, Inc. v. Broudo, 542 U.S. 936, 124 S.Ct. 2904, 159 L.Ed.2d 811 (2004)—**§ 12.11, n. 77**.
Dura Pharmaceuticals, Inc. v. Broudo, 544 U.S. 336, 125 S.Ct. 1627, 161 L.Ed.2d 577 (2005)—**§ 12.11, n. 54, 78, 81**.
Durham v. Kelly, 810 F.2d 1500 (9th Cir. 1987)—**§ 7.12, n. 40**.
DVI Inc. Seurities. Litigation, In re, 249 F.R.D. 196 (E.D. Pa. 2008)—**§ 12.25, n. 114**.
Dyer v. Eastern Trust & Banking Co., 336 F.Supp. 890 (D.Me.1971)—**§ 11.4, n. 20**.

E

Eagletech Communications, Inc., Matter of, Sec. Exch. Act Rel. No. 34–54095, Admin. Proc. File No. 3–11832, 2006 WL 1835958 at *2 (SEC 2006)—**§ 14.22, n. 107**.
eBay, Inc. Shareholders Litigation, In re, 2004 WL 253521(Del.Ch.2004)—**§ 6.3, n. 92**.
Ebbers, United States v., 458 F.3d 110 (2d Cir.2006)—**§ 16.2, n. 317**.
Eberhardt v. Waters, 901 F.2d 1578 (11th Cir. 1990)—**§ 1.6, n. 22**.
Eckstein v. Balcor Film Investors, 8 F.3d 1121 (7th Cir.1993)—**§ 12.10, n. 140**.
Edelson v. Ch'ien, 405 F.3d 620 (7th Cir. 2005)—**§ 11.2, n. 5**.
Edgar v. MITE Corp., 457 U.S. 624, 102 S.Ct. 2629, 73 L.Ed.2d 269 (1982)—**§ 11.12; § 11.12, n. 8, 32, 44; § 11.13; § 11.13, n. 34, 39**.
Edge Partners, L.P. v. Dockser, 944 F.Supp. 438 (D.Md.1996)—**§ 12.15, n. 11**.
Edward J. Mawod & Co. v. SEC, 591 F.2d 588 (10th Cir.1979)—**§ 12.1, n. 30**.
E.F. Hutton & Co., In re, 1988 WL 239506 (SEC 1988)—**§ 14.13, n. 8, 31**.
E.F. Hutton Southwest Properties II, Ltd., In re, 953 F.2d 963 (5th Cir.1992)—**§ 19.2, n. 32**.
Ehlert v. Singer, 245 F.3d 1313 (11th Cir. 2001)—**§ 12.15, n. 141**.
Eichler v. SEC, 757 F.2d 1066 (9th Cir.1985)—**§ 6.3, n. 127, 138; § 14.10, n. 56, 81**.
E.I. du Pont de Nemours & Co. v. Collins, 432 U.S. 46, 97 S.Ct. 2229, 53 L.Ed.2d 100 (1977)—**§ 20.7, n. 2, 3**.
Eirman v. Olde Discount Corp., 697 So.2d 865 (Fla.App.1997)—**§ 14.14, n. 69**.
Eisenstadt v. Allen, 113 F.3d 1240 (9th Cir. 1997)—**§ 12.9, n. 244**.
Eldridge v. Ward, 174 F. 402 (2d Cir.1909)—**§ 14.18, n. 25**.
Electronic Data Systems Corp., 2005 WL 171966 (SEC 2005)—**§ 10.8, n. 104**.
Electronic Shareholder Forums, 2008 WL 170875 (SEC 2008)—**§ 10.2, n. 31, 33**.
Electronic Specialty Co. v. International Controls Corp., 409 F.2d 937 (2d Cir.1969)—**§ 12.9, n. 318; § 12.19, n. 80**.
Elgindy, Matter of, 2004 WL 865791 (SEC 2004)—**§ 14.10, n. 127**.
Eliasberg v. Standard Oil Co., 23 N.J.Super. 431, 92 A.2d 862 (1952)—**§ 17.1, n. 49**.
Elkind v. Liggett & Myers, Inc., 635 F.2d 156 (2d Cir.1980)—**§ 12.9, n. 244; § 12.17, n. 82; § 12.19, n. 88**.
Elliott, United States v., 62 F.3d 1304 (11th Cir.1995)—**§ 21.2, n. 18, 23, 25**.
Elliott v. SEC, 36 F.3d 86 (11th Cir.1994)—**§ 16.2, n. 415**.
Emergency Order Pursuant to Section 12(k)(2) of the Securities Exchange Act of 1934 Taking Temporary Action to Respond To Market Developments, 2008 WL 2743880 (SEC 2008)—**§ 14.22, n. 36**.
Emergent Capital Investment Management, LLC v. Stonepath Group, Inc., 343 F.3d 189 (2d Cir. 2003)—**§ 12.11, n. 72**.
Emerson Electric Co., In re, 16 Sec.Reg. & L.Rep. (BNA) 1982 (SEC 1984)—**§ 10.8, n. 642**.
Enron Corp. Securities, Derivative and ERISA Litigation, In re, 235 F.Supp.2d 549 (S.D. Tex. 2002)—**§ 12.25, n. 96**.
Envirokare Tech, Inc. v. Pappas, 420 F. Supp.2d 291 (S.D.N.Y. 2006)—**§ 9.3, n. 206**.
E.ON AG v. Acciona, S.A., 468 F.Supp.2d 537 (S.D.N.Y. 2006)—**§ 11.9, n. 40**.
E.ON AG v. Acciona, S.A, 468 F.Supp.2d 559 (S.D.N.Y. 2007)—**§ 11.4, n. 48**.
EP Medsystems, Inc. v. EchoCath, Inc., 235 F.3d 865 (3d Cir.2000)—**§ 12.9, n. 274**.
Epstein v. MCA, Inc., 50 F.3d 644 (9th Cir. 1995)—**§ 11.5, n. 112, 125**.
Ernst & Ernst v. Hochfelder, 425 U.S. 185, 96 S.Ct. 1375, 47 L.Ed.2d 668 (1976)—**§ 2.2, n. 14; § 10.3, n. 31; § 12.1, n. 22, 31, 32; § 12.2, n. 5; § 12.3, n. 33; § 12.4, n. 22, 41; § 12.8; § 12.8, n. 2, 16; § 12.22, n. 6; § 14.3, n. 349**.
Errion v. Connell, 236 F.2d 447 (9th Cir. 1956)—**§ 12.3, n. 42**.
Escott v. BarChris Construction Corp., 283 F.Supp. 643 (S.D.N.Y.1968)—**§ 7.3, n. 140; § 7.4; § 7.4, n. 21**.
Esplin v. Hirschi, 402 F.2d 94 (10th Cir. 1968)—**§ 12.10, n. 57**.
Ettinger v. Merrill Lynch, Pierce, Fenner & Smith, Inc., 835 F.2d 1031 (3d Cir.1987)—**§ 14.10, n. 84**.
Euronext Favors NYSE Proposal But Shareholders May Want Higher Offer, 38 Sec. Reg. & L. Rep. (BNA) 914 (2006)—**§ 1.1, n. 30**.
Europe & Overseas Commodity Traders v. Banque Paribas London, 147 F.3d 118 (2d Cir.1998)—**§ 20.1, n. 30**.

F

G

H

I

J

K

L

M

Marks v. CDW Computer Centers, Inc., 122 F.3d 363 (7th Cir.1997)—**§ 10.3, n. 45**.
Marquette Cement Manufacturing Co. v. Andreas, 239 F.Supp. 962 (S.D.N.Y.1965)—**§ 13.3, n. 40**.
Marquit v. Williams, 229 F.3d 1135 (2d Cir. 2000)—**§ 20.6, n. 84**.
Marshall v. Green Giant Co., 16 Sec.Reg. & L.Rep. (BNA) 1157 (D.C.Minn.1984)—**§ 22.7, n. 43**.
Marshel v. AFW Fabric Corp., 533 F.2d 1277 (2d Cir.1976)—**§ 12.20, n. 11**.
Marsh Group v. Graff, 46 Fed.Appx. 140 (4th Cir. 2002)—**§ 12.9, n. 128**.
Marsh & McClennan Cos. Securities Litigation, In re, 501 F. Supp.2d 452 (S.D.N.Y. 2006)—**§ 12.8, n. 150**.
Martin v. T.V. Tempo, Inc., 628 F.2d 887 (5th Cir.1980)—**§ 1.6, n. 135, 181**.
Mary S. Krech Trust v. Lakes Apartments, 642 F.2d 98 (5th Cir.1981)—**§ 4.20, n. 66; § 4.24, n. 23**.
Master Financial, Inc., 1999 WL 343087 (SEC 1999)—**§ 4.12, n. 18**.
Mastrobuono v. Shearson Lehman Hutton, Inc., 128 F.R.D. 243 (N.D.Ill.1989)—**§ 15.1, n. 28**.
Mastrobuono v. Shearson Lehman Hutton, Inc., 514 U.S. 52, 115 S.Ct. 1212, 131 L.Ed.2d 76 (1995)—**§ 12.12, n. 20; § 15.1, n. 43**.
Matassarin v. Lynch, 174 F.3d 549 (5th Cir. 1999)—**§ 1.6, n. 220**.
Mathers Fund, Inc. v. Colwell Co., 564 F.2d 780 (7th Cir.1977)—**§ 20.10, n. 13**.
Mathews v. Kidder, Peabody & Co., 161 F.3d 156 (3d Cir.1998)—**§ 12.15, n. 11**.
Matter of (see name of party)
Matthews, United States v., 34 Sec. Reg. & L. Rep. (BNA) 601 (S.D.N.Y.2002)—**§ 14.10, n. 104**.
Mayaja v. Bodkin, 824 F.2d 439 (5th Cir. 1987)—**§ 15.1, n. 25**.
Mayer v. Chesapeake Ins. Co. Ltd., 877 F.2d 1154 (2d Cir.1989)—**§ 13.2, n. 89; § 13.3, n. 52**.
Mayer v. Oil Field Systems Corp., 803 F.2d 749 (2d Cir.1986)—**§ 7.6, n. 38**.
Maynard Oil Co. v. Deltec Panamerica S.A., 630 F.Supp. 502 (S.D.N.Y.1985)—**§ 11.8, n. 12, 55**.
Mayo v. Apropos Technology, Inc., 2002 WL 193393 (N.D.Ill.2002)—**§ 12.15, n. 93**.
Mayo v. Dean Witter Reynolds, Inc., 258 F.Supp.2d 1097 (N.D. Cal. 2003)—**§ 15.1, n. 43**.
McAdam v. Dean Witter Reynolds, Inc., 896 F.2d 750 (3d Cir.1990)—**§ 14.15, n. 18**.
McCowan v. Dean Witter Reynolds, Inc., 682 F.Supp. 741 (S.D.N.Y.1987)—**§ 15.1, n. 28**.
McDonald's Corp., 2007 WL 895066 (SEC 2007)—**§ 10.8, n. 344**.
McFarland v. Memorex Corp., 493 F.Supp. 631 (N.D.Cal.1980)—**§ 7.3, n. 60, 138, 139**.
McGill v. American Land & Exploration Co., 776 F.2d 923 (10th Cir.1985)—**§ 1.6, n. 102, 358**.
McGraw Hill Cos., 2008 WL 376143 (SEC 2008)—**§ 10.8, n. 341**.
McKey v. Charles Schwab & Co., 67 Cal. App.4th 731, 79 Cal.Rptr.2d 213 (Cal.App. 1998)—**§ 14.14, n. 69**.
McKowan Lowe & Co. v. Jasmine, Ltd., 976 F.Supp. 293 (D.N.J.1997)—**§ 12.15, n. 11**.
McMahan & Co. v. Wherehouse Entertainment, Inc., 65 F.3d 1044 (2d Cir.1995)—**§ 7.5, n. 23; § 12.12, n. 48**.
McMahan & Co. v. Wherehouse Entertainment, Inc., 859 F.Supp. 743 (S.D.N.Y. 1994)—**§ 12.23, n. 6**.
McMahan & Co. v. Wherehouse Entertainment, Inc., 900 F.2d 576 (2d Cir.1990)—**§ 12.9, n. 11**.
Meason v. Bank of Miami, 652 F.2d 542 (5th Cir.1981)—**§ 1.6, n. 398**.
Mecca v. Gibraltar Corp., 746 F.Supp. 338 (S.D.N.Y.1990)—**§ 7.12, n. 41**.
Mechigian v. Art Capital Corp., 612 F.Supp. 1421 (S.D.N.Y.1985)—**§ 1.6, n. 105**.
Media General, Inc., 2001 WL 138964 (SEC 2001)—**§ 10.8, n. 40**.
Medimmune, Inc. Securities Litigation, In re, 873 F.Supp. 953 (D.Md.1995)—**§ 12.9, n. 134**.
Medtox Scientific, Inc. v. Morgan Capital, L.L.C., 258 F.3d 763 (8th Cir.2001)—**§ 13.3, n. 92, 93, 94**.
Meehan, Matter of, 1937 WL 1551 (SEC 1937)—**§ 14.3, n. 353**.
Merck & Co., 2008 WL 162838 (SEC 2008)—**§ 10.8, n. 225**.
Merck & Co. Securities Litigation, In re, 432 F.3d 261 (3d Cir. 2005)—**§ 12.10, n. 65; § 12.15, n. 92**.
Mercury Air Group, Inc. v. Mansour, 237 F.3d 542 (5th Cir.2001)—**§ 12.9, n. 315**.
Merrill Lynch & Co., 2008 WL 384380 (SEC 2008)—**§ 10.8, n. 339**.
Merrill Lynch & Co. Inc. v. Allegheny Energy, Inc., 500 F.3d 171 (2d Cir. 2007)—**§ 12.11, n. 56**.
Merrill Lynch, Pierce, Fenner & Smith, Inc., 1997 WL 720940 (SEC 1997)—**§ 10.2, n. 23**.
Merrill Lynch, Pierce, Fenner & Smith, Inc., Matter of, 2005 WL 1993862 (NYSE 2005)—**§ 2.5, n. 91**.
Merrill Lynch, Pierce, Fenner & Smith, Inc., Matter of, Sec. Exch. Act Rel. No. 3414149 (SEC 1977)—**§ 14.16, n. 7**.
Merrill Lynch, Pierce, Fenner & Smith, Inc. v. Bobker, 636 F.Supp. 444 (S.D.N.Y.1986)—**§ 11.6, n. 92**.
Merrill Lynch, Pierce, Fenner & Smith, Inc. v. Bobker, 808 F.2d 930 (2d Cir.1986)—**§ 11.6, n. 96**.
Merrill Lynch, Pierce, Fenner & Smith, Inc. v. Curran, 456 U.S. 353, 102 S.Ct. 1825, 72 L.Ed.2d 182 (1982)—**§ 22.7, n. 37**.
Merrill Lynch, Pierce, Fenner & Smith v. Dabit, 547 U.S. 71, 126 S.Ct. 1503, 164 L.Ed.2d 179 (2006)—**§ 12.5; § 12.5, n. 63, 65; § 12.7, n. 17, 121; § 12.15, n. 336**.
Mesa Petroleum Co. v. Cities Service Co., 715 F.2d 1425 (10th Cir.1983)—**§ 11.13, n. 39**.
Metcalf & Eddy, United States v., No. 1:99CV125666 (D. Mass. 1999)—**§ 22.2, n. 26**.

N

O

P

Q

R

S

SEC v. Forex Asset Management LLC, 242 F.3d 325 (5th Cir.2001)—**§ 16.2, n. 158**.
SEC v. Franklin, 265 Fed. Appx. 644 (9th Cir. 2008)—**§ 21.2, n. 116**.
SEC v. Friendly Power Co., 49 F.Supp.2d 1363 (S.D.Fla.1999)—**§ 1.6, n. 138, 187, 291; § 16.2, n. 167**.
SEC v. Gallard, 1997 WL 767570 (S.D.N.Y. 1997)—**§ 1.6, n. 70**.
SEC v. Gann, 2006 WL 616005 (N.D.Tex. 2006)—**§ 20.5, n. 87**.
SEC v. General Time Corp., 407 F.2d 65 (2d Cir.1968)—**§ 20.10, n. 15**.
SEC v. George, 426 F.3d 786 (6th Cir. 2005)—**§ 1.6, n. 74; § 16.2, n. 171**.
SEC v. Ginsburg, 362 F.3d 1292 (11th Cir. 2004)—**§ 12.17, n. 80**.
SEC v. Glenn W. Turner Enterprises, Inc., 474 F.2d 476 (9th Cir.1973)—**§ 1.6, n. 14, 127, 131, 183**.
SEC v. Glen–Arden Commodities, Inc. [1973 Transfer Binder] Fed.Sec.L.Rep. (CCH) ¶ 94,142 (E.D.N.Y.1973)—**§ 1.6, n. 13**.
SEC v. Global Telecom Services LLC, 325 F.Supp.2d 94 (D. Conn. 2004)—**§ 1.6, n. 365**.
SEC v. Goldfield Deep Mines Co., 758 F.2d 459 (9th Cir.1985)—**§ 1.6, n. 108**.
SEC v. Gold–Ventures Club, 2002 WL 1058847 (N.D. Ga. 2002)—**§ 17.4, n. 7**.
SEC v. Great Lakes Equities Co., 1990 WL 260587 (E.D.Mich.1990)—**§ 14.15, n. 102; § 17.4, n. 74**.
SEC v. Guild Films Co., 279 F.2d 485 (2d Cir.1960)—**§ 4.27; § 4.27, n. 48**.
SEC v. Haffenden–Rimar International, Inc., 362 F.Supp. 323 (E.D.Va.1973)—**§ 1.6, n. 13**.
SEC v. Harwyn Industries Corp., 326 F.Supp. 943 (S.D.N.Y.1971)—**§ 5.1, n. 33; § 5.3; § 5.3, n. 40, 44**.
SEC v. Hasho, 784 F.Supp. 1059 (S.D.N.Y. 1992)—**§ 14.10, n. 101**.
SEC v. Heartland Group, Inc., 2003 WL 103015 (N.D.Ill. 2003)—**§ 16.2, n. 17**.
SEC v. Hickey, 322 F.3d 1123 (9th Cir.2003)—**§ 16.2, n. 154**.
SEC v. Holschuh, 694 F.2d 130 (7th Cir. 1982)—**§ 4.1, n. 50; § 4.26, n. 10, 17; § 4.36, n. 32**.
SEC v. Homa, 2000 WL 1468726 (N.D.Ill. 2000)—**§ 16.2, n. 12, 14**.
SEC v. Infinity Group Co., 212 F.3d 180 (3d Cir.2000)—**§ 1.6, n. 96**.
SEC v. Interlink Data Network of Los Angeles, Inc., 1993 WL 603274 (C.D.Cal.1993)—**§ 4.20, n. 22, 62, 73; § 4.25, n. 9**.
SEC v. International Heritage, Inc., 4 F.Supp.2d 1368 (N.D.Ga.1998)—**§ 16.2, n. 99, 105**.
SEC v. International Mining Exchange, Inc., 515 F.Supp. 1062 (D.Colo.1981)—**§ 1.6, n. 188**.
SEC v. I–2001, 2002 WL 14394 (SEC 2002)—**§ 1.6, n. 45**.
SEC v. Johnson, 174 Fed. Appx. 111 (3d Cir. 2006)—**§ 2.2, n. 105**.
SEC v. Jones, 476 F.Supp.2d 374 (S.D.N.Y. 2007)—**§ 16.2, n. 168**.
SEC v. Joseph Schlitz Brewing Co., 452 F.Supp. 824 (E.D.Wis.1978)—**§ 3.8, n. 15; § 3.9, n. 23; § 12.9, n. 41, 306; § 16.2, n. 152**.
SEC v. Kenton Capital, Ltd., 69 F.Supp.2d 1 (D.D.C.1998)—**§ 21.2, n. 2, 71**.
SEC v. Kern, 425 F.3d 143 (2d Cir. 2005)—**§ 4.27, n. 94**.
SEC v. Kimmes, 799 F.Supp. 852 (N.D.Ill. 1992)—**§ 6.3, n. 55**.
SEC v. King, Civ. Action No. 7:00CV00622, 32 Sec. Reg. & L. Rep. (BNA) 1140 (W.D. Va. 2000)—**§ 12.17, n. 9**.
SEC v. Kirkland, 521 F.Supp.2d 1281 (M.D. Fla. 2007)—**§ 1.6, n. 261**.
SEC v. KMPG, LLP, 2005 WL 3540252 (S.D.N.Y. 2005)—**§ 9.6, n. 101**.
SEC v. Kornman, 391 F.Supp.2d 477 (N.D. Tex. 2005)—**§ 12.17, n. 212; § 16.2, n. 87**.
SEC v. Koscot Interplanetary, Inc., 497 F.2d 473 (5th Cir.1974)—**§ 1.6, n. 15, 131, 183**.
SEC v. Lambert, 38 F.Supp.2d 1348 (S.D.Fla. 1999)—**§ 12.17, n. 244**.
SEC v. Lange, 2002 WL 475130 (E.D.Pa. 2002)—**§ 16.2, n. 172**.
SEC v. Lauer, 52 F.3d 667 (7th Cir.1995)—**§ 1.6, n. 70**.
SEC v. Lavigne, 2000 WL 1643954 (E.D.N.Y. 2000)—**§ 6.3, n. 56**.
SEC v. Life Partners, Inc., 87 F.3d 536 (D.C.Cir.1996)—**§ 1.6, n. 129, 143, 145**.
SEC v. Lipson, 278 F.3d 656 (7th Cir.2002)—**§ 12.17, n. 104**.
SEC v. Lund, 570 F.Supp. 1397 (C.D.Cal. 1983)—**§ 12.17, n. 245**.
SEC v. Lybrand, 200 F.Supp.2d 384 (S.D.N.Y. 2002)—**§ 4.27, n. 18, 86; § 5.3, n. 43, 51**.
SEC v. Macon, 28 F.Supp. 127 (D.Colo.1939)—**§ 14.18, n. 52**.
SEC v. Madden, 2000 WL 781334 (E.D.N.Y. 2000)—**§ 6.3, n. 48**.
SEC v. Maio, 51 F.3d 623 (7th Cir.1995)—**§ 12.17, n. 248, 260**.
SEC v. M.A. Lundy Associates, 362 F.Supp. 226 (D.R.I.1973)—**§ 1.6, n. 13**.
SEC v. Management Dynamics, Inc., 515 F.2d 801 (2d Cir.1975)—**§ 16.2, n. 102**.
SEC v. Manor Nursing Centers, Inc., 458 F.2d 1082 (2d Cir.1972)—**§ 2.5, n. 24, 25; § 3.7, n. 15, 16; § 7.1, n. 14; § 16.2, n. 95, 96**.
SEC v. Markowski, 277 Fed.Appx. 903 (11th Cir. 2008)—**§ 14.3, n. 83**.
SEC v. Materia, 745 F.2d 197 (2d Cir.1984)—**§ 12.17, n. 7, 158**.
SEC v. Mayhew, 121 F.3d 44 (2d Cir.1997)—**§ 12.17, n. 273**.
SEC v. McCaskey, 2002 WL 850001 (S.D.N.Y. 2002)—**§ 16.2, n. 170**.
SEC v. McDonald Investment Co., 343 F.Supp. 343 (D.Minn.1972)—**§ 4.12, n. 17**.
SEC v. Meltzer, 440 F.Supp.2d 179 (E.D.N.Y. 2006)—**§ 14.18, n. 3**.
SEC v. Merchant Capital, LLC, 483 F.3d 747 (11th Cir. 2007)—**§ 1.6, n. 290**.
SEC v. Mersky, 1993 WL 387105 (E.D.Pa. 1993)—**§ 14.18, n. 32**.
SEC v. Michel, 521 F.Supp.2d 795 (N.D. Ill. 2007)—**§ 12.17, n. 241**.

Smaller Reporting Company Regulatory Relief and Simplification, 2007 WL 4440393 (SEC 2007)—**§ 9.3, n. 41**.
Smallwood v. Pearl Brewing Co., 489 F.2d 579 (5th Cir.1974)—**§ 11.4, n. 50**.
Smith, United States v., 155 F.3d 1051 (9th Cir.1998)—**§ 12.17, n. 109, 209**.
Smith Barney Fund Management LLC, Matter of, 2005 WL 1278368 (SEC 2005)—**§ 21.4, n. 14**.
Smith Barney, Inc. v. Painters Local Union No. 109 Pension Fund, 254 Neb. 758, 579 N.W.2d 518 (1998)—**§ 14.14, n. 67**.
Smith v. Ayres, 845 F.2d 1360 (5th Cir.1988)—**§ 12.7, n. 49**.
Smith v. SEC, 129 F.3d 356 (6th Cir.1997)—**§ 16.2, n. 10**.
Smith v. Slade & Co., 1982 WL 1341 (D.D.C. 1982)—**§ 14.20, n. 31**.
Smoky Greenhaw Cotton Co. v. Merrill Lynch, Pierce, Fenner & Smith, Inc., 785 F.2d 1274 (5th Cir.1986)—**§ 14.3, n. 89; § 22.7, n. 18**.
Smolowe v. Delendo Corp., 136 F.2d 231 (2d Cir.1943)—**§ 13.2, n. 86**.
Snap–On Inc. v. Ortiz, 1999 WL 592194 (N.D. Ill. 1999)—**§ 3.9, n. 53**.
Soderberg v. Gens, 652 F.Supp. 560 (N.D.Ill. 1987)—**§ 12.12, n. 69**.
Sofonia v. Principal Life Insurance Co., 465 F.3d 873 (8th Cir. 2006)—**§ 12.15, n. 241**.
Software Toolworks, Inc. Securities Litigation, In re, 50 F.3d 615 (9th Cir.1994)—**§ 7.4, n. 36, 67**.
Software Toolworks, Inc. Securities Litigation, In re, 789 F.Supp. 1489 (N.D.Cal.1992)—**§ 7.4, n. 17**.
Sonoma Valley Bancorp, 2007 WL 582651 (SEC 2007)—**§ 10.8, n. 540**.
Sony Corp. & Sumio Sano, In re, 1998 WL 439898 (SEC 1998)—**§ 3.9, n. 143**.
Southland Sec. Corp. v. INSpire Ins. Solutions, Inc., 365 F.3d 353 (5th Cir. 2004)—**§ 12.8, n. 155**.
Sparta Surgical Corp. v. NASD, Inc., 159 F.3d 1209 (9th Cir. 1998)—**§ 7.17, n. 117**.
Spartek, Inc., In re, 1979 WL 173653 (1979)—**§ 16.2; § 16.2, n. 356**.
Speck v. Oppenheimer & Co., Inc., 583 F.Supp. 325 (W.D.Mo.1984)—**§ 15.1, n. 157**.
Spicer v. Chicago Board Options Exchange, Inc., 977 F.2d 255 (7th Cir.1992)—**§ 14.26, n. 29**.
SPIC v. Vigman, 74 F.3d 932 (9th Cir.1996)—**§ 14.3, n. 414**.
Spike Financial Services, LLC, 2001 WL 1512715 (SEC 2001)—**§ 14.5, n. 6**.
Spitzer v. McLeod, 38 Sec Reg. & L. Rep. (BNA) 298 (N.Y. Supp. Ct. 2006)—**§ 6.3, n. 75**.
Sprecher, United States v., 783 F.Supp. 133 (S.D.N.Y.1992)—**§ 4.29, n. 36**.
Stahl v. Gibraltar Financial Corp., 967 F.2d 335 (9th Cir.1992)—**§ 10.3, n. 14, 29, 53**.
Stalvey & Associates, Inc., In re, 750 F.2d 464 (5th Cir.1985)—**§ 14.24, n. 24**.
Starr ex rel. Estate of Sampson v. Georgeson Shareholder, Inc., 412 F.3d 103 (2d Cir. 2005)—**§ 12.10, n. 157**.
Statement of the Securities and Exchange Commission Concerning Financial Penalties, 2006 WL 14406 (SEC 2006)—**§ 16.2, n. 248**.
State v. ______ (see opposing party)
Steadman v. SEC, 450 U.S. 91, 101 S.Ct. 999, 67 L.Ed.2d 69 (1981)—**§ 16.2, n. 422**.
Stead v. SEC, 444 F.2d 713 (10th Cir.1971)—**§ 16.2, n. 415**.
Steckman v. Hart Brewing, Inc., 143 F.3d 1293 (9th Cir.1998)—**§ 3.9, n. 155**.
Steel Partners II, L.P. v. Aronson, 2006 WL 1044818 (D.N.J. 2006)—**§ 11.2, n. 37**.
Steiner v. Southmark Corp., 734 F.Supp. 269 (N.D.Tex.1990)—**§ 7.3, n. 138**.
Steinhardt Group v. Citicorp, 126 F.3d 144 (3d Cir.1997)—**§ 1.6, n. 128**.
Stella v. Graham–Paige Motors Corp., 104 F.Supp. 957 (S.D.N.Y.1952)—**§ 13.3, n. 58**.
Stephens, Inc., 30 Sec. Reg. & L. Rep. (BNA) 1795 (SEC 1998)—**§ 4.17, n. 46**.
Stephenson v. Paine Webber Jackson & Curtis, Inc., 839 F.2d 1095 (5th Cir.1988)—**§ 12.21, n. 16**.
Sterling Foster & Co. Securities Litigation, In re, 222 F.Supp.2d 216 (E.D.N.Y. 2002)—**§ 7.3, n. 4**.
Stevens v. Liberty Packing Corp., 111 N.J.Eq. 61, 161 A. 193 (1932)—**§ 1.6, n. 19**.
Stewart, United States v., 305 F.Supp.2d 368 (S.D.N.Y. 2004)—**§ 12.8, n. 5**.
Stock Exchanges Options Trading Antitrust Litigation, In re, 317 F.3d 134 (2d Cir. 2003)—**§ 14.1, n. 216**.
Stockwell v. Reynolds & Co., 252 F.Supp. 215 (S.D.N.Y.1965)—**§ 12.7, n. 114**.
Stoneridge Investment Partners, LLC v. Scientific–Atlanta, Inc., ___ U.S. ___, 128 S.Ct. 761, 169 L.Ed.2d 627 (2008)—**§ 12.4, n. 35; § 12.11, n. 29; § 12.25, n. 110, 111, 137**.
Stone v. Kirk, 8 F.3d 1079 (6th Cir.1993)—**§ 1.6, n. 289**.
Stone & Webster, Inc., In re, Securities Litigation, 414 F.3d 187 (1st Cir. 2005)—**§ 12.9, n. 224**.
Stransky v. Cummins Engine Co., 51 F.3d 1329 (7th Cir.1995)—**§ 12.9, n. 316; § 12.19, n. 66**.
Strategic Resource Management, Inc., 52 S.E.C. 542 (1995)—**§ 14.10, n. 62**.
Strauss v. Kopp Investment Advisors, Inc., 1999 WL 787818 (S.D.N.Y.1999)—**§ 13.3, n. 79**.
Streeter v. Lowe, 184 F. 263 (1st Cir.1911)—**§ 14.18, n. 24**.
Strong/Corneliuson Capital Management, Matter of, 1994 WL 361971 (SEC 1994)—**§ 14.3, n. 354; § 20.7, n. 3**.
Strougo v. Bassini, 1 F.Supp.2d 268 (S.D.N.Y. 1998)—**§ 20.6, n. 20, 37**.
Strougo v. Bassini, 282 F.3d 162 (2d Cir. 2002)—**§ 20.10, n. 20, 50**.
Strougo v. BEA Associates, 188 F.Supp.2d 373 (S.D.N.Y.2002)—**§ 20.6, n. 40**.
Strougo v. BEA Associates, 1999 WL 147737 (1999)—**§ 20.10, n. 77**.
Strougo v. BEA Associates, 2000 WL 45714 (2000)—**§ 20.6, n. 16, 18, 20, 37, 38**.

T

U

V

W

Y

*

Index

We have included references to material that appears only in the Practitioner's Edition in order to guide the reader to sources beyond this Hornbook.

Including references to the Practitioner's Edition